Department of Defense Sponsored

Information Security Research

New Methods for Protecting Against Cyber Threats

Department of Defense

Editors

Cliff Wang, PhD
Steven King, PhD
Ralph Wachter, PhD
Robert Herklotz, PhD
Chris Arney, PhD
Gary Toth
David Hislop, PhD
Sharon Heise, PhD
Todd Combs, PhD

WILEY PUBLISHING, INC.

Department of Defense Sponsored Information Security Research: New Methods for Protecting Against Cyber Threats

Published by
Wiley Publishing, Inc.
10475 Crosspoint Boulevard
Indianapolis, IN 46256
www.wiley.com

Copyright © 2007 by Wiley Publishing, Inc., Indianapolis, Indiana

Published simultaneously in Canada

ISBN: 978-0-471-78756-3

Manufactured in the United States of America

10 9 8 7 6 5 4 3 2 1

Credits

Executive Editor
Carol Long

Senior Development Editor
Tom Dinse

Production Editor
Angela Smith

Copy Editor
Michael Koch

Editorial Manager
Mary Beth Wakefield

Production Manager
Tim Tate

Vice President and Executive Group Publisher
Richard Swadley

Vice President and Executive Publisher
Joseph B. Wikert

Proofreader
Ian Golder, Word One

Anniversary Logo Design
Richard Pacifico

Contents

Foreword

In recent years, critical infrastructure protection and cyber security has moved from a relatively obscure research topic into a practical concern for anyone who uses a laptop or PC for a task such as online banking or purchases. The Department of Defense has been at the forefront of research in these areas as it moves toward a network-centric vision of global operations.

Many books have been written for the general public, for the operational practitioners, and for the research community to explain the information technology problems that face us in the beginning of the twenty-first century. This book represents the culmination of five years and nearly $80 million of focused academic research in support of the technology challenges faced by the Department of Defense as well as the federal government.

This book encapsulates the results of the Critical Infrastructure Protection and High Confidence Software University Research Initiative. The Office of the Deputy Under Secretary of Defense for Science and Technology initiated this program in 2000 in response to a Presidential Decision Directive on Critical Infrastructure Protection. The program was created in coordination with the White House Office of Science and Technology Policy. Recently, there have been significant increases in university cyber security research in the National Science Foundation and other agencies; but at the start of this program, DoD was the primary source of academic research funds in this area.

This book brings together a collection of reprinted best-of-breed technical papers in information technology, cyber security, and information assurance that are the results of research by many of the top universities and researchers in the country. Moreover, these papers are accompanied by overviews and summaries written specifically to help readers understand each of the university projects. The results represent many important research advances and present new opportunities for developing innovative technologies and businesses to significantly enhance our national security.

The Army, Navy, and Air Force research program managers, university principal investigators, and the many researchers engaged in this research are to be commended for their sustained efforts and impressive results of this initiative.

Dr. Charles Holland
Director, Information Processing Technology Office
Defense Advanced Research Projects Agency
Former Deputy Under Secretary of Defense for Science and Technology

Acknowledgments

The Deputy Under Secretary of Defense for Science and Technology and the Army, Navy, and Air Force Program Managers acknowledge and thank all who contributed to this book, including the members of the DoD teams who developed the research topics, previous program managers who have moved to other positions, and government researchers who participated in annual reviews of the research. This book reflects the hard work and high-caliber research performed by the principal investigators, researchers, and students who have participated in the program in the past five years. In addition, we thank Maj. James Sweeney, OSD who helped develop the original Broad Agency Announcement, Mr. Terry Bollinger who contributed to much of the strategic and technical planning for the book and compiled the project successes, Ms. Audrey Haar who provided technical editing and workshop planning, Mr. Michael Dingman who provided meeting planning, organizational, and administrative support to the project, and Mr. Bill Newhouse who updated and verified the program statistics. Finally, we would like to thank Julie Infantino, Bill Heinbockel, Rosalie McQuaid, Wesley Snyder, Lindsey Spriggs, Joanne Ventola, and Jim Watters for final proofreading.

Introduction

Steven King

Initiative Origins

In recent years there has been a growing recognition of the criticality of our information infrastructure to our national well-being in general and in particular, our national security. However, the potential national impact of attacks or natural disasters on this infrastructure and the interdependencies created by our dependence on the information infrastructure began to be recognized and gained significant attention in the late 1990s. The release of the Report of the President's Commission on Critical Infrastructure Protection (*Critical Foundations, 1997*), the Critical Infrastructure Protection Presidential Decision Directive 63 (PDD-63), and the National Research Council's Report, *Trust in Cyber Space (1999),* highlighted the need for additional innovative research to secure cyber space.

Critical Infrastructures are defined as those that are so vital that their incapacitation or destruction would have a *debilitating impact on defense or economic security (Critical Foundations, October, 1997).* They include:

- Information and Communications
- Water Supply
- Banking and Finance
- Transportation
- Emergency Health Services
- Power, Oil, and Gas Production
- Law Enforcement
- Government and Emergency Services

PDD-63 and, subsequently, the December 17, 2003 Homeland Security Presidential Directive (HSPD-7) on Critical Infrastructure Identification, Prioritization, and Protection established policies intended to assure the continuity and viability of critical infrastructures and to take all necessary measures to swiftly eliminate any significant vulnerabilities to both physical and cyber attacks on our critical infrastructures. At the time, it was noted that advances in information technology were greatly increasing the linkages between previously independent or loosely coupled systems and infrastructures. In particular, the Internet is now providing the command and control functions for the other infrastructures replacing many previously dedicated communication paths. A particular concern was the increasing potential for cascading failures; where a failure in one infrastructure triggers failures in other infrastructures.

From the perspective of the national defense community, achieving a high level of information connectivity and corresponding operational enhancements, known as net-centricity, is regarded as a critical enabler for the Department of Defense (DoD) to "accelerate business processes, operational decision-making and subsequent action" (*Quadrennial Defense Review Report,* February 2006). In addition, as explained in the DoD planning document Joint Vision 2020, Information Superiority, is a critical element of evolving DoD operational concepts. In a net-centric environment, Information Superiority implies that the warfighter has the ability to securely obtain the appropriate information, as needed, when needed and wherever needed to perform their assigned mission. The underlying assumption of the DoD's strategic vision is a reliable, secure information and communications infrastructure that supports all DoD operations. This need has been recognized for some time and considerable effort has gone into defining, architecting, designing, and implementing this infrastructure. The Global Information Grid (GIG) defines the core concepts and architecture for DoD's global, protected, robust network that will enable the strategic visions of Information Superiority and Net-Centric Operations.

The DoD networks must be defended from a wide range of attacks. DoD faces the same range of threats prevalent on the Internet, including attacks by script-kiddies, sophisticated hackers, and organized crime. However, DoD's primary concerns are the potential for sophisticated nation-state or transnational attacks. These attacks could take the form of espionage, deception, direct cyber attacks on DoD networks, cyber attacks on the supporting national infrastructure, physical attacks on DoD's networked command, control and communications infrastructure, or any combination of attacks. Furthermore, DoD must be able to defend its mobile network infrastructure while under hostile fire in battlefield environments. A foundational requirement for developing protection of the critical information infrastructure is the ability to create, validate, protect, and use high confidence, adaptable software.

In order to achieve its strategic goals and to protect its own networks, the DoD has been at the forefront of research in Information Assurance, Cyber Security and High Confidence Software, funding research in academia, industry, and government laboratories for many years. However, the growing cyber threat led to an effort to expand DoD's research funding focused on the critical information infrastructure. As a result, in coordination with the White House Office of Science and Technology Policy, the Office of the Director for Defense Research and Engineering began a focused effort within the Multidisciplinary University Research Initiative (MURI). The effort, starting in 2001, focused on the technical areas of Critical Infrastructure Protection and High Confidence, Adaptable Software. Advances in both research areas are required to achieve the national and DoD strategic security goals. The principal goal of this initiative was to enhance U.S. universities' capabilities to perform innovative, unclassified science and engineering research supporting the emerging national priority of Critical Infrastructure Protection. This targeted university research competition focused on information technology's role in Critical Infrastructure Protection and on providing the High Confidence, Adaptable Software that underpins both critical infrastructures' and DoD's extensive reliance on embedded information technology. A second, equally important goal was to train and educate researchers to expand the long-term capabilities across the research base. This research program is generally referred to by its abbreviation: CIP/SW URI.

When developing the scope of this university research initiative, the primary focus of the research topics was the protection of the rapidly expanding information and communications infrastructure sector. In a separate but related problem, DoD operations increasingly depend on software-intensive, distributed, and integrated embedded information systems. Our ability to affordably develop these complex warfighter systems requires new assured development technology, increased assurance in heterogeneous distributed computing systems and assured software quality throughout the development and operational life-cycle. Thus, the second part of this research initiative focused on the foundational research, core technologies, and tools needed to develop, assess, and assure software-intensive systems.

The MURI is a research program designed to support university research teams composed of more than one science or engineering discipline. These team efforts can often accelerate research progress by idea cross-fertilization and can also hasten the transition of research findings to practical application. By supporting team efforts, MURIs complement other DoD programs that support university research through single-investigator awards. The grants are structured as three-year awards funded between a half million to one million dollars per year, and can be extended by two one-year renewal options for a maximum award period of five years. The teams represent collaborations of multiple universities and the research projects are overseen by program managers at the Army Research Office, the Office of Naval Research and the Air Force Office of Scientific Research.

In 2001, a key concern in the research area of Critical Infrastructure Protection was the small cadre of cutting-edge researchers in this interdisciplinary field. More opportunities were needed to enable entry into the field at the post-doctoral and faculty level. DoD sponsored 20 Critical Infrastructure Protection and Information Assurance Fellowships to jump-start the research community. These fellowships were designed to enable researchers to apply their expertise in computer science, electrical engineering, physics, and other fields to cyber security and information assurance problems. Each fellowship recipient was mentored by a DoD-funded researcher who was already working in the field. These two-year fellowship positions were at twelve top cyber security research universities. A survey of the recipients at the end of their fellowships indicated that all the fellows intended to continue in the field (75% in academia and the rest split between government and industry). This resulted in a quick infusion of talent at a time when the number of academic researchers was small. With the fellowships and the large number of faculty, post-docs, graduate students, and undergraduate students working on the competitively selected CIP/SW URI projects, our goal of expanding the research community was well met.

This book is the culmination of a successful five-year university research effort to advance the state-of-understanding as a foundation for defending our information infrastructure and building complex software-intensive systems. This book highlights the sustained work of this five-year research program. While the initiative focus was on high quality, multidisciplinary, basic research, we have already seen a number of efforts to incorporate the results into DoD systems, develop commercial spin-offs, apply the tools developed for identifying security vulnerabilities, and patent the resulting technology. The research presented in this book addresses many of the key components needed to secure both DoD's GIG and the Internet.

Research Topics

Based on national and DoD priorities, 13 research topics were identified. These topics were developed jointly by representatives of the Army, Navy, Air Force, the Defense Advanced Research Projects Agency (DARPA), the National Security Agency (NSA), and the Office of the Secretary of Defense. The topics capitalized on the work of the INFOSEC Research Council (IRC) [http://www.infosec-research.org/] in its 1999 version of the IRC *Hard Problems List* and the work of the IRC's Mobile Code Working Group.

Proposals were solicited through a Broad Agency Announcement. The grants were awarded under the supervision of the Research Topic Chiefs from the Army Research Office, the Office of Naval Research, and the Air Force Office of Scientific Research.

In 2001, DoD awarded 23 grants to university research consortia. In 2004, five additional grants were awarded in two new topic areas. Over the five year course of the initiative, DoD funded approximately $80 million of university research ending in 2006. This work reflects the collective effort of hundreds of professors, researchers, post-docs, graduate, and undergraduate students. The following are the research topics:

CIP/SW URI Research Topics
2001:
- Topic 1 Network Surveillance
- Topic 2 Information Assurance for Wireless Networks
- Topic 3 CIP Performance Assessment
- Topic 4 Assured Development Technology for High-Confidence Embedded Systems
- Topic 5 Understanding Mobile Code
- Topic 6 Protecting COTS from the Inside
- Topic 7 Heterogeneous Distributed Computing Systems
- Topic 8 Digital Libraries for Constructive Mathematical Knowledge
- Topic 9 Assuring Software Quality
- Topic 10 Dynamic Network Management
- Topic 11 Understanding and Countering Deception
- Topic 12 Novel Network Architectures
- Topic 13 Protecting Infrastructures from Themselves

2004:
- Topic 14 High Confidence Real-Time Anomaly and Misuse Detection
- Topic 15 Policy-Based Enterprise-Wide Services

CIP/SW URI Program Results

The results of this focused program have been impressive. As of July 2006, 121 Ph.D. degrees and 125 Masters of Science degrees have been awarded to students funded by this program. Fifty-eight post-doctoral and faculty fellows were also trained. In addition the program has provided research topics and Information Assurance (IA)-focused research for another 157 Ph.D. students, 52 Masters students, and 84 undergraduates. It has led to the creation of 63 working and prototype security and software tools. An indication of the emerging practical implications of this research is that it has produced at least 16 patent applications, even though the majority of the research has been oriented toward basic topics that do not typically produce patents in their early stages. An even stronger indication of the impact and positive interactions of the researchers with industry is a total of 97 working engagements between the research groups and user communities in both industry and the Department of Defense. Often these activities have led to the evaluation and use of the above mentioned prototypes and tools. In at least seven cases, the CIP/SW URI technology is in trial field use. One commercial product, Grammatech's CodeSurfer™ static analysis tool has also resulted from this research.

Another indication of the breadth and success of the CIP/SW URI program has been the number of honors and publications it has helped engender. To date, the participating university researchers have received at least 33 awards and special honors, including numerous Best Paper awards and invitations to brief at Congressional hearings. Researchers have been further honored by 127 invitations to speak and 50 invitations to write on their work, 9 requests to be the special editors of special issues on information assurance/software related topics, and 30 invitations to organize conferences on information assurance/software topics. In terms of publications, the production of CIP/SW MURI has been even more impressive. To date it has produced at least 229 peer-reviewed journal papers. Researchers have also written 45 book chapters and 4 complete books. Finally, 982 less formal papers for conferences (many peer reviewed), proceedings, and technical reports were produced. Since the publication of technical papers often lags the completion of the research by a year or more, many more papers are ultimately expected as the research results are finalized. The net result is that DoD investments in these basic research areas have formed the foundation for future applied research and technology development.

The CIP & IA Fellows contributed an additional 95 papers, a book on securing Linux, the development of a safer, bug-tolerant version of the programming language, C, and the development of CyberSleuth™, a framework to gather and disseminate computer security related information (https://www.ists.dartmouth.edu/cybersleuth/) to cite just a few examples.

While each of the research projects has noteworthy successes, a few are given here as representative examples of the research achievements.

- University of Nebraska in Lincoln (Principal Investigator: Matthew Dwyer) led the *Software Model Checking for Embedded Systems* research program, which was used to eliminate a potential safety problem for small business planes. By using their Java PathFinder (JPF) tool, a subtle error in the new IMA-based DEOS real-time operating system was discovered. This software is used in the inertial guidance systems. The error had escaped detection during conventional testing.

- University of Wisconsin in Madison (Principal Investigator: Somesh Jha) led the *Protecting COTS from the Inside* research effort, which developed a superior multi-path ("static") analysis technique for uncovering security holes and built-in malware in off-the-shelf Windows software. The methods developed are simultaneously more comprehensive than ordinary testing, and much more efficient than earlier multi-path analysis methods. A version of this tool is now a commercial product from Grammatech.

- University of Maryland (Principal Investigator: John Baras) led the *Distributed Immune Systems for Wireless Networks Information Assurance* research program, which transitioned group communication security results to Lockheed Martin and Hughes Network Systems for satellite networks.

- Carnegie Mellon University (Principal Investigator: Greg Ganger) led the *Enabling Dynamic Security Management of Networked Systems via Device-Embedded Security* research program, which developed new concepts and prototypes of how to build self-securing devices and storage and provided persuasive arguments on how such work could provide the underlying basis for fundamental future changes in how system and network architectures are made secure.

- University of Arizona (Principal Investigator: Judee Burgoon) led the *Detecting Deception in the Military Infosphere: Improving and Integrating Human Detection Capabilities with Automated Tools* research program, which briefed at a Congressional hearing on research progress in automated identification of human threats.

- Stony Brook University (Principal Investigator: R. Sekar) led the *Model-Carrying Code: A New Approach to Mobile-Code Security* research program, received additional funding from Computer Associates, a major vendor of enterprise security software, to develop an industry standard based on their MURI research.

- Florida Institute of Technology (Principal Investigator: James Whittaker) led the *Neutralizing Malicious Mobile Code* research program, which created a fully functional prototype of a behavior-based approach to virus detection and prevention that has proven capable of identifying previously unknown virus threats as effectively as traditional "signature based" virus checkers found previously identified viruses. This research spawned a small business for the commercialization of the technology. Elements of the early research have been incorporated into the Harris Corporation's Security, Threat, Avoidance Technology (STAT) suite of security software tools.

- Stanford University (Principal Investigator: Sanjay Lall) led the *Architectures for Secure and Robust Distributed Infrastructures* research program, which developed a strategy for increasing the efficiency of the Internet called "Approximate Fair Dropping" (AFD). ADF helps avoid chaotic behaviors and ensure fair allocation of network bandwidth.

- University of California Santa Barbara (Principal Investigator: Richard Kemmerer) led the *Hi-DRA High-speed, Wide-area Network Detection, Response, and Analysis* research program, which developed a comprehensive intrusion detection framework that provides monitoring, intrusion detection, and response for both computer system and network system. The Intrusion Detection (IDS) framework and the set of *State Transition Analysis Technique* (STAT) toolkits have been transitioned to Air Force Research Laboratory, Army Research Laboratory, DARPA, and Argonne National Laboratory.

Book Structure and Goals

The bulk of this book is composed of 22 paired articles written by the university researchers funded by the initiative. The first of each pair of papers is a context paper that provides an overview of each of the research projects and helps set the stage for the more technical second paper. The context paper describes the work of the project, provides a limited description of the research area in general, and places the project's results and accomplishments in context of the research field. The second paper reprints the authors' self-selected "best paper." The intent is two-fold: to provide a comprehensive survey of this large, sustained research program and to provide selected in-depth technical information and results from the program.

The papers are grouped in five chapters, each of which is introduced by the DoD program managers who have overseen the research. The five chapters are:

Chapter 1 Architecting Information Infrastructures for Security
- Infrastructure protection, defense, and response
- Service assurance of infrastructure
- Resilient and robust infrastructure
- Highly assured mobile communication

Chapter 2 At the Edges of the Critical Information Infrastructure
- Trusted edge devices
- High confidence embedded systems
- Effective verification and benchmarking for embedded systems
- Building resilience and self-recovery

Chapter 3 Software Engineering for Assurance
- COTS protection and defense
- Policy driven, high confidence software design
- Shaping policy for software performance and assurance
- Trade-off among assurance properties
- Modeling and simulation

Chapter 4 Malicious Mobile Code
- Effective detection and response to malicious code
- Understanding of threat and vulnerability
- Building resilience and self-recovery
- Establishing safe environment for mobile code
- Trusted and authenticated mobile code

Chapter 5 Dependable Critical Information Infrastructure for Command and Control
- Establishment of full situation awareness
- Effective networked control and command
- Deceptive data detection and deceptive behavior modeling

The goals of this book are to promulgate the results of an outstanding body of research, to expose this research to a broader technical, industrial, and policy community with an interest in the field, and to provide a record of the results of a large, focused research effort in a technical area critical to our national defense. After five years of research, many of the results described herein are ready for transition to applied research, technology development, or commercialization. It is hoped that this book may provide additional exposure to help enable this future development. To this end, the intent is to have the researchers speak for themselves.

CHAPTER 1

Architecting Information Infrastructures for Security

Cliff Wang

The current Internet started with an implicit assumption of trust among the parties making up the infrastructure of the network. This assumption might have been valid during the earlier days of the Internet when it was a self-policing organization of academic, military, and corporate users, but it began to falter when millions of new users were added to the Internet on a yearly basis and the Internet became an unregulated territory. Today, hackers of various levels of sophistication freely exploit the vulnerabilities and weakness of the Internet. Numerous large-scale attacks and intrusions have resulted in billions of dollars of damage. Maintaining the security of our information infrastructure has become a top priority in recent years.

There have been constant efforts to retrofit security into the existing Internet. However, such approaches have largely been hampered by the fundamentally open nature of the Internet architecture and the lack of good security principles in the existing Internet architecture. There is a critical need to develop a novel architecture that allows robust, thorough security to be easily implemented on a network designed with different assumptions than those of the existing Internet. The next generation information and communications infrastructure must provide authentic, accurate, secure, and reliable services, even under a full range of threats or attacks. These qualities must be assured across a heterogeneous information infrastructure that provides interconnectivity via both wired and wireless links, at a wide range of link speeds. This new architecture will enable many emerging applications such as mobile computing or virtual office. In this new architecture, an individual user could rely on networking technologies to perform various tasks (from business transactions to research experiments) at any place and time, with the confidence that a high level of information assurance will be guaranteed.

For the next generation communication infrastructure, managing security and maintaining trust are critical challenges. Contrary to the initial assumption of trust in place, the new network architectures will operate on an implicit assumption of mistrust. The architecture will enable the trust level to be dynamically modified over time based upon the characteristics and behaviors of the network itself. The network will have the capability to operate in degraded mode at all times, while trading off performance with security continually in response to the threat environment.

In the past decade, we have experienced an explosive growth in both the scale of the infrastructure and the speeds of the networks. In addition, mobile devices are widely in use today with wireless connections to the Internet. Maintaining a high level of security for the infrastructure is an enormous technical challenge that demands the development of new capabilities in many areas. For example, innovative approaches and techniques to defend against sophisticated intrusions have always been a top priority. Currently available techniques have severe limitations. For example, they:

- Can detect only the most common attacks,
- Do not adapt to changing conditions,
- Inadequately detect sophisticated multi-stage, multi-level attacks against network infrastructure elements,
- Do not perceive indirect attacks,
- Exhibit high false alarm rates.

We need both host-based and network-based defenses against attacks and intrusions. These require the development of breakthrough technologies in the areas of anomaly based detection, correlation, fusion methods, adaptive response mechanisms, and automatic generation of responses. Furthermore, new techniques and tools are required to scale to very high-speed, dynamic networks and to provide a real-time or near real-time, network-wide capability to accurately detect, analyze, and respond to intrusions, intrusion attempts, suspicious network activities, and anomalies.

Military tactical communication relies on a dynamic and mobile wireless infrastructure to support a heterogeneous mixture of individual soldiers, ground vehicles, airborne platforms, unmanned aerial vehicles, robotics, and unattended sensor networks. A tactical mobile ad hoc network works in a challenging environment of noisy wireless channels, high mobility of individual nodes, and a mobile network infrastructure. Tactical networks also need to perform self-configuration and dynamic addressing while maintaining interoperability with non-wireless infrastructures. Techniques designed for fixed infrastructures may not work for highly mobile, wireless, high-bit error-rate communications. Protection techniques for this type of wireless infrastructure must be resilient and fault tolerant against communication channel interruption, data loss, or even malicious attacks or intrusions.

To support critical missions of network-centric operations and to achieve information superiority, the next generation Internet must be a high-performance network infrastructure that can serve as a reliable, high-capacity information backbone to make information resources readily available. This requires that the infrastructure provide a quality-of-service (QoS) guarantee in terms of timeliness, precision, and accuracy. To establish and maintain a high level of QoS assurance, the next generation architecture needs to incorporate advanced techniques and technologies that can effectively and intelligently monitor and allocate the available resources and meet QoS requirements dynamically and at different levels.

In this chapter, we have contributed technical papers from six Critical Infrastructure Protection (CIP) MURI teams working on the following aspects of next-generation Internet and secure information infrastructure:

- Communication infrastructure protection, defense, and response,
- Service assurance of communication infrastructure,
- Resiliency and robustness of communication infrastructure,
- Highly assured mobile communication systems,
- Distributed system security and assurance.

The paper "Overview of the ASRDI (Architectures for Secure and Robust Distributed Infrastructures) Project" discusses the development of new theoretical tools for analysis of the dynamics of large-scale networked infrastructures. The Stanford MURI team focused on unifying mathematical principles, ideas, and frameworks from communications, controls, computation, and dynamical systems theory, with an emphasis on attempting to reduce the use of ad hoc methods and capture more fundamental notions of limits on performance. Another paper, "Quality of Service Assurance for Dependable Information Infrastructures," summarizes the work carried out by the Arizona State University researchers on providing QoS service assurance at different levels, ranging from local service assurance to global service assurance, along with security assurance for the next-generation communication infrastructure.

The paper "Summary of the Hi-DRA Project: A System for High-Speed, Wide-Area Network Detection, Response, and Analysis" summarizes the University of California Santa Barbara MURI project on developing a network surveillance, analysis, and response infrastructure for high-speed, wide-area networks, whereas the paper "Anomaly and Misuse Detection in Network Traffic Streams—Checking and Machine Learning Approaches" presents the University of Pennsylvania MURI team's latest work on building effective defenses against malware, including both network-based and host-based approaches.

The MURI team at University of Maryland has been working on developing innovative distributed methods and algorithms to secure wireless communication. The paper "Distributed Immune Systems for Wireless Networks Information Assurance" summarizes their scientific achievements. The MURI project at Carnegie Mellon University has been focusing on advancing security in distributed systems. The paper "Distributed System Security via Logical Frameworks" provides a detailed description of the application of logical frameworks to distributed systems.

Overview of the ASRDI (Architectures for Secure and Robust Distributed Infrastructures) Project*

Sanjay Lall, Aeronautics and Astronautics, Stanford
Carolyn Beck, General Engineering, UIUC
Stephen Boyd, Electrical Engineering, Stanford
John Doyle, Control and Dynamical Systems, Caltech
Geir Dullerud, Mechanical Engineering, UIUC
Chris Hadjicostis, Electrical and Computer Engineering, UIUC
Muriel Medard, Electrical Engineering and Computer Science, MIT
Balaji Prabhakar, Electrical Engineering and Computer Science, Stanford
Rayadurgam Srikant, General Engineering UIUC
George Verghese, Electrical Engineering and Computer Science, MIT

Abstract

The major barrier constraining the successful management and design of large-scale distributed infrastructures is the conspicuous lack of knowledge about their *dynamical* features and behaviors. Up until very recently analysis of systems such as the Internet, or the national electricity distribution system, have primarily relied on the use of non-dynamical models, which neglect their complex, and frequently subtle, inherent dynamical properties. These traditional approaches have enjoyed considerable success while systems are run in predominantly cooperative environments, and provided that their performance boundaries are not approached. With the current proliferation of applications using and relying on such infrastructures, these infrastructures are becoming increasingly stressed, and as a result the incentives for malicious attacks are heightening. The stunning fact is that the fundamental assumptions under which all significant large-scale distributed infrastructures have been constructed and analyzed no longer hold; the invalidity of these non-dynamical assumptions is witnessed with the greater frequency of catastrophic failures in major infrastructures such as the Internet, the power grid, the air traffic system, and national-scale telecommunication systems.

This project is about network, reliability and robustness in large-scale systems. The major vision of this program is ubiquitous: we have distributed computing and information and would like to link these via secure communications to allow coordination of limited resources to achieve

*This research was supported by AFOSR DoD award number 49620-01-1-0365

global objectives that can be both predicted and guaranteed. The objective is to ensure that incorrect local decisions, due to dynamical effects, do not cause large-scale failures.

To address the challenges posed by dynamical behavior of large-scale network infrastructures, we bring to bear the tools and techniques of control theory together with those from communication networks and queuing theory. In particular, the algorithms and analytical approaches of control used for developing control strategies and logic are combined with protocol design methods to construct new, secure architectures for distributed networks. We focus on the dominant issues of complex dynamic behavior, local rather than global information and state, distributed rather than centralized decision making, secure, robust performance in an uncertain environment, and dynamic network connectivity.

1   Introduction

The objective of this project is to advance the security and reliability of large-scale network infrastructures. The research is specifically targeted at the most critical medium- and long-term security and performance issues facing current and future military networks, as well as homeland installations. The program is focused both on fundamental scientific understanding of the mechanisms by which single attacks can lead to catastrophic cascading failures caused by dynamic effects of propagation, misprioritization and instability, as well as development of new protocols which eliminate such vulnerabilities. The research of this URI is already having significant impact on the commercial sector, affecting the router designs of Cisco, and the protocol designs of Microsoft and Nokia, as well as the open protocols behind TCP and AQM.

The program 1) analyzes the decisions made by routers and layer protocols to see how they lead to network-level consequences; 2) studies the propagation dynamics of the network to characterize instabilities; 3) has developed protocols that eliminate these instabilities; 4) studies the measurable indicators of high-throughput data streams that can be used to detect attempted attacks in real-time and monitor network performance; 5) formulates new methods, such as combining routing and coding over multiple paths, that make certain classes of attack much more difficult; 6) develops information-based randomized algorithms that prevent attacks which depend on distributed, multi-source simultaneous attack and response; 7) re-examines the basic protocols of the network to suggest modifications that can be incrementally deployed, without requiring all users to simultaneously change software systems; 8) understands the parallels and distinctions between data networks and transportation and energy networks, noting that each of these three infrastructures has witnessed large-scale catastrophic failures of similar nature in recent years; and 9) has worked on a fundamental rethinking of how such networks function, to guide designers of the next generation of systems.

Traditional approaches to increasing network security have primarily focused on protecting the integrity of nodes at the edge of the network rather than systematic and robust design of the network itself. In these traditional approaches the emphasis has been on improving encryption, key-exchange protocols and intelligent attack detection, so as to achieve nodes with extremely fortified defenses. This does not however protect against the catastrophic failures we have witnessed in recent years on the Internet and the National Power Grid, where nodes misinform each other, or under- or over-react to remote events, causing large-scale cascading failures. In current networks knowledge of which nodes to rely upon to make mission-critical decisions is being passed through and fed back via increasingly long chains of intermediaries, each of which inherently decreases the reliability of the global system. A secure layer is important, but in order to have more than a secure layer on top of a fragile foundation layer it is necessary to design security and robustness into the system interactions. The Internet requires end-user protocol-based cooperation, and the Power Grid requires multiple control centers; the Stanford URI is working on architectures which require neither of these limitations. In particular, this URI program is developing sophisticated mathematical models and systematic tools, and using them not only for post-mortem analysis of attacks and failures but also to design and implement new protocols which are resistant to these modes of failure.

This work is undergoing transition to current communication networks, and will have significant application to future military mixed wired and wireless command and control networks. The focus is on attacks at the network infrastructure level, not on attacks on the computers at the edge of the network.

2   Congestion and Buffering in Wired networks

We have studied the problem of designing globally stable, scalable congestion control algorithms for the Internet. Prior work primarily used linear stability as the criterion for such a design. Global stability has been studied only for single node, single source problems. In our work, we have obtained conditions for a general topology network accessed by sources with heterogeneous delays. We obtain a sufficient condition for global stability in terms of the increase and decrease parameters of the congestion control algorithm and the price functions used at the links.

The key idea in our recent work is to first show that the source rates are both upper and lower bounded, and then use these bounds in Razumikhin's theorem to derive conditions for global stability. However, a stumbling block in extending earlier results to a general network is the difficulty in obtaining reasonable bounds on the source rates and in finding an appropriate Lyapunov-Razumikhin function. We take a significant step in this direction by finding a Lyapunov-Razumikhin function that provides global stability conditions for a general topology network with heterogeneous delays.

The global stability condition derived thereby is delay-independent, and is given in terms of the increase and decrease parameters and a parameter of the price function. When the condition holds, the network is globally stable for all values of fixed communication delays and controller gains. It is different from most prior works, where the conditions are given in term of the gains and the delays. Since our global stability condition is delay-independent, the network is robust to the delays and the gains used by users in the network. On the other hand, our stability condition restricts the possible choices for the utility functions and the price functions, whereas earlier stability conditions like work for general utility functions. Characterizing the stability region when our condition is violated, but the local stability condition still holds, is still an open problem. Our simulation results indicate that the region of attraction could be large under such a scenario.

We show that one can obtain conditions for global stability that relate the parameters of the congestion algorithm to the parameters of the price functions used at the links of the network. We further considered a two-phase algorithm, with a slow-start phase followed by a congestion-avoidance phase, as in today's version of TCP-Reno, and showed that a three-phase approximation of this two-phase algorithm is still globally, asymptotically stable under the same conditions on the congestion control parameters.

2.1   Sizing issues in buffer routers

Large buffers in Internet routers often limit achievable throughput, requiring the use of off-chip DRAMs. A standard guideline used for buffer size design is $B = RTT \times C$, where C is the capacity of the link and RTT is the round trip time. Recently, this design rule has been questioned and the use of small buffer routers was validated based on statistical multiplexing effects.

However, these results have been based on *static* network simulations with *fixed number of flows*. In our work, we have completed far more extensive network simulations evaluating the accuracy of these results in a *dynamic* environment where file flows arrive and depart, i.e., flow numbers are not fixed. More specifically, we assess the performance of dynamic networks with very small buffers, with the end-user in mind. As flows arrive and depart, link utilization should not be considered as the most important factor in the design of the network. In a static network, where the number of flows is fixed, utilization and goodput have a direct correspondence as each user sees an average throughput of $\frac{C \times U}{N}$. In a dynamic network, the number of flows is time-varying: there is no such correspondence between the link utilization and the end-to-end throughput. Therefore, we directly calculate end-to-end throughput seen by the users and use this as a metric for evaluating performance.

For completeness we first completed simulations with fixed number of long flows. We then showed that in this case smaller buffers can indeed be used without any significant effects on throughput. We then further showed that Poisson pacing of TCP is not necessary. In fact, our simulations demonstrate that the effect of short flows and RTT variations create sufficient randomness to ensure high link utilization.

The current Internet consists of extremely fast core routers and slow edge routers. The edge routers switch packets at a rate which is several orders of magnitude smaller than the core routers.

Our simulations show that in this case, very small buffers can be used without affecting the throughput, even in a dynamic network.

We have also considered the case where edge routers switch packets at a rate comparable to that of core routers, that is, there are no access bandwith constraints. In this case, our simulation results demonstrate that if the network is moderately congested, then increasing the buffer size will in fact result in a substantial increase in overall throughput. As an example, when the load on a 100Mbps link is approximately 80%, we find an increase in average throughput of between 60%-100% as the buffer size is increased from 20 to 1000 packets. We have now showed that TCP-pacing does not improve average throughput significantly.

Considering the same architecture as in the preceding discussion, we show that under mildly loaded conditions (load less than 50%), increased buffer sizes do not lead to increased throughput. That is, small buffers are adequate only when the core router is guaranteed to operate at 50% load, or less. In summary, in contrast to previous work, our simulations show that actual performance of routers with small buffers depends on the type of Internet architecture assumed.

2.2 Fluid model development and analysis of priority processing schemes in the Internet

Previous simulation studies have shown that providing a simple priority to short flows in Internet routers can dramatically reduce their mean delay while having little impact on the long flows that carry the bulk of the Internet traffic. We have proposed simple fluid models that can be used to quantify these observations. These fluid models are justified by showing that stochastic models of resource-sharing among TCP flows converge to these fluid models when the router capacity and the number of users is large.

We showed that a Shortest Remaining Processing Time (SRPT) scheme dramatically improves short flow performance, while having little impact on long flows. This scheme requires the router to estimate whether the flow is short or long, which is not feasible given that routers do not have access to per-flow information. Alternatively, using simple sampling techniques, it can be determined fairly accurately whether a flow is long or short. Assuming such a mechanism exists and can be easily implemented, we evaluate the performance of such priority processing schemes analytically, and further strengthen our conclusions via simulations.

Without priorities, the nature of bandwidth sharing in the Internet favors long flows. A more equitable sharing discipline can be approximated by discriminatory processor sharing (DPS). Stochastic analysis of DPS is extremely difficult and closed-form solutions exist only for exponentially distributed service times. However, in a system with a large number of files and a large server capacity, such as the Internet, some form of the law of large numbers can be applied and the resulting stochastic system can be approximated by a deterministic system that can be modeled by a set of differential equations. We have proposed such fluid flow models to capture the resource sharing character of TCP flows in the Internet. These models consider the impact of access bandwidth constraints. Using these models, we showed analytically that a stochastic model for DPS converges to the fluid limit in a large system. This further characterizes the speed of convergence of the fluid limit to equilibrium.

2.3   Connection-level stability analysis in the Internet

In this work, we have studied connection-level models of file transfer requests in the Internet, where connection arrivals to each route occur according to Poisson processes and the file-sizes have phase-type distributions. We use Sum-of-Squares techniques to construct Lyapunov functions statisfying Foster's condition for stochastic stability.

3   Scheduling and Resource Allocation in Wireless Networks

3.1   A Large Deviations Analysis of Scheduling

In [37] we consider a cellular network consisting of a base station and N receivers. The channel states of the receivers are assumed to be identical and independent of each other. The goal is to compare the throughput of two different scheduling policies (a queue-length-based policy and a greedy scheduling policy) given an upper bound on the queue overflow probability or the delay violation probability. We consider a multi-state channel model, where each channel is assumed to be in one of L states. Given an upper bound on the queue overflow probability or an upper bound on the delay violation probability, we show that the total network throughput of the queue-length-based policy is no less than the throughput of the greedy policy for all N. We also obtain a lower bound on the throughput of the queue-length-based policy. For sufficiently large N, the lower bound is shown to be tight, strictly increasing with N, and strictly larger than the throughput of the greedy policy. Further, for a simple multi-state channel model (on-off channel), we prove that the lower bound is tight for all N.

Multiuser wireless scheduling has received much attention in recent years. Consider a cellular network consisting of a base station and N users (receivers), where the base station maintains N separate queues, one corresponding to each user. Assume time is slotted and the channel states of the receivers at each time slot are known at the base station. Then, the base station can decide which queues to serve according to their channel states. We considered the case where the base station operates in a TDMA fashion, i.e., the base station can serve only one queue in each time slot. Two scheduling policies have been widely studied in the literature: (i) the base station serves the user with the best (weighted) channel state (opportunistic scheduling) [34, 19]; or (ii) serve the one with the best queue-length-weighted channel state (queue-length based (QLB) scheduling)

[31, 11, 26, 27, 7, 4, 21]. While the QLB scheduling is throughput optimal (i.e., can stabilize any set of user throughputs that can be stabilized by any other algorithm), opportunistic scheduling maximizes the total network throughput if all queues are continuously backlogged. If the arrival rates to the users are identical and the channel state distributions to the receivers are identical, then these two scheduling policies have the same stability region.

While stability is the first concern of scheduling policies, quality-of-service (QoS) is equally important in applications. For example, we may require the queue overflow probability to be small or require small delays. The performance of different scheduling policies under QoS constraints has received much attention recently. For reasons of analytical tractability, much of the prior work assumes that the channels to all the receivers are independent and statistically identical. Under this assumption, and assuming identical user utilities, opportunistic scheduling policies become greedy policies in which the base station transmits to the receiver with the best channel state. In [25], the author studies a simple network consisting of two users where the channels are assumed to be independent, identically distributed ON-OFF channels. Using large-deviations techniques, it is shown that the total network throughput of the QLB policy is larger than the throughput of the greedy policy under the queue overflow constraint. In [11], a wireless network with N users and ON-OFF channels is considered. It is assumed that the arrivals are identical and Poisson, and the capacity when the channel is ON is one packet per time slot. It is then shown that, when the number of users increases from N to $2N$, the expected sum of queue lengths is non-increasing under the QLB policy, while it increases linearly under the greedy policy. Further, in [8], the behavior of the greedy policy for Rayleigh fading channels is studied and it is shown that under a delay constraint, the total network throughput of the greedy policy increases initially with the number of users, but eventually decreases and goes to zero when the number of the users is sufficiently large.

Motivated by these prior results, in our work reported in [37], we study the performance of the two scheduling policies (greedy and QLB) for a wireless network with multi-state channels and constant arrivals. Using sample-path large-deviations techniques that have been used in [5], [25] and [29], we obtain the following results:

1. Assuming a multi-state channel model and a constant arrival rate in each time slot, under the QLB policy, we compute a lower bound on the large-deviations exponent of the probability that at least one queue in the network exceeds a large threshold. We obtain lower bounds on the maximum network throughput under the QoS constraints, and for large N, the lower bounds are tight, strictly increasing, and strictly greater than the throughput of the greedy policy. For the ON-OFF channel model, we prove that the lower bounds are tight for all N. It was conjectured that in [25] that, for the ON-OFF channel model, the complexity of the calculation of the large-deviations exponent increases exponentially with increasing N, but we show here that a simple closed-form expression can be obtained.

2. Consider ON-OFF channels and the QLB policy. In [11], under the assumption that the channel capacity is one packet per time slot, for a different model, it is shown the expected sum of the queue lengths is nondecreasing when the number of users increases from N to $2N$. For the ON-OFF channel model, we show that the maximum network throughput is strictly increasing in N under the delay-violation constraint or queue overflow constraint. Our result does not only compare performance with N users and $2N$ users, but at all intermediate values as well. Our result also holds even when the capacity of the network is greater than one packet-per-slot. Further, for the general multi-state channel model, the maximum throughput is shown to be strictly increasing with N for large N.

3. For the greedy policy, we analytically show that the throughput goes to a constant under the queue overflow constraint, and decreases to zero under the delay violation constraint. This result holds for the general multi-state channel model, and is consistent with the numerical results for Rayleigh fading channels in [8].

4. Under the QoS constraints, we show that the throughput of the QLB scheduling policy is no less than the throughput of the greedy policy. This conclusion was also obtained in [25] for a two-user system and under the queue overflow constraint. Here, we prove that it is true for networks with N users ($N \geq 2$) and multi-state channels.

3.2   Distributed Fair Resource Allocation in Cellular Networks in the Presence of Heterogeneous Delays

In [38] we consider the problem of allocating resources at a base station to many competing flows, where each flow is intended for a different receiver. The channel conditions may be time-varying and different for different receivers. It has been shown in [8] that in a delay-free network, a combination of queue-length-based scheduling at the base station and congestion control at the end users can guarantee queue-length stability and fair resource allocation. We extended this result to wireless networks where the congestion information from the base station is received with a feedback delay at the transmitters. The delays can be heterogenous (i.e., different transmitters may have different round-trip delays) and time-varying, but are assumed to be upper-bounded, with possibly very large upper bounds. We showed that the joint congestion control-scheduling algorithm continues to be stable and continues to provide a fair allocation of the network resources.

We have studied the problem of fair allocation of resources in the downlink of a cellular wireless network consisting of a single base station and many receivers (see Figure 1). The data destined for each receiver is maintained in a separate buffer. The arrivals to the buffers are determined via a congestion control mechanism. We assume that the time is slotted. The channels between the base station and the receivers are assumed to have random time-varying gains which are independent from

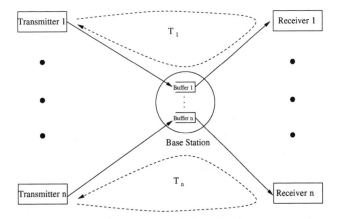

Figure 1: Network with feedback delays. The channel from the base station to the receivers is time-varying.

one time-slot to the next. The independence assumption can be relaxed easily, but we use it here for ease of exposition. The goal is to allocate the network capacity fairly among the users, in accordance with the needs of the users, while exploiting the time-variations in the channel conditions. We associate a utility function with each user that is a concave, increasing function of the mean service that it receives from the network. In an earlier paper [8], it was shown that a combination of Internet-style congestion control at the end-users and queue-length based scheduling at the base station achieves the goal of fair and stabilizing resource allocation. This result is somewhat surprising since the resource constraints in the case of a wireless network are very different from the linear constraints in the case of the Internet [28]. The relative merits of congestion control-based resource allocation scheme as compared to other resource allocation schemes for cellular networks are discussed in [8]. Several other works in the same context are [30, 18, 20]. However, none of these works explicitly include the effect of feedback delay in their analysis. One of the reasons that delay is not important in these other works is that a specific scheduling algorithm is used in the network which allows the congestion control to be based only on the queue length at the entry node of each source. However, we considered a situation where such scheduling is not used and where the bottleneck is at the cellular network while the sources may be located far away from the base station. An example of such a situation is a file transfer from a remote host over the downlink of a cellular network. We aim to consider the effect of this essential parameter on the fairness and stability properties of the algorithm presented in [8].

In [8], it is assumed that there are no delays in the transmission of packets from an end-user (transmitter) to the base station and in the transmission of congestion information from the base station back to the end users. But if we consider the case where the end users are connected to the base station through the Internet, then delays exist in both directions: there is a propagation delay τ_i^f from the end user i to the base station — we call it the forward delay of the end user i, and a propagation delay τ_i^b from the base station to the end user i — we call it the backward delay. It is well-known that the presence of delays may affect the performance of the network. For example, Internet congestion controllers which are globally stable for the delay-free network may become unstable if the feedback delays are large [28]. In our problem, when delays exist, the information the end users obtain will be "outdated" information. So the congestion information the users obtain at time t does not reflect the queue status at the base station at time t. So it is interesting to study a wireless network with delays and ask whether the conclusions of [8] still hold for wireless networks with heterogeneous delays. We answer this question by showing that for a network with uniformly-bounded delays, which are potentially heterogeneous and time-varying, the algorithm of [8] is stable and can be used to approximate weighted-m fair allocation arbitrarily closely. We emphasize that the results hold for networks with arbitrarily large, but bounded time-varying delays. So even if the end users can only get very old feedback information from the base station, the network is still stable and can eventually reach the fair resource allocation.

3.3   Simultaneous Routing and Resource Allocation

In wireless data networks the optimal routing of data depends on the link capacities which, in turn, are determined by the allocation of communications resources (such as transmit powers and signal bandwidths) to the links. The optimal performance of the network can only be achieved by simultaneous optimization of routing and resource allocation.

The paper [120] studies the simultaneous routing and resource allocation problem and exploits problem structure to derive efficient solution methods. We use a capacitated multicommodity flow model for the data flows in the network. We assume that the capacity of a wireless link is a concave and increasing function of the communications resources allocated to the link (TDMA and FDMA systems), and the communications resources for groups of links are limited. These assumptions allow us to formulate the simultaneous routing and resource allocation problem as a convex optimization problem over the network flow variables and the communications variables. These two sets of variables are coupled only through the link capacity constraints. We exploit this separable structure by dual decomposition. The resulting solution method attains the optimal coordination of data routing in the network layer and resource allocation in the radio control layer via pricing on the link capacities.

In [118], we generalize the simultaneous routing and resource allocation formulation to include CDMA wireless systems. Although link capacity constraints of CDMA systems are not jointly convex in rates and powers, we show that by using coordinate projections or transformations, the simultaneous routing and power allocation problem can still be formulated as (in systems with interference cancellation) or approximated by (in systems without interference cancellation) a convex optimization problem which can be solved very efficiently. We also propose a heuristic link-removal procedure based on the convex approximation to further improve the system performance.

4 Fault Diagnosis over Packet Dropping Networks

There are several challenges that arise when trying to perform management and control over unreliable, possibly heterogeneous networks. The major concern is the fact that, due to the nature of network links, observations may be delayed, lost or received out of order. In such case, diagnosers or controllers that use this underlying network infrastructure need to be able to cope with the unreliability of the communication links in an effective and reliable manner. Within the context of this URI project, we have been exploring a number of directions that aim to achieve this ultimate goal.

4.1 Probabilistic Fault Detection and Identification

Another direction that we have been pursuing is along the lines of our work on systematic and efficient methodologies for fault management in dynamic systems. For example, we have developed probabilistic schemes for detecting permanent or transient functional changes (faults) in large-scale discrete event systems that can be modeled as finite-state machines. In one particular setup, the detector observes the frequencies with which states are occupied and detects faults by analyzing the deviation between the expected frequencies and the actual measurements. These features can be useful in distributed or networked settings where the input-state order may not be known and, at this point, we are considering applications of these ideas in the context of statistical methods for network security and intrusion detection. This work appeared as an invited paper during the 2002 Conference on Decision and Control; an extended version of it also appeared in the IEEE Transactions on Automatic Control.

More recently, we have began the investigation of schemes for observing/diagnosing/controlling systems or networks under unreliable information that might arise due to permanent or transient faults in the system sensors. More specifically, we have developed a probabilistic methodology for failure diagnosis in finite state machines given a sequence of unreliable (possibly corrupted) observations. Assuming prior knowledge of the input probability distribution but no knowledge of the actual input sequence, the core problem we considered aimed at choosing from a pool of known, deterministic finite state machines (FSMs) the one that most likely matches a given (output) sequence of observations. The main challenge is that errors, such as symbol insertions, deletions, and transpositions, may corrupt the observed output sequence; the cause of these errors could be a faulty sensor or problems encountered in the communication channels or network links connecting the system sensors with the diagnoser/observer. Given the possibly erroneous output sequence of observations, we have proposed an efficient recursive algorithm for obtaining the most likely underlying FSM. We have illustrated the proposed methodology using as an example the diagnosis (identification) of a communication protocol.

Along these lines, we have also been able to make connections with the literature on hidden

Markov models. To this end, we are currently trying to understand the role of reduced-order models and the role of modeling methodologies such as hidden Markov models or the influence model. We believe that this work will have important practical implications because it relates directly to the issue of sensor reliability and cost (i.e., the task of determining the required levels of reliability for the system sensors in order to guarantee a certain level of performance).

4.2   Distributed Symmetric Function Computation in Noisy Wireless Sensor Networks with Binary Data

With the wide availability of inexpensive wireless technology and sensing hardware, wireless sensor networks are expected to become commonplace because of their broad range of potential applications. A wireless sensor network consists of sensors that have sensing, computation and wireless communication capabilities. Each sensor monitors the environment surrounding it, collects and processes data, and when appropriate transmits information so as to cooperatively achieve a global detection objective. We have considered the common situation where there is a single fusion center, and the network goal is to cooperatively provide information to this fusion center so it can compute some function of the sensor measurements.

We have investigated this problem in multi-hop networks with noisy communication channels where the measurement of each sensor consists of one bit. We consider a sensor network consisting of n sensors, each having a recorded bit, the sensor's measurement, which has been set to either "0" or "1". The goal of the fusion center is to compute a symmetric function of these bits; i.e., a function that depends only on the number of sensors that have a "1". Specifically, distributed symmetric function computation with binary data, which is also called a counting problem, is as follows: each node is in either state "1" or "0", and the fusion center needs to decide, using information transmitted from the network, the number of sensors in state "1".

The sensors convey information to the fusion center in a multi-hop fashion to enable the function computation. The problem studied is to minimize the total transmission energy used by the network when computing this function, subject to the constraint that this computation is correct with high probability.

When nothing is known about the structure of the function to be computed, all bits must to be transmitted to the fusion center, and this is purely a routing problem when the channels are reliable. When the wireless channels are unreliable, the use of channel coding (see, for example, [9]) makes it possible to convey information in a point-to-point fashion with arbitrarily small amounts of error. However, the use of point-to-point error-correction coding without any in-network processing may result in high energy cost and delay. Our focus is computation of symmetric functions in a noisy wireless sensor network when total energy consumption *is* a major concern.

The algorithms considered are related to the algorithms for distributed computation over noisy networks, which are studied in [10, 23, 24, 22, 17], and references within. In both problems, the goal is to compute the value of some function based on the information of the nodes. Our work is closely related to parity computation and threshold detection in noisy radio networks studied in [10] and [17], respectively, where a broadcast network is assumed, in which all nodes can hear all transmissions, and each node has a "1" or a "0". The goal in [10, 17] was to investigate the minimum number of transmissions required to compute the parity or decide whether the number of nodes in state "1" has exceeded the threshold value. Note that parity and threshold detection are special cases of counting, since both of these are determined if we know how many nodes have "1".

While the problems considered in [10] and [17] are similar to our problem, a major difference is that in our model, each node may not be able to hear every other node in the network. The reason for this is that energy consumption can be an important consideration in wireless networks and it is well-known that it can be reduced significantly if the transmissions are carried out in a multi-hop fashion. This is a consequence of the well-known propagation model used to model wireless communication channels, whereby the energy required to transmit over a distance of r is proportional to r^α, where $\alpha \geq 2$ is a constant depending upon the environment. Thus, instead of each sensor sending its information to the fusion center directly, it is more efficient from an energy consumption point of view to send the information through relay nodes. It may be possible to reduce energy consumption even further by using some form of in-network data processing. This may have further benefits; for instance, if all the sensor measurements are to be transmitted from the sensors to the fusion center, then relay nodes closer to the fusion center would be depleted of their energy faster than nodes that are further away from the fusion center. Thus, in-network processing to reduce the number of transmissions could be beneficial for eliminating hotspots. Fundamentally, this is the distinction between multi-hop wireless networks used for communication and multi-hop wireless networks used for sensing. In multi-hop wireless communication networks, the protocols are designed so that they are not application-specific, and therefore the network can support a constantly evolving set of applications. Contrasting this, in multi-hop sensor networks, the architecture and protocols can be designed for each specific application, exploiting its structure, to reduce the energy usage within the network. This is the motivation for the recent works reported in [12] and [15]. In [12], the authors have designed a block coding scheme to compress the amount of information to be transmitted in a sensor network computing some functions. In [15], the authors investigate the optimal computation time and the minimum energy consumption required to compute the maximum of the sensor measurements. However, the in-network processing that we consider is different from the processing considered in [12] and [15], where the communication channels are assumed to be reliable, and the processing is to primarily exploit the spatial correlation [15] or the spatio-temporal correlations [12]. In our problem, processing is required not only to reduce the redundancy in the information to be conveyed in the fusion center, but also to introduce some redundancy to combat the effect of the noisy channels in the sensor network. Our results show that the additional redundancy required to combat channel errors does not significantly negate the benefits of in-network computation used to eliminate redundancy in the information, and the combination of in-network computation and channel coding could reduce the number of transmissions required in multi-hop networks to the same order as the number required in single-hop networks.

We use the routing protocol in [12] along with ideas from distributed parity computation in noisy networks ([10]) to devise near energy-optimal algorithms for counting in sensor networks. A key difference between our work and the work in [10] is that, in the case of sensor networks, the fusion center does not communicate directly with each of the sensors. Thus, local computation is necessary before conveying some aggregate information in a multi-hop fashion to the fusion center. The local computation in our case is not a simple parity computation as in [10] but as we will see later, the network needs to compute the number of sensors in each local neighborhood (called a *cell*) that have seen a "1". Further, we require that the computation be accurate uniformly over all cells. In addition, we will show that error-correction coding is required in the algorithms to minimize the energy required for counting.

We assume the wireless channels are binary symmetric channels with a probability of error p, and that each sensor uses r^α units of energy to transmit each bit, where r is the transmission range of the sensor. Using the above ideas, we first study the case where each sensor has only one observation to report, and show that the amount of energy required for counting (i.e., detecting the number of sensors seeing a "1") is $O\left(n(\log\log n)\left(\sqrt{\frac{\log n}{n}}\right)^\alpha\right)$, where n is the number of sensors in the network. We also show that any algorithm satisfying the performance constraints must necessarily have energy usage $\Omega\left(n\left(\sqrt{\frac{\log n}{n}}\right)^\alpha\right)$. Then, we consider the case where the sensor network observes N events, and each node records one bit per event, thus having N bits to convey. The fusion center now wants to compute N symmetric functions, one for each of the events. We then extend to the case where each sensor has N binary observations, and the symmetric function needs to be computed for each observation. We show that the total transmission energy consumption can be reduced to $O\left(n\left(\max\left\{1, \frac{\log\log n}{N}\right\}\right)\left(\sqrt{\frac{\log n}{n}}\right)^\alpha\right)$ per observation. When $N = \Omega(\log\log n)$, the energy consumption is $\Theta\left(n\left(\sqrt{\frac{\log n}{n}}\right)^\alpha\right)$ per observation, which is a tight bound. If we only want to know roughly (a notion made precise in [39]) how many sensors have "1". The answer can be obtained with the transmission energy consumption $\Theta\left(n\left(\sqrt{\frac{\log n}{n}}\right)^\alpha\right)$.

5 Decentralized Control

5.1 Control over Networks

The first line of research we have been pursuing relates to the study of the fundamental performance limitations of control methodologies that use existing network infrastructure as their communications backbone. For instance, by modeling a packet dropping network as an erasure channel and by focusing on bounded variance stabilization schemes, one can study the problem of plant stabilization despite message delays, packet drops, quantization noise and measurement noise. Our initial work on this problem appeared as an invited paper in the 2002 Conference on Decision and Control and focused on the case when the system to be stabilized is a discrete-time linear time-invariant system, the communication links (between sensors, controller(s) and actuators) are part of a packet dropping network in which transmissions are independent, and the network packets are large enough so that the effect of measurement quantization can be modeled by an additive white noise process. This work, which has been referenced extensively by many researchers, has also been extended to settings where the system to be stabilized is a continuous-time system, in which case one additional parameter that needs to be chosen is the sampling rate at which the sample-data controller is operating. We have been able to determine ways to optimally choose this and other parameters of this control problem, and our results are currently under revision in the IEE Proceedings on Control Theory and Applications.

Related to the task described above is our study of the effects of roundoff noise on our ability to detect and identify transient faults that affect the operation of control systems. This roundoff noise could arise due to finite precision limitations of our controllers or due to quantization that takes place when sending information of the underlying communication network (e.g., the Internet). Our analysis has provided insight that allows us to handle roundoff noise via explicit bounds on the precision needed to guarantee the correct identification of the number of errors. Our analytical bounds can be very tight for certain choices of design parameters and can be used to provide guidance about the design of fault-tolerant systems.

More recently, our group has been focusing its efforts in extending these ideas to settings where the network delays between different packets are not independent. To this end, we have been trying to make connections with work on linear jump Markov systems. We are also interested in understanding how different network protocols (e.g., forward error correction or path diversity techniques) can be used to enable more effective controllers.

5.2 Decentralized Observation and Monitoring

Another direction that we have been pursuing within the context of this project relates to the construction of observers for switched systems under unknown or partially known inputs. This is a situation that arises frequently in practice as unknown inputs are used to represent uncertain system dynamics and faults or, in the case of decentralized systems, control signals generated by other controllers. Within this line of work, we have obtained methods for constructing reduced-order state observers for linear systems with unknown inputs. Apart from making connections with existing work on system invertibility and fault detection and identification, our approach provides a characterization of observers with delay, which eases the established necessary conditions for existence of unknown input observers with zero-delay. Our techniques are quite general in that they encompass the design of full-order observers via appropriate choices of design matrices.

Our work has also looked at challenges that arise in monitoring and controlling discrete event systems over unreliable networks. For instance, we have looked at decentralized failure diagnosis schemes for systems that can be modeled as finite state machines. The specific scenario we considered consists of multiple local diagnosers, each with partial access to the outputs of the system under diagnosis. Our focus has been on designing a global coordinator which synchronizes with the local diagnosers at unspecified time intervals, and combines the local estimates in order to reach a final diagnosis. Under the assumption that the system and the local diagnosers are known, we have been able to analyze the effectiveness of simple types of global coordinators that operate without knowledge of the functionality of the system or the local diagnosers. In each case, we were able to derive conditions for finite-delay and zero-delay diagnosability, and to explore the trade-offs between the various schemes in terms of processing power and memory requirements on the global coordinator.

5.3   Decentralized Control

In order to develop systems that can coordinate with each other via communication the research in this program targets many new issues which are not present in the traditional feedback control scenario. These include distributed control decision based on local rather than global information, asynchronous information transmission, dynamic network topology, and scalability of algorithms to networks with large-numbers of nodes. Separate idealizations of the first two of these aspects of the problem have been possible in the past, although even these model problems lead to substantial difficulties in analysis. For example, one may use an idealized model of communication, and consider the simplest *decentralized control* problem. A general formulation of this problem can be reduced to one of structured control synthesis, a problem for which a systematic approach is lacking in the current literature.

Conversely, one may assume a centralized information pattern and consider the centralized control problem subject to *asynchronous communication*. In this case, instead of data consisting of continuous signals, data is now transmitted in packets. Furthermore, packets are subject to loss or delay, large packets may be fragmented and require reassembly, and packet streams may be received out of order. Control systems must be designed which are robust to these occurrences.

Given a particular plant and a constraint set of allowable decentralized controllers, one would like to determine if the associated control problem is, in a certain sense, easily solvable. The paper [121] develops a clear and precise characterization of when this is so. The notion of *quadratic invariance* is introduced in that paper, and is outlined here.

We suppose we have a linear plant G, and a subspace of admissible controllers S, which captures any sparsity constraints on the controller. The set S is called quadratically invariant if KGK is an element of S for all K in S. The paper shows that, if the constraint set has this property, then a controller which minimizes any norm of the closed-loop system may be efficiently found.

The area of decentralized control systems has been a source of challenging problems for many years. Starting with work on team theory, there have been many results showing that problems with certain information structures may be solved, and recently many papers have developed specific optimization methods to address these problems. Examples include decentralized control where the systems are chained in a particular way, as well as arrays of systems where information satisfies certain delay requirements. Our work provides a unifying framework in which to analyze these systems. So far, all of the known solvable problems to which we have applied this theory have been found to be quadratically invariant.

There are many links here to other active areas of research within this project, in particular to the work on the decentralized congestion control mechanisms used by TCP in the Internet. Further work remains, as there are important questions of computational complexity, since many decentralized control problems are known to be intractable. It is also known that many decentralized linear control systems have optimal controllers which are nonlinear. Our work addresses some extremely fundamental issues which are a central concern, and produces results which are both theoretically important and practically relevant.

5.4   Monitoring and Control of Power System Dynamics

We have addressed monitoring and control of system-wide electromechanical (or 'swing') dynamics in power systems, as well as the dynamics of auction-based electricity markets. We showed that observer-based power system monitors can be used to estimate the full state of the system as well as identify and isolate a number of events (e.g., faults) using only sparse local measurements, all in the presence of various system disturbances. This work also develops and exploits a spatio-temporally integrated view of electromechanical dynamics. This contrasts with the traditional approach of either studying temporal variations at fixed spatial points or investigating spatial variations of specified (e.g., modal) temporal behavior. We use a continuum model of the swing dynamics to expose the wave-like propagation of electromechanical disturbances and to gain insight for the design of controls. This leads to strategies for decentralized control of these electromechanical waves, drawing on prototype controllers found in electromagnetic transmission line theory (e.g., matched-impedance terminations) and active vibration damping (e.g., energy-absorbing controllers and vibration isolators). Finally, we have proposed various controllers to realize quenching or confining-and-quenching strategies, and tested these in simulations of a 179-bus reduced-order representation of the power grid of the western US and Canada.

6   Complexity and robustness in complex networks

Recent progress in systems biology and network-based technological systems, together with new mathematical theories, has revealed generalized principles that shed new light on complex networks, and confirmed the observations that an inherent feature of complex multiscale systems is that they are "robust yet fragile" (RYF). They are both intrinsically robust under most normative conditions and yet can be extremely sensitive to certain perturbations in their environment and component parts. This RYF feature provides a new paradigm for thinking about complexity and evolution across a broad range of phenomena and scales from computer networks to immune systems, from power grids and cancers to ecosystems, financial markets and human societies. While this research draws heavily on systems and control theory, most papers have appeared in biology, networking, and physics journals. In this section, we will review recent progress in theory and applications aimed at an engineering audience.

This research builds on insights about the fundamental nature of complex biological and technological networks that can now be drawn from the convergence of three research themes. 1) Molecular biology has provided a detailed description of much of the components of biological networks, and with the growing attention to systems biology the organizational principles of these networks are becoming increasingly apparent. 2) Advanced technology has provided engineering examples of networks with complexity approaching that of biology. While the components differ from biology, we have found striking convergence at the network level of architecture and the role of layering, protocols, and feedback control in structuring complex multiscale modularity. Our research is leading to new theories of the Internet and to new protocols that are being tested and deployed for high performance scientific computing. 3) Most importantly, there is a new mathematical framework for the study of complex networks that suggests that this apparent network-level evolutionary convergence both within biology and between biology and technology is not accidental, but follows necessarily from the requirements that both biology and technology be efficient, adaptive, evolvable, and robust to perturbations in their environment and component parts. This theory builds on and integrates decades of research in pure and applied mathematics with engineering, and specifically with robust control theory.

Through evolution and natural selection or by deliberate design, such systems exhibit highly functional and symbiotic interactions of extremely heterogeneous components, the very essence of "complexity". At the same time this resulting organization allows, and even facilitates, severe fragility to cascading failure triggered by relatively small perturbations. Thus robustness and fragility are deeply intertwined in biological systems, and in fact the mechanisms that create their extraordinary robustness are also responsible for their greatest fragilities. Our highly regulated and efficient metabolism evolved when life was physical challenging and food was often scarce. In a modern lifestyle, this robust metabolism can contribute to obesity and diabetes. More generally, our highly controlled physiology creates an ideal ecosystem for parasites, who hijack our robust cellular machinery for their own purposes. Our immune system prevents most infections but can cause devastating autoimmune diseases, including a type of diabetes. Our complex physiology requires robust development and regenerative capacity in the adult, but this very robustness at the cellular level is turned against us in cancer. We protect ourselves in highly organized and complex societies which facilitate spread of epidemics and destruction of our ecosystems. We rely on ever advancing technologies, but these confer both benefits and horrors previously unimaginable. This universal "robust yet fragile" (RYF) nature of complex systems is well-known to experts such as physicians and systems engineers, but has been systematically studied in any unified way only recently. It is now clear that it must be treated explicitly in any theory that hopes to explain the emergence of biological complexity, and indeed is at the heart of complexity itself.

These RYF features appear on all time and space scales, from the tiniest microbes and cellular subsystems up to global ecosystems, and also -we believe- to human social systems, and from the oldest known history of the evolution of life through human evolution to our latest technological innovations. Typically, our networks protect us, which is a major reason for their existence. But in addition to cancer, epidemics, and chronic auto-immune disease, the rare but catastrophic market crashes, terrorist attacks, large power outages, computer network virus epidemics, and devastating fires, etc, remind us that our complexity always comes at a price. Statistics reveal that most dollars and lives lost in natural and technological disasters happen in just a small subset of the very largest events, while the typical event is so small as to usually go unreported. The emergence of complexity can be largely seen as a spiral of new challenges and opportunities which organisms exploit, but lead to new fragilities, often to novel perturbations. These are met with increasing complexity and robustness, which in turn creates new opportunities but also new fragilities, and so on. This is not an inexorable trend to greater complexity, however, as there are numerous examples of lineages evolving increasing simplicity in response to less uncertain environments. This is particularly true of parasites that rely on their hosts to control fluctuations in their microenvironment, thus shielding them from the larger perturbations that their hosts experience.

It is only fairly recently, and particularly the last few decades, that human technology has become focused not just on robustness, but on architectures that facilitate the evolution of new capabilities and the scaling to large system sizes. Protocol-based multilayer modular design is permeating advanced technologies of all kinds, but the Internet remains perhaps the most well-known example. It is also particularly suitable for our purposes for several reasons. The Internet, and cybertechnology generally, are unprecedented in the extent to which their features parallel biology. Their most salient features are often hidden from the user and thus as metaphors are often terribly misleading, yet are extremely useful when right. Only cybertechnology has the potential to rival biotechnology in accelerating the human/technology evolution, and the combined RYF spiral could have profound consequence. The most consistent, coherent, and salient features of all complex technologies are their protocols. To engineers, the term "protocol" is the set of rules by which components interact to create system-level functionality. Indeed, in advanced technologies, and we believe in the organization of cells and organisms, the protocols are more fundamental than the modules whose interconnection they facilitate, although they often are obscured by the overwhelming details that now characterize experimental results in biology. A central feature of efficient, protocol-based systems is that, provided they obey the protocols, modules can be exchanged. The details are less important here than the consequences, which are the system-level robustness and evolvability that these protocols facilitate. New and even radically different hardware is easily incorporated at the lowest physical layers, and even more radically varying applications are enabled at the highest layers. Ironically as in biology, it is these transient elements of hardware and application software that are most visible to the user, while the far more fundamental and persistent infrastructure is the core protocols, which by design remain largely hidden from the user.

A protocol-based organization facilitates coordination and integration of function to create coherent and global adaptation to variations in their components and environments on a vast range of time scales despite implementation mechanisms that are largely decentralized and asynchronous. The parallels here between the Internet and biology are particularly striking. The TCP/IP protocol suite enables adaptation and control on time scale from the sub-microsecond changes in physical media, to the millisecond-to-second changes in traffic flow, to the daily fluctuations in user interactions, to evolving hardware and application modules over years and decades. The remarkable robustness to changing circumstances and evolution of Internet-related technology could only have come about as the result of a highly structured and organized suite of relatively invariant and universally-shared, well-engineered protocols.

Similarly, a protocol-based architecture in biology and its control mechanisms facilitate both robustness and evolvability, despite massive impinging pressures and variation in the environment. With the most obvious example involving the table of codons, biology's universally shared set of protocols are more fundamental and invariant than the modules whose control and evolution they facilitate. Allostery, a huge suite of post-translational modifications, and the rapid changes in location of macromolecular modules enable adaptive responses to environmental signals or alterations on rapid time scales. Translational and transcriptional control and regulation of alternative splicing and editing act on somewhat longer time scales. On still longer time scales within and across generations, the sequences of the DNA itself can change, not only through random mutation, but also through highly structured and evolved mechanisms that facilitate the generation of adaptive diversity. Furthermore, as biologists dig deeper past the superficiality of sequence data into the complexity of regulation, they unearth additional layers of control that are fundamentally similar to those in advanced technologies. There is seemingly no limit to the ingenuity that biology uses in creating additional layers of sophisticated control. Now familiar examples range from RNA editing and alternative splicing to transposons, mismatch repair, and repetitive sequences to the cutting and pasting in the "arms race" of the immune system versus spirochete and trypanosome coat proteins.

Perhaps the most familiar example of lateral gene transfer in bacteria is possible because bacteria have a shared set of protocols that have even been quite appropriately described by some as the "bacterial Internet." Bacteria can simply grab DNA encoding new genes from other bacteria and incorporate it into their genome, just like computer users can buy a new computer and plug it into home or office networks. This "plug and play" modularity works because there is a shared set of protocols that allow even novel genetic material to be functional in an entirely new cellular setting. Plug and play DNA mobility and expression is further facilitated by integrons and plasmids. Thus, for example, bacteria can acquire antibiotic resistance on time-scales that would be vanishingly improbable by point mutations, an example of how rapid evolution of complexity is possible by Darwinian mechanisms. Natural selection can favor the evolution of whole protocol suites, and their interactions, which in turn massively accelerate the acquisition and sharing of functional adaptive change. Thus evolvability itself can be seen as the robustness of lineages, rather than organisms, on long time scales and to possibly large changes in the environment, indeed ones that would be lethal to organisms if they occurred rapidly. An important insight is that robustness and evolvability are generally not in conflict, and both are the product of systematic and organized control mechanisms.

The framework being developed here is radical in both its methodology and philosophical implication. Methodologically it draws on mathematics that is often not well known outside expert circles and in many cases had not traditionally been thought of as "applied." The mathematics tells us that robustness and fragility have conserved quantities, and we believe these will ultimately be of as much importance to understanding biological complexity as energy and entropy were to understanding the steam engine and mitochondria. The above views of "organized complexity" motivated by biology and engineering contrast sharply with that of "emergent complexity" that is more popular within the physical sciences. Highly Optimized/Organized Tolerance/Tradeoffs (HOT) has aimed to explain the issues of organized complexity, but emphasizing models and concepts such as lattices, cellular automata, spin glasses, phase transitions, criticality, chaos, fractals, scale-free networks, self-organization, and so on, that have been the inspiration for the "emergent" perspective. A side benefit of this largely pedagogical effort is it has led to apparently novel insights into RYF aspects of longstanding mysteries in physics, from coherent structures in shear flow turbulence and coupled oscillators, to the ubiquity of power laws, to the nature of quantum entanglement, to the origin of dissipation. Finally, the underlying mathematics may offer new tools to explore other problems in physics where RYF features may play a role, particularly involving multiple scales and organized structures and phenomena.

7 Network Reliability

We have investigated the reliability of networks operated in a distributed manner to changes in the network. Our work is based on the use of network coding, which allows both distributed coding and distributed implementations of cost optimization for the subgraphs used for network coding. We have considered two main issues: 1) the reliability of networks to packet losses 2) the cost efficiency of distributed coding and optimization under changes of topology, cost and traffic.

Packet losses in networks result from a variety of causes, which include congestion, buffer over-flows, and, in wireless networks, link outage due to fading. Thus a method to ensure reliable communication is necessary, and the prevailing approach is for the receiver to send requests for the retransmission of lost packets over some feedback channel. There are, however, a number of drawbacks to such an approach, which are evident most notably in high-loss environments and for multicast connections. In both instances, many requests for retransmissions are usually required, which place an unnecessary load on the network and which may overwhelm the source. In the latter instance, there is the additional problem that retransmitted packets are often only of use to a subset of the receivers and are therefore redundant to the remainder. An approach that overcomes these drawbacks is to use erasure-correcting codes. Under such an approach, the original packets are reconstructed from those that are received and little or no feedback is required. This approach has been recently exemplified by digital fountain codes, which are fast, near-optimal erasure codes. Such codes can approach the capacity of connections over lossy packet networks, provided that the connection as a whole is viewed as a single channel and coding is performed only at the source node. But in lossy packet networks where all nodes have the capability for coding, such as overlay networks using UDP and wireless networks, there is no compelling reason to adopt this view, and a greater capacity can in fact be achieved if we do not.

We have developed a capacity-approaching coding scheme for unicast or multicast over lossy packet networks. In the scheme, all nodes perform coding, but do not wait for a full block of packets to be received before sending out coded packets. Rather, whenever they have a transmission opportunity, they form coded packets with random linear combinations of previously received packets. All coding and decoding operations in the scheme have polynomial complexity. Our analysis of the scheme has shown that it is not only capacity-approaching, but that the propagation of packets carrying innovative information follows that of a queueing network where every node acts as a stable MM1 queue. We are able to consider networks with both lossy point-to-point and broadcast links, allowing us to model both wireline and wireless packet networks.

In the area of distributed optimization, we have presented decentralized algorithms that compute minimum-cost subgraphs for establishing multicast connections in networks that use coding. These algorithms, coupled with existing decentralized schemes for constructing network codes, constitute a fully decentralized approach for achieving minimum cost multicast. Our approach is in sharp contrast to the prevailing approach based on approximation algorithms for the directed Steiner tree problem, which is suboptimal and generally assumes centralized computation with full network knowledge. We also have developed extensions beyond the basic problem of fixed-rate multicast in networks with directed point-to-point links, and consider the case of elastic rate demand as well as the problem of minimum energy multicast in wireless networks. For the case of optimization under changing conditions, we have given a formulation of the dynamic multicast problem for coded networks that lies within the framework of dynamic programming. Our formulation addresses the desired objective of finding minimum-cost time-varying subgraphs that can deliver continuous service to dynamic multicast groups in coded networks and, because it lies within the framework of dynamic programming, can be approached using methods developed for general dynamic programming problems. The solution that we propose uses such methods to approximate the optimal cost function, which is used to modify the objective function of an optimization that determines the multicast subgraph to use during each time interval. Depending upon the approximation that is used for the optimal cost function, this optimization conducted every time interval may be tractable and may even be amenable to decentralized computation.

7.1 Graph Structure and Similarity

We have investigated measures of graph similarity, developed a new measure, and applied it to the matching of graph fragments to their original locations in a parent graph. Measures of graph similarity have a broad array of applications, including comparing chemical structures, navigating complex networks like the World Wide Web, and more recently, analyzing different kinds of biological data. The research focuses on an interesting class of iterative algorithms that use the structural similarity of local neighborhoods to derive pairwise similarity scores between graph elements. Our new similarity measure uses a linear update to generate both node-node and edge-edge similarity scores, and has desirable convergence properties. The research also explores the application of our similarity measure to graph matching. We attempt to correctly position a subgraph within a parent graph using a maximum-weight matching algorithm applied to the similarity scores between the two graphs. Significant performance improvements are observed when the 'topological' information provided by the similarity measure is combined with additional information — such as partial labeling — about the attributes of the graph elements and their local neighborhoods. Further work is needed to explore various extensions of these ideas, including to the case of dynamically evolving graphs.

In other work, we study synchronization of complex random networks of nonlinear oscillators, with identical oscillators at the nodes interacting through 'diffusive' coupling across edges of the interconnection graph. Our random network is constructed by a generalized Erdos-Renyi method, so as to have specifiable expected-degree distribution. We present a sufficient condition for synchronization and a sufficient condition for desynchronization, stated in terms of the coupling strength and the extreme values of the distribution of nontrivial eigenvalues of the graph Laplacian. We then determine the Laplacian eigenvalue distribution for the case of large random graphs through computation of the moments of the eigenvalue density function. The analysis is illustrated using a random network with a power-law expected-degree distribution and chaotic dynamics at each node. The mathematical structure of our problem is closely related to that of consensus problems in networks of agents, as well as the task of analyzing flocking/swarming conditions in a group of autonomous agents.

8   Impact of research and transitions

1) The first important algorithm to be transitioned is Approximate Fair Dropping (AFD). This is a new randomized algorithm that partitions the bandwidth of a link among the flows traversing the link. It builds on the CHOKe (choose and keep or choose and kill) algorithm, which is a simple algorithm for protecting TCP flows from UDP flows and enables the detection of flows which attempt to take up a disproportionate share of resources. The randomized nature of the algorithms not only make them simpler to implement, but also prevents users from predicting and attempting to spoof their behavior. The AFD algorithm is in discussion for implementation in the CISCO GSR12000 series of core routers.

2) Secondly, the FAST (Fast AQM, Scalable TCP) protects the TCP protocol from instabilities which currently occur at high link speeds. These instabilities cause network throughput to drop to an extremely low level, and affect fast networks dramatically. Building on research from both the controls and networking community has led to this new protocol, which is both provably robust and scalable as well as incrementally deployable. In an experiment in November 2002, a speed of 8,609 megabits per second (Mbps) was achieved by using 10 simultaneous flows of data over routed paths, which is the largest aggregate throughput ever accomplished in such a configuration. FAST has been developed in significant part by Caltech, and has been transitioned through the Stanford Linear Accelerator Center (SLAC), working in partnership with the European Organization for Nuclear Research (CERN), and DataTAG, StarLight, TeraGrid, Cisco, and Level3.

3) This program has developed Distributed Random Coding (DRC), which combines the benefits of coding and routing into a single protocol. Here, instead of simply forwarding packets, nodes construct and forward algebraic combinations of inputs. This results in a network which has both significantly increased throughput as well as making it impossible for an observer to decode data transmitted by simply observing the network at a single point. This protocol has been implemented in a large-scale network testbed by Microsoft, working with Sprint.

All of the above protocols are backed up by theoretical analysis, with, for example, associated proofs of stability and convergence. The program has developed several further protocols for network security, including mechanisms for covert message transmission via timing channels, protection against SYN flooding, the SIFT algorithm for prioritization in caches and buffers, and the SHRiNK method for monitoring extremely large-scale networks.

References

[1] R. Pan, B. Prabhakar, K. Psounis: "CHOKe - A stateless active queue management scheme for approximating fair bandwidth allocation". *INFOCOM 2000.*

[2] R.Pan, L.Breslau, B.Prabhakar, S.Shenker: "Approximate fairness through differential dropping," *ACM Computer Communications Review,* January 2002.

[3] R.Pan, L.Breslau, B.Prabhakar, S.Shenker: "Approximate fair allocation of link bandwidth," *IEEE Micro,* January 2003.

[4] M. Andrews, K. Kumaran, K. Ramanan, A.L. Stolyar, R. Vijayakumar, and P. Whiting. CDMA data QoS scheduling on the forward link with variable channel conditions. Bell Laboratories Tech. Rep., April 2000.

[5] D. Bertsimas, I. Ch. Paschalidis, and J. N. Tsitsiklis. Asymptotic buffer overflow probabilities in multiclass multiplexers: An optimal control approach. In *IEEE Transactions on Automatic Control,* 43:315-335, March 1998.

[6] S. Deb and R. Srikant. Global stability of congestion controllers for the internet. *IEEE Transactions on Automatic Control,* 48(6):1055–1060, June 2003.

[7] A. Eryilmaz and R. Srikant, and J. Perkins. Stable scheduling policies for fading wireless channels. In *IEEE/ACM Transactions on Networking,* April 2005, pp. 411-424.

[8] A. Eryilmaz and R. Srikant. Scheduling with Quality of Service Constraints over Rayleigh Fading Channels In *Proceedings of IEEE Conference on Decision and Control,* Dec. 2004.

[9] R. G. Gallager. Information Theory and Reliable Communication. John Wiley & Sons, New York, 1968.

[10] R. G. Gallager. Finding parity in a simple broadcast network. In *IEEE Transactions on Information Theory,* vol. 34, pp 176-180, 1988.

[11] A. Ganti, E. Modiano and J. Tsitsiklis. Optimal Transmission Scheduling in Symmetric Communication Models with Intermittent Connectivity, 2004 Preprint.

[12] A. Giridhar and P. R. Kumar. Computing and communicating functions over sensor networks. In *IEEE Journal on Selected Areas in Communications,* pp. 755–764, vol. 23, no. 4, April 2005.

[13] P. Gupta and P. Kumar. Critical power for asymptotic connectivity in wireless network. In *Stochastic Analysis, Contrtol, Optimization and Applicaitons: a Volume in Honor of W.H.Fleming,* W. McEneaney, G. Yin and Q. Zhang, Eds., 1998

[14] P. Gupta and P. Kumar. The capacity of wireless networks. In *IEEE transactions of Information Theory,* vol. 46, no.2, pp. 388-404, 2000.

[15] N. Khude, A. Kumar and A. Karnik. Time and Energy Complexity of Distributed Computation in Wireless Sensor Networks. In *Proceedings of the IEEE Infocom,* 2005.

[16] S. R. Kulkarni and P. Viswanath. A Deterministic Approach to Throughput Scaling in Wireless Networks. In *IEEE Trans. on Information Theory,* Vol. 50, No.6, pp. 1041-1049, June 2004.

[17] E. Kushilevitz and Y. Mansour. Computation in Noisy Radio Networks In *Proceedings of the ninth annual ACM-SIAM symposium on Discrete algorithms,* pp. 236-243, 1998.

[18] X. Lin and N. Shroff. The impact of imperfect scheduling on cross-layer rate control in wireless networks. In *Proceedings of IEEE Infocom 2005,* Miami, Florida, March 2005.

[19] X. Liu, E. Chong, and N. Shroff. Opportunistic transmission scheduling with resource-sharing constraints in wireless networks. In *IEEE Journal on Selected Areas in Communications,* 19(10):2053 − 2064, October 2001.

[20] M. Neely, E. Modiano, and C. Li. Fairness and optimal stochastic control for heterogeneous networks. In *Proceedings of IEEE Infocom 2005,* Miami, Florida, March 2005.

[21] M. J. Neely, E. Modiano, and C. E. Rohrs. Power and server allocation in a multi-beam satellite with time varying channels. In *Proceedings of IEEE Infocom,* New York, NY. June 2002

[22] S. Rajagopalan and L. J. Schulman. A Coding Theorem for Distributed Computation. In Proc. 26th STOC 790-799, 1994.

[23] L. J. Schulman. Communication on Noisy Channels: A Coding Theorem for Computation. In *Proceeding of 33rd FOCS,* pp. 724-733, 1992.

[24] L. J. Schulman. Deterministic Coding for Interactive Communication. In *Proceeding of the 25th Annual Symposium on Theory of Computing,* pp. 747-756, 1993.

[25] S. Shakkottai. Effective Capacity and QoS for Wireless Scheduling, 2004 Preprint.

[26] S. Shakkottai, R. Srikant, and A. Stolyar. Pathwise optimality of the exponential scheduling rule for wireless channels. In *Advances in Applied Probability,* 1021-1045, Dec. 2004.

[27] S. Shakkottai and A. Stolyar. Scheduling for multiple flows sharing a time-varying channel: The exponential rule. In *Translations of the American Mathematical Society,* Series 2,A volume in memory of F. Karpelevich, Yu. M. Suhov, Editor, Vol. 207, 2002.

[28] R. Srikant. *The Mathematics of Internet Congestion Control.* Birkhauser, 2004.

[29] A. Stolyar and K. Ramanan. Largest weighted delay first scheduling: Large deviations and optimality. In *Ann. Appl. Probab.* 11:1-48, 2001.

[30] A. Stolyar. Maximizing queueing network utility subject to stability: Greedy primal-dual algorithm. Submitted.

[31] L. Tassiulas and A. Ephremides. Dynamic server allocation to parallel queues with randomly varying connectivity. In *IEEE Transactions on Information Theory*, 39:466-478, March 1993.

[32] S. Toumpis and A. J. Goldsmith Large wireless network under fading, mobility, and delay constraints. In *Procedings of IEEE INFOCOM*, 2004.

[33] G. Vinnicombe. On the stability of networks operating TCP-like congestion control. In *Proceedings of the IFAC World Congress*, Barcelona, Spain, 2002. University of Cambridge Technical Report CUED/F-INFENG/TR.398. Available at http://www.eng.cam.ac.uk/~gv.

[34] P. Viswanath, D. Tse, and R. Laroia. Opportunistic beamforming using dumb antennas. In *IEEE Transactions on Information Theory*, 48(6):1277C1294, June 2002.

[35] F. Xue and P. R. Kumar. The number of neighbors needed for connectivity of wireless networks. Wireless Networks, pp. 169–181, vol.10, no. 2, March 2004.

[36] Ying, L., G. E. Dullerud, and R. Srikant, "Global Stability of Internet Congestion Controllers with Heterogeneous Delays," IEEE Transactions on Networking; to appear June 2006.

[37] Ying, L. , R. Srikant, A. Eryilmaz, and G. E. Dullerud, "A Large Deviations Analysis of Scheduling in Wireless Networks", submitted to IEEE Transactions on Information Theory; conference version in *Proceedings of the IEEE Conference on Decision and Control*, 2005.

[38] Ying, L. , R. Srikant, A. Eryilmaz, and G. E. Dullerud, "Distributed Fair Resource Allocation in Cellular Networks in the Presence of Heterogeneous Delays", submitted to IEEE Transactions on Automatic Control; conference version in *Proceedings of the Intl. Symposium on Modelling and Optimization in Mobile, Ad Hoc, and Wireless Networks*, 2005.

[39] Ying, L. , R. Srikant, and G. E. Dullerud, "Distributed Symmetric Function Computation in Noisy Wireless Sensor Networks with Binary Data", *Proceedings of the Intl. Symposium on Modelling and Optimization in Mobile, Ad Hoc, and Wireless Networks*, 2006.

[40] C. N. Hadjicostis, "Coding Approaches to Fault Tolerance in Combinational and Dynamic Systems." Kluwer Academic Publishers, 2002.

[41] S. Sundaram and C. N. Hadjicostis, "Non-Concurrent Error Detection and Correction in Switched Linear Controllers." International Workshop on Hybrid Systems: Computation and Control (Series Lecture Notes in Computer Science, vol. 2993), pp. 585-599, Springer-Verlag, 2004.

[42] S. Sundaram and C. N. Hadjicostis, "Error Detection and Correction in Switched Linear Controllers via Periodic and Non-Concurrent Checks." To appear in Automatica.

[43] S. Sundaram and C. N. Hadjicostis, "Comments on "Time-Delayed State Estimator for Linear Systems with Unknown Inputs"," International Journal on Control, Automation and Systems, vol. 3, no. 4, pp. 646-647, December 2005.

[44] C. N. Hadjicostis, "Probabilistic Fault Detection in Finite-State Machines Based on State Occupancy Measurements," IEEE Transactions on Automatic Control, vol. 50, no. 12, pp. 2078-2083, December 2005.

[45] Y. Wu and C. N. Hadjicostis, "Algebraic Approaches for Centralized and Distributed Fault Identification in Discrete Event Systems," IEEE Transactions on Automatic Control, vol. 50, no. 12, pp. 2048-2053, December 2005.

[46] C. N. Hadjicostis, "Aliasing Probability Calculations for Arbitrary Compaction under Independently Selected Random Test Vectors," IEEE Transactions on Computers, vol. 54, no. 12, pp. 1614-1627, December 2005.

[47] E. Athanasopoulou and C. N. Hadjicostis, "Probabilistic Approaches to Fault Detection in Networked Discrete Event Systems," IEEE Transactions on Neural Networks, vol. 16, no. 5, pp. 1042-1053, September 2005 (Special Issue on Adaptive Learning Systems in Communication Networks).

[48] C. N. Hadjicostis, "Finite-State Machine Embeddings for Non-Concurrent Error Detection and Identification," IEEE Transactions on Automatic Control, vol. 50, no. 2, pp. 142-153, February 2005.

[49] C. N. Hadjicostis and G. C. Verghese, "Coding Approaches to Fault Tolerance in Linear Dynamic Systems," IEEE Transactions on Information Theory, vol. 51, no. 1, pp. 210-228, January 2005.

[50] C. N. Hadjicostis, "Non-Concurrent Error Detection and Identification in One-Hot Encoded FSMs," Automatica, vol. 40, pp. 1665-1676, 2004.

[51] C. N. Hadjicostis, "Coding Techniques for Fault-Tolerant Parallel Prefix Computations in Abelian Groups," The Computer Journal, vol. 47, no. 3, pp. 329-341, 2004.

[52] C. N. Hadjicostis, "Non-Concurrent Error Detection and Correction in Fault-Tolerant Linear Finite-State Machines," IEEE Transactions on Automatic Control, vol. 48, no. 12, pp. 2133-2140, December 2003.

[53] C. N. Hadjicostis, "Non-Concurrent Error Detection and Correction in Fault-Tolerant Discrete-Time LTI Dynamic Systems," IEEE Transactions on Circuits and Systems (I), vol. 50, no. 1, pp. 45-55, January 2003.

[54] C. N. Hadjicostis and G. C. Verghese, "Encoded Dynamics for Fault Tolerance in Linear Finite-State Machines," IEEE Transactions on Automatic Control, vol. 47, no. 1, pp. 189-192, January 2002.

[55] R. Touri, P. G. Voulgaris and C. N. Hadjicostis, "Time-Varying Power-Limited Preprocessing for Perfect Reconstruction of Binary Signals." To appear in the Proceedings of ACC 2006, the 2006 American Control Conference.

[56] E. Athanasopoulou and C. N. Hadjicostis, "Decentralized Failure Diagnosis in Discrete Event Systems." To appear Proceedings of ACC 2006, the 2006 American Control Conference.

[57] P. G. Voulgaris, C. N. Hadjicostis and R. Touri, "Encoder-Decoder Design for Perfect Reconstruction: A Robust Control Perspective." Proceedings of CDC/ECC 2005, the joint 44th IEEE Conference on Decision and Control and the European Control Conference 2005 (invited), pp. 2536-2541, Seville, Spain, 2005.

[58] S. Sundaram and C. N. Hadjicostis, "On Delayed Observers for Linear Systems with Unknown Inputs." Proceedings of CDC/ECC 2005, the joint 44th IEEE Conference on Decision and Control and the European Control Conference 2005, pp. 7210-7215, Seville, Spain, 2005.

[59] Athanasopoulou and C. N. Hadjicostis "Maximum Likelihood Diagnosis in Partially Observable Finite-State Machines." Proceedings of MED 2005, the 13th IEEE Mediterranean Conference on Control and Automation (invited), Limassol, Cyprus, 2005.

[60] G. Takos and C. N. Hadjicostis, "Hierarchical Decentralized Fusion from Correlated Sensor Measurements." Proceedings of ICNSC 2005, the 2005 IEEE International Conference on Networking, Sensing and Control.

[61] E. Athanasopoulou and C. N. Hadjicostis "Synchronization-Based Fault Detection in Discrete Event Systems." Proceedings of CDC 2004, the 43rd IEEE Conference on Decision and Control, Atlantis, Paradise Island, Bahamas, 2004.

[62] Lingxi Li, C. N. Hadjicostis and R. Sreenivas, "Fault Detection and Identification in Petri Net Controllers." Proceedings of CDC 2004, the 43rd IEEE Conference on Decision and Control, Atlantis, Paradise Island, Bahamas, 2004.

[63] C. N. Hadjicostis, "Finite-State Machine Embeddings for Non-Concurrent Error Error Detection and Identification," Proceedings of CDC 2003, the 42nd IEEE Conference on Decision and Control, vol. 4, pp. 3215-3220, Maui, Hawai, 2003.

[64] P. G. Voulgaris, C. N. Hadjicostis and R. Touri, "A Perfect Reconstruction Paradigm for Digital Communication," Proceedings of CDC 2003, the 42nd IEEE Conference on Decision and Control, vol. 4, pp. 4196-4201, Maui, Hawaii, 2003.

[65] Y. Wu and C. N. Hadjicostis, "Distributed Non-Concurrent Fault Identification in Discrete Event Systems." Proceedings of CESA 2003, the Multiconference on Computational Engineering in Systems Applications (invited), Lille, France, 2003.

[66] E. Athanasopoulou and C. N. Hadjicostis, "Aliasing Probability Calculations in Testing Sequential Circuits." Proceedings of MED 2003, the 11th IEEE Mediterranean Conference on Control and Automation, Rhodes, Greece, 2003.

[67] C. N. Hadjicostis, "Encoded Finite-State Machines for Non-Concurrent Error Detection and Identification." Proceedings of ISCAS 2003, the 2003 IEEE International Symposium on Circuits and Systems (invited), vol. 3, pp. 858-861, Bangkok, Thailand, 2003.

[68] C. N. Hadjicostis, "Aliasing Probability Calculations in Nonlinear Compactors." Proceedings of ISCAS 2003, the 2003 IEEE International Symposium on Circuits and Systems, vol. 5, pp. 529-532, Bangkok, Thailand, 2003.

[69] C. N. Hadjicostis and R. Touri, "Feedback Control utilizing Packet Dropping Network Links." Proceedings of CDC 2002, the 41st IEEE Conference on Decision and Control (invited), vol. 2, pp. 1205-1210, Las Vegas, NV, 2002.

[70] Y. Wu and C. N. Hadjicostis, "Non-Concurrent Fault Identification in Discrete Event Systems using Encoded Petri Net States." Proceedings of CDC 2002, the 41st IEEE Conference on Decision and Control (invited), vol. 4, pp. 4018-4023, Las Vegas, Nevada, 2002.

[71] C. N. Hadjicostis, "Probabilistic Fault Detection in Finite-State Machines Based on State Occupancy Measurements." Proceedings of CDC 2002, the 41st IEEE Conference on Decision and Control (invited), vol. 4, pp. 3994-3999, Las Vegas, Nevada, 2002.

[72] Papachristodoulou, A; Li, L; Doyle, JC, 2004. Methodological frameworks for large-scale network analysis and design, Computer Communication Review, Jul 2004

[73] Li, L., D. Alderson, J. Doyle, and W. Willinger. 2004. A First-Principles Approach to Understanding the Internet's Router-level Topology. Proc. ACM Sigcomm, Computer Communication Review, Oct. 2004.

[74] Csete M.E. and J.C. Doyle, 2004, Bow ties, metabolism, and disease, Trends in Biotechnology, Vol 22, Issue 9, pg. 446-450

[75] J. Stelling, U. Sauer, Z. Szallasi, F. J. Doyle III, and J. Doyle, 2004, Robustness of cellular functions, Cell, October, 2004.

[76] Willinger, W, D. Alderson, J.C. Doyle, and L.Li., 2004. More "Normal" Than Normal: Scaling Distributions and Complex Systems. Proceedings of the 2004 Winter Simulation Conference.

[77] Shapiro, BE; Hucka, M; Finney, A; Doyle, J. 2004. MathSBML: a package for manipulating SBML-based biological models, Bioinformatics, Nov 1, 2004

[78] Doyle, J; Csete, M, 2004. Imitation of life: How biology is inspiring computing, Nature. Oct 21 2004

[79] Kitano, H; Oda, K; Kimura, T; Matsuoka, Y; Csete, M; Doyle, J; Muramatsu, M, 2004 .Metabolic syndrome and robustness tradeoffs, DIABETES 53: S6-S15 Suppl. 3, Dec 2004

[80] H. El-Samad, H. Kurata , J.C. Doyle , C.A. Gross, and M. Khammash, 2005, Surviving Heat Shock: Control Strategies for Robustness and Performance, PNAS (8): 2736-2741 Feb 22, 2005

[81] Jin C, Wei D, Low SH, Bunn J, Choe HD, Doyle JC,et al, FAST TCP: From theory to experiments IEEE Network 19 (1): 4-11 Jan-Feb 2005

[82] Paganini F, Wang ZK, Doyle JC, et al. Congestion control for high performance, stability, and fairness in general networks, IEEE-ACM Transactions On Networking 13 (1): 43-56 Feb 2005

[83] W. Willinger, J Doyle, Robustness and the Internet: Design and evolution, in Robust Design: A Repertoire of Biological, Ecological, and Engineering Case Studies (Santa Fe Institute Studies on the Sciences of Complexity), Erica Jen, Editor

[84] L. Chen, S. H. Low and J. C. Doyle. Joint congestion control and media access control design for wireless ad hoc networks, IEEE Infocom, Miami, FL, March 2005.

[85] Wang JT, Li L, Low SH, Doyle JC. (2005) Cross-layer optimization in TCP/IP networks, IEEE-ACM Transactions On Networking 13 (3): 582-595 Jun 2005

[86] Manning M, Carlson JM, Doyle J (2005) Highly optimized tolerance and power laws in dense and sparse resource regimes Physical Review E 72 (1): Art. No. 016108 Part 2 Jul 2005

[87] R. Tanaka, T-M Yi, and J. Doyle (2005) Some protein interaction data do not exhibit power law statistics, FEBS letters, 579 (23): 5140-5144 Sep 26 2005

[88] Doyle et al, (2005), The "Robust Yet Fragile" Nature of the Internet, P Natl Acad Sci USA. vol. 102 no. 41, October 11, 2005

[89] Zhou T, Carlson JM, Doyle J (2005) Evolutionary dynamics and highly optimized tolerance, Journal Of Theoretical Biology 236 (4): 438-447 Oct 21 2005

[90] L Li, D Alderson, JC Doyle, W Willinger (2005) Towards a Theory of Scale-Free Graphs: Definition, Properties, and Implications, Internet Math, to appear

[91] D Alderson, L Li, W Willinger, JC Doyle (2005) Understanding Internet Topology: Principles, Models, and Validation, IEEE/ACM Transactions On Networking, Dec. 2005.

[92] MA Moritz, ME Morais, LA Summerell, JM Carlson, J Doyle (2005) Wildfires, complexity, and highly optimized tolerance, P Natl Acad Sci USA, December 13, 2005; 102 (50),

[93] T Brookings, JM Carlson, and J Doyle (2005) Three mechanisms for power laws on the Cayley tree, Phys. Rev. E 72, 056120

[94] S. Boyd, P. Diaconis, P. Parrilo, and L. Xiao. Symmetry analysis of reversible Markov chains. To appear in *Internet Mathematics*, 2005.

[95] S. Boyd, P. Diaconis, J. Sun, and L. Xiao. Fastest mixing Markov chain on a path. To appear in *The American Mathematical Monthly*, 2005.

[96] S. Boyd, P. Diaconis, and L. Xiao. Fastest mixing Markov chain on a graph. *SIAM Review*, 46(4):667–689, 2004.

[97] S. Boyd, A. Ghosh, B. Prabhakar, and D. Shah. Gossip algorithms: Design, analysis and applications. Presented at *INFOCOM 2005*.

[98] S. Boyd, A. Ghosh, B. Prabhakar, and D. Shah. Mixing times for random walks on geometric random graphs. Presented at *SIAM ANALCO 2005*.

[99] S. Boyd, A. Ghosh, B. Prabhakar, and D. Shah. Analysis and optimization of randomized gossip algorithms. In *Proceedings of IEEE Conference on Decision and Control (CDC)*, volume 5, pages 5310–5315, Bahamas, December 2004.

[100] S. Boyd, A. Ghosh, B. Prabhakar, and D. Shah. Randomized gossip algorithms. Submitted to *IEEE Transactions on Information Theory*, March 2005.

[101] C. Langbort, L. Xiao, R. D'Andrea, and S. Boyd. A decomposition approach to distributed analysis of networked systems. In *Proceedings of IEEE Conference on Decision and Control (CDC)*, volume 4, pages 3980–3985, Bahamas, December 2004.

[102] J. Sun, S. Boyd, L. Xiao, and P. Diaconis. The fastest mixing Markov process on a graph and a connection to a maximum variance unfolding problem.

[103] L. Xiao and S. Boyd. Fast linear iterations for distributed averaging. *Systems and Control Letters*, 53(1):65–78, 2004.

[104] L. Xiao and S. Boyd. Optimal scaling of a gradient method for distributed resource allocation. Revised for publication in *Journal of Optimization Theory and Applications*, February 2005. Available at `http://www.stanford.edu/~boyd/fast_redstb.html`.

[105] L. Xiao, S. Boyd, and S.-J. Kim. Distributed average consensus with least-mean-square deviation. Submitted to *Journal of Parallel and Distributed Computing*, May 2005. Available at `http://www.stanford.edu/~boyd/lms_consensus.html`.

[106] L. Xiao, S. Boyd, and S. Lall. A scheme for robust distributed sensor fusion based on average consensus. In *Proceedings of the Fourth International Conference on Information Processing in Sensor Networks (IPSN)*, pages 63–70, Los Angeles, CA, April 2005.

[107] D. S. Lun, M. Medard, and R. Koetter. Efficient operation of wireless packet networks using network coding.. In Proc. International Workshop on Convergent Technologies (IWCT) 2005, June 2005. Invited paper.

[108] S. Deb, M. Effros, T. Ho, D. R. Karger, R. Koetter, D. S. Lun, M. Medard, and N. Ratnakar. Network coding for wireless applications: A brief tutorial. In Proc. International Workshop on Wireless Ad-hoc Networks (IWWAN) 2005, May 2005. Invited paper.

[109] D. S. Lun, N. Ratnakar, R. Koetter, M. Medard, E. Ahmed, and H. Lee. Achieving minimum cost multicast: A decentralized approach based on network coding. In Proc. IEEE Infocom 2005, March 2005.

[110] D. S. Lun, M. Medard, and M. Effros. On coding for reliable communication over packet networks. In Proc. 42nd Annual Allerton Conference on Communication, Control, and Computing, September-October 2004. Invited paper.

[111] Laura Zager, Graph Similarity and Matching, Masters thesis, EECS Department, MIT, May 2005.

[112] Victor Preciado and George Verghese, "Synchronization in Generalized Erdos-Renyi Networks of Nonlinear Oscillators," IEEE Conf. on Decision and Control, Sevilla, Spain, December 2005.

[113] Ernst Scholtz, Observer-Based Monitors and Distributed Wave Controllers for Electromechanical Disturbances in Power Systems, PhD thesis, EECS Department, MIT, August 2004.

[114] Ernst Scholtz, Bernard Lesieutre and GeorgeVerghese, "Decentralized Controllers for Electromechanical Waves in Power Networks," Proc. 36th North American Power Symposium, August 2004, Moscow, Idaho.

[115] Ernst Scholtz, George Verghese and Bernard Lesieutre, "Observer-Based Monitors for Electromechanical Dynamics in Power Networks," Proc. 15th Power System Computation Conference, August 2005, Liege, Belgium.

[116] Teruo Ono, Game Theoretic Analysis and Agent-Based Simulation of Electricity Markets, Masters thesis, EECS Department, May 2005.

[117] Teruo Ono and George Verghese, "Replicator Agents for Electricity Markets," 13th International Conf. on Intelligent Systems Application to Power Systems (ISAP 2005), Washington DC, November 2005.

[118] M. Johansson, L. Xiao, and S. Boyd. Simultaneous routing and resource allocation in CDMA wireless data networks. Submitted to *The 2003 IEEE International Conference on Communications*, August 2002.

[119] S. Lall and C. Beck. Error bounds for balanced model reduction of linear time-varying systems. *IEEE Transactions on Automatic Control*, 48(6):946–956, June 2003.

[120] L. Xiao, M. Johansson, and S. Boyd. Simultaneous routing and resource allocation via dual decomposition. Submitted to *IEEE Transactions on Communications*, August 2002.

[121] M. Rotkowitz and S. Lall. Decentralized control information structures preserved under feedback. In *Proceedings of the IEEE Conference on Decision and Control*, pages 569–575, December 2002.

[122] R. Cogill and S. Lall. Topology independent controller design for networked systems. In *Proceedings of the IEEE Conference on Decision and Control (CDC)*, pages 1788–1793, 2004.

[123] M. Rotkowitz and S. Lall. On computation of optimal controllers subject to quadratically invariant sparsity constraints. In *Proceedings of the American Control Conference (ACC)*, pages 5659–5664, June 2004.

[124] B.-D. Chen and S. Lall. Control of distributed discrete-time systems on graphs. In *Proceedings of the American Control Conference (ACC)*, pages 2251–2256, June 2004.

Approximate Fairness through Differential Dropping

Rong Pan   Lee Breslau   Balaji Prabhakar   Scott Shenker
Stanford University   AT&T Research Labs   Stanford University   ACIRI

Abstract—**Many researchers have argued that the Internet architecture would be more robust and more accommodating of heterogeneity if routers allocated bandwidth fairly. However, most of the mechanisms proposed to accomplish this, such as Fair Queueing [16], [6] and its many variants [2], [23], [15], involve complicated packet scheduling algorithms. These algorithms, while increasingly common in router designs, may not be inexpensively implementable at extremely high speeds; thus, finding more easily implementable variants of such algorithms may be of significant practical value. This paper proposes an algorithm that – similar to FRED [13], CSFQ [24], and several other designs [17], [14], [5], [25] – combines FIFO packet scheduling with *differential dropping* on arrival. Our design, called *Approximate Fair Dropping* (AFD), bases these dropping decisions on the recent history of packet arrivals. AFD retains a simple forwarding path and requires an amount of additional state that is small compared to current packet buffers. Simulation results, which we describe here, suggest that the design provides a reasonable degree of fairness in a wide variety of operating conditions. The performance of our approach is aided by the fact that the vast majority of Internet flows are slow but the fast flows send the bulk of the bits. This allows a small sample of recent history to provide accurate rate estimates of the fast flows.**

I. INTRODUCTION

Since the pioneering observations of Nagle [16], many researchers have argued that the Internet architecture would be more robust (in the face of ill-behaved flows) and more accommodating of heterogeneity (by no longer requiring adherence to a single congestion control algorithm) if routers allocated bandwidth fairly. This viewpoint is not universally shared,[1] but even among adherents of this approach the question of feasibility has been a major concern. This is because most of the proposed mechanisms, such as Fair Queueing [16], [6] and its many variants [2], [23], [15], involve complicated packet scheduling algorithms. These algorithms, while increasingly common in router designs, may not be inexpensively implementable at extremely high speeds; thus, finding more easily implementable variants of such algorithms may be of significant practical value. This paper focuses on the design of a

router mechanism that combines approximately fair bandwidth allocations with relatively low implementation complexity.

We have three basic requirements of our design. First, it should achieve reasonably fair bandwidth allocations, and by "fair" we mean the max-min definition of fairness [6]. We make no pretense at being able to match the packet-by-packet fairness of Fair Queueing or other schemes that use intricate packet scheduling algorithms to ensure that perfect fairness is achieved on very short time scales. Instead, we aim for approximate fairness over longer time scales, on the order of several roundtrip times.

Second, we require that the design be easily amenable to high speed implementations. To this end we limit ourselves to FIFO packet scheduling algorithms with probabilistic drop-on-arrival; as in RED [8], when a packet arrives either the packet is dropped or placed on a FIFO queue. The dropping decisions must be simple with $O(1)$ complexity (that is, the complexity must not increase with the number of flows or packets). The amount of state required to make these dropping decisions must be small; the point of reference we choose to define "small" is the amount of memory which is already devoted to the packet buffers.

Third, the algorithm must employ some form of active queue management (AQM). It need not mimic RED or any other form of AQM precisely, but it should embody AQM's fundamental principles of responding early (and gently) to congestion while absorbing small bursts of traffic.[2]

To achieve these goals, we propose an algorithm called Approximate Fair Dropping (AFD). Its structure is similar to RED in that it uses a FIFO queue with probabilistic

---

[1] We discuss other viewpoints in Section VII.

[2] There is a fourth requirement that, for lack of space, we do not discuss in this paper; this is the requirement that the scheme be able to *punish* unresponsive flows. That is, the scheme should not just allocate bandwidth fairly, but should be able to shut down (by dropping all their packets) flows that incur high drop rates for long periods of time. The rationale for this is persuasively described in [10]; [24] discusses the role of fair bandwidth allocation in implementing this. We are easily able to augment our design to meet this goal and, as we see in Section V, one of the designs we present here already (but unintentionally!) achieves this goal.

drop-on-arrival. In contrast to RED, however, these probabilistic dropping decisions are based not only on the past measurements of the queue size but also on the recent history of a packet's flow.[3] AFD uses the history to estimate the flow's current sending rate, and then drops with a probability designed to limit that flow's throughput to the fair share.

Thus, dropping is not applied uniformly across flows (as in RED) but is applied differentially based on an estimate of the flow's current sending rate. The exact form of differential dropping is chosen to approximate fair bandwidth allocations. Several recent designs have advocated such FIFO-based *differential dropping* designs, including FRED [13], CSFQ and its several extensions [24], [5], [25], and RED-PD [14]. AFD adopts many aspects of these proposals.

Our design might initially appear to be seriously misguided. The state required to keep enough history to accurately estimate each flow's rate is quite large, and grows linearly with the number of flows. This is clearly not a feasible approach. However, note that our design only needs to estimate the rates of flows whose packets are likely to be dropped. Thus, we need only keep enough state to estimate rates when those rates are comparable to (or larger than) the fair share rate. This is a crucial difference.

It is well known that the distribution of the sizes of flows (the total number of bytes transferred) has a long tail, and that most flows are small – the mice – but a large fraction of the bytes are sent by large flows – the elephants.[4] As we show using trace data in Section VI, and has been observed in [14], the distribution of flow *rates* has a similar property. While perhaps not as long-tailed as the size distribution, initial evidence suggests that the flow rate distribution (measured on the time scale of a second) is long-tailed. Most flows are *slow* (in bits/sec) – we will call them *turtles* – but most of the bytes are sent by fast flows – we will call them *cheetahs*.

In AFD, we only need state for the fast flows and can ignore the slow flows because they won't be dropped; the amount of state required is roughly proportional to the number of fast flows, which is manageable. However, the challenge is how to keep state only on the fast flows when one doesn't know, in advance, which flows are fast or slow. A record of the very recent packet arrivals contains mostly packets from the fast flows (because they send most of the bytes), while most of the slow flows won't show up in the

recent history. This is the approach we take.

This paper has VII sections. We describe a conceptual version of our design in Section II, and then use analysis to develop guidelines for the various parameters in Section III. We then present the practical design in Section IV. We evaluate this design using simulation in Section V, and use trace data and other measurements to estimate the state requirements for the design in Section VI. We conclude in Section VII with a discussion of related work.

II. CONCEPTUAL DESIGN

We first present a high level conceptual design of AFD. Consider a link of speed C shared by n flows, each sending at rate r_i. Assume, for convenience, that all packets are the same size P. The total load on the link is $R = \sum_i r_i$. The fair share r_{fair} is given by the solution to $C = \sum_i \min(r_i, r_{fair})$. We can use differential dropping to accomplish our goal of fair bandwidth allocations if we use dropping probabilities for each flow, d_i, given by the relation $d_i = (1 - \frac{r_{fair}}{r_i})_+$.[5] The resulting throughput of each flow is bounded by the fair share: $r_i(1 - d_i) = \max(r_i, r_{fair})$.

The key design question is: how can we estimate r_i and r_{fair}. To estimate r_i we keep a *shadow buffer* of b recent packet headers. When a packet arrives, with probability $\frac{1}{s}$, where s is the sampling interval, we copy its header and insert it into the shadow buffer; thus, we sample roughly 1 in s packets. When a packet is inserted into the shadow buffer, we remove another packet at random to keep the total number of packets at b.[6] Thus, at all times the shadow buffer has a record of b recent packet arrivals. Note that the shadow buffer contains copies of the packet headers, and the insertion and deletion of packets from the shadow buffer is parallel to the main forwarding of packets. The shadow buffer is used to guide the dropping decisions in the following manner. When a packet (from, say, flow i) arrives (regardless of whether its header is copied into the packet buffer) we compute the number of packets from that flow in the shadow buffer; we call this the number of *matches*, m_i. We then estimate the rate of that flow to be $r_i^{est} = R\frac{m_i}{b}$ (recall that R is the aggregate arrival rate).

To avoid having to scan the shadow buffer each time a packet arrives, we keep a table of the flows and their current packet counts; we call this the *flow table*. A hash table is one natural data structure for the flow table that has $O(1)$ lookup time. Each time a packet is inserted into the shadow buffer, the appropriate counter in the flow ta-

---

[3]In this paper, we define a flow as a stream of packets with the same source-destination addresses. However, one could use any definition of flow discernible from an IP packet header.

[4]As we discuss later in Section VI, we use the term "long-tail" to describe distributions that decay slower than exponentially.

[5]We use the notation that $z_+ = \max(0, z)$.

[6]Random removal avoids synchronization problems. We could also remove packets in a FIFO manner; it turns out that this does not affect performance greatly.

ble is incremented, each time a packet is removed the appropriate count is decremented, and every time a packet arrives the match count is looked up in the flow table. Insertions and deletions can be somewhat slow (because we need only insert and delete every s packets) but the lookup has to done at linespeed (because it is done on every packet arrival).

Estimating the rate of a single flow requires only the recent activity of that flow and so is fairly straightforward. Estimating r_{fair} is more complicated because the definition of r_{fair} depends on all the r_i. We use an approach borrowed from [24]. Upon each packet arrival we apply the dropping probability $d_i = (1 - \frac{r_{fair}}{r_i^{est}})_+$, which can be rewritten as $d_i = (1 - \frac{m_{fair}}{m_i})_+$ with $m_{fair} = b\frac{r_{fair}}{R}$. Note that if we vary m_{fair} the total throughput, $\sum_i r_i d_i$, varies from R when $m_{fair} = \infty$, to C when $m_{fair} = b\frac{r_{fair}}{R}$, to 0 when $m_{fair} = 0$. Thus, we can approximate r_{fair} by varying m_{fair} so that the link is fully utilized but not overloaded.

In our approach, we vary m_{fair} to ensure that the average queue length stabilizes around the target value of $0.5(min_{th} + max_{th})$ where min_{th} and max_{th} are the threshold values defined in RED. We borrow the AQM approach described in [12], which employs a proportional-integral controller. Since this form of AQM is very effective at keeping the links fully utilized, the resulting values of $m_{fair}\frac{R}{b}$ will be a good approximation to r_{fair}.

Our basic approach has borrowed liberally from CSFQ [24], FRED [13], and CHOKe [18], and is quite similar to the concurrently developed RED-PD [14].[7] FRED uses the number of packets from each flow in the packet buffer to guide its dropping decisions; thus, our design can be seen as an extension of FRED to use more history and a different dropping function (which is the same as used in CSFQ).

Does AFD achieve the goals we laid out in the Introduction? AFD's probabilistic drop-on-arrival can be implemented with a very simple forwarding path. The dropping decision has complexity $O(1)$ and involves few computations. In addition, AFD incorporates active queue management. Fairness and feasibility (in terms of the state required) are the two remaining questions. If the rate estimates are accurate, we expect AFD to allocate bandwidth fairly. While we delay the bulk of our simulation results, and all of the simulation details, until Section V, we now show initial evidence that this expected fairness is actually achieved. Figure 1 shows the result of 50 CBR sources

---

[7]In fact, we had several design discussions with the RED-PD designers while both algorithms were being developed. While the two schemes have some similarities, they are targeted at slightly different goals. See Section VII.

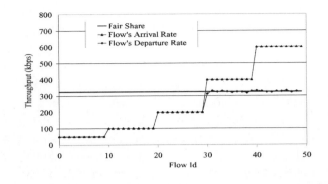

Fig. 1. Offered Load and Throughput for 50 CBR Flows under AFD

sending at five different rates (some above the fair share, some below) over a single link. The bandwidth allocations are quite fair; flows sending below the fair share incur no drops, and flows sending above the fair share have their excess packets dropped.

Fairness depends on the accuracy of the rate estimations, and the rate estimations depend on the size of the shadow buffer. Without sufficient history the rate estimations will fluctuate wildly and lead to quite unpredictable (and unfair) results. Rate estimation improves with larger b (the size of the shadow buffer) and, to some extent, with larger s (because s increases the time interval represented by the contents of the shadow buffer). The question is how large do b and s have to be in order to achieve reasonable fairness. This is crucial because we want the state required for this algorithm to be small (at least compared to the packet buffers). The viability of our scheme comes down to whether fairness can be achieved without too much state, and we explore that issue in the next few sections.

In Section III we develop three guidelines for how to set b and s. After describing a more practical (as opposed to the conceptual version just presented) version of AFD in Section IV, we evaluate the fairness that results from such parameter settings in Section V. Finally, in Section VI we estimate the state requirements of AFD when using the parameter-setting guidelines.

III. SETTING THE BASIC PARAMETERS

In this conceptual model, there are two basic parameters that we need to set: the shadow buffer size b and sampling interval s. Our goal is to achieve a reasonable degree of fairness, and in this section we develop three *guidelines* on what values of b and s achieve that goal. To do so, we consider three scenarios and analyze them using very simple models. These models are unrealistic but our hope is that the resulting guidelines provide useful order-of-magnitude estimates for the parameters of interest.

A. Static Scenario

We first consider the static case of n sources sharing a single link of bandwidth C. All flows are Poisson sources sending at a constant rate r_i and all packets are the same size. The overall drop rate D is given by $D = \frac{(R-C)_+}{R}$ where, as above, $R = \sum_i r_i$. Let $P_i(m)$ be the probability that when a packet from flow i arrives, there are m packets from flow i in the shadow buffer. In our simple model,

$$P_i(m) = \binom{b}{m}(1 - \frac{r_i}{R})^{b-m}(\frac{r_i}{R})^m$$

For the purposes of this model, we assume that m_{fair} is fixed to be the appropriate value: $m_{fair} = b\frac{r_{fair}}{R}$. We denote the *ideal* dropping rate by $\tilde{d}_i$: $\tilde{d}_i = (1 - \frac{r_{fair}}{r_i})_+$. $d_i(b)$ is the average dropping rate of the i'th flow for a given size of shadow buffer:

$$d_i(b) = \sum_{m=0}^{b} P_i(m)(1 - \frac{m_{fair}}{m})_+$$

The relative error in the throughput of the i'th flow is

$$\Delta_i(b) = |\frac{r_i(1 - d_i(b)) - r_i(1 - \tilde{d}_i)}{r_i(1 - d_i)}| = |\frac{\tilde{d}_i - d_i(b)}{1 - d_i}|$$

Note that the sampling interval s drops out of all of these quantities. This is not surprising given that a random sampling of a Poisson process remains a Poisson process.

Our goal is to choose the size of the shadow buffer so that we achieve some reasonable degree of fairness. We seek to determine how large the shadow buffer must be so that the maximal error, $\max_i \Delta_i(b)$, is below some target error tolerance E. Analysis and numerical calculations (which we do not have space for here) indicate the maximal error occurs when $r_i \approx r_{fair}$. Consider a flow with $r_i = r_{fair}$; we can approximate the relative error, call it Δ, in the limit of large b for this flow as follows (noting that the ideal dropping rate for this flow is zero, $\tilde{d}_i = 0$, and so $\Delta(b) = d_i(b)$). Letting $\alpha = \frac{r_{fair}}{R}$, we have:

$$\Delta(b) = \sum_{m=0}^{b} \binom{b}{m}(1 - \alpha)^{b-m}\alpha^m(1 - \frac{b\alpha}{m})_+$$

$$= \sum_{m=\lceil b\alpha \rceil}^{b} \binom{b}{m}(1 - \alpha)^{b-m}\alpha^m(1 - \frac{b\alpha}{m})$$

For sufficiently large b, we can approximate the binomial form as a normal distribution with average αb and variance $b\alpha(1 - \alpha)$. Using an integral formulation, we find:

$$\Delta(b) \approx \frac{1}{\sqrt{2\pi b\alpha(1 - \alpha)}} \int_{b\alpha}^{\sim} dx \, e^{-\frac{(x-b\alpha)^2}{2b\alpha(1-\alpha)}} (1 - \frac{b\alpha}{x})_+$$

$$< \frac{1}{\sqrt{2\pi b\alpha(1 - \alpha)}} \int_{0}^{\infty} dy \, e^{-\frac{y^2}{2b\alpha(1-\alpha)}} \frac{y}{b\alpha}$$

$$= \sqrt{\frac{2(1 - \alpha)}{\pi b\alpha}} \int_{0}^{\infty} dz \, ze^{-z^2} \approx .40\sqrt{\frac{(1 - \alpha)}{b\alpha}}$$

Thus, we can bound the asymptotic expression for the relative error from above by the formula

$$\Delta(b) \leq .40(b\alpha)^{-0.5}$$

A choice of b that will always meet the error tolerance of E (in this asymptotic limit) is:

$$b\frac{r_{fair}}{R} > (\frac{E}{0.40})^{-2}$$

Note that $b\frac{r_{fair}}{R} = m_{fair}$ where, as defined above, m_{fair} is the expected number of shadow buffer matches for a flow with $r_i = r_{fair}$. One can meet the error tolerance merely by making the shadow buffer big enough to make sure that $m_{fair} > (\frac{E}{0.40})^{-2}$. For our purposes, we choose $E \approx .15$. This might seem quite unambitious, but recall that we are calculating an upper bound on the worst-case error (that is, of flows sending at a constant rate right at the fair share); the errors for rates well above and well below the fair share are significantly smaller. Setting $E = 0.15$ results in $m_{fair} \approx 10$. This is our first guideline.

Guideline 1: $b \gtrsim 10\frac{R}{r_{fair}}$ or, equivalently, $m_{fair} \gtrsim 10$

B. Dynamic Scenario

Even if routers allocate bandwidth fairly on the time scale over which they measure usage, flows that respond slowly when excess bandwidth is available are at a disadvantage when competing with flows that respond more rapidly. We can illustrate this with a simple model involving flows with different roundtrip times (RTTs).

Consider flows competing for bandwidth with differing roundtrip times τ_i. All packets are the same size P. Each flow adjusts its window size w_i in a TCP-like fashion (with all the details of TCP omitted); the window (measured in terms of packets) increases by one in time τ_i when there is no packet loss during that RTT, and the window is halved if there is a packet loss (and we neglect the case of multiple packet losses, or of timeouts, in an RTT). The rates r_i of the flows are roughly $r_i = \frac{w_i P}{\tau_i}$. The router has a shadow buffer of size b and a sampling interval of s; the time interval T over which the shadow buffer measures usage is $T = \frac{bsP}{R}$. We assume that the fair share rate r_{fair} is constant and that the fair share expected number of matches $m_{fair} = b\frac{r_{fair}}{R}$ is roughly 10 (as suggested by guideline 1). Consider a flow i and let m_i denote the average number of its matches in the shadow buffer. Because the fair share is fixed, we can approximate the dynamics of each flow as independent.[8] We consider a series of time slots $t = 1, 2, \ldots$, each of length τ_i. For convenience, we assume that $T = k_i \tau_i$ for some integer k_i. The average number of matches m_i in the shadow buffer at some time t is roughly $m_i(t) = \frac{1}{s} \sum_{j=0}^{k_i-1} w_i(t-j)$. Thus, the window dynamics can be written as:

$$w_i(t+1) = w_i(t) + 1 \quad (m_i \leq m_{fair})$$

$$w_i(t+1) = \frac{w_i(t)}{2} \quad (m_i > m_{fair})$$

$$m_i(t) = \frac{1}{s} \sum_{j=0}^{k_i-1} w_i(t-j)$$

If we start off with $w_i(t=0) = 1$, the first drop for flow i occurs (approximately) when $w_i(t) = s\frac{m_{fair}}{k_i} + \frac{k_i}{2}$ (which we assume is an integer). At that point, the window is halved to $w_i(t) = \frac{sm_{fair}}{2k_i} + \frac{k_i}{4}$. If this halving of the window brings the number of matches down below m_{fair} in the next time period then the increasing process starts again. If not, the window is halved again (and again) until $m_i(t)$ is below m_{fair}. Let's assume that the window is halved only once; in this case $w_i(t)$ becomes a repeating series of values starting at $w_i(t) = \frac{sm_{fair}}{2k_i} + \frac{k_i}{4}$ and increasing by 1 until the value $w_i(t) = \frac{sm_{fair}}{k_i} + \frac{k_i}{2}$ is reached. The average window over this periodic cycle of flow i, $\bar{w}_i$, is:

$$\bar{w}_i = \frac{3}{4}\left(\frac{sm_{fair}}{k} + \frac{k_i}{2}\right)$$

The average window size that yields the fair share is $\frac{sm_{fair}}{k_i}$. w_i reaches that level when $sm_{fair} = \frac{3}{2}k_i^2$. Thus, if we set $m_{fair} = 10$ we have, approximately,

$$k_i \approx \sqrt{\frac{20s}{3}}$$

For $s = 1$, $k_i \approx 2.6$, and for $s = 10$, $k_i \approx 8$.

[8]The error occurs because the timescale τ has R in the denominator; if we replace that by C then the dynamics are completely independent in this simple model.

This model is vastly oversimplified – in particular, the impact of multiple drops per round-trip times and possible time-outs are not modeled and it is assumed that dropping starts as soon as the number of matches is over m_{fair} – and it probably significantly underestimates the hardship imposed on flows with long RTTs. We therefore choose to be conservative and increase (almost double) the ratio to be closer to $k_i \approx 5\sqrt{s}$. Moreover, we choose to accommodate roundtrips on the order of $150msec$. Recalling that $T = k_i \tau$ and $T = \frac{bsP}{R}$, we adopt as our guideline 2 the following inequality:

Guideline 2: $b\sqrt{s}\frac{P}{R} \gtrsim 750msec$

C. Burst Scenario

Consider a flow that, after being quiescent, sends h packets (of size P) back to back. If h is smaller than $m_{fair}s$ then it is likely that none of the incoming packets will be dropped, and if h is significantly larger than this amount then the latter packets will probably be dropped. We want the quantity $m_{fair}s$ to be large enough to absorb the packet bursts typical of TCP and other window-based congestion control algorithms. If we take τ to be a typical RTT, and assume that a flow might send an entire window's worth of packets back-to-back (where the window size corresponds to the fair share), then we would want $m_{fair}sP > r_{fair}\tau$. For a link of capacity C with $R \approx C$, this becomes $bs > \frac{C\tau}{P}$.

We must also ensure that $m_{fair}sP$ is not so large that bursts of that size dominate the packet buffer. If the packet buffers are sized to be $C\tau$ where C is the link speed and τ is some nominal delay (on the order of 250msec) used to size the packet buffers, and as above we assume the dropping rate is low (so $R \approx C$), then we require that $m_{fair}sP \ll C\tau$ or, equivalently, $bs \ll \frac{C^2\tau}{Pr_{fair}}$.

The previous two guidelines presented lower bounds for b and s. Our third guideline yields both upper and lower bounds on the product bs.

Guideline 3: $\frac{C\tau}{P} < bs \ll \frac{C^2\tau}{Pr_{fair}} = \frac{C\tau}{P}\frac{b}{m_{fair}}$

We treat these three guidelines not as hard-and-fast rules but rather as general rules-of-thumb to guide how the parameters are set. There is no need for getting the parameters b and s exactly right. If they are too small, the fairness will be less than ideal; if they are too big, the network may be more vulnerable to bursts. But in both cases, as we see in Section V, the degradation is gradual. We also note that compliance with these guidelines can be easily checked by operators. For the first guideline, one need only record the historical values of m_{fair} (which, as we describe in Section IV, the algorithm sets automatically) to ensure that it is well above 10. The second guideline is computable from the link capacity. The third can be checked by using the values of m_{fair}.

With these guidelines, we now see how the algorithm works in practice. In the next section we describe two practical versions of the algorithm, one that follows directly from our conceptual model and one that requires less state.

IV. PRACTICAL DESIGNS

Our description of the conceptual design glossed over several aspects of the algorithm. First, the algorithm for adjusting m_{fair} is borrowed from [12]. We sample the queue length at a rate f_s; upon each sample we adjust the value of m_{fair} according to the following equation:

$$m_{fair}(t) = m_{fair}(t-1) + \alpha(q(t-1) - q_{target})$$

$$-\beta(q(t) - q_{target})$$

where $q(t)$ is the queue length at the t'th sample, $q(t-1)$ is the queue length at the previous sample, and $q_{target} = 0.5(min_{th} + max_{th})$ is the target queue size. This procedure not only stabilizes the average queue length around the target value and provides active queue management, but also estimates m_{fair} implicitly. We choose $f_s = 160Hz$, which is the same as in [12], and α , β are 1.7 and 1.8, respectively. Our algorithm does not seem terribly sensitive to small changes in the parameter values, but we have not done a systematic study of these parameters.[9]

Second, we will use a hash table for the flow table. In so doing, we need not store entire packet headers in the shadow buffer but merely enough bits to accurately identify the flow in the hash table. In practice we will store a k-bit hash of the source-destination addresses (or whatever flow signature is chosen). Third, the design must be modified to accommodate variable size packets. This entails keeping byte counts in the shadow buffer, and measuring matches in bytes rather than packets in the hash table. When removing packets from the shadow buffer (which are picked randomly), we seek to keep the total number of bytes in the shadow buffer constant (but tolerate some jitter). We call this design AFD-SB, with the SB standing for *shadow buffer*.

AFD-SB stores flow information in two places, the shadow buffer and the flow table. A natural way to reduce the state requirements of AFD would be to eliminate one of these. We can't eliminate the flow table, since it is required to make the packet lookups $O(1)$, so we seek instead to

eliminate the shadow buffer. We argue in Section VI that if a hash table is used, the hash table and shadow buffer require similar amounts of state; eliminating the shadow buffer would thereby reduce the state requirements by half. However, if we used CAM memory for the flow table the state reduction would be far greater (since hash tables need to be sized an order of magnitude larger than the number of flows to avoid collisions).

The question is whether we can perform the correct operations on the flow table without the shadow buffer. Incrementing the flow table upon packet insertions is straightforward. However, decrementing is hard. When we eliminated packets from the shadow buffer, we picked one at random (or in a FIFO order); all packets had equal chance to be eliminated. Choosing a *flow* at random with uniform probability in the flow table is easy, but it isn't clear how to pick a *packet* at random with uniform probability without linearly traversing the flow entries.

To solve this problem, we adopt an approximation. Note that one could choose a packet with uniform probability if one chose flows (from which to eliminate a packet) according to probabilities $\frac{m_i}{\sum_j m_j}$. However, choosing among all n flows in this manner requires a linear search. We propose picking k flows at random, where $k \ll n$ and choosing among them with the same probability function: $\frac{m_i}{\sum_{j \in S} m_j}$ where S is the set of flows chosen at random. We use $k = 5$ in our simulations.[10]

We call this AFD-FT (with the FT standing for *flow table*). We propose AFD-FT as an example of how one could introduce approximations into AFD in order to make it more easily implementable (by requiring less state). However, we expect that there are many other ways to implement the flow table; in particular, each router design will have its own hardware constraints and to maximize implementability it will be important to adapt AFD to each situation. We offer AFD-FT as an existence proof that AFD's performance is reasonably robust to approximations.

We now proceed to explore the performance of our two designs – AFD-SB and AFD-FT – through simulation.

V. SIMULATION

A. Simulation Preliminaries

We used the *ns* [28] simulator to evaluate our two designs in a variety of scenarios. We compare our designs to two other schemes: RED [8] and FRED [13]. RED provides a baseline comparison with an algorithm that makes

---

[9]Our particular AQM design choice, borrowed from [12], seemed particularly easy to adapt to the AFD algorithm. However, we assume that there are countless ways to incorporate AQM in our differential dropping design.

[10]To accommodate varying size packets, we decrement the chosen flow by the number of bytes in the arriving packet. If the chosen flow doesn't have enough bytes, we remember the deficit and subtract more upon the next packet.

no attempt to allocate bandwidth fairly.[11] FRED provides a useful guidepost of how much fairer the allocations are when the dropping decisions are informed by the current packet buffer occupancy.[12] AFD keeps a longer history than FRED, and so the relative performance can be seen as an indication of how important this additional state is. FRED is easier to implement than AFD and requires less state, and so our simulation results should be taken as illustrating the fairness vs. complexity/state tradeoffs provided by the two algorithms.[13]

We envision AFD operating in an environment where flows use many forms of congestion control. In our simulations, we used the following different congestion control algorithms:

TCP: We use TCP-sack as provided in the *ns* release. The TCP flows sometimes have different RTTs, or different file sizes, as described below.

AIMD: We modify the increase parameter a and decrease parameter b in TCP's Additive-Increase/Multiplicative-Decrease algorithm. Standard TCP has $(a, b) = (1, 0.5)$. In addition, we use sources with the following parameters: $(1, 0.9)$, $(0.75, 0.31)$, $(2.0, 0.5)$. We refer to these as AIMD1, AIMD2 and AIMD3, respectively. The first and third are more aggressive than normal TCP, and the second is slightly less aggressive than TCP.

Binomial: Recently Bansal and Balakrishnan [1] introduced a more general family of increase/decrease algorithms. Increases are of the form $w + aw^{-k}$ and decreases are of the form $w - bw^\iota$ for constants (a, b, k, ι). We used two versions: $(1.5, 1.0, 2, 0)$ and $(1.0, 0.5, 0, 1)$. The first is roughly comparable to TCP and the second is much more aggressive than TCP. We refer to these as Binomial1 and Binomial2.

CBR: These are constant rate flows that do not perform congestion control.

Most of our simulations are run on the topology depicted in Figure 2(a), and a few are run on the topology in Figure 2(b). The congested links have transmission latencies of 20 msec, and unless otherwise stated the uncongested links have latencies of 2 msec. The routers on the congested link(s) have buffers that hold 600 packets. The simulations are run for 10 minutes of simulation time, with the first 100 seconds discarded for warmup. Unless otherwise stated, all data packets are 1000 bytes, and AFD is run with $b = 500$ and $s = 5$.

---

[11] We use RED in *gentle* mode with the parameter settings of $min_{th} = 25$ and $max_{th} = 125$ for a 10Mbps link. The thresholds are scaled proportionaly for higher speed links.

[12] We simulated FRED with $min_q = 4$ and other parameters as in the RED simulations.

[13] Other algorithmic differences, such as the manner in which drop probabilities are computed, differentiate AFD from RED.

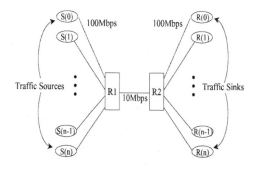

(a) Single Link Topology

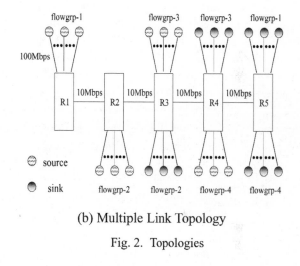

(b) Multiple Link Topology

Fig. 2. Topologies

B. Simulation Results

Mixed Traffic: In Section II we showed that AFD provides equal bandwidth shares to CBR flows sending at different rates. We now consider the more challenging case of a mixture of flows using different congestion control algorithms. The basic scenario we present consists of 7 groups of flows, each with five flows, sharing the bottleneck link in Figure 2(a). The 7 groups are AIMD1, AIMD2, AIMD3, Binomial1, Binomial2, TCP, and TCP with a higher latency of 24.5msec on the 100Mbps access links (yielding a roundtrip latency, without queueing, of 100msec for this flow group, as compared to 10msec for the other flows). Figure 3(a) shows the throughput received by each group of flows (we average within each group so that the data is more easily presentable; the fluctuations within groups are quite small, as was seen in Figure 1 for the CBR simulation). The bar chart shows the bandwidth allocations for the flow groups in the following order: AIMD1, AIMD2, AIMD3, Binomial1, Binomial2,

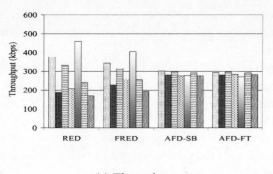

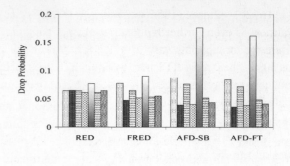

(a) Throughput   (b) Drop Rates

Fig. 3. Mixed Traffic

TCP, and TCP with increased latency.[14]

The throughput allocations for RED and FRED are substantially uneven, showing that this set of flows includes several rather aggressive congestion control algorithms. Therefore, this presents a reasonable test of the fairness properties of the various algorithms. AFD-SB and AFD-FT both have reasonably fair allocations. Figure 3(b) shows the average drop rate for each group of flows; RED has uniform drop rates, FRED has somewhat uneven drop rates, and both AFD algorithms have extremely uneven drop rates. This demonstrates that applying differentiated drop rates can lead to fairness for different flows.

We now check how well this scenario compares with the guidelines. With $b = 500$ and 35 flows, the average share of the shadow buffer is roughly 14 packets which is in line with the recommendation of 10 packets in Guideline 1. It turns out that due to the fluctuations induced by the window based flow control, in which packets tend to be bunched, the average of m_{fair} is closer to 1. Guideline 2 sets bounds on $b\sqrt{s}\frac{P}{R}$; the guideline calls for this quantity to be larger than 750msec and our scenario has 890msec. Lastly, Guideline 3 calls for $300 < bs \ll 15,000$ if we choose $\tau = 250$msec. Our scenario has $bs = 2,000$.

High Speed Link: To ensure that the fairness in this initial simulation scales, we increased the speed of the congested link, the size of the shadow buffer, and the number of flows by a factor of 10. Figure 4 shows the throughput levels that result.

Increased Multiplexing: Next we tested what happens if the number of flows is increased by a factor of three (retaining the same mixture of flows and the same b). Results for AFD-SB are shown in Figure 5; results for AFD-FT are similar. Even though this scenario violates Guideline 1 (because now the fair number of matches is less than 5),

the fair throughput levels are preserved. The conservative assumptions used in deriving the guidelines provide a margin for error.

Reduced Shadow Buffer: If we return to our canonical scenario and reduce the size of the shadow buffer, does fairness suffer? Figure 6 shows the throughput levels for AFD-SB (similar results hold for AFD-FT) for buffer sizes of $b = 250$ and $b = 125$ (the latter violates Guideline 1 significantly) in addition to the canonical case of $b = 500$. In this case, fairness degrades slightly as the shadow buffer size decreases, but AFD still outperforms the baseline algorithms.

While these cases establish that AFD-SB and AFD-FT can provide fair bandwidth allocations when faced with a diverse set of sources, there are cases when the AFD algorithms do not perform as perfectly. We now present three such cases.

Long RTTs: First, consider the case where there are 4 flow groups, each with 10 TCP flows. The flow groups have different RTTs, as determined by the latencies of the connecting 100Mbps links. The latency of the central congested link remains the same (20msec), and the latencies of the connecting links are (followed in parentheses by the resulting total latency of the path, not counting queueing delays): 2msec (48msec), 7msec (68msec), 12msec (88msec), 17msec (108msec). The congested link has queueing delays of roughly 60msec which should be added to the total latency numbers to compute estimates of the RTTs. For each algorithm, the resulting bandwidth allocations for each flow group are shown in the bar chart in Figure 7(a) ordered from smallest to largest latency. The AFD designs provide much better fairness than RED or FRED. The throughput values differ from the fair share by as much as 4%. We chose parameters that were designed (according to Guideline 2) to accommodate RTTs of up to 150msec, and this scenario is just a bit over that limit. If we increase the latency values to 2msec (48msec), 22msec

---

[14]Unless otherwise noted, we use the same ordering of flow groups in the remaining bar charts.

(111msec), 42msec (175msec) and 62msec(238msec), the fairness is even further reduced, as shown in Figure 7(b). Here the throughputs vary from the fair share by as much as 20%. The largest RTT here (roughly 300msec including queueing delay) is larger than our b and s can accommodate (by guideline 2), and the resulting decrease in fairness is evident.[15]

Unresponsive Flow: Next, we return to the latency values and traffic mix used in Figure 3. To this traffic mix we add a CBR flow sending at 15% of the link capacity. Figure 8 shows that the throughput allocations in AFD-SB are not perfectly fair, with the CBR receiving roughly 15% more than the fair share. The CBR under AFD-FT receives very little throughput at all, only about 15% of the fair share. This was not our intention when designing AFD-FT. However, we are not unhappy with this result; as we observed in Section I, punishing unresponsive flows that tolerate high persistent high drop rates is an important design goal (see [10] for the rationale). We have to (and can easily) add additional mechanism (which we do not discuss in this paper) to AFD-SB to accomplish this goal but AFD-FT does this by default. This occurs because the CBR flow occupies 15% of the shadow buffer (packets are selected to be inserted into the shadow buffer whether or not they are destined to be dropped), which is 5 times larger than the share of any other flow. The approximate packet deletion scheme in AFD-FT is biased against larger flows; when the differences between flows is small this bias is negligible, but when the difference is a factor of five, the bias dominates the results. We believe this phenomenon is also responsible for AFD-FT performing better than AFD-SB in the RTT tests (see Figure 7).

Multiple Congested Links: The third challenging scenario for AFD is when there are multiple congested links. This scenario used the topology in Figure 2(b). There are four different source-destination pairs: three that traverse a single congested link and one that traverses the long path through 3 congested links. Each link has a latency of 5ms. In the first scenario we consider, each of these flow groups consists of 20 standard TCP flows, so that every congested link is traversed by the same number (i.e., 40) of flows. Figure 9(a) shows that the flows that traverse the long path (the fourth group shown for each algorithm in the bar chart) receive substantially less bandwidth than the others, roughly 83% of the fair share. While the throughputs are much fairer than RED or FRED, these results are troubling. If we double the number of flows in the group that traverses the link between R4 and

R5, which reduces the fair share on that link, then the results become much fairer. These results are shown in Figure 9(b), with the first group of two bars showing the throughput for the flow groups traversing each of the first two congested links, respectively, and the second group of two bars showing the throughput of the group traversing R4-R5 and the throughput of the group traversing the long path, respectively. Bandwidth allocation for pairs of flow groups that share the same bottleneck link is much fairer for the AFD algorithms relative to the previous scenario. These results suggest, and simple analysis confirms, that AFD does not perform well when there are multiple congested links with *exactly* the same fair share. Flows that are sending right at their fair share experience probabilistic dropping at multiple hops, and therefore receive less than flows that traverse only one congested link. However, if flows pass through multiple congested links that have different fair shares, then when sending at around the fair share the multi-hop flow only suffers drops at one link. We conjecture (not based on any special insight but just based on common sense) that traversing paths with multiple congested links with approximately the same fair shares will be an unusual case.

We tested many other scenarios in simulation, including different traffic mixes and variable size packets, that we do not present here. In all cases, the fairness properties of AFD were maintained. Before concluding the description of our simulations, we briefly mention 3 additional experiments.

Many Small Flows: In the simulations described above, all of our sources had an unlimited amount of data to send. In the next scenario, keeping our basic mixture of 7 flow groups (with infinite sources), we introduce approximately 22,000 short TCP flows representing, for example, shorter web transactions. We use a Pareto distribution of flow lengths. The average number of packets per flow is 15 with a shape parameter of 1.2. We ask two questions: does the presence of many short flows interfere with the fairness properties of the longer-lived flows, and does AFD allow the shorter flows to finish sooner? Figure 11(a) shows the throughput received by the infinite source flow groups under RED, AFD-SB and AFD-FT. AFD-SB and AFD-FT still provide very good fairness in this scenario. Figure 11(b) shows a histogram of the finishing times of the short-lived flows under AFD-SB and RED. Note that this is on a logarithmic scale, so that while the difference in heights between the bars representing the fastest finishing times is small, it represents a difference of approximately 2000 flows. In all the other histogram bins, RED has more flows. Thus, AFD-SB (and the same applies to AFD-FT) aids short flows by lowering their drop rates and allowing

---

[15]The analysis leading to guideline 2 suggests that $v\sqrt{s}\frac{\overline{P}}{R}$ should be greater than 5 times the maximal RTT. In this case, that would call for $b\sqrt{s}\frac{P}{R} \approx 1.55$sec whereas in this scenario $b\sqrt{s}\frac{P}{R} = 890$msec.

them to finish sooner. With RED, the short flows see the same ambient drop rate as all other flows.

Two-Way Traffic: When two-way traffic is present, the traffic can become burstier due to ACK-compression [27]. In this scenario, we have the 7 flow groups from our basic scenario sending in both directions. The congested link has a latency of 5ms. Figure 10 shows the throughput for each flow group. AFD-SB and AFD-FT both provide much better fairness than RED and FRED. AFD-FT punishes one particularly aggressive group of flows (for reasons we discussed in the Unresponsive Flow section above). The additional queueing delay incurred in the reverse direction is enough to cause the performance of the TCP flow group with longer RTT (the 7th group) to suffer under AFD-SB (their RTT with queueing delay is roughly 180msec, which is larger than the 150msec our parameters were intended for).

Changing Traffic: We also tested the performance of AFD under changing traffic conditions. In this scenario, three flow groups (AIMD1, AIMD2, TCP) begin sending data at the start of the simulation. After 100 seconds, three additional groups (of the same kinds) start transmitting, doubling the offered load. At time 200 seconds, the first 3 groups stop sending. Figure 12 shows that the AFD-SB algorithm is able to adapt to the changing traffic, cutting the allocations in half when the offered load doubles, and increasing them again when the load is reduced.

Bursty Flows: We also examined the performance of AFD in the presence of on-off sources. These sources exhibit maximally bursty behavior by sending a burst at the speed of the access link (100Mbps) for a brief period and then going idle. The burstiness of these on-off sources is varied by adjusting their burst times while holding the burst rate and idle period constant. An on-off source can be characterized by the ratio of its average sending rate, $\frac{r_{burst} \times t_{burst}}{t_{burst} + t_{idle}}$, to the fair share rate, r_{fair}.

The results of these experiments are shown in Figure 13. Each group of bars in the figure represents one experiment. In each experiment, there are 5 flows in each of the original 7 groups of flows (i.e., those used in the Mixed Traffic experiments above), and a single on-off source. The ratio of the average sending rate of the on-off flow to the fair share rate is indicated on the X-axis (ranging from .5 to 16.) For each experiment, the first seven bars show the average throughput for the flows in each of the 7 flow groups. The eighth bar shows the throughput of the on-off source.

There are three things to note in this figure. First, the bursty flows are not punished for their burstiness. When the average rate of the on-off source is one-half the fair share, its packets are not dropped. When its average sending rate is equal to the fair share, it experiences some

packet drops and its throughput is approximately 90% of the fair share rate.[16] The second point to note is that as the sending rate of the bursty flow increases (up to 16 times the fair share rate), it does not receive more than the fair share. Finally, as the sending rate of the bursty flow increases, the fairness among the other flow groups is maintained. When the on-off source sends at 16 times the fair share rate, all the other flow groups receive between 95% and 100% of the fair share. Hence, these results indicate that AFD performs well in the face of very bursty flows, neither punishing nor rewarding flows for their burstiness while preserving the basic fairness among all flows.

C. Discussion of Simulation Results

We now review the general conclusions that can be drawn from our set of simulations. In most scenarios, as long as the guidelines are followed AFD-SB and AFD-FT provide very good approximations to fair bandwidth allocations. The level of fairness is far superior to RED (which does not attempt to provide fairness) and FRED (which uses a very restricted amount of state to guide the dropping decisions). The performance of AFD-SB and AFD-FT seemed fairly robust to varying parameters and conditions. In those scenarios where b was not large enough, or the RTTs were too large, the level of fairness degraded gracefully. Thus, AFD appears to not need precise parameter tuning, and fails softly when the parameters are far out of alignment.

As we saw with the unresponsive CBR flow, and in many of our other simulations not shown here, AFD-FT responds quite punitively when flows are not responsive. We judge this a good thing, but ultimately this is a policy question. With AFD-SB we can turn this policy on or off depending on the desires of the network operator;[17] in AFD-FT this policy is hardwired in. Moreover, the choice of $k = 5$ in our version of AFD-FT (where k is the number of other flows that must be compared before a packet is eliminated from the flow table) will probably need to be made larger when the number of persistent fast flows is larger. AFD-FT dealt quite well with the many small flows, but if the number of fast flows is on the order of thousands the number of comparisons will probably have to be on the order of 10 or more. We have not yet investigated how this parameter will scale.

---

[16]Recall that deviations from the fair share are most likely to occur for flows sending at or near the fair share rate.

[17]Again, we don't present the algorithm which implements this policy in AFD-SB, but it is straightforward and requires only that the shadow buffer and flow table keep separate track of matches that were dropped and matches that were not dropped.

VI. STATE REQUIREMENTS AND RATE DISTRIBUTIONS

These simulations show that when using the guidelines to set the parameters, AFD provides reasonably fair bandwidth allocations. However, can this algorithm be feasibly implemented? All the operations on the forwarding path are $O(1)$, so the main barrier to implementation would be if AFD required an impractical amount of state. This feasibility requirement is economic, not technical. Clearly routers could be built with vast amounts of additional storage; however, that would come at a steep price, and we are looking to achieve fairness without greatly increasing the complexity or the cost of future routers. We use, as our standard, the requirement that the additional state required by AFD should be small compared to the memory already required by the packet buffer. We compute the state requirements, with the aid of two measurements, in Section VI-A. In Section VI-B we discuss how these state requirements depend crucially on the rate distribution and, in Section VI-C, present some trace data on current rate distributions.

A. Calculation of State Requirements

We compute the state requirements of our two designs – AFD-SB and AFD-FT – separately. We start with AFD-SB, whose state consists of two parts: the shadow buffer and the hash table.

Guideline 1 (Section III-A) states that the shadow buffer should hold roughly $10 \frac{R}{r_{fair}}$ packets. This estimate assumed that all packets were the same size. To adjust this for variable packet sizes, we first define $\tilde{R}$ as the packet arrival rate in terms of packets/sec, and $\tilde{r}_{fair}$ as the arrival rate of a flow sending at the fair share rate; also, let P_{max} and P_{ave} denote the maximal and average packet sizes. The proper sizing of the shadow buffer in terms of packets, when you have variable sized packets, is then $b = 10 \frac{\tilde{R}}{\tilde{r}_{fair}}$. The worst case, the lowest value, for $\tilde{r}_{fair}$ is when a fair share flow is sending maximal sized packets: $\tilde{r}_{fair} \geq \frac{r_{fair}}{P_{max}}$. The expression for R is simply $R = \frac{R}{P_{ave}}$. To represent each packet in the shadow buffer we use, roughly 6 bytes.[18] Assuming that $P_{max} = 1500$ bytes and $P_{ave} = 300$ bytes,[19] we then find that b_{bit}, the shadow buffer size in bits, should be roughly:

$$b_{bit} = 10 * 48 * \frac{\frac{R}{300}}{\frac{r_{fair}}{1500}} = 2400 \frac{R}{r_{fair}}$$

Similarly, we can estimate the storage required for a hash table to keep track of the number of bytes sent by each flow. We describe our trace data in Section VI-C, but for now we use the fact that, in the various traces we have seen and for the shadow buffer sizes we are proposing, the number of flows in the hash table is typically less than a fourth the number of packets in the shadow buffer (See Figure 14). Let's assume that we need 2 bytes per entry for counting (assuming we count matches at the granularity of 40 byte units and ignore roundoff errors), and that we use a hash table 12 times larger than the expected number of flows to reduce the chance of collisions in the hash table. The size of the hash table h_{bit}, in bits, is then:

$$h_{bit} = 10 * 16 * 12 * \frac{1}{4} \frac{\frac{R}{300}}{\frac{r_{fair}}{1500}} = 2400 \frac{R}{r_{fair}}$$

Thus, to a first approximation, these two data structures require similar amounts of memory. Many router vendors recommend having on the order of 250 msec's worth of memory in the packet buffers. We compare the memory required by AFD to the memory already recommended for the packet buffer, which is roughly $\frac{C}{4}$ where C is the speed of the link (in bps). The ratio, call it ρ_{SB}, of AFD-SB's state requirement to the size of the packet buffers is given by:

$$\rho_{SB} = \frac{4800 \frac{R}{r_{fair}}}{\frac{1}{4}C} = \frac{19.2 kbits/sec}{(1-D)r_{fair}} \approx \frac{19.2 kbits/sec}{r_{fair}}$$

where the last approximation is because $C = R(1 - D)$ and we suspect the aggregate dropping rate will typically be low. Thus, the fraction of extra memory, ρ_{SB}, required by AFD-SB depends on the typical size of the fair share rate on a link.

We now calculate the state requirements of AFD-FT. If the flow table is implemented using a hash table, then we merely use the state requirements above (only the hash table part) and so the state requirements are roughly half that of AFD-SB. If the flow table is implemented using CAM then we no longer need a table 12 times the number of flows (as we did with the hash table). The CAM-based design needs roughly 64 bits per flow (48 bits for the hashed flow-id and 16 bits for a counter). Modifying the calculations above to reflect these changes, we find that the AFD-FT ratio is:

$$\rho_{FT} \approx \frac{3.2 kbits/sec}{r_{fair}}$$

---

[18]We need not store the full header in the shadow buffer, merely the hash of the source-destination addresses. 6 bytes is a sufficiently large hash to comfortably accommodate roughly 10^8 flows with small chance of collision.

[19]See [3] for measurements of average packet size. We've used a fairly conservative estimate, as the average packet size reported in [3] is over 400bytes. The average packet size over our three traces that we report on in Section VI-C is almost 500 bytes.

which is one-sixth of the AFD-SB requirements.

Note that these estimates of the ratios ρ depend only on the fair share of a link and not directly on its bandwidth. For slow links, the fair share will be quite small (and thus ρ could be 1 or larger), but the amount of memory required for these slow links is insignificant; if the fair share is 19.2kbps, so $\rho = 1$, on a T3 link, the required extra memory for AFD-SB is roughly 1.5Mbytes. Thus, we care mostly about these ratios ρ on faster links where the absolute amount of memory devoted to the packet buffers is quite large. We assume that faster links will have larger fair shares, and these ratios ρ estimating the relative memory requirements of AFD will be smaller on such links.

We are not aware of many studies of the typical fair shares on current Internet links.[20] One can't infer the fair share merely by taking a packet trace; without fair bandwidth allocation one can't tell which flows are constrained by that link, and which flows are constrained elsewhere. One would have to find a link whose router has Fair Queueing (or some equivalent algorithm) on which to take traces (and even these traces would be misleading because of the lack of fair bandwidth allocations elsewhere along in the network). Lacking a solidly grounded method for measuring typical fair shares, we turned to an available dataset that has some bearing on the question.

One way to obtain a very rough estimate of the fair share on a path is to measure the end-to-end throughput obtained by a TCP connection that traverses that path. This is a very imperfect measure, since TCP throughput varies as a function of RTT and not all traffic is TCP-friendly. We obtained a dataset of measured end-to-end throughputs of transfers between NIMI measurement sites.[21] 47 sites participated in this measurement by periodically transferring a 1MB file with another randomly chosen NIMI site. The dataset contains roughly ʋ5,000 transfers. For lack of space we do not show the distribution here, but in over 90% of the transfers the rate is greater than 250kbps. These measurements are not focused on high-speed links. However, most of the NIMI boxes are at universities and other sites that are well-connected to the Internet, and none of them are behind very slow modems, so the measurements are probably indicative of moderate speed links. If we take 250kbps as a rough estimate of the fair share then $\rho_{SB} \approx \frac{1}{13}$ and $\rho_{FT} \approx \frac{1}{78}$. That is, the extra memory required by AFD-SB is less than a tenth of the memory already devoted to packet buffers. We view these estimates as being a very

conservative lower bound, in that the fair shares on very fast links may be much larger, and thus the ratios ρ_{SB} and ρ_{FT} much smaller. As one moves up the network hierarchy towards the backbone links, it is likely that a larger fraction of flows are bottlenecked somewhere else in the network. That means that the fair share available to flows unconstrained elsewhere could be quite large. If backbone links had $r_{fair} \approx 2Mbps$ then $\rho_{SB} \approx \frac{1}{100}$ and $\rho_{FT} \approx \frac{1}{600}$. However, the level of fair shares remains an open question, and we hope in the future to find better ways to estimate the fair share on high-speed links.

This paper does not address detailed implementation issues. However, since we've used the storage requirements of the packet buffer as a yardstick for the state requirements of AFD, we would be remiss if we did not point out that this comparison is somewhat misleading. Packet buffers make heavy use of slower (and cheaper) DRAM with a smaller amount of faster (and more expensive) SRAM. We can do likewise with the shadow buffer state. However, the flow table will probably require SRAM or CAM. Thus, we cannot conclude that AFD imposes a cost that is a fraction ρ of the packet buffer cost. We leave the detailed implementation issues for future work (by others); our goal here is to provide a rough estimate of the state requirements.

The estimates above are very rough in nature. On any particular choice, such as the 250msecs for packet buffers or the numbers of bits for counters, one could argue that we are off by a factor of two. But we believe these calculations give us an order-of-magnitude estimate of the state requirements of our design, and suggest that AFD, in either of its incarnations, is likely able to achieve reasonable levels of fairness without exorbidant amounts of extra state.

We now argue that the distribution of rates greatly aids the AFD approach.

B. Impact of the Rate Distribution

Our state calculations depended critically on the value of r_{fair}, and in particular on the ratio $\frac{r_{fair}}{R}$. One intuitive way understanding this ratio is the following. Let's call a flow a *cheetah* if it is sending above or near the fair share, and let n_c denote the number of such flows. We call the other flows, the slow ones, *turtles*. Let $\gamma = \sum_{turtles} \frac{r_i}{R}$ denote the fraction of the offered load that comes from these slow flows. The equation defining the fair share $\sum_i \min(r_i, r_{fair}) = C$ becomes: $R\gamma + r_{fair}n_c = C$. We can write this as

$$\frac{R}{r_{fair}} = \frac{n_c}{(1-D) - \gamma}$$

---

[20] The *available bandwidth*, which is a somewhat different concept, was studied in [19].

[21] NIMI is the National Internet Measurement Infrastructure; see [20] for a more detailed description. See [26] for details of the measurement process.

where D is the overall drop rate. The quantity $\frac{R}{r_{fair}}$ is minimized when both the number of cheetahs is small *and* the fraction of bandwidth consumed by the turtles is quite small: in short, when most of the bandwidth is being sent by a very few fast flows. It is in this regime that AFD requires very little state to perform well.

To make this more precise, we now look at how r_{fair} varies under different rate distributions in a simple analytical model. We consider a continuum of flows whose rates are given by a density function $h(r)$. We will consider four continuum distributions that all have the same average rate (of 1 in arbitrary units) and normalize the distribution by n (representing the number of flows), so the total load offered by each distribution is n. For each distribution we have $n = \int_0 h(r)dr$ and $1 = \frac{1}{n}\int_0 h(r)rdr$. We assume that the router allocates bandwidth fairly, and that flows respond by restraining their flow to the fair share if their assigned rate (by the distribution) is larger than the fair share. As we vary the capacity C between 0 and n we compute the fair share $r_{fair}(C)$ from the constraint: $C = \int_0^\infty h(r)\min(r, r_{fair}(C))dr$. The question is how $r_{fair}(C)$ compares for the various distributions we consider.

We consider four distributions, in order of increasing variance. For a *point* distribution, where all flows are the same rate, the fair share is merely $r_{fair}^{int} = \frac{C}{n}$. For a distribution where rates are uniformly distributed between 0 and 2, the fair share is $r_{fair}^{uni} = 2(1 - \sqrt{1 - \frac{C}{n}})$. For an exponential distribution, $h(r) = ne^{-r}$, the fair share is $r_{fair}^{ex} = -\ln(1 - \frac{C}{n})$. Finally, for a power-law distribution $h(r) = \frac{n}{2}r^{-3}$ for $r \geq \frac{1}{2}$ (and 0 otherwise; this restriction is to avoid the divergence at the origin), we have $r_{fair}^{pl} = \frac{1}{4}(1 - \frac{C}{n})^{-1}$. The point of this exercise is that as the tail of the distributions got larger (that is, the number of very fast flows increases) the fair share as a function of C became larger. While the fair share diverges for both the exponential and the cubic power-law distributions as $\frac{C}{n}$ approaches 1, the fair share is dramatically larger in the power-law case.

Guideline 1 calls for the buffer size to be roughly $b = 10\frac{R}{r_{fair}}$. If the rate distribution is such that r_{fair} is larger (for a given R) then the shadow buffer size, and all the state requirements, become smaller. Note that if the fair share remains the same then the state requirements increase linearly with the speed of the link (and the offered load R). However, if we keep the same offered load and let the fair share increase to its natural level as we increase C, and study $b(C) = 10\frac{C}{r_{fair}(C)}$, then we find two cases. For the point and uniform distributions, $b(C)$ increases; this is what we expect, more state is required on faster links.

For the exponential and power-law distributions, however, $b(C)$ decreases; as the speed of the link increases the state requirements of the algorithm go down! Note this is not a decrease in the ratio ρ, this is a decrease in the absolute amount of state.

We have no way of judging with any certainty what the fair share rates will be in the future on high-speed links. However, the arguments above suggest that AFD will operate best when the distribution of flow rates has a long tail. We now turn to empirical evidence to see if this is currently the case.

C. Trace Data

We obtained traces of traffic from three separate locations: a 100Mbps link at a national laboratory, a T3 peering link between two providers, and a FDDI ring connecting a modem bank at a dial up provider to a backbone network.[22] We refer to these traces as Trace 1, Trace 2, and Trace 3, respectively. Trace 1 consists of approximately 22 million packets collected during a two hour interval. Trace 2 consists of 34 million packets over a 45 minute span. Trace 3 collected approximately 6 million packets in 70 minutes.

Guideline 2 calls for keeping state of about 1 second in order to estimate the rates. For a variety of different time intervals, Figure 14 shows the average ratio between the number of packets in the shadow buffer and the number of distinct flows represented in the shadow buffer; this ratio was used in Section VI-A to estimate the state requirements for AFD.

For each of the traces we estimated individual flow rates based on the packets seen in the last second; see [14] for similar data and related discussions. Figure 15 shows the complementary distribution of flow rates for each of the three traces. Trace 3 is not obviously inconsistent with a slowly decaying exponential distribution, but the other two clearly have long tails.[23] This is even more pronounced on a log-linear plot, which for space reasons we do not show here. Figure 16 shows the cumulative distributions of the 1-second flow rates. Note 10% or less of the flows represent roughly 60% of the bytes in the worst case, and roughly 90% of the bytes in the best case. This is in contrast to the fastest 10% of the flows carrying 33% of the bytes for an exponential distribution. Thus, based on the very preliminary evidence presented here and in [14] we

---

[22]To preserve anonymity, we omit further details about these sites.

[23]We use the term *long tailed* to refer to distributions that decay slower than exponentially. Power-law distributions are examples of this, but so are Weibull and other distributions. We do not intend to enter the rather lengthy and subtle debates about whether or not a particular distribution is a power law or Weibull or some other form. We merely observe that it obviously decays slower than an exponential.

conjecture that rate distributions are usually long-tailed. In the language of Section VI-B, we expect that the number of cheetahs will typically be small, but they will represent the bulk of the bytes.

Similar statements have long been made about the distribution of flow sizes. Figures 17 and 18 show the analogous data for flow sizes as measured by the total number of bytes transferred. These distributions are significantly more skewed than the rate distributions. Figure 19 shows the total flow size plotted against the flow's rate (as measured by total bytes over completion time) for flows in Trace 2 that are larger than 10,000 bytes (the other traces have similar results). No correlation is visually apparent, and when we compute the correlation it is quite small; the correlations between rate and size are .0075, .0031 and .00088 for the three traces, and are .11, .22 and −.0045 when we correlate the logarithms of the rate and size. This shows that the distinction between cheetahs and turtles is different from the historical distinction between elephants and mice. The long-tailed distribution of rates is clearly not directly driven by the long-tailed distribution in sizes. Their underlying mechanisms are presumably different.

We are not aware of work that analyzes the mechanisms responsible for the distribution of flow rates. We assume that the rates on a link, at least for longer-lasting flows, reflects the available bandwidth at that flow's bottleneck link. However, it is not clear to us why the distribution of these bottleneck rates should have a long tail. Much more work remains to be done to characterize these rate distributions, and explain their origin.

VII. CONTEXT, RELATED WORK, AND DISCUSSION

This paper starts with the assumption that routers should allocate bandwidth fairly. While this is a familiar and oft-told story, for context we once again briefly review the rationale for fairness. We then discuss related work and conclude with some comments on AFD's underlying design principles.

Congestion control is one of the Internet's most fundamental architectural problems. In the current Internet, most routers do not actively manage per-flow bandwidth allocations, and so the bandwidth received by a flow depends on the congestion control algorithms used by other competing flows. To achieve relatively equitable bandwidth allocations, all flows must be TCP-compatible [4] (also known as TCP-friendly); that is, they must use a congestion control algorithm that results in bandwidth allocations similar to TCP's. This approach requires uniformity and cooperation, both of which might be problematic.

By restricting the world of congestion control algorithms to those that are TCP-compatible, some applica-

tions may be impaired. This would be the case if some applications required radically different forms of congestion control that are inherently unfriendly to TCP. However, recent advances in *Equation-Based Congestion Control* (EBCC) [11] and other TCP-compatible algorithms [22], [21] gives hope that a very wide variety of application requirements could be fulfilled within the sphere of TCP-compatibility. Thus, the uniformity requirement, while potentially a problem, may in fact be tolerable.

As for cooperation, any host can obtain more bandwidth simply by using a more aggressive congestion control algorithm. Thus, the current approach relies on end-hosts (and their users) voluntarily adopting the TCP-compatible guidelines. There has been some initial work to penalize flows that violate the rules [9], but so far the goal of reliably identifying *ill-behaved* flows has proved elusive.[24]

In response to these problems, there has been a long history (dating back to Nagle [16]) of proposing that routers play a more active role in allocating bandwidth. If the routers ensure fair bandwidth allocations[25] then end-hosts are no longer required to adhere to any particular form of congestion control and the problems of uniformity and cooperation mentioned above no longer exist.[26] The proposals to accomplish this fair bandwidth allocation, such as Fair Queueing [6] and related algorithms [15], [23], [2], all involve complicated packet scheduling algorithms and require per-flow state. High-speed implementations of these algorithms are just now becoming available. If such implementations continue to scale to the highest speeds without causing undue costs, then the contents of this paper are probably moot. However, it isn't yet clear that these implementations will scale *inexpensively* to increasingly higher speeds. If the cost of adding this extra functionality is significant, designs with lower complexity but similar functionality may be preferable in commercial designs. This was our goal in designing AFD, to provide fairness at a significantly reduced level of complexity.

Core-Stateless Fair Queueing (CSFQ) [24] and the subsequently proposed variations [5], [25] share the same goal. While they achieve high degrees of fairness with

---

[24]There has been more success with identifying high-bandwidth flows, and unresponsive flows, but that still leaves flows a large leeway to cheat.

[25]To give users an incentive to use some form of responsive congestion control we add the requirement that flows are punished if they incur persistent high drop rates. See [10], [24] for discussions of this topic.

[26]Some claim that such fair allocation mechanisms open the door to denial-of-service attacks through flow-spoofing; while we do not believe such arguments are sufficient to nullify the desirability of fair bandwidth allocations, and that this paper is not the place to delve into such arguments at length, we did want to note the existence of objections to the fair bandwidth allocation paradigm.

scalable mechanisms in the core routers, these schemes require a change in the packet format (to accommodate another field) and the careful configuration of routers into core, edge, and peripheral regions. Thus, while CSFQ delivers a high degree of fairness, it faces significant deployment hurdles.

There are several other proposals for low-complexity approximations to fairness, such as FRED, [13], SRED [17], SFB [7], CHOKe [18] and RED-PD [14]. These present a spectrum of possible designs, differing in the extent to which they carefully manage the bandwidth allocation. The extremes of the spectrum are complete fairness (Fair Queueing) on one end and unmanaged allocation (RED) on the other; in between, some algorithms carefully manage the bandwidth of a few flows (*e.g.* RED-PD) while others attempt to manage all flows at the same time, but do a less careful job on each one (*e.g.* AFD). Different choices along this spectrum embody different expectations about the set of congestion algorithms deployed. One possible view is that in the future almost all flows will use a TCP-compatible congestion control algorithm, and that there will only be a very few malicious (or broken) flows that are substantially more aggressive. In this scenario, routers only need to detect these few outlying flows and restrain their usage to an appropriate level. RED-PD is an example of an algorithm well-suited to this task. Another possible view is that flows will use a very wide variety of congestion control algorithms, not necessarily TCP-compatible, and that routers will need to allocate bandwidth to flows as the common case. AFD is designed for this scenario. Which of these two approaches – identifying a few outlying flows and treating them as special or treating allocation as the common case – depends on how the future of congestion control unfolds.[27] Our purpose in this paper is not to argue that one vision is more likely than another, merely to design an algorithm that would be suitable if the second scenario comes to pass.

The spectrum of approximate fairness designs also presents us with different tradeoffs between increased fairness and reduced complexity. The desirability of one spot on the spectrum versus another depends greatly on the nature of Internet traffic and on router design constraints, both of which change over time. We based AFD on the assumption that while traffic characteristics and hardware capabilities will evolve, there will be three enduring truths. First, FIFO packet scheduling will be significantly easier to implement than certain non-FIFO scheduling algorithms; it uses cheaper hardware that scales to faster speeds. Second, the distribution of rates on high-speed

links will be long-tailed. We don't expect this to necessarily be a power-law or any other particular form, but we do expect that the majority of flows will be slow but the fast (high-rate) flows will send the bulk of the bytes. Third, we assume that memory – fast, slow, and CAM – will continue to decrease in price relative to the special logic needed to implement non-FIFO packet scheduling. AFD's main implementation burden is additional memory; we assume that the marginal cost of equipping routers with AFD will shrink (relative to packet scheduling designs) as these commodity products become cheaper over time. If these three assumptions hold, then we believe AFD may be a cost-effective scheme for providing approximately fair bandwidth allocations.

REFERENCES

[1]   Bansal, D., and Balakrishnan, H., "Binomial Congestion Control Algorithms " *Proceedings of Infocom '01*.

[2]   Bennett, J. and Zhang, H., "Hierarchical Packet Fair Queueing Algorithms", *SIGCOMM Symposium on Communications Architectures and Protocols*, pp. 143–156, Aug. 1996.

[3]   http://www.caida.org/analysis/AIX/plen_hist/

[4]   Braden, B., Clark, D., Crowcroft, J., Davie, B., Deering, S.,Estrin, D., Floyd, S., Jacobson, V., Minshall, G., Partridge, C., Peterson, L.,Ramakrishnan,K., Shenker,S., Wroclawski, J., Zhang, L., "Recommendations on queue management and congestion avoidance in the internet", *IETF RFC (Informational) 2309*, April 1998.

[5]   Cao, Z., Wang, Z. and Zegura, E., "Rainbow Fair Queueing: Fair Bandwidth Sharing Without Per-Flow State", *Proceedings of INFOCOM'00* March 2000.

[6]   Demers, A., Keshav, S. and Shenker, S., "Analysis and simulation of a fair queueing algorithm", *Journal of Internetworking Research and Experience*, pp 3-26, Oct. 1990. Also in Proceedings of ACM SIGCOMM'89, pp 3-12.

[7]   Feng, W., Shin, K., Kandlur, D. and Saha, D., "Stochastic Fair Blue: A Queue Management Algorithm for Enforcing Fairness", *Proceedings of INFOCOM'2001 (to appear)*, April, 2001.

[8]   Floyd, S. and Jacobson, V., "Random Early Detection Gateways for Congestion Avoidance", *IEEE/ACM Transaction on Networking*, 1(4), pp 397-413, Aug. 1993.

[9]   Floyd, S., and Fall, K., "Router Mechanisms to Support End-to-End Congestion Control", *LBL Technical report*, February 1997.

[10]   Floyd, S., and Fall, K., "Promoting the Use of End-to-End Congestion Control in the Internet", To appear in *IEEE/ACM Transactions on Networking*, August 1999.

[11]   Floyd, S., Handley, M., Padhye, J., and Widmer, J., "Equation-Based Congestion Control for Unicast Applications", *Proceedings of ACM SIGCOMM'2000*, August 2000.

[12]   Hollot, C.V., Misra, V., Towsley, D. and Gong, W., "On Designing Improved Controllers for AQM Routers Supporting TCP Flows", *Proceedings of Infocom '01*.

[13]   Lin, D. and Morris, R., "Dynamics of random early detection", *Proceedings of ACM SIGCOMM'97*, pp 127-137, Oct. 1997.

[14]   Mahajan, R. and Floyd, S. "Controlling High-Bandwidth Flows at the Congested Router", ACIRI, Berkeley, California, Nov. 2000.

[15]   McKenny, P., "Stochastic Fairness Queueing", *Proceedings of INFOCOM'90*, pp 733-740.

[16] Nagle, J., "On packet switches with infinite storage", *Internet Engineering Task Force*, RFC-970, December, 1985.

[17] Ott, T., Lakshman, T. and Wong, L., "SRED: Stabilized RED", *Proceedings of INFOCOM'99*, pp 1346-1355, March 1999.

[18] Pan, R., Prabhakar, B. and Psounis, K., "CHOKe - A Stateless Active Queue Management Scheme For Approximating Fair Bandwidth Allocation", *Proceedings of INFOCOM'00* March 2000.

[19] Paxson, V., "End-to-End Internet Packet Dynamics", *IEEE/ACM Transactions on Networking*, vol. 7, no. 3, pp. 277-292, 1999.

[20] Paxson, V., Mahdavi, J., Adams, A. and Mathis, M., "An Architecture for Large-Scale Internet Measurement", *IEEE Communications Magazine*, vol. 36, no. 8, pp. 48-54, August 1998.

[21] Rajaie, R., Handley, M. and Estrin, D., "An End-to-end Rate-based Congestion Control Mechanism for Realtime Streams in the Internet", *Proceedings of INFOCOM'99*, March, 1999.

[22] Rhee, I., Ozdemir, V. and Yi, Y., "TEAR: TCP emulation at receivers – flow control for multimedia streaming", *Technical Report, Department of Computer Science, NCSU*, April, 2000.

[23] Shreedhar, M., and Varghese, G., "Efficient Fair Queueing using Deficit Round Robin", *ACM Computer Communication Review*, vol. 25, no. 4, pp. 231–242, October, 1995.

[24] Stoica, I., Shenker, S. and Zhang, H., "Core-Stateless Fair Queueing: Achieving Approximately Fair Bandwidth Allocations in High Speed Networks", *Proceedings of ACM SIGCOMM'98*.

[25] Venkitaraman, N., Mysore, J., Srikant R.,and Barnes, R. "Stateless Prioritized Fair Queueing", *Internet Engineering Task Force* July 2000.

[26] Zhang, Y., Paxson, V., and Shenker, S., "The Stationarity of Internet Path Properties: Routing, Loss, and Throughput", ACIRI Technical Report, May 2000.

[27] Zhang, L., Shenker, S. and Clark, D., "Observations on the Dynamics of a congestion control Algorithm: The Effects of Two-Way Traffic", *Proceedings of ACM SIGCOMM'91*.

[28] ns - Network Simulator (Version 2.1b6).

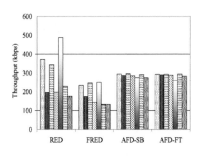

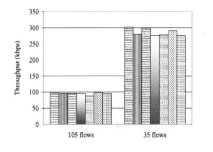

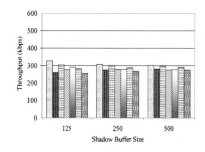

Fig. 4. High-Speed Link   Fig. 5. Increased Multiplexing   Fig. 6. Reduced Shadow Buffer

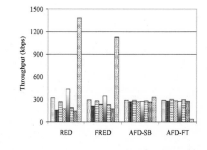

Fig. 7. Long RTTs (a) Max Latency = 200 msec (b) Max Latency = 300 msec   Fig. 8. Unresponsive Flow

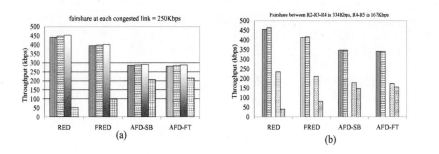

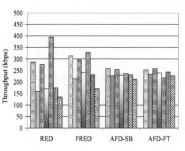

Fig. 9. Multiple Congested Links (a) same Fair Share (b) different Fair Share   Fig. 10. Two-Way Traffic

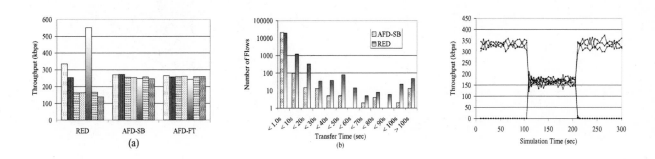

Fig. 11. Web Traffic – (a) throughput of large flows (b) transfer time of small flows   Fig. 12. Changing Traffic

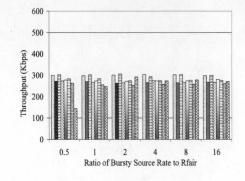

Fig. 13. Bursty Traffic

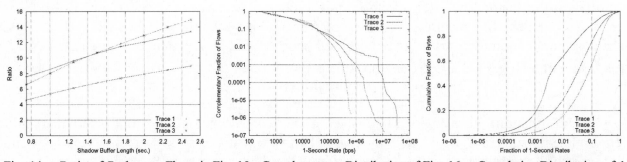

Fig. 14. Ratio of Packets to Flows in Fig. 15. Complementary Distribution of Fig. 16. Cumulative Distribution of 1-
Shadow Buffers   1-Second Rates   Second Rates

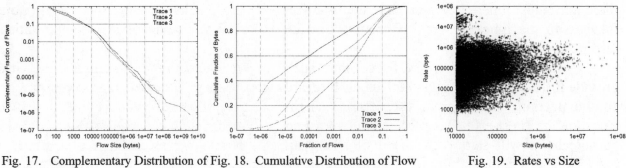

Fig. 17. Complementary Distribution of Fig. 18. Cumulative Distribution of Flow   Fig. 19. Rates vs Size
Flow Sizes   Sizes

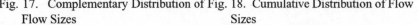

Quality of Service Assurance for Dependable Information Infrastructures

Nong Ye, Ying-Cheng Lai and Toni Farley
ARIZONA STATE UNIVERSITY
{nongye@asu.edu}

Abstract

The information infrastructure has enabled a networked computing and communication environment. Although many DoD organizations depend on network-centric information operations to support critical missions, the current information infrastructure provides little guarantee of their dependability. In this paper, we first discuss some drawbacks of existing information infrastructures, such as the Internet and Computational Grids, in Quality of Service (QoS) assurance. Next, we present the objective of our project in the Critical Infrastructure Protection (CIP) program to assure end-to-end QoS for individual high-priority jobs on the information infrastructure with minimum traffic congestion through local, regional, and global level QoS models. In each section, we summarize our research accomplishments to date, present the outcomes of some representative work, and point to published papers for more details.

Introduction

Information infrastructures enable a networked computing and communications environment, such as those used by many DoD organizations, to perform network-centric information operations for critical missions. Network-centric information operations are characterized by information moving between computational nodes on the network with the goal of information superiority -- 100% relevant content, along with data accuracy and timely delivery. Such operations depend on network-centric operational architectures that provide desired QoS assurance. For example, a high-performance information infrastructure that provides a speedy, dependable backplane sharing of various resources (including data, computation, communication, and visualization) on the computing and communications network. QoS has three attributes: timeliness, precision, and accuracy (Ye, 2002; Chen, et al., 2003). This project focuses on the timeliness of information operations and time management of computational resources on the network.

Existing information infrastructures, such as the Internet and Computational Grids, provide little dependability guarantees, with regards to timeliness, for networked computing and communication. The Internet supports the sharing of computational resources on a network based on the "best-effort" model, in which trust among participating parties is assumed. That is, participant A will satisfy the need of other participants as long as the current capacity of participant A's computational resources can do so. Hence, resources are made available for use by anyone regardless of the state of the resources until those resources are depleted. This "best-effort" model has provided an environment for crafty exploits and denial-of-service attacks that have occurred and presented a significant threat to the realm of information superiority. Moreover, QoS for a user's application is not guaranteed because other users may emerge at any time to compete for and share computational resources, causing time delay. Thus, little resource management and QoS guarantees exist for dependable information operations on the Internet.

Computational Grids (Foster and Kesselman, 1999) address the resource management problem by using centralized brokers or mating agents to assign networked computational resources to users' applications. The centralized authority of resource management (top-down, command-directed synchronization of network-centric information operations) works only within a small-scale networking environment of closely-coupled administrative domains, such as a network of several national supercomputing centers, as currently demonstrated (National Science Foundation, 2000). Centralized authority of resource management does not scale to an information infrastructure where many independent administrative domains exist, as these domains may not necessarily obey this authority. First of all, administrative domains for different organizations likely act on their own to rapidly respond to local situations and meet local contingencies as they see them. Secondly, information operations through interactions among different administrative domains are typically complex and non-linear. These two factors make even local influences from closely-coupled, friendly administrative domains hard to predict. The top-down, centralized synchronization of resource management in Computational Grids is not scalable to large-scale, complex, adaptive information infrastructures in dynamically changing environments.

Most existing research work on computer network QoS is aimed towards population-based performance objectives concerning the mean, worst-case, or statistically bounded performance of time delay, execution time, or other timeliness measures; with little consideration for the end-to-end timelines assurance of an individual job on the network. For example, consider a message that needs to be sent from a command center to a battle field with a certain timeliness requirement. The mean time delay property of a computer network or the statistical bound on the percentage of jobs experiencing extended delay on the network tells little about the specific time delay that this particular message experiences. The lowest bound set by the worst-case time delay property of the network may be short of meeting the timeliness requirement of this message. To achieve information superiority, it is important to assure end-to-end QoS for each individual high-priority job. This project focuses on end-to-end performance objectives for individual high-priority jobs on information infrastructures.

Integrated Service (IntServ) and Differentiated Service (DiffServ) are two existing models that address QoS on information infrastructures (Almquist, 1992; Blake et al., 1998; Braden et al., 1994). The IntServ model relies on bandwidth reservation for each flow on a computer network. This model has an extremely high overhead from managing the reservations made for many flows on large-scale computer networks, such as information infrastructures, and thus is not scalable. The DiffServ model classifies jobs on computer networks into groups of different priorities and, given these groups, different QoS treatments. However, the DiffServ model does not consider the performance objectives of individual jobs.

The objective of this project is to achieve end-to-end QoS assurance for individual high-priority jobs on an information infrastructure. To accomplish this objective, we work on QoS models at the local, regional, and global levels of the information infrastructure. A local level QoS model aims at providing service stability and dependability on an individual resource, of an information infrastructure, by minimizing the waiting time variance (WTV) of jobs admitted for service by that resource. A regional level QoS model aims at providing service stability and dependability from a collection of multiple resources on the information infrastructure under a centralized control environment, (e.g., computational resources shared within the administrative domain of one organization). A global level QoS model is built on service stability and dependability at the local and regional levels of the information infrastructure to provide assurance for the end-to-end QoS requirement of an individual high-priority job that flows across multiple administrative domains, without a centralized control authority.

In the following sections of this paper, we describe our major research for the local, regional and global level QoS models. In these sections we reference only some of our publications, but still include all publications related to this project in the reference section.

Local Level QoS Models

The local level QoS model manages a computer or network system with a single resource that services processes (jobs) initiated by user requests for service. Timeliness is an important attribute of Quality of Service (Ye, 2002; Chen et al., 2003). Timeliness measures the time it takes a computer or network system to respond to, process, and complete a service request (job). In general, when a job arrives at a system requesting service, the system admits the job and places it in a waiting queue if the resource is busy processing another job. The time that a job spends in the system includes waiting time and processing time, which is the time it takes the resource to process the job after it is taken from the waiting queue. Processing time is usually determined by the size of a job and thus out of our control. Waiting time depends on admission control (which determines if a job is admitted into the system) and job scheduling (which determines job servicing order).

We aim to reduce the variance of job waiting times for service stability and dependability. Ultimately we would like to see the waiting time of any job in a computer or network system, at any given time, remain the same. That is, the objective of our local level QoS model is service stability and dependability by minimizing job WTV. Service stability of individual resources at the local level of an information infrastructure makes them become "standard parts", enabling predictable performance of each job passing through each individual resource, which in turn will greatly simplify QoS assurance problems at the regional and global levels. Otherwise regional and global level QoS assurance becomes extremely difficult to plan and manage.

Our local level QoS model focuses on admission control, job scheduling and their effects on job waiting time. Our research in this area has led to the following:

1) Batch Scheduled Admission Control (BSAC) – a method that controls the admission of jobs into a local level system in batches
2) Verified Spiral (VS) and Balanced Spiral (BS) - job scheduling methods to determine the sequence of admitted jobs for receiving service one by one, leading to:
   - Job scheduling method for the weighted WTV problem in which each job has a priority weight
   - Inventory control method that reserves the capacity of a resource to further stabilize job WTV
   - Mathematical relationship of WTV with buffer size and job processing time distribution such that a system administrator can use this relationship to set the buffer size according to the desired WTV and job processing time distribution for desired service stability and dependability
3) Implementation of BSAC and BS on a working hardware router
4) Discovery and geometric interpretation of an eye-shape pattern revealing the relationship between job waiting time variance and mean, leading to:

- Mathematical method for deriving an optimal job sequence for minimizing the waiting time variance of a given problem
- Mathematical derivation of the optimal job sequence for the WTV problem

5) Weighted Shortest Processing Time – Adjusted (WSPT-A) - another job scheduling method to stabilize service on an individual resource (Ye et al., 2005)

6) Feedback control mechanism for service stability and dependability from an individual resource (Ye et al., 2003)

In the remainder of this section, we briefly overview items 1-4, and point to publications on this research for further details. We refer the reader to the respective references for details on items 4 and 5.

BSAC for Admission Control

Most computer and network systems (e.g., web servers and routers) on the Internet currently do not use any type of admission control for jobs requesting service. For example, a router usually admits all arriving data packets (jobs) and places them in a waiting queue if the bandwidth (resource) is being used by other data packets, or drops it if the waiting queue is full. Since a job's waiting time depends on the number of other jobs waiting, it varies greatly. With no admission control, the number of jobs waiting in a system is unpredictable, waiting time is unstable, and the timeliness of service undependable. Additionally, the job waiting time variable has a negative impact on QoS and user satisfaction.

There is little existing work that investigates the impact of admission control on the variance of job waiting times. We develop an admission control method, called Batch Scheduled Admission Control (BSAC), to reduce WTV (Ye et al, in Review). A computer/network system with BSAC makes a decision of whether or not to admit an incoming job. Using the BSAC method, dynamically arriving jobs are admitted into the system in batches. Many criteria can be considered to determine the size of each batch. For example, the number of jobs in the batch can be used to define the batch size if the processing time does not vary much among jobs. The total load of the processing times of all the jobs in the batch can also be used to define the batch size if there is a large variance in the processing times of jobs. System administrators can set the batch size based on memory capacity, desired upper bound on waiting time (since a larger batch causes more jobs waiting for longer time), and so on.

To assure QoS on computers and networks, we can classify jobs into two groups with different priorities: high and low (Almquist, 1992; Blake et al., 1998; Braden et al., 1994). The system we design is for high priority jobs. We assume that lower priority jobs are processed whenever the system is not busy, or by another resource. At any given time, the system maintains current batch and a waiting batch. The resource is taking jobs in the current batch one by one for service according to their scheduled order. During the processing of jobs in the current batch, arriving jobs, if admitted, are placed in the waiting batch. For an incoming job, the system admits it if adding it to the waiting batch does not produce a batch whose length exceeds the batch size, and rejects it otherwise. A rejected job may be advised by the system to come back at a later time or turn to another system with a similar resource.

A time slot, *T*, for processing one batch can be set according to the maximum time required to process all jobs in any batch of a given size. At times *T*, *2T*, *3T*, etc. the resource has finished processing all jobs in the current batch, and moves jobs in the waiting batch into the current batch for processing. The length of the current batch may be less than the batch size since there may not have been enough jobs that arrived during a time interval of T to fill it up. When this occurs, low-priority jobs can fill up the current batch. So, any residual time is spent processing lower priority jobs, maintaining a time synchronized schedule for high priority jobs.

Since current computer and network systems admit all jobs, waiting time depends on the variable job arrival times. As a result the number or load of jobs waiting is unbounded. We expect that BSAC reduces WTV because it bounds and stabilizes the number or total load of jobs in each batch processed for service. Waiting time consists of waiting time in the waiting and current batches. Time in the waiting batch is the same for all jobs. Time in the current batch is bounded by the batch size. Hence, the total waiting time of each job is bounded and stabilized.

We test and compare WTV between BSAC and no admission control for two test problems with 30 and 3000 jobs respectively that arrive in two different arrival patterns: bursty and steady. All jobs must be scheduled for service by the resource. Among existing job scheduling methods in the literature, we select five representative methods to implement in this study: First Come First Serve (FCFS), Shortest Processing Time first (SPT), Weighted SPT first (WSPT), Earliest Due Date (EDD), Highest Levels First with Estimated Times (HLFWET) and Smallest Co-Levels First with Estimated Times (SCFWET).

The results in Table 1 show that BSAC provides a smaller variance and thus better stability of job waiting times when compared to no admission control. This holds for both bursty and steady job arrival conditions, regardless of the job scheduling method or problem size.

Table 1. Variance of job waiting times for BSAC and no admission control.

Scheduling method	No admission control and bursty pattern	No admission control and steady pattern	BSAC and both arrival patterns
FCFS, Problem 1	148.8	89.06	21.16
FCFS, Problem 2	240.5122	30.9732	11.9975
SPT, Problem 1	10257	3080.62	282
SPT, Problem 2	93.0607	19.193	3.752
WSPT, Problem 1	11973.67	4095.51	355.28
EDD, Problem 1	10944.73	5092.29	361.23
HLFWET, Problem 1	11291.42	4619.90	450.54
SCFWET, Problem 1	10941.06	3806.60	323.30

Spiral Methods for Job Scheduling

Although jobs arrive dynamically at an individual computer or network resource, the application of BSAC allows job admission into a resource in batches. Hence, we investigate the problem of scheduling a batch of jobs, with given processing times, to minimize WTV for service stability and dependability. When scheduling jobs, we may take into account several factors of individual jobs, such as their processing times, priorities, due dates, and so on (Pinedo, 1995). In this project, we develop two job scheduling methods, Verified Spiral and Balanced Spiral, to reduce the WTV of jobs without priorities in a given batch on a single computer or network resource. (Li, 2005; Ye, in Review). This project also consider the factors influencing WTV (e.g. sum and distribution of job processing times, and scheduling methods), as well as the weighted WTV problem, in which jobs have different weights (priorities), related job scheduling methods are Weighted Verified Spiral and Weighted Simplified Spiral (Li, 2005).

In this section, we first describe the mathematical formulation of the scheduling problem. Next we outline the scheduling methods: Verified Spiral and Balanced Spiral. We include some results comparing our Spiral methods to other scheduling methods, with regards to minimizing WTV. We refer the reader to respective references for details and work not outlined here.

Given n jobs in a batch all available at time zero, there are $n!$ possible job sequences. Assume that there is no set-up time for each job to be processed by a resource. We formulate a WTV problem as an Integer Programming problem. The decision variables are s_{ij}'s, for $i = 1, \ldots, n$ and $j = 1, \ldots, n$, representing a job sequence as well as the position of each job in the sequence. The binary integer, s_{ij}, is 1 if job j is scheduled at position i, and 0 otherwise. There are n positions in the job sequence since there are n jobs. The job to be scheduled and thus processed first is placed at position 1, the job to be scheduled second is placed at position 2, and so on. The processing time of job j is p_j, which is given. The waiting time of the job at position i is w_i.

Objective Function:

$$\text{Minimize: } \frac{1}{n-1}\sum_{k=1}^{n}(w_k - \frac{1}{n}\sum_{i=1}^{n}w_i)^2 \tag{1}$$

Subject to:

$$\sum_{j=1}^{n}s_{ij} = 1, i = 1,\ldots,n; \tag{2}$$

$$\sum_{i=1}^{n}s_{ij} = 1, j = 1,\ldots,n; \tag{3}$$

$$s_{ij} = 0 \text{ or } 1; i, j = 1,\ldots,n; \tag{4}$$

$$w_1 = 0; \tag{5}$$

$$w_i = w_{i-1} + \sum_{j=1}^{n}s_{i-1,j} * p_j, i = 2,\ldots,n. \tag{6}$$

The objective function of the WTV problem (Equation 1) is to minimize the sample variance of waiting times of n jobs. Equation 2 describes the constraint that there can be only one job assigned to each position. Equation 3 indicates that one job can be placed at only one position. Equation 4 gives the integer constraint. The waiting time of the first job to be processed is 0, which is given in equation 5. Equation 6 defines the waiting time of the job at position i ($i \geq 2$), which is the waiting and processing time of the job at position $i\text{-}1$.

Since the WTV problem is NP-hard (Kubiak, 1993), there are no efficient search algorithms to find the optimal sequence(s). Among four heuristic job scheduling methods for the WTV problem developed by Eilon and Chowdhury, two methods produce better performance for a number of small data sets: E&C1.1 and E&C1.2 (Eilon and Chowdhury, 1977). We select these two methods for further testing on large data sets and comparison with our scheduling methods, which make further improvement of E&C1.1 and E&C1.2. In addition to these methods, we compare our methods to that of SPT.

Verified Spiral (VS)

In Verified Spiral we modify E. &. C. 1.1 by first incorporating Schrage's conjecture and Hall and Kubiak's proof about the placement of the first, second and third longest jobs (Schrage, 1975; Hall and Kubiak, 1991). And then, modifying the spiral placement of remaining jobs by adding a selection of two positions to place the next job, either before the tail or after the head of the job sequence, based on which position produces a smaller variance of waiting times for jobs already in the sequence, as follows.

Suppose an arbitrary job set $P = \{p_1, p_2, K, p_n\}$ needs to be scheduled for a single resource. Assume that the jobs are numbered such that $p_1 \leq p_2 \leq \Lambda \leq p_n$.

1. To start, first place job p_n in the last position, job p_{n-1} in the last-but-one position, job p_{n-2} in the first position, and job p_1 in the second position. Now the job sequence becomes $\{p_{n-2}, p_1, p_{n-1}, p_n\}$. The job pool has the remaining jobs $\{p_2, K, p_{n-3}\}$.

2. Remove the longest job from the job pool, place the job either exactly before job p_1 or exactly after job p_1 in the job sequence, depending on which position produces a smaller WTV of the job sequence so far.

3. Repeat Step 2 until the job pool is empty.

Balanced Spiral (BS)

To reduce the computational cost associated with the VS method, the BS method replaces the verification of WTV during the placement selection (Step 2). In BS, we maintain the balance of the total processing time of jobs in the left (L) and right (R) side of the sequence, while placing a job from the job pool, as follows:

1. To start, first place job p_n in the last position, and job p_{n-1} in the last-but-one position, and then job p_{n-2} in the first position. Let sequence $L = \{p_{n-2}\}$ and sequence $R = \{p_{n-1}\}$. Note that p_n is not included in R. We denote the sum of the processing times of the jobs in L and R as SUM_L and SUM_R respectively. The job pool has the remaining jobs $\{p_1, p_2, K, p_{n-3}\}$.

2. If $SUM\_L < SUM\_R$, remove the largest job from the job pool, append the job to the last position of L, and update SUM_L; else if $SUM\_L \geq SUM\_R$, remove the largest job from the job pool, add the job to the first position of R, and update SUM_R.

3. Repeat Step 2 until the job pool is empty.

We develop the BS method based on an observation of balanced L and R in the optimal sequence of a special case, and the near-balanced L and R that we obtain at each step when placing a job to construct the optimal sequence for some small-size WTV problems.

Comparison Testing

We test and compare VS and BS with three other job scheduling methods: SPT, E&C1.1 and E&C1.2. Table 2 shows the percentage deviation from the lower bound job WTV on nine small problems (S1-S9) and four large problems (L1-L4). The results demonstrate that VS and BS give comparable or better performance in minimizing WTV for these problems.

Table 2. Deviation from lower bound WTV for SPT, E&C1.1, E&C1.2, VS and BS.

Test Problem	SPT	E& C1.1	E&C1.2	VS	BS
S1	13.72%	0.36%	0.00%	0.00%	0.00%
S2	19.15%	0.27%	0.00%	0.00%	0.00%
S3	31.07%	0.23%	0.03%	0.00%	0.00%
S4	34.08%	0.19%	0.09%	0.00%	0.00%
S5	48.07%	0.11%	0.09%	0.00%	0.00%
S6	66.45%	2.41%	0.01%	0.00%	1.37%
S7	17.90%	0.02%	0.01%	0.00%	0.00%
S8	35.31%	1.30%	0.01%	0.00%	0.01%
S9	51.14%	0.40%	0.17%	0.01%	0.01%
L1	15.7%	0.00%	0.00%	0.00%	0.00%
L2	99.3%	0.02%	0.01%	0.00%	0.00%
L3	62.8%	0.00%	0.00%	0.00%	0.00%
L4	49.7%	0.11%	0.07%	0.07%	0.41%

Hardware Implementation of BSAC and BS

To show the feasibility and performance of our BSAC and BS algorithms, we implement them on a research router using the Intel IXP1200 network processor. The router is able to run both algorithms for minimizing the WTV of jobs arriving for service. In initial experiments we process 1,000 packets in the router grouped in batches of size 10. Our results show that the WTV for a batch under the FCFS scheme with no admission control is 44,645. With BSAC added for admission control, and still using FIFO scheduling, we get a better WTV of 43,433. When we add BSAC and BS together, the WTV reduces even more to 36,770.

Thus, we find that our initial tests of implementing our methods on real hardware show that the algorithms are feasible and can improve performance with respect to minimizing job WTV. The details of our implementation, extended experimental results, and further analysis on performance metrics, such as WTV and running time, will be reported in future publications.

A Universal Pattern in the Optimization of Waiting Time Variance

During our investigation of WTV minimization, we discover an interesting eye shape pattern when we plot the waiting time variance over mean of all possible job sequences for a given problem, as shown in Figure 1. The eye shape pattern has several important implications for the WTV minimization problem. This pattern allows us to evaluate the sacrifice of the mean waiting time while pursuing the minimum WTV, and possibly develop a mathematical method to estimate the minimum WTV and derive the optimal job sequence.

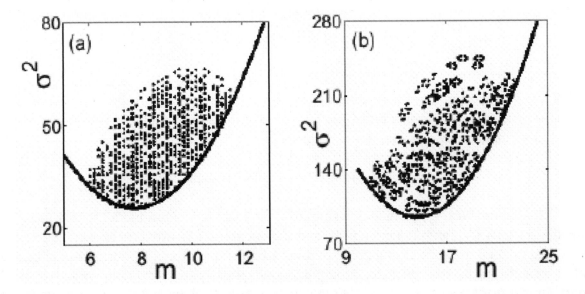

Figure 1. Examples of the eye-shape pattern: (a) P = (1,2,3,4,5,6), and (b) P= (2,3,5,9,10,11). The lower contour of the eye shape can be fit by a quadratic curve.

To evaluate the sacrifice of the mean waiting time while pursuing the minimum WTV, for the nine small-size problems in Table 2, S1-S9, we examine and compare the mean waiting times of three data points in each of the eye-shape plots for these problems:

1. the data point with the minimum WTV that is located at the lowest point on the y-axis of the eye shape pattern (if there are multiple data points with that minimum WTV value, the data point with the smallest mean waiting time among these data points is examined)
2. the data point with the minimum mean waiting time that is located at the left corner of the eye shape pattern
3. the data point with the maximum mean waiting time that is located at the right corner of the eye shape pattern

It is shown that data point 2 corresponds to the job sequence produced by SPT and 3 corresponds to the job sequence produced by the job scheduling method of placing the job with the Longest Processing Time (LPT) first (Pinedo, 1995). Data points 2 and 3 define the range of the mean waiting times from all the possible job sequences. From Figure 1, we observe that data point 1 is closer to 2 (minimum mean) than to 3 (maximum mean) on the x-axis. We examine the distances between the data points on the x-axis and the ratio of this distance to the range. We find that, on average, for these nine problems the optimal job sequence with minimum WTV (data point 1) sacrifices the mean waiting time by about 28.73% of the entire range of mean waiting times. Hence, while pursuing WTV minimization, we do not sacrifice much from the optimal waiting time mean.

Two other important implications of the eye shape pattern lie in the lower contour and the use of this contour to find the minimum WTV and derive the job sequence that produces it. If we can mathematically derive the minimum WTV using the lower contour, one implication is that we can compute the minimum WTV without knowing the exact job sequence that produces it. This allows us to evaluate the WTV of a job sequence produced by a heuristic job scheduling method. Further deriving the job sequence that produces the minimum WTV leads to another implication; we will have a mathematical method of deriving the optimal sequence for a given problem, rather than using a space search or heuristic method to find a sequence with good or near optimal WTV. In our study, we have provided a geometric interpretation of the eye shape pattern. We have also inferred the mathematical form of the function for the lower contour of the eye shape pattern to be a quadratic function of waiting time variance over mean, and have verified this function through a number of examples.

Regional Level QoS Models

The regional level QoS model is similar to the local level QoS model in that the objective is to minimize WTV for service stability and dependability. However, the regional level QoS model deals with a network of computers with shared computational resources in the centralized control environment, like that for computational grids. Since existing research work on computational grids does not address the objective of service stability through minimizing WTV, we work on the multiple-resource job scheduling problem to schedule jobs on multiple resources of same or different capacities for minimizing WTV. Our research has produced the following:

1) Mathematical proof of the equivalence of the completion time variance (CTV) problem and the WTV problem involving multiple shared resources of the same capacity; the identical parallel machine problem (Xu)
2) Mathematical proof of certain properties of the optimal sequence(s) for the multiple-resource WTV problem (Xu)
3) Five heuristic algorithms for the identical parallel machine problem: First in First Out (FIFO)+VS, SPT+VS, LPT+VS, Dynamic VS (DVS) and Dynamic BS (DBS) (Xu).
4) Job scheduling methods for the WTV problem involving multiple resources of different capacities.

In this section we overview item 3 above. Items 1 and 2, add additional information on 3, can be found in the associated reference. Item number 4 is in progress.

Heuristic algorithms for the Identical Parallel Machine WTV Problem

The identical parallel machine CTV and WTV problems are NP-complete (Cai and Cheng, 1998; Xu). Hence, the use of a heuristic algorithm for computational efficiency is justified. In this section, five heuristic algorithms are presented for the identical parallel machine WTV problem: FIFO+VS, SPT+VS, LPT+VS, DVS and DBS (Xu). We compare these five algorithms with FIFO, SPT and LPT alone. These 8 algorithms are described in this section.

1. FIFO (First-In-First-Out)
   FIFO is considered in this study because it is one of the most commonly used dispatching rules in scheduling and is widely used for a variety of Internet services. In FIFO, we assume the jobs arrive in a random order and all jobs have arrived. All machines are idle at the beginning. The first job is served by an idle machine. The next job will be served by another idle machine. If all machines are busy, then the next job will be served on a

machine that becomes free next. That is, in FIFO both job dispatching to machines and job scheduling on each machine follow the FIFO order.

2. SPT (Shortest Processing Time)

    SPT is presented here because it is optimal to a related measure as presented in Pinedo, 1995. In the SPT heuristic, jobs are first sorted in increasing order of their processing times. The smallest m jobs are assigned to the first position on each machine, and then whenever a machine is freed, the next smallest job is assigned to that machine. That is, both job dispatching to machines, and scheduling on each machine, follow the order of SPT first.

3. LPT(Longest Processing Time)

    LPT is considered in this study because it is also optimal to a related measure. In LPT jobs are sorted in a decreasing order of their processing times. The largest m jobs will be assigned to the first position on each machine, and then whenever a machine is freed, the next largest job will be assigned to that machine. Hence, in LPT, job dispatching to machines and job scheduling on each machine follows the order of LPT first.

4. FIFO+VS (FIFO + Verified Spiral)

    FIFO+VS is shown in Figure 2.

5. SPT+VS (SPT + Verified Sprial)

    This is similar to FIFO + VS except that FIFO is replaced by SPT for job dispatching to machines in Step 1.

6. LPT+VS (LPT + Verified Sprial)

    This is similar to FIFO + VS except that FIFO is replaced by LPT for job dispatching to machines in Step 1.

7. DVS (Dynamic Verified Spiral)

    DVS checks and compares the waiting time variances from the possible assignments of a given job to a possible machine. The DVS heuristic is presented in Figure 3.

8. DBS (Dynamic Balance Spiral)

    DBS is similar to DVS except that VS is replaced by BS to schedule the jobs assigned to each machine $i \in M$. The BS method is shown in Figure 4.

FIFO+VS

1   $\overline{w}_{max} \leftarrow 0$

2   Use FIFO to assign jobs to m machines.

3   **for** $i \leftarrow 1$ **to** m

4   **do**

5   Apply Verified Spiral (VS) [4] to schedule the jobs assigned to machine i

6   Calculate $\overline{w_i}$

7   **if** $\overline{w_i} > \overline{w}_{max}$

8   **then** $\overline{w}_{max} = \overline{w_i}$

9   **for** $i \leftarrow 1$ **to** m

10   **do**

11          $r_i = \overline{w}_{max} - \overline{w_i}$

12 Let the current schedule be $\lambda_{current}$

13 Calculate the variance $var(\lambda_{current})$

14 PRINT $\lambda_{current}$, $var(\lambda_{current})$

Ye et al. [4] show that the schedule from Verified Spiral (VS) for a single machine is very close to the optimal solution of $1\|WTV$. VS is briefly described below.

VERIFIED SPIRAL

1   $J \leftarrow \{p_1, p_2, \ldots, p_n\}$, where $p_1 \leq p_2 \leq p_3 \leq \ldots \leq p_n$

2   $L \leftarrow [p_{n-2}]$, $R \leftarrow [p_{n-1}, p_n]$

3   Place the smallest job, p_1, in between L and R.

4   $J \leftarrow J - \{p_1, p_{n-2}, p_{n-1}, p_n\}$

5   $j \leftarrow n - 3$

6   **while** $J \neq \emptyset$

7   **do**

8           $S_R \leftarrow [L, p_1, p_j, R]$, calculate $Var(S_R)$.

9           $S_L \leftarrow [L, p_j, p_1, R]$, calculate $Var(S_L)$

10   **if** $Var(S_R) \leq Var(S_L)$

11   **then**

12                  $R \leftarrow [p_j, R]$

13   **else**

14                  $L \leftarrow [L, p_j]$

15          $j \leftarrow j - 1$

16          $J \leftarrow J - \{p_j\}$

Figure 2. FIFO+VS Heuristic

DYNAMIC VERIFIED SPIRAL(DVS)

1   $J \leftarrow \{p_1, p_2, \ldots, p_n\}$, where $p_1 \leq p_2 \leq p_3 \leq \ldots \leq p_n$

2   $j \leftarrow 1$, $\lambda \leftarrow \emptyset$, $\lambda_{current} = \emptyset$

3   while $J \neq \emptyset$

4   do

5   for $i \leftarrow 1$ to m

6   do

7                   $VAR_{min} \leftarrow \infty$, $\overline{w}_{max} \leftarrow 0$

8   Add p_j to machine i under schedule λ

9   for $i \leftarrow 1$ to m

10   do

11   Apply Verified Spiral (VS) to schedule the jobs assigned to machine i

12   Calculate $\overline{w_i}$

13   if $\overline{w_i} > \overline{w}_{max}$

14   then

15                                  $\overline{w}_{max} \leftarrow \overline{w_i}$

16   for $i \leftarrow 1$ to m

17   do

18                              $r_i \leftarrow \overline{w}_{max} - \overline{w_i}$

19   Let $\lambda_{current}$ be the current schedule, calculate the variance $var(\lambda_{current})$

20   if $var(\lambda_{current}) < VAR_{min}$

21   then

22                              $VAR_{min} \leftarrow var(\lambda_{current})$

23                              $\lambda_{min} \leftarrow \lambda_{current}$

24          $\lambda \leftarrow \lambda_{min}$

25          $J \leftarrow J - \{p_j\}$

26          $j \leftarrow j + 1$

27   PRINT λ_{min}, VAR_{min}

Figure 3: Dynamic Verified Spiral Heuristic

BALANCED SPIRAL

1    $J \leftarrow \{p_1, p_2, \ldots, p_n\}$, where $p_1 \leq p_2 \leq p_3 \leq \cdots \leq p_n$

2   Place job p_n in the last position

3    $L = [p_{n-2}]$, $R = [p_{n-1}]$

4    $J \leftarrow J - \{p_{n-2}, p_{n-1}, p_n\}$

5    $j \leftarrow n - 3$

6    $SUM_L = \sum_{k \in L} p_k$, $SUM_R = \sum_{k \in R} p_k$

7   while $J \neq \emptyset$

8   do

9   if $SUM_L < SUM_R$

10   then

11                $L \leftarrow [L, p_j]$

12   Update SUM_L

13   else

14                $R \leftarrow [p_j, R]$

15   Update SUM_R

16        $J \leftarrow J - \{p_j\}$

17        $j \leftarrow j - 1$

Figure 4. Scheduling Method used in Dynamic Balanced Spiral

Comparison of Heuristics

Table 3 shows the results for six small-size WTV problems, where WTVD is the Waiting Time Variance Deviation from the optimal solution and WTMD is the Waiting Time Mean deviation from optimal. We find the optimal solution by enumerating all possible schedules. For each problem, FIFO, SPT and LPT are the worst among all the heuristics in waiting time variance. However, a significant improvement is made when VS is added to these three heuristics. DVS has the best performance in waiting time variance among all heuristics, and in 2 out of 6 problems it gives the optimal solution. The performance of DBS is very close to DVS, and DBS gives the optimal solution for one out of six problems. Further results on larger problems and varying distributions are given by Xu.

Table 3: Comparison Results for 8 methods on 6 small-size WTV problems

Heuristic	Measurement	Problem 1	Problem 2	Problem 3	Problem 4	Problem 5	Problem 6
FIFO	WTVD	29.40%	50.35%	705.91%	12.57%	338.41%	51.99%
	WTMD	13.33%	62.85%	196.25%	18.65%	91.62%	41.53%
SPT	WTVD	20.90%	28.97%	36.54%	10.01%	14.32%	31.66%
	WTMD	0.00%	0.00%	0.00%	0.00%	0.00%	0.00%
LPT	WTVD	115.30%	143.48%	838.49%	49.48%	569.12%	180.99%
	WTMD	88.89%	117.71%	521.61%	39.45%	282.20%	142.37%
FIFO+VS	WTVD	4.70%	0.65%	29.34%	0.91%	24.61%	3.03%
	WTMD	22.22%	51.61%	96.38%	13.58%	58.56%	54.66%
SPT+VS	WTVD	0.82%	1.91%	5.91%	0.42%	0.79%	1.77%
	WTMD	28.89%	43.20%	58.21%	15.53%	23.56%	42.37%
LPT+VS	WTVD	0.15%	0.03%	11.57%	0.02%	53.06%	0.00%
	WTMD	22.22%	24.96%	108.93%	9.90%	107.18%	25.00%
DVS	WTVD	0.15%	0.03%	3.58%	0.00%	0.13%	0.00%
	WTMD	22.22%	24.43%	81.92%	9.67%	19.37%	25.00%
DBS$_\lambda$	WTVD	0.15%	0.03%	4.39%	0.00%	0.13%	0.14%
	WTMD	22.22%	24.43%	87.32%	9.67%	19.37%	25.71%

Global Level QoS Assurance

At the global level, we investigate providing end-to-end QoS on general networks. Our objectives are to assure end-to-end QoS of high-priority individual jobs and minimize traffic congestion. In this area we have achieved the following:

1) Review of existing decentralized resource management methods (Wu et al., 2005) and existing work on QoS in the application fields of computers and networks, air traffic management, postal mail delivery, and so on.
2) Metrics of QoS requirements for various applications on the information infrastructure towards QoS standards, using human factors and technology data.
3) Network simulation experiments to reveal sensitive points of data collection and measures, and emergence of network hierarchy.
4) A job reservation and execution protocol and supporting algorithms to assure the end-to-end QoS of an individual high-priority job, and minimize traffic congestion.
5) Mathematical theories of scale free networks, probabilistic methods of generating scale free networks, and empirical results on attack resistance and infection.

In this section we overview the above items and refer to our publications for further reading and research results. Research that is ongoing is briefly overviewed based on goals and initial directions.

QoS Metrics

Concise specification of QoS requirements is vital to realizing QoS assurance on the information infrastructure. Since different applications have different service features, each application should specify its explicit QoS requirements to a computer network in order to achieve the desired QoS. If there are no requirements given, the network will take for granted that any level of service is acceptable, and therefore can provide any level of QoS support. The types of QoS support provided, such as bandwidth and priority in a router's queue, may lead to delay and jitter that can then render QoS unacceptable. Consequently, if we want to satisfy QoS of various applications, the first step is to identify the QoS metrics of each application on the information infrastructure.

In this study, we first analyze the influence of two key factors, human factors and technology attributes, on QoS requirements. Next, we classify an application based on the application's different service characteristics resulting mainly from these two key factors. Finally, based on existing literature, we systematically propose numerical measures, which can quantitatively represent the QoS requirements of various applications (including web browsing, enhanced web browsing, email, ftp, telnet, Internet relay chat, audio broadcasting, video broadcasting, interactive audio on demand, interactive video on demand, telemetry, audio conferencing, audiographic conferencing, video conferencing, videophony, and voice over IP) with different service characteristics in Multi Service Networks, along with the rational behind these choices. More details of the QoS metrics for various applications are presented in (Chen et al, 2003).

Table 4. QoS metrics for web browsing

Appl. Class	Technology Attributes	QoS Metrics						
		Timeliness			Preciseness			Accuracy
		Response time Expected by Users	Delay (ms)	Jitter (ms)	Data Rate (bps)	Required Bandwidth (bps)	Loss Rate	Error Rate
Web Browsing	Non Real Time and Asymmetric	2-5 Seconds	< 400	N/A	< 30.5 K	< 30.5 K	Zero	*Zero*

Data Collection and Measures

At the global level, we investigate detecting emergent behavior on a network of networks modeled as the Internet. We determine that the Internet is a scale free network, and build our internet model using the two key characteristics: preferential attachment and growth. We run experiments using various levels and types of attacks and failures, and collect data to determine which metric best describes the state of the system, and at which points to collect this metric. Details and results of this research work are currently in the publishing process (Ye, Farley and Aswath, accepted).

End-to-end QoS Assurance Problem

We first define and formalize the end-to-end QoS assurance problem. Next, we introduce a simulation design to investigate the application of our research work at the local and regional levels to this global QoS problem.

Definition and formulation of the end-to-end QoS assurance problem

We define end-to-end QoS assurance as a fixed path problem of self-interest only. Given the following, determine the arrival time of each flow at each hop along the path of the flow:

    a. *n* flows
    b. a fixed end-to-end path of each flow
    c. end-to-end timeliness target of each flow
    d. *m* resources required by all *n* flows
    e. service capacity and waiting time at each resource from local-level and regional-level QoS models

We make the fixed path assumption based on existing evidences of a stable primary path of an end-to-end flow. For more than 50% of destinations there is only one dominant path, and for 25% of destinations there are exactly two domain-level paths (Govindan and Reddy, 1997). The reason for this is that routing policy is usually set by bi-lateral transit agreements. In most cases, a domain keeps a primary and a back-up transit to a collection of destinations. It is also shown that the likelihood of observing a dominant route is 82% at the host level, 97% at the city level and 100% at the autonomous system (AS) level (Paxson, 1996). In EGP (Exterior Gateway Protocol) for inter-AS routing, almost 90% of recorded updates contain close to 0% new information, indicating stable routes (Chinoy, 1993). The Border Gateway Protocol (BGP), contains only incremental updates. Injecting just 10% of the total inter-AS reachability information (about 200 entries) into the inter-AS routing permits the forwarding of at least 85% of the transit traffic without resorting to encapsulation (Rekhter and Chinoy, 1992) More than 80% of prefixes are reachable through a primary path for more than 95% of time.

In our ongoing work we consider subproblems of the fixed path problem of self-interest only. First, we allow each flow to determine its own arrival time by considering shortest possible time along with slack time. Next, we resolve timing conflicts at each resource while making the slack time of each flow ≥ zero. And finally, coordinate the resolutions at various resources. We also consider finding solutions for the open path problem. Such as assuring end-to-end QoS of some flows, expanding the set of *m* resources by pursuing alternative paths for those flows. Subproblems here include selecting alternative resources for those flows and solving a fixed path problem with an expanded set of resources. For both fixed and open path problems, we consider self-interest and global interest of minimizing global traffic congestion (e.g., minimizing traffic bottlenecks).

A Job Reservation and Execution Protocol

To address the end-to-end QoS assurance problem, we incorporate our work at the local and regional levels. Consider a network where variance in job waiting times is minimized. The processing time of a job depends on its size and can be calculated. By minimizing waiting time variance, we can predict the completion time (waiting time + processing time) of a job at each point in a network. Our network model considers only high priority jobs and assumes low priority jobs are handled whenever resources are idle.

In addition to incorporating our work at the local and regional levels, our experimental framework uses the concept of path reservation, as seen in the Resource ReSerVation Protocol (RSVP) proposal (Braden et al., 1997). However, we aim to overcome some problems with RSVP. We briefly overview RSVP and our protocol.

RSVP reserves a path for a flow on the Internet. This reservation is made at intermediate routers along the path. After a reservation for a flow is made, the jobs (in the form of a set of individual packets) in that flow travel along the reserved path. The idea behind this method is that by reserving resources to manage a flow, its QoS requirements can be assured. Some of the key points to RSVP are:

1. RSVP is receiver oriented, i.e., the receiver initiates the reservation request.
2. RSVP does not perform its own routing; it uses underlying routing protocols to determine where it should carry reservation requests, i.e., RSVP runs on top of the Internet Protocol.
3. Once the path is determined, the receiver sends a RESV packet with the bandwidth requirement along the determined path.
4. Each intermediate node on the path then makes a decision about accepting or rejecting the RESV request.
   a. Fail – NACK or error sent to the originator of the RESV packet.
   b. Success – set parameters in packet classifier and packet scheduler to achieve required QoS.

Our protocol is also based on path reservation and incorporates our work at the local and regional levels to minimize the variance of job waiting times at each point along the reserved path. We briefly outline the two phases (probe and job) of our protocol.

1. Probe Phase:
   a. At the source node, find the best path among n possible paths based on historic information and current state information. The source node subscribes to the historic performance and current state information from intermediate routers along n possible paths.
   b. Source initiated: source sends a probe packet along the best path. The probe packet carries the parameters (job_id, start_time, J, D_{ee}), where J is the job (packet) size, D_{ee} is the end to end delay requirement.
   c. Every intermediate router i has three parameters (B_{ij}, P_i, D_i), where B_{ij} is the size of batch j at the router, P_i is the processing power of the router, D_i is the max (worst) possible delay that a packet can experience at this router. Each router also maintains a variable $B_{residual}$ that keeps track of how much resource is left at the router as reservations are made.
   d. For each router i, upon receiving a probe packet:
      If ($B_{residual} \geq J$),
        $D_{ee} = D_{ee} - D_i$
        If ($D_{ee} > 0$)
            Forward probe packet
            $B_{residual} = B_{residual} - J$
            Add *(job_id, probe_reply_timeout)* to reservation list of batch j.
      Else
            drop probe packet
      (probe_reply_timeout = arrival time + timeout based on the avg roundtrip time)
   e. Upon destination receiving a probe packet:

If (D_{ee}–transportation time of the probe packet per job size unit * job size > 0)

Return *probe_reply* packet

Else

Drop probe packet

f.　For each router *i*,

If (*probe_reply* packet not received by the time *probe_reply_timeout*)

Drop the corresponding job from the list of jobs scheduled for batch *j*.

If (*probe_reply* packet arrives without a corresponding *job_id* in the list)

Drop probe_reply packet

g.　Source receives the probe_reply packet and enters Job Phase

2.　Job Phase:

a.　Source sends the job (packets) along the reserved path

b.　Each intermediate router *i*, receiving the job checks to see if the job is in the job list for batch *j*

　　a.　If yes

　　　　i.　If the complete job arrives within its corresponding batch start time, schedule the job using BS

　　　　ii.　If the job does not arrive before its corresponding batch's start time, drop the job from high priority queue

　　b.　If no

　　　　i.　Keep the job in the best-effort queue

From the brief outline given, observe that our protocol assumes admission control in batches. For this we use the BSAC method from our local and regional level work. During the job phase, jobs are scheduled using the BS algorithm from our local and regional level work to minimize the waiting time variance of jobs, which gives us the ability to determine the amount of time it will take a job to travel along a path, because we can compute its completion time at each router along the path (waiting time+processing time). Without stabilizing the waiting time variance, it would not be possible to make close predictions of the completion time at each point, thereby complicating the issue of maintaining timing along the path.

Our method uses a type of resource reservation that is different than RSVP. We compare our method to that of RSVP and list some of the main advantages of our method:

1.　Non-Persistent reservation. RSVP reserves a path for an entire flow, we make the reservation for a specific job (set of packets) in a flow. Some advantages of this are:

a.　Resources are not wasted if the flow is not active. Consider the case of Voice over IP (VoIP) where there are distinct active and inactive periods. If we consider an active period as a job, then RSVP reserves the path for the duration of the call, whereas our protocol only reserves the path during the active periods.

b.　We target all types of applications, and the reservations are therefore valid only as long as they are needed irrespective of whether it's a short-term or a long-term connection.

c.　We may know all of the characteristics of a job, but not of a flow which has characteristics that may change over time.

2. Less State Info: Unlike RSVP, we store less state information. We store state information corresponding to two batches, the current batch and the next batch. The state information includes only job ids and the residual capacity of a batch.

3. Parallels Routing Algorithm: RSVP runs on top of IP. Our solution is integrated parallel to the routing algorithm to incorporate adjustments based on network dynamics. For example, a path that was good at the beginning of a VoIP session may at some point become congested. In our solution, a new path may be selected mid-session since path selection is done on a per job (active period) basis.

4. Light weight and Distributed: Our solution is light weight as it does not carry much state information and distributed as each router makes its own independent decision about accepting or rejecting a job.

One of the key benefits of our method is reducing resource wastage in a reservation. There are 3 ways to look at reserving paths. Reservation per packet, reservation per job (our method) and reservation per flow (RSVP). The first case, per packet, is clearly impractical as the reservation mechanism would significantly slow down network traffic. The last case, per flow, wastes too much resource along a path when a flow is inactive. We attempt to find a middle ground between the two by defining a job (set of packets) and making the reservation for that job.

Since we consider a network based on BSAC, we investigate batch sizes with respect to the number of packets in a job. The size of a batch is a variable that can be changed, adding flexibility to the framework. Another variable is the number of batches to reserve (persistence of reservation). For this, we consider the following optimization problem:

1. Let $C_{probe,i}$ be the cost of sending probe i
2. Let $C_{resv,i}$ be the cost of holding reservation for batch i
3. Let y be the optimum reservation persistance
4. Let a_i be the number of packets in job i
5. Minimize $\sum (a_i / y) * C_{probe,i} + (y - a_i \% y) * C_{resv,i}$
6. s.t. $y > 1$

Our proposed solution is currently in development. The ideas presented here are preliminary. We do not claim this as a complete solution for solving end-to-end QoS. However, we aim to provide a solution that is flexible, proactive, and secure. Flexibility is inherent in the variable parameters we allow (path selection, batch size, persistence of reservation) and the ability to change these parameters dynamically. As an example of proactive, consider sending packets in a flow, and stopping the flow after finding its QoS cannot be met (reactive), we do not release packets for a job until we know the QoS can be met (proactive). Our solution is more secure in that various "pieces" of a flow may not travel along the same path, thereby increasing the difficulty in eavesdropping. The use of BSAC and BS allows the overall benefits of time synchronization on a network, for which the implications are numerous.

In addition to the benefits we are continuing to explore, we also consider the tradeoffs. Obviously adding such synchronization and reservation to a network will consume resources and add processing time. Our ongoing efforts consider the advantages of our solution and weigh them against the shortcomings. We view this problem from a framework point of view, and are not currently actively trying to integrate it into existing protocols on the Internet.

Dynamics and Security of Computer Networks

Complex networks arise in natural systems and they are also an essential part of modern society. Many real complex networks were found to be heterogeneous with power-law degree distribution (Barabasi and Albert, 1999, Albert and Barabasi, 2002, Newman, 2003): $P(k) : k^{-\gamma}$, where k is the number of links of a randomly chosen node in the network and γ is the scaling exponent. This power-law, or algebraic, distribution means that the probability for a subset of nodes to possess a large number of links is not exponentially small, in contrast to random networks. Mathematically, the power-law distribution means that statistical moments of the degree variable are generally not defined, hence the name of scale-free networks. Because of the ubiquity of scale-free networks in natural and man-made systems, the security of these networks, i.e., how failures or attacks affect the integrity and operation of the networks, has been of great interest since the discovery of the scale-free property. The work by Albert et al. demonstrated that scale-free networks possess the robust-yet-fragile property, in the sense that they are robust against random failures of nodes but fragile to intentional attacks (Albert et al, 2000). However, the term fragility here means that a scale-free network can become disintegrated under attacks on a small but still appreciable set of nodes that include a substantial fraction of links in the network (Cohen, et al, 2000). An attack on a single or very few nodes will in general not bring down the network. This interesting result was actually obtained based purely on the scale-free architecture of the network. In other words, dynamics in the network, i.e., how information or load is distributed in the network, was not taken into account.

An intuitive reasoning based on the load distribution would suggest that, for a scale-free network, the possibility of breakdown triggered by an attack on or failure of even only a single node cannot be ignored. Imagine such a network that transports some physical quantities, or load. Nodes with large numbers of links receive relatively heavier load. Each node, however, has a finite capacity to process or transport load. In order for a node to function properly, its load must be less than the capacity at all time; otherwise the node fails. If a node fails, its load will be directed to other nodes, causing a redistribution of load in the network. If the failing node deals with a small amount of load, there will be little effect on the network because the amount of load that needs to be redistributed is small. This is typically the situation of random failure of nodes. However, if the failing node carries a large amount of load, the consequence could be serious because this amount of load needs to be redistributed and it is possible that for some nodes, the new load exceeds their capacities. These nodes will then fail, causing further redistributions of load, and so on. As a consequence, a large fraction of the network can be shutdown.

Cascading failures can occur in many physical systems. In a power transmission grid, for instance, each node (a generator) deals with a load of power. Removal of nodes in general can cause redistribution of loads over all the network, which can trigger a cascade of overloading failures. The recent massive power blackout caused by a series of seemingly unrelated events on August 14, 2003 in the northeastern United States and Canada seemed to have the characteristics of cascading breakdown. Another example is the Internet, where the load represents data packets a node (router) is requested to transmit and overloading corresponds to congestion (Arenas et al, 2001). The rerouting of data packets from a congested router to another may spread the congestion to a large fraction of the network. Internet collapses caused by congestion have been reported (Jacobson, 1988). With the possibility of cascading failures, a realistic concern is attacks on complex networks. In particular, for a scale-free network, the majority of the nodes deal with small amount of load, so the probability for a node with a large amount of load to fail randomly is small. This, of course, will not be the case of intentional attacks that usually target one or a few of the most heavily linked nodes.

There have been a few recent studies on cascading failures in complex networks (Motter and Lai, 2002, Holme and Kim, 2002). In Motter and Lai, 2002, a simple mechanism was proposed to incorporate the dynamics of load in both random and scale-free networks. The model generates results that are completely consistent with the above intuition on cascading failures. For instance, it was demonstrated that random networks are robust against cascading breakdown but it can be easily triggered by intentional attacks in scale-free networks. The existing results are, however, largely descriptive and qualitative. We have addressed theoretically and numerically the fundamental mechanism of cascading breakdown. To make analysis amenable, we focused on scale-free networks, use the load model in Motter and Lai, 2002 that captures the essential features of cascading failures, and investigated cascades triggered by attack on a single node. Our finding is that cascading breakdown in scale-free networks can be understood in terms of a phase transition. In particular, let α be the tolerance parameter characterizing the capacity of nodes in the network. Cascading breakdown due to attack on a single node is possible only when α is below a critical value α_c. By making use of the degree distribution of scale-free networks and the concept of betweenness (Newman, 2001) to characterize the load distribution, we were able to derive a theoretical formula for estimating the phase-transition point α_c, which was verified by numerical experiments. In terms of practical utility, our result enables a possible implementation of predicting and preventing mechanism for cascading breakdown in scale-free networks.

The load dynamics in scale-free networks can be modeled, as follows. For a given network, suppose that at each time step one unit of the relevant quantity, which can be information, energy, etc., is exchanged between every pair of nodes and transported along the shortest path. To characterize the load distribution, the concept of betweenness is useful (Newman, 2001). The load (or betweenness) at a node i is defined as the total number of shortest paths passing through this node. The capacity of a node is the maximum load that the node can handle. In man-made networks, the capacity is severely limited by cost. Thus, it is natural to assume that the capacity C_i of node i is proportional to its initial load L_i (Motter and Lai, 2002),

$$C_i = (1+\alpha)L_i, \tag{7}$$

where the constant $\alpha \geq 0$ is the tolerance parameter. When all nodes are on, the network operates in a free flow state insofar as $\alpha \geq 0$. But, the removal of nodes in general changes the distribution of shortest paths. The load at a particular node can then change. If it increases and becomes larger than the capacity, the node fails. Any failure leads to a new distribution of load and, as a result, subsequent failures can occur. The failures can stop without affecting too much the connectivity of the network but it can also propagate and shutdown a considerable fraction of the whole network. Cascading failures can be conveniently quantified by the relative size of the largest connected component

$$G = \frac{N'}{N}, \tag{8}$$

where N and N' are the numbers of nodes in the largest component before and after the cascade, respectively. The integrity of the network is maintained if $G \approx 1$, while breakdown occurs if $G \approx 0$.

To obtain an analytic estimate of the critical value of the tolerance parameter, we focus on the situation where cascading failures are caused by attack on the node with the largest number of links and the failures lead to immediate breakdown of the network. That is, G becomes close to zero after one redistribution of the load. For a node in the network, its load is a function of the degree variable k. For scale-free networks, we have (Goh et al, 2001, Park et al, accepted),

$$L(k): k^\eta, \tag{9}$$

where $\eta > 0$ is a scaling exponent. To proceed, we write the degree distribution as $P(k) = ak^{-\gamma}$ and the load distribution as $L(k) = bk^\eta$, where a and b are positive constants. Let k_{max} be the largest degree in the network. Before the attack, we have

$$\int_1^{k_{max}} P(k)dk = N \text{ and} \tag{10}$$

$$\int_1^{k_{max}} P(k)L(k)dk = S,$$

where S is the total load of the network. These two equations give

$$a = \frac{(1-\gamma)N}{[k_{max}^{1-\gamma} - 1]} \text{ and} \tag{11}$$

$$b = \frac{\beta S}{a(1 - k_{max})^{-\beta}},$$

where $\beta \equiv \gamma - \eta - 1$. After the removal of the highest degree node (it is only the first step of the whole cascading process), the degree and load distributions become $P'(k) = a'k^{-\gamma'}$ and $L'(k) = b'k^{\eta'}$, respectively. Since only a small fraction of nodes are removed from the network, we expect the changes in the algebraic scaling exponents of these distributions to be negligible. We thus write $P'(k) \approx a'k^{-\gamma}$ and $L'(k) \approx b'k^\eta$, where the proportional constants a' and b' can be calculated in the same way as for a and b. We obtain $a' = (1-\gamma)(N-1)/[k_{max}^{1-\gamma} - 1]$ and $b' = \beta S'/a'(1 - k_{max})^{-\beta}$, where S' is the total load of the network after the attack. For nodes with k links, the difference in load before and after the attack can be written as $\Delta L(k) \approx (b' - b)k^\eta = (\frac{b'}{b} - 1)L(k)$. Given the capacity $C(k)$, the maximum load increase that the nodes can handle is $C(k) - L(k) = \alpha L(k)$. The nodes still function if $\alpha > (\frac{b'}{b} - 1)$ but they fail if $\alpha < (\frac{b'}{b} - 1)$. The critical value α_c of the tolerance parameter is then

$$\alpha_c = \frac{b'}{b} - 1 \tag{12}$$

$$\approx (\frac{k_{max'}^{1-\gamma} - 1}{k_{max}^{1-\gamma} - 1})(\frac{1 - k_{max}^{-\beta}}{1 - k_{max'}^{-\beta}})(\frac{S'}{S}) - 1$$

$$\approx (\frac{1 - k_{max}^{-\beta}}{1 - k_{max'}^{-\beta}})(\frac{S'}{S}) - 1$$

$$\approx \{1 - (k_{max}^{-\beta} - k_{max'}^{-\beta})\}(\frac{S'}{S}) - 1$$

$$= \{1 - k_{max'}^{-\beta}(-1 + (\frac{k_{max}}{k_{max'}})^{-\beta})\}(\frac{S'}{S}) - 1,$$

where the third line of Eq. (12) is obtained from the second line by using the fact $(k_{max'}^{1-\gamma} - 1)/(k_{max}^{1-\gamma} - 1) \approx 1$. This is so because both $k_{max'}^{1-\gamma}$ and $k_{max'}^{1-\gamma}$ approach zero when $N \to \infty$ and $\gamma > 1$. In the limit $N \to \infty$, we have $k_{max'}^{-\beta} : 0$, $k_{max}/k_{max'} :$ constant, and $S'/S \to 1$, so $\alpha_c \approx 0$, indicating that an infinite scale-free network cannot be brought down by a single attack if $\alpha > 0$. On the other hand, for finite size network, since $k_{max'}^{-\beta} > 0$, we have $\alpha_c > 0$, suggesting that breakdown can occur for $\alpha < \alpha_c$. The practical usage of Eq. (12) is that it provides a way to monitor the state of a (finite) network to assess the risk of cascading breakdown. In particular, the critical value α_c can be computed in time and comparison with the pre-designed tolerance parameter value α can be made. If α_c shows a tendency of increase and approaches α, early warning can be issued to signal an immediate danger of network breakdown.

References

R. Albert and A.-L. Barabsi. Statistical mechanics of complex networks. Rev. of Mod. Phys., 74(47), 2002.

R. Albert, H. Jeong, and A.-L. Barabasi. Error and attack tolerance of complex networks. Nature, 406:378–382, 2000.

P. Almquist. Type of service in the internet protocol suite. Request for Comments 1349, Internet Engineering Task Force. URL: http://www.ietf.org/rfc.html, July 1992.

A. Arenas, A. Das-Guilera, and R. Guimer. Communication in networks with hierarchical branching. Phys. Rev. Lett., 86:3196–3199, 2001.

A.-L. Barabasi and R. Albert. Emergence of scaling in random networks. Science, 509, 1999.

S. Blake, D. Black, M. Carlson, E. Davies, Z. Wang, and W. Weiss. An architecture for differentiated service. Request for Comments (Informational) 2475, Internet Engineering Task Force. URL: http://www.ietf.org/rfc.html, Dec 1998.

R. Braden, D. Clark, and S. Shenker. Integrated services in the internet architecture: an overview. RFC 1633, IETF, proposed standard, June 1994.

R. Braden, L. Zhang, S. Berson, S. Herzog and S. Jamin. Resource ReSerVation Protocol (RSVP) -- Version 1 Functional Specification. RFC 2205, IETF, proposed standard, September 1997.

X. Cai and T.C.E. Cheng, Multi-machine scheduling with variance minimization. Discrete Applied Mathematics, 84: 55–70, 1998.

Y. Chen, T. Farley, and N. Ye. Qos requirements of network applications on the internet. Information, Knowledge, Systems Management, 4(1):55–76, 2003.

B. Chinoy. Dynamics of internet routing information. Proc. ACM SIGCOMM, 45-52, 1993.

R. Cohen, K. Erez, D. b Avraham, and S. Havlin. Resilience of the internet to random breakdowns. Phys. Rev. Lett., 85:4626–4628, 2000.

S. Eilon and I.G. Chowdhury. Minimizing waiting time variance in the single machine problem. Management Science, 23:567–574, 1977.

Ian Foster and C. Kesselman. The Grid: Blueprint for a New Computing Infrastructure. Morgan Kaufmann, San Francisco, California, 1999.

K.-I. Goh, B. Kahng, and D. Kim. Universal behavior of load distribution in scale-free networks. Phys. Rev. Lett., 87:278701, 2001.

R. Govindan and A. Reddy. An analysis of inter-domain topology and route stability. Proc. IEEE INFOCOM, 1997.

N.G. Hall and W. Kubiak. Proof of a conjecture of schrage about the completion time variance problem. Operations Research Letters, 10:467–472, 1991.

P. Holme and B. J. Kim. Vertex overload breakdown in evolving networks. Phys. Rev. E, 65:066109, 2002.

V. Jacobson. Congestion avoidance and control. Comput. Commum. Rev, 18:314–329, Aug 1988.

W. Kubiak. Completion time variance minimization on a single machine is difficult. Operations Research Letters, 14:49–59, 1993.

Y.-C. Lai, Z. Liu, and N. Ye. Infection dynamics on growing networks. International Journal of Modern Physics B, 17:4045–4061, 2003.

Y.-C. Lai and N. Ye. Recent developments in chaotic time series analysis. International Journal of Bifurcation and Chaos, 13(6):1383–1422, 2003.

X. Li. Minimizing waiting time variance for stable quality of service on local computer and network resources. PhD Dissertation, Arizona State University, Tempe, AZ, April, 2005.

Z. Liu, Y.-C. Lai, and N. Ye. Statistical properties and attack tolerance of growing networks with algebraic preferential attachment. Physical Review E, 66:036112/1–7, 2002.

Z. Liu, Y.-C. Lai, and N. Ye. Propagation and immunization of infection on general networks with both homogeneous and heterogeneous components. Physical Review E, 67:031911/1–5,

2003. This work was selected by the Virtual Journal of Biological Physics Research for the April 1, 2003 issue.

Z. Liu, Y.-C. Lai, N. Ye, and P. Dasgupta. Connectivity distribution and attack tolerance of general networks with both preferential and random attachments. Physics Letters A, 303:337–344, 2002.

A. E. Motter, A. P. S. de Moura, Y.-C. Lai, and P. Dasgupta. Topology of the conceptual network of language. Physical Review E (Rapid Communications), 65:065102, 2002. This work was featured in New Scientists (July 13, page 22) AND Nature Science Update AND Wissenschaft in German AND in newspapers in Europe, Brazil, and China. This work was also selected by the Virtual Journal of Biological Physics Research for the July 1, 2002 issue.

A.E. Motter and Y.-C. Lai. Cascade-based attacks on complex networks. Phys. Rev. E, 66:065102(R), 2002.

National Science Foundation. New grid portal to improve u.s. researchers' access to advanced computing resources. URL: http://www.nsf.gov/cgi-bin/getpub?pr0088, 2000.

M.E.J. Newman. The structure of scientific collaboration networks. Proc. Natl. Acad. Sci., 98:404–409, 2001.

M.E.J. Newman. Who is the best connected scientist? A study of scientific coauthorship networks. Phys. Rev. E, 64:016131/32, 2001.

M.E.J. Newman. The structure and function of complex networks. SIAM Review, 45:167–256, 2003.

K. Park, Y.-C. Lai, and N. Ye. Self-organized scale-free networks. Physical Review Letters, accepted.

K. Park, Y.-C. Lai, and N. Ye. Characterization of weighted complex networks. Physical Review E, 70(2):026109/1–4, 2004.

K. Park, L. Zhao, Y.-C. Lai, and N. Ye. Jamming in complex gradient networks. Physical Review E, accepted.

V. Paxson. End-to-end routing behavior in the internet. Proc. ACM SIGCOMM, 1996.

M. Pinedo. Scheduling Theory, Algorithms, and Systems. Prentice-Hall, Inc., 1995.

Y. Rekhter and B. Chinoy. Injecting inter-autonomous system routes into intro-autonomous system routing: a performance analysis. Computer Communcations Review, January, 1992.

L. Schrage. Minimizing the time-in-system variance for a finite jobset. Management Science, 21:540–543, 1975.

T. Wu, N. Ye, and D. Zhang. Comparison of distributed methods for resource allocation. International Journal of Production Research, 43(3):515–536, 2005.

X. Xu and N. Ye. Minimization of Job Waiting Time Variance on Identical Parallel Machines. In review.

Z. Yang, N. Ye, and Y.-C. Lai. Qos model of a router with feedback control. Quality and Reliability Engineering International, accepted.

N. Ye. Qos-centric stateful resource management in information systems. Information Systems Frontiers, 4(2):149–160, 2002.

N. Ye. Network security and quality of service. In McGraw-Hill Yearbook of Science & Technology 2005, New York, New York: McGraw Hill, 232-235, 2005.

N. Ye, T. Farley, and D. Aswath. Data measures and collection points to detect traffic changes on large-scale computer networks. Information, Knowledge, Systems Management, accepted.

N. Ye, E. Gel, X. Li, T. Farley, and Y.-C. Lai. Web-server qos models: Applying scheduling rules from production planning. Computers & Operations Research, 32(5):1147–1164, 2005.

N. Ye, B. Harish, X. Li, and T. Farley. Batch scheduled admission control for service dependability of computer and network systems. In review.

N. Ye, Y.-C. Lai, and T. Farley. Dependable information infrastructures as complex adaptive systems. Systems Engineering, 6(4):225–237, 2003.

N. Ye, X. Li, and T. Farley. Job scheduling methods to reduce the variance of job waiting times on computers and networks. In review.

N. Ye, Z. Yang, Y.-C. Lai, and Toni Farley. Enhancing router qos through job scheduling with weighted shortest processing time-adjusted. Computers & Operations Research, 32(9):2255–2269, 2005.

L. Zhao, Y.-C. Lai, K. Park, and N. Ye. Onset of traffic congestion in complex networks. Physical Review E, 71(2):026125/1–8, 2005.

L. Zhao, K. Park, Y.-C. Lai, and N. Ye. Tolerance of scale-free networks against attack-induced cascades. Physical Review Letters, submitted.

Onset of traffic congestion in complex networks

Liang Zhao,[1,2] Ying-Cheng Lai,[1,3] Kwangho Park,[1] and Nong Ye[4]

[1]*Department of Mathematics and Statistics, Arizona State University, Tempe, Arizona 85287, USA*
[2]*Institute of Mathematics and Computer Science, University of São Paulo, São Carlos, Brazil*
[3]*Department of Electrical Engineering and Department of Physics, Arizona State University, Tempe, Arizona 85287, USA*
[4]*Department of Industrial Engineering and Department of Computer Science and Engineering, Arizona State University,
Tempe, Arizona 85287, USA*

(Received 30 August 2004; revised manuscript received 11 November 2004; published 24 February 2005)

Free traffic flow on a complex network is key to its normal and efficient functioning. Recent works indicate that many realistic networks possess connecting topologies with a scale-free feature: the probability distribution of the number of links at nodes, or the degree distribution, contains a power-law component. A natural question is then how the topology influences the dynamics of traffic flow on a complex network. Here we present two models to address this question, taking into account the network topology, the information-generating rate, and the information-processing capacity of individual nodes. For each model, we study four kinds of networks: scale-free, random, and regular networks and Cayley trees. In the first model, the capacity of packet delivery of each node is proportional to its number of links, while in the second model, it is proportional to the number of shortest paths passing through the node. We find, in both models, that there is a critical rate of information generation, below which the network traffic is free but above which traffic congestion occurs. Theoretical estimates are given for the critical point. For the first model, scale-free networks and random networks are found to be more tolerant to congestion. For the second model, the congestion condition is independent of network size and topology, suggesting that this model may be practically useful for designing communication protocols.

DOI: 10.1103/PhysRevE.71.026125
PACS number(s): 89.75.Hc, 89.20.Hh, 05.10.−a

I. INTRODUCTION

Free, uncongested traffic flows on networks are critical for a modern society as its normal and efficient functioning relies on such networks as the internet, the power grid, and transportation networks, etc. To ensure free traffic flows on a complex network is naturally of great interest. The aim of this paper is to address this problem via modeling. Our particular interest is to understand under what conditions traffic congestion can occur on a complex network and to explore possible ways of control to alleviate the congestion. The models we have constructed are based on the setting of information transmission and exchange on the internet. There have been many previous works in this direction [1–14]. A basic assumption used in these studies is that the network possesses a regular and homogeneous structure. Recent works reveal, however, that many realistic networks including the internet are complex with scale-free and small-world features [15,16]. It is thus of paramount interest to study the effect of network topology on traffic flow, which is the key feature that distinguishes our work from the existing ones. While our model is for computer networks, we expect it to be relevant to other practical networks in general, such as the postal service network or the airline transportation network. Our studies may be useful for designing communication protocols for complex networks.

The structure and dynamics on complex networks have attracted a tremendous amount of recent interest [16–18] since the seminal works on scale-free networks by Barabási and Albert [15] and on the small-world phenomenon by Watts and Strogatz [19]. Large networks in nature are always evolving in that nodes and links are continuously added to and/or deleted from the network. Networks are growing if, on average, the numbers of nodes and links increase with time. Most large networks are sparse, that is, the average number of links per node is much smaller than the total number of nodes in the network. Growing and complex networks may be classified according to whether there exists a hierarchy of organized structures. In particular, in a scale-free network, the number of links of various nodes follows a power-law (or algebraic) probability distribution, indicating that nodes in the network are organized into a hierarchy of connected clusters in terms of their numbers of links. In a random network [20], nodes are connected to each other in a completely random fashion and, as such, there is no organized hierarchy of structures in links. Regular networks possess only a few types of linking structures, in contrast to scale-free networks that have an infinite number of possibilities of linking. In this sense, the class of small-world networks studied by Watts and Strogatz [19] is constructed by randomly rewiring only a small fraction of links in a regular network and, hence, they are only a perturbed version of the "backbone" regular network.

Mathematically, a way to characterize a complex network is to examine the degree distribution $P(k)$, where k is the realization of a random variable K measuring the number of links at a node. Scale-free networks are characterized by

$$P(k) \sim k^{-\gamma}, \tag{1}$$

where $\gamma > 0$ is the algebraic scaling exponent. For random networks, the degree distributions are exponential,

$$P(k) \sim \exp(-ak), \tag{2}$$

where $a > 0$ is a constant. The specific class of small-world networks proposed by Watts and Strogatz [19] also assumes the exponential distribution. It should be noticed that strictly scale-free networks are idealized. Realistic networks always contain both scale-free and random components. This "mixed" characteristic is the case for many networks in nature such as the scientific-collaboration network [18,21], the movie-actor network [22,23], and the conceptual network of languages [24].

Models of traffic flow on computer networks have been studied extensively [1–14]. In this context, the information processors are routers which have the same function as, say, workers in the postal service. Routers route the data packets to their destinations. In a computer network, a node may be a host or a router. A host can create packets with addresses of destination and receive packets from other hosts. A router finds, for each packet, the shortest path between the host and the destination and forward the packet along this path in each time step. Here, by "shortest" we mean the path with the smallest number of links. Previous studies focus on two different classes of computer network models. The first class treats all nodes as both hosts and routers [7,10–12], and for the second class [5,8,13,14], some nodes are hosts and others are routers. However, all existing models assume regular network topology, such as two-dimensional lattices [5,7,8,13] or Cayley trees [9–12]. In view of the recent evidence that the internet and many other realistic networks are complex to a significant extent [15,16,18], there is a need to investigate the dynamics of traffic flow on these networks.

In this paper, we construct two dynamical models, each with two parameters: the information creation rate λ and a control parameter β that measures the capacity of nodes to process information. In the first model, the capacity of packet delivery of each node is proportional to its degree, while in the second model, it is proportional to the number of shortest paths passing through the node (betweenness [21]). The quantity of interest is the critical rate λ_c of information generation (as measured by the number of packets created within the network in unit time) at which a phase transition occurs from free to congested traffic flow. In particular, for $\lambda < \lambda_c$, the numbers of created and delivered packets are balanced, resulting in a steady state, or free flow of traffic. For $\lambda > \lambda_c$, congestions occur in the sense that the number of accumulated packets increases with time, due to the fact that the capacities of nodes for delivering packets are limited. We are interested in determining the phase-transition point λ_c, given a network topology, in order to address which kind of network is more susceptible to phase transition and therefore traffic congestion. For this purpose, we study four kinds of networks: Cayley trees, regular, random, and scale-free networks. Our main result is that, in model I, λ_c is larger for networks that have a larger connectivity to betweenness ratio for the small set of nodes with the largest betweenness. Specifically, congestion is easier to occur in Cayley trees, then regular networks, then scale-free networks, and random networks are most tolerant to congestion. We give a theoretical argument to explain this phenomenon, based on identifying the existence of a subset of relatively heavily linked nodes in a network as the key. This is further supported by examining the effect of enhancing the capacities of these nodes to process information. From another standpoint, this result suggests a way to alleviate traffic congestions for scale-free networks: making heavily linked nodes [12] as powerful and efficient as possible for processing information. In the second model, we find that the congestion condition is independent of network size and topology and it thus represents a more useful protocol for alleviating traffic congestion on networks, especially for trees and regular networks.

One recent work that is particularly relevant to our study is the one addressing optimal network topologies for local search on networks [12]. This paper addressed the problem of searchability in complex networks with or without congestion. The focus was on optimal network configurations in terms of search cost, with the conclusion that there are only two classes of optimal networks: starlike or homogeneous-isotropic configurations, depending on the number of parallel searches. Our interest here is in the phase transition from free traffic to congestion and how it occurs with respect to the most representative types of complex networks found in realistic applications: regular, random, and scale-free networks. Despite the difference in the objective, the idea about the definition and analysis of congestion in Ref. [12] is very useful, which we have adopted here.

In Sec. II, we describe our traffic flow models. In Sec. III, we present a theoretical analysis for estimating the critical point for phase transition. Simulation results are given in Sec. IV and a discussion is offered in Sec. V.

II. TRAFFIC-FLOW MODELS

Our traffic-flow model is based on the routing algorithm in computer networks. To account for the network topology, we assume that the capacities for processing information are different for different nodes, depending on the numbers of links (model I) or the number of shortest paths (model II) passing through them. Our routing algorithm consists of the following steps.

(1) At each time step, the probability for node i to generate a packet is λ.

(2) At each time step, a node i delivers C_i packets one step toward their destinations, where $C_i = (1 + \text{int}[\beta k_i])$ in model I and $C_i = (1 + \text{int}[\beta B_i / N])$ in model II, $0 < \beta < 1$ is a control parameter, k_i is the degree of node i, and B_i is its betweenness. A packet, once reaching its destination, is removed from the traffic.

(3) Once a packet is created, it is placed at the end of the queue if this node already has several packets waiting to be delivered to their destinations. The existing packets may be created at some previous time steps or they are transmitted from other nodes. At the same time, a destination node, different from the original one, is chosen at random in the network. The router finds a shortest path between the node with the newly created packet and its destination and, the packet is forwarded along this path during the following time steps. If there are several shortest paths for one packet, the one is chosen whose next station (selected node) has the smallest

number of waiting packets or the shortest queueing length.

(4) At each time step, the first C_i packets at the top of the queue of node i, if it has more than C_i packets in its queue, are forwarded one step toward their destinations and placed at the end of the queues of the selected nodes. Otherwise, all packets in the queue are forwarded one step. This procedure applies to every node at the same time. As a result, the delivering time that a packet needs to reach its destination is related not only to the distance (number of time steps) between the source and the destination, but also to the number of existing packets along its path. Note that, here, the quantity C_i measures the forwarding capacity of node i.

Since N is the total number of nodes in the network, the total number of created packets at each time step is λN, and the total number of delivered packets at each time step is approximately $\Sigma_{i=1}^{N} C_i$ if every node has a sufficient number of packets, which is greater than the total number of created packets provided that $\lambda < 1$. Due to the network complexity, packets are more likely to be routed to the nodes with higher betweenness on their way to the final destinations. As a result, packets are more likely to be accumulated at these nodes, resulting in traffic congestion.

Qualitatively, the dynamics of traffic flow on a network is then as follows. For small values of the creation rate λ, the number of packets on the network is small so that every packet can be processed and delivered in time. Typically, after a short transient time, a steady state for the traffic flow is reached in which the instantaneous number $\langle n(t) \rangle$ of packets, averaged over all nodes in the network, fluctuates about a constant. That is, on average, the total numbers of packets created and delivered are equal, resulting in a free-flow state. This is in fact the well-known Little's law in queueing theory [25]. For larger values of λ, the number of packets created is more likely to exceed that which can be processed in time. In this case, $\langle n(t) \rangle$ grows in time and traffic congestion becomes possible. As λ is increased from zero, we thus expect to observe two phases: free flow for small λ and a congested phase for large λ, with a phase transition from the former to the latter at λ_c. To observe the phase transition and to determine λ_c, given a network structure, are main goals of this paper.

III. THEORETICAL ESTIMATION OF CRITICAL POINT

Here we give a heuristic theory for determining the phase-transition point λ_c, given a particular network structure. Because the node with the largest betweenness can be easily congested and the congestion can quickly spread to the entire network, it is necessary to consider only the traffic balance of this node. Since the packets are transmitted along the shortest paths from the source to the destination, the probability that a created packet will pass through the node with the largest betweenness i is $B_i / \Sigma_{j=1}^{N} B_j$. At each time step, on average, λ packets are generated. Thus, the average number of packets that the node with the largest betweenness receives at each time step is

$$Q_{in} = \lambda ND \frac{B_{L_{max}}}{N \sum\limits_{j=1}^{N} B_j}, \tag{3}$$

where D is the average shortest path length of the network and L_{max} is the index of the node with the largest betweenness. On the other hand, the total number of packets that the node with the largest betweenness can deliver at each time step is

$$Q_{out} = C_{L_{max}}. \tag{4}$$

Congestion occurs when the number of incoming packets is equal to or larger than the outgoing packets at the node with the largest betweenness, i.e.,

$$Q_{in} \geq Q_{out}. \tag{5}$$

Then,

$$\lambda_c ND \frac{B_{L_{max}}}{N \sum\limits_{j=1}^{N} B_j} = C_{L_{max}}. \tag{6}$$

Since $\Sigma_{j=1}^{N} B_j = N(N-1)D$, Eq. (6) can be simplified to

$$\lambda_c = \frac{C_{L_{max}}(N-1)}{B_{L_{max}}}. \tag{7}$$

Equation (7) can be applied to general networks, which is the same result as in Ref. [12].

For model I, Eq. (7) turns out to be

$$\lambda_c = \frac{(1 + \text{int}[\beta k_{L_{max}}])(N-1)}{B_{L_{max}}}. \tag{8}$$

To gain insight, we consider two special cases, regular networks and Cayley trees. First, for regular networks, all nodes have the same structure and the same number of links. We thus have

$$B_{L_{max}} = (N-1)D. \tag{9}$$

The congestion condition can then be estimated by the following equation:

$$\lambda_c \approx \frac{1 + \beta k}{D}. \tag{10}$$

For regular networks $D = N/2k$, we have

$$\lambda_{c,reg} \approx \frac{2k(1 + \beta k)}{N}. \tag{11}$$

Now consider a special kind of regular network, square lattices with periodic boundary condition. For such a lattice with $L \times L$ nodes, $D = L/2$, we have

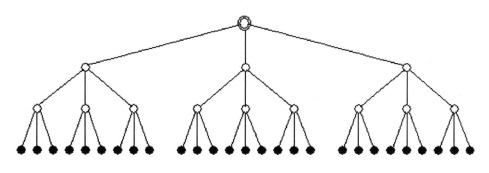

FIG. 1. Illustration of a Cayley tree with the branching factor z =3 and the level of the leaves l =3. The root is on level 0 and the depth of the tree is thus $l+1=4$. Solid circles, circles, and double circle represent leaves, intermediate nodes, and root, respectively.

$$\lambda_{c,lattice} \approx \frac{2(1+\beta k)}{L}. \qquad (12)$$

If $\beta=0$, Eq. (12) recovers the estimate of Ref. [13] and the estimate from the mean field model of Fŭks and Lawniczak [7].

A schematic illustration of a Cayley-tree network is shown in Fig. 1. Since the root has the highest betweenness and a small number of links, it is easy for congestion to occur at the root, which has a major impact on the whole tree. For these reasons, λ_c can be conveniently estimated by only considering the traffic flow through the root.

The total number of nodes in the tree is

$$N=z^0+z^1+z^2+\cdots+z^l=\frac{z^{l+1}-1}{z-1}. \qquad (13)$$

The betweenness B_r of the root can be calculated by counting the routes from any node in the tree to different first-order subtrees, which must pass through the root. We obtain

$$B_r=\frac{1}{2}\frac{(N-1)}{z}\frac{(z-1)(N-1)}{z}z \qquad (14)$$

$$=\frac{z(z^l-1)^2}{2(z-1)}. \qquad (15)$$

In Eq. (14), the factor $(N-1)/z$ is the number of nodes in one chosen first-order subtree and the factor $(N-1)(z-1)/z$ is the number of nodes in all other $z-1$ first-order subtrees. The number of shortest paths from the chosen first-order subtree to any other first-order subtree is the multiplication of these two factors. The factor z means that we have precisely z ways to choose a first-order subtree. The factor $1/2$ is included because each shortest path has been counted twice.

Since the number of links of the root is z, the number of packets that the root can deliver per unit time is

$$Q_{out}=C_r \approx 1+\beta z. \qquad (16)$$

Putting B_r and C_r in Eq. (7), $\lambda_{c,Cayley}$ is estimated to be

$$\lambda_{c,Cayley} \approx \frac{2(1+\beta z)}{z^l-1}. \qquad (17)$$

For model II, the delivery capacity of each node is proportional to its betweenness, i.e., $C_i=1+\text{int}[\beta B_i/N]$. In this case, the critical generating rate for general networks becomes

$$\lambda_c = \frac{(1+\text{int}[\beta B_{L_{max}}/N])(N-1)}{B_{L_{max}}} \qquad (18)$$

$$\approx \frac{(N-1)}{B_{L_{max}}}+\beta \qquad (19)$$

$$\approx \beta, \qquad (20)$$

where, because $B_{L_{max}} \gg N$ in all networks considered in this work, the second term in Eq. (19) dominates. Equation (20) shows that the critical generating rates are roughly independent of the network size and topology.

By comparing Eq. (20) to Eqs. (11) and (17), we see that, although model II makes no significant improvement on random and scale-free networks, it can increase λ_c for regular networks and Cayley trees. A practical significance is that protocols designed based on model II can generally be robust against traffic congestion, regardless of the network topology.

IV. SIMULATION RESULTS

The primary goal of our simulation is to understand the behavior of the phase transition, which leads to traffic congestion, with respect to the network topology. Thus we focus on examining the value of the critical point λ_c for Cayley trees, regular, random, and scale-free networks. Another goal is to explore the effect of adjusting the capacity parameter β. In particular, we are interested in the possibility of increasing the capacities of a small subset of nodes with higher betweenness to improve the network's tolerance to traffic congestions. In order to characterize the transition, we use the order parameter introduced in Ref. [9]:

$$\eta = \lim_{t \to \infty} \frac{\langle \Delta\Theta \rangle}{\lambda \Delta t}, \qquad (21)$$

where $\Delta\Theta=\Theta(t+\Delta t)-\Theta(t)$, $\Theta(t)$ is the total number of packets in the network at time t, and $\langle \cdots \rangle$ indicates the average over time windows of Δt. When $\lambda < \lambda_c$, the network is in the free-flow state; then $\Delta\Theta \approx 0$ and $\eta \approx 0$. For $\lambda > \lambda_c$, $\Delta\Theta$ increases with Δt.

In our simulations, the networks are generated as follows. For all kinds of networks, each node points to a linked list, which contains its nearest neighbors. For a Cayley tree with depth $l+1$ and branching factor z, there are $N=\text{int}[(z^{l+1}-1)/(z-1)]$ nodes, which are labeled as

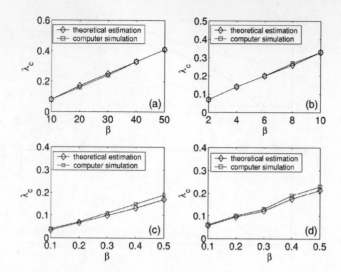

FIG. 2. (Color online) For model I, the order parameter η versus the packet-generating rate λ for the following. (a) Cayley tree, z =3, l=6, $\langle k \rangle$=2, and thus N=1093. Square, triangle, dot, circle, and cross curves correspond to the simulations of β=10,20,30,40,50, respectively. (b) Regular network, N=1000, $\langle k \rangle$=4, square, triangle, dot, circle, and cross curves correspond to the simulations of β =2,4,6,8,10, respectively (c) Scale-free network and (d) random network, N=1000, $\langle k \rangle$=4, where square, triangle, dot, circle, and cross curves correspond to the simulations of β =0.1,0.2,0.3,0.4,0.5, respectively. In all simulations, 50 realizations are averaged.

$\{0,1,2,\ldots,N-1\}$. Thus the list pointed to by node i at level $j \in \{0,1,\ldots,l-1\}$ contains the following node labels as children: $\{i \times Z+1, i \times Z+2,\ldots, i \times Z+Z\}$. At the same time, node i is inserted in the lists pointed to by each of its children. This process begins from the root with node label 0 and ends at the last node at level $l-1$. To generate a regular network with degree k and the label set $\{1,2,\ldots,N\}$, each node i points to a list containing the node labels $\{i-k/2,\ldots,i-2,i-1,i+1,i+2,\ldots,i+k/2\}$. However, if $i+j>N$, the label is replaced by $i+j-N$, and if $i-j<1$, it is replaced by $i-j+N$. Scale-free and random networks are generated by using the general network model proposed in Ref. [26].

First, we present simulation results with model I. Figure 2 shows the order parameter η versus λ for different capacity parameters β for the (a) Cayley tree, (b) regular network, (c) scale-free network, and (d) random network. We see that, for all cases considered, η is approximately zero when λ is small; it suddenly increases when λ is larger than a critical value λ_c. We also observe that λ_c increases with β, which means that enhanced capacity for processing packets can help alleviate possible congestions that are most likely to occur at the heavily linked nodes. As a result, phase transition can be delayed in the sense that the network can be more tolerant to traffic congestions for larger values of λ. Figure 2 also indicates that, in order to get the same order of λ_c, a large value of the capacity parameter β is required for Cayley trees and regular networks; however, small β is needed for random and scale-free networks. This means that Cayley trees and regular networks are significantly more susceptible

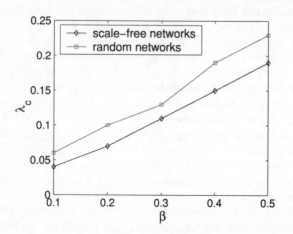

FIG. 3. (Color online) For model I, comparison of theoretical prediction (diamond curves) and simulation (square curves) of λ_c values for (a) Cayley trees, z=3, l=6, $\langle k \rangle$=2; for (b) regular networks, (c) scale-free networks, and (d) random networks, N=1000, $\langle k \rangle$=4.

to traffic congestion. This is because, in Cayley trees and regular networks, the most congested nodes have large betweenness, but very small number of links, i.e., the ratio $k_{L_{max}}/B_{L_{max}}$ is much smaller than those in random and scale-free networks. Equation (8) then indicates that the λ_c for Cayley trees and regular networks is much smaller than that for random and scale-free networks.

Figure 3 shows the critical generating rate λ_c from theoretical predictions and from simulations. The theoretical results are obtained by Eqs. (17), (11), and (8) for Cayley trees, regular, random, and scale-free networks, respectively. In all cases, a good agreement is observed. From Fig. 2, we see that the critical packet generation rates λ_c of scale-free and random networks are of the same order. However, a direct comparison of simulation results (Fig. 4) shows that λ_c for random networks is actually larger than that for scale-free networks. As mentioned, scale-free networks are heterogeneous in links, which causes heterogeneity in betweenness.

FIG. 4. (Color online) For model I with N=1000, $\langle k \rangle$=4, simulation results of λ_c versus β for scale-free and random networks.

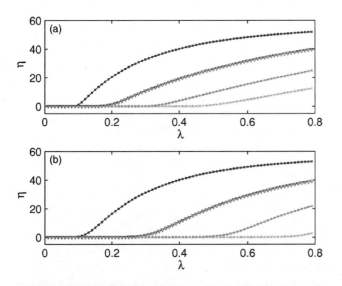

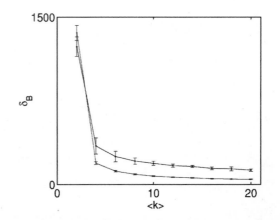

FIG. 6. (Color online) For $N=1000$ and 50 realizations, the standard deviation of betweenness δ_B versus the average degree $\langle k \rangle$ for scale-free (upper trace) and random (lower trace) networks.

FIG. 5. (Color online) For model I with $N=1000$, $\beta=0.2$, order parameter η versus the packet-generating rate λ for (a) scale-free networks, (b) random networks. Square, triangle, circle, and cross curves correspond to the simulations of $\langle k \rangle=4,6,8,10$, respectively. In all simulations, 50 realizations are averaged.

This means that there is a small group of nodes which have large betweenness but majority of nodes in the network have small betweenness. Thus, most generated packets will have a high probability to pass through this small number of high betweenness nodes, making them vulnerable to congestion. Qualitatively, we may think that the packet transmission routes are relatively better distributed for random networks than for scale-free networks.

How does the congestion condition change with the network's average degree $\langle k \rangle$? Figure 5 shows that in both scale-free and random networks, λ_c increases as the average degree increases. This is because increasing the average degree makes nodes in the networks more connected and hence the shortest paths are less dependent on the heavily linked nodes. Consequently, congestion on the heavily linked nodes can be delayed. As mentioned, betweenness homogeneity is an important factor for traffic congestion. In order to characterize this feature, we calculate the standard deviation of betweenness defined as

$$\delta_B = \frac{1}{N} \sqrt{\sum_{i=1}^{N} (B_i - \langle B \rangle)^2}, \qquad (22)$$

where $\langle B \rangle$ is the average betweenness of the network in consideration. Figure 6 shows the decreasing of the standard deviation of betweenness for both the scale-free and random networks as the average degree increases, indicating that the distribution of betweenness is more homogeneous with increasing $\langle k \rangle$. Thus, packet loads of the nodes with the largest betweenness are reduced and congestion triggered by these nodes is delayed. From the same figure, we see that, except for $\langle k \rangle=2$, the betweenness deviation in random networks is smaller than that in scale-free networks. That is, the betweenness distribution in random networks is in general more homogeneous. This is another supporting factor for the

explanation as to why random networks are more tolerant to congestion.

We now present simulation results with model II. Here, the delivery capacity of each node is proportional to its betweenness, i.e., $C_i = 1 + \text{int}[B_i/N]$. Figure 7 shows the order parameter η versus λ for different capacity parameters β for (a) Cayley tree, (b) regular, (c) scale-free, and (d) random network. We see that values of λ_c are roughly the same for all kinds of networks considered here, confirming our prediction by Eq. (20).

Figure 8 shows the critical generating rate λ_c from theoretical predictions and simulations for the four kinds of networks. In all cases, good agreement is observed. These simu-

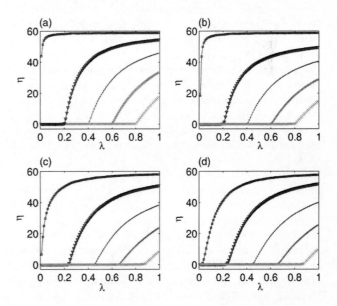

FIG. 7. (Color online) For model II, order parameter η versus the packet-generating rate λ for (a) Cayley tree, $z=3$, $l=6$, $\langle k \rangle=2$, thus $N=1093$; for (b) regular network, (c) scale-free network, and (d) random networks, $N=1000$, $\langle k \rangle=4$. In all of the four cases, square, triangle, dot, circle, and cross curves correspond to the simulations of $\beta=0.0,0.2,0.4,0.6,0.8$, respectively. The capacity of delivery of each node is proportional to its betweenness. In all simulations, 50 realizations are averaged.

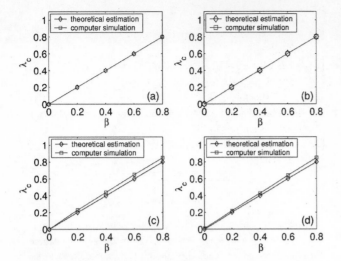

FIG. 8. (Color online) For model II, comparison of theoretical prediction (diamond curves) and computer simulation (square curves) of λ_c versus the capacity parameter β for (a) Cayley trees, $z=3$, $l=6$, $\langle k \rangle=2$; for (b) regular, (c) scale-free, and (d) random networks, $N=1000$, $\langle k \rangle=4$.

lation results thus show that protocols based on our model II are more tolerant to congestion for all kinds of networks studied here, especially for Cayley trees and regular networks.

V. DISCUSSION

We live in a modern world supported by large, complex networks. Examples range from financial markets to internet, communication, and transportation systems. Recently there has been a tremendous effort to study the general structure of these networks [16–18]. Universal features such as the small-world [19] and scale-free [15] properties, which can be characterized at a quantitative level, have been discovered in almost all realistic networks. The discoveries suggest that, to understand the dynamics on complex networks, their structures have to be taken into account.

This paper addresses the dynamics of traffic flow on complex networks. Our motivation comes from the desire to understand the influence of topological structure on the traffic dynamics on a network, as existing works in this direction often assume regularity and homogeneity for the underlying network [1–14]. We consider general network structures to couple with simple traffic-flow models determined by the rate of information generation and a parameter to describe the average capacity of nodes to process information. Our study indicates that phase transition can generally occur in the sense that free traffic flow can be guaranteed for low rates of information generation but large rates above a critical value can result in traffic congestions. Our models enable the critical value for the phase transition to be estimated theoretically and computed, given a particular network topology. We present computational results and analysis, which indicate that, in case the delivery capacity of each node is proportional to its degree, the critical value is smaller for networks of smaller ratio of degree to betweenness for the set of most easily congested nodes (the set of nodes with the largest betweenness). In this case, random and scale-free networks are more tolerant to congestion than trees and regular networks. This is further supported by examining the effect of enhancing the capacities of these nodes to process information on the global traffic flow. These results suggest a way to alleviate traffic congestions for protocol based on model I for networks with a significant heterogeneous component: making nodes with large betweenness as powerful and efficient as possible for processing and transmitting information. For protocol based on model II, the capacity of delivery of each node is proportional to its betweenness. In this case, the critical value λ_c is independent of the network topology. Compared with model I, while model II can improve a little the performance for scale-free and random networks, it can improve significantly the performance for trees and regular networks against congestion.

ACKNOWLEDGMENTS

Z. Liu provided assistance in the initial phase of this project. The work was supported by AFOSR under Grant No. F49620-01-1-0317 and by NSF under Grant No. ITR-0312131.

[1] H. Li and M. Maresca, IEEE Trans. Comput. **38**, 1345 (1989).

[2] W. E. Leland, M. S. Taqqu, W. Willinger, and D. V. Wilson, Comput. Commun. Rev. **23**, 183 (1993).

[3] M. S. Taqqu, W. Willinger, and R. Sherman, Comput. Commun. Rev. **27**, 5 (1997).

[4] M. E. Crovella and A. Bestavros, IEEE/ACM Trans. Netw. **5**, 835 (1997).

[5] T. Ohira and R. Sawatari, Phys. Rev. E **58**, 193 (1998).

[6] M. Faloutsos, P. Faloutsos, and C. Faloutsos, Comput. Commun. Rev. **29**, 251 (1999).

[7] H. Fŭks and A. T. Lawniczak, Math. Comput. Simul. **51**, 101 (1999).

[8] R. V. Solé and S. Valverde, Physica A **289**, 595 (2001).

[9] A. Arenas, A. Díaz-Guilera, and R. Guimerà, Phys. Rev. Lett. **86**, 3196 (2001).

[10] R. Guimerà, A. Arenas, and A. Díaz-Guilera, Physica A **299**, 247 (2001).

[11] R. Guimerà, A. Arenas, A. Díaz-Guilera, and F. Giralt, Phys. Rev. E **66**, 026704 (2002).

[12] R. Guimerà, A. Díaz-Guilera, F. Vega-Redondo, A. Cabrales, and A. Arenas, Phys. Rev. Lett. **89**, 248701 (2002).

[13] M. Woolf, D. K. Arrowsmith, R. J. Mondragón-C, and J. M. Pitts, Phys. Rev. E **66**, 046106 (2002).

[14] S. Valverde and R. V. Solé, Physica A **312**, 636 (2002).

[15] A.-L. Barabási and R. Albert, Science **286**, 509 (1999); A.-L. Barabási, R. Albert, and H. Jeong, Physica A **272**, 173 (1999);

281, 69 (2000).

[16] R. Albert and A.-L. Barabási, Rev. Mod. Phys. **74**, 47 (2002).

[17] S. H. Strogatz, Nature (London) **410**, 268 (2001).

[18] M. E. J. Newman, SIAM Rev. **45**, 167 (2003).

[19] D. J. Watts and S. H. Strogatz, Nature (London) **393**, 440 (1998).

[20] P. Erdös and A. Rényi, Publ. Math., Inst. Hungarian Acad. Sci. **5**, 17 (1960); B. Bollobaás, *Random Graphs* (Academic, London, 1985).

[21] M. E. J. Newman, Phys. Rev. E **64**, 016131 (2001).

[22] R. Albert and A.-L. Barabási, Phys. Rev. Lett. **85**, 5234

(2000).

[23] J.-W. Kim, B. Hunt, and E. Ott, Phys. Rev. E **66**, 046115 (2002).

[24] A. E. Motter, A. P. S. de Moura, Y.-C. Lai, and P. Dasgupta, Phys. Rev. E **65**, 065102(R) (2002).

[25] See, for example, O. Allen, *Probability, Statistics and Queueing Theory with Computer Science Application*, 2nd ed. (Academic, New York, 1990).

[26] Z. Liu, Y.-C. Lai, N. Ye, and P. Dasgupta, Phys. Lett. A **303**, 337 (2002).

Anomaly and Misuse Detection in Network Traffic Streams — Checking and Machine Learning Approaches

Sampath Kannan*,   Insup Lee   Wenke Lee   Oleg Sokolsky   Diana Spears
William Spears

December 7, 2005

Abstract

The prevalence of security holes in programs and protocols, the increasing size and complexity of the Internet, and the sensitivity of the information stored throughout have made the problem of network security of paramount importance and attracted newspaper headlines[17]. Viruses and worms can spread rapidly wreaking havoc on the hosts they infect. Other types of *malware* (the generic name we use to describe any kind of program that engages in unauthorised behavior) can consume network resources, acquire disallowed privileges, and breach the confidentiality and integrity of sensitive data. The diversity of possible attacks entails a variety of techniques to counter them. One the most important defenses is a network intrusion detection system (NIDS). Such a system is deployed at routers or other intermediate points on the network to monitor traffic and detect attacks or anomalies in traffic patterns and to activate alarms when they are detected. Host-based defenses monitor and/or patch vulnerabilities that can be exploited by malware, perform formal analyses of software to detect potential problems, and observe the behavior of running software to raise alarms if warranted. In this paper we explore a variety of approaches to improve defenses against malware, including both network-based and host-based approaches.

Keywords: Network Intrusion Detection, Host-based Intrusion Detection, Anomaly Detection, Malware, Botnets, Case-based reasoning.

Categories: Network security, Intrusion Detection Systems, Run-time monitoring, Streaming algorithms, Semantic analogy-based reasoning.

1 Preliminaries

To make networks secure against such attacks we need a combination of techniques such as firewalls, strongly typed languages, secure protocols such as IP-sec and https, intrusion and anomaly detection systems, and decoys and honey pots. Furthermore, each of these protection mechanisms has to be continually adapted to combat new and increasingly sophisticated attacks.

At the network level, defense mechanisms try to detect *intrusions* and *anomalies*, terms that are defined below. "Intrusion" refers to a hacker — who may be a legitimate user or an outsider — getting privileges s/he is not entitled to, and using them to steal confidential data, misuse system resources, deface webpages, corrupt files, set up programs with backdoors for future access, or attack other systems. Intrusions usually follow a "script" or scenario, wherein the hacker first probes a system for vulnerabilities such as web pages with CGI scripts, programs with buffer overflow problems, etc. Buffer overflow occurs when a program stores a data item that is too big to fit within the space allocated for it. Without adequate protection, the

---

*Point of Contact: Sampath Kannan, email: kannan@cis.upenn.edu, tel: (215) 898-9514, fax: (215) 898-0587

data item simply overflows into adjacent space which may contain information that is critical to the correct behavior of a program, such as the address to which the program should jump to execute the next instruction. Malware can exploit this vulnerability by providing such oversized data to important programs in the system, and using the resulting buffer overflow to hijack the execution of the program to locations containing part of the malware code. They might also ping all machines to detect which machines are up and running, do port scans to find port numbers for various protocols, and check for the services offered by a machine. This exploration might reveal holes which they then exploit to gain access to the system, after which they try to gain further privileges. Because of this pattern of behavior, there is a "signature" or sequence of events associated with each type of intrusion and databases of such signatures are used to detect intrusions.

In anomaly detection, we analyze statistical information about network traffic and raise alarms when we see "aberrant" statistics. This definition is general and can include a variety of different tests and techniques.

Both intrusion detection and anomaly detection can be performed at routers and other intermediate points on the network (systems that do this are called Network Intrusion Detection Systems (NIDS)) or at hosts (such systems are called Host-Based Intrusion Detection Systems).

2   Research Summary

In order to produce systematic and comprehensive Network and Host-Based Intrusion Systems that are capable of detecting and adapting to new attacks as they occur major improvements are needed in the algorithmic and systems infrastructure for processing traffic. While we have been working on this larger question, we are simultaneously tackling specific problems that will be important "plug-ins" into this infrastructure. Listed below are our solutions to two important problems that arise in Network Intrusion Detection.

- We learn new signatures based on known attacks and apply them to the traffic. This will greatly reduce the false negative rate that results if we simply check for intrusions against a static database.

- We detect attacks by "botnets" (which are networks of automated and coordinated attackers) by extracting anomalies in traffic patterns.

Viruses and worms are specific types of malware that have gained notoriety in recent years. These programs are spread by a variety of means – email attachments, IRC protocols, software downloads, etc. While attempts have been made to detect viruses and worms at the network level by observing anomalous traffic patterns[18, 10], and by learning signatures[14], the more sophisticated and novel attacks will need a host-based detection component as well. While fundamentally novel viruses are difficult to create, a common approach used by hackers is to mutate the code for a virus so as to retain its functionality while evading detection. Thus, one can group viruses into families with common origins which are referred to as polymorphic families of viruses. Further complicating the situation is the possibility that the virus code exists in encrypted form and is only decrypted at the time of execution.

- We define and compute measures for the similarity of two programs viewed as control-flow graphs. We have initiated an experimental study of such an approach for detecting polymorphic families of viruses.

In addition to working on the specific problems above, we seek to improve the infrastructure for intrusion and anomaly detection. The Monitoring and Checking (MaC) framework is a framework for run-time monitoring of software systems. We have designed and implemented a prototype of this framework called JavaMaC that monitors running Java programs. In JavaMaC, the user provides information associating low-level program variables with more abstract events. The user also specifies properties to be satisfied by the running system using a formal framework such as temporal logic or automata. The MaC system instruments the Java program to extract information about the low-level variables of interest at run-time, feeds the extracted information to an event recognizer that detects the occurrence of abstract events and then sends this sequence of abstract events to an automaton that detects violations of the desired properties. This infrastructure is natural and convenient to use in the context of intrusion and anomaly detection. The instrumentation here will extract relevant features from network traffic. The choice of the features themselves is an interesting research question. Each anomaly or intrusion detection module can then use this stream of extracted features to determine if events of interest to that module have occurred. The sequence of events is then used by the module to raise an alarm when an intrusion or anomaly is detected. Putting a number of such modules on the same platform also allows us to combine the inferences made by the individual modules to reduce false positive and false negative rates. Using statistical techniques to find the best way to combine the output of modules is another important research question.

Another infrastructure improvement necessary for intrusion detection systems is in the area of streaming algorithms. Such algorithms process massive amounts of data generated at a rapid rate. They are incapable of storing any more than a negligible amount of the observed data but must nevertheless compute various functions on the data stream. Perforce these computations will be approximate for all but the most trivial functions. Such a data stream model applies at the routers in a network. To implement signature-based intrusion detection systems at a high volume router at the backbone of a network requires being able to compute sophisticated functions on the traffic stream. This problem is difficult enough that current systems deal with very limited signatures, usually matched with one packet in the traffic stream. To deal with signatures that span multiple packets one needs algorithms that can use memory very efficiently without having to remember state for each of the currently active traffic flows. To deal with problems of this nature, basic research is needed on algorithmic questions that can be solved in the streaming model.

3　A Closer Look at Three Results

3.1　Detecting Botnets

Increasingly, attackers are using the resources of their victims. Whereas previous generations of malware merely caused harm to individual computers, attackers are now pooling their victims into large networks, and using these for malicious purposes. The resulting victim clouds constitute a more significant, growing threat on the Internet. Common examples include botnets (which perform arbitrary tasks), proxynets (which anonymize attacker communications), and zombie distributed denial-of-service (DDoS) armies (used to consume network resources).

Unlike individual infections, victim networks are difficult to effectively remediate. Further, the networks of infected individuals facilitate attacks (such as DDoS, distributed network scanning) that are more effective using large numbers of victims. More ominously, a large pool of victims creates an effective malware launching platform, so that new vulnerabilities are exploited instantaneously by numerous attackers [21]. This significantly shortens the response time and patch window that network administrators need to perform basic maintenance.

3.1.1　Motivation and Goals

Attacking networks (e.g., botnets) constitute a growing, urgent problem for information security researchers. Botmasters are creating complex, large, and mature networks of victims. Warning signs include the following:

- Botnet Complexity We are witnessing a growing list of victim networks structured with bewildering complexity. Some recent examples include: distributed phishing sites [8], which rotate the fake web page among victims in the cloud, distributed spam armies [16], which make response (e.g., patching, blacklisting) more difficult than stopping a single machine, and distributed denial of service zombies [12].

- Botnet Size The victim networks are not only complex, but also large. The scale of the botnet problem is simply staggering. Botnets can easily approach 50,000 victim members [20]. Our large-scale project at Georgia Institute of Technology [3] has captured botnets with 350,000 members. One reliable estimate is that some 170,000 new victim infections occur per day [2]. The research effort in [3] has cataloged nearly 200 individual major bot versions (or families), each with dozens of different variations and minor version.

- Botnet Maturity Botnets have undergone years of development and use, and are currently quite robust. Whereas previous botnets used IRC networks to coordinate communication between victims and the botmaster [5], current generations of botnets use non-standard protocols, or customized versions of IRC servers running on victim computers.

An important problem is the detection of the attacking network. Existing intrusion detection techniques can identify discrete "side-effects" of a botnet (e.g., detecting a scan or phishing attack), but fail to identify the *entire network* of victims performing the attacks.

Thus, in order to handle botnet attacks we must:

1. Identify the command-and-control (C&C) traffic. Without coordination, botnets are merely clusters of discrete, unorganized infections, for which there are existing orthogonal solutions. If we can identify the command-and-control traffic, we can disrupt the botnet, anticipate attacks, and perform tracebacks.

2. Identify the victims in a botnet. If all of the victims in an attacking network are enumerated, upstream providers can block their traffic, and network owners can be notified to start patching. Since most victims have multiple infections (and participate in many botnets) identifying victim clouds lets one anticipate the propagation potential of similar malware.

3.1.2 Approaches and Results

A solution to the problem posed by botnets begins with an understanding of the command and control infrastructure of botnets. This is used to design corresponding detection and response capabilities. More specifically, we define a taxonomy of botnets based on how they perform command and control over victim hosts. We have implemented and tested a next-generated technique for detecting and responding to botnets, which is described below.

Detection

We have developed several *anomaly detection* approaches to identify botnets. The main idea is to look for *abnormal* traffic behaviors caused by the command and control activities of the botnets. In this research, we focus on a class of botnets that use Dynamic DNS (DDNS) service.

The general pattern of botnet creation is detailed in Fig. 1. To start, a malware author, VX in the diagram, will purchase one or several domain names (perhaps using stolen accounts). The newly purchased domains are initially "parked" at 0.0.0.0, reserved for unknown addresses. The malware author then hardcodes the string names of their domains into a dropper, and spreads the binary, as shown in steps 1 and 2 of Fig. 1.

While the virus spreads, the malware author also creates a C&C "rallying" box for the victims. This is typically one of two types: a high-bandwidth compromised machine, or (more frequently) a high-capacity co-located box (perhaps rented with stolen funds). The C&C box is set up to run an IRC service (often a modified version), to provide a medium for the bots to communicate.

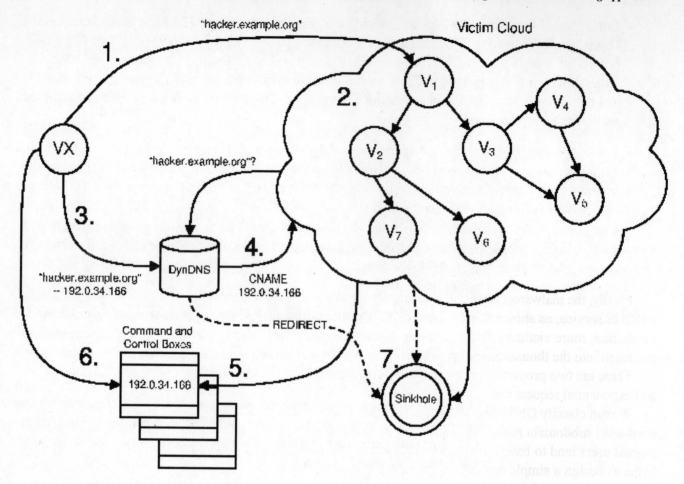

Figure 1: General spread of a botnet.

(1) A malware author writes a virus, hardcoding an address (here, "hacker.example.org") that victims should contact after infection (called "command and control" or C&C). (2) The virus spreads, reaching unknown victims. (3) The malware author purchases an inexpensive DDNS service to link the string name to the C&C box's IP address, often another compromised machine. (4) The bots lookup the IP of the C&C box from the DDNS server, and (5) rally at the C&C box. Eventually, the DDNS provider detects the abuse and revokes the account, redirecting all traffic to (6) the KarstNet sinkhole. In some fortuitous cases, prompt reverse engineering of binary samples (obtained from honeypots) let us sinkhole botnets even before they become active.

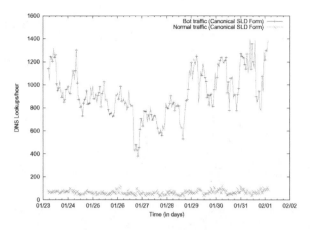

Figure 2: Comparison of Canonical DNS Request Rates

Finally, the malware author will also arrange for DNS resolution of the domain names, and register with a DDNS service, as shown at step 3 in Fig. 1. The IP address they provide is for the C&C box. As DNS propagates, more victims join the network, and within a day, the bot army swells. Overnight, the bot army can reach into the thousands, even for a novice Visual Basic virus.

There are two properties of botnet DNS behavior that help distinguish their traffic: use of subdomains, and exponential request rates.

We can classify DNS requests as either second-level domain (SLD) requests, such a "example.com", or third-level subdomain requests ($3LD$), such as "foo.example.com". From extensive empirical observations, normal users tend to have a single domain name, while bots tend to use mostly subdomains [15]. This fact helps us design a simple detection system. We define the *canonical SLD request rate* as the total number of requests observed for all the $3LD$s present in a SLD, plus any requests to the SLD. We use the term $|SLD|$ to represent the number of $3LD$s observed in a given SLD. (Thus, if the SLD "example.com" has two subdomains, then its $|SLD| = 2$.) For a given SLD_i, with rate R_{SLD_i} we calculate its canonical rate C_{SLD_i} as:

$$C_{SLD_i} = R_{SLD_i} + \sum_{j=1}^{|SLD_i|} R_{3LD_j}$$

We ran a modified version of `dnstop` on a DDNS provider's busy network for a week, and sampled approximately 1.28 million DNS requests. We filtered out all bot traffic (by hand, with the help of the DDNS provider), and calculated a mean lookup rate for normal traffic. Fig. 2 shows the average lookup rate for normal hosts, in requests per hour.

When put in canonical form, distinguishing the normal and bot traffic is straight forward. We simply set an expected mean for the rate of normal traffic, $E(X) = \mu$. We then use Chebyshev's inequality, Eq.(1), to fix an appropriate threshold for the normal request rates and request anomalous (i.e., bot) lookups.

$$P(|X - \mu| \geq t) \leq \frac{\sigma^2}{t} \tag{1}$$

The above simple threshold based approach using canonical SLD scores is very useful, and created no false positives in our test data set. We can imagine situations, however, where the botmasters could attempt to evade such detection. We developed a secondary detection filter based on *sorted request rate densities*. This second detection layer is also useful for noisy networks where short-term normal and bot DNS rates may be very similar. To reduce the chance of false positives, the second filter can be used to examine just the hosts who have excessive canonical SLD scores.

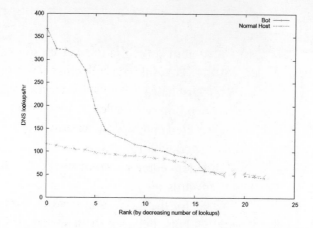

Figure 3: Comparison of Sorted DNS Rates

A key distinguishing feature for this second filter is that botnet DNS requests rates are usually exponential over a 24 hour period. The diurnal nature of bot behavior means that there are periodic spikes in bot requests. These spikes are caused by infected hosts who turn on their computers in the morning, releasing a sudden burst of DNS traffic as the bots reconnect to the C&C box. This spike is not present in normal DNS request rates, which require (usually slower and random) user interaction to generate a DNS request. In some cases, flash crowds of users visiting a popular site may behave like a botnet [9], but this is rare, and likely not sustained as seen in botnets.

We can use the sorted rates of normal DNS requests over a 24 hour period to create a distribution, or density signature for normal traffic. Figure 3 shows the sorted 24-hour average rates for normal traffic. Compared to the sorted botnet traffic, the two distributions are quite different. Because of the diurnal spikes in traffic, the botnet traffic exhibits an exponential distribution.

We can then use any standard distance metric to compare the two distributions. Mahalanobis distance is one useful measure of the distance between request rate distributions and a normal model. (Though the results obtained using the Mahalanobis distance have been encouraging, one could also imagine using one of a plethora of other notions of distance between distributions.)

The Mahalanobis distance, d, is:

$$d^2(x, \bar{y}) = (x - \bar{y})' C^{-1}(x - \bar{y}) \tag{2}$$

x and $\bar{y}$ are variable vectors (features) of the new observation and the trained (normal) profile, respectively. C is the inverse covariance matrix for each member of the training data set.

As noted in [22], the Mahalanobis distance metric considers the variance of request rates in addition to the average request rate. This detects outliers, and measures the consistency of the observed request rates with the trained (normal) samples. As in [22], we can simplify the Mahalanobis distance metric by assuming the independence of each sample in the normal traffic (and therefore removing the covariance matrix).

$$d(x, \bar{y}) = \sum_{i=0}^{n-1} \left(\frac{|x_i - \bar{y}_i|}{\bar{\sigma}_i} \right) \tag{3}$$

As with the canonical SLD request rate, we can train using the normal model, and pick an appropriate threshold. If observed traffic for a host has too great a distance score from the normal, it is deemed an outlier, and flagged as a bot.

Response

We have developed, `KarstNet`, a collection of sinkholes located at different addresses on the Internet as a response mechanism to the detected botnets. The sinkhole collection is used by third party networks that need to redirect abusive traffic. `KarstNet` coordinates exchanges between sinkhole providers and DDNS owners, letting them arrange for sinkholes, swap binary samples and logs, and monitor botnet activity. An extensive database back end lets users track infected machines, Classless Inter-Domain Routing (CIDR) [6] blocks, and even geographical locations associated with infections.

Specifically, `KarstNet` lets DDNS providers enter a canonical name (CNAME) or other appropriate DNS record responses (RR) to direct bots towards an available `KarstNet` sinkhole. Once redirected, the DDNS server no longer returns the CNAME for the C&C, and instead points all traffic to the sinkhole. The sinkhole then plays "TCP games" with the bots, delaying them in routing- or application-level tarpits, blackhole routing (where no replies are sent at all), and generally passively consuming victim resources. Victim join limits, sinkhole responses, and other behaviors are also controlled by the systems exchange site.

In a four month period, `KarstNet` has trapped nearly 6 million unique victims and disrupted the C&C for dozens of botnets, all in size of 100K+ victims.

3.2   Quantitative Bisimulation for Program Similarity

The state of the art in virus programming has progressed to the point when novice hackers can quickly put together new viruses from available building blocks. Several toolkits, such as DREG and NGVCK [19], are readily available on the Internet. Their widespread use leads to the proliferation of new viruses and worms that belong to several well-known families, but at the same time are different enough that signature-based methods do not detect these new viruses using existing signatures. Development of a new signature for each new variant and propagating these new signatures to virus checking software becomes prohibitively expensive and inefficient.

We describe a different approach to detection of new viruses that belong to existing virus families. The approach exploits the fact that viruses are built from standard building blocks and thus exhibit substantial similarity. In order to tell whether a new program may be a new virus, we measure its similarity to known representatives of virus families.

The similarity measure is defined by generalizing *simulation* and *bisimulation* [13], two well-known process relations. These relations are widely used in the behavioral modeling of computer systems. A system is modeled as a *labeled transition system*, which describes how the system evolves from one execution state to another by performing certain actions that appear as labels on transitions between states. These relations capture the intuition that systems that are related can perform the same actions – in other words, one can simulate the other. A state s in one system simulates a state t in another system if, whenever the system in the state t can perform an action a and move to the state t', the other system in the state s can also perform the action a and move to the state s' that simulates t'. If this relation is symmetric, that is, t also simulates s, the relation is called bisimulation.

Although simulation and bisimulation capture the right intuition for comparison of two systems, they cannot be applied for the purpose of detecting similarity between virus programs because they call for exact matches between the steps of two systems, and evaluate to a boolean value rather than to a quantitative similarity rank.

We generalize the simulation relation to a function $Q(s, t)$ that takes its values in the interval $[0, 1]$. We then apply the function to the control flow graphs of the two programs. Program S is the known representative of a virus family. Program T is the suspected virus. If s_0 and t_0 are the initial nodes of the control flow graphs of S and T, respectively, the high value of $Q(s_0, t_0)$ indicates that T exhibits a high degree of similarity to S and is likely to be a member of the virus family derived from S.

To define the function Q, we assume two *local similarity* functions and a parameter $p \in [0, 1]$. The first local similarity function establishes similarity of two states in the transition systems, disregarding their transitions. For example, when we are comparing control flow graphs, nodes are labeled with fragments of assembly code that are executed when the system is in that state. The local node similarity compares how similar the two assembly fragments are. The node similarity function takes values in the interval $[0, 1]$. We assume that the function is symmetric, that is, $N(s, t) = N(t, s)$ and that a node is perfectly similar to itself, that is, $N(s, s) = 1$. In a similar way, we define the edge similarity function $L(a, b)$, which computes the similarity between two actions performed by the two systems. The parameter p reflects the relative importance we assign to local similarity of the two nodes compared to the similarity of the steps that can be taken from the nodes and of the nodes that can be reached by these steps.

Now, we are ready to define the quantitative similarity function with the parameter p, Q_p. It is the function that satisfies the following condition:

$$Q_p(s_1, s_2) = \begin{cases} N(s_1, s_2) & \text{if } \forall a, s_1 \overset{a}{\nrightarrow} \\ (1 - p) \cdot N(s_1, s_2) + p \cdot \frac{1}{n} \cdot \sum_{s_1 \overset{a}{\to} s_1'} \max_{s_2 \overset{b}{\to} s_2'} L(a, b) \cdot Q_p(s_1', s_2') & \text{otherwise,} \end{cases} \quad (4)$$

where n is the number of transitions leaving s_1. For each transition of s_1, the definition finds the best match provided by a transition of s_2, and computes the average of these matches. This corresponds to the expected value of the match for a randomly selected transition of s_1. Thus obtained "step" similarity value is assigned weight p, while the "local" similarity value, given by the node similarity function, is assigned weight $1 - p$. If s_1 does not have any outgoing transitions, quantitative similarity is given by the local similarity function.

The values of Q_p for all state pairs in the two transition systems can be computed using linear programming. We have started experimental evaluation of the utility of Q_p for the comparison of virus control flow graphs and obtained encouraging initial results.

Quantitative simulation can be extended to quantitative bisimulation B_p by making the definition symmetric. Intuitively, bisimilarity between states s and t equals to the minimum of the similarities between s and t and, conversely, t and s. Formally, $B_p(s_1, s_2) = \min(B_p^-(s_1, s_2), B_p^-(s_2, s_1))$,, where $B_p^-(s_1, s_2)$ is defined as

$$B_p^-(s_1, s_2) = \begin{cases} N(s_1, s_2) & \text{if } \forall a, s_1 \overset{a}{\nrightarrow} \\ (1 - p) \cdot N(s_1, s_2) + p \cdot \frac{1}{n} \cdot \sum_{s_1 \overset{a}{\to} s_1'} \max_{s_2 \overset{b}{\to} s_2'} L(a, b) \cdot B_p(s_1', s_2') & \text{otherwise.} \end{cases}$$

Computation of quantitative bisimulation is closely related to finding the value of an *infinite-horizon 2-player stochastic game with imperfect information* [1]. While no polynomial algorithms are known for this problem, there is an approximate solution that can be computed in polynomial time and guarantees the required degree of precision.

Other generalizations for bisimulation and simulation of labeled transition systems can be found in the literature. In [4] several metrics have been proposed for *quantitative transition systems*, which are labeled with tuples of numbers instead of more conventional symbolic labels. The quantity computed (representing the degree to which some state simulates another state) is *extremal* In other words, it is the worst simulated transition from state s by a transition from state t that determines the simulation score of s by t. In [7] a notion of *approximate bisimulation* is defined for linear systems. Here again, a label matches labels within an ϵ ball and we need *every* transition from s to match in this approximate sense with a transition from t in order for s and t to be assigned a high bisimulation score. In contrast, our measure is *cumulative* in that it uses a (weighted) average of the extent to which each transition is simulated. Cumulative measures seem more appropriate for detecting similarity between virus programs since it is easy to defeat extremal measures by introducing dummy transitions that do not match with any others.

3.3   Learning Malware Signatures through Case-Based Reasoning

The purpose of *intrusion detection* is to recognize malicious computer hacking, i.e., malware, based on evidential traces. Intrusion end-goals include, for example, corruption, disablement, and identity-theft. The traditional approach to intrusion detection consists of matching, as early as possible, a new script/scenario against known prior attacks, called "signatures." Signatures are typically stored in a database. If the new script is similar enough to a known former attack signature, then it is labeled "positive" (an attack) by the network intrusion detection system (NIDS); otherwise, it is labeled "negative" (not an attack). This project assumes that each script or signature has the form of a sequence of commands.

Typically, NIDS try to find an exact match between a new ongoing script and a prefix of a stored attack signature. Unfortunately in practice an exact match is rarely possible to find, even though the new script may be the beginning of an attack that is nearly identical semantically to a prefix of a previous attack. For example, the attacker might use recently invented, disguised commands that perform the same function as previous commands.

The most significant and prevalent problem for intrusion detection systems occurs when a true attack is in progress, but the NIDS fails to recognize it as an attack. This is called a *false negative*, or an *error of omission*. The primary contribution of our research is to address and substantially mitigate this problem of false negatives. In particular, a case-based reasoning (CBR) [11] approach is applied, which allows the NIDS to attempt a "flexible," rather than an exact match between a new script and a prior attack signature in the database. It is the *analogy* portion of CBR systems that provides flexibility in matching. The particular type of analogy that we use is semantic, rather than syntactic. The latter is more traditional for analogy; however, semantic analogies enable greater flexibility in matching. For example, by matching semantically, a NIDS is not deceived by deliberately camouflaged commands.

Our innovation is to convert a script or signature from syntax to semantics using an artificial intelligence (AI) technique called *plan recognition*. Our plan recognition approach infers the hacker's knowledge and goals from the hacker's ongoing sequence of commands. The output of our program is designated a *knowledge script*, which is annotated with hypothesized knowledge and is eventually stored in the database as a *knowledge signature*. It consists of a temporal sequence of inferred information tidbits assumed to be gained by the hacker while typing in commands. A knowledge script/signature is the semantic equivalent of the original script/signature. For example, after typing the command "ping," a hacker has knowledge of whether or not the pinged computer is up and running. This information is stored explicitly in a knowledge script. As expected, a semantic knowledge script/signature is substantially easier to match than the original syntactic script/signature. The matching process is flexible because it is done by analogy. If, for example, *Computer 1* and *Computer 13* play the same role in two different attacks, they are considered analogous, or synonymous, and a match between them will succeed despite the fact that their names differ. By reducing the number of false negatives, the number of *false positives* may inadvertently be increased. A false positive is defined to occur if a non-attack is incorrectly labeled "positive," i.e., as an attack, by the NIDS. This problem of false positives is also addressed using Artificial Intelligence techniques.

In summary, our semantic analogy-based approach using case-based reasoning is an appropriate solution to the problem of false negatives. We have implemented and tested our approach, and initial experimental results have demonstrated a dramatic reduction in the number of errors of omission (false negatives).

Current research on the artificial intelligence approach is focused on four major directions. First, we are running extensive, rigorous experimental comparisons between several alternative *similarity metrics* used in analogy, in order to select the one that performs the best in the context of intrusion detection. Second, we are developing novel similarity metrics that can not only label a script as a "positive" attack, but can also designate a label regarding the hypothesized *type* of attack. Third, we are working toward a formalization of similarity that is well adapted to intrusion detection, but is also "universal," in the sense that it will not depend on the representation of attacks (e.g., one might wish to compare the similarity between a script and a stored signature that are in different computer languages). Theoretical results will be developed regarding the universality of this similarity. Finally, if our system concludes that a new script is indeed an ongoing attack (based on similarity to a stored signature), then the next step will be to use Artificial Intelligence techniques to predict the attacker's next move(s). Predictions could be extremely valuable for designing countermeasures to attacks, such as decoys or honeypots.

4   Conclusions and Future Work

We have described three results in the areas of network intrusion detection and malware detection. We are also refining the infrastructural framework that can serve as a platform on which different intrusion and anomaly detection modules reside.

Further research on the highlighted problems is focused on (1) the deployment and refinement of Karst-Net, (2) Variations and extensions of the notion of quantitative simulation to allow for imperfect synchrony between the two systems and to deal with an input consisting of more than 2 systems, and (3) The search for a notion of similarity for analogy-based reasoning that best fits the intrusion detection context.

References

[1] K. Chatterjee, M. Jurdziński, and T.A. Henzinger. Quantitative stochastic parity games. In *SODA '04: Proceedings of the 15th annual ACM-SIAM Symposium on Discrete Algorithms*, pages 121–130, 2004.

[2] CipherTrust. Ciphertrust's zombiemeter. http://www.ciphertrust.com/resources/statistics/zombie.php, 2005.

[3] David Dagon, Cliff Zou, Sanjeev Dwivedi, Julian Grizzard, and Wenke Lee. Karstnet: Countering the attacking networks. Technical report, Georgia Institute of Technology, May 2005.

[4] L. de Alfaro, M. Faella, and M. Stoelinga. Linear and branching metrics for quantitative transition systems. In *ICALP '04: 31st International Colloquium on Automata, Languages, and Programming*, volume 3142 of *LNCS*, pages 97–109, 2004.

[5] Felix C. Freiling, Thorsten Holz, and Georg Wicherski. Botnet tracking: Exploring a root-cause methodology to prevent distributed denial-of-service attacks. Technical Report ISSN-0935-3232, RWTH Aachen, April 2005.

[6] V. Fuller, T. Li, J. Yu, and K. Varadhan. Classless inter-domain routing (cidr): an address assignment and aggregation strategy. http://www.faqs.org/rfcs/rfc1519.html, 1993.

[7] A. Girard and G.J. Pappas. Approximate bisimulation relations for constrained linear systems. Technical Report MS-CIS-05-19, Dept. of CIS, University of Pennsylvania, September 2005.

[8] Cody Hatch. Distributed phishing. http://marc.theaimsgroup.com/?l=dailydave&m=111505651308364, 2005.

[9] Srikanth Kandula, Dina Katabi, Matthias Jacob, and Arthur W. Berger. Botz-4-sale: Surviving organized ddos attacks that mimic flash crowds. In *2nd Symposium on Networked Systems Design and Implementation (NSDI)*, May 2005.

[10] H.A. Kim and B.Karp. Autograph: toward automated, distributed worm signature detection. In *Proc. 13th USENIX Security Symposium*, 2004.

[11] David B. Leake, editor. *Case-Based Reasoning: Experiences, Lessons, and Future Directions.* AAAI/MIT Press, 2000.

[12] Jun Li, J. Mirkovic, Mengqiu Wang, P. Reiher, and Lixia Zhang. Save: source address validity enforcement protocol. In *INFOCOM 2002. Twenty-First Annual Joint Conference of the IEEE Computer and Communications Societies*, pages 1557–1566, 2002.

[13] Robin Milner. *Communication and Concurrency.* Prentice Hall Intl., 1989.

[14] J. Newsome, B. Karp, and D. Song. Polygraph: Automatically generating signatures for polymorphic worms. In *Proc. IEEE Symp. Security and Privacy (Oakland 2005)*, 2005.

[15] Prof. Randy Vaughn (Baylor Univ). Personal correspondence. April 5 2005.

[16] S.E. Schechter and M.D. Smith. Access for sale. In *2003 ACM Workshop on Rapid Malcode (WORM'03)*. ACM SIGSAC, October 2003.

[17] John Schwartz. Computer vandals clog antivandalism web site. *New York Times*, 2001.

[18] S.Singh, C. Estan, G. Varghese, and S. Savage. Automated worm fingerprinting. In *Proc. 6th ACM/USENIX Symp. Operating Systems Design and Implementation*, 2004.

[19] Peter Szor. *The Art of Computer Virus Research and Defense.* Addison Wesley Professional, 2005.

[20] The Honeynet Project and Research Alliance. Know your enemy: Tracking botnets. `http://www.honeynet.org/papers/bots/`, 2005.

[21] United States Government Accounting Office. Emerging cybersecurity issues threaten federal information systems. `http://www.gao.gov/new.items/d05231.pdf`, May 2005.

[22] Ke Wang and Sal Stolfo. Anomalous payload-based network intrusion detection. In *Proceedings of the 7th International Symposium on Recent Advances in Intrusion Detection (RAID 2004)*, 2004.

An Ensemble of Anomaly Classifiers for Identifying Cyber Attacks[*]

Carlos Kelly[†]   Diana Spears[‡]   Christer Karlsson[§]   Peter Polyakov[¶]

Abstract

A novel approach is presented that bridges the gap between anomaly and misuse detection for identifying cyber attacks. The approach consists of an ensemble of classifiers that, together, produce a more informative output regarding the class of attack than any of the classifiers alone. Each classifier classifies based on a limited subset of possible features of network packets. The ensemble classifies based on the union of the subsets of features. Thus it can detect a wider range of attacks. In addition, the ensemble can determine the probability of the type of attack based on the results of the classifiers. Experimental results demonstrate an increase in the rate of detecting attacks as well as accurately determining their type.

Keywords: intrusion detection, classifier ensemble

1 Problem Description.

In our current information age, and with the timely issue of national security, network security is an especially pertinent topic. One important aspect of computer network security is *network intrusion detection*, i.e., the detection of malicious traffic on a computer network.

There are two main approaches to designing Network Intrusion Detection Systems (NIDS): *anomaly detection* and *misuse detection*. Both are essentially classifiers, i.e., they label incoming network packets as "attack," "non-attack," and if an attack perhaps what type of attack. Anomaly and misuse detection are complementary approaches to intrusion detection. Anomaly detection consists of building a model of normal computer usage, and tagging outliers as "anomalies." Such systems are typically computationally efficient, but only yield a binary classification – "attack" or "non-attack" [5, 12]. Misuse detection systems match potential attacks (e.g., network packets) against a database of known attacks (called *signatures*). If there is a match, then the data (packet) is labeled an "attack," and the class of attack is considered to be the same as that of the matching signature. Unfortunately, misuse detection systems tend to be slow, especially if their database of signatures is large [10].

The main thrust of our research is to bridge the gap between anomaly and misuse detection. Anomaly NIDS classify packets quickly in comparison to misuse based NIDS, but without as much information about the attack. We have created an ensemble of anomaly-based NIDS that refines the binary classification of each ensemble member and yields more detailed classification information than each member alone. Therefore, if anomaly detection precedes misuse detection, then our system will partially refine the output of anomaly detection, thereby accelerating the processing of the misuse detection system. The pipeline can be summarized as: (1) anomaly detection, (2) refinement by ensemble, and (3) misuse detection. If the computational cost of the second step, refinement by ensemble, is lower than the computational benefit that it yields by shortening the run-time of the misuse detection system, then our approach will be beneficial overall. Whether this is the case, depends on the size of the database of signatures that one maintains. Over time, as people (and systems) increase their knowledge base of attacks, we expect our approach to become increasingly more useful.

This paper describes only steps (1) and (2) of the pipeline above. Step (3) will be addressed as part of future work. In the remainder of this paper, we describe our ensemble approach, as well as experimental evaluation results that show its effectiveness for intrusion detection. Here, it is assumed that the data consists of Transmission Control Protocol (TCP) packets, sent over the network. The data we used is from the DARPA/MIT Lincoln Laboratory database (see http://www.ll.mit.edu/IST/ideval/index.html).

---

[*]Supported by the ONR URI grant "Anomaly and misuse detection in network traffic streams," subcontract PENUNV48725.
[†]Mathematics Department, University of Wyoming.
[‡]Computer Science Department, University of Wyoming.
[§]Computer Science Department, University of Wyoming.
[¶]Mathematics Department, University of Wyoming.

2   A Novel Ensemble Approach.

An *ensemble* of classifiers is a collection of classifiers that are combined into a single classifier. Most of the research conducted on classifier ensembles assumes homogeneous ensembles of binary classifiers, and assumes that the ensemble also outputs a binary classification. The purpose of such ensembles is to increase classification accuracy, e.g., with voting, *bagging*, or *boosting* [1]. One notable exception is the *stacked generalization* approach of Wolpert [13]. Stacked generalization assumes a heterogeneous ensemble of different classifiers, each with its own "area of expertise." Nevertheless, the purpose of stacked generalization is also to increase classification accuracy, without changing the set of classes.

To the best of our knowledge, *our approach to ensembles is the first to utilize a heterogeneous set of classifiers for the purpose of increasing information (refined classification), rather than classification accuracy.* Specifically, our approach takes a suite of classifiers (currently two), each of which outputs a binary classification, and combines them to output a probability distribution over *seven* classes. We expect the ensemble output to be increasingly more informative as the number of classifier components is increased beyond two. Furthermore, if the classifiers run on the data in parallel, adding more classifiers to the ensemble would not increase the overall time to apply the method, i.e., it is highly scalable. However, this is our first investigation into such an ensemble, so we begin with two classifiers.

The essence of our approach is to empirically build an *ensemble probability classification matrix*, abbreviated as *EPCM*, based on system performance on test data. In other words, in machine learning one typically trains the system on training data, and then tests its performance on test data. We instead partition the data into three sets: the training data, the testing data, and the validation data. Each individual classifier is trained separately on the training data. Note that the training data is attack-free – because anomaly detection systems learn models of normal (friendly) user data, and then use these models to detect anomalies, which are labeled "attacks." After training, each system has a hypothesis regarding the nature of "non-attack" data. These hypotheses are applied to the testing data, to make predictions regarding whether each system thinks each packet is an "attack" or a "non-attack." We also use the known information (from the DARPA website) on the test data regarding whether each packet is an attack or not, and if it is an attack then what class of attack (from the seven known classes). All of this information is automatically combined into an EPCM, which predicts a probability distribution over the seven classes, based on the outputs of the systems in the ensemble and the true classes of the packets (as defined by DARPA/MIT). The last step is to test the performance of the ensemble on a set of validation data, for which there is no advance knowledge given to the system regarding the (true) data classification.

Why do we expect our novel approach to work? The key to our success is the notion of *inductive bias*, or simply *bias*. Mitchell defines *bias* as "any basis for choosing one generalization over another, other than strict consistency with the observed training instances" [9]. The hypotheses output by our classifiers are special instances of what Mitchell calls "generalizations." An example of a bias is the choice of what attributes the classifier system considers. For instance, one system might only look at the header information in a packet when classifying the packet as a type of attack, whereas another system might only look at the packet payload. Certainly the choice of attributes will affect the types of attacks that the system is able to identify. One system might be able to detect some classes of attacks; another system might be able to detect other classes. In general, the classes of attacks detectable by two systems could be disjoint or overlap. By combining two systems with very different biases, we increase the set of detectable attacks. Furthermore, by exploiting known differences in system biases, we can further refine our classification knowledge. For example, if one system says "attack" and the other says "non-attack," then this combined information can tell us (with high probability) what *kind* of attack it is most likely to be. To better understand the synergistic effects of combining the information, we formalized the biases of each of the two systems. From this formalization, one can understand the classes of attacks for which each system is best suited to identify. This is the essential rationale behind our ensemble approach.

3   Ensemble Components.

Our ensemble is composed of two anomaly NIDS, LERAD [5] and PAYL [12]. LERAD's hypotheses are rule sets of expected (normal) user behavior, and PAYL's hypotheses are byte distributions derived from normal packets. Each of these systems is described in greater detail, below.

Some preprocessing of the raw network dump data was necessary for LERAD and PAYL to be able to process packets. A tool (te.cpp) provided on Mahoney's web site http://www.cs.fit.edu/mmahoney/dist preprocessed the raw network data into streams for LERAD. A Perl script (a21.p1), also provided by Mahoney, transformed the streams into a LERAD-readable database format. The preprocessing tool te.cpp was altered so that it also produced a file of packets readable by PAYL.

Also, some postprocessing was required. LERAD and PAYL produce a list of packets that the systems consider to be "attacks" (anomalies). We created a tool that produces alarm statistics by comparing the output of LERAD and PAYL to the DARPA/MIT labeled attacks. For further details on this postprocessing stage, see Section 5 below.

Finally, before we describe each system, note that we used LERAD unmodified as found on Mahoney's web site, listed above. However, the source code for PAYL is not currently available, and therefore we re-implemented the algorithms based on [12].

3.1   LERAD and Its Biases. As mentioned above, LERAD learns a set of classification rules. Rules take the following general form: $(a_i = v_j \wedge \cdots \wedge a_n = v_m) \rightarrow (a_k = v_p \vee \cdots \vee a_q = v_s)$ where the a's are attributes and the v's are values of these attributes. Only conjunction is allowed in the rule antecedent and only disjunction is allowed in the rule consequent. An example rule might be:

If the destination port number is 80 and the source port number is 80, then the first word in the payload is GET or the first word in the payload is SET or the number of bytes in the payload is greater than 60.

Recall that each of these rules describes normal (benign) system use.

LERAD's classification algorithm is the following. Each new example (packet) receives a score, which is the sum of rule violations. If the score exceeds a threshold, T_L, defined below, then the packet is classified as an "attack."

LERAD's training algorithm inputs a set of attack-free training examples, and outputs a rule set, R. The algorithm begins with rule creation, then does rule sorting and, finally, rule pruning.

LERAD has many implicit inductive biases embedded within the system. We selected those that are most relevant to the construction of our ensemble and formalized them. By doing this, we were better able to understand and predict the types of attacks for which LERAD is best suited to detect.

What are these relevant biases of LERAD? One is the set of attributes considered by LERAD, called S_L. We know that $|S_L| = 23$, and the specific attributes are the packet date, time, last two bytes of the destination IP address, last four bytes of the source IP address, the source and destination port numbers, the TCP flags for the first, next to last and last TCP packets, the duration in seconds, the number of payload bytes, and the first eight words in the payload.

A second bias is the threshold, T_L, used by LERAD during classification. Before formalizing this threshold, we first repeat the formula for the anomaly score for each new example (packet), which we consider a bias. From [5] this is: $score_{anomaly} = \sum_{i=1}^{m} \frac{n_i \cdot t_i}{e_i} F_{r_i}$ where F_{r_i} is 0 if rule r_i is satisfied and 1 if it is not satisfied, m is $|R|$ (i.e., the number of rules), n_i is the rule support for rule r_i (defined above), e_i is the number of expressions in the antecedent of rule r_i, and t_i is the time that has elapsed since the rule was last violated. Then the threshold, T_L, is: $ln(score_{anomaly})/ln(10) > 4.5$. Finally, the last bias that we considered relevant in LERAD is the fact that its hypotheses take the form of rules, which we already formalized syntactically above.

3.2   PAYL and Its Biases. The classification hypotheses of PAYL are byte distributions, derived from the training data (see Figure 1).distribution is an empirically-derived approximation of a probability distribution $P(b_0, b_2, \ldots, b_{255})$, i.e., the probability of seeing each ASCII byte in a packet of a certain type. The types of packets are those that have a particular destination port number or a particular payload length. In other words, for each unique port number and payload length, PAYL associates (and learns) a probability distribution over the individual bytes in the payload. In fact, the full hypothesis of PAYL consists of a set of *profiles*. Each profile consists of a pair of 256-valued vectors (one for each byte). The first element of the pair is an average byte distribution, $P(b_0, b_1, \ldots b_{255})$, and the second element of the pair is a vector of standard deviations from the means, i.e., $(\sigma_0, \sigma_1, \ldots, \sigma_{255})$. Classification involves both a distance function and a threshold. If the distance between the byte distribution of a new example and the byte distribution of the hypothesis (which represents a profile of normal behavior) exceeds the threshold, then the new example is labeled an "attack."

PAYL's training algorithm consists of first classifying the training examples (packets) according to their destination port number and payload length. Then, the mean and standard deviation are calculated for each byte.

PAYL also has implicit inductive biases embedded within the system, and we selected those that are most

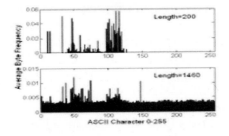

Figure 1: Sample byte distributions for different payload lengths of port 80 on the same host server.

relevant to the construction of our ensemble. The first bias is the set of attributes considered by PAYL, called S_P. Note that $|S_P| = 3$. These attributes are the destination port number, the number of bytes in the payload, and the distribution of bytes in the payload.

The second aspect of PAYL that we consider to be a bias is its distance function for computing the distance between two distributions. The function used by PAYL is (from [12]): $d(e, \overline{y}) = \sum_{i=0}^{255} \frac{|e_i - \overline{y_i}|}{\sigma_i + \alpha}$ where $\overline{y}$ and σ are the average and standard deviation, i.e., elements of the profile that constitutes PAYL's hypothesis, e is an example, and α is a conditioning variable needed to prevent divide-by-zero errors.

The threshold, T_P, was not formalized. It was derived empirically, as described in Section 5, below.

3.3   Example Application of the System Biases. By making LERAD and PAYL's biases explicit, we have been able to analyze and understand them better. From this process, we have drawn the following conclusions about the suitability of these two systems to detecting different attack characteristics:

- LERAD is sensitive to only a subset of the information in a packet, namely, the packet header and the first eight words.

- Two packets that differ by even a single byte (among the attribute fields that LERAD examines) are likely to be classified differently by LERAD. A packet that satisfies both the antecedent and consequent of a rule can be made to violate the rule by changing a single byte in one of the fields (attributes) of the consequent.

- PAYL is sensitive to only a subset of the information in a packet, namely, the packet payload and the destination port number.

- Two packets that differ by a single byte are unlikely to be classified by PAYL as being different – because the byte distributions of the two packets will probably be very similar.

The following example illustrates how these biases of LERAD and PAYL translate into specialized detection capabilities:

EXAMPLE 1. Consider the *Denial of Service* attack called "Back." This attack is a malformed web request to an HTTP port with the payload, "Get //// ..." followed by 6000-7000 slashes. One of the biases of PAYL is that it examines the byte distributions. For this particular attack, the byte distribution of the payload is almost exclusively centered on the "/" character in the ASCII table. This implies that PAYL will almost surely detect the attack. One of the biases of LERAD is that it examines the relationships of the first eight words in the payload of a message. Since "GET" followed by 6000-7000 slashes is an unusual relationship, we would also expect LERAD to detect this attack. Therefore, the "Back" attack is a specific type of attack that would be detected by both systems.

4   The Network Data.

As mentioned above, we are working with the DARPA/MIT Lincoln Laboratory database of packets. We decided to only work with the 1999 data, since the 1998 data does not include a key to differentiate normal packets from attack packets. The data from 1999 is five weeks long. The first and third weeks are attack free, whereas the second, fourth and fifth weeks contain attacks. Each TCP packet is a binary sequence not exceeding 64,000 bytes in length. The DARPA web site classifies attacks into five categories: 1.**Denial of Service (DoS)**, 2.**User to Root (U2R)**, 3.**Remote to User (R2U)**, 4.**Probes.**, and 5. **Data.**

This classification is standard, comprehensive, and still modern [11]. Nevertheless, this DARPA classification does not result in mutually exclusive classes. Therefore, we have expanded the classification to include overlaps as two additional classes, thus resulting in a total of seven attack classes. The two additional attack classes are: 6. **Data and User to Root** and 7. **Data and Root to Local**. The 1999 DARPA data was divided into three sets. The training set consisted of all the data that was attack free. Training data: 03/08-03/12 (week one) and 03/22-03/26 (week three). Of the remaining data, the test and validation data sets were divided as follows: test data: 03/29-03/31, 04/02, 04/05 and 04/09; validation data: 04/01, 04/06-04/08. Both the test and validation data sets contain many attacks, though some attacks occur only in the test set and other attacks occur only in the validation set. There are slightly more attacks in the test set than in the validation set.

5   Ensemble Implementation.

In this section we describe in detail step (2) of the pipeline, introduced in Section 1, and called the "refinement by ensemble" step. The purpose of the ensemble is to produce a classification vector associated with a new packet, which could be an attack. For the ensemble, we concentrate only on test data that consists of attacks, i.e., non-attack packets are ignored.[1] There are a couple of reasons that we did this. For one, these are the only packets whose classification needs to be refined. Second, segmenting the data to determine the temporal boundaries of non-attacks proved to be very difficult – it proved challenging to determine the exact duration of non-attack packets. Therefore, our test data and validation data focused on attack packets only, and how to refine their classification.

When combining LERAD and PAYL, there are four possibilities for the combined outputs of the two systems: L-yes and P-yes, L-yes and P-no, L-no and P-yes, and L-no and P-no, where "yes" means the packet is labeled an "attack" and "no" means the packet is labeled a "non-attack." One of these pairs becomes the input to the ensemble system, for each new example/packet. The output of the ensemble for one pair is a probability distribution, called the *probability classification vector*, which gives the probabilities that the new example falls into each of the seven possible attack classes, described in Section 4 above. In summary, given a new packet, which we also call a *sample* to be consistent with statistical definitions, there are four possible events corresponding to the four possible class labels given by the pair of classifier systems. These input events need to be converted to an output probability distribution over the seven attack classes. Recall that this process is performed on the test data set. In other words, the training data is used for LERAD and PAYL to learn their hypotheses, and then these hypotheses make predictions over the test data to discover anomalies that are different from the hypotheses about normal user behavior. We combine LERAD and PAYL's predictions on the test data with the true (based on the DARPA web site) classifications of the test data packets. Then, we convert this information into a probability classification vector for each pair of outcomes from LERAD and PAYL. These vectors are joined together in an ensemble probability classification matrix (EPCM), and output by the ensemble (see Table 2).

To accomplish this, the first step is to formalize, in probability terminology, what precisely we are trying to find during step (2), i.e., what is the formal representation of an ensemble probability classification matrix (EPCM)? The answer is that we want to find $P(C|E)$, where C is a classification vector, i.e., a probability distribution over the seven classes, and E is an input event, i.e., the pair of labels given by LERAD and PAYL, such as L-yes and P-no. This probability value cannot be approximated directly from the results of the test data. We need to use a conditional probability rule to calculate this conditional probability. The conditional probability rule that we use is: $P(Y|X) = (P(Y, X)/P(X))$.

For example, suppose we have the results from the test data in Table 1. Each table entry that is not listed under "Sum" represents $P(Y, X)$, i.e., the frequency (which is an estimate of the probability based on the test data) of a packet giving a certain pair of binary outputs by LERAD and PAYL *and* being in a particular attack class (based on the DARPA/MIT web site classification of the test data). Furthermore, the "Sum" entry at the bottom of each column represents $P(X)$, i.e., the frequency of a certain pair of binary outputs by LERAD and PAYL. Using the conditional probability rule, given above, we calculate $P(Y|X)$, which is the output of the ensemble. Continuing our example from Table 1, by applying the conditional probability rule we get Table 2.

---

[1]We use the same criteria as DARPA did to label packets as "attacks."

Attack	y/y	y/n	n/y	n/n	Sum
Class 1	4	8	5	6	23
Class 2	6	4	2	1	13
Class 3	1	16	1	10	28
Class 4	0	0	2	1	3
Class 5	0	6	0	7	13
Class 6	2	1	1	0	4
Class 7	0	0	1	0	1
Sum	13	35	12	25	85

Table 1: Matrix of frequencies of attack events and classifier labels for LERAD/PAYL.

Attack	y/y	y/n	n/y	n/n
Class 1	0.3077	0.2286	0.4167	0.2400
Class 2	0.4615	0.1143	0.1667	0.0400
Class 3	0.0770	0.4571	0.0833	0.4000
Class 4	0	0	0.1667	0.0400
Class 5	0	0.1714	0	0.2800
Class 6	0.1538	0.0286	0.0833	0
Class 7	0	0	0.0833	0

Table 2: An ensemble probability classification matrix (EPCM), which is output by the ensemble. Each column is a probability classification vector.

Note that this is a matrix consisting of vectors (the columns) – one for each input event/sample, giving the vector output that is a probability distribution over the seven possible attack classes. This is what we call the "ensemble probabilistic classification vector."

For each new packet in the final validation data we can now use these vectors for classification. In particular, we run LERAD and PAYL on this new packet. If we get L-yes and P-no, then the ensemble predicts (using Table 2) the probability that the attack is of type Denial of Service is approximately 0.2268. The probability that the attack is of type User to Root is approximately 0.1143, and similarly for the remaining classes of attacks.

Given this ensemble output information, a misuse detection system could restrict its search and computations to a small subset of possible attack signatures when trying to find the most similar previous attack. The reasons for continuing with a misuse detection system are that our ensemble outputs probabilities – however a match with a signature could give further confirmation of the attack class, and also a stored signature could be used for predicting the attacker's next move.

We conclude this section by noting the role that the system inductive biases played in determining the probability classification vectors. Note that if the ensemble input is L-yes and P-yes, then the ensemble will conclude that the highest probability is that we either have an attack of Class 1 (Denial of Service) or an attack of Class 2 (User to Root). Having a high probability of being an attack of Class 1 can be explained in terms of the system biases. Recall Example 1 from Section 3.3, which was an example of a Denial of Service attack. In that case, the large number of slashes indicated that such an attack would be manifested as an unusual byte distribution and would therefore be likely to be detected by PAYL. Furthermore, the usual relationship between the slashes and one of the keywords indicated that such an attack would also probably be detected by LERAD. Based on the system biases, we therefore predicted that Denial of Service attacks would frequently result in L-yes and P-yes. Table 2 indeed confirms our prediction.

In summary, our analysis of system biases was quite helpful for both predicting and understanding the output of our ensemble. Future versions of our ensemble approach will investigate building an ensemble from first principles, based on bias analyses, rather than using a purely empirical approach.

5.1   Parameter Tuning. LERAD's process of learning a rule set involves a random element (see Section 3.1). Nevertheless, our experimental investigations revealed that there are not significant differences in performance

Attack	y/y	y/n	n/y	n/n	Sum
Class 1	5	9	8	1	23
Class 2	6	4	2	1	13
Class 3	1	13	9	5	28
Class 4	1	1	0	1	3
Class 5	2	8	2	1	13
Class 6	1	2	1	0	4
Class 7	0	0	1	0	1
Sum	16	37	23	9	85

Table 3: A random frequency matrix with the same row sums as in Table 1.

arising as a result of alternating the random seed. Therefore, we fixed LERAD's random seed to be 0, and all results described in this paper assume this same seed.

We ran extensive empirical experiments to find optimal settings for the parameters of PAYL: $T_P = 256$ and $\alpha = 0.1$. These are the values that are used in all of the empirical experiments, described below.

6   A Matrix-Matrix Comparison.

6.1   Another Matrix for Comparison. To evaluate the quality of our ensemble output, we require a comparison against a reasonable standard. For this purpose, we decided to use a *random frequency matrix*. Such a matrix is created using randomly-chosen matrix entries that are weighted based on the relative frequency of each class of attack in the test data. In other words, it is not purely random, but contains useful information about attack frequencies, and it is constructed from the test data – just like our ensemble is.

The particular methodology for creating the random frequency matrix was to use the test data to determine both the attack frequencies and to ensure that the random frequency matrix has the same row sums as the actual frequency matrix created from the test data (which was shown in Table 1 and was used directly for building the ensemble). In other words, *both* the ensemble probability classification matrix (EPCM) and the random frequency matrix are constructed based on information from the actual frequency matrix derived from the test data set. The difference between them is that the EPCM has probability entries that directly reflect the test data, whereas the random frequency matrix has characteristics that reflect those of the test data, but includes some randomness. An example of a transformation of an actual frequency matrix to a random frequency matrix is shown in Table 3. Then, we convert the random frequency matrix into entries that are probabilities, just like we did for the EPCM in Section 5. We call this final matrix a *weighted random probability classification matrix*, abbreviated *WRPCM*.

Finally, observe that the WRPCM is randomly created. Therefore comparing the EPCM with one WRPCM is statistically meaningless. To resolve this issue, we created 10,000 WRPCMs to compare with one EPCM, and took the mean and standard deviation of the differences as our evaluation.

6.2   Evaluation Metric. We created a *validation probability matrix (VPM)* over the validation data set – for the validation data set this is "ground truth" and is used as the performance standard. To measure the distance between the EPCM or a WRPCM and the VPM, we used the standard *Euclidean metric*, which sums distances between pairs of matrix entries.

We applied the Euclidean evaluation metric to compare the EPCM-VPM distance versus WRPCM-VPM distance, on the validation data set. The following section describes the results of these comparisons.

6.3   Experimental Results. The average distance from the EPCM-VPM distance value to the 10,000 WRPCM-VPM distance values is 0.7264, and the standard deviation is 0.1516. Using the Euclidean metric, we find that the distance between the EPCM-VPM value and the mean of the WRPCM-VPM values is 0.3463, and the EPCM-VPM value is 2.507 standard deviations from the mean of the WRPCM-VPM values.

6.4   Interpretation of Results. The EPCM is more than 2.5 standard deviations closer (which is better) to the VPM (considered "ground truth") on the validation set than the average of the 10,000 WRPCMs. In other words, a weighted random guess has a very low chance of being more accurate than the EPCM. In particular, the probability that a random accuracy variable X is less than the ensemble accuracy is $P(X \leq 0.3463) = P(((X - \mu)/\sigma) \leq ((0.3463 - \mu)/\sigma) = P(z \leq -2.5075) = F(-2.5073) = 0.0062$, assuming distances are normally distributed. From the experimental results, we found that only 24 of the 10,000 WRPCM accuracies were better than those of the ensemble, which is quite low.

7 Summary and Future Work.

In summary, we have introduced a novel approach to an ensemble of classifiers that is designed for classification refinement, rather than for improving classification accuracy. Our experimental results indicate that our approach is very promising, and applicable to intrusion detection. In particular, our ensemble increased the number of attack classes from one to seven. Furthermorecloser (which is better) to the correct VPM on the validation data than the average of its competitors (the WRPCMs).

Our ensemble has an important role to play in refining the binary classifications output by the anomaly detection systems, prior to running a misuse detection system. The final step of the pipeline process described in Section 1, that of feeding the ensemble output into a misuse detection system, needs to be accomplished as part of future work. For example, we might use SNORT [10], which is the most widely available commercial misuse detection system. SNORT has a rule associated with each attack, so we might consider using our ensemble to partition the rule set according to attack class, and then check a potential attack packet with the rules from the class to which there is the greatest probability (according to the ensemble) that the attack belongs. This would increase SNORT's classification speed. It is interesting to note that for this paradigm, valuable information would be produced by the ensemble even if all classifiers (members) of the ensemble individually classified the candidate packet as a "non-attack." This is because even if its component classifiers label a packet as a "non-attack," the ensemble still predicts a class of attack for the packet. Therefore, if the packet does indeed turn out to be an attack, the ensemble will be especially helpful.

Finally, recall that we mentioned earlier that this ensemble approach is not only scalable, but is likely to benefit in performance from the incorporation of additional classifiers. We intend to explore this fruitful future direction for our research.

References

[1] E. Alpaydin, *Introduction to Machine Learning*, MIT Press: Cambridge, MA, 2004.

[2] Defense Advanced Research Projects Agency, *DoD Standard Transmission Control Protocol*, Information Processing Techniques Office, Arlington, VA (1990).

[3] R. Durst and T. Champion and B. Witten and E. Miller and L. Spagnuolo, *Testing and evaluating computer intrusion detection systems*, Comm. of the ACM, 42(7), (1999), pp. 53–61.

[4] J. W. Haines and R. P. Lippmann and D. J. Fried and E. Tran and S. Boswell and M. A. Zissman, *1999 DARPA Intrusion detection system evaluation: Design and procedures*, MIT Lincoln Laboratory Tech. Report.

[5] M. V. Mahoney, *A machine learning approach to detecting attacks by identifying anomalies in network traffic*, Ph.D. dissertation, Florida Tech., 2003.

[6] M. V. Mahoney and P. K. Chan, *An analysis of the 1999 DARPA/Lincoln Laboratory evaluation data for network anomaly detection*, Proc. RAID, (2003), pp. 220–237.

[7] ———, *Learning rules for anomaly detection of hostile network traffic*, Proc. Third International Conference on Data Mining (ICDM), (1987).

[8] J. S. Milton and J. C. Arnold, *Introduction to Probability and Statistics Principles and Applications for Engineering and the Computer Sciences*, Third Ed., McGraw-Hill: NY, 1995.

[9] T. M. Mitchell, *Machine Learning*, McGraw-Hill: Boston, MA, 1997.

[10] L. Schaelicke and K. Wheeler and C. Freeland, *SPANIDS: A scalable network intrusion detection loadbalancer*, Proc. Comp. Frontiers, (2005), pp. 315–332.

[11] J. Wang, *Loss-sensitive rules for intrusion detection and response*, Ph.D. dissertation, Univ. of Pennsylvania, 2004.

[12] K. Wang and S. J. Stolfo, *Anomalous payload-based network intrusion detection*, Proc. RAID, (2004), pp. 1–12.

[13] D. H. Wolpert, *Stacked generalization*, Neural networks 5, (1992), pp. 241–259.

Distributed System Security via Logical Frameworks

Lujo Bauer, Frank Pfenning, and Michael K. Reiter
Carnegie Mellon University

August 2005

Abstract

We describe a project to advance security in distributed systems via the application of logical frameworks. At the heart of the effort lies an *authorization logic* which plays a triple role: (1) to specify an access-control policy as a logical theory, (2) to enforce the policy by mechanically verifying proofs in the logic, and (3) to reason about the policy by characterizing the space of all possible proofs. We are deploying a security infrastructure based on these ideas using mobile phones as a universal access-control device at Carnegie Mellon University.

ACM subject classifiers: C.2.0 General—*Security and protection*; D.4.6 Security and Protection—*Access controls*; F.4.1 Mathematical Logic—*Computational Logic*; K.6.5 Security and Protection—*Authentication*

Keywords: Security, logical frameworks, authorization, access control.

1   Introduction

Our goal is to advance security in distributed systems via the application of logical frameworks. Our research targets multiple facets of the life-cycle of a distributed system, ranging from design through execution, and from sound mechanism design through sound policy enforcement. It consists of three major interconnected thrusts.

First, we use logical frameworks for encoding and enforcing access-control policies in a practical distributed system. Access-control mechanisms today, whether it be physical keys for doors or password protection for computer accounts, reflect access-control policies that are explicit only in the manual procedures of the organization that manages these resources. As such, any change in policy, e.g., creating a new computer account, or permitting a person to unlock a door, is effected through a manual process. We utilize logical frameworks to encode organizational policies within computer systems, thereby harnessing the power of these frameworks to support the management and enforcement of access-control policy, and gaining security and flexibility by doing so. We have demonstrated this capability in a ubiquitous computing test-bed that we are developing at Carnegie Mellon called Grey [6]. In this test-bed we use "smart" mobile phones as a universal access control device, for example, to open an office door or logging into a machine when approaching it.

Second, we exploit existing technologies to mechanically reason about security policies as specified in a logical framework. This closes an important security gap, helping users and managers understand the consequences of their policies. We are particularly interested in verifying non-interference properties of policies which guarantee that some principals' assertions can have no bearing on access to a a certain resource.

Third, we are developing and implementing a framework for the specification of distributed and concurrent systems and their implementations, specifically targeting the architecture outlined in the remainder of this paper. This work extends a collaboration between NRL and Carnegie Mellon that resulted in the design of CLF, an innovative logical language for the specification of concurrent systems. CLF incorporates ideas from logical frameworks, linear logic, and monads into an expressive meta-language.[1] CLF is now fully specified and has been successfully validated on mainstream concurrency formalisms (e.g., Petri nets, the π-calculus), advanced concurrent programming languages (Concurrent ML), and security protocol specification languages (MSR). The goal of our current research is to facilitate the transition of CLF from a foundational language into an implemented tool that can be applied to the specification of complex distributed and concurrent systems. The current prototype is called LolliMon [21].

2 A Logic-Based Approach

Distributed systems are notoriously error-prone in virtually all phases of their life-cycle, including design, implementation and management. They are particularly susceptible to security breaches; since distributed systems are more complex than their centralized counterparts, modes of attack may be difficult to foresee, and defenses are often subtle and fragile. As such, distributed system security is an area that demands rigor, and there is a well-documented history of security failures resulting from informal design, implementation and management.

The last several years have witnessed substantial progress in verification methodologies based on formal logic. Nevertheless, there remain significant gaps between verifying specifications on the one hand, and translating these specifications into verified implementations and policy enforcement on the other. We have made progress toward closing this gap, through three related but complementary research thrusts. First, we are developing and deploying a system for day-to-day use in which access-control policy is expressed in and enforced via a logical framework, permitting us to utilize the sound footing of the framework to reason about the correctness of the access-control decisions it renders. Second, we are applying tools based on LF to reasoning about formally specified security policies. Third, we are developing an extended logical framework in which we can in addition formalize our distributed enforcement mechanism.

2.1 Logical Frameworks

A *logical framework* is a meta-language for specification and implementation of logical systems. Logical frameworks have a rich history and numerous applications in programming languages, logic, and automated reasoning [29, 27]. The particular logical framework most relevant to this application is LF [18] and its implementation in Twelf [31]. One of its central characteristics is that *formal proofs* with respect to a specified set of inference rules are *first-class objects*, and that checking if a given proof is well-formed is efficiently decidable.

The use of a logical framework in such applications as proof-carrying code [26, 2] or proof-carrying authorization [5] can be sketched broadly as followed.

1. Principal A would like to convince principal B of a certain claim C, such as his right to access a resource.

2. Principal B has announced what he is willing to accept as evidence of such a claim by publishing rules of proof for establishing claims. These rules of proof embody a certain *security policy*.

---

[1]This prior work was supported by ONR Grants N00014-01-1-0432 and N00173-00-C-2086 – *Efficient Logics for Reasoning about Security Protocols and Their Implementations*.

3. Principal A constructs a formal proof of C, represents this proof as an object in LF, and transmits it to B.

4. Principal B checks the proof of claim C with respect to his rules (and therefore with respect to his security policy). If the proof is correct, he accepts the claim C, otherwise he rejects it.

We will explain the particular variation of this general scenario adopted for our work in the next section, but it should already be clear that it is critical that *formal proofs* are *objects*.

This methodology is well established and there are several practically efficient implementations. However, how do we know that a given set of proof rules correctly implements an intended security policy? One of the central items of our work has been to exploit the recently developed meta-reasoning facilities of the Twelf implementation [32, 33] in order to formally reason about the policies that are specified and enforced by the access-control architecture sketched in the next section. Successes in reasoning about standard classical [28] and modal logics [25] provide some hints, but access-control logics are more complex along certain dimensions and remain a significant challenge for automated tools. Initial results in this direction have been reported in [30].

Another use for logical frameworks is explained in Section 2.3.

2.2   Implementation of Access Control via Logical Frameworks

Distributed authorization systems (e.g., [9, 15, 19]) provide a way to implement and use complex security policies that are distributed across multiple hosts. The methods for distributing and assembling pieces of these security policies can be described using formal logics [20, 17]—such formalization can dramatically increase confidence in the systems' correctness. Distributed authorization systems have been built by first designing an appropriate logic and then implementing the system around it [1, 4].

Most distributed authorization systems try to provide support for notions such as the ability to delegate privileges and aggregate principals into groups. While these systems strive to be as expressive as possible—that is, to be able to represent as many security policies as possible—they are constrained by how they choose to implement these ideas. The SPKI/SDSI [15] notion of delegation, for example, includes a Boolean flag that describes whether the delegated privilege may be redelegated by the recipient. PolicyMaker [9], on the other hand, requires any redelegation to be explicitly approved by the security policy. Each choice may be the best one for a particular situation, but no one particular choice can be the ideal one for *all* situations. The necessity of making these design choices limits the generality and expressivity of each such system. A system may be well suited for a particular environment but cannot scale to all plausible distributed-authorization scenarios, and systems developed for use in different environments may not be able to interoperate.

Proof-carrying authorization (PCA), a particularly promising, recent approach to distributed authorization, follows a different strategy to achieving generality [3, 8]. Unlike other systems, in which axioms that define ideas like delegation are part of the logic which describes the system, PCA is based on a standard, and completely general, higher-order logic (HOL) [13]. Higher-order logic is undecidable—there is no algorithm which will always be able to prove the truth of every true statement—which raises the question: how can such a logic can be used in an authorization system? A server is typically presented with a list of credentials and has to decide whether they are sufficient for access to be granted. If the logic that models this is undecidable, the server might not be able to come to the correct conclusion.

PCA solves this problem by making it the client's responsibility to prove that access should be granted. The server's task then becomes to verify that the client's proof is valid, which can be done efficiently even if the proof is expressed in an undecidable logic. Transferring the burden of proof from the server to the client ensures that the server's task is tractable, but doesn't explain how the client is able to construct a proof. What makes the client's task possible is that any particular client doesn't need the full expressivity of the undecidable logic. Instead, a particular client is probably content to construct proofs in some decidable subset of higher-order logic—an application-specific subset that corresponds to a particular notion of delegation, a particular way of defining groups or roles, etc. This application-specific subset can be exposed to a client as a regular authorization logic, for example, a logic that models SPKI/SDSI. The client can manipulate this logic and construct proofs without knowledge of the underlying, more general (and more confusing) framework. The server verifying the proof, on the other hand, doesn't care which particular application-specific logic the client uses. As long as the application-specific logic is presented as a subset of higher-order logic, the server sees the client's proof as just another higher-order logic proof, which it knows how to verify.

This approach gives PCA great flexibility. Unlike traditional distributed authorization systems, a PCA-based system can be customized to describe many different sets of authorization scenarios. At the same time, because the different scenarios are expressed in the same underlying framework, all of these components can be made to inter-operate.

Logical frameworks, such as LF and CLF, are ideal tools for describing and reasoning about security logics including PCA and the higher-order logic on which it is based, and thus for providing assurance that certain security properties are achieved. However, inconsistencies between the model of an authorization system and its implementation can negate some of the conclusions of such reasoning. It is thus worthwhile to consider integrating logical frameworks directly into the implementation of a system, i.e., so that the implementation of a distributed system explicitly uses the data structures and proof-generation and proof-checking techniques of logical frameworks. An earlier proof-of-concept experiment [5, 8] suggested this to be feasible, and we are in the process of extending the use of logical frameworks in the implementation of access-control mechanisms in real systems.

Technology has evolved to the point where it is no longer necessary for access control in the physical world and access control on computers to be separate domains. The development and proliferation of high-powered and relatively inexpensive mobile computing devices (PDAs and "smart" mobile phones) and abundance of local communications options (Bluetooth and WiFi) have extended the reach of computers into everyday life. At the same time, recent advances in logic-based access-control suggest that it is possible to build practical access-control systems with nearly unlimited flexibility. The convergence of these developments makes it possible to introduce powerful new paradigms in which mobile devices take the place of both physical keys and computer passwords, eliminating the need for many separate access-control systems and introducing into the world of physical access-control drastic advances in flexibility, convenience, and security.

In particular, we envision an environment in which a Bluetooth-enabled, "smart" mobile phone will be the sole access-control token that a person will need to carry, replacing keys, smart cards, and passwords. The mobile phone will enable its bearer to enter his car, unlock his office door, and log onto his computer. To make this possible the mobile phone will generate PCA proofs that demonstrate that the bearer of the phone is authorized to access his office, computer, etc. The office door and computer logon program will contain a proof checker that will verify proofs prior to allowing access. The policy itself, which must be reflected in the proof of access, may remain distributed until the moment of proof construction, with each piece housed on a different device or provided by a different entity. In addition to the convenience of having to carry only one device, such a system greatly increases security by permitting the use of flexible, distributed, and precise policies. In practice, for example, the policy authorizing an employee access to his office often culminates in handing to the employee a key, which he can then use as he sees fit; in our system, on the other hand, the policy could be evaluated at the time of access, perhaps permitting accesses that a physical key could not and denying others, in response to pieces of the policy that have been dynamically changed.

Such uses of mobile devices will vastly increase the importance of preventing their misuse, as is particularly of concern if the device is physically captured. Ultimately the utility of a PCA proof rests on the protection of cryptographic keys from unintended disclosure, and those stored on a mobile device are especially vulnerable to an attacker who physically reverse-engineers this device. An aspect of the system currently under development are "capture protection" services to render devices far less susceptible to misuse if captured, by utilizing a remote "capture protection server" to confirm that a device remains in its proper owner's possession before permitting its cryptographic key to be used. This can be accomplished without disclosing the device's key to the servers; while permitting the device to move the capture protection server it is utilizing as convenient; and in the face of arbitrary efforts to obtain the key from the device by reverse-engineering [23, 22].

We have deployed this access-control system for our own daily use, with a limited set of resources (e.g., our own office doors, computer logins) and users. As the system matures, we intend to broaden its use to a larger user base and a range of resources and activities on the CMU campus (e.g., purchases). Deploying such a system for everyday use involved solving or making progress on a range of issues that had not been fully addressed in such applications before, some specific to our logic-based approach and others merely exacerbated by it:

- Utilizing such a general approach for access control requires that the unintended consequences of this generality can be constrained. For example, in such a logic-based approach, authority is proved in a formal framework to which a variety of parties (users, computers) contribute "statements" (credentials). This raises the question of what unintended consequences result from participants who behave unexpectedly, e.g., by uttering contradictory statements. This issue is fundamental to the viability of this approach, but remained largely unexplored until recently [30], as sketched in Section 2.1.

- Logic-based approaches have previously been demonstrated in narrow contexts, where proof-generation strategies were neatly laid out with human assistance. This does not scale, and we further conjecture that different proof strategies may be appropriate for different environments. We have developed an approach in which the task of generating a proof is automatically distributed among the set of entities best qualified to construct it. Additionally, we are designing mechanisms that permit the proof-generation infrastructure to learn from experience, i.e., in which proof generation strategies are discovered and refined automatically, over time, and made available for use by other devices as needed. Initial results are reported in [7].

- Previous work on implementing distributed authorization systems has typically been in the context of networks of well-connected machines with plentiful computational abilities. A practical system such as the one we are deploying must explicitly account for the limitations of severely resource-constrained devices (e.g., smartphones) that communicate via a range of protocols with highly variable capacity, latency, and availability (e.g., GPRS, SMS). We have developed several strategies for coping with these difficulties, including designing a modular and lightweight communications framework well suited to such a heterogeneous environment, and intuitive and streamlined user interfaces that facilitate interaction between users and smartphones. We report on the design and describe the initial implementation of our system in [6].

- Keeping authorization credentials within a device obviously raises concerns surrounding the device's capture. We are experimenting with the aforementioned techniques for "capture resilience" in our setting, i.e., techniques that render devices largely invulnerable to capture and misuse, despite their not being physically tamper-resistant [23, 22].

2.3 Distributed Architecture Specification with a Framework Extension

With the techniques sketched in the previous section we can formally specify security policies, reason about their correctness, and enforce them in a distributed implementation. However, we cannot reason about the distributed implementation itself.

We are currently taking the first critical step towards formally reasoning about the distributed implementation by designing and implementing an extension of the logic framework LF that directly supports the specification of distributed and concurrent systems. This builds on prior research on the Concurrent Logical Framework (CLF) [34, 10]. CLF allows specifying a distributed system at a high level of abstraction. It is based on a novel combination of linear logic [16], type theory [14], and monads [24]. Our current work follows two related threads in pursuing this goal:

- We have resolved some implementation challenges of CLF, resulting in a prototype called LolliMon [21], but more remain. Specifically, the efficiency of concurrent simulation does not yet allow larger-scale experiments. Nonetheless, LolliMon has been very useful for describing implementations in CLF, as the resulting programs are too large for visual inspection, while type-checking and simulation would provide at least partial assurance.

- While the LolliMon implementation allows simulation of a distributed system, it is not suited to testing reachability. This requires a theorem prover or, in some fragments, a model checker. The initial design and implementation of a theorem prover for linear logic is described in [11, 12]; current research is aimed at making it more easily applicable to CLF.

We are in the process of formally specifying the evolving PCA architecture described in the previous section in CLF. A future direction of research would be to also formalize the meta-reasoning about the architecture itself (and not just specific policies as proposed in Section 2.1). The above items of current research are promising pre-requisites for this planned future work.

3   Conclusion

We have described a distributed security architecture based on a logical framework. The logical framework plays several roles: it serves to specify the security policy as a logical theory in an authorization logic, enforce it via checking of formal proofs, and reason about it by proof-theoretic analysis. We have realized a prototype for our framework at Carnegie Mellon University, exploiting the computational power and communication capabilities of "smart" cell phones for flexible distributed access control. Our experience so far has been positive: while the logical machinery provides a sound, uniform, and inherently extensible foundation, typical situations do not require to understand this underlying machinery for day-to-day tasks.

Acknowledgments. We gratefully acknowledge contributions by Kevin Bowers, Kaustuv Chaudhuri, Deepak Garg, Scott Garriss, Jonathan M. McCune, Jason Rouse, Peter Rutenbar, and Kevin Watkins to both the theory and implementation of the system.

This ongoing research is supported by the Office of Naval Research under grant N00014-04-1-0724: *Distributed System Security via Logical Frameworks*, the National Science Foundation grant number CNS-0433540, and the U.S. Army Research Office contract number DAAD19-02-1-0389.

References

[1] M. Abadi, E. Wobber, M. Burrows, and B. Lampson. Authentication in the Taos Operating System. In *Proceedings of the 14th ACM Symposium on Operating System Principles*, pages 256–269. ACM Press, Dec. 1993.

[2] A. Appel. Foundational proof-carrying code. In J. Halpern, editor, *Proceedings of the 16th Annual Symposium on Logic in Computer Science (LICS'01)*, pages 247–256. IEEE Computer Society Press, June 2001. Invited Talk.

[3] A. W. Appel and E. W. Felten. Proof-carrying authentication. In *Proceedings of the 6th ACM Conference on Computer and Communications Security*, Singapore, Nov. 1999.

[4] D. Balfanz, D. Dean, and M. Spreitzer. A security infrastructure for distributed Java applications. In *21th IEEE Computer Society Symposium on Research in Security and Privacy*, Oakland, CA, May 2000.

[5] L. Bauer. *Access Control for the Web via Proof-carrying Authorization*. PhD thesis, Princeton University, Nov. 2003.

[6] L. Bauer, S. Garriss, J. M. McCune, M. K. Reiter, J. Rouse, and P. Rutenbar. Device-enabled authorization in the Grey system. In *Proceedings of the 8th Information Security Conference (ISC'05)*, Sept. 2005. An extended version of this paper appears as CMU Computer Science Department Tech Report 05-111.

[7] L. Bauer, S. Garriss, and M. K. Reiter. Distributed proving in access-control systems. In *Proceedings of the 2005 IEEE Symposium on Security & Privacy*, May 2005.

[8] L. Bauer, M. A. Schneider, and E. W. Felten. A general and flexible access-control system for the web. In *Proceedings of the 11th USENIX Security Symposium*, San Francisco, CA, Aug. 2002.

[9] M. Blaze, J. Feigenbaum, and M. Strauss. Compliance checking in the PolicyMaker trust-management system. In *Proceedings of the 2nd Financial Crypto Conference*, volume 1465 of *Lecture Notes in Computer Science*, Berlin, 1998. Springer.

[10] I. Cervesato, F. Pfenning, D. Walker, and K. Watkins. A concurrent logical framework II: Examples and applications. Technical Report CMU-CS-02-102, Department of Computer Science, Carnegie Mellon University, 2002. Revised May 2003.

[11] K. Chaudhuri and F. Pfenning. A focusing inverse method prover for first-order linear logic. In R.Nieuwenhuis, editor, *Proceedings of the 20th International Conference on Automated Deduction (CADE-20)*, pages 69–83, Tallinn, Estonia, July 2005. Springer Verlag LNCS 3632.

[12] K. Chaudhuri and F. Pfenning. Focusing the inverse method for linear logic. In L.Ong, editor, *Proceedings of the 14th Annual Conference on Computer Science Logic (CSL'05)*, pages 200–215, Oxford, England, Aug. 2005. Springer Verlag LNCS 3634.

[13] A. Church. A formulation of the simple theory of types. *Journal of Symbolic Logic*, 5:56–68, 1940.

[14] R. L. Constable et al. *Implementing Mathematics with the Nuprl Proof Development System*. Prentice-Hall, Englewood Cliffs, New Jersey, 1986.

[15] C. M. Ellison, B. Frantz, B. Lampson, R. L. Rivest, B. M. Thomas, and T. Ylonen. *SPKI Certificate Theory*, Sept. 1999. RFC2693.

[16] J.-Y. Girard. Linear logic. *Theoretical Computer Science*, 50:1–102, 1987.

[17] J. Y. Halpern and R. van der Meyden. A logic for SDSI's linked local name spaces. In *Proceedings of the 12th IEEE Computer Security Foundations Workshop*, pages 111–122, Mordano, Italy, June 1999.

[18] R. Harper, F. Honsell, and G. Plotkin. A framework for defining logics. *Journal of the Association for Computing Machinery*, 40(1):143–184, Jan. 1993.

[19] R. Housley, W. Polk, W. Ford, and D. Solo. *Internet X.509 Public Key Infrastructure Certificate and CRL Profile*, Apr. 2002. RFC3280.

[20] B. Lampson, M. Abadi, M. Burrows, and E. Wobber. Authentication in distributed systems: Theory and practice. *ACM Trans. Comp. Sys.*, 10(4):265–310, Nov. 1992.

[21] P. López, F. Pfenning, J. Polakow, and K. Watkins. Monadic concurrent linear logic programming. In A.Felty, editor, *Proceedings of the 7th International Symposium on Principles and Practice of Declarative Programming (PPDP'05)*, pages 35–46, Lisbon, Portugal, July 2005. ACM Press.

[22] P. MacKenzie and M. K. Reiter. Delegation of cryptographic servers for capture-resilient devices. *Distributed Computing*, 16(4):307–327, December 2003.

[23] P. MacKenzie and M. K. Reiter. Networked cryptographic devices resilient to capture. *International Journal of Information Security*, 2(1):1–20, November 2003.

[24] E. Moggi. Notions of computation and monads. *Information and Computation*, 93(1):55–92, 1991.

[25] T. Murphy VII, K. Crary, R. Harper, and F. Pfenning. A symmetric modal lambda calculus for distributed computing. Technical Report CMU-CS-04-105, Carnegie Mellon University, Feb. 2004.

[26] G. C. Necula. Proof-carrying code. In N. D. Jones, editor, *Conference Record of the 24th Symposium on Principles of Programming Languages (POPL'97)*, pages 106–119, Paris, France, Jan. 1997. ACM Press.

[27] F. Pfenning. The practice of logical frameworks. In H. Kirchner, editor, *Proceedings of the Colloquium on Trees in Algebra and Programming*, pages 119–134, Linköping, Sweden, Apr. 1996. Springer-Verlag LNCS 1059. Invited talk.

[28] F. Pfenning. Structural cut elimination I. intuitionistic and classical logic. *Information and Computation*, 157(1/2):84–141, Mar. 2000.

[29] F. Pfenning. Logical frameworks. In A. Robinson and A. Voronkov, editors, *Handbook of Automated Reasoning*, chapter 17, pages 1063–1147. Elsevier Science and MIT Press, 2001.

[30] F. Pfenning. Constructive authorization logics. 4th Workshop on Foundations of Computer Security (FCS'05), Chicago, Illinois, July 2005. Invited Talk.

[31] F. Pfenning and C. Schürmann. System description: Twelf — a meta-logical framework for deductive systems. In H. Ganzinger, editor, *Proceedings of the 16th International Conference on Automated Deduction (CADE-16)*, pages 202–206, Trento, Italy, July 1999. Springer-Verlag LNAI 1632.

[32] C. Schürmann. *Automating the Meta Theory of Deductive Systems*. PhD thesis, Department of Computer Science, Carnegie Mellon University, Aug. 2000. Available as Technical Report CMU-CS-00-146.

[33] C. Schürmann and F. Pfenning. A coverage checking algorithm for LF. In D. Basin and B. Wolff, editors, *Proceedings of the 16th International Conference on Theorem Proving in Higher Order Logics (TPHOLs 2003)*, pages 120–135, Rome, Italy, Sept. 2003. Springer-Verlag LNCS 2758.

[34] K. Watkins, I. Cervesato, F. Pfenning, and D. Walker. A concurrent logical framework I: Judgments and properties. Technical Report CMU-CS-02-101, Department of Computer Science, Carnegie Mellon University, 2002. Revised May 2003.

Device-Enabled Authorization in the Grey System*

Lujo Bauer, Scott Garriss, Jonathan M. McCune,
Michael K. Reiter, Jason Rouse, and Peter Rutenbar

Carnegie Mellon University, Pittsburgh, Pennsylvania, USA

Abstract. We describe the design of Grey, a set of software extensions that convert an off-the-shelf smartphone-class device into a tool by which its owner exercises and delegates her authority to both physical and virtual resources. We focus on the software components and user interfaces of Grey, highlighting the features of each. We also discuss an initial case study for Grey, in which we are equipping over 65 doors on two floors of office space for access control using Grey-enabled devices, for a population of roughly 150 persons. Further details of Grey, and this and other applications, can be found in a companion technical report.

1 Introduction

Access control today is characterized by an expanse of mechanisms that do not interoperate and that are highly inflexible. Access to physical resources (e.g., home, office) is most commonly tied to the possession of a hardware key, and in office environments possibly a swipe card or RFID card. By contrast, access to virtual resources is typically tied to the knowledge of a password and/or possession of a physical token (e.g., SecureID) for producing time-varying passwords.

In this paper we introduce the Grey system, which utilizes converged mobile devices, or "smartphones", as the technology of choice for unifying access control to both physical and virtual resources. We focus on smartphones for two central reasons. First, their nearly ubiquitous adoption is inevitable, as in the long term they stand to inherit the vast cellular phone market, which in 2004 shipped over 648 million units [30]. Second, the hardware capabilities of smartphones and the maturity of application programming environments for them have advanced to a stage that enables applications to take full advantage of rich computation, communication, and interface capabilities (e.g., a camera).

This convergence of market trends and technological advances points to a future marked by pervasive adoption of highly capable and always-in-hand smartphones. Grey is an effort to use this platform to build a ubiquitous access-control technology spanning both physical and virtual resources. This vision is not ours alone: several groups have experimented with the use of mobile phones as digital

---

* We gratefully acknowledge support from the National Science Foundation grant number CNS-0433540, the Office of Naval Research grant number N00014-04-1-0724, and the U.S. Army Research Office contract number DAAD19-02-1-0389.

keys [9, 26]; NTT Docomo is conducting trials on the use of mobile phones to authorize entry to apartments*; and mobile phones can already be used to purchase items from vending machines in several countries. However, to the extent that we can infer the capabilities of these systems, we believe that Grey presents a more sound and flexible platform for building a ubiquitous access-control system and, eventually, for experimenting with advanced mobile applications.

As an example of the type of flexibility not possible in other solutions, with Grey a user will be able to easily create and lend to her friend a temporary, virtual key to her car or apartment; this will happen seamlessly regardless of whether the user and her friend are standing next to each other or thousands of miles apart. Similarly, a manager could give to her secretary temporary access to her email without revealing any information (e.g., passwords) that could be used at a later time or to access a different resource. Going further, a user could specify that his office may be accessed by any three of his colleagues acting together, but at least three would have to cooperate to gain access.

Grey is a novel integration of several technologies that results in a single tool for exercising and delegating authority that we believe is far more secure, flexible and usable than any alternative available today. At the core of Grey is a flexible and provably sound authorization framework based on *proof-carrying authorization* (PCA) [3], extended with a new distributed proving technique that offers significant efficiency advances [7]. In addition to enabling a user to exercise her authority, PCA provides a framework in which users can delegate authority in a convenient fashion. For protection of phone-resident cryptographic keys in the event of phone capture, Grey incorporates *capture resilience* [22], which renders a lost or stolen phone resistant to misuse. And, on the user-interface front, we employ a technique for conveying key material and network addresses, that is as simple as taking a picture with the phone's built-in camera [23, 29]. Phone-to-phone and phone-to-infrastructure data communication utilizes an asynchronous messaging layer that we have developed to take advantage of the myriad networking technologies available to modern smartphones, including Bluetooth, cellular data service (e.g., GPRS), and messaging protocols (e.g., SMS and MMS).

In this paper we describe the adaptation of these components into a practical access-control system called Grey. At the time of this writing, we are deploying Grey to create a platform for future research on practical smartphone-based access-control systems. Our initial deployment on two floors of a new building on our university campus will involve roughly 150 users and consist of two applications: (1) controlling access to 65 offices by Grey-enabled phones; (2) using Grey for accessing Windows XP sessions. In these applications, Grey offers a more secure, flexible and convenient basis for access control than existing solutions.

Due to space limitations, we were forced to omit the descriptions of several important aspects of Grey. For more detail, including a thorough discussion of related work, a more comprehensive description of the software architecture, more extensive performance results, and a description of the Grey Windows XP login plugin, please see our companion technical report [6].

---

* `http://www.i4u.com/article960.html`

2   Component Technologies

Grey is a novel integration of a number of recently-developed technologies that utilize the capabilities of modern smartphones; we summarize these component technologies here.

2.1   Graphical Identifiers

A common feature of modern smartphones is a camera. In Grey we utilize this camera as a data input device for the smartphone, e.g., by asking the user to take a picture of an item she intends to interact with. Information conveyed by photographing two-dimensional barcodes is a theme common to several ubiquitous computing efforts (e.g., [13, 28]), typically to convey service information or a URL where such information can be obtained. In Grey, there are two types of identifiers that are commonly input via the camera:

An identifier for a public key. A useful identifier for a key is the collision-resistant hash of the key (e.g., [20]). In Grey, a two-dimensional barcode is used to encode the hash of a public key and can be displayed on a sticker attached to an item (e.g., on a door) or, for a device with a display (e.g., smartphone or computer), presented on the display. A camera-equipped smartphone can then photograph this identifier and authenticate the public key obtained by other means (e.g., over a wireless link) [23]. This provides a natural and user-friendly way for obtaining an authentic public key.

A network address. A barcode can also be used to encode a network address. As above, a camera-equipped smartphone can then obtain the network address by photographing the barcode. This idea has been utilized to circumvent high-latency device discovery in Bluetooth [29], and we use it in this way in Grey. In addition, this idea offers similar usability advantages to that above, as it is an intuitive operation for a user to photograph the device with which she intends to communicate.

The pervasiveness of graphical identifiers in Grey lends itself well to graphical management interfaces for collecting identifiers and managing access. We will provide an overview of the interfaces we have developed in Section 4.

2.2   Capture-Resilient Cryptography

A user's Grey-enabled smartphone utilizes a private signature key in the course of exercising the user's authority. The capture of a smartphone thus risks permitting an attacker who reverse-engineers the smartphone to utilize this private key and, as a result, the user's authority. To defend against this threat, Grey *capture protects* the phone's private key [22]. At a high level, capture protection utilizes a remote *capture-protection server* to confirm that the device is being held by the person who initialized the device (e.g., using a PIN, face recognition via the phone's camera, or other biometric if the phone supports it), before it permits the key on the phone to be used. This server can also disable the use of the key permanently when informed that the device has been lost, or temporarily to protect the key from an online dictionary attack on the PIN (or other authentication technique). At the same time, this capture-protection server is untrusted in that it gains no information about the user's key.

In keeping with the theme that Grey is a wholly decentralized system, the capture-protection server is not a centralized resource. That is, each user can utilize her own capture-protection server (e.g., her desktop computer), and indeed there is no management required of this server in the sense of establishing user accounts. Rather, this server need only have a public key that is made available to the user's phone when the phone's key is created—perhaps by taking a picture of it displayed on the server's screen, as described in Section 2.1—and must to be reachable when the phone needs to utilize its private key.

A concern that arises with the use of a phone for exercising personal authority is the sheer inconvenience of losing one's phone, in the sense of being unable to exercise one's own authority. While this can occur with any form of access control that utilizes a token or other hardware, we note that capture protection provides a remedy. Since the capture-protection server ensures that a key can be used only by a device in possession of the person present when the key was created, a user may back up her key with little risk of exposing it in an indefensible way.

2.3 Proof-Carrying Authorization

Prior research in distributed authorization has produced a number of systems [27, 16, 15, 10] that provide ways to implement and use complex security policies that are distributed across multiple entities. Gaining access to a resource typically involves locating and gathering credentials and verifying that a set of credentials satisfies some access-control policy. Both the gathering and the verification is typically carried out by the entity or host that is trying to decide whether to allow access.

These credentials and the algorithms for deciding whether a set of credentials satisfies some security policy can be described using formal logics (e.g., [1, 18]). In early work in this vein, the design of access-control systems starts with the specification of a security logic, after which a system is built that implements as exactly as possible the abstractions and algorithms that the logic describes [31, 5]. While this approach can dramatically increase confidence in the systems' correctness [2], at best the system *emulates* the access-control ideal as captured in the formal logic. That is, since the correspondence between the formal logic and the implementation is only informal, any guarantees derived from the formal logic might fail to extend to the implemented system.

An alternative introduced in the concept of *proof-carrying authorization* (PCA) [3, 8] is to utilize this formal logic directly in the implementation of the system. In PCA the system directly manipulates fragments of logic that represent credentials; the proofs of access are likewise constructed directly in formal logic. This integration of formal logic into the implemented system provides increased assurance that the system will behave as expected. This is the high-level approach that we adopt in Grey. As such, each Grey component (including a smartphone) includes an automated theorem prover for generating proofs in the logic, and a checker for verifying proofs.

A fundamental tension in access control is that the more expressive a system is (that is, the greater the range of security policies that its credentials can describe), the more difficult it becomes to make access-control decisions. To ensure that the access-control decision can always be made, most systems restrict the range of security policies that can be expressed, ruling out many potentially useful policies. Since Grey is meant to be used in a highly heterogeneous environment and supports ad-hoc creation of policy components, this type of inflexibility could be very limiting. An insight behind PCA is that the access-control policy concerning any particular client is likely to be far simpler to reason about than the sum of all the policies of all clients. PCA takes advantage of this insight by making it the client's responsibility to prove that access should be granted. To gain access, a client must provide the server with a logical proof that access should be allowed; the server must only verify that the proof is valid, which is a much simpler task. The common language in which proofs are expressed is a higher-order logic [11]; when constructing proofs, each client uses only a tractable subset of the higher-order logic that fits its own needs. The mechanism for verifying proofs is lightweight, which increases confidence in its correctness [4] and also enables even computationally impoverished devices to be protected by Grey.

3   A Usage Scenario

Grey's integration of the technologies described in Section 2 (and others) enables a range of interactions that enhance access control to render it more user friendly, decentralized and flexible. To illustrate this, we describe an example scenario that utilizes several of the pieces we have introduced.

The scenario we consider begins with two researchers, Alice and Bob, who meet at a conference and begin a research collaboration. Anticipating communicating electronically when they return to their home institutions, each enters the other in his/her smartphone "address book". To populate her address book entry for Bob, Alice needs merely to snap a picture of the two-dimensional barcode displayed on Bob's phone. The barcode encodes both the Bluetooth address of Bob's phone, enabling Alice's phone to connect to it, and a hash of Bob's public key, which can be used to authenticate the full key that is transferred via Bluetooth along with Bob's contact information. After Alice returns to her home institution, her phone automatically synchronizes its address book with her PC. This could permit her, for example, to authenticate electronic mail from Bob using standard protocols (e.g., [25]).

As their submission deadline approaches, Alice and Bob decide to meet in person, and so Bob makes plans to visit Alice. On the day that Bob arrives at Alice's institution, Alice is delayed at home. Bob thus arrives to Alice's locked office door. Inside the glass next to Alice's door is a barcode sticker that encodes the Bluetooth address of a computer that can actuate Alice's door to open, if convinced to do so. Bob photographs the barcode, prompting his smartphone to connect to the computer, which challenges Bob's phone to prove his rights to access the door—a feat which his phone cannot do alone, since Bob lacks the needed credentials. The theorem prover in his phone, however, discerns that Alice's phone could assist, and initiates a communication with it.

Upon receiving Bob's phone's request, the theorem prover in Alice's phone automatically generates several options by which Alice can permit Bob to enter the door, based on credentials that she has previously created and that are stored in the phone: she can (i) simply grant him a credential to open the door only this time; (ii) add him to a group `visitors` that she previously cre-

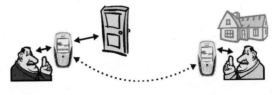

Fig. 1. Bob entering Alice's office. In the course of proving access, Bob's phone contacts Alice's phone for help.

ated and granted rights to, among other things, open her door; or (iii) give him the rights of her secretary, to whom she also granted the ability to open her door. Alice's phone presents this list to Alice, who selects (ii). The phone then signs a credential to this effect and returns it to Bob's phone, enabling it to complete the proof of access.

It is worthwhile to reflect on the presentation of this process to each of Alice and Bob. Bob, upon photographing the door barcode, is asked to enter a PIN in order to utilize his private key to sign a request to open the door—an operation protected by capture protection; see Section 2.2—and the door opens with no further interaction (albeit with some waiting while Alice makes her decision). Alice is consulted merely with a list offering her several options by which she can permit Bob to enter her office. Upon selecting one and also typing her PIN—again to activate her capture-protected key—her task is completed.

Bob's credential indicating that he is a member of Alice's `visitors` group turns out to be handy while he awaits Alice's arrival. In addition to permitting him to open Alice's office, it could grant his laptop access to the campus 802.11 network, to the floor printer, and to a back room where there is a vending machine with snacks and sodas. All these privileges are afforded to Bob due to Alice's prior creation of credentials that grant these privileges to her `visitors`.

4 Software Architecture

At a high level of abstraction, every Grey host or device is composed of some subset of the following elements: a compact and trustworthy *verifier* that mediates access to a protected resource; an extensible *prover* that attempts to construct proofs of access; a lightweight, asynchronous *communication framework* that facilitates the distributed construction of proofs and management of certificates (for details please see our companion technical report [6]); and a collection of *graphical interfaces* that allows the convenient and seamless integration of Grey into everyday life. Grey is implemented in Java, which allows it to easily extend across multiple platforms (workstations, smartphones, embedded PCs, etc.) and operating systems.

4.1   Graphical User Interfaces

An emphasis in Grey is usability. In this subsection we describe the primary user interfaces involved in Grey at the time of this writing.

In order to maximize our user population, we have targeted Grey for the widest range of smartphones possible, including those of modest size—and correspondingly modest screen size. For example, our primary development platform to date has been the Nokia 6620, a smartphone with dimensions $4.28 \times 2.29 \times 0.93$ inches and a 176×208 pixel display. Due to the limited screen size on this class of smartphones, we have divided tasks into those performed on the phone by necessity, and those that can be offloaded to a companion tool run on a personal computer, after which the necessary state can be transferred to the phone via a synchronization operation. At a high level, tasks such as the creation of groups and roles (as defined in [20]), and proactive policy creation, are offloaded to the companion tool. Because these tasks are standard in a variety of access-control settings, here we focus on the phone-resident interfaces, as these are the ones that we believe to be more innovative.

The tasks performed on the smartphone with user interaction include: collecting identifiers (of persons, keys, or addresses); making an access request to a resource; and reactive policy creation, i.e., responding to a request for a credential to permit another person to complete an access proof.

Address book The first of these tasks, building an address book of identifiers and bindings among them, is performed using the camera and the keypad of the phone. As described in Section 2.1, the identifiers that can be input via the camera include pictures of public keys (and of network addresses, but these are not involved in address-book creation). The keypad permits the input of text strings. The address-book interface enables the creation of speaks-for relationships between names and keys: a user photographs the key and then either selects an already-present identifier for which the key speaks or inputs the identifier at that time. After a user photographs the two-dimensional barcode encoding a key, the key is permanently hidden from the her. While user-friendly representations of keys using "snowflakes" [17, 21], flags [14] or random art [24] have been proposed, we believe that exposing keys in the interface is unnecessary and potentially confusing.

Requesting access to a resource A user requesting access to a resource for the first time must obtain the network address of the computer that controls access to that resource. Collecting this network address can presently be done in two ways: either with Bluetooth discovery or, as discussed in Section 2.1, using the phone's camera to photograph a two-dimensional barcode encoding the Bluetooth address (Figure 2). The latter technique is more reliable, since Bluetooth discovery can net multiple devices, and selecting the proper device is a user choice that is vulnerable to misinterpretation or the user being misled. Once the network address for a resource is captured, it is kept in a resource menu on the phone. A single click on a resource in this menu initiates an attempt to connect to the corresponding computer and start the sequence to access the resource (see Figure 3).

Perhaps the most innovative aspect of this part of the user interface is its use of learned patterns of resource accesses. Most users exhibit a pattern of accesses; e.g., a typical workday begins with the user opening a building door, then a door on the floor on which she works, then her office door, and finally logging into her desktop computer. If all these resources are ac-

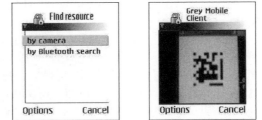

Fig. 2. Bob learns the Bluetooth address of Alice's door by taking a picture of the two-dimensional barcode visible near Alice's door.

cessed using Grey, the user's smartphone will learn the temporal proximity and order of these accesses as a pattern, and can offer this pattern as an option when the user initiates the first access in the pattern (e.g., Work_Garage to HH_D202_PC in Figure 3 is such a pattern). If the user selects the pattern, the phone will attempt to connect to and access each of the resources in sequence, with each step contingent on the previous access in the pattern succeeding. In this way, merely two clicks and a PIN entry as the user approaches her building will enable her to reach her office and will log her into her desktop.

Reactive policy creation The third type of interface presented by the phone to the user permits the reactive creation of policy. This interface is launched by the prover in the user's smartphone after the prover has generated a list of credentials to which the user could consent to enable an access that is being attempted by another person. For ex-

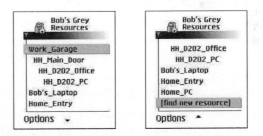

Fig. 3. Resource list on Bob's phone.

ample, in the usage scenario of Section 3, this is the interface by which Alice adds Bob to her visitors group by selecting this option from the menu generated by the prover (see Section 4.2).

Because this interface interrupts the user (unlike the other interfaces, which are user driven), it is important that the user can apply access control to this step and silence these interrupts at times she prefers to not be interrupted. For the former (access control), we employ the same access-control infrastructure that we use for other resources, utilizing a default, but user-configurable, policy that permits only those in the phone's address book to request assistance. The latter, i.e., silencing all such requests, is a simple toggle, and, once activated, received requests will be silently queued for the user to handle later. The party requesting credentials from her will be informed that a response is not forthcoming, and will not be able to access the requested resource (or at least not with her help). However, if she later consents to the request, the appropriate credential will still be sent to the requester for use in the future.

4.2 Prover

As described in the example in Section 3, after arriving at Alice's office, Bob instructs his phone to unlock the door. The door's first reply contains a *challenge*— a statement, in logic, of the theorem that Bob's phone must prove before the door will unlock. The challenge that typically needs to be proved is that the door's owner believes that it is OK for access to be granted. In this case, expressed in logic, the challenge is *Alice* **says goal**(A-111), i.e., Bob must prove that Alice believes that it is OK to access her office, A-111.**

The straightforward way for Bob to answer the door's challenge is to scour the network for useful credentials and then attempt to form them into a proof; most distributed authorization systems use a close facsimile of this approach. There are some inherent problems, however, with this method of constructing a proof. Bob might guess, for example, that Alice has credentials that he could use, but he does not know exactly which of the credentials that she possesses will be helpful for this particular proof. It would be inefficient for Alice to send Bob *all* her credentials, since she might have hundreds. Moreover, sending all her credentials to Bob would reveal exactly the extent of Alice's authority, which is unlikely to meet with Alice's approval. Finally, there may be cases, such as in our example, when the credential that Bob needs has not yet been created; in these situations a simple search, no matter how thorough, would fail to yield sufficient credentials for Bob to access Alice's office.

An answer to these problems can be found in *distributed proving*—a scheme in which Bob's phone does not just search for individual credentials, but also solicits help in proving simpler subproofs that he can assemble into a proof of the challenge [7]. Using this approach, Bob's phone might ask Alice's phone to prove a theorem like *Bob* **says goal**(...) → *Alice* **says goal**(...). Alice's phone now has the opportunity to decide which of her credentials to use or which new credentials to create in order to prove this theorem; these credentials will be returned to Bob's phone along with the proof. This scheme of farming out subproofs to other entities spans two extremes: *eager* proving, in which a client farms out a theorem only if he is completely unable to make progress on it himself; and *lazy* proving, in which the client asks for help as soon as he isolates a theorem that

---

** In order to enforce the timeliness of Bob's response and to protect against replay attacks, the logical statement that must be proved also contains a nonce. This and other low-level details that are not novel are described elsewhere; we omit them from this paper in order to focus on the more abstract ideas.

someone else might be able to help with. Distributed proving can be combined with several optimizations, including caching of credentials and subproofs and deriving proof strategies based on the shape of previously encountered proofs [7].

The use of distributed proving in Grey and the details of constructing proofs in general are largely out of the view of the user. Bob's phone processes the door's challenge until it arrives at a potentially useful subtheorem; at that point, the phone consults the address book to determine how Alice can be reached (by phone or by URL, for example). Since Bob might have to pay for the communication (typically, some combination of SMS and GPRS connectivity is needed, and use of either may incur some cost) and to prevent other users from being unintentionally disturbed, Bob's phone prompts Bob to approve the help request. Alice may need reminding or convincing before she will be willing to help, and so Bob is given the option of annotating his request for a subproof with a recorded or text message.

Upon receiving Bob's request, Alice's phone first verifies that Alice is in fact willing to help Bob (Figure 4). If Alice agrees, her phone begins to compute the subproof, which can in many cases be done without further input from Alice. Sometimes, however, construction of the subproof will require Alice to gener-

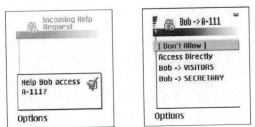

Fig. 4. Alice is given the opportunity to chose the type of credential to grant to Bob.

ate a new credential. In these cases, Alice is shown a list of the credentials that can be used to complete the subproof. Alice can either choose the credential she wishes to create, or decide that none of them are appropriate. When Alice makes her selection, her smartphone finishes constructing the subproof and sends it to Bob. Bob's phone incorporates Alice's subproof into the main proof and sends the proof to the door.

Although a single help request is sufficient for our example with Alice and Bob, Bob's phone may in general need to request subproofs from several other users; in addition, each of those users may in turn also need to solicit help. Through a combination of optimizations derived from observing both successful and unsuccessful past behaviors, a user's Grey smartphone can guide proof search to minimize the number of times help is requested. If multiple avenues can lead to constructing a proof, the ones most likely to be successful and quick will be the ones pursued first [7].

Figure 5 depicts the structure of the Grey application that runs on Bob's phone. The entire application is implemented in Java Micro Edition (J2ME), the restricted flavor of Java that runs on many smartphones. The process of generating proofs is managed by different components depending on whether Bob is trying to access a resource himself (ProofTalker) or help another user (HelpTalker). In addition to directing a Prolog engine to traverse the space of possible proofs, these components manage communication with the resource Bob is trying to access and with other users via the communication framework. They also create and manage credentials using the Crypto module.

Grey makes use of a rich set of standard extensions to the core J2ME APIs to enable use of Bluetooth and other communications protocols (JSR-82 and JSR-120) and the phone's camera (JSR-135). In addition, we use the Bouncy-Castle libraries*** to implement the higher-level Grey cryptographic primitives.

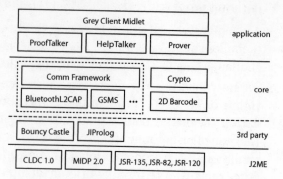

Fig. 5. The structure of the Grey application that runs on smartphones.

4.3 Verifier

One of the goals of Grey is to encompass many diverse resources that a user might wish to access. Some of these resources, such as doors and computer logins, we traditionally associate with the need for access control. Others, like thermostats, are not normally thought of the same way. However, with the ability to actuate such resources remotely, via the network or via a smartphone, also comes the need to regulate access. For example, Alice may want to adjust her office temperature before she arrives at work, but she most likely does not want passers-by to do the same.

To enable Grey to conveniently apply to a wide range of devices, it was necessary for its verification module—the component that mediates access to resources—to be simple, relatively lightweight, and device independent. At the same time, we wanted to maintain a high level of assurance that access is not granted improperly. The proof-carrying authorization paradigm fits our needs well; in PCA, access to a resource is allowed if the client presents a proof that he is authorized to use it. The verification of such proofs is a straightforward mechanical process, with none of the complexity and potential intractability of generating proofs. This distinction is fortunate, since the verifier is in the trusted computing base, while proof generation is not. Moreover, the verification process itself is independent of the security policy protecting the resource, and so also of the resource's type (e.g., door, login).

Figure 6 shows the components and control flow of the verification module, which are described in more detail in the following paragraphs. The process of gaining ac-

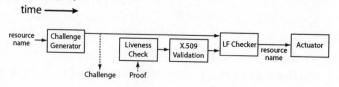

Fig. 6. Flow of the verification process.

cess to a resource is initiated by a user request. In response to the request, a *challenge* is generated. The challenge is the statement, in formal logic, of the

*** http://www.bouncycastle.org

theorem whose proof a potential user must provide. As described in Section 2.3, the challenge is specified in higher-order logic; this in turn is encoded in LF, the notation of one of the most widely used frameworks for specifying logics [19].

When Bob attempts to access Alice's office, the verification module generates a challenge that includes the name of the resource, A-111, and a nonce. This challenge is sent to Bob, but also recorded for use in later stages of verification.

Bob's eventual reply to the challenge will contain a set of credentials (e.g., Bob is a member of `visitors`), and a proof, in formal logic, that the credentials satisfy the door's challenge. The first step of verifying the proof is to ensure (using the nonce) that it was created within a brief period after the door issued the challenge. Next, the credentials, which are X.509v3 certificates with customized extensions, are verified: their digital signatures and expiration times are checked. Finally, the formal proof is passed to an LF type checker, which ensures that the structure of the proof is valid (e.g., that it contains no false implications) and that the correct theorem (the one that was issued as the challenge) was proved. This algorithm is widely studied and well understood, providing high assurance that an invalid proof will never be accepted [12, 4]. If this proof is successfully verified, the LF checker signals an actuator to open the door.

Figure 7 shows the structure of the Grey application that controls access to a door. Similarly to the prover application described in Section 4.3, this application is constructed in a modular fashion—the only customization necessary was the front end (DoorTalker) that encapsulates these modules and the actuator module (Strike-Controller) that sends commands specific to the relay controller we use.

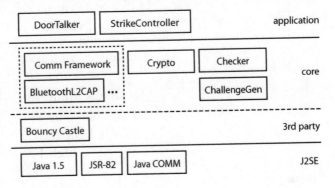

Fig. 7. The structure of the Java application that allows office doors to be Grey-enabled.

The required physical infrastructure for Grey-enabling a door is relatively minimal: a standard electric door strike actuated by an embedded PC located in the wall near each door. Our prototype embedded PC measures $4.55 \times 3.75 \times 1.70$ inches—small enough to fit *within* each door, an option we seriously considered. It is equipped with a Bluetooth adapter and an RS-485 relay controller, and to improve reliability has no moving parts (i.e., cooling is passive, and flash memory is used for non-volatile storage). The prototype embedded PC uses a commodity Pentium M on a PC-104+ mainboard; for a wide deployment of Grey a significantly more compact, custom embedded system could be designed.

Enabling a door with Grey does not preclude legacy access technologies (e.g., keys, proximity cards) from being used; Grey merely provides a parallel way to unlock the door. Of course, Grey can also be used as the sole method of controlling access.

4.4   Performance on Smartphones

In this section we provide performance measurements for certain tasks in Grey. Our primary interest is measuring delays as experienced by the user to access a resource in the common case. We report such numbers here, and additionally measure costs associated with underlying operations to shed light on the sources of these delays.

Our first macrobenchmark is the time required to open a door. The computer controlling the door lock was an embedded PC with a 1.4GHz Pentium M processor; more detail on this pilot application is given in our companion technical report [6]. Each timing was measured starting when the user selected the door from the resource list on her phone (a Nokia 6620), and ended when the door unlocked. On average, this delay was 5.36 seconds excluding any user interaction (more on this below), with an variance of 0.33 due to background work on the phone. The second macrobenchmark is the time required for a user to log into a 2GHz Windows XP workstation using Grey [6]. The methodology in this experiment was similar to that for the door. This delay averaged to 9.31 seconds, with a variance of 2.20. The bulk of the extra time was taken up by the load time for `explorer.exe` and desktop preparation.

We emphasize that these are common-case numbers in three senses. First, neither of these tests involved a remote help request. Help requests can take significantly longer (e.g., a minute), and vary depending on cellular network conditions and user responsiveness. Second, these measurements did not involve the use of a capture-resilient signing key on the phone, and as such the signing operation by the phone did not involve user input (i.e., a PIN) or interaction with a capture-protection server. In our present implementation, we have adopted a design by which the user can configure the frequency with which she is prompted for her PIN (and the capture-protection server is contacted), rather than being prompted per resource access. Her capture-resilient key is then used at these intervals to create a short-lived certificate for a non-capture-resilient public key (a step which does require PIN entry) that is used to sign access requests. As such, the common case incurs only the latency of a signature with this non-capture-resilient key. Third, the network address for each of the computers regulating access was already stored in the resource list of the phone and so, e.g., the one-time barcode-processing overhead incurred if it is first captured via the camera (roughly 1.5 sec.) is not reflected in these numbers.

Typical latencies of under six seconds to open a door and roughly nine seconds to complete a computer login are already comparable to the latencies of more traditional access control (e.g., physical keys and passwords). However, we emphasize that Grey permits these latencies to be hidden from the user more effectively than alternatives. Our current systems utilize class 2 Bluetooth devices, meaning that, e.g., a smartphone could initiate an access once it is within 10 meters of the resource (the door or computer). By the time the user reaches the resource in order to make use of it, the access typically would have completed. In our own experience with using the system, access is consequently far quicker than with the alternatives that Grey replaces for us.

5   Conclusion and Status

Smartphones offer a number of features that make them attractive as a basis for pervasive-computing applications, not the least of which is their impending ubiquity. Grey is an effort to leverage these devices beyond the games, personal information management, and basic communication (voice, email) for which they are primarily used today. We believe, in particular, that these devices can form the basis of a sound access-control infrastructure offering both usability and unparalleled flexibility in policy creation.

Grey is a collection of software extensions to commodity mobile phones that forms the basis for such an infrastructure. At the core of Grey is the novel integration of several new advances in areas ranging from device technologies (e.g., cameras) and applications thereof, to theorem proving in the context of access-control logics. This integration yields, we believe, a compelling and usable tool for performing device-enabled access control to both physical and virtual resources.

Grey is being deployed to control access to the physical space on two floors of a building recently constructed on our university campus. Construction of this building was completed in June 2005, and Grey is being phased into the building on an opt-in basis. This deployment will serve as a platform for continued research on usability, credential management, theorem proving and other technologies in the function of access control.

References

1. M. Abadi. On SDSI's linked local name spaces. *J. Computer Security*, 1998.
2. M. Abadi, M. Burrows, B. Lampson, and G. D. Plotkin. A calculus for access control in distributed systems. *ACM Trans. Prog. Lang. and Sys.*, Sept. 1993.
3. A. W. Appel and E. W. Felten. Proof-carrying authentication. In *Proc. 6th ACM Conference on Computer and Communications Security*, Nov. 1999.
4. A. W. Appel, N. Michael, A. Stump, and R. Virga. A trustworthy proof checker. *J. Automated Reasoning*, 31(3-4):231–260, 2003.
5. D. Balfanz, D. Dean, and M. Spreitzer. A security infrastructure for distributed Java applications. In *Proc. 21st IEEE Symposium on Security and Privacy*, 2002.
6. L. Bauer, S. Garriss, J. M. McCune, M. K. Reiter, J. Rouse, and P. Rutenbar. Device-enabled authorization in the Grey system. Technical Report CMU-CS-05-111, Computer Science Department, Carnegie Mellon University, Feb. 2005.
7. L. Bauer, S. Garriss, and M. K. Reiter. Distributed proving in access-control systems. In *Proc. 2005 IEEE Symposium on Security and Privacy*, May 2005.
8. L. Bauer, M. A. Schneider, and E. W. Felten. A general and flexible access-control system for the Web. In *Proc. 11th USENIX Security Symposium*, Aug. 2002.
9. A. Beaufour and P. Bonnet. Personal servers as digital keys. In *Proc. 2nd IEEE International Conference of Pervasive Computing and Communications*, Mar. 2004.
10. M. Blaze, J. Feigenbaum, and M. Strauss. Compliance checking in the PolicyMaker trust-management system. In *Proc. 2nd Financial Crypto Conference*, 1998.
11. A. Church. A formulation of the simple theory of types. *J. Symbolic Logic*, 1940.
12. T. Coquand. An algorithm for testing conversion in type theory. In G. Huet and G. Plotkin, editors, *Logical Frameworks*, pages 255–280. 1991.

13. D. L. de Ipiña, P. Mendonça, and A. Hopper. TRIP: a low-cost vision-based location system for ubiquitous computing. *Pers. and Ubiq. Comp.*, 6(3), 2002.

14. S. Dohrmann and C. Ellison. Public key support for collaborative groups. In *Proc. First Annual PKI Research Workshop*, Apr. 2002.

15. C. Ellison, B. Frantz, B. Lampson, R. Rivest, B. Thomas, and T. Ylonen. SPKI certificate theory. RFC 2693, Sept. 1999.

16. C. M. Ellison, B. Frantz, B. Lampson, and R. Rivest. Simple public key certificate. Internet Engineering Task Force Draft, July 1997.

17. I. Goldberg. Visual key fingerprint code. Available at `http://www.cs.berkeley.edu/iang/visprint.c`, 1996.

18. J. Y. Halpern and R. van der Meyden. A logic for SDSI's linked local name spaces. In *Proc. 12th IEEE Computer Security Foundations Workshop*, 1999.

19. R. Harper, F. Honsell, and G. Plotkin. A framework for defining logics. *J. ACM*, 40(1):143–184, Jan. 1993.

20. B. Lampson, M. Abadi, M. Burrows, and E. Wobber. Authentication in distributed systems: Theory and practice. *ACM Trans. Comp. Sys.*, 10(4):265–310, Nov. 1992.

21. R. Levin. PGP snowflake. Personal communication, 1996.

22. P. MacKenzie and M. K. Reiter. Networked cryptographic devices resilient to capture. *International Journal of Information Security*, 2(1):1–20, Nov. 2003.

23. J. M. McCune, A. Perrig, and M. K. Reiter. Seeing-is-believing: Using camera phones for human-verifiable authentication. In *Proc. 2005 IEEE Symposium on Security and Privacy*, May 2005.

24. A. Perrig and D. Song. Hash visualization: A new technique to improve real-world security. In *Proc. 1999 Intern. Work. Crypto. Techn. and E-Comm.*, July 1999.

25. B. Ramsdell. Secure/multipurpose internet mail extensions (S/MIME) version 3.1: Message specification. RFC 3850, July 2004.

26. N. Ravi, P. Stern, N. Desai, and L. Iftode. Accessing ubiquitous services using smart phones. In *Proc. 3rd Intern. Conf. Pervasive Comp. and Comm.*, 2005.

27. R. L. Rivest and B. Lampson. SDSI—A simple distributed security infrastructure. Presented at CRYPTO '96 Rumpsession, Apr. 1996.

28. M. Rohs and B. Gfeller. Using camera-equipped mobile phones for interacting with real-world objects. *Advances in Pervasive Computing*, pages 265–271, Apr. 2004.

29. D. Scott, R. Sharp, A. Madhavapeddy, and E. Upton. Using visual tags to bypass Bluetooth device discovery. *Mobile Comp. and Comm. Review*, 1(2), Jan. 2005.

30. A. Slawsby and A. Leibovitch. Worldwide mobile phone 2004–2008 forecast update and 1H04 vendor shares, Dec. 2004. `http://www.idc.com/getdoc.jsp?containerId=32336`.

31. E. Wobber, M. Abadi, M. Burrows, and B. Lampson. Authentication in the Taos operating system. *ACM Trans. Comp. Sys.*, 12(1):3–32, Feb. 1994.

Distributed Immune Systems for Wireless Networks Information Assurance

John S. Baras
Institute for Systems Research
University of Maryland College Park

Introduction

The theme of the research program summarized in this paper, is the development of innovative distributed methods and algorithms for network security and information assurance that are designed to work well in the demanding wireless mobile communications environment. When possible we have tried to take advantage of the special nature of wireless networks to improve assurance and security, while keeping the disadvantages of wireless to a minimum. Our goal is to *design 'robust' information assurance systems*, i.e. systems capable of maintaining some degree of assurance even under high levels of noise and node capture or destruction. The research program under our CIP URI was organized around three interrelated thrusts:

(1) Distributed Autonomous Immune Systems
(2) Assurance Via Distributed Physical Layer Signal Processing and Routing
(3) Distributed Computing Formalisms and Systems

Our research on methods, algorithms, modeling and analytical methods is supported by: Mobile wireless network simulation testbeds; Real experimentation with mobile wireless network testbeds

This integration is achieved by innovative ideas and schemes that focus on the following principles: Distributed automatic classification of intrusions in real-time; Automatic generation of responses for containing and nullifying an intrusion faster than it spreads; Attacking intrusions close to the 'network edge'; Utilization of synergy between physical layer and network layer assurance schemes; Hierarchical methods and schemes in both the physical and logical domain for efficiency and scalability. Furthermore we have adopted a "systems view" of security and information assurance; that is security and information assurance belongs to network management and control.

The major motivation for our methods and ideas comes from: the operational principles of biological immune systems; recent successful development of 'digital immune systems' for the protection of commercial networks from virus attacks; recent advances in complex waveform generation which can be profitably utilized to secure wireless communications in a variety of yet unexplored ways.

The research summarized here was performed by seven faculty investigators from diverse areas of engineering, computer science and mathematics (J.S. Baras, C. A. Berenstein, A. Ephremides, V. Gligor, K.J.R. Liu, H. Papadopoulos, N. Roussopoulos, M.Wu), twenty three graduate research assistants, two postdoctoral fellows and one research engineer, in the period 2001 to 2004. The project created many new interactions between the participants and cross-fertilized the group on issues of wireless security and information assurance.

1. Distributed Autonomous Immune Systems

1.1 Finite Automata Models for Anomaly Detection

A fundamental problem in intrusion detection is the fusion of dependent information sequences. We investigated the fusion of two such sequences, namely the sequences of system calls and the values of the instruction pointer. We introduced FAAD, a finite automaton representation defined for the product alphabet of the two sequences where dependencies are implicitly taken into account by a matching procedure. Our learning algorithm captures these dependencies through the application of certain parameterized functions. Through the choice of thresholds and inner product structures, we were able to produce a compact representation of the normal behavior of a program.

Intrusion detection methods can be divided into two categories: misuse detection and anomaly detection. Anomaly detection is based on an approximate representation of normal behavior of the system. A behavior which significantly deviates from this normal representation is flagged as an intrusion. We developed a new technique for program-based anomaly detection. Forrest and her collaborators have shown that the sequence of system calls can be used to represent the normal behavior of a program. Learning this behavior is accomplished by the use of the "N-grams" which are strings of length N observed during the normal use of the program. This approach is inspired by the intrinsic ability of biological immune systems to distinguish between "self" (the organism) and pathogens.

Finite Automata (FA) or Finite State Machines (FSM) have been suggested as an alternative to N-grams. Once a finite automaton is constructed, combinations of all allowed transitions can generalize it to strings not used in the learning phase but "similar" to the ones used. We developed a novel algorithm, proved its properties and evaluated its performance. The rate of false positives is non-increasing with training for FAAD. An attractive feature of FAAD is that training can continue after its use for intrusion detection begins. We performed evaluation of our algorithm with various attacks. Our new algorithm performed very well in all tests we did.

1.2 Intrusion Detection with Support Vector Machines and Generative Models

We investigated the development of algorithms for intrusion detection using Support Vector Machines (SVM). Based on the formal models we developed intrusion detection was formulated as the problem of detection and classification of symbolic strings (attack tree model), given small amounts of data. Our main objective in this research was to combine use of formal models (like attack trees) and parallel clustering algorithms of the Support Vector Machine (SVM) type, to develop fast distributed algorithms for identification of components of intrusions and abnormal behaviors. Our approach and methods are somewhat inspired from similar successful combination of formal (logic) models and SVM in genomics and proteomics, and in particular for the problem of partial identification using side logical information. These are the so-called "generative models based SVM" schemes. They have excellent learning properties for unknown patterns and generalization capabilities.

We addressed the problem of detecting intrusions in the form of malicious programs on a host computer system by inspecting the trace of system calls made by these programs. We used 'attack-tree' type generative models for such intrusions to select features that are used by a Support Vector Machine Classifier. Our approach combines the ability of an HMM generative model to handle variable-length strings, i.e. the traces, and the non asymptotic nature of Support Vector Machines that permits them to work well with small training sets. The central problem is to decide whether a computer program that runs on a single host computer system is a *normal* program that does not compromise the security of the host or a *malicious* program that is a threat to the host. To decide on the nature of a program, we examine the string (trace) of system calls that it makes and operate under the assumption that this trace contains all the information we need to make this decision. A relatively large number of training examples especially of programs that are malicious is hard to come by. Therefore we seek to use non-parametric discriminative classifiers such as Support Vector Machines that, of all learning techniques are designed to work well with small training sets.

Real attacks have a finite (and not too long) underlying *attack* sequence of system calls because they target specific vulnerabilities of the host. This and the padding are represented in a 'plan of attack' called the *Attack Tree*. The basic attack scheme encoded in the Attack Tree is not changed by modifications such as altering the padding scheme or the amount of padding (time spent in the padding nodes). Given an attack tree, it is straightforward to find the list of all traces that it can generate. Our intrusion detection executes the following steps: (1) Learn about A from the training set T; (2) Form a rule to determine the likelihood of a given trace being generated by A . These objectives can be met by a probabilistic modeling of the Attack Tree. We used parametric HMMs to derive a real valued feature vector of fixed dimension for these variable length strings that enables us to use Support Vector Machines for classification.

1.3 Detection and Classification of Network Intrusions Using Hidden Markov Models

We developed and evaluated algorithms for detection and classification of intrusions using Hidden Markov Models (HMM). We demonstrated that it is possible to model attacks with a low number of states and classify them using Hidden Markov Models with very low False Alarm rate and very few False Negatives. Hidden Markov Model training was performed on normal and anomalous sequences (traces). We tested several algorithms, applied different rules for classification and evaluated the relative performance of these. Several of the attack examples presented exploit buffer overflow vulnerabilities, due to availability of data for such attacks. We emphasize that the purpose of our algorithms is not only the detection and classification of buffer overflows, but they are targeted for detecting and classifying a broad range of attacks.

Among the attacks we studied were: *eject, ps, ffbconfig* and *fdformat* and all of them belong to the class of User to Root exploits. User to Root exploits belong to the class of attacks where the attacker gains access to a normal user account on the system and by exploiting some vulnerability obtains the root access. Certain regularities were captured in behavior of exploited programs by comparing them against normal instances of those programs, other instances of attacks detected at different periods of time and by searching for certain events in the behavior of a program that were expected to happen by using the knowledge about the mechanism of those attacks and their goals. The studied examples show that each attack is characterized with a very simple distinguishing sequence of system calls and accompanying parameters (like size, PID, path, etc.), which can be used for recognition and identification of different attacks.

In the framework of intrusion detection the problem can be formulated as follows: *given M attack models in the form of Hidden Markov Models with known parameters, detect the one that matches the incoming sequence with the highest probability.* However, in the case of detecting an attack the incoming sequence may or may not match one of the HMM models of attack. In case it does not match one of the attack models we need to consider two cases: either the incoming sequence is not an attack or it is an unknown attack that we don't have in our database. The problem of M-ary detection was solved by calculating log-likelihoods for each of the possible models given the observed sequence and finding the maximum. One of our significant contributions is reflected in the area of classification. For known attacks our approach is based on training on anomalous sequences. Training is performed on a couple of files, each of length 100 system calls. Testing is performed on around 2-4 % of the total number of sequences of the initial data set. The strength of this approach is that it chooses only potential attacks in both the training and testing sets. Another advantage of this approach is that the attacker cannot change the behavior of normal over time by slowly adding more and more abnormal sequences since we are using anomalous sequences for training. This algorithm has been used successfully for detection of already known attacks.

1.4 On-line Adaptive IDS Scheme for Detection of Unknown Network Attacks Using Probabilistic Models and Logic

The main focus was to design a scheme that can incorporate both misuse and anomaly detection and hence be used to detect known network attacks (instances of which might not have been seen before), but more importantly, unknown network attacks. Since misuse detection introduces false negatives and anomaly detection introduces false positives, we need to be able to find a good trade-off. The idea is to set a desirable detection rate (which, in our case was 100%), and then minimize the false positive rate by filtering false positives through stages.

It is important to emphasize that this scheme's goal is to get as good results as possible with *limited* information. This means that we do not know signatures of all the attacks. If we knew that, we could just use signature detection. By incorporating probabilistic models and the administrator's knowledge about possible vulnerabilities, we can achieve very optimistic results. There are five stages in our scheme: Initialization, Parallel testing and training, Logic, Verification and Adaptive phase.

The process is as follows: Partition the probabilistic space into normal behavior, known attacks and (everything else is) unknown attacks. This is done through offsetting log-likelihoods of each model space. In the Parallel testing and training phase, we do trace detection and classification (normal, known attack, unknown attack) and if the classified sequence is not normal we go to the Logic phase (note that in this phase we also train new HMM with the incoming sequence for possible future use – in the Verification phase). In the Logic phase, we use the administrator's knowledge databases containing possibly malicious events - sequences of (in our case) system calls. We scan the trace for those events (sequentially!). In case there are none, the decision is made that the trace is normal, so the HMM model of the trace (created in the previous phase) is forwarded to the Adaptive phase. In case there is a malicious event (or several events, depending of how many of them are needed to raise an alarm), the execution goes to the next, Verification phase. This phase does probabilistic testing (analog to the probabilistic testing in the beginning). Since all the attacks we used in our simulations belong to the same group of attacks (Buffer Overflow attacks), this represents the worst-case scenario for the scheme, since the attacks tend to look alike. With 100% detection rate, we were also able to achieve a very good false positive rate – 0.08%.

1.5 On-Line Distributed Detection of Self-Propagating Code

Worms are programs that self-propagate across a network by exploiting security flaws in widely-used services offered by vulnerable computers in the network. Worms are popular attacks because no other mechanism allows for the rapid and widespread distribution of malicious code, with virtually no way to trace the attacker. It has been stated that the spread of the theoretical flash or Warhol worms will be so fast that no human-driven communication will suffice for adequate identification of an outbreak before nearly complete infection is achieved. The appearance of such a worm was voted the greatest security threat. There is therefore great need to develop automated mechanisms for detecting worms based on their traffic patterns. In our work we completed the development and evaluation of such algorithms. In our research we focused on the fact that the self propagating code will try to use specific vulnerabilities that can be identified with certain port numbers. So we used as the traffic monitoring variable the connection attempts (probes) to a given TCP/UDP port number(s). We also assumed most of the times a probability distribution on the traffic observations. So in our framework we assume that there is a baseline of connections to the given monitored port in all sensors (computers) of the network. The observations can be made at different participating nodes enforcing policies for blocking self-propagating code once it is detected. We explored the effect of aggregation from distributed sensors. This approach is motivated by the current infrastructure of distributed Intrusion Detection Systems such as myNetwatchman, Dshield and Symantec's DeepSight Threat Management System.

We developed a novel formulation of these problems using change detection as the foundation of our approach. We developed methods that are valid without the standard i.i.d. assumption on the observations after the change, which is not true because each infected host will try in general to scan the same number of hosts in a given interval of time, and as more and more hosts become infected the observation data volume will increase fast with time. We have developed, implemented, simulated and evaluated a variety of methods using our framework. These include detection of a change in the mean, change detection in distributed sensor systems, CUSUM of aggregated traffic, exponential signal detection in noise, exponential change in the mean, nonparametric regression detection (which allows situations where the number of probes seen exhibits long range dependence and multifractal behavior), and new fully nonparametric algorithms in order to deal with some of the more complicated problems, in particular those where no clear mean can be established. We developed algorithms based on the sequential probability ratio test (SPRT), where the goal is to optimize a hypothesis testing problem given a trade-off between the probability of errors and the observation time. We also formulated these problems as quickest change detection problems, where the trade-off is between the delay of detection and the false alarm rate. The methodologies we used to analyze these problems proceed along two main ideas: developing generalized likelihood ratio (GLR) algorithms for on-line algorithms; developing filter bank algorithms (using HMMs). We also investigated the development of robust non-parametric algorithms using cumulative sum (CUSUM) and Girshik-Rubin-Shiryaev (GRSh) statistics. In sequential versions of the problem the sequential probability ratio test (SPRT) was used.

We performed extensive analytic and experimental (based on synthetic networks and attack data) performance evaluation of the various schemes we developed. Our evaluation results seem to strongly suggest that in scale-free networks a very small set of the highly connected nodes is sufficient for detection and aggregation only improves the performance of the nonparametric statistics. If we select sensors at random or if we monitor a random network then aggregation is very important for detection. We also developed and evaluated collaborative distributed algorithms for these worm detection problems.

1.6 On-Line Distributed Detection of Distributed Denial of Service Attacks

A denial of service attack (DoS) can be defined as an attack designed to disrupt or completely deny legitimate users' access to networks, servers, services or other resources. The most common DoS attack involves sending a large number of packets to a destination causing excessive amounts of network endpoint bandwidth to be consumed and (or) cpu processing rate at the destination. In a distributed denial of service (DDoS) typically an attacker compromises a set of Internet hosts (using manual or semiautomated methods like a worm) and installs a small attack daemon on each host, producing a group of "zombies". There are various techniques and ideas for mitigation of denial of service attacks that require the identification of the routers participating (involuntarily) in the attack. Most of these techniques consume a significant amount of router resources so it is advisable to use them only when needed. A reasonable assumption for transit networks carrying a lot of traffic which cannot be analyzed at line rate, is that routers do not keep the number of packets to a specific destination, as this might be too expensive during operation. Thus we are interested only in monitoring passively the network.

We completed a novel formulation and approach to the problem of detecting when a distributed denial of service is taking place in one sub-network of a transit (core) network comprised only on routers. We assumed the transit network itself is not the target of the attack, but it is being used by the attack to reach the victim. We developed a novel formulation of the problem as sequential space-time change detection on a graph. The mathematical techniques we use for detecting an attack are thus based on change detection theory. In a distributed environment a small change in local nodes can be correlated with the state at different nodes to provide a global view and early warning about the state of the network. We developed and applied parametric and nonparametric change detection algorithms to the problem of detecting changes in the "direction" of traffic flow. We investigated also the quickest detection problem when the attack is distributed and coordinated from several nodes against a targeted one. We developed and used a "directionality framework", which gives us a way to compute the severity and directionality of the change.

One of the main advantages in having several nodes under monitoring is that we can perform a correlation of the statistics between the different nodes in order to decrease the detection delay given a fixed false alarm rate probability. The alarm correlation can be performed by several methods. We developed and evaluated a simple algorithm that only requires the knowledge of the routing tables for the nodes being monitored. Selecting which statistics to correlate (add) is a key issue. Our algorithm not only can detect the attack (depending on the new correlation threshold), but also it can diminish the impact of the false alarm originating at some node. However another important conclusion is that without the need to extract or store header information from the packets transmitted through the network, we are able to infer (from the intersection of the two routing tables for the "winning" correlated statistic of the links) the "best" possible targets (estimated).

1.7 Detection of Attacks Against the MAC Protocol in Wireless Networks

Selfish behavior at the MAC layer can have devastating side effects on the performance of wireless networks, similar to the effects of DoS attacks. One of the most challenging detection tasks is that of detecting backoff manipulation. Due to the randomness introduced in the choice of the backoff, it is difficult to detect when a node has chosen small backoff values by chance or not. In our work we focused on prevention and detection of the manipulation of the backoff mechanism of 802.11's MAC protocol, although our approach can be extended to any probabilistic distributed MAC protocol.

Our main contributions are the introduction of two algorithms. The first one is an algorithm that prevents cheating in the backoff stage of 802.11 DCF for noncolluding nodes. The protocol is called ERA-802.11 for Ensuring Randomness in 802.11. ERA-802.11 appends a couple of bits to the RTC/CTS reservation mechanism of 802.11. In it, the sender commits to a random backoff. Once the receiver obtains this commitment it sends back an honest backoff value. Finally when the sender receives the backoff of the receiver it replies with the information required to open the commitment. Once the receiver checks the correctness of the committed value, the final backoff value, agreed among sender and receiver, is the *XOR* of the backoffs selected by both of them. This algorithm is based on Blum's flipping coins over the telephone protocol and it ensures honest backoffs when at least one, either the receiver or the sender is honest.

The second algorithm is a misbehavior detection procedure to deal with the problem of colluding selfish nodes (a pair of misbehaving sender and receivers can override ERA-802.11's prevention mechanism). We first explored the problems with previous solutions attempting to detect backoff manipulation. We showed how intelligent selfish nodes can overrride previous detection schemes while still providing high throughput by swithcing between a large backoff and a small backoff. Finally we presented a new algorithm that detects several attempts of intelligent nodes to gain more access to the medium.

Although we have focused on the MAC layer of 802.11, our approach is general and can serve as a guideline for the design of any probabilistic distributed MAC protocol.

1.8 On-Line Detection of Routing Attacks in MANETs

Mobile -wireless- ad hoc networks (MANETS) are particularly vulnerable to attacks on their routing protocols. Unlike fixed networks, the routers usually do not reside in physically protected places and can fall under the control of an attacker more easily. Such an attacker can then send incorrect routing information. Furthermore messages can be eaves dropped and faked messages can be injected into the network without the need to compromise nodes. General attacks are misrouting, false message propagation, packet dropping, packet generation with faked source address, corruption on packet contents and denial-of-service.

One of the attacks exploiting the wireless medium is the wormhole attack. The wormhole attack can be devastating to a routing protocol. We developed a formulation and a novel approach for the detection of such attacks. Our approach builds a model capturing the dynamics of a highly mobile ad hoc network. The basic idea is that an attacker will change the routing information in such a way that our perceived mobility of the nodes will differ from our previous experience. We want to learn the allowable state transitions (which depend in our sampling interval.) We performed various simulation experiments which validated this promise. We used as the observation variable the hop count distribution at a given node. For simplicity we assumed a proactive distance vector routing protocol such as DSDV in order to have all hop counts at any time. In the change detection setup we used a CUSUM procedure applicable to the case of dependent observations.

We performed analytical and simulation evaluations of the performance of the new algorithm. Although the attacks introduced by very different and easy means, the principle of detecting an unknown attack to the routing protocol with different characteristics was demonstrated. In particular some attacks produced a change in the variance of the hop count distribution, while others produced a change in the mean of the hop count distribution. Both attacks were detected by simply testing the likelihood of our learned model.

1.9 Software Systems for Attack Detection and Defense in MANET

We have investigated a highly extensible intrusion detection system to determine its utility in solving problems of identifying previously unidentified attacks, with special interest in its application in wireless ad hoc networks. The STAT system (developed by Richard Kemmerer and his group at the University of California Santa Barbara) is a state-based detection system: each attack is mapped into a set of states called an attack scenario. Certain behaviors trigger transitions between states - these transitions represent either the progression of a possible attack or the recognition and quelling of a false alarm.

When a series of behaviors cause the final state to be reached, an attack is said to have occurred. The power of this approach lies in the identification of only the essential elements of attacks - hence if the goals of the attackers are known, it should be possible to construct attack scenarios abstract enough to capture new methods of attaining those same goals.

We extended STAT and STATL, and implemented several and tested several of our intrusion detection algorithms in STAT: buffer overflow, timing disruption, sequence falsification, wormhole, routing misbehavior and others. We are setting up a wireless testbed to analyze extensively feasibility and performance of STAT in wireless ad hoc networks by identifying energy requirements and adaptability to a dynamic attack environment.

2. Assurance Via Distributed Physical Layer Signal Processing and Routing

2.1 Physical Layer Secrecy over Wireless Channels via Chaotic CDMA

Our main objective has been to design chaotic CDMA systems that provide uncoded $Pr(e)$ advantages to intended users in the context of multiuser communication over fading channels. The systems we have considered and optimized exploit linear modulation of a digital information-bearing signal on a chaotic sequence, *i.e.*, a sequence generated by iterating an initial condition through a chaotic mapping. The $Pr(e)$ advantages offered to intended users are achieved by providing side information to these users in the form of the initial condition. These systems are attractive alternatives to conventional CDMA systems, *i.e.*, systems that exploit modulation on binary-valued pseudonoise (PN) spreading sequences generated by feedback shift-register structures. Indeed, chaotic CDMA systems can provide additional $Pr(e)$ performance advantages to intended users by exploiting the inherent sensitivity to initial conditions of chaotic systems, with minimal increase in transmitter and intended receiver complexity and without the need for additional side information with respect to what is required by conventional CDMA systems.

We have designed tools for characterizing the differences in attainable performance between intended and unintended users in single-user settings (corresponding to only one transmitting user), as a function of processing gain and SNR for a large class of PC maps. In particular, we have determined the performance characteristics of DS/SS schemes with signatures generated by various families of chaotic piecewise-linear maps, in the context of signaling over AWGN and frequency nonselective fading channels and have recently started exploring the multiuser setting. As our investigative efforts have revealed, even in the single-user setting, these systems can be designed to provide secrecy benefits to intended receivers in the form of uncoded $Pr(e)$ performance advantages. In particular, chaotic spreading can provide substantial improvement in terms of the $Pr(e)$ advantages offered to intended users with respect to conventional DS/SS systems that make the PN sequence seed available only to intended receivers.

We developed optimized digital implementations of the underlying chaotic DS/SS as well as quantifying the extent to which these implementations preserve the important properties of the underlying chaotic DS/SS of interest. We have shown that by properly choosing the precision depth in the implementation, the pseudochaotic DS/SS systems we developed can achieve the performance characteristics of the underlying chaotic DS/SS over an arbitrarily wide (yet finite) range of channel SNR values. As a result we were able to show that 16-bit precision depths suffice to provide effectively private communication over a very wide SNR range (that includes the SNR range of practical settings) even for processing gains well below those used in practical systems. We also considered the privacy provided by chaotic DS/CDMA, i.e., the multiuser extensions of DS/SS systems.

2.2 Distributed Coding-Based Protocols for Private Computation with Intrusion Detection over Wireless Channels

We designed distributed algorithms for networks of nodes/sensors that wish to compute functions of their data with privacy, while maintaining the ability to detect intrusions with high probability. In particular, we considered multinode settings, whereby the nodes wish to effectively use resources, such as bandwidth and transmit and processing power, to compute a function of their individual data over a common wireless channel – making the desired function output, in the process, available to an arbitrary subset of the participating nodes – while achieving the following objectives:

(i) no additional information is revealed by the protocol about each participant's individual data, other than what is made available through the result of the desired computation;

(ii) intruders, actively participating in the computation in an effort to alter its end result, can be detected by means of the protocol with high probability.

We focused our efforts on a driving example involving source localization (estimation of the location of a target) by fusing noisy target range information available at spatially dispersed sensor nodes. In a typical setting, each sensor node may possess measurements which can be used to derive such information about the relative range between the target and that particular sensor. In this area, we are leveraging our recent findings of distributed algorithms that can be used to compute functions of the node data in a wireless network by using distributed locally constructed fusion rules at each node.

2.3 Communication-Friendly Encryption of Multimedia

We investigated means of protecting the confidentiality and achieving access control of multimedia information, which is one of the crucial security elements for many applications. More specifically we researched efficient and effective encryption of multimedia with a focus on communication and compression issues. We identified a set of domains along the representation and communication process of multimedia where encryption can be applied, and proposed three encryption operations through elegant combinations of multimedia signal processing and contemporary cryptography.

By moving the encryption domain from the bit stream to upper levels and therefore preserving standard compliance, more sophisticated intermediate processing can be applied directly on the encrypted data. Under such a framework, we proposed an encryption tool via a generalized index mapping, which can be applied to any scalar or vector symbols with a finite value range. The compression overhead of this scheme can be adjusted and confined to a moderate amount. The three fundamental schemes we developed can be used as building blocks and combined to form an encryption system for multimedia data. Our designs of these proposed encryption operations take into consideration the inherent structure and the underlying syntax of multimedia sources to achieve improved friendliness to communications, compression, and computation.

2.4 Topology-Aware Key Management Schemes for Wireless Multicast
Technological advancements have created the potential for many new applications that will allow users to simultaneously share content and collaborate. The most relevant enabling network technology for group communication is multicast. The problem of access control has received extensive attention in the recent literature and many solutions for the generic problem have been proposed. However, the traditional literature does not address network-specific issues.

In tree-based multicast key management schemes, most rekeying messages are only useful to a subset of users, who are always neighbors on the key management tree. This observation motivates us to design a key tree that matches the network topology in such a way that the neighbors on the key tree correspond to the topology of the wireless LAN, which consists of mobile users and access points. This key tree design proceeds in two steps:

Step 1: Design a subtree for the users connecting to each access point (AP). These subtrees are called *user subtrees*.

Step 2: Design a subtree which governs the key hierarchy between the APs and the key distribution center (KDC). This subtree shall be called the *AP subtree*.

By delivering the rekeying messages only to the users who need them, we may take advantage of the fact that the key tree matches the network topology, and localize the delivery of rekeying messages to small regions of the network.

2.5 Secure and Cost-Efficient Contributory Group Key Agreement Protocols
In contributory key agreements, every group member makes its own contribution independently when establishing group keys, and each member's personal key is not disclosed to any other entities. Compared with centralized key management schemes, the contributory key agreement schemes also have the advantages that they do not rely on centralized servers and secure communication channels. In our research we investigated methods for reducing the cost associated to key updates in contributory group key agreement protocols. We developed TCGK, a suite of cost-efficient Tree-based Contributory Group Key agreement protocols for secure group communication with dynamic membership changes. We designed a novel logical key tree structure, based on which the rekeying cost per user join or leave event can be dramatically reduced. To our

best knowledge, TCGK has the lowest cost among the existing tree-based contributory key agreement schemes, and achieves better scalability. The simulation results have also confirmed the superiority of TCGK to the existing schemes in term of cost savings.

In secure group communications, the time cost associated with key updates for member join and departure is an important aspect of quality of service, especially in large groups with dynamic membership. In time-sensitive applications, a timely key update during member join or departure assures that secure group communications can be established in a timely manner. We developed a new scheme called Join-Exit Tree (JET) Group Key Agreement. Our analytical results show that our proposed scheme achieves an average asymptotic time of $O(\log (\log n))$ for a join event, and also $O(\log (\log n))$ for a departure event when group dynamics are known a priori. We have extensively studied the performance of our scheme under different user activity scenarios, including sequential user join, the MBone (Multicast Backbone) multicast session data, and a probabilistic user behavior model. In all these scenarios, our proposed scheme has outperformed the existing schemes in terms of rekeying time complexity. In addition to the improved time efficiency, our scheme also has low communication and computation complexity.

2.6 Attacks and Protection of Dynamic Membership Information in Secure Group Communications

In secure group communications, key management is employed to prevent unauthorized access to multicast content. We discovered that the rekeying process associated with multicast key management can disclose information about the dynamics of the group membership to both insiders and outsiders. We collectively refer to group dynamics information (GDI) as the number of users in the multicast group as a function of time, and the number of users who join or leave the service during a time interval. The leakage of GDI from the rekeying process can lead to serious security and privacy problems. For centralized key management schemes, we have developed two effective strategies to steal the GDI. These strategies involve:

(1) obtaining membership dynamics from the format of rekeying messages;
(2) estimating the number of users, $N(t)$, from the size of rekeying messages.

Many popular centralized key management schemes are vulnerable to these attacks. Our simulations show that these passive-attack strategies result in accurate estimation of the GDI.

To protect the GDI, we developed an anti-attack technique utilizing batch rekeying and phantom users. The combined effects of the phantom users and the real users lead to a new rekeying process, called the *observed rekeying process*, which would be monitored by the attackers. The goal is to produce an observed rekeying process that reveals the least amount of information about the real GDI. We derived performance criteria that describe the security level of the proposed scheme using mutual information. The proposed anti-attack scheme is evaluated based on the data obtained from real MBone sessions. We also developed the analysis of the vulnerability of various contributory key management schemes and investigated techniques that can be used to protect dynamic group membership information in distributed environments.

2.7 Key Management Schemes for Distributed Sensor Networks

Distributed sensor networks (DSN) are of central importance to military operations. Our interest in this work is very large distributed sensor networks using inexpensive sensors. We have developed innovative key management schemes for such networks. This addresses an important information assurance problem for such wireless sensor networks. These very large sensor networks have significant differences from more conventional sensor networks. First, in scale, we are interested in size of 10,000 nodes as opposed to 100. Second, they have dynamic topology. Third, due to the method of deployment, like deployment by scattering no prior knowledge of sensor-node location can be assumed. Fourth they should be able to accommodate incremental addition / deletion of nodes after deployment. Fifth and most significant, they face hostile environments of operation, where they must operate unattended, and are subject to sensor nodes monitoring, capture and manipulation. Physical capture and tampering by adversary is possible, which requires tamper-detection technology, disable sensor and erase keys, detection of data inputs alteration, detection of input manipulation via data correlation.

From the perspective of key management these constraints imply that key exchange/distribution via third party is not possible: unknown network topology, intermittent operations, network scale and dynamics. Key pre-distribution is the only viable solution (to date). We have developed and analyzed a new scheme based on a *probabilistic key sharing* approach. Each node has been given k keys from a pool of P keys. If two nodes share a common key then a link exists between them. These secure links provide an overlay secure network. This overlay network has to be connected. Our new basic scheme consists of the following three steps: (1) Key pre-distribution; (2) Shared-key discovery; (3) Path-key establishment. We have analyzed this scheme and developed analytically its performance evaluation.

2.8 Attacks and Defenses Utilizing Cross-Layer Interactions in MANET

Cross-layer protocol design is one of the prevailing methodologies that have recently been adopted in networking research and leads to significant performance benefits. We assessed the performance of cross-layer interaction and investigated its effects with regard to security and information assurance of mobile ad hoc wireless networks. Using attacks in realistic wireless networks as a prototype, we found that natural cross-layer interactions between physical, MAC and network layer protocols in MANET can turn out to be a weak point, causing various attacks and intrusions. However, by allowing a controlled synergy between the affected layers, we facilitate timely detection of such attacks that are otherwise difficult to detect and may have devastating effects on network functionality and operation.

We demonstrated that natural interactions between physical layer and MAC, as well as MAC and routing protocols in MANET can lead to a variety of attacks and intrusions. We showed that without purposeful collaboration between the layers affected by such attacks, they are very difficult to detect while at the same time can have catastrophic effects on the MANET functionality and operation. To illustrate the impact of MAC layer attacks we first described the effects of a dishonest user in the MAC layer to the performance of the network and later we concentrated on malicious users. For the majority of the work we focused on attacks involving interactions between the MAC and routing protocols and described detection and defense mechanisms we have developed for such attacks. We described several DoS attacks in realistic MANET that explicitly exploit cross-layer interactions. We used the realistic scenario, where each node initially employs legal communication patterns that prevent other nodes from communicating and after some time they start misbehaving in order to maintain priority in the network.

We used IEEE 802.11 MAC layer and by using several different scenarios we showed that attacks that originate in the MAC layer easily propagate to the routing layer causing breaking of existing routes. We also showed that attack propagation can cause not only breaking of selected routes, but can also be used to include the attackers in the new routes. We showed that the attack with colluding attackers is more powerful than the attacks using only single attacker or multiple non-colluding attackers. We proved using a game-theoretic approach that the scenario in which each attacker attempts to maximize his own gain results in minimal gain for each of the attackers.

2.9 Key and Node Revocation in Distributed Sensor Networks

Sensor network security poses a unique challenge due to the large numbers of sensor nodes involved and the limitations of sensor node hardware. A variety of techniques to bootstrap security in sensor networks have been developed using key pre-distribution techniques based on our original scheme. However, the problem of key and node revocation in sensor networks has received relatively little attention. Distributed revocation protocols pose new design challenges since these protocols need to account for the presence of active adversaries pretending to be legitimate protocol participants via compromised sensor nodes. Revocation protocols that function correctly in such environments are essential to secure sensor network operation. In the absence of such protocols, an adversary could effectively take control of the sensor network's operation by using compromised nodes which retain their network connectivity for extended periods of time. In our research, we defined a set of basic properties that distributed sensor-node revocation protocols must satisfy, and presented a protocol for distributed node revocation that satisfies these properties under general assumptions and a standard attacker model.

The low-cost, off-the-shelf hardware components in unshielded sensor-network nodes leave them vulnerable to compromise. With little effort, an adversary may capture nodes, analyze and replicate them, and surreptitiously insert these replicas at strategic locations within the network. Such attacks may have severe consequences; they may allow the adversary to corrupt network data or even disconnect significant parts of the network. Pervious node replication detection schemes depend primarily on centralized mechanisms with single points of failure, or on neighborhood voting protocols that fail to detect distributed replications. To address these fundamental limitations, we proposed two new algorithms based on emergent properties, i.e., properties that arise only through the collective action of multiple nodes. Randomized Multicast distributes node location information to randomly-selected witnesses, exploiting the birthday paradox to detect replicated nodes, while Line-Selected Multicast uses the topology of the network to detect replication. Both algorithms provide globally-aware, distributed node-replica detection, and Line-Selected Multicast displays particularly strong performance characteristics.

2.10 Covert Channel Attacks on MANET Routing and MAC Protocols

We have demonstrated the possibility of Covert Communication imbedded at the Network Layer (through Routing) in an Ad Hoc wireless Network. We have evaluated the performance of the Covert Channel when the routing protocol is AODV; we have shown that the covert channel is almost undetectable and is capable of transmitting information at the level of a few bits per second. We have shown that such covert communication is possible for any reactive routing protocol. In addition we have developed a superior and totally undetectable covert channel that can be implemented at the MAC layer superposed on a standard collision resolution protocol and have evaluated its performance as well.

We have also investigated Anonymous Communication in Ad Hoc Networks that can protect local membership information, provide robustness against DoS Attacks, and assist in Intrusion Detection. In parallel with the above, we have launched an investigation of sensor networks that are deployed for the purpose of detection of targets or events. We have studied distributed, centralized, and hybrid processing schemes and evaluated detection performance as well as energy consumption for both RF communication and processing. We have also evaluated the robustness of these schemes with respect to loss of nodes and measurements. Also, we have considered the possibility of sequential detection and the exploitation of correlation (spatial and temporal) among the measurements. In addition we formulated the routing issue and we have developed routing link metrics that capture residual battery levels and energy consumption as well as the effect of the routing tree structure on detection performance. We are exploring several extensions of the basic model and we are formulating alternative variants that share the same cross-layer properties as our basic model.

We have extended the investigation of Covert Communication in Ad Hoc wireless networks to the MAC Layer. We have demonstrated implementation of covert channels utilizing MAC protocols based on splitting algorithms. We have developed three different covert transmission strategies; we have evaluated their performance under different variations of the MAC protocols, we have shown that when the conservative transmission strategy is used, the covert channel is totally undetectable, and that the channel is able to transmit information at the level of 0.3 bit per slot

2.11 Vertical Protocol Integration for Enhanced Security in Wireless Sensor Networks

Making upper-layer protocol choices (MAC and routing) contingent on QoS at the physical layer can increase network robustness against threats such as jamming, denial of services, etc. In our past work, we have argued that the inherent interdependencies among protocol layers dictate the joint design across multiple layers. We have focused on the lower three layers in which these interactions are strongest. We have further focused on the resulting benefits from such integration for wireless network security and information assurance. This integration provides flexibility in designing protocols and networks.

The central thesis of our work is that flexible networking enhances significantly the capabilities of wireless networks to withstand threats. During this reporting period, we investigated the use of flexible MAC/routing protocols to enhance security of wireless sensor networks (or, more generally, any type of wireless ad hoc networks). The basic premise in this line of investigation is the exploitation of the separate degrees of freedom that MAC and routing provide for the transmission of information. In a nutshell, if the routing protocol is attacked and certain routes get congested, the MAC protocol can alleviate congestion by allocating more bandwidth to the congested nodes. Similarly, if the MAC protocol is attacked (which means some nodes are flooded with packets that block reception of desired information), the routing protocol can reroute around the congested bottlenecks. Sensor networks are especially interesting as special cases of ad hoc networks because they provide additional means of flexibility and security trade-offs.

We have focused first on the performance (i.e., the probability of correct detection) as a function of how the sensor data are processed and sent on. Specifically, we have considered the extreme case in which all the data by all sensors are sent to a single control node for processing, versus the other extreme case in which each sensor performs detection and transmits only the result of its detection. We have also considered the intermediate cases of each sensor transmitting a quantized value of its local likelihood ratio for final processing at the control node. In addition to sensing performance analysis, we are also considering the energy expenditures involved in these three options and we plan to evaluate the effectiveness of different threats on each of these alternatives.

Our method uses a novel "coloring" problem that differs from previously considered ones. Typical "coloring" problems have involved the link activation problem that minimizes the length of time needed for the transmission of given numbers of packets between pairs of nodes. Some of these problems are NP-complete and others can be solved in polynomial time. The coloring problem that results from our formulation can be viewed as a "node-group" activation problem by means of identifying sets of receivers that can be enabled simultaneously without full knowledge of the traffic demands. Our initial formulation has led to relatively straight-forward linear programs that yield time-division schedules for best "time-reuse" across the network of a given set of receiving nodes.

3. Distributed Computing Formalisms and Systems

3.1 Formal Modeling of Ad Hoc Routing Protocols for Security Analysis and Testing

Model checking routing protocols for security flaws may assist protocol designers by identifying vulnerabilities automatically. However, model checking has always suffered from the state space explosion problem as more details are added to the model. Using symbolic representations in conjunction with partial order reduction can shrink this state space in a generic fashion, however, not enough to make this approach practical. Our new approach that may be used in conjunction with those listed above derives from careful consideration of timing. The route discovery flood, and depending on the protocol, the route reply phase, contains race conditions. Since MAC protocols are nondeterministic, it is impossible to pre-determine the results of such a race. The nondeterminism can be modeled probabilistically.

We may soften the problem of model checking to require that only a specified percentage of executions is formally established, using redundancy in implementation to cover the uncertain aspects, given that this percentage is high enough. Intuitively, this should eliminate many states because there are many unlikely race outcomes. Proceeding along these ideas leads to an interesting relationship between the probability of certain causal meshes and the volume of a corresponding class of polytopes whose half-plane contstraint coefficients obey a shortest path distance matrix. A tailored version of Lasserre's dimensional recursion has been formulated, yielding faster results than available tools. We have also investigated the integration of these ideas with human in the loop theorem provers.

3.2 Dynamic and Distributed Trust for Mobile Wireless Ad-Hoc Networks

Future battlefield networks will involve thousands of heterogeneous nodes operating under rapidly changing connectivity, and resource (bandwidth, energy, computation, etc.) constraints. Mobile Ad-hoc networks (MANET) form the basis for current and future military networks. Trust and trust establishment among communicating nodes (soldiers, vehicles, UAVs, satellites) and sensor nodes is the absolute starting point for establishing any such network. The essential and unique properties of trust management in this new paradigm of wireless networking, as opposed to traditional centralized approaches are: (1) *Uncertainty* of trust value. Trust value is represented as subject probability ranging from 0 to 1; (2) *Locality* in trust information exchange; (3) *Distributed computation*.

The main ingredients of our innovative solution of the trust management problem are: (i) An efficient, resilient, distributed scheme for distributing trust evidence documents; (ii) A distributed scheme for "spreading" trust to validated nodes; (iii) A new concept of topology control that helps trust propagation (speed) and minimizes resources (number of links and bandwidth); (iv) Fundamental analytical results, backing experimental evidence of performance, based on techniques from mathematical physics of spin glasses and phase transitions and on the mathematics of dynamic cooperative games on graphs. Our goal is to build a trust computation model based only on *local interactions*, and to investigate the global effects of these interactions. We demonstrated how phase transitions (in this case they mean node transitions from non-trusted to trusted) can appear within a MANET. We linked the existence and analysis of such phase transitions to dynamic cooperative games. The cooperative game framework we developed is useful for investigating other emergent properties of MANET: route connectivity, security, resource allocation. Agents are self-interested, and usually face a frustrated interaction. Normally outcomes without cooperation are worse than those with cooperation. Thus, it is desirable to analyze rules that force all entities to cooperate. Inspiration for our analytical methods comes from the Ising and spin glass models in physics. The Ising model describes the interaction of magnetic moments or spins, where some spins seek to align (ferromagnetism), while others try to anti-align (antiferromagnetism). Inspired by the Ising model, we developed an interesting cooperative game, where nodes in the network correspond to spins and all nodes only interact with their neighbors, and where each player aims to maximize his payoff.

We analyze the effects of local interactions, which are realized by local policies in our scheme, on global features and dynamics of the system. One of the most important properties is the existence of trusted paths (i.e. paths where all nodes are trusted) between trusted sources and destinations. We analyzed trust dynamics within a MANET, i.e. how trust spreads and/or is revoked between nodes. We investigated and answered questions such as: Does trust spread to a *maximum* set of nodes? What parameters speed up or slow down this transition?

We investigated the effects of the physical and logical (trust) topologies on the performance of distributed trust schemes. The desired properties are: fast spreading and fast revocation of trust even with failing nodes. An important requirement is to achieve high performance efficiently, which in the framework of MANET translates to sparsity of the logical (trust) topology. In this context we showed that topologies with the so-called "*small world*" characteristic are the most efficient. This leads to simple schemes for controlling the trust graph topology so as to maintain this desirable characteristic. We provided interesting interpretations and properties of these topologies: Nodes few "trust" hops from each other; Scalable: local map is like global map.

3.3 Pathwise Trust Computation for MANET

Trust between nodes depends on their past interactions, and future interactions depend on established trust. However, when two nodes have had no direct interaction, they can base their trust estimates for each other on other nodes' experiences (second-hand evidence). In this way, one or more *trust paths* are formed. We modeled the situation as a weighted graph, in which edges represent direct trust relations. We captured and formalized two fundamental intuitive notions of trust: First, long trust paths are less reliable than short ones. Second, many trust paths are more reliable than just a few. Each trust relation takes into account not only the amount of trust that a node places on another, but also the amount of evidence that this estimate is based on.

Our formal model is based on a mathematical structure called a *semiring*. It allows us to model the trust relations, interpret the intuitive notions in a rigorous way, propose algorithms for the solution, and analyze their behavior when problem parameters change. We have developed two semirings that estimate the (indirect) trust relation between two nodes. The first is simpler, more bandwidth-efficient, faster, but less accurate than the second since it bases the estimates on the single best trust path available. The second uses all available information (weighted according to its importance), so the trust decision is perfectly accurate. However, it requires longer waiting times and more message exchanging. So, we have identified a tradeoff between accuracy and cost (which quantifies wireless network constraints such as limited bandwidth and energy).

We evaluated a solution that takes advantage of the good points of both semirings. We keep the information that influences the result the most. Therefore, we compute an accurate result, without wasting resources. We also placed great emphasis on the robustness of our solution, i.e. what happens when malicious nodes infiltrate the system. The scenario we used partitions the nodes into Good and Bad. Good nodes interact with other nodes (both Good and Bad) and gradually identify their one-hop neighbors correctly. Bad nodes always give the worst opinions for Good nodes, and the best opinions for other Bad nodes. As we increase the percentage of Bad nodes, we expect the situation to deteriorate but a graceful degradation is preferred to a catastrophe. What happens is that Good nodes only identify (Good and Bad) nodes that are close to them (in the trust graph). They reach no decision when it comes to nodes that are many hops away. Even when there are 90% Bad nodes, no Bad node is misidentified as Good, or vice-versa.

Our model is expressive enough to describe the trust computations of PGP. We believe that it can provide a platform for the design and comparison of various trust metrics that can potentially satisfy a number of different constraints.

3.4 Network Tomography for Dynamic Network Monitoring and Information Assurance

The fundamental problem addressed by Network Tomography is to obtain a spatio-temporal picture of a network from end-to-end views and measurements such as delay or packet loss. These measurements can be performed in an active fashion via probes or in a passive fashion (non-intrusive). The implementation can be either via unicast or multicast communications. An interesting such example problem involves using measured end-to-end delays, which can be thought of as representing distances in a graph. Another interesting example is to measure end-to-end packet loss. The problem is then: can we reconstruct the entire graph from a subset of these distances? This problem is an example of an *inverse problem.*

A repetitive application of these concepts leads to the problem of monitoring the status of a network by observations from the "edge". A realistic formulation of these problems must account for the fact that only partial information can be obtained by setting up monitors at a relatively small subset of the nodes. From these monitors, data can be collected and examined. The problem of discovering the detailed inner structure of the network from the collection of end to end measurements can be seen as a type of inverse problem, analogous to those arising in conventional tomography, but discrete this time.

One of the ways to try to understand what's going on, is to visualize the directed graph representing the network by laying it out in 3D hyperbolic space or even 2D hyperbolic space, since in these spaces the volume of a ball increases exponentially with the radius, as opposed to the familiar geometric increase of the volume of a ball in Euclidean 3-D space, respectively 2D Euclidean space. We have developed an innovative mathematical formulation of these problems using this representation of the network as embedded in the real hyperbolic plane. In this representation paths between nodes become the geodesics of the hyperbolic geometry. Thus our innovative formulation and solution methodology reinforce that the *correct* tomography to use is not the Euclidean one but that in the 2-D or 3-D real hyperbolic space.

A key objective of our research is to obtain computationally efficient algorithms for solving such inverse problems. Our approach is based on our previous work, where we have studied a classical inverse problem of partial differential equations, the Inverse Conductivity Problem, also called EIT (Electrical Impedance Tomography) in the engineering literature. Our earlier work demonstrated a close relation between tomography and EIT. For the EIT problem we have obtained a very efficient computationally solution that involved Radon Transform in hyperbolic space. The EIT problems arising out of network tomography problems are more akin to discrete electrical network inverse problems as those investigated and solved by Curtis and Morrow. Our approach combines the methods of Curtis and Morrow with our earlier tomographic methods on trees and graphs, while extending these methods to probabilistic models and situations.

3.5 Dissemination and Discovery of Information Assurance Models and Data in Wireless Networks

The proliferation of wireless technologies along with the large volume of data available online are forcing us to rethink existing data dissemination techniques and in particular for aggregate data. In addition to scalability and response time, data delivery to mobile clients with wireless connectivity must also consider energy consumption. We developed a hybrid scheduling algorithm (DV-ES) for broadcast-based data delivery of aggregate data over wireless channels. Our algorithm efficiently "packs" aggregate data for broadcast delivery and utilizes view subsumption at the mobile client, which allow for faster response times and lower energy consumption.

Object location is a major part in the operation of distributed networks. We investigated and analyzed the performance of several search methods for unstructured networks. We analyzed the performance of the algorithms relative to various metrics, giving emphasis on the success rate, bandwidth-efficiency and adaptation to dynamic network conditions. Simulation results were used to empirically evaluate the behavior of nine representative schemes under a variety of different environments. We developed the Adaptive Probabilistic Search method (APS). Other proposed search methods either depend on network-disastrous flooding and its variations or utilize indices too expensive to maintain. Our scheme utilized feedback from previous searches to probabilistically guide future ones. It performs efficient object discovery while inducing zero overhead over dynamic network operations, such as new node arrivals/departures or object relocation. Extensive simulation results show that APS achieves high success rates, increased number of discovered objects, very low bandwidth consumption and good adaptation to changing topologies.

We have developed an *Adaptive Group Notification* (*AGNO*) scheme on top of APS. *AGNO* efficiently contacts large peer populations in unstructured Peer-to-Peer networks and defines a novel implicit approach towards group membership by monitoring demand for content as this is expressed through lookup operations. Utilizing search indices, together with a small number of soft-state shortcuts, *AGNO* achieves effective and bandwidth-efficient content dissemination, without the cost and restrictions of a membership protocol. The method achieves high-success content transmission at a cost at least two times smaller than other proposed techniques for unstructured networks.

4. Publications

1. J.S. Baras and M. Rabi, "Intrusion Detection with Support vector Machines and Generative Models", *Proc. of 5th Information Security Conference*, ISC 2002, LNCS Vol. 2433, pp. 32-47.

2. J.S. Baras, A.A. Cardenas and V. Ramezani, "On-Line Detection of Distributed Attacks from Space-Time Network Flow Patterns" , *Proceedings of 23rd Army Science Conference*, Orlando, Florida, December 2-5, 2002. This paper received the **Best Paper Award** *in IT/C4ISR* (Information Technology, Information Technology/Command, Control, Communications, Computers, Intelligence, Surveillance and Reconnaissance) at the 23rd Army Science Conference.

3. V.R. Ramezani, Shah-An Yang and J.S. Baras, "Finite Automata Models for Anomaly Detection", *Proceedings of 37th Conference on Information Sciences and Systems*, Johns Hopkins University, Baltimore, Maryland, March 12-14, 2003.

4. A.A. Cardenas, J. S. Baras and V. Ramezani, "Distributed Change Detection for Worms, DDoS and other Network Attacks", invited paper, *Proceedings of the 2004 American Control Conference (ACC04)*, Volume 2 pages 1008-1013, Boston, MA, June 30 - July 2, 2004.

5. S. Radosavac and J. S. Baras, "Detection and Classification of Network Intrusions Using Hidden Markov Models," *Proc. of 37th Conference on Information Sciences and Systems (CISS)*, Baltimore, March 2003.

6. S. Radosavac, J. S. Baras and N. Benammar, "Cross-Layer Attacks in Wireless Ad Hoc Networks", *Proceedings of the 38th Annual Conference on Information Sciences and Systems (CISS 2004)*, pp. 1266-1271, Princeton, New Jersey, March 17-19, 2004

7. J. Baras and S. Radosavac, "Attacks and Defenses Utilizing Cross-Layer Interactions in MANET," *Workshop on Cross-Layer Issues in the Design of Tactical Mobile Ad Hoc Wireless Networks: Integration of Communication and Networking Functions to Support Optimal Information Management*, June 2–3, 2004, Naval Research Laboratory, Washington, DC.

8. A. A. Cardenas, S. Radosavac and J. S. Baras, "Detection and Prevention of MAC Layer Misbehavior for Ad Hoc Networks," *Proceedings of the 2004 ACM Workshop on Security of Ad Hoc and Sensor Networks (SASN'04),* pp. 17-22, Washington, DC, October 25, 2004.

9. S. Radosavac, J. S. Baras and I. Koutsopoulos, "A Framework for MAC Protocol Misbehavior Detection in Wireless Networks", *Proceedings of ACM Workshop on Wireless Security (WiSe 2005)*, Cologne, Germany, September 2, 2005..

10. S. Radosavac, K. Seamon and J. S. Baras, "bufSTAT – A Tool for Early Detection and Classification of Buffer Overflow Attacks", *Proceedings of the First IEEE/Createnet SecureCom 2005,* Athens, Greece, September 5-9, 2005.

11. G. Theodorakopoulos and J. S. Baras, "On Trust Models and Trust Evaluation Metrics for Ad-Hoc Networks", accepted by *IEEE Journal of Selected Areas in Communications, special issue on Security in Wireless Ad-Hoc Networks,* June 2005.

12. G. Theodorakopoulos, J. S. Baras, "Trust Evaluation in Ad-Hoc Networks", *Proceedings of ACM Workshop on Wireless Security (WiSe 2004),* pp. 1-10, Philadelphia, Pennsylvania, October 1, 2004. (**Best Paper Award**).

13. M. Karir, J. S. Baras, "LES: Layered Encryption Security", *Proceedings of the 3rd International Conference on Networking (ICN'04),* pp. 382-388, Gosier, Guadeloupe, French Caribbean, February 29 – March 4, 2004.

14. Roy-Chowdhury, J. S. Baras, "Framework for IP Multicast Routing in Satellite ATM Networks", *Proceedings of 22nd AIAA International Communication Satellite Systems Conference & Exhibit 2004, (ICSSC),* Monterey, California, May 9-12, 2004.

15. Roy-Chowdhury, J. S. Baras, " Key Management for Secure Multicast in Hybrid Satellite Networks", *Proceedings of the 18th International Information Security Conference (IFIP/SEC 2004), Security and Protection in Information Processing Systems,* pp. 533-548, August 23-26, 2004.

16. L. Eschenauer, V. Gligor and J. S. Baras, "On Trust Establishment in Mobile Ad-Hoc Networks", *Proc. 10th International Workshop on Security Protocols*, April 2002, Cambridge, UK; in *Security Protocols*, Lecture Notes in Computer Science, Springer, 2003.

17. L. Eschenauer, J. S. Baras and V. Gligor, ``Distributed Trust Establishment in MANETs: Swarm Intelligence," *CTA Conference,* April 29 - May 1, 2003, pp. 125-129.

18. T. Jiang, J.S. Baras, "Ant-based Adaptive Trust Evidence Distribution in MANET", *Proceedings of MDC'04,* pp. 4392-4396, Tokyo, Japan, March 23-26, 2004.

19. J. S. Baras and T. Jiang, "Cooperative Games, Phase Transitions on Graphs and Distributed Trust In MANET", invited paper, in *Proc of 2004 IEEE Conference on Decision and Control,* Dec. 2004.

20. J.S. Baras and T. Jiang, "Dynamic and Distributed Trust for Mobile Ad-Hoc Networks", in *Proc. 24th Army Science Conference*, Orlando, Florida, Nov. 2004.

21. J. S. Baras and T. Jiang, "Managing Trust in Self-organized Mobile Adhoc Networks", invited paper, *Proc. Wireless and Mobile Security Workshop, Network and Distributed Systems Security Symposium*, February 2005, San Diego, USA.

22. T. Jiang and J. S. Baras, "Autonomous Trust Establishment", *Proc. 2nd International Network Optimization Conference (INOC)*, February 2005, Lisbon, Portugal.

23. J. S. Baras and T. Jiang, "Cooperation, Trust and Games in Wireless Networks", invited paper, in *Proceedings of Symposium on Systems, Control and Networks*, honoring Professor P. Varaiya, Birkhauser, June 2005.

24. A. A. Cardenas, N. Benammar, G. Papageorgiou and J.S. Baras, "Cross-Layered Security Analysis of Wireless Ad-Hoc Networks", *Proc. 24th Army Science Conference* , Orlando, Florida, Nov. 2004.

25. S. Yang and J.S. Baras, *"TORA, Verification, Proofs and Model Checking", Proceedings of WiOpt '03: Modeling and Optimization in Mobile, AdHoc and Wireless Networks*, Sophia-Antipolis, France, March 3-5, 2003.

26. S. Yang, J.S. Baras, "Correctness Proof for a Dynamic Adaptive Routing Algorithm for Mobile Ad-hoc Networks" *Proceedings of IFAC Workshop – Modeling and Analysis of Logic Controlled Dynamic Systems,* Irkutsk , Lake Baikal, Russia, July 30 – August 1, 2003.

27. S. Yang and J. S. Baras, "Modeling Vulnerabilities of Ad Hoc Routing Protocols," *Proceedings of the SASN 2003 Conference*, George Mason University, Fairfax, Virginia, October 31, 2003.

28. L. Eschenauer and V. Gligor, "A Key-Management Scheme for Distributed Sensor Networks," *Proceedings of the 9th ACM Conference on Computer and Communications Security*, pp. 41-47, ACM Press, 2002.

29. H. Chan, A. Perrig, V. Gligor and G. Muralidharan, "On the Distribution and Revocation of Cryptographic Keys in Sensor Networks", to appear in *IEEE Trans. On Dep. And Secure Computations*, 2005.

30. B. Parno, A. Perrig and V. Gligor, "Distributed Detection of Node Replication Attacks in Sensor Networks", to appear in *IEEE Journal on Security and Privacy*, 2005.

31. H. Chan, G. Muralidharan, V. Gligor, and A. Perrig, "On the Distribution and Revocation of Keys in Sensor Networks," invited paper, for the Inaugural Issue of the *IEEE Transactions on Dependable and Secure Computing*.

32. A. Perrig, G. Muralidharan and V. Gligor, "On the Distribution and Revocation of Hyptographic Keys in Sensor Networks," to appear in *IEEE Transaction on Dependable and Secure Computing*.

33. B. Parno, A. Perrig and V. Gligor, "Distributed Detection of Node Replication Attacks in Sensor Networks," *Proceedings of the 2005 IEEE Symposium on Security and Privacy (IEEE S&P 2005)*, pp. 49-63, Oakland, California, May 8-11, 2005.

34. I. Haitner, O. Horvitz, J. Katz, C.Y. Koo, R. Morselli, and R.Shaltiel, "Reducing Complexity Assumptions for Statistically-Hiding Commitment", *Proceedings Eurocrypt 2005*.

35. O. Horvitz and J. Katz, "Lower Bounds on the Efficiency of 'Black-Box' Commitment Schemes," *Proc. of International Colloquium on Automata, Languages, and Programming (ICALP) 2005*.

36. C. A. Berenstein and S-Y. Chung, "*w*-Harmonic Functions and Inverse Conductivity Problems on Networks," *SIAM J. Appl. Math.* 65, 2005, no. 4, 1200-1226.

37. J. Baras, C. A. Berenstein and F. Gavilánez, "Continuous and Discrete Inverse Conductivity Problems," *AMS, Contemporary Math*, Vol. 362, pp. 33-51, June 2004.

38. J. Baras, C. A. Berenstein and F. Gavilánez, "Network Tomography," *Proceedings of 2004 AMS meeting at Ryder Univ., Special Session on Tomography*, to appear in Contemporary Math.

39. Y. Sismanis, A. Deligiannakis, N. Roussopoulos, and Y. Kotidis, "Dwarf: Shrinking the PetaCube", Proc. of *ACM SIGMOD International Conference on Management of Data*, June 3-6 2002, pp.464-475.

40. Y. Sismanis, A. Deligiannakis, Y. Kotidis and N. Roussopoulos, "Hierarchical Dwarfs for the Roll-Up Cube," In Proc. of the *DOLAP Workshop* (held in conjunction with ACM CIKM'03), New Orleans, LA, USA, November 2003.

41. M. A. Sharaf, Y. Sismanis, A. Labrinidis, P. K. Chrysanthis and N. Roussopoulos, "Efficient Dissemination of Aggregate Data over the Wireless Web," In Proc. of the *Sixth International Workshop on the Web and Databases* (held in conjunction with ACM SIGMOD'03), June 12-13 2003, San Diego, CA, USA.

42. D. Tsoumakos and N. Roussopoulos, "Adaptive Probabilistic Search for Peer-to-Peer Networks," in Proc. of the 3rd *IEEE International Conference on P2P Computing*, Sept 1-3 2003, Linkoping, Sweden.

43. D. Tsoumakos and N. Roussopoulos: "A Comparison of Peer-to-Peer Search Methods," in Proc. of the *Sixth International Workshop on the Web and Databases* (held in conjunction with ACM SIGMOD'03), June 12-13 2003, San Diego, CA, USA

44. Y. Sismanis and N. Roussopoulos, "The Polynomial Complexity of Fully Materialized Coalesced Cubes," in *Proc. 30th International Conference on Very Large Databases, Toronto,* August 29th-September 3rd, 2004.

45. D. Tsoumakos and N. Roussopoulos, "A Framework for Sharing Voluminous Content in P2P Systems," in *Proc. 2004 International MultiConference in Computer Science & Computer Engineering,* Las Vegas, Nevada, June 21-24, 2004.

46. S. Kantere and D. Tsoumakos and N. Roussopoulos, "Querying Structured Data in an Unstructured P2P System," *Proceedings of the 6th ACM International Workshop on Web Information and Data Management* (WIDM 2004), November 12-13, 2004, Washington, DC, USA.

47. D. Tsoumakos and N. Roussopoulos, "AGNO: An Adaptive Group Communication Scheme for Unstructured P2P Networks," to appear in *Proc. of 2005 Euro-Par Conference.*

48. K. Bitsakos, D. Tsoumakos, N. Roussopoulos and Y. Aloimonos, "A Framework for Distributed Human Tracking," to appear in *Proc. of the 2005 International Conference on Parallel and Distributed Processing Techniques and Applications (PDPTA'05).*

49. L. Yu and A. Ephremides, "Detection Performance and Energy Efficiency Trade-off in a Sensor Network," *Proceedings 41st Annual Allerton Conference on Communication, Control, and Computing,* Monticello, Illinois, October 2004.

50. A. Ephremides and L. Yu, "Detection, Energy, and Robustness in Wireless Sensor Networks," invited paper, *Proceedings of Mobwiser*, Singapore, March 2004.

51. S. Li and A. Ephremides, "A Covert Channel in MAC Protocols Based on Splitting Algorithms", invited paper, in *Proceeding of 43rd IEEE Wireless Communication and Networking Conference(WCNC)*, 2005, New Orleans, LA USA.

52. S. Li and A. Ephremides, "A Network Layer Covert Channel in Ad-hoc Wireless Networks", in *Proceedings of 1st IEEE Communications Society Conference on Sensor and Ad Hoc Communications and Network(SECON)*, Santa Clara, CA, October 2004.

53. Y. Sun, W. Trappe, and K. J. R. Liu, "An Efficient Key Management Scheme for Secure Wireless Multicast," in *Proc. 2002 IEEE Int. Conference on Communications*, Vol 2, pp. 1236-1240, April 2002, New York City.

54. W. Trappe, Y. Wang, and K.J.R. Liu, "Establishment of Conference Keys in Heterogeneous Networks", *Proc of 2002 IEEE International Conference on Communications*, ICC 2002., Vol. 4 , pp. 2201 -2205.

55. B. Sun, W. Trappe, Y. Sun, and K.J.R. Liu, "A Time-Efficient Contributory Key Agreement Scheme for Secure Group Communications", *Proc of 2002 IEEE International Conference on Communications*, ICC 2002., Vol. 2, pp. 1159 -1163.

56. M. Wu and Y. Mao, "Communication-Friendly Encryption of Multimedia," *Proc. IEEE Multimedia Signal Processing Workshop (MMSP'02)*, St. Thomas, U.S. Virgin Islands, Dec. 2002.

57. W. Trappe, M. Wu, Z.J. Wang, K.J.R. Liu, "Anti-collusion Fingerprinting for Multimedia", *IEEE Transactions on Signal Processing*, Volume: 51 Issue: 4 , Apr 2003, Page(s): 1069 -1087

58. W. Trappe, J. Song, R. Poovendran, and K.J.R. Liu, "Key Management and Distribution for Secure Multimedia Multicast," *IEEE Trans. on Multimedia*, Vol. 5, No. 4, pp.544-557, Dec 2003.

59. Yan Sun, and K.J. Ray Liu, "Securing Dynamic Group Membership Information over Multicast: Attacks and Immunization", in Proc. *IEEE GLOBECOM,* San Francisco, CA, Dec. 2003.

60. Yan Sun, Wade Trappe, and K.J. Ray Liu, "Topology-aware Key Management Schemes for Wireless Multicast", in Proc. *IEEE GLOBECOM,* San Francisco, CA, Dec. 2003.

61. Yan Sun, and K.J. Ray Liu, "Multi-layer Management for Secure Multimedia Multicast Communications", in Proc. *IEEE International conferences on Multimedia and Expo (ICME'03)*, vol. II, pp 205-208, Baltimore, MD, July 2003.

62. Y. Sun, and K. J. Ray Liu, "Securing Dynamic Membership Information in Multicast Communications", in *Proc. IEEE INFOCOM'04*, Hong Kong, March 2004.

63. Sun, and K. J. Ray Liu, "Scalable Hierarchical Access Control in Secure Group Communications", in *Proc. IEEE INFOCOM'04*, Hong Kong, March 2004.

64. Y. Mao, Y. Sun, M. Wu and K. J. Ray Liu, "Dynamic Join and Exit Amortization and Scheduling for Time-Efficient Group Key Agreement", in *Proc. IEEE INFOCOM'04*, Hong Kong, March 2004.

65. Y. Sun, W. Trappe, and K. J. R. Liu, "A Scalable Multicast Key Management Scheme for Heterogeneous Wireless Networks," *IEEE/ACM Transactions on Networking*, Vol. 12, No. 4, pp. 653-666, August 2004.

66. W. Trappe, Y. Wang, and K.J.R. Liu, "Resource-Aware Conference Key Establishment for Heterogeneous Networks," *IEEE/ACM Trans. on Networking*, vol 13, no 1, pp.134-146, Feb 2005.

67. W. Yu and K.J.R. Liu, "Attack-Resistant Cooperation Stimulation in Autonomous Ad Hoc Networks", a*ccepted by IEEE JSAC special issue on Autonomic Communication Systems, June 2005.*

68. W. Yu, Y. Sun and K.J.R. Liu, "HADOF: Defense Against Routing Disruptions in Mobile Ad Hoc Networks", *Proc. IEEE INFOCOM'05*, Miami, March 2005.

69. Y. Sun, W. Yu, Z. Han and K. J.R. Liu, "Information Theoretic Framework of Trust Modeling and Evaluation for Ad Hoc Networks", *accepted by IEEE JSAC special issue on Security in Wireless Ad Hoc Networks,* June 2005.

70. Y. Mao, Y. Sun, M. Wu, and K. J.R. Liu, "Join-Exit Scheduling for Contributory Group Key Agreement", accepted by *IEEE/ACM Transactions on Networking*, May 2005.

71. Y. Hwang and H. C. Papadopoulos, "Partial-encryption analysis of a class of pseudo-chaotic spread spectrum systems," in *Proc. 40th Allerton Conf. on Comm. Control Comput*, Sep. 2002.

72. Y. Hwang and H. C. Papadopoulos, "Physical-layer secrecy with DS/SS from piecewise linear chaotic Markov maps: analysis and design," in *Proc. IEEE Wireless Commun. Net. Conf.*, pp. 642-647, March 2003.

73. Y. Hwang and H. C. Papadopoulos, "Physical-layer Secrecy in AWGN Via a Class of Chaotic {DS/SS} Systems: Analysis and Design," accepted for publication *in IEEE Trans. Signal Processing 2004.*

74. Y. Hwang and H. C. Papadopoulos, "Physical-layer Secrecy with Chaotic DS/SS: Unintended Receiver Performance Analysis and System Design," in Proc. 2004 *IEEE Int. Conf. Communications (ICC), June 2004.*

75. Y. Hwang and H. C. Papadopoulos, "Private Communication over Fading Channels with Chaotic DS/SS," in Proc. 2004 *IEEE Int. Conf. Acoust. Speech, Signal Processing (ICASSP), pp. 957-960, May 2004.*

76. D. S. Scherber and H. C. Papadopoulos, "Locally Constructed Algorithms for Distributed Computations in Ad-hoc Networks," in Proc. 2004 *Conf. Inform. Proc. Sens. Net. (IPSN).*

77. T. Pham, D. S. Scherber, and H. C. Papadopoulos, "Distributed Source Localization Algorithms for Acoustic Ad-hoc Sensor Networks," in Proc. *IEEE SAM'2004 Workshop.*

A Key Management Scheme for Distributed Sensor Networks

Laurent Eschenauer and Virgil D. Gligor

Electrical and Computer Engineering Department

University of Maryland, College Park, MD. 20742

{laurent, gligor}@eng.umd.edu

Abstract — Distributed Sensor Networks (DSNs) are ad-hoc, mobile, networks that include sensor nodes with very limited computation, memory and communication capabilities. DSNs are dynamic in the sense that they allow addition and deletion of sensor nodes after deployment to grow the network or replace failing and unreliable nodes. DSNs may be deployed in hostile areas where communication is monitored and nodes are subject to capture and surreptitious use by an adversary. Hence DSNs require cryptographic protection of communications and sensor-capture detection, sensor disabling, and key revocation. In this paper, we present a key management scheme designed to satisfy both the operational and the security requirements of DSNs. The scheme includes selective distribution and revocation of keys to sensor nodes as well as node re-keying, and requires neither on-line, trusted authorities nor substantial communication, computation, and memory capabilities. It relies on probabilistic key sharing among the nodes of a random graph and uses simple, secure shared-key discovery and path-key establishment protocols for key distribution, revocation, re-keying, and incremental additions of nodes. The security and network connectivity characteristics supported by the key management scheme are discussed and simulation experiments presented.

Index Terms— distributed sensor networks, key distribution and revocation, node re-keying, connectivity of random graphs, secure shared-key discovery, path-key establishment.

I. INTRODUCTION

Distributed Sensor Networks (DSNs) share several characteristics with the more traditional embedded wireless networks [11]. Both include: arrays of sensor nodes that are battery powered, have limited computational capabilities and memory, rely on intermittent wireless communication via radio frequency and, possibly, optical links; data-collection nodes that cache sensor data and make it available for processing to application components of the network; control nodes that monitor the status of and broadcast simple commands to sensor nodes; and some mobile nodes (e.g., data collection and control nodes placed on humans, vehicles, aircraft). However, DSNs differ from the traditional embedded wireless networks in several important areas, namely: their scale is orders of magnitude larger than that of embedded wireless networks (e.g., tens of thousands as opposed to just tens of sensor nodes); they are dynamic in the sense that they allow addition and deletion of sensor nodes after deployment to grow the network or replace failing and unreliable nodes without physical contact; and they may be deployed in hostile areas where communication is monitored and sensor nodes are subject to capture and manipulation by an adversary. These challenging operational requirements place equally challenging security constraints on DSN design. (For a detailed analysis of the operational and security constraints of DSNs, the reader is referred to the work of Carman, Kruus and Matt [3].)

Communication Security Constraints. The extreme power, computational and memory limitations of sensor nodes we are considering for large-scale DSNs preclude the use of some of the traditional cryptographic tools for securing network communication. For example, the implementation of the Smart Dust project [5,8] uses sensors that have only 8Kb of program memory and 512 bytes for the data memory, and processors with 32 8-bit general registers that run at 4 MHz and 3.0V, such as the ATMEL 90LS8535. For such DSNs, asymmetric (public-key) cryptosystems and random-number are impractical since they are computationally intensive and consume a significant amount of power. Use of symmetric-key ciphers, low-power encryption modes, and hash functions becomes the only viable means of protecting communication against DSN adversaries; e.g., on limited-capability processors, block ciphers and hash functions are three to four order of magnitude faster than asymmetric operations, such as digital signatures [6].

Although sensor nodes trust each other, physical capture of, and tampering with, a sensor node or a subset of nodes by an adversary is possible due to their ad-hoc deployment in hostile areas. This requires that tamper-detection technologies [7,13] be used to shield sensors such that detection of physical sensor manipulation disables a sensor's operation and erases its keys. Furthermore, active manipulation of a captured sensor's data inputs by an adversary must be detectable. However, since the captured sensor nodes may not necessarily communicate in an erratic or anomalous manner, traditional anomaly detection techniques may not apply. Detecting a sensor's data input manipulation may require data correlation analysis and anomaly detection, possibly off-line, by collection and processing nodes. While such analysis can detect active insertion of bogus data by an adversary, it requires redundant sensor coverage of deployment areas and, hence, sufficient sensor-node density in the DSN.

Key Management Constraints. Traditional Internet style key exchange and key distribution protocols based on infrastructures using trusted third parties are also ruled out by sensor-node processing limitations, unknown network topology, intermittent sensor-node operation, network scale and dynamics. To date, the only practical options for the distribution of keys to sensor nodes of large-scale DSNs whose physical topology is unknown prior to deployment would have to rely on *key pre-distribution.* Keys would have to be installed in sensor nodes to accommodate secure connectivity between nodes. However, traditional key pre-distribution offers two inadequate solutions: either a single *mission key* or a set of separate *n-1 keys*, each being pair-wise privately shared with another node, must be installed in every sensor node.

The single mission-key solution is inadequate because the capture of any sensor node may compromise the entire DSN since selective key revocation is impossible upon sensor-capture detection. In contrast, the pair-wise private sharing of keys between every two sensor nodes avoids the wholesale DSN compromise upon node capture since selective key revocation becomes possible. However, this solution requires pre-distribution and storage of n-1 keys in each sensor node, and n(n-1)/2 per DSN, which renders it impractical for large-scale DSNs using, say, more than 10,000 nodes, for both intrinsic and technological reasons. First, pair-wise private key sharing between any two sensor nodes would be unusable since such connectivity is achievable only in small node neighborhoods delimited by wireless communication ranges and sensor density (e.g., of the order of tens of nodes but not tens of thousands). Second, incremental addition and deletion as well as re-keying of sensor nodes would become both expensive

and complex as they would require multiple keying messages to be broadcast network-wide to all nodes during their non-sleep periods (i.e., one broadcast message for every added/deleted node or re-key operation). Third, storing *n-1* keys would push sensor-memory limits for the foreseeable future, even if only short, 64-bit, keys are used,[1] and would complicate fast key erasure upon detection of physical sensor tampering.

Our Approach. We propose a simple key pre-distribution scheme that requires memory storage for only few tens to a couple of hundred keys, and yet has similar security and superior operational properties compared to those of the pair-wise private key-sharing scheme. Our scheme relies on probabilistic key sharing among the nodes of a random graph and uses a simple secure shared-key discovery protocol for key distribution, revocation and node re-keying. We distribute a ring of keys to each sensor node, each key ring consisting of randomly chosen k keys from a very large pool of P keys, which is generated off-line, prior to DSN deployment. Because of the random choice of keys on key rings, a shared key may not exist between some pairs of nodes. Although two nodes may or may not share a key, if a path of nodes sharing pair-wise private keys exists between the two nodes at network initialization, the two nodes can use that path to exchange a key that will establish a direct link. We use random graph analysis and simulation to show that what really matters in key pre-distribution is the shared-key connectivity of the resulting network. Therefore, full shared-key connectivity offered by pair-wise private key sharing between every two nodes becomes unnecessary. For example, we show that to establish "almost certain" shared-key connectivity for a 10,000-node network, a key ring of only 250 keys have to be pre-distributed to every sensor node where the keys were drawn out of a pool of 100,000 keys, leaving a substantial number of keys available for DSN expansion (viz., Sections III and IV). We also show that the security characteristics of probabilistic key distribution and revocation based on random graphs are suitable for solving the key management problem of DSNs.

Related Work. Symmetric key pre-distribution has been used in past research, but with a focus on group and broadcast communication. For group communication [1,2], this research tries to accommodate any set of up to k users while being secure against collusion of some of

---

[1] Adding approximately 64K-bit *key* memories to sensors of large-scale DSNs may become feasible in a couple sensor-node generations from now.

them. Pre-distribution is used to alleviate the cost of communication between group members and to setup a common secret key; however, memory constraints are not placed on group members. Other work on broadcast encryption [4] focuses on key distribution to support broadcast communication between slave nodes and a master node – an impractical approach for DSNs.

II. OVERVIEW OF THE BASIC SCHEME

In this section, we present the basic features of our scheme, deferring its analysis for the next section.

A. Key Distribution

In our scheme, key distribution consists of three phases, namely key pre-distribution, shared-key discovery, and path-key establishment.

The *key pre-distribution* phase of our scheme consists of five off-line steps, namely generation of a very large pool of P keys and of their key identifiers; random drawing of k keys out of P without replacement to establish the key ring of a sensor; loading of the key ring into the memory of each sensor; saving of the key identifiers of a key ring and associated sensor identifier on a trusted control node; and for each node, loading the *i*th controller with the key shared with that node. (Note that the key shared by a node with the *i*th controller, K^{ci}, can be computed as $K^{ci} = E_{Kx}(ci)$, where $Kx = K_1 \oplus, ..., \oplus K_k$), K_i are the keys of the node's key ring, ci is the controller's identity, and E_{Kx} denotes encryption with node key Kx. Hence, the keys shared by a node with controllers, which are only infrequently used, need not take any space on the key ring.) As shown in the next section, the key pre-distribution phase ensures that only a small number of keys need to be placed on each sensor node's key ring to ensure that any two nodes share (at least) a key with a chosen probability. For example, for 0.5 probability only 75 keys drawn out of a pool of 10,000 keys need to be on any key ring.

The *shared-key discovery* phase takes place during DSN initialization in the operational environment where every node discovers its neighbors in wireless communication range with which it shares keys. In this phase, every node broadcasts a short, securely encoded message to its neighbors in wireless range and each node decodes every other node's message in a secure manner to discover the shared keys.[2] We adapt a method by

Trappe et al. [9,12] for secure re-keying in broadcast groups to the secure shared-key discovery (viz., Appendix A). To discover its keys shared with its neighbors, each node X computes two B-bit random seeds μ_1 and μ_2 which, unlike in the original proposal, need not be random. Then, node X broadcasts a *hello* message that contains random seeds μ_1, μ_2 and parameter α, where

$$\alpha = \mu_2 + \prod_{i=1}^{k} f(K_i^X, \mu_1),$$

K_i^X, i= 1,...,k, are the keys present on node X's key ring, and function f is a public *parametric one-way function*. Note that the use of the parametric one-way function does not reveal any of the keys used in the *hello* message. All nodes neighboring X in wireless communication range compute

$$\mu'_2(j) = \alpha \pmod{f(K_j, \mu_1)}$$

for all K_j, j= 1,...,k, on their own key ring. If a key K_j on a neighbor's key ring matches one of node X's keys K_i, the computation of $\alpha \pmod{f(K_j, \mu_1)}$ produces a value $\mu'_2(j)$ that would match the received seed μ_2. Therefore, a neighboring node of X would know that its key K_j for which the computation of α produced the correct μ_2 is shared with the node X. The cost of shared-key discovery is k times the cost of one f computation plus one modular division and is small because the size of a key ring, k, is small (viz., analysis of Section III).

The shared-key discovery phase establishes the topology of the sensor array as seen by the routing layer of the DSN. A *link* exists between two sensor nodes only if they share a key; and if a link exists between two nodes, all communication on that link is secured by link encryption. Note that it is possible that the same key is shared by more than a pair of sensor nodes, since the key rings consist of keys drawn randomly from the same pool. This does not cause a link-security exposure because, in normal mode of operation sensor nodes trust each other and, during the revocation phase following node-capture detection, revocation of a captured node's key ring ensures that the small set of (k) keys on that ring are removed network-wide. (Potential damage caused by sensor node capture is limited to the feeding of bogus data to that sensor node's inputs since common tamper-detection shielding of each node is assumed to ensure key-ring erasure.)

The *path-key establishment* phase assigns a *path-key* to selected pairs of sensor nodes in wireless communication range that do not share a key but are connected by two or more (i.e., a path of) links at the end of the shared-key discovery phase. Path keys need

---

[2] The simplest way for any two nodes to discover if they share a key is that each node broadcast, in clear text, the list of identifiers of the keys on their key ring. The drawback of this simple approach is that if an attacker captures a node, the attacker knows immediately which link he can decrypt and which links he cannot.

not be generated by sensor nodes. The design of the DSN ensures that, after the shared-key discovery phase is finished, a number of keys on a key ring are left unassigned to any link. For example, both analysis (Section III) and simulations (Section IV) show that even without special provisioning a substantial number of keys are left unused on key rings. Provisioning for sufficient ring keys that are left unassigned by the determination of key-ring size (k) can also anticipate both the effects of revocation and those of incremental addition of new sensor nodes, since both may require the execution of the path key establishment phase after shared-key discovery. The analysis and simulations presented in the next sections indicates that such provisioning is especially simple.

B. Revocation

Whenever a node is detected as being compromised it is essential to be able to revoke the entire key ring of that node. To effect revocation, a controller node (which has a large communication range and may be mobile) broadcasts a single revocation message containing signed list of k key identifiers for the key ring to be revoked followed by the random seed μ and α. (We use the same secure scheme as that of Trappe *et al.* briefly presented in Appendix A.) To sign the list of key identifiers, the controller generates a key K_e and α:

$$\alpha = K_e + \prod_{i=1}^{n} f(K_i, \mu),$$

where the K_i are unique, randomly chosen, secret keys shared by the controller with each sensor node n_i during key pre-distribution phase. Each sensor node can obtain key K_e to verify the signature on the key identifier list by computing:

$$\alpha \,(\text{mod } f(K_i,\mu)\,) = K_e.$$

Note that the cost of obtaining the signature key is a single network-wide broadcast of a short, $k+2$ word message[3] during the non-sleep period of each node. The computation cost is similar to that for shared-key discovery operation.

After obtaining the signature key, each node verifies the signature of the signed list of key identifiers, locates those identifiers in its key ring, and removes the corresponding keys (if any). Once the keys are removed from key rings, some links may disappear, and the affected nodes need to reconfigure those links by restarting the shared-key discovery and, possibly path-key establishment, phase for them. Because only k out of

P keys are removed from the pool for every revoked node, revocation affects only a few other nodes and a small part of their key ring but it disables all connectivity of the compromised node.

C. Incremental Addition of Sensor Nodes

In our scheme, the incremental addition of sensor nodes is especially simple. That is, a new node has a key ring of k keys drawn from the same pool of P random keys loaded. Then its keys shared with the controller nodes K^{ci} are securely multicast to the controller nodes (via a similar scheme as that used by each controller to broadcast its signature key used at revocation, as discussed above) and the node is deployed. Finally, the node simply initiates shared-key discovery and, possibly path-key establishment. Network-wide broadcasts are unnecessary.

D. Re-Keying

Although it is anticipated that in most DSNs the lifetime of a key shared between two nodes exceeds that of the two nodes, it is possible that in some cases the lifetime of keys expires and re-keying must take place. Re-keying is equivalent with a self-revocation of a key by a node. As such, it does not involve any network-wide broadcast message from a controller and, hence, is especially simple. After expired-key removal, the affected nodes restart the shared-key discovery and, possibly path key establishment, phase.

E. Effect of Compromising Unshielded Sensor Nodes

Although we assume tamper-detection, sensor-node shielding that erases the keys of captured nodes, we note that our key distribution scheme is more robust than the those based on a single mission key or on pair-wise private sharing of keys even in the face of physical attacks against captured unshielded sensor nodes. In such attacks, an adversary can obtain access to a sensor's keys, and then both eavesdrop on and insert bogus messages in DSN communication. In the single mission key scheme, *all* communication links are compromised, whereas in the pair-wise private key sharing, all $n-1$ links to the captured unshielded node are compromised. In contrast, in our scheme only the $k \ll n$ keys of a single ring are obtained, which means that the attacker has a probability of approximately k/P to attack successfully any DSN link (viz., simulation results of Section IV). The node's shared keys with controllers could also be re-created by the adversary, but this does not affect any other sensor nodes.

---

[3] The alternative of broadcasting n identical lists of k identifiers encrypted in n different node keys shared with the controller would be substantially more expensive.

III. ANALYSIS

A. DSN Connectivity with Random Graphs

The limits of the wireless communication ranges of sensor nodes, not just the security considerations, preclude use of DSNs that are fully connected by shared-key links between all sensor nodes. Moreover, it is unnecessary for the shared-key discovery phase to guarantee full connectivity for a sensor node with all its neighbors in wireless communication range, as long as multi-link paths of shared keys exist among neighbors that can be used to setup a path key as needed. We use these two observations and the requirement for shared-key provisioning for new links suggested by incremental network growth, revocation and re-keying, and to establish DSN connectivity requirements based on random graph connectivity properties.

Let p be the probability that a shared key exists between two sensor nodes, n be the number of network nodes, and $d = p*(n-1)$ the degree of a node (i.e., the number of edges connecting that node with its graph neighbors). In particular, to establish the DSN shared-key connectivity, we need to answer the following two questions:

- what should the degree of a node, d, be so that a DSN of n nodes is connected? and,

- given d and the neighborhood connectivity constraints imposed by wireless communication (e.g., the number of nodes n' in a neighborhood), what values should the key ring size, k, and pool, P, have for a network of size n? In particular, if memory capacity of each sensor limits the key ring size to a given value of k, what should the size of the key pool, P, be?

Random graph theory helps answer the first question. A random graph G(n, p) is a graph of n nodes for which the probability that a link exists between two nodes is p. When p is zero the graph does not have any edge, while for p equals one, the graph is fully connected. The first question of interest to us is what is the value of p for which it is "almost certainly true" that the graph is connected.

Erdős and Rényi [10] showed that for monotone properties, there exists a value of p such that the property moves from "nonexistent" to "certainly true" in a very large random graph. The function defining p is called the *threshold function* of a property. For the property "the graph is connected," the threshold function P_c is:

$$Pc = \lim_{n \to \infty} \Pr[G(n,p) \text{ is connected}] = e^{-e^{-c}}$$

where

$$p = \frac{\ln n}{n} + \frac{c}{n}, \text{ and } c \text{ is any real constant.}$$

Therefore, given n we can find p and $d = p*(n-1)$ for which the resulting graph is connected with a desired probability P_c.

Figure 1 illustrates the plot of the degree of a node, d, as a function of the network size, n, for various values of Pc. This figure shows that, to increase the probability that a random graph is connected by one order, the degree of a node only increases by 2. Moreover, the curves of this plot are almost flat when n is large, indicating that the size of the network has insignificant impact on the degree of a node required to have a connected graph.

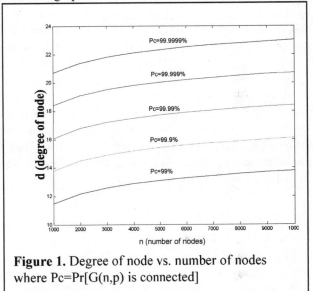

Figure 1. Degree of node vs. number of nodes where Pc=Pr[G(n,p) is connected]

To answer the second question above, we note that the wireless connectivity constraints may limit neighborhoods to $n' \ll n$ nodes, which implies that the probability of sharing a key between any two nodes in a neighborhood becomes $p' = d/(n'-1) \gg p$. Hence, we set the probability that two nodes share at least one key in their key rings of size k chosen from a given pool of P keys to p' and then derive P as a function of k. This derivation takes into account that the size of the key pool, P, is not a sensor-design constraint. In contrast with k, which is limited by the sensor memory size, the key-pool of size P is generated and used off-line and hence can be very large. To derive the value of P, given constraint k for a p' that retains DSN connectivity with node degree d, we note that

$p' = 1 - \Pr[\text{two nodes do not share any key}]$,

and thus

$$p' = 1 - \frac{((P-k)!)^2}{(P-2k)!\, P!}$$

(viz., derivation in Appendix B). Since P is very large, we use the Stirling's approximation for n!,

$$n! \approx \sqrt{2\pi} \cdot n^{n+\frac{1}{2}} \cdot e^{-n},$$

to simplify the expression of p', and obtain:

$$p' = 1 - \frac{(1-\frac{k}{P})^{2(P-k+\frac{1}{2})}}{(1-\frac{2k}{P})^{(P-2k+\frac{1}{2})}}.$$

Figure 2 illustrates a plot of this function for various values of P. For example, one may see that for a pool size P = 10,000 keys, only 75 keys need to be distributed to any two nodes to have the probability $p = 0.5$ that they share a key in their key ring. If the pool is ten times larger, namely P = 100,000, the number of keys required is 250, which is only 3.3 times the number of keys distributed in the case P = 10,000. This provides intuition for the scalability of our approach. Of course, to determine the final the size of the key ring we need to provision for additions of new nodes, revocation and re-keying. The scalablity properties of our solution indicate that such provisioning will have minimal impact on the size of key rings.

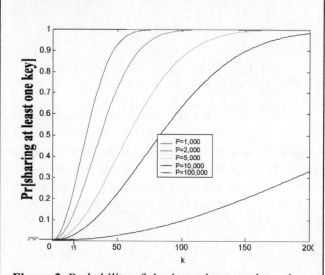

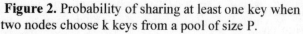

Figure 2. Probability of sharing at least one key when two nodes choose k keys from a pool of size P.

B. An example

To understand how the scheme works we present a simple numerical example. Let us assume that a DSN has n=10,000 nodes and that we want the resulting network to be connected with probability $Pc = 0.99999$.

This means the network will "almost certainly be connected." Further, assume that that each node in the DSN has a wireless communication range that requires a neighborhood connectivity of 40 nodes.

Using the Erdős and Rényi's formula for $Pc = 0.99999 = e^{-e^{-c}}$ we find that $c = 11.5$. For this value of c we obtain $p=2*10^{-3}$ and $d = 2*10^{-3} * 9999$ other nodes. It follows that if in our network each node can communicate with 20 other nodes out of the n=10,000 nodes, the network will be (almost certainly) connected. The formula of p' above shows by setting $p' = p = 2*10^{-3}$ and selecting an especially small value of k, say k = 15, we must have a pool size P=100,000 (also viz., Figure 2). Of course, larger values of k can be accommodated by a pool size P = 100,000, as seen below.

The requirement that each neighborhood consists of $n' = 40$ sensor nodes implies that instead of $p = 2*10^{-3}$ we now have $p' = d/(n'-1) = 20/(40-1) \approx 0.5$. This means that either the memory size of the key ring, k, or the pool size, P, or both, must increase. For example, the formula for p' above indicates that we now need to increase the key ring size k from 15 to 250 if we intend to use the same pool size P = 100,000. Furthermore, if the neighborhood size is increased to $n' = 60$, then $p' = 20/(60-1) \approx 0.33$. The formula for p' above indicates that we now need only a key ring size of k = 200 for a pool size of P=100,000 keys.

IV. SIMULATIONS

We used simulations to investigate the effect of the various parameters on different DSN sizes. We were interested in understanding the efficiency and scalability of our scheme and also to characterize some parameter values that cannot be easily computed, such as the diameter of the resulting secure network.

The simulations assume a network of 1,000 nodes, having an average density of 40 sensor nodes in a neighborhood. Each simulation experiment is reproduced 10 times with different seeds for the random number generator, and the results presented represent the average values on the 10 experiments, unless otherwise noted.

A. Effect on the network topology

The fact that two nodes may not share a key during the shared-key discovery phase means that, from a network router's point of view, a link does not exist between those two nodes. This has an effect on the average path length (number of links) between two nodes after shared-key discovery. We computed this value for various size of the key ring and show the result on Figure 3. This figure indicates that the average path length of the network depends on the size of the key ring. The smaller k is the higher the probability that a link does not have a key and, therefore, longer paths need to be found between nodes. In this example, the network gets disconnected for small k.

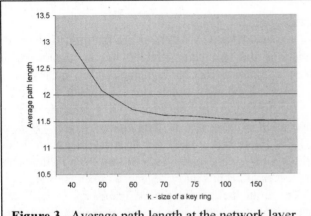

Figure 3. Average path length at the network layer

Because some links may not be keyed, a node may need to use a multi-link path to communicate with one of its wireless neighbor. Although this path would be used only once (to send the key to use for the link encryption), it should not be too long; otherwise the delay and communication cost to setup a path key with a neighbor may be high. In this example, we show how the multi-link path from a node to one of its neighbor varies with k.

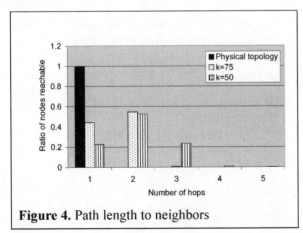

Figure 4. Path length to neighbors

Figure 4 shows us that the effect traversing multiple links to set up a path key is negligible. If a neighborhood node cannot be reached via a shared key (i.e., one link or hop), it will take at most two or three links (hops) to contact it. Since this has to be done only once to setup the path key, the effects are negligible. With $k=75$, only

half of the neighbors are reachable over a single link (hop), but most of the other may be reachable over in three-link (hop) paths. While for $k=50$ only one third of the nodes are reachable over a single link, but at most four links (hops) are needed for a path to contact all of them.

B. Effect of an Attack against Unshielded Sensor Nodes

We suggested that capture of an unshielded node leads to the compromise of only k keys and that an adversary could only attack k/P links. We verified this fact by observing how many keys are used to secure links in the simulated DSN and how many links are secured with the same key.

Figure 5 shows that out of the pool of 10,000 keys, only 50% of the keys are used to secure links, only 30% are used to secure one link, 10% are used to secure two links, and only 5% are used to secure 3 links. This suggests that compromise of one key does lead to the compromise of another link with probability .3, of two other link with probability .1, and so on.

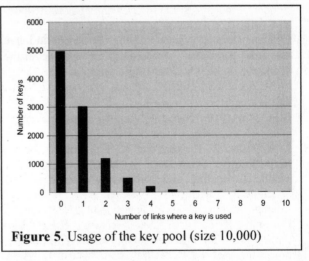

Figure 5. Usage of the key pool (size 10,000)

V. Conclusions

We presented a new key management scheme for large-scale DSNs. All such schemes must be extremely simple given the sensor-node resource limitations. Our approach is also scalable and flexible: trade-offs can be made between sensor-memory cost and connectivity, and design parameters can be adapted to fit the operational requirements of a particular environment. We illustrated the effect of the modifying design parameters using both analysis and simulations. The results indicate that our scheme is superior to the traditional key pre-distribution schemes.

ACKNOWLEDGEMENTS

REFERENCES

[1] C. Blundo, A. De Santis, A. Herzberg, S. Kutten, U. Vaccaro and M. Yung, "Perfectly Secure Key Distribution for Dynamic Conferences", in Advances in Cryptology --- CRYPTO '92, Springer-Verlag, Berlin, 1993, pp. 471--486.

[2] C. Blundo, L. A. Frota Mattos and D. R. Stinson, "Tradeoffs Between Communication and Storage in Unconditionally Secure Schemes for Broadcast Encryption and Interactive Key Distribution", Lecture Notes in Computer Science 1109 (1996), pp. 387--400 (Advances in Cryptology --- CRYPTO '96).

[3] D. W. Carman, P. S. Kruus and B. J. Matt,"Constraints and Approaches for Distributed Sensor Network Security", dated September 1, 2000. NAI Labs Technical Report #00-010, available at *http://download.nai.com /products/media/nai/zip/nailabs-report-00-010-final.zip*

[4] A. Fiat and M. Naor, "Broadcast Encryption", in Advances in Cryptology --- CRYPTO '93, Springer-Verlag, Berlin, 1994, pp. 480--491.

[5] J. Hill, R. Szewczyk, A. Woo, S. Hollar, D. Culler, K. Pister, "System architecture directions for network sensors", Proc. of ASPLOS-IX, Cambridge, Mass. 2000.

[6] Y.-C. Hu, D. B. Johnson and A. Perrig, "SEAD: Secure Efficient Distance Vector Routing for Mobile Wireless Ad Hoc Networks", Proceedings of the 4th IEEE Workshop on Mobile Computing Systems & Applications (WMCSA 2002), IEEE, Calicoon, NY, June 2002 (to appear).

[7] IBM, *IBM 4758 General Information Manual*, available at *http://www.ibm.com/security/cryptocards/*

[8] J. M. Kahn, R. H. Katz and K. S. J. Pister, "Mobile Networking for Smart Dust", ACM/IEEE Intl. Conf. on Mobile Computing and Networking (MobiCom 99), Seattle, WA, August 17-19, 1999, pp. 271 – 278.

[9] J. Song, R. Poovendran, W. Trappe, and K. J. R. Liu, "A Dynamic Key Distribution Scheme Using Data Embedding for Secure Multimedia Multicast"', Proceedings of SPIE Security and Watermarking for Multimedia, Vol. 4314, pg. 618-628, 2001

[10] J. Spencer, *The Strange Logic of Random Graphs*, *Algorithms and Combinatorics 22*, Springer-Verlag 2000, ISBN 3-540-41654-4

[11] F. Stajano, *Security for Ubiquitous Computing*, John Wiley and Sons, New York, Feb. 12, 2002, ISBN: 0-470-84493-0, 267 pp.

[12] W. Trappe, J. Song, R. Poovendran, and K. J. R. Liu, "A Dynamic Key Distribution Scheme Using Data Embedding for Secure Multimedia Multicast", Submitted to *IEEE Transactions on Multimedia*, available at http://www.eng.umd.edu/~wxt/papers/spiekey1.pdf.

[13] S.R. White and L. Comerford, ABYSS: A Trusted Architecture for Software Protection., Proc. of IEEE Security and Privacy, Oakland, CA, 1987, pp. 38-51.

APPENDIX A

In this section we briefly review the method of Trappe et al. [12] for re-keying in a broadcast environment. We adopt this method both for the discovery of shared keys and for broadcasting a controller's signature key. The security of this method relies on *parametric one-way functions* (POWFs).

Definition. *A parametric one-way function (POWF) h is a function from $K \times Y \to Z$, such that given $z = h(k, y)$ and parameter y it is computationally difficult to determine x.*

Parametric one-way functions are families of one-way functions that are parameterized by the parameter y. Such a function can be implemented by means of a symmetric encryption cipher. For example, if we let g be a suitable hash function and E_k a symmetric cipher invocation with a key k, then $h(k,y) = g(E_k(y))$ is a POWF. [Note that g need not be a cryptographic hash function.] It is easy to see that efficient POWFs that map sequences of 2B bits into a sequence of B bits exist.

We outline the construction of Trappe *et al.*'s only for signature-key broadcasting as our adaptation to shared-key discovery follows immediately.

1) Signature-key broadcasting

A POWF h that maps a sequence (k,y) of 2B bits to B bits is made available to every user. A new POWF f is defined by prepending a single 1 bit to the output of $h(k,y)$, that is $f(k,y)=1 \parallel h(k,y)$. Assume that a controller wants to broadcast a new signature key K_e to all network nodes with which it shares keys K_i. The controller first broadcasts a B-bit random seed μ. Next, it generates the new key K_e and computes the broadcast message α as:

$$\alpha = K_e + \prod_{i=1}^{n} f(K_i,\mu).$$

Any node sharing secret key K_i with the controller may decode α by computing:

$$\alpha \,(\mathrm{mod}\, f(K_i,\mu)) = K_e.$$

2) Security of signature key broadcasting

We only need to show the security of the signature key distribution. Trappe *et al.* show that it is computationally difficult for a node to recover the secret key of another node from the public messages exchanged. First, they consider a variation of the controller's broadcast message:

$$\alpha = K_e + \prod_{i=1}^{n-1} K_i .$$

This variation requires that $K_e < min_i\{K_i\}$. This scheme would successfully distribute the message to all nodes, however it would be possible for a node n_i to recover the another node's key K_j by computing:

$$A_i = \frac{\alpha - K_e}{K_i} = \prod_{j \neq i} K_j$$

and then factor A_i to recover the other K_j's.

The complete scheme, using function f and μ broadcast in the clear only allows an adversary to compute

$$A_i = \prod_{j \neq i} f(K_j, \mu),$$

whose factoring reveals information only about $f(K_j, \mu)$. It is computationally infeasible for an adversary to retrieve K_j given μ and $f(K_j, \mu)$.

Appendix B

The probability that two key rings share a key is $1 -$ Pr[two nodes do not share any key]. To compute the probability that two key rings do not share any key, we note that each key of a key ring is drawn out of a pool of P keys without replacement. Thus, the number of possible key rings is:

$$\frac{P!}{k!(P-k)!}$$

Pick the first key ring. The total number of possible key rings that do not share a key with this key ring is the number of key-rings that can be drawn out of the remaining P-k unused key in the pool, namely:

$$\frac{(P-k)!}{k!(P-2k)!}$$

Therefore, the probability that no key is shared between the two rings is the ratio of the number of rings without a match by the total number of rings:

$$\frac{k!(P-k)!(P-k)!}{P!k!(P-2k)!}.$$

Thus, the probability that there is at least a shared key between two key rings is:

$$p' = 1 - \frac{((P-k)!)^2}{(P-2k)!P!}.$$

Summary of the Hi-DRA Project
A System for High-Speed, Wide-Area Network Detection, Response, and Analysis

Richard A. Kemmerer Giovanni Vigna
Reliable Software Group
University of California, Santa Barbara
Email: {kemm,vigna}@cs.ucsb.edu

Antonio Carzaniga Alexander L. Wolf
University of Colorado
Boulder, Colorado
Email: {carzanig,alw}@cs.colorado.edu

Abstract

The goal of the Hi-DRA project is to develop a system for network surveillance, analysis, and response for high-speed, wide-area networks. The Hi-DRA approach advocates that the protection of the network infrastructure must rely on *local surveillance* and *global coordination and control*. Local surveillance addresses the problem of securing a protection domain by means of proactive security measures, extensive monitoring, and real-time response. Global coordination and control enables the correlation of security-related information coming from different subsystems to obtain a global view of the security state of the infrastructure. To achieve its goals, the Hi-DRA approach relies on five key concepts: high-speed network monitoring and analysis; highly configurable intrusion detection sensors; comprehensive correlation; advanced network modeling; and a scalable infrastructure for global command and control. This paper presents an overview of the Hi-DRA project and provides a description of key ideas underlying the approach.

Keywords: *Intrusion Detection, Misuse Detection, Anomaly Detection, Alert Correlation, Security, Computer Security, Network Security, High-Speed Networks.*

I. INTRODUCTION

The incredible growth of networking technology has been driven by the immediate need for higher bandwidths and advanced services. This trend has delivered a number of promising results, but has also produced solutions that are only partially satisfactory. Security is one aspect that has often been overlooked in the design and implementation of new network services. The pressure created by users' needs and the reduced time-to-market has not allowed for thorough security analysis and the sound design of protocols, services, and applications.

In the last ten years new mechanisms have been designed and implemented to support privacy and integrity of network services. Examples of these solutions are firewalls [9], [10], virtual private networks (VPNs) [19], and intrusion detection systems (IDSs) [1]. Even though they represent a first step towards improved security, the solutions proposed so far suffer from a number of limitations in terms of performance, configurability, completeness, and scalability. The research carried out on the Hi-DRA project at the University of California, Santa Barbara (UCSB) and at the University of Colorado, Boulder (UCB) over the last four years addresses these limitations. Hi-DRA is a network surveillance, analysis, and response infrastructure for high-speed, wide-area networks.

a) Addressing performance issues in high-speed networks: As networks become faster, delivering bandwidths of gigabits per second to end nodes, there is a need for new techniques that can keep up with the increased network throughput. Existing network sensors can barely keep up with bandwidths of hundreds of Mbps. Furthermore, there is also a need to better handle attacks directed at the network infrastructure. More efficient monitoring solutions based on load balancing techniques have been proposed, but these solutions concentrate only on the traffic load and do not take into account the target network's characteristics and the parameters of the security analysis being performed on the network data. A more effective approach would rely on semantic-rich descriptions of both the protected targets (e.g., what services are deployed and what the network topology is) and the intrusion patterns (e.g., what type of events may be involved in the attacks to be detected).

To be able to perform a broader range of traffic analysis in high-speed networks, we have developed an intelligent network traffic partitioning technique that enables parallel execution of the network analysis process. Our partitioning approach to network security analysis supports in-depth, stateful intrusion detection on high-speed links. The approach is centered around a *slicing* mechanism that divides the overall network traffic into subsets of manageable size. The traffic partitioning is done so that a single slice contains all the evidence necessary to detect a specific attack, making sensor-to-sensor interactions unnecessary.

b) Addressing configurability issues of surveillance sensors: The protection of the national information infrastructure requires a means to dynamically configure the infrastructure's security posture as a reaction to detected attacks. This reaction may vary from recording information, to raising the level of concern, to rerouting traffic, etc. For this reason, there is a need for the dynamic reconfiguration of surveillance sensors in terms of positioning of the sensors, types of attacks to be detected, and the types of response.

We have developed a highly configurable "web of sensors" that supports dynamic configuration. Our web of sensors research built on the State Transition Analysis Technique (STAT) [21] previously developed at UCSB. The STAT approach describes computer attacks at a high level. Attack scenarios are abstracted into *states*, which describe the security status of a system, and *transitions*, which model the evolution between states. By modeling an attack as an evolving scenario it is possible to preempt ongoing attacks and perform responses in real-time. To address the complexity of intrusion detection infrastructures, we developed the STAT framework, which overcomes the limitations of current approaches. Instead of providing yet another system tailored to some domain-specific requirements, STAT provides a software framework for the development of new intrusion detection functionality in a modular fashion. When using the STAT framework, intrusion detection sensors are built by dynamically composing domain-specific components with a domain-independent runtime. The resulting intrusion detection sensors represent a software family. Each sensor has the ability to reconfigure its behavior dynamically. The reconfiguration functionality is supported by a component model and by a control infrastructure, called MetaSTAT. The final product of the STAT framework is a highly-configurable, well-integrated intrusion detection infrastructure.

c) Addressing alert correlation issues: As more IDSs are developed, network security officers (NSOs) are faced with the task of analyzing an increasing number of alerts resulting from the analysis of different event streams. In addition, IDSs are far from perfect and may produce both false positives and non-relevant positives. Non-relevant positives are alerts that correctly identify an attack, but the attack fails to meet its objective. For instance, the attack may be exercising a vulnerability in a service that is not provided by the victim host. As an example, consider a "Code Red" worm that attacks a Linux Apache server. Although an actual attack is seen on the network, this attack will fail, because Apache is not vulnerable to the exploit utilized by the worm. Clearly, there is a need for tools and techniques that allow an NSO to aggregate and combine the outputs of multiple IDSs, filter out spurious or incorrect alerts (such as "Code Red" attacks against Apache installations), and provide a high-level view of the security state of the protected network.

We have developed an alert correlation process that produces a succinct overview of security-related activity on the network. Our process uses a set of components that focus on different aspects of the overall correlation task. We have also designed and implemented a tool, called AlertSTAT, which uses the MetaSTAT infrastructure to collect the alerts produced by the intrusion detection sensors and then performs correlation on the resulting data using a number of different components.

d) Addressing network security modeling issues: Security analysis should take advantage of a reliable knowledge base that contains semantically-rich information about a protected network. Unfortunately, existing network security solutions rely on incomplete data models. Networks are complex systems and most approaches oversimplify their target models in an effort to limit the problem space. For example, firewall technologies often consider a limited subset of security mechanisms and do not take into account specific characteristics of the network being protected, such as the interactions among different protocols and services, or the particular architecture and operating systems installed on the protected nodes. In addition, network management protocols (e.g., SNMP) do not consider important aspects of the managed hosts such as trust relationships or protection domains. There is a need for a comprehensive model that can be the basis for coordinated security analysis and infrastructure status monitoring.

We have developed a network reference model and a tool based on the model to support sophisticated network discovery, validation, and analysis. The model is not limited to a specific network level, but integrates network information throughout the layers. The model contains information about topology, infrastructure, and deployed services. In addition, the relationships among different entities in different layers of the model are made explicit. For example, the model includes trust relationships between service clients and servers, as well as relationships between services and configuration objects (e.g., files) used to define the application behavior.

The model served as the basis for NetMap, which is a security tool for network modeling, discovery, and analysis. The modeled information is managed by using a suite of composable network tools that can determine various aspects of network configurations through scanning techniques and heuristics. Tools in the suite are responsible for a single, well-defined task. Each tool has an abstract specification of the input, the output, the type of processing, and the requirements for carrying out a task. Tool descriptions are expressed in a Network Tool Language. The tool descriptions are then stored in a database. By using the network model and the tool descriptions, NetMap is able to automatically determine which tools are needed to perform a particular complex task and how the tools should be scheduled to obtain the requested results.

e) Addressing scalability and survivability issues for global command and control: Surveillance of protected networks is the basis for securing the information infrastructure, but there is also the need to take into account infrastructure-wide security issues. This was made clear in the many distributed denial-of-service attacks, which were coordinated aggressions targeting a number of different companies. The attacks were detected singularly by each target site and the tasks of analysis and response were carried out locally. Coordination among the attacked sites, when there was any, was performed through an *ad hoc* spontaneous network composed of system administrators communicating through email (when possible) or by phone. It is clear that in order to be able to assess and respond to more serious attacks, the scope of the deployed infrastructure protection mechanisms should be national and even international.

An emergency response capability with international scope can only be realized if the protection mechanisms can take advantage of a scalable communication and coordination infrastructure. Existing solutions have evolved from local-area network scale to enterprise-wide scale by extending and replicating local solutions. This approach has already shown its limitations and cannot be pursued further for the creation of an Internet-scale protection infrastructure. New general, scalable mechanisms must be devised to support coordination and communication on a larger scale.

We developed a ubiquitous event notification service as the basis for communication and coordination among the components of the protection infrastructure. To realize this service, we adapted and extended Siena [3], [4], which is a publish/subscribe event notification service developed at UCB. Siena is designed specifically to operate in the context of wide-area networks such as the Internet. Scalability is achieved by performing efficient content-based routing of alerts and control messages. In particular, Siena takes advantage of commonalities among subscriptions to reduce the network and computational cost of propagating notifications from publishers to subscribers. In using Siena as the Internet-scale event notification infrastructure, we employed the network reference model described above as a common ontology for fusing and correlating alerts coming from different sensors in different network domains. Siena offers an expressive and generic data model on top of which we instantiated alerts and control messages in compliance with this common ontology. In addition to employing the shared data model in this way, we also extended Siena to recognize a wider range of event patterns in order to support the kinds of alert fusion and correlation required by the data model.

This paper is intended as a summary of the research carried out as part of the Hi-DRA project. The material presented in this paper has appeared in other publication venues, all of which are referenced or cited here. The five reprinted articles that accompany this summary [8], [14], [20], [23], [24] are a good starting point to understand the details of the Hi-DRA research project.

The remainder of this paper is organized in five sections, which overview the five approaches presented above. Each section also gives a pointer to where more complete information can be obtained on the research being summarized. More specifically, Section II presents our approach to high-speed monitoring and analysis, Section III presents the web of sensors, Section IV presents our component-based approach to alert correlation, Section V overviews our advanced network modeling approach, and Section VI presents our work on information dissemination and classification. The final section of the paper summarizes the papers that we have published in each of these areas.

II. HIGH SPEED MONITORING AND ANALYSIS

To perform in-depth, stateful analysis it is necessary to divide the traffic volume into smaller portions that can be thoroughly analyzed by intrusion detection sensors. This approach has often been advocated by the high-performance research community as a way to distribute the service load across many nodes. In contrast to the case for standard load balancing, the division (or slicing) of the traffic for intrusion detection has to be performed in a way that guarantees the detection of all the threat scenarios considered. If a random division of traffic is used, sensors may not receive sufficient data to detect an intrusion, because different parts of the manifestation of an attack may have been assigned to different slices. Therefore, when an attack scenario consists of a number of steps, the slicing mechanism must assure that all of the packets that could trigger those steps are sent to the sensor configured to detect that specific attack.

The problem of intrusion detection analysis in high-speed networks can be effectively attacked only if a scalable solution is available. We specified the requirements for a scalable solution in [14]. These requirements were used as the basis for the design of our network-based intrusion detection system. The system consists of a *network tap*, a *traffic scatterer*, a set of m *traffic slicers*, a *switch*, a set of n *stream reassemblers*, and a set of p *intrusion detection sensors*.

The network tap component monitors the traffic stream on a high-speed link. Its task is to extract the sequence F of link-layer frames $\langle f_0, f_1, ..., f_t \rangle$ that are observable on the wire during a time period. This sequence of frames is passed to the scatterer which partitions F into m sub-sequences $F_j : 0 \leq j < m$. Each F_j contains a (possibly empty) subset of the frame sequence F. Every frame is an element of exactly one sub-sequence and therefore $\cup_{j=0}^{j<m} F_j = F$. The scatterer can use any algorithm to partition F. Hereafter, it is assumed that the scattering algorithm simply cycles over the m sub-sequences in a round-robin fashion. As a result, each F_j contains an m-th of the total traffic.

Each sub-sequence F_j is transmitted to a different traffic slicer S_j. The task of the traffic slicers is to route the frames they receive to the sensors that may need them to detect an attack. This task is not performed by the scatterer, because frame routing may be complex, requiring a substantial amount of time, while the scatterer has to keep up with the high traffic throughput and can only perform very limited processing per frame.

The traffic slicers are connected to a switch component, which allows a slicer to send a frame to one or more of n outgoing channels C_i. The set of frames sent to a channel is denoted by FC_i. Each channel C_i is associated with a stream reassembler component R_i and a number of intrusion detection sensors. The set of sensors associated with channel C_i is denoted by IC_i. All the sensors that are associated with a channel are able to access all the packets sent on that channel. A problem that could occur with this approach is that the original order of two packets could be lost if the two frames took different paths over distinct slicers to the same channel. Therefore, the reassemblers associated with each channel make sure that the packets appear on the channel in the same order that they appeared on the high-speed link. That is, each reassembler R_i must make sure that for each pair of frames $f_j, f_k \in FC_i$, $(f_j$ before $f_k)$ $\iff j < k$.

Each sensor component I_j is associated with q different attack scenarios, and each attack scenario has an associated *event space*. The event space specifies which frames are candidates to be part of the manifestation of the attack. For example, consider an attack targeting a Web server called `dino` within the network protected by the intrusion detection system. In this case, the event space for that attack is composed of all the TCP traffic that involves port 80 on host `dino`.

Event spaces are expressed as disjunctions of *clauses*, where each clause is an expression of the type xRy. x denotes a value derived from the frame (e.g., a part of the frame header) while R specifies an arithmetic relation (e.g., $=$, $! =$, $<$). y can be a constant, the value of a variable, or a value derived from the same frame. Clauses and event spaces may be derived automatically from the attack descriptions, for example from signatures written in attack languages such as Bro [16], Sutekh [17], STATL [11], or Snort [18].

The effectiveness of the scatterer/slicer/ reassembler architecture were experimentally evaluated on a system using three traffic slicers ($m = 3$) and four stream reassemblers ($n = 4$) with one intrusion detection sensor per stream with favorable results. The details of the implementation and of these experiments can be found in the accompanying reprint [14].

III. WEB OF SENSORS

We have developed a novel approach to distributed intrusion detection. The idea is that a protected network is instrumented with a "web of sensors" composed of distributed components integrated by means of a local communication and control infrastructure. The task of the web of sensors is to provide fine-grained surveillance inside the protected network. The web of sensors implements local surveillance against both outside attacks and local misuse by insiders in a way that is complementary to the mainstream approach where a single point of access (e.g., a gateway) is monitored for possible malicious activity. The outputs of the sensors, in the form of alerts, are collected by a number of "meta-sensor" components. Each meta-sensor is responsible for a subset of the deployed sensors, and may coordinate its activities with other meta-sensors. The meta-sensors are responsible for storing the alerts, for routing alerts to other sensors and meta-sensors (e.g., to perform correlation to identify composite attack scenarios), and for exerting control over the managed sensors.

Control is the most challenging (and most overlooked) functionality of distributed surveillance. Most existing approaches simply aggregate the outputs of distributed sensors and focus mainly on the intuitive presentation of alerts to the network security officer. This is not enough. There is a need for fine-grained control of the deployed sensors in terms of scenarios to be detected, tailoring of the sensors with respect to the protected network, and dynamic control over the types of response. These are requirements that can be satisfied only if the surveillance sensors are *highly configurable* and if configuration can be performed dynamically, without stopping and restarting sensors when a reconfiguration is needed.

We have designed a suite of highly configurable surveillance sensors and a command and control meta-sensor that allows the network security officer to exert a very fine-grained control over the deployed surveillance infrastructure. Meta-sensors can be organized hierarchically to achieve scalability and can be replicated to support fault-tolerance. This web of sensors is built around the State Transition Analysis Technique (STAT) framework developed by the Reliable Software Group at UCSB. The STAT framework provides a platform for the development of highly configurable probes in different domains and environments. The resulting set of applications is a software family whose members share a number of features, including dynamic reconfigurability and a fine-grained control over a wide range of characteristics [22].

The STAT approach is centered around five key concepts: the STAT technique, the STATL language, the STAT Core, the CommSTAT communication infrastructure, and the MetaSTAT control system.

The approach provides the basic mechanisms to reconfigure, at run-time, which input event streams are analyzed by each sensor, which scenarios have to be used for the analysis, and what types of responses must be carried out for each stage of the detection process. In addition, the approach explicitly models the dependencies among the modules composing a sensor so that it is possible to automatically identify the steps that are necessary to perform a reconfiguration of the deployed sensing infrastructure. In addition, the possibility of retrieving current configurations from remote sensors allows one to determine if a reconfiguration is valid or meaningful.

The STAT framework is the only known framework-based approach to the development of intrusion detection systems. Our experience with the framework shows that by following this approach it is possible to develop intrusion detection systems with reduced development effort, with respect to an *ad hoc* approach. In addition, the approach is advantageous in terms of the increased reuse that results from using an object-oriented framework and a component-based approach. The details of the web of sensors approach can be found in the accompanying reprint [23].

IV. Alert Correlation

To address the issue of analyzing a large number of alerts, researchers and vendors have proposed *alert correlation*, which is an analysis process that takes the alerts produced by intrusion detection systems and produces compact reports on the security status of the network under surveillance. Although a number of correlation approaches have been suggested, there is no consensus on what this process is or how it should be implemented and evaluated. In particular, most existing correlation approaches operate on only a few aspects of the correlation process, such as the fusion of alerts that are generated by different intrusion detection systems in response to a single attack, or the identification of multi-step attacks that represent a sequence of actions performed by the same attacker. In addition, correlation tools that do cover multiple aspects of the correlation process are evaluated "as a whole," without an assessment of the effectiveness of each component of the analysis process. As a result, it is not clear if and how the different parts of the correlation process contribute to the overall goals of correlation.

Another problem is that many existing approaches operate under the assumption that the alert stream is composed of detections of successful attacks. Unfortunately, experience shows that this assumption is wrong. Intrusion detection systems are very noisy, and, in addition to false positives, they produce alerts with different levels of relevance. As a consequence, the effectiveness of alert correlation is negatively affected by the poor quality of the input alert stream.

The process of alert correlation consists of a collection of components that transform intrusion detection sensor[1] alerts into intrusion reports. Because alerts can refer to different kinds of attacks at different levels of granularity, the correlation process cannot treat all alerts equally. Instead, it is necessary to provide a set of components that focus on different aspects of the overall correlation task.

The AlertSTAT correlation tool that we implemented uses a pipeline architecture, consisting of ten different components. The process starts with a *normalization* component that translates every alert that is received into a standardized format that is understood by all other correlation components. This is necessary because alerts from different sensors can be encoded in different formats. Next, a *pre-processing* component augments the normalized alerts so that all required alert attributes (such as start-time, end-time, source, and target of the attack) are assigned meaningful values.

The core of the correlation process consists of components that implement specific functions, which operate on different spatial and temporal properties. That is, some of the components correlate events that occur close in time and space (e.g., alerts generated on one host within a small time window), while

---

[1] We use *intrusion detection system* and *intrusion detection sensor* (or just *sensor*) interchangeably.

others operate on events that represent an attack scenario that evolves over several hours and that includes alerts that are generated on different hosts (e.g., alerts that represent large-scale scanning activity). It is natural to combine events that are closely related (spatially and temporally) into composite alerts, which are in turn used to create higher-level alerts.

The next four correlation components of our process all operate on single, or closely related, events. The *fusion* component is responsible for combining alerts that represent the independent detection of the same attack instance by different intrusion detection systems. The *verification* component takes a single alert and determines the success of the attack that corresponds to this alert. The idea is that alerts that correspond to failed attacks should be appropriately tagged and their influence on the correlation process should be decreased. The *thread reconstruction* component combines a series of alerts that refer to similar attacks launched by a single attacker against a single target. The *attack session reconstruction* component associates network-based alerts with host-based alerts that are related to the same attack.

The next two components in our process operate on alerts that involve a potentially large number of different hosts. The *focus recognition* component has the task of identifying hosts that are either the source or the target of a substantial number of attacks. This is used to identify denial-of-service (DoS) attacks or port scanning attempts. The *multi-step correlation* component has the task of identifying common attack patterns, such as an island-hopping attack (i.e., an attack where an intruder breaks into a host and uses it as a launch pad for more attacks). These patterns are composed of a sequence of individual attacks, which can occur at different points in the network.

The final components of the correlation process contextualize the alerts with respect to a specific target network. The *impact analysis* component determines the impact of the detected attacks on the operation of the network being monitored and on the assets that are targeted by the malicious activity. The results of this analysis are then used by the *prioritization* component to assign an appropriate priority to every alert. This priority information is important for quickly discarding information that is irrelevant or of less importance to a particular site.

In its current configuration, alerts that are correlated by one AlertSTAT component are input to the next component. Although this process is sequential, all alerts are not required to pass through components sequentially. Some components could operate in parallel, and it is even possible that alerts output by a sequence of components could be fed back as input to a previous component of the process.

We have applied our correlation tool to a large number of diverse data sets, to analyze if and how each component contributes to the overall correlation process. These experiments demonstrate that the effectiveness of each component of the process is dependent on the data sets being analyzed. To be more precise, these experiments show that the performance of the correlation process is significantly influenced by the network topology, the characteristics of the attack, and the available meta-data. Thus, one cannot, in general, determine a ranking among components with respect to their effectiveness. The details of the AlertSTAT tool and of the experiments can be found in the accompanying reprint [20].

V. ADVANCED NETWORK MODELING AND ANALYSIS

Network security is achieved by composing the functionality of a number of security applications, such as firewalls and intrusion detection systems. Deploying and configuring security applications requires an in-depth knowledge of the network to be protected. In addition, continuous monitoring of both the network and the configuration of the security applications is the basis for determining the current network security posture.

Unfortunately, knowledge about the network being protected often exists only in the "mind" of the network administrator, and this knowledge is obtained by using a number of tools, each of which can only provide a subset of the information about the protected network. For example, the information about the services active on a host could be determined by scanning the ports of the host. In addition, the results obtained from the execution of one tool are often used as the basis for additional analysis and possibly as input for the execution of other tools. In the previous example, once the open ports have been determined, banner-grabbing tools can help to determine the type and version of the server applications. The coordination of tool executions and the composition of their results is usually a human-intensive task. This is the case even when ad-hoc scripts and procedures developed by network administrators through years of experience in integrating the results of network monitoring and analysis are available.

NetMap is a novel approach that provides support for automated network discovery and security analysis. NetMap is centered around a model of both the network to be analyzed and the tools to be used for analysis. The network model has been designed by taking into account the models used by existing network management and vulnerability scanning tools. The model is not limited to a specific network level; it integrates network information throughout the layers, and it contains information about topology, infrastructure, and deployed services. In addition, the security-relevant relationships between different entities in different layers of the model are made explicit. For example, the model includes trust relationships between clients and servers for specific services, as well as relationships between services and configuration objects (e.g., files) used to define the application behavior. The network model is implemented as a database management system, called NetDB.

In addition to the network model, we have developed a tool model that supports the abstract description of a suite of network discovery and scanning tools using a Network Tool Language (NTL). Each tool in the suite is responsible for a single, well-defined task. Each tool has a specification of the input, the output, the type of processing, and the requirements for carrying out a task. The tool descriptions are stored in a tool repository, called the Network Tool Database (NTDB).

NetMap allows a network administrator to specify high-level discovery/analysis tasks in a query language, called NetScript. Tasks range from pure network discovery, to the validation of existing information, to vulnerability scanning. Given a task description, a query processor component uses the tool descriptions to determine which tools are needed to perform a particular complex task, what their schedule should be, and how the results should be inserted into an instance of the network model that represents the protected network. The details of the NetMap tool can be found in the accompanying reprint [24].

In addition to the NetMap approach, we developed a number of tools to support the monitoring and analysis of the network routing infrastructure. These tools analyze the events associated with the reconfiguration of traffic distribution to identify both anomalous behavior and inconsistencies [13], [15].

VI. Information Dissemination and Classification

Our work on information dissemination and classification concentrated on integrating intrusion-detection sensors through a scalable, loosely-coupled communication service, called Siena, and on developing a generic, flexible, and high-performance data classifier called SFF. These are discussed in the following two subsections.

A. High-Level Integration of Intrusion-Detection Sensors

Enterprise-wide dynamic response and countermeasure requires a non-traditional communication mechanism to distribute alerts, and to control and configure sensors deployed throughout the network. The Siena content-based communication service [5] is ideally suited to this application, since it has been designed specifically to support loosely coupled communication among components distributed across a wide-area network. Moreover, it has been designed for scalability in terms of the number of participants and the number of messages they exchange.

The model of communication underlying Siena is *publish/subscribe*, whereby the service delivers messages, not through an explicit destination-addressing scheme as in a point-to-point service, but instead by matching the content of messages generated by publishers against the interests expressed by subscribers. Thus, the service does not require the sender to know the set of receivers, and in fact, that set can vary over time without any intervention by the sender.

A message carries information in the form of a set of attribute/value pairs. For example, the message displayed in Figure 1a represents a portscan alarm. A *filter*, which represents the interests of a subscriber, selects messages by specifying a conjunction of constraints on the values of some attributes. The operators available for use within filters include all the common equality and ordering relations ($=, \neq, <, >$, etc.), the substring ($*$), prefix ($>*$), and suffix ($*<$) operators for strings, and an operator *any* that matches any value. With these selection operators, Siena achieves the expressiveness of a significant subset of SQL. Figure 1b shows a filter that matches any security alarm for hosts "*.bar.com".

```
string       class = network/security/alarm
time          date = Mar 4 11:43:37 MST 1998
string       tohost = foo.bar.com
string     fromhost = pub32.internetcafe.com
string       attack = portscan
```

(a)

```
string    class    >*    network/security/
string    tohost   *<    .bar.com
string    attack   any
```

(b)

Fig. 1.   Example of a Message (a) and a Filter (b).

Siena comes with a complete, fully-documented API, with language mappings for Java and C++. This API allows applications to publish and subscribe, and also offers some value-added services, including message buffers and support for mobile client applications [2]. In addition to this primary, functional interface, Siena implements a management interface that allows applications to remotely control some server parameters and operations.

These two interfaces are the basis for the integration of higher-level components of the Hi-DRA infrastructure. In particular, a Siena client can be used as an alert generator within the STAT framework (see Section III). This is done using a module called SienaSTAT, which feeds Siena-based IDMEF alert messages into the AlertSTAT correlator. SienaSTAT uses a Siena-XML interface API called SXML. This value-added API automates the process of publishing XML documents (such as IDMEF alerts) as Siena messages. Applications can subscribe for XML information by posing subscriptions in the form of XPath expressions, as well as publish XML documents. The XML publication mechanism and XPath subscription mechanism are completely parameterized and integrated. This means that both processes are controlled by a set of translation rules that determine how XML data are represented within a Siena message.

Siena was conceived as a federation of servers, each of which is responsible for dispatching messages passed to it either from clients or from other servers. However, its design has inspired the development of a true network architecture that we call *content-based networking* [7]. The service interface of this network eschews receiver addresses in favor of more powerful *receiver predicates* (disjunctions of what are called "filters" in Siena), with the flow of messages from senders to receivers determined by the evaluation of message content against receiver predicates. As with any network-level service, the fundamental challenge is the design of highly efficient and reliable routing and forwarding functions to support message delivery. The routing function we developed is based on the use of symmetric broadcast trees pruned by content-based predicates [6]. The forwarding function provides a means to index predicates so that the content of messages can be quickly compared to large numbers of predicates and thereby determine to which next-hop router a given message should be forwarded. Content-based networking provides an advanced infrastructure upon which to implement a publish/subscribe service, as well as related high-level services such as query/advertise [12]. The details of content-based forwarding can be found in the accompanying reprint [8].

B. High-Performance Classification

The problem of forwarding in a content-based network turns out to share many characteristics with the problem of data or packet classification found in the domain of intrusion detection. In this context, the forwarding function can be used to enhance the capabilities of the high-performance monitor architecture discussed in Section II.

Recall that in the monitor architecture a traffic *scatterer* distributes network packets to a battery of traffic *slicers* using a simple round-robin scheduling policy. The advantage of this design is that the most performance-critical component of the architecture can be implemented using a simple algorithm and, in fact, this component can be easily implemented using specialized hardware. The disadvantage is that related packets (i.e., packets that must be taken together to match a specific attack signature) must be eventually processed by a single sensor, which in turn means that traffic flows that are initially spread out by the round-robin scatterer, must be reassembled and reordered in the correct arrival sequence at a later stage.

To overcome the need to reassemble, we can instead treat the problem as a flow problem, sieving traffic through a hierarchical network of *splitters* (rather than "scatterers"). In this architecture, each splitter makes an informed decision as to where to forward each packet, either dropping the packet or forwarding it along to one or more downstream splitters or sensors. The rules that determine the behavior of a splitter are derived from a combination of the rules defined by the IDS sensors downstream, with the root splitter using a few simple rules, and with other splitters at each level applying progressively refined and more specific rules. Intuitively, a splitter achieves its ideal effectiveness in filtering traffic when its rules partition its input stream evenly over its output (downstream) links.

The implementation of each splitter is based on the algorithms developed for the content-based forwarding function, together with network-specific input and output interfaces. The input interface presents network packets as messages, each one containing a set of attribute/value pairs, to the forwarding engine. For example, the network message interface translates packet data into attributes such as `ARP.Sender.IP`, `IP.Source`, `IP.Protocol`, `ICMP.Type`, and `TCP.SourcePort`. The output interface operates simply by forwarding the packet to one or more other splitters or sensors for further processing. Each splitter is loaded with a set of rules expressing conditions over the attributes.

The splitter algorithm, which we refer to as SFF, is a generic *multiclassifer* in that it can be used to classify a stream of input data of any kind (e.g., network packets, security alerts, log entries, and practically anything that can be expressed as a set of attributes and values) into any number of possibly overlapping categories.

Of course, genericity comes at a price. Our goal was to support gigabit and greater line speeds, so a software implementation on a commodity platform, such as FreeBSD on x86, was limiting the performance of the algorithm, especially when applying the algorithm to network intrusion detection. The time spent in kernel space, instead of running the classification algorithm, mostly consisted of managing network I/O buffers, which dominated the processing time for packets. Thus, we designed and developed a port of the SFF algorithm to the Intel IXP 1200 network processor.

VII. PAPERS PUBLISHED

A. High Speed Monitoring and Analysis

- C. Kruegel, F. Valeur, G. Vigna, and R.A. Kemmerer, **Stateful Intrusion Detection for High-Speed Networks**, in *Proceedings of the IEEE Symposium on Research on Security and Privacy*, pp. 285-293, IEEE Press, Oakland, CA, May 2002.
- C. Kruegel and T. Toth, **Using Decision Trees to Improve Signature-based Intrusion Detection**, in *Proceedings of the 6th Symposium on Recent Advances in Intrusion Detection (RAID)*, Lecture Notes in Computer Science, Springer Verlag. Pittsburgh, PA, September 2003.

B. Web of Sensors

- G. Vigna, R.A. Kemmerer, and P. Blix, **Designing a Web of Highly-Configurable Intrusion Detection Sensors**, in *Proceedings of the 4th International Symposium on Recent Advances in*

Intrusion Detection (RAID 2001), pp. 69-84, LNCS 2212, Springer-Verlag, Davis, CA, October 2001.

- R.A. Kemmerer and G. Vigna, **Intrusion Detection: A Brief History and Overview**, in *IEEE Computer, Special Issue on Security and Privacy*, pp. 27-30, IEEE Press, April 2002.

- G. Vigna, B. Cassell, and D. Fayram, **An Intrusion Detection System for Aglets**, in *Proceedings of the International Conference on Mobile Agents (MA '02)*, pp. 64-77, LNCS 2535, Springer-Verlag, Barcelona, Spain, October 2002.

- S.T. Eckmann, G. Vigna, and R.A. Kemmerer, **STATL: An Attack Language for State-based Intrusion Detection** in *Journal of Computer Security*, vol. 10, no. 1/2, pp. 71-104, IOS Press, 2002.

- S. Soman, C. Krintz, and G. Vigna, **Detecting Malicious Java Code Using Virtual Machine Auditing**, in *Proceedings of the 12th USENIX Security Symposium*, pp. 153-167, Washington, DC, August 2003.

- G. Vigna, F. Valeur, and R.A. Kemmerer, **Designing and Implementing A Family of Intrusion Detection Systems**, in *Proceedings of the European Conference on Software Engineering (ESEC)*, Helsinki, Finland, September 2003.

- G. Vigna, W. Robertson, V. Kher, and R.A. Kemmerer, **A Stateful Intrusion Detection System for World-Wide Web Servers**, in *Proceedings of the Annual Computer Security Applications Conference (ACSAC)*, pp. 34-43, Las Vegas, NV, December 2003.

- J. Zhou and G. Vigna, **Detecting Attacks That Exploit Application-Logic Errors Through Application-Level Auditing**, in *Proceedings of the Annual Computer Security Applications Conference (ACSAC)*, pp. 168-178, Tucson, AZ, December 2004.

- G. Vigna, S. Gwalani, K. Srinivasan, E. Belding-Royer, and R. Kemmerer, **An Intrusion Detection Tool for AODV-based Ad Hoc Wireless Networks**, in *Proceedings of the Annual Computer Security Applications Conference (ACSAC)*, pp. 16-27, Tucson, AZ, December 2004.

- R.A. Kemmerer and G. Vigna, **Sensor Families for Intrusion Detection Infrastructures**, in *Managing Cyber Threats: Issues, Approaches and Challenges*, Springer-Verlag, January 2005.

Alert Correlation

- F. Valeur, G. Vigna, C. Kruegel, and R. Kemmerer, **A Comprehensive Approach to Intrusion Detection Alert Correlation**, in *IEEE Transactions on Dependable and Secure Computing*, vol. 1, no. 3, pp. 146-169, July-September 2004.

- C. Kruegel and W. Robertson, **Alert Verification - Determining the Success of Intrusion Attempts**, in *Proceedings of the Workshop on Detection of Intrusions and Malware and Vulnerability Assessment (DIMVA)*, Germany, July 2004.

- C. Kruegel, W. Robertson, and G. Vigna, **Using Alert Verification to Identify Successful Intrusion Attempts**, in *Practice in Information Processing and Communication (PIK)*, vol. 27, no. 4, pp. 219-227, October/December, 2004.

- C. Kruegel and F. Valeur, and G. Vigna, **Intrusion Detection and Correlation: Challenges and Solutions**, Springer-Verlag, ISBN 0-387-233398-9, 2005.

Advanced Network Modeling and Analysis

- G. Vigna, F. Valeur, J. Zhou, and R.A. Kemmerer, **Composable Tools For Network Discovery and Security Analysis**, in *Proceedings of the Annual Computer Security Applications Conference (ACSAC)*, pp. 14-24, IEEE Press, Las Vegas, NV, December 2002.

- V. Mittal and G. Vigna, **Sensor-Based Intrusion Detection for Intra-Domain Distance-Vector Routing**, in *Proceedings of the ACM Conference on Computer and Communication Security (CCS'02)*, pp. 127-137, ACM Press, Washington, DC, November 2002.

- G. Vigna and A. Mitchell, **Designing and Implementing Network Short-Term Memory**, in *Proceedings of ICECCS '02*, pp. 91-100, IEEE Press, Greenbelt, MD, December 2002.

- G. Vigna, **A Topological Characterization of TCP/IP Security**, in *Proceedings of the 12th International FME Symposium*, pp. 914-940, LNCS 2805, Springer-Verlag, Pisa, Italy, September 2003.
- C. Kruegel, D. Mutz, W. Robertson, and F. Valeur, **Topology-based Detection of Anomalous BGP Messages**, in *Proceedings of the 6th Symposium on Recent Advances in Intrusion Detection (RAID)*, Lecture Notes in Computer Science, Springer Verlag. USA, September 2003.

E. Information Dissemination and Classification

- A. Carzaniga, M.J. Rutherford, and A.L. Wolf, **A Routing Scheme for Content-Based Networking**, in *Proceedings of IEEE INFOCOM 2004*, Hong Kong, China, March 2004.
- M. Caporuscio, A. Carzaniga, and A.L. Wolf, **Design and Evaluation of a Support Service for Mobile, Wireless Publish/Subscribe Applications**, in *IEEE Transactions on Software Engineering*, vol. 29, no. 12, pp. 1059–1071, December 2003.
- N. Arshad, D. Heimbigner, and A.L. Wolf, **Deployment and Dynamic Reconfiguration Planning for Distributed Software Systems**, in *15th International Conference on Tools with Artificial Intelligence (ICTAI '03)*, pp. 39–46, Sacramento, California, November 2003.
- A. Carzaniga and A.L. Wolf **Forwarding in a Content-Based Network**, in *Proceedings of ACM SIGCOMM 2003*, p. 163–174. Karlsruhe, Germany, August 2003.
- M. Castaldi, A. Carzaniga, P. Inverardi and A.L. Wolf, **A Lightweight Infrastructure for Reconfiguring Applications**, in *SCM 2001/2003*, pp. 231–244, LNCS 2649, Springer-Verlag, Portland, Oregon, May 2003.
- A. Carzaniga and A. Orso, **Continuous Remote Analysis for Improving Distributed Systems Performance**, in *RAMSS'03, 1st International Workshop on Remote Analysis and Measurement of Software Systems*, pp. 21–24, Portland, Oregon, May 2003.
- M. Caporuscio, A. Carzaniga, and A.L. Wolf, **An Experience in Evaluating Publish/Subscribe Services in a Wireless Network**, *Third International Workshop on Software and Performance*, Rome, Italy, July 2002.
- C. Wang, A. Carzaniga, D. Evans, and A.L. Wolf, **Security Issues and Requirements for Internet-scale Publish-Subscribe Systems**, In *Proceedings of the Thirty-Fifth Annual Hawaii International Conference on System Sciences (HICSS-35)*, Big Island, Hawaii, January 2002.
- D. Heimbigner, **Adapting Publish/Subscribe Middleware to Achieve Gnutella-Like Functionality**, in *Proceedings of the ACM Symposium on Applied Computing*, pp. 11–14, March 2001.

ACKNOWLEDGMENTS

This research was supported by the Army Research Laboratory and the Army Research Office, under agreement DAAD19-01-1-0484. The U.S. Government is authorized to reproduce and distribute reprints for Governmental purposes notwithstanding any copyright annotation thereon.

REFERENCES

[1] E. Amoroso. *Intrusion Detection: An Introduction to Internet Surveillance, Correlation, Trace Back, Traps, and Response.* Intrusion.Net Books, February 1999.

[2] Mauro Caporuscio, Antonio Carzaniga, and Alexander L. Wolf. Design and evaluation of a support service for mobile, wireless publish/subscribe applications. *IEEE Transactions on Software Engineering*, 29(12):1059–1071, December 2003.

[3] Antonio Carzaniga, David S. Rosenblum, and Alexander L. Wolf. Interfaces and algorithms for a wide-area event notification service. Technical Report CU-CS-888-99, Department of Computer Science, University of Colorado, October 1999. revised May 2000.

[4] Antonio Carzaniga, David S. Rosenblum, and Alexander L. Wolf. Achieving scalability and expressiveness in an internet-scale event notification service. In *Proceedings of the Nineteenth Annual ACM Symposium on Principles of Distributed Computing*, pages 219–227, Portland OR, USA, July 2000.

[5] Antonio Carzaniga, David S. Rosenblum, and Alexander L. Wolf. Design and evaluation of a wide-area event notification service. *ACM Transactions on Computer Systems*, 19(3):332–383, August 2001.

[6] Antonio Carzaniga, Matthew J. Ruterford, and Alexander L. Wolf. A routing scheme for content-based networking. In *Proceedings of the IEEE Conference on Computer Communications (INFOCOM)*, pages 918–928, March 2004.

[7] Antonio Carzaniga and Alexander L. Wolf. Content-based networking: A new communication infrastructure. In *Proceedings of the NSF Workshop on an Infrastructure for Mobile and Wireless Systems*, number 2538 in Lecture Notes in Computer Science, pages 59–68. Springer-Verlag, 2002.

[8] Antonio Carzaniga and Alexander L. Wolf. Forwarding in a content-based network. In *Proceedings of the Conference on Applications, Technologies, Architectures, and Protocols for Computer Communication (SIGCOMM)*, pages 163–174, August 2003.

[9] B. Chapman and E. Zwicky. *Building Internet Firewalls*. O'Reilly & Associates, 1995.

[10] W. Cheswick, S. Bellovin, and A. Rubin. *Firewalls and Internet Security: Repelling the Wily Hacker*. Addison-Wesley, second edition, 2003.

[11] S.T. Eckmann, G. Vigna, and R.A. Kemmerer. STATL: An Attack Language for State-based Intrusion Detection. In *Proceedings of the ACM Workshop on Intrusion Detection Systems*, Athens, Greece, November 2000.

[12] Dennis M. Heimbigner. Adapting publish/subscribe middleware to achieve gnutella-like functionality. In *Proceedings of the ACM Symposium on Applied Computing*, pages 11–14. ACM Press, March 2001.

[13] C. Kruegel, D. Mutz, W. Robertson, and F. Valeur. Topology-based Detection of Anomalous BGP Messages. In *Proceedings of the 6th International Symposium on Recent Advances in Intrusion Detection (RAID)*, Pittsburgh, PA, September 2003.

[14] C. Kruegel, Fredrik Valeur, G. Vigna, and R.A. Kemmerer. Stateful Intrusion Detection for High-Speed Networks. In *Proceedings of the IEEE Symposium on Research on Security and Privacy*, Oakland, CA, May 2002. IEEE Press.

[15] V. Mittal and G. Vigna. Sensor-Based Intrusion Detection for Intra-Domain Distance-Vector Routing. In R. Sandhu, editor, *Proceedings of the ACM Conference on Computer and Communication Security (CCS'02)*, Washington, DC, November 2002. ACM Press.

[16] V. Paxson. Bro: A System for Detecting Network Intruders in Real-Time. In *Proceedings of the 7th USENIX Security Symposium*, San Antonio, TX, January 1998.

[17] J. Pouzol and M. Ducassé. From Declarative Signatures to Misuse IDS. In W. Lee, L. Mé, and A. Wespi, editors, *Proceedings of the RAID International Symposium*, volume 2212 of *LNCS*, pages 1 – 21, Davis, CA, October 2001. Springer-Verlag.

[18] M. Roesch. *Writing Snort Rules: How To write Snort rules and keep your sanity.* http://www.snort.org.

[19] C. Scott, P. Wolfe, M. Erwin, and A. Oram. *Virtual Private Networks*. O'Reilly, second edition, December 1998.

[20] F. Valeur, G. Vigna, C.Kruegel, and R. Kemmerer. A Comprehensive Approach to Intrusion Detection Alert Correlation. *IEEE Transactions on Dependable and Secure Computing*, 1(3):146–169, July-September 2004.

[21] G. Vigna, S. Eckmann, and R. Kemmerer. The STAT Tool Suite. In *Proceedings of DISCEX 2000*, Hilton Head, South Carolina, January 2000. IEEE Computer Society Press.

[22] G. Vigna, R.A. Kemmerer, and P. Blix. Designing a Web of Highly-Configurable Intrusion Detection Sensors. In W. Lee, L. Mè, and A. Wespi, editors, *Proceedings of the 4th International Symposiun on Recent Advances in Intrusion Detection (RAID 2001)*, volume 2212 of *LNCS*, pages 69–84, Davis, CA, October 2001. Springer-Verlag.

[23] G. Vigna, F. Valeur, and R.A. Kemmerer. Designing and Implementing a Family of Intrusion Detection Systems. In *Proceedings of the European Software Engineering Conference and ACM SIGSOFT Symposium on the Foundations of Software Engineering (ESEC/FSE 2003)*, Helsinki, Finland, September 2003.

[24] G. Vigna, F. Valeur, J. Zhou, and R.A. Kemmerer. Composable Tools For Network Discovery and Security Analysis. In *Proceedings of the 18th Annual Computer Security Applications Conference (ACSAC '02)*, pages 14–24, Las Vegas, NV, December 2002. IEEE Press.

Stateful Intrusion Detection for High-Speed Networks

Christopher Kruegel   Fredrik Valeur
Giovanni Vigna   Richard Kemmerer

Reliable Software Group
University California, Santa Barbara
{kruegel,fredrik,vigna,kemm}@cs.ucsb.edu

Abstract

As networks become faster there is an emerging need for security analysis techniques that can keep up with the increased network throughput. Existing network-based intrusion detection sensors can barely keep up with bandwidths of a few hundred Mbps. Analysis tools that can deal with higher throughput are unable to maintain state between different steps of an attack or they are limited to the analysis of packet headers. We propose a partitioning approach to network security analysis that supports in-depth, stateful intrusion detection on high-speed links. The approach is centered around a slicing mechanism that divides the overall network traffic into subsets of manageable size. The traffic partitioning is done so that a single slice contains all the evidence necessary to detect a specific attack, making sensor-to-sensor interactions unnecessary. This paper describes the approach and presents a first experimental evaluation of its effectiveness.

Keywords: Intrusion Detection, High-Speed Networks, Security Analysis.

1 Introduction

Network-based intrusion detection systems (NIDSs) perform security analysis on packets obtained by eavesdropping on a network link. The constant increase in network speed and throughput poses new challenges to these systems. Current network-based IDSs are barely capable of real-time traffic analysis on saturated Fast Ethernet links (100 Mbps) [3]. As network technology presses forward, Gigabit Ethernet (1000 Mbps) has become the de-facto standard for large network installations. In order to protect such installations, a novel approach for network-based intrusion detection is necessary to manage the ever-increasing data volume.

Network speeds have increased faster than the speed of processors, and therefore centralized solutions have reached their limit. This is especially true if one considers in-depth, stateful intrusion detection analysis. In this case, the sensors have to maintain information about attacks in progress (e.g., in the case of multi-step attacks) or they have to perform application-level analysis of the packet contents. These tasks are resource intensive and in a single-node setup may seriously interfere with the basic task of retrieving packets from the wire.

To be able to perform in-depth, stateful analysis it is necessary to divide the traffic volume into smaller portions that can be thoroughly analyzed by intrusion detection sensors. This approach has often been advocated by the high-performance research community as a way to distribute the service load across many nodes. In contrast to the case for standard load balancing, the division (or slicing) of the traffic for intrusion detection has to be performed in a way that guarantees the detection of all the threat scenarios considered. If a random division of traffic is used, sensors may not receive sufficient data to detect an intrusion, because different parts of the manifestation of an attack may have been assigned to different slices. Therefore, when an attack scenario consists of a number of steps, the slicing mechanism must assure that all of the packets that could trigger those steps are sent to the sensor configured to detect that specific attack.

This paper presents an approach to in-depth, stateful intrusion detection analysis and a tool based on this approach. The approach allows for meaningful slicing of the network traffic into portions of manageable size. The slicing approach and a tool based on the approach are presented in Section 3, after a discussion of related work in Section 2. Section 4 presents the results of the quantitative evaluation of the first prototype of the tool. Section 5 presents some final remarks and outlines future research.

Reprinted with permission from *Proceedings of the IEEE Symposium on Security and Privacy*, May 2004, 285–294.

2   Related Work

The possibility of performing network-based intrusion detection on high-speed links (e.g., on OC-192 links) has been the focus of much debate in the intrusion detection community. A common position is to state that high-speed network-based intrusion detection is not practical because of the technical difficulties encountered in keeping pace with the increasing network speed and the more widespread use of encrypted traffic. Others advocate locating highly distributed network-based sensors at the periphery of computer networks; the idea being that the traffic load is, possibly, more manageable there.

Even though both of the advocated approaches above have good points, analysis of network traffic on high-speed links still represents a fundamental need in many practical network installations. The commercial world attempted to respond to this need and a number of vendors now claim to have sensors that can operate on high-speed ATM or Gigabit Ethernet links. For example, ISS [4] offers *Net-ICE Gigabit Sentry*, a system that is designed to monitor traffic on high-speed links. The company advertises the system as being capable of performing protocol reassembly and analysis for several application-level protocols (e.g. HTTP, SMTP, POP) to identify malicious activities. The tool claims to be the "first network-IDS that can handle full Gigabit speeds." However, the authors of the tool also state that "GigaSentry handles a full Gigabit in lab conditions, but real-world performance will likely be less. [...] Customers should expect at least 300 Mbps real-world performance, and probably more depending up the nature of their traffic. [...] GigaSentry can only capture slightly more than 500,000-packets/second." These comments show the actual difficulties of performing network-based intrusion detection on high-speed links. Other IDS vendors (like Cisco [1]) offer comparable products with similar features. Unfortunately, no experimental data gathered on real networks is presented. TopLayer Networks [11] presents a switch that keeps track of application-level sessions. The network traffic is split with regard to these sessions and forwarded to several intrusion detection sensors. Packets that belong to the same session are sent through the same link. This allows sensors to detect multiple steps of an attack within a single session. Unfortunately, the correlation of information between different sessions is not supported. This could result in missed attacks when attacks are performed against multiple hosts (e.g., ping sweeps), or across multiple sessions.

Very few research papers have been published that deal with the problem of intrusion detection on high-speed links. Sekar et al. [10] describe an approach to perform high-performance analysis of network data, but unfortunately they do not provide experimental data based on live traffic analysis. Their claim of being able to perform real-time

intrusion detection at 500 Mbps is based on the processing of off-line traffic log files. This estimate is not indicative of the real effectiveness of the system when operating on live traffic.

3   A Slicing Approach to High-Speed Intrusion Detection

The problem of intrusion detection analysis in high-speed networks can be effectively attacked only if a scalable solution is available. Let us consider the traffic on the monitored network link as a bi-directional stream of link-layer frames (e.g., Ethernet frames). This stream contains too much data to be processed in real-time by a centralized entity and has to be divided into several smaller streams that are fed into a number of different, distributed sensors. Each sensor is only responsible for a subset of all detectable intrusion scenarios and can therefore manage to process the incoming volume in real-time. Nevertheless, the division into streams has to be done in a way that provides each sensor with enough information to detect exactly the same attacks that it would have witnessed when operating directly on the network link.

3.1   Requirements

The overall goal is to perform stateful intrusion detection analysis in high-speed networks. The approach presented in this paper can be characterized by the following requirements.

- The system implements a misuse detection approach where *signatures* representing attack scenarios are matched against a stream of network events.

- Intrusion detection is performed by a set of sensors, each of which is responsible for the detection of a subset of the signatures.

- Each sensor is autonomous and does not interact with other sensors.

- The system partitions the analyzed event stream into slices of manageable size.

- Each traffic slice is analyzed by a subset of the intrusion detection sensors.

- The system guarantees that the partitioning of traffic maintains detection of all the specified attack scenarios. This implies that sensors, signatures, and traffic slices are configured so that each sensor has access to the traffic necessary to detect the signatures that have been assigned to it.

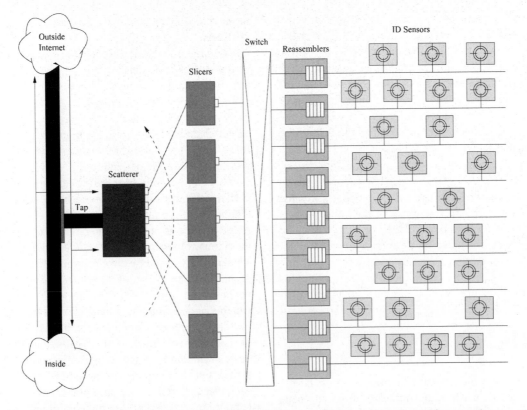

Figure 1. High-level architecture of the high-speed intrusion detection system.

- Components can be added to the system to achieve higher throughput. More precisely, the approach should result in a scalable design where one can add components as needed to match increased network throughput.

3.2 System Architecture

The requirements listed in the previous section have been used as the basis for the design of a network-based intrusion detection system. The system consists of a *network tap*, a *traffic scatterer*, a set of m *traffic slicers* $S_0, ..., S_{m-1}$, a *switch*, a set of n *stream reassemblers* $R_0, ..., R_{n-1}$, and a set of p *intrusion detection sensors* $I_0, ..., I_{p-1}$. A high-level description of the architecture is shown in Figure 1.

The network tap component monitors the traffic stream on a high-speed link. Its task is to extract the sequence F of link-layer frames $\langle f_0, f_1, ..., f_t \rangle$ that are observable on the wire during a time period Δ. This sequence of frames is passed to the scatterer which partitions F into m sub-sequences $F_j : 0 \leq j < m$. Each F_j contains a (possibly empty) subset of the frame sequence F. Every frame f_i is an element of exactly one sub-sequence F_j and therefore $\cup_{j=0}^{j<m} F_j = F$. The scatterer can use any algorithm to partition F. Hereafter, it is assumed that the splitting algorithm simply cycles over the m sub-sequences in a round-robin

fashion, assigning f_i to $F_{i \bmod (m)}$. As a result, each F_j contains an m-th of the total traffic.

Each sub-sequence F_j is transmitted to a different traffic slicer S_j. The task of the traffic slicers is to route the frames they receive to the sensors that may need them to detect an attack. This task is not performed by the scatterer, because frame routing may be complex, requiring a substantial amount of time, while the scatterer has to keep up with the high traffic throughput and can only perform very limited processing per frame.

The traffic slicers are connected to a switch component, which allows a slicer to send a frame to one or more of n outgoing channels C_i. The set of frames sent to a channel is denoted by FC_i. Each channel C_i is associated with a stream reassembler component R_i and a number of intrusion detection sensors. The set of sensors associated with channel C_i is denoted by IC_i. All the sensors that are associated with a channel are able to access all the packets sent on that channel. The original order of two packets could be lost if the two frames took different paths over distinct slicers to the same channel. Therefore, the reassemblers associated with each channel make sure that the packets appear on the channel in the same order that they appeared on the high-speed link. That is, each reassembler R_i must make sure that for each pair of frames $f_j, f_k \in FC_i$ it holds that $(f_j \text{ before } f_k) \iff j < k$.

Each sensor component I_j is associated with q different attack scenarios $A_j = \{A_{j0}, ..., A_{jq-1}\}$. Each attack scenario A_{jk} has an associated *event space* E_{jk}. The event space specifies which frames are candidates to be part of the manifestation of the attack. For example, consider an attack targeting a Web server called `spider` within the network protected by the intrusion detection system. In this case, the event space for that attack is composed of all the TCP traffic that involves port 80 on host `spider`.

Event spaces are expressed as disjunctions of *clauses*, that is, $E_{jk} = c_{jk_0} \vee c_{jk_1} \vee ... \vee c_{jk_n}$, where each clause c_{jk} is an expression of the type xRy. x denotes a value derived from the frame f_i (e.g., a part of the frame header) while R specifies an arithmetic relation (e.g., $=$, $!=$, $<$). y can be a constant, the value of a variable, or a value derived from the same frame. Clauses and event spaces may be derived automatically from the attack descriptions, for example from signatures written in attack languages such as Bro [6], Sutekh [7], STATL [2], or Snort [8].

3.3   Frame Routing

Event spaces are the basis for the definition of the filters used by the slicers to route frames to different channels. The filters are determined by composing the event spaces associated with all the scenarios that are "active" on a specific channel. More precisely, the set of active scenarios is $AC_i = U_{j=0}^{j<u} A_j$ where A_j is the set of scenarios of $I_j \in IC_i$. The event space EC_i for a channel C_i is the disjunction of the event spaces of all active scenarios, which corresponds to the disjunction of all the clauses of all the active scenarios. The resulting overall expression is the filter that each slicer uses to determine if a frame has to be routed to that specific channel. Note that it is possible that a certain frame will be needed by more than one scenario. Therefore, it will be sent on more than one channel.

The configuration of the slicers as described above is static; that is, it is calculated off-line before the system is started. The static approach suffers from the possibility that, depending on the type of traffic, a large percentage of the network packets could be forwarded to a single channel. This would result in the overloading of sensors attached to that channel. The static configuration also makes it impossible to predict the exact number of sensors that are necessary to deal with a Gigabit link. The load on each sensor depends on the scenarios used and the actual traffic. The minimum requirement for the slicers is that the capacity of their incoming and outgoing links must be at least equal to the bandwidth of the monitored link.

One way to prevent the overloading condition is to perform dynamic load balancing. This is done by reassigning scenarios to different channels at run-time. This variant obviously implies the need to reconfigure the filter mechanism at the traffic slicers and update the assignment of clauses to channels.

In addition to the reassignment of whole scenarios to different channels, it is also possible to split a single scenario into two or more refined scenarios. The idea is that each refined scenario catches only a subset of the attacks that the original scenario covered, but each can be deployed on a different channel. Obviously, the union of attacks detectable by all refined scenarios has to cover exactly the same set of attacks as the original scenario did.

This can be done by creating additional constraints on certain attributes of one or more basic events. Each constraint limits the number of attacks a refined scenario can detect. The constraints have to be chosen in a way such that every possible value for a certain attribute (of the original scenario) is allowed by the constraint of at least one refined scenario. Then the set of all refined scenarios, which each cover only a subset of the attacks of the original one, are capable of detecting the same attacks as the original.

A simple mechanism to partition a particular scenario is to include a constraint on the destination attribute of each basic event that represents a packet which is sent by the attacker. One has to partition the set of possible destinations such that each refined scenario only covers attacks against a certain range of hosts. When the union of these target host ranges covers all possible attack targets, the set of refined scenarios is capable of finding the same attacks as the original scenario.

Such an approach is necessary when a single scenario causes too much traffic to be forwarded to a single channel.

In addition, obviously innocent or hostile frames could be filtered out before the scenario clauses are applied, thereby eliminating traffic that needs no further processing. This could be used, for instance, to prevent the system from being flooded by packets from distributed denial-of-service slaves that produce traffic with a unique, known signature.

4   Evaluation

The initial set of experiments were primarily aimed at evaluating the effectiveness of the scatterer/slicer/ reassembler architecture. For these experiments, we deployed three traffic slicers ($m = 3$) and four stream reassemblers ($n = 4$) with one intrusion detection sensor per stream. The next section presents the details of the hardware and software used to realize the initial prototype, and the section after that gives the details of each experiment and presents the corresponding results.

4.1   Prototype Architecture

The prototype is composed of a number of hosts responsible for the analysis of the traffic carried by a Gigabit link.

The Gigabit link is realized as a direct connection (crossover cable) between two machines equipped with Intel Xeon 1.7 GHz processors, 512 MB RAM and 64-bit PCI 3Com 996-T Gigabit Ethernet cards running Linux 2.4.2 (Red Hat 7.1). One of the two machines simulates the network tap and is responsible for creating the network traffic (via `tcpreplay` [12]). The other machine acts as the traffic scatterer and is equipped with three additional 100 Mbps 3Com 905C-TX Ethernet cards.

The scatterer functionality itself is realized as a kernel module attached to the Linux kernel bridge interface. The bridge interface provides a hook that allows the kernel to inspect the incoming frames before they are forwarded to the network layer (e.g., the IP stack). The scatterer module intercepts frames coming from the Gigabit interface and immediately forwards them to one of the outgoing links through the corresponding Fast Ethernet card. The links are selected in a round-robin fashion. The scatterer also attaches a sequence number to each packet, which is later used by the reassemblers. In order to overcome the problem of splitting Ethernet frames with a length close to the maximum transferable unit (MTU), the sequence number has to be integrated into the Ethernet frame without increasing its size. To leave the data portion untouched, we decided to modify the Ethernet header. We also wanted to limit the modifications of the Ethernet frame to a minimum in order to be able to reuse existing hardware (e.g., network interface cards, network drivers). Therefore, the MTU had to remain unchanged. For this reason, we decided to use the six-byte Ethernet source address field for sequence numbers. As a result, before the traffic scatterer forwards a frame, it writes the current sequence number into the source address field and increments it.

The experimental setup demonstrates that the partitioning of traffic is possible and that it allows for the detailed analysis of higher traffic volume (including defragmentation, stream reassembly, and content analysis). Because we only use three traffic slicers (with an aggregated bandwidth of 300 Mbps), sustained incoming traffic of 1 Gbps would overload our experimental setup. However, the introduction of additional traffic slicers would allow us to handle higher traffic inputs.

The traffic slicers (Intel Pentium 4 1.5 GHz, 256 MB RAM, 3Com 905C-TX fast Ethernet cards running Linux 2.4.2 - Redhat 7.1) have the NIC of the link that connects them to the traffic scatterer set to promiscuous mode, in order to receive all incoming frames. The data portion of each incoming frame is matched against the clauses stored for each channel. Whenever a clause for a channel is satisfied, a copy of the frame is forwarded to that channel. Note that this could (and usually does) increase the total number of frames that have to be processed by the intrusion detection sensors. Nevertheless, a sufficiently large number of sensors combined with sophisticated partitioning enable one to keep the amount of traffic at each sensor low enough to handle. In our test setup, the partitioning (i.e., the clauses) was determined as follows. Similar to Snort [9], we distinguished between an inside network and an outside network, representing the range of IP addresses of the protected network and its complement, respectively. The protected network address range is divided according to the existing class C subnetworks. The network addresses are then grouped into four sets, each of which is assigned to a different channel. This partitioning allows the system to detect both attacks involving a single host and attacks spanning a subnetwork. As explained in Section 3.3 more sophisticated schemes are possible by analyzing additional information in the packet headers or even by examining the frame payload.

Once the filters have been configured, the frames have to be routed to the various channels. As in the case for the transmission between the scatterer and the traffic slicers, we want to prevent frames from being split when sent to the channels. This makes it necessary to include the destination address information of the intended channel in the Ethernet frame itself without increasing its size and without modifying the payload. To do this we use the Ethernet destination address. Therefore, the destination address is rewritten with values `00:00:00:00:00:01`, `00:00:00:00:00:02`, etc., depending on the destination channel. There were two reasons for using a generic link number instead of the actual Ethernet addresses as the target address for sensors. First, a number of sensors may be deployed on each channel, processing portions of the traffic in parallel. Since each sensor has to receive all packets on the channel where it is attached, selecting the Ethernet address of a single sensor is not beneficial. Second, whenever the NIC of a sensor has to be replaced, the new Ethernet address would have to be updated at each traffic slicer. In order to save this overhead, each traffic slicer simply writes the channel number into the target address field of outgoing frames.

The actual frame routing is performed by a switch (a Cisco Catalyst 3500XL) that connects traffic slicers with reassemblers. The MAC address-port table of the switch holds the static associations between the channel numbers (i.e., the target Ethernet addresses set by the traffic slicers) and the corresponding outgoing ports. In general backplanes of switches have very high bandwidth compared to Ethernet links, so they are not likely to be overloaded by traffic generated by the scatterer.

In our setup, the stream reassemblers are located at each sensor node (using the same equipment as the traffic slicers), and they provide the intrusion detection sensors with a temporally sorted sequence of frames by using the encapsulated sequence numbers. The reassembly procedure

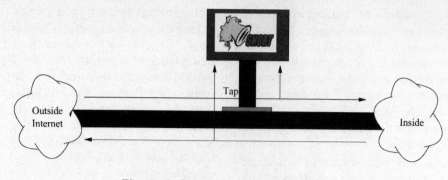

Figure 2. Single-node Snort setup.

has been integrated into `libpcap` so that every sensor that utilizes these routines to capture packets can be run unmodified. For each frame, we assume that no other frame with a smaller sequence number can arrive after a certain time span (currently 500 ms). This means that when an out-of-order packet is received, it is temporarily stored in a queue until either the missing packets are received and the correctly-ordered batch of packets is passed to the application, or the reassembler decides that some packets have been lost because a timeout expired and the packet is passed without further delay. Therefore, each received packet is passed to the sensors with a worst case delay being the timeout value. The timeout parameter has to be large enough to prevent the situation where packets with smaller sequence numbers arrive after subsequent frames have already been processed but small enough so that the reaction lag of the system is within acceptable limits. Since the processing and transmission of frames is usually very fast and no retransmission or acknowledgments are utilized, one can expect frames to arrive at each reassembler in the correct order most of the time. In principle, this allows one to safely choose a very short time span. We expect to have no problems in reducing the current timeout value, but at the moment we have no experimental evaluation of the effect of different timeout values on the effectiveness of intrusion detection.

The network cards of the nodes would normally be receiving traffic at rates close to their maximum capacity. If administrative connections, such as dynamically setting clauses, reporting alarms, or performing maintenance work were to go through the same interfaces, these connections could potentially suffer from packet loss and long delays. To overcome this problem, each machine is connected to a second dedicated network that provides a safe medium to perform the tasks mentioned above. An additional communication channel decoupled from the input path has the additional benefit of increasing the resiliency of the system against denial-of-service attacks. That is, alarms and reconfiguration commands still reach all intended receivers, since they do not have to compete against the flood of incoming packets for network access.

4.2 Experimental Results

The goal of the set of experiments described in this section is to get a preliminary evaluation of the practicality and effectiveness of our approach. The general assumption is that we are interested in in-depth, stateful, application-level analysis of high-speed traffic. For this reason, we chose Snort as our "reference" sensor and we enabled reassembling and defragmenting.

To run our experiments we used traffic produced by MIT Lincoln Labs as part of the DARPA 1999 IDS evaluation [5]. More precisely, we used the data from Tuesday of the fifth week. The traffic log was injected on the Gigabit link using `tcpreplay`. To achieve high speed traffic we had to "speed up" the traffic. We assumed that this would not affect the correctness of our experiment. We also assumed that the LL/MIT traffic is a reasonable approximation of real-world traffic. This assumption has often been debated, but we think that for the extent of the tests below this assumption is reasonable.

The first experiment was to run Snort on the tcpdump traffic log. The results of this "off-line" run are: 11,213 detections in 10 seconds with an offline throughput of 261 Mbps. The ruleset used included 961 rules.

The second experiment was to run Snort on a single-node monitor. The setup is shown in Figure 2. In practice, Snort is run on the scatterer host and it reads directly from the network card. We measured the decrease in effectiveness of the detection when the traffic rate increases[1]. The ruleset used included only the 18 rules that actually fired on the test data. Figure 3 shows the results of this experiment. The reduced performance is due to packet loss, which becomes substantial at approximately 150 Mbps. This experiment identifies the saturation point of this setup.

The third experiment was to run Snort in the simple setup of Figure 2 with a constant traffic rate of 100 Mbps and an increasing number of signatures. The experiment starts with only the eighteen signatures that are needed to achieve

---

[1]The limit of 200 Mbps in the graphs is the maximum amount of traffic that `tcpreplay` is able to generate.

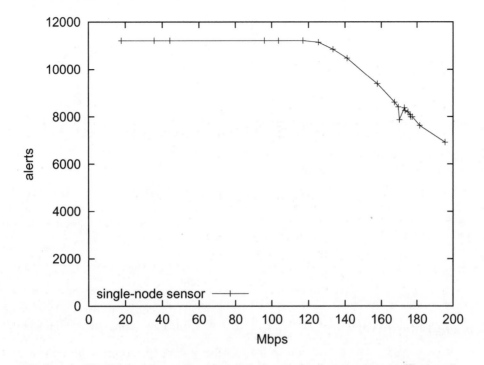

Figure 3. Single-host monitor detection rate for increasing traffic levels.

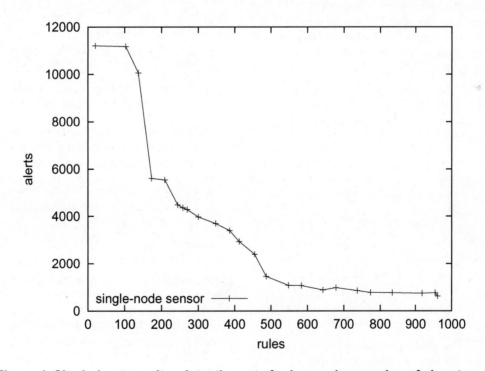

Figure 4. Single-host monitor detection rate for increasing number of signatures.

maximum detection for the given data. The plot in Figure 4 shows how the performance decreases as more signatures are added to the sensor. This experiment demonstrates that such a setup is limited by the number of signatures that can be used to analyze the traffic stream.

The fourth and fifth experiments repeated the previous two experiments using Snort sensors in the proposed architecture. Figure 5 and 6 present the results of these experiments. The performance of the single-node experiments are included for comparison. The drop in detection rate at high speeds by the distributed sensor, which can be seen in Figure 5, is caused by packet loss in the scatterer. The network cards currently used for the output traffic are not able to handle more than about 170 Mbps. The experimental results show that the proposed architecture has increased throughput and is much less sensitive to the number of signatures used.

5   Conclusion and Future Work

This paper presents the design, implementation, and experimental evaluation of a distributed network monitor. The system supports stateful, in-depth analysis of network traffic on high-speed links. The evaluation of the first prototype showed that the approach is more scalable than the single-host monitor approach. The current results are very preliminary and a thorough evaluation will require experimentation in a real-world environment.

Future work will include a more thorough evaluation of the trade-offs when configuring the system, the development of a mechanism for dynamic load balancing, and the use of hierarchically structured scatterers/slicers to achieve higher throughput levels.

Acknowledgments

This research was supported by the Army Research Office, under agreement DAAD19-01-1-0484 and by the Defense Advanced Research Projects Agency (DARPA) and Rome Laboratory, Air Force Materiel Command, USAF, under agreement number F30602-97-1-0207. The U.S. Government is authorized to reproduce and distribute reprints for Governmental purposes notwithstanding any copyright annotation thereon.

The views and conclusions contained herein are those of the authors and should not be interpreted as necessarily representing the official policies or endorsements, either expressed or implied, of the Army Research Office, the Defense Advanced Research Projects Agency (DARPA), Rome Laboratory, or the U.S. Government.

References

[1] CISCO. CISCO Intrusion Detection System. Technical Information, Nov 2001.

[2] S.T. Eckmann, G. Vigna, and R.A. Kemmerer. STATL: An Attack Language for State-based Intrusion Detection. In *Proceedings of the ACM Workshop on Intrusion Detection Systems*, Athens, Greece, November 2000.

[3] NSS Group. Intrusion Detection and Vulnerability Assessment. Technical report, NSS, Oakwood House, Wennington, Cambridgeshire, UK, 2000.

[4] ISS. BlackICE Sentry Gigabit. http://www.networkice.com/products/sentry_gigabit, November 2001.

[5] MIT Lincoln Laboratory. DARPA Intrusion Detection Evaluation. http://www.ll.mit.edu/IST/ideval/, 1999.

[6] V. Paxson. Bro: A System for Detecting Network Intruders in Real-Time. In *Proceedings of the 7th USENIX Security Symposium*, San Antonio, TX, January 1998.

[7] J. Pouzol and M. Ducassé. From Declarative Signatures to Misuse IDS. In W. Lee, L. Mé, and A. Wespi, editors, *Proceedings of the RAID International Symposium*, volume 2212 of *LNCS*, pages 1 – 21, Davis, CA, October 2001. Springer-Verlag.

[8] M. Roesch. Writing Snort Rules: How To write Snort rules and keep your sanity. http://www.snort.org.

[9] M. Roesch. Snort - Lightweight Intrusion Detection for Networks. In *Proceedings of the USENIX LISA '99 Conference*, November 1999.

[10] R. Sekar, V. Guang, S. Verma, and T. Shanbhag. A High-performance Network Intrusion Detection System. In *Proceedings of the 6th ACM Conference on Computer and Communications Security*, November 1999.

[11] Toplayer networks. http://www.toplayer.com, November 2001.

[12] M. Undy. tcpreplay. Software Package, May 1999.

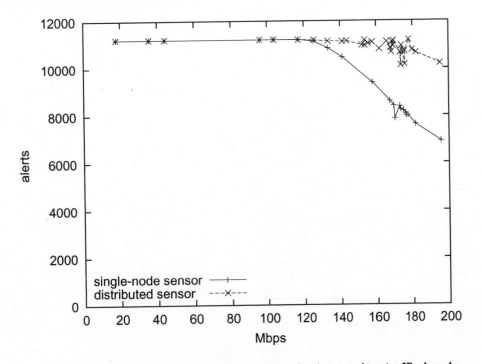

Figure 5. Distributed monitor detection rate for increasing traffic levels.

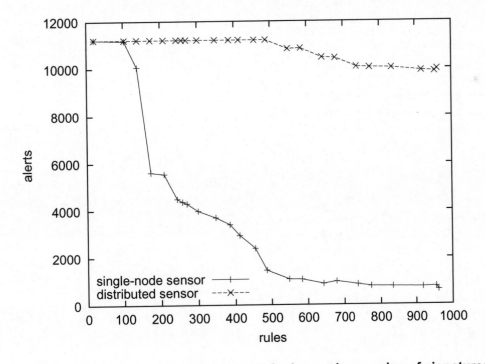

Figure 6. Distributed monitor detection rate for increasing number of signatures.

CHAPTER 2

At the Edges of the Critical Information Infrastructure

David Hislop and Todd Combs

In this chapter, we have contributed technical papers from four CIP MURI teams working on the following aspects of next generation edge devices of Internet and secure information infrastructure:

- Trusted edge devices
- High confidence embedded systems
- Effective verification and benchmarking for embedded systems
- Building resilience and self-recovery

The abstracts of the High Confidence Embedded Systems (HCES) research papers, contained in this chapter, clearly highlight the focused efforts to enable the implementation of a tool-based environment for modern system and software engineering.

It is important to note that although the approaches are varied, there is a strong commonality in the overall objectives. This is reflected in the general agreement on the need for suites of compatible tools to span the totality of the critical engineering tasks; that is from the establishment of the requirements to the implementation of the system.

The Kansas State University/University of Nebraska–Lincoln/University of Massachusetts team has developed tools and techniques for the construction, analysis, and verification of embedded systems. Specifically, the team has focused on overcoming inflexibilities in earlier model-checking techniques, and on providing frameworks that better support formal description and development of software product-line architectures for large-scale distributed systems. Although earlier model-checking techniques have been successfully applied to verify hardware and software designs, their scalability and applicability has been limited because the associated modeling languages, core algorithms, and optimization strategies are fixed and cannot be tailored to particular application domains. These limitations are especially troubling in the area of software systems, where scale and use of dynamic data and threading makes them more challenging to analyze than hardware systems. One of the primary contributions of the team has been the development of Bogor—a powerful, customizable, and extensible model-checking framework. Bogor's modeling language can be extended with new primitives that enable domain-specific behaviors to be captured directly. Moreover, Bogor's modular architecture allows core algorithm and optimization modules to be unplugged and replaced with customized modules that leverage particular domain properties and characteristics. By customizing Bogor, the MURI team has demonstrated orders of magnitude improvement in model-checking performance for a number of application areas, including checking designs of distributed real-time systems built using component middleware and model-checking current Java systems. The team's overview paper in this chapter, "Customizable Model Checking for Embedded Software," argues that sophisticated reasoning techniques like model checking can be made much more effective if they are customized to particular application domains; this paper describes how a class of model-checking optimizations can be dramatically improved by domain customization when model checking Java programs.

The Carnegie Mellon team, led by Professor Clarke, focuses on making formal methods part of the standard designer's toolbox for developing high-confidence embedded systems. Formal methods offer a sound alternative to ad hoc approaches to systems and software engineering, which must rely on extensive simulation and testing to guarantee that performance and safety requirements are satisfied. Advances made at Carnegie Mellon in model-checking technologies—including bounded model checking, compositional reasoning, and the exploitation of counter-examples to guide the efficient construction of source code abstractions—make it possible to apply formal methods to realistically scaled systems. These techniques have been extended to incorporate models of the continuous dynamic environments of embedded systems for feedback control applications. Carnegie Mellon researchers have also developed new methods for incorporating statistical data into model-checking formalisms so that traditional probabilistic measures of system failure and security can be computed efficiently for software and networked systems. To address the enormous problem of legacy systems, the Carnegie Mellon team has also developed algorithms and tools that extract formal architectural models from existing software. Their research efforts are presented in the summary paper titled "Formal Verification for High Confidence Embedded Systems."

A second Carnegie Mellon team led by Professor Ganger has focused on research enabling better security via smarter devices. Security compromises are a fact of life and a major concern for national defense as well as corporate America. No single defense is adequate, and this project develops and explores a model in which security functionality is distributed among physically distinct components. Inspired by siege warfare, the project explores the value of individual devices erecting their own security perimeters and defending their own critical resources (for example, network link or storage media). Together with conventional OS and firewall defenses, such self-securing devices promise greater survivability for network infrastructures and flexibility for security administrators dealing with intrusions. The paper "Better Security via Smarter Devices" summarizes their latest work. By having each device erect an independent security perimeter, the network environment gains many outposts from which to act when under attack. Devices not only protect their own resources, but they can observe, log, and react to the actions of other nearby devices. Infiltration of one security perimeter will compromise only a small fraction of the environment—other devices can work to dynamically identify the problem, alert still-secured devices about the compromised components, and raise the security levels of the environment. The team has created models for quantifying the effects of worm/attack mitigation techniques, such as NIC-embedded isolation and aggressive host inoculation, on worm/attack propagation. They have discovered additional uses for device-embedded data protection and versioning mechanisms—most notably for efficient, survivable storage protocols—strengthening the case for their inclusion in future storage infrastructures. They have also developed NIC-embedded intrusion detection, isolation, and propagation mechanisms capable of, for example, slowing Internet worm propagation speeds by orders of magnitude. They have introduced self-securing storage approaches for protecting data from intruders, enhancing diagnosis of and recovery from intrusions, and they have demonstrated functional prototypes of self-securing storage, self-securing network interface cards, and storage-based intrusion detection—all managed by a common administrative console.

The paper "Overview of the HASTEN (High Assurance Systems Tools and Environments) Project" presents the work carried out by the University of Pennsylvania team. The researchers have focused their efforts on tool environments. The HASTEN project aimed at extending the state of the art in embedded system development in all phases of the development cycle, starting from informal requirements, through high-level specification and model-driven design, to code generation, verification, and validation, as well as post-deployment run-time monitoring. Significant progress has been made in all of these areas. Additionally, in the AIRES (Automatic Integration of Reusable Embedded Software) tool, the detailed design techniques allow more efficient and thorough exploration of design alternatives for allocation of application software to hardware platforms, task formation, and priority assignment. Advances in code generation from hybrid systems models allow us, for the first time, to provide formal guarantees that behavior of the generated code follows the behavior of the model within fixed bounds. In the field of verification, significant improvements have been made both in expressive power of model-checking technology and in scalability of model-checking tools with the help of compositional assume-guarantee methods. Significant advances have been made in the automatic extraction of verification models from Java code. Runtime monitoring capabilities have also seen an increase in expressive power, with added support for monitoring regular expressions and dynamically changing sets of properties.

Better Security via Smarter Devices

Gregory R. Ganger, Dawn Song, Chenxi Wang
Carnegie Mellon University

Abstract

High-profile computer security failures have become regular news items. This article describes why today's approach to computer security continues to fail and a more promising approach on the horizon. Inspired by constructs from siege warfare, this approach extends the many devices in a computing infrastructure such that they each treat their interfaces as security perimeters and participate in defending the infrastructure. Together with conventional border defenses, like firewalls, such self-securing devices can provide dynamic prevention, detection, diagnosis, isolation, and repair when intruders get past an outer perimeter.

1. Overview

Computer security breaches are a huge and growing challenge for digital infrastructures. Since such infrastructures play critical roles in our economic, government, and military interests, we must find ways of better preventing intrusions and mitigating the damage that they can do. Doing so, however, is going to require fundamental change in the approaches taken to computer security.

Today's main security tools provide border defenses and watch for attempts to breach them. The most common border defense is the network "firewall," which sits between a managed network and the rest of the Internet. It examines packets going in each direction, allowing only those that conform to rules defined by the network's administrator. A border exists within most computer systems, as well, in the form of the operating system's kernel and administrative roles. Behind each of these borders, intrusion detection systems can look for attempts to breach the border defense.

This conventional security architecture is fundamentally brittle, because it relies on a small number of border protections to protect a large number of resources and services with many users. This reliance comes with three major difficulties: (1) the many interfaces and functionalities needed to support many services make correct implementation and administration extremely difficult; the practical implications are daily security alerts for popular OSs and network applications; (2) once they bypass a border protection, attackers can freely manipulate everything it protects, which greatly complicates most phases of security management, including intrusion detection, isolation, diagnosis, and recovery; intruders commonly disable intrusion detection systems and remove traces of their presence after breaking into a system; (3) having a central point of security checks creates performance, fault-tolerance, and flexibility limitations for large-scale environments.

In practice, it is impossible to completely prevent intrusions into a network of any size and function. There are simply too many humans and too much software (created by humans) involved. Humans are fallible. They make mistakes when building software, when configuring systems, and when giving trust. All of these open doorways for intruders. And, the doorways get wider as systems become more flexible, since it becomes harder and harder to distinguish good uses of the flexibility from bad.

Users of computer systems are not going to allow a reverse in the trend towards greater functionality, so a different security approach is needed. This article promotes an alternative architecture in which individual system components erect their own security perimeters and protect their resources (e.g., network, storage, or video feed) from intruder tampering. This "self-securing devices" architecture distributes security functionality amongst *physically isolated* components, avoiding much of the fragility and unmanageability inherent in today's border-based security. Specifically, this architecture addresses the three fundamental difficulties by: (1) simplifying each security perimeter (e.g., consider network card or disk interfaces), (2) reducing the power that an intruder gains from compromising just one of the perimeters, and (3) distributing security enforcement checks among the many components of the system.

Conventional CPUs will still run application programs, but they won't dictate which packets are transferred onto network wires and they won't dictate which disk blocks are overwritten. Instead, self-securing network interface cards (NICs) will provide firewall and proxy server functionality for a given host, as well as throttling or labelling its outbound traffic when necessary. Likewise, self-securing storage devices will detect and protect their data from compromised client systems, and self-securing user interface com-

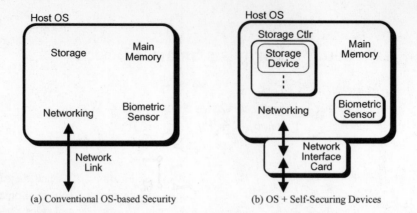

(a) Conventional OS-based Security   (b) OS + Self-Securing Devices

Figure 1. Two security approaches for a computer system. On the left, (a) shows the conventional approach, which is based on a single perimeter around the set of system resources. On the right, (b) shows our new approach, which augments the conventional security perimeter with perimeters around each self-securing device. These additional perimeters offer additional protection and flexibility for defense against attackers. Firewall-enforced network security fits a similar picture, with the new architecture providing numerous new security perimeters within each system on the internal network.

ponents can assist with end-to-end trust in the sources of user input and system output. In a system of self-securing devices, compromising the OS of the main CPU won't give a malicious party complete control over all system resources — to gain complete power, an intruder must also compromise the disk's OS, the network card's OS, etc. Similarly, getting past the outer firewall will not give unchecked access to the internal network; self-securing switches, NICs, and routers will still be in the way.

Augmenting current border protections with self-securing devices promises much greater flexibility for security administrators. By having each device erect an independent security perimeter, the network environment gains many outposts from which to act when under attack. Devices not only protect their own resources, but they can observe, log, and react to the actions of other nearby devices. Infiltration of one security perimeter will compromise only a small fraction of the environment, allowing other devices to dynamically identify the problem, alert still-secured devices about the compromised components, raise the security levels of the environment, and so forth.

Self-securing devices will require more computational resources in each device. However, with rapidly shrinking hardware costs, growing software development costs, and astronomical security costs, it makes no sense to not be throwing hardware at security problems. A main challenge has been identifying the best ways to partition (and replicate) functionality across self-securing components in order to enhance security and robustness. A corollary challenge is to re-marshall the distributed functionality to achieve acceptable levels of performance and manageability. After de-

scribing our inspiration for this architecture (medieval siege warfare), this article overviews some of our experiences and success stories from years of research.

2. Siege Warfare in the Internet Age

Despite enormous effort and investment, it has proven nearly impossible to prevent computer security breaches. To protect our critical information infrastructures, we need defensive strategies that can survive determined and successful attacks, allowing security managers to dynamically detect, diagnose, and recover from breaches in security perimeters. Borrowing from lessons from historical warfare, we promote a new network security architecture analogous to medieval defense constructs.

Current security mechanisms are based largely on singular border protections. This roughly corresponds to early defense practices in which defenders erected walls around their camps and homes to provide protective cover during attacks. Once inside the walls, however, attackers faced few obstacles to gaining access to all parts of the enclosed area. Likewise, a hacker who successfully compromises a firewall or OS has complete access to the resources protected by these border defenses—no additional obstacles are faced.[1] Of course, border defenses were a large improve-

_____

[1]This is not quite correct in the case of a firewall protecting a set of hosts that each run a multi-program OS, such as Windows NT or Linux. Such an environment is more like a town of many houses surrounded by a guarded wall. Each house affords some protection beyond that provided by the guarded wall, but not as much in practice as might be hoped. In particular, most people in such an environment will simply open the door when

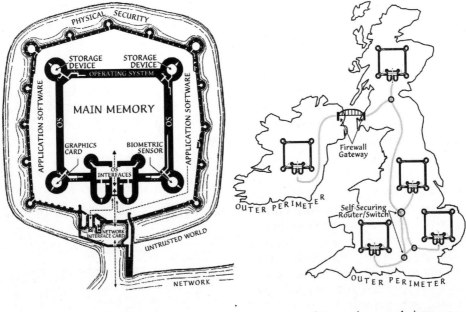

(a) a siege-ready computer system   (b) two siege-ready intranets

Figure 2. The self-securing device architecture illustrated via the siege warfare constructs that inspired it. On the left, (a) shows a siege-ready system with layered and independent tiers of defense enabled by device-embedded security perimeters. On the right, (b) shows two small intranets of such systems, separated by firewall-guarded entry points. Also note the self-securing routers/switches connecting the machines within each intranet.

ment over open camps, but they proved difficult to maintain against determined attackers — border protections can be worn down over time and defenders of large encampments are often spread thin at the outer wall.

As the size and sophistication of attacking forces grew, so did the sophistication of defensive structures. The most impressive such structures, constructed to withstand determined sieges in medieval times, used multiple tiers of defenses. Further, tiers were not strictly hierarchical in nature — rather, some structures could be defended independently of others. This latter advancement in defense capabilities provided defenders with significant flexibility in defense strategy, the ability to observe attacker activities, and the ability to force attackers to deal with multiple independent defensive forces.

Applying the same ideas to computer and network security, border protections (i.e., firewalls and host OSs) can be augmented with security perimeters erected at many points within the borders. Enabled by low-cost computation (e.g., embedded processors, ASICs), security functionality can be embedded in most device microcontrollers, yielding "better

security via smarter devices." We refer to devices with embedded security functionality as *self-securing devices*.

Self-securing devices can significantly increase network security and manageability, enabling capabilities that are difficult or impossible to implement in current systems. For example, independent device-embedded security perimeters guarantee that a penetrated boundary does not compromise the entire system. Uncompromised components continue their security functions even when other system components are compromised. Further, when attackers penetrate one boundary and then attempt to penetrate another, uncompromised components can observe and react to the intruder's attack; from behind their intact security perimeters, they can send alerts to the security administrator, actively quarantine or immobilize the attacker, and wall-off or migrate critical data and resources. Pragmatically, each self-securing device's security perimeter is simpler because of specialization, which should make correct implementations more likely. Further, distributing security checks among many devices reduces their performance impact and allows more checks to be made.

By augmenting conventional border protections with self-securing devices, this new security architecture promises substantial increases in both network security and

---

they hear a knock, assuming that the wall keeps out attackers. Worse, in the computer environment, homogeneity among systems results in a single set of keys (attacks) that give access to any house in the town.

security manageability. As with medieval fortresses, well-defended systems conforming to this architecture could survive protracted sieges by organized attackers.

3. Device-embedded security examples

This section overviews some prime examples of self-securing devices and what can be done with them. By embedding intrusion survival functionality into devices, one enjoys their benefits even when host OSes, user accounts, and other devices are compromised.

Network interface cards (NICs): The role of NICs in a computer system is to move packets between the system's components and the network. Thus, the natural security extension is to enforce security policies on packets forwarded in each direction, looking for and potentially blocking malicious network activity [1, 2, 3].

Like a firewall, a self-securing NIC can examine packet headers and simply not forward unacceptable packets into or out of the computer system; in fact, 3Com has recently started selling firmware extensions to NICs that allow them to do exactly this. In addition to avoiding the bottleneck imposed by current centralized approaches, NIC-based firewalls can also protect systems from some insider attacks as well as Internet attacks, since only the one host system is inside the NIC's boundary.

Most interestingly, a self-securing NIC can watch its own host system for signs of compromise, helping administrators to identify and contain compromised machines within their intranet. Given its closeness to its host, a NIC can have a much clearer view of its host's network interactions, more easily identifying denial-of-service attacks and propagation attempts, including many explicitly designed to defeat network intrusion detection systems. By throttling suspicious behavior, self-securing NICs can reduce damage and give administrators time to react—notably, rapid-propagation worms like Code Red and Slammer within the intranet can be quickly identified by self-securing NICs and throttled at their source. If all machines on the Internet were so equipped, such worms could not spread rapidly in the way that they do—our analyses [2, 3, 10] indicate such throttling could extend the spread time from 15 minutes to over six months.

Storage devices: The role of storage devices in computer systems is to persistently store data. Thus, natural security extensions are to watch the access stream for signs of misbehavior, keep a record of storage activity, and prevent compromised clients from destroying stored data.

Storage-based intrusion detection is a new approach that can spot several common intruder actions, such as adding backdoors, inserting Trojan horses, and removing traces of their presence [7]; as a simple form of this, some high-end file servers now come with built-in support for virus scan-

ning. (A virus scanner in the file server cannot be disabled by viruses that compromised clients machines, like scanners within those clients can.) Experiments show that most real intrusion tools (15 of the 18 studied) are quickly detected by a storage IDS.

A self-securing storage device can also protect stored data from attackers, preventing undetectable tampering and permanent deletion [8]. It does so by managing storage space from behind its security perimeter, keeping an audit log of all requests, and keeping previous versions of data modified by attackers. Since a storage device cannot distinguish compromised user accounts from legitimate users, the latter requires keeping all versions of all data. Finite capacities will limit how long such comprehensive versioning can be maintained, but 100% per year storage capacity growth will allow modern disks to keep several weeks of all versions. If intrusion detection mechanisms reveal an intrusion within this multi-week *detection window*, security administrators will have this valuable audit and version information for diagnosis and recovery. This information will enable diagnosis by not allowing system audit logs to be doctored, exploit tools to be deleted, or back doors to be hidden—the common steps taken by intruders to disguise their presence. This information will also simplify recovery by allowing rapid restoration of pre-intrusion versions and incremental examination of intermediate versions for legitimate updates. Finally, self-securing storage devices can be a critical component of survivable storage systems [4, 11].

Routers and switches: The role of routers and switches in a network environment is to forward packets from one link to an appropriate next link. Thus, natural security extensions for such devices are traffic monitoring (e.g., attack detection), control (e.g., firewalls), and isolation (e.g., VLANs). Many current routers now provide such functions.

More advanced mechanisms combine the information and capabilities of multiple network switches and routers to enable distributed monitoring. Traffic monitoring at different vantage points allow us to detect anomalous traffic patterns and hence detect attacks at an early stage. For example, traffic monitoring on routers/switches in internal networks allows us to detect a compromised internal machine when it tries to probe and login to other machines that the compromised machine does not usually connect to. Such anomolous traffic patterns would not be caught using the traditional firewall approach because the traffic is solely internal. On the other hand, large scale Internet attacks such as distributed Denial-of-Service (DDoS) attacks and fast worm propagation often cause drastic changes in Internet traffic patterns, and traffic monitoring on the routers on the Internet could detect such traffic pattern change and hence the attacks at an early stage. While traffic monitoring on low bandwidth links or internal networks could use detailed profiling information, traffic monitoring on high bandwidth links and on the Internet often has stringent speed and memory requirements that require the design of more efficient and less fine-grained mechanisms to detect traffic pattern changes. For example, monitoring with per-flow state is not possible for high-bandwidth routers.

We have designed efficient algorithms to detect DDoS attacks and worm propagations at an early stage on high-speed routers [6, 9, 13, 12]. Such traffic monitoring can not only detect attacks, but also automatically develop appropriate filters to stop or throttle attacks. For example, we have developed efficient traffic monitoring mechanisms to enable detection of the victims and attackers in DDoS attacks and compromised machines that try spread worms in real time. By dropping or delaying the traffic from attackers and to the victims, we could defend against or mitigate large scale Internet attacks. Traffic monitoring can not only be applied to the header information in the packets, but also to the content of the packets. Viruses and worms often have distinct signatures in the packet payload. Traffic monitoring can also be used to identify such signatures and throttle packets according to the signatures.

Virtual Machines: Following on our work, several groups have noted that virtual machine technology offers boundaries that can be as strong as physical isolation. A virtual machine monitor is a small piece of software that works within a host's main CPU to provide "virtual machines" in which OSs and applications can execute. To the code within them, each virtual machine can look just like a complete hardware system, isolated from the other virtual machines. At the University of Michigan, researchers are exploring intrusion diagnosis based on complete machine replay based on a log of all input events (network packets, keystrokes, etc.). With such replay, a forensic analyst can replay and watch the actions of an intrusion in a controlled environment, examining what they did and how. At Stanford, researchers are exploring intrusion detection within a virtual machine monitor, using techniques similar to those described above, but with the extra benefit of being able to examine the host's main memory contents. Self-securing virtual machine monitors have all of the features of other self-securing devices, so long as the isolation implementation has no exploitable bugs.

User interface devices: An important emerging form of self-securing device is used for trusted computing. Controversial efforts like the TCPA (Trusted Computing Platform Alliance) and Microsoft's Palladium project seek to increase "trust" in computing: users should be able to trust the apparent source of output, software should be able to trust its runtime environment and the sources of input, and remote systems should be able to trust the sources of information. Each of these is largely impossible in today's systems, where digital intruders (or misbehaving users) can completely control and manipulate all software and data on their machines. Let's consider an example of each type of trust:

Users trusting output: an intruder who compromises your desktop computer can make it display anything it wants. So, for example, it can manipulate the stock quote, trick you into typing in your passwords or credit card numbers, or show you fake news stories. With trusted computing, output devices could be taught to ignore (or visibly tag) output that does not come from trusted sources.

Software trusting input: an intruder who compromises your desktop computer can manipulate (or fabricate) input signals conveyed to the software running on the system. So, for example, it could replay your password to authentication services to gain access to "secure data." Often-touted biometric sensors, which promise to distinguish between users based on measurements of their physical features, would do nothing to change this unless there is evidence (e.g., a digital signature) of the source and timeliness. Such evidence of when and where readings were taken is needed because, unlike passwords, biometrics are not secrets [5]. For example, anyone can lift fingerprints from a laptop with the right tools or download facial images from a web page. Thus, the evidence is needed to prevent straightforward forgery and replay attacks.

Remote system trusting source: an identity thief who gains access to your personal information and any relevant passwords can use Internet services as you. Likewise, an intruder who compromises your desktop computer can conduct transactions using your credentials from your actual computer. A trusted computing component could assure remote systems that transactions come from you—they could ensure that the right software (which they trust) ran on your actual machine and that you actually typed commands into the machine (using the input trust discussed above). This form of trusted computing is the one most frequently discussed, because it makes e-commerce more secure by allowing service providers to trust that their software runs as desired on customer systems—in fact, the best product name we've heard for this is EMBASSY (from Wave Systems), evoking the image of a trusted outpost in a foreign land. It is also the most controversial form, since some worry that it will allow powerful corporations or governments to dictate the software running on everyone's computers.

The "secure coprocessors" often used to achieve trusted computing functions can also be used for intrusion detection and diagnosis functions.

4 Summary

This article promotes a new security architecture in which traditional boundary protections are coupled with security functionality embedded into self-securing devices.

The resulting collection of independent security perimeters enables a flexible infrastructure for dynamic prevention, detection, diagnosis, isolation, and repair of successful intrusions. Much progress has been made in developing the self-securing device concept, core technologies, and case studies. Although challenges remain, self-securing devices have been shown a promising and viable approach to making digital infrastructures much more intrusion-tolerant.

Acknowledgments

We thank the members and companies of the PDL Consortium (including EMC, Engenio, Hewlett-Packard, HGST, Hitachi, IBM, Intel, Microsoft, Network Appliance, Oracle, Panasas, Seagate, Sun, and Veritas) for their interest, insights, feedback, and support. We thank IBM and Intel for hardware grants supporting our research efforts. This material is based on research sponsored by the Air Force Research Laboratory, under agreement number F49620-01-1-0433.[2]

References

[1] David Friedman and David F. Nagle. *Building Scalable Firewalls with Intelligent Network Interface Cards*. CMU-CS-00-173. Technical Report, Carnegie Mellon Univeristy School of Computer Science, December 2000.

[2] Gregory R. Ganger, Gregg Economou, and Stanley M. Bielski. *Self-securing network interfaces: what, why and how*. CMU-CS 02-144. August 2002.

[3] Gregory R. Ganger, Gregg Economou, and Stanley M. Bielski. *Finding and Containing Enemies Within the Walls with Self-securing Network Interfaces*. Carnegie Mellon University Technical Report CMU-CS-03-109. January 2003.

[4] Garth R. Goodson, Jay J. Wylie, Gregory R. Ganger, and Michael K. Reiter. Efficient Byzantine-tolerant erasure-coded storage. *International Conference on Dependable Systems and Networks* (Florence, Italy, 28 June – 01 July 2004), 2004.

[5] Andrew J. Klosterman and Gregory R. Ganger. *Secure Continuous Biometric-Enhanced Authentication*. CMU-CS-00-134. Technical Report, Carnegie Mellon Univeristy School of Computer Science, May 2000.

[6] James Newsome, Brad Karp, and Dawn Song. Polygraph: Automatic Signature Generation for Polymorphic Worms. *IEEE Symposium on Security and Privacy* (Oakland, CA, 08–11 May 2005), pages 226–241. IEEE Computer Society, 2005.

[7] Adam G. Pennington, John D. Strunk, John Linwood Griffin, Craig A. N. Soules, Garth R. Goodson, and Gregory R. Ganger. Storage-based intrusion detection: watching storage activity for suspicious behavior. *USENIX Security Symposium* (Washington, DC, 06–08 August 2003), 2003.

[8] John D. Strunk, Garth R. Goodson, Michael L. Scheinholtz, Craig A. N. Soules, and Gregory R. Ganger. Self-securing storage: protecting data in compromised systems. *Symposium on Operating Systems Design and Implementation* (San Diego, CA, 23–25 October 2000), pages 165–180. USENIX Association, 2000.

[9] Shobha Venkataraman, Dawn Song, Phil Gibbons, and Avrim Blum. New Streaming Algorithms for Superspreader Detection. *Network and Distributed System Security Symposium* (San Diego, CA, 03–04 February 2005), 2005.

[10] Cynthia Wong, Chenxi Wang, Dawn Song, Stan Bielski, and Gregory R. Ganger. Dynamic Quarantine of Internet Worms. *International Conference on Dependable Systems and Networks* (Florence, Italy, 28 June 2004). IEEE Computer Society, 2004.

[11] Jay J. Wylie, Michael W. Bigrigg, John D. Strunk, Gregory R. Ganger, Han Kiliccote, and Pradeep K. Khosla. Survivable information storage systems. *IEEE Computer*, **33**(8):61–68. IEEE, August 2000.

[12] Abraham Yaar, Adrian Perrig, and Dawn Song. FIT: Fast Internet Traceback. *IEEE INFOCOM* (Miami, FL, 13–16 March 2005), 2005.

[13] Avi Yaar, Adrian Perrig, and Dawn Song. Pi: A Path Identification Mechanism to Defend against DDoS Attacks. *IEEE Symposium on Security and Privacy* (Oakland, CA, 11–14 May 2003). IEEE Computer Society, 2003.

[2]The U.S. Government is authorized to reproduce and distribute reprints for Governmental purposes notwithstanding any copyright notation thereon. The views and conclusions contained herein are those of the authors and should not be interpreted as necessarily representing the official policies or endorsements, either expressed or implied, of the Air Force Research Laboratory or the U.S. Government.

Storage-based Intrusion Detection:
Watching storage activity for suspicious behavior

Adam G. Pennington, John D. Strunk, John Linwood Griffin,
Craig A.N. Soules, Garth R. Goodson, Gregory R. Ganger
Carnegie Mellon University

Abstract

Storage-based intrusion detection allows storage systems to watch for data modifications characteristic of system intrusions. This enables storage systems to spot several common intruder actions, such as adding backdoors, inserting Trojan horses, and tampering with audit logs. Further, an intrusion detection system (IDS) embedded in a storage device continues to operate even after client systems are compromised. This paper describes a number of specific warning signs visible at the storage interface. Examination of 18 real intrusion tools reveals that most (15) can be detected based on their changes to stored files. We describe and evaluate a prototype storage IDS, embedded in an NFS server, to demonstrate both feasibility and efficiency of storage-based intrusion detection. In particular, both the performance overhead and memory required (152 KB for 4730 rules) are minimal.

1 Introduction

Many intrusion detection systems (IDSs) have been developed over the years [1, 23, 29], with most falling into one of two categories: network-based or host-based. Network IDSs (NIDS) are usually embedded in sniffers or firewalls, scanning traffic to, from, and within a network environment for attack signatures and suspicious traffic [5, 25]. Host-based IDSs (HIDS) are fully or partially embedded within each host's OS. They examine local information (such as system calls [10]) for signs of intrusion or suspicious behavior. Many environments employ multiple IDSs, each watching activity from its own vantage point.

The storage system is another interesting vantage point for intrusion detection. Several common intruder actions [7, p. 218][34, pp. 363–365] are quite visible at the storage interface. Examples include manipulating system utilities (e.g., to add backdoors or Trojan horses), tampering with audit log contents (e.g., to eliminate evidence), and resetting attributes (e.g., to hide changes). By design, a storage server sees all changes to persistent data, allowing it to transparently watch for suspicious changes and issue alerts about the corresponding client systems. Also, like a NIDS, a storage IDS must be compromise-independent of the host

OS, meaning that it cannot be disabled by an intruder who only successfully gets past a host's OS-level protection.

This paper motivates and describes storage-based intrusion detection. It presents several kinds of suspicious behavior that can be spotted by a storage IDS. Using sixteen "rootkits" and two worms as examples, we describe how fifteen of them would be exposed rapidly by our storage IDS. (The other three do not modify stored files.) Most of them are exposed by modifying system binaries, adding files to system directories, scrubbing the audit log, or using suspicious file names. Of the fifteen detected, three modify the kernel to hide their presence from host-based detection including FS integrity checkers like Tripwire [18]. In general, compromises cannot hide their changes from the storage device if they wish to persist across reboots; to be re-installed upon reboot, the tools must manipulate stored files.

A storage IDS could be embedded in many kinds of storage systems. The extra processing power and memory space required should be feasible for file servers, disk array controllers, and perhaps augmented disk drives. Most detection rules will also require FS-level understanding of the stored data. Such understanding exists trivially for a file server, and may be explicitly provided to block-based storage devices. This understanding of a file system is analogous to the understanding of application protocols used by a NIDS [27], but with fewer varieties and structural changes over time.

As a concrete example with which to experiment, we have augmented an NFS server with a storage IDS that supports online, rule-based detection of suspicious modifications. This storage IDS supports the detection of four categories of suspicious activities. First, it can detect unexpected changes to important system files and binaries, using a rule-set very similar to Tripwire's. Second, it can detect patterns of changes like non-append modification (e.g., of system log files) and reversing of inode times. Third, it can detect specifically proscribed content changes to critical files (e.g., illegal shells inserted into /etc/passwd). Fourth, it can detect the appearance of specific file names (e.g., hidden "dot" files) or content (e.g., known viruses or attack tools). An administrative interface supplies the

Originally published in the *Proceedings of the 12th USENIX Security Symposium* (Berkeley, CA: USENIX Association, 2003).
Reprinted by permission.

199

detection rules, which are checked during the processing of each NFS request. When a detection rule triggers, the server sends the administrator an alert containing the full pathname of the modified file, the violated rule, and the offending NFS operation. Experiments show that the run-time cost of such intrusion detection is minimal. Further analysis indicates that little memory capacity is needed for reasonable rulesets (e.g., only 152 KB for an example containing 4730 rules).

The remainder of this paper is organized as follows. Section 2 introduces storage-based intrusion detection. Section 3 evaluates the potential of storage-based intrusion detection by examining real intrusion tools. Section 4 discusses storage IDS design issues. Section 5 describes a prototype storage IDS embedded in an NFS server. Section 6 uses this prototype to evaluate the costs of storage-based intrusion detection. Section 7 presents related work. Section 8 summarizes this paper's contributions and discusses continuing work.

2   Storage-based Intrusion Detection

Storage-based intrusion detection enables storage devices to examine the requests they service for suspicious client behavior. Although the world view that a storage server sees is incomplete, two features combine to make it a well-positioned platform for enhancing intrusion detection efforts. First, since storage devices are independent of host OSes, they can continue to look for intrusions after the initial compromise, whereas a host-based IDS can be disabled by the intruder. Second, since most computer systems rely heavily on persistent storage for their operation, many intruder actions will cause storage activity that can be captured and analyzed. This section expands on these two features and identifies limitations of storage-based intrusion detection.

2.1   Threat model and assumptions

Storage IDSs focus on the threat on of an attacker who has compromised a host system in a managed computing environment. By "compromised," we mean that the attacker subverted the host's software system, gaining the ability to run arbitrary software on the host with OS-level privileges. The compromise might have been achieved via technical means (e.g., exploiting buggy software or a loose policy) or non-technical means (e.g., social engineering or bribery). Once the compromise occurs, most administrators wish to detect the intrusion as quickly as possible and terminate it. Intruders, on the other hand, often wish to hide their presence and retain access to the machine.

Unfortunately, once an intruder compromises a machine,

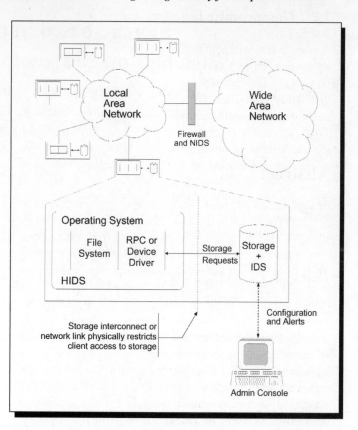

Figure 1: **The compromise independence of a storage IDS.** The storage interface provides a physical boundary behind which a storage server can observe the requests it is asked to service. Note that this same picture works for block protocols, such as SCSI or IDE/ATA, and distributed file system protocols, such as NFS or CIFS. Also note that storage IDSs do not replace existing IDSs, but simply offer an additional vantage point from which to detect intrusions.

intrusion detection with conventional schemes becomes much more difficult. Host-based IDSs can be rendered ineffective by intruder software that disables them or feeds them misinformation, for which many tools exist. Network IDSs can continue to look for suspicious behavior, but are much less likely to find an already successful intruder—most NIDSs look for attacks and intrusion attempts rather than for system usage by an existing intruder [11]. A storage IDS can help by offering a vantage point on a system component that is often manipulated in suspicious ways *after* the intruder compromises the system.

A key characteristic of the described threat model is that the attacker has software control over the host, but does not have physical access to its hardware. We are not specifically trying to address insider attacks, in which the intruder would also have physical access to the hardware and its storage components. Also, for the storage IDS to be effective, we assume that neither the storage device nor the admin console are compromised.

2.2   Compromise independence

A storage IDS will continue watching for suspicious activity even when clients' OSes are compromised. It capitalizes on the fact that storage devices (whether file servers, disk array controllers, or even IDE disks) run different software on separate hardware, as illustrated in Figure 1. This fact enables server-embedded security functionality that cannot be disabled by any software running on client systems (including the OS kernel). Further, storage devices often have fewer network interfaces (e.g., RPC+SNMP+HTTP or just SCSI) and no local users. Thus, compromising a storage server should be more difficult than compromising a client system. Of course, such servers have a limited view of system activity, so they cannot distinguish legitimate users from clever impostors. But, from behind the physical storage interface, a storage IDS can spot many common intruder actions and alert administrators.

Administrators must be able to communicate with the storage IDS, both to configure it and to receive alerts. This administrative channel must also be compromise-independent of client systems, meaning that no user (including root) and no software (including the OS kernel) on a client system can have administrative privileges for the storage IDS. Section 4 discusses deployment options for the administrative console, including physical consoles and cryptographic channels from a dedicated administrative system.

All of the warning signs discussed in this paper could also be spotted from within a HIDS, but host-based IDSs do not enjoy the compromise independence of storage IDSs. A host-based IDS is vulnerable to being disabled or bypassed by intruders that compromise the OS kernel. Another interesting place for a storage IDS is the virtual disk module of a virtual machine monitor [39]; such deployment would enjoy compromise independence from the OSes running in its virtual machines [4].

2.3   Warning signs for storage IDSs

Successful intruders often modify stored data. For instance, they may overwrite system utilities to hide their presence, install Trojan horse daemons to allow for re-entry, add users, modify startup scripts to reinstall kernel modifications upon reboot, remove evidence from the audit log, or store illicit materials. These modifications are visible to the storage system when they are made persistent. This section describes four categories of warning signs that a storage IDS can monitor: data and attribute modifications, update patterns, content integrity, and suspicious content.

2.3.1   Data/attribute modification

In managed computing environments, the simplest (and perhaps most effective) category of warning signs consists of data or meta-data changes to files that administrators expect to remain unchanged except during explicit upgrades. Examples of such files include system executables and scripts, configuration files, and system header files and libraries. Given the importance of such files and the infrequency of updates to them, any modification is a potential sign of intrusion. A storage IDS can detect all such modifications on-the-fly, before the storage device processes each request, and issue an alert immediately.

In current systems, modification detection is sometimes provided by a checksumming utility (e.g., Tripwire [18]) that periodically compares the current storage state against a reference database stored elsewhere. Storage-based intrusion detection improves on this current approach in three ways: (1) it allows immediate detection of changes to watched files; (2) it can notice short-term changes, made and then undone, which would not be noticed by a checksumming utility if the changes occurred between two periodic checks; and (3) for local storage, it avoids trusting the host OS to perform the checks, which many rootkits disable or bypass.

2.3.2   Update patterns

A second category of warning signs consists of suspicious access patterns, particularly updates. There are several concrete examples for which storage IDSs can be useful in watching. The clearest is client system audit logs; these audit logs are critical to both intrusion detection [6] and diagnosis [35], leading many intruders to scrub evidence from them as a precaution. Any such manipulation will be obvious to a storage IDS that understands the well-defined update pattern of the specific audit log. For instance, audit log files are usually append-only, and they may be periodically "rotated." This rotation consists of renaming the current log file to an alternate name (e.g., `logfile` to `logfile.0`) and creating a new "current" log file. Any deviation in the update pattern of the current log file or any modification of a previous log file is suspicious.

Another suspicious update pattern is timestamp reversal. Specifically, the data modification and attribute change times commonly kept for each file can be quite useful for post-intrusion diagnosis of which files were manipulated [9]. By manipulating the times stored in inodes (e.g., setting them back to their original values), an intruder can inhibit such diagnosis. Of course, care must be taken with IDS rules, since some programs (e.g., `tar`) legitimately set these times to old values. One possibility would be to only set off an alert when the modification time is set back long after a file's creation. This would exclude `tar`-style activity but would catch an intruder trying to obfuscate a modified file. Of course, the intruder could now delete the file, create a new one, set the date back, and hide from the storage IDS—a more complex rule could catch this, but such escalation is the nature of intrusion detection.

Detection of storage denial-of-service (DoS) attacks also falls into the category of suspicious access patterns. For example, an attacker can disable specific services or entire systems by allocating all or most of the free space. A similar effect can be achieved by allocating inodes or other metadata structures. A storage IDS can watch for such exhaustion, which may be deliberate, accidental, or coincidental (e.g., a user just downloaded 10 GB of multimedia files). When the system reaches predetermined thresholds of unallocated resources and allocation rate, warning the administrator is appropriate even in non-intrusion situations—attention is likely to be necessary soon. A storage IDS could similarly warn the administrator when storage activity exceeds a threshold for too long, which may be a DoS attack or just an indication that the server needs to be upgraded.

Although specific rules can spot expected intruder actions, more general rules may allow larger classes of suspicious activity to be noticed. For example, some attribute modifications, like enabling "set UID" bits or reducing the permissions needed for access, may indicate foul play. Additionally, many applications access storage in a regular manner. As two examples: word processors often use temporary and backup files in specific ways, and UNIX password management involves a pair of inter-related files (/etc/passwd and /etc/shadow). The corresponding access patterns seen at the storage device will be a reflection of the application's requests. This presents an opportunity for anomaly detection based on how a given file is normally accessed. This could be done in a manner similar to learning common patterns of system calls [10] or starting with rules regarding the expected behavior of individual applications [19]. Deviation from the expected pattern could indicate an intruder attempting to subvert the normal method of accessing a given file. Of course, the downside is an increase (likely substantial) in the number of false alarms. Our focus to date has been on explicit detection rules, but anomaly detection within storage access patterns is an interesting topic for future research.

2.3.3   Content integrity

A third category of warning signs consists of changes that violate internal consistency rules of specific files. This category builds on the previous examples by understanding the application-specific semantics of particularly important stored data. Of course, to verify content integrity, the device must understand the format of a file. Further, while simple formats may be verified in the context of the write

operation, file formats may be arbitrarily complex and verification may require access to additional data blocks (other than those currently being written). This creates a performance vs. security trade-off made by deciding which files to verify and how often to verify them. In practice, there are likely to be few critical files for which content integrity verification is utilized.

As a concrete example, consider a UNIX system password file (/etc/passwd), which consists of a set of well-defined records. Records are delimited by a line-break, and each record consists of seven colon-separated fields. Further, each of the fields has a specific meaning, some of which are expected to conform to rules of practice. For example, the seventh field specifies the "shell" program to be launched when a user logs in, and (in Linux) the file /etc/shells lists the legal options. During the "Capture the Flag" information warfare game at the 2002 DEF CON conference [21], one tactic used was to change the root shell on compromised systems to /sbin/halt; once a targeted system's administrator noted the intrusion and attempted to become root on the machine (the common initial reaction), considerable down-time and administrative effort was needed to restore the system to operation. A storage IDS can monitor changes to /etc/passwd and verify that they conform to a set of basic integrity rules: 7-field records, non-empty password field, legal default shell, legal home directory, non-overlapping user IDs, etc. The attack described above, among others, could be caught immediately.

2.3.4   Suspicious content

A fourth category of warning signs is the appearance of suspicious content. The most obvious suspicious content is a known virus or rootkit, detectable via its signature. Several high-end storage servers (e.g., from EMC [24] and Network Appliance [28]) now include support for internal virus scanning. By executing the scans within the storage server, viruses cannot disable the scanners even after infecting clients.

Two other examples of suspicious content are large numbers of "hidden" files or empty files. Hidden files have names that are not displayed by normal directory listing interfaces [7, p. 217], and their use may indicate that an intruder is using the system as a storage repository, perhaps for illicit or pirated content. A large number of empty files or directories may indicate an attempt to exploit a race condition [2, 30] by inducing a time-consuming directory listing, search, or removal.

2.4   Limitations, costs, and weaknesses

Although storage-based intrusion detection contributes to security efforts, of course it is not a silver bullet.

Like any IDS, a storage IDS will produce some false positives. With very specific rules, such as "watch these 100 files for any modification," false positives should be infrequent; they will occur only when there are legitimate changes to a watched file, which should be easily verified if updates involve a careful procedure. The issue of false alarms grows progressively more problematic as the rules get less exact (e.g., the time reversal or resource exhaustion examples). The far end of the spectrum from specific rules is general anomaly detection.

Also like any IDS, a storage IDS will fail to spot some intrusions. Fundamentally, a storage IDS cannot notice intrusions whose actions do not cause odd storage behavior. For example, three of the eighteen intrusion tools examined in the next section modify the OS but change no files. Also, an intruder may manipulate storage in unwatched ways. Using network-based and host-based IDSs together with a storage IDS can increase the odds of spotting various forms of intrusion.

Intrusion detection, as an aspect of information warfare, is by nature a "game" of escalation. As soon as one side takes away an avenue of attack, the other starts looking for the next. Since storage-based intrusion detection easily sees several common intruder activities, crafty intruders will change tactics. For example, an intruder can make any number of changes to the host's memory, so long as those modifications do not propagate to storage. A reboot, however, will reset the system and remove the intrusion, which argues for proactive restart [3, 16, 43]. To counter this, attackers must have their changes re-established automatically after a reboot, such as by manipulating the various boot-time (e.g., `rc.local` in UNIX-like systems) or periodic (e.g., `cron` in UNIX-like systems) programs. Doing so exposes them to the storage IDS, creating a traditional intrusion detection game of cat and mouse.

As a practical consideration, storage IDSs embedded within individual components of decentralized storage systems are unlikely to be effective. For example, a disk array controller is a fine place for storage-based intrusion detection, but individual disks behind software striping are not. Each of the disks has only part of the file system's state, making it difficult to check non-trivial rules without adding new inter-device communication paths.

Finally, storage-based intrusion detection is not free. Checking rules comes with some cost in processing and memory resources, and more rules require more resources. In configuring a storage IDS, one must balance detection efforts with performance costs for the particular operating environment.

3 Case Studies

This section explores how well a storage IDS might fare in the face of actual compromises. To do so, we examined eighteen intrusion tools (Table 1) designed to be run on compromised systems. All were downloaded from public websites, most of them from Packet Storm [26].

Most of the actions taken by these tools fall into two categories. Actions in the first category involve hiding evidence of the intrusion and the rootkit's activity. The second provides a mechanism for reentry into a system. Twelve of the tools operate by running various binaries on the host system and overwriting existing binaries to continue gaining control. The other six insert code into the operating system kernel.

For the analysis in this section, we focus on a subset of the rules supported by our prototype storage-based IDS described in Section 5. Specifically, we include the file/directory modification (Tripwire-like) rules, the append-only logfile rule, and the hidden filename rules. We do not consider any "suspicious content" rules, which may or may not catch a rootkit depending on whether its particular signature is known.[1] In these eighteen toolkits, we did not find any instances of resource exhaustion attacks or of reverting inode times.

3.1 Detection results

Of the eighteen toolkits tested, storage IDS rules would immediately detect fifteen based on their storage modifications. Most would trigger numerous alerts, highlighting their presence. The other three make no changes to persistent storage. However, they are removed if the system reboots; all three modify the kernel, but would have to be combined with system file changes to be re-inserted upon reboot.

Non-append changes to the system audit log. Seven of the eighteen toolkits scrub evidence of system compromise from the audit log. All of them do so by selectively overwriting entries related to their intrusion into the system, rather than by truncating the logfile entirely. All cause alerts to be generated in our prototype.

System file modification. Fifteen of the eighteen toolkits modify a number of watched system files (ranging from 1 to 20). Each such modification generates an alert. Although three of the rootkits replace the files with binaries that match the size and CRC checksum of the previous files, they do not foil cryptographically-strong hashes. Thus, Tripwire-like systems would be able to catch them

---

[1]An interesting note is that rootkit developers reuse code: four of the rootkits use the same audit log scrubbing program (sauber), and another three use a different program (zap2).

ist [14]. This type of infrastructure is already common for administration of other network-attached security components, such as firewalls or network intrusion detection systems. For direct-attached storage devices, cryptographic channels can be used to tunnel administrative requests and alerts through the OS of the host system, as illustrated in Figure 2. Such tunneling simply treats the host OS as an untrusted network component.

For small numbers of dedicated servers in a machine room, either approach is feasible. For large numbers of storage devices or components operating in physically insecure environments, cryptography is the only viable solution.

4.3   Checking the detection rules

Checking detection rules can be non-trivial, because rules generally apply to full pathnames rather than inodes. Additional complications arise because rules can watch for files that do not yet exist.

For simple operations that act on individual files (e.g., READ and WRITE), rule verification is localized. The device need only check that the rules pertaining to that specific file are not violated (usually a simple flag comparison, sometimes a content check). For operations that affect the file system's namespace, verification is more complicated. For example, a rename of a directory tree may impact a large number of individual files, any of which could have IDS rules that must be checked. Renaming a directory requires examining all files and directories that are children of the one being renamed.

In the case of rules pertaining to files that do not currently exist, this list of rules must be consulted when operations change the namespace. For example, the administrator may want to watch for the existence of a file named /a/b/c even if the directory named /a does not yet exist. However, a single file system operation (e.g., mv /z /a) could cause the watched file to suddenly exist, given the appropriate structure for z's directory tree.

4.4   Responding to rule violations

Since a detected "intruder action" may actually be legitimate user activity (i.e., a false alarm), our default response is simply to send an alert to the administrative system or the designated alert log file. The alert message should contain such information as the file(s) involved, the time of the event, the action being performed, the action's attributes (e.g., the data written into the file), and the client's identity. Note that, if the rules are set properly, most false positives should be caused by legitimate updates (e.g., upgrades) from an administrator. With the right information in alerts, an administrative system that also coordinates legitimate upgrades could correlate the generated alert (which can

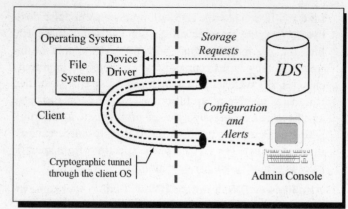

Figure 2: **Tunneling administrative commands through client systems.** For storage devices attached directly to client systems, a cryptographic tunnel can allow the administrator to securely manage a storage IDS. This tunnel uses the untrusted client OS to transport administrative commands and alerts.

include the new content) with the in-progress upgrade; if this were done, it could prevent the false alarm from reaching the human administrator while simultaneously verifying that the upgrade went through to persistent storage correctly.

There are more active responses that a storage IDS could trigger upon detecting suspicious activity. When choosing a response policy, of course, the administrator must weigh the benefits of an active response against the inconvenience and potential damage caused by false alarms.

One reasonable active response is to slow down the suspected intruder's storage accesses. For example, a storage device could wait until the alert is acknowledged before completing the suspicious request. It could also artificially increase request latencies for a client or user that is suspected of foul play. Doing so would provide increased time for a more thorough response, and, while it will cause some annoyance in false alarm situations, it is unlikely to cause damage. The device could even deny a request entirely if it violates one of the rules, although this response to a false alarm could cause damage and/or application failure. For some rules, like append-only audit logs, such access control may be desirable.

Liu, et al. proposed a more radical response to detected intrusions: isolating intruders, via versioning, at the file system level [22]. To do so, the file system forks the version trees to sandbox suspicious users until the administrator verifies the legitimacy of their actions. Unfortunately, such forking is likely to interfere with system operation, unless the intrusion detection mechanism yields no false alarms. Specifically, since suspected users modify different versions of files from regular users, the system faces a difficult reintegration [20, 41] problem, should the updates be judged legitimate. Still, it is interesting to consider embedding this approach, together with a storage IDS, into storage systems for particularly sensitive environments.

A less intrusive storage-embedded response is to start versioning all data and auditing all storage requests when an intrusion is detected. Doing so provides the administrator with significant information for post-intrusion diagnosis and recovery. Of course, some intrusion-related information will likely be lost unless the intrusion is detected immediately, which is why Strunk et al. [38] argue for always doing these things (just in case). Still, IDS-triggered employment of this functionality may be a useful trade-off point.

Metadata	
• inode modification time	• data modification time
• access time	• file permissions
• link count	• device number
• file owner	• inode number
• file type	• file owner group
• file size	

Data	
• any modification	• append only
• password structure	

Table 2: **Attribute list.** Rules can be established to watch these attributes in real-time on a file-by-file basis.

5 Storage-based intrusion detection in an NFS server

To explore the concepts and feasibility of storage-based intrusion detection, we implemented a storage IDS in an NFS server. Unmodified client systems access the server using the standard NFS version 2 protocol [40][2], while storage-based intrusion detection occurs transparently. This section describes how the prototype storage IDS handles detection rule specification, the structures and algorithms for checking rules, and alert generation.

The base NFS server is called S4, and its implementation is described and evaluated elsewhere [38]. It internally performs file versioning and request auditing, using a log-structured file system [32], but these features are not relevant here. For our purposes, it is a convenient NFS file server with performance comparable to the Linux and FreeBSD NFS servers. Secure administration is performed via the server's console, using the physical access control approach.

5.1 Specifying detection rules

Our prototype storage IDS is capable of watching for a variety of data and metadata changes to files. The administrator specifies a list of Tripwire-style rules to configure the detection system. Each administrator-supplied rule is of the form: {*pathname, attribute-list*}—designating which attributes to monitor for a particular file. The list of attributes that can be watched is shown in Table 2. In addition to standard Tripwire rules, we have added two additional functions that can be specified on a per-file basis. The first watches for non-append changes, as described earlier; any truncation or write anywhere but at the previous end of a file will generate an alert. The second checks

a file's integrity against the password file integrity rule discussed earlier. After every write, the file must conform to the rigid structure of a password file (7 colons per line), and all of the shells must be contained in the "acceptable" list.

In addition to per-file rules, an administrator can choose to enable any of three system-wide rules: one that matches on any operation that rolls-back a file's modification time, one that matches on any operation that creates a "hidden" directory (e.g., a directory name beginning with '.' and having spaces in it), and one that looks for known (currently hard-coded) intrusion tools by their sizes and SHA-1 digests. Although the system currently checks the digests on every file update, periodic scanning of the system would likely be more practical. These rules apply to all parts of the directory hierarchy and are specified as simply ON or OFF.

Rules are communicated to the server through the use of an administrative RPC. This RPC interface has two commands (see Table 3). The setRule() RPC gives the IDS two values: the path of the file to be watched, and a set of flags describing the specific rules for that file. Rules are removed through the same mechanism, specifying the path and an empty rule set.

5.2 Checking the detection rules

This subsection describes the core of the storage IDS. It discusses how rules are stored and subsequently checked during operation.

5.2.1 Data structures

Three new structures allow the storage IDS to efficiently support the detection rules: the reverse lookup table, the inode watch flags, and the non-existent names table.

Reverse lookup table: The reverse lookup table serves two functions. First, it serves as a list of rules that the server

---

[2]The use of the NFSv2 protocol is an artifact of the server implementation the IDS is built into, but makes no difference in the areas we care about.

Command	Purpose	Direction
`setRule(path, rules)`	Changes the watched characteristics of a file. This command is used to both set and delete rules.	admin⇒server
`listRules()`	Retrieves the server's rule table as a list of {`pathname, rules`} records.	admin⇒server
`alert(path, rules, operation)`	Delivers a warning of a rule violation to the administrator.	server⇒admin

Table 3: **Administrative commands for our storage IDS.** This table lists the small set of administrative commands needed for an administrative console to configure and manage the storage IDS. The first two are sent by the console, and the third is sent by the storage IDS. The pathname refers to a file relative to the root of an exported file system. The *rules* are a description of what to check for, which can be any of the changes described in Table 2. The *operation* is the NFS operation that caused the rule violation.

is currently enforcing. Second, it maps an inode number to a pathname. The alert generation mechanism uses the latter to provide the administrator with file names instead of inode numbers, without resorting to a brute-force search of the namespace.

The reverse lookup table is populated via the `setRule()` RPC. Each rule's full pathname is broken into its component names, which are stored in distinct rows of the table. For each component, the table records four fields: *inode-number*, *directory-inode-number*, *name*, and *rules*. Indexed by *inode-number*, an entry contains the *name* within a parent directory (identified by its *directory-inode-number*). The *rules* associated with this *name* are a bitmask of the attributes and patterns to watch. Since a particular inode number can have more than one name, multiple entries for each inode may exist. A given inode number can be translated to a full pathname by looking up its lowest-level name and recursively looking up the name of the corresponding directory inode number. The search ends with the known inode number of the root directory. All names for an inode can be found by following all paths given by the lookup of the inode number.

Inode `watchflags` field: During the `setRule()` RPC, in addition to populating the reverse lookup table, a rule mask of 16 bits is computed and stored in the `watchflags` field of the watched file's inode. Since multiple pathnames may refer to the same inode, there may be more than one rule for a given file, and the mask contains the union. The inode `watchflags` field is a performance enhancement designed to co-locate the rules governing a file with that file's metadata. This field is not necessary for correctness since the pertinent data could be read from the reverse lookup table. However, it allows efficient verification of detection rules during the processing of an NFS request. Since the inode is read as part of any file access, most rule checking becomes a simple mask comparison.

Non-existent names table: The non-existent names table lists rules for pathnames that do not currently exist. Each entry in the table is associated with the deepest-level (ex-

isting) directory within the pathname of the original rule. Each entry contains three fields: *directory-inode-number*, *remaining-path*, and *rules*. Indexed by *directory-inode-number*, an entry specifies the *remaining-path*. When a file or directory is created or removed, the non-existent names table is consulted and updated, if necessary. For example, upon creation of a file for which a detection rule exists, the *rules* are checked and inserted in the `watchflags` field of the inode. Together, the reverse lookup table and the non-existent names table contain the entire set of IDS rules in effect.

5.2.2 Checking rules during NFS operations

We now describe the flow of rule checking, much of which is diagrammed in Figure 3, in two parts: changes to individual files and changes to the namespace.

Checking rules on individual file operations: For each NFS operation that affects only a single file, a mask of rules that might be violated is computed. This mask is compared, bitwise, to the corresponding `watchflags` field in the file's inode. For most of the rules, this comparison quickly determines if any alerts should be triggered. If the "password file" or "append only" flags are set, the corresponding verification function executes to determine if the rule is violated.

Checking rules on namespace operations: Namespace operations can cause watched pathnames to appear or disappear, which will usually trigger an alert. For operations that create watched pathnames, the storage IDS moves rules from the non-existent names table to the reverse lookup table. Conversely, operations that delete watched pathnames cause rules to move between tables in the opposite direction.

When a name is created (via CREATE, MKDIR, LINK, or SYMLINK) the non-existent names table is checked. If there are rules for the new file, they are checked and placed in the `watchflags` field of the new inode. In addition, the corresponding rule is removed from the non-existent

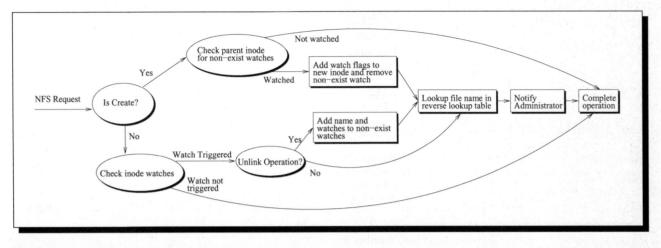

Figure 3: **Flowchart of our storage IDS.** Few structures and decision points are needed. In the common case (no rules for the file), only one inode's `watchflags` field is checked. The picture does not show RENAME operations here due to their complexity.

names table and is added to the reverse lookup table. During a MKDIR, any entries in the non-existent names table that include the new directory as the next step in their remaining path are replaced; the new entries are indexed by the new directory's inode number and its name is removed from the remaining path.

When a name is removed (via UNLINK or RMDIR), the `watchflags` field of the corresponding inode is checked for rules. Most such rules will trigger an alert, and an entry for them is also added to the non-existent names table. For RMDIR, the reverses of the actions for MKDIR are necessary. Any non-existent table entries parented on the removed directory must be modified. The removed directory's name is added to the beginning of each remaining path, and the directory inode number in the table is modified to be the directory's parent.

By far, the most complex namespace operation is a RENAME. For a RENAME of an individual file, modifying the rules is the same as a CREATE of the new name and a REMOVE of the old. When a directory is renamed, its subtrees must be recursively checked for watched files. If any are found, and once appropriate alerts are generated, their rules and pathname up to the parent of the renamed directory are stored in the non-existent names table, and the `watchflags` field of the inode is cleared. Then, the non-existent names table must be checked (again recursively) for any rules that map into the directory's new name and its children; such rules are checked, added to the inode's `watchflags` field, and updated as for name creation.

5.3 Generating alerts

Alerts are generated and sent immediately when a detection rule is triggered. The alert consists of the original detection rule (pathname and attributes watched), the specific attributes that were affected, and the RPC operation that

triggered the rule. To get the original rule information, the reverse lookup table is consulted. If a single RPC operation triggers multiple rules, one alert is sent for each.

5.4 Storage IDS rules in a NIDS

Because NFS traffic goes over a traditional network, the detection rules described for our prototype storage IDS could be implemented in a NIDS. However, this would involve several new costs. First, it would require the NIDS to watch the LAN links that carry NFS activity. These links are usually higher bandwidth than the Internet uplinks on which most NIDSs are used.[3] Second, it would require that the NIDS replicate a substantial amount of work already performed by the NFS server, increasing the CPU requirements relative to an in-server storage IDS. Third, the NIDS would have to replicate and hold substantial amounts of state (e.g. mappings of file handles to their corresponding files). Our experiences checking rules against NFS traces indicate that this state grows rapidly because the NFS protocol does not expose to the network (or the server) when such state can be removed. Even simple attribute updates cannot be checked without caching the old values of the attributes, otherwise the NIDS could not distinguish modified attributes from reapplied values. Fourth, rules cannot always be checked by looking only at the current command. The NIDS may need to read file data and attributes to deal with namespace operations, content integrity checks, and update pattern rules. In addition to the performance penalty, this requires giving the NIDS read permission for all NFS files and directories.

Given all of these issues, we believe that embedding storage IDS checks directly into the storage component is more appropriate.

---

[3] Tapping a NIDS into direct-attached storage interconnects, such as SCSI and FibreChannel, would be more difficult.

6 Evaluation

This section evaluates the costs of our storage IDS in terms of performance impact and memory required—both costs are minimal.

6.1 Experimental setup

All experiments use the S4 NFS server, with and without the new support for storage-based intrusion detection. The client system is a dual 1 GHz Pentium III with 128 MB RAM and a 3Com 3C905B 100 Mbps network adapter. The server is a dual 700 MHz Pentium III with 512 MB RAM, a 9 GB 10,000 RPM Quantum Atlas 10K II drive, an Adaptec AIC-7896/7 Ultra2 SCSI controller, and an Intel EtherExpress Pro 100 Mb network adapter. The client and server are on the same 100 Mb network switch. The operating system on all machines is Red Hat Linux 6.2 with Linux kernel version 2.2.14.

SSH-build was constructed as a replacement for the Andrew file system benchmark [15, 36]. It consists of 3 phases: The unpack phase, which unpacks the compressed tar archive of SSH v. 1.2.27 (approximately 1 MB in size before decompression), stresses metadata operations on files of varying sizes. The configure phase consists of the automatic generation of header files and makefiles, which involves building various small programs that check the existing system configuration. The build phase compiles, links, and removes temporary files. This last phase is the most CPU intensive, but it also generates a large number of object files and a few executables. Both the server and client caches are flushed between phases.

PostMark was designed to measure the performance of a file system used for electronic mail, netnews, and web based services [17]. It creates a large number of small randomly-sized files (between 512 B and 16 KB) and performs a specified number of transactions on them. Each transaction consists of two sub-transactions, with one being a create or delete and the other being a read or append. The default configuration used for the experiments consists of 100,000 transactions on 20,000 files, and the biases for transaction types are equal.

6.2 Performance impact

The storage IDS checks a file's rules before any operation that could possibly trigger an alert. This includes READ operations, since they may change a file's last access time. Additionally, namespace-modifying operations require further checks and possible updates of the non-existent names table. To understand the performance consequences of the storage IDS design, we ran PostMark and SSH-Build tests. Since our main concern is avoiding a per-

Benchmark	Baseline	With IDS	Change
SSH untar	27.3 (0.02)	27.4 (0.02)	0.03%
SSH config.	42.6 (0.68)	43.2 (0.37)	1.3%
SSH build	85.9 (0.18)	86.8 (0.17)	1.0%
PostMark	4288 (11.9)	4290 (13.0)	0.04%

Table 4: **Performance of macro benchmarks.** All benchmarks were run with and without the storage IDS functionality. Each number represents the average of 10 trials in seconds (with the standard deviation in parenthesis).

Benchmark	Baseline	With IDS	Change
Create	4.32	4.35	0.7%
Remove	4.50	4.65	3.3%
Mkdir	4.36	4.38	0.5%
Rmdir	4.52	4.59	1.5%
Rename file	3.81	3.91	2.6%
Rename dir	3.91	4.04	3.3%

Table 5: **Performance of micro benchmarks.** All benchmarks were run with and without the storage IDS functionality. Each number represents the average of 1000 trials in milliseconds.

formance loss in the case where no rule is violated, we ran these benchmarks with no relevant rules set. As long as no rules match, the results are similar with 0 rules, 1000 rules on existing files, or 1000 rules on non-existing files. Table 4 shows that the performance impact of the storage IDS is minimal. The largest performance difference is for the configure and build phases of SSH-build, which involve large numbers of namespace operations.

Microbenchmarks on specific filesystem actions help explain the overheads. Table 5 shows results for the most expensive operations, which all affect the namespace. The performance differences are caused by redundancy in the implementation. The storage IDS code is kept separate from the NFS server internals, valuing modularity over performance. For example, name removal operations involve a redundant directory lookup and inode fetch (from cache) to locate the corresponding inode's watchflags field.

Rules take very little time to generate alerts. For example, a write to a file with a rule set takes 4.901 milliseconds if no alert is set off. If an alert is set off the time is 4.941 milliseconds. These represent the average over 1000 trials, and show a .8% overhead.

6.3 Space efficiency

The storage IDS structures are stored on disk. To avoid extra disk accesses for most rule checking, though, it is important that they fit in memory.

Three structures are used to check a set of rules. First, each inode in the system has an additional two-byte field for the bitmask of the rules on that file. There is no cost for this, because the space in the inode was previously unused. Linux's ext2fs and BSD's FFS also have sufficient unused space to store such data without increasing their inode sizes. If space were not available, the reverse lookup table can be used instead, since it provides the same information. Second, for each pathname component of a rule, the reverse lookup table requires $20 + N$ bytes: a 16-byte inode number, 2 bytes for the rule bitmask, and $N+2$ bytes for a pathname component of length N. Third, the non-existent names table contains one entry for every file being watched that does not currently exist. Each entry consumes 274 bytes: a 16-byte inode number, 2 bytes for the rule bitmask, and 256 bytes for the maximum pathname supported.

To examine a concrete example of how an administrator might use this system, we downloaded the open source version of Tripwire [42]. Included with it is an example rule file for Linux, containing (after expanding directories to lists of files) 4730 rules. We examined a Red Hat Linux 6.1 [31] desktop machine to obtain an idea of the number of watched files that actually exist on the hard drive. Of the 4730 watched files, 4689 existed on our example system. Using data structure sizes from above, reverse lookup entries for the watched files consume 141 KB. Entries in the non-existent name table for the remaining 41 watched files consume 11 KB. In total, only 152 KB are needed for the storage IDS.

6.4 False positives

We have explored the false positive rate of storage-based intrusion detection in several ways.

To evaluate the file watch rules, two months of traces of all file system operations were gathered on a desktop machine in our group. We compared the files modified on this system with the watched file list from the open source version of Tripwire. This uncovered two distinct patterns where files were modified. Nightly, the user list (`/etc/passwd`) on the machine was overwritten by a central server. Most nights it does not change but the create and rename performed would have triggered an alert. Additionally, multiple binaries in the system were replaced over time by the administrative upgrade process. In only one case was a configuration file on the system changed by a local user.

For alert-triggering modifications arising from explicit administrative action, a storage IDS can provide an added benefit. If an administrator pre-informs the admin console of updated files before they are distributed to machines, the IDS can verify that desired updates happen correctly. Specifically, the admin console can read the new contents

via the admin channel and verify that they are as intended. If so, the update is known to have succeeded, and the alert can be suppressed.

We have also performed two (much) smaller studies. First, we have evaluated our "hidden filename" rules by examining the entire filesystems of several desktops and servers—we found no uses of any of them, including the '.' or '..' followed by any number of spaces discussed above. Second, we evaluated our "inode time reversal" rules by examining lengthy traces of NFS activity from our environment and from two Harvard environments [8]—we found a sizable number of false positives, caused mainly by unpacking archives with utilities like `tar`. Combined with the lack of time reversal in any of the toolkits, use of this rule may be a bad idea.

7 Additional Related Work

Much related work has been discussed within the flow of the paper. For emphasis, we note that there have been many intrusion detection systems focused on host OS activity and network communication; Axelsson [1] recently surveyed the state-of-the-art. Also, the most closely related tool, Tripwire [18], was used as an initial template for our prototype's file modification detection ruleset.

Our work is part of a recent line of research exploiting physical [12, 44] and virtual [4] protection boundaries to detect intrusions into system software. Notably, Garfinkel et al. [13] explore the utility of an IDS embedded in a virtual machine monitor (VMM), which can inspect machine state while being compromise independent of most host software. Storage-based intrusion detection rules could be embedded in a VMM's storage module, rather than in a physical storage device, to identify suspicious storage activity.

Perhaps the most closely related work is the original proposal for self-securing storage [38], which argued for storage-embedded support for intrusion survival. Self-securing storage retains every version of all data and a log of all requests for a period of time called the *detection window*. For intrusions detected within this window, security administrators have a wealth of information for post-intrusion diagnosis and recovery.

Such versioning and auditing complements storage-based intrusion detection in several additional ways. First, when creating rules about storage activity for use in detection, administrators can use the latest audit log and version history to test new rules for false alarms. Second, the audit log could simplify implementation of rules looking for patterns of requests. Third, administrators can use the history to investigate alerts of suspicious behavior (i.e., to check for supporting evidence within the history). Fourth, since the history is retained, a storage IDS can delay checks until the device is idle, allowing the device to avoid performance penalties for expensive checks by accepting a potentially longer detection latency.

8   Conclusions and Future Work

A storage IDS watches system activity from a new viewpoint, which immediately exposes some common intruder actions. Running on separate hardware, this functionality remains in place even when client OSes or user accounts are compromised. Our prototype storage IDS demonstrates both feasibility and efficiency within a file server. Analysis of real intrusion tools indicates that most would be immediately detected by a storage IDS. After adjusting for storage IDS presence, intrusion tools will have to choose between exposing themselves to detection or being removed whenever the system reboots.

In continuing work, we are developing a prototype storage IDS embedded in a device exporting a block-based interface (SCSI). To implement the same rules as our augmented NFS server, such a device must be able to parse and traverse the on-disk metadata structures of the file system it holds. For example, knowing whether /usr/sbin/sshd has changed on disk requires knowing not only whether the corresponding data blocks have changed, but also whether the inode still points to the same blocks and whether the name still translates to the same inode. We have developed this translation functionality for two popular file systems, Linux's ext2fs and FreeBSD's FFS. The additional complexity required is small (under 200 lines of C code for each), simple (under 3 days of programming effort each), and changes infrequently (about 5 years between incompatible changes to on-disk structures). The latter, in particular, indicates that device vendors can deploy firmware and expect useful lifetimes that match the hardware. Sivathanu et al. [37] have evaluated the costs and benefits of device-embedded FS knowledge more generally, finding that it is feasible and valuable.

Another continuing direction is exploration of less exact rules and their impact on detection and false positive rates. In particular, the potential of pattern matching rules and general anomaly detection for storage remains unknown.

Acknowledgments

We thank the members and companies of the PDL Consortium (including EMC, Hewlett-Packard, Hitachi, IBM, Intel, Microsoft, Network Appliance, Oracle, Panasas, Seagate, Sun, and Veritas) for their interest, insights, feedback, and support. We thank IBM and Intel for hardware grants supporting our research efforts. This material is based on research sponsored by the Air Force Research Laboratory, under agreement number F49620-01-1-0433, and by DARPA/ITO's OASIS program, under Air Force contract number F30602-99-2-0539-AFRL.[4] Craig Soules was supported by a USENIX Fellowship. Garth Goodson was supported by an IBM Fellowship.

References

[1] S. Axelsson. *Research in intrusion-detection systems: a survey*. Technical report 98–17. Department of Computer Engineering, Chalmers University of Technology, December 1998.

[2] M. Bishop and M. Dilger. Checking for race conditions in file accesses. *Computing Systems*, **9**(2):131–152, Spring 1996.

[3] M. Castro and B. Liskov. Proactive recovery in a Byzantine-fault-tolerant system. Symposium on Operating Systems Design and Implementation, pages 273–287. USENIX Association, 2000.

[4] P. M. Chen and B. D. Noble. When virtual is better than real. Hot Topics in Operating Systems, pages 133–138. IEEE Comput. Soc., 2001.

[5] B. Cheswick and S. Bellovin. *Firewalls and Internet security: repelling the wily hacker*. Addison-Wesley, Reading, Mass. and London, 1994.

[6] D. Denning. An intrusion-detection model. *IEEE Transactions on Software Engineering*, **SE-13**(2):222–232, February 1987.

[7] D. E. Denning. *Information warfare and security*. Addison-Wesley, 1999.

[8] D. Ellard, J. Ledlie, P. Malkani, and M. Seltzer. Passive NFS tracing of an email and research workload. Conference on File and Storage Technologies, pages 203–217. USENIX Association, 2003.

[9] D. Farmer. What are MACtimes? *Dr. Dobb's Journal*, **25**(10):68–74, October 2000.

[10] S. Forrest, S. A. Hofmeyr, A. Somayaji, and T. A. Longstaff. A sense of self for UNIX processes. IEEE Symposium on Security and Privacy, pages 120–128. IEEE, 1996.

[11] G. R. Ganger, G. Economou, and S. M. Bielski. *Finding and Containing Enemies Within the Walls with Self-securing Network Interfaces*. Carnegie Mellon University Technical Report CMU-CS-03-109. January 2003.

[12] G. R. Ganger and D. F. Nagle. Better security via smarter devices. Hot Topics in Operating Systems, pages 100–105. IEEE, 2001.

---

[4]The U.S. Government is authorized to reproduce and distribute reprints for Governmental purposes notwithstanding any copyright notation thereon. The views and conclusions contained herein are those of the authors and should not be interpreted as necessarily representing the official policies or endorsements, either expressed or implied, of the Air Force Research Laboratory or the U.S. Government.

[13] T. Garfinkel and M. Rosenblum. A virtual machine introspection based architecture for intrusion detection. NDSS. The Internet Society, 2003.

[14] H. Gobioff. *Security for a high performance commodity storage subsystem.* PhD thesis, published as TR CMU–CS–99–160. Carnegie-Mellon University, Pittsburgh, PA, July 1999.

[15] J. H. Howard, M. L. Kazar, S. G. Menees, D. A. Nichols, M. Satyanarayanan, R. N. Sidebotham, and M. J. West. Scale and performance in a distributed file system. *ACM Transactions on Computer Systems,* **6**(1):51–81, February 1988.

[16] Y. N. Huang, C. M. R. Kintala, L. Bernstein, and Y. M. Wang. Components for software fault-tolerance and rejuvenation. *AT&T Bell Laboratories Technical Journal,* **75**(2):29–37, March-April 1996.

[17] J. Katcher. *PostMark: a new file system benchmark.* Technical report TR3022. Network Appliance, October 1997.

[18] G. H. Kim and E. H. Spafford. The design and implementation of Tripwire: a file system integrity checker. Conference on Computer and Communications Security, pages 18–29. ACM, 1994.

[19] C. Ko, M. Ruschitzka, and K. Levitt. Execution monitoring of security-critical programs in distributed systems: a specification-based approach. IEEE Symposium on Security and Privacy, pages 175–187. IEEE, 1997.

[20] P. Kumar and M. Satyanarayanan. Flexible and safe resolution of file conflicts. USENIX Annual Technical Conference, pages 95–106. USENIX Association, 1995.

[21] R. Lemos. Putting fun back into hacking. ZDNet News, 5 August 2002. `http://zdnet.com.com/2100-1105-948404.html`.

[22] P. Liu, S. Jajodia, and C. D. McCollum. Intrusion confinement by isolation in information systems. IFIP Working Conference on Database Security, pages 3–18. IFIP, 2000.

[23] T. F. Lunt and R. Jagannathan. A prototype real-time intrusion-detection expert system. IEEE Symposium on Security and Privacy, pages 59–66. IEEE, 1988.

[24] McAfee NetShield for Celerra. EMC Corporation, August 2002. `http://www.emc.com/pdf/partnersalliances/einfo/McAfee_netshield.pdf`.

[25] NFR Security. `http://www.nfr.net/`, August 2002.

[26] Packet Storm Security. Packet Storm, 26 January 2003. `http://www.packetstormsecurity.org/`.

[27] V. Paxson. Bro: a system for detecting network intruders in real-time. USENIX Security Symposium, pages 31–51. USENIX Association, 1998.

[28] J. Phillips. *Antivirus scanning best practices guide.* Technical report 3107. Network Appliance Inc. `http://www.netapp.com/tech_library/3107.html`.

[29] P. A. Porras and P. G. Neumann. EMERALD: event monitoring enabling responses to anomalous live disturbances. National Information Systems Security Conference, pages 353–365, 1997.

[30] W. Purczynski. GNU fileutils – recursive directory removal race condition. BugTraq mailing list, 11 March 2002.

[31] Red Hat Linux 6.1, 4 March 1999. `ftp://ftp.redhat.com/pub/redhat/linux/6.1/`.

[32] M. Rosenblum and J. K. Ousterhout. The design and implementation of a log-structured file system. *ACM Transactions on Computer Systems,* **10**(1):26–52. ACM Press, February 1992.

[33] V. Samar and R. J. Schemers III. *Unified login with pluggable authentication modules (PAM).* Open Software Foundation RFC 86.0. Open Software Foundation, October 1995.

[34] J. Scambray, S. McClure, and G. Kurtz. *Hacking exposed: network security secrets & solutions.* Osborne/McGraw-Hill, 2001.

[35] B. Schneier and J. Kelsey. Secure audit logs to support computer forensics. *ACM Transactions on Information and System Security,* **2**(2):159–176. ACM, May 1999.

[36] M. I. Seltzer, G. R. Ganger, M. K. McKusick, K. A. Smith, C. A. N. Soules, and C. A. Stein. Journaling versus Soft Updates: Asynchronous Meta-data Protection in File Systems. USENIX Annual Technical Conference, 2000.

[37] M. Sivathanu, V. Prabhakaran, F. I. Popovici, T. E. Denehy, A. C. Arpaci-Dusseau, and R. H. Arpaci-Dusseau. Semantically-smart disk systems. Conference on File and Storage Technologies, pages 73–89. USENIX Association, 2003.

[38] J. D. Strunk, G. R. Goodson, M. L. Scheinholtz, C. A. N. Soules, and G. R. Ganger. Self-securing storage: protecting data in compromised systems. Symposium on Operating Systems Design and Implementation, pages 165–180. USENIX Association, 2000.

[39] J. Sugerman, G. Venkitachalam, and B.-H. Lim. Virtualizing I/O Devices on VMware Workstation's Hosted Virtual Machine Monitor. USENIX Annual Technical Conference, pages 1–14. USENIX Association, 2001.

[40] Sun Microsystems. *NFS: network file system protocol specification,* RFC–1094, March 1989.

[41] D. B. Terry, M. M. Theimer, K. Petersen, A. J. Demers, M. J. Spreitzer, and C. H. Hauser. Managing update conflicts in Bayou, a weakly connected replicated storage system. ACM Symposium on Operating System Principles. Published as *Operating Systems Review,* **29**(5), 1995.

[42] Tripwire Open Souce 2.3.1, August 2002. `http://ftp4.sf.net/sourceforge/tripwire/tripwire-2.3.1-2.tar.gz`.

[43] K. Vaidyanathan, R. E. Harper, S. W. Hunter, and K. S. Trivedi. Analysis and implementation of software rejuvenation in cluster systems. ACM SIGMETRICS Conference on Measurement and Modeling of Computer Systems. Published as *Performance Evaluation Review,* **29**(1):62–71. ACM Press, 2002.

[44] X. Zhang, L. van Doorn, T. Jaeger, R. Perez, and R. Sailer. Secure Coprocessor-based Intrusion Detection. ACM SIGOPS European Workshop. ACM, 2002.

Customizable Model Checking for Embedded Software

Xianghua Deng, John Hatcliff, Matthew Hoosier, Robby
Department of Computing and Information Sciences,
Kansas State University *

Matthew B. Dwyer
Department of Computer Science and Engineering,
University of Nebraska †

February 1, 2006

Keywords

model checking, program analysis, embedded software, real-time software

Abstract

Software plays a critical role in the correct operation of the nation's power, water, financial, transportation, medical and military infrastructure. In the future, our society's critical infrastructure will only become more dependent on sophisticated sofware capabilities. It is essential that we develop methods for developing highly-reliable software systems and for assuring high-levels of confidence in their correct operation. As part of the Army Research Office's High-Confidence Embedded Systems program, we have explored the application of an emerging automated system verification technique, called model checking, to reason about crucial correctness properties of software operating in embedded computer-based systems. We have concluded that a single approach to model checking such software is incapable of scaling to realistic software. Instead what is needed is a flexible model checking framework that can be customized to the application, run-time environment, and correctness properties under analysis to maximize performance. In this paper, we describe such a framework and several customizations of that framework that are able to reason effectively about the behavior of complex embedded software.

1   Introduction

Computer-based systems are an indispensable component of nearly all of modern society's infrastructures. Power, water, transportation, medical, and military systems all rely heavily on the use of computers and the trend is towards more fully-automated sensing and control in system operation. With humans playing a less immediate role in determining correct system operation, methods for assuring the correctness of control software in those systems becomes an essential element in protecting the world's critical infrastructure.

Testing embedded software is extremely difficult. Modern embedded software, such as the mission computing software on an F-18 E fighter which is comprised of thousands of components and implemented with several millions lines of multi-threaded C++ code, is as large and complex as many non-embedded applications. Furthermore, this software operates in a context where many streams of sensor data, reflecting the physical environment, are fed as input to the software. Thus, even generating inputs for such software is difficult since they must reflect not only the proper input values but the ordering and timing of the delivery

---

*Manhattan KS, 66506, USA. {deng,hatcliff,matt,robby}@cis.ksu.edu
†Lincoln NE, 68588-0115, USA. dwyer@cse.unl.edu

those values. Testing across this input space is impractical, but deploying embedded software for critical missions without confidence in their operation is risky.

For the past four years, we have been investigating analysis techniques that are capable of providing high-levels of assurance of the correctness of embedded software as part of the Army Research Office's High-Confidence Embedded Systems (HCES) program. Our work is set more broadly in the context of the United States' Department of Defense University Research Initiative on Critical Infrastructure Protection and High Confidence, Adaptable Software and has as its primary objective the adaptation of model checking technologies, which have emerged as a widely-used means of verifying correctness properties of hardware circuits, to reason about the correctness of embedded software. Rather than focus solely on implementation-level reasoning about software behavior, we believe that model checking has the potential to be applied broadly throughout the software development process. This philosophy aligns our work closely with emerging approaches to model-driven development of embedded software and has led us to the development of model checking-based analyses of artifacts ranging from high-level requirements models, architectural and component-level design models, as well as implementations of software running on modern embedded systems computing platforms.

To provide some background, model checking [7] is a powerful algorithmic technique for reasoning about the behavior of finite-state system descriptions, such as functional designs of hardware circuits. The foundations of model checking were established in the 1980s and research in the 1990s focused on developing model checking tools and steadily increasing their performance. The past decade has seen the transfer of model checking into practice for hardware systems and early work on applying existing model checking tools to reason about a wide-variety of development artifacts for general software systems. For example, model checking frameworks have been applied to reason about software process models (e.g., [22]), software requirements models (e.g., [5]), architectural frameworks (e.g., [16, 23]), design models (e.g., [1, 19]), and system implementations (e.g., [3, 8, 17]). The effectiveness of these efforts has relied on: (1) detailed knowledge of a particular model checking framework, (2) an understanding of the semantics of notations for describing a software artifact, and (3) knowledge of how such artifacts are used to encode information about a class of software systems. The first of these is necessary if one to wants leverage an existing state-of-the-art checking tool since implementing a highly-tuned model checker of one's own is a significant engineering task. The second is needed to map the software models and code into the input language of the model checking tool. The third is needed to customize or optimize the performance of the model checking tool to yield scalable and effective analysis for realistic software systems.

We have a significant base of experience working in each of these areas and have been among the leaders in applying existing model checking tools to reason about software, but model checking embedded software presents several new and complicating challenges that we believe requires a new approach. Existing model checkers, such as SPIN [21], FDR2 [14], and NuSMV [6], were designed to support a fixed input language using a fixed collection of state-space representations, reduction and exploration algorithms. The capabilities of these tools have evolved over time, but that evolution has been limited to the capabilities that the tool developer found useful or desirable. While these model checkers are in widespread use, there are multiple difficulties in applying them to reason about design and implementation artifacts related to embedded software. Our approach has been to design a new model checking framework, called Bogor, from the ground up that: (a) implements state-of-the-art data structures and algorithms for efficient model checking, (b) defines mechanisms that allow the framework to be extended to analyze new software artifacts, and (c) defines interfaces that allow optimizations specific to those artifacts to be easily defined and integrated. To achieve this, Bogor supports five orthogonal *dimensions of extension*.

(1) **Extensible system modeling:** Semantic primitives used in defining software artifacts cover a broad range from typical arithmetic and logical operations, which are well-supported by existing model checkers, to domain-specific large-grain operations [16, 19]. It is not always possible to map domain constructs efficiently onto model checker input languages. For example, most model checking frameworks do not support the kinds of event-driven processing that is common in embedded systems. *Bogor allows developers to define domain-specific primitives to express the data and control structures used in a variety of embedded software modeling notations and implementation infrastructures.*

(2) **Extensible property specification:** Model checking frameworks typically come with the ability to check implicit properties, such as deadlock, system-specific invariants, and state-oriented temporal logic formulae. It is often the case, however, that the correctness properties of a family of software systems is

more naturally phrased in a different property language, for example, the sequencing of event flow in a real-time distributed design or pre/post-condition specifications for component implementations in such a system. Encoding such properties with the limited features of existing model checker languages can lead to significant inefficiencies [9]. *Bogor allows developers to customize property checking to optimize performance for targeted properties.*

(3) Extensible state encodings: Most model checking frameworks, with the exception of [4], employ a small fixed set of strategies for encoding system data. Knowledge about domain-specific data, components and properties may suggest opportunities for particularly efficient encodings that cannot be easily incorporated in existing model checking frameworks. For example, in many real-time embedded systems certain implementation details are hidden behind middleware interfaces and a customized analysis would benefit by also *hiding* those details in its representation of program state. *Bogor allows developers to tailor the encoding of system data to achieve state space reductions.*

(4) Extensible search algorithms: Model checking typically involves a stateful search of a system's reachable state-space. For defect detection one may perform a less complete heuristic search [13, 18] and for certain classes of systems state-less search may be an attractive alternative [17]. Well-understood faults in systems motivate the development of customized searches targeted for those faults. For example, in priority-scheduled embedded systems one may bias the search to analyze schedules that are more likely to give rise to priority-inversion errors. *Bogor allows developers to configure the search mode of the model checker based on the kinds of reasoning desired and on the nature of the software artifact under analysis.*

(5) Extensible reduction strategies: There exists an enormous body of literature on state space reduction strategies. For example, partial order reductions which exploit information about independence between transitions (e.g., [7, Chapter 10]) have proved quite effective in reducing model checking costs. Interestingly, the theoretical presentation of such techniques are often parameterized (e.g., by an independence relation), but actual implementations are usually hard-wired to a particular parameter setting (e.g., a particular notion of independence). We have found many instances where the ability to customize these parameters in the implementation can yield dramatic, multiple-order-of-magnitude, reductions in analysis cost. *Bogor allows developers to combine collections of reductions to target a specific family of software systems and thereby maximize state-space reduction without incurring unnecessary overhead.*

We have used Bogor to implement a number of model checking based analyses customized for different software domains. The companion paper [11], describes how Bogor has been adapted to exploit the semantics of the Java memory model to provide state-of-the-art partial order reductions [7] for analyzing multi-threaded Java programs; this customization has yielded up to a ten-thousand fold reduction in the time needed to analyze real programs. We have also developed customizations for a variety of specification forms, for example, very expressive pre/post-condition specifications of Java programs [25] and focused method atomicity specifications [20]. The above efforts focus on reasoning about program implementations, but we have developed customizations of Bogor that reason about correctness properties of component-oriented designs of middleware-based distributed real-time embedded software that have been applied to realistic models of avionics mission computing systems [10, 12]. Rather than recount the details of these efforts, in this paper we illustrate how Bogor can be customized to reason about real-time software implemented in Ravenscar-Java [24], a subset of the Real-time Specification for Java (RTSJ) [2]. These customizations, along with the experiences of more than ten other Bogor customization efforts, provide solid evidence of the generality and utility of Bogor as a platform for building customized software analyses.

The next Section provides background on the design of Bogor. Section 3 presents details on the semantics of Ravenscar-Java, how we customized Bogor to analyze such programs, and the effort needed to perform that customization. We discuss future directions for research in the area of customizable model checking for embedded systems in Section 4.

2   Bogor : A Customizable Model Checking Framework

Our experience applying and adapting existing model checkers to reason about properties of embedded software led us to develop a new model checking framework that is explicitly designed to be easily customized to (a) represent a wide range of system and software models, (b) check a variety of correctness specifications, and (c) apply data structures and algorithms that are specialized to a class of embedded systems to reduce

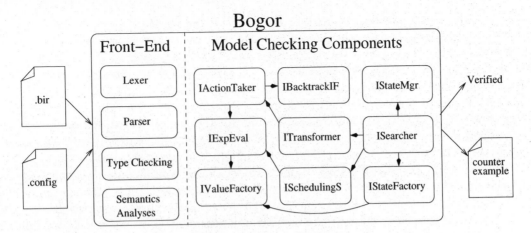

Figure 1: Bogor Architecture

the cost of analysis. In this section, we describe the basic architecture of this framework, which we call Bogor [26], and explain how its design supports the five dimensions of extension outlined above.

Explicit state model checkers share much in common with program interpreters. They both execute sequences of program statements updating a representation of the current program state as they proceed. Unlike an interpreter, however, a model checker records the sequence of statements in the execution and records all of the program states that have been encountered along that execution; this allows it to detect when the execution cycles back on itself. Furthermore, when a model checker encounters a state it has seen before, it backs up and attempts to execute a different sequence of statements. It accumulates the set of program states that have been seen along any of the executed statement sequences, and, in this way, a model checker can be thought of as interpreting a set of acyclic program executions. In its purest form a model checker will interpret *all possible* program executions, but this is intractable for many real systems since the number of possible program runs is enormous, if not infinite. Even without considering all possible program executions the stateful search of a subset of all program executions can provide a degree of coverage of program behavior that is significantly greater than traditional testing.

Figure 1 presents a high-level view of Bogor's architecture. The architecture can be divided into two parts: a front-end that processes a given model expressed in Bogor's modeling language (BIR), and the functional components of the model checker. The front-end is similar to that of any translator or interpreter in that it builds an intermediate representation that is used for analysis, and checks the well-formedness of that representation, for example, by type checking. BIR defines a guarded assignment language with built-in scalar and dynamically allocated *record* types that define a system's state and guarded-assignment transition systems that describe the evolution of a system's state; software artifacts are translated to BIR which is then processed by Bogor. The front-end is designed to easily support syntactic extensions to express new modeling and specification language features (in support of dimensions (1) and (2)). Figure 6 illustrates the syntax for introducing new primitive types (via `typedef`), new state changing operations (via `actiondef`), and new side-effect free operations (via `expdef`) into the model checker input. Figure 8 illustrates a fragment of a guarded transition system that moves through a series of states (defined via named `locations`) and executes operations including making calls to extensions (named with the `Ravenscar` prefix).

To support the desired extensibility dimensions, we have factored the design of the functional components of the model checker as shown in Figure 1. While all model checking tools include these essential components in their implementations, those implementations are often tangled, and thus insertion of alternate strategies or customization of existing strategies is often quite difficult. Bogor is not just the realization of an implementation that decouples model checker functional components. It embodies a component-based model checker design that employs widely-used and well-documented design patterns [15] to hide implementation details by encapsulation (to reduce dependences between components) and to build in strategies for parameterization, adaptation, and extension. Bogor modules need to interact with each other, however, a module should only be dependent on the interfaces of other modules. We will describe each Bogor module and the intuition behind its interface, and we will frequently refer to design patterns (or their variations) from [15] using a small caps font (e.g., ABSTRACT FACTORY). We will only describe the basic capability of each module. Modules can be extended to provide more capabilities via DECORATORS. A complete listing of the Bogor module APIs and examples of their use can be found on the Bogor web-site [26].

BIR values are divided into two categories (reflecting BIR types): primitive values and non-primitive values. When a primitive (non-primitive) type extension is declared, then its corresponding value should implement the `IPrimitiveExtValue` (`INonPrimitiveExtValue`) interface. Non-extension values, their creation, and the determination of their default values are managed by the `IValueFactory` interface. Thus, the specific implementation of the values depends on the implementation of the value factory. However, Bogor requires that a primitive value implementation be immutable (i.e., once created, it cannot be changed). Immutability opens the opportunity for object pooling (via the FLYWEIGHT pattern) whenever appropriate. A BIR state interface (`IState`) is a FACADE providing the interface to access the global values, thread locations and local values at each of a thread's stack frame. Modeling and specification language extensions (supporting dimensions (1) and (2)) make use of these value and state interfaces to implement the semantics of introduced operations. For example, a specification `expdef` may perform complex traversals of the program state to evaluate an *atomic proposition* on states used in a user defined property; this level of generality is not available in existing model checkers.

The Bogor model checker core consists of three major modules: the search module, the scheduling module, and the state manager module, as well as several other support modules.

The `ISearcher` is a STRATEGY for the search method used. For example, if depth-first search is used, then at any given state, its children states will be explored first before exploring its sibling states. This module directly supports extensibility dimension (4).

The `IStateManager` is a FACADE for managing states. Specifically, the interface dictates that given a state, the module determines whether the state has been visited before. There is no constraint on how it achieves that as long as it does not make an assumption that the instance of each state is different. For example, in depth-first search mode there is only one active state at any given time; this is analogous to having one state at runtime. The state is modified by each action and the search relies on the backtracking ability (i.e., undo) to restore the state to the previously visited state. Thus, the module cannot rely on the actual state representation because it changes as program traces are explored during the search. This module directly supports extensibility dimension (3).

The `ISchedulingStrategist` is a STRATEGY for the scheduler. The most basic scheduling strategy employed by model checkers is to generate all possible interleavings of thread executions. Other strategies include incorporation of support for priority based scheduling. In addition, when processing any intra-thread non-deterministic choice (e.g., associated with multiply-enabled transitions within the same thread), this module should be consulted to determine which transition to execute next. For example, in a full-state exploration mode, the scheduler should make sure that every branch of a non-deterministic choice should be explored. This module is also consulted to determine which transformations are enabled in a given state. This module supports both extensibility in terms of search (4) and provides the framework for implementing different reduction strategies (5).

The `IActionTaker` is an INTERPRETER for BIR actions such as assignment actions. The module is also a VISITOR for BIR actions, which enables new actions to be incorporated easily if necessary. Given the context of the action (e.g., the state in which it is being interpreted, the thread that executes it, etc.), the module is responsible for executing the action — thus, this module potentially changes the state. For a depth-first search, the module is required to produce backtracking information for each action it executes. It is also responsible for managing invocations of all the action extensions that are defined. The `IExpEvaluator` and the `ITransformer` are similar to `IActionTaker` except that they are responsible for executing BIR expressions and transformations, respectively. Furthermore, the `ITransformer` is also responsible for exception handling. These modules are overridden to implement extension primitives to achieve extensibility in dimensions (1) and (2).

The `IBacktrackingInfoFactory` is an ABSTRACT FACTORY for creating backtracking information for each BIR non-extension action. For example, for a depth-first search, backtracking information consists of a method that implements the "undo-ing" of a particular action. The `IStateFactory` and the `IValueFactory` are similar to the `IBacktrackingInfoFactory` except that they are responsible for creating BIR states and values, respectively.

Finally, cross-cutting this modular design is a custom publish-subscribe infrastructure that allows analysis developers to trigger processing when different activities during model checking are performed (e.g., whenever backtracking occurs, whenever a specific thread executes an action). This `Listener` framework provides a

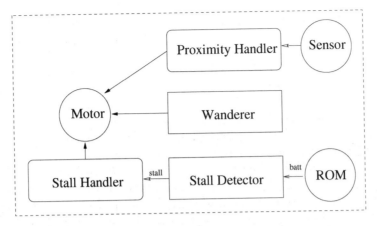

Figure 2: RockerBoogie Components

very flexible mechanism for adapting the base behavior of existing model checker module implementations to realize new forms of reduction (and thus supports extensibility dimension (5)). In fact, this framework is used in implementing the advanced partial-order reductions described in the companion paper [11].

3 Customizing Bogor for Ravenscar-Java

Bogor is not designed as a framework that practicing software developers building embedded software will employ. Rather it is a framework to be employed by a single trained validation and verification engineer to develop customized tools to provide effective debugging and validation support to such software developers. In this section, we relate our experiences performing one specific customization of Bogor. Our goal is to convey both (a) the insight that is needed to identify aspects of a class of embedded software systems that can be leveraged for reducing the cost of system analysis and (b) the ease with which those insights can be integrated into the Bogor framework to produce such an analysis.

The specific analysis we are considering explores the set of all execution sequences of program statements[1] for multi-threaded programs written in a subset of the Real-time Specification for Java that allows for both time-triggered and aperiodic interrupts from the environment and time-scheduled and prioritized thread execution. These features are not supported natively in Bogor, nor are they supported by any other model checking framework that we are aware of, and we use Bogor's extensibility to develop an analysis capable of checking state reachability and invariant properties of such systems.

In the remainder of this section we introduce the Ravenscar-Java subset of RTSJ by way of example, describe how features of Ravenscar-Java are mapped onto Bogor extensions, describe in detail various aspects of the semantics of those features and how they can be exploited to reduce the cost of model checking-based analyses, and conclude with an assessment of the effort required to customize Bogor.

3.1 Ravenscar-Java by Example

Ravenscar-Java is designed for real-time high-integrity systems, therefore, it emphasizes predictability. It eliminates a number of complex features in RTSJ that make static prediction of execution time difficult – for example, asynchronous transfer of control (ATC) and asynchronous thread termination. It also limits the use of some other RTSJ features, for example, restricting the set of thread types and memory management approaches. Moreover, it supports a predictable two phase computation model consisting of an initialization phase and a mission phase. During the initialization phase, all the threads and memory areas are allocated, but thread execution is not started. During the mission phase, threads are run, but no further threads or memory areas are allocated.

To illustrate the features of Ravenscar-Java, we present a small real-time event-driven robot control program. RockerBoogie[2] is the control software for a leJOS robot model of a simplified Mars lander. The robot moves around its local environment until either: its proximity sensor detects an obstacle or its motor stalls.

---

[1] Technically, we reason about sequences of bytecodes that correspond to program statements.
[2] http://lejos.sourceforge.net/robots.html

When it detects an obstacle, it attempts to navigate around the obstacle. When it senses its motor has stalled (by reading battery voltage), it reflexively moves backward in an attempt to free itself. RockerBoogie was originally written in multi-threaded Java using primitives of the leJOS operating system, but we mapped its implementation onto the subset of RTSJ features present in Ravenscar-Java[3]. The components of the adapted RockerBoogie are illustrated in Figure 2 where circles denote physical entities and rectangles denote software components. There are three functional components of the software: `Wanderer` controls the movement of the robot around its environment, `Stall Detector` and `Stall Handler` detect and respond to motor stall indications, and `Proximity Handler` detects obstacles and effects avoidance.

Figure 3 shows part of the initialization phase of the example in Ravenscar-Java. Initialization and mission phase can be delineated using different mechanisms, in this code the start times of all threads are set to variable `epoch`, which is set to 1000 ms, thus defining the initialization phase as the first 1000 ms of system execution. After that time elapses the mission phase commences.

```
1   public   class Main extends Initializer {
2      AbsoluteTime epoch = new AbsoluteTime(Clock.getRealtimeClock().getTime());
3      epoch.set(epoch.getMilliseconds() + 1000, 0);
4      PriorityParameters wanderPriority = new PriorityParameters(1);
5      PeriodicParameters wanderPeriod = new PeriodicParameters
6                      (epoch,new RelativeTime (1200,0));
7      Wander wander = new Wander();
8      PeriodicThread wanderThread = new PeriodicThread
9                      (wanderPriority, wanderPeriod, wander);
10     PriorityParameters sshPriority = new PriorityParameters(4);
11     HandleStall hs = new HandleStall(sshPriority,
12                     new SporadicParameters(new RelativeTime (600,0)));
13     SporadicEvent senseStallEvent = new SporadicEvent(hs);
14     PriorityParameters ssPriority = new PriorityParameters(3);
15     PeriodicParameters ssPeriod = new PeriodicParameters(
16                     epoch, new RelativeTime (600,0));
17     SenseStall ss = new SenseStall(senseStallEvent);
18     PeriodicThread senseStallThread = new PeriodicThread(
19                     ssPriority, ssPeriod,ss);
20     PriorityParameters proximityPriority = new PriorityParameters(2);
21     HandleProximity proximityHandler = new HandleProximity(proximityPriority,
22                     new SporadicParameters(new RelativeTime (800,0),1));
23     SporadicInterrupt proximityInterrupt = new SporadicInterrupt(hwHandler,
24                     ''PROXIMITY_INTERRUPT'');
25     wanderThread.start();
26     senseStallThread.start();
```

Figure 3: Part of Initialization of Rocker Boogie

Ravenscar-Java supports two kinds of threads: periodic threads, which model periodic tasks, and sporadic event handlers (SEH), which model aperiodic tasks. SEH have an associated minimum-inter-arrival time (MIT) which limits the frequency of event triggering. The modified RockerBoogie has four threads : two periodic tasks and two SEHs. The two periodic tasks implement the `Wanderer` and `Stall Detector` capabilities and the two SEHs implement the `Stall Handler` and `Proximity Handler` capabilities. In Figure 3, lines 14-19 show the creation of stall detector (`senseStallThread`) as a `PeriodicThread` with priority 3 and a period of 600 ms; Figure 4 presents the implementation of this thread as an instance of the `SenseStall` class. The stall handler is created as a SEH at lines 10-13 of Figure 3 with a priority of 4 and a MIT of 600 ms. In order to detect motor stall, the stall detector performs local computation requiring the allocation of a temporary object as shown on line 22 of class `ComputeSenseStall.run()`. Figure 5 shows the simple logic of the SEH stall handler in class `HandleStall`.

Ravenscar-Java greatly simplifies the RTSJ memory model. Programs can only use two kinds of memory areas: immortal memory and LTMemory. Immortal memory is a portion of the heap that is accessible from

---

[3]Several changes were required to the RockerBoogie software to track version changes in leJOS, for example, battery voltage is no longer provided by `ROM` class but by `Battery` class.

```
1   class SenseStall implements Runnable {
2       SpordicEvent senseStallEvent;
3       LTMemory scratchMemory;
4       ComputeSenstall compute;
5       SenseStall(SpordicEvent sse) {
6           senseStallEvent = sse;
7           scratchMemory = new LTMemory(1000);
8           compute = new ComputeSenseStall();
9       }
10      public void run() {
11          scratchMemory.enter(compute);
12          if(compute.stalled){
13              SenseStallEvent.fire();
14          }
15          ...
16      }}
17
18  public class ComputeSenseStall implements Runnable {
19      boolean stalled;
20      public void run() {
21          int bv = ROM.getBatteryPower();
22          StallData tmp = new StallData(bv);
23  ....
```

Figure 4: Part of the stall detector

```
1   class HandleStall extends SpordicEventHandler {
2       public HandleStall(PriorityParameters pri,
3                          SporadicParameters sp) {
4           super(pri,sp);
5       }
6       public void handlerAsyncEvent(){
7           Motor.A.reverseDirection();
8       }}
```

Figure 5: SenseStall Handler Logic

any program thread but is never garbage collected (i.e., all data allocated in this memory pool exists for the duration of the program execution). An LTMemory is a program-controlled approach to region-based memory allocation. A program explicitly enters the region and establishes an LTMemory as the current working heap. All subsequent object allocations are made to that LTMemory up to the point where the region is exited, at which point all objects in the LTMemory are reclaimed. LTMemory is used whenever a thread needs to allocate objects to perform local computation (i.e., it functions as a scratch memory). Figure 4 shows a typical usage of LTMemory the memory area is created on line 7 in the constructor of SenseStall which is invoked in the initialization phase. The periodic thread, SenseStall.run(), enters the LTMemory at line 11 to perform local computation on object compute. This causes the ComputeSenseStall.run() method to execute and when it returns the LTMemory region is exited and all the objects allocated in the region will be reclaimed.

For asynchronous event handling, Ravenscar-Java defines sporadic events. Pairs of sporadic events and the SEH that responds to them are related to each other during the initialization phase; this relation remains fixed during the mission phase. There are two kinds of sporadic events: SporadicEvents and SporadicInterrupts. The former is for asynchronous communication between threads and the latter is to handle external happenings which are outside of JVM (i.e., interrupts). In the RockerBoogie software there is one SporadicEvent and one SporadicInterrupt. The creation of the sporadic event is shown in lines 11-13 of Figure 3. The SporadicEvent, senseStallEvent, is fired from SenseStall.run(), as shown in Figure 4, and the handled in the HandleStall class implementation. The SporadicInterrupt is fired from outside of the JVM (e.g., triggered by a hardware sensor) its handling by the `HandleProximity` class implementation is established in lines 20-24.

3.2   Mapping Ravenscar Primitives To Bogor

As a subset of RTSJ, Ravenscar-Java inherits the design decision to implement all of its primitives as Java classes. For each class and method in the Ravenscar-Java we define a Bogor extension. Figure 6 illustrates some of these extensions. The `typedefs` correspond to Ravenscar-Java class definitions, for example, `LTMemory` or `SporadicEvent`. For methods in those classes, such as `LTMemory.enter()`, we introduce `actiondefs` with the appropriate types, `enterLTMemory(Ravenscar.LTMemory)`. An `actiondef` is used whenever the method effects a state change and returns no value. If a method returns a value then it is defined using an `expdef`, for example `createPeriodicThread(int, int, string)`. Since BIR distinguishes between side-effect-free expressions and side-effecting actions, modeling a side-effecting value-returning Ravenscar-Java method requires a pair of expression and action; action `addPeriodicThreadToSystem()` is paired with `createPeriodicThread()` in this way. Bogor extension definitions can be parameterized by type. The last two `expdefs` illustrate the parameterization of create methods for sporadic events and interrupts by the type of sporadic event.

```
1    extension Ravenscar for edu.ksu.cis.rtsjCheck.Ravenscar {
2        typedef LTMemory;
3        typedef PeriodicThread;
4        typedef SpordicEventHandler;
5        typedef SpordicEvent;
6        typedef SpordicInterrupt;
7        actiondef enterLTMemory(Ravenscar.LTMemory);
8        actiondef exitLTMemory(Ravenscar.LTMemory);
9        actiondef putObjectInCurrentMemoryArea( (|java.lang.Object|) );
10       expdef Ravenscar.PeriodicThread createPeriodicThread(int,int,string);
11       actiondef addPeriodicThreadToSystem(Ravenscar.PeriodicThread);
12       expdef Ravenscar.SpordicEventHandler
13                         createSpordicEventHandler(int,int,string);
14       actiondef addSpordicEventHandlerToSystem
15                         (Ravenscar.SpordicEventHandler);
16       expdef Ravenscar.SpordicEvent createSpordicEvent<'enum$a>
17                         ('enum$a,Ravenscar.SpordicEventHandler);
18       expdef Ravenscar.SpordicInterrupt createSpordicInterrupt <'enum$a>
19                         ('enum$a,Ravenscar.SpordicEventHandler,string);
```

Figure 6: Ravenscar extension for Bogor

With these extensions the Ravenscar-Java initialization code shown in Figure 3 can be mapped to the BIR shown in Figure 7. Each Ravenscar-Java thread, whether periodic or SEH, is modeled by a thread in BIR.

As mentioned above, our goal is to analyze sequences of program statements and, of course, this is influenced heavily in Ravenscar-Java programs by the timing of thread scheduling, event firing and interrupts. We observe, however, that to preserve the ordering of program statements it is not necessary to track the passage of time precisely during our analysis, rather we need only keep track of the relative passage of time in the different threads in the system. To do this, we normalize all thread periods and MITs by their greatest common divisor; in the RockerBoogie example that value is 200 ms. In doing this, we can no longer rely on system timers to trigger when thread scheduling or event firing may occur. We model all legal schedules and event firings by introducing an additional thread, called the `timerThread`, into the BIR system that explicitly executes threads and event handlers based on the passage of normalized periods and MITs.

Creation of a periodic thread is modeled by action `createPeriodicThread()` with three parameters: normalized period, thread priority and the name of the BIR thread which implements its `run()` method. On line 6 of Figure 7, `senseStall` is created with a normalized period of 3 (600 ms/200 ms), a priority of 3 and the name of the BIR thread `senseStallThread` which implements the `SenseStall.run()` method of Figure 4 as the guarded transition system that is excerpted in Figure 8. Once created the thread needs to be added to the state of the system to be analyzed which is achieved by a call to `addPeriodicThreadToSystem()`. The creation of an SEH in BIR is similar to the creation of periodic thread with one additional parameter : the normalized MIT. The `proximityHandler` is created in line 3 of Figure 7 with a priority of 2 and a normalized MIT of 4 (800 ms/200 ms).

Since each sporadic event has only one fixed handler, SporadicEvents are created by calling action `createSporadicEvent` with two arguments: an event type and the name of the BIR handler thread. Line 11 of Figure 7 shows the creation of the SporadicEvent, `stallEvent`. SporadicInterrupt creation needs one more argument: the name of the external happening that triggers it. Line 13 shows the creation of SporadicInterrupt, `proximityEvent` which is bound to the hardware generated interrupt `PROXIMITY_INTERRUPT`.

Creation of an LTMemory area in the initialization phase maps directly onto our Bogor extensions as shown in line 15-16 of Figure 7.

```
1   wander := Ravenscar.createPeriodicThread(6,1,"wanderThread");
2   Ravenscar.addPeriodicThreadToSystem(wander);
3   proximityHandler := Ravenscar.createSpordicEventHandler
4                       (2,4,"proximityHandlerThread");
5   Ravenscar.addSpordicEventHandlerToSystem(proximityHandler);
6   senseStall := Ravenscar.createPeriodicThread(3,3,"senseStallThread");
7   Ravenscar.addPeriodicThreadToSystem(senseStall);
8   stallHandler := Ravenscar.createSpordicEventHandler
9                       (4,3,"senseStallHandlerThread");
10  Ravenscar.addSpordicEventHandlerToSystem(stallHandler);
11  stallEvent := Ravenscar.createSpordicEvent<SpordicEventType>
12      (SpordicEventType.stall, stallHandler);
13  proximityEvent := Ravenscar.createSpordicInterrupt<SpordicEventType>
14    (SpordicEventType.proximity, proximityHandler,"PROXIMITY_INTERRUPT");
15  scratchMemory := Ravenscar.createLTMemory(1000);
16  Ravenscar.addLTMemoryToSystem(scratchMemory);
```

Figure 7: Rocker Boogie initialization in BIR

Figure 8 shows a fragment of the `SenseStall.run()` method of Figure 4. Entering the `scratchMemory` LTMemory scope to perform the local computation defined by `ComputeSenseStall.run()` and then exiting the memory scope is illustrated on lines 1 through 12. The BIR implementing the object allocation on line 22 of `ComputeSenseStall.run()`, in Figure 8, is shown on lines 14 through 24. Note that since our analysis only considers sequencing of statement we only maintain a logical two-way mapping between objects and memory areas; physical addresses of LTMemory and objects allocated in it are abstracted.

3.3   Ravenscar/Java Reduction Techniques

In this section we outline the modeling of SporadicInterrupts and customized reduction techniques that exploit the semantics of SporadicInterrupts. We subsequently describe a reduction technique that exploits properties of the overall timing of Ravenscar-Java programs. We note also that our model enforces thread priorities in scheduling which is easily achieved by overriding the `SchedulingStrategist` module in Bogor.

3.3.1   Sporadic Interrupts and the Hardware Environment

SporadicInterrupts are bound to happenings (interrupts) that are generated outside the software. To perform analysis, we model the hardware environment that generates SporadicInterrupts by BIR *environment threads*. Ravenscar-Java programs may be designed to operate in a wide-variety of environments, and we would like these threads to capture the behavior of all of those environments. A Ravenscar-Java program does not precisely describe the hardware environment it is designed to operate in, rather it states the weak assumption that SporadicInterrupts will not occur too frequently – expressed as the MITs. Consequently, we analyze

```
 1      loc  loc1 : live {}
 2          when true do {
 3              Ravenscar.enterLTMemory(scratchMemory); }
 4          goto loc2;
 5      loc  loc2 : live {}
 6          when true
 7              invoke    {| Computation.<run>()|}()
 8          goto loc3;
 9      loc  loc3 : live {}
10          when true do {
11              Ravenscar.exitLTMemory(scratchMemory);}
12          goto loc4;
13      . . . . .
14      loc  loc0 : live  {temp}
15          when true do {
16              temp := new (| RockerBoogie.StallData |);}
17          goto loc1;
18      loc  loc1 : live {temp}
19              invoke {| RockerBoogie.StallData.<init>()|}(temp, bv)
20          goto loc2;
21      loc  loc2 : live {temp}
22          when true do {
23              Ravenscar.putObjectInCurrentMemoryArea(temp);}
24          goto loc3;
```

Figure 8: Part of stall detector in BIR

the BIR model of a Ravenscar-Java program combined with threads that generate SporadicInterrupts no more frequently than the MIT.

We achieve this by assigning to each SporadicInterrupt (SI) a separate environment thread and a clock, C_{si}, which elapses at the same rate as the system clock and records the amount of time that has elapsed since the SI's most recent firing; since our model of time is normalized so are these clocks. If the time of C_{si} is greater or equal to the MIT of the SI (MIT_{si}), the environment thread for SI will nondeterministically choose to fire SI or not. This nondeterministic behavior of the environment for each SI can be further simplified to a thread which loops executing statements of the form $\langle \textbf{await}\, C_{si} \geq MIT_{si} \rightarrow SI.fire(); \text{reset}\, C_{si}\rangle$. This effectively pushes nondeterminism up to the scheduling level, by disabling the environment thread until the time constraint has been met. Note that by letting an environment thread remain enabled after the guard is true ($C_{si} \geq MIT_{si}$), the model checker will explore all possible sequences of SporadicEvent firings and system statements.

An environment thread may choose to never fire a given SI, which is consistent with any MIT, but has the negative consequence that C_{si} may grow without bound; this will render model checking intractable. We note, however, that once C_{si} has reached the value of MIT_{si} the await guard in the environment thread remains true regardless of further increments of C_{si}. Thus, C_{si} can be realized as a bounded counter in the range $[0, MIT_{si} - 1]$. We note, however, that these bounds may grow very large; we have seen examples with MITs of one minute which yielded a normalized value of 300.

Large MITs can have a negative impact on the performance of analysis which, in the worst case, is proportional to $\Pi_{i=1}^{n} MIT_i$ where n is the number of SIs in the system. For systems with large MIT values, we can mitigate the increase in analysis cost by introducing a sound approximate environment model that is guaranteed to produce all of the behaviors of the model described above, but may be significantly less expensive. Figure 9 illustrates the concept of this approximation. The figure shows the skeleton of a transition system for a SI with $MIT_{si} = n$ (a) and $MIT_{si} = n - 1$ (b). Clearly the (b) model includes all the paths in (a), but it may include some extra paths. In essence, (b) can be seen as weakening the MIT_{si} constraint by simply reducing the normalized MIT value. In Ravenscar-Java $MIT \geq 0$, but if $MIT = 0$ the environment can send infinitely many consecutive SI which is clearly not feasible in a real environment; thus the minimal feasible value for MIT is one. Reducing the enforced MIT value reduces analysis cost, but it also introduces infeasible paths into the analysis which may yield false negative results. The environment threads we use to model Ravenscar-Java hardware environments easily accommodate the definition of arbitrary MIT values, thereby giving the analysis user flexibility in controlling the trade-off between analysis cost and precision for different systems.

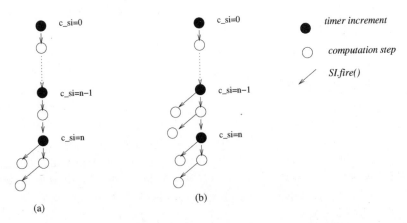

Figure 9: Cost reduction via MIT approximation

3.3.2   The System Timing Model

To reason about statement sequences in Ravenscar-Java programs, we must account for the influence of system timing in controlling the execution of threads and aperiodic events. In contrast to platform specific approaches that estimate the duration of program actions and the progress of system time, we adopt the abstract model of time from [10] which is able to detect the impossibility of certain actions in a program execution.

In the models generated from Ravenscar-Java programs, there will be a `timerThread` (as shown in Figure 10) that advances normalized system time. For the periodic subsystem, there is a `timeOutSender` thread which releases periodic tasks according to their periods, start times, and current system time. To model the physical device timer, the system always schedules the `TimeOutSender` thread immediately after `timerThread`. Since the sole purpose of system time is to release periodic tasks, we treat time as a bounded counter that is reset based on the hyper-period of the periodic tasks in the program. To achieve soundness with respect to all sequences of Ravenscar-Java program statements, the timer thread nondeterministically interleaves with all transitions of program threads.

```
1   thread timerThread() {
2     loc loc0: live {}
3       when true do invisible { time := (time + 1) % 6;  } goto loc1;
4     loc loc1: live{}
5       when proximityInterval >= proximityMIT do {} goto loc0;
6       when proximityInterval < proximityMIT do {
7         proximityInterval := proximityInterval + 1;} goto loc0;}
```

Figure 10: Timer Thread in the RockerBoogie Model

Timing model semantics

While sound, the approach described above is somewhat inefficient. To motivate several optimizations, we briefly sketch the semantics of timing in Ravenscar-Java BIR models. Let an execution of the system, after projecting out transitions in the `timeOutSender` thread, be:

$$s_0 \xrightarrow{\tau_0} s_1 \xrightarrow{\tau_1} s_2 \ldots s_n \xrightarrow{\tau_n} s_{n+1} \cdots$$

where s_i are states and τ_i is either the timer transition T_k (i.e., the (k+1)st timer transition) or a non-timer transition nt_j (i.e., the (j+1)st non-timer transition.) The model is setup so that the first transition τ_0 is T_0; we can use the occurrence of T_i to denote system time i. If we project out the states and only leave the transitions, we have a string of transitions

$$T_0 \ldots nt_i \ldots nt_{i+1} \ldots T_k \ldots$$

Let the running time of transition nt_i be Δt_i, then

$$k - 1 \leq \Sigma_{j=0}^{i} \Delta t_j < k \qquad (1)$$

where $k = min\{m \mid T_m \text{ occurred after } nt_{i+1}\}$. For example, a string of $T_0 nt_0 nt_1 \ldots$ yields $0 \leq \Delta t_0 < 1$ and a string of $T_0 nt_0 T_1 nt_1 T_2 \ldots$ yields $1 \leq \Delta t_0 < 2$. Intuitively, the number of timer transitions T_i serves to provide upper and lower bounds on the duration of transitions in terms of normalized clock ticks.

Timing based reduction techniques

We can use use Equation 1 to calculate a constraint for Δt_{i+1}. Let a string of transitions be

$$T_0 \ldots nt_i \ldots nt_{i+1} \ldots nt_{i+2} \ldots T_l \ldots$$

where $k = min\{m \mid T_m \text{ occurred after } nt_{i+1}\}$ and $l = min\{m \mid T_m \text{ occurred after } nt_{i+2}\}$. By equation 1, we get

$$k - 1 \leq \Sigma_{j=0}^{i} \Delta t_j < k$$

and

$$l - 1 \leq \Sigma_{j=0}^{i+1} \Delta t_j < l.$$

By subtracting these inequations, we get $\Delta t_{i+1} > l - 1 - k$. By definition $l \geq k$, but there are two cases to consider. If $l = k$, nt_{i+1} and nt_{i+2} execute without any intervening timer transition the string is

$$T_0 \ldots nt_i \ldots nt_{i+1} nt_{i+2} \ldots T_l \ldots$$

If $l > k$, then there are timer transitions between nt_{i+1} and nt_{i+2} and the number of T occurring between them equals $l - k$, in which case the string is

$$T_0 \ldots nt_i \ldots nt_{i+1} T_k T_{k+1} \ldots T_{l-1} nt_{i+2} \ldots T_l \ldots$$

In most systems, each transition is much smaller than a normalized clock tick (e.g., the system clock tick in RockerBoogie is 200 ms). Thus, for a transition nt_i, $\Delta nt_i < 1$ so $l - k - 1 < 1$ and $l - k < 2$. This means that timer transitions can not be scheduled consecutively. This is a simple optimization that is implemented in a few lines of code in a customized `SchedulingStrategist` Bogor module. This implementation easily accommodates heuristics relating the expected ratio of normalized clock ticks to transition durations to provide further, albeit unsound, reductions.

Another timing related reduction technique is to leverage the overrun of deadlines as discussed in [10]. Ravenscar-Java is designed to deal with hard real-time system, thus there should be no deadline overruns; this will typically be guaranteed by a schedulability analysis. If we take this as an assumption then we can further constrain the sequence of allowable system actions, for example, so that no two consecutive releases of a periodic thread are issued without scheduling the thread. A minor modification to the `SchedulingStrategist` module describe above implements this optimization.

3.4   Discussion

We have described how Ravenscar-Java primitives are mapped onto an extended set of BIR primitives. Our basic strategy was to start with a direct mapping that preserved the sequencing of Ravenscar-Java program statements. We then considered a series of features of Ravenscar-Java, analyzed their semantics and generated insight into how those semantics could be safely approximated and captured in our analysis. We use five different mechanisms to develop a customized analysis for Ravenscar-Java programs using Bogor.

BIR Extension We supported the Ravenscar-Java primitives as first-class primitives in BIR by introducing types, actions and expressions that model their semantics. A total of 33 lines of code were needed to define the syntactic extensions for Ravenscar-Java and an additional 146 lines of code were needed to implement the semantics of those extensions in the `ExpEval` and `ActionTaker` modules. This modest effort resulted in a customized version of BIR that serves as an effective target for translating Ravenscar-Java application code.

Application Mapping We mapped Ravenscar-Java application code to the extended BIR by what amounts to a syntactic translation. This translation performs certain transformations, like normalization of periods and MITs, that are required by our analysis.

Environment Threads We added additional threads to model the hardware environment that a Ravenscar-Java program executes in. This was necessary to reflect the true behavior of these programs in their execution environments.

Timing Threads We added threads that model the passage of time and the decisions of the Ravenscar-Java run-time system in performing thread scheduling. These threads incorporate optimizations that arise due to the fact that our analysis is only considering the sequencing of Ravenscar-Java statements.

Module Overriding We overrode several modules of the core Bogor model checking engine to optimize analysis. The bulk of our efforts involved optimizing the representation of program state, by exploiting the fixed nature of certain portions of the data in the mission phase; we implemented 286 lines of code spread across the `StateMgr` and `StateFactory` modules. We implemented a total 145 lines of code in the `SchedulingStrategist` module and 19 lines of code in the `Searcher` module to enforce priority scheduling and our abstract timing model and to apply the optimizations that eliminate consecutive timer transitions and periodic thread releases.

Our experience in this customization effort reflects our experience in developing other Bogor customizations as well as the experience of users of Bogor who are outside of our group. A mixture of extension mechanisms is usually needed to effectively customize an analysis to a particular class of systems. While multiple mechanisms are needed, the size and complexity of changes to existing Bogor components is relatively modest – for the Ravenscar-Java customization less than 600 lines of code were needed. It is important to emphasize, however, that the insight needed to drive such customizations may be non-trivial; an experienced domain expert is clearly needed for this activity.

4 Future Directions

Construction of embedded systems is increasingly based on *model-driven development* techniques in which customizable modeling frameworks are used to construct graphical abstractions of system architecture and behavior that can be leveraged for a variety of activities including analysis, simulation, and automatic code generation. These approaches often emphasize the concept of *meta-modeling* – which enables system architects to define domain-specific modeling languages that ease development tasks by incorporating as first-class elements in the modeling language various data types, communication mechanisms, attributes, and software building blocks that are specific to a particular domain. Despite significant progress, these modeling frameworks often provide minimal support for capturing precise semantics and for deep semantic reasoning. The need to incorporate domain-specific semantic information is a further hindrance to developing tool support, because this requires a rich extensible framework capable of supporting definition of domain-specific semantics declarations.

We believe that Bogor is an ideal vehicle for support of abstract semantics capture and reasoning in the context of meta-modeling. In particular, its extensible modeling language allows domain-specific semantic abstractions to be defined to match the modeling elements introduced by meta-modeling. We have carried out initial work in this area by defining extensions to Bogor to support simulation and model checking of component-based systems built in the context of Boeing's Bold Stroke product-line architecture for avionics mission control systems. Specifically, we incorporated Bogor into our Cadena [19, 10] model-driven development environment for component-based systems, and used it to model check system descriptions derived from component transition system models and customized Bogor representations of CORBA Real-Time middleware services. By tailoring Bogor's state-space search strategy and state storage mechanisms to periodic computation patterns specific to the Bold Stroke infrastructure, we were able to achieve orders of magnitude of reduction in the cost of model checking [12].

An essential element of future model-driven development approaches will be the availability of a suite of analysis techniques to reason about a wide-range of correctness, robustness, security, and performance properties of embedded software and systems early in the development lifecycle. Model-based analysis, like our customizations of Bogor, must be tailored to the class of systems, the details of modeling notations, and the properties being analyzed in order to maximize their effectiveness. We believe that the lessons learned in developing and applying Bogor can set the stage for the next phase of development of customizable system analysis frameworks.

Acknowledgements

Our work has benefited from long-running interactions with two additional members of our HCES project: George Avrunin and Stephen Siegel at the University of Massachusetts. They have focused their efforts on analyzing explicitly parallel programs written using the MPI, but recent work has begun to explore how Bogor can be used to support such analyses. Feedback from David Hislop, the HCES program manager at the Army Research Office, and his efforts to foster collaboration among the three HCES project teams have also helped shape the broader goals of our work. In addition, our colleagues Venkatesh Prasad Ranganath, Todd Wallentine, and Georg Jung have participated in many discussions on the design and application of Bogor and helped it to mature into a stable and useful framework for analysis. Finally, there is a growing community of Bogor users who have initiated efforts to develop a wide-range of customized software analyses based on Bogor. The feedback and technical interchange with this community has been extremely valuable and we thank them for it.

References

[1] R. Alur and M. Yannakakis. Model checking of hierarchical state machines. In *Proceedings of the Sixth ACM SIGSOFT Symposium on Foundations of Software Engineering*, pages 175–188, Nov. 1998.

[2] G. Bollela, J. Gosling, B. Brosgol, P. Dibble, S. Furr, D. Hardin, and M. Turnbull. *The Real-Time Specification for Java*. Addison-Wesley, 2000.

[3] G. Brat, K. Havelund, S. Park, and W. Visser. Java PathFinder – a second generation of a Java model-checker. In *Proceedings of the Workshop on Advances in Verification*, July 2000.

[4] T. Bultan, R. Gerber, and C. League. Composite model-checking: verification with type-specific symbolic representations. *ACM Transactions on Software Engineering and Methodology*, 9(1):3–50, Jan. 2000.

[5] W. Chan, R. J. Anderson, P. Beame, D. Notkin, D. H. Jones, and W. E. Warner. Optimizing symbolic model checking for statecharts. *IEEE Transactions on Software Engineering*, 27(2):170–190, 2001.

[6] A. Cimatti, E. Clarke, F. Giunchiglia, and M. Roveri. NuSMV : a new symbolic model checker. *International Journal on Software Tools for Technology Transfer*, 2(4):410–425, 2000.

[7] E. Clarke, O. Grumberg, and D. Peled. *Model Checking*. MIT Press, Jan. 2000.

[8] J. C. Corbett, M. B. Dwyer, J. Hatcliff, S. Laubach, C. S. Păsăreanu, Robby, and H. Zheng. Bandera : Extracting finite-state models from Java source code. In *Proceedings of the 22nd International Conference on Software Engineering*, June 2000.

[9] J. C. Corbett, M. B. Dwyer, J. Hatcliff, and Robby. Expressing checkable properties of dynamic systems: The Bandera Specification Language. *International Journal on Software Tools for Technology Transfer*, 4(1):34–56, 2002.

[10] X. Deng, M. B. Dwyer, J. Hatcliff, G. Jung, and Robby. Model-checking middleware-based event-driven real-time embedded software. In *Proceedings of the 1st International Symposium on Formal Methods for Components and Objects*, Nov. 2002.

[11] M. B. Dwyer, J. Hatcliff, Robby, and V. R.Prasad. Exploiting object escape and locking information in partial order reduction for concurrent object-oriented programs. *Formal Methods in System Design*, 25(2–3):199–240, September–November 2004.

[12] M. B. Dwyer, Robby, X. Deng, and J. Hatcliff. Space reductions for model checking quasi-cyclic systems. In *Proceedings of the 3rd International Conference on Embedded Software (EMSOFT 2003)*, volume 2855 of *Lecture Notes in Computer Science*, pages 173–189. Springer, October 2003.

[13] S. Edelkamp, A. L. Lafuente, and S. Leue. Directed explicit model checking with hsf-spin. In *Model Checking Software, Proceedings of the 8th International SPIN Workshop*, volume 2057 of *Lecture Notes in Computer Science*, May 2001.

[14] FormalSystems. FDR2 website. `http://www.fsel.com/`, 2003.

[15] E. Gamma, R. Helm, R. Johnson, and J. Vlissides. *Design Patterns*. Addison-Wesley Pub. Co., Jan. 1995.

[16] D. Garlan, S. Khersonsky, and J. S. Kim. Model checking publish-subscribe systems. In *Proceedings of the 10th International SPIN Workshop on Model Checking of Software*, May 2003.

[17] P. Godefroid. Model-checking for programming languages using VeriSoft. In *Proceedings of the 24th ACM Symposium on Principles of Programming Languages (POPL'97)*, pages 174–186, Jan. 1997.

[18] A. Groce and W. Visser. Model checking java programs using structural heuristics. In *Proceedings of the International Symposium on Software Testing and Analysis*, pages 12–21. ACM Press, 2002.

[19] J. Hatcliff, W. Deng, M. Dwyer, G. Jung, and V. Prasad. Cadena: An integrated development, analysis, and verification environment for component-based systems. In *Proceedings of the 25th International Conference on Software Engineering*, 2003.

[20] J. Hatcliff, Robby, and M. B. Dwyer. Verifying atomicity specifications for concurrent object-oriented software using model checking. In M. Young, editor, *Proceedings of the Fifth International Conference on Verification, Model Checking, and Abstract Interpretation (VMCAI 2004)*, volume 2937 of *Lecture Notes In Computer Science*, pages 175–190, Jan 2004.

[21] G. J. Holzmann. The model checker SPIN. *IEEE Transactions on Software Engineering*, 23(5):279–294, May 1997.

[22] C. T. Karamanolis, D. Giannakopolou, J. Magee, and S. M. Wheather. Model checking of workflow schemas. In *Proceedings of the 4th International Enterprise Distributed Object Computing Conference*, pages 170–181, Sept. 2000.

[23] N. Kaveh. Model checking distributed objects design. In *Proceedings of the 23rd International Conference on Software Engineering*, May 2001.

[24] J. Kwon, A. Wellings, and S. King. Ravenscar-java: a high integrity profile for real-time java. In *Proceedings of the 2002 joint ACM-ISCOPE conference on Java Grande*, pages 131–140, 2002.

[25] Robby, E. Rodríguez, M. B. Dwyer, and J. Hatcliff. Checking strong specifications using an extensible software model checking framework. In *Proceedings of the 10th International Conference on Tools and Algorithms for the Construction and Analysis of Systems*, volume 2988 of *Lecture Notes in Computer Science*, pages 404–420, Mar. 2004.

[26] Bogor Website. `http://bogor.projects.cis.ksu.edu`, 2003.

Exploiting Object Escape and Locking Information in Partial-Order Reductions for Concurrent Object-Oriented Programs*

MATTHEW B. DWYER   dwyer@cis.ksu.edu
JOHN HATCLIFF   hatcliff@cis.ksu.edu
ROBBY   robby@cis.ksu.edu
VENKATESH PRASAD RANGANATH   rvprasad@cis.ksu.edu
Department of Computing and Information Sciences, Kansas State University, 234 Nichols Hall, Manhattan KS, 66506, USA

Received July 20, 2003; Revised March 23, 2004; Accepted March 30, 2004

Abstract. Explicit-state model checking tools often incorporate partial-order reductions to reduce the number of system states explored (and thus the time and memory required) for verification. As model checking techniques are scaled up to software systems, it is important to develop and assess partial-order reduction strategies that are effective for addressing the complex structures found in software and for reducing the tremendous cost of model checking software systems.

In this paper, we consider a number of reduction strategies for model checking concurrent object-oriented software. We investigate a range of techniques that have been proposed in the literature, improve on those in several ways, and develop five novel reduction techniques that advance the state of the art in partial-order reduction for concurrent object-oriented systems. These reduction strategies are based on (a) detecting heap objects that are *thread-local* (i.e., can be accessed by a single thread) and (b) exploiting information about patterns of lock-acquisition and release in a program (building on previous work). We present empirical results that demonstrate upwards of a hundred fold reduction in both space and time over existing approaches to model checking concurrent Java programs. In addition to validating their effectiveness, we prove that the reductions preserve LTL_{-X} properties and describe an implementation architecture that allows them to be easily incorporated into existing explicit-state software model checkers.

Keywords: software model checking, software verifcation, partial order reduction, escape analysis, locking discipline

1. Introduction

State-space exploration techniques such as model checking verify a property ϕ of a concurrent system Σ by exploring all possible interleavings of thread transitions from Σ while looking for violations of ϕ. This exhaustive exploration is very expensive with respect to both the time and space required to store visited system states. In many cases, the exploration process searches paths that differ only in unimportant ways—e.g., in the intermediate states

*This work was supported in part by the U.S. Army Research Office (DAAD190110564), by DARPA/IXO's PCES program (AFRL Contract F33615-00-C-3044), by NSF under grant CCR-0306607, by Rockwell-Collins, and by Intel Corporation (Grant 11462).

Reprinted with kind permission of Springer Science and Business Media from *Formal Methods in System Design*. Vol 25, Issue 2–3, September–November 2004. 199–240. Copyright Springer-Verlag 2004.

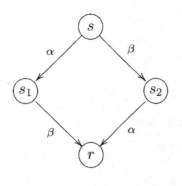

Figure 1.   Independent transitions.

produced or in the ordering of transitions—that cannot be distinguished by the property ϕ. Exploring multiple paths that are indistinguishable by ϕ is not necessary for verification, and techniques called *partial-order reductions* (POR), e.g. [6, Chapter 10], have been widely applied to avoid this form of unnecessary exploration.

Figure 1 presents a state s with two outgoing transitions α and β. These transitions are *independent* in the sense that they *commute*: both paths $\alpha\beta$ and $\beta\alpha$ arrive at the same state r. If the property ϕ being verified cannot distinguish the intermediate states s_1 and s_2 nor the ordering of the transitions, then α and β are said to be *invisible* to ϕ, and it is safe to explore one path only. For example, α might represent the assignment of a constant value v_1 to variable x that is local to thread t_1, and β might represent the assignment of a constant value v_2 to variable y that is local to thread t_2. If the primitive propositions in ϕ do not refer to x and y, and if they do not refer to the control points associated with assignment states to x and y, then transitions are invisible to ϕ and the resulting sub-paths are ϕ-*equivalent*. Partial-order reduction strategies reduce both time and space for storing states by detecting independent transitions and by exploring a single representative sub-path (e.g., $\alpha\beta$) from a set of ϕ-equivalent sub-paths (e.g., $\{\alpha\beta, \beta\alpha\}$).

Recent work [7, 9, 33] has demonstrated the effectiveness of state-space exploration techniques for verifying temporal properties of concurrent object-oriented (OO) software systems. Exhaustive exploration of such systems is expensive due not only to the presence of concurrency, but also to the potentially large and complex heap structures that arise in OO systems. The semantics of OO languages, such as Java, require that heap-allocated data be treated by a concurrent thread as if other threads may access it, but Java programs may manipulate significant amounts of heap-allocated data that can be considered *local* to a thread. For conventional transition systems, strategies like partial-order reductions have proven effective in exploiting local data to significantly reduce cost of state-space search. In existing work on partial-order reductions, the transition independence conditions that enable reductions can be identified in static descriptions of transition system (e.g., in the Promela [20] model of a system) by a syntactic scan of the description (e.g., two transitions from different processes access program variables that are declared as locals in a thread [6, p. 157] as in the example above). However, independence of program actions is much more difficult to recognize in object-oriented systems where heap-allocated data are referenced through chains of dereferences, where aliasing makes it hard to determine ownership and visibility of objects, and where locking can enforce exclusive access to shared objects.

There is a rich body of work from the compiler community on reducing the run-time cost of heap-allocated data in programs. For example, recent work on object stack allocation [10] and synchronization removal [29] have identified a number of opportunities for exploiting the results of *escape analysis* to improve performance by eliminating object dereferencing, reducing garbage collection, and eliminating Java monitor statements. Escape analyses can be used to determine that an object instance is only manipulated by a single thread and thus can be treated as local to that thread. Those analyses can also be used to enable partial-order reductions for model checking OO programs. However, as originally designed, they make cost-benefit trade-offs that are appropriate for compilation speed and performance optimization, but are sub-optimal for model checking reductions. Specifically, the lack of context and object-sensitivity in many existing escape analyses means they will miss opportunities to identify objects as thread local. More fundamentally, for an object to be classified as thread-local, these analyses require *all* accesses to the object to come from a single thread. Exploiting information about the *run time* state of the program can enable significantly more precise analyses, as evidenced for a variety of analyses in [17]. For example, in our context, although an object is accessed by more than one thread over its lifetime, run time information can determine that it can still be classified as thread-local if no more than one thread can access the object in any given state encountered in the program execution. With this type of on-the-fly analysis and optimization, one must balance the run-time overhead against the potential benefit. For model checking, the size of the state-space is the dominant factor in the cost of analysis. Exponential state-space growth means that the potential benefit of precise on-the-fly analysis will often be significant and more than outweigh any increase in the analysis cost.

Another line of work has studied the extent to which the locking disciplines used in implementing concurrent object-oriented programs can be used to drive state-space reductions. Inspired by the work of Lipton [26], recent work [14, 31] exploits locking information to identify regions of program execution that can safely be modeled as executing atomically. These methods rely on programmer annotations to identify the objects in the program that are governed by a specific locking discipline. Once annotated, the program can be analyzed on-the-fly to assure that the discipline is maintained. If the discipline is maintained, atomicity can be exploited to reduce the state-space during model checking [31].

In this paper, we propose a variety of partial-order reduction strategies for model checking concurrent object-oriented software that are based on detecting heap objects that are *thread-local* (i.e., can be accessed by a single thread only). Transitions that access such objects are independent, and identifying these allows the model checker to avoid exploring unnecessary interleavings. Locality of actions can be determined using both (a) analysis of the program heap structure to determine object escape information and (b) analysis of the locking patterns used to coordinate object access. We define and evaluate both a static and dynamic technique for approach (a) and several strategies for approach (b) as well as combinations of these techniques. Furthermore, we define and evaluate an additional atomicity-based reduction that can be combined with any of the preceding techniques.

We have implemented these reduction techniques in Bogor [27][1]—a novel model checker that is the core of the next generation of the Bandera tool set for model checking concurrent Java systems [7]. Bogor is an extensible model checker designed to support checking of

OO software with state-of-the-art strategies for heap-state representations and for achieving heap [22] and thread symmetry reductions [3]. This allows us to justify the effectiveness of our reductions empirically and to directly compare them with existing approaches to software model checking.

We begin our presentation in Section 2 with a collection of examples that provides the intuition behind our reduction strategies. Section 3 recalls the basic definitions of the *ample set* [6] partial-order reduction framework. The sections that follow provide the contributions of our paper.

- (Section 4) We recall how the traditional notion of transition independence (which requires transitions to be independent for all states) can be generalized to the notion of *conditional independence* [23] (which allows transitions to be independent in some states but not in others). We believe that this generalization to *state-sensitive independence* is necessary to treat effectively the dynamic nature of object-oriented software systems. Appendix 10 presents modifications to the correctness proofs for the ample set framework in [6] that account for the generalization to conditional independence.
- (Section 5) We describe how Java transition systems and independence properties for heap-based data can be cast in the ample sets partial-order reduction framework using both *static* and *dynamic* escape analysis. For static escape analysis, we summarize how Ruf's escape analysis [29] developed for removal of unnecessary synchronization can be adapted to provide information about object-sharing suitable for identifying independent transitions and driving partial-order reductions. For dynamic escape analysis, we give a novel technique for carrying out escape analysis on-the-fly during model checking that substantially improves upon the optimization enabled by the static escape analysis.
- (Section 6) We recall Stoller's locking-discipline based reduction approach [31] and then present alternate lock-based strategies that also incorporate dynamic thread-locality information. We note that neither our approach nor Stoller's subsumes the other, and then we present a strategy that combines Stoller's strategy with the best of our alternate strategies.
- (Section 7) We describe how to incorporate additional optimizations that avoid storage of unnecessary intermediate states—essentially by dynamically determining sequences of transitions such that each of these sequences can be expanded in a single atomic step.
- (Section 8) We report on experimental studies that show the relative performance of these reduction techniques. These techniques in combination they can provide multiple order of magnitude state-space reductions over that provided by existing highly-optimized software model checking frameworks.

Section 9 presents related work, and Section 10 concludes. Appendix 10 presents the static analysis that we used to detect thread-local objects. Appendix 10 presents modifications to the correctness proofs for the ample set framework in [6] that account for the generalization to conditional independence. Appendix 10 presents the proofs that the thread-local and lock-based reductions we propose satisfy the conditions of the ample set framework. Appendix 10 recasts Stoller's reduction approach into the ample set framework and describes our implementation of the strategy, which we use as a point of comparison in our experimental studies.

Our approach and results are described in the context of Bogor, however, we believe that the relative simplicity of integrating the approach with explicit-state model checking algorithms and the potential for significant reductions that it brings, suggest that other software model checkers should incorporate similar ideas.

2.   Motivating examples

In the following subsections, we give examples to provide the intuition behind our reduction strategies.

2.1.   Detecting independence using object escape information

Figure 2 presents two Java programs that we will use to illustrate why we want to consider both static and dynamic detection of thread-local objects. Both programs are similar: the main thread creates two `Process` threads, and for each `Process`, a list is built and then traversed while incrementing each list node's x field.

The difference: in figure 2(a), the list is both built and traversed in the `run` method of the `Process` thread; in figure 2(b), the list is built in the `Process` object's constructor, but the list is traversed in the `run` method of the `Process` thread. We would like an analysis to tell us if the lists in these examples are thread-local.

```
          (a) Independent Work (version 1)              (b) Independent Work (version 2)
public class IndependentWork1 {              public class IndependentWork2 {
  public static void main                      public static void main
      (String[] args) {                            (String[] args) {
    new Process().start();                       new Process().start();
    new Process().start();                       new Process().start();
  }                                            }
}                                            }
class Node {                                  class Node {
  int x; Node next;                            int x; Node next;
  public Node(int x) {                         public Node(int x) {
    this.x = x;                                  this.x = x;
  }                                            }
}                                            }
class Process extends Thread {                class Process extends Thread {
  Node head;                                   Node head;
  public void run() {                          public Process() {
    head = new Node(0);                          head = new Node(0);
    Node temp = head;                            Node temp = head;
    for (int i = 1; i < 10; i++) {               for (int i = 1; i<10; i++) {
      temp.next = new Node(i);                     temp.next = new Node(i);
      temp = temp.next;                            temp = temp.next;
    }                                            }
    while (head != null) {                     }
      head.x++;                                public void run() {
      head = head.next;                          while (head != null) {
    }                                              head.x++;
  }                                              head = head.next;
}                                              }
                                             }
                                           }
```

Figure 2.   Java examples illustrating static vs. dynamic escape analysis.

A conventional static escape analysis would establish the fact that the list does not escape the Process thread in figure 2(a), and thus it is thread-local. This information allows a model checker to apply partial-order reductions and avoid exploring interleavings with other threads at any transitions that access thread-local data—since the actions of other threads cannot interfere with the thread-local data, it is safe to explore only a path where there are no context switches, i.e., the current thread continues to execute. In fact, for Independent Work (version 1), static analysis is able to determine that the entire run method of the Process thread may execute as a sequence of thread-local transitions without considering any interleavings. This ends up reducing the number of states explored by a factor of twelve.

In contrast, the list in figure 2(b) actually gets manipulated by two threads: the main thread executes the Process constructor (and thus builds the list), but the Process thread traverses the list. Thus, a conventional static escape analysis would tell us that the list does escape the control of both the main and the Process thread, and based on that information we could not consider the list to be thread-local. Thus, no reduction in the number of states explored is possible based on conventional static escape analysis information.

The dynamic escape analysis that we have implemented checks for the thread-local condition after each execution step. It clearly detects that the list of figure 2(a) is thread-local at every program state. Moreover, it reveals an interesting fact about the list of figure 2(b): the list is never reachable by more than one thread at any state in the program. When the main thread executes the Process constructor, it is the only thread that can reach the list. Furthermore, when the constructor's execution is complete, the main thread cannot reach the list anymore. Thus, when a Process thread is started, it is the only thread that can reach the list.[2] Thus, we can consider the list thread-local at all program states of figure 2(b). This information allows the model checker to apply reductions and to process the run method of the Process as a sequence of thread-local transitions without considering any interleavings. We will demonstrate that the cost of dynamic escape analysis is negligible, and is almost always dramatically dominated by cost savings in number of states explored/stored, etc.

There are many other common coding patterns where dynamic escape analysis provides significant optimization of model checking costs. For example, many objects are often thread-local at the beginning of their life-times (and thus partial-order reductions can be applied during this portion of the execution) and then only later do they escape. In Section 5, we give a more rigorous explanation of the notions of thread-local object and state-sensitive transition independence that enable effective optimizations based on partial-order reductions.

2.2. Detecting independence using object locking information

Figure 3 presents a bounded-buffer implementation of a first-in first-out (FIFO) data structure that we use to illustrate the usefulness of lock-based partial-order reductions in addition to the thread-local object-based reductions of the previous example. There are two threads that are exchanging messages (objects) via the two instances of bounded-buffers. A thread can only take a message from a non-empty buffer; otherwise, it will block. Conversely, a thread can only add a message to a non-full buffer.

```
public class BBDriver {                     class BoundedBuffer {
  public static                               protected Object [] buffer;
      void main(String[] args) {              protected int bound;
    BoundedBuffer b1 =                         protected int head;
        new BoundedBuffer(3);                  protected int tail;
    BoundedBuffer b2 =
        new BoundedBuffer(3);                  public BoundedBuffer(int b) {
                                                 bound = b;
    b1.add(new Object());                        buffer = new Object[bound];
    b1.add(new Object());                        head = 0;
                                                 tail = bound - 1;
    (new InOut(b1, b2)).start();             }
    (new InOut(b2, b1)).start();
  }                                           public synchronized
}                                                 void add(Object o) {
                                               while (tail == head) {
class InOut extends Thread {                      try {
  BoundedBuffer in;                                wait();
  BoundedBuffer out;                             } catch (InterruptedException e) {
                                                 }
  public InOut(BoundedBuffer in,               }
              BoundedBuffer out) {             buffer[head] = o;
    this.in = in;                              head = (head + 1) % bound;
    this.out = out;                            notifyAll();
  }                                           }

  public void run() {                         public synchronized Object take() {
    Object tmp;                                 while (head == ((tail+1) % bound)) {
                                                 try {
    while (true) {                                 wait();
      tmp = in.take();                           } catch (InterruptedException e) {
      out.add(tmp);                             }
    }                                          }
  }                                            tail = (tail + 1) % bound;
}                                              notifyAll();
                                               return buffer[tail];
                                             }
                                           }
                                         }
```

Figure 3.   BoundedBuffer example illustrating locking-discipline.

Because of the high degree of object-sharing in this example, escape-based information does not yield dramatic reductions. Conventional static escape analysis does not reveal any objects that are thread-local. Dynamic escape analysis reveals that the BoundedBuffer objects are thread-local during the execution of the associated constructors, and reductions based on this information reduces the number of explored states from 4641 to 3713. However, considering locking information and state storage heuristics can reduce the states stored by a factor of 57 (bringing the number of stored states down to 81).

The BoundedBuffer class is *thread-safe,*[3] i.e., all accesses to its instance are mutually exclusive. The mutual exclusion is guaranteed by using the Java synchronize modifier on all of its methods. This style of implementation is commonly used, e.g., the java.util.Vector class and the java.util.Hashtable class in the Java Collection Framework. The java.lang.Object.wait() method and the java.lang.Object. notifyAll() method are used to implement the blocking behavior of the bounded-buffer.

Notice that all accesses to the fields of a bounded-buffer object take place through its (synchronized) methods. Thus, when any field of a bounded-buffer is accessed by a thread *t*, this means that *t* holds the lock of the bounded-buffer object. This disciplined use of locks guarantees that no other threads can access the fields until the bounded-buffer's lock is released. We call an object that uses this pattern of locking *self-locking* since the object's fields are protected by acquiring the lock associated with the object. Based on this information, many interleavings can be safely avoided when exploring the state-space of this system. For example, there is no need to consider any interleaving of thread actions before the assignments to `head` in the `add` method and to `tail` in the `take` method since locking guarantees that no other threads would be able to execute statements that change the values of the `head` and `tail` fields.

Furthermore, notice also that all accesses to the array `buffer` that provides the storage for the buffer occur only in the bounded-buffer (synchronized) methods, because the array does not escape the bounded-buffer. Specifically, all access paths to the array are dominated by a `BoundedBuffer` object—no other object holds a direct reference to the array. Thus, a `BoundedBuffer` object lock must be acquired before the array is accessed. We refer to this pattern of locking as *monitor-based* locking discipline. In addition to the reductions due to self-locking above, this means that there is no need to consider interleavings before the assignments to the `buffer` arrays in the `add` and `take` methods.

For both the `BoundedBuffer` object fields and buffer array, threads follow a locking discipline to access data—there is always a specific lock (whether in the object itself or in an associated object) that must be acquired before accessing the data. In Stoller's lock-based reductions [31], users annotate the objects that satisfy this general notion of locking discipline. Then, the model checking algorithm with partial-order reductions uses this information to avoid interleavings as described above while simultaneously checking that the locking discipline is not violated.

While Stoller's approach covers most cases that yield opportunities for lock-based reductions, there are several common locking idioms that dynamically re-associate locks with a set of objects being protected. Some of these examples can be handled by our dominated/monitor based approach but not by Stoller's method. On the other hand, there are also examples where there is no link via references from a protecting object to the object being protected, and in these cases, Stoller's method enables reductions whereas ours does not. Finally, we have observed that combining lock-based reductions with thread-local-based reductions almost always yields some improvements over either type of strategy alone, and further combining these with heuristics for avoiding state storage yields dramatic reductions. Furthermore, we discuss how Stoller's approach can be combined with ours. In the latter sections of this paper, we attempt to clarify the relationships between these approaches, and we aim to determine which strategies should be considered for implementation in explicit-state software model checkers.

2.3. Heuristics to avoid state storage

In addition to reducing interleavings based on independence information derived from escape analysis and locking discipline, we propose variants to our algorithms that also apply heuristics to avoid storing states produced when there are no interleavings. Using these additional heuristics, for example, the number of states explored for Independent Work (version 2) drops from 6770 states using algorithm that does not consider escape information to a total of 2 states.

3. Background

3.1. State transition systems

We present our reduction strategies using the well-known partial-order reduction framework based on *ample sets* as presented in [6]. The presentation in [6] phrases systems in terms of *state transition systems* (Kripke structures with slight modifications). Transitions and state structures in Java systems are substantially more complex than those found in traditional model checking since Java systems include notions such as heap-allocated data, dynamic thread creation, exceptions, etc. Nevertheless, previous formal presentations on partial-order reductions for Java systems, e.g., the work of Stoller [31], provide strategies for phrasing Java systems (with a few simplifying constraints) as transition systems. Accordingly, in our work, we will assume the existence of strategies for phrasing Java semantics in the form of state transition systems. We believe that the conditions on the state structure and transitions that are needed to describe the enabling/disabling of our reductions are simple enough to be accurately described without exposing significant details of the Java execution model in the formal structures we use for presenting our ideas.

A *state transition system* [6] Σ is a quadruple (S, T, S_0, L) with a set of states S, a set of transitions T such that for each $\alpha \in T$, $\alpha \subseteq S \times S$, a set of initial states S_0, and a labeling function L that maps a state s to a set of primitive propositions that are true at s.

For the Java systems that we consider, each state s holds the stack frames for each thread (program counters and local variables for each stack frame), global variables (i.e., static class fields), and a representation of the heap. Intuitively, each $\alpha \in T$ represents a statement or step (e.g., execution of a bytecode) that can be taken by a particular thread t. In general, α is defined on multiple "input states," since the transition may be carried out, e.g., not only in a state s but also in another state s' that only differs from s in that it presents the result of another thread t' performing a transition on s.

For a transition $\alpha \in T$, we say that α is *enabled* in a state s if there is a state s' such that $\alpha(s, s')$ holds. Otherwise, α is disabled in s. Intuitively, a transition α for a thread t may be disabled if the program counter for t is not at the bytecode represented by α, if α represents an entermonitor bytecode step that is blocked waiting to acquire a lock, or if t is currently in the *wait set* of an object o (i.e., t has surrendered the lock of o and put itself to sleep by calling wait on o). The set of transitions enabled in s is *enabled*(s), and the set of transitions enabled in s belonging to thread t is *enabled*(s, t). We denote the program counter of a thread t in a state s by $pc(s, t)$. We write *current*(s, t) for the set of transitions associated the current control point $pc(s, t)$ of thread t (this set will include *enabled*(s, t) as well as any transitions of t at $pc(s, t)$ that may be disabled). Also, *current*(s) represents the union of current transitions at s for all active threads.

A transition is *deterministic* if for every state s there is at most one state s' such that $\alpha(s, s')$. When α is deterministic, we write $s' = \alpha(s)$ instead of $\alpha(s, s')$. Following [6], we will only consider deterministic transitions. Note that this does *not* eliminate non-determinism in a thread (e.g., as might result from abstraction)—the non-determinism is simply represented by multiple enabled transitions for a thread. For each transition α, we assume that we can determine, among other things, a unique identifier for a thread t that executes α, and the set of variables or heap-allocated objects that are read or written by α. A *path* π from a state s is a finite or infinite sequence such that $\pi = s_0 \overset{\alpha_0}{\to} s_1 \overset{\alpha_1}{\to} \cdots$ such that $s = s_0$ and for every i, $\alpha_i(s_i) = s_{i+1}$.

In order to simplify the presentation of some of the lock-based reduction algorithms described in the latter part of the paper, we make the following assumption.

Assumption 1. We assume that at each control-point for a thread t and for any state s, if we take O to be the set of objects accessed in s by all transitions of t that are current for that control point, then O contains at most one object. This reflects the granularity of Java transitions at the bytecode level (i.e., each Java bytecode accesses at most one object).

3.2. Partial-order reductions

POR techniques based on ample sets can be summarized as follows. For each state s where $enabled(s) = \{\alpha_0, \alpha_1, \ldots, \alpha_m, \beta_0, \beta_1, \ldots, \beta_n\}$, one attempts to determine a subset $ample(s) = \{\alpha_0, \alpha_1, \ldots, \alpha_m\}$ of $enabled(s)$ such that it is sufficient to only explore paths out of s that begin with transitions α_i from $ample(s)$. The fact that exploring these paths alone is sufficient can be established by showing that each of the other possible paths out of s (i.e., those beginning with one or more β_j) is equivalent (with respect to the property ϕ being checked) to one of the explored paths (i.e., those beginning with one or more α_i). Showing this equivalence relies on establishing three basic notions: (1) showing that ample transitions α_i are *independent* of (i.e., commute with) non-ample transitions β_j, which allows the α_i to be "moved to the front" of paths considered from s (the α_i are allowed to be dependent on each other), (2) showing that the relative ordering of α_i with respect to β_j and the intermediate states generated by α_i are *invisible* to the property ϕ, and (3) showing that no transition β with a ϕ-observable effect is delayed forever by a cycle in the ample transitions α_i.

We now consider both *independence* and *invisibility* in more detail, and then proceed with an outline of the ample sets state-exploration algorithm and conditions that guarantee that strategies for defining *ample* result in correct reductions.

3.2.1. Independence.
In presentations of POR [6, p. 144], the notion of independent transition is usually expressed using an *independence relation* I between transitions. Specifically, $(\alpha, \beta) \in I$ if *for all states* s the execution order of α and β can be interchanged when they are both enabled in s. An independence relation is required to be symmetric and anti-reflexive and to satisfy the two conditions in the definition below. The first ensures that one transition does not disable the other (note the 'symmetric' requirement on I ensures that this condition only needs to be stated in one direction). The second ensures that executing the transitions in any order will lead to the same state.

Definition 1 (Independence conditions). For each $(\alpha, \beta) \in I$, and for all states $s \in S$:

- Preservation of Enabledness: If $\alpha, \beta \in enabled(s)$ then $\alpha \in enabled(\beta(s))$,
- Commutativity: If $\alpha, \beta \in enabled(s)$ then $\alpha(\beta(s)) = \beta(\alpha(s))$.

It is convenient to refer to the *dependence relation D* that is defined as the complement of I.

Note that if a thread has multiple enabled transitions $\{\alpha_1, \ldots, \alpha_n\}$ at a particular control-point, this definition implies that those transitions cannot be independent of each other. This follows from the fact that if one of the α_i is executed, it will change the program counter for that thread and will thus disable the remaining transitions (violating the first condition of the definition). Heuristics based on this observation play an important role in the choice of transitions to consider in partial-order reduction strategies.

3.2.2. Invisibility.

The correctness of POR depends not only on the ability of certain transitions to commute with another, but also on the inability of the property ϕ being checked to distinguish the ordering of commuting transitions or the intermediate states generated by them. Let $L : S \rightarrow 2^{AP}$ be the function from a system Σ that labels each state with a set of atomic propositions. A transition $\alpha \in T$ is *invisible* with respect to a set of propositions $AP' \subseteq AP$ if α does not change the value of the propositional variables in AP', i.e., if for each pair of states $s, s' \in S$ such that $s' = \alpha(s)$, $L(s) \cap AP' = L(s') \cap AP'$. A transition is *visible* if it is not invisible [6, p. 144].

The well-studied property of *stuttering equivalence* can be used to establish that if a path π_2 can be obtained from path π_1 by commuting, adding, or removing invisible transitions, then no LTL$_{-X}$ (i.e., LTL without the 'next state' operator) formula can distinguish π_1 and π_2 [6, p. 146]. We do not present the details of stuttering equivalence here. Instead, we simply note that the conditions in the following section guarantee that only invisible transitions are included in *ample*(s) and that any path omitted as a result of following the POR strategy is stuttering equivalent to some path that is included in the reduced system. Thus, preservation of verification and refutation of LTL$_{-X}$ properties is guaranteed.

We previously used stuttering equivalence to prove the correctness of Bandera's approach to LTL$_{-X}$ property-preserving slicing [18], and notions of visibility/invisibility defined there along with their correctness justifications carry over to the present setting. Bandera's specification language [8] includes two forms of primitive propositions: location predicates and data state predicates. A location predicate P_l for control point l holds when a thread is at l. Thus, both the transition of a thread into l is visible (because the proposition value shifts from *false* to *true*) and the transition of thread out of l is visible (because the proposition shifts from *true* to *false*)—all other transitions are invisible to P_l. A data state predicate that refers to a set of memory cells holds when the values of those cells satisfy the predicate. Thus, any transition that modifies one or more of those cells is visible, and all others are invisible. In each of the two types of predicates, Bandera uses a simple static analysis to form a conservative approximation of the set of visible/invisible transitions.

3.3. Ample set conditions

Algorithm 1 presents the familiar depth-first search algorithm extended to include the ample-sets-based partial-order reduction [6, p. 143]. As we have noted, the essence of the idea

```
1 seen := {s_0}
2 pushStack(s_0)
3 DFS(s_0)


DFS(s)
4 workSet(s) := ample(s)
5 while workSet(s) is not empty
6     let α ∈ workSet(s)
7     workSet(s) := workSet(s) \ {α}
8     s' := α(s)
9     if s' ∉ seen then
10        seen := seen ∪ {s'}
11        pushStack(s')
12        DFS(s')
13        popStack()
end DFS
```

Algorithm 1. Depth-first search with partial-order reduction [6, p. 143].

is, for a given state s, only explore transitions from s that are in $ample(s) \subseteq enabled(s)$. When $ample(s) = enabled(s)$, s is said to be *fully expanded*.

Building on the notions of independence and invisibility above [6, pp. 147–151] gives four conditions that $ample(s)$ must satisfy to achieve correct reductions when checking LTL_{-X}.

Condition C0 requires that a state has no successor in the full search iff it has no successors in the reduced search. This simple condition is satisfied by any natural approach to computing $ample(s)$.

C0: For all $s \in S$, $ample(s) = \emptyset$ if and only if $enabled(s) = \emptyset$.

Of the four conditions, C1 is the most interesting with respect to justifying our conditions for thread-local and lock-based independence. As shown in [6, p. 148], it guarantees that every transition $\beta \in (enabled(s) - ample(s))$ is independent of the transitions in $ample(s)$. This (along with the subsequent conditions) enables one to show that every path π_f from s in a full (non-reduced) exploration can be shown equivalent to a path π_r in the reduced exploration by commuting independent transitions in π_f to obtain π_r.

C1: For all $s \in S$, every path that starts at s has one of the following forms:

- the path has a prefix $\beta_1 \beta_2 \ldots \beta_m \alpha$ where $m \geq 0$ and $\alpha \in ample(s)$ and each β_i is not in $ample(s)$ and is independent of all transitions in $ample(s)$, or
- the path is an infinite sequence of transitions $\beta_1 \beta_2 \ldots$ where each β_i is independent of all transitions in $ample(s)$.

The intuition behind condition C2 is simple: if we omit some paths that contain different orderings of the transitions in *ample(s)*, then all transitions in *ample(s)* should be invisible.

C2: For all $s \in S$, if s is not fully expanded, then every $\alpha \in ample(s)$ is invisible.

Condition C3 ensures that an enabled transition β is never infinitely postponed due to a cycle of ample transitions.

C3: A cycle (in the reduced state graph) is not allowed if it contains a state in which some transition β is enabled, but is never included in *ample(s)* for any state s on the cycle.

A sufficient condition for C3 is that at least one state along each cycle is fully expanded [6, p. 155].

[6, Chapter 10] gives several strategies for implementing *ample(s)* so that the conditions above are satisfied. We will refer to these strategies when outlining our implementation in subsequent sections.

4.   State-sensitive independence

In conventional systems considered for model checking, requiring that the independence condition for (α, β) hold for *all* states (as in Definition 1 of the previous section) is reasonable since independence is usually detected by doing a *static* scan of the system description as written in, e.g., Promela, to detect that, e.g., two transitions from different processes are not interacting with the same channel or the same program variable [6, p. 157].

In our setting, due to the changing structure of the heap, it is useful to weaken the notion of independence relation to allow a pair of transitions to be independent in some states and dependent in others. For example, there will be situations where (a) a thread t is manipulating a non-escaped object o at control point p (and the manipulating transition will be independent of the transitions of other threads), (b) subsequent execution causes o to escape so that it can be accessed by other threads, and (c) control of t returns to p and now the transition at p is not guaranteed independent since o is now visible from other threads. Thus, we follow the notion of *conditional independence* introduced in [23] and modify the notion of independence relation to allow *state-sensitive independence* conditions by considering a family of relations $I_s \subseteq T \times T$ indexed by states $s \in S$. We write $I_s(\alpha)$ for the set of transitions related to α by I_s. Following the criteria for conventional independence relations [6, p. 144], we require each I_s to be symmetric and anti-reflexive and to satisfy the following three conditions below. The first two conditions are identical to those of Definition 1. The third condition, which we have added to incorporate conditional independence into the ample set reduction framework, ensures that the independence property between two transitions α and β_1 is not dissolved by a transition β_0 from another thread that is independent of α (if β_0 and β_1 are from the same thread, they are not independent of each other, and thus one is allowed to dissolve independence properties of the other).

Definition 2 (State-sensitive independence conditions). For each state $s \in S$, and for each $(\alpha, \beta) \in I_s$, $thread(\alpha) \neq thread(\beta)$ and

- Preservation of Enabledness: If $\alpha, \beta \in enabled(s)$ then $\alpha \in enabled(\beta(s))$.
- Commutativity: If $\alpha, \beta \in enabled(s)$ then $\alpha(\beta(s)) = \beta(\alpha(s))$.
- Preservation of Independence: If $\{\beta_0, \beta_1\} \subseteq I_s(\alpha)$ and $thread(\beta_0) \neq thread(\beta_1)$ and $s' = \beta_0(s)$, then $\{\beta_1\} \subseteq I_{s'}(\alpha)$.

Of the conditions C0–C1 for ample set corrections, only C1 refers the concept of independence. Accordingly, we need to modify it to account for the notion of state-sensitive independence (the underlined text indicates the additions to the condition).

C1: For all $s \in S$, every path that starts at s has one of the following forms:

- the path has a prefix $\beta_1 \beta_2 \ldots \beta_m \alpha$ where $m \geq 0$ and $\alpha \in ample(s)$ and each β_i is not in $ample(s)$ and is independent <u>at s</u> of all transitions in $ample(s)$, or
- the path is an infinite sequence of transitions $\beta_1 \beta_2 \ldots$ where each β_i is independent <u>at s</u> of all transitions in $ample(s)$.

Note that the [Preservation of Independence] condition of I_s ensures that transitions in $ample(s)$ continue to be independent of the β_i at each of the intermediate states generated in the paths given in Condition C1 of the preceding section. Appendix 10 gives a proof of this claim, along with modifications to proofs of [6] that justify that this modified version of C1 together with the notion of state-sensitive independence give rise to correct reductions.

5. Partial-order reduction for unshared objects using escape analyses

In this section, we present our approach for detecting independent transitions using static and dynamic escape analysis. We first introduce some terminology related to Java-specific transition systems. Memory cells in Java can be partitioned into three categories: local (these correspond to local variables of methods, which are stack-allocated), global (these correspond to static fields of classes), and heap (these correspond to explicit and implicit instance fields of dynamically allocated created objects and array components). Note that implicit instance data includes data structures to represent locks, waiting thread sets, blocked thread sets, etc. for each object instance. A transition is said to *access* a memory cell if it performs one of the following actions associated with particular Java bytecodes [25]. Local accesses include a number of different bytecodes associated with accessing local slots in the current stack frame (e.g., iload, istore). Global (i.e., static field) accesses are reads from a static field (getstatic) and stores to a static field (putstatic). Heap (i.e., object instance) accesses are reads from an instance field (getfield), stores to an instance field (putfield), locking (entermonitor), unlocking (exitmonitor), and invocations of wait, notify, notifyAll methods of an object (java.lang.Object, note that arrays in Java are also objects). Array accesses (also included in heap accesses) are reads from an array element (bytecodes $x$aload) and stores to an array index (bytecodes $x$astore), where x is either b, c, s, i, l, f, d, or a.

To reason about whether thread transitions can fail to be independent due to accesses to heap memory cells that are visible by multiple threads, we will conservatively approximate *visibility* by *reachability along object references*. First, the *reference-type memory cells* of an object o include all static fields, instance fields, and array cells (if o is an array) of non-primitive type. An object o is *reachable from a memory cell* (i.e., a local variable, an array element, an instance field, or a static field) if and only if the cell holds the reference for o or if the cell holds the reference for an object o' and o is reachable from any of o''s reference-type memory cells. An object o is *reachable from a thread* t at a certain state s if and only if there exists a stack frame of t in s that holds a local variable v such that o is reachable from v (note that the stack frames include the this variable, which will allow the thread to reach the instance fields of the thread object associated with the thread), or if o is reachable from a static field of any class. Note that approximating 'visibility' by reachability as defined above is conservative in several ways. For example, the lock of an object o held by thread t prevents another thread t' that also synchronizes on o from accessing o's fields. In addition, certain instance fields may be reachable but never actually touched by a particular thread.

A heap-allocated object o is said to be *thread-local with respect to thread t at state s* if o is reachable only from thread t. A transition $\alpha \in current(s, t)$ is said to be *thread-local at s* if it does not access a global memory cell (static field), or if all of its accesses are either to local data or to objects that are thread-local to t at s.

Based on the notion of "thread-local", which we will detect by both static and dynamic analyses in the following sections, we can now define an independence relation that will be the key element of the correctness argument for our reduction strategy.

Definition 3 (Thread-local transition independence).   Let $s \in S$, t_1 and t_2 be threads, $\alpha \in current(s, t_1)$, and β be any transition of t_2. Then both $(\alpha, \beta) \in I_s^{tl}$ and $(\beta, \alpha) \in I_s^{tl}$ hold iff $t_1 \neq t_2$ and α is thread-local at s.

We now argue that our independence relation satisfies the three criteria for independence relations given in Definition 2. Let $(\alpha, \beta) \in I_s^{tl}$. For the [Preservation of Enabledness] condition, note that if $\alpha, \beta \in enabled(s)$ the only situation where β could disable α is one in which α corresponds to an entermonitor instruction on object o (α is ready to grab o's lock), and β also corresponds to entermonitor on o (β actually acquires o's lock). However, this cannot be the case since α is thread-local and thus o is not reachable from any other thread. For all other cases of disabledness (i.e., t_1 is in a wait set, t_1's program counter does not match α, etc.), it is t_1 itself that must move to shift into a disabled state.

For the [Commutativity] condition, it is clear that if α can only access memory cells that are thread-local to t_1, then both $\alpha(\beta(s))$ and $\beta(\alpha(s))$ yield states s_1 and s_2 (respectively) that cannot be distinguished by subsequent transitions. However, it is not obvious that $s_1 = s_2$. For example, consider that if both α and β correspond to allocations of objects o_a and o_b, respectively, then $\alpha(\beta(s))$ and $\beta(\alpha(s))$ could result in two different heap shapes (in one, o_a could be positioned first in the memory address space of the heap, while o_b could be positioned first in the other). The fact that $s_1 = s_2$ in our setting relies on the fact that Bogor's heap representation is *canonical* in the sense that any two program states that have observationally equivalent heaps (i.e., heaps that cannot be distinguished by any program context) are represented by a single canonical structure in the model checker [28].

The satisfaction of the [Preservation of Independence] condition relies on the fact that if a transition α of thread t is thread-local due to the fact that it is manipulating an object o that is local to t, then α can lose its thread-local status only if t itself takes an action to cause o to escape (i.e., if o is local to t, no other threads can make o escape—only t-actions can). Appendix 10 presents a more rigorous justification of this condition.

5.1.   Thread-locality by static analysis

Quite a few static analyses [5, 29] have been proposed to determine thread-locality of objects via *escape analysis* in languages such as Java. In general, the results of an escape analysis are used to remove unnecessary synchronization and stack allocation of objects which in turn improves runtime performance.

To statically detect thread-local objects, we use an adaptation of Erik Ruf's escape analysis [29]. Ruf's analysis detects objects that are guaranteed to be *locked* by a single thread only. Any synchronization statements that are only applied to such objects are unnecessary and can safely be removed from the program. We adapt Ruf's analysis to obtain a variant that detects objects that are guaranteed to be *accessed* by a single thread only.

The results of the analysis are available via an interface that allows one to query each variable (field or local) to determine if that variable always refers to objects that are thread-local for the lifetime of the program execution. A transition in the model is annotated as thread-local if calls to the analysis interface indicate that all variables accessed in the transition refer to only thread-local objects. We write *static-thread-local*(α) to denote the fact that transition α such an annotation.

Given this static escape information that allows us to detect thread-local objects and independent transitions, we now explain our approach for constructing the ample sets. Algorithm 1 (along with the ample set conditions C0–C3) reveal that it is always safe to include the entire set of currently enabled transitions in *ample*(s). The main idea is to improve on this by including only invisible thread-local transitions in *ample*(s).

We adopt the strategy of [6, Section 10.5.2, p. 157], which suggests that one considers the set *enabled*(s, t_i) of transitions enabled in s for some thread t_i as a candidate for *ample*(s). The rationale for this is as follows. Recall that we explained under Definition 1 that enabled transitions from the same control point of a thread cannot be independent. Also, the intuition behind ample set condition C1 reveals that that transitions chosen for *ample*(s) should be independent of all other transitions omitted from *ample*(s). Therefore, when choosing candidates for *ample*(s), either all enabled transitions from thread t at s must be included in *ample*(s) or all must be excluded.

Algorithm 2 presents the algorithm to compute the ample set. Following the discussion in the previous paragraph, the algorithm considers as possible values of *ample*(s) the enabled transitions of each thread t. If the *ample* function finds a thread whose transitions satisfies *checkC1*, *checkC2*, and *checkC3*, then the set of enabled transitions of that thread is returned. If no such set is found, the result *ample*(s) is defined to be set of enabled transitions from all threads (i.e., the state is fully expanded).

```
checkC1(s, t)
1 for each α of t in s do
2    if ¬static-thread-local(α) then return FALSE
3 return TRUE
end checkC1


checkC2(X)
4 for each α ∈ X do
5    if visible(α) then return FALSE
6 return TRUE
end checkC2


checkC3(s, X)
7 for each α ∈ X do
8    if onStack(α(s)) then return FALSE
9 return TRUE
end checkC3


ample(s)
10 for each t such that enabled(s, t) ≠ ∅ do   /* enforcing C0 */
11    if checkC1(s,t) ∧ checkC2(enabled(s, t)) ∧ checkC3(s,enabled(s, t)) then
12       return enabled(s, t)
13 return enabled(s)
end ample
```

Algorithm 2.   Ample set construction algorithm using static escape analysis.

The function *checkC1* checks to see if *all* transitions of thread t in s are classified as thread-local by static escape analysis. Note that we check *all* transitions of t for thread-locality instead of just the enabled transitions of t. This is necessary to cover the case where a thread has enabled transitions that are all thread-local but also has one or more disabled transitions β_i that are not thread-local. In such a case, it is possible that another thread t' can execute while t remains at its current control point and t' may enable t's disabled (and non-dependent) transitions. This can lead to a violation of C1: an execution trace exists in the unreduced system where a β_i that is not independent of the transitions in *ample*(s) is executed before a transition from *ample*(s).[4]

The function *checkC2* determines whether all transitions in a set are invisible [6]. The function *checkC3* enforces Condition C3.

5.2.   *Thread-locality by dynamic analysis*

Algorithm 3 presents the function *checkC1* that uses dynamic escape analysis to determine whether all transitions of a thread are thread-local. Intuitively, the dynamic escape analysis inspects the current state of the model checker to determine whether the transitions of a

checkC1(s, t)
1 $G := \emptyset$ /* static fields accessed from t in s */
2 $O := \emptyset$ /* heap objects/arrays accessed by t's enabled transitions in s */
3 for each α of t in s do
4   *collectAccessed*(s,t,α,G,O)
5 if $G \neq \emptyset$ then return FALSE
6 for each thread t' in s such that $t' \neq t$ do
7   if *reachable*(s,t',O) then return FALSE
8 return TRUE
end *checkC1*

Algorithm 3. Ample set construction algorithm using dynamic escape analysis.

given thread are reachable by some other threads at that particular state. The functions *checkC2*, *checkC3*, and *ample* are the same as listed in Algorithm 2.

We briefly describe the steps in function *checkC1* which are easily implemented using Bogor's state representation interface. *checkC1* first collects all the static fields, objects, or arrays that are accessed by the transitions of thread t in state s (lines 1–4). If some globals are accessed, the algorithm returns FALSE since one or more transitions are not thread-local (line 5). If some heap objects accessed by t are reachable by the other threads (note that objects reachable through static fields are reachable by all the threads), then one or more transitions are not thread-local (lines 6–7). Otherwise, all enabled transitions of t at s are thread-local (line 8).

6. Partial-order reduction for shared objects using locking-discipline

Having established how thread-locality information can drive partial-order reductions, we now turn to the idea of exploiting locking information in partial-order reductions as emphasized by recent work of Stoller [31, 32]. Stoller showed how it is unnecessary to explore some interleavings for objects that are accessed according to a *locking discipline* (i.e., a systematic use of locks to obtain mutually exclusive access to object fields).

Our goals are to illustrate several lock-based strategies that take a different approach than that of Stoller and to illustrate how lock-based strategies can be enhanced when they are combined with the previously introduced thread-locality strategies. After summarizing Stoller's approach, we begin with a strategy based on what we call the *weak self-locking discipline* that is conceptually simpler (and thus easier to implement) and covers many common patterns of lock usage. With this strategy providing the basic intuition, we then proceed with a more general strategy called *weak self-locking domination* that captures monitor-based locking strategies. We note that neither this strategy nor Stoller's subsumes the other, and this leads us to a strategy that combines Stoller's approach and the weak self-locking domination strategy. Our experiments in Section 8 will illustrate the relative effectiveness of each of these approaches.

6.1. *Stoller's lock-based reductions*

In well-designed Java programs, mutually exclusive access to fields of shared objects is achieved by having threads acquire the implicit locks associated with Java objects. *Race conditions* can occur when a thread accesses a shared object without first acquiring an associated lock. In such conditions, the order of thread accesses/updates to an unprotected memory cell is difficult or impossible to predict, and this often leads to erroneous functional behavior.

The Eraser algorithm [30] introduced by Savage et.al. performs a run-time analysis to detect violations of a particular locking discipline, which we refer to as LD. Such violations indicate the possibility of race conditions. Assume that there is some static annotation system that indicates the set of objects *LD-Objects* that should be accessed according to LD. For example, a reasonable annotation system might be a per-class system that indicates that all objects from a particular class should satisfy LD.

Definition 4 (Locking discipline (LD)).   An execution of a system satisfies LD iff for all objects $o \in$ *LD-Objects*, one of the following conditions hold:

- LD-RO: o is read-only after it is initialized.
- LD-lock: o is lock-protected after initialization, i.e., there exists an object o' such that for all threads t and for all execution states s in which t accesses o, t owns the lock of o' in s.

The Eraser algorithm assumes initialization to be completed when an object becomes *accessed* by two different threads.

In this paper, we are interested in reduction strategies relating to the LD-lock case (i.e., reduction strategies that are driven by *locking* patterns). The reduction strategies that we are considering are orthogonal to LD-RO, and thus, they can be easily combined. Throughout the rest of the paper, we liberally use LD to refer to LD-lock in order to simplify the presentation.

Stoller proposed reduction strategies that capitalize on independence properties that result when objects satisfy LD. The essence of his method (ignoring several technical conditions for now) as implemented in the JPF model-checker is as follows. Users are required to give annotations to classify objects into the following categories: (a) objects that are not shared between threads, (b) *communication objects*—shared objects that do not obey LD, and (c) objects that obey LD (this category can be viewed as the complement of the union of (a) and (b)). During state-space exploration, if a transition α does not access a communication object and does not perform a lock acquire on an LD object, then there is no need to consider interleavings before α.

Stoller also establishes an important point related to the correct classification of LD objects: the Eraser lock-set algorithm can be modified and applied simultaneously while performing reductions during state-space exploration to detect situations where a declared LD-object actually violates LD. If undetected, such situations lead to unsafe reductions in the sense that some interleavings are omitted that should actually be explored. When LD violations are detected in Stoller's approach, the user is expected to shift the object from the LD to the communication-object classification, then restart the model-check.

The basic idea of the run-time monitoring lock-set algorithm is to associate a table with each LD object that maps each thread to the set of locks that it holds when it accesses the object. As the model checker executes transitions, when a thread t accesses an object field, the lock set associated with the object for t is intersected with the set of locks currently held by t. An empty intersection value implies that LD has been violated.

As we relate this approach to our escape-analysis-based strategies, there are several issues to bring forward. First, Stoller suggests that static analysis may be applied to avoid having the user manually identify the set of unshared objects [31, Section 8]. This is essentially what we have done with the static escape analysis of Section 5.1. Note that this follows Stoller's conditions where an object's classification (e.g., as unshared) is fixed throughout the lifetime of the system. Our dynamic escape-analysis of Section 5.2 moves beyond this to lift the restriction that objects must have a fixed classification.

Next, note that LD and the associated Eraser lock-set algorithm do not require that an object be lock-protected until after initialization has completed (where "initialization completed" is defined to be a state where the object is accessed by a second thread). This treatment is designed to cover the common situation where a single thread runs the constructor of an object (which initializes the object) without locking the object, and then the object escapes and is lock-protected after the constructor completes. With our dynamic escape analysis, it is easy to enforce different variants of this approach.

Finally, Stoller based his reductions on the persistent-set/sleep-set framework [15]— the style of partial-order reductions used in Verisoft [16]. Verisoft implements stateless search, and does not support checking of LTL properties. Thus, Stoller's proofs do not try to establish the extra conditions (e.g., as embodied in conditions C2 and C3 of the ample set reductions) that are required to preserve LTL_{-X}. However, these conditions are orthogonal to notions of independence, etc., and could be easily added to Stoller's presentation.

Appendix D recasts Stoller's LD-based reduction strategy in the ample set framework and describes our implementation of it. We use this implementation as a point of comparison with the alternate strategies that we propose.

6.2. Weak self locking-based reductions

We now consider several different reduction strategies that combine thread-locality and lock-based reduction. We begin with a simple strategy that covers common usage of locks, and then consider other approaches building on this in the following subsections.

An object o satisfies what we call the *self-locking discipline* if, for any thread t that performs a non-lock-acquiring access on o, t holds o's lock. This discipline corresponds to the simplest type of locking used in Java programs, and it is typically achieved by declaring all the methods of a particular class to be `synchronized` and by making its field accessible only through its methods.

As noted above, the constructor of an object will typically access its fields without locking the object—thus, technically violating the self-locking discipline. For instance, in the bounded-buffer example of figure 3, instances of the class `BoundedBuffer` would satisfy the self-locking discipline (since methods of the class are declared as synchronized) except for the fact that these instances are not locked in the constructor. Accordingly, previous work on race condition detection and other verification oriented type systems (e.g., [14]) relies on making various unchecked assumptions about the behavior of relevant object constructors—namely, that the objects being initialized do not escape the constructor (thereby disallowing the possibility that other threads could generate conflicting accesses to the object). It is easy in our framework to check this assumption using thread-locality information. Moreover, it is natural to weaken the self-locking discipline to allow arbitrary (non-lock-protected) accesses to an object as long as the object is unshared. We call this weaker version the *weak self-locking discipline*. Specifically, an object o satisfies the *weak self-locking discipline* if *in any state s in which it is not thread-local*, for any thread t that performs a non-lock-acquiring access on o, t holds o's lock (the italicized phrase distinguishes this definition from the definition of *self-locking discipline*).

The following independence relation that exploits both thread-local information and self-locking information.

Definition 5 (Weak self-locking transition independence (WSL)).   Let $s \in S$, t_1 and t_2 be threads, $\alpha \in current(s, t_1)$, and β be any transition of t_2. Then both $(\alpha, \beta) \in I_s^{wsl}$ and $(\beta, \alpha) \in I_s^{wsl}$ hold iff $t_1 \neq t_2$ and either:

1. for each object o that α accesses, o is a thread-local object, or
2. both of the following conditions hold:

   (a) α does not access global memory cells (static fields), and
   (b) for each object o that α accesses, o satisfies the weak self-locking discipline and o is locked by t_1 in s.

We now argue that this relation satisfies the three properties of an independence relation given in Definition 2. Since we already proved the case for thread-local transitions when considering Definition 3, we consider only the second case.

For the [Preservation of Enabledness] condition, note that if t_1 holds the lock on an object o that it is accessing, then there is no action from α on o that can disable β. Only the acquiring of a previously unheld lock on o by t_1 can disable β (when β is also attempting to acquire o's lock), and this cannot be the case since t_1 is already holding all the locks on the objects that α is accessing.

For the [Commutativity] condition, it is clear that if both α and β are enabled and t_1 already holds the lock of o, then β does not access o (since o satisfies the weak self-locking discipline, t_2 would have to hold the lock of o, but this is not the case). Thus, α and β commute.

For the [Preservation of Independence] condition, we need to show that t_2 can never cause α to lose its independence status. For that to happen, t_2 must lock o first, but this can not happen until t_1 releases the lock on o. Appendix C.1 presents a more rigorous justification of this condition.

Algorithm 4 presents the ample-set $checkC1$ function that exploits the weak self-locking discipline. We only present the additional computations from Algorithm 3 (inserting 5.1–5.6 in between line 5 and line 6).

checkC1(s, t)

. . .

5.1 if none of t's transitions at state s is acquiring a lock on any $o \in O$ then

5.2 $O_{WSL} := \{o \in O \mid o$'s type is in $T_{WSL}\}$

5.3   for each thread $t' \in threads(s)$ such that $t' \neq t$ do

5.4   if some objects $O'_{WSL} \subseteq O_{WSL}$ are not locked by $t \wedge reachable(s, t', O'_{WSL})$ then

5.5   signal condition on O'_{WSL} is violated by t' at s

5.6   if $O = O_{WSL}$ then return TRUE

. . .

end *checkC1*

Algorithm 4.   Ample set construction algorithm using weak self-locking discipline.

Similar to the LD-based implementation of Stoller, we require the user to indicate which objects are weak self-locking objects. However, there are different approaches for providing this information. We require the user to indicate the Java classes whose instances are weak self-locking objects. For example, for the bounded buffer program in figure 3, the user can specify that the `BoundedBuffer` class instances are weak self-locking objects. Note that this pattern in software design is common, for example, many classes in the Java collection framework have the same synchronization structure such as `java.util.Vector` and `java.util.Hashtable`, and it does not put a significant burden on the user to supply such annotations.

Given a set T_{WSL} of classes, the algorithm checks if a thread t at state s only (non-lock-acquiring) accesses instances of a class in T_{WSL}. If it does, then the reduction may be applied. It proceeds by checking that none of t's transitions acquire locks on the objects (line 5.1). If that is the case, the algorithm collects the set O_{WSL} of objects that are accessed by thread t and whose types are in T_{WSL} (line 5.2). The objects in O_{WSL} are then checked to see if they satisfy the weak self-locking discipline (line 5.3–5.5). Specifically, if some objects from O_{WSL} are not thread-local to t and are not locked, then the user is notified that a locking-discipline violation has occurred and applied reductions may be unsafe. Note that the notification is conservative, i.e., the reductions may be safe because it may be the case that the other threads never actually access the objects in the future. Regardless of the notification, if O_{WSL} are equal to O (line 5.6), then TRUE is returned. Since the objects are assumed to satisfy O_{WSL}, they cannot be accessed by other threads even though they are reachable. Therefore, the basic "possibility of interference" condition that we realized as reachability in Section 5 (i.e., accesses to object o can possibly interfere with each other when o is reachable from two or more different threads) is now realized as accessibility.

6.3. *Weak self-locking domination-based partial-order reduction*

We now consider the case where monitors are used to guard accesses to certain objects in addition to locking the objects directly. We use the term *monitors* as described in [1, p. 203]:

First and foremost, monitors are a data abstraction mechanism. A monitor encapsulates the representation of an abstract object and provides a set of operations that are the *only* means by which that representation is manipulated. In particular, a monitor contains variables that store the object's state and procedures that implement operations on the object. A process can access the variables in a monitor only by calling one of the monitor's procedures. Mutual exclusion is provided implicitly by ensuring that procedures in the same monitor are not executed concurrently.

For example, in the bounded buffer program in figure 3, an instance of the `BoundedBuffer` class protects (monitors) the array object that implements the buffer.

We will automatically discover the relationship of monitors and the objects being monitored instead of requiring the user to supply it. That is, instead of requiring an annotation that explicitly specifies the monitoring relation, the relationship is inferred. We only require that the user supplies annotations indicating weak self-locking objects as described in the previous subsection. Given a state s and the set of weak self-locking objects $O_{WSL} \subseteq objects(s)$ (where $objects(s)$ returns the set of all objects in state s) for which locks are being held by a thread t in s, one can detect the objects that are protected by the objects O_{WSL} from another thread t'. Specifically, we look for situations in which, on all reference chains from t' to the objects being accessed, there exists an object in O_{WSL} whose lock is held by t (i.e., the paths from t' to objects being accessed are *dominated* by weak self-locking objects locked by t). We revise the independence relation to exploit this observation as follows.

Definition 6 (Weak self-locking dominated transition independence (WSL^{dom})).   Let $s \in S$, t_1 and t_2 be threads, $\alpha \in current(s, t_1)$, and β be any transition of t_2. Then both $(\alpha, \beta) \in I_s^{wsl,dom}$ and $(\beta, \alpha) \in I_s^{wsl,dom}$ hold iff $t_1 \neq t_2$ and either:

1. for each object o that α accesses, o is a thread-local object, or
2. both of the following conditions hold:

    (a) α does not access global memory cells (static fields), and
    (b) either one of the following condition holds:

        i. for each object o that α accesses, o satisfies the weak self-locking discipline and o is locked by t_1 in s, or
        ii. for each object o that α accesses, o can only be reached by t_2 from some weak self-locking objects O_{WSL} and t_1 locks all objects in O_{WSL} at s.

We now argue that the definition of the WSL^{dom} independence relation satisfies the three properties of Definition 2. We only consider the last case (2.b.ii) as the other cases are the same as for the WSL relation.

For the [Preservation of Enabledness] condition, note that if t_1 holds the lock for all objects in O_{WSL} that protect o, then it is not possible for t_2 to access, and thus, be disabled by actions on o.

For the [Commutativity] condition, since t_2 does not access o, α and β commute.

checkC1(s, t)

...

5.1 if none of t's transitions at state s is acquiring a lock on any $o \in O$ then

5.2 $O_{WSL} := \{o \in O \mid o$'s type is in $T_{WSL}\}$

5.3   for each thread $t' \in threads(s)$ such that $t' \neq t$ do

5.4   if some objects $O'_{WSL} \subseteq O_{WSL}$ are not locked by $t \wedge reachable(s,t',O'_{WSL})$ then

5.5   signal condition on O'_{WSL} is violated by t' at s

5.6   if $O = O_{WSL}$ then return TRUE

5.7 $O_{SL} := \{o \mid o$'s type is in $T_{WSL} \wedge o$ is locked by $t\}$

5.8 $O_{SL^{dom}} := \emptyset$

5.9   for each thread $t' \in threads(s)$ such that $t' \neq t$ do

5.10 $O_{SL^{dom}} := O_{SL^{dom}} \cup \{o \in objects(s) \mid \neg reachable_{\downarrow O_{SL}}(s, t', \{o\})\}$

5.11   if $O \subseteq O_{SL^{dom}}$ then return TRUE

...

end *checkC1*

Algorithm 5. Ample set construction algorithm using weak self-locking dominated discipline.

For the [Preservation of Independence] condition, relies on the fact that t_2 can never make α lose its independence because it cannot access O_{WSL} since objects O_{WSL} are weak self-locking objects and o is protected by O_{WSL}. Appendix 10 presents the formal justification of this condition.

Algorithm 5 presents the ample-set *checkC1* function that exploits the weak self-locking dominated discipline. As stated before, the user is only required to specify which objects are weak self-locking objects. The algorithm begins by applying the weak self-locking discipline similar to Algorithm 4 (line 5.1-5.6). It then computes the set of objects $O_{SL^{dom}}$ that are dominated by self-locking objects that are locked by t (O_{SL}) from the other threads (line 5.6–5.10). If each element $o \in O$ is in $O_{SL^{dom}}$, i.e., all accessed objects are dominated, then TRUE is returned (line 5.11).

6.4. Combining LD and WSL^{dom} disciplines

We now describe how the two locking discipline-based strategies can be combined. To see why this combination is useful, we first show that neither discipline subsumes the other.

Figure 4 presents an example where WSL^{dom} works better than LD. There are two synchronized containers (i.e., the containers are self-locking objects) and two threads. Each thread transfers the element of its left container to its right. The transfer can happen if the container is non-empty, otherwise the thread is blocked. Before the element is actually transferred, its x field is incremented. Thus, the element is accessed during the transfer.

Figure 5 illustrates the state after the thread $P1$ has locked the container $C1$ (denoted $C1_{P1}$) and when the thread is incrementing $E1$'s x field. The dotted arrow from $P1$ to $E1$ illustrates the reference to $E1$ that resides in the JVM stack when the increment happens.

```
public class WSLdom {                     class Container {
  public static                            private Element element;
      void main(String [] args) {
    Container c1 = new Container();         public void put(Element e) {
    Container c2 = new Container();           element = e;
    c1.put(new Element());                  }
    (new Process(c1, c2)).start();
    (new Process(c2, c1)).start();          public synchronized void
  }                                             transfer(Container other) {
}                                             while (element == null) {
                                                try {
class Process extends Thread {                    wait();
  Container left;                               } catch
  Container right;                                 (InterruptedException ie) {}
                                              }
  public Process(Container left,              element.x++;
                 Container right) {           synchronized(other) {
    this.left = left;                           other.element = element;
    this.right = right;                         other.notify();
  }                                             element = null;
                                              }
  public void run() {                       }
    while (true) {                        }
      left.transfer(right);
    }                                     class Element {
  }                                         public byte x;
}                                         }
```

Figure 4.   An example showing LD does not subsume WSL^{dom}.

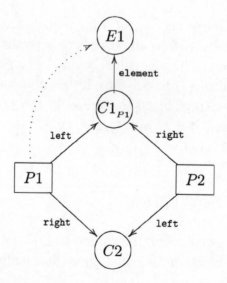

Figure 5.   A state of the example in figure 4.

Notice that $P2$ can reach $E1$ only by going through $C1$ which is locked by $P1$. Thus, the increment by $P1$ is protected by $C1$. This state satisfies the conditions of WSL^{dom}. Once the element is transferred, then $P2$ can transfer the element from $C2$ to $C1$. As with $P1$, $P2$ increments the data in $E1$ first. However, this increment is now protected by $C2$ instead of $C1$. While this satisfies WSL^{dom}, it does not satisfy LD (i.e., $\{C1\} \cap \{C2\} = \emptyset$—there does not exist a lock l such that l protects every access to $E1$).

```
public class LDlock {                    class Process extends Thread {
  public boolean b;                        Object sync;
                                           LDlock ldlock;
  public static                           public Process(Object sync,
      void main(String[] args) {                          LDlock ldlock) {
    Object sync = new Object();             this.sync = sync;
    LDlock ldlock = new LDlock();           this.ldlock = ldlock;
    new Process(sync, ldlock)             }
        .start();                         public void run() {
    new Process(sync, ldlock)               while (true) {
        .start();                             synchronized(sync) {
  }                                             ldlock.b = !ldlock.b;
}                                             }
                                            }
                                          }
                                        }
```

Figure 6.   An example showing LD is not subsumed by WSL^{dom}.

Furthermore, because WSL^{dom} is using the notion of state-specific independence, it does not require that the conditions to be satisfied for all of the states. Analogous to the partial-order reduction using the dynamic escape analysis, the partial-order reduction by WSL^{dom} is applied only when the conditions hold.

Figure 6 illustrates that LD is not subsumed by WSL^{dom}. Basically, there is no reference relationship between the monitor (i.e., the object referred by sync in Process) and the object being monitored (i.e., the object referred by ldlock). Therefore, WSL^{dom} can not be applied for this example while LD can.

We can combine the two approaches by weakening the condition of LD using WSL^{dom}. We only intersect the set of locks being held by the thread that accesses LD objects if the WSL^{dom} conditions do not hold at that state. In other words, we apply the WSL^{dom} discipline before applying LD. This combination subsumes both LD and WSL^{dom}. Furthermore, it *potentially* reduces the space requirement for the lock-set algorithm because WSL^{dom} is applied first. Thus, we potentially reduce the number of objects for which we should maintain the lock-set.

7.   Optimizing by avoiding state storage

In the previous sections, we focused on reducing the space required for model checking by reducing the number of interleavings explored. In this section, we focus on reducing the space required by not inserting certain visited states into the *seen* set of Algorithm 1(b). We have already noted that when one has independent transitions α and β as in figure 1, it does not matter whether one visits s_1 or s_2 on the way to r. The reduction that we now consider is based on the following heuristic: intermediate states like s_1 and s_2 are more likely to be encountered multiple times due to actions of different threads when all interleavings were included, but now that we are "thinning out" the interleavings, it is less likely that states generated from independent transitions will be arrived at from multiple paths. In addition, if there is only a single thread t enabled in a state s, it is less likely that the states generated from s by t will be arrived at from paths other than the one through s via t's action. Thus, we avoid storing a state $s' = \alpha(s)$ in *seen* when at least one of the following conditions holds: (1) α is an independent transition, or (2) α represents an action by thread t and t is the only thread enabled at s. Note that there may be several transitions that satisfy the first condition (i.e., independent). In choosing between these transitions, we prefer the one whose executing thread is the same as the last transition's executing thread. This reduces the amount of context switches, thus, it increases the sequentiality of counterexamples. Therefore, they are easier to understand.

This technique is basically the *transition aggregation* technique commonly used in model checking. It is similar to using Promela's `atomic` command on independent transitions (or a single thread's transitions) as mentioned above. However, we aggregate the transitions on-the-fly instead of categorizing the transitions statically. This technique is also similar to state-caching techniques [21] that drops states as the *seen* state set starts to become too large. One difference is that our reduction technique does not *remove* states from the *seen* set. Instead, we avoid storing particular states that we believe are unlikely to be encountered in any way other than moving along the path we are currently traversing. In the case where the states are encountered again, their children states are going to be revisited. Thus, this technique does not lead to unsafe reduction, but it may introduce time overhead.

Of course, any time one omits storing visited states in *seen*, it becomes more difficult to guarantee termination of the model checking algorithm. In our setting, for example, if there is a non-terminating loop whose body consists of thread-local transitions, then model checking with our above heuristic incorporated will not terminate. Fortunately, for such models, this problem can be solved by *always* storing states that are produced from control-flow graph back-edge transitions, and this is the strategy that we implement.

A similar technique [2] is applied for model checking real-time systems using covering sets. The authors noted that their algorithm works well with a BFS state-space exploration, but perform poorly with a DFS algorithm due to large time overhead. As shown in the next section, our algorithm works really well with a DFS algorithm, and it significantly reduces the cost of model checking (both time and space).

8. Evaluating reduction methods

Tables 1 and 2 show the results of evaluating our reduction strategies using six examples. For each example, we give data for each reduction strategy presented in the previous sections (whenever applicable). (**B**) is our base case that represents the state of our tools before incorporating thread-local object and lock-based reductions. It already applies a variety of sophisticated optimization techniques including collapse compression, and heap and process symmetry reductions [28], and it aggregates transitions that only access local variables [7] which in effect implements partial-order reductions for local variable accesses. Each of the remaining strategies represents an *addition* of reductions to (B). (**S**) adds the static approach for discovering thread-locality (Section 5.1). The timing numbers reported in this column do not include the costs of performing the static analysis and the associated annotating transformations, since our numbers clearly indicate that the static approach cannot compete with the dynamic approach in any case. (**D**) adds the dynamic approach for discovering thread-locality (Section 5.2). (**DA**) is like (D), but uses the strategy to avoid

Table 1. Experiment data.

Example		**(B)**	**(S)**	**(D)**	**(DA)**	**(SDA)**
Independent Work 1	**trans**	23302	1008	402	402	404
Threads: 3	**states**	6670	565	230	2	2
Locations: 36	**time**	6.63	.52	.32	.16	.13
Max. Objects: 22	**mem**	1.08	.41	.39	.36	.37
Independent Work 2	**trans**	18822	◁	402	402	◁
Threads: 3	**states**	5810	◁	230	2	◁
Locations: 48	**time**	5.56	◁	.47	.18	◁
Max. Objects: 22	**mem**	.96	◁	.4	.36	◁
Deadlock	**trans**	288	◁	178	253	◁
Threads: 3	**states**	142	◁	113	36	◁
Locations: 31	**time**	.26	◁	.26	.23	◁
Max. Objects: 6	**mem**	.37	◁	.36	.36	◁
Bounded Buffer	**trans**	10298	◁	7176	13488	◁
Threads: 3	**states**	4641	◁	3713	2473	◁
Locations: 64	**time**	4.11	◁	3.44	2.88	◁
Max. Objects: 10	**mem**	.89	◁	.72	.62	◁
Readers Writers	**trans**	1788086	◁	391191	700566	◁
Threads: 5	**states**	313331	◁	103638	79554	◁
Locations: 314	**time**	00:11:26	◁	00:03:42	00:03:46	◁
Max. Objects: 14	**mem**	30.5	◁	10.18	8.89	◁
Replicated Workers	**trans**	25557571	4376590	2076823	2535696	2661545
Threads: 4	**states**	4594721	1344215	827763	231219	231219
Locations: 509	**time**	09:00:54	01:12:35	00:39:48	00:21:47	00:21:10
Max. Objects: 44	**mem**	434.99	117.38	71.21	24.99	23.34

state storage described in Section 7. (**SDA**) is a combination of (S) and (DA): for transitions that are statically annotated as thread-local (as described in Section 5.1) the scan of the heap required for dynamic escape analysis is omitted; for non-annotated transitions the heap scan is employed as described in Section 5.2. (**WSL**) adds reduction by the weak self-locking discipline described in Section 6.2. (**WSL**^{dom}) adds reduction by the weak self-locking dominated discipline described in Section 6.3. (**LD**) adds reduction by Stoller's locking discipline reduction. As discussed in Section 6.4, these lock-based reductions cover different patterns of program locking so we have experimented with their combination (**LD + WSL**^{dom}).

For each example, we give metrics on the size of the example including the number of threads, control locations and the maximum number of objects allocated in a single program run across all runs of the program. For each reduction strategy, we present the number of

Table 2.   Experiment data 2.

Example		(WSL)	(WSL^{dom})	(LD)	(LD + WSL^{dom})
Bounded Buffer	**trans**	3731	2914	4410	2914
Threads: 3	**states**	140	81	341	81
Locations: 64	**time**	.59	.54	.76	.56
Max. Objects: 10	**mem**	.46	.44	.49	.45
Readers Writers	**trans**	272680	262480	739570	262480
Threads: 5	**states**	20826	18924	86499	18924
Locations: 314	**time**	00:00:45	00:00:47	00:02:51	00:00:44
Max. Objects: 14	**mem**	3.38	3.25	9.42	3.25
Replicated Workers	**trans**	994007	994007	2908147	806863
Threads: 4	**states**	49354	49354	200947	36724
Locations: 509	**time**	00:04:08	00:05:06	00:16:39	00:03:52
Max. Objects: 44	**mem**	6.52	7.12	21.87	6.41

transitions **trans**, **states**, **time** (seconds or hh:mm:ss), and memory consumption **mem** (Mb) at the end of the search; ◁ indicates that numbers are identical to the numbers reported for the strategy to the immediate left. The reductions were implemented as extensions to Bogor [27] (which is implemented in Java), and the experiments were run on an Opteron 1.8 GHz (32-bit mode) with maximum heap of 1 Gb using the Java 2 Platform. In all runs, Bogor performed a full state-space search and found equivalent sets of errors across all strategies.

The *Independent Work (version 1)* example of figure 2 represents a best-case reduction scenario where all heap-allocated data are obviously thread-local. As described in Section 3, both (S) and (D) are able to detect that the Process lists are thread-local, and that the entire run method may execute as a sequence of thread-local transitions. (D) improves on (S) because the dynamic escape analysis can determine that the instances of Process are thread-local before they are started, whereas (S) can not. Therefore, the creation and initialization of the second Process is not interleaved with the execution of the first Process in (D). In contrast, the interleavings happen in (S). When atomicity reductions are used (DA), the run() method bodies are executed atomically and the size of the resulting state-space contains only an initial and final state (i.e., the smallest possible state-space). Adding static escape information to (DA) consequently yields no further reduction. Since this example has no locking, the other methods have no impact and hence we did not run them.

The *Independent Work (version 2)* example of figure 2 is identical to version 1 except that the thread local lists are allocated in the main() method. The static escape analysis (S) fails to identify the lists as thread local for the Process instances and consequently no reduction was gained. The dynamic (D) and atomicity (DA) had essentially the same performance as for version 1. As with version 1, the locking-based reductions yield no further reductions. It is interesting to note that both *Independent Work* examples could be scaled to have arbitrary numbers of threads with local lists of arbitrary length and the (DA) state-space would still remain at size 2.

In contrast, the *Deadlock* and *BoundedBuffer* examples represent nearly worst-case (thread-local) reduction scenarios where all heap-allocated data are manipulated by multiple program threads. In the *Deadlock* example, a pair of threads share objects on which locks are acquired, but there are no accesses to or through those objects. Static escape analysis (S) classifies objects that are unshared in some program states but not in others as non-thread-local; this is the case during initialization in *Deadlock*. Consequently it yields no reduction. Dynamic analysis (D) is able to detect independent transitions in the initialization phase, but that only yields minor reductions. Atomicity reductions (DA) yield a more significant reduction since many of the thread transitions are local. Despite the presence of locking, the *Deadlock* example does not contain object field reads or writes on which locking-based reductions are based. They provide no benefit over (B) without their combination with escape-based methods, and for this reason we do not report the statistics.

The *BoundedBuffer* example is more interesting. It has a pair of threads that share bounded buffer objects through which data are passed and on which the threads block waiting for available data to read or available space to write. All of the approaches presented in the paper provide reductions for this example except for the static escape analysis-based reductions. Just as for *Deadlock*, the static analysis-based technique is unable to leverage objects that are thread-local in only part of the program, and thus they yield no reduction. Dynamic (D) and atomicity (DA) approaches identify initialization states with independent actions and drive modest reductions. Locking disciplines play an important role in this system as the weak self-locking discipline is used (e.g., to update *head* and *tail* fields of the `BoundedBuffer` instances) and monitors are used (e.g., to access the array contained in the `BoundedBuffer`). All of the locking-discipline approaches provide additional reductions over (DA), and, as expected, the combined approach yields the best state space reduction, although in this case it is no better than (WSL^{dom}).

The *Readers Writers* example provides a flexible approach to implementing policies governing access to shared program regions [24]; reader or writer preference can easily be achieved. While these policies may change the conditions under which locks are acquired or released, the basic monitor relationships between objects and locks are established dynamically through heap references using the *specific notification* pattern. The dynamism in this example renders static escape analysis (S) ineffective. As for previous examples, dynamic (D) and atomicity (DA) approaches identify initialization states with independent actions and drive modest reductions and all of the locking-discipline approaches provide additional reductions over (DA). Dominated weak-self locking (WSL^{dom}) is also quite effective here yielding the best reduction.

The *Replicated Worker* example is a parallel programming framework written in Java that has been used in dozens of real scientific and engineering applications [12]. It reflects a more realistic balance between shared and local heap data; there are several shared objects, including an instance of `java.util.Vector`, and each thread in the system has several local vector instances and instances of `java.util.VectorEnumeration`. Furthermore, there are multiple locking patterns used in the implementation to govern access to shared `Vector` instances. Static escape analysis (S) is able to detect independent transitions that can be exploited for nearly a four-fold reduction in states. The rest of the reduction techniques present data that is largely consistent with that seen for the *Bounded Buffer*. In this example, the combined approach exploits the strengths of both (LD) and (WSL^{dom}) improving on each of them to yield an overall 125-fold reduction in states over (B).

We make the following observations from these results:

- Dynamic escape analysis is quite effective. We have demonstrated that the overhead is small, and that any cost is completely outweighed by the savings achieved (which in many cases are substantial). For model-checkers such as Bogor that permit an easy implementation, it seems that this approach should always be considered for implementation.

- In model-checkers where dynamic escape analysis can be implemented easily, considering static escape analysis is not worthwhile given the effectiveness of dynamic escape analysis. However, in model-checkers that do not admit an implementation of dynamic analysis, static escape analysis can be applied with good effect (as demonstrated by the numbers for the *Replicated Workers* example). Beforehand, we imagined that static analysis in combination with dynamic analysis might be useful to reduce the overhead associated with dynamic analysis (many thread-local transitions can be recognized once before model checking begins, as opposed to checking for thread-locality in every state). However, dynamic escape analysis in Bogor is so cheap, that there seems to be little point in trying to amortize some of the costs with a static analysis.

- It is easy to combine lock-based reductions with thread-local object reductions, and the resulting combination is much more effective than either approach alone.

- Applying simple heuristics to avoid storing states can be quite effective. Atomicity reductions (e.g., (DA)) can increase the number of transitions that are explored as seen in the *Replicated Workers* data. This can degrade run-time performance of the model checks, but the reduction of the state-space size in our experiments more than compensates that loss of performance. It seems quite possible that additional heuristics can be applied for effective reduction of state storage, and we are exploring other opportunities along these lines [11].

- It is unclear how to provide a general lock-based reduction strategy. We have taken the approach of identifying different patterns of program locking, targeting those patterns with reduction strategies, and then combining those strategies to maximize the degree of reduction. This has proven quite effective with the LD, WSL^{dom}, DA combination. We are studying strategies that target additional locking patterns that might be added to the framework.

- The empirical evaluation to date has demonstrated the potential for significant reduction. It is quite encouraging that the degree of reduction appears to be greatest for the largest, most complex example (*Replicated Workers*). We are applying our reductions to additional examples to gain a deeper understanding of the breadth of effectiveness of our techniques and the degree to which they enable scaling of software model checking.

9. Related work

We have already discussed in detail how our work is related to existing work on partial-order reductions and escape analysis. Here we discuss several approaches that adapt partial-order reduction to target dynamic and concurrent software such as Java programs.

Iosif [22] combines heap and process symmetry reductions with partial-order reduction. This approach exploits the fact that heap allocation statements are independent transitions. The heap symmetry ensures that for any execution order of enabled allocations the result be the same state. Our dynamic analysis subsumes this because Bogor uses the same heap symmetry reduction and new objects are only reachable from the thread that allocates it.

Stoller [31] exploits a common pattern in Java synchronization, i.e., locking of shared data structures. He also exploits transitions that access only thread-local objects. However, the user is required to indicate which objects are thread-local by specifying which bytecode instructions allocate thread-local objects. The tool uses this information during the search by making transitions that accesses thread-local objects invisible, and it also checks the validity of the user supplied information. In contrast, our static analysis approach automatically computes a safe approximation of the thread-local objects, and our dynamic analysis computes the most-precise objects thread-locality information automatically on-the-fly. We introduce similar locking discipline to Stoller's approach to exploit synchronization patterns in Java programs. Furthermore, we illustrate how our approach can be combined with Stoller's to achieve the best known reduction.

Brat et al. [4] use alias analysis to establish which transitions are independent for partial-order reductions. This approach introduces an iterative algorithm where the model checker starts with an unsafe under-approximation of the alias set and refines the alias set on each iteration as the state exploration uncovers more aliasing. The iteration proceeds to a fix point in which a safe reduced state-space is constructed. In contrast, our dynamic approach does not require iteration to build a *safe* reduced state-space of the system. We can construct it on the fly because our notion of independence is state-sensitive instead of using the traditional global independence.

Flanagan and Qadeer have developed an approach for detecting when thread interleavings can be avoided using Lipton's theory of reduction [26] based on the notion of left- and right-movers. In [14], they present a type system for verifying that Java methods annotated as `atomic` are free from any interference due to interleaving, and thus clients of those methods can safely assume that the methods execute "in one step". This idea presents an interesting alternative for leveraging notions of independence: instead of using independence information to reduce the number of state explored in model checking, it is used to check that a developer has used locking in a correct way to achieve an interference-free method implementation. The type system relies on developer-supplied annotations that indicate which lock is used to protect fields. In addition, developers supply annotations to indicate which locks are held upon entry to a method and upon exit of a method. We believe that the ability to check a user-supplied annotation that a method is "atomic" is quite useful. The type system approach allows one to obtain efficient and scalable checking at the cost of a fair amount of user supplied annotations. In recent work [19], we have shown that model checking using the algorithms described in this paper can be effective for checking atomicity specifications. In particular, the approaches introduced here for detecting thread-locality and non-interference due to proper locking are applied to automatically discover properties that would otherwise need to be reported with annotations, and the increased precision of model checking yields fewer false positives when detecting atomicity violations. Of course, the tradeoff for this increased automation and precision is greater costs associated with state space exploration compared to type-checking. However, our experiments in [19] show that the state-space reductions described here enable relatively efficient checking for software units (as opposed to whole programs).

Flanagan and Qadeer have also proposed to use the theory of movers in a partial-order reduction strategy for state-space exploration [13]. They note that the partial-order reductions considered by ourselves and Stoller only incorporate reductions that move transitions in left-oriented fashion, and they argue that incorporate right-moving as well as left-moving transitions should result in better reduction techniques. Their framework relies on developer-supplied *access predicates* that indicate the conditions under which it is safe to access an object. They also show how access predicates can be automatically inferred by iterating the model checking. It is unclear how expensive this approach is since no performance numbers are given. We are currently investigating the extent to which this alternate view of partial-order reduction can be incorporated in our implementation. Note that since neither the atomic type system [14] nor the state-space reduction strategy [14] incorporates automatic detection of escape information, it is likely that incorporation of such information could provide additional benefits in the form of reducing the annotation burden or increasing the amount of reduction.

10.   Conclusion

The application of model checking to reason about object-oriented programs is growing. Given the significant body of research on static analysis and transformations targeted at improving the run-time of such programs, it is natural to attempt to adapt those techniques to reduce the state-space of a system. In this paper, we have illustrated how both static and dynamic escape analysis can be applied to gather information that can be used effectively to reduce the state-space of a system. We have shown how reductions can be accomplished by adapting the previously developed partial-order reduction framework of ample sets. Further, we have shown how escape information can be combined with other lock-based reduction strategies and with heuristics for avoiding state-space storage. We believe that these techniques represent a significant step forward in the state-of-the-art of partial-order reductions for software model checking. Based on our experience thus far, the relative ease with which dynamic escape analysis results can be exploited in explicit state model checking algorithms combined with the power of its reduction suggests that it ought to become a standard component of model checkers for systems with dynamic memory allocation. Further experimental studies will be beneficial in revealing the breadth and significance of these reductions across a range of realistic concurrent Java programs.

Appendix A: Overview of static escape analysis

To statically detect thread-local objects, we use an adaptation of Erik Ruf's escape analysis [29]. Ruf's analysis detects objects that are guaranteed to be *locked* by a single thread only. Any synchronization statements that are only applied to such objects are unnecessary and can safely be removed from the program. We adapt Ruf's analysis to obtain a variant that detects objects that are guaranteed to be *accessed* by a single thread only. After giving a brief summary of Ruf's analysis, we describe in greater detail how we adapt it for our setting.

Ruf's analysis builds an abstraction of the heap by forming equivalence classes of expressions (i.e., reference variable names or names with field selectors) that refer to the same set of objects. Attributes recorded for each equivalence class capture information about threads which may synchronize on objects from the equivalence class. The equivalence classes are represented as *alias sets*, which are tuples of the form ⟨*fieldmap, synchronized, syncThreads, global*⟩ in which *fieldmap* is a function from field names to alias sets (giving alias information for member fields), *synchronized* is a boolean that indicates whether the objects represented by the current equivalence class may be synchronized, *syncThreads* is a set of threads that may synchronize on the object, and *global* is a boolean to track the escape status of the object. Unification (merging) on alias sets is defined as the join operation on boolean (*true* is top), set, and function lattices. Alias sets support creation of new instances which are isomorphic to the existing one. *Alias contexts* $\langle \langle p_0, p_1, \ldots, p_n \rangle, r, e \rangle$ are used to capture the flow of information across method call/returns. They are composed of a sequence of alias sets, $p_0, p_1, \ldots p_n$ corresponding to the parameter list of the method along with an alias set r for return values r and another set e for thrown exceptions. The alias used at a method call-site is called a *site-context* and the set used for the method itself is called a *method-context*. Similar to alias sets, alias contexts support unification which is defined as the point-wise extension of alias set unification to tuples. Alias contexts support creation of new instances such that all relations between the original alias sets are preserved in the among the new instances of alias sets.

Ruf's analysis proceeds in three phases. In Phase 1, it identifies the thread allocation sites in the system and the methods executed in each thread instance. It also determines if each thread allocation site can produce multiple thread instances at run-time. In Phase 2, each global variable is associated with an alias set. It is assumed that all alias sets reachable from a global alias set (i.e., one which has its *global* field set to *true*) are global too. The analysis then does a bottom-up intra-procedural analysis on strongly-connected components (SCCs) in the system. The intra-procedural analysis involves creating alias sets for local variables and unifying them at suitable program points. The interesting cases occur at synchronization points and call-sites. At synchronization points, the *synchronized* element of the synchronized alias set is set to *true* and if it is *global* is *true* then thread allocation sites of the enclosing method is added to *syncThreads*. At call-sites, a *site-context* is created with the alias sets for receiver, arguments, return value and exception variables. For each callee at the call-sites, this site-context is then unified with the method context of the callee if the callee and the caller occur in the same SCC. If not, a new instance of the method context of the callee is created and unified with the site-context. In Phase 3, the analysis processes the SCCs in top-down topological order to process each synchronization point and call-sites. At each synchronization point, if the synchronized alias set is *contention-free*, i.e., $|sycnThreads| < 2$, then the synchronization is marked for removal. At each call-site, a new instance, M', of the callee's method-context, M, is created. If M' is synchronized, *S.syncThreads* is injected into *M'.syncThreads*, recursively. M and M' are compared recursively to determine if the method should be specialized and called or a previous specialized instance can be called. The comparison evaluates to true when the contention-free status of corresponding alias sets in the alias contexts is same.

In our adaptation of this analysis we use a slightly altered alias set in which *synchronized* and *syncThreads* elements are absent. Instead there are two boolean elements named *accessed* and *shared* which indicate if the object was accessed and if it is shared between threads, respectively. The assumptions about globalness is unchanged.

Our analysis proceeds in three phases similar to Ruf's analysis but focuses on read/write access points in the system rather than synchronization points. Phase 1 is similar to that of the Ruf's analysis except that we use information from Object/Value flow analysis to determine the call hierarchy (instead of the Rapid Type Analysis used by Ruf) and to identify the `java.lang.Thread.start` call-sites which may be executed multiple times during the execution of the system. In Phase 2, at each object access point, the *accessed* attribute of the corresponding alias set is set to *true*. The processing of call-sites is identical to Ruf's analysis except for when the called method is `java.lang.Thread.start`. In this case, if *accessed* element of two alias sets being unified is *true* then the *shared* element of the resulting alias set is set to *true*. The rational for this is that all objects reachable from a thread are reachable from objects created in that thread and/or from objects created by the parent thread. Hence, it suffices to determine escapism at `start` call-sites. In Phase 3, the information from the callers is propagated to the callees. When using the calculated information, if the object marked as *non-shared* is accessed in a method in a thread started at a call-site which is executed multiple time as determined in Phase 2 then that object is marked as *shared* or *escaping*.

Appendix B: Modifications to ample set framework proofs

We have cast our reduction strategies in terms of the ample set partial-order reduction framework as presented in [6, Chapter 10]. That framework requires transitions marked as independent to be remain independent for all states. Our only change to ample set framework has been to relax this notion of independence to obtain the notion of *state-sensitive independence* based on *conditional independence* [23] as presented in the body of the paper.

Almost all of the proofs from [6, Chapter 10] go through unchanged. In this section, we give the "patches" to the proofs [6, Chapter 10] that are necessary to establish the correctness of the ample set reductions using state-sensitive independence.

The proofs of [6, Section 10.6] are based on a construction that aims to show that in a given transition sequence, the transitions in the sequence can be reordered by moving transitions from ample sets ahead of those transitions that are not in ample sets. We need to show that this construction is still valid when one moves to state-sensitive independence. The construction relies on the fact that in the traditional notion of independence, the independence property is not "lost" as one proceeds through the steps of the sequence (in the traditional notion of independence, a pair of transitions marked as independent are independent in all states). The following properties show that the property of state-sensitive independence is preserved in a way that allows the construction of [6, Section 10.6] to still be applied (specifically, the properties below justify the steps **B1** and **B2** in the construction [6, Section 10.6, p. 161]).

Property 1. *Let $s_0 \xrightarrow{\beta_0} s_1 \xrightarrow{\beta_1} \cdots \xrightarrow{\beta_n} s_{n+1}$ be a path such that $\alpha \in enabled(s_0)$ and $I_{s_0}(\alpha) \supseteq \{\beta_0, \beta_1, \ldots, \beta_n\}$, then $\alpha \in enabled(s_{k+1})$ and $I_{s_k}(\alpha) \supseteq \{\beta_k, \beta_{k+1}, \ldots, \beta_n\}$, for $0 \le k \le n$.*

Proof 1: This is proved by induction on k:

- Case $k = 0$: Assume a path $s_0 \xrightarrow{\beta_0} s_1 \xrightarrow{\beta_1} \cdots \xrightarrow{\beta_n} s_{n+1}$, $\alpha \in enabled(s_0)$, and $I_{s_0}(\alpha) \supseteq \{\beta_0, \beta_1, \ldots, \beta_n\}$. Trivially, $\alpha \in enabled(s_0)$ and $I_{s_0}(\alpha) \supseteq \{\beta_0, \beta_1, \ldots, \beta_n\}$.
- Induction hypothesis (case $k = i$): If $\alpha \in enabled(s_0)$ and $I_{s_0}(\alpha) \supseteq \{\beta_0, \beta_1, \ldots, \beta_n\}$ for a path $s_0 \xrightarrow{\beta_0} s_1 \xrightarrow{\beta_1} \cdots \xrightarrow{\beta_n} s_{n+1}$, then $\alpha \in enabled(s_{i+1})$ and $I_{s_i}(\alpha) \supseteq \{\beta_i, \beta_{i+1}, \ldots, \beta_n\}$.
- Case $k = i + 1$: Assume a path $s_0 \xrightarrow{\beta_0} s_1 \xrightarrow{\beta_1} \cdots \xrightarrow{\beta_n} s_{n+1}$, $\alpha \in enabled(s_0)$, and $I_{s_0}(\alpha) \supseteq \{\beta_0, \beta_1, \ldots, \beta_n\}$. By induction hypothesis, we have $\alpha \in enabled(s_{i+1})$ and $I_{s_i}(\alpha) \supseteq \{\beta_i, \beta_{i+1}, \ldots, \beta_n\}$. By pair-wise application of the preservation of independence property of I_s (Definition 2), $I_{s_{i+1}}(\alpha) \supseteq \{\beta_{i+1}, \beta_{i+2}, \ldots, \beta_n\}$. By the preservation of enabledness property of I_s (Definition 2), $\alpha \in enabled(s_{i+2})$.

$\square$

Property 2. *Given a path $s_0 \xrightarrow{\beta_0} s_1 \xrightarrow{\beta_1} \cdots \xrightarrow{\beta_{k-2}} s_{k-1} \xrightarrow{\beta_{k-1}} s_k \xrightarrow{\alpha} s_{k+1}$ where $\alpha \in enabled$ (s_0) and $I_{s_0}(\alpha) \supseteq \{\beta_0, \beta_1, \cdots, \beta_{k-1}\}$, then there is also a path $s_0 \xrightarrow{\alpha} \alpha(s_0) \xrightarrow{\beta_0} \alpha(s_1) \xrightarrow{\beta_1} \cdots \xrightarrow{\beta_{k-2}} \alpha(s_{k-1}) \xrightarrow{\beta_{k-1}} \alpha(s_k)$, where $s_{k+1} = \alpha(s_k)$.*

Proof 2: This is proved by induction on k (the number of β transitions):

- Case $k = 1$: Assume $s_0 \xrightarrow{\beta_0} s_1 \xrightarrow{\alpha} s_2$, where $\alpha \in enabled(s_0)$ and $\{\beta_0\} \subseteq I_{s_0}(\alpha)$. By commutativity property of I_s (Definition 2), and because of $s_2 = \alpha(s_1)$, thus, $s_0 \xrightarrow{\alpha} \alpha(s_0) \xrightarrow{\beta_0} \alpha(s_1)$.
- Induction hypothesis (case $k = i$): Given a path $s_0 \xrightarrow{\beta_0} s_1 \xrightarrow{\beta_1} \cdots \xrightarrow{\beta_{i-2}} s_{i-1} \xrightarrow{\beta_{i-1}} s_i \xrightarrow{\alpha} s_{i+1}$ where $\alpha \in enabled(s_0)$ and $I_{s_0}(\alpha) \supseteq \{\beta_0, \beta_1, \ldots, \beta_{i-1}\}$, then there is also a path $s_0 \xrightarrow{\alpha} \alpha(s_0) \xrightarrow{\beta_0} \alpha(s_1) \xrightarrow{\beta_1} \cdots \xrightarrow{\beta_{i-2}} \alpha(s_{i-1}) \xrightarrow{\beta_{i-1}} \alpha(s_i)$, where $s_{i+1} = \alpha(s_i)$.
- Case $k = i + 1$: Assume a path $s_0 \xrightarrow{\beta_0} s_1 \xrightarrow{\beta_1} \cdots \xrightarrow{\beta_{i-2}} s_{i-1} \xrightarrow{\beta_{i-1}} s_i \xrightarrow{\beta_i} s_{i+1} \xrightarrow{\alpha} s_{i+2}$ where $\alpha \in enabled(s_0)$ and $I_{s_0}(\alpha) \supseteq \{\beta_0, \beta_1, \ldots, \beta_i\}$. By Property 1, we have $\beta_i \in I_{s_i}(\alpha)$. By commutativity property of I_s (Definition 2), we have $s_i \xrightarrow{\alpha} \alpha(s_i) \xrightarrow{\beta_i} s_{i+2}$. Thus, we have a path $s_0 \xrightarrow{\beta_0} s_1 \xrightarrow{\beta_1} \cdots \xrightarrow{\beta_{i-2}} s_{i-1} \xrightarrow{\beta_{i-1}} s_i \xrightarrow{\alpha} \alpha(s_i) \xrightarrow{\beta_i} s_{i+2}$. By induction hypothesis, there is a path $s_0 \xrightarrow{\alpha} \alpha(s_0) \xrightarrow{\beta_0} \alpha(s_1) \xrightarrow{\beta_1} \cdots \xrightarrow{\beta_{i-2}} \alpha(s_{i-1}) \xrightarrow{\beta_{i-1}} \alpha(s_i) \xrightarrow{\beta_i} s_{i+2}$.

$\square$

Appendix C: Ample set condition proofs

C.1. Justification of independence relations (Definition 3, Definition 5, and Definition 6)

C.1.1. Justification of thread-local independence. In Section 3.2, we give informal arguments to justify that the conditions for state-sensitive independence are indeed achieved by our notion of independence based on thread-local transformation. Below, we give more rigorous arguments to justify that claim.

Property 3.   *For each state $s \in S$, if there exists a transition $\alpha \in current(s)$ that is thread-local at s and a transition $\beta \in enabled(s)$ such that $s' = \beta(s)$ and α is not thread-local at s' then it must be the case that $thread(\alpha) = thread(\beta)$ and β is not thread-local at s.*

Proof 3:   Suppose that at a state $s \in S$, there exists a transition α that is thread-local and a transition $\beta \in enabled(s)$ such that $s' = \beta(s)$ and α is *not* thread-local at s'.

- Assume that $thread(\alpha) \neq thread(\beta)$. This cannot be the case since α is thread-local at s. That is, α does not access objects that are reachable from other threads. In other words, no other threads can cause the objects that α accesses to be reachable by a thread other than $thread(\alpha)$.
- Assume that β is thread-local. This also cannot be the case since a thread-local transition cannot make some objects to be reachable by other threads. In other words, the only way a thread-local object o can become non-thread-local is by executing a transition δ that assigns o's reference to a static field or the field of an object o' that is already non-thread-local. In either case, such a transition δ is non-thread-local by definition.

Therefore, by contradiction, it must be the case that $thread(\alpha) = thread(\beta)$ and β is not thread-local.   □

Preservation of independence: For each state $s \in S$, and for each $(\alpha, \beta) \in I_s^{tl}$, if $\{\beta_0, \beta_1\} \subseteq I_s^{tl}(\alpha)$ and $thread(\beta_0) \neq thread(\beta_1)$ and $s' = \beta_0(s)$, then $\{\beta_1\} \subseteq I_{s'}^{tl}(\alpha)$.

Proof 4:   Since $(\alpha, \beta_0) \in I_s^{tl}$ either α or β_0 (or both) is current at s and a thread-local transition at s:

- If α is a thread-local transition or both α and β_0 are thread-local transitions, then since $thread(\alpha) \neq thread(\beta_0)$ by Property 3, it must be the case that α is thread-local at s' (and note that α must be current at s' since its thread did not move in the transition to s'). Since we also have $thread(\alpha) \neq thread(\beta_1)$, then $(\alpha, \beta_1) \in I_{s'}^{tl}$ by definition of I_s^{tl}.
- If β_0 is a thread-local transition and α is not thread-local, then β_1 is also thread-local. Since we have $thread(\beta_0) \neq thread(\beta_1)$, then again by Property 3, it must be the case that β_1 is thread-local at s' (and note β_1 must be current at s' since its thread did not move in the transition to s') and thus $(\alpha, \beta_1) \in I_{s'}^{tl}$.

□

The proofs for both the weak self-locking independence and weak self-locking dominated independence are similar to the thread-local independence, and thus, they are not shown.

C.2. Proofs for Condition C1

In Sections 5 and 6, we introduced several *checkC1* functions using several reduction strategies. We now prove that the functions satisfy Condition C1. We only prove the *checkC1* function using the weak self-locking dominated discipline because the other functions (using the dynamic escape analysis and the weak self-locking) are subsumed by this one. We do not consider the case where the *checkC1* function notifies the user because of locking discipline annotation violation, because in that case the current model checking run is abandoned, the user corrects the annotation, and the run is restarted (note that these steps can also be taken automatically).

Property 4. *If the checkC1 function using the weak self-locking dominated discipline at figure 5 returns TRUE for a thread t at state s, then $current(s, t) \subseteq enabled(s, t)$ (i.e., $current(s, t) = enabled(s, t)$).*

Proof 5: (By contradiction): Suppose that there exists $\alpha \in current(s, t)$ such that $\alpha \notin enabled(s, t)$. There are three cases that can cause the *checkC1* function to return TRUE, and we show that each of these leads to a contradiction:

- It returns TRUE at line 5.6. This means that the objects O that are accessed by *current(s, t)* are self-locking objects. By definition of self-locking objects, t must hold all the locks of objects O at s. This leads to a contradiction, because $\alpha \in current(s, t)$ and thus, it cannot be disabled at s because α can be disabled only if α is a lock acquire operation and some other thread t' holds the lock of some of the objects in O.
- It returns TRUE at line 5.10. This means that the objects O that are accessed by *current(s, t)* are protected by self-locking objects O_{WSL}. By definition of self-locking objects, t must hold all the locks of objects O_{WSL} at s. This leads to a contradiction, because $\alpha \in current(s, t)$ and thus, it cannot be disabled at s because α can be disabled only if some other thread t' holds the lock of some object in O. However, t' cannot access O without accessing O_{WSL} that are locked by t.
- It returns TRUE at line 8. This means that the objects O that are accessed by *current(s, t)* are thread-local objects. By definition of thread-locality, only t can reach the objects O. This leads to a contradiction, because $\alpha \in current(s, t)$ and thus, it cannot be disabled at s because α can be disabled only if some other thread t' holds the lock of some object in O. However, none of the objects in O is reachable from t'.

Therefore, by contradiction, it must be the case that if the *checkC1* function using the weak self-locking dominated discipline at figure 5 returns TRUE for a thread t at state s, then $current(s, t) \subseteq enabled(s, t)$ (i.e., $current(s, t) = enabled(s, t)$). $\qquad\square$

Lemma 1. *The checkC1 function using the weak self-locking dominated discipline at figure 5 satisfies Condition C1.*

Proof 6: The discussion in [6, p. 157–158] notes that there are two conditions that are sufficient for establishing Condition C1 when selecting $ample(s) = enabled(s, t)$: (1)

checkC1(s, t)
1 $G := \emptyset$ /* static fields accessed from *t* in *s* */
2 $O := \emptyset$ /* heap objects/arrays accessed by *t*'s enabled transitions in *s* */
3 for each α of *t* in *s* do
4   *collectAccessed(s, t, α, G, O)*
5 if $\exists o \in O.o \in O_{commun}$ or $\exists g \in G.g \in G_{commun}$ then return FALSE
6 if $O \subseteq O_{unsh}$ then return TRUE
7 for each $g \in G$ do
8   if *intersectIfNotEmpty(g, collectAllLocksHeldBy(t, s))* = $\emptyset$ then
9   signal condition on *g* is violated by *t*
10 for each $o \in O$ do
11   if $\neg inInitialization(o, s)$ then
12   if *intersectIfNotEmpty(o, collectAllLocksHeldBy(t, s))* = $\emptyset$ then
13   signal condition on *o* is violated by *t*
14 return TRUE
end *checkC1*

intersectIfNotEmpty(e, S)
15 if *lockSetTable* maps *e* then
16    $S' := lockSetTable(e) \cap S$
17   *lockSetTable* := *lockSetTable*$[e \mapsto S']$
18   return S'
19 else
20   *lockSetTable* := *lockSetTable*$[e \mapsto S]$
21   return *S*
end *intersectIfNotEmpty*

Algorithm 6.   Ample set construction algorithm using LD.

enabled(s, t) should be independent from transitions in all of threads, and (2) no transitions from other threads should be able to enable any transitions of *t* that are disabled at *s*. We now show that these conditions are satisfied by *checkC1*.

If the *checkC1* function returns TRUE for a thread *t* at state *s*, then for all threads *t'* where $t \neq t'$:

- It must be the case that for all $\alpha \in current(s, t)$ and for all β of *t'*, we have that $(\alpha, \beta) \in I_s^{wsl,dom}$. This is true by the properties established in Appendix C.1.
- It must be the case that *current(s, t)* \ *enabled(s, t)* = $\emptyset$. This is true by Property 4.

□

Appendix D: Stoller's LD-based strategy in the ample set framework

In Section 6.1, we describe how Stoller's approach for LD can be recast in the ample set framework. The *checkC1* function that uses LD is illustrated in Algorithm 6. The algorithm begins with collecting accessed static fields and objects (line 1–4). If any accessed fields or objects are communication objects, then FALSE is returned (line 5). If all the fields or objects accessed are unshared objects, then TRUE is returned (line 6). For each static field

g, if the intersection of the set of locks being held at s with the set of locks being held at the states where g was accessed previously is empty, then the user is signaled that the search may be unsafe (line 7–9). This is done similarly for objects (line 10–13), except that the signaling is done if the objects are not currently being initialized at s.

Given an element e and a set S, the *intersectIfNotEmpty* function (line 16–21) intersects S with the set obtained by a look-up of the element from a global table *lockSetTable* (i.e., *lockSetTable(e)*). It then maps e to the result in the table, and then the result is returned. If the element e is not in the table, then, the e is mapped to S and S is returned.

Given an object o and a state s, the *inInitialization* determines whether the object is currently being initialized (e.g., we have not yet reached a state where o is accessed by a thread other than the thread that created it). This can be implemented by keeping the state of o. When it is first created, we keep track of the thread that creates it and we also note that o is in the initialization phase. For each access to o, we check the threads that access it. If it is different than the thread that created it, then we noted that o is no longer in its initialization phase. Given a thread t and a state s, the function *collectAllLocksHeldBy* collects all the objects that are locked by t at state s. This can be done simply by heap traversal of the state. We do not show the algorithms for *inInitialization* and *collectAllLocksHeldBy* due to space constraint.

Notes

1. http://bogor.projects.cis.ksu.edu.
2. This is due to the fact that we optimize the model by using information from a dead variable analysis. After each `Process` is started, the JVM stack element that holds a reference of the `Process` object is considered dead.
3. A term that is usually used in the Java community for synchronized classes.
4. Interestingly, for transition systems arising from Java programs as we generate them in Bandera, it is enough to check for only the enabled transitions of t since the problematic enabled/disabled transition structure described above does not arise. However, we use the definitions above for generality.

References

1. G.R. Andrews, *Concurrent Programming: Principles and Practice*. Addison-Wesley, 1991.
2. G. Behrmann, K.G. Larsen, and R. Pelánek, "To store or not to store," in W.A.H. Jr. and F. Somenzi (Eds.), *Proceedings of the 15th International Conference on Computer Aided Verification*, Vol. 2725 of Lecture Notes in Computer Science, Springer, July 2003, pp. 433–445.
3. D. Bosnacki, D. Dams, and L. Holenderski, "Symmetric SPIN," *International Journal on Software Tools for Technology Transfer*, 2002.
4. G. Brat and W. Visser, "Combining static analysis and model checking for software analysis," in *Proceedings of the 16th IEEE Conference on Automated Software Engineering*, Nov. 2001.
5. J.-D. Choi, M. Gupta, M.J. Serrano, V.C. Sreedhar, and S.P. Midkiff, "Escape analysis for object oriented languages application to Java," in *OOPSLA'99 ACM Conference on Object-Oriented Systems, Languages and Applications*, Vol. 34(10) of ACM SIGPLAN Notices, Denver, CO, ACM Press, Oct. 1999, pp. 1–19.
6. E. Clarke, O. Grumberg, and D. Peled, *Model Checking*. MIT Press, 2000.
7. J.C. Corbett, M.B. Dwyer, J. Hatcliff, S. Laubach, C.S. Păsăreanu, Robby, and H. Zheng, "Bandera: Extracting finite-state models from Java source code," in *Proceedings of the 22nd International Conference on Software Engineering*, June 2000.

8. J.C. Corbett, M.B. Dwyer, J. Hatcliff, and Robby, "Expressing checkable properties of dynamic systems: The Bandera specification language," *International Journal on Software Tools for Technology Transfer*, 2002.

9. C. Demartini, R. Iosif, and R. Sisto, "dSPIN: A dynamic extension of SPIN," in *Theoretical and Applied Aspects of SPIN Model Checking*, LNCS 1680, Sept. 1999.

10. J. Dolby and A.A. Chien, "An automatic object inlining optimization and its evaluation," In *Proceedings of the ACM SIGPLAN '00 Conference on Programming Language Design and Implementation (PLDI-00)*, June 2000, pp. 345–357.

11. M.B. Dwyer, Robby, X. Deng, and J. Hatcliff, "Space reductions for model checking quasi-cyclic systems," in *Proceedings of the Third International Conference on Embedded Software*, 2003.

12. M.B. Dwyer and V. Wallentine, "A framework for parallel adaptive grid simulations," *Concurrency: Practice and Experience*. Vol. 9, No. 11, pp. 1293–1310, 1997.

13. C. Flanagan and S. Qadeer, "Transactions: A new approach to the state-explosion problem in software model checking," in *Proceedings of the 2nd Workshop on Software Model Chekcing*, 2003.

14. C. Flanagan and S. Qadeer, "A type and effect system for atomicity," in *Proceedings of the ACM SIGPLAN 2003 Conference on Programming Language Design and Implementation*, 2003.

15. P. Godefroid, *Partial Order Methods for the Verification of Concurrent Systems*, Vol. 1032 of Lecture Notes in Computer Science, Springer Verlag, 1996.

16. P. Godefroid, "Model-checking for programming languages using VeriSoft," in *Proceedings of the 24th ACM Symposium on Principles of Programming Languages (POPL'97)*, Jan. 1997, pp. 174–186.

17. B. Grant, M. Philipose, M. Mock, C. Chambers, and S.J. Eggers, "An evaluation of staged run-time optimizations in DyC," in *Proceedings of the ACM SIGPLAN '99 Conference on Programming Language Design and Implementation (PLDI-99)*, May 1999, pp. 293–304.

18. J. Hatcliff, M.B. Dwyer, and H. Zheng, "Slicing software for model construction," *Higher-order and Symbolic Computation*, Vol. 13, No. 4, 2000.

19. J. Hatcliff, Robby, and M.B. Dwyer, "Verifying atomicity specifications for concurrent object-oriented software using model checking," in M. Young (Ed.), *Proceedings of the Fifth International Conference on Verification, Model Checking, and Abstract Interpretation (VMCAI 2004)*, No. 2937 in Lecture Notes in Computer Science, Jan. 2004.

20. G.J. Holzmann, "The model checker SPIN," *IEEE Transactions on Software Engineering*, Vol. 23, No. 5, pp. 279–294, 1997.

21. G.J. Holzmann, "State compression in SPIN: Recursive indexing and compression training runs," in *Proceedings of Third International SPIN Workshop*, Apr. 1997.

22. R. Iosif, "Symmetry reduction criteria for software model checking," in *Proceedings of Ninth International SPIN Workshop*, Vol. 2318 of Lecture Notes in Computer Science, Springer-Verlag, Apr. 2002, pp. 22–41.

23. S. Katz and D. Peled, "Defining conditional independence using collapses," *Theoretical Computer Science*, Vol. 101, pp. 337–359, 1992.

24. D. Lea, *Concurrent Programming in Java*, 2nd edn., Addison-Wesley, 2000.

25. T. Lindholm and F. Yellin, *The Java Virtual Machine Specification*. Addison-Wesley, 1999.

26. R.J. Lipton, "Reduction: A method of proving properties of parallel programs," *Communications of the ACM*, Vol. 18, No. 12, 1975.

27. Robby, M.B. Dwyer, and J. Hatcliff, "Bogor: An extensible and highly-modular model checking framework," in *Proceedings of the 9th European Software Engineering Conference held jointly with the 11th ACM SIGSOFT Symposium on the Foundations of Software Engineering*, 2003.

28. Robby, M.B. Dwyer, J. Hatcliff, and R. Iosif, "Space-reduction strategies for model checking dynamic software," in *Proceedings of the 2nd Workshop on Software Model Chekcing*, 2003.

29. E. Ruf, "Effective synchronization removal for java," in *Proceedings of the ACM SIGPLAN '00 Conference on Programming Language Design and Implementation (PLDI-00)*, June 2000, pp. 203–213.

30. S. Savage, M. Burrows, G. Nelson, P. Sobalvarro, and T. Anderson, "Eraser: A dynamic data race detector for multithreaded programs," *ACM Transactions on Computer Systems*, Vol. 15, No. 4, pp. 391–411, 1997.

31. S. Stoller, "Model-checking multi-threaded distributed Java programs," in *International Journal on Software Tools for Technology Transfer*. Springer-Verlag, 2002.

32. S. Stoller and E. Cohen, "Optimistic synchronization-based state-space reduction," in *Proceedings of the 9th International Conference on Tools and Algorithms for the Construction and Analysis of Systems, LNCS 2619*, 2003.

33. W. Visser, K. Havelund, G. Brat, and S. Park, "Model checking programs," in *Proceedings of the 15th IEEE Conference on Automated Software Engineering*, Sept. 2000.

Overview of the HASTEN (High Assurance Systems Tools and Environments) Project *

Insup Lee*, Rajeev Alur*, Bob Cook†, Carl Gunter‡, Elsa Gunter‡,
Sampath Kannan*, Kang Shin⋆, and Oleg Sokolsky*

*Department of Computer and Information Science, University of Pennsylvania,
†Department of Computer Science, Georgia Southern University,
‡Department of Computer Science, University of Illinois at Urbana Champaign,
⋆Department of Electrical Engineering and Computer Science, University of Michigan

July 29, 2005

Abstract

Embedded systems consist of a collection of components that interact with each other and with their environment through sensors and actuators. Embedded systems are characterized by the nature of resource limitations and constraints that need to be considered during development and deployment. Embedded systems have been developed traditionally in an ad-hoc manner by practicing engineers and programmers. The existing technology for embedded systems does not effectively support the development of reliable and robust embedded systems. The effective development of embedded systems requires a collection of tools to capture requirements, to construct, analyze and simulate specifications, to generate and test implementations, and to monitor and check implementations at run-time.

The goal of this research project is to develop a framework for the integrated use of a suite of methods and tools for the specification, analysis, development, testing, prototyping, simulation and monitoring of embedded software. The framework is called HASTEN (High Assurance Systems Tools and Environments) and is based on systems that the proposers have been studying separately for some time and also includes systems that are developed elsewhere. The primary methods of interest are: formal specifications, test generation from specifications, automated verification, prototyping and simulation, and run-time monitoring and checking. Each of the methods has its own strengths. Taken within the context of an 'end-to-end' view of the software life cycle they can achieve together more than any one of them could do. However, these methods traditionally have been applied to different representations of the system at different points in its development and deployment. Furthermore, some of these methods are enhanced to handle the resource limitation and constraint characteristics of embedded systems. The significant effort of the proposed work has been to enchance individual methods to support embedded systems. We

---

*This research was supported in part by ARO DAAD19-01-1-0473.

have evaluated the proposed techniques on a collection of DoD embedded system applications to be chosen to represent domains requiring high assurance and real-time requirements.

1   Introduction

An embedded system consists of a collection of components that interact with each other and with their environment through sensors and actuators. Many embedded systems are part of safety-critical applications, e.g., avionic systems, manufacturing, automotive controllers, and medical devices.

There are several factors that complicate the design and implementation of embedded systems. First, the software complexity of embedded systems increases steadily as microprocessors become more powerful. To mitigate the development cost of software, embedded systems are being designed to flexibly adapt to different environments. The requirements for increased functionality and adaptability make the development of embedded software complex and error-prone. Second, tight resource constraints distinguish embedded systems from most other computer-based systems. The need to satisfy the system requirements and still stay within the resource constraints makes the design space more complicated. Multi-dimensional trade-offs among different resources are hard to quantify within existing design technologies. Third, embedded systems are increasingly networked to improve functionality, reliability and maintainability. Networking makes embedded software even more difficult to develop, since composition and abstraction principles are poorly understood.

Embedded software systems have been developed traditionally in an ad-hoc manner by practicing engineers and programmers. Knowledge of system behavior and functionality is contained in the mind of the domain-expert, and is only imperfectly captured and translated into system products by the engineers and programmers.

Design based on mathematical modeling plays a critical role in other engineering disciplines, such as structural engineering. Although much progress in developing formalisms and tools based on them has been made during the last three decades, their use has been limited by the expense (i.e., time, computational resources, and expertise) required to employ them. The complexity of embedded software systems has increased to a point where it is not possible to envision the development of high-confidence embedded software systems without using such techniques in the future. The effective development of embedded systems requires a collection of tools to capture requirements, to construct, analyze and simulate specifications, to generate and test implementations, and to monitor and check implementations at run-time. Moreover, for these tools to be effective, they should be designed to operate within a uniform framework that spans all stages of the embedded application life cycle.

A number of methods and tools that enhance design, analysis, and implementation have been developed over the years. Each of the methods and tools has its own strengths. Taken within the context of an 'end-to-end' view of the software life cycle they can achieve together more than any one of them could do.

We have developed a framework for the integration of a suite of methods and tools for the specification, analysis, development, testing, prototyping, simulation and monitoring of embedded software. The framework is called HASTEN (High Assurance Systems Tools and Environments) and is based on systems that support formal specification and verification, test generation from specifications, prototyping and simulation, and run-time monitoring and checking.

Figure 1 shows the overall structure of the HASTEN environment. A software engineering process is centered around the development of two entities, requirements artifacts and system artifacts (shown in the middle column of Figure 1) and the validation of system artifacts with respect to requirements artifacts. Requirement artifacts, initially constructed informally through the requirements elicitation, are gradually refined into more rigorous representations. System artifacts can range from design documents such as UML diagrams, to prototypes and specifications, to executable code. Each of them are developed to satisfy some of the requirements. As shown in Figure 1, techniques such as prototyping, simulation, verification, testing, and monitoring can be used to evaluate that a system artifact meets its requirements during development and deployment of the system. Evaluation results are used as feedback to modify the system artifacts, and sometimes the requirements. Any changes to the system and requirement artifacts, in turn, necessitates a new round of analysis.

The important distinguishing feature of HASTEN is the use of formal methods in all parts of the framework. The underlying philosophy of HASTEN is that formal methods bring the most benefit when their use spans several stages of software lifecycle, such as user requirements specification, design of software requirements, architectural design, detailed design and coding, transfer of the software to production, operation and maintenance [44]. Since we expect that the scale of embedded designs will exceed the capabilities of formal methods tools in the near future, formal methods are complemented in the HASTEN environment with traditional development and validation methods such as rapid prototyping and testing. However, test suites are automatically generated from the requirements and the specification and can be used to validate an implementation. Code generation is used to provide a connection between formal models of the system and its implementation. Finally, to ensure correctness of the implementation during the operation phase, we derive checkers that can be executed by a run-time support system and raise alarms when an inconsistency is detected.

In this paper, we show how our research on different aspects of embedded systems design and analysis populates the HASTEN framework with concrete tools and techniques. Section 2 deals with requirements artifacts. We explore formalization of requirements and analysis of requirements specifications. In Section 3 we turn to the problem of construction and verification of system artifacts. Section 4 considers simulation of formal models as a rigorous prototyping technique and code generation from the formal models as means of system implementation. Finally, Sections 5

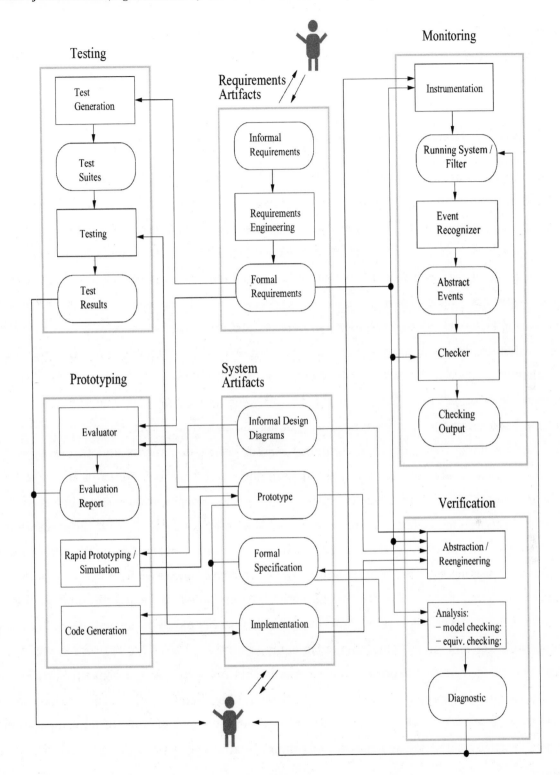

Figure 1: The HASTEN Environment

and 6 discuss validation of implementations derived using traditional methods for compliance with the system models. We consider generation of tests from formal specifications and generation of checkers and run-time monitoring.

2   Requirements Formalization and Analysis

Computer-based systems are becoming increasingly important in safety critical domains such as process control, transport and medicine. Though researchers have long advocated precise, unambiguous formal approaches to describing such systems, much commercial development, and even federal regulations, continue to be based on informal requirements documents. These documents describe various aspects of the system including functional requirements, design specifications, usage scenarios, interfaces, hardware platforms, *etc.*, and their correctness and completeness will have a direct bearing on the safety and reliability of derived implementations.

To combat cost overruns and system failures related to inconsistencies and incompleteness in requirements specifications, researchers have long emphasized the need for more formality in requirements description. To address the gap between engineering practice and the capabilities of formal methods techniques, we have been developing integrated methods, techniques, and tools to extract formal models from informal computer system design documents and to use these models to improve the quality of end products. It is important for the process to be intuitive for the domain engineers. Furthermore, the resulting requirements specification should be amenable to analysis and refinement during subsequent stages of the design process. During the translation the description will then be checked for ambiguities (*i.e.*, can it be interpreted in more than one way?), potential inconsistencies (*i.e.*, are contradictory requirements presented in different places?), and incompleteness (*i.e.*, has the requirements gathering process failed to adequately specify all cases?) With formal requirements, it is possible to apply analysis tools based on formal methods to detect potential problems and aid system designers in eliminating them before errors occur in deployment. Further, if extracted models represent both requirements properties and design specifications, the latter can be model checked with respect to the former. And finally, design specifications can also be used to generate tests, which can be used to evaluate the conformance of implementations to their specifications. The type and number of tests generated will depend on the level of assurance demanded.

The effectiveness of formal methods in the requirements analysis of medical systems is explored with the two case studies performed within the scope of the HASTEN project.

FDA: Blood Bank Policy. The first case study [43] considers the FDA regulation 21 CFR 610.40, "Hepatitis B Testing Protocols" [48] that contains guidelines for the nation's blood bank industry. This industry encompasses the collection, testing, distribution, and management of blood products. The systems managing these blood products may be categorized as very large, partial real-time, distributed inventory systems. It has been established that blood product management system developers are having difficulty translating regulatory requirements into their operational management systems [36], and that the complexity of these systems makes them subject to errors and unforeseen consequences.

The goal of the case study was to assess the feasibility of the model extraction process. We concentrated on the first several sentences of the policy, and most of the translation tasks were done manually. The NLP phase included parsing and co-referencing steps and translation of the document into a collection of frames. By encoding the frames in a restricted version of Java programming language, we obtained an object-oriented domain model. From the object-oriented model, we extracted an extended finite state machine (EFSM) specification in a format suitable for analysis by such tools as SMV, SPIN [30]. The case study allowed us to better understand the stages in the process of model extraction and was instrumental in shaping our research direction.

Infusion Pump. Army medics have observed that two thirds of combat fatalities involve significant blood loss due to hemorrhaging. WRAIR (Walter Reed Army Institute for Research) has developed CARA, an algorithm for controlling an infusion pump to allow rapid stabilization of a patient's blood pressure. The system consists of an infusion pump, the CARA software and a blood pressure measurement unit.

WRAIR provided us with a set of informal requirements for CARA consisting of a tagged requirements document and a listing of questions and answers which amended that document. The tagged requirements document mixed user, system, and environmental requirements.

We used these documents to create manually a formal model of the CARA system, which consisted of a number of EFSM's [11]. This EFSM model was used as an unambiguous reference specification for modeling the system using a variety of analysis tools. We also constructed a hardware-in-the loop simulation of the infusion process. The case study allowed us to gain a better understanding of the model features that need to be extracted from informal documents and helped shape the model validation component of modelical devices.

2.1 Analysis of CARA requirements

To analyze the EFSM model of the CARA system, we encoded parts of the the EFSM model of CARA in the the Design Oriented Verification and Evaluation (DOVE) tool [47]. DOVE consists of a graphical user interface for modeling a system as EFSMs, and a reasoning engine for automated and interactive verification of properties expressed in Linear Temporal Logic (LTL). DOVE was originally developed by the Defense Science and Technology Organization (DSTO) in Australia. Using DOVE, we were able to directly encode the HASTEN EFSM specifications for the pump monitors, and model an abstraction of the pump and the environment in which the pump will operate.

To be able to reason about the composition of the separate pump monitors and the pump and environment, we needed to extend DOVE with the ability to make product automata from components. This included clarifying how to specify when actions of two automata should be synchronous versus when they should be asynchronous. Previously, DOVE required that the design of a system be given as a single EFSM. To facilitate automatic communication between DOVE and other tools in the HASTEN project, we also implemented a translation between the internal language for EFSMs in DOVE and the HASTEN EFSM format.

Following the phase of encoding the EFSM models of the CARA system, we translated some of the English language specifications from WRAIR into LTL formulae and verified that the EFSM specifications satisfied these LTL formulae. Some difficulties arose in translating the English specifications into LTL formulae. A common specification would say that if certain conditions were met, that some action was to happen. A difficulty in encoding such a requirement in LTL is that the English does not say when the action is to happen. LTL gives only two possibilities for this: Next and Eventually. It may seem obvious that the intended interpretation is that the action should happen Next. However, Next is not compositional. The use of Next would rule out the possibility of some other independent process in the system, or the environment, being able to commit an interleaved intervening action. This typically cannot be guaranteed, and in the composite model is typically false. What is probably generally meant is that the next thing the component dealing with the specified condition does is the given action. Other components may commit independent actions in between the time that the condition is first met and the specified action is taken. To handle this problem we introduced a notion of "Locally Next". This version of Locally Next is a short-hand for the LTL formula expressing that no action of the effected component EFSM is to take place until the desired action takes place. We also extended DOVE to incorporate liveness conditions as well.

Subsequent to the work in DOVE, we modeled the same components of the CARA system in PET (Path Exploration Tool) [26] as we had done in DOVE. PET enables programs written in a simple imperative programming language to be verified with respect to LTL formulae. Thus we gave a prototype implementation of the EFSMs as simple concurrent imperative programs. Doing so highlighted that there were atomicity assumptions implicit in the EFSM specifications that had to be made explicit in the prototype implementation, as they would in any real implementation.

2.2   Modeling and integrating policies for embedded applications

Embedded computer systems are now routinely deployed in a wide range of engineered products such as appliances, medical devices, communication devices, and automobiles. Increasingly, embedded devices, such as smart cards and cell phones, are *programmable*, and offer an open API for software applications. While this offers the user the much coveted flexibility to customize and enhance functionality, it underscores the need for formal assurances about system operation as many embedded devices are used in safety-critical and security-critical contexts. We believe that the model-based design paradigm, with its promise for greater design automation and formal guarantees of reliability, is particularly relevant for this purpose. We have developed a model-based approach to adding policies to payment cards.

Smart cards are personal cards with an embedded processor, and are commonly used for identification, payment, and access control. Java cards are programmable smart cards with an API that supports a restricted subset of Java (see java.sun.com/products/javacard). The global platform architecture provides a runtime environment for these cards, and allows installation of certified applets that run in restricted contexts or security domains (see www.globalplatform.org). This enabling technology, together with the obvious need for assurances of security and integrity for downloading applications on such cards, prompted us to explore formal and model-based development.

We focus on a specific form of programs called *policies*. A policy specifies whether or not a transaction should be approved, possibly based on the history of transactions. Sample policies are "the total amount of money spent during the past month should not exceed a specified limit," and "transactions involving a specified list of emergency services is always allowed." These policies can be written by multiple parties, and installed at any time. While this offers flexibility, it is necessary to detect and resolve conflicts among different policies. Also, a new policy needs to be integrated with existing policies, possibly with checks for redundancy since on-card memory is limited. For this purpose, we present *policy automata* as a formal model for specifying policies. A policy automaton is an extended finite-state machine that examines the requested transaction, and votes on it. A vote can be yes, no, maybe, or in general, a value from some domain of votes that can capture priorities or complex constraints. The domain of votes is also equipped with a decision rule that collects the votes of all the policy automata to either approve the transaction, reject it, or declare a conflict. The individual policy automata update their states based on this global resolution. Using this framework one can specify policies in a modular fashion. Note that the constraints imposed by these policies are *non-monotonic* (as policies are added approval of a transaction can switch from yes to no and back to yes), and *stateful* (approval of a transaction depends on decisions on previous transactions). We show that static techniques such as model checking can be used to detect potential conflicts among a set of policy automata, and also to check whether a new policy is redundant with respect to a set of existing policy automata. Our policy description framework is relevant in other contexts such as firewall policies, where multiple parties wish to independently add rules governing approval of requests.

In [45] we defined a policy description language suitable for our approach. We also implemented a prototype tool POLARIS. Polaris provides a graphical editor for specifying policies as extended state machines, and an enumerative reachability checker to detect conflicts and redundancy. We have modified the development kit from Oberthur Card Systems that allows us to install applets onto Java cards. To install a policy onto the card, Polaris compiles a policy automaton into a Java class instance, downloads it onto the card, and registers the new policy with the main routine that polls all the registered policies before deciding on a transaction. We believe that this architecture for dynamically adding policies to a Java card is an advance in the state-of-the-art for smart cards technology.

3   Design Specification, Modeling, and Analysis

An embedded system can be modeled on a variety of levels and using a plethora of formalisms. Some visual formalisms, such as Statecharts [27], are targeted at easy comprehension of the model by the users. Other formalisms may facilitate analysis of the model, sometimes at the expense of readability. Yet others may be suitable for code generation, often at the expense of formal sophistication. It is commonly believed that no single formalism will solve all the modeling problems. Different modeling assumptions are suitable for each modeling task. For example, hybrid systems formalisms often used in behavioral analysis of embedded systems (for example, CHARON [3]), abstract away computation time, assuming that sensor readings, actuation, mode switches, etc., happen instantaneously. This assumption greatly simplifies analysis, but may make the model physically unrealizable. Furthermore, a hybrid system model usually models both the embedded system and its environment. Such a model, when used for code generation, has to "forget" the environment part. On the other hand, a formalism for schedulability analysis, such as ACSR [42], does not have to model details of computation, instead capturing only computation times and periodicity of task executions. Such a model, of course, cannot be used, for example, in code generation.

3.1   Charon: Modeling and analysis of hybrid systems

We have been developing the modeling language CHARON, a design environment for specification and analysis of embedded systems [4]. In CHARON, the building block for describing the system architecture is an *agent* that communicates with its environment via shared variables. The language supports the operations of *composition* of agents to model concurrency, *hiding* of variables to restrict sharing of information, and *instantiation* of agents to support reuse. The building block for describing flow of control inside an atomic agent is a *mode*. A mode is basically a hierarchical state-machine, that is, a mode can have sub-modes and transitions connecting them. Variables can be declared locally inside any mode with standard scoping rules for visibility. Modes can be connected to each other only via well-defined entry and exit points. We allow *sharing* of modes so that the same mode

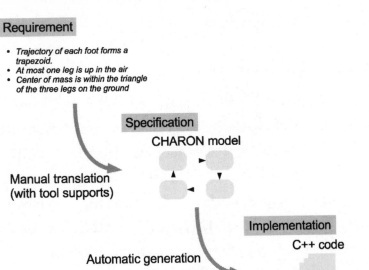

Figure 2: Requirement, modeling, and implementation of the walking process of a four-legged robot

definition can be instantiated in multiple contexts. Discrete updates in CHARON are specified by *guarded actions* labeling transitions connecting the modes. Some of the variables in CHARON can be declared *analog*, and they flow continuously during continuous updates that model passage of time. The evolution of analog variables can be constrained in three ways: differential constraints, algebraic constraints, and invariants which limit the allowed durations of flows. CHARON supports compositional trace semantics for both modes and agents [8]. For analysis it supports simulation, and formal verification of safety properties for a restricted subset (where discrete state is finite, and continuous dynamics is linear) [4].

To demonstrate our framework, we use a case study of the walking process of a four-legged robot. The requirement of the system can be informally described as follows: (1) the control objective for each leg is to ensure that the leg moves in such a way that the trajectory of the paw (i.e., the end of the knee joint) forms a trapezoid; (2) the global control objective is to ensure that only one leg is up in the air at any moment; and (3) the center of mass for the robot is within the triangle given by the three legs on the ground.

Such requirements can be formally specified by using the CHARON language. First, the trajectory of the paw can be specified by using a set of differential equations switched upon some conditions over the position of the paw. Second, a shared variable can be used to control which leg can be lifted next. Third, the constraint of the center of mass for the robot can be specified as the invariant over the position of the paws.

Once the CHARON specification is done, model checking techniques can be applied to ensure if it satisfies the requirement. Finally, the CHARON specification can be converted into an implementation automatically through the code generation tool.

3.1.1   Model Checking of Hybrid Systems

Inspired by the success of model checking in hardware verification and protocol analysis [20, 31], there has been increasing research on developing algorithms and tools for automated verification of hybrid (mixed discrete-continuous) models of embedded controllers [2, 7, 14, 17, 23, 29, 40]. Model checking requires the computation of the set of reachable states of a model, and in presence of continuous dynamics, this is typically undecidable. Consequently, contemporary tools for model checking of hybrid systems, such as CHECKMATE [17] and d/dt [14], focus on hybrid systems with linear dynamics, and approximate the set of reachable states by polyhedra.

We have shown that effectiveness of the reachability computation techniques for hybrid systems can be enhanced using predicate abstraction [5]. Predicate abstraction is a powerful technique for extracting finite-state models from complex, potentially infinite state, discrete systems (see, for instance, [22, 49]), and tools such as Bandera [21], SLAM [15], and Feaver [32] have successfully used it for analysis of C or Java programs. The input to our verification tool consists of the concrete system modeled in CHARON, the safety property to be verified, and a finite set of predicates over system variables to be used for abstraction. For the sake of efficiency, we require that all invariants, switching guards, and discrete updates of the hybrid model are specified by linear expressions, the continuous dynamics is linear, possibly with bounded input, and the property as well as the abstraction predicates are linear. An abstract state is a valid combination of truth values to the predicates, and thus, corresponds to a polyhedral set of the concrete state-space. The verifier performs an on-the-fly search of the abstract system by symbolic manipulation of polyhedra.

The core of the verifier is the computation of the transitions between abstract states that capture both discrete and continuous dynamics of the original system. Computing discrete successors is relatively straightforward, and involves computing weakest preconditions, and checking non-emptiness of intersection of polyhedral sets. For computing continuous successors of an abstract state A, we use a strategy inspired by the techniques used in CHECKMATE and d/dt. The basic strategy computes the polyhedral slices of states reachable at fixed times $r, 2r, 3r, \ldots$ for a suitably chosen r, and then, takes convex-hull of all these polyhedra to over-approximate the set of all states reachable from A. However, while tools such as CHECKMATE and d/dt are designed to compute a "good" approximation of the continuous successors of A, we are interested in testing if this set intersects with a new abstract state, and this permits many optimizations. Postulating the verification problem for hybrid systems as a search problem in the abstract system has many benefits compared to the traditional approach of computing approximations of reachable sets of hybrid systems, and our experiments indicate significant improvements in time and space requirements.

The success of our scheme crucially depends on the choice of the predicates used for abstraction.

We have proposed techniques for identifying such predicates automatically by analyzing spurious counter-examples generated by the search in the abstract state-space. Counter-example guided refinement of abstractions has been used in multiple contexts before, for instance, to identify the relevant timing constraints in verification of timed automata [9], to identify the relevant boolean predicates in verification of C programs [15], and to identify the relevant variables in symbolic model checking [19]. In a recent paper, we present the basic techniques for analyzing counter-examples, techniques for discovering new predicates that will rule out spurious counter-examples, optimizations of these techniques, implementation of these in our verifier, and case studies demonstrating the promise of the approach [6].

The abstract counter-example consists of a sequence of abstract states leading from an initial state to a state violating the property. The analysis problem is to check if the corresponding sequence of modes and discrete switches can be traversed in the concrete system. We perform a forward search from the initial abstract state following the given counter-example in the abstract state space. The analysis relies on techniques for polyhedral approximations of the reachable sets under continuous dynamics. To speed up the feasibility analysis, we have also implemented a local test that checks for feasibility of pair-wise transitions, and this proves to be effective in many cases. If the counter-example is found to be infeasible, then we wish to identify one or more new predicates that would rule out this sequence in the refined abstract space. This reduces to the problem of finding one or more predicates that *separate* two sets of polyhedra. We present a greedy strategy for identifying the separating predicates. After discovering new predicates, we include these to the set of predicates used before, and rerun the search in the refined abstract state space defined by the enriched predicate set.

We have demonstrated the feasibility of our approach using three case studies. The first one involves verification of a parametric version of Fischer's protocol for timing-based mutual exclusion. The second one involves analysis of a thermostat model. The third case study analyses a model of an adaptive cruise controller.

3.2 End-to-end design and analysis of embedded systems

AIRES (Automatic Integration of Reusable Embedded Software) [25] is a software toolkit to assist in high-level design and analysis of embedded/real-time systems. In AIRES application software and hardware platforms are modeled in the Generic Modeling Environment (GME) developed by Vanderbilt University. AIRES uses the models in the GME environment and provides tools to import new models into GME, allocate application software to the hardware platform, help designers make design decisions such as task formation and priority assignment, and perform a schedulability analysis.

The software model in AIRES, called the structural model, is a directed acyclic graph where each node in the graph is a software component and each link represents interactions between different components. An individual component performs some functionality for the application and can be basically viewed as a function call. Each component has characteristics associated with it, including worst-case execution time, minimum rate of invocation (also called the period), deadline, and the amount of memory that is needed for the code and during its execution. A component can be triggered to execute by either a timer, an outside event, or by the completion of another component. It is assumed that a component is triggered at either a fixed frequency, or there is some bounded amount of time between consecutive invocations of the component which is defined by its minimum rate of invocation. Furthermore, if the task is triggered by the completion of another task, then it will inherit the minimum rate of invocation from that task.

A link in the structural model is used to signify either data passing from one component to another, one component triggering the execution of another, or both. Links can be defined to be asynchronous or synchronous. An asynchronous link will send data to the destination component once the source component has completed and the destination component will use this information the next time that it executes. A synchronous link will send data to the destination component once the source component has completed, and once this data has been received the destination component will use this information and begin execution. A synchronous link may set the data size to be zero in which case the link is simply used to tell the destination component to begin execution. However, if the data size is set to zero for an asynchronous task then the link has no meaning. Currently, there are constraints that models do not contain synchronous loops (e.g., a component A has a synchronous connection both to and from component B) since this appears as an infinite loop. Furthermore, a component may only have one input synchronous connection since problems may arise if a component has more than one input synchronous connection where the source components have different periods.

The hardware model in AIRES, called the platform model, consists of one or more processors connected by a single bus. Each processor has an OS associated with it along with certain resource capacity and timing characteristics. The resource capacity characteristics include: how much the processor can be utilized, the amount of memory that each processor can have, and the memory unit size for the processor. The bus connecting each of the processors similarly has a bit transfer rate and a utilization capacity associated with it.

The structural model can either be manually created in GME, or it can be imported from a Simulink model. To translate a Simulink model into AIRES, the user specifies which subsystems will be translated into software components through a naming convention. This convention is specified by the user and is defined by a prefix and/or suffix in the subsystems name. Subsystems that match this name are called atomic level models or atomic level functions. The signals that are passed from atomic level models can be put into buses, multiplexers, goto blocks or from blocks in the Simulink model. However, these are not present in AIRES, so the model needs to be first translated into an equivalent model by replacing these blocks with the equivalent connections without these blocks. Finally, models in Simulink can have a number of different levels of hierarchy which are disallowed in AIRES, and hence, the Simulink model needs to be translated into an equivalent flattened one. Once this translation is done, the Simulink model can be directly translated into the AIRES structural model.

The first step in translating the structural model into a system that is known to meet all of its timing and resource constraints [39] is component allocation [51]. Component allocation is to map each component in the structural model to one of the processors in the platform model. This needs to be done in such a way that the timing analysis may be done easily. Furthermore, if resource constraints are provided (e.g., processor utilization bound, bus utilization bound, processor memory bound, etc.) it is also necessary to make sure that the allocation does not violate these constraints. There are different allocation algorithms, each of which has a different strategy or goal in mind. There are also "Second Order Mapping" options where the algorithm will have a primary goal defined by the "First Order Mapping" algorithm, but will also try to achieve the goal defined by the Second Order Mapping. Note that these goals may create conflicts, e.g. minimizing the amount of traffic across the bus and balancing the loads of the processors.

The second step is to group the components together to form OS processes or tasks. Tasks can be formed between components that (1) are allocated to the same CPU, (2) have the same period, and (3) will not form a dependency loop if they are grouped together. There is a performance tradeoff between forming large tasks (tasks containing many components) and forming small tasks (tasks containing a few components). If large tasks are formed then there are fewer context switches reducing overhead. However, if smaller tasks are used then there is finer granularity in communicating messages and assigning task priorities, both of which may reduce the overall response times. AIRES takes an aggressive approach, and as long as a group of components satisfy the above three conditions, a task is formed with these components.

The third step in translating the structural model into a system that is known to meet all of its timing and resource constraints is to assign priority to each task [46]. After this is done, the resulting model is called the runtime model and the timing analysis can be performed. Different algorithms are given for assigning priorities including rate-monotonic (RM), deadline monotonic (DM), latest completion time (LCT), and user-defined priority assignment. Deadline monotonic can be run using the given deadlines or a deadline distribution algorithm can be run where the deadlines given by this algorithm are used for priority assignment.

Once the runtime model has been generated, the timing analysis can be run to determine if each task meets its timing constraints. The schedulability test begins by assigning directed concurrent links between tasks that have potential to preempt each other (i.e., the source task of the link may preempt the destination task). These links are formed between tasks that (1) are on the same processor, (2) one task does not trigger (directly or indirectly) the other, and (3) the source task has higher priority than the destination task. The schedulability test will begin by scheduling an input task and will then schedule each task that it triggers after it completes, and each of these tasks will schedule their successors after they complete, etc. When a task is being scheduled it looks at the tasks that could possibly preempt it and the number of times that these tasks have preempted the task's predecessors to determine the number of times that the task being scheduled could be preempted in the worst case. Furthermore, when a message is sent across the network, the message is modeled as a task and the network is modeled as a CPU. This accurately models message scheduling and the overhead incurred by sending messages from one CPU to another.

If the timing analysis is successful then the system will be able to meet all of its timing and resource constraints. However, if the analysis yields a timing failure then AIRES can initiate a design refinement. Design refinement is a way to go back to previous stages and undo previous decisions to make the system schedulable. Currently, design refinement is under development, and it is only implemented for priority assignment. However, in the long run we would like to provide design refinement for task/component allocation and task formation. In priority refinement a modified simulated annealing algorithm is used to reassign priorities in an attempt to reduce the overall time by which tasks miss their deadlines. If at any time the design refinement algorithm finds a successful system then algorithm terminates.

3.3 Implementation validation with respect to models

There is a gap between design and implementation since the implementation contains a lot more details than the design. In particular, there is no guarantee that an implementation is consistent with a design model unless the implementation is derived automatically from the design model. Since it is not yet possible to completely generate an implementation from design, it is important to ensure the implementation is consistent with the design model. There are two ways to use a design model to validate an implementation: model-based testing and model-based run-time monitoring and checking. The former is to generate a test suite from a design model and then apply tests to an implementation. The latter is to observe the execution of a running system and ensure that its run-time behavior is consistent with those described in the design specification, and is also known as run-time verification.

Synthesis of interfaces for Java classes. Model-based development emphasizes components with clearly specified APIs. In current practice, components such as Java library classes have a clearly specified static interface that consists of all the (public) methods, along with the types of input parameters and returned values, that the component supports. Usually, there are constraints on the sequencing of method calls for the intended use of the component. For example, for a file system, the method *open* should be invoked before the method *read*, without an intervening call to *close*. While such interfaces can be made precise using, for instance, regular expressions as types, these kinds of precise specifications are typically missing. Such dynamic interfaces for components can help applications programmers, and can possibly be used by program analysis tools to check automatically whether the component is being correctly invoked. In the JIST project, we are developing a rigorous and automated approach to extracting dynamic interfaces from existing code for Java classes [1].

Formally, an *interface I* for a Java class C maps a history of method calls and returned values to the methods that can be invoked after this history. Given a set S of *safe* valuations for the class variables, we say that the interface I is *correct* with respect to the requirement S if invoking any of the methods allowed by I maintains the state of C within S. Typically, the safe set will correspond to requirements such as "the exception E is never raised," or "an error value is never returned." Different applications can employ the same class with different requirements, and different interfaces can be correct for different requirements. There is a natural notion of the *most permissive* interface for a given class C with respect to a given requirement S. Needless to say, typical decision problems concerning this most permissive interface are undecidable. Our tool algorithmically constructs a correct, but not necessarily most permissive, interface that can be represented as a finite-state machine.

The first step of our solution employs *predicate abstraction*, a powerful and popular technique for extracting finite-state models from complex and potentially infinite state models [22, 49]. Given a (concrete) Java class C and a finite set $\mathcal{P}$ of boolean predicates over the class variables, the corresponding abstract class $A(C, \mathcal{P})$ has the same set of methods as C, but the input parameters, returned values, and the abstract states are (finitely many) valid combinations of truth values to the boolean predicates. The abstract transition relation over-approximates the concrete one in the standard way. As a result, the abstract class $A(C, \mathcal{P})$ is nondeterministic: whenever one of its methods is called, there are multiple possible executions that can result in different abstract states and returned values. The interface computation for the abstract class is then formulated as a two-player partial information game. Player 0, the user of the class, chooses to invoke one of the methods. Player 1, the abstract class, chooses a corresponding possible execution through the abstract state-transition graph which results in an abstract return value. A strategy for player 0 is *winning* if the game always stays within the abstract states that satisfy the requirement S. A winning strategy for player 0 in this game is a correct interface for the original class C with respect to the requirement S.

The second step of our solution corresponds to computing a winning strategy in the two-player partial information game over the abstract class $A(C, \mathcal{P})$ with respect to the safety requirement.

From the classical results concerning partial information safety games, it follows that the most general winning strategy in this game can be represented by a deterministic finite-state automaton (DFA) I of size exponential in the number of states of $A(C, \mathcal{P})$ (which, in turn, is exponential in the number of predicates used for abstraction). We compute the strategy automaton using the L^* algorithm for learning a regular language using membership and equivalence queries [13]. We use an existing BDD-based symbolic model checker NuSMV [18] to answer the queries. The membership query is to test whether all runs of the abstract class $A(C, \mathcal{P})$ corresponding to a given sequence of method calls and returned values, stay within the safe set S, and can be posed as an invariant verification problem for the composed model. The equivalence test is to check whether the current strategy automaton J has the same language as the most general winning strategy I for $A(C, \mathcal{P})$ with respect to S. To test $L(I) = L(J)$, we first use the subset query $L(J) \subseteq L(I)$ (i.e., is J safe?). This test is also an invariant verification problem, and if the test fails, NuSMV returns a counter-example that can be used by the learning algorithm to update J. We also approximate the superset query $L(J) \supseteq L(I)$ (i.e., is J maximal?) using membership queries. In summary, our approach terminates with a deterministic finite-state automaton J such that (1) J is the minimal DFA accepting $L(J)$, (2) the number of model checking queries is polynomial in the size of J, (3) J is correct for $A(C, \mathcal{P})$ with respect to S, and (4) either J is declared to be the most permissive interface for $A(C, \mathcal{P})$, or J is declared to be approximate (and in this case, the most permissive interface is guaranteed to have 2 more states than J).

The solution is implemented in a prototype tool called *JIST, the Java Interface Synthesis Tool.* The JIST abstractor processes *Jimple,* an intermediate representation of Java byte code used by the Soot framework [50]. Given an input Jimple class, and a set of predicates, the abstractor transforms the input class line by line producing a class with only boolean (or enumerated) variables. Currently, only a subset of Jimple is supported and only those abstraction predicates that compare a variable to a constant are handled. The transformed class then is rewritten to a symbolic representation compatible with the input format of the model checker NuSMV. The JIST synthesizer implements the L^* learning algorithm via CTL model checking queries on this symbolic representation using the model checker NuSMV.

The tool has been applied on a variety of libarary classes in Java2SDK. In each case, the initial class file has a few (less than 20) methods with about a hundred lines of code. As a requirement, we choose a particular exception, and as abstraction predicates, we include all conditions of the form "a variable is equal to a constant" that are checked before raising the exception. After the transformations, the input to the symbolic model checker has 20–50 boolean variables. The interface is computed by the synthesizer within a few minutes. More importantly, the interfaces computed by the tool are the maximally permissive interfaces, and in practice, seem to capture useful information.

4 Prototyping and Code Generation

In this section, we are concerned with the ultimate product of the development process: the implementation of the system. We consider the use of models as early prototypes of the system and their use in the rigorous development of the final system implementation.

A model-based approach is an emerging paradigm for developing robust software, and has been the focus of increasing research effort. Models are used during the design phase to ensure systems under consideration have desired properties. Benefits of high-level modeling can be significantly improved if models can be used for code generation as well as the validation of implementation.

We have developed a code generation tool for hybrid systems [10, 37, 35, 12]. Our code generation tool accepts hybrid systems specifications written in CHARON and produces C++ code. The generated code can be mapped to periodic tasks of the target platform to approximate the continuous-time semantics of the hybrid model.

Intuitively, the behavior of the generated C++ code becomes closer to the model as the period becomes smaller, although small errors due to the discreteness of the code cannot be entirely eliminated in general. In a purely continuous model, such errors may be acceptable since the model is generally designed to be robust to a certain degree of errors (e.g., noise in sensored data).

In hybrid systems, however, the consequence of such a straightforward approximation may be rather significant. First, small errors in the continuous state may cause an erroneous discrete transition, leading to a state that is otherwise not reachable. This renders the safety property proven in the model level no longer guaranteed. Second, discrete transitions are performed only at some time instances depending on the sampling rates, and thus some urgent transition that must be taken immediately to satisfy the invariant may be missed. Even worse, the violation of the invariant may remain undetected. Third, if the code is decomposed into multiple tasks that are executed concurrently, the progress of each component may become different, giving rise to another source of errors. In particular, if the tasks are executed at different rates, it is not possible to enforce the same progress for different tasks regardless of scheduling.

To address the discrepancy between the model and the generated code formally, we define a series of formal models that are derived from the original hybrid model and gradually become closer to the generated code as the above mentioned concerns are considered.

Discretized Hybrid Systems. Given that the code is executed in a discrete fashion, the correctness of generated code can be relaxed as follows: Given a hybrid model A and a discrete time domain $T = \{t_i | t_i \in \Re, i = 0, 1, 2, \ldots, t_i < t_{i+1}\}$, we define the discrete-time abstraction of A over T, denoted by A/T, as an extended finite state machine with an equivalent set of variables x_T and discrete states P_T, and $x_T(t_{i+1}) = x_T(t_i) + \int_{t_i}^{t_{i+1}} f_p(x_T) \, dt$. We say that A/T abstracts A, if $x_T(t) = x(t)$ for all $t \in T$, provided that A satisfies $x(t') \in I(p_i)$ for all $t' \in [t_i, t_{i+1}]$ for all $i \geq 0$. Then, an implementation $\text{prog}(A/T)$ of A/T, is a program that computes $x(t_{i+1})$ using $\text{prog}(f_p)$ that numerically solves the equation $x(t_{i+1}) = x(t_i) + \int_{t_i}^{t_{i+1}} f_p(x)\, dt$, and determines the next discrete state p', on or before time t_{i+1}.

We say that $\text{prog}(A/T)$ is a precise implementation of A/T if the following two requirements are met: (1) there is a precise algorithm $\text{prog}(f_p)$ to solve $\int_{t_i}^{t_{i+1}} f_p(x)\, dt$, and (2) the execution of the algorithm and decision of the next discrete state can be done within the time constraint $(t_{i+1} - t_i)$. The latter requirement is a classic real-time computing problem. For the special case of $t_{i+1} - t_i = h$ for all $i \geq 0$, $\text{prog}(A/T)$ can easily be mapped to a periodic task of real-time operating systems with a period h. On the other hand, the former requirement can be satisfied only for a limited class of differential equations (e.g., zero-order differential equations) and a sampling rate carefully selected to avoid floating-point errors. Thus, there still exists a gap from the code.

Sequential Hybrid Systems. To eliminate behaviors that are not possible in the original hybrid system model, but can occur during execution due to numerical computation errors, we have developed a technique, called Instrumented Hybrid Automata (IHA). IHA allows one to contract intervals denoted by invariants and transition guards so that their evaluations are sound even with numerical computation errors [16]. The current approach is to determine the static worst-case bound and use for all the states. It is then possible to prove that erroneous discrete transitions due to numerical errors are prevented. However, a maximum error bound that is evaluated too conservatively may exclude possibly valid behaviors, and lead to a deadlock in the worst case. So, we plan to extend the approach as follows. First, instead of using a single global error bound β, it should be possible to instrument guards and invariants based on position-specific bound β_p for each position p. Furthermore, it may even be possible to get a tighter β_p for each position p if it determined at run-time. Second, if we are given a bound on the largest allowable local error, the bound can be used to determine the smallest k-th RK method that guarantees the bound.

Communicating Hybrid Systems. When a model consists of a set of communicating hybrid systems, it is natural to map code generated from different components to concurrent tasks. Then, code generation needs to consider issues such as synchronization between tasks and different sampling rates for components. For example, given a composite hybrid model $A = A_1 \| A_2 \| \dots \| A_n$, $\text{prog}(A/T)$ would consist of concurrent programs $\text{prog}(A_1/T), \text{prog}(A_2/T), \dots, \text{prog}(A_n/T)$ such that each program $\text{prog}(A_l/T)$ roughly follows the following steps: (1) execute a numerical method to solve $x_{A_l}(t_{i+1}) = x_{A_l}(t_i) + \int_{t_i}^{t_{i+1}} f_{p_{A_l}}(x_{A_l})\, dt$ where x_{A_l} is a vector of variables with dynamics constrained by A_l, (2) wait for A_k for all $k \neq l$ to finish computation of $x_{A_k}(t_{i+1})$, and (3) decide on the next discrete state. This implies that components are executing at the same rate. Such restriction may be quite costly if the programs are executed in a distributed system where communication is an expensive operation. However, if the concurrent tasks execute at different rates, the relationship between the model and the code is not obvious. For example, modeling tools, such as SIMULINK, support code generation with different sampling rates (assuming they are harmonic) for different components of a single model to improve the CPU utilization, but there does not seem to be any formal semantics relationship between the implementation and the model.

We define a formal model for communicating hybrid systems that allows each of which being executed at different rates, but still guarantee that their behaviors are the ones allowed by the original model. Note that, in general, a set of concurrent programs, $\text{prog}(A_1/T_1), \text{prog}(A_2/T_2), \ldots, \text{prog}(A_n/T_n)$ for $A = A_1 \| A_2 \| \ldots \| A_n$, may not implement A/T precisely for any T if $T_k \neq T_l$ for some k, l. The reason is that, to evaluate a guard set $G(p, p')$ of A_l at time t, valuation $x_k(t)$ should be available for all $1 \leq k \leq n$, which is true only when $T_1 = T_2 = \ldots = T_n$. The evaluation of guards based on valuations from different time instances may lead to an erroneous discrete transition that is not allowed in the original hybrid model. We call this type of error *synchronization error*. For example, suppose a hybrid model consisting of two variables x_1, x_2 and code generated is such that the two variables are updated at different rates. Assume further that, at time t, the generated code has valuation $x_1(t)$ (i.e., x_1 at time t), but only valuation $x_2(t')$ at time $t' < t$ is available for x_2. If $(x_1(t), x_2(t')) \in G((p, p'))$ for some p', where p is the discrete state at time t, then the generated code may take the transition (p, p') since it *appears* to be enabled. However, if $x(t) = (x_1(t), x_2(t)) \notin G((p, p'))$ in the original hybrid model, then the transition should not be taken at time t. Here, the generated code is not consistent to the model due to a synchronization error.

We apply the same idea used in IHA to prevent the synchronization error. That is, the maximum asynchrony can be determined from the worst case schedule of the components. Then the maximum asynchrony can be projected to the error bound by considering the dynamics. The resulting error bound can be used to construct IHA to prevent erroneous discrete transitions.

Figure 3 shows the overall approach of our framework. We start with communicating hybrid automata defined in the continuous time domain. The continuous model is transformed to *discretized communicating hybrid automata* by projecting to a discrete time domain. The states of discretized communicating hybrid automata are defined only at time instances belonging to the given time domain. The semantics of discretized communicating hybrid automata are defined to generate exact snapshots of communicating hybrid automata in a discrete fashion; that is, they are equivalent to those of the original communicating hybrid automata at the same discrete time instances. Note that the discrete time domain is shared by all the components of discrete communicating hybrid automata. That is, the components are assumed to be synchronized at every time instance of the discrete time domain. To relax this constraint, we have defined *Instrumented Communicating Hybrid Automata* that allows heterogeneous discrete time domains between components [35]. The states of instrumented communicating hybrid automata are defined at the time instances belonging to the

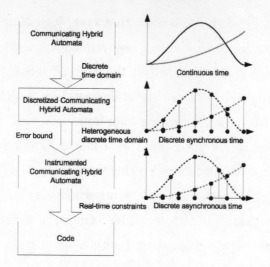

Figure 3: Steps in Code Generation from Hybrid System Models

union of all the discrete time domains of the components. It is then possible to show that, for every trace of discrete transitions of instrumented communicating hybrid automata, there exists an equivalent trace of discrete transitions in the original communicating hybrid automata.

5   Model-Driven Test Generation

Testing is the most widely used validation technique in practice. Although testing cannot provide an absolute guarantee on correctness as it is possible with formal verification, a disciplined use of testing can greatly increase the effectiveness of system validation, especially when performed by suitable tools. Testing does not try to exercise all possible behaviors of the system. Instead, the testing process observes the execution of the systems on a number of representative test cases. To ensure that the system is thoroughly explored during testing, careful selection of test cases should ensure that, on the one hand, no important behaviors are omitted and, on the other hand, execution of the selected use cases does not take unnecessarily long. We can improve the rigor of testing-based validation by using system models as the source of test cases. For embedded systems, testing is usually performed in a controlled environment; therefore, the most natural medium for test generation is a model that captures the expected behavior of the environment as well as the prescribed behavior of the implementation. Our approach uses *extended finite state machines* (EFSMs) as the modeling language. EFSMs are finite state machines extended with data variables that can be assigned new values when a transition is taken. Expressions over the data variables can then be used to specify when a transition can be taken.

Coverage criteria are used to decide when we have enough test cases. A wide variety of coverage criteria have been introduced in the literature and applied in practice. We consider several commonly used coverage criteria based on control flow and data flow in the system. Control coverage criteria such as statement and transition coverage require that every node (resp. transition) is visited by some execution of a test case. Data flow-based coverage criteria aim to capture dependencies between variables in the program. If one variable can affect the value of another variable, then the effect of every assignement to the first variable of every use of the variable has to be tested by some test case.

We show in [33] that the problem of test generation from EFSMs based on control flow and data flow oriented coverage criteria can be formulated as a model checking problem. Given a system model and a temporal logic formula, model checking establishes whether the model satisfies the formula. If so, model checkers are capable of supplying a witness that explains the success of the formula. Conversely, if the model fails to satisfy the formula, a counterexample is produced. In our approach, each coverage criterion is associated with a set of temporal logic formulas and the problem of test generation satisfying the criterion is reduced to the problem of finding witnesses for every formula in the set with respect to a given EFSM. The capability of model checkers to construct witnesses and counterexamples allows test generation to be automatic. The problem is further generalized in [34].

6 Run-Time Verification of Embedded Systems

Run-time verification is a novel assurance technology for computer-based systems that has gained significant attention in recent years. The underlying premise of the run-time verification approach is that correctness of a system cannot be fully guaranteed by design-time methods. On the one hand, complexity of real-world systems will always exceed capabilities of analysis tools. On the other hand, design-time analysis is usually applied to system models, and there is always a possibility of a mismatch between the system model and its implementation. Unpredictable environments make design-time analysis even more complex for embedded systems.

Run-time verification offers the possibility of checking the system implementation that is operating on real inputs from its environment. This eliminates all effects of model mismatches, since no model is involved in the analysis process. Several methodologies for run-time verification have emerged recently, most notably [24, 28, 38]. Over several years, we have developed a run-time verification architecture called MaC and defined a property specification language MEDL for use in MaC [38]. Most of these approaches, including MaC, target single-processor systems and may not be suitable, in their present form, for checking of networked embedded systems. Our current research tries to overcome this deficiency. When checking a distributed system, a centralized checking approach is not feasible because it will overload the network, and the checker will necessarily be a bottleneck. At the same time, fully distributed checkers tend to be very hard to design. This is because user-specified properties are usually specified in the network-oblivious, end-to-end fashion. Decomposing such a monolithic property into several properties that can be locally checked and collectively guarantee the global property is a provably hard problem [41]. We are taking the middle ground between fully centralized and fully distributed approaches. We notice that the properies are internally evaluated over tree-like data structures, and most of computation is done close to the leaves. We then use the structure of these trees to decompose them in such a way that low levels of the tree are evaluated locally at the system nodes, and the root of the structure, along with a few high levels are evaluated centrally, which does not require frequent communication between the system nodes and the checker node.

A major concern for run-time verification of embedded systems is monitoring overhead. There are two main components to the run-time verification overhead. One is due to the computation needed to perform checking, while the other relates to instrumentation. Most run-time verification approaches rely on instrumentation of the system code to extract observations. Tight real-time constraints found in some embedded systems may not allow for extensive instrumentation. The overhead of instrumentation can make the system violate its timing constraints or even make it unschedulable. The challenge is to reliably predict the effect of run-time verification on the system performance and find systematic ways to reduce overhead.

We have studied two approaches to reducing the overhead of monitoring checking. One approach, advocated in [38], aims at removing the computational overhead completely by running the checker on a separate platform, either dedicated to checking or shared with less constrained applications. While this approach has been shown effective in many situations, it may not always be suitable for checking embedded systems. On the one hand, the system may not have enough processing nodes to run the checker separately from the system. On the other hand, a separate checker involves communication between the system and the checker that increases checking latency and ties up communication resources. This may not be suitable for network-centric embedded systems. A new approach, targeted specifically at embedded systems aims at reduction of both checking overhead and instrumentation overhead by compiling the checker into a special automaton and tightly integrating it with the rest of the system. Checking overhead is now relatively small and highly predictable, since a known number of automaton steps is required for each observation, and each step is very inexpensive. On top of that, the tight integration of the checker into the system allows to reduce instrumentation overhead by turning of the instrumentations that are irrelevant for a particular checking state.

7   Conclusions

The goal of the HASTEN project is to develop a framework for integrated development and analysis of embedded systems, and to populate the framework with efficient methods and tools for the specification, analysis, development, testing, prototyping, simulation and monitoring of embedded software. This paper provides an overview of the overall framework as well as individual projects. These projects cover all stages of the embedded systems life cycle, from requirements formalization, through design specification, analysis, and model-based code generation implementation validation, to model-driven testing and post-deployment run-time verification.

The framework and individual tools have been evaluated in a number of case studies and spurred several technology transfer efforts. The methods and tools have been utilized on embedded systems projects at Boeing, Ford, Lockheed Martin Advanced Technology Labs, among others. To make presentation concrete, we describe two case studies from the domain of medical systems: one on an infusion pump system developed by the U.S. Army, and and the other on FDA blood bank management sytsem.

References

[1] R. Alur, P. Cerny, P. Madhusudan, and W. Nam. Synthesis of interface specifications for Java classes. 2005.

[2] R. Alur, C. Courcoubetis, N. Halbwachs, T.A. Henzinger, P. Ho, X. Nicollin, A. Olivero, J. Sifakis, and S. Yovine. The algorithmic analysis of hybrid systems. *Theoretical Computer Science*, 138:3–34, 1995.

[3] R. Alur, T. Dang, J. Esposito, R. Fierro, Y. Hur, F. Ivancic, V. Kumar, I. Lee, P. Mishra, G. Pappas, and O. Sokolsky. Hierarchical modeling and analysis of embedded systems. *Proceedings of the IEEE*, 90(1):11–28, January 2003.

[4] R. Alur, T. Dang, J. Esposito, Y. Hur, F. Ivancic, V. Kumar, I. Lee, P. Mishra, G. Pappas, and O. Sokolsky. Hierarchical modeling and analysis of embedded systems. *Proceedings of the IEEE*, 91(1), 2003.

[5] R. Alur, T. Dang, and F. Ivancic. Reachability analysis of hybrid systems via predicate abstraction. In *Hybrid Systems: Computation and Control, Fifth International Workshop*, LNCS 2289, pages 35–48, 2002.

[6] R. Alur, T. Dang, and F. Ivancic. Counter-example guided predicate abstraction of hybrid systems. In *TACAS'03: Ninth International Conference on Tools and Algorithms for the Construction and Analysis of Software*, LNCS 2619, pages 208–223, 2003.

[7] R. Alur and D.L. Dill. A theory of timed automata. *Theoretical Computer Science*, 126:183–235, 1994.

[8] R. Alur, R. Grosu, I. Lee, and O. Sokolsky. Compositional refinement of hierarchical hybrid systems. In *Hybrid Systems: Computation and Control, Fourth International Workshop*, LNCS 2034, pages 33–48, 2001.

[9] R. Alur, A. Itai, R.P. Kurshan, and M. Yannakakis. Timing verification by successive approximation. *Information and Computation*, 118(1):142–157, 1995.

[10] R. Alur, F. Ivančić, J. Kim, I. Lee, and O. Sokolsky. Generating embedded software from hierarchial hybrid models. In *Proceedings of ACM Conference on Languages, Compilers, and Tools for Embedded Systems (LCTES)*, 2003.

[11] Rajeev Alur, David Arney, Elsa L. Gunter, Insup Lee, Jaime Lee, Won Hong Nam, Frederick Pearce, Steve Van Albert, and Jiaxiang Zhou. Formal specifications and analysis of the computer assisted resuscitation algorithm (cara) infusion pump control system. *International Journal in Software Tools for Technology Transfer*, 4, 2004. (Special Issue on CARA).

[12] M. Anand, J.Kim, and I.Lee. Code generation from hybrid systems models for distributed embedded systems. In *Proceedings of the IEEE ISORC*, pages 166–173, 2005.

[13] D. Angluin. Learning regular sets from queries and counterexamples. *Information and Computation*, 75:87–106, 1987.

[14] E. Asarin, O. Bournez, T. Dang, and O. Maler. Approximate reachability analysis of piecewise-linear dynamical systems. In *Hybrid Systems: Computation and Control, Third International Workshop*, LNCS 1790, pages 21–31. 2000.

[15] T. Ball and S. Rajamani. Bebop: A symbolic model checker for boolean programs. In *SPIN 2000 Workshop on Model Checking of Software*, LNCS 1885, pages 113–130. Springer, 2000.

[16] J.-Y. Choi, Y. Hur, and I. Lee. IHA: Ensuring sound numerical simulation of hybrid automata. Technical Report MS-CIS-03-06, University of Pennsylvania, March 2003.

[17] A. Chutinan and B.K. Krogh. Verification of polyhedral-invariant hybrid automata using polygonal flow pipe approximations. In *Hybrid Systems: Computation and Control, Second International Workshop*, LNCS 1569, pages 76–90, 1999.

[18] A. Cimatti, E. Clarke, E. Giunchiglia, F. Giunchiglia, M. Pistore, M. Roveri, R. Sebastiani, and A. Tacchella. NuSMV Version 2: An OpenSource Tool for Symbolic Model Checking. In *Proc. International Conference on Computer-Aided Verification (CAV 2002)*, LNCS 2404. Springer, 2002.

[19] E. Clarke, O. Grumberg, S. Jha, Y. Lu, and H. Veith. Counterexample-guided abstraction refinement. In *Computer Aided Verification*, pages 154–169, 2000.

[20] E.M. Clarke and R.P. Kurshan. Computer-aided verification. *IEEE Spectrum*, 33(6):61–67, 1996.

[21] J.C. Corbett, M.B. Dwyer, J. Hatcliff, S. Laubach, C.S. Pasareanu, Robby, and H. Zheng. Bandera: Extracting finite-state models from Java source code. In *Proceedings of 22nd International Conference on Software Engineering*, pages 439–448. 2000.

[22] P. Cousot and R. Cousot. Abstract interpretation: a unified lattice model for static analysis of programs by construction or approximation of fixpoints. In *Proceedings of the 4th ACM Symposium on Principles of Programming Languages*, pages 238–252, 1977.

[23] C. Daws, A. Olivero, S. Tripakis, and S. Yovine. The tool KRONOS. In *Hybrid Systems III: Verification and Control*, LNCS 1066, pages 208–219. Springer-Verlag, 1996.

[24] D. Drusinsky. The Temporal Rover and the ATG Rover. In *Proceedings of $7^t h$ International SPIN Workshop, LNCS 1885*, volume 1885, pages 323–329, 2000.

[25] Z. Gu, S. Wang, S. Kodase, and K.G. Shin. An end-to-end tool chain for multi-view modeling and analysis of avionics mission computing software. In *Proceedings of 24th IEEE International Real-Time Systems Symposium (RTSS 2003)*, December 2003.

[26] E. L. Gunter and D. Peled. Path exploration tool. In *TACAS '99: Proceedings of the $5^t h$ International Conference on Tools and Algorithms for Construction and Analysis of Systems*, volume 1579 of *LNCS*, pages 405–419, 1999.

[27] D. Harel. Statecharts: A visual formalism for complex systems. *Science of Computer Programming*, 8:231–274, 1987.

[28] K. Havelund and G. Rosu. Monitoring Java programs with JavaPathExplorer. In *Proceedings of the Workshop on Runtime Verification*, volume 55 of *Electronic Notes in Theoretical Computer Science*. Elsevier Publishing, 2001.

[29] T.A. Henzinger, P. Ho, and H. Wong-Toi. HyTech: a model checker for hybrid systems. *Software Tools for Technology Transfer*, 1, 1997.

[30] G. Holzmann. *Design and Validation of Computer Protocols*. Prentice Hall, 1991.

[31] G.J. Holzmann. The model checker SPIN. *IEEE Transactions on Software Engineering*, 23(5):279–295, 1997.

[32] G.J. Holzmann and M.H. Smith. Automating software feature verification. *Bell Labs Technical Journal*, 5(2):72–87, 2000.

[33] H. Hong, I. Lee, O. Sokolsky, and H. Ural. A temporal logic based theory of test coverage and generation. In *Proceedings of the International Conference on Tools and Algorithms for Construction and Analysis of Systems (TACAS 02)*, April 2002.

[34] Hyoung Seok Hong, Sung Deok Cha, Insup Lee, Oleg Sokolsky, and Hasan Ural. Data Flow Testing as Model Checking. In *Proceedings of the Intl. Conference on Software Engineering*, May 2003.

[35] Y. Hur, J. Kim, I. Lee, and J.-Y. Choi. Sound code generation from communicating hybrid models. In *Proceedings of HSCC*, volume 2993 of *LNCS*, pages 432–447, 2004.

[36] Paul Jones. Problems with blood bank, personal communication, fda. June 2002.

[37] Jesung Kim and Insup Lee. Modular code generation from hybrid automata based on data dependency. In *Proceedings of RTAS*, 2003.

[38] M. Kim, S. Kannan, I. Lee, O. Sokolsky, and M. Viswanathan. Java-MaC: a run-time assurance approach for Java programs. *Formal Methods in Systems Design*, 24(2):129–155, March 2004.

[39] S. Kodase, S. Wang, and K.G. Shin. Transforming structural model to runtime model of embedded software with real-time constraints. In *Proceedings of Design, Automation and Test in Europe Conference (DATE 2003)*, 2003.

[40] K. Larsen, P. Pettersson, and W. Yi. Uppaal in a nutshell. *Springer International Journal of Software Tools for Technology Transfer*, 1, 1997.

[41] Kim Guldstrand Larsen and Liu Xinxin. Compositionality through an operational semantics of contexs. In *Proceedings of ICALP '90*. LNCS 443, 1990.

[42] I. Lee, P. Brémond-Grégoire, and R. Gerber. A Process Algebraic Approach to the Specification and Analysis of Resource-Bound Real-Time Systems. *Proceedings of the IEEE*, pages 158–171, Jan 1994.

[43] Insup Lee and David Arney. Formal model of the management of donors and units initially reactive for hbsag. RTG Internal Memo, 2003.

[44] C. Mazza, J. Fairclough, B. Melton, D. de Pablo, A. Scheffer, and R. Stevens. *Software Engineering Standards*. Prentice Hall, 1994.

[45] M. McDougall, R. Alur, and C.A. Gunter. A model-based approach to integrating security policies for embedded devices. In *EMSOFT '04: Proceedings of the fourth ACM international conference on Embedded software*, pages 211–219, 2004.

[46] J.R. Merrick, S. Wang, and K.G. Shin. Priority refinement for dependent tasks in large embedded real-time software. In *Proceedings of IEEE Real-Time and Embedded Technology and Application Symposium (RTAS 2005)*, March 2005.

[47] M.A. Ozols, K. A. Eastaughffe, and A. Cant. Dove: A tool for design oriented verification and evaluation. In *Proceedings of AMAST'97*, volume 1349 of *Lecture Notes in Computer Science*, pages 574–575, December 1997.

[48] Federal Register. 21 cfr part 610.40. http://www.access.gpo.gov/nara/cfr/index.html, 2003.

[49] S. Graf and H. Saidi. Construction of abstract state graphs with PVS. In *Proc. 9th International Conference on Computer Aided Verification (CAV'97)*, volume 1254, pages 72–83. Springer Verlag, 1997.

[50] R. Vallée-Rai, L. Hendren, V. Sundaresan, P. Lam, and P.Co. Soot – a Java optimization framework. In *Proc. of CASCON*, pages 125–135, 1999.

[51] S. Wang, J.R. Merrick, and K.G. Shin. Component allocation with multiple resource constraints for embedded real-time software design. In *Proceedings of IEEE Real-Time and Embedded Technology and Applications Symposium (RTAS 2004)*, pages 219–226, May 2004.

Hierarchical Modeling and Analysis of Embedded Systems

RAJEEV ALUR, MEMBER, IEEE, THAO DANG, JOEL ESPOSITO, YERANG HUR, FRANJO IVANČIĆ, STUDENT MEMBER, IEEE, VIJAY KUMAR, INSUP LEE, FELLOW, IEEE, PRADYUMNA MISHRA, GEORGE J. PAPPAS, MEMBER, IEEE, AND OLEG SOKOLSKY

Invited Paper

This paper describes the modeling language CHARON for modular design of interacting hybrid systems. The language allows specification of architectural as well as behavioral hierarchy and discrete as well as continuous activities. The modular structure of the language is not merely syntactic, but is exploited by analysis tools and is supported by a formal semantics with an accompanying compositional theory of refinement. We illustrate the benefits of CHARON in the design of embedded control software using examples from automated highways concerning vehicle coordination.

Keywords—*Embedded control systems, formal analysis tools, hybrid systems, modular design.*

I. INTRODUCTION

An embedded system typically consists of a collection of digital programs that interact with each other and with an analog environment. Examples of embedded systems include manufacturing controllers, automotive controllers, engine controllers, avionic systems, medical devices, microelectromechanical systems, and robots. As computing tasks performed by embedded devices become more sophisticated, the need for a sound discipline for writing embedded software becomes more apparent (cf. [1]). An embedded system consisting of sensors, actuators, plant, and control software is best viewed as a *hybrid* system. The relevance of hybrid modeling has been demonstrated in various applications such as coordinating robot systems [2], automobiles [3], aircraft [4],

and chemical process control systems [5]. A model-based design paradigm is particularly attractive because of its promise for greater design automation and formal guarantees of reliability.

Traditionally, control theory and related engineering disciplines have addressed the problem of designing robust control laws to ensure optimal performance of processes with continuous dynamics. This approach to system design largely ignores the problem of implementing control laws as a piece of software and issues related to concurrency and communication. Computer science and software engineering, on the other hand, have an entirely discrete view of the world, which abstracts from the physical characteristics of the environment to which the software is reacting and is typically unable to guarantee safety and/or performance of the embedded device as a whole. Hybrid modeling combines these two approaches and is natural for specification of embedded systems.

We have been developing a modeling language, CHARON, that is suitable for specification of interacting embedded systems as communicating agents. CHARON has been used in the modeling and analysis of a wide range of hybrid systems, such as automotive power trains, vehicle-to-vehicle control systems [6], biological cells [7], multiagent systems [8], [9], and infusion pump and inverted pendulum systems [10]. The two salient aspects of CHARON are that it supports modular specifications and that it has a well-defined formal semantics.

Hierarchical, Modular Modeling: Modern software design paradigms promote *hierarchy* as one of the key constructs for structuring complex specifications. They are concerned with two distinct notions of hierarchy. In *architectural hierarchy*, a system with a collection of communicating agents is constructed by parallel composition of atomic agents; in *behavioral hierarchy*, the behavior of an individual agent is described by hierarchical sequential composition. The former

Manuscript received December 20, 2001; revised August 31, 2002. This work was supported in part by the Defense Advanced Research Projects Agency under Model-Based Integrated Embedded Software Contract F33615-00-C-1707; in part by the Army Research Office under Contract DAAD19-01-1-0473; in part by the National Science Foundation under Grant CCR-9970925, Grant CCR-9988409, Grant CCR-0086147, Grant CISE-9703220, and Grant ITR CCR01-21431; and in part by the Office of Naval Research under Contract N00014-97-1-0505.

The authors are with the Department of Computer and Information Science, University of Pennsylvania, Philadelphia, PA 19104, USA.

Digital Object Identifier 10.1109/JPROC.2002.805817

Reprinted from *Proceedings of the IEEE*. Vol. 91, Issue 1. January 2003. 11–28.

297

hierarchy is present in almost all concurrency formalisms, and the latter, while present in all block-structured programming languages, was introduced for state-machine-based modeling in STATECHARTS [11]. CHARON supports both architectural and behavioral hierarchies.

Early formal models for hybrid systems include phase transition systems [12] and hybrid automata [13]. Although modularity in hybrid specifications has been addressed in languages such as hybrid input–output (I/O) automata [14], CHARON allows richer specifications. Discrete updates in CHARON are specified by *guarded actions* labeling transitions connecting the modes. Some of the variables in CHARON can be declared *analog*, and they flow continuously during continuous updates that model the passage of time. The evolution of analog variables can be constrained in three ways: *differential* constraints (e.g., by equations such as $\dot{x} = f(x, u)$), *algebraic* constraints (e.g., by equations such as $y = g(x, u)$), and *invariants* (e.g., $|x - y| \leq \varepsilon$) which limit the allowed durations of flows.

Compositional Semantics: Formal semantics leads to definitions of *semantic* equivalence (or refinement) of specifications based on their observable behaviors. *Compositional* here means that semantics of a component can be constructed from the semantics of its subcomponents. Such formal compositional semantics is a cornerstone of concurrency frameworks such as communicating sequential processes (CSP) [15] and the calculus of communicating systems (also referred to as CCS) [16], and is a prerequisite for developing modular reasoning principles such as compositional model checking and systematic design principles such as stepwise refinement.

Two aspects of CHARON make it difficult to adopt existing techniques. First, the global nature of time makes it challenging to define semantics of hybrid components in a modular fashion. Second, features such as group transitions, exceptions, and history retention supporting rich hierarchical specifications cause additional difficulties. The compositional semantics of CHARON supports observational trace semantics for both modes and agents [17]. The key result is that the set of traces of a mode can be constructed from the traces of its submodes. This result leads to a compositional notion of refinement for modes.

This paper is organized as follows. Section II gives a short overview of related work. In Section III, we present the features of the language CHARON, and in Section IV we describe the formal semantics and accompanying compositional refinement calculus, using examples from the automotive experimental platform of DARPA's MoBIES project. Section V gives an overview of ongoing research on formal analysis. We conclude in Section VI with a summary of the CHARON design toolkit.

II. BACKGROUND

Software Design Notations: Modern object-oriented design paradigms such as the Unified Modeling Language (UML) allow specification of the architecture and control at high levels of abstraction in a modular fashion and bear great promise as a solution to managing the complexity at all stages of the software design cycle [18]. Emerging tools such as RationalRose (available: www.rational.com) support modeling, simulation, and code generation and are becoming increasingly popular in domains such as automotive software and avionics.

Tool Support for Control System Design: Traditionally, control engineers have used tools for continuous differential equations such as MATLAB (available: www.mathworks.com) for modeling of the plant behavior, for deriving and optimizing control laws, and for validating functionality and performance of the model through analysis and simulation. Tools such as SIMULINK recently augmented the continuous modeling with state-machine-based modeling of discrete control.

Modeling Languages for Hybrid Systems: To benefit from object-oriented design, several languages that support object-oriented modeling of complex dynamical systems have been proposed. Omola [19], Dymola [20], and Modelica [21] provide noncausal models; that is, there is no notion of causality in the equations in the models. Those three have been used mostly for describing physical objects, whereas SHIFT [22] is more like a programming language and has been used extensively to specify automated vehicle highway systems. PTOLEMY II [23] supports the modeling, simulation, and design of concurrent systems. It incorporates a number of models of computation (such as synchronous/reactive systems, CSP, finite state machines, continuous time, etc) with semantics that allow domains to interoperate.

All the above languages were proposed for modeling and simulation purposes and have not been used for formal verification of systems. CHARON has compositional formal semantics required to reason about systems in a modular way while incorporating many features of the aforementioned languages. Two features that are not supported by CHARON are model inheritance and dynamic creation of model instances.

Model Checking: Inspired by the success of model checking in hardware verification and protocol analysis [24], [25], there has been increasing research on developing techniques for automated verification of hybrid (mixed discrete-continuous) models of embedded controllers [13], [26]–[29]. The state-of-the-art computational tools for model checking of hybrid systems are of two kinds. Tools such as KRONOS [30], UPPAAL [31], and HYTECH [32] limit the continuous dynamics to simple abstractions such as rectangular inclusions (e.g., $\dot{x} \in [1, 2]$) and compute the set of reachable states exactly and effectively by symbolic manipulation of linear inequalities. On the other hand, emerging tools such as CHECKMATE [33], d/dt [34], and level-sets method [35], [36] approximate the set of reachable states by polyhedra or ellipsoids [37] using optimization techniques. Even though these tools have been applied to interesting real-world examples after appropriate abstractions, scalability remains a challenge.

III. MODELING LANGUAGE

In CHARON, the building block for describing the system architecture is an *agent* that communicates with its environment by means of shared variables. The language supports the operations of *composition* of agents to model concurrency, *hiding* of variables to restrict sharing of information, and *instantiation* of agents to support reuse. The building block for describing flow of control inside an atomic agent is a *mode*. A mode is basically a hierarchical state machine; that is, a mode can have submodes and transitions connecting them. Variables can be declared locally inside any mode with standard scoping rules for visibility. Modes can be connected to each other only by well-defined entry and exit points. We allow *sharing* of modes so that the same mode definition can be instantiated in multiple contexts. To support *exceptions*, the language allows group transitions from default exit points that are applicable to all enclosing modes; to support *history retention*, the language allows default entry transitions that restore the local state within a mode from the most recent exit.

Case Study: Throughout this paper, we will use a recent case study to illustrate the modeling and analysis concepts within the proposed framework. The case study is based on the longitudinal control system for vehicles moving in an Intelligent Vehicle Highway System (IVHS) [38]. A detailed description of the system can be found in [39]. Before proceeding with the modeling of the problem, we present a brief informal description of the control system.

In the context of IVHS, vehicles travel in platoons; inside a platoon, all vehicles follow the leader. We consider a platoon i and its preceding platoon $(i - 1)$. Let v_i and a_i denote the velocity and acceleration, respectively, of the platoon i, and let d_i be its distance to the platoon $(i - 1)$. The most important task of a longitudinal controller for the leader car of each platoon i is to maintain the distance d_i equal to a safety distance $D_i = \lambda_a a_i + \lambda_v v_i + \lambda_p$; in the nominal operation, $\lambda_a = 0s^2$, $\lambda_v = 1s$ and $\lambda_p = 10m$. Other tasks the controller should perform are to track an optimal velocity and trajectories for certain maneuvers. Without going into details, the controller for the leader car of platoon i proposed in [39] consists of four control laws u, which are used in different regions of the state space. These regions are defined based on the values of the relative velocity $v_i^e = 100(v_{i-1} - v_i)/v_i$ and the error between the actual and the safe inter-platoon distances $e_i = d_i - D_i$. When v_i^e and e_i change from one region to another, the control law should change accordingly. One important *property* we want to verify is that a *collision between platoons never happens*, that is, $d_i > 0m$. To this end, we consider a system with four continuous variables (d_i, v_{i-1}, v_i, a_i). The dynamics of these variables are as follows:

$$\begin{cases} \dot{d}_i & = v_{i-1} - v_i \\ \dot{v}_{i-1} & = a_{i-1} \\ \dot{v}_i & = a_i \\ \dot{a}_i & = u \end{cases} \tag{1}$$

where u is the control. One can see that the dynamics of each platoon depends on the state of its preceding platoon. We consider a pair of platoons $(i - 1)$ and i and prove that the controller of the leader car of platoon i can guarantee that no collision happens regardless of the behavior of platoon

$(i-1)$. More precisely, the acceleration a_{i-1} of the platoon in front is treated as *uncertain input* with values in the interval $[a_{\min}, a_{\max}]$ where $a_{\min}$ and $a_{\max}$ are the maximal possible deceleration and acceleration.

A. Agents and Architectural Hierarchy

The architectural hierarchy of the above platoon control system is shown in Fig. 1. The agent PLATOON-i consists of two subagents, namely VELOCITY and CONTROLLER. The subagent CONTROLLER models the control laws and outputs the acceleration a_i of the platoon i. The subagent VELOCITY takes as input the variable acc and updates the variable vel of the platoon i. The agent PLATOON-$(i - 1)$, whose role is to model all possible behaviors of the platoon in front, outputs its own velocity (variable vel) to the agent PLATOON-i. In other words, the velocity (or acceleration) of the platoon $(i - 1)$ can be seen as *uncertain input* (or external disturbance) to the agent PLATOON-i.

Each agent has a well-defined interface consisting of its typed input and output variables, represented visually as blank and filled squares, respectively. The two variables vel of the agents PLATOON-$(i - 1)$ and PLATOON-i are inputs to the agent DISTANCE, which outputs the distance between the two platoons. The subagent CONTROLLER of PLATOON-i computes the desired acceleration a_i based on the inter-platoon distance and the velocity of the platoon in front.

Formally, an *agent*, $A = \langle TM, V, I \rangle$, consists of a set V of variables, a set I of initial states and a set TM of modes. The set V is partitioned into *local* variables V_l and *global* variables V_g; global variables are further partitioned into input and output variables. Type correct assignments of values to variables are called valuations and denoted Q_V. The set of initial states $I \subseteq Q_V$ specifies possible initializations of the variables of the agent. The modes, described in more detail below, collectively define the behavior of the agent. An *atomic* agent has a single top-level mode. *Composite* agents are constructed from other agents and have many top-level modes. For example, the behavior of the agent PLATOON-i is given by the top-level modes of its atomic subagents, VELOCITY and CONTROLLER.

Fig. 1 illustrates the three operations defined on agents. Agents can be *composed* in parallel with each other. The parallel agents execute concurrently and communicate through shared variables. To enable communication between agents, global variables are *renamed*. For example, variables vel of agents PLATOON-$(i - 1)$ and PLATOON-i are renamed into velFirst and velOther, respectively, so that the agent DISTANCE can read them without confusion. Finally, the communication between the vehicles can be *hidden* from the outside world. In our example, only the variable vel is the output of the PLATOON-i agent. The variable acc, used internally by the agent PLATOON-i, cannot be accessed from the outside.

B. Modes and Behavioral Hierarchy

Modes represent behavioral hierarchy in the system design. The behavior of each atomic agent is described by a

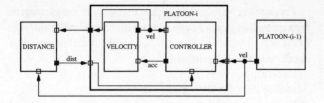

Fig. 1 The architectural hierarchy of the platoon controller.

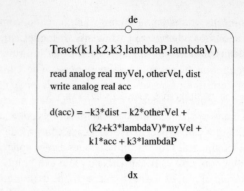

Fig. 2 Mode `Track`.

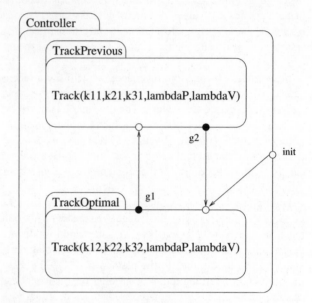

Fig. 3 Behavior of the agent `Controller`.

mode, which corresponds to a single thread of discrete control. Each mode has a well-defined data interface consisting of typed global variables used for sharing state information and also a well-defined control interface consisting of entry and exit points, through which discrete control enters and exits the mode. Entry and exit points are denoted as blank and filled circles, respectively. A top-level mode, which is activated when the corresponding agent comes into existence and is never deactivated, has a special entry point init.

At the lowest level of the behavioral hierarchy are atomic modes. They describe continuous behaviors. For example, Fig. 2 illustrates the behavior of the mode `Track`, which specifies a control law by means of a differential constraint that asserts the relationship between desired acceleration `acc` and input variables of the mode, representing the velocities of the platoon, the platoon in front of it and the distance between platoons. CHARON also supports algebraic constraints on variable values. In addition, an *invariant* may be used to specify how long the mode can remain active. Once an invariant is violated, the mode has to be exited by taking one of the transitions leaving the mode.

The values of `k1`, `k2`, `k3`, `lambdaP`, and `lambdaV` are parameters of the mode. The mode can be instantiated with different values for the parameters several times in the same model, yielding different control laws. This will be illustrated later.

Composite modes contain a number of submodes. During execution, a composite mode performs discrete transitions that connect its control points and control points of its submodes. For example, the behavior of the agent `Controller` is captured by the mode shown in Fig. 3. To avoid cluttering the figure, we omit the guards on mode transitions.

Formally, a mode $M = \langle SM, V, E, X, T, Cons \rangle$ consists of a set of submodes SM, a set of variables V, a set of *entry control points* E, a set of *exit control points* X, a set of transitions T, and a set of constraints $Cons$. As in agents, variables are partitioned into global and local variables. For the submodes of M, we require that each global variable of a submode is a variable (either global or local) of M. This induces a natural scoping rule for variables in a hierarchy of modes: a variable introduced as local in a mode is accessible in all its submodes but not in any other mode. Every mode has two distinguished control points, called default entry (de) and exit (dx) points. They are used to represent such high-level behavioral notions as interrupts and exceptions, which will be discussed in more detail in Section IV.

Constraints of a mode define continuous behavior of a mode in three ways. Continuous trajectories of a variable x

can be given by either an algebraic constraint A_x, which defines the set of admissible values for x in terms of values of other variables, or by a differential constraint D_x, which defines the admissible values for the first derivative of x with respect to time. Additionally, only those trajectories are allowed that satisfy the invariant of the mode, which is a predicate over the mode variables.

Transitions of a mode M can be classified as *entry transitions*, which connect an entry point of M with an entry point of one of its submodes; *exit transitions*, connecting exit points of submodes to exit points of M; and *internal transitions* that lead from an exit point of a submode to an entry point of another submode. In the example, the entry transition of `Controller` specifies that the mode starts in the TrackOptimal submode, which will be used to "catch up" with the platoon in front. There are no exit transitions, since it is a top-level mode and must execute forever. Every transition has a *guard*, which is a predicate over the valuations of mode variables that specifies when the transition can be executed. When a transition occurs, it executes a sequence of assignments, changing values of the mode variables. A transition that originates at a default exit point of a submode is called a group transition of that submode. A group transition can be executed to interrupt the execution of the submode.

In CHARON, transitions and constraints can refer to externally defined Java classes, thus allowing richer discrete and continuous specifications.

IV. FORMAL SEMANTICS AND COMPOSITIONAL REFINEMENT

In this section, we first define the operational semantics of modes and agents that makes the notion of executing a CHARON model precise and can be used, say, by a simulator. Second, we define observational semantics for modes and agents. The observational semantics hides the details about internal structure and retains only the information about inputs and outputs. Informally, the observational semantics consists of the static interface (such as the global variables and entry/exit points) and dynamic interface consisting of the *traces*, that is, sequences of updates to global variables. Third, for modularity, we show that our semantics is compositional. This means that the set of traces of a component can be defined from the set of traces of its subcomponents. Intuitively, this means that the observational semantics captures *all* the information that is needed to determine how a component interacts with its environment. Finally, we define a notion of refinement (or equivalence) for modes/agents. This allows us to relate different models of the same system. We can establish, for instance, that an abstract (simplified) version of a platoon refines a detailed version, and then analyze control of platoons using the abstract version instead of the detailed one, significantly simplifying analysis. The compositional rules about refinement form the basis for analysis in a system with multiple components, each with a simplified and a detailed model.

A. Formal Semantics of Modes

Intuitive Semantics: Before presenting the semantics formally, we give the intuition for mode executions. A mode can engage in discrete or continuous behavior. During an execution, the mode and its environment either take turns making discrete steps or take a continuous step together. Discrete and continuous steps of the mode alternate. During a continuous step, the mode follows a continuous trajectory that satisfies the constraints of the mode. In addition, the set of possible trajectories may be restricted by the environment of the mode. In particular, when the mode invariant is violated, the mode must terminate its continuous step and take one of its outgoing transitions. A discrete step of the mode is a finite sequence of discrete steps of the submodes and enabled transitions of the mode itself. A discrete step begins in the current state of the mode and ends when it reaches an exit point or when the mode decides to yield control to the environment and lets it make the choice of the next step. Technically, when the mode ends its discrete step in one of its submodes, it returns control to the environment via its default exit point. The closure construction, described later, ensures that the mode can yield control at appropriate moments and that the discrete control state of the mode is restored when the environment schedules the next discrete step.

Preemption: An execution of a mode can be preempted by a *group* transition. A group transition of a mode originates at the default exit of the mode. During any discrete step of the mode, control can be transferred to the default exit, and an enabled group transition can be selected. There is no priority between the transitions of a mode and its group transitions. When an execution of a mode is preempted, the control state of the mode is recorded in a special *history* variable, a new local variable that we introduce into every mode. Then, when the mode is entered through the default entry point next time, the control state of the mode is restored according to the history variable.

The History Variable and Active Submodes: To record the location of discrete control during executions, we introduce a new local variable h into each mode that has submodes. The history variable h of a mode M has the names of the submodes of M as values, or a special value ϵ that is used to denote that the mode is not active. A submode N of M is called *active* when the history variable of M has the value N.

Flows: To precisely define continuous trajectories of a mode, we introduce the notion of a *flow*. A flow for a set V of variables is a differentiable function f from a closed interval of nonnegative reals $[0, \delta]$ to Q_V. We refer to δ as the *duration* of the flow. We denote a set of flows for V as $\mathcal{F}_V$.

Syntactic Restrictions on Modes: To ensure that the semantics of a mode is well-defined, we impose several restrictions on mode structure. First, we assume that the set of differential and algebraic constraints in a mode always has a nonempty set of flows that satisfy them. This is needed to ensure that the set of behaviors of a mode is nonempty. Furthermore, we require that the mode cannot be blocked at any of its nondefault control points. This means that the disjunction of all guards originating from a control point evaluates to `true`.

State of a Mode: We define the state of a mode in terms of all variables of the mode and its submodes, including the local variables on all levels. We use V_* for the set of all variables. The local variables of a mode together with the local variables of the submodes are called the private variables; this set of variables is denoted as V_p.

The state of a mode M is a pair (c, s), where c is the location of discrete control in the mode and $s \in Q_{M.V_*}$. Whenever the mode has control, it resides in one of its control points, that is, $c \in M.C$. Given a state (c, s) of M, we refer to c as the *control state* of M and to s as the *data state* of M.

Closure of a Mode: Closure construction is a technical device to allow the mode to interrupt its execution and to maintain its history variable. Transitions of the mode are modified to update the history variable h after a transition is executed. Each entry or internal transition assigns the name of the destination mode to h, and exit transitions assign ϵ to h. In addition, default entry and exit transitions are added to the set of transitions of the mode. These default transitions do not affect the history variable and allow us to interrupt an execution and then resume it later from the same point.

The default entry and exit transitions are added in the following way. For each submode N of M, the closure adds a default exit transition from $N.dx$ to $M.dx$. This transition does not change any variables of the mode and is always enabled. Default entry transitions are used to restore the local control state of M. A default entry transition that leads from a default entry of M to the default entry of a submode N is enabled if $h = N$. Furthermore, we make sure that the default entry transitions do not interfere with regular entry transitions originating from de. The closure changes each such transition so that it is enabled only if $h = \epsilon$. The closure construction for the mode Controller introduced in Section III-B is illustrated in Fig. 4.

Operational Semantics: An operational view of a closed-mode M with the set of variables V consists of a *continuous* relation R^C and, for each pair $c_1 \in E$, $c_2 \in X$, a *discrete* relation $R^D_{c_1, c_2}$.

The relation $R^C \subseteq Q_V \times \mathcal{F}_V$ gives, for every data state of the mode, the set of flows from this state. By definition, if the control state of the mode is not at dx, the set of flows for the state is empty. R^C is obtained from the constraints of a mode and relations $SM.R^C$ of its submodes. Given a data state s of a mode M, $(s, f) \in R^C$ iff f satisfies the constraints of M and, if N is the active submode at s, (s, f), restricted to the global variables of N, belongs to $N.R^C$.

The relation $R^D_{e,x}$, for each entry point e and exit point x of a mode, is composed of *macrosteps* of a mode starting at e and ending at x. A macrostep consists of a sequence of *microsteps*. Each microstep is either a transition of the mode or a macrostep of one of its submodes. Given the relations $R^D_{e,x}$ of the submodes of M, a *microexecution* of a mode M is a sequence of the form $(e_0, s_0), (e_1, s_1), \ldots, (e_n, s_n)$ such that every (e_i, s_i) is a state of M and for even i, $((e_i, s_i), (e_{i+1}, s_{i+1}))$ is a transition of M, while for odd i, (s_i, s_{i+1}) is a macrostep of one of the submodes of M. Given such a microexecution of M with $e_0 = e \in E$ and $e_n = x \in X$, we have $(s_0, s_n) \in R^D_{e,x}$. To illustrate the notion of macrosteps, consider the closed-mode Controller from Fig. 4. Let s be such that $h = \epsilon$ and g_1 is false. Then there is a microexecution for Controller : init, TrackOptimal.de, TrackOptimal.dx, and dx (we show only the control points of the microexecution for clarity). This means that $(s, s[h := \texttt{TrackOptimal}]) \in R^D_{\text{init}, dx}$. If g_1 is true in a state s', then $(s', s'[h := \texttt{TrackPrevious}]) \in R^D_{init, dx}$ corresponding to the microexecution init, TrackOptimal.de, TrackOptimal.dx, TrackOptimal.de, TrackOptimal.dx, and dx.

The *operational semantics* of the mode M consists of its control points $E \cup X$, its variables V and relations R^C and $R^D_{e,x}$. The operational semantics of a mode defines a transition system $\mathcal{R}$ over the states of the mode. We write $(e_1, s_1) \overset{o}{\rightarrow} (e_2, s_2)$ if $(s_1, s_2) \in R^D_{e_1, e_2}$ and $(dx, s_1) \overset{f}{\rightarrow} (dx, s_2)$ if $(s_1, f) \in R^C$, where f is defined on the interval $[0, t]$ and $f(t) = s_2$. We extend $\mathcal{R}$ to include *environment* steps. An environment step begins at an exit point of the mode and ends at an entry point. It represents changes to the global variables of the mode by other components while the mode is inactive. Private variables of the mode are unaffected by environment steps. Thus, there is an

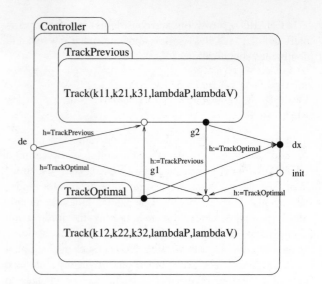

Fig. 4 The closure of a mode.

environment step $(x, s) \overset{\varepsilon}{\rightarrow} (e, t)$ whenever $x \in X$, $e \in E$ and $s[V_p] = t[V_p]$. We let λ range over $\mathcal{F}_V \cup \{o, \varepsilon\}$. An *execution* of a mode is now a path through the graph of $\mathcal{R}$

$$(e_0, s_0) \overset{\lambda_1}{\rightarrow} (e_1, s_1) \overset{\lambda_2}{\rightarrow} \ldots \overset{\lambda_n}{\rightarrow} (e_n, s_n). \qquad (2)$$

Trace Semantics: To be able to define a refinement relation between modes, we consider trace semantics for modes. A *trace* of the mode is a projection of its executions onto the global variables of the mode. The *trace semantics* for M is given by its control points E and X, its global variables V_g, and its set of its traces L_M.

In defining compositional and hierarchical semantics, one has to decide what details of the behavior of lower-level components are observable at higher levels. In our approach, the effect of a discrete step that updates only local variables of a mode is not observable by its environment, but stoppage of time introduced by such a step *is* observable. For example, consider two systems, one of which is always idle, while the other updates a local variable every second. These two systems are different, since the second one does not have flows more than one second long. Defining modular semantics in a way that such distinction is not made seems much more difficult.

B. Trace Semantics for Agents

An execution of an agent $A = \langle TM, V, I \rangle$ follows a trajectory, which starts in one of the initial states and is a sequence of flows interleaved with discrete updates to the variables of the agent. An execution of A is constructed from the relations R^C and R^D of its top-level mode. For a fixed initial state s_0, each mode $M \in TM$ starts out in the state (init_M, s_M), where init_M is the nondefault entry point of M and $s_0[M.V] = s_M$. Note that as long as there is a mode M whose control state is at init_M, no continuous steps are possible. However, any discrete step of such a mode will come from $R^D_{\text{init}_M, dx}$ and bring the control state of M to dx. Therefore, any execution of the agent A with $|TM| = k$

will start with exactly k discrete initialization steps. At that point, every top-level mode of A will be at its default exit point, allowing an alternation of continuous steps from R^C and discrete steps from $R^D_{de,dx}$. The choice of a continuous step involving all modes or a discrete step in one of the modes is left to the environment. Before each discrete step, there is an environment step, which takes the control point of the chosen mode from dx to de and leaves all the private variables of all top-level modes intact. After that, a discrete step of the chosen mode happens, bringing control back to dx. Thus, an execution of A with $|TM| = k$ is a sequence $s_0 \overset{o}{\to} s_1 \overset{o}{\to} \ldots s_k \overset{\lambda_1}{\to} s_{k+1} \overset{\lambda_2}{\to} \ldots$ such that:

1) the first k steps are discrete and initialize the top-level modes of A.
2) for every $i \geq k$, one of the following holds:
   a) the ith step is a continuous step, in which every mode takes part;
   b) the ith step is a discrete environment step;
   c) the ith step is a discrete step by one of the modes and the private variables of all other modes are unchanged.

Note that environment steps in agents and in modes are different. In an agent, an environment step may contain only discrete steps, since all agents participate in every continuous step. The environment of a mode can engage in a number of continuous steps while the mode is inactive.

A trace of an agent A is an execution of A, projected onto the set of its global variables. The denotational semantics of an agent consists of its set of global variables V_g and its set of traces L_A.

Trace semantics for modes and agents can be related to each other in an obvious way. Given an atomic agent A whose behavior is given by a mode M, we can obtain a trace of A by taking a trace of M and erasing the information about the control points from it.

C. Compositionality Results

As shown in [17], our semantics is compositional for both modes and agents as follows. First, the set of traces of a mode can be computed from the definition of the mode itself and the semantics of its submodes. Second, the set of traces of a composite agent can be computed from the semantics of its subagents.

Mode Refinement: The trace semantics leads to a natural notion of refinement between modes. A mode M and a mode N are said to be *compatible* if $M.V_g = N.V_g$, $M.E = N.E$, and $M.X = N.X$, i.e., they have the same global variables and control points. For two compatible modes M and N, we say that M refines N, denoted $M \preceq N$, if $L_M \subseteq L_N$, i.e., every trace of M is a trace of N.

The refinement operator is compositional with respect to the encapsulation. If, for each submode N_i of M there is a mode N'_i such that $N_i \preceq N'_i$, then we have that $M \preceq M'$, where M' is obtained from M by replacing every N_i with N'_i. The refinement rule is explained visually in the left side of Fig. 5.

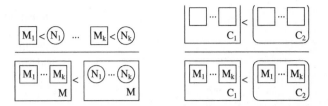

Fig. 5 Compositionality rules for modes.

A second refinement rule is defined for contexts of modes. Informally, if we consider a submode N within a mode M, the remaining submodes of M and the transitions of M can be viewed as an environment or *mode context* for N.

As with modes, refinement of contexts is also defined by language inclusion and is also compositional. If a context C_1 refines another context C_2, then inserting modes $M_1, \ldots, M_k$ into the two contexts preserves the refinement property. A visual representation of this rule is shown in the right side of Fig. 5. Precise statements of the results can be found in [17].

Compositionality of Agents: An agent is, in essence, a set of top-level modes that interleave their discrete transitions and synchronize their flows. The compositionality results for modes lift in a natural way to agents too. The operations on agents are compositional with respect to refinement. An agent A and an agent B are said to be *compatible* if $A.V_g = B.V_g$. Agent A refines a compatible agent B, denoted $A \preceq B$, if $L_A \subseteq L_B$. Given compatible agents such that $A \preceq B$, $A_1 \preceq B_1$ and $A_2 \preceq B_2$, let $V_1 = \{x_1, \ldots, x_n\}$, $V_2 = \{y_1, \ldots, y_n\}$ be indexed sets of variables with $V_1 \subseteq A.V$ and let $V_h \subseteq A.V$. Then $A \setminus \{V_h\} \preceq B \setminus \{V_h\}$, $A[V_1 := V_2] \preceq B[V_1 := V_2]$ and $A_1 \| A_2 \preceq B_1 \| B_2$.

V. ANALYSIS

Since CHARON models have a precise semantics, they can be subjected to a variety of analyzes. In this section, we give a brief overview of our ongoing research efforts in formal analysis methods for hybrid systems. These include new techniques in accurate event detection for simulation, efficient simulation, reachability analysis to detect violations of safety requirements and abstraction methods for enhancing the applicability of analysis techniques.

A. Simulation Techniques

Numerical simulation is an important tool for designing and analyzing many types of control systems, including hybrid systems. In addition to pure simulation, numerical approximation techniques are increasingly being used in reachability computations, verification, and other forms of automated analysis [33], [36], [40].

All numerical simulators operate based on some assumptions about the nature of the systems being simulated. The degree to which the system adheres to these assumptions determines how accurate the results are and what computational effort is required to generate them. Traditional numerical integration techniques typically make assumptions that tend to be violated by hybrid system models.

In addition, the hierarchical structure of the models yields the following two observations. Often, high-level modes have very slow changing dynamics, while low-level detailed models may possess fast changing dynamics. Multiple agents in a model may be decoupled in the continuous sense, yet interact through discrete messaging. Both observations may be used to increase efficiency of simulators.

Therefore, novel simulation techniques, specific to hierarchical hybrid systems are warranted. The need for specialized simulation tools has been recognized to some degree in the literature [41], [42]. Several hybrid system simulators have been introduced (see, for example, Modelica [43], ABACUSS [44], 20-sim [45], SHIFT [22], and χ [46], as well as others reviewed in [42]). Most of the previous research has focused on properly detecting and locating discrete transitions, while largely ignoring the remaining issues. In this section, we describe three techniques that exploit the hierarchical structure of hybrid system models to provide increased accuracy and efficiency during simulation.

1) Accurate Event Detection: The problem of accurately detecting and localizing the occurrence of transitions when simulating hybrid systems has received an increased amount of attention in recent years. Formally, the *event detection problem* is posed as follows. Given a system

$$\dot{s} = \begin{cases} f^{M_1}(s), & \text{if } g(s) < 0 \\ f^{M_2}(s), & \text{if } g(s) \geq 0 \end{cases} \tag{3}$$

where the mode $M \in \{M_1, M_2\}$ and $s \in Q_{M.V_*}$ is the continuous (or data) state, one would like to simulate the flow of s according to f^{M_1} until the *first* time, t', that the event $g(s(t')) = 0$ occurs. We assume that initially $M = M_1$ meaning that f^{M_1} is the active flow. Additionally we assume that the guard $g(s) < 0$ is true initially.

It is generally agreed that any algorithm that addresses this problem should possess the following attributes:

1) The algorithm should be guaranteed to detect an event if one occurs and guaranteed to not return false positives.
2) If more than one event occurs in a given time interval, the algorithm ought to be capable of determining and reporting the *first* event.
3) Once it is determined that an event has occured, the algorithm should be able to localize precisely the time t' at which it occured.
4) Provided all of the above criteria are fulfilled, the algorithm should be as efficient as possible.

Early event detection methods, such as [47]–[50], lack rigor and are not guaranteed to correctly detect an event in many situations. More recent approaches (see [51] and [52], for example) satisfy the first three objectives in most situations while being reasonably efficient. However, a situation in which nearly all current simulators fall short is when switches occur near model singularities. Since the step-size selection scheme for the integration is typically independent of the event detection algorithm, it is entirely possible that the integrator will take a step into the region where $f^{M_1}(x)$ is undefined. If the particular integration method has an in-

Fig. 6 Cases 1 and 2 illustrate situations in which naive simulators can fail to detect transitions by selecting integration points which completely "miss" the guard set; Case 3 depicts a situation in which even sophisticated methods fail, when the event occurs near a region where the differential equation has a singularity at which the right side cannot be evaluated.

termediate step that requires evaluating the derivative at this state inside the singular region, a floating point exception is generated and the simulation fails abruptly. Some of these problematic situations are illustrated in Fig. 6.

We have developed a method [53] guaranteed to detect enabling of all transitions, including those occuring near singular regions. We attempt to overcome this problem by treating the event detection problem as a control system design problem. We consider the continuous dynamics of the system and the numerical integration method (we use Linear Multistep Methods—see [54] for further details)

$$s_{k+1} = s_k + h \left\{ \sum_{j=1}^{m} \beta_j f_{k-j+1} \right\} \tag{4}$$

as our collective dynamic system, where t_k is the time of the kth simulation step, s_k is the value of the state at t_k, $h = t_{k+1} - t_k$ is the simulation step size, and $\sum_{j=1}^{m} \beta_j f_{k-j+1}$ is some weighted combination of past values of the derivative which approximates the flow on $[t_k, t_{k+1}]$.

Returning to our control system analogy, the integration step size h is treated as an input and the value of the transition guard, $g_k = g(s_k)$, or switching function is the output. The task at hand is to integrate the ordinary differential equation (ODE) until the boundary of the guard set is reached, taking care to never evaluate the right side of the ODE inside the guard set. In terms of our control system analogy, the problem can be rephrased as: design a feedback law that zeros the output with no overshoot. The resulting solution is essentially an Input/Output Linearization in discrete time. For a linear guard the output dynamics would be

$$g_{k+1} = g_k + h \frac{\partial g}{\partial s} \left\{ \sum_{j=1}^{m} \beta_j f_{k-j+1} \right\} \tag{5}$$

selecting the step size h as

$$h = \frac{(\gamma - 1) g_k}{\frac{\partial g}{\partial s} \left\{ \sum_{j=1}^{m} \beta_j f_{k-j+1} \right\}} \tag{6}$$

results in (5) appearing as $g_{k+1} = \gamma g_k$. By selecting the constant $0 < \gamma < 1$ we are ensured $g_k \to 0$ while maintaining $g_k \leq 0$. Thus, the simulation settles to the transition surface without overshooting it and crossing into the singular

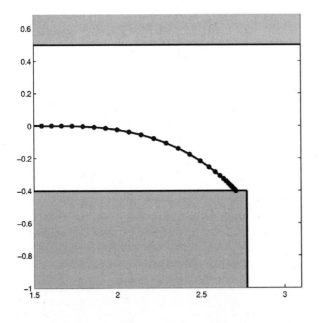

Fig. 7 The simulation takes successively smaller steps to properly locate the point at which the vehicle clips the corner.

region. This technique is illustrated in Fig. 7 where a vehicle is trying to go around a corner and the simulation must detect if it clears the corner. One can see how the simulation converges onto the exact point at which the collision occured.

2) Multirate Simulation: Many systems, especially hierarchical ones, naturally evolve on different time scales. For example, the center of mass of an automobile may be accelerating relatively slowly compared with the rate at which the crankshaft angle changes; yet the evolution of the two are intimately coupled. Despite this disparity, traditional numerical integration methods force all coupled differential equations to be integrated using the same step size. The idea behind multirate integration methods [55], [56] is to use larger step sizes for the slow changing sets of differential equations and smaller step sizes for the differential equations evolving on the fast time scale. Such a strategy increases efficiency without compromising accuracy. Areas of application include simulating integrated circuits and molecular and stellar dynamics [57]–[59]. Despite the seemingly natural connection, they have never previously been used in hierarchical hybrid systems simulation. In [60], we introduce a multirate algorithm for simulating hierarchical hybrid systems.

3) Multiagent Simulation: Multiagent hybrid systems are sets of interacting hybrid systems. In the case of the automated highway example, each vehicle may be modeled as an individual agent; however, one may like to consider the dynamics of an entire group of vehicles collectively to see how they interact. The continuous dynamics of each vehicle is physically decoupled from that of the other agents, and typically they operate independently. However, certain important discrete events may depend on the state of two or more agents. Examples of this would be when two cars come dangerously close, one car informs a group of vehicles that it is merging into the platoon, etc. Most multiagent

systems of this form, when modeled in CHARON, have the following mathematical structure:

$$\dot{x} = f_x(x) \tag{7}$$
$$\dot{y} = f_y(y) \tag{8}$$
$$g(x, y) \leq 0 \tag{9}$$

where x and y are the continuous states of agent 1 and agent 2, their dynamics are given by the flows $f_x : \mathbb{R}^n \to \mathbb{R}^n$ and $f_y : \mathbb{R}^m \to \mathbb{R}^m$, and the predicate $g(x, y) < 0$ guards a transition for one or both agents. Note that each agent's ODEs are decoupled; however, coupling is introduced through the guards.

From the point of view of simulating the continuous dynamics, it is not necessary to synchronize the integration rates of the two cars, since they are decoupled. Each set of ODEs should maximize the tradeoff between accuracy and efficiency by selecting the largest possible integration step size that is able to recreate that agents' dynamics within some acceptable user-specified error tolerance. Unfortunately, properly detecting the occurrence of events, $g(x, y) = 0$, requires that the value of the state be reported in a synchronized fashion. Traditionally, simulators compute the best step size for each agent and then take the minimum as a global step size. This can result in significant inefficiencies.

Our goal is to simulate each agent with a different step size while still ensuring proper event handling. The idea is to allow the simulation for each agent to proceed independently when no events are about to occur. Only when events seem likely do we adaptively select the step sizes to bring all of the agents into synchronization to properly detect the event.

In the case of N agents, our approach to this problem, reported in [61], is to define N local clocks, $t_1, \ldots, t_N$ and N step sizes $h_1, \ldots, h_N$, one for each agent. The step sizes are selected based on the system dynamics so as to simultaneously synchronize the local clocks and detect the event using the control theoretic technique of I/O linearization.

Fig. 8 and 9 illustrate how the simulation for two agents might proceed. Fig. 8 shows the trajectories of the two cars. The simulation tries to detect when the cars collide. Fig. 9 displays how the step sizes are selected independently throughout most of the simulation. When the system approaches an event, the local clocks automatically synchronize.

4) Distributed Simulation: The main idea behind distributed simulation is to get speedup by using multiple computing resources, since simulations of complex systems are normally very slow. Distributed simulation techniques are categorized as conservative or optimistic based on how local clocks are synchronized. If the local clock of the agent always advances and does not go backward, it is *conservative simulation*; otherwise, it is *optimistic simulation*. Conservative simulation techniques ensure that the local clock l_c of the agent either advances or stops, but does not roll back. In optimistic simulation, the focus is to exploit possible parallelism as much as possible by allowing each agent to run at a different speed without the guarantee that

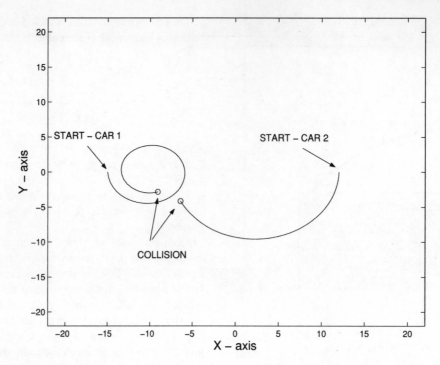

Fig. 8   The trajectories of the two cars in the plane.

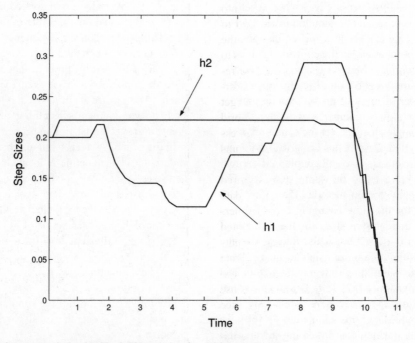

Fig. 9   Step sizes used for the two cars depicted in Fig. 8. The step sizes h_1 and h_2 are selected independently away from the constraint, but are brought into synchronization when an event is impending.

no event occurs between t_1 and t_2 when its local clock l_c is advanced from t_1 to t_2. If an event e that occurred at time t_e gets recognized by the agent at t_r, where $t_r > t_e$, the simulator provides a rollback operation by restoring the local clock l_c to an earlier time such that the event e can be handled if and when it occurs. Note that the event e may not occur at all if rollbacks are propagated to other agents so that the event e becomes no longer possible.

Our approach to simulate hybrid systems in a distributed fashion is to use more computing resources by exploiting

inherent modularity of systems described in CHARON. By modularity, we mean two things. One is behavioral modularity captured by mode and the other is architectural modularity by agent. One way to exploit mode-level modularity within a single agent is to use multiple rates for the simulation of the same agent as described in Section V-A2. Another way is to distribute atomic agents to exploit agent-level modularity. When the agents are distributed, they need to synchronize to update their states as the agents share information. Here, the challenge is how to reduce synchronization

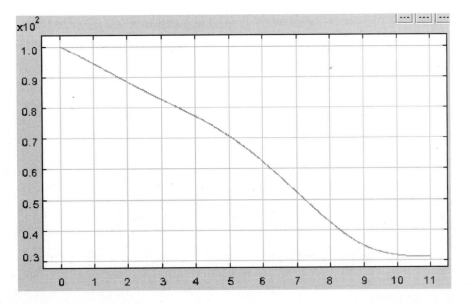

Fig. 10 The distance d_i between the two platoons.

overheads among distributed agents. We briefly describe our conservative algorithm and optimistic algorithms.

In a conservative approach, we decompose functions into subfunctional blocks, and the simulator allows the agent to execute the next block only when all the agents complete the current block. Although our conservative approach allows to simulate hybrid systems, the disadvantage is that overhead resulting from communications degrades the possible performance gain from distributing computations. Thus, we can get speedup only in simulating very computation-oriented hybrid systems. Our optimistic simulation algorithms are to address the overhead problems. The main features of the algorithms are as follows. First, to reduce communication overhead, we let agents synchronize just before the new value of a shared variable is necessary instead of communicating every update round. Second, to reduce computation overhead due to numerical integration, we simulate the agent with its approximated polynomial dynamics and resolve the possible misses of events with a rollback operation. This allows each agent to execute its computation without integrating the shared variables controlled by other agents. Our approach is *optimistic* in the sense that each agent goes forward even when there is no guarantee that their clocks do not have to go backward.

5) Case Study: We now consider simulation of the platoon controller under normal conditions. Fig. 10–12 are snapshots of the CHARON plotter and show the simulation results for the following scenario. Initially, the distance between the two platoons is large, and the platoon i is moving faster than the platoon in front ($i-1$) and is therefore closing the gap. We let the velocity of the platoon in front be a sinusoidal function of time starting at an initial value 20. One can see from the figures that the controller of platoon i, initially in the mode "track optimal velocity," first decreases the gap between the two platoons by accelerating. When its distance to the preceding platoon becomes small, the controller slowly decelerates and switches to mode "track velocity of previous car" approximately at time 8.2. The controller then tries to

follow the platoon in front at some constant distance. Additional simulation trace plots of this example can be found in [6].

B. State-Space Exploration Techniques

1) Exact Reachability Using Requiem: Formal verification of safety requirements of hybrid systems requires the computation of reachable states of continuous systems. **Requiem** is a Mathematica package that, given a nilpotent linear differential equation and a set of initial conditions, symbolically computes the exact set of reachable states. Given various classes of linear differential equations and semialgebraic sets of initial conditions, the computation of reachable sets can be posed as a quantifier elimination problem in the decidable theory of reals as an ordered field [62]. Given a nilpotent system and a set defined by polynomials inequalities, **Requiem** automatically generates the quantifier elimination problem and invokes the quantifier elimination package in Mathematica 4.0. If the computation terminates, it returns the quantifier free formula describing the reachable set. More details can be found in [62]. The entire package is available at www.seas.upenn.edu/hybrid/requiem.html.

Parametric analysis using Requiem: We demonstrate the use of **Requiem** on the platoon controller described earlier. The experimental nature of the current quantifier elimination package makes it impossible to apply it to the system described by (1). We thus simplify the controller with equivalent dynamics, which controls the acceleration of the platoon i instead of its derivative. This approximation results in the three dimensional system described by

$$\begin{cases} \dot{d}_i & = v_{i-1} - v_i \\ \dot{v}_{i-1} & = a_{i-1} \\ \dot{v}_i & = u \end{cases} \tag{10}$$

We treat the acceleration of the preceding platoon a_{i-1} as a parametric disturbance and control the acceleration $\dot{v}_i$ of

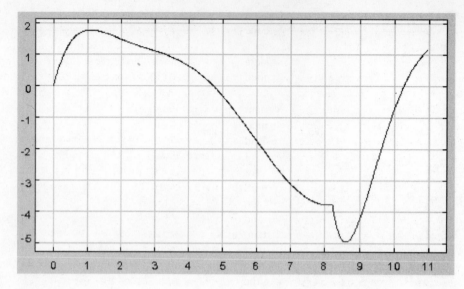

Fig. 11   The acceleration a_i of the platoon i.

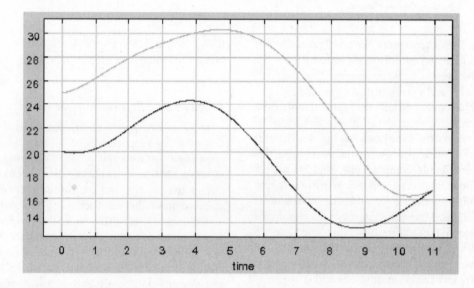

Fig. 12   The velocity of the platoon i and the preceding platoon $(i-1)$ (the platoon i moves faster).

the following platoon. The problem is to find the set of conditions on the parameter set $\{a_{i-1}, b, c\}$ and the state variables, which would lead to a collision ($d_i \leq 0$) when we apply a control u of the form $bt + c$ where b and c are integer constants. We use **Requiem**'s parametric backward reachability function to obtain the quantifier free formula. By giving specific values to the parameters and initial conditions, we can see whether the formula reduces to *true* or *false*. For example, we can prove the expected result that when the vehicles are started close to each other ($d = 1$) and the control parameters b and c are positive, collision is unavoidable, whereas if b and c are negative, collision does not occur. The entire example and the output is available at www.seas.upenn.edu/hybrid/requiem/ReqIEEE.html.

2) Predicate Abstraction: In the world of program analysis, predicate abstraction has emerged to be a powerful and popular technique for extracting finite-state models from complex, potentially infinite state, discrete systems (see [63]–[66] for a sampling of this active research area).

A verifier based on this scheme requires three inputs, the (concrete) system to be analyzed, the property to be verified, and a finite set of predicates over system variables to be used for abstraction. An abstract state is a valid combination of truth values to the predicates, and thus corresponds to a set of concrete states. There is an abstract transition from an abstract state A to an abstract state B, if there is a concrete transition from some state corresponding to A to some state corresponding to B. The job of the verifier is to compute the abstract transitions and to search in the abstract graph looking for a violation of the property. If the abstract system satisfies the property, then so does the concrete system. If a violation is found in the abstract system, then the resulting counterexample can be analyzed to test if it is a viable execution of the concrete system. This approach, of course, does not solve the verification problem by itself. The success crucially depends on the ability to identify the "interesting" predicates, either manually or by some automated scheme and on the ability of the verifier to compute abstract transitions efficiently. Nevertheless, it has led to opportunities to bridge the gap between code and models and to combine automated search with user's intuition about interesting predicates. Tools such as Bandera [67], SLAM [68], and Feaver [69] have successfully applied predicate abstraction for analysis of C or Java programs.

Inspired by this trend, we develop algorithms for invariant verification of hybrid systems using discrete approximations based on predicate abstractions. Consider a hybrid automaton with n continuous variables and a set L of locations. Then the continuous state-space is $L \times \mathbb{R}^n$. For the sake of efficiency, we restrict our attention where all invariants, switching guards, and discrete updates of the hybrid automaton are specified by linear expressions and the continuous dynamics is linear, possibly with uncertain, bounded input. For the purpose of abstraction, the user supplies initial predicates $p_1, \ldots, p_k$, where each predicate is a polyhedral subset of $\mathbb{R}^n$. In the abstract program, the n continuous variables are replaced by k discrete Boolean variables, one Boolean variable b_i for each predicate p_i. A combination of values to these k Boolean variables represents an abstract state corresponding to a set of continuous states and the abstract state space is $L \times \mathbb{B}^k$. Our verifier performs an on-the-fly search of the abstract system by symbolic manipulation of polyhedra.

The core of the verifier is the computation of the transitions between abstract states that capture both discrete and continuous dynamics of the original system. Computing discrete successors is relatively straightforward and involves computing weakest preconditions and checking nonemptiness of an intersection of polyhedral sets. The implementation attempts to reduce the number of abstract states examined by exploiting the fact that each abstract state is an intersection of k linear inequalities. For computing continuous successors of an abstract state A, we use a strategy inspired by the techniques used in CHECKMATE [33] and d/dt [34]. The basic strategy computes the polyhedral slices of states reachable from A at fixed times $r, 2r, 3r, \ldots$ for a suitably chosen r, then takes the convex-hull of all these polyhedra to overapproximate the set of all states reachable from A. However, while tools such as CHECKMATE and d/dt are designed to compute a "good" approximation of the continuous successors of A, we are interested in testing if this set intersects with a new abstract state. Consequently, our implementation differs in many ways. For instance, it checks for nonempty intersection with other abstract states of each of the polyhedral slices and omits steps involving approximations using orthogonal polyhedra and termination tests (see [34]).

Postulating the verification problem for hybrid systems as a search problem in the abstract system has many benefits compared to the traditional approach of computing approximations of reachable sets of hybrid systems. First, the expensive operation of computing continuous successors is applied only to abstract states and not to intermediate polyhedra of unpredictable shapes and complexities. Second, we can prematurely terminate the computation of continuous successors whenever new abstract transitions are discovered. Finally, we can explore with different search strategies aimed at making

progress in the abstract graph. For instance, our implementation always prefers computing discrete transitions over continuous ones. Our early experiments indicate that improvements in time and space requirements are significant compared to a tool such as d/dt. A more detailed description of our predicate abstraction technique for hybrid systems can be found in [70].

Verification of the platoon controller using predicate abstraction: To formally prove the safety property of this longitudinal controller, we make use of the reachability method using predicate abstraction. Here, we focus only on two regions which are critical from a safety point of view: "track optimal velocity" ($v_i^e \leq -10$ and $e_i \geq -1m - \epsilon$) and "track velocity of previous car" ($v_i^e \leq -10$ and $e_i \leq -1m$). We include a thickening parameter $\epsilon > 0m$ into the model to add nondeterminism to it. The two regions under consideration overlap allowing the controller to either use the "track optimal velocity" controller or the "track velocity of previous car" controller in this ϵ-thick region. Besides adding some nondeterminism to the model, the thickening parameter also provides improved numerical stability to the simulation and reachability computation, as it is numerically hard to determine the exact time at which a switch occurs.

The respective control laws u_1 and u_2 are as follows:

$$u_1 = \frac{1}{8}d_i + \frac{3}{4}v_{i-1} - \left(\frac{3}{4} + \frac{1}{8}\lambda_v\right)v_i - \frac{3}{2}a_i - \frac{1}{8}\lambda_p \quad (11)$$

$$u_2 = d_i + 3v_{i-1} - (3 + \lambda_v)v_i - 3a_i - \lambda_p. \quad (12)$$

Note that these regions correspond to situations where the platoon in front moves considerably slower; moreover, the second region is particularly safety critical because the interplatoon distance is smaller than desired.

To construct the discrete abstract system, in addition to the predicates of the invariants and guards, we include some predicates over the distance variable to be able to separate the bad region from the reachable set: $d_i \leq 0, d_i \geq 2, d_i \geq 10, d_i \geq 20$. The total number of initial predicates is 11. For the initial set specified as $20 \leq d_i \leq 100 \land 15 \leq v_{i-1} \leq 18 \land 20 \leq v_i \leq 25$, the tool found 14 reachable abstract states and reported that the system is safe. Note this property has been proven in [71] using optimal control techniques for individual continuous modes without mode switches. Here, we prove the property for all possible behaviors of the controller.

VI. THE CHARON TOOLKIT

In this section, we describe the CHARON toolkit. Written in Java, the toolkit features an easy-to-use graphical user interface (GUI), with support for syntax-directed text editing, a visual input language, a powerful type-checker, simulation, and a plotter to display simulation traces. The CHARON GUI uses some components from the model checker JMOCHA [72], and the plotter uses a package from the modeling tool PTOLEMY [23].

The editor windows highlight the CHARON language keywords and comments. *Parsing on the fly* can be enabled or disabled. In case of an error while typing, the first erroneous token

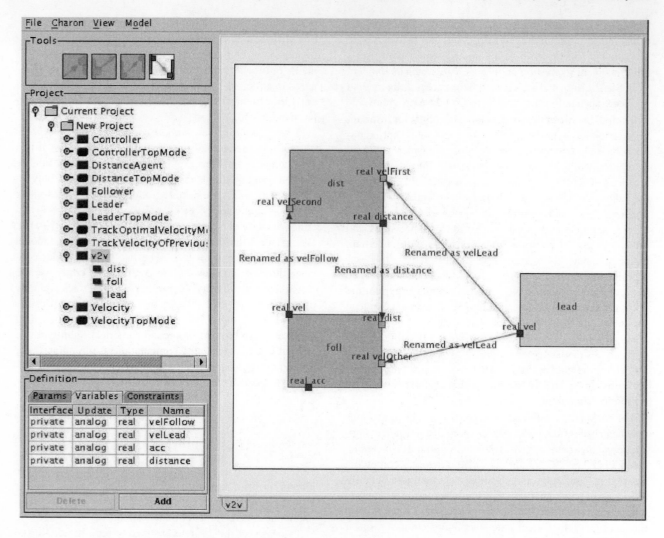

Fig. 13   The visual input tool of CHARON. The arrows depict variable renamings.

will be highlighted in red. Further, a pop-up window can be enabled that tells the user what the editor expects next. Clicking one of the pop-up options, the associated text is automatically inserted at the current cursor position. This allows the user not only to correct almost all syntactic errors at typing but also to learn the CHARON language.

The CHARON toolkit also includes a visual input language capability. It allows the user to draw agent and mode definitions at a given level of hierarchy. The visual input tool is depicted in Fig. 13, showing one level of the platoon controller from Fig. 1. By clicking on the subagents, the user can explore the lower levels of hierarchy. The interpreter of the visual input translates the specification into text-based CHARON source code using an intermediate XML-based representation.

Once a set of edited and saved CHARON language files exists, the user can simulate the hybrid system. In this case, the CHARON toolkit calls the parser and the type-checker. If there are no syntactic errors, it generates a *project context* that is displayed in a separate project window that appears on the left side of the desktop, as shown in Fig. 14, which displays the same model as Fig. 13.

The project window displays the internal representation of CHARON in a convenient tree format. Each node in the tree may be expanded or collapsed by clicking it. The internal representation tree consists of two nodes: `agents` and `modes`. They are initially collected from the associated CHARON files.

A CHARON specification describes how a hybrid system behaves over time. CHARON's simulator provides a means to visualize a possible behavior of the system. This information can be used for debugging or simply for understanding in detail the behavior of the given hybrid system description.

The simulation methodology used in the CHARON toolkit, which is depicted in Fig. 15, resembles concepts in code generation from a specification. Since CHARON allows the user to provide external Java source code, the simulator needs to be an executable Java program. CHARON has a set of Java files that represent a core simulator. Given a set of CHARON files, Java files are automatically generated that represent a Java interpretation of the CHARON specification of a hybrid system. They are used in conjunction with the predefined simulator core files and the external Java source code to produce a simulation trace.

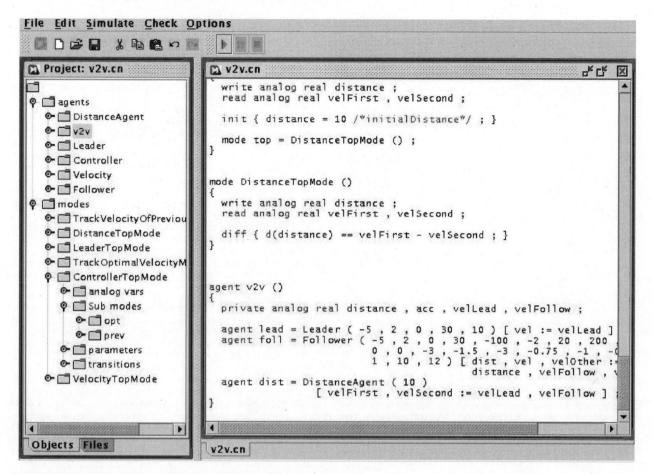

Fig. 14 The editor frame on the right side of the CHARON desktop and the corresponding project frame on the left.

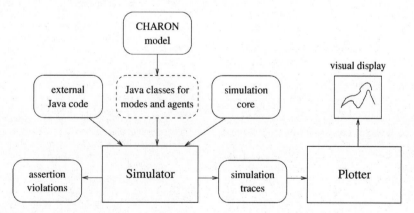

Fig. 15 The simulation methodology of CHARON.

The CHARON plotter allows the visualization of a simulation trace generated by the simulator. It draws the value of all selected variables using various colors with respect to time. It also highlights the time that selected transitions have been taken. The simulation results obtained in Fig. 10–12 have been produced using the CHARON plotter.

In addition, the simulator checks *assertions* that are placed in the CHARON model by the user. Assertions can be added to any mode or agent in the model. They are state predicates over the variables of the mode or agent and are supposed to be true whenever the mode is active or, for agents, always.

If an assertion is violated during a simulation, the simulator stops and the trace produced by the simulator can be used to find the source of the violation.

More information on the CHARON toolkit, along with a preliminary release, is available for free at www.cis.upenn.edu/mobies/charon/.

ACKNOWLEDGMENT

The authors would like to thank D. Huber and M. Mc-Dougall for their work on the CHARON visual interface,

U. Sammapun for her contribution to the simulator generator, and V. Sokolskaya for the implementation of the typechecker. In addition, the authors would like to thank R. Fierro and R. Grosu for their various contributions during the initial development of CHARON.

REFERENCES

[1] E. A. Lee, "What's ahead for embedded software," *IEEE Comput.*, pp. 18–26, Sept. 2000.

[2] R. Alur, J. Esposito, M. Kim, V. Kumar, and I. Lee, "Formal modeling and analysis of hybrid systems: A case study in multirobot coordination," in *Lecture Notes in Computer Science, FM'99—Formal Methods*. Heidelberg, Germany: Springer-Verlag, 1999, vol. 1708, pp. 212–232.

[3] A. Balluchi, L. Benvenuti, M. Di Benedetto, C. Pinello, and A. Sangiovanni-Vicentelli, "Automotive engine control and hybrid systems: Challenges and opportunities," *Proc. IEEE*, vol. 88, pp. 888–912, July 2000.

[4] C. Tomlin, G. J. Pappas, and S. Sastry, "Conflict resolution for air traffic management: A study in muti-agent hybrid systems," *IEEE Trans. Automat. Contr.*, vol. 43, pp. 509–521, Apr. 1998.

[5] S. Engell, S. Kowalewski, C. Schulz, and O. Stursberg, "Continuous-discrete interactions in chemical processing plants," *Proc. IEEE*, vol. 88, pp. 1050–1068, July 2000.

[6] F. Ivančić, "Report on Verification of the MoBIES Vehicle-Vehicle Automotive OEP Problem," Univ. of Penn., MS-CIS-02-02, 2002.

[7] R. Alur, C. Belta, F. Ivančić, V. Kumar, M. Mintz, G. Pappas, H. Rubin, and J. Schug, "Hybrid modeling and simulation of biomolecular networks," in *Lecture Notes in Computer Science, Hybrid Systems: Computation and Control*, M. D. Di Benedetto and A. Sangiovanni-Vincentelli, Eds. Heidelberg, Germany: Springer-Verlag, 2001, vol. 2034, pp. 19–32.

[8] E. Aaron, F. Ivančić, and D. Metaxas, "Hybrid models of navigation strategies for games and animations," in *Lecture Notes in Computer Science, Hybrid Systems: Computation and Control*, C. Tomlin and M. Greenstreet, Eds. Heidelberg, Germany: Springer-Verlag, 2002, vol. 2289, pp. 7–20.

[9] E. Aaron, F. Ivančić, O. Sokolsky, and D. Metaxas, "A framework for reasoning about animation systems," in *Lecture Notes in Computer Science, Intelligent Virtual Agents*. Heidelberg, Germany: Springer-Verlag, 2001, vol. 2190, pp. 47–60.

[10] R. Fierro, Y. Hur, I. Lee, and L. Sha, "Modeling the simplex architecture using CHARON," in *Proc. 21st IEEE Real-Time Systems Symp. WIP Sessions*, 2000, pp. 77–80.

[11] D. Harel, "Statecharts: A visual formalism for complex systems," *Sci. Comput. Program.*, vol. 8, pp. 231–274, 1987.

[12] O. Maler, Z. Manna, and A. Pnueli, "From timed to hybrid systems," in *Lecture Notes in Computer Science, Real-Time: Theory in Practice*. Heidelberg, Germany: Springer-Verlag, 1991, vol. 600, pp. 447–484.

[13] R. Alur, C. Courcoubetis, N. Halbwachs, T. A. Henzinger, P. Ho, X. Nicollin, A. Olivero, J. Sifakis, and S. Yovine, "The algorithmic analysis of hybrid systems," *Theor. Comput. Sci.*, vol. 138, pp. 3–34, 1995.

[14] N. Lynch, R. Segala, F. Vaandrager, and H. Weinberg, "Hybrid I/O automata," in *Hybrid Systems III: Verification and Control*, 1996, vol. 1066, pp. 496–510.

[15] C. A. R. Hoare, *Communicating Sequential Processes*. Englewood Cliffs, NJ: Prentice-Hall, 1985.

[16] R. Milner, *Lecture Notes in Computer Science, A Calculus of Communicating Systems*. Heidelberg, Germany: Springer-Verlag, 1980, vol. 92.

[17] R. Alur, R. Grosu, I. Lee, and O. Sokolsky, "Compositional refinement for hierarchical hybrid systems," in *Lecture Notes in Computer Science, Hybrid Systems: Computation and Control*. Heidelberg, Germany: Springer-Verlag, 2001, vol. 2034, pp. 33–48.

[18] G. Booch, I. Jacobson, and J. Rumbaugh, *Unified Modeling Language User Guide*. Boston, MA: Addison-Wesley, 1997.

[19] S. E. Mattsson and M. Anderson, "The ideas behind omola," in *CACSD 92: IEEE Symp. Comput. Aided Control Syst. Design*, 1992, pp. 23–29.

[20] H. Elmqvist, F. E. Cellier, and M. Otter, "Object-oriented modeling of hybrid systems," in *Proc. Eur. Simulation Symp.*, 1993, pp. 31–41.

[21] H. Elmqvist, S. E. Mattsson, and M. Otter, "Modelica—The new object-oriented modeling languague," in *Proc. 12th Eur. Simulation Multiconf.*, 1998, pp. 127–131.

[22] A. Deshpande, A. Gollu, and L. Semenzato, "The Shift Programming Language and Run-Time System for Dynamic Networks of Hybrid Automata," Univ. California Berkeley, UCB-ITS-PRR-97-7, 1997.

[23] J. Davis, M. Goel, C. Hylands, B. Kienhuis, E. A. Lee, J. Liu, X. Liu, L. Muliadi, S. Neuendorffer, J. Reekie, N. Smyth, J. Tsay, and Y. Xiong, "Overview of the Ptolemy Project," Univ. California Berkeley, UCB/ERL M99/37, 1999.

[24] E. M. Clarke and R. P. Kurshan, "Computer-aided verification," *IEEE Spectr.*, vol. 33, pp. 61–67, June 1996.

[25] G. J. Holzmann, "The model checker SPIN," *IEEE Trans. Software Eng.*, vol. 23, pp. 279–295, May 1997.

[26] R. Alur and D. L. Dill, "A theory of timed automata," *Theor. Comput. Sci.*, vol. 126, pp. 183–235, 1994.

[27] R. Alur, T. Henzinger, G. Lafferriere, and G. Pappas, "Discrete abstractions of hybrid systems," *Proc. IEEE*, vol. 88, pp. 971–984, July 2000.

[28] N. Halbwachs, Y. Proy, and P. Raymond, "Verification of linear hybrid systems by means of convex approximations," in *Lecture Notes in Computer Science, Static Analysis*. Heidelberg, Germany: Springer-Verlag, 1994, vol. 864.

[29] T. A. Henzinger, "The theory of hybrid automata," in *Proc. 11th IEEE Symp. Logic in Comput. Sci.*, 1996, pp. 278–293.

[30] C. Daws, A. Olivero, S. Tripakis, and S. Yovine, "The tool KRONOS," in *Lecture Notes in Computer Science, Hybrid Systems III: Verification and Control*. Heidelberg, Germany: Springer-Verlag, 1996, vol. 1066, pp. 208–219.

[31] K. Larsen, P. Pettersson, and W. Yi, "UPPAAL in a nutshell," *Springer Int. J. Softw. Tools Technol. Transfer*, vol. 1, 1997.

[32] T. A. Henzinger, P. Ho, and H. Wong-Toi, "Hytech: The next generation," in *Lecture Notes in Computer Science, Tools and Algorithms for the Construction and Analysis of Systems*. Heidelberg, Germany: Springer-Verlag, 1995, vol. 1019, pp. 41–71.

[33] A. Chutinan and B. K. Krogh, "Verification of polyhedral-invariant hybrid automata using polygonal flow pipe approximations," in *Lecture Notes in Computer Science, Hybrid Systems: Computation and Control*. Heidelberg, Germany: Springer-Verlag, 1999, vol. 1569, pp. 76–90.

[34] E. Asarin, O. Bournez, T. Dang, and O. Maler, "Approximate reachability analysis of piecewise-linear dynamical systems," in *Lecture Notes in Computer Science, Hybrid Systems: Computation and Control*. Heidelberg, Germany: Springer-Verlag, 2000, vol. 1790, pp. 21–31.

[35] M. Greenstreet and I. Mitchell, "Reachability analysis using polygonal projections," in *Lecture Notes in Computer Science, Hybrid Systems: Computation and Control*. Heidelberg, Germany: Springer-Verlag, 1999, pp. 103–116.

[36] I. Mitchell and C. Tomlin, "Level set methods for computation in hybrid systems," in *Lecture Notes in Computer Science, Hybrid Systems: Computation and Control*. Heidelberg, Germany: Springer-Verlag, 2000, vol. 1790, pp. 310–323.

[37] A. Kurzhanski and P. Varaiya, "Ellipsoidal techniques for reachability analysis," in *Lecture Notes in Computer Science, Hybrid Systems: Computation and Control*. Heidelberg, Germany: Springer-Verlag, 2000, vol. 1790, pp. 202–214.

[38] P. Varaiya, "Smart cars on smart roads: Problems of control," *IEEE Trans. Automat. Contr.*, vol. 38, Feb. 1993.

[39] D. Godbole and J. Lygeros, "Longitudinal control of a lead card of a platoon," *IEEE Trans. Veh. Technol.*, vol. 43, no. 4, pp. 1125–1135, 1994.

[40] T. Dang and O. Maler, "Reachability analysis via face lifting," in *Lecture Notes in Computer Science, Hybrid Systems: Computation and Control*, T. Henzinger and S. Sastry, Eds. Heidelberg, Germany: Springer-Verlag, 1998, vol. 1386, pp. 96–109.

[41] S. Kowalewski, M. Fritz, H. Graf, J. Preubig, S. Simon, O. Stursberg, and H. Treseler, "A case study in tool-aided analysis of discretely controled continuous systems: The two tanks problem," in *Lecture Notes in Computer Science, Hybrid Systems V*. Heidelberg, Germany: Springer-Verlag, 1999, vol. 1567.

[42] P. Mosterman, "An overview of hybrid simulation phenomena and their support by simulation packages," in *Hybrid Systems: Computation and Control*, F. Varager and J. H. van Schuppen, Eds. Heidelberg, Germany: Springer-Verlag, 1999, vol. 1569, pp. 163–177.

[43] P. Fritzson and V. Engelson, "Modelica—A unified object-oriented language for system modeling and simulation," in *ECOOP 98: The 12th Eur. Conf. Object-Oriented Program.*, 1998, pp. 67–90.

[44] R. Allgor, P. Barton, and W. Feehery, "A large scale differential-algebraic and parametric sensitivity solver," *ABACUSS Project Rep.*, vol. 97, no. 1, pp. 1–4, 1997.

[45] J. Broenink, "Modeling, simulation and analysis with 20-sim," *Journal A*, vol. 38, no. 3, pp. 22–25, 1995.

[46] D. van Beek, G. Fabian, and J. Rooda, "Integration of the discrete and the continuous behavior in the hybrid chi simulator," in *Proc. 1998 Eur. Simulation Multiconf.*, 1998, pp. 252–257.

[47] M. B. Carver, "Efficient integration over discontinuities in ordinary differential equation simulations," *Math. and Comput. Simulation*, vol. XX, pp. 190–196, 1978.

[48] F. Cellier, "Combined discrete/continuous system simulation by use of digital computers: techniques and tools," Ph.D. dissertation, ETH Zurich, Zurich, Switzerland, 1979.

[49] C. W. Gear and O. Osterby, "Solving ordinary differential equations with discontinuities," Dept. Comput. Sci., Univ. Ill., 1981.

[50] L. F. Shampine, I. Gladwell, and R. W. Brankin, "Reliable solution of special event location problems for ODE's," *ACM Trans. Math. Softw.*, vol. 17, no. 1, pp. 11–25, Mar. 1991.

[51] V. Bahl and A. Linninger, "Modeling of continuous-discrete processes," in *Hybrid Systems: Computation and Control*. Heidelberg, Germany: Springer-Verlag, 2001, vol. 2034, pp. 387–402.

[52] T. Park and P. Barton, "State event location in differential-algebraic models," *ACM Trans. Model. Comput. Simulation*, vol. 6, no. 2, pp. 137–165, 1996.

[53] J. Esposito, V. Kumar, and G. Pappas, "Accurate event detection for simulating hybrid systems," in *Hybrid Systems: Computation and Control*. Heidelberg, Germany: Springer-Verlag, 2001, vol. 2034, pp. 204–217.

[54] U. Ascher and L. Petzold, *Computer Methods for Ordinary Differential Equations and Differential-Algebraic Equations*. Philadelphia, PA: Soc. for Ind. and Applied Math., 1998.

[55] C. W. Gear and D. R. Wells, "Multirate linear multistep methods," *BIT*, vol. 24, pp. 484–502, 1984.

[56] R. C. Rice, "Split Runge-Kutta methods for simultaneous equations," *J. Res. Nat. Bur. Stand.*, vol. 64B, pp. 151–170, 1960.

[57] C. Engstler and C. Lubich, "Multirate extrapolation methods for differential equations with different time scales," *Computing*, vol. 58, pp. 173–185, 1996.

[58] M. Gunther and P. Rentrop, "Multirate row methods and latency of electrical circuits," *Appl. Numer. Math.*, vol. 13, pp. 83–102, 1993.

[59] J. Sand and S. Skelboe, "Stability of backward euler multirate methods and convergence of waveform relaxation," *BIT*, vol. 32, pp. 350–366, 1992.

[60] J. Esposito and V. Kumar, "Efficient dynamic simulation of robotic systems with hierarchy," in *IEEE Int. Conf. Robotics Automation*, May 2001, pp. 2818–2823.

[61] J. Esposito, G. Pappas, and V. Kumar, "Multi-agent hybrid system simulation," in *Proc. 40th IEEE Conf. Decision and Contr.*, Dec. 2001, pp. 780–786.

[62] G. Lafferriere, G. Pappas, and S. Yovine, "Symbolic reachability computation for families of linear vector fields," *J. Symbol. Comput.*, vol. 32, no. 3, pp. 231–253, Sept. 2001.

[63] E. Clarke, O. Grumberg, S. Jha, Y. Lu, and H. Veith, "Counterexample-guided abstraction refinement," in *Lecture Notes in Computer Science, Computer Aided Verification*. Heidelberg, Germany: Springer-Verlag, 2000, vol. 1855, pp. 154–169.

[64] P. Cousot and R. Cousot, "Abstract interpretation: A unified lattice model for static analysis of programs by construction or approximation of fixpoints," in *Proc. 4th ACM Symp. Principles Program. Lang.*, 1977, pp. 238–252.

[65] S. Das, D. Dill, and S. Park, "Experience with predicate abstraction," in *Computer Aided Verification*, 1999, vol. 1633, pp. 160–171.

[66] S. Graf and H. Saidi, "Construction of abstract state graphs with PVS," in *Computer Aided Verification*, 1997, vol. 1254, pp. 72–83.

[67] J. C. Corbett, M. B. Dwyer, J. Hatcliff, S. Laubach, C. S. Pasareanu, Robby, and H. Zheng, "Bandera: Extracting finite-state models from Java source code," in *Proc. 22nd Int. Conf. Software Eng.*, 2000, pp. 439–448.

[68] T. Ball and S. Rajamani, "Bebop: A symbolic model checker for Boolean programs," in *Lecture Notes in Computer Science, SPIN Model Checking and Software Verification*. Heidelberg, Germany: Springer-Verlag, 2000, vol. 1885, pp. 113–130.

[69] G. J. Holzmann and M. H. Smith, "Automating software feature verification," *Bell Labs Tech. J.*, vol. 5, no. 2, pp. 72–87, 2000.

[70] R. Alur, T. Dang, and F. Ivančić, "Reachability analysis of hybrid systems via predicate abstraction," in *Lecture Notes in Computer Science, Hybrid Systems: Computation and Control*, C. Tomlin and M. Greenstreet, Eds. Heidelberg, Germany: Springer-Verlag, Mar. 2002, vol. 2289, pp. 35–48.

[71] A. Puri and P. Varaiya, "Driving Safely in Smart Cars," Cal. PATH, Univ. Cal., Berkeley, UBC-ITS-PRR-95-24, 1995.

[72] R. Alur, L. de Alfaro, R. Grosu, T. A. Henzinger, M. Kang, R. Majumdar, F. Mang, C. M. Kirsch, and B. Y. Wang, "Mocha: A model checking tool that exploits design structure," in *Proc. 23rd Int. Conf. Softw. Eng.*, 2001, pp. 835–836.

Rajeev Alur (Member, IEEE) received the B.Tech. degree in computer science from the Indian Institute of Technology, Kanpur, India, in 1987 and the Ph.D. degree in computer science from Stanford University, Stanford, CA, in 1991.

He was previously with Bell Laboratories, Lucent Technologies, Murray Hill, NJ. He is currently a Professor of Computer and Information Science at the University of Pennsylvania, Philadelphia. He has published more than 70 articles in refereed journals and conference proceedings and served on numerous scientific committees. He serves on the editorial board of Formal Methods in System Design, Kluwer. His research interests include software engineering, design automation for embedded systems, and applied formal methods. He is well known for his research on timed and hybrid automata, a framework for specification and analysis of real-time systems.

Dr. Alur has won such awards as the Sloan Faculty Fellowship and the NSF CAREER award. He co-organized and cochaired the 1995 Workshop on Hybrid Systems and the 1996 Conference on Computer-Aided Verification.

Thao Dang received the *Diplôme d'Ingénieur* degree and the M.Sc. degree in electrical engineering from Ecole Nationale Supérieure d'Ingénieurs Electriciens, Grenoble, France, in 1996. She received the Ph.D. degree in automatic control from the Verimag Laboratory, Grenoble, France, in 2000.

From 2001 to 2002, she was a Postdoctoral Research Associate at the Department of Computer and Information Science, University of Pennsylvania, Philadelphia. She is currently a research scientist at the Centre National de la Recherché Scientifique (CNRS) (the French National Center of Scientific Research) and a member of the Verimag Laboratory. Her research interests are modeling, verification, and control of hybrid systems, and their applications in design and analysis of embedded real-time systems.

Joel Esposito is currently a Ph.D. degree candidate at the General Robotic and Active Sensory Perception (GRASP) Lab at the University of Pennsylvania, Philadelphia.

His research interests include simulation of hybrid and embedded systems as well as developing other numerical and computational tools for control system design. He also works on motion planning and control for mobile robotics.

Yerang Hur received the B.S. and M.S. degrees in computer engineering from Seoul National University, Seoul, South Korea, in 1994 and 1996, respectively. He is currently a Ph.D. degree candidate in the Department of Computer and Information Science, University of Pennsylvania, Philadelphia.

His research interests are in the areas of design automation, modeling and analysis of hybrid systems, parallel and distributed simulation, programming language support for system designs, real-time operating systems, mobile computing, distributed systems, and computer architecture.

Franjo Ivančić (Student Member, IEEE) received the *Diplom* degree in computer science from Rheinische Friedrich-Wilhelms University, Bonn, Germany, in 1999 and the M.S.E. degree in computer science from the University of Pennsylvania, Philadelphia, in 2000.

From 1997 to 1999, he was a Research Associate at the German National Research Center for Information Technology, Sankt Augustin, Germany. He is currently a Ph.D. candidate in the Department of Computer and Information Science, University of Pennsylvania. His research interests include software design automation techniques for embedded systems and formal methods for the analysis of hybrid systems.

Vijay Kumar received the M.Sc. and Ph.D. degrees in mechanical engineering from Ohio State University, Columbus, in 1985 and 1987, respectively.

From 1987 to present, he has been on the faculty in the Department of Mechanical Engineering and Applied Mechanics with a secondary appointment in the Department of Computer and Information Science at the University of Pennsylvania, Philadelphia. He is currently a Professor and the Deputy Dean for research in the School of Engineering and Applied Science. He has served on the Editorial Board of the *Journal of Franklin Institute* and the *ASME Journal of Mechanical Design*. His research interests include robotics, dynamics, control, design, and biomechanics.

Dr. Kumar is a member of the American Society of Mechanical Engineers and the Robotics International Society of Manufacturing Engineers. He is the recipient of the 1991 National Science Foundation Presidential Young Investigator award and the 1997 Freudenstein Award for significant accomplishments in mechanisms and robotics. He has served on the editorial board of the IEEE TRANSACTIONS ON ROBOTICS AND AUTOMATION.

Insup Lee (Fellow, IEEE) received the B.S. degree in mathematics from the University of North Carolina, Chapel Hill, in 1977 and the Ph.D. degree in computer science from the University of Wisconsin, Madison, in 1983.

From 1983 to present, he has been with the Department of Computer and Information Science, University of Pennsylvania, Philadelphia. He is currently Professor in that department. He has been on the editorial boards of *Formal Methods in System Design* and *Journal of Electrical Engineering and Information Science*. His research interests include real-time systems, formal methods, and software engineering. He has been developing programming concepts, language constructs, and operating systems for real-time systems. In recent years, he has been developing specification, analysis, and testing techniques based on real-time process algebra (ACSR) and hybrid systems. Furthermore, he has been implementing and evaluating software engineering tools based on formal techniques. He has also developed the MaC framework, which can be used to assure the correctness of a running system through monitoring and checking of safety properties.

Dr. Lee has been on the editorial board of IEEE TRANSACTIONS ON COMPUTERS. From 1994 to 1997, he was Computer Science and Engineering Undergraduate Curriculum Chair at the University of Pennsylvania. He has served on numerous program committees and has also chaired or cochaired several conferences and workshops.

Pradyumna Mishra received the B.Tech. degree from the Department of Electrical Engineering at the Indian Institute of Technology, Kharagpur, India, in 2000.

He is currently a Ph.D. degree candidate in the Department of Computer and Information Science at the University of Pennsylvania, Philadelphia. His research interests are in the areas of embedded control systems, hybrid systems, distributed robotics, and air traffic management systems.

George J. Pappas (Member, IEEE) received the B.S. degree in computer and systems engineering and the M.S. degree in computer and systems engineering from the Rensselaer Polytechnic Institute, Troy, NY, in 1991 and 1992, respectively. He received the Ph.D. degree from the Department of Electrical Engineering and Computer Sciences, University of California, Berkeley, in 1998.

In 1994, he was a Graduate Fellow at the Division of Engineering Science of Harvard University, Cambridge, MA. He is currently an Assistant Professor and Graduate Group Chair in the Department of Electrical Engineering at the University of Pennsylvania, Philadelphia, where he also holds a Secondary Appointment in the Department of Computer and Information Sciences. His research interests include embedded hybrid systems, hierarchical control systems, nonlinear control systems, geometric control theory, flight and air traffic management systems, robotics, and unmanned aerial vehicles.

Dr. Pappas is the recipient of the 2002 NSF CAREER award and the 1999 Eliahu Jury Award for Excellence in Systems Research from the Department of Electrical Engineering and Computer Sciences at the University of California, Berkeley.

Oleg Sokolsky received the M.Sc. degree in computer science from St. Petersburg Technical University, St. Petersburg, Russia, in 1988 and the Ph.D. degree in computer science from the State University of New York, Stony Brook, in 1996.

He is currently a Research Assistant Professor at the University of Pennsylvania, Philadelphia, where he has held research staff positions since 1998. His research interests include formal methods for the analysis of real-time and hybrid systems, model checking, and run-time verification.

Formal Verification for High Confidence Embedded Systems

Edmund Clarke[1]   David Garlan[1]   Bruce H. Krogh[2]   Reid Simmons[1]   Jeannette Wing[1]

[1]School of Computer Science
[2]Department of Electrical and Computer Engineering
Carnegie Mellon University
5000 Forbes Avenue
Pittsburgh, PA 15213

Abstract

This paper describes recent advances in the development of formal verification methods for embedded systems, including new techniques for dealing with probabilistic specifications and hybrid dynamic systems, and architecture-level descriptions, and methods for evaluating survivability and security. Current simulation and testing methods cover only a small fraction of the operating conditions that will be encountered in today's embedded computing systems, which are becoming increasingly complex to provide more demanding functionality. Particularly for safety-critical applications, new methods are needed to provide the high confidence that required for commercial and military systems. Formal verification methods offer the possibility of certifying the correctness of embedded system designs for complete ranges of operating conditions. The paper concludes with a discussion of the issues that need to be addressed to incorporate these techniques into tools used every day by embedded system design engineers.

Acknowledgment. This paper describes research supported in part by the US Army Research Office (ARO) High Confidence Embedded Systems Multidisciplinary Research Initiative, under contract no. DAAD19-01-1-0485.

1. Introduction

In virtually all of the technologies we use in government, industry, and daily life, there is an increasing reliance on embedded computers to augment capabilities, improve performance, and enhance safety. To meet the demands for high-confidence in these increasingly complex embedded systems, testing has become the most time-consuming and costly aspect of development for many commercial and military systems. There is a crucial need for better tools that make it possible to guarantee the correctness of embedded systems when they are designed, before they are deployed on target platforms. The availability of such tools could contribute to significant savings in the time and cost developing and certifying systems. For safety-critical applications, these tools could save lives.

Assuring embedded systems will operate correctly and safely is becoming increasingly difficult because:

- embedded systems have become highly distributed, multi-task, real-time systems, wrought with all the problems that can arise due to concurrency in complex real-time systems;
- embedded systems are controlling increasingly sophisticated and complex physical systems, which makes it necessary to take into account the continuous physical dynamics and feedback interactions in determining their correctness;
- embedded systems must operate with more autonomy under increasingly unpredictable conditions, making fault tolerance and survivability key requirements that must be assessed using models of uncertainty in the system components and the environment; and
- embedded systems are being developed with a wider, more sophisticated array of models and tools, making it more difficult to abstract essential features for verification and provide useful insight to the engineers.

These factors contribute to the growing concern that current methods for designing and evaluating complex embedded systems are inadequate.

The degree of assurance provided today is based on extensive simulation and testing. In some cases, simulation is the only option; testing may be impossible because the system's intended effect is irreversible, or because the environment is inaccessible. Both simulation and testing suffer from being incomplete: they evaluate the system for only selected operating conditions and inputs. In most of today's applications, it is impossible to cover even a small fraction of the total operating space that an embedded system will actually encounter when it is deployed.

The goal of the research described in this paper is to complement traditional methods of embedded system verification (simulation and testing) with formal verification methods, that is, with methods that analyze the behavior of a system over a complete (possibly infinite) set of operating conditions without resorting to exhaustive simulation. Our long-term vision is to see a "row of buttons" on the desktop of the design engineer's workstation that provide immediate access to formal verification procedures that are practical and efficient. Each button might be specific to a class of properties relevant to the engineer's application. For example, for the design of an automobile intelligent cruise control system, the engineer would be able to invoke a procedure to verify that collisions will be avoided with other vehicles under a full range of speed, traffic, and road conditions. The invocation of this verification procedure by a simple selection on a screen would hide from the engineer the details of the sophisticated operations on the specification and engineering model required to apply the algorithms described in this paper. We envision similar buttons to check for deadlock freedom, race conditions, maximum resource usage, minimum delay time, and so on. We believe such property-specific and domain-specific tools based on formal verification methods will make it possible to design and deploy complex embedded systems with a level of confidence that far exceeds what can be achieved today using simulation and testing. This paper describes recent advances in fundamental research that address many technical challenges, pragmatic and theoretical, that need to be addressed to realize our vision.

Verification is the process of determining whether a system satisfies a given property of interest. In formal verification, we use an abstract mathematical model of the system to be checked, and describe the desired behavioral properties with precise, mathematical rigor. Today the best known verification methods are model checking and theorem proving, both of which have sophisticated tool support and have been applied to non-trivial systems, including the design and debugging of microprocessors, cache coherence protocols, and Internet working protocols. Model checking in particular has enjoyed huge success in industry for verifying digital circuit designs. In recent years, companies such as Fujitsu, IBM, Intel, and Motorola have started in-house model checking groups. Companies such as Cadence, IBM, Lucent, and Siemens market formal verification tools to hardware designers.

Despite these successes, formal verification has not been used to a great extent in the development of embedded systems. One reason for this lack of use is that the formalisms and techniques have not been distilled into tools that are accessible to the practicing design engineer. Too much expertise is required to construct the abstract models and formal specifications, making formal verification practical only for applications that merit the attention of personnel with specialized advanced training. Making formal verification part of the embedded system tool kit is more than simply "technology transition," however. The techniques themselves require further research to alleviate existing limitations: at present, they do not scale well to problems with large state spaces and they do not handle important features of embedded systems applications.

Our research initiative sponsored by the Army Research Office High Confidence Embedded Systems program is organized around the following broad themes:

Verifying System Integrity. By system integrity we mean correct behavior involving interactions between different components of an embedded system implementation. There are special classes of bugs that frequently arise in embedded system architectures, stemming from synchronization violations, resource constraints, and real-time constraints. These problems are particularly difficult to find using traditional testing because of the large number of situations that must be tried and because the problems often arise only after particular sequences of events occur, which are often not reproducible. Real-time performance affects the integrity of an embedded system, particularly when tasks are executed on a distributed hardware platform. Recent efforts in the design of embedded systems have resulted in defining architectural frameworks to support system development. The constraints inherent in these classes of architectures make the formal verification of real-time and decisional problems more tractable. The advances to address many of these issues builds on techniques—primarily model checking (see Sect. 2)—originally developed for formal verification of large-scale digital circuits and computer communication protocols, where similar problems of concurrency are prevalent.

Modeling the Environment. In many applications, crucial aspects of correct behavior are defined in terms of the interactions between the embedded computing system and its environment. These aspects include both the dynamics of physical systems being controlled and the inherent uncertainty of the environments in which these systems operate. To deal with physical systems, it is necessary for the formal model to include features of the environment, which typically involves continuous-valued variables and continuous dynamics. To deal with uncertainty, it is necessary to assess a system's survivability and fault tolerance with respect to the likelihood of failure events and other contingencies. Security against malicious intrusion into the embedded systems has also become an issue of major concern in recent year. In this paper, we describe new methods for addressing these issues, including methods for formal verification of probabilistic models, techniques for verifying properties of systems interactions between discrete and continuous dynamic system (so-called hybrid dynamic systems), and new approaches to evaluating system survivability and security.

Usability. To develop "push-button" verification tools that can be used routinely by engineers (non-specialists in formal verification), innovative work is needed to make effective connections to the design environments and languages currently used for embedded system development. This paper describes work on tools for specifying and analyzing architectures for embedded systems, and a new method for extracting the architectural structure of a given implementation to provide a structured view of the design and to enhance the analyzability of the system. The concluding section of the paper discusses remaining issues to be addressed in the area of usability as well as other work that needs to be done to realize our "push-button" vision for formal verification.

The remainder of this paper is organized as follows. Section 2 provides a brief introduction to model checking, the algorithmic approach to formal verification developed over the past 25 years that underlies much of the work described in the subsequent sections. Section 3 describes several advances in fundamental model checking techniques made during the course of our recent research. Significant extensions of model checking to new types of systems and specifications are described in Sections 4 and 5, which concern model checking for probabilistic systems and hybrid dynamic systems, respectively. Section 6 describes new methods for evaluating the survivability and security of embedded system, which are based on generalizations of model checking concepts and algorithms. Section 7 concerns the specification, analysis, and evaluation of architectures for embedded system designs, which will ultimately provide the context for applying the formal verification techniques described in the previous sections. The concluding section discusses directions for future work aimed at transitioning the results of the fundamental research described in this paper into engineering tools for embedded system design.

2. Model Checking

Model checking refers to a collection of methods and tools for verifying properties of a system algorithmically, that is, without human intervention or the use of heuristics [CGP99]. Model checking requires two formalisms. First, the behaviors of the system for which properties are to verified must be specified using a precise mathematical formalism. Second, there must be a formal mathematical language for specifying the properties of interest unambiguously.

Many embedded systems can be modeled formally using a finite-state *transition system*, augmented by a set of *conditions* that are either true or false depending on the state of the transition system. This mathematical structure that represents the possible behaviors a system as its state (and consequently the conditions) evolve over time through state transitions is called a Kripke structure. For example, the computer program in a cell phone that establishes a connection when a telephone number is entered goes through a sequence of states with the transitions between states determined by the cell phone communication hardware, which can also be modeled as a transition system. Some state transition sequences lead to a successful connection, whereas other sequences lead to error conditions that display messages on the screen.

Given a transition system modeling an embedded system, properties to be verified by a model checker characterize the collection of desirable, or undesirable, behaviors. For the cell phone application, it might be of interest to verify that the cell phone computer program always makes a successful connection whenever its environment (the cell phone communication hardware) goes through particular sequences of state transitions. An undesirable behavior would be to reach a program state from which it would be impossible to the initial state, allowing the user make another call. In general, the specifications of interest are *sets* of possible behaviors rather, than a single sequence of state transitions and conditions. Therefore, the language for specifying properties to be verified must provide an efficient and intuitive method for describing entire classes of behaviors. Two common formalisms for specifying a property to be verified are: (i) an additional transition system constructed so that its behaviors correspond precisely to the set of desired or undesired behaviors; or (ii) some form of *temporal logic*, which refers to a formal mathematical language for describing possible sequences of conditions that can occur as a system behavior evolves in time.

Model checking tools start with the finite state model of the system under consideration and examine all possible behaviors, without a bound on time, to expose any violations of task synchronization constraints. The key to model checking is a set of algorithms to evaluate whether or not given specifications are true for all possible behaviors without simulating each behavior (which would be impossible, since there is no bound on time). When specifications are not satisfied, these algorithms provide the user with *counter examples*, which are explicit behaviors that violate the specification. Counter examples give the designer insight into why the system does not satisfy design requirements and what needs to be done to fix the problem.

The challenge in model checking is to deal with the state-space explosion that occurs in real systems because they are made through the composition of many components. Given a set of N components each with M states, the state space for their composite behavior can be as large as M^N, a number that quickly exceeds the memory of any current or foreseeable computer for real systems. Therefore, the technical challenge in model checking is in devising algorithms and data structures that make it possible to handle large state spaces. In the mid-80s Carnegie Mellon researchers made a major breakthrough in the state space explosion challenge of model checking. McMillan, a Carnegie Mellon graduate student, used Bryant's ordered binary decision diagrams to represent the states and state transitions in Clarke's model checking technique, enabling model checkers to go from handling 104 states to 10^{20} states and beyond. BDDs became the data structure of choice for building symbolic model checkers throughout the next two decades of research.

Researchers throughout the world have develop new algorithms, data structures and tools for model checking, including techniques for compositional reasoning, counterexample explanation, counterexample-guided abstraction and refinement, generation of graphs of counterexamples, model checking real-time systems, parameterized model checking, and predicate abstraction. Compositional reasoning makes it possible to verify properties of systems composed of many interacting components by evaluating properties of the individual components, thereby avoiding the construction of the full system which may have a prohibitive number of states. Abstraction refers to the construction of models that have fewer states the model under consideration that may be sufficient to solve the verification problem. The basic idea is to hide details of the behaviors that might be irrelevant. If the abstraction is too conservative, that is, if too many details have been eliminated, a more refined (i.e., less conservative) abstraction is constructed, often through insight and guidance provided by a counter example from the initial abstraction. A recent trend has been to integrate and augment model checking with other verification techniques, such as boolean satisfiability solvers (so-called SAT solvers), decision procedures, and proof checking.

Model checking is fast, automatic, and supports partial specifications; above all, its tour de force is that it produces counterexamples, which can represent subtle errors in design, and thus can be used to aid in debugging. Model checking is a proven success in the design of digital hardware and protocol verification; a current trend is to apply model checking to software. In the following sections, we describe research aimed at applying model checking techniques to a number of problems arising in embedded systems.

3. Advances in Model Checking for Embedded Systems

Applying model checking to embedded systems is complicated by several factors, ranging from the difficulty to model computer programs—due to the complexity of programming languages as compared to hardware description languages—to difficulties in specifying meaningful properties of embedded systems using the usual temporal logical formalisms of model checking. A third reason is the perennial state space explosion problem, whereby the complexity of verifying an implementation against a specification becomes prohibitive.

The most common instantiations of model checking to date have focused on finite-state models and either computation tree logic (CTL) [ClE81], a form of so-called branching-time temporal logic, or linear-time logic (LTL) [LiP85]. To apply model checking to embedded systems, it is necessary to specify (often complex) properties on the finite-state abstracted models of embedded computer programs. The difficulties in doing so are even more pronounced when reasoning about modular software, such as the concurrent or component-based sequential programs in embedded systems. Indeed, in modular programs, communication among modules proceeds via events (or actions), which can represent function calls, requests and acknowledgments, etc. Moreover, such communication is commonly data dependent. Behavioral claims, therefore, are often specifications defined over combinations of events and data valuations in embedded systems.

Existing modeling techniques usually represent finite-state machines as finite annotated directed graphs, using either state-based or event-based formalisms. Although both frameworks are interchangeable (an event can be encoded as a change in state variables, and likewise one can equip a state with different events to reflect different values of its internal variables), converting from one representation to the other often leads to a significant enlargement of the state space. Moreover, neither approach on its own is practical when it comes to modular embedded software. Considerable domain expertise is usually required to generate the appropriate models for verification and to specify proper claims.

To address the requirements for verification of embedded systems, we have developed a framework in which both state-based and event-based properties can be expressed, combined, and verified. The models are directed graphs in which states are labeled with logical conditions and transitions are labeled with events. The specification logic is a state/event derivative of LTL. This allows us to represent both embedded software and specifications directly and intuitively.

We have extended existing model checking algorithms to help reason about state/event-based systems without increasing requirements for memory or time. Moreover, the verification algorithm uses compositional abstraction refinement procedures developed for the efficient verification of concurrent systems. These procedures are embedded within a counterexample-guided abstraction refinement framework (CEGAR) [CGJ00]. CEGAR lets us investigate the validity of a given specification through a sequence of increasingly refined abstractions of the system, until the property is either established or a real counterexample is found. Moreover, thanks to compositionality, the abstraction, counterexample validation, and refinement steps can all be carried out component-wise, thereby alleviating the need to build the full state space of the distributed system.

The verification of state/event specifications on concurrent systems requires that the global composed system be deadlock free. Deadlocks can occur, for example, when several embedded components communicate via blocking message passing. That is, if the embedded processes stop progress while waiting for certain messages, a circular wait condition could occur where each process in the circle is waiting for a message from the next process. Deadlock freedom is often a vital specification, especially for safety-critical embedded systems, which are expected always to service requests within a fixed time limit or be responsive to external stimuli. One of the main advances in our work is the development of new, non-standard abstraction schemes that preserve deadlock and are (in an appropriate sense) compositional [CCO04]. As a result, we have been able to devise a compositional CEGAR-based framework for deadlock detection, which has led to substantial time and space improvements over corresponding classical approaches found in the literature.

We have applied this new modeling and verification procedure to an inter-process communication protocol (IPC) developed by ABB Corporation, used to mediate information in a multi-threaded robotics control automation system [CC005]. The implementation is required to satisfy various safety-critical properties, in particular, deadlock-freedom. The IPC protocol supports multiple modes of communication, including synchronous point-to-point, broadcast, publish/subscribe, and asynchronous communication. Each of these modes is implemented in terms of messages passed between queues owned by different threads. The protocol handles the creation and manipulation of message queues, synchronizing access to shared data using various operating system primitives (e.g., semaphores), and cleaning up internal states when a communication fails or times out. We successfully verified the absences of deadlocks in this industrial embedded system application.

Recently, we have also made progress in so-called bounded model checking. In contrast to conventional model checking that evaluates a specification for all possible behaviors, bounded model checking evaluates the correctness of a specification over a fixed number of transitions. Distinct variables are introduced for the conditions and states at each transition the bounded this bounded time horizon. This makes it possible to use SAT solvers to evaluate whether or not the specification is satisfied for all possible sequences of state transitions for the transition relation defining the finite-state transition system. The model checking problem is solved with a negative result if a behavior of finite length violates the specification. On the other hand, if all behaviors up to a given length satisfy the specification, the time horizon needs to be increased to see if some longer behavior violates the specification. We have derived bounds on the number of steps that need to be considered for bounded model checking to be conclusive for LTL specifications, and have considered the implications for the computational complexity of this approach [CKO04,CKO05].

4. Probabilistic Model Checking

In many embedded system applications, standard model checking is too stringent, either because the system is too complex to verify properties using current tools or because a design that satisfies a property in all cases will be too conservative in dealing with normal operating situations. Probabilistic model checking relaxes the requirements by check to see if properties will hold with a given probability, rather than in all cases. For example, it might be desirable to guarantee that a robot control system avoids a particular situation that will require human intervention at least 95% of the time. This would be a reasonable specification when a human operator can deal with the difficult operating conditions, provided they are sufficiently infrequent so as to not overload the human operator or slow down the automatic operation of the system in most circumstances.

To perform probabilistic model checking, probabilities need to be in introduced into (1) the models that generate the possible system behaviors and (2) the formalism used to describe the sets of desired or undesired behaviors (the specifications). The first issue is addressed by assigning probabilities to the transitions that can be made from each state, which results in a continuous-time Markov chain (CTMC), or in the case of interacting transition systems, a so-called generalized semi-Markov process (GSMP) [Gly89]. To create probabilistic specifications, temporal logic statements are augmented to prescribe a bound on the probability that the behavior of the system will satisfy or not satisfy the given temporal logic statement [ASS00, BHH03].

Given a probabilistic model and a probabilistic specification, there are two alternatives for evaluating where or not the specification is satisfied. The first approach is to compute numerically the probability that the given specified property will be satisfied, using analytical methods for evaluating the probabilities of events in a CTMC, and then compare this probability with the bound given in the specification [KNP02]. This approach is attractive for relatively small systems and simple specifications, but it becomes more difficult and even impossible to compute the probabilities of interest numerically when the systems become very large and the specifications become complex, for example, when there are many nested conditions in the specification.

The second approach to probabilistic model checking combines the speed of simulation and with statistical sampling theory to evaluate whether or not a probabilistic specifications is true [YoS02]. The principal advantage of this statistical approach is a specification may be quickly satisfied with a relatively low number of simulations. This occurs when the probabilistic confidence intervals provided by the sampling theory, which can be computed after each simulation run, are sufficient to demonstrate the correctness of the probabilistic specification.

We have developed a tool, YMER, for verifying properties of probabilistic transient properties that uses a blend of numerical and statistical techniques [You05]. To handle the generality of stochastic discrete event systems, YMER implements the statistical model checking techniques, based on discrete event simulation and acceptance sampling. YMER uses discrete event simulation to generate sample execution paths. The verification result over a sample execution path is the outcome of a chance experiment (Bernoulli trial), which is used as an observation for an acceptance sampling procedure. YMER implements both sampling with a fixed number of observations and sequential acceptance sampling. YMER includes support for distributed acceptance sampling, i.e. the use of multiple machines to generate observations, which can result in significant speedup as each observation can be generated independently. YMER can use numerical techniques CTMCs as it includes the hybrid engine from the PRISM tool for CTMC model checking [KNP02]. Numerical and statistical techniques can be used in combination to solve nested CSL queries for CTMCs.

Empirical results show numerical and statistical approaches are linear in the time bound in basic CSL specifications, but the statistical approach scales better with the size of the state space and requires considerably less memory. The numerical method can be more accurate, but the statistical approach can provide results much more quickly, albeit with a specified uncertainty that is costly to reduce [YKN05]. A direction for future research would be to obtain a better understanding of the number of samples required for verifying properties of varying complexity. It may also be possible to increase performance when verifying conjunctions by considering heuristics for ordering the terms in the specification. Another problem to consider is that of verifying CSL formulas with unrestricted temporal operators and the steady-state operator, which requires developing techniques for evaluating the long-run behavior of a discrete event system.

5. Hybrid Dynamic Systems

Embedded systems interacting with continuous dynamic environments are hybrid dynamic systems, that is, systems with both continuous and discrete state variables. Hybrid dynamics can also appear in the environment itself when the continuous dynamics change depending on discrete conditions, such as changes that occur in robotic mechanisms depending on whether or not certain surfaces are in contact. Tools for formal verification are based on models of computation that are inherently discrete state/event models, whereas the interactions of embedded systems with the physical world are governed by the laws of continuous dynamics, usually modeled by differential and algebraic equations.

In contrast to model checking for finite-state systems, algorithmic verification is possible for hybrid dynamic systems with only very simple classes of continuous dynamics. Consequently, the best one can hope for is the verification of properties of conservative models that represent outer or inner approximations to the families of exact system behaviors. The standard approach to hybrid system verification is to construct a finite-state abstraction so that methods for verifying properties of discrete-state systems can be applied to hybrid dynamic systems [AHL00, ChK01]. To apply these methods, the designer would typically use engineering insight and simulation studies to identify the appropriate level of detail needed in the model and the operating conditions that need to be investigated [FeK04]. Similar scoping of the problem is necessary for purely discrete-state systems.

The fundamental problem in obtaining discrete models of hybrid systems is the computation and representation of reachable sets for the continuous dynamics. Current methods for computing these reachable sets are effective only when there are only a few (less than 10) continuous state variables. Even for low-dimensional systems, numerical errors inherent in floating point computations often thwart attempts to verify properties of embedded control systems. To deal with this problem, we have developed methods for decomposing the continuous dynamic models into low-dimensional interacting subsystems, each of which can be handled effectively with our computational tools [HaK04]. Formally, this approach corresponds to projecting the full state vector into lower-dimensional subspaces. We have also developed a new hybrid systems verification tool called PHAVer that uses integer representations of rational numbers as an alternative to floating point numbers, thereby avoiding the numerical problems encountered in other hybrid system verification tools [Fre05]. PHAVer support compositional reasoning so that properties of a hybrid system made of several components can be inferred from properties of the individual components [FHK04].

Another approach to reducing the time to verify hybrid systems leverages the concept of counter-example-guided abstraction refinement (CEGAR), developed originally for discrete-state systems [Kur94,CGJ00]. CEGAR uses information from so-called counterexamples, which are behaviors in the abstract model of the system that violate the specification, to guide the construction of a less conservative abstraction (a refinement) to determine if the specification is actually violated in the original model. We have developed CEGAR for hybrid systems and applied it to small examples, including a model of an automobile cruise control system [CFH03]. The concept of CEGAR for hybrid systems makes it possible to use a variety of methods for computing the reachable sets for the continuous dynamics [SFH03] and to explore the behaviors of the system for parts of counterexamples (so-called fragments) without evaluating the behaviors for entire counterexamples [FCJ05].

6. Survivability and Security

Survivability refers to the capability of a networked computing system to continue to function and provide services at a sufficient level of performance and safety when there are faults and failures in certain system components. Security generally refers to the ability of a computing system to ward off malicious attempts to gain inappropriate access to information or to diminish the ability of the system to perform effectively. Although it is agreed that survivability and security refer to different aspects of a system's performance, these terms both concern operation under conditions that are not normal. Therefore, there are similarities in the methods and tools needed to evaluate survivability and security. This section describes recent research that has lead to tools for evaluating survivability and security based on a common set of concepts and algorithms.

Concerns about survivability and security have grown as embedded systems have become more complex, with networks of embedded processors playing increasingly significant roles in safety-critical applications. Moreover, although embedded systems have been traditionally dedicated, isolated systems, they are becoming more accessible, and therefore more vulnerable, through wireless access and other connections to sources outside the specific domain for which the embedded system has been designed. For example, it would be useful for automotive companies to have remote, wireless access to the networked embedded systems on automobiles to perform monitoring, maintenance and software upgrades. This introduces a potential point of vulnerability, however, to unwanted intrusion into the automotive control system.

Analysis of the survivability and security of networked systems involves the modeling of the operating modes and characteristics of the system nodes and communication channels, followed with an analysis of how the performance is affected under various abnormal operating conditions. These modeling and analysis activities are often performed manually for many computer systems, but the complexity of networked systems quickly exceeds the capacity of manual analysis. What is needed are: (1) a method for generating the models automatically from simple, manageable models of the system components; and (2) computational tools to evaluated the likelihood that that the system will be able to function properly when components fail (survivability) or that adversarial actions will be thwarted effectively (security).

We have shown recently how the technologies developed for formal verification can be used as the basis for the modeling and analysis of survivability and security in networked embedded systems [JhW00,SHJ02]. The first observation is that the formalism of concurrent, communicating transition systems used to describe systems for model checking tools are a natural, intuitive way to model networked embedded systems. Each component of the networked embedded system, including its behaviors under normal and faulty conditions or malicious attacks, can be modeled as a transition system. The interactions of the systems are then modeled by the natural mechanisms for composition available in model checking tools such as NuSMV and SPIN.

The key idea for evaluating survivability and security using these models is to generalize the algorithms used by model checkers to generated counter examples to demonstrate particular ways in which a given specification can be violated. This generalization is described as follows. The system designer creates a specification (using the temporal logic CTL, for example) that describes the successful avoidance of an undesired behavior of the system. For example, a specification could describe the condition that an automotive control system always delivers correct ignition and fuel injection commands to the engine. Then, the model checker will identify the set of states and transitions that could lead to a violation of this specification, but rather than generate a single counter-example, the new algorithms create a *scenario graph* that represent *all* state-transition sequences that could lead to a violation of the specification. In general, in a large networked embedded system there could be several ways in which undesirable conditions could occur, which is why it is difficult to construct manually. Using our algorithms, the scenario graphs generated by the model checking tools are guaranteed to be complete and correct.

Given the scenario graph, one can perform a variety of analyses that provide insight in to the survivability and security of a system and how to make design modifications that will increase survivability and security [JSW02,ShW04]. For example, probabilities can be introduced on the transitions in the scenario graph to represent the relative likelihoods of various events. Decision strategies for responding to different conditions can also be introduced to influence the way the system would behave under active control. The theory of Markov decision processes can then be invoked to compute quantitative measures of the survivability and security of the system. The designer can also play "what-if" games with the scenario graph, but removing or changing various transitions to evaluate the effectiveness of various alternatives to change the system architecture. Finally, the graph can be analyzed using numerical optimization methods to evaluate what could or should be made to achieve optimal survivability and security subject the availability of limited resources. A promising direction for future developments is to include models of an adversary in security analyses. One step in that direction that uses game theory is reported in [LyW05].

7. Architectures for Embedded Software

A well-defined software architecture is critical for the success of a complex embedded system. An architecture provides a high-level view of the system in terms of its principal runtime components, their interactions, and their properties. As an abstract representation of a system, an architecture permits many forms of high-level inspection and analysis, allowing the designer to determine if the system will satisfy its critical quality specifications. Recently, there has been considerable interest in these methods in the *model-driven architecture* (MDA) initiative of the Object Management Group [OMG05]. A toolset to support the MDA approach in the automotive industry is described in [SGB04].

Architectures are described using *architecture description languages* (ADLs). Trade-offs among the features of several ADLs proposed during the past decade evaluated in [RSM04]. Many features of software for embedded systems can be dealt with at the architectural level, including software re-use, dependability and even run-time adaptivity for new applications [GCS03,CHG04]. In this section we describe recent research on using architectural descriptions to generate embedded code (Sect. 7.1) and a new approach to recovering the architectural structure from existing code (Sect. 7.2).

7.1 Automatic Code Generation

One theme of our research on software architectures reported in the paper [GRS05] included in this volume addresses a long-term goal of software engineering, which is to establish systematic techniques for generating code directly from such high-level specifications or models. This line of research has led to a long stream of results in areas of formal refinement and automatic code generation The attraction of automatic code generation stems from the observation that considerable leverage can be obtained by separating software design into two levels. At the top level one describes a system in terms of a "platform-independent" model (PIM). Then one reifies that model into a lower-level "platform-specific" model (PSM) that binds abstract components and connectors to concrete mechanisms and code. This separation allows one to focus initially on abstract structure and functionality of a system, binding implementation issues later, and potentially allowing the same abstract model to be targeted to different platforms.

In [GRS05] we describe our experience of developing an approach and supporting tool set to support an MDA-like approach to NASA Space Systems Software. The key elements of the approach are (a) the use of formal architectural modeling to capture the abstract system description; (b) the clear separation of essential component functionality (described using pure functions) from incidental (or platform-specific) code; and (c) a retargetable code generator and reuse repository to translate architectural designs to one of many possible deployment platforms.

Bridging the gap between the system design and working code is manual, brittle, and error prone. Programmers may not fully understand the intentions of system designers, and there is no verifiable relationship between system design and code. This situation is compounded by the fact that for most space missions multiple versions of the software must be created. Some are full-featured, used during development, simulation, and testing on-ground; other leaner versions are needed for resource-constrained flight platforms.

Our work unifies two separate streams of research to produce a new synthetic approach. The first stream is formal representation of software architecture and tools to analyze those descriptions [AlG97],[GMW00]. The second is a proposal to define control systems from components specified as pure functions [DvR04]. In this work we show how to use architectural descriptions combined with pure functions to create a tool that generates deployable code.

Working with engineers at NASA JPL, we developed an approach, and a tool called MDS Studio, that is centered on three significant changes to their current practice:

1. Use a formal architectural modeling language to represent a system design and its constraints. Linked to existing NASA system design databases, a formal architectural description provides an explicit representation of a system configuration, and permits automated analyses such as conformance to architectural style, as well as system-specific constraints. (For example, if a system engineer determines that in the system under design a state A depends on state B, a rule is automatically created in the architectural modeling tool to check that the estimator for state variable A is also connected to state variable B.)

2. Define high-level components as pure functions (stateless mappings of inputs to outputs), thereby abstracting from details of timing, synchronization, communication, and data representation, while still retaining the ability to describe critical algorithms for state estimation and control.

3. Provide a retargetable compiler that can produce multiple versions of deployable code from the abstract architectural design. The compiler leverages the substantial body reusable framework code to map the "essential" computations defined in the abstract configuration to specific implementations, but does so in a way that preserves the design constraints.

This approach is applied in the following process:
1. Systems engineer conduct a state effects analysis, to determine the states required to achieve a mission.
2. Software engineers write essential code to implement these states as pure functions, which just implement the steps of the various control loops, but not how they are put together or scheduled.
3. This essential code is uploaded to a state database, which is then used to generate architectural styles, which are used to:
4. Compose the system in an architectural model that specifies instances of the essential code and how they relate.
5. This architectural model is fed into code generators that weave the essential code with framework code and other incidental code, such as connections and schedulers, to produce code that can be deployed. The aim is that code can be generated for different deployments without affecting the pure functions or the architectural model.

The architectural modeling tool provides a platform for reasoning about the correctness of the model developed by the software engineers. Whenever new rules about the desired behavior of the system are discovered, the system engineer can express this as a rule in the architectural modeling tool, ensuring that this check becomes a part of the build process of the system. Another benefit of this approach is a side effect of the reuse library; as components accumulate over time, the amount of testing that any one component might experience will increase, providing more confidence in the reliability of the components. Finally, the functional approach to developing the essential components is amenable to the design and maintenance of an automated suite of unit tests. The simplicity of the pure function signature specification ensures that writing unit tests for these functions is a straightforward practice; each pure function can be tested in complete isolation from all other pure function components. Further details of this work and the NASA case study are reported in the paper.

7.2 Inferring Architectures from Run-Time Behavior

Despite considerable progress in developing an engineering basis for software architecture, a persisting difficult problem is determining whether a system as implemented has the architecture as designed. Without some form of consistency guarantees, the validity of any architectural analysis will be suspect, at best, and completely erroneous, at worst. Currently two general techniques are used to determine or enforce relationships between a system's software architecture and its implementation. The first is to ensure consistency by construction. This can be done by embedding architectural constructs in an implementation language where program analysis tools can check for conformance. Or, it can be done through code generation, using tools to create an implementation from a more abstract architectural definition. Ensuring consistency by construction is effective when it can be applied, since tools can guarantee conformance. Unfortunately, this approach has limited applicability since it requires the use of specific architecture-based development tools, languages, and implementation strategies.

We have developed a technique to determine the architecture of a system by examining its runtime behavior. The key idea is that a system's execution can be monitored and observations about its runtime behavior can then, in principal, be used to infer its dynamic architecture. This approach has the advantage that it applies to any system that can be monitored, it gives an accurate image of what is actually going on in the real system, it can accommodate systems with architectures that change dynamically, and it imposes no a priori restrictions on system implementation or architectural style. This capability is realized in the DiscoSTEP tool, which uses mappings based on regularities in run-time observations to construct an architectural view of an implemented system to dynamically verify conformance to a pre-existing architectural specification [SAG05]. This mapping is defined conceptually as a Colored Petri Net [Jen94] that are used at runtime to track the progress of the system and output architectural events when predefined runtime patterns are recognized. Thus the mapping provides a kind of behavior modeling, where it is used to identify just those behaviors of a system that are "architecturally significant."

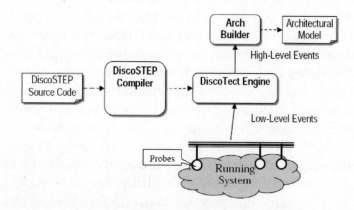

Figure 7.1. The DiscSTEP architecture from [SAG05].

Figure 7.1 illustrates the main components of the DiscoSTEP tool. The DiscoSTEP language allows for the specification of the mappings between low-level events and architecture events. The run-time engine deploys probes to collect events from the program to produce architecture events, which are then analyzed by DiscoSTEP to recognize interleaved patterns of runtime events to generate sets of architectural events. A run-time event is a message that indicates something has happened: method calls, CPU utilization, network bandwidth consumption, memory usage, etc. The Architecture Builder incrementally constructs the architectural description, which can be displayed to the user or processed by other architectural analysis tools. This approach applies to systems that follow specified coding conventions.

In a case study reported in [SAG05], DiscoSTEP was used to determine the run-time architecture of a simulation testbed for adaptive mobile systems [Kaz03]. Current research aims to expand the applicability of this technology to a broader range of languages and architectural styles, and to create effective metrics to identify the coverage of the architectural analysis.

8. Conclusions

This paper describes several recent advances in developing the fundamental algorithms and techniques that will lead to effective tools for formal verification of embedded systems. We have worked with several industrial and government research groups developing case studies to apply these methods as they have been developed. Applications include automotive control systems, robotic systems, (list) with citations.

To realize the vision of "push-button" verification in the designers' tool box, more research and development is needed to transfer the advances described in this paper into the design flow for high-confidence embedded systems. Toward this end, issues being addressed in on-going research include:

- automatic translations between models currently used by designers and the formal models required by the verification algorithms;
- generation of formal specifications from domain-specific requirements definitions that are more intuitive to design engineers
- Our research in this area will emphasize: (i) translators that can produce formal models automatically for embedded system software; and (ii) techniques for presenting verification results to the user so that they can be interpreted easily and to provide effective information for correcting and modifying designs.

References

[AHL00] R. Alur, T. A. Henzinger, G. Lafferriere, G. J. Pappas. Discrete abstractions of hybrid systems. Proceedings of the IEEE, 88(7), 2000, pp. 971-84.

[AlG97] R. Allen and D. Garlan. A formal basis for architectural connection. ACM Transactions on Software Engineering and Methodology, 6(3), July 1997.

[ASS00] A. Aziz, K. Sanwal, V. Singhal, R. Brayton. Model checking continuous-time Markov chains. ACM Trans. Comput. Logi 1(1). pp. 162-170, 2000.

[BHH03] C. Baier, B. R. Haverkort, H. Hermanns, J.-P. Katoen. Model checking algorithms for continuous-time Markov chains. IEEE Trans. on Software Engineering. 29(6), pp. 524-541, 2003.

[CC005] S. Chaki, E. M. Clarke, J. Ouaknine, N. Sharygina, and N. Sinha. Concurrent software verification with states, events, and deadlocks. Formal Aspects of Computing, 2005.

[CCO04] S. Chaki, E. M. Clarke, J. Ouaknine, and N. Sharygina. Automated, compositional and iterative deadlock detection. Proceedings of MEMOCODE 04, 2004.

[CFH03] E. Clarke, A. Fehnker, Z. Han, B. Krogh, J. Ouaknine, O. Stursberg and M. Theobald. Abstraction and counterexample-guided refinement in model checking of hybrid systems. International Journal of Foundations of Computer

Science (IJFCS) special issues on Verification and Analysis of Infinite State Systems, 2003.

[CGJ00]   E. M. Clarke, O. Grumberg, S. Jha, Y. Lu, and H. Veith. Counterexample-guided abstraction re.nement. In Proceedings of CAV, volume 1855 of Lecture Notes in Computer Science, pages 154–169. Springer, 2000.

[CGJ00]   E.M. Clarke, O. Grumberg, S. Jha, Y. Lu, and H. Veith. Counterexample-guided abstraction refinement. in CAV, volume 1855 of LNCS, pages 154–169. Springer, 2000.

[CGP99]   E. Clarke, O. Grumberg, and D. Peled. Model Checking. MIT Press, 1999.

[CHG04]   S.-W. Cheng, A.-C. Huang, D. Garlan, B. Schmerl, and P. Steenkiste. Rainbow: Architecture-based self adaptation with reusable infrastructure. IEEE Computer Vol. 37 Num. 10, October 2004.

[CHG04]   S-W Cheng, A-C Huang, D. Garlan, B. Schmerl, and P. Steenkiste. Rainbow: Architecture-based self adaptation with reusable infrastructure. IEEE Computer Vol. 37 Num. 10, October 2004.

[ChK01]   A. Chutinan, B. H. Krogh. Verification of infinite-state dynamic systems using approximate quotient transition systems. IEEE Trans. on Automatic Control 46 (9), 1401-10, 2001.

[CKO04]   E. M. Clarke, D. Kroening, J. Ouaknine, and O. Strichman. Completeness and complexity of bounded model checking. Proceedings of VMCAI 04, LNCS 2937, 2004.

[CKO05]   E. M. Clarke, D. Kroening, J. Ouaknine, and O. Strichman. Computational challenges in bounded model checking. International Journal on Software Tools for Technology Transfer 7(2), 2005.

[ClE81]   E. M. Clarke and E. A. Emerson. Design and synthesis of synchronization skeletons using branching time temporal logic. Lecture Notes in Computer Science, 131, 1981.

[DvR04]   D. Dvorak and K. Reinholtz. Separating essential from incidentals: an execution architecture for real-time control systems. Proc. 7th IEEE International Symposium on Object-Oriented Real-Time Distributed Computing. Austria, 2004.

[FeK04]   A. Fehnker and B. H. Krogh. Hybrid system verification is not a senecure: The electronic throttle control case study. 2nd International Symposium on Automated Technology for Verification and Analysis (ATVA 2004), National Taiwan University, November 2004.

[FHK04]   G. Frehse, Z. Han, B. H. Krogh, Assume-guarantee reasoning for hybrid I/O-automata by over-approximation of continuous interaction. IEEE Conf. on Decision and Control. Dec. 2004.

[Fre05]   G. Frehse. PHAVer: Algorithmic verification of hybrid systems past HyTech. M. Morari and L. Tiele (eds.). Hybrid Systems: Computation and Control (HSCC'05). Lecture Notes in Computer Science, vol. 3414. pp. 258-273. Springer, 2005.

[GCS03] D. Garlan, S-W Cheng, and B. Schmerl. Increasing system dependability through architecture-based self-repair. *Architecting Dependable Systems*, R. de Lemos, C. Gacek, A. Romanovsky (Eds), Springer-Verlag, 2003.

[GKK03] D. Garlan, S. Khersonsky, and J. S. Kim, Model checking publish-subscribe systems. Proc. 10th International SPIN Workshop on Model Checking of Software (SPIN 03), Portland, Oregon, May 2003.

[Gly89] P. W. Glynn. A GSMP formalism for discrete event sytsems. Proc. of the IEEE, 77(1):14-23, Jan 1989.

[GMW00] D. Garlan, R. Monroe, and D. Wile. ACME: Architectural description of component-based systems. Foundations of Component-Based Systems, Cambridge University Press, 2000.

[GRS05] D. Garlan, W. K. Reinholtz, B. Schmerl, N. Sherman, and T. Tseng. Bridging the gap between systems design and space systems software. 29th Annual IEEE/NASA Software Engineering Workshop (SEW-29), Greenbelt, MD, USA, April 2005.

[HaK04] Z. Han and B. H. Krogh, Reachability analysis of hybrid control systems using reduced-order models, 2004 American Control Conference, June 2004.

[How71] R. A. Howard. *Dynamic Probabilistic Systems*, Vol. II. John Wiley & Sons, New York, NY, 1971.

[Jen94] K. Jensen. An introduction to the theoretical aspects of coloured Petre nets. In J. D. de Bakker, W.-P. de Roever, G. Rozenberg (eds.) A Decade of Concurrency, Lecture Notes in Computer Science, vol. 803, Springer, pp. 230-272, 1994.

[JhW00] S. Jha and J. M. Wing. Survivability analysis of networked systems. Proceedings of the International Conference on Software Engineering, Toronto, May 2001.

[JSW02] S. Jha, O. Sheyner, and J. M. Wing. Minimization and reliability analyses of attack graphs. Proceedings of the Computer Security Foundations Workshop, Nova Scotia, June 2002, pp. 49-63.

[Kaz03] R. Kazman, J. Asundi, J.S. Kim, and B. Sethananda. A simulation testbed for mobile adaptive architectures. Computer Standards and Interfaces, 2003.

[KNP02] M. Kwiatkowska, G. Norman, D. Parker. PRISM: Probabilistic symbolic model checker. in T. Field, P. G. Harrison, J. Brakely, U. Harder (eds.). Proc. 12th International Conf. on Modelling Techneques and Tools for Computer Performance Evaluation. Lecture Notes in Computer Science, vol. 2324, pp. 200-204. Springer, 2002.

[Kur94] R. Kurshan. Computer-Aided Verification of Coordinating Processes: The Automata-Theoretic Approach. Princeton University Press, 1994.

[Lai01] T. L. Lai. Sequential analysis: some classical problems and new challenges. Statistica Sinica 11(2), pp. 303-408, 2001.

[LiP85] O. Lichtenstein and A. Pnueli. Checking that finite state concurrent programs satisfy their linear specification. In Proceedings of POPL, 1985.

[LyW05]   K-W Lye and J. M. Wing. Game strategies in network security. International Journal of Information Security, February 2005.

[OMG05]   Object Management Group. MDA: The Architecture of Choice for a Changing World. http://www.omg.org/mda.

[RSM04]   R. Roshandel, B. Schmerl, N. Medvidovic, D. Garlan, and D. Zhang. Understanding tradeoffs among different architectural modelling approaches. Proc. 4th Working IEEE/IFIP Conference on Software Architectures, Oslo, Norway, June 11-14, 2004.

[RSM04]   R. Roshandel, B. Schmerl, N. Medvidovic, D. Garlan, and D. Zhang. Understanding Tradeoffs among Different Architectural Modelling Approaches. Proceedings of the 4th Working IEEE/IFIP Conference on Software Architectures, Oslo, Norway, June 11-14, 2004.

[SAG05]   B. Schmerl, J. Aldrich, D. Garlan, R. Kazman, and H. Yan. Discovering architectures from running systems using colored Petri nets. Submitted for publication.

[SFH04]   O. Stursberg, A. Fehnker, Z. Han, B. H. Krogh, Verification of a cruise control system using counterexample-guided search, Control Engineering Practice, Special Issue on Analysis and Design of Hybrid Systems, Vol. 12, Issue 10 , Oct. 2004, Pages 1269-1278.

[SGB04]   K. Steppe, D. Garlan, G. Bylenok, B. Schmerl, K. Abirov, and N. Shevchenko. Tool support for model based architectural design for automotive control systems. First European Workshop on Model Driven Architecture with Emphasis on Industrial Application, Enschede, The Netherlands, March 17-19, 2004.

[SGB04]   K. Steppe, D. Garlan, G. Bylenok, B. Schmerl, K. Abirov, and N. Shevchenko Tool support for model based architectural design for automotive control systems. First European Workshop on Model Driven Architecture with Emphasis on Industrial Application, Enschede, The Netherlands, March 17-19, 2004.

[SHJ02]   O. Sheyner, J. Haines, S. Jha, R. Lippmann, and J. M. Wing. Automated generation and analysis of attack graphs. Proceedings of the IEEE Symposium on Security and Privacy, Oakland, CA, May 2002.

[ShW04]   O. Sheyner and J. Wing. Tools for generating and analyzing attack graphs, Proceedings of Formal Methods for Components and Objects, Lecture Notes in Computer Science, 2004, pp. 344-371.

[Wal47]   A. Wald. *Sequential Analysis*. Wiley, New York, 1947.

[YKN05]   H. L. S. Younes, M. Kwiatkowska, G. Norman, and D. Parker. Numerical vs. statistical probabilistic model checking. International Journal on Software Tools for Technology Transfer, to appear 2005..

[YoS02]   H. L. S. Younes and R. G. Simmons. Probabilistic verification of discrete event systems using acceptance sampling. In E. Brinksma and K. Guldstrand Larsen (eds), Proc. 14th International Conference on Computer-Aided Verification, Lecture Notes in Computer Science, vol. 2404, Copenhagen, Denmark, July 2002. Springer.

[You05]   H. L. S. Younes. YMER: A statistical model checker. In K. Etessami and S. Rajamani (eds.), Proc. 17th International Conference on Computer Aided Verification, Lecture Notes in Computer Science, vol. 3576, pp. 429--433, Edinburgh, Scotland. Springer. 2005.

Bridging the Gap between Systems Design and Space Systems Software

David Garlan[*], William K. Reinholtz[**], Bradley Schmerl[*], Nicholas D. Sherman[*], Tony Tseng[*]

School of Computer Science
Carnegie Mellon University
Pittsburgh, PA 15213 USA
{garlan,schmerl,nds,tttseng}@cs.cmu.edu

** *Jet Propulsion Laboratory*
California Institute of Technology
Pasadena, CA 91109 USA
William.K.Reinholtz@jpl.nasa.gov

Abstract

A challenging problem for software engineering practitioners is moving from high-level system architectures produced by system engineers to deployable software produced by software engineers. In this paper we describe our experience working with NASA engineers to develop an approach and toolset for automating the generation of space systems software from architectural specifications. Our experience shows that it is possible to leverage the space systems domain, formal architectural specifications, and component technology to provide retargetable code generators for this class of software.

1. Introduction

A long-term goal of software engineering has been to establish systematic techniques for developing systems from high-level specifications or models. This line of research has led to a long stream of results in areas of formal refinement, automatic code generation, and, perhaps most recently, model-driven architecture (MDA) [8]. The attraction of the later stems from the observation that considerable leverage can be obtained by separating software design into two levels. At the top level one describes a system in terms of a "platform-independent" model (PIM). Then one reifies that model into a lower-level "platform-specific" model (PSM) that binds abstract components and connectors to concrete mechanisms and code. This separation allows one to focus initially on abstract structure and functionality of a system, binding implementation issues later, and potentially allowing the same abstract model to be targeted to different platforms.

While a great idea in principle, it is currently unclear how one should instantiate MDA in practice. In particular, what exactly is meant by "platform independence?" Which details should go in a PIM and which in the PSM? Can one apply a component-based approach to a PIM? If so, how should one describe components at that level so they can be "refined" into working code in more detailed models? What is the nature of code generation in such a scheme? How automated can it be? Where does the concrete code come from, and to what extent can one really target the same PIM to different PSMs?

The answers to such questions are likely to be domain-specific. At the very least, the nature of the reification process is likely to vary considerably depending on whether we are talking about a large scale-distributed information system (with platforms such as CORBA and J2EE), as compared to a resource-constrained embedded system (with real-time OS platforms concerned with scheduling, memory footprint, power consumption, etc.)

In this paper we describe our experience of developing an approach and supporting tool set to support MDA-like approach to NASA Space Systems Software. The key elements of the approach are (a) the use of formal architectural modeling to capture the abstract system description; (b) the clear separation of essential component functionality (described using pure functions) from incidental (or platform-specific) code; and (c) a retargetable code generator and reuse repository to translate architectural designs to one of many possible deployment platforms.

2. The Challenge for Space Systems

Space systems are a natural candidate for an MDA-like approach. In current practice at NASA, systems engineers typically develop the high-level design for a space mission based on knowledge of the mission goals, the target environment, and system resources. This design is specified in part as a high-level architecture in terms of components such as sensors actuators, estimators, controllers, etc., and their pathways of interaction (including shared variables). Later that architecture is translated into working code by software engineers who take into consideration details such as scheduling priorities, communication mechanisms, storage policies, etc.

Unfortunately, bridging the gap between the system design and working code is manual, brittle, and error prone. Programmers may not fully understand the intentions of system designers, and there is no verifiable relationship between system design and code.

This situation is compounded by the fact that for most space missions multiple versions of the software must be

Reprinted from *29th Annual IEEE/NASA Software Engineering Workshop* (April 6–7, 2005). 34–46.

336

created. Some are full-featured, used during development, simulation, and testing on-ground; other leaner versions are needed for resource-constrained flight platforms.

An MDA-like approach could in principle have a strong impact on this kind of development by providing a more rigorous connection between abstract designs and deployed code, by helping to automate the production of code from those designs, and by reducing the effort to target the same abstract system design to multiple deployments. Such a solution, however, would need to

1. support existing systems engineering models and methods, including the ability for systems engineers to specify detailed algorithms for such things as estimation, mission planning, and actuation;

2. provide a formal enough representation of the system design to support analyses and check conformance to design constraints;

3. allow software engineers to produce code preferably automatically) targeted to radically different deployments;

Note that the desired separation of concerns for NASA space systems has a very different flavor from those in many other domains. For most systems the distinction between a PIM and a PSM is that the former excludes details about the physical deployment environment (e.g., the location and number of servers). For space systems, however, the nature of the physical platform (e.g., sensors, actuators) and its detailed characteristics (failure rates, jitter, power consumption, etc.) are central to the systems design process and the resulting high-level design, and must appear in the PIM. Lower-level variability for a particular deployment would include things like quality of monitoring and debugging code, target programming language, and storage policies.

3. Related Work

The problem of moving from abstract designs to code has a long history of research and development. Most researchers have examined this from a theoretical perspective, providing theories of correctness-preserving refinement in languages like CSP [6], Z [12], algebraic specifications [5], and many others. However, these have had limited impact on industrial practice, since they tend to require levels of formal training and large investments in up-front system specification.

A number of researchers have looked at the more constrained problem of moving from architectural models to code. [7] proposed a form of "correct" architectural refinement, based on the use of transformational patterns. This work focused on moving from high-level architectures to lower-level ones, as opposed to code. Aldrich has proposed the ArchJava language [1] as a staging point for

transforming architectures to code. This is a promising avenue, but requires the use of a specialized programming language extension to work. Moreover, it does not directly address the problem of targeting multiple code deployments. [11] addresses code generation from architectures, but also does not provide alternative deployments, and is limited to very specific forms of connection.

The closest branch of related work is the recent flurry of activity in the area of "Model-Driven Architecture" (MDA), proposed by the OMG as a method and set of notations for moving between high-level and low-level designs [8]. As noted earlier, MDA proscribes a two-level process, in which deployment details are added at the low-level so that the same abstract design can be used in different concrete settings.

While attractive in principle, as noted, there remain many details about the MDA approach that remain unanswered. This paper can be viewed as shedding light on some of those answers for the specific domain of space systems software. This domain has some distinct characteristics that make it both challenging and tractable. One of the distinguishing aspects is the need to have precise representations of component functions at an abstract level. Another is the need to model the physical setting (actuators, sensors, environmental and system state) at the high level. This is in contrast to most MDA approaches which leave such details to the lower-level model (PSM).

The work reported here also builds on previous work by the authors, unifying two separate streams of research to produce a new synthetic approach. The first stream is formal representation of software architecture and tools to analyze those descriptions [2][4]. The second is a proposal to define control systems from components specified as pure functions [3]. In this work we show how to use architectural descriptions combined with pure functions to create a tool that generates deployable code.

4. Current Practice

At the start of our collaboration, NASA was well aware of the problems outlined above, and had developed a number of processes and technologies to ameliorate some of the problems: (a) a well-defined system design process and repository to store the results; (b) an architectural style well-matched to space systems development; (c) a large body of reusable code for creating deployments of a system. We consider each, together with comments about their limitations.

Design Process: The success of most NASA missions depends critically on up-front design by system engineers who consider (a) the goals of the mission (b) scenarios of use (c) resource concerns (d) failure modes to produce a systems design. This process, called *state effects analysis*, determines the relevant state variables for the system and their dependencies, as well as the algorithms used by the various system components that examine and change that state. Results of this process are stored in a *state database*, which records both the resulting design and the rationale behind the design decisions.

While state effects analysis and the state database help space systems domain experts to design effective systems, balancing complex requirements for functionality, resource usage, and failure handling, there are a number of limitations. First, the design decisions are largely informal. For example, the database may note a dependency between two states, but that dependency is not represented in a way that can be automatically checked against a resulting design. Second, and more importantly, components in the design must be represented using the concrete notations of a programming language: C++ in this case. While programming languages allow engineers to be concrete about the algorithms to be used, they tend to overconstrain the implementations. In particular, they force premature decisions about things such as order of processing of input variables, synchronization mechanisms, communication polices, and data representation decisions.

Software Architecture: Over the past few years engineers at NASA's Jet Propulsion Lab (JPL) had developed a new architectural style for space systems, called Mission Data Systems (MDS) [9]. MDS adopts a product-line approach to space software, by providing a generic architectural framework for space systems design, providing a vocabulary of design (sensors, actuators, state variables, etc.) together with rules for how these elements can be combined. This is coupled with a reusable code base (described below) for instantiating the framework for specific missions.

While the creation of an architectural style for space systems is an important step towards regularizing development, and providing opportunities for analysis and reuse, at the start of our project this style was largely described informally. As we illustrate later, rules for composition were expressed in English, and there was no way to either represent a full design in the MDS style formally, or to check for conformance to that style.

Reuse: Taking advantage of commonalities in space systems (as characterized by the MDS style), over the past few years NASA engineers had developed a large body of reusable code for creating specific deployments. This code covered areas like data structures for state representation, communications infrastructure, event logging, timing services, units of measurement, and visualization. In fact, in its current state there are over 250K lines of (potentially) reusable framework code.

While providing excellent opportunities for reuse, the existing body of framework code had several limitations. First was the sheer complexity of it. For a given target

deployment, knowing which packages to use, in which combinations, was not a trivial matter. Second, since framework code had to be combined with mission-specific code manually, there were many opportunities for error, and very little that one could do to check that the resulting system continued to respect the abstract design. Third, as noted, components written in C++ could potentially conflict with the use of particular framework code, by prematurely binding implementation decisions.

5. Our Approach

Working with engineers at NASA JPL, we developed an approach, and a tool called MDS Studio, that is centered on three significant changes to their current practice:

1. Use a formal architectural modeling language to represent a system design and its constraints. Linked to existing NASA system design databases, a formal architectural description provides an explicit representation of a system configuration, and permits automated analyses such as conformance to architectural style, as well as system-specific constraints. (For example, if a system engineer determines that in the system under design a state A depends on state B, a rule is automatically created in the architectural modeling tool to check that the estimator for state variable A is also connected to state variable B.)
2. Define high-level components as pure functions (stateless mappings of inputs to outputs), thereby abstracting from details of timing, synchronization, communication, and data representation, while still retaining the ability to describe critical algorithms for state estimation and control.
3. Provide a retargetable compiler that can produce multiple versions of deployable code from the abstract architectural design. The compiler leverages the substantial body reusable framework code to map the "essential" computations defined in the abstract configuration to specific implementations, but does so in a way that preserves the design constraints.

This approach is applied in the following process:

1. Systems engineer conduct a state effects analysis, to determine the states required to achieve a mission.
2. Software engineers write essential code to implement these states as pure functions, which just implement the steps of the various control loops, but not how they are put together or scheduled.
3. This essential code is uploaded to a state database, which is then used to generate architectural styles, which are used to:

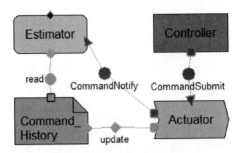

Figure 1. A *Controller/Actuator/Estimator* pattern in MDS

4. Compose the system in an architectural model that specifies instances of the essential code and how they relate.

5. This architectural model is fed into code generators that weave the essential code with framework code and other incidental code, such as connections and schedulers, to produce code that can be deployed. The aim is that code can be generated for different deployments without affecting the pure functions or the architectural model.

In the remainder of the section we elaborate on these three innovations.

5.1.   Architectural Modeling and Analysis

The architectural modeling tool allows the user to create instances of components, both pure functions and state variables. The distinction between essential and incidental is valuable to understand in this process: the components are essential code, whereas the connectors are incidental. The architectural model primarily encapsulates the knowledge of the instances of components, and the communication patterns between components. The architectural model is built according to a set of architectural styles. An architectural style captures the component, connector, and interface types that can be used to compose an architecture, in addition to rules about their composition.

The base architectural style used for MDS consists of the following component types:

- *StateVariableT*: Contains the value history record of the state over time and goals associated with the state.
- *EstimatorT*: Is responsible for examining all of the available cues (other states, sensors, or goals) and updating state variables periodically to provide a current best estimate of the states value based on available evidence (command history, other states, sensor values, etc.).
- *ControllerT*: If there are goals associated with a state variable, this component is responsible for delegating the goals to other states, or for issuing commands to adaptors to achieve the state.

- *ActuatorT*: Represents the interface between a controller and the hardware. Commands are issued to actuators to get the spacecraft to do something.
- *SensorT*: Represents an interface between an estimator and hardware, for use by estimators.
- *ValueHistoryT*: Store a discrete set of data. For example, they may be used to store the history of commands sent to an actuator by a controller.

In addition to the above component types, there are connector types for communicating between components (e.g., *Command Submit, Measurement Request, State Update*), and port and role types for component and connector interfaces. Figure 1 illustrates a small segment of an architecture written in this style. This segment depicts interaction between a *Controller*, an *Actuator*, and an *Estimator*. In this interaction, the *Controller* submits a command to an *Actuator* via its *Command Submit* connector. The *Actuator* then notifies the *Estimator* that it received a command and writes that command to a *Value History*. Subsequently, the *Estimator* queries the *Value History* to find out what the command was.

In addition to a set of types, the MDS style also defines rules about the composition of an MDS system. These rules were expressed in English by JPL engineers, but needed to be translated into formal architectural rules that can be checked automatically with architectural tools. In developing the architectural style, we were given ten informal rules, which were translated into 39 architectural rules. Examples of the MDS rules:

1. If an *Estimator* can be notified of a command by an *Actuator*, then that *Estimator* must be able to read the *Value History* that the *Actuator* updates.
2. An *Actuator* must have exactly one *Controller* connected to it.
3. An *Actuator* must have the same number of *Command Submit, Command Notification*, and *Value History Update* ports (one for each type of command that it receives).

The first MDS rule above can be captured in Acme with the following predicate:[1]

invariant (forall e :! EstimatorT **in** self.*components* |
  (forall cnp :! CmdNotProvT **in** e.*ports* |
    (forall a :! ActuatorT **in** self.*components* |
      (forall cnr :! CmdNotReqrT **in** a.*ports* |
        (*connected* (cnp, cnr) ->
        (exists vh :! ValueHistoryT in self.components |
          reading (e, vh) and updating (a, vh))))))[2];

---

[1] In this rule, self refers to the system, *italicized* words refer to predefined Acme functions, and the clause <name> :! <type> means that <name> declares the type <type>

[2] reading and updating are defined elsewhere in the style.

In addition to this base MDS style, our approach takes advantage of the use of specializations of the MDS style that are tailored to both the particular mission and code generation. Specializations of this style must satisfy all of the rules of the original MDS style, but may add rules and structure. For example, if the mission requires a wheel state variable, then there will likely be specializations of the state variable type tailored to this wheel, in addition to specializations of wheel estimators, wheel controllers, etc. For example, a *WheelVelEstT* would be a subtype of *EstimatorT*, and might have additional required ports or properties. Furthermore, if state analysis specifies a dependency between a wheel state variable and a power state variable, then the corresponding mission style would check that the estimator associated with one state variable queries the state of the other state variable. A rule of this type would look like the following:

```
invariant (forall e :! WheelVelEstT in self.components |
  (exists s :! PowerStateVar in self.components |
    connected (e, s));
```

5.2.   Component Specification

Whereas in MDS as implemented by NASA JPL the components of the system (controllers, estimators, and hardware adaptors) are C++ objects, in MDS Studio the components are implemented as pure stateless functions. This means that everything that is needed for a function is provided through the interface to the function, and the result is returned by the function, i.e., the function does not read or change any global variables.

Consider for example a Controller function. The goal of a controller is to update the state of any pending or current goals, as needed, and to issue commands to actuators to achieve goals. The generic header for a controller pure function would look like:

```
ControllerFunc (Goals, StateVar, Config) → messages
```

The algorithm for the controller would calculate what it needs to do to achieve the goals, based on the value of the state variable, as well as when the goals need to be achieved. It may use the configuration parameter to help in its calculations. The configuration parameter will contain information that is needed for the controller to accurately calculate what it needs to do, such as the diameter of the wheel being controlled. If it needs to actuate the hardware, then it returns the required messages that need to be sent to an actuator. Where it receives the information from, and the particular actuators to which its messages are sent, are completely independent of the controller code. The author of the controller code needs to know the type of actuator that is being controlled so that it know what message need to be sent, as well as to calculate how to achieve goals.

The suggested benefits of using pure stateless functions include making the components easier to write, test, and integrate in a code generation system. For example, while it is possible to write an OO component with a race condition depending on the order of invocation of the methods on the object, that category of defect is not possible in a pure function. Additionally, a testing suite no longer has to be savvy of the internal state of the object; the return value of the pure function is a function of its inputs alone. Finally, it is easier to capture the knowledge of how to interact with a pure function in the state database; by adopting certain constraints on the signature of the pure function, the process of generating the code to invoke the pure function becomes much simpler and easier to inspect for correctness.

Essential and Incidental Code

A critical aspect of our approach is the separation of the software into essential and incidental code. Essential code is broadly defined as software that is specific to the physical platform, the specific mission, or the physical environment in which the rover is operating. For example, essential code associated with a *Power* state on the spacecraft would include the code for recording the *Power* state variable, and pure functions for the *Power* estimator, controller, sensor, and actuator.

Incidental code is everything else. Essential code is strictly defined as the state variables with the important system state, and the pure functions representing components. Incidental code is subdivided into several types:

- A space system's reuse library; for example, classes for time reckoning and memory management are in this category.
- Platform-specific code for interacting with particular hardware on a particular space craft.
- Code for communicating between components, which is weaved in by the code generator.
- Classes and types to support the essential code, such as message and command types specific to a particular mission.

In order to have a clean division between the essential and incidental code, essential code is implemented using pure functions as described above, but may use classes and types in the incidental code. Furthermore essential code is freed from having to be concerned with scheduling or thread-safety (e.g., locking a mutex before accessing a variable). In fact, essential code is not permitted to handle this – but rather, it is the responsibility of the incidental code to handle these issues.

Generating Mission-specific Architectural Styles

Once the essential code elements have been written for a particular mission, they are added to the state database for the mission. The architectural style specializations corresponding to a particular mission are generated from the state database. An engineer can then assemble the architectural model for the mission using these styles. Consider the Power example introduced earlier. The architectural style for the mission will include a *PowerStateVariableT* and a *PowerEstimatorT* type (in addition to other component types). The software engineer can then assemble the architectural model from these types, and may include multiple instances of these types (one for each battery on the spacecraft, for example).

5.3. Compilation

The code generation system is responsible for translating the component instances and communication patterns in the architectural model to the appropriate representations in code. For every component, it generates a wrapper around the associated pure function that handles the selection of correct objects to pass to the pure function, and where to pass messages. The code generator also produces code to ensure that the components are scheduled, as well as any code for logging or debugging.

Different code generators can be plugged in to generate code for different platforms, without having to change the architectural model. For example, a code generator for a simulation may choose to log all messages that are sent, to aid in debugging.

It is possible to write incidental code generators with a high degree of variability in the generated software. Attributes that can be modified include, but are not necessarily limited to, the following list.

- *Threading model*: single-threaded or multi-threaded systems are possible. The incidental code is responsible for taking any precautions (e.g. locking mutexes) necessary in a multithreaded environment.
- *Debugging code*: The incidental code may include debugging software to examine messages or state while the system is executing.
- *Scheduler implementation*: the implementation of the scheduler is not dictated by the architectural model.
- *Style of implementation*. This is the example difference implementation constructed over the course of this project. In one incidental code generator, procedural code is produced, with globally accessible data and wrapper functions; in another incidental code generator, wrappers are classes, and connectors between the components are also full-fledged classes.

Figure 2 shows a pseudo-code example of the wrapper that may be generated by a code generator for calling a controller. The wrapper handles thread-safety and logging, making sure that it acquires and releases the appropriate locks, and sends the appropriate logging messages.

```
void controller17_wrapper () {
    pthread_mutex_lock (stateVar17_mutex);
    pthread_mutex_lock (stateVar17_goals_mutex);
    pthread_mutex_lock (actuator17_config_mutex);
    pthread_mutex_lock (actuator17_inputQ_mutex);
    log.out ("Calling controller17 function");
    message =
        controllerFunc (stateVar17_goals, stateVar17,
                        actuator17_config);
    log.out (messages);
    actuator17_inputQ.put (message);
    pthread_mutex_unlock ()...
}
```

Figure 2. Example of Generated Code.

6. Example

To illustrate how this approach works in practice, consider a simple example of a wheel motor "control loop." The wheel motor control loop controls an actuator that adjusts the current sent to a wheel motor, and receives data from a sensor that reports encoder values, which count how far the wheel has turned. The goal is to construct a system that controls the motion of a wheel. It should be possible to set a goal (for example, for a particular velocity) on the state variable associated with the wheel; it should also be possible to read data such as the current velocity from the wheel's state variable. (For the purposes of this example, we will not discuss the interaction between this control loop and other control loops that may exist on the space craft.)

6.1. Writing the Essential Code

The essential code is written based on the results of the state effects analysis. For each important state that is identified during state analysis, essential code components associated with it need to be written.

In the wheel control loop, the following mission-specific components are created:

- Wheel State Variable: This state variable contains the value history of the wheel position and its derivatives, such as the wheel velocity and the wheel acceleration.
- Wheel Controller: This pure function component is responsible for handling goals placed on the Wheel State Variable. It achieves the goals by issuing commands to the wheel actuator, such as increasing the amount of current sent to the hardware by the actuator to affect the speed at which the wheel turns.
- Wheel Motor Actuator: This pure function component is responsible for accepting commands from the Wheel Controller, relaying the commands to the actuator, and storing them in a command history.

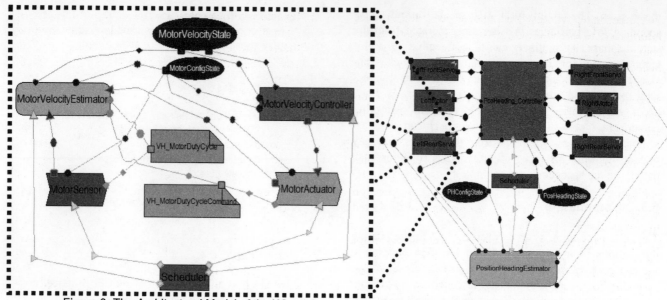

Figure 3. The Architectural Model of the Wheel Controller, and its Context in the Larger Robot Architecture.

- Wheel Encoder Sensor: This pure function component is responsible for reading the data sent by the encoders (encoders measure the number of times the wheel has turned) and storing these measurements in a measurement history.
- Wheel Estimator: This pure function component is responsible for analyzing the available cues (current state of the Wheel State Variable, command history, measurement history, and goal record) and updating the state function in the Wheel State Variable with a new, best estimate of the value history of the wheel. This estimate is represented as a state function; this continuous function returns the state at any time in the past or future; different times will have different levels of the uncertainty for that time. Entities that use the state need to be savvy of the uncertainty associated with any state they read.
- Wheel Configuration State Variable: This state variable is responsible for holding information about the wheel. For example, the diameter of the wheel would be a good candidate for capturing in a configuration state variable, as opposed to hard-coding the value; this allows for easy reuse of the code for different size wheels.

6.2. Putting Essential Code in the State DB

The next step is to describe the essential code in the State Database. Every essential function is named; the arguments and their associated order and types are described; and the return values are described. In addition, every state variable is described, along with its associated member variables.

For the wheel motor control loop example, all of the pure functions and state variables are entered into the state database. Our tool then generates architectural styles to represent the pure functions as components in an architectural model. The types generated for the wheel example would be: MotorVelocityStateT, MotorConfigurationStateT, MotorVelocityEstT, MotorSensorT, MotorActuatorT, and MotorVelocityCntrlT.

6.3. Developing the Architectural Model

The architectural model is then developed, allowing the software engineer to connect the various pure function components. In addition to the component types generated as part of the previous step, the software engineer uses the following types of generic MDS connectors to connect instances of these components:

- Connectors between Pure Functions and State Variable members: these connectors represent that member of the state variable being passed into the pure function as an argument. There are two subtypes of this connector, representing read-only and read-write semantics, respectively.
- Connectors between Pure Functions and Standalone Value Histories: these connectors represent that standalone value history being passed into the pure function as an argument. There are two subtypes of this connector, representing read-only and read-write semantics, respectively.
- Connectors between Pure Functions and Pure Functions: these connectors represent a message being passed from one Pure Function to another.

Furthermore, the software engineer needs to introduce information to aid the code generator in scheduling the components. The software engineer can instantiate a Scheduled Rate Group component and an appropriate connector to connect those components that must be scheduled. This is used to specify the rate at which components are scheduled, and which components should be scheduled in that rate group.

Once the architectural model has been developed, it can be checked for conformance to architectural rules prior to code generation. For example, the model can be checked to ensure that ports on either side of a connection are compatible, and that every pure function is connected to a scheduler.

The left of Figure 3 shows the architectural model for the wheel controller example. It shows that the MotorVelocityEstimator, MotorVelocityController, MotorActuator, and MotorSensor are all in the same rate group, that the MotorVelocityEstimator uses information from the MotorVehicleState, the MotorSensor, and the MotorActuator to calculate the new states for the MotorVelocity. If the estimator also required information from other states (such as a power state), then this would also be indicated in the architectural model.

The wheel motor controller is actually part of a larger system for a robot with four wheels. The full architectural model is presented to the right of Figure 3. This allows for scalability of the architectural model, and also allows for reuse. For example, the RightMotor component is decomposed with a similar control loop for the LeftMotor.

6.4. Generating the Code

Once the architectural model is developed, a code generator is chosen by the software engineer to produce the code for a particular deployment. For example, the code could be generated from this model for deployment on a Personal Exploration Robot (PER) hardware, or for simulation in a software environment.

7. Implementation and Evaluation
7.1. Implementation

We have implemented the above approach in a toolset that consists of the following components:

- A cleanroom MDS Framework implementation in C++. Because of security restrictions, we were at the time unable to view actual MDS code. We implemented our own version of the framework that is a subset of the existing MDS framework, but doesn't include some of the utility packages (such as units of measurement).
- API interfaces for the pure functions.
- MDS Studio, an MDS architectural modeling tool that extends AcmeStudio [10], an architecture devel-

opment environment. It is built on top of Eclipse, an open extensible integrated development environment.[3] The extensions provide access to the code generators, as well as actions that are specific to the MDS architectural style.

- Two types of code generators to generate code in different platform styles:
  - The procedural incidental code generator wraps each pure function (corresponding to the component type) with a wrapper function (corresponding to the component instance) that is responsible for accessing a shared data structure and selecting the correct data structures to interact with each other in the pure function. In other words, there is a global data structure containing state, and wrapper functions that maintain the structure and communication patterns in the network.
  - The object-oriented incidental code uses C++ classes to wrap each pure function. These classes are responsible for supporting the communication patterns described in the architectural model.

We have successfully generated code that runs on the Personal Exploration Rover (PER),[4] that is a robot designed to be similar to the Mars Sojourner.

7.2. Evaluation

Having asserted that the tool developed in this project provides several benefits to JPL Engineers, it is appropriate to describe the benefits that have been observed.

7.2.1 Reduced Costs
In this system, there are the following opportunities for reuse of code:

- MDS Framework code (schedulers, memory management, etc) may be reused across all missions.
- Essential code may be reused if a different mission is using the same hardware, or in cases where the robots are operating in a similar physical environment (for example, estimators for time-of-day and solar radiation levels on Mars will be reusable across different robot platforms).
- Type definitions for stateful objects may be reused across systems, if system and software engineers choose to. They contain no program logic, merely data. For example, a TemperatureKelvin class definition likely will find use in many circumstances.
- Incidental code generators can be reused across different platforms.

In addition, the code generation system saves having to write a significant amount of code. It takes approxi-

---

[3] http://www.eclipse.org
[4] http://www.cs.cmu.edu/~personalrover/PER

mately one hour to assemble the architectural model of the PER, resulting in a system of approximately 50 components. The incidental code generated for the PER consists of approximately 542 lines of code. This is a good productivity level. However, this incidental code represents the very simplest of the incidental code generators that can be imagined. As incidental code generators become more capable, and generate more sophisticated code, the productivity gains will be even greater.

7.2.2   Increased Reliability

The architectural modeling tool provides a platform for reasoning about the correctness of the model developed by the software engineers. Whenever new rules about the desired behavior of the system are discovered, the system engineer can express this as a rule in the architectural modeling tool, ensuring that this check becomes a part of the build process of the system. One example of a potential rule would be a check that a state cannot depend on itself for estimation (this would cause instability in estimation), even if separated by many intermediate states.

Another benefit of this approach is a side effect of the reuse library; as components accumulate over time, the amount of testing that any one component might experience will increase, providing more confidence in the reliability of the components.

Finally, the functional approach to developing the essential components is amenable to the design and maintenance of an automated suite of unit tests. The simplicity of the pure function signature specification ensures that writing unit tests for these functions is a straightforward practice; each pure function can be tested in complete isolation from all other pure function components.

7.2.3   Usability

This project was developed in collaboration with engineers at the NASA Jet Propulsion Laboratory, in multiple meetings. As a part of this project, the tool was demonstrated to several engineers at JPL. Initial reactions to the tool were quite positive, indicating that such a tool for their system would be helpful in their work.

8.   Technical Challenges

Having described the approach and briefly illustrated it, we now consider some of the specific technical challenges that arose in carrying out the work.

8.1.   Adding implementation choices

One of the critical issues in an MDA-like approach is how to introduce implementation choices that are not directly relevant at the PIM model, but are needed to produce working code. In the case of MDS Studio there were two categories of extra detail. First was scheduling information: as real-time control systems specification and analysis of timing properties are critical for the final system, even though they are not part of the essential code produce for the high-level model.

To handle this we introduced a special architectural construct called *scheduled rate groups.* Components in the same rate group are scheduled together as periodic tasks at a specified rate defined by the group. Putting this in the architecture has the benefit that timing analysis can be performed over the architectural model.

The second class of implementation choices concerned the nature of the code produced. MDS Studio permits variability along the dimensions outlined earlier. The choice of value within each of those dimensions is determined by the choice of compiler. For example, in our prototype one compiler produces code appropriate for large-footprint testing and debugging; another produces smaller run-time code that can operate in a resource constrained environment.

8.2.   Scalability

The most significant issue concerning the user interface in this project was the issue of scalability. In order to address this, the team used the concept of compositions, or logical groupings of entities that may be captured as new types in the system. These represent replicable structural patterns that can be instantiated and visualized as first class entities. For example, the wheel controller described in this paper could be captured as a composition, given a type name, and then instantiated anew at the discretion of the software engineer.

8.3.   Fitting a Functional Style of Code into a State-Oriented Environment

In this project, a functional style of code for the essential code must be integrated with a state-oriented system, in which globally accessible stateful objects are the most important elements in both the architecture and implementation of the system. The functional style is important from a system point of view, but may not be enforced by the semantics of the target deployment language (e.g., C++). Therefore, while the essential functions are not themselves stateful, they manipulate stateful objects in the system. Thus persistent system state is factored out of the components that access or change that state. The benefit of this is that it becomes easy to understand the interactions between components. Pure functions have only two ways of interacting with the external world: they can return messages; or they may read or modify stateful objects that are passed in as arguments.

8.4.   Interfacing to Essential Code

One of the key challenges that had to be addressed for the pure functions was finding the right interface to the pure functions. The trade-off is that we required the interface to allow engineers full expressive power to implement the functions, while making the interfaces simple enough to understand and to reliably and simply generate code around them. If the interfaces were complex, this would require a greater number of connections in the architectural model, in addition to more complex code generation for each of these new types of connections.

We addressed this challenge in close consultation with JPL engineers, conducting interviews to simplify the interface and ensure that the engineers could still write the necessary code in the pure functions. In the end, we settled on the interfaces to pure functions essentially being value histories and messages. Once we got this right, implementing the code generators was quite straightforward.

9. Conclusions

This paper has described our experience of adapting two research threads to develop a new tool for NASA space systems engineers that allows them to move from high level system specifications to multiple deployments. Those threads were formal architectural representation within a domain-specific style for spaces systems, and pure functional representations of component capability.

Although the tool we developed addresses a particular audience and domain, we believe there are a number of important general lessons that can be applied more generally to create tools for moving from architectural designs to working systems.

1. *Augmentation (not replacement) of existing capabilities*: For this work to be successful we had to fit into an existing development process and use predetermined technologies. These included the architectural style rules, the state database, and the MDS framework code. This meant that we had to design our tools so that they worked with current practices, rather than mandating a set of new technologies that would fit seamlessly with our approach. This is something that will need to be addressed when applying the MDA approach more generally.

2. *Use of formal models*: The formal architectural style that we used is a benefit in this work because it is reasonably complex. This means that certain errors can be caught at the architectural modeling phase and not propagated to implementation. Less interesting styles would not produce the same benefits.

3. *Style specialization*: We used two related architectural styles for this work. The first style is a generic style that captures mission-independent rules about MDS composition. This was specialized to contain types representing particular specializations of the generic components for particular missions (for example, a WheelControllerT became a subtype of Control-

lerT), and additional rules about composition. In fact, we are currently experimenting with additional styles to factor out some additional implementation details, such as scheduling, rather than including it in the one substyle. This use of successively detailed styles should prove useful in other areas where abstract architectures need to be mapped into implementations.

4. *Separation of essential from incidental code*. A key to making the refinement successful was to find the sweet-spot between what goes into the architectural model and what goes into the code generators. We suggest that any similar refinement process will need to involve both architects and developers, in order to define this interface. However, once this work is done, the actual implementation of the process in another domain should be straightforward.

While still a prototype system, the work to date shows promise for becoming a major advance in space systems engineering. In particular, the combination of component specification clarity, automatic generation of code, and formal checking of architectural constraints provides a powerful combination of new capabilities beyond existing practices of NASA engineers.

References

[1] Aldrich, J., Chambers, C., and Notkin, D. ArchJava: Connecting Software Architecture to Implementation. Proc. ICSE 24, Orlando, Florida, 2002.

[2] Allen, R. and Garlan, D. A Formal Basis for Architectural Connection. ACM Transactions on Software Engineering and Methodology, 6(3), July 1997.

[3] Dvorak, D., and Reinholtz, K. Separating Essential from Incidentals, An Execution Architecture for Real-Time Control Systems. Proc. 7th IEEE International Symposium on Object-Oriented Real-Time Distributed Computing. Austria, 2004.

[4] Garlan, D., Monroe, R., and Wile, D. "Acme: Architectural Description of Component-Based Systems." Foundations of Component-Based Systems, Cambridge University Press, 2000.

[5] Guttag, J.V., and Horning, J.J. (Eds) *Larch: Languages and Tools for Formal Specification*. Springer-Verlag, 1993.

[6] Hoare, C.A.R. Communicating Sequential Processes. Prentice Hall, 1985.

[7] Moriconi, M., Quian, X., and Riemenschneider, R. Correct Architecture Refinement. IEEE Trans. Soft. Eng. **21**(4), 1995.

[8] Object Management Group. MDA: The Architecture of Choice for a Changing World. http://www.omg.org/mda.

[9] Rasmussen, R. Goal-Based Fault Tolerance for Space Systems using the Mission Data Systems. Proc. 2001 IEEE Aerospace Conference, Big Sky, MT, 2001.

[10] Schmerl, B. and Garlan, D. Supporting Style-Centered Architecture Development. ICSE 26, Edinburgh, Scotland, 2004.

[11] Shaw, M., DeLine, R., Klein, D.V., Ross, T.L., Young, D.M., Zelesnik, G. Abstractions for Software Architectures and Tools to Support Them. *IEEE Transactions on Software Engineering*, 21(4):314-335, 1995.

[12] Woodcock, J. and Davies, J. Using Z: Specification, Refinement, and Proof. Prentice Hall International, 1996.

CHAPTER 3

Software Engineering for Assurance

Ralph Wachter and Gary Toth

Software engineering is essential to building and operating software-intensive applications that form the basis of critical infrastructures. Software engineering for assurance encompasses software engineering, knowledge management, and network systems administration. The network is not only a communications conduit, but also a fundamental component of today's warfighting operations.

Software engineering concerns the creation and maintenance of software applications utilizing tools, techniques, and practices derived from many scientific and technical disciplines as well as from relevant application domains. In the past, assurances in building, operating, and maintaining these software-enabled systems largely focused on functional correctness; ensuring that the software conforms to and operates according to its input-output specification. Today, that is no longer sufficient. Interconnections and interdependencies among infrastructures, both explicit and implicit, present new vulnerabilities not present only a few years ago.

To address these vulnerabilities, assurance must be integrated system wide and built into the software from the beginning. Assurances need to be adapted to the operational environment and encompass the firmware electronics and application-level protocols for information exchange. Without trust in the software at all levels, in all stages of development, and in all applications of use, there can be no trust in the information crisscrossing the global information infrastructures.

The papers in this chapter address only a few of the challenges in software engineering for assurance. We have contributed technical papers from five CIP MURI teams working on the following aspects of software engineering for assurance:

- COTS protection and defense
- Policy-driven, high-confidence software design
- Shaping policy for software performance and assurance
- Trade-off among assurance properties
- Modeling and simulation

With the mandate for the Department of Defense to use commercial off-the-shelf products, there is less opportunity to oversee software development. As a result, only the software code may be available for inspection. Research projects at Carnegie Mellon University and the University of Wisconsin focus on new approaches to program code analysis, vulnerability detection and remediation. Their research results are presented in the papers "Static Analysis to Enhance the Power of Model Checking for Concurrent Software" by the Carnegie Mellon University team, and "Analysis of COTS for Security Vulnerability Remediation" by the University of Wisconsin team.

Modeling and simulation are part of the software engineering toolbox for testing and evaluation. The understanding derived from using these tools often leads to better decisions for software development and maintenance. At times, elaborate test beds are the only means to safely study vulnerabilities and responses, and to assess whether a system will work as intended before it is released into a critical environment. The multi-university project with Florida State University, the George Washington University, the University of Central Florida, and the University of Wisconsin-Madison focuses on several research areas in analysis, modeling, and simulation with the goal of providing a framework for making informed decisions about protection of critical infrastructures. The paper "Analysis, Modeling, and Simulation for Networked Systems" captures the research accomplishment of this MURI team.

When software is deployed, its use must be controlled, interactions mediated, and its overall operation managed. Policies that govern allowable behavior provide administrative controls over software and information in enterprise settings. The implementation of policy mechanisms is accomplished with software and can be quite varied, ranging from middleware-level to code-level controls where the original code is automatically adapted to reflect enforceable policies. The research project at Michigan State University explores adaptive middleware for achieving dependability in networked applications. Their latest results are presented in their summary paper, "RAPIDware: Component-Based Development of Adaptive and Dependable Middleware."

Policies might be used to enforce access restrictions or allowable resource usage. Policies may define tradeoffs among system properties, including those of assurance, and reflect the preferences and priorities of decision-makers for allowable roles and operations. The project at the State University of New York at Stony Brook explores role-based access controls and policy analysis algorithms for decentralized policy administration. The paper "Generating Efficient Security Software from Policies" provides a good summary of this MURI project on security policies.

The results of these projects are transitioning into commercial practice and DoD systems development. Often the transition arose from technical collaborations with software developers in industry and government. In addition, because of their research, students on these projects have found employment with companies that are adopting that technology.

The sponsored research reported in this chapter spans disciplines, including computer science, mathematics, and logic. This research has provided valuable new insight into software assurance and critical infrastructure protection but many difficult challenges remain.

Static Analysis to Enhance the Power of Model Checking for Concurrent Software*

Edmund Clarke
Carnegie Mellon University
Pittsburgh

Daniel Kroening
ETH
Zurich

Thomas Reps
University of Wisconsin
Madison

Abstract. Errors in software products can increase development cost and in some cases cause serious damage. Such errors are often very hard to diagnose. This is especially true when multiple programs interact with each other simultaneously. Manual inspection or testing of large programs may fail to uncover subtle faults. We describe an automated technique called *Model Checking*, and show how it can be applied to concurrent software written in widely used programming languages. We discuss scalability problems that arise when model checking is applied to large programs, as well as challenges presented by the constructs and datatypes that modern programming languages support.

1 Introduction

Correctness of computer software is critical in today's information society. This is especially true of software that runs on computers embedded in our transportation and communication infrastructure. Examples of serious software errors are easy to find. For instance, in 1997, the propulsion system of the Aegis missile cruiser USS Yorktown failed for over two hours due to a software bug [1]. The cause turned out to be a division by zero within a database system, which resulted in an exception and crashed all computer consoles and terminal units. The software of the USS Yorktown operated on a network of Windows NT machines and was quite complex, consisting of several millions of lines of C code.

Another instance is the development of the F/A-22 as part of the Joint Strike Fighter program. The project was delayed multiple times. Many times, it was the software running on the F/A-22 that was not ready yet. Pilots often had to re-boot computers while in the air [2, 3]. The F/A-22 has about 2.5 million lines

* This research was sponsored by the Gigascale Systems Research Center (GSRC) under contract no. 9278-1-1010315, Semiconductor Research Corporation (SRC) under contract no. 99-TJ-684, the National Science Foundation (NSF) under grant no. CCR-9803774, the Office of Naval Research (ONR), the Naval Research Laboratory (NRL) under contract no. N00014-01-1-0796, the Army Research Office (ARO) under contract no. DAAD19-01-1-0485, and the General Motors Collaborative Research Lab at CMU. The views and conclusions contained in this document are those of the author and should not be interpreted as representing the official policies, either expressed or implied, of GSRC, NSF, ONR, NRL, ARO, GM, or the U.S. government.

of software written in Ada. This number is expected to rise to 6 million lines of C/C++ code on the F-35.

Computer software also plays an important role in other parts of our infrastructure. On August 14, 2003, a blackout affected more than 50 million people in large areas on the US east coast, causing an estimated damage between $4 billion and $10 billion [4]. While the blackout was triggered by trees hitting local power transmission lines, it was a software bug that made it devastating. A bug in GE Energy's XA/21 power control system allowed the blackout to spread. The software had been in use since 1990, but the bug had never before become apparent. The flaw was discovered by an audit of over 4 million lines of C/C++ code after the blackout and was identified as a "race condition."

Programs in imperative languages like C or C++ are executed line-by-line in what is called the *thread of control*. It is tempting to hope that a line-by-line inspection of the code, following this thread of control, will uncover all the flaws in a program. The problem is that complex systems have many software components running in parallel, so that there are many different threads of control that run simultaneously. While one of these threads may currently be executing some statement in its program, another thread with exactly the same program, may be executing an entirely different line of code. Consequently, in the presence of multiple threads, one has to consider any combination of program lines the threads can execute.

The *State* of the program is the location of the control in each thread, and the values of the program variables. In order to discover flaws, it is necessary to explore the possible states of the program. To illustrate the large number of states that concurrency can cause, consider the little program in Fig. 1. It has one variable x, which is initialized with zero. It has two threads A and B of control, and only four lines of code in total. The first line in both threads simply idles until x becomes zero. The second line set x to 1 or 2, respectively. Despite its tiny size, the program has 10 reachable states. These states are shown in Figure 2. The blowup is due to the different combinations of program locations in the two threads A and B. Thus, a manual search for errors in large concurrent programs is infeasible.

```
        Thread A                        Thread B

    1   while(x!=0) skip;          1   while(x!=0) skip;
    2   x=1;                        2   x=2;
    3                               3
```

Fig. 1. A small program with two threads of control

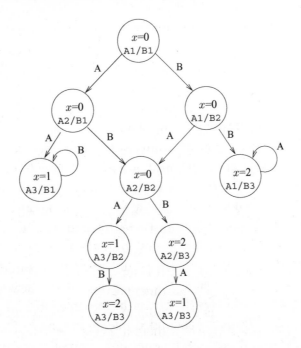

Fig. 2. The states of the program in Fig. 1. In each state, the first line contains the values of the program variable x, whereas the second line contains the current program location in thread A and B, respectively. The variable x is initialized with 0.

Model Checking [5, 6] is an automated technique for exploring all the states of a system. Introduced in 1981, it has become a standard verification technique in the hardware industry. It has been successfully used to find bugs in circuitry that would have been hard to find by inspection.

Model Checking has the potential to produce major enhancements in the reliability and robustness of software as well. The basic idea of software model checking is to explore all the states of the software system systematically. The states are checked for errors. Such an error may be division by zero as in the case of the USS Yorktown, a race condition as in the case of GE's XA/21, or a violated assertion. Once such an erroneous state is found, it can be reported to the programmer together with a counterexample, i.e., an error trace, which demonstrates the flaw. Counterexamples can be very helpful for understanding the nature of the error and fixing it.

However, the effectiveness of Model Checking of such systems is severely constrained by the state space explosion problem, i.e., by the sheer number of states a program can be in. If there are too many states, it becomes impossible to explore all of them, even on a powerful computer.

Much of the research in this area is therefore targeted at reducing the state-space of the model used for verification. One principal method in state space reduction of software systems is *abstraction*. Abstraction techniques reduce the program state space by generating a smaller set of states in a way that preserves the relevant behaviors of the system. Abstractions are most often performed in an informal, manual manner, and require considerable expertise.

Manual abstraction is error-prone, too. The person performing the abstraction will often capture the intended behavior when abstracting, and not the behavior of the actual code, and thus, could hide a bug. Industrial applications of model checking therefore favor automated ways to compute the abstract model. One such method, called *Predicate Abstraction* [7, 8], has proven to be particularly successful when applied to large software programs. We describe the background and applications of predicate abstraction in section 2.

Reasoning about the correctness of programs is a central topic at the heart of computer science. Computer scientists formulate claims about the values particular program variables can have. Many researchers, familiar with mathematical reasoning, adopt a very high level view of the variables in a program: they treat integer program variables like unbounded integer numbers. This assumption is used to justify the use of theorem provers for arithmetic over unbounded integers.

These theorem provers are made by mathematicians for mathematicians. Computers, on the other hand, represent numbers using a finite number of bits, which implies that the range of numbers that can be represented is restricted. Figure 3 shows a small C program, which, due to the finite 8-bit range of the `unsigned char` type, may return a surprising result: when represented with 8 bits by a computer, 200 is stored as 11001000. Adding 100 results in an overflow, as the ninth bit of the result is discarded.

$$
\begin{array}{r}
11001000 = 200 \\
+\ 01100100 = 100 \\
\hline
= 00101100 = 44!
\end{array}
$$

Programmers also often use bit-level operators, which manipulate single bits in the representation of a number. Thus, tools that search for bugs in program code must take the bit-level nature of the program variables into account when reasoning about arithmetic, and cannot rely on tools for reasoning about unbounded integers. A *propositional satisfiability* (SAT) solver is a tool that decides whether a formula that only uses Boolean variables (i.e., variables that can either be **true** or **false**) has a solution or not. We describe how a SAT solver can be used to enable such proper reasoning in section 3.

In order to allow flexible and expressive data structures, programmers often use *pointers*. A pointer is a program variable that permits redirection of read or write accesses to another location. This also makes line-by-line code analysis difficult, since it is often unclear from the context what location is being

```
unsigned char number=200;
number=number+100;
printf("Sum: %d\n", number);
```

Fig. 3. Program variables are not integers: arithmetic overflow in a short C program. On most architectures, the result is 44, not 300, since `unsigned char` only represents numbers from 0 to 255.

```
int number;

void f(int *p) {
  number=200;
  *p=0;
  number=number+100;
  printf("Sum: %d\n", number);
}
```

Fig. 4. Program analysis requires accurate information about the pointers in the program: The output of this function depends on whether p points to `number`. If so, the result is 100, and 300 otherwise.

accessed. Program analysis tools must, therefore, implement a sound means to reason about the values of pointer variables. We describe the challenges that arise in the context of pointers and pointer arithmetic within C-programs in section 4.

2 Abstraction

Even simple computer programs keep track of many million bytes of data. However, for many properties of interest, most of this data is irrelevant. As an example, consider a search for a division-by-zero error. When checking this property, the particular value of the divisor can be disregarded as long it is not zero. If it is zero, an error is found, but otherwise, the actual value of the divisor is of little interest.[1] Thus, the state-space can be reduced by merging states in which the divisor is non-zero.

This idea is exploited by a technique called *Predicate abstraction* [7, 8]. Predicate abstraction is one of the most popular and widely applied methods for systematic abstraction of programs. It abstracts data by only keeping track of certain predicates on the data, such as "the divisor is not zero". Each predicate is represented by a Boolean variable in the abstract program, while the original

---

[1] Strictly speaking, this cannot always be done, because the result of the division may be used in subsequent calculations that compute the denominator of another division operation.

data variables are eliminated. This abstract model is again a program, and its control structure matches that of the original program, but since all the variables are either **true** or **false**, the size of the state-space is greatly reduced.

Typically, this abstract program is created using *Existential Abstraction* [9]. This method defines the instructions in the abstract program so that it is guaranteed to be a *conservative* over-approximation of the original program for reachability properties. Thus, in order to show that no erroneous state is reachable, it is sufficient to show that the abstract model does not contain it.

As an example, consider the small program and its abstraction in Figure 5. In line 1, an input x is read, e.g., from an operating console. In lines 2 and 3, the program checks if x is zero, and if so, sets x to one. In line 6, a division is performed with x as divisor. Line 5 asserts that the divisor is non-zero. The abstraction on the right hand side keeps track of a predicate *p1*, which holds if x is non-zero. Since the input may be both zero or non-zero, *p1* is set to a non-deterministically chosen value (denoted by *) in line 1 of the abstract program. Lines 2 and 3 in the abstract program set the predicate to **true** if it was **false** before.

	Original Program		Abstraction
1	`x=input();`	1	`p1=*;`
2	`if(x==0)`	2	`if(p1)`
3	`  x=1;`	3	`  p1=true;`
4		4	
5	`assert(x!=0);`	5	`assert(p1);`
6	`z=100/x;`	6	`skip;`

Fig. 5. A small program together with its existential abstraction using the predicate $x \neq 0$

The original program on the left hand side may have many million states, depending on the range of x. In contrast to that, the reachable states of the abstract program on the right hand side are easily examined, since only two valuations of *p1* have to be considered.

The drawback of such a conservative abstraction is that when model checking of the abstract program fails, it may produce a counterexample that does not correspond to any counterexample on the original program. This is usually called a *spurious counterexample* [10]. When a spurious counterexample is encountered, *refinement* is performed by adjusting the set of predicates in a way that eliminates this counterexample from the abstract program.

This abstraction refinement process has been automated by the *Counterexample Guided Abstraction Refinement* paradigm [11, 12, 10, 13], or CEGAR for short. One starts with a coarse abstraction. If it is found that an error-trace reported by the model checker is unrealistic, the error trace is used to refine the abstract program, and the process proceeds until no spurious error traces can be found. The actual steps of the loop follow the *abstract-verify-refine* paradigm and depend on the abstraction and refinement techniques used.

This method is promoted by the success of the SLAM [12] project at Microsoft. The goal of the SLAM project is to automatically identify errors in Windows device drivers. These device drivers are written in ANSI-C. Engineers at Microsoft formulated a set of rules that a device driver has to follow in order to interoperate correctly with the other drivers and the rest of the operating system.

Abstraction and Bit-vectors One component of the CEGAR loop abstracts the program into a Boolean program, which can then be verified by exhaustive search. This abstraction can be done line-by-line. Assume the line to be abstracted is

$$x=x+1;$$

and consider the predicate $x > 0$, called *p1*. The abstract program state consists of the value of the predicate *p1*. An abstract transition is a pair of abstract states. The first state is the state before the execution of a statement and the second state is the state after the execution of the statement.

There are altogether four potential abstract transitions (Figure 6) for this example, corresponding to the two possible values of the predicate before and after the execution of the line of code. We denote the value of x after the execution by x'. As an example, the transition from $x=0$ to $x'=1$ corresponds to the abstract transition *p1*=false to *p1'*=true.

p1:	false $\longrightarrow$ false	false $\longrightarrow$ true	true $\longrightarrow$ false	true $\longrightarrow$ true
x:	-10 $\longrightarrow$ -9	0 $\longrightarrow$ 1	127 $\longrightarrow$ -128	20 $\longrightarrow$ 21

Fig. 6. Abstract transitions

However, most existing program analysis tools will disregard one particular abstract transition. Integers are usually represented by computers using a bit-encoding called *two's complement*. In case of an 8-bit variable, one of the bits is used to encode the sign of the value. If this sign bit is one, the number is negative, and if the sign bit is zero, the number is positive. The largest number that an 8-bit two's complement encoding can represent is 127, and the smallest is -128. If 127 is incremented, the result is -128 due to the overflow.

$$
\begin{array}{r}
01111111 = 127 \\
+\; 00000001 = 1 \\
\hline
= 10000000 = \text{-}128!
\end{array}
$$

Thus, the abstract program must contain a transition from *p1*=true (127) to *p1'*=false (-128). Program analysis tools that treat program variables as unbounded integers disregard this transition, and thus, may fail to find bugs. The next section describes a technique that permits a sound treatment of the bit-vector semantics of software programs.

3   Abstraction using SAT

A propositional satisfiability (SAT) solver is a tool that given a Boolean formula decides whether the formula has a solution or not. The performance of such solvers has improved tremendously in the past few years. Modern solvers such as ZChaff [14] are now able to solve some instances with hundreds of thousands of variables and millions of clauses. We describe how such a SAT solver can be used to reason properly about bit-level representations of program variables.

This section provides a short overview of the algorithm for abstracting a program using a SAT solver. For more information on the algorithm in the case of sequential code, we refer the reader to [15]. The algorithm is extended to concurrent programs with asynchronous interleaving semantics in [16].

The SAT solver is used in order to compute the abstract program. An abstract transition from the abstract state $\hat{x}$ to the abstract state $\hat{x}'$ exists in the abstract program if there is a transition in the original program from x to x' and x is abstracted to $\hat{x}$ and x' is abstracted to $\hat{x}'$. This relationship can be represented by a formula. The formula is then transformed to a Boolean formula by replacing the bit-vector arithmetic operators by arithmetic circuits. Every solution to the formula that the SAT solver finds corresponds to one abstract transition.

The abstract model is passed to a model checker. We experimented with a variety of model checkers, e.g., MOPED, SPIN, NUSMV, and the SAT-based symbolic simulator BOPPO [17]. If the model checker returns a counterexample, it has to be simulated on the original code to check if it is spurious.

Using SAT for Simulation   Given an abstract error trace, the algorithm checks if it is spurious. The algorithm forms another SAT instance using the original program, but following the control flow given by the abstract error trace. This corresponds to Bounded Model Checking [18] on the original program. In Bounded Model Checking, the transition system and the property are jointly unwound until given depth is reached to form a Boolean formula which has a solution if an error is reachable within the bound.

If the formula has a solution, the algorithm builds an error trace from the solution given by the SAT solver, which shows the path to the error. In contrast to other methods, the path contains valuations of the program variables. If the instance is unsatisfiable, the simulation was unable to follow a particular branch that was taken in the abstract model. Thus, the trace obtained from the model checker is spurious.

Refinement If a spurious path is found, the algorithm refines the abstract model by adding some detail that will prevent that this particular spurious path is taken again. The algorithm computes weakest preconditions beginning with the guard of the branch that caused the simulation failure. The atomic expressions found in these preconditions are added as new predicates to the abstract model.

A main advantage of the SAT-based abstraction technique is that most ANSI-C constructs can be handled during the program abstraction. This differs from other model checking approaches that operate only on a small subset of the C language. The SAT-based approach permits model checking of realistic programs by supporting complex features of C, such as multiplication/division, pointers, bit-wise operations, type conversion and shift operators.

One of the most successful industrial software model checkers, SLAM, has been recently integrated with our method to reason about bit-vector constructs [19]. The integration resulted in a speed up of the verification of previously checked safety properties of Windows device drivers. The speedup was caused by the improved accuracy of the abstraction engine. Moreover, the SAT-based model checker made it possible to verify new properties that made use of bit-level constructs. The SAT-based version of SLAM has found a previously unknown bug in a Windows device driver due to SLAM's improved accuracy.

4   Programs with Pointers

Programs written in C and C++ make frequent use of pointers and references. A pointer is a program variable which is used to refer to another variable, which may be an integer, or even another pointer. *Dereferencing* a pointer corresponds to first reading the pointer value and then accessing the variable the pointer refers to.

Pointers are a challenge for program analysis tools for two reasons: First of all, if a pointer contains a bad value, the second access may cause a failure or destroy valuable data that is needed elsewhere. Thus, keeping track of the possible values the pointer variables can have is crucial.

The second problem is the size of the state-space: A pointer can potentially refer to an arbitrary memory cell of the computer. Thus, each statement that contains a pointer dereferencing operation is able to modify all the data of the program, which multiplies the number of states the program can potentially be in.

In the context of predicate abstraction, pointers complicate the construction of the abstract model tremendously. Again, consider a predicate x=0, and the following line of code, where p is a pointer that refers to a variable of the same type that x has:

$$*p=0;$$

It is unclear whether this line of code will result in a state in which the predicate x=0 holds, as this depends on the value of the pointer p. If p contains the address of the variable x, the predicate holds; otherwise, the predicate is not affected by the statement. Thus, an abstraction using this predicate will be very imprecise, as we can hardly rule out any behavior at all.

This motivates the need for stronger abstraction techniques once pointers are present. If the pointers point to static objects only, additional predicates that capture this relationship are sufficient. For the example above we would need a predicate p=&x. If it holds, the abstraction is performed as if the statement were x=0; otherwise, we could conclude that the predicate x=0 is not affected by the statement.

However, this approach fails as soon as dynamic objects are introduced, e.g., by allowing memory-allocating functions such as malloc() in C or new in C++. The number of dynamically-allocated objects is usually not bounded a priori, and thus, predicates of the form above will not be sufficient.

Abstractions that are capable of recovering properties of programs that use pointers and unbounded amounts of dynamically-allocated storage have been investigated in [20, 21]. This work was originally motivated by the problem of *shape analysis* for programs written in languages that permit destructive updating of dynamically allocated storage. The aim of shape analysis is to discover information (in a conservative way) about the possible "shapes" of the dynamically allocated linked data structures to which a program's pointer variables can point.

A *parametric* analysis framework is one that can be instantiated in different ways to create different program-analysis algorithms that provide answers to different questions, with varying degrees of efficiency and precision. The framework described in [20, 21] is capable of expressing rich properties of memory configurations, and confirming such behavioral properties as (i) when the input to a list-insert program is an acyclic list, the output is an acyclic list, and (ii) when the input to a list-reversal program that uses destructive-update operations is an acyclic list, the output is an acyclic list. Moreover, as we investigated the shape-analysis problem more deeply, we discovered methods that allowed us to deal with memory configurations other than just linked data structures. For instance, recent work has concerned concurrency [22, 23] and numeric properties [24, 25].

An interesting aspect of the approach is the way that it makes use of 2-valued and 3-valued logic: 2-valued and 3-valued *logical structures*—i.e., collections of relations—are used to represent concrete and abstract stores, respectively; individuals represent entities such as memory cells, threads, locks, etc.; unary and binary relations encode the contents of variables, pointer-valued structure fields, and other aspects of memory states; and first-order formulas with transitive closure are used to specify properties such as sharing, cyclicity, reachability, etc. Formulas are also used to specify how the store is affected by the execution of the different kinds of statements in the programming language.

The analysis framework can be instantiated in different ways by varying the relation symbols of the logic, and, in particular, by varying which of the unary relations control how nodes are folded together. The specified set of relations determines the set of properties that will be tracked, and consequently what properties of stores can be discovered to hold at different points in the program by the corresponding instance of the analysis. The approach ensures that abstract (i.e., 3-valued) structures have an *a priori* bounded size, which guarantees that an analysis will always terminate. The abstractions obtained in this way are similar to—but strictly more general than [21]—the ones obtained via predicate abstraction. A prototype tool that implements this approach has been created, called TVLA (**T**hree-**V**alued-**L**ogic **A**nalyzer) [26, 27].

5 Conclusion

Concurrent software is safety-critical, and manual inspection is infeasible. We have described an automated technique for the analysis of highly-concurrent systems called *Model Checking*. The state space explosion is the major challenge in this research area. A key technique that makes model checking feasible on large programs is *Abstraction*. Sound abstraction of realistic C programs is a challenge due to bit-level number representations and complex dynamic data structures.

References

1. http://appserv.gcn.com/17_17/news/33727-1.html.
2. F-35 joint strike fighter program. http://www.jsf.mil/.
3. David Nellemann. Air Force F-22 embedded computers, September 1994. http://archive.gao.gov/t2pbat2/152615.pdf.

4. U.S.-Canada power system outage task force final report on the August 14th blackout in the United States and Canada, April 2004. https://reports.energy.gov/.

5. E. M. Clarke and E. A. Emerson. Synthesis of synchronization skeletons for branching time temporal logic. In *Logic of Programs: Workshop*, volume 131 of *LNCS*. Springer-Verlag, 1981.

6. E. Clarke, O. Grumberg, and D. Peled. *Model Checking*. MIT Press, 1999.

7. S. Graf and H. Saïdi. Construction of abstract state graphs with PVS. In O. Grumberg, editor, *Proc. 9th INternational Conference on Computer Aided Verifi cation (CAV'97)*, volume 1254, pages 72–83. Springer Verlag, 1997.

8. M. Colon and T.E. Uribe. Generating finite-state abstractions of reactive systems using decision procedures. In *Computer Aided Verifi cation*, pages 293–304, 1998.

9. E. Clarke, O. Grumberg, and D.E. Long. Model checking and abstraction. In *POPL*, 1992.

10. E. Clarke, O. Grumberg, S. Jha, Y. Lu, and Veith H. Counterexample-guided abstraction refinement. In *CAV*, pages 154–169. Springer-Verlag, 2000.

11. R.P. Kurshan. *Computer-aided verifi cation of coordinating processes: the automata-theoretic approach*. Princeton University Press, 1994.

12. T. Ball and S.K. Rajamani. Boolean programs: A model and process for software analysis. Technical Report 2000-14, Microsoft Research, February 2000.

13. Satyaki Das and David L. Dill. Successive approximation of abstract transition relations. In *Proceedings of the Sixteenth Annual IEEE Symposium on Logic in Computer Science*, 2001. June 2001, Boston, USA.

14. Matthew W. Moskewicz, Conor F. Madigan, Ying Zhao, Lintao Zhang, and Sharad Malik. Chaff: Engineering an efficient SAT solver. In *Proceedings of the 38th Design Automation Conference (DAC'01)*, pages 530–535, June 2001.

15. E. Clarke, D. Kroening, N. Sharygina, and K. Yorav. Predicate abstraction of ANSI–C programs using SAT. *Formal Methods in System Design*, 25:105–127, September–November 2004.

16. Himanshu Jain, Edmund Clarke, and Daniel Kroening. Verification of SpecC and Verilog using predicate abstraction. In *Proceedings of MEMOCODE 2004*, pages 7–16. IEEE, 2004.

17. Byron Cook, Daniel Kroening, and Natasha Sharygina. Symbolic model checking for asynchronous boolean programs. In P. Godefroid, editor, *Proceedings of SPIN 2005*, number 3639 in Lecture Notes in Computer Science, pages 75–90. Springer Verlag, 2005.

18. A. Biere, A. Cimatti, E. M. Clarke, M. Fujita, and Y. Zhu. Symbolic model checking using SAT procedures instead of BDDs. In *Design Automation Conference (DAC'99)*, 1999.

19. Byron Cook, Daniel Kroening, and Natasha Sharygina. Cogent: Accurate Theorem Proving for Program Analysis. Technical Report 473, ETH Zurich, Computer Science, 2004.

20. M. Sagiv, T. Reps, and R. Wilhelm. Parametric shape analysis via 3-valued logic. *Trans. on Prog. Lang. and Syst.*, 24(3):217–298, 2002.

21. T. Reps, M. Sagiv, and R. Wilhelm. Static program analysis via 3-valued logic. In *Computer Aided Verif.*, pages 15–30, 2004.

22. E. Yahav. Verifying safety properties of concurrent Java programs using 3-valued logic. In *Princ. of Prog. Lang.*, pages 27–40, January 2001.

23. E. Yahav, T. Reps, M. Sagiv, and R. Wilhelm. Verifying temporal heap properties specified via evolution logic. In *European Symp. on Programming*, 2003.

24. D. Gopan, F. DiMaio, N.Dor, T. Reps, and M. Sagiv. Numeric domains with summarized dimensions. In *Tools and Algs. for the Construct. and Anal. of Syst.*, pages 512–529, 2004.

25. D. Gopan, T. Reps, and M. Sagiv. A framework for numeric analysis of array operations. In *Princ. of Prog. Lang.*, pages 338–350, 2005.

26. T. Lev-Ami and M. Sagiv. TVLA: A system for implementing static analyses. In *Static Analysis Symp.*, pages 280–301, 2000.

27. TVLA system. "http://www.cs.tau.ac.il/~tvla/".

Abstraction Refinement via Inductive Learning

Alexey Loginov[1], Thomas Reps[1], and Mooly Sagiv[2]

[1] Comp. Sci. Dept., University of Wisconsin; {alexey,reps}@cs.wisc.edu
[2] School of Comp. Sci., Tel-Aviv University; msagiv@post.tau.ac.il

Abstract. This paper concerns how to automatically create abstractions for program analysis. We show that inductive learning, the goal of which is to identify general rules from a set of observed instances, provides new leverage on the problem. An advantage of an approach based on inductive learning is that it does not require the use of a theorem prover.

1 Introduction

We present an approach to automatically creating abstractions for use in program analysis. As in some previous work [12, 4, 13, 18, 5, 2, 8], the approach involves the successive refinement of the abstraction in use. Unlike previous work, the work presented in this paper is aimed at programs that manipulate pointers and heap-allocated data structures. However, while we demonstrate our approach on shape-analysis problems, the approach is applicable in any program-analysis setting that uses first-order logic.

The paper presents an abstraction-refinement method for use in static analyses based on 3-valued logic [21], where the semantics of statements and the query of interest are expressed using logical formulas. In this setting, a memory configuration is modeled by a *logical structure*; an individual of the structure's universe either models a single memory element or, in the case of a *summary individual*, it models a collection of memory elements. Summary individuals are used to ensure that abstract descriptors have an *a priori* bounded size, which guarantees that a fixed-point is always reached. However, the constraint of working with limited-size descriptors implies a loss of information about the store. Intuitively, certain properties of concrete individuals are lost due to abstraction, which groups together multiple individuals into summary individuals: a property can be true for some concrete individuals of the group, but false for other individuals. The TVLA system is a tool for creating such analyses [1].

With the method proposed in this paper, refinement is performed by introducing new *instrumentation relations* (defined via logical formulas over core relations, which capture the basic properties of memory configurations). Instrumentation relations record auxiliary information in a logical structure, thus providing a mechanism to fine-tune an abstraction: an instrumentation relation captures a property that an individual memory cell may or may not possess. In general, the introduction of additional instrumentation relations refines an abstraction into one that is prepared to track finer distinctions among stores. The choice of instrumentation relations is crucial to the precision, as well as the cost, of the analysis. Until now, TVLA users have been faced with the task of identifying an instrumentation-relation set that gives them a definite answer to the query, but does not make the cost prohibitive. This was arguably the key remaining challenge in the TVLA user-model. The contributions of this work can be summarized as follows:

- It establishes a new connection between program analysis and machine learning by showing that *inductive logic programming* (ILP) [19, 17, 14] is relevant to the problem of creating abstractions. We use ILP for learning new instrumentation relations that preserve information that would otherwise be lost due to abstraction.

- The method has been implemented as an extension of TVLA. In this system, all of the user-level obligations for which TVLA has been criticized in the past have been addressed. The input required to specify a program analysis consists of: (i) a transition system, (ii) a query (a formula that identifies acceptable outputs), and (iii) a characterization of the program's valid inputs.

- We present experimental evidence of the value of the approach. We tested the method on sortedness, stability, and antistability queries for a set of programs that perform destructive list manipulation, as well as on partial-correctness queries for two binary-search-tree programs. The method succeeds in all cases tested.

Inductive learning concerns identifying general rules from a set of observed instances—in our case, from relationships observed in a logical structure. An advantage of an approach based on inductive learning is that it does not require the use of a theorem prover. This is particularly beneficial in our setting because our logic is undecidable.

The paper is organized as follows: §2 introduces terminology and notation. Readers familiar with TVLA can skip to §2.2, which briefly summarizes ILP. §3 illustrates our goals on the problem of verifying the partial correctness of a sort-

Fig. 1. A possible store for a linked list.

ing routine. §4 describes the techniques used for learning abstractions. (Further details can be found in [16].) §5 presents experimental results. §6 discusses related work.

2 Background

2.1 Stores as Logical Structures and their Abstractions

```
typedef struct node {
    struct node *n;
    int data;
} *List;
```

(a)

Relation	Intended Meaning
$eq(v_1, v_2)$	Do v_1 and v_2 denote the same memory cell?
$q(v)$	Does pointer variable q point to memory cell v?
$n(v_1, v_2)$	Does the n field of v_1 point to v_2?
$dle(v_1, v_2)$	Is the data field of v_1 less than or equal to that of v_2?

(b)

Table 1. (a) Declaration of a linked-list datatype in C. (b) Core relations used for representing the stores manipulated by programs that use type List.

Our work extends the program-analysis framework of [21]. In that approach, concrete memory configurations (i.e., *stores*) are encoded as logical structures in terms of a fixed collection of *core relations*, C. Core relations are part of the underlying semantics of the language to be analyzed. For instance,

Fig. 2. A logical structure S_2 that represents the store shown in Fig. 1 in graphical and tabular forms.

Tab. 1 gives the definition of a C linked-list datatype, and lists the relations that would be used to represent the stores manipulated by programs that use type List, such as the store in Fig. 1. 2-valued logical structures then represent memory configurations: the individuals are the set of memory cells; in this example, unary relations represent pointer variables and binary relation n represents the n-field of a List cell. The data field is modeled indirectly, via the binary relation *dle* (which stands for "data less-than-or-equal-to") listed in Tab. 1.   Fig. 2 shows 2-valued structure S_2, which represents the store of Fig. 1 (relations t_n, $r_{n,x}$, and c_n will be explained below).

Let $\mathcal{R} = \{eq, p_1, \ldots, p_n\}$ be a finite vocabulary of relation symbols, where $\mathcal{R}_k$ denotes the set of relation symbols of arity k (and $eq \in \mathcal{R}_2$). A *2-valued logical structure* S over $\mathcal{R}$ is a set of *individuals* U^S, along with an *interpretation* that maps each relation symbol p of arity k to a truth-valued function: $p^S : (U^S)^k \rightarrow \{0, 1\}$, where eq^S is the equality relation on individuals. The set of 2-valued structures is denoted by $\mathcal{S}_2[\mathcal{R}]$.

In 3-valued logic, a third truth value—$1/2$—is introduced to denote uncertainty. For $l_1, l_2 \in \{0, 1/2, 1\}$, the *information order* is defined as follows: $l_1 \sqsubseteq l_2$ iff $l_1 = l_2$ or $l_2 = 1/2$. A *3-valued logical structure* S is defined like a 2-valued logical structure, except that the values in relations can be $\{0, 1/2, 1\}$. An individual for which $eq^S(u, u) = 1/2$ is called a *summary individual*. A summary individual abstracts one or more fragments of a data structure, and can represent more than one concrete memory cell. The set of 3-valued structures is denoted by $\mathcal{S}_3[\mathcal{R}]$.

Concrete and Abstract Semantics A concrete operational semantics is defined by specifying a structure transformer for each kind of edge e that can appear in a transition system. A structure transformer is specified by providing *relation-update formulas* for the core relations.[3] These formulas define how the core relations of a 2-valued logical structure S that arises at the source of e are transformed by e to create a 2-valued logical structure S' at the target of e. Edge e may optionally have a *precondition formula*, which filters out structures that should not follow the transition along e.

However, sets of 2-valued structures do not yield a suitable abstract domain; for instance, when the language being modeled supports allocation from the heap, the set of individuals that may appear in a structure is unbounded, and thus there is no a priori upper bound on the number of 2-valued structures that may arise during the analysis.

To ensure termination, we abstract sets of 2-valued structures using 3-valued structures. A set of stores is then represented by a (finite) set of 3-valued logical structures. The abstraction is defined using an equivalence relation on individuals: each individual of a 2-valued logical structure (representing a concrete memory cell) is mapped to an individual of a 3-valued logical structure according to the vector of values that the concrete individual has for a user-chosen collection of unary abstraction relations:

Definition (Canonical Abstraction). Let $S \in \mathcal{S}_2$, and let $\mathcal{A} \subseteq \mathcal{R}_1$ be some chosen subset of the unary relation symbols. The relations in $\mathcal{A}$ are called *abstraction relations*; they define the following equivalence relation $\simeq_\mathcal{A}$ on U^S:

$$u_1 \simeq_\mathcal{A} u_2 \iff \text{for all } p \in \mathcal{A}, p^S(u_1) = p^S(u_2),$$

and the surjective function $f_\mathcal{A} : U^S \rightarrow U^S / \simeq_\mathcal{A}$, such that $f_\mathcal{A}(u) = [u]_{\simeq_\mathcal{A}}$, which maps an individual to its equivalence class. The *canonical abstraction* of S with respect to $\mathcal{A}$ (denoted by $f_\mathcal{A}(S)$) performs the join (in the information order) of predicate values, thereby introducing $1/2$'s. $\square$

If all unary relations are abstraction relations ($\mathcal{A} = \mathcal{R}_1$), the canonical abstraction of 2-valued logical structure S_2 is S_3, shown in Fig. 3, with $f_\mathcal{A}(u_1) = u_1$ and $f_\mathcal{A}(u_2) =$

---

[3] Formulas are first-order formulas with transitive closure: a *formula* over the vocabulary $\mathcal{R}$ is defined as follows (where $p^*(v_1, v_2)$ stands for the reflexive transitive closure of $p(v_1, v_2)$):

$p \in \mathcal{R},$ $\qquad \varphi ::= \mathbf{0} \mid \mathbf{1} \mid p(v_1, \ldots, v_k) \mid (\neg\varphi_1) \mid (v_1 = v_2)$

$\varphi \in \textit{Formulas},$ $\qquad \mid (\varphi_1 \wedge \varphi_2) \mid (\varphi_1 \vee \varphi_2) \mid (\varphi_1 \rightarrow \varphi_2) \mid (\varphi_1 \leftrightarrow \varphi_2)$

$v \in \textit{Variables}$ $\qquad \mid (\exists v \colon \varphi_1) \mid (\forall v \colon \varphi_1) \mid p^*(v_1, v_2)$

$f_{\mathcal{A}}(u_3) = u_{23}$. S_3 represents all lists with two or more elements, in which the first element's data value is lower than the data values in the rest of the list. The following graphical notation is used for depicting 3-valued logical structures:

- Individuals are represented by circles containing their names and (non-0) values for unary relations. Summary individuals are represented by double circles.
- A unary relation p corresponding to a pointer-valued program variable is represented by a solid arrow from p to the individual u for which $p(u) = 1$, and by the absence of a p-arrow to each node u' for which $p(u') = 0$. (If $p = 0$ for all individuals, the relation name p is not shown.)
- A binary relation q is represented by a solid arrow labeled q between each pair of individuals u_i and u_j for which $q(u_i, u_j) = 1$, and by the absence of a q-arrow between pairs u_i' and u_j' for which $q(u_i', u_j') = 0$.
- Relations with value $1/2$ are represented by dotted arrows.

Canonical abstraction ensures that each 3-valued structure is no larger than some fixed size, known *a priori*. Moreover, the meaning of a given formula in the concrete domain ($\wp(\mathcal{S}_2)$) is consistent with its meaning in the abstract domain ($\wp(\mathcal{S}_3)$), although the formula's value in an

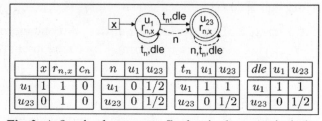

	x	$r_{n,x}$	c_n		n	u_1	u_{23}		t_n	u_1	u_{23}		dle	u_1	u_{23}
u_1	1	1	0	u_1	0	1/2		u_1	1	1		u_1	1	1	
u_{23}	0	1	0	u_{23}	0	1/2		u_{23}	0	1/2		u_{23}	0	1/2	

Fig. 3. A 3-valued structure S_3 that is the canonical abstraction of structure S_2.

abstract structure $f_{\mathcal{A}}(S)$ may be less precise than its value in the concrete structure S.

Abstract interpretation collects a set of 3-valued structures at each program point. It can be implemented as an iterative procedure that finds the least fixed point of a certain collection of equations on variables that take their values in $\wp(\mathcal{S}_3)$ [21].

p	IntendedMeaning	ψ_p
$t_n(v_1, v_2)$	Is v_2 reachable from v_1 along n fields?	$n^*(v_1, v_2)$
$r_{n,x}(v)$	Is v reachable from pointer variable x along n fields?	$\exists\, v_1 : x(v_1) \wedge t_n(v_1, v)$
$c_n(v)$	Is v on a directed cycle of n fields?	$\exists\, v_1 : n(v_1, v) \wedge t_n(v, v_1)$

Table 2. Defining formulas of some commonly used instrumentation relations. There is a separate reachability relation $r_{n,x}$ for every program variable x.

Instrumentation Relations The abstraction function on which an analysis is based, and hence the precision of the analysis defined, can be tuned by (i) choosing to equip structures with additional *instrumentation relations* to record derived properties, and (ii) varying which of the unary core and unary instrumentation relations are used as the set of abstraction relations. The set of instrumentation relations is denoted by $\mathcal{I}$. Each relation symbol $p \in \mathcal{I}_k \subseteq \mathcal{R}_k$ is defined by an *instrumentation-relation definition formula* $\psi_p(v_1, \ldots, v_k)$. Instrumentation relation symbols may appear in the defining formulas of other instrumentation relations as long as there are no circular dependences.

The introduction of unary instrumentation relations that are used as abstraction relations provides a way to control which concrete individuals are merged together, and thereby control the amount of information lost by abstraction. Tab. 2 lists some instrumentation relations that are important for the analysis of programs that use type List.

2.2 Inductive Logic Programming (ILP)

Given a logical structure, the goal of an ILP algorithm is to learn a logical relation (defined in terms of the logical structure's other relations) that agrees with the classification of input examples. ILP algorithms produce the answer in the form of a logic program. (Non-recursive) logic programs correspond to a subset of first-order logic.[4] A logic program can be thought of as a disjunction over the program rules, with each rule corresponding to a conjunction of literals. Variables not appearing in the head of a rule are implicitly existentially quantified.

Definition (ILP). Given a set of positive example tuples E^+, a set of negative example tuples E^-, and a logical structure, the goal of ILP is to find a formula ψ_E such that all $e \in E^+$ are satisfied (or *covered*) by ψ_E and no $e \in E^-$ is satisfied by ψ_E. □

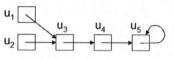

Fig. 4. A linked list with shared elements.

For example, consider learning a unary formula that holds for linked-list elements that are pointed to by the n fields of more than one element (as used in [11, 3]). We let $E^+ = \{u_3, u_5\}$ and $E^- = \{u_1, u_4\}$ in the 2-valued structure of Fig. 4. The formula $\psi_{isShared}(v) \stackrel{\text{def}}{=} \exists v_1, v_2 :$ $n(v_1, v) \wedge n(v_2, v) \wedge \neg eq(v_1, v_2)$ meets the objective, as it covers all positive and no negative example tuples.

Fig. 5 presents the ILP algorithm used by systems such as FOIL [19], modified to construct the answer as a first-order logic formula in disjunctive normal form. This algorithm is capable of learning the formula $\psi_{isShared}(v)$ (by performing one iteration of the outer loop and three iterations of the inner loop to successively choose literals $n(v_1, v)$, $n(v_2, v)$, and

```
Input: Target relation E(v₁,...,vₖ),
       Structure S ∈ S₃[R],
       Set of tuples Pos, Set of tuples Neg
[1]  ψ_E := 0
[2]  while (Pos ≠ ∅)
[3]      NewDisjunct := 1
[4]      NewNeg := Neg
[5]      while (NewNeg ≠ ∅)
[6]          Cand := candidate literals using R
[7]          Best := L ∈ Cand with max Gain(L, NewDisjunct)
[8]          NewDisjunct := NewDisjunct ∧ L
[9]          NewNeg := subset of NewNeg satisfying L
[10]     ∃-quantify NewDisjunct variables ∉ {v₁,...,vₖ}
[11]     ψ_E := ψ_E ∨ NewDisjunct
[12]     Pos := subset of Pos not satisfying NewDisjunct
```

Fig. 5. Pseudo-code for FOIL.

$\neg eq(v_1, v_2)$). It is a sequential covering algorithm parameterized by the function *Gain*, which characterizes the usefulness of adding a particular literal (generally, in some heuristic fashion). The algorithm creates a new disjunct as long as there are positive examples that are not covered by existing disjuncts. The disjunct is extended by conjoining a new literal until it covers no negative examples. Each literal uses a relation symbol from the vocabulary of structure S; valid arguments to a literal are the variables of target relation E, as well as new variables, as long as at least one of the arguments is a variable already used in the current disjunct. In FOIL, one literal is chosen using a heuristic value based on the information gain (see line [7]). FOIL uses information gain to find the literal that differentiates best between positive and negative examples.

3 Example: Verifying Sortedness

---

[4] ILP algorithms are capable of producing recursive programs, which correspond to first-order logic plus a least-fixpoint operator (which is more general than transitive closure).

Given the static-analysis algorithm defined in §2.1, to demonstrate the partial correctness of a procedure, the user must supply the following program-specific information:

- The procedure's control-flow graph.
- A *data-structure constructor* (DSC): a code fragment that non-deterministically constructs all valid inputs.
- A query; i.e., a formula that identifies the intended outputs.

The analysis algorithm is run on the DSC concatenated with the procedure's control-flow graph; the query is then evaluated on the structures that are generated at exit.

Consider the problem of establishing that InsertSort shown in Fig. 6 is partially correct. This is an assertion that compares the state of a store at the end of a procedure with its state at the start. In particular, a correct sorting routine must perform a permutation of the input list, i.e. all list elements reachable from variable x at the start of the routine must be reachable from x at the end. We can express the permutation property as follows:

```
[1]  void InsertSort(List x){
[2]  List r, pr, rn, l, pl;
[3]  r = x;
[4]  pr = NULL;
[5]  while (r != NULL) {
[6]    l = x;
[7]    rn = r->n;
[8]    pl = NULL;
[9]    while (l != r) {
[10]     if (l->data > r->data){
[11]       pr->n = rn;
[12]       r->n = l;
[13]       if (pl == NULL) x = r;
[14]       else pl->n = r;
[15]       r = pr;
[16]       break;
[17]     }
[18]     pl = l;
[19]     l = l->n;
[20]   }
[21]   pr = r;
[22]   r = rn;
[23] }
[24] }
```

Fig. 6. A stable version of insertion sort.

$$\forall v : r^0_{n,x}(v) \leftrightarrow r_{n,x}(v), \tag{1}$$

where $r^0_{n,x}$ denotes the reachability relation for x at the beginning of InsertSort. If Formula (1) holds, then the elements reachable from x after InsertSort executes are exactly the same as those reachable at the beginning, and consequently the procedure performs a permutation of list x. In general, for each relation p, we have such a *history relation p^0*.

Fig. 7 shows the three structures that characterize the valid inputs to InsertSort (they represent the set of stores in which program variable x points to an acyclic linked list). To verify that InsertSort produces a *sorted* permutation of the input list, we would check to see whether, for all of the structures that arise at the procedure's exit node, the following formula evaluates to 1:

$$\forall v_1 : r_{n,x}(v_1) \rightarrow (\forall v_2 : n(v_1, v_2) \rightarrow dle(v_1, v_2)). \tag{2}$$

If it does, then the nodes reachable from x must be in non-decreasing order.

Abstract interpretation collects 3-valued structure S_3 shown in Fig. 3 at line [24]. Note that Formula (2) evaluates to $1/2$ on S_3. While the first list element is guaranteed to be in correct order with respect to the remaining elements, there is no guarantee that all list nodes represented by the summary node are in correct order. In particular, because S_3 represents S_2, shown in Fig. 2, the analysis admits the possibility that the (correct) implementation of insertion sort of Fig. 6 can produce the store shown in Fig. 1. Thus, the abstraction that we used was not fine-grained enough to establish the partial correctness of InsertSort. In fact, the abstraction is not fine-grained enough to separate the set of sorted lists from the lists not in sorted order.

In [15], Lev-Ami et al. used TVLA to establish the partial correctness of `InsertSort`. The key step was the introduction of instrumentation relation $inOrder_{dle,n}(v)$, which holds for nodes whose `data`-components are less than or equal to those of their n-successors; $inOrder_{dle,n}(v)$ was defined by:

$$inOrder_{dle,n}(v) \stackrel{\text{def}}{=} \forall v_1 : n(v, v_1) \rightarrow dle(v, v_1). \tag{3}$$

The sortedness property was then stated as follows (cf. Formula (2)):

$$\forall v : r_{n,x}(v) \rightarrow inOrder_{dle,n}(v). \tag{4}$$

After the introduction of relation $inOrder_{dle,n}$, the 3-valued structures that are collected by abstract interpretation at the end of `InsertSort` describe all stores in which variable x points to an acyclic, *sorted* linked list. In all of these structures, Formulas (4) and (1) evaluate to 1. Consequently, `InsertSort` is guaranteed to work correctly on all valid inputs.

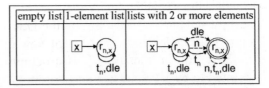

Fig. 7. The structures that describe possible inputs to `InsertSort`.

4   Learning an Abstraction

In [15], instrumentation relation $inOrder_{dle,n}$ was defined explicitly (by the TVLA user). Heretofore, there have really been two burdens placed on the TVLA user:

 (i) he must have insight into the behavior of the program, and

(ii) he must translate this insight into appropriate instrumentation relations.

The goal of this paper is to automate the identification of appropriate instrumentation relations, such as $inOrder_{dle,n}$. For `InsertSort`, the goal is to obtain definite answers when evaluating Formula (2) on the structures collected by abstract interpretation at line [24] of Fig. 6. Fig. 8 gives pseudo-code for our method, the steps of which can be explained as follows:

 – (Line [1]; [16, §4.3]) Use a data-structure constructor to compute the abstract input structures that represent all valid inputs to the program.

```
Input:  a transition system,
         a data-structure constructor,
         a query φ (a closed formula)
[1]   Construct abstract input
[2]   do
[3]      Perform abstract interpretation
[4]      Let S_1,...,S_k be the set of
          3-valued structures at exit
[5]      if for all S_i, ⟦φ⟧_3^{S_i}(∅) ≠ 1/2 break
[6]      Find formulas ψ_{p_1},...,ψ_{p_k} for new
          instrumentation rels p_1,...,p_k
[7]      Refine the actions that define
          the transition system
[8]      Refine the abstract input
[9]   while (true)
```

Fig. 8. Pseudo-code for iterative abstraction refinement.

 – Perform an abstract interpretation to collect a set of structures at each program point, and evaluate the query on the structures at exit. If a definite answer is obtained on all structures, terminate. Otherwise, perform abstraction refinement.

 – (Line [6]; §4.1 and §4.2) Find defining formulas for new instrumentation relations.

 – (Line [7]) Replace all occurrences of these formulas in the query and in the definitions of other instrumentation relations with the use of the corresponding new instrumentation relation symbols, and apply finite differencing [20] to generate refined relation-update formulas for the transition system.

— (Line [8]; [16, §4.3]) Obtain the most precise possible values for the newly introduced instrumentation relations in abstract structures that define the valid inputs to the program. This is achieved by "reconstructing" the valid inputs by performing abstract interpretation of the data-structure constructor.

A first attempt at abstraction refinement could be the introduction of the query itself as a new instrumentation relation. However, this usually does not lead to a definite answer. For instance, with InsertSort, introducing the query as a new instrumentation relation is ineffective because no statement of the program has the effect of changing the value of such an instrumentation relation from $1/2$ to 1.

In contrast, when unary instrumentation relation $inOrder_{dle,n}$ is present, there are several statements of the program where abstract interpretation results in new definite entries for $inOrder_{dle,n}$. For instance, because of the comparison in line [10] of Fig. 6, the insertion in lines [12]–[14] of the node pointed to by r (say u) before the node pointed to by l results in a new definite entry $inOrder_{dle,n}(u)$.

An algorithm to generate new instrumentation relations should take into account the sources of imprecision. §4.1 describes subformula-based refinement; §4.2 describes ILP-based refinement. At present, we employ subformula-based refinement first, because the cost of this strategy is reasonable (see §5) and the strategy is often successful. When subformula-based refinement can no longer refine the abstraction, we turn to ILP.

Because a query has finitely many subformulas and we currently limit ourselves to one round of ILP-based refinement, the number of abstraction-refinement steps is finite. Because, additionally, each run of the analysis explores a bounded number of 3-valued structures, the algorithm is guaranteed to terminate.

4.1   Subformula-Based Refinement

When the query φ evaluates to $1/2$ on a structure S collected at the exit node, we invoke function *instrum*, a recursive-descent procedure to generate defining formulas for new instrumentation relations based on the subformulas of φ responsible for the imprecision. The details of function *instrum* are given in [16, §4.1].

Example. As we saw in §3, abstract interpretation collects 3-valued structure S_3 of Fig. 3 at the exit node of InsertSort. The sortedness query (Formula (2)) evaluates to $1/2$ on S_3, triggering a call to *instrum* with Formula (2) and structure S_3, as arguments. Column 2 of Tab. 3 shows the instrumentation relations that are created as a result of the call. Note that $sorted_3$ is defined exactly as $inOrder_{dle,n}$, which was the key insight for the results of [15]. □

p	ψ_p (after call to *instrum*)	ψ_p (final version)
$sorted_1()$	$\forall v_1 : r_{n,x}(v_1) \rightarrow (\forall v_2 : n(v_1, v_2) \rightarrow dle(v_1, v_2))$	$\forall v_1 : sorted_2(v_1)$
$sorted_2(v_1)$	$r_{n,x}(v_1) \rightarrow (\forall v_2 : n(v_1, v_2) \rightarrow dle(v_1, v_2))$	$r_{n,x}(v_1) \rightarrow sorted_3(v_1)$
$sorted_3(v_1)$	$\forall v_2 : n(v_1, v_2) \rightarrow dle(v_1, v_2)$	$\forall v_2 : sorted_4(v_1, v_2)$
$sorted_4(v_1, v_2)$	$n(v_1, v_2) \rightarrow dle(v_1, v_2)$	$n(v_1, v_2) \rightarrow dle(v_1, v_2)$

Table 3. Instrumentation relations created by subformula-based refinement.

The actions that define the program's transition relation need to be modified to gain precision improvements from storing and maintaining the new instrumentation relations. To accomplish this, refinement of the program's actions (line [7] in Fig. 8) replaces all occurrences of the defining formulas for the new instrumentation relations in the query and in the definitions of other instrumentation relations with the use of the corresponding new instrumentation-relation symbols.

Example. For InsertSort, the use of Formula (2) in the query is replaced with the use of the stored value $sorted_1()$. Then the definitions of all instrumentation relations are scanned for occurrences of $\psi_{sorted_1}, \ldots, \psi_{sorted_4}$. These occurrences are replaced with the names of the four relations. In this case, only the new relations' definitions are changed, yielding the definitions given in Column 3 of Tab. 3.

In all of the structures collected at the exit node of InsertSort by the second run of abstract interpretation, $sorted_1() = 1$. The permutation property also holds on all of the structures. These two facts establish the partial correctness of InsertSort. This process required one iteration of abstraction refinement, used the basic version of the specification (the vocabulary consisted of the relations of Tabs. 1 and 2, together with the corresponding history relations), and needed no user intervention. □

4.2 ILP-Based Refinement

Shortcomings of Subformula-Based Refinement To illustrate a weakness in subformula-based refinement, we introduce the stability property. The stability property usually arises in the context of sorting procedures, but actually applies to list-manipulating programs in general: the stability query (Formula (5)) asserts that the relative order of elements with equal data-components remains the same.[5]

$$\forall v_1, v_2 : (dle(v_1, v_2) \land dle(v_2, v_1) \land t_n^0(v_1, v_2)) \to t_n(v_1, v_2) \qquad (5)$$

Procedure InsertSort consists of two nested loops (see Fig. 6). The outer loop traverses the list, setting pointer variable r to point to list nodes. For each iteration of the outer loop, the inner loop finds the correct place to insert r's target, by traversing the list from the start using pointer variable l; r's target is inserted before l's target when l->data > r->data. Because InsertSort satisfies the invariant that all list nodes that appear in the list before r's target are already in the correct order, the data-component of r's target is less than the data-component of *all* nodes ahead of which r's target is moved. Thus, InsertSort preserves the original order of elements with equal data-components, and InsertSort is a stable routine.

However, subformula-based refinement is not capable of establishing the stability of InsertSort. By considering only subformulas of the query (in this case, Formula (5)) as candidate instrumentation relations, the strategy is unable to introduce instrumentation relations that maintain information about the *transitive* successors with which a list node has the correct relative order.

Learning Instrumentation Relations Fig. 9 shows the structure S_9, which arises during abstract interpretation just before line [6] of Fig. 6, together with a tabular version of relations t_n and dle. (We omit reachability relations from the figure for clarity.) After the assignment l = x;, nodes u_2 and u_3 have identical vectors of values for the unary abstraction relations. The subsequent application of canonical abstraction produces structure S_{10}, shown in Fig. 10. Bold entries of tables in Fig. 9 indicate definite

---

[5] A related property, antistability, asserts that the order of elements with equal data-components is reversed: $\forall v_1, v_2 : (dle(v_1, v_2) \land dle(v_2, v_1) \land t_n^0(v_1, v_2)) \to t_n(v_2, v_1)$

Our test suite also includes program InsertSort_AS, which is identical to InsertSort except that it uses $\geq$ instead of $>$ in line [10] of Fig. 6 (i.e., when looking for the correct place to insert the current node). This implementation of insertion sort is antistable.

values that are transformed into $1/2$ in S_{10}. Structure S_9 satisfies the sortedness invariant discussed above: every node among $u_1, ..., u_4$ has the *dle* relationship with all nodes appearing later in the list, except r's target, u_5. However, a piece of this information is lost in structure S_{10}: $dle(u_{23}, u_{23}) = 1/2$, indicating that some nodes represented by summary node u_{23} might not be in sorted order with respect to their successors. We will refer to such abstraction steps as *information-loss points*.

An abstract structure transformer may temporarily create a structure S_1 that is not in the image of canonical abstraction [21]. The subsequent application of canonical abstraction transforms S_1 into structure S_2 by grouping a set U_1 of two or more individuals of S_1 into a single summary individual of S_2. The loss of precision is due to one or both of the following circumstances:

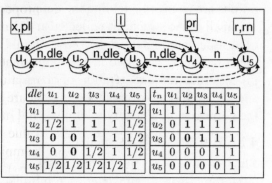

dle	u_1	u_2	u_3	u_4	u_5
u_1	1	1	1	1	1/2
u_2	1/2	1	1	1	1/2
u_3	0	0	1	1	1/2
u_4	0	0	1/2	1	1/2
u_5	1/2	1/2	1/2	1/2	1

t_n	u_1	u_2	u_3	u_4	u_5
u_1	1	1	1	1	1
u_2	0	1	1	1	1
u_3	0	0	1	1	1
u_4	0	0	0	1	1
u_5	0	0	0	0	1

Fig. 9. Structure S_9, which arises just before line [6] of Fig. 6. Unlabeled edges between nodes represent the *dle* relation.

- One of the individuals in U_1 possesses a property that another individual does not possess; thus, the property for the summary individual is $1/2$.
- Individuals in U_1 have a property in common, which cannot be recomputed precisely in S_2.

In both cases, the solution lies in the introduction of new instrumentation relations. In the former case, it is necessary to introduce a unary abstraction relation to keep the individuals of U_1 that possess the property from being grouped with those that do not. In the latter case, it is sufficient to introduce a non-abstraction relation of appropriate arity that captures the common property of individuals in U_1. The algorithm described in §2.2 can be used to learn formulas for the following three kinds of relations:[6]

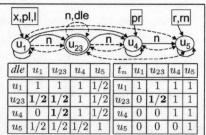

dle	u_1	u_{23}	u_4	u_5
u_1	1	1	1	1/2
u_{23}	**1/2**	**1/2**	1	1/2
u_4	0	**1/2**	1	1/2
u_5	1/2	1/2	1/2	1

t_n	u_1	u_{23}	u_4	u_5
u_1	1	1	1	1
u_{23}	0	**1/2**	1	1
u_4	0	0	1	1
u_5	0	0	0	1

Fig. 10. Structure S_{10}, corresponding to the transformation of S_9 by the statement on line [6] of Fig. 6. Unlabeled edges between nodes represent the *dle* relation.

Type I: Unary relation r_1 with $E^+ = \{u\}$ for one $u \in U_1$, and $E^- = U_1 - \{u\}$.

Type II: Unary relation r_2 with $E^+ = U_1$.

Type III: Binary relation r_3 with $E^+ = U_1 \times U_1$.

Type I relations are intended to prevent the grouping of individuals with different properties, while Types II and III are intended to capture the common properties of individuals in U_1. (Type III relations can be generalized to higher-arity relations.)

For the logical structure that serves as input to ILP, we pass the structure S_1 identified at an information-loss point. We restrict the algorithm to use only non-history

---

[6] These are what are needed for our analysis framework, which uses abstractions that generalize predicate-abstraction domains. A fourth use of ILP provides a new technique for predicate abstraction itself: ILP can be used to identify nullary relations that differentiate a positive-example structure S from the other structures arising at a program point. The steps of ILP go beyond merely forming Boolean combinations of existing relations; they involve the creation of new relations by introducing quantifiers during the learning process.

relations of the structure that lose definite entries as a result of abstraction (e.g., t_n and *dle* in the above example). Definite entries of those relations are then used to learn formulas that evaluate to 1 for every positive example and to 0 for every negative example.

We modified the algorithm of §2.2 to learn multiple formulas in one invocation of the algorithm. Our motivation is not to find a single instrumentation relation that explains something about the structure, but rather to find all instrumentation relations that help the analysis establish the property of interest. Whenever we find multiple literals of the same quality (see line [7] of Fig. 5), we extend distinct copies of the current disjunct using each of the literals, and then we extend distinct copies of the current formula using the resulting disjuncts.

This variant of ILP is able to learn a useful binary formula using structure S_9 of Fig. 9. The set of individuals of S_9 that are grouped by the abstraction is $U = \{u_2, u_3\}$, so the input set of positive examples is $\{(u_2, u_2), (u_2, u_3), (u_3, u_2), (u_3, u_3)\}$. The set of relations that lose definite values due to abstraction includes t_n and *dle*. Literal $dle(v_1, v_2)$ covers three of the four examples because it holds for bindings $(v_1, v_2) \mapsto (u_2, u_2), (v_1, v_2) \mapsto (u_2, u_3)$, and $(v_1, v_2) \mapsto (u_3, u_3)$. The algorithm picks that literal and, because there are no negative examples, $dle(v_1, v_2)$ becomes the first disjunct. Literal $\neg t_n(v_1, v_2)$ covers the remaining positive example, (u_3, u_2), and the algorithm returns the formula

$$\psi_{r_3}(v_1, v_2) \stackrel{\text{def}}{=} dle(v_1, v_2) \vee \neg t_n(v_1, v_2), \tag{6}$$

which can be re-written as $t_n(v_1, v_2) \rightarrow dle(v_1, v_2)$.

Relation r_3 allows the abstraction to maintain information about the transitive successors with which a list node has the correct relative order. In particular, although $dle(u_{23}, u_{23})$ is $1/2$ in S_{10}, $r_3(u_{23}, u_{23})$ is 1, which allows establishing the fact that all list nodes appearing prior to r's target are in sorted order.

Other formulas, such as $dle(v_1, v_2) \vee t_n(v_2, v_1)$, are also learned using ILP (cf. Fig. 12). Not all of them are useful to the verification process, but introducing extra instrumentation relations cannot harm the analysis, aside from increasing its cost.

5 Experimental Evaluation

We extended TVLA to perform iterative abstraction refinement, and applied it to three queries and five programs (see Fig. 11). Besides `InsertSort`, the test programs included sorting procedures `BubbleSort` and `InsertSort_AS`, list-merging procedure `Merge`, and *in-situ* list-reversal procedure `Reverse`.

At present, we employ subformula-based refinement first. During each iteration of subformula-based refinement, we save logical structures at information-loss points. Upon the failure of subformula-based refinement, we invoke the ILP algorithm described in §4.2. To lower the cost of the analysis we prune the returned set of formulas. For example, we currently remove formulas defined in terms of a single relation symbol; such formulas are usually tautologies (e.g., $dle(v_1, v_2) \vee dle(v_2, v_1)$). We then define new instrumentation relations, and use these relations to refine the abstraction by performing the steps of lines [7] and [8] of Fig. 8. Our implementation can learn relations of all types described in §4.2: unary, binary, as well as nullary. However, due to the present cost of maintaining many unary instrumentation relations in TVLA, in the experiments reported here we only learn binary formulas (i.e., of Type III). Moreover, we define new instrumentation relations using only learned formulas of a simple form (currently, those with two atomic subformulas). We are in the process of extending our techniques for pruning useless instrumentation relations. This should make it practical for us to use all types of relations that can be learned by ILP for refining the abstraction.

Example. When attempting to verify the stability of `InsertSort`, ILP creates nine formulas including Formula (6). The subsequent run of the analysis successfully verifies the stability of `InsertSort`. □

Test Program	*sorted*	*stable*	*antistable*
BubbleSort	1	1	1/2
InsertSort	1	1	1/2
InsertSort_AS	1	1/2	1
Merge	1/2	1	1/2
Reverse	1/2	1/2	1

Fig. 11. Results from applying iterative abstraction refinement to the verification of properties of programs that manipulate linked lists.

Fig. 11 shows that the method was able to generate the right instrumentation relations for TVLA to establish all properties that we expect to hold. Namely, TVLA succeeds in demonstrating that all three sorting routines produce sorted lists, that `BubbleSort`, `InsertSort`, and `Merge` are stable routines, and that `InsertSort_AS` and `Reverse` are antistable routines.

Indefinite answers are indicated by 1/2 entries. *It is important to understand that all of the occurrences of 1/2 in Fig. 11 are the most precise correct answers.* For instance, the result of applying `Reverse` to an unsorted list is usually an unsorted list; however, in the case that the input list happens to be in non-increasing order, `Reverse` produces a sorted list. Consequently, the most precise answer to the query is 1/2, not 0.

Test Program	*sorted* # instrum rels total/ILP	*stable* # instrum rels total/ILP	*antistable* # instrum rels total/ILP
BubbleSort	31/0	32/0	41/9
InsertSort	39/0	49/9	43/3
InsertSort_AS	39/0	43/3	40/0
Merge	30/3	28/0	31/3
Reverse	26/3	27/3	24/0

Fig. 12. The numbers of instrumentation relations (total and learned by ILP) used during the last iteration of abstraction refinement.

Fig. 12 shows the numbers of instrumentation relations used during the last iteration of abstraction refinement. The number of ILP-learned relations used by the analysis is small relative to the total number of instrumentation relations.

Fig. 13 gives execution times that were collected on a 3GHz Linux PC. The longest-running analysis, which verifies that `InsertSort` is stable, takes 8.5 minutes. Seven of the analyses take under a minute. The rest take between 70 seconds and 6 minutes. The total time for the 15 tests is 35 minutes. These numbers are very close to how long it takes to verify the sortedness queries when the user carefully chooses the right instrumentation relations [15].[7] The maximum amount of memory used by the analyses varied from just under 2 MB to 32 MB.[8]

The cost of the invocations of the ILP algorithm when attempting to verify the antistability of `BubbleSort` was 25 seconds (total, for 133 information-loss points). For all other benchmarks, the ILP cost was less than ten seconds.

Three additional experiments tested the applicability of our method to other queries and data structures. In the first experiment, subformula-based refinement successfully verified that the *in-situ* list-reversal procedure `Reverse` indeed produces a list that is the reversal of the input list. The query that expresses this property is $\forall v_1, v_2 : n(v_1, v_2) \leftrightarrow n^0(v_2, v_1)$. This experiment took only 5 seconds and used less than 2 MB of memory. The second and third experiments involved two programs that manipu-

---

[7] Sortedness is the only query in our set to which TVLA has been applied before this work.

[8] TVLA is written in Java. Here we report the maximum of total memory minus free memory, as returned by Runtime.

late binary-search trees. `InsertBST` inserts a new node into a binary-search tree, and `DeleteBST` deletes a node from a binary-search tree. For both programs, subformula-based refinement successfully verified the query that the nodes of the tree pointed to by variable `t` remain in sorted order at the end of the programs:

$$\forall v_1 \colon r_t(v_1) \rightarrow (\forall v_2 \colon (left(v_1, v_2) \rightarrow dle(v_2, v_1)) \wedge (right(v_1, v_2) \rightarrow dle(v_1, v_2))) \quad (7)$$

The initial specifications for the analyses included only three standard instrumentation relations, similar to those listed in Tab. 2. Relation $r_t(v_1)$ from Formula (7), for example, distinguishes nodes in the (sub)tree pointed to by `t`. The `InsertBST` experiment took 30 seconds and used less than 3 MB of memory, while the `DeleteBST` experiment took approximately 10 minutes and used 37 MB of memory.

6   Related Work

The work reported here is similar in spirit to counterexample-guided abstraction refinement [12, 4, 13, 18, 5, 2, 8, 6]. A key difference between this work and prior work in the model-checking community is the abstract domain: prior work has used abstract domains that are fixed, finite, Cartesian products of Boolean values (i.e., predicate-abstraction domains), and hence the only relations introduced are nullary relations. Our work applies to a richer class of abstractions—3-valued structures—that generalize predicate-abstraction domains. The abstraction-refinement algorithm described in this paper can introduce unary, binary, ternary, etc. relations, in addition to nullary relations. While we demonstrated our approach using shape-analysis queries, this approach is

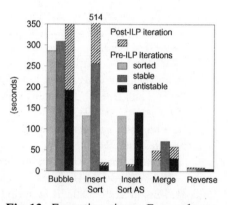

Fig. 13. Execution times. For each program, the three bars represent the sorted, stable, and antistable queries. In cases where subformula-based refinement failed, the upper portion of the bars shows the cost of the last iteration of the analysis (on both the DSC and the program) together with the ILP cost.

applicable in any setting in which first-order logic is used to describe program states.

A second distinguishing feature of our work is that the method is driven not by counterexample traces, but instead by imprecise results of evaluating a query (in the case of subformula-based refinement) and by loss of information during abstraction steps (in the case of ILP-based refinement). There do not currently exist theorem provers for first-order logic extended with transitive closure capable of identifying infeasible error traces [9]; hence we needed to develop techniques different from those used in SLAM, BLAST, etc. SLAM identifies the shortest prefix of a spurious counterexample trace that cannot be extended to a feasible path; in general, however, the first information-loss point occurs before the end of the prefix. Information-loss-guided refinement can identify the earliest points at which information is lost due to abstraction, as well as what new instrumentation relations need to be added to the abstraction at those points. A potential advantage of counterexample-guided refinement over information-loss-guided refinement is that the former is goal-driven. Information-loss-guided refinement can discover many relationships that do not help in establishing the query. To alleviate this problem, we restricted the ILP algorithm to only use relations that occur in the query.

Abstraction-refinement techniques from the abstract-interpretation community are capable of refining domains that are not based on predicate abstraction. In [10], for example, a polyhedra-based domain is dynamically refined. Our work is based on a different abstract domain, and led us to develop some new approaches to abstraction refinement, based on machine learning.

In the abstract-interpretation community, a strong (albeit often unattainable) form of abstraction refinement has been identified in which the goal is to make abstract interpretation complete (a.k.a. "optimal") [7]. In our case, the goal is to extend the abstraction just enough to be able to answer the query, rather than to make the abstraction optimal.

References

1. TVLA system. http://www.cs.tau.ac.il/ tvla/.
2. T. Ball and S. Rajamani. Automatically validating temporal safety properties of interfaces. In *SPIN*, pages 103–122, 2001.
3. D.R. Chase, M. Wegman, and F. Zadeck. Analysis of pointers and structures. In *PLDI*, pages 296–310, 1990.
4. E.M. Clarke, O. Grumberg, S. Jha, Y. Lu, and H. Veith. Counterexample-guided abstraction refinement. In *CAV*, pages 154–169, 2000.
5. S. Das and D. Dill. Counter-example based predicate discovery in predicate abstraction. In *FMCAD*, pages 19–32, 2002.
6. C. Flanagan. Software model checking via iterative abstraction refinement of constraint logic queries. In *CP+CV*, 2004.
7. R. Giacobazzi, F. Ranzato, and F. Scozzari. Making abstract interpretations complete. *J. ACM*, 47(2):361–416, 2000.
8. T. Henzinger, R. Jhala, R. Majumdar, and K. McMillan. Abstractions from proofs. In *POPL*, pages 232–244, 2004.
9. N. Immerman, A. Rabinovich, T. Reps, M. Sagiv, and G. Yorsh. The boundary between decidability and undecidability for transitive closure logics. In *CSL*, pages 160–174, 2004.
10. B. Jeannet, N. Halbwachs, and P. Raymond. Dynamic partitioning in analyses of numerical properties. In *SAS*, pages 39–50, 1999.
11. N. Jones and S. Muchnick. Flow analysis and optimization of Lisp-like structures. In *Program Flow Analysis: Theory and Applications*, pages 102–131. Prentice-Hall, 1981.
12. R. Kurshan. *Computer-aided Verification of Coordinating Processes*. Princeton University Press, 1994.
13. Y. Lakhnech, S. Bensalem, S. Berezin, and S. Owre. Incremental verification by abstraction. In *TACAS*, pages 98–112, 2001.
14. N. Lavrač and S. Džeroski. *Inductive Logic Programming: Techniques and Applications*. Ellis Horwood, 1994.
15. T. Lev-Ami, T. Reps, M. Sagiv, and R. Wilhelm. Putting static analysis to work for verification: A case study. In *ISSTA*, pages 26–38, 2000.
16. A. Loginov, T. Reps, and M. Sagiv. Learning abstractions for verifying data-structure properties. report TR-1519, Comp. Sci. Dept., Univ. of Wisconsin, January 2005. Available at "http://www.cs.wisc.edu/wpis/papers/tr1519.ps".
17. S. Muggleton. Inductive logic programming. *New Generation Comp.*, 8(4):295–317, 1991.
18. C. Pasareanu, M. Dwyer, and W. Visser. Finding feasible counter-examples when model checking Java programs. In *TACAS*, pages 284–298, 2001.
19. J.R. Quinlan. Learning logical definitions from relations. *Mach. Learn.*, 5:239–266, 1990.
20. T. Reps, M. Sagiv, and A. Loginov. Finite differencing of logical formulas with applications to program analysis. In *ESOP*, pages 380–398, 2003.
21. M. Sagiv, T. Reps, and R. Wilhelm. Parametric shape analysis via 3-valued logic. *TOPLAS*, 24(3):217–298, 2002.

Analysis of COTS for Security Vulnerability Remediation

Gogul Balakrishnan   Mihai Christodorescu   Vinod Ganapathy
Jonathon T. Giffin   Shai Rubin   Hao Wang
Somesh Jha*   Barton P. Miller[†]   Thomas Reps[‡]

Computer Sciences Department, University of Wisconsin
1210 West Dayton Street, Madison, Wisconsin 53706

Abstract

The increased use of untrusted, externally-developed program code is reshaping our notions of privacy and organizational boundaries. The use of such public domain and *commercial off-the-shelf* (*COTS*) components offers an organization several advantages, such as decreased development time and increased flexibility during implementation. However, their rash deployment poses two critical risks. First, COTS components may contain or enable vulnerabilities that can be successfully exploited by malicious attackers. Second, COTS components may accidentally or deliberately leak sensitive information. Vulnerability analysis and information-flow analysis address these two risks respectively. In the WiSA project at the University of Wisconsin–Madison, we are developing analysis techniques to address these risks.

Categories and Subject Descriptors

D.3.3 [**Programming Languages**]: Language Constructs and Features
D.4.6 [**Operating Systems**]: Security and Protection
F.3.1 [**Logics and Meanings of Programs**]: Specifying and Verifying and Reasoning about Programs
K.6.5 [**Management of Computing and Information Systems**]: Security and Protection

General Terms

Experimentation, Languages, Measurement, Security

Keywords

Static binary analysis, commercial off-the-shelf components, malware detection, virus detection, intrusion detection

1   Introduction

The increased use of untrusted, externally-developed program code is reshaping our notion of privacy and organizational boundaries. The use of such public domain and *commercial off-the-shelf* (*COTS*) components has obvious advantages, such as reduced development time. However, COTS components expose an organization to risks. A component should be given enough access to do its job, but no more (this is known as the *principle of least privilege*). Moreover, organizations that deal with sensitive information should protect this information: organizations should

---

*jha@cs.wisc.edu
[†]bart@cs.wisc.edu
[‡]reps@cs.wisc.edu

create an *information enclave* that enforces privacy policies. In a closed software process, it is possible to enforce the principle of least privilege and the policies of an information enclave through strict code inspection and coding practices. However, COTS components are by definition developed by other groups, and therefore the organization that uses these components has no control over the coding practices of the developers. Therefore, there is a need for analysis tools to scrutinize COTS components to ensure that they do not contain harmful vulnerabilities or leak sensitive information. There are two classes of analysis techniques: vulnerability analysis and information-flow analysis.

The *Wisconsin Safety Analysis (WiSA)* project lead by S. Jha, B. Miller, and T. Reps is developing analysis techniques especially suited for COTS components.[1] First, we identify requirements for the task of analyzing COTS components. These requirements drive our technical approaches. Our techniques are designed to be multi-lingual (capable of handling multiple languages), handle a wide range of security and privacy policies, and balance accuracy and scalability. We achieve these goals by combining techniques from static analysis (such as program slicing, shape analysis, and alias analysis), model checking, specifications for expressing security policies (such as security automata), and formalisms for expressing information flow (such as secure flow typing and decentralized labels). Combinations of these techniques are required to address the challenges posed by vulnerability and information flow analysis of COTS components. These analysis techniques provide a comprehensive analysis of COTS components and thus reduce the risk due to COTS deployment.

The basic goals of the WiSA project are:

- **Multi-lingual analysis**
  COTS components, by definition, are developed by remote organizations. Therefore, analysis techniques cannot assume that all COTS components will be written in one programming language. Hence, techniques for analyzing COTS components should be multi-lingual, i.e., capable of working with several different languages. We achieve this goal by analyzing binary code directly or by compiling untrusted source code into an intermediate form which is then analyzed.

- **Balance accuracy and scalability**
  The analysis techniques should be able to handle COTS components of realistic size. We have designed techniques that balance accuracy with scalability. Accuracy is achieved by combining several sophisticated program analysis techniques, such as shape analysis, aliasing analysis, and type inferencing. Scalability is addressed by using techniques for handling composition of components and targeting the analysis to any properties of interest.

- **Support a wide range of safety and privacy policies**
  Security requirements of COTS components depend on the context of their use. As part of this project we plan to develop specification languages that can express safety and privacy related policies. Specifications related to safety express *discretionary access control* policies. *Mandatory access control* policies control flows of sensitive information and can also be expressed in our specification language. Hence, an analyst can express a variety of properties in our specification language.

- **Potential for analyzing composition of components**
  Most real systems are composed of several components. We plan to develop a framework so that components can be analyzed separately and then the analysis results can be integrated. For this purpose, we will base our methodology on *rely-guarantee* reasoning. Rely-guarantee reasoning has been used in software engineering and verification of concurrent systems exactly for this purpose. This will also address the scalability issue.

We have made partial progress towards some of these goals. We have developed a static-analysis and rewriting infrastructure for x86 binaries. This infrastructure can be used for a variety of tasks, such as model-based intrusion detection, testing malware detectors, and semantics-aware malware detection. A short description of this infrastructure appears in the following section.

2 Binary Analysis Infrastructure

A considerable amount of recent research activity [2–4, 7, 8, 11, 12, 17] has developed analysis tools to find bugs and security vulnerabilities in source code. When attempting to apply such analysis techniques to executables, investigators already encounter a challenging program-analysis problem. The model-checking community would consider

---

[1] Detailed information about WiSA can be found at http://www.cs.wisc.edu/wisa.

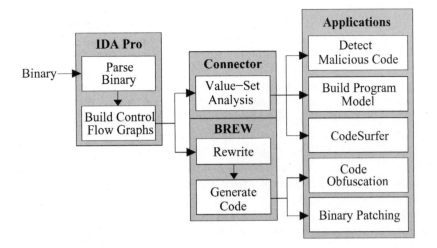

Figure 1: Architecture.

the problem to be that of *model extraction*: the tools need to extract a suitable model from the executable. From the perspective of the compiler community, the problem is one of *IR recovery*: tools need to recover Intermediate Representations (IR) from the executable that are similar to those that would be available from source code analysis.

Successful analysis of binary code requires new solutions to this problem. The commercial disassembler IDAPro is a start: IDAPro provides an initial estimate of the IR. However, the IR that IDAPro constructs is incomplete in critical ways that limits its ability to serve as a foundation for further analysis.

- Binary programs frequently transfer control via indirect jumps whose targets are not computed until program run time. IDAPro uses heuristics to resolve indirect jumps. Consequently, it may not resolve all indirect jumps correctly, i.e., it may not find all possible targets of an indirect jump and it even occasionally identifies incorrect targets. Therefore, the control-flow graph constructed by IDAPro is frequently incomplete or outright incorrect. Similar problems occur with IDAPro's resolution of indirect calls; therefore, the call graph is also often incomplete or incorrect. Call graphs and control-flow graphs form the basis of further program analysis. Incorrectness in these graphs will propagate through the analysis and produce bad results.

- IDAPro does not provide a safe estimate of what memory locations are used or modified by each instruction in the executable. Such information is important for tools that aid in program understanding or bug finding; its omission limits the success of these tools.

Hence, IDAPro cannot produce a suitable IR for automated program analysis.

We have been developing a static analysis algorithm called *value-set analysis* (VSA) that augments and corrects the information provided by IDAPro in a safe way [1]. Specifically, VSA provides the following information:

- Complete, correct control-flow graphs with indirect jumps resolved safely.

- A call graph with indirect calls resolved safely.

- A set of variable-like entities called *a-locs*.

- Values for pointer variables.

- Used, killed, and possibly-killed variables for nodes in control-flow graphs.

This information is emitted in a format that is suitable for subsequent program analysis applications such as the commercial tool CodeSurfer.

VSA is a flow-sensitive, context-sensitive, abstract-interpretation algorithm parameterized by call-string length [15] that determines a safe over-approximation of the set of numeric values and addresses that memory locations hold at each program point. A key feature of VSA is that it tracks integer-valued and address-valued quantities simultaneously. This is crucial for analyzing executables because numeric values and addresses are indistinguishable in an executable.

VSA has similarities with the pointer-analysis problem that has been studied in great detail for programs written in high-level languages. For each variable v, pointer analysis determines an over-approximation of the set of variables whose addresses v can hold. Similarly, VSA determines an over-approximation of the set of addresses that each a-loc can hold at each program point. On the other hand, VSA also has some of the flavor of numeric static analyses, like constant propagation and interval analysis, where the goal is to over-approximate the integer values that each variable can hold. In addition to information about addresses, VSA determines an over-approximation of the set of integer values that each a-loc can hold at each program point. The result is a safe and correct IR that enables further static program analyses to produce meaningful results for binary programs.

Figure 1 shows how VSA and IDAPro cooperate to produce a base that static analysis application can use to analyze binary programs. IDAPro first processes a binary executable, producing the initial IR that may be incomplete or incorrect. VSA then executes as part of a tool called the *connector*, as it connects IDAPro with static analysis tools in a safe way. The complete, correct IR produced by VSA can then be used by applications performing static program analysis, such as the commercial tool CodeSurfer or research techniques detecting malicious code in executables or building models of expected execution for programs. We will consider these last two applications momentarily.

Alternatively, the IR can be used for binary rewriting, a process that changes the binary code of a program to produce a new executable with altered behavior. Our tool, called *BREW*, alters the IR in the connector and regenerates binary code for the modified program. Binary rewriting applies to tools such as code obfuscators that change program code to increase the difficulty of reverse engineering, and to binary patching tools that repair program bugs without requiring recompilation of source code.

2.1   Applications

Malware detectors, such as virus scanners, identify malicious code hidden within off-the-shelf code and in code shared over communications networks. Despite the importance of malware detectors, there is a dearth of testing techniques to evaluate them. We introduced a technique based on program obfuscation to generate tests for malware detectors [5]. Our technique is geared towards evaluating the resilience of malware detectors to various obfuscation transformations commonly used by hackers to disguise malware. We also demonstrated that a hacker can leverage a malware detector's weakness in handling obfuscation transformations and can extract the signature used by a detector for a specific malware. We evaluated three widely-used commercial virus scanners using our techniques and discovered that the resilience of these scanners to various obfuscations is very poor.

The fundamental deficiency of these commercial virus scanners is their use of pattern-matching approaches to malware detection: these approaches are purely syntactic and ignore the semantics of binary instructions. We developed a malware-detection algorithm that addressed this deficiency by using instruction semantics to detect malicious program traits [6]. Experimental evaluation demonstrated that, with a relatively low run-time overhead, our malware-detection algorithm can detect variants of malware embedded within COTS code. Moreover, our semantics-aware malware detection algorithm is resilient to common obfuscations used by hackers.

Just as a misuse detector identifies attacks contained in program code, a network intrusion detection system (NIDS) detects attacks contained in network traffic. Using network-level obfuscation transformations, we used black-box testing to evaluate the ability of COTS misuse-NIDS products to detect attacks and secure an organization's networks. A misuse-NIDS defines penetration via a table of malicious signatures: if the network traffic matches a signature in the table, an alarm is raised. Both researchers and industry professionals accept that the effectiveness of current off-the-shelf NIDS is questionable. Current NIDS generate many false alarms, and worse (although not always publicized), they miss many real attacks. Our research strives to bring us closer to an effective NIDS: an intrusion detection system that detects the attacks we specify and only those attacks. In our research, we developed formal models and tools that can increase our confidence in NIDS. In the last two years, we have addressed two fundamental problems of NIDS effectiveness: NIDS testing and signature construction.

We formulated a computational model that describes how attackers can generate attack instances that evade a NIDS. Based on this model, we implemented a testing tool that automatically generated new attack instances from known ones [13]. We used this tool to find attack instances that evaded two well-known COTS NIDS: *Snort*, which is a popular NIDS publicly available from SourceFire, and *UnityOne*, which is a commercial NIDS from TippingPoint used by highly secured sites such as the Los Alamos National Lab. In both cases, we exposed vulnerabilities that would have enabled attackers to evade these systems for any TCP-based attack. In response to our findings, both Sourcefire and TippingPoint issued patches to fix their systems.

The signatures that a NIDS uses determine its ability to recognize attacks. We developed a method to systematically construct and evaluate signatures [14]. First, we formally defined the ability of attackers to obfuscate attacks. Then, we combined this formal model with language-based techniques to find loopholes in signatures. To the best of our knowledge, this was the first method that enabled NIDS developers to systematically "debug" the signatures they developed. We showed that, under certain assumptions, the signatures produced are loophole free.

As a complement to network-based intrusion detection, host-based intrusion detection systems identify attempts to exploit program vulnerabilities, frequently by monitoring the program's execution. A model-based or behavioral-based anomaly detector restricts execution to a precomputed model of expected behavior. An execution monitor verifies a stream of system calls generated by the executing program and rejects any call sequences deviating from the model. Constructing a model via static binary program analysis that balances the competing needs of detection ability and efficiency is a challenging task. Non-deterministic finite automaton (NFA) models are efficient to operate, but fail to detect attacks because they do not model the call-return semantics of the program. Pushdown automaton (PDA) models detect more attacks by additionally modeling the program's call stack, but they are inefficient to operate. New models of correct program execution are needed.

We developed a new formal model called the *Dyck model* that preserves the correctness of PDA models but operates with efficiency close to that of NFA models [10, 16]. Our model determinizes previously costly PDA operations modeling the program's call stack [9]. Techniques for determinizing the PDA models essentially incorporate additional program state, such as the program counter and stack activity, into the model. Our results showed that the Dyck model enabled construction of precise program models with performance suitable for online security monitoring. These results vindicated context sensitive models, showing that reasonable efficiency needs not be sacrificed for model precision.

3   Conclusions

We have made good progress towards some of our goals. However, there are some important tasks that should be addressed in the future. We want to improve the robustness and enhance the capabilities of our static-analysis and rewriting infrastructure. Information-flow analysis also remains an important goal which we have not addressed. Compositional analysis of COTS also remains an important goal.

References

[1] G. Balakrishnan and T. Reps. Analyzing memory accesses in x86 executables. In *13th International Conference on Compiler Construction (CC)*, Barcelona, Spain, Apr. 2004.

[2] T. Ball and S. K. Rajamani. The slam toolkit. In *International Conference on Computer Aided Verification (CAV)*, 2001.

[3] W. Bush, J. Pincus, and D. Sielaff. A static analyzer for finding dynamic programming errors. *Software—Practice & Experience*, 30:775–802, 2000.

[4] H. Chen and D. Wagner. MOPS: An infrastructure for examining security properties of software. In *ACM Conference on Computer and Communications Security*, Nov. 2002.

[5] M. Christodorescu and S. Jha. Testing malware detectors. In *International Symposium on Software Testing and Analysis (ISSTA)*, Boston, MA, July 2004.

[6] M. Christodorescu, S. Jha, S. A. Seshia, D. Song, and R. E. Bryant. Semantics-aware malware detection. In *2005 IEEE Symposium on Security and Privacy*, Oakland, CA, May 2005.

[7] M. Das, S. Lerner, and M. Seigle. ESP: path-sensitive program verification in polynomial time. In *Programming Language Design and Implementation (PLDI)*, New York, NY, 2002.

[8] D. R. Engler, B. Chelf, A. Chou, and S. Hallem. Checking system rules using system-specific, programmer-written compiler extensions. In *Operating System Design and Implementation (OSDI)*, 2000.

[9] H. H. Feng, J. T. Giffin, Y. Huang, S. Jha, W. Lee, and B. P. Miller. Formalizing sensitivity in static analysis for intrusion detection. In *IEEE Symposium on Security and Privacy*, Oakland, CA, May 2004.

[10] J. T. Giffin, S. Jha, and B. P. Miller. Efficient context-sensitive intrusion detection. In *11th Network and Distributed System Security Symposium (NDSS)*, San Diego, CA, Feb. 2004.

[11] K. Havelund and T. Pressburger. Model checking Java programs using Java PathFinder. *Software Tools for Technology Transfer*, 2(4), 2000.

[12] T. A. Henzinger, R. Jhala, R. Majumdar, and G. Sutre. Lazy abstraction. In *Principles of Programming Languages (POPL)*, 2002.

[13] S. Rubin, S. Jha, and B. P. Miller. Automatic generation and analysis of NIDS attacks. In *20th Annual Computer Security Applications Conference (ACSAC)*, Tuscon, AZ, Dec. 2004.

[14] S. Rubin, S. Jha, and B. P. Miller. Language-based generation and evaluation of NIDS signatures. In *IEEE Symposium on Security and Privacy*, Oakland, CA, May 2005.

[15] M. Sharir and A. Pnueli. Two approaches to interprocedural data flow analysis. In S. S. Muchnick and N. D. Jones, editors, *Program Flow Analysis: Theory and Applications*, chapter 7, pages 189–233. Prentice-Hall, 1981.

[16] W. von Dyck. Gruppentheoretische studien. *Mathematische Annalen*, 20:1–44, 1882.

[17] D. Wagner, J. Foster, E. Brewer, and A. Aiken. A first step towards automated detection of buffer overrun vulnerabilities. In *Network and Distributed System Security Symposium*, Feb. 2000.

Formalizing Sensitivity in Static Analysis for Intrusion Detection

Henry Hanping Feng*, Jonathon T. Giffin†, Yong Huang*,
Somesh Jha†, Wenke Lee‡, and Barton P. Miller†

*Department of Electrical and Computer Engineering
University of Massachusetts–Amherst
{hfeng,yhuang}@ecs.umass.edu

†Computer Sciences Department
University of Wisconsin–Madison
{giffin,jha,bart}@cs.wisc.edu

‡College of Computing
Georgia Institute of Technology
wenke@cc.gatech.edu

Abstract

A key function of a host-based intrusion detection system is to monitor program execution. Models constructed using static analysis have the highly desirable feature that they do not produce false alarms; however, they may still miss attacks. Prior work has shown a trade-off between efficiency and precision. In particular, the more accurate models based upon pushdown automata (PDA) are very inefficient to operate due to non-determinism in stack activity. In this paper, we present techniques for determinizing PDA models. We first provide a formal analysis framework of PDA models and introduce the concepts of determinism and stack-determinism. We then present the VP-Static model, which achieves determinism by extracting information about stack activity of the program, and the Dyck model, which achieves stack-determinism by transforming the program and inserting code to expose program state. Our results show that in run-time monitoring, our models slow execution of our test programs by 1% to 135%. This shows that reasonable efficiency need not be sacrificed for model precision. We also compare the two models and discover that deterministic PDA are more efficient, although stack-deterministic PDA require less memory.

1. Introduction

A typical *host-based intrusion detection system (HIDS)* monitors execution of a process to identify potentially malicious behavior. An anomaly detection HIDS identifies variations from a preconstructed model of normal program behavior. Such a system interposes a monitor between a process and the operating system. All events (usually system calls) that flow from the program to the operating system are validated against the model. Events that do not conform to the model are rejected by the monitor. Figure 1 shows a typical HIDS architecture.

There are several techniques to construct the program model used in an anomaly detection HIDS. Learning-based techniques [4, 5, 8, 12, 14, 15, 22, 26] construct the program model by training on a set of execution traces. Sometimes a specification of the program provided by a domain expert is also used as a program model [11]. This paper focuses on program models constructed using static analysis [6, 23, 24]. In the context of static analysis, there is a trade-off between efficiency and precision. Non-deterministic finite automaton (NFA) models are efficient to operate, but introduce impossible paths because they do not model the call-return semantics of the program. Pushdown automaton (PDA) models eliminate impossible paths by incorporating the program's stack, but they are inefficient to operate. The inefficiency in the PDA models occurs because the stack activity of the program is hidden from the model and results in non-determinism. Therefore, the state space of the PDA model can become prohibitively large during operation. We call this the *curse of non-determinism*. This paper formally presents several techniques to handle this problem. Specifically, we make the following contributions:

- **Formal framework.** Formal models in intrusion detection research have received scant attention, and we address this shortcoming. Investigating formalisms drives the discovery of why certain program models do or do not exhibit reasonable performance. Our primary purpose is to formally analyze recently proposed models rather than to in-

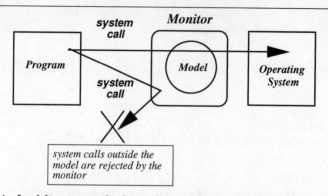

Figure 1. Architecture of a host-based intrusion detection system.

troduce all-new models. A commonality of these models is the exposure of process execution state beyond a simple system call stream. For example, Sekar *et al.* [19] proposed using program counter information. Feng *et al.* [2] and Giffin *et al.* [7] exposed the stack activity of a program. We show that a context-free language (CFL) is homomorphic to a deterministic CFL. The proof of this result is similar to that of Chomsky [1] and provides intuition about techniques that expose program state. Non-determinism in stack activity is the major factor contributing to the time and space complexity of operating PDA models. Motivated by this observation, we define a stack-deterministic PDA model in which the stack activity is deterministic. Section 3 discusses these formalisms.

‣ **Model determinizing techniques.** Techniques for determinizing the PDA models essentially incorporate additional program state (such as the program counter and stack activity) into the model. We describe two techniques incorporating additional state of the program. In the *observational technique*, the monitor extracts the relevant information from the program. For example, the monitor can extract information about the stack activity of the program by walking the call stack. Our VPStatic model, a statically-constructed variant of the VtPath model [2], implements this technique. The rewriting or *instrumentation technique* transforms the program to introduce additional code that exposes program state. For example, additional system calls introduced before a call to function f indicate to the model that a call to f is about to happen. Our recent Dyck model implements this approach [7]. We also compare the observational and rewriting approaches to determinizing the PDA model. Sections 4 and 5 present the two models.

‣ **Evaluation.** Our results show that the formalisms of deterministic and stack-deterministic push-down automata enable construction of context-sensitive program models suitable for online security monitoring. The VPStatic automaton operation slows execution of our test programs by 0% to 17%, although the unoptimized stack walking algorithm adds up to 80% additional overhead. The Dyck model is slightly less efficient due to state non-determinism, with overheads of 8% to 135%. However, the Dyck model has a compact representation, requiring only 38% to 49% more memory for program instrumentation and the state machine. These results vindicate context sensitive models, showing that reasonable efficiency needs not be sacrificed for model precision. Complete results are given in Section 6.

2. Related Work

Significant intrusion detection systems research has focused upon static and dynamic analysis techniques to automatically generate program models. Wagner *et al.* produced models via static analysis of C source code [23, 24]. They described the precise *abstract stack* model, which is a non-deterministic pushdown automaton (PDA). Due to the stack state maintained in a PDA, this model captured the precise call and return behavior of function calls. Unfortunately, runtime automaton operation in the monitor was prohibitively high for some programs, reaching several tens of minutes per transaction. We observed similar results with PDA models extracted using static binary analysis of SPARC executables [6]. Both papers concluded that imprecise, context-insensitive models must be used for reasonable performance.

However, only context-sensitive models, such as the PDA, can detect the impossible path exploits described by Wagner *et al.* [23,24]. Such attacks force control flow to enter a function from one call site but to return to a different call site, presumably in a portion of the program code suitable for the attack. A context-sensitive model detects this illicit control flow by modeling the state of a program's call stack.

Our experience indicates that severe non-determinism in this stack state is the major contributing factor to the time and space complexity of PDA operation. The Dyck model proved this: by eliminating non-determinism on stack transitions, a context-sensitive model could be efficiently operated [7]. This paper formalizes the Dyck model and proves that it is a stack deterministic PDA. We further improve the model by eliminating the additional system calls required by the previous model construction. Our VPStatic model goes further. It is a fully deterministic PDA and requires no modifications to the original, analyzed binary.

Dynamic analysis extends the original work of Forrest *et al.* [3] and constructs a program model based upon observed system call traces from numerous training runs [4,5,8,12,14,15,22,26,27]. Sekar *et al.* showed that learning a deterministic automaton is possible by associating each system call with its corresponding program counter [19]. This model does not monitor context information and may miss attacks due to this imprecision. It may also miss attacks on dynamically linked libraries due to its oversimplified handling of dynamic objects.

Our previous VtPath model improved the precision of dynamically constructed models [2]. This model additionally monitors return addresses on the call stack. Our VPStatic model is a natural extension of VtPath constructed using static analysis techniques. Again, we add formalism to the previous work. The VtPath model calculates an ad-hoc virtual path from the call stacks of two adjacent system calls and verifies the validity of that path. VPStatic is a provably deterministic PDA. The use of an automaton localizes transitions to states, making VPStatic more precise. Moreover, the VPStatic model does not suffer the false alarms of VtPaths due to its conservative static analysis.

Others have pioneered work outside of static and dynamic analysis. These approaches monitor execution based upon specifications of system calls [10] or of expected program behavior [11]. When provided by a domain expert, these specifications can likely enhance the quality of automatically generated models.

The VPStatic model has an *anomaly recovery* property not considered by previous approaches. After an anomaly occurs, we can still uniquely determine the expected state and stack context for the next valid system call by monitoring its program counter and call stack. Thus, we can continue to operate the automaton and potentially detect more attacks such as a root-level exploit following a probe. This also allows for a greater variety of security policies by enabling the system to fail an anomalous system call and continue execution rather than terminate the program. For example, a monitor that terminates a network daemon after an anomalous system call could be used for a denial of service attack. We can instead prevent just the anomalous call and allow process execution and monitoring to continue.

3. Formal Models

We begin by formally describing pushdown automata, deterministic pushdown automata, and stack-deterministic pushdown automata. These finite state machines are the underlying constructs of our program models used for intrusion detection.

Definition 1 *[PDA and DPDA]*

A pushdown automaton *(PDA)* P is 7-tuple $P = (Q, \Sigma, \Gamma, \delta, q_0, z_0, F)$, where Q is the set of states, Σ is the input alphabet, Γ is the stack alphabet, δ is the transition relation mapping $Q \times (\Sigma \cup \{\epsilon\}) \times \Gamma$ to finite subsets of $Q \times (\Gamma \cup \{\epsilon\})^\star$, $q_0 \in Q$ is the unique initial state, $z_0 \in \Gamma$ is the initial stack start symbol, and $F \subseteq Q$ is the set of accepting states. There are three types of transitions in δ:

1. *(Input consumption or ϵ transition):* $(p, z) \in \delta(q, a, z)$ where $a \in \Sigma \cup \{\epsilon\}$.
   The top of the stack is z and stack contents do not change. If $a = \epsilon$, then this represents a transition from q to p that consumes no input. If $a \in \Sigma$ and P is in state q, then consume input a and move to state p.

2. *(Push transition; pushes z' onto the stack):* $(p, zz') \in \delta(q, a, z)$ where $a \in \Sigma \cup \{\epsilon\}$.
   The explanation is the same as (1), but now z' is pushed onto the stack.

3. *(Pop transition; pops z from stack):* $(p, \epsilon) \in \delta(q, a, z)$ where $a \in \Sigma \cup \{\epsilon\}$.
   The explanation is the same as (1), but now z is popped from the stack.

A PDA $P = (Q, \Sigma, \Gamma, \delta, q_0, Z_0, F)$ is called *deterministic if the transition relation δ satisfies the following conditions* [9]:

- **(Condition 1):** *For all $q \in Q$ and $z \in \Gamma$, whenever $\delta(q, \epsilon, z)$ is nonempty, then $\delta(q, a, z)$ is empty for all $a \in \Sigma$.*

- **(Condition 2):** *For all q in Q, $a \in \Sigma \cup \{\epsilon\}$ and $z \in \Gamma$, $\delta(q, a, z)$ contains at most one element.*

A deterministic PDA is abbreviated as DPDA.

Our definition allows only one stack symbol to be pushed onto or popped from the stack. The most general definition of a PDA (as found in [9]) allows more than one stack symbol to be pushed on the stack. However, it is easy to see that a PDA P (according to the general definition) can always be converted into a PDA which conforms to our definition (the construction essentially transforms pushing many symbols on the stack into a sequence of pushes of one symbol.)

Given a PDA $P = (Q, \Sigma, \Gamma, \delta, q_0, z_0, F)$, a *configuration* c is a tuple (q, γ), where $q \in Q$ is the current state and

γ is a string of stack symbols representing the stack contents. Given two configurations c and c' and $a \in \Sigma$, we say that $c \Rightarrow_P^a c'$ if c is transformed into c' by a sequence of transitions of the PDA P while consuming input a. The relation $\Rightarrow_P^a$ can be extended to words $w \in \Sigma^\star$, i.e., given two configurations c and c' and $w \in \Sigma^\star$, $c \Rightarrow_P^w c'$ if c is transformed into c' by a sequence of transitions of the PDA P while consuming input from string w. When P is clear from the context, we simply write $\Rightarrow^w$ instead of $\Rightarrow_P^w$. The language $L(P)$ accepted by $P = (Q, \Sigma, \Gamma, \delta, q_0, z_0, F)$ is defined as

$$\{w | (q_0, z_0) \Rightarrow_P^w (p, \gamma) \text{ for some } p \in F \text{ and } \gamma \in \Gamma^\star\}$$

PDAs accept context free languages (CFL). If a language L is accepted by DPDA, it is called a *deterministic context free language* or *DCFL*. Theorem 1 proves that every CFL L is homomorphic [9] to a DCFL L'. Moreover, the proof of the theorem gives a procedure for determinizing a PDA by expanding the input alphabet. This proof is similar to that of Chomsky [1].

Theorem 1 *Let L be a CFL. There exists a DCFL L_D and a homomorphism h such that $h(L_D) = L$.*

Proof: *Let $P = (Q, \Sigma, \Gamma, \delta, q_0, z_0, F)$ be a PDA accepting L. We will construct a new input alphabet Σ_D. There are three types of symbols in Σ_D.*

- **Input:** *For each $a \in \Sigma \cup \{\epsilon\}$ and $p \in Q$, there is an input symbol $e_{a,p}$. The input symbol $e_{a,p}$ represents consuming input a and transitioning to state p.*

- **Push:** *For each $a \in \Sigma \cup \{\epsilon\}$, $p \in Q$ and $z \in \Gamma$, there is an input symbol $f_{a,p,z}$. The input symbol $f_{a,p,z}$ represents consuming input a, pushing z on to the stack, and transitioning to state p.*

- **Pop:** *For each $a \in \Sigma \cup \{\epsilon\}$, $p \in Q$ and $z \in \Gamma$, there is an input symbol $g_{a,p,z}$. The input symbol $g_{a,p,z}$ represents consuming input a, popping z from the stack, and transitioning to state p.*

Next, we will construct a DPDA $P_D = (Q, \Sigma_D, \Gamma, \delta_D, q_0, z_0, F)$. Notice that the only components different between P and P_D are the input alphabet and the transition relation. The transition relation for the DPDA P_D is defined as follows:

- *For each transition $(p, z) \in \delta(q, a, z)$ in P, we have the transition $\delta_D(q, e_{a,p}, z) = \{(p, z)\}$.*

- *For each transition $(p, zz') \in \delta(q, a, z)$ in P, we have the transition $\delta_D(q, f_{a,p,z'}, z) = \{(p, zz')\}$.*

- *For each transition $(p, \epsilon) \in \delta(q, a, z)$ in P, we have the transition $\delta_D(q, g_{a,p,z}, z) = \{(p, \epsilon)\}$.*

It is easy to see that P_D is deterministic. Consider the following homomorphism h:

$$\begin{aligned} h(e_{a,p}) &= a \\ h(f_{a,p,z}) &= a \\ h(g_{a,p,z}) &= a \end{aligned}$$

Let $L(P_D)$ be the language accepted by the DPDA P_D. Then $h(L(P_D)) = L(P) = L$. $\square$

The construction used in the proof of Theorem 1 expands the input alphabet by exposing the stack operations and the target state of the transition. For example, the input symbol $f_{a,p,z}$ indicates to the DPDA P_D that it should consume input a, push z on the stack, and transition to state p. Suppose that a PDA P models a program Pr. In this case, the DPDA P_D models the program Pr, where internal state of the program Pr (such as stack activity) is exposed. In other words, exposing program state corresponds to the input alphabet expansion used in Theorem 1.

3.1. Intrusion Detection using PDAs and DPDAs

In *model-based intrusion detection*, one constructs a model $M(Pr)$ of a program Pr (see Figure 1). Pr generates a sequence of symbols (usually a sequence of system calls). After receiving a symbol a from the program, the model $M(Pr)$ determines whether there exist transitions on symbol a. If there *does not* exist a transition on the input symbol a, the monitor reports an intrusion. Otherwise, the model processes symbol a and updates its state.

PDA models. Suppose that the model $M(Pr)$ is a PDA $(Q, \Sigma, \Gamma, \delta, q_0, z_0, F)$. The state of the model is the set of configurations. The model's initial state is $\{(q_0, z_0)\}$. Let C be the set of possible configurations for $M(Pr)$ after processing a sequence of symbols w from Pr. Suppose the next symbol that Pr generates is a. The new state of the program is $succ(C, a)$, which represents all configurations that result from configurations in C after processing input a. Formally, $succ(C, a)$ is defined as $\{c' | \exists c \in C. c \Rightarrow^a c'\}$. If $succ(C, a)$ is empty, the monitor reports an intrusion. Otherwise, the new state of the model $M(Pr)$ is $succ(C, a)$ and the processing continues.

In general, the state of the model can be infinite. For example, suppose the model is in the state $C = \{(p, z)\}$ and receives a symbol a. Assume that the model has the following transitions:

$$\begin{aligned} \delta(p, \epsilon, z) &= \{(p, zz)\} & (1) \\ \delta(p, a, z) &= \{(q, \epsilon)\} & (2) \end{aligned}$$

It is easy to see that $succ(C, a)$ is the infinite set $\{(q, z^i) \mid i \geq 0\}$. Notice that the infiniteness arises from rule 1, which corresponds to left recursion in a program. However, it turns out that the state of the model (which is a set of configurations) is regular and can be represented as a finite-state automaton [18, 23]. The time and space complexity of updating the state of the model after receiving a symbol is unfortunately cubic in the size of the model. Wagner and Dean concluded that operating a PDA model for intrusion detection was prohibitively expensive [23, 24].

DPDA models. Suppose the model $M(Pr)$ is a DPDA. Given an input symbol $a \in \Sigma$, a configuration c, and a DPDA $M(Pr)$, there exists *at most one configuration c'* such that $c \Rightarrow^a c'$. Therefore, it is easy to see that during monitoring the set of configurations C has at most one configuration. The time and space complexity of updating the state of the model after receiving a symbol is $O(1)$.

Stack-deterministic PDA models. In our experience, nondeterminism in stack activity is the major contributing factor to the time and space complexity of operating PDA models. This motivates our definition of a stack-deterministic PDA model, which allows non-determinism but requires the state of the stack be left unchanged at points of nondeterminism. Formally, a PDA $P = (Q, \Sigma, \Gamma, \delta, q_0, z_0, F)$ is called a *stack-deterministic PDA* or *sDPDA* if it satisfies the following two conditions:

- **(Condition 1):** *No stack activity on ϵ-transitions.*
  There is no push or pop transition $\delta(q, a, z)$ such that $a = \epsilon$.

- **(Condition 2):** *Stack activity only depends upon the input symbol and the top of the stack.*
  For all $a \in \Sigma$ and $z \in \Gamma$, there *does not exist* two states q_1 and q_2 (not necessarily different), such that

$$(p_1, w_1) \in \delta(q_1, a, z),$$
$$(p_2, w_2) \in \delta(q_2, a, z),$$

where $w_1 \neq w_2$.

Assume that we use an sDPDA model $M(Pr)$ of a program Pr for intrusion detection. Let C be the set of configurations obtained after processing a sequence of symbols w. From the two conditions given above, all configurations in C must have the same stack. Formally, $C \in 2^Q \times \Gamma^\star$, where Q and Γ are the set of states and stack alphabets for the model $M(Pr)$. Since the size of C can be at most $n = |Q|$, the time and space complexity for processing a new symbol a is $O(n)$. If a language L is accepted by sDPDA, it is called a *stack-deterministic context free language* or *sD-CFL*. Theorem 3 in Appendix A proves that the language accepted by a sDPDA is a DCFL. Therefore, an sDPDA is not fundamentally more powerful than a DPDA.

Theorem 2 *Let L be a CFL. There exists a sDCFL L_D and a homomorphism h such that $h(L_D) = L$.*

Proof: *Let $P = (Q, \Sigma, \Gamma, \delta, q_0, Z_0, F)$ be a PDA accepting L. We will construct a new set of input symbols Σ_{sD}. There are three types of symbols in Σ_{sD}.*

- **Input:** *This is simply the input alphabet Σ of the PDA P.*

- **Push:** *For each $a \in \Sigma \cup \{\epsilon\}$ and $z \in \Gamma$, there is an input symbol $f_{a,z}$. The input symbol $f_{a,z}$ represents consuming input a and pushing z onto the stack.*

- **Pop:** *For each $a \in \Sigma \cup \{\epsilon\}$ and $z \in \Gamma$, there is an input symbol $g_{a,z}$. The input symbol $g_{a,z}$ represents consuming input a and popping z from the stack.*

Next, we will construct a sDPDA $P_{sD} = (Q, \Sigma_{sD}, \Gamma, \delta_{sD}, q_0, z_0, F)$. Notice that the only components different between P and P_{sD} are the input alphabet and the transition relation. The transition relation for the sDPDA P_{sD} is defined as follows:

- *For each transition $(p, z) \in \delta(q, a, z)$ in P, we have the transition $(p, z) \in \delta_{sD}(q, a, z)$.*

- *For each transition $(p, zz') \in \delta(q, a, z)$ in P, we have the transition $(p, zz') \in \delta_{sD}(q, f_{a,z'}, z)$.*

- *For each transition $(p, \epsilon) \in \delta(q, a, z)$ in P, we have the transition $(p, \epsilon) \in \delta_{sD}(q, g_{a,z}, z)$.*

It is easy to see that P_{sD} is stack-deterministic. Consider the following homomorphism h:

$$\begin{aligned} h(a) &= a \\ h(f_{a,z}) &= a \\ h(g_{a,z}) &= a \end{aligned}$$

Let $L(P_{sD})$ be the language accepted by P_{sD}. Then $h(L(P_{sD})) = L(P) = L$. $\square$

The construction used in the proof of Theorem 2 expands the input alphabet by exposing the stack operations. For example, the input alphabet $f_{a,z}$ indicates to the sDPDA P_D that it should consume input a and push z onto the stack. Recall that in the proof of Theorem 1 we expanded the input alphabet to expose the stack activity and the target of the transition, e.g., $f_{a,p,z}$ indicated that it should consume input a, push z on the stack, and transition to state p. In constructing an sDPDA, we exposed the stack activity of the PDA but not the target of the transition.

Table 1 summarizes the time and space complexity of processing a new symbol for the three models. The size of input alphabet for the three models is also shown. From Theorems 1 and 2 it is clear that the size of the input alphabets for DPDA and sDPDA models is larger than for the corresponding PDA.

Model	Time complexity	Space complexity	Input alphabet size
PDA	$O(nm^2)$	$O(nm^2)$	k
DPDA	$O(1)$	$O(1)$	$\Theta(knr)$
sDPDA	$O(n)$	$O(n)$	$\Theta(kr)$

Table 1. Time and space complexities for processing an input symbol with various models. The number of states and transitions in the model are denoted by n and m respectively. The size of the input and stack alphabets in the PDA are denoted by k and r respectively.

3.2. Connection to Existing Techniques

Several authors have proposed exposing program state to improve the precision of the models. For example, Sekar *et al.* [19] propose using program counter information. This is equivalent to expanding the input alphabet to expose the target of the transition. Giffin *et al.* [7] and Feng *et al.* [2] expose the stack activity of a program. In our context, this is equivalent to expanding the input alphabet by exposing the stack activity (this is very similar to the homomorphism demonstrated in the proof of Theorem 2). Therefore, the formal framework of PDA, DPDA, sDPDA, and homomorphisms provides a systematic way of understanding and evaluating techniques that expose additional program state.

4. The VPStatic Model: Determinizing via Stack Exposure

The VPStatic model is a statically-constructed variant of the context-sensitive VtPath model [2]. Like its dynamic counterpart, it uses stackwalks during execution to determine the call stack state of the monitored process. Combined with program counter monitoring, this produces the extra symbols necessary to fully determinize the model.

4.1. Model Generation by Static Analysis

The VPStatic model is generated by statically analyzing the binary executable of a program. We first introduce notation. There is a function entry state $Entry(f)$ and exit state $Exit(f)$ for each function f in the executable, system call state S for each system call instruction, and call site entry state C (state right before the call) and exit state C' (state right after the return) for each function call site. $Addr(S)$, $Addr(C)$, and $Addr(C')$ denote the address of the corresponding system call or function call instruction $(Addr(C) = Addr(C'))$. $Func(a)$ is the function containing the instruction at address a.

```
char* filename;                                States
pid_t[2] pid;
int prepare(int index) {                       Entry(prepare
  char buf[20];
  pid[index] = getpid();                       S_getpid
  strcpy(buf, filename);
  return open(buf, O_RDWR);                    S_open
}                                              Exit(prepare)
void action() {                                Entry(action)
  uid_t uid = getuid();                        S_getuid
  int handle;
  if (uid != 0) {
    handle = prepare(1);                       C1, C1'
    read(handle, ...);                         S_read
  } else {
    handle = prepare(0);                       C0, C0'
    write(handle, ...);                        S_write
  }
  close(handle);                               S_close
}                                              Exit(action)
```

Figure 2. A simple code fragment example.

We use a simple program fragment, shown in Figure 2, as a running example. The automaton and the left side list of transitions in Figure 3 describe a non-deterministic PDA for the example program that is quite similar to the callgraph model [24]. As for the callgraph model, system call numbers are the only observed inputs to simulate the automaton. We use "none" (or more commonly ε) as a place holder when transitions are not associated with any system call. This PDA is non-deterministic since we have not exposed stack activities and targets of transitions. To make the PDA deterministic, we extract address information from the binary to expose internal state. The automaton and the right side list of transitions in Figure 3 describe the final DPDA.

The input symbols of the DPDA have the forms in the proof of Theorem 1, with slight modifications. Namely, for system call and call site states, we use $Addr(p)$ instead of p to expose the state, since the address information is what we can extract from program counter and call stack when dynamically monitoring program executions. For example, $g(a, Addr(p), z)$ or $g(a, p, z)$ means the automaton consumes the input symbol, pops z from the stack, and transitions to state p. This is equivalent to the transition $g_{a,p,z}$ used in the proof of Theorem 1. Other symbols can be similarly explained. All three forms of input symbols $e(\ldots)$, $f(\ldots)$ and $g(\ldots)$ appear in Figure 3. The formal models section proved this pushdown automaton is deterministic. A detailed description of the model is in Appendix B.

4.2. Online Detection by Dynamic Monitoring

After the profile is generated, we can simulate the automaton during online program monitoring. When each sys-

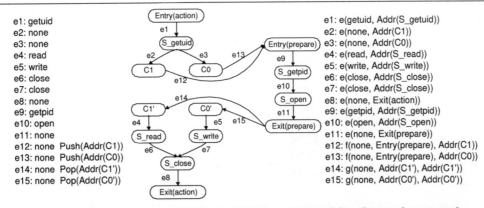

Figure 3. The PDA and VPStatic DPDA generated for the code example.

$$e(none, Exit(Func(a_{m+1})))$$
$$g(none, a_m, a_m)$$
$$e(none, Exit(Func(a_m)))$$
$$g(none, a_{m-1}, a_{m-1})$$
$$\vdots$$
$$e(none, Exit(Func(a_{l+1})))$$
$$g(none, a_l, a_l) \qquad (3)$$
$$e(none, b_l) \qquad (4)$$
$$f(none, Entry(Func(b_{l+1})), b_l)$$
$$e(none, b_{l+1})$$
$$f(none, Entry(Func(b_{l+2})), b_{l+1})$$
$$\vdots$$
$$e(none, b_n)$$
$$f(none, Entry(Func(b_{n+1})), b_n) \qquad (5)$$
$$e(s_B, b_{n+1}) \qquad (6)$$

Figure 4. VPStatic input symbol sequence generated for system call S_B.

tem call is made, we extract all the call site addresses for the functions that have not returned yet into a *virtual stack list (VSL)*, ordered from the outermost function to the innermost function. The definition of VSL is similar to that in [2].

Assume $A = a_1, a_2, \ldots, a_m$ and $B = b_1, b_2, \ldots, b_n$ are the virtual stack lists of the last and the current system calls, respectively. Also, assume s_B is the current system call and b_{n+1} is its address (the current program counter), and s_A and a_{m+1} are the last system call and its address, respectively. Suppose l is the first index for A and B so that the corresponding items are not equal, namely, $a_i = b_i$ for $i = 1, 2, \ldots, l-1$, and $a_l \neq b_l$. For the current system call, we generate a sequence of input symbols and feed them to the automaton one by one. The input symbol sequence generated is shown in Figure 4.

For example, assume an ordinary user (not root) exe-

cutes the example program and runs to the getpid line in Figure 2. The virtual stack list A here should look like "*prefix*, $Addr(C1)$", where *prefix* is a sequence of addresses corresponding to the functions that lead to action. The system call S_A is getpid. If the program executes to open, the virtual stack list B here is the same as A since the call stack does not change, and system call S_B is open. So from Figure 4, the symbol sequence generated is $e(open, Addr(S_{open}))$, which successfully leads the automaton to the next state S_{open}. However, if an attacker overflows a buffer using strcpy, she could change the return address of prepare to $Addr(C0)$, to gain unauthorized write access to the file after prepare returns. In that case, the virtual stack list B changes to "*prefix*, $Addr(C0)$". Since $Addr(C0) \neq Addr(C1)$, from Figure 4, the symbol sequence generated will be:

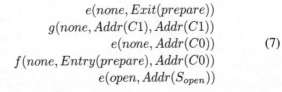

$$e(none, Exit(prepare))$$
$$g(none, Addr(C1), Addr(C1))$$
$$e(none, Addr(C0)) \qquad (7)$$
$$f(none, Entry(prepare), Addr(C0))$$
$$e(open, Addr(S_{open}))$$

However, since state S_{getpid} does not have a transition associated with $e(none, Exit(prepare))$, an alarm will be triggered and the intrusion is detected.

After all input symbols generated for a system call are processed, the current state should be the state corresponding to the system call, and the current automaton stack context is just the VSL of this system call. Namely, the current state and stack context can be uniquely decided for a valid system call. If there is no corresponding transition to follow for an input symbol, then anomalous execution indicative of an intrusion attempt has occurred.

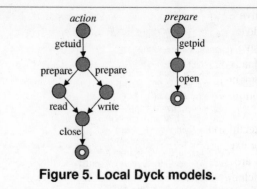

Figure 5. Local Dyck models.

5. The Dyck Model: Determinizing via Instrumentation

As shown in Section 3, adding stack determinism to a PDA requires additional alphabet symbols to make stack-modifying transitions deterministic. Statically constructed program models use the PDA stack to model the running process's call stack. Stack operations then occur at function call sites and returns. The *Dyck model* [7] uses binary rewriting to insert code before and after each function call site to generate the extra symbols needed for stack-determinism.

5.1. Static Model Construction

The Dyck static analyzer reads a binary program image and produces both an Dyck model and an instrumented version of the binary. This requires four steps:

1. For each function, construct a control flow graph (CFG).

2. Convert each CFG into a *local model*: a non-deterministic finite automaton that accepts all sequences of function calls and kernel traps that the function could generate under correct execution.

3. Classify function calls and insert code around function call sites to generate symbols necessary for stack-determinism. This instrumentation adds new events into the call stream, so we update local models to match.

4. Combine the collection of modified local models into a single sDPDA modeling the entire rewritten program.

Recall that Figure 2 shows code for two example functions, `prepare` and `action`. Although we show C source code for readability, we analyze SPARC binary code.

We convert each function's CFG into a local model. This is straightforward: a CFG is already a non-deterministic finite state machine with all edges unlabeled. If a basic block contains a user call or kernel trap site, we label all outgoing

```
void action () {
    uid_t uid = getuid();
    int handle;
    if (uid != 0) {
        precall(A);
        handle = prepare(1);
        postcall(A);
        read(handle, ...);
    } else {
        precall(B);
        handle = prepare(0);
        postcall(B);
        write(handle, ...);
    }
    close(handle);
}
```

Figure 6. Example Code With Dyck Instrumentation. Inserted code appears in boldface.

edges of that block with the call name. We label all other edges ϵ and convert all basic blocks into automaton states. The ϵ-reduced and minimized local automata for the example code are shown in Figure 5. Appendix C.1 gives the formal definition of a local model.

Next, we add edges to the local models around function call transitions that model the call stack changes occurring at runtime. An edge before each call transition pushes a unique identifier onto the PDA stack kept in the runtime monitor; an edge after the call pops that identifier off. Each call site has a unique push and pop symbol, so the monitor can differentiate between different call sites to the same function. The NFA local models are now PDAs.

To add stack-determinism to these PDA models, we must add symbols to the event stream that distinguish each stack operation. The analyzer rewrites the binary image of the program by inserting a *history stack* into the program's data space and adding code immediately before and after each call site. The history stack records stack changes occurring since the last kernel trap. *Precall* code before call site A pushes the symbol $f_{\epsilon,A}$ onto the history stack. If the call generates a kernel trap before returning, then the monitor reads all collected symbols from the history stack to identify the execution path followed in the program. If the call returns without generating a kernel trap, then the *postcall* code pops $f_{\epsilon,A}$ from the history stack and discards it. Otherwise, it adds the symbol $g_{\epsilon,A}$ to the history stack. Figure 6 shows the rewritten code for `action` with instrumented call sites to `prepare`.

Adding code instrumentation at recursive call sites has potentially high runtime cost. We add neither stack transitions to the local models nor code to the binary image around call sites that may recurse.

Lastly, we compose the collection of modified local automata at points of function calls to form the global model

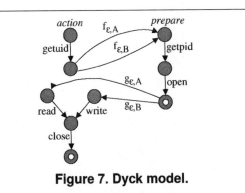

Figure 7. Dyck model.

of the entire program. The analyzer replaces each function call transition with ϵ-edges entering and returning from the model of the target function. Figure 7 shows the completed Dyck model for the example functions. Note the similarity to the VPStatic model described earlier. Here, the input symbol $f_{\epsilon,A}$ additionally pushes the identifier A onto the PDA stack. The symbol $g_{\epsilon,A}$ is an input symbol that pops A. Appendix C.1 formally defines the model using language theory. The Dyck model is an sDPDA (see Appendix C.2).

5.2. Runtime Monitoring

The user executes the rewritten binary in her security-critical environment, with the *runtime monitor* tracing its execution at system calls. The monitor enforces the model, guaranteeing that process execution does not deviate from the possible sequences of system call streams.

Dyck model operation is more straightforward than VP-Static operation. Although the model is a PDA, the monitor keeps only one PDA stack due to stack-determinism. When the traced process generates a kernel trap, the monitor reads all saved symbols from the process's history stack. Each symbol is an input to the automaton that modifies the stack state and corresponds to a return from or a call to another function. These symbols are equivalent to the virtual path symbols calculated from stack walks in the VPStatic model. The monitor then processes the kernel trap symbol, permitting execution only if the symbol has a valid transition in the model.

6. Performance Measurements

To compare the performance of the VPStatic and Dyck models, we measured two costs of execution monitoring. First, we measured the increase in execution time when monitoring. Second, we calculated the increased memory use due to the program models and Dyck instrumentation.

We analyzed performance for three test programs. Our tools currently build models only for statically-linked programs. As a result, the set of test programs is not repre-

sentative of those with greatest security concern, although they do contain a mix of computation-intensive and syscall-intensive programs. Table 2 lists the three programs and workloads and statistics for each. `htzipd` is a proprietary implementation of `httpd` which is the only httpd implementation we successfully compiled statically under Solaris.

Execution time overheads are calculated by subtracting a base execution time from monitored execution time. All times are averaged over several runs. Execution times do not include setup time in the monitor during which the program model is read from disk. The current implementation of both the VPStatic and Dyck monitors execute in user space and detect system call events via Solaris process tracing. To better evaluate the cost of operating each model, the base execution time is measured with process tracing enabled. At each system call stop, the monitor does nothing but resume the execution of the stopped process. The difference between base time and monitored time then captures exactly the overhead of model operation.

We calculated memory usage similarly. The value of interest is the increase in state required for each process. In particular, the static code of the monitoring process is of little meaning as it may be shared among all audited processes. For the VPStatic model, we compute the per process state by taking the difference between memory use with full auditing enabled and with an empty profile loaded with auditing disabled. The memory used by the Dyck model also includes the cost of binary code inserted into the original application.

This section does not include measurements with the previously used average branching factor metric [23]. This metric is poorly suited for measurements of context-sensitive languages as stack transitions entering system call wrapper functions obscure the reachable system calls. Lacking an appropriate metric, we rely instead upon our theoretical discussions in the previous sections as an evaluation of the strength of our models. Strength metrics may be applied in the future if new research develops reasonable measurement algorithms.

6.1. Execution Time Overhead Results

Table 3 contains execution time overheads for the VPStatic and Dyck models. Base execution times are presented twice because differences in monitor implementations result in somewhat different base times. Due to the high cost of the stack walk operation in the VPStatic model, we separate the model's runtime into two components: the time to operate the automaton and the time to perform the stack walk. The Dyck model does not walk the call stack, so no such separation is presented.

Program	Workload	Instructions	Functions	Call Sites
htzipd	Service 500 client requests, transferring 151.7 MB in total.	110,096	1455	6928
gzip	Compress a 23.5 MB tar file.	57,271	884	2844
cat	Concatenate 38 files totalling 500 MB to a file.	52,601	838	2728

Table 2. Test programs, workloads, and statistics.

Program	Untraced	VPStatic					Dyck		
		Base	Automaton	%	Stackwalk	%	Base	Automaton	%
htzipd	16.66	22.06	3.80	17	17.54	80	20.50	27.72	135
gzip	13.72	14.69	0.03	0	0.17	1	13.99	1.17	8
cat	46.20	59.14	2.56	4	15.81	28	54.84	30.60	56

Table 3. Model execution times in seconds. Base execution time includes system call tracing without automaton operation. Percentages compare against base execution.

Program	VPStatic	Dyck
htzipd	225	300
gzip	389	415
cat	170	289

Table 4. Average system call verification time, in microseconds.

Table 4 shows the average monitor execution time, in microseconds, per system call event received. Each system call requires the monitor to update its calling context information and to verify that the system call is a valid operation in the program model. The times to perform these operations remained relatively constant even as the number of stack symbols read from the monitored process changed, although outlying points did occur.

The tables show two interesting results. First, these deterministic or stack-deterministic models are efficient to operate. Automaton operations in the deterministic VPStatic model are extremely fast. Second, the VPStatic model is more efficient to operate than the Dyck model.

This second result occurs for two reasons. First, it illustrates the operational differences between deterministic and stack-deterministic automata. The DPDA used with the VPStatic model operates in constant time, but the sDPDA underlying the Dyck model requires linear time operation (Table 1). This effect is clearly visible in the respective runtimes of the two models. Second, the Dyck model has additional execution at many function call sites due to the injected code. This cost arises even if the process follows an execution path that does not generate system calls. The VPStatic model incurs monitoring cost only at system call events.

6.2. Memory Use Overhead Results

Table 5 presents the memory needs of execution monitoring for the two models. We divide the memory costs of the Dyck model into the cost of the current rewriting infrastructure, which doubles the size of each program's code segment, and the cost of our code insertions and state machine representation. The infrastructure cost is excessive, but could be significantly reduced by shifting to a more efficient rewriter.

The VPStatic state machine cost is greater than the corresponding Dyck models. Again, this highlights differences between DPDA and sDPDA models. An automaton allowing non-determinism in state transitions naturally has a more compact representation. Hence, the Dyck model will produce smaller automaton structures than the VPStatic model. Moreover, we have not yet optimized the VPStatic model size. For example, we could remove all the function entry and exit nodes using techniques similar to the automaton reduction used for Dyck model. We kept the original format of the model since it is a recent development and is conceptually clearer this way.

6.3. Discussion

We draw two primary conclusions from this work. First, the formalisms of deterministic and stack-deterministic push-down automata result in highly accurate and highly efficient program models. Non-deterministic context-sensitive models produced overheads orders of magnitude worse than base execution [6, 23, 24] and would never be suitable for real-world operation. Our automaton operation overheads, while not yet as low as we would like, show that context-sensitivity and precise program models need not be sacrificed for performance.

Second, the differences in these models suggests that hybridization of the two construction and monitoring tech-

Program	Unmonitored	VPStatic		Dyck				
		State Machine	%	Infrastructure	%	Instrumentation	State Machine	%
htzipd	568	1040	183	504	89	48	168	38
gzip	600	560	93	288	48	48	232	47
cat	280	544	194	272	97	32	104	49

Table 5. Memory use in KB due to monitoring. Percentages are increases over unmonitored execution.

niques may be beneficial. The Dyck model produces no context information at points of recursion or dynamic linking to non-instrumented binaries. The VPStatic model can identify this missing information by inspecting existing program state. If instrumented libraries are available, the Dyck model can more easily use these libraries at runtime as memory offsets of return addresses are not an issue. The Dyck model can also successfully reveal context information in optimized binaries where stack walking may be difficult or impossible. On the other hand, binary rewriting does occasionally fail. We can then rely on the stack walk technique to recover state information. Likewise, we may wish to limit instrumentation to some set of critical program points and rely upon stack walking elsewhere. A hybrid model would combine both state recovery mechanisms to capture the complete context of a system call. The hybrid would gain from the strengths of both models while minimizing the drawbacks of each.

7. Limitations

Although our approaches produce more sensitive and more accurate models than other approaches, there are still limitations. It is well documented [16, 17, 25] that attackers can exploit weaknesses and limitations of intrusion detection models to avoid detection. Short of complete instrumentation, which amounts to essentially interpreting the program, our statically-generated models do not have complete information about the state of the executing program. An attacker can exploit incomplete information in the model to evade the HIDS.

7.1. Incomplete Sensitivity

Models discussed in this paper incorporate information about the stack activity of the program. Thus, our models are context sensitive. However, since our model does not track predicates used in branches, they are neither flow nor path sensitive. This incompleteness can result in our model allowing extraneous behavior. For example, consider the following code fragment:

```
char *str, *user;

str = (char *) calloc (...);
user = (char *) calloc (...);
...

if (strncmp (user, "admin", 5)) {
    sys_1 ();
} else {
    sys_2 ();
}
strcpy (str, someinput);
if (strncmp (user, "admin", 5)) {
    sys_3 ();
} else {
    sys_4 ();
}
```

There are two possible system call sequences for the code fragment:

`sys 1`, `sys 3`, and

`sys_2`, `sys_4`.

The sequences correspond to the predicate `strncmp(user,"admin",5)` being true or false respectively. Notice that the predicates used in both the branches are the same. However, since our models do not track the values of branch predicates, they will allow the following four sequences:

`sys_1`, `sys_3`,

`sys_1`, `sys_4`,

`sys_2`, `sys_3`, and

`sys_2`, `sys_4`.

An attacker can exploit this limitation to avoid detection. In the example given above, an attack uses a large `someinput` in `strcpy` to overflow `str` on the heap to change the value of `user`. If `user` is "guest" and the overflow in `strcpy` changes `user` to "admin", then the illegal sequence `sys_1`, `sys_4` is executed, which is accepted by our model and hence the attack is not detected.

7.2. Incomplete Set of Events

Events monitored by our model are system calls. As pointed out by Wagner and Soto [25] and Tan *et al.* [20,21], an attacker can evade detection if it generates sequence of events accepted by our model. We previously presented such an attack using the following code segment [2]:

```
...
f(); //f has no system calls, a buffer-overflow occurs
     // so that after f the program jumps to IP

if (regular_user) {
  return ();
}

IP: //super user privileges
  execve (''/bin/sh'');
```

An attack that uses a buffer overflow in `f` to force the program to jump to `IP` can (illegally) obtain a root shell. Without inserting code instrumentation before and after `f`, our models will miss this attack because there is no system call in the code segment between the call to `f` and `IP`. In other words, no matter how the program control flow is illegally modified within the code segment, there is no observable events to our models. However, when code instrumentation is added right before and after the call to `f`, the attack will be detected by our model.

An attack can also evade detection if it simply replaces the system call parameters [25]. We recover some arguments of system calls using static analysis, but there are several system calls where we have incomplete information about the arguments.

7.3. Playing Inside the Sandbox: Mimicry Attacks

We assume that attackers have complete knowledge about our model-construction algorithm. In *mimicry* attacks, an adversary transforms her attack in such a way that the resulting sequence is accepted by the detection model [25]. For example, the attacker can mimic the legal program behavior by generating (legal) system calls and inserting them in the original attack sequence. An attacker can use a different attack sequence that is semantically equivalent to the original attack sequence. These attacks are very serious and can easily evade simple detection models, such as the n-gram model proposed by [3]. However, incorporating additional information about the program in the model makes it difficult to mount mimicry attacks. Our models monitors information about system calls, program counter, and call stack. Therefore, to mount a successful mimicry attack an adversary is required to produce correct call stack and program counter information along with the sequence of system calls which is equivalent to the attack.

8. Conclusions

We formally described statically-constructed context-sensitive program models for host-based intrusion detection. Seeking to add efficiency to the precision of these models, we examined deterministic PDAs and introduced stack-deterministic PDAs. The proofs of language equivalence between the homomorphic image of a DCFL or sD-CFL and a CFL give rise to monitoring techniques that make these models possible. The VPStatic model walks a process's call stack to harvest return addresses revealing context information enabling a deterministic model. Using program instrumentation, the Dyck model eliminates stack non-determinism. Experiments demonstrate that context-sensitivity and efficiency can coexist in these program models, benefiting all such intrusion detection systems.

Acknowledgments

We thank the anonymous referees for their useful comments. The members of the WiSA security group at Wisconsin provided ongoing feedback to this work. We also acknowledge Dr. Weibo Gong at the University of Massachusetts for discussion and support. Mr. Prahlad Fogla and Mr. Oleg Kolensnikov at Georgia Institute of Technology provided ongoing feedback to this work. We use EEL [13] to analyze SPARC binary code.

This work is supported in part by Army Research Office contract DAAD19-01-1-0610, Office of Naval Research grant N00014-01-1-0708, NSF grants CCR-0133629 and CCR-0208655, and Department of Energy grants DE-FG02-93ER25176 and DE-FG02-01ER25510. The U.S. Government is authorized to reproduce and distribute reprints for Governmental purposes, notwithstanding any copyright notices affixed thereon. The views and conclusions contained herein are those of the authors and should not be interpreted as necessarily representing the official policies or endorsements, either expressed or implied, of the above government agencies or the U.S. Government.

References

[1] N. Chomsky. Context-free grammars and pushdown storage. In *Quarterly Progress Report No. 65*, pages 187–194. Massachusetts Institute of Technology Research Laboratory of Electronics, April 1962.

[2] H. Feng, O. Kolesnikov, P. Fogla, W. Lee, and W. Gong. Anomaly detection using call stack information. In *IEEE Symposium on Security and Privacy*, Oakland, California, May 2003.

[3] S. Forrest, S. A. Hofmeyr, A. Somayaji, and T. A. Longstaff. A sense of self for Unix processes. In *IEEE Symposium on Security and Privacy*, pages 120–128, Los Alamitos, California, May 1996.

[4] T. Garvey and T. Lunt. Model-based intrusion detection. In *14th National Computer Security Conference (NCSC)*, Baltimore, Maryland, June 1991.

[5] A. Ghosh, A. Schwartzbard, and M. Schatz. Learning program behavior profiles for intrusion detection. In *1st USENIX Workshop on Intrusion Detection and Network Monitoring*, Santa Clara, California, April 1999.

[6] J. Giffin, S. Jha, and B. Miller. Detecting manipulated remote call streams. In *11th USENIX Security Symposium*, San Francisco, California, August 2002.

[7] J. Giffin, S. Jha, and B. Miller. Efficient context-sensitive intrusion detection. In *11th Annual Network and Distributed Systems Security Symposium (NDSS)*, San Diego, California, February 2004.

[8] S. Hofmeyr, A. Somayaji, and S. Forrest. Intrusion detection system using sequences of system calls. *Journal of Computer Security*, 6(3):151–180, 1998.

[9] J. Hopcroft, R. Motwani, and J. Ullman. *Introduction to Automata Theory, Languages, and Computation.* Addison-Wesley, 2nd edition, 2001.

[10] K. Ilgun, R. Kemmerer, and P. Porras. State transition analysis: A rule-based intrusion detection approach. *IEEE Transactions on Software Engineering*, 21(3):181–199, March 1995.

[11] C. Ko, G. Fink, and K. Levitt. Automated detection of vulnerabilities in privileged programs by execution monitoring. In *10th Annual Computer Security Applications Conference (ACSAC)*, Orlando, Florida, December 1994.

[12] T. Lane and C. Brodley. Temporal sequence learning and data reduction for anomaly detection. *ACM Transactions on Information and System Security*, 2(3):295–331, August 1999.

[13] J. Larus and E. Schnarr. EEL: Machine independent executable editing. In *SIGPLAN Conference on Programming Language Design and Implementation (PLDI)*, La Jolla, California, June 1995.

[14] W. Lee, S. Stolfo, and K. Mok. A data mining framework for building intrusion detection models. In *IEEE Symposium on Security and Privacy*, Oakland, California, May 1999.

[15] T. Lunt. Automated audit trail analysis and intrusion detection: A survey. In *11th National Computer Security Conference (NCSC)*, Baltimore, Maryland, October 1988.

[16] V. Paxson. Bro: A system for detecting network intruders in real-time. *Computer Networks*, 31(23-24), December 1999.

[17] T. H. Ptacek and T. N. Newsham. Insertion, evasion, and denial of service: Eluding network intrusion detection. Technical report, Secure Networks Inc., January 1998. http://www.aciri.org/vern/Ptacek-Newsham-Evasion-98.ps.

[18] S. Schwoon. *Model-Checking Pushdown Systems*. Ph.D. dissertation, Technische Universität München, June 2002.

[19] R. Sekar, M. Bendre, P. Bollineni, and D. Dhurjati. A fast automaton-based method for detecting anomalous program behaviors. In *IEEE Symposium on Security and Privacy*, Oakland, California, May 2001.

[20] K. Tan, K. Killourhy, and R. Maxion. Undermining an anomaly-based intrusion detection system using common exploits. In *Recent Advances in Intrusion Detection (RAID) 2002, LNCS #2516*, pages 54–73, Zurich, Switzerland, October 2002. Springer-Verlag.

[21] K. Tan, J. McHugh, and K. Killourhy. Hiding intrusions: From the abnormal to the normal and beyond. In *5th International Workshop on Information Hiding, LNCS #2578*, Noordwijkerhout, Netherlands, October 2002. Springer-Verlag.

[22] H. Teng, K. Chen, and S.-Y. Lu. Adaptive real-time anomaly detection using inductively generated sequential patterns. In *IEEE Symposium on Security and Privacy*, Oakland, California, May 1990.

[23] D. Wagner. *Static Analysis and Computer Security: New Techniques for Software Assurance.* Ph.D. dissertation, University of California at Berkeley, Fall 2000.

[24] D. Wagner and D. Dean. Intrusion detection via static analysis. In *IEEE Symposium on Security and Privacy*, Oakland, California, May 2001.

[25] D. Wagner and P. Soto. Mimicry attacks on host-based intrusion detection systems. In *9th ACM Conference on Computer and Communications Security (CCS)*, November 2002.

[26] C. Warrander, S. Forrest, and B. Pearlmutter. Detecting intrusions using system calls: Alternative data models. In *IEEE Symposium on Security and Privacy*, Oakland, California, May 1999.

[27] A. Wespi, M. Dacier, and H. Debar. Intrusion detection using variable-length audit trail patterns. In *Recent Advances in Intrusion Detection (RAID) 2000, LNCS #1907*, pages 110–129, Toulouse, France, October 2000. Springer-Verlag.

A. Proof for Section 3

Theorem 3 *The language L accepted by an sDPDA is a DCFL.*

Proof: *First, remove ϵ transitions. Let $P = (Q, \Sigma, \Gamma, \delta, q_0, z_0, F)$ be an sDPDA. Recall that an sDPDA does not have stack activity on ϵ-transitions. Given states q and q' and a stack symbol $z \in \Gamma$, we say that $(q, z) \Rightarrow_\epsilon (q', z)$ if there exists an ϵ-transition such that $(q', z) \in \delta(q, \epsilon, z)$. Let $\Rightarrow_\epsilon^\star$ be the reflexive and transitive closure of $\Rightarrow_\epsilon$. Notice that $\Rightarrow_\epsilon^\star$ can be computed in polynomial time using standard graph reachability algorithms. We will transform the transition relation δ of P to δ' to remove ϵ transitions. First, δ' will contain all the non-ϵ transitions $\delta(q, a, z)$. For each transition, $(q', z) \in \delta(q, a, z)$ (where $a \neq \epsilon$), $\delta'(q, a, z)$ contains all (q'', z) such that $(q', z) \Rightarrow_\epsilon^\star (q'', z)$.*

Second, remove state non-determinism. Due to the step given above, we can assume that the sDPDA P does not contain ϵ-transitions. Next we can remove the "state" non-determinism of P using the standard subset construction used in determinizing a NFA. Let $P = (Q, \Sigma, \Gamma, \delta, q_0, z_0, F)$ be an sDPDA without ϵ-transitions. We will construct a DPDA $DP = (Q_1, \Sigma, \Gamma, \delta_1, q_0^1, z_0, F_1)$, where $Q_1 = 2^Q$, $q_0^1 = \{q_0\}$, F_1 are all subsets of Q such that $F_1 \cap F \neq \emptyset$, and δ_1 is defined as follows: $\delta_1(q_1, a, z)$ contains (q_2, z'), where q_2 is the following set:

$$\{q' \mid \exists q \in q_1 : (q', z') \in \delta(q, a, z)\}$$

Recall that because of condition 2 in the definition of sDPDA the stack activity is completely determined by the input a and top of the stack z. Therefore, the definition of δ_1

is well defined. It is easy to see that DP is a DPDA and accepts the same language as the sDPDA P.   □

B. Definition of VPStatic Model

We expand the notation in Section 4. $SysCall(S)$ is the system call made at S, and $Target(C) = Target(C')$ is the target function of the call site C/C'.

The computation model is a DPDA $(Q, \Sigma, \Gamma, \delta, q_0, z_0, F)$. We still use the simple program fragment, shown in Figure 2, as a running example. Its corresponding automaton is shown in Figure 3.

Q is the set of states. The example program has 14 states. Note we have five different kinds of states in the automaton: function entry states ($Entry(action)$ and $Entry(prepare)$), function exit states ($Exit(action)$ and $Exit(prepare)$), system call states (S_getuid, S_read and so on), call site entry states ($C1$ and $C0$) and call site exit states ($C1'$ and $C0'$).

Σ is the input alphabet. The input symbols of this DPDA have the forms in the proof of Theorem 1, with slight modifications. Namely, for system call and call site states, we use $Addr(p)$ instead of p to expose the state. For example, $g(a, Addr(p), z)$ or $g(a, p, z)$ means the automaton consumes the input symbol, pops z from the stack, and transitions to state p. This is equivalent to the transition $g_{a,p,z}$ used in the proof of Theorem 1. Other symbols can be similarly explained using the proof of Theorem 1. During online detection, we monitor the call stack and program counter to expose address information $Addr(p)$. We use *none* as the placeholder when no system call is involved for the transition. All three forms of input symbols $e(\ldots)$, $f(\ldots)$ and $g(\ldots)$ appear in Figure 3.

Γ is the stack alphabet. For our model, Γ is

$$\{Addr(p) | p \in Q \text{ and } p \text{ is a function call site state}\} \cup \{z_0\}$$

where z_0 is the initial stack start symbol. We use the automaton stack of the DPDA to simulate the program call stack.

The start state q_0 is the entry state of the program entry function. F is the set of accepting states. If we require the program to exit normally, F is the set of all states for `exit` system calls. If the program can be killed anytime, F is the set of all states, or $F = Q$. Since the example program is only a program fragment, the start and the accept state set are not shown in Figure 3.

δ is the transition function. The automaton is constructed by interconnecting the transformed control flow graph of each function. If both the states connected by a transition e are in the same function, we call e an *intra-function* transition. Otherwise, we call e an *inter-function* transition. Intra-function transitions are always marked with input symbols of the form $e(\ldots)$ since they do not deal with

automaton stack. For example, in Figure 3, transition $e6$: $e(close, Addr(S\_close))$ means that if the current state is S_read, the program issues a system call *close*, and we observe that its program counter is $Addr(S\_close)$, then the current state is moved to S_close.

Inter-function transitions modify the automaton stack. They only exist between a call site entry state and its target function entry state, and between a target function exit state and a corresponding call site exit state. If T_1 is a call site entry state and T_2 is the corresponding target function entry state, we add a transition from T_1 to T_2 and label it with $f(none, T_2, Addr(T_1))$, which means the program is calling a function, and we push the address of the corresponding call site into the automaton stack. In Figure 3, transitions e_{12} and e_{13} belong to this case. If T_2 is a call site exit state, and T_1 is the corresponding target function exit state, we add a transition from T_1 to T_2 and label it with $g(none, Addr(T_2), Addr(T_2))$, which means we only follow this transition if the address of the call site the program is returning to matches the top symbol on automaton stack, and we pop this address. In Figure 3, transitions e_{14} and e_{15} belong to this case.

This completes our model definition. The formal models section proved this pushdown automaton is deterministic. Note recursive function call and return transitions are handled just like non-recursive ones.

C. Definitions and Proofs for Section 5

C.1. Definition of Dyck Model

Let $\mathcal{S}$ be the set of system call sites (traps to the operating system) and $\mathcal{C}$ be the set of function call sites. Let $\theta(c)$ denote the target function of call site c. Note that two different call sites $c_1, c_2 \in \mathcal{C}$ are unique, even if $\theta(c_1) = \theta(c_2)$.

Definition 2 *[Local Model]*
Let $G = \langle V, E \rangle$, $E \subseteq V \times V$ be the control flow graph of program Pr. Let $a \triangleleft v$ indicate that vertex $v \in V$ contains call site a. The local model for each function $i \in Pr$ is $A_i = (Q_i, \Sigma_i, \delta_i, q_{0,i}, F_i)$, where:

- $Q_i = V$

- $\Sigma_i = S_i \cup C_i \cup \{\epsilon\}$ *where $S_i \subseteq \mathcal{S}$ and $C_i \subseteq \mathcal{C}$*

- $q_{0,i} \in V$ *is the unique CFG entry state*

- $F_i = \{v \in V \setminus q_{0,i} | v \text{ is a CFG exit }\}$

- $q \in \delta_i(p, a)$ *if $a \triangleleft p$ and $(p, q) \in E$*

- $q \in \delta_i(p, \epsilon)$ *if $\forall a \in S_i \cup C_i : a \ntriangleleft p$ and $(p, q) \in E$*

This definition simply labels CFG edges as described in Section 5.1. All local models are ϵ-reduced and minimized to reduce their storage requirements.

The definition of the global Dyck model depends upon a classification of function call sites. Let C_1, C_2, C_3, and C_4 partition C as follows:

- $a \in C_1$ if a does not recurse and $\theta(a)$ must generate at least 1 system call before returning.

- $a \in C_2$ if a does not recurse and $\theta(a)$ may conditionally generate a system call before returning.

- $a \in C_3$ if a does not recurse and $\theta(a)$ will never generate a system call before returning.

- $a \in C_4$ if a may recurse.

We write C_{12} to denote $C_1 \cup C_2$.

Definition 3 *[Dyck Program Model]*

Let i range over all functions in Pr with τ the entry point function. Let f and g be the symbols used in the proof of Theorem 2, with $\mathcal{F} = \{f_{\epsilon,\gamma} : \gamma \in C_{12}\}$ and $\mathcal{G} = \{g_{\epsilon,\gamma} : \gamma \in C_{12}\}$. Then D is a Dyck model if there exists $D_\epsilon = (Q, \Sigma \cup \{\epsilon\}, \Gamma, \delta_\epsilon, q_0, z_0, F)$ with:

1. *$Q = \bigcup_i Q_i$*

2. *$\Gamma = C_{12}$*

3. *$\Sigma = \mathcal{S} \cup \mathcal{F} \cup \mathcal{G}$*

4. *$q_0 = q_{0,\tau}$*

5. *$z_0 = \epsilon$*

6. *$F = F_\tau$*

7. *$(q, z) \in \delta_\epsilon(p, a, z)$ if $a \in \mathcal{S}$ and $\exists i : q \in \delta_i(p, a)$*

8. *$(q, z) \in \delta_\epsilon(p, \epsilon, z)$ if*

   (a) *$\exists a \in C_2 \cup C_3 \,\exists i : q \in \delta_i(p, a)$; or*

   (b) *$\exists a \in C_4 \,\exists i \,\exists r \in Q_i : r \in \delta_i(p, a) \wedge q = q_{0,\theta(a)}$; or*

   (c) *$\exists a \in C_4 \,\exists i \,\exists r \in Q_i : q \in \delta_i(r, a) \wedge p \in F_{\theta(a)}$*

9. *$(q, za) \in \delta_\epsilon(p, f_{\epsilon,a}, z)$ if $a \in C_{12} \wedge \exists i \,\exists r \in Q_i : r \in \delta_i(p, a) \wedge q = q_{0,\theta(a)}$*

10. *$(q, \epsilon) \in \delta_\epsilon(p, g_{\epsilon,a}, a)$ if $a \in C_{12} \wedge \exists i \,\exists r \in Q_i : q \in \delta_i(r, a) \wedge p \in F_{\theta(a)}$*

and $D = (Q, \Sigma, \Gamma, \delta, q_0, z_0, F)$ is D_ϵ under ϵ-reduction.

Several properties of the definition require explanation. Property 3 adds push and pop symbols to the alphabet of system calls. Property 7 maintains the system call transition property of the local automata: a system call will not modify stack state. Property 8(a) adds ϵ-edges around call sites that may not generate a system call. Properties 8(b) and (c) link automata at recursive call sites with ϵ-edges rather than with edges that update the PDA stack. Properties 9 and 10 describe transitions for precalls and postcalls that modify stack state.

C.2. Stack-determinism of Dyck Model

Theorem 4 *The Dyck model is an sDPDA.*

Proof: *Clearly, the Dyck model is a PDA.*

$\epsilon \notin \Sigma \Rightarrow \forall z \in \Gamma \;\not\exists p \in Q : \delta(p, \epsilon, z) \neq \emptyset$, so sDPDA condition 1 is satisfied.

Suppose $\exists q_1, q_2 \in Q$ so that for some $\sigma \in \Sigma$ and $z \in \Gamma$, $\delta(q_1, \sigma, z) = (p_1, w_1)$ and $\delta(q_2, \sigma, z) = (p_2, w_2)$ with $w_1 \neq w_2$. Proof by contradiction in three cases:

1. *If $\sigma \in \mathcal{S}$, then $w_1 = z = w_2$ by Property 7.*

2. *If $\sigma \in \mathcal{F}$, then $\exists \gamma \in C_{12} : \sigma = f_{\epsilon,\gamma}$ and $w_1 = z\gamma = w_2$ by Property 9.*

3. *If $\sigma \in \mathcal{G}$, then $\exists \gamma \in C_{12} : \sigma = g_{\epsilon,\gamma}$. Then $z = z'\gamma$ and $w_1 = z' = w_2$ by Property 10.*

Thus, sDPDA condition 2 holds. $\qquad\square$

RAPIDware: Component-Based Development of Adaptive and Dependable Middleware

(www.cse.msu.edu/rapidware)

Philip. K. McKinley, R. E. Kurt Stirewalt, Betty H. C. Cheng,
Laura K. Dillon and Sandeep Kulkarni

Software Engineering and Network Systems Laboratory
Department of Computer Science and Engineering
Michigan State University
East Lansing, Michigan 48824

August 2005

Abstract

Society depends increasingly on cyberinfrastructure for some of its most important functions. However, today's cyberinfrastructure is brittle and insecure, due in large part to the quality of the underlying software. A robust cyberinfrastructure must be able to adapt to changing conditions and protect itself from component failures and security attacks. Moreover, the design of such software systems should be grounded in rigorous software engineering techniques to assure their integrity and security under extreme conditions. This paper overviews the RAPIDware project, which investigates the design of high-assurance adaptive middleware, a critical step toward a robust cyberinfrastructure. Contributions of the project are reviewed, and experimental case studies are described.

Keywords: adaptive software, compositional adaptation, middleware, pervasive computing, autonomic computing, computational reflection, separation of concerns, component-based design, aspect-oriented programming, object-oriented programming, contract-based design, safe adaptation.

1 Introduction

Computing technology now affects nearly every dimension of modern society: managing critical infrastructure such as power grids and telecommunication networks; supporting electronic commerce and medical information systems; and controlling the operation of aircraft and automobiles. In addition, the "wireless edge" of the Internet continues to expand its reach, not only to support communication among mobile users, but also in the form of sensor networks for monitoring the physical environment. The increasing complexity of computing systems, and their interaction with the physical world, gives rise to the need for systems capable of self-management. *Autonomic computing* [1] refers to systems that are able to adapt to changing conditions, compensate for hardware and software failures, fend off attacks, and optimize performance, all with minimal human intervention. This capability is especially important to systems such as defense systems and communication networks, which must continue to operate correctly during exceptional situations. Such systems require run-time adaptation, including the ability to modify and replace components, in order to survive hardware component failures and security attacks.

We say a software application is *adaptable* if it can change its behavior dynamically (at run time) in response to transient changes in its execution environment (*e.g.,* to address dynamic network conditions) or to permanent changes in its requirements (*e.g.,* to upgrade long-running mission-critical systems). Developing and maintaining adaptable software are nontrivial tasks. An adaptable application comprises functional code, which implements the imperative behavior of the application (sometimes referred to as the *business logic*), and adaptive code, which implements the adaptive behavior of the application. The difficulty in developing and maintaining adaptable applications comes from the nature of the adaptive code, which tends to *crosscut* the functional code. Example crosscutting concerns include quality-of-service (QoS), fault tolerance, security, and energy management. Even more challenging than developing new adaptable applications is enhancing *existing* applications, such that they execute effectively in dynamic environments not envisioned during their original design and development. For example, many non-adaptive applications are being ported to mobile computing environments where they require dynamic adaptation.

One approach to designing adaptive software systems focuses on *middleware*, the layer of services between applications and underlying operating systems and network protocols. Middleware typically executes within the address space of the application, and therefore it can be "customized" using information specific to the particular application. On the other hand, middleware is designed to operate transparently with respect to the business logic of the application. In recent years, numerous studies have addressed the issue of how middleware can adapt to dynamic, heterogeneous environments to better serve applications [2]. The adaptive functionality in such systems can encompass not only changes in program flow, but also run-time changes to the composition of the software itself. Dynamic recomposition is needed when resource limitations (for example, memory in small devices) restrict the number of responding components that can be deployed simultaneously, or when adding new behavior to deployed systems to accommodate unanticipated conditions or requirements (for example, detection of and response to a new security attack). However, support for dynamic adaptation exacerbates the problem of assuring system integrity and security. As the demand for adaptive systems increases, a pressing challenge to the research community is to build a foundation of development technologies and tools, grounded in rigorous software engineering, that will enable the design and maintenance of high-assurance adaptive software systems.

The RAPIDware project investigates three overlapping aspects of this problem. First, we explore ways to enhance existing applications with new adaptive behavior, effectively providing a migration path to hardening existing software infrastructure. We focus primarily on approaches that can be realized through generative programming techniques [3]. We evaluate these mechanisms through case studies in both wired and wireless network testbeds. Second, we investigate design technologies that support assurance in adaptation. Specific topics include contract-based software design, safe adaptation, and analysis and verification of adaptive software. Third, we investigate technologies needed to enable robust and secure software adaptation across a network-centric infrastructure. Key topics include design of secure communication protocols and use of machine learning techniques to support decision-making for adaptation. In the remainder of this paper, we provide an overview of the work in each of these areas.

2   Adaptive Middleware: Background and Challenges

The interest in dynamically adaptive software systems has increased significantly during the past decade, in part due to advances in three supporting technologies: computational reflection, separation of concerns, and component-based design. *Computational reflection* refers to the ability of a program to reason about, and possibly alter, its own behavior [4]. Reflection enables a system to "open up" its implementation details for such analysis without compromising portability or revealing parts unnecessarily. In this approach, the program contains one or more *meta* levels, which enable reconfiguration of the underlying *base*-level code. *Separation of concerns* [5] enables the separate development of an application's functional behavior and its adaptive behavior involving crosscutting concerns (e.g., quality of service, fault tolerance, security). This separation simplifies development and maintenance, while promoting software reuse [6]. A widely used technique is aspect-oriented programming (AOP) [7], where the code implementing a crosscutting concern, called an *aspect*, is developed separately from other parts of the system and *woven* with the business logic at compile- or run-time. Finally, *component-based design* [8] enables different parts of the system to be developed independently, potentially by different parties. Popular component-based platforms include COM/DCOM, .NET, CCM, and EJB. Compatible service clients and providers are coupled at run time through a process known as *late binding*. Component-based design facilitates reuse of software by enabling the assembly of off-the-shelf components provided by different vendors. Moreover, maintaining the component structure of a program after the initial deployment, when combined with late binding, facilitates dynamic recomposition [9].

With these technologies in hand, there are different ways to implement adaptive programs. One is to extend programming languages with explicit constructs for adaptation and reconfiguration. Open Java [10], R-Java [11], Handi-Wrap [12], and PCL [13] are examples. While this approach is an effective means to develop new adaptive programs, the developer needs to learn and understand the language extensions. Moreover, adding adaptive behavior to an *existing* non-adaptive program requires modifying the program source code directly. In other words, this approach is well suited to the development of new adaptable applications, but cannot be applied transparently to existing ones. An alternative approach is to use *middleware*, which provides a means to implement adaptation separately from the business logic of the application. Many adaptive middleware approaches are based on an object-oriented programming paradigm and are extensions of popular object-oriented middleware platforms such as CORBA, Java RMI, and DCOM/.NET. These approaches work by intercepting and modifying messages passing through the middleware. Examples include TAO [14], DynamicTAO [15], Open ORB [16], QuO [17], Squirrel [18], and IRL [19]. Other approaches implement adaptive behavior by extending a virtual machine with facilities to intercept and redirect interactions in the functional code. Examples of extensions to the Java Virtual Machine (JVM) include Iguana/J [20], metaXa [21] (previously called Meta Java), Guaraná [22], PROSE [23], and R-Java [11]. In general, approaches in this category are very flexible with respect to dynamic reconfiguration, in that new code can be introduced to the application at run time. However, while these methods provide transparency with respect to the application source code, they are applicable only to programs that are written for a specific middleware platform or virtual machine, thus limiting their applicability.

In the RAPIDware project, we focus on three complementary issues in the design of adaptive middleware. First, recognizing that many parts of the cyberinfrastructure already exist and will persist for many years, we investigate technologies that enable the *migration* from existing systems to those that are adaptive. A key research issue is how to do this in a manner that is both transparent to the application business logic and avoids dependencies on the underlying platforms. Second, we investigate techniques to improve the assurance of both new and existing adaptive middleware. The design of reconfigurable software must be supported by a programming paradigm that lends itself to *automated* checking of both functional and nonfunctional properties of the system [24]. In RAPIDware, we are developing tools and methods that apply rigorous software engineering to the entire software lifecycle of an adaptive system, from requirements, to design, to code generation, to run-time execution. Third, while middleware plays a key role in adaptive systems, adaptation often involves coordination across multiple system layers and among different platforms. Therefore, we are investigating techniques to facilitate such interoperation across different parts of the cyberinfrastructure.

3   Software Adaptation Mechanisms

At the core of most approaches to software adaptation is a level of indirection, with respect to object references and method invocations, that enables interception and redirection of interactions among program entities. An example is the use of a software *proxy*, whereby method calls to a target object must pass through a surrogate object that might redirect the calls to a different object. This indirection enables software components and control flow to be dynamically reconfigured, or replaced entirely, in response to changes in the execution environment [2].

Transparent Shaping. In RAPIDware we are exploring a variety of ways to enhance existing programs with new adaptive behavior. Collectively, these techniques comprise a new programming model, called *transparent shaping* [25–27], that enables new adaptive behavior to be woven into existing programs without modifying the application source code. Integration of the adaptive code is a two-phase process that combines aspect-oriented programming and computational reflection. In the first phase, the application is transformed into a new *adapt-ready* application by weaving "hooks" into the application code as needed. In the second phase, usually executed at run-time, an "adaptation infrastructure" is inserted dynamically using these hooks. Although this process incurs a (one-time) overhead, our experiments show the effect on the application is small. Once in place, the adaptation infrastructure supports insertion and removal of specific software sensors and actuators, enabling run-time adaptation and response to specific conditions.

We have designed and implemented transparent shaping tools for several commonly used programming languages and middleware platforms. First, we developed *Adaptive Java* [28], an extension to Java that contains constructs to support dynamic recomposition, and *MetaSockets* [29], an adaptable communication substrate for distributed applications. Second, we improved Adaptive Java by developing transparent reflective aspect programming (TRAP), which enables new adaptive behavior to be incorporated into existing programs automatically using code generation techniques. We have developed TRAP instances for Java [27] and for C++ [30]; a version for C# is under development. Third, we developed the Adaptive Corba Template (ACT) [31], which enables transparent shaping within existing middleware frameworks. Currently, we are exploring the relationship between adaptive systems and Parnas' program families [32, 33]. Specifically, we are investigating how transparent shaping can be used to generate one member of a *family* of adaptable programs given another program in the same family [34]. Placing these transformations under a formal umbrella enables reasoning about both software migration paths and dynamic reconfiguration during execution.

Experimental Case Studies. We have used transparent shaping to realize dynamic adaptation in existing applications. Several of our case studies address challenges arising in mobile computing settings: balancing quality-of-service and energy consumption on wearable and handheld computers [35–38], supporting autonomic handoff and QoS adaptation in heterogeneous multi-cell wireless networks [26, 27, 39], and dynamic configuration of "transient proxies" to enhance audio/video streaming across mobile ad hoc networks [40]. Other case studies focus on issues related to application integration: seamless interoperation of otherwise incompatible adaptive middleware frameworks [31], and development of composite Internet applications by (transparently) enabling them to interact using Web Services [41]. Recently, we proposed Service Clouds [42], a distributed infrastructure designed to facilitate rapid prototyping and deployment of autonomic communication services on the Internet. We have implemented a prototype of Service Clouds atop the PlanetLab Internet testbed [43] and used it to construct services for fast bulk data transfer and fault-tolerant multimedia conferencing.

4 Assurance in Adaptation

A major issue in the use of adaptive software mechanisms is *assurance*, namely how to specify, analyze, test, or otherwise verify that a system will always exhibit safety, liveness, and quality-of-service properties when it is deployed. In the RAPIDware project, we are investigating three main approaches to this problem: contract-based design; techniques to guarantee safe adaptation; and formal methods to specify and analyze adaptive systems.

Contract-Based Design of Adaptive Systems.   Adaptive logic can often be separated from an application's business logic, where the separated concern is not completely orthogonal to the business logic. In RAPIDware, we are investigating two approaches to reasoning about application functionality when the logic for one or more concerns has been separated. The first and most mature approach extends Meyer's *design by contract* method [44] for reasoning about the interaction of application functionality and the separated concern. Beugnard and others [45] previously extended Meyer's approach from static specifications that are used at design time to entities that can be renegotiated at run-time as conditions change. We have developed a model of *synchronization contracts* [46], which declare an application's resource-usage patterns and which are negotiated by dynamically granting exclusive access to shared resources [46,47]. As an active process cycles through its synchronization states, resources are automatically acquired and/or released in order to keep the process in compliance with its contract. When an active process enters a state whose resource needs cannot be satisfied (e.g., because other processes already hold the needed resources) the process blocks until these resources become available. Our underlying middleware uses deadlock- and starvation-avoidance algorithms to fully automate negotiation of contracts, thereby separating synchronization and scheduling concerns from the business logic. We have used synchronization contracts to guard against serialization vulnerabilities, which pose serious security risks to multi-threaded applications [46, 48, 49]. Our second, more recent approach, exploits recent developments in formally-specified architecture description languages (ADLs) such as Wright [50] and connector wrappers [51], to reason about the orthogonality of concerns, such as reliability. We are using connector specifications to guide the development of a common-services middleware framework called Theseus, which supports highly asynchronous distributed systems [52, 53].

Safe Adaptation.   A key issue when adding new adaptive behavior to an existing system is to ensure that a given adaptive action does not put the system into an inconsistent state. We are exploring two complementary approaches to addressing this problem. The first approach uses a distributed configuration management technique [54, 55], where dependency analysis is used to determine which software elements are affected by the candidate adaptive component. Using this dependency information, a safe adaptation graph (SAG) is constructed depicting all of the safe intermediate configurations. This SAG depicts more than one sequence of intermediate actions that can yield the intended adaptive action. As such, costs can be associated with various links, thus enabling optimization decisions to be made for selecting the most cost-effective approach to achieving a given adaptation. Once a request for adaptation is made, the software execution is directed to an appropriate safe point, at which the adaptation is made. If, during the adaptation process, an unexpected event or error occurs, then the system execution is rolled back to a point prior to the beginning of the adaptation process. The second approach uses a state-based representation for the intermediate states for a given adaptation. Specifically, a distributed application is modeled as a state-transition system and safe sequences of intermediate adaptive actions during adaptation process are identified [56]. A *transitional invariant lattice* is used to model the invariants that should be satisfied by the behavior of the intermediate adaptive actions. Once a safe sequence is identified, a program is instrumented to guarantee local adaptations do not occur out of order.

Specification and Analysis of Adaptive Systems.   Adaptive systems typically adapt by adding, removing or replacing components. Component-based adaptation [2] allows for separation of concerns and independent development of components, and is essential towards building autonomic systems. As discussed earlier, transparent shaping offers adaptive mechanisms to support adaptation within program families (at the *implementation level*). Moving up one level of abstraction to the *design level*, we describe a *component family* as comprising components that provide similar functionality. Thus, depending upon the environment conditions and system requirements, one component may be replaced by another component in the family. In designing such a family of components, we separate *adapt-active* parts of each component from its functionality, thereby simplifying the specification and verification of adaptation. Only this adapt-active part is responsible for ensuring the correctness during adaptation [57]. We have found that the design of component families also helps in independent development of components and enhances reusability of components. Moreover, the use of the transitional-invariant lattice can be used to ensure that the adaptations between components in a family are indeed performed correctly [56].

At an even more abstract level, we have also introduced an approach for formally specifying adaptation *requirements* [58] in temporal logic [59]. We introduce A-LTL , an adaptation-based extension to linear temporal logic, and we use this logic to specify three commonly used adaptation semantics. We introduce adaptation semantics graphs to visually present the adaptation semantics. Specifications for adaptive systems can be automatically generated from adaptation semantics graphs. Leveraging this specification capability and using the separation of concerns approach for modeling adapt-active and functional portions of the system, we have developed a systematic process for specifying and analyzing the requirements of adaptive systems, including global system invariants [60]. We also support the automatic generation of executable prototypes to validate the requirements. We have applied this approach to a broad range of state-based modeling languages, including Petri nets, LOTOS, UML state diagrams and Z. Once the requirements have been validated and analyzed, then we can refine the specifications into components for design-level specification and verification, and eventually refine the specifications into code using transparent shaping code generation techniques.

5   Toward an Adaptive Network-Centric Infrastructure

Adaptation is not confined to middleware. An adaptive cyberinfrastructure requires interaction among applications, middleware, operating systems and networks, as well as coordination of adaptive behavior across different physical platforms. Moreover, it is imperative that these adaptive operations are carried out in a secure manner across the set of participating processes. In addition, the means by which the system decides how and when to adapt must be robust and capable of learning from past experience. In RAPIDware, we are addressing all three issues.

Distributed Collaborative Adaptation.   Although middleware is very effective in realizing many types of adaptive behavior, others require cooperation among multiple system layers (vertical adaptation) and among distributed platforms (horizontal adaptation). We have investigated several techniques and protocols to support such interactions, including efficient monitoring protocols for overlay networks [61,62], an informed mobility protocol for managing energy in mobile ad hoc networks [63], cross-layer cooperation between middleware and the operating system kernel [40], and techniques to balance QoS and energy consumption in wireless networks [37]. The Service Clouds framework [42], mentioned earlier, supports vertical and horizontal adaptation by using overlay networks as a vehicle for distributed coordination. The framework is designed to be extensible: a suite of low-level UAF services for local and remote interactions can be used to construct higher-level adaptation services.

Secure Group Communication. Adaptability is also desired in network-centric group communication, where a group of users are collaborating on a common task. Encryption of the data is necessary to secure it from unauthorized access. However, to protect the security of the current users when the group membership changes, new keys must be distributed to users. We first developed a family of algorithms that enables the tradeoff between critical cost (the messages/encryptions ratio) and overall cost of rekeying [64]. Next, we investigated tradeoffs between storage cost and rekeying cost for secure multicast [65]. We developed a family of algorithms that provide a tradeoff between the number of keys maintained by users and the time required for rekeying due to revocation of multiple users. We showed that these methods can reduce the cost of rekeying by $43\% - 79\%$ when compared with previous solutions. We are currently evaluating these protocols using existing protocol analyzers [66, 67] to formally verify the adaptive properties. Finally, we investigated the problem of distributing key updates in secure dynamic groups [68] and proposed algorithms that reduce bandwidth by up to 55% when compared with previous algorithms.

Decision Making. In addition to software adaptation mechanisms and approaches to facilitating their correct and secure operation, an autonomic system also requires some means of *deciding* when conditions warrant a responsive adaptive action. Such decisions can be extremely complex, as software must process input not only on the state of its execution environment but, with the advent of pervasive computing, must also assess relative importance of different input from the physical world. In order for systems to "learn" from past experience and respond to unexpected situations, they must be able to filter an enormous number of input that may affect the decision. Moreover, many systems must make decisions in real time to prevent damage or loss of service. We are pursuing a two-pronged approach to the investigation of decision making for adaptive systems. The first approach explores how feature interaction analysis techniques can be applied to the decision-making process for adaptation [69]. The second approach uses statistical learning algorithms, previously used to help robots learn tasks, to aid decision-making in adaptive software [70].

Conclusions

As the complexity of computing systems increases, research in distributed autonomic computing is essential to the design of future systems that are robust, secure, adaptive and self-managing. Such software is likely to play a critical role in a variety of applications related to national defense and public safety. The RAPIDware project addresses several key aspects of high-assurance adaptive systems: adaptation mechanisms, assurance techniques, and network-centric infrastructure issues. Our ongoing investigations focus on the integration of these methods to support a wide variety of autonomic distributed systems. Moreover, this experimental research, combined with case studies involving industrial partners, will facilitate technology transfer and help to maximize the impact of this research on the state of the practice.

Further Information. Related papers and technical reports of the Software Engineering and Network Systems Laboratory can be found at the SENS website: `http://www.cse.msu.edu/sens`. Additional details on the RAPIDware project, including papers and software downloads, can be found at: `http://www.cse.msu.edu/rapidware`.

Acknowledgements. The RAPIDware project is supported in part by the U.S. Department of the Navy, Office of Naval Research under Grant No. N00014-01-1-0744. The authors would like to acknowledge the contributions of several students and other researchers: Reimer Behrends, Bru Bezawada, Karun Biyani, Eric Kasten, Masoud Sadjadi, Jesse Sowell, Chiping Tang, Zhenxiao Yang, Ji Zhang, Zhinan Zhou, Matthew Wallace, Jesus Bisbal, Peng Ge, Farshad Samimi, Mahesh Arumugam, Ali Ebnenasir, and David Knoester.

References

[1] J. O. Kephart and D. M. Chess, "The vision of autonomic computing," *IEEE Computer*, vol. 36, no. 1, pp. 41–50, 2003.

[2] P. K. McKinley, S. M. Sadjadi, E. P. Kasten, and B. H. C. Cheng, "Composing adaptive software," *IEEE Computer*, vol. 37, no. 7, pp. 56–64, 2004.

[3] K. Czarnecki and U. Eisenecker, *Generative programming*. Addison Wesley, 2000.

[4] P. Maes, "Concepts and experiments in computational reflection," in *Proceedings of the ACM Conference on Object-Oriented Languages (OOPSLA)*, pp. 147–155, ACM Press, December 1987.

[5] P. Tarr and H. Ossher, eds., *Workshop on Advanced Separation of Concerns in Software Engineering at ICSE 2001 (W17)*, May 2001.

[6] K. J. Lieberherr, *Adaptive Object-Oriented Software: The Demeter Method with Propagation Patterns*. PWS Publishing Company, Boston, 1996. ISBN 0-534-94602-X.

[7] G. Kiczales, J. Lamping, A. Mendhekar, C. Maeda, C. Videira Lopes, J. M. Loingtier, and J. Irwin, "Aspect-oriented programming," in *Proceedings of the European Conference on Object-Oriented Programming (ECOOP)*, Springer-Verlag LNCS 1241, June 1997.

[8] C. Szyperski, *Component Software: Beyond Object-Oriented Programming*. Addison-Wesley, 1999.

[9] I. Ben-Shaul, O. Holder, and B. Lavva, "Dynamic adaptation and deployment of distributed components in Hadas," *IEEE Transactions on Software Engineering*, vol. 27, no. 9, pp. 769–787, 2001.

[10] M. Tatsubori, S. Chiba, K. Itano, and M.-O. Killijian, "OpenJava: A class-based macro system for Java," in *Proceedings of OORaSE*, pp. 117–133, 1999.

[11] J. de Oliveira Guimarães, "Reflection for statically typed languages," in *Proceedings of 12th European Conference on Object-Oriented Programming (ECOOP'98)*, pp. 440–461, 1998.

[12] J. Baker and W. Hsieh, "Runtime aspect weaving through metaprogramming," in *Proceedings of the first International Conference on Aspect-Oriented Software Development*, (Enschede, The Netherlands), 2002.

[13] V. Adve, V. V. Lam, and B. Ensink, "Language and compiler support for adaptive distributed applications," in *Proceedings of the ACM SIGPLAN Workshop on Optimization of Middleware and Distributed Systems (OM 2001)*, (Snowbird, Utah), June 2001.

[14] D. C. Schmidt, D. L. Levine, and S. Mungee, "The design of the TAO real-time object request broker," *Computer Communications*, vol. 21, pp. 294–324, April 1998.

[15] F. Kon, M. Román, P. Liu, J. Mao, T. Yamane, L. C. Magalhães, and R. H. Campbell, "Monitoring, security, and dynamic configuration with the dynamicTAO reflective ORB," in *Proceedings of the IFIP/ACM International Conference on Distributed Systems Platforms (Middleware 2000)*, (New York), April 2000.

[16] G. S. Blair, G. Coulson, P. Robin, and M. Papathomas, "An architecture for next generation middleware," in *Proceedings of the IFIP International Conference on Distributed Systems Platforms and Open Distributed Processing (Middleware'98)*, (The Lake District, England), September 1998.

[17] J. A. Zinky, D. E. Bakken, and R. E. Schantz, "Architectural support for quality of service for CORBA objects," *Theory and Practice of Object Systems*, vol. 3, no. 1, 1997.

[18] R. Koster, A. P. Black, J. Huang, J. Walpole, and C. Pu, "Thread transparency in information flow middleware," in *Proceedings of the International Conference on Distributed Systems Platforms and Open Distributed Processing*, Springer Verlag, Nov. 2001.

[19] R. Baldoni, C. Marchetti, and A. Termini, "Active software replication through a three-tier approach," in *Proceedings of the 22th IEEE International Symposium on Reliable Distributed Systems (SRDS02)*, (Osaka, Japan), pp. 109–118, October 2002.

[20] B. Redmond and V. Cahill, "Supporting unanticipated dynamic adaptation of application behaviour," in *Proceedings of the 16th European Conference on Object-Oriented Programming*, June 2002.

[21] M. Golm and J. Kleinoder, "metaXa and the future of reflection," in *Proceedings of Workshop on Reflective Programming in C++ and Java*, pp. 1–5, 1998.

[22] A. Oliva and L. E. Buzato, "The implementation of Guaraná on Java," Tech. Rep. IC-98-32, Universidade Estadual de Campinas, Sept. 1998.

[23] A. Popovici, T. Gross, and G. Alonso, "Dynamic homogenous AOP with PROSE," tech. rep., Department of Computer Science, Federal Institute of Technology, Zurich, 2001.

[24] N. Venkatasubramanian, "Safe 'composability' of middleware services," *Communications of the ACM*, vol. 45, pp. 49–52, June 2002.

[25] Z. Yang, B. H. C. Cheng, R. E. K. Stirewalt, J. Sowell, S. M. Sadjadi, and P. K. McKinley, "An aspect-oriented approach to dynamic adaptation," in *Proceedings of the ACM SIGSOFT Workshop on Self-Healing Systems (WOSS02)*, (Charleston, South Carolina), November 2002.

[26] S. M. Sadjadi and P. K. McKinley, "Transparent self-optimization in existing CORBA applications," in *Proceedings of the International Conference on Autonomic Computing (ICAC-04)*, (New York, NY), May 2004.

[27] S. M. Sadjadi, P. K. McKinley, B. H. C. Cheng, and R. E. K. Stirewalt, "TRAP/J: Transparent generation of adaptable java programs," in *Proceedings of the 2004 International Symposium on Distributed Objects and Applications*, (Agia Napa, Cyprus), October 2004.

[28] E. Kasten, P. K. McKinley, S. Sadjadi, and R. Stirewalt, "Separating introspection and intercession in metamorphic distributed systems," in *Proceedings of the IEEE Workshop on Aspect-Oriented Programming for Distributed Computing (with ICDCS'02)*, (Vienna, Austia), July 2002.

[29] S. M. Sadjadi, P. K. McKinley, and E. P. Kasten, "Architecture and operation of an adaptable communication substrate," in *Proceedings of the Ninth IEEE International Workshop on Future Trends of Distributed Computing Systems (FTDCS'03)*, (San Juan, Puerto Rico), pp. 46–55, May 2003.

[30] S. Fleming, B. H. C. Cheng, R. E. K. Stirewalt, and P. K. McKinley, "An approach to implementing dynamic adaptation in c++," in *Proceedings of the ICSE Workshop on Design and Evolution of Autonomic Application Software (DEAS)*, (St. Louis, Missouri), May 2005.

[31] S. M. Sadjadi and P. K. McKinley, "ACT: An adaptive CORBA template to support unanticipated adaptation," in *Proceedings of the 24th IEEE International Conference on Distributed Computing Systems (ICDCS)*, (Tokyo, Japan), March 2004.

[32] D. L. Parnas, "On the design and development of program families," *IEEE Transactions on Software Engineering*, March 1976.

[33] D. L. Parnas, P. C. Clements, and D. M. Weiss, "The modular structure of complex systems," in *Proceedings of the 7th International Conference on Software engineering*, pp. 408–417, 1984.

[34] S. M. Sadjadi, P. K. McKinley, and B. H. C. Cheng, "Transparent shaping of existing software to support pervasive and autonomic computing," in *Proceedings of the ICSE Workshop on Design and Evolution of Autonomic Application Software (DEAS)*, (St. Louis, Missouri), May 2005.

[35] P. K. McKinley, E. P. Kasten, S. M. Sadjadi, and Z. Zhou, "Realizing multi-dimensional software adaptation," in *Proceedings of the ACM Workshop on Self-Healing, Adaptive and self-MANaged Systems (SHAMAN), held in conjunction with the 16th Annual ACM International Conference on Supercomputing*, (New York City), June 2002.

[36] P. K. McKinley, S. Sadjadi, E. P. Kasten, and R. Kalaskar, "Programming language support for adaptable wearable computing," in *Proceedings of the Sixth International Symposium on Wearable Computers*, (Seattle, Washington), October 2002.

[37] Z. Zhou, P. K. McKinley, and S. M. Sadjadi, "On quality-of-service and energy consumption tradeoffs in FEC-enabled audio streaming," in *Proceedings of the 12th IEEE International Workshop on Quality of Service (IWQoS 2004)*, (Montreal, Canada), June 2004. selected as Best Student Paper).

[38] Z. Yang, Z. Zhou, B. H. C. Cheng, and P. K. McKinley, "Enabling collaborative adaptation across legacy components," in *Proceedings of the Third Workshop on Reflective and Adaptive Middleware (with Middleware'04)*, (Toronto, Ontario, Canada), October 2004.

[39] S. M. Sadjadi, P. K. McKinley, R. E. K. Stirewalt, and B. H. C. Cheng, "Generation of self-optimizing wireless network applications," in *Proceedings of the International Conference on Autonomic Computing (ICAC-04)*, (New York, NY), May 2004.

[40] F. Samimi, P. K. McKinley, S. M. Sadjadi, and P. Ge, "Kernel-middleware interaction to support adaptation in pervasive computing environments," in *Proceedings of the Second International Workshop on Middleware for Pervasive and Ad-Hoc Computing (with Middleware'04*, (Toronto, Ontario, Canada), October 2004.

[41] S. M. Sadjadi and P. K. McKinley, "Using transparent shaping and web services to support self-management of composite systems," in *Proceedings of the Second IEEE International Conference on Autonomic Computing (ICAC)*, (Seattle, Washington), June 2005.

[42] P. K. McKinley, F. A. Samimi, J. K. Shapiro, and C. Tang, "Service Clouds: A distributed infrastructure for composing autonomic communication services," Tech. Rep. MSU-CSE-05-31, Department of Computer Science, Michigan State University, East Lansing, Michigan, November 2005.

[43] L. Peterson, T. Anderson, D. Culler, and T. Roscoe, "A Blueprint for Introducing Disruptive Technology into the Internet," in *Proceedings of HotNets–I*, (Princeton, New Jersey), October 2002.

[44] B. Meyer, *Object-Oriented Software Construction*. Prentice Hall, 1997.

[45] A. Beugnard *et al.*, "Making components contract aware," *IEEE Computer*, vol. 32, pp. 38–45, July 1999.

[46] R. Behrends, R. E. K. Stirewalt, and L. K. Dillon, "Avoiding serialization vulnerabilities through the use of synchronization contracts," in *Proc. of the Workshop on Specification and Automated Processing of Security Requirements*, pp. 207–219, Austrian Computer Society, Sept. 2004.

[47] R. Behrends, *Designing and Implementing a Model of Synchronization Contracts in Object-Oriented Languages.* PhD thesis, Michigan State University, East Lansing, Michigan USA, Dec. 2003.

[48] R. Behrends, R. E. K. Stirewalt, and L. K. Dillon, "A component-oriented model for the design of safe multi-threaded applications," in *Proceedings of the 8th International SIGSOFT Symposium on Component-based Software Engineering (CBSE 2005): Software Components at Work*, May 2005.

[49] R. E. K. Stirewalt, R. Behrends, and L. K. Dillon, "Safe and reliable use of concurrency in multi-threaded shared memory sytems," in *Proceedings of the 29th Annual IEEE/NASA Software Engineering Workshop*, 2005.

[50] R. Allen and D. Garlan, "A formal basis for architectural connection," *ACM Transactions on Software Engineering and Methodology*, vol. 6, pp. 213–248, July 1997.

[51] B. Spitznagel and D. Garlan, "A Compositional Formalization of Connector Wrappers," in *Proceedings of the 2003 International Conference on Software Eng ineering*, (Portland, Oregon, USA), May 2003.

[52] J. H. Sowell and R. E. K. Stirewalt, "Middleware reliability implementations and connector wrappers," in *Proc. of the ICSE Workshop on Architecting Dependable Systems (WADS'04)*, May 2004.

[53] J. H. Sowell and R. E. K. Stirewalt, "A feature-oriented alternative to implementing reliability connector wrappers," in *Architecting Dependable Systems III* (R. de Lemos, C. Gacek, and A. Romanovsky, eds.), Springer, 2005.

[54] J. Zhang, Z. Yang, B. H. C. Cheng, and P. K. McKinley, "Adding safeness to dynamic adaptation techniques," in *Proceedings of the ICSE 2004 Workshop on Architecting Dependable Systems*, (Edinburgh, Scotland), May 2004.

[55] J. Zhang, B. H. C. Cheng, Z. Yang, and P. K. McKinley, "Enabling safe dynamic component-based software adaptation," in *Architecting Dependable Systems III, Springer Lecture Notes for Computer Science* (A. R. Rogerio de Lemos, Cristina Gacek, ed.), Springer-Verlag, 2005.

[56] S. Kulkarni and K. Biyani, "Correctness of component-based adaptation," in *Proceedings of the International Symposium on Component-based Software Engineering*, May 2004.

[57] K. N. Biyani and S. S. Kulkarni, "Building component families to support adaptation," in *Proceedings of the ICSE Workshop on Design and Evolution of Autonomic Application Software (DEAS)*, (St. Louis, Missouri), May 2005.

[58] D. M. Berry, B. H. C. Cheng, and J. Zhang, "The four levels of requirements engineering for and in dynamic adaptive systems," in *11th International Workshop on Requirements Engineering Foundation for Software Quality (REFSQ)*, (Porto, Portugal), June 2005.

[59] J. Zhang and B. H. C. Cheng, "Specifying adaptation semantics," in *Proceedings of the IEEE ICSE Workshop on Architecting Dependable Systems (WADS)*, (St. Louis, Missouri), IEEE, May 2005.

[60] J. Zhang and B. H. C. Cheng, "Model-based development of dynamically adaptive software," in *IEEE International Conference on Software Engineering (ICSE06)*, (Shanghai, China), IEEE, May 2006. (accepted to appear).

[61] C. Tang and P. K. McKinley, "On the cost-quality tradeoff in topology-aware overlay path probing," in *Proceedings of the 11th IEEE International Conference on Network Protocols (ICNP)*, (Atlanta, Georgia), pp. 268–279, November 2003.

[62] C. Tang and P. K. McKinley, "A distributed approach to topology-aware overlay path monitoring," in *Proceedings of the 24th IEEE International Conference on Distributed Computing Systems (ICDCS)*, (Tokyo, Japan), March 2004.

[63] C. Tang and P. K. McKinley, "iMobif: An informed mobility framework for energy optimization in wireless ad hoc networks," in *Proceedings of the Second International Workshop on Wireless Ad Hoc Networking (WWAN), in conjunction with the 25th IEEE International Conference on Distributed Computing Systems*, (Columbus, Ohio), June 2005.

[64] S. S. Kulkarni and B. Bruhadeshwar, "Adaptive rekeying for secure multicast," *IEEE/IEICE Special Issue on Communications: Transactions on Communications*, vol. E86-B, pp. 2948–2956, October 2003.

[65] S. S. Kulkarni and B. Bruhadeshwar, "Rekeying and storage cost for multiple user revocation," in *Proceedings of The 12th Annual Network and Distributed System Security Symposium*, (San Diego, California), 2005.

[66] P. Syverson and C. Meadows, "A formal language for cryptographic protocol requirements," *Designs, Codes, and Cryptography*, vol. 7, pp. 27–59, January 1996.

[67] C. Meadows, P. Syverson, and I. Cervesato, "Formal specification and analysis of the Group Domain Of Interpretation Protocol using NPATRL and the NRL Protocol Analyzer," *Journal of Computer Security*, vol. 12, no. 6, pp. 893–931, 2004.

[68] S. S. Kulkarni and B. Bruhadeshwar, "Distributing key updates in secure dynamic groups," in *Proceedings of the First International Conference on Distributed Computing and Internet Technology*, vol. 3347 of *Lecture Notes in Computer Science*, (Bhubaneswar, India), Springer, December 2004.

[69] J. Bisbal and B. H. C. Cheng, "Resource-based approach to feature interaction in adaptive software," in *ACM SIGSOFT Workshop on Self-Managing Systems (WOSS04)*, November 2004.

[70] E. P. Kasten and P. K. McKinley, "Meso: Perceptual memory to support online learning in adaptive software," in *Proceedings of the 3rd International Conference on Development and Learning (ICDL'04)*, (La Jolla, California), October 2004.

Composing Adaptive Software

Compositional adaptation enables software to modify its structure and behavior dynamically in response to changes in its execution environment. A review of current technology compares how, when, and where recomposition occurs.

Philip K. McKinley

Seyed Masoud Sadjadi

Eric P. Kasten

Betty H.C. Cheng
Michigan State University

Interest in adaptive computing systems has increased dramatically in the past few years, and a variety of techniques now allow software to adapt dynamically to its environment. Two revolutions in the computing field are driving this development. First is the emergence of *ubiquitous computing*,[1] which focuses on dissolving traditional boundaries for how, when, and where humans and computers interact. For example, mobile computing devices must adapt to variable conditions on wireless networks and conserve limited battery life. Second is the growing demand for *autonomic computing*,[2] which focuses on developing systems that can manage and protect themselves with only high-level human guidance. This capability is especially important to systems such as financial networks and power grids that must survive hardware component failures and security attacks.

There are two general approaches to implementing software adaptation. *Parameter adaptation* modifies program variables that determine behavior. The Internet's Transmission Control Protocol is an often-cited example: TCP adjusts its behavior by changing values that control window management and retransmissions in response to apparent network congestion. But parameter adaptation has an inherent weakness. It does not allow new algorithms and components to be added to an application after the original design and construction. It can tune parameters or direct an application to use a different existing strategy, but it cannot adopt new strategies.

By contrast, *compositional adaptation* exchanges algorithmic or structural system components with others that improve a program's fit to its current environment. With compositional adaptation, an application can adopt new algorithms for addressing concerns that were unforeseen during development. This flexibility supports more than simple tuning of program variables or strategy selection. It enables dynamic recomposition of the software during execution—for example, to switch program components in and out of a memory-limited device or to add new behavior to deployed systems.

Dynamic recomposition of software dates back to the earliest days of computing, when self-modifying code supported runtime program optimization and explicit management of physical memory. However, such programs were difficult to write and debug. Several new software tools and technologies now help address these problems. Given the increasing pace of research in compositional adaptation, we offer a review of the supporting technologies, proposed solutions, and areas that require further study.

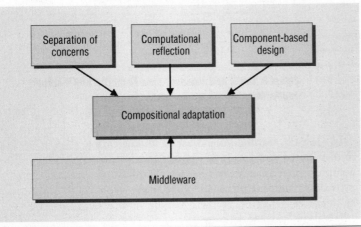

Figure 1. Main technologies supporting compositional adaptation: separation of concerns, computational reflection, and component-based design.

Reprinted with permission from *Computer*. Vol. 37, Issue 7. July 2004. 56–64.

Middleware and Adaptation

Much recent research in adaptive software focuses on middleware—the layers of services separating applications from operating systems and network protocols.

Douglas Schmidt decomposes middleware into four layers,[1] shown in Figure A:

- *Host-infrastructure middleware* resides atop the operating system and provides a high-level API that hides the heterogeneity of hardware devices, operating systems, and—to some extent—network protocols.
- *Distribution middleware* provides a high-level programming abstraction, such as remote objects, enabling developers to write distributed applications in a way similar to stand-alone programs. Corba, DCOM, and Java RMI all fit in this layer.
- *Common middleware* services include fault tolerance, security, persistence, and transactions involving entities such as remote objects.
- *Domain-specific middleware* services are tailored to match a particular class of applications.

Most adaptive middleware is based on an object-oriented programming paradigm and derived from popular middleware platforms such as Corba, Java RMI, and DCOM/.NET.

Many adaptive middleware approaches work by intercepting and modifying messages. Figure B shows the flow of a request-reply sequence in a simplified Corba client-server application. This application comprises two autonomous programs hosted on two computers connected by a network.

Assume that the *client* has a valid Corba reference to the *servant* object. The client request to the servant goes first to the *stub*, which represents the Corba object on the client side. The stub marshals the request and sends it to the client *object request broker*. The client ORB sends the request to the server ORB, where a *skeleton* unmarshals the request and delivers it to the servant. The servant replies to the request, by way of the server ORB and skeleton. The client ORB will receive the reply and dispatch it to the client.

In recent years, numerous studies have addressed the issue of how middleware can adapt to dynamic, heterogeneous environments to better serve applications.[2,3] Middleware traditionally hides resource distribution and platform heterogeneity from the application business logic. Thus it is a logical place to put adaptive behavior that is related to crosscutting concerns such as QoS, energy management, fault tolerance, and security policy.

References

1. D.C. Schmidt, "Middleware for Real-Time and Embedded Systems," *Comm. ACM*, June 2002, pp. 43-48.
2. *Comm. ACM*, special issue on adaptive middleware, June 2002, pp. 30-64.
3. *IEEE Distributed Systems Online*, special issue on reflective middleware, June 2001; http://dsonline.computer.org/0105/features/gei0105.htm.

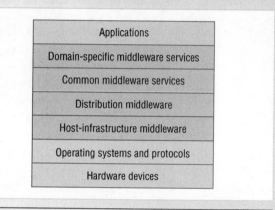

Figure A. Four-layer decomposition of middleware to bridge the gap between an application program and the underlying operating systems, network protocols, and hardware devices.

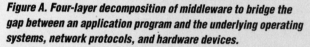
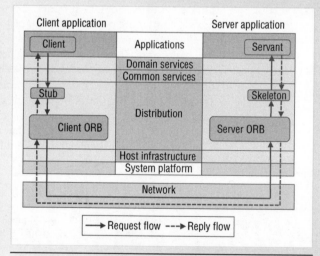

Figure B. Corba call sequence for a simplified client-server application.

ENABLING TECHNOLOGIES

At the core of all approaches to compositional adaptation is a level of indirection for intercepting and redirecting interactions among program entities. Figure 1 shows three technologies—separation of concerns, computational reflection, and component-based design—that we consider as key to reconfigurable software design. Programmers can use these technologies to construct self-adaptive systems in a systematic and principled—as opposed to ad hoc—manner.[3]

In addition, the widespread use of middleware in distributed computing has been a catalyst for compositional adaptation research. Middleware provides a natural place to locate many types of adaptive behavior, as the "Middleware and Adaptation" sidebar describes.

Separation of concerns

Separation of concerns[4] enables the separate development of an application's functional behavior—that is, its business logic—and the code for

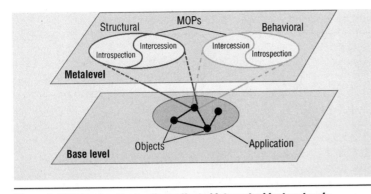

Figure 2. Metalevel understanding collected into metaobject protocols.

crosscutting concerns, such as quality of service (QoS), energy consumption, fault tolerance, and security. An application cannot implement a crosscutting concern at a single program location; instead, it must add the code at many places. Separating crosscutting concerns from functional behavior simplifies development and maintenance, while promoting software reuse.

Separation of concerns has become an important principle in software engineering.[5] Presently, the most widely used approach appears to be aspect-oriented programming.[6] AOP provides abstraction techniques and language constructs to manage crosscutting concerns. The code implementing these concerns, called *aspects,* is developed separately from other parts of the system. In AOP, *pointcuts* are sets of locations in the code where the developer can weave in aspects. Pointcuts are typically identified during development. Later, for example during compilation, the developer uses a specialized compiler, called an *aspect weaver,* to combine different aspects with an application's business logic to create a program with new behavior. An example is the AspectJ compiler. AOP proponents argue that disentangling crosscutting concerns leads to simpler software development, maintenance, and evolution.

AOP is important to dynamic recomposition because most adaptations are relative to some crosscutting concern, such as QoS. AOP enables these concerns to be isolated from the rest of the program. However, in traditional AOP the compiled program is still tangled. To support dynamic recomposition, the programmer needs a way to maintain this separation at runtime.

Computational reflection

Computational reflection refers to a program's ability to reason about, and possibly alter, its own behavior.[7] Reflection enables a system to reveal selected details of its implementation without compromising portability.

Reflection comprises two activities: *introspection* to let an application observe its own behavior, and *intercession* to let a system or application act on

these observations and modify its own behavior. In a self-auditing distributed application, for example, software "sensors" could use introspection to observe and report usage patterns for various components. Intercession would allow the system to insert new types of sensors, as well as components that implement corrective action, at runtime.

As Figure 2 shows, a reflective system (represented as base-level objects) and its self-representation (represented as metalevel objects) are causally connected, meaning that modifications to either one will be reflected in the other.

A metaobject protocol (MOP) is an interface that enables "systematic" introspection and intercession of the base-level objects. MOPs support either structural or behavioral reflection.[3] *Structural reflection* addresses issues related to class hierarchy, object interconnection, and data types. As an example, a metalevel object can examine a base-level object to determine what methods are available for invocation. Conversely, *behavioral reflection* focuses on the application's computational semantics. For instance, a distributed application can use behavioral reflection to select and load a communication protocol well suited to current network conditions.

A developer can use reflective services that are either native to a programming language—such as Common Lisp Object System (CLOS), Python, or various Java derivatives—or provided by a middleware platform. When combined with AOP, reflection enables a MOP to weave code for crosscutting concerns into an application at runtime. However, dynamically loading and unloading adaptive code requires the target software modules to exhibit a "plug-and-play" capability.

Component-based design

The third major technology supporting compositional adaptation is component-based design. *Software components* are software units that third parties can independently develop, deploy, and compose.[9] Popular component-based platforms include COM/DCOM, .NET, Enterprise Java Beans, and the Corba Component Model.

Component-based design supports two types of composition. In *static* composition, a developer can combine several components at compile time to produce an application. In *dynamic* composition, the developer can add, remove, or reconfigure components within an application at runtime. To provide dynamic recomposition, a component-based framework must support late binding, which enables coupling of compatible components at run-

Table 1. Example research projects, commercial packages, and standard specifications that provide compositional adaptation.

Project	Institution/Organization
Language-based projects	
AspectJ	Xerox Palo Alto Research Center
Composition filters	Universiteit Twente, The Netherlands
Program Control Language (PCL)	University of Illinois
Open Java	IBM Research
R-Java	University Federal de São Carlos, Brazil
Kava	University of Newcastle, UK
Adaptive Java	Michigan State University
Transparent Reflective Aspect Programming in Java (TRAP/J)	Michigan State University
Middleware-based projects	
Domain-specific services layer:	
Boeing Bold Stroke (BBS)	Boeing
Common services layer:	
CorbaServices	Object Management Group
Quality objects (QuO)	BBN Technologies
Adaptive Corba Template (ACT)	Michigan State University
Interoperable Replication Logic (IRL)	University of Rome, Italy
Distribution layer:	
.NET remoting	Microsoft
Open ORB and Open COM	Lancaster University, UK
The ACE ORB (TAO) and Component Integrated ACE ORB (CIAO)	Distributed Object Computing Group
DynamicTAO and Universally Interoperable Core (UIC)	University of Illinois
Orbix, Orbix/E, and ORBacus	Iona Technologies
Squirrel	University of Kaiserslautern, Germany
AspectIX	Friedrich-Alexander University, Germany
Host infrastructure layer:	
Java virtual machine (JVM)	Sun Microsystems
Common Language Runtime (CLR)	Microsoft
Iguana/J	Trinity College, Dublin
Prose	Swiss Federal Institute of Technology
Adaptive Communication Environment (ACE)	Distributed Object Computing Group
Ensemble	Cornell University
Cross-layer projects	
Distributed Extensible Open Systems (DEOS)	Georgia Institute of Technology
Grace	University of Illinois

time through well-defined interfaces used as contracts. In addition, to provide consistency with other applications, a component-based framework must support coexistence of multiple versions of components.

By enabling the assembly of off-the-shelf components from different vendors, component-based design promotes software reuse. Moreover, mechanisms for maintaining a program's component structure after the initial deployment, when combined with late binding, facilitate compositional adaptation.

Middleware and other factors

In addition to the three main technologies supporting dynamic recomposition, many other factors have contributed to the growth in this area. Perhaps the most important is middleware's

increasing role in distributed computing. Middleware provides a layer that developers can exploit to implement adaptive behavior. Indeed, many approaches to compositional adaptation are realized in various middleware layers.

Other technologies important to adaptive software design include software design patterns, mobile agents, generative programming, adaptive programming, and intentional programming.[5]

COMPOSITIONAL ADAPTATION TAXONOMY

Researchers and developers have proposed a wide variety of methods for supporting compositional adaptation. Table 1 lists several research projects, commercial software packages, and standard specifications that support some form of compositional adaptation. The list is by no means exhaustive. Rather, it includes projects that exemplify the

Table 2. Software recomposition techniques.

Technique	Description	Examples
Function pointers	Application execution path is dynamically redirected through modification of function pointers.	Vtables in COM, delegates and events in .NET, callback functions in Corba
Wrappers	Objects are subclassed or encapsulated by other objects (wrappers), enabling the wrapper to control method execution.	ACE, R-Java, PCL, QuO, TRAP/J
Proxies	Surrogates (proxies) are used in place of objects, enabling the surrogate to redirect method calls to different object implementations.	ACT, AspectIX
Strategy pattern	Each algorithm implementation is encapsulated, enabling transparent replacement of one implementation with another.	DynamicTAO and UIC
Virtual component pattern	Component placeholders (virtual components) are inserted into the object graph and replaced as needed during program execution.	ACE and TAO
Metaobject protocol	Mechanisms supporting intercession and introspection enable modification of program behavior.	Open Java, Kava, TRAP/J, Open ORB, Open COM, Iguana/J
Aspect weaving	Code fragments (aspects) that implement a crosscutting concern are woven into an application dynamically.	AspectJ, Composition Filters, TRAP/J, AspectIX, Iguana/J, Prose
Middleware interception	Method calls and responses passing through a middleware layer are intercepted and redirected.	ACT, IRL, Prose
Integrated middleware	An application makes explicit calls to adaptive services provided by a middleware layer.	Adaptive Java, Orbix, Orbix/E, ORBacus, BBS, CIAO, Iguana/J, Ensemble

distinctions in a taxonomy we have developed based on how, when, and where software composition takes place. We have applied the taxonomy to many additional projects.[10]

How to compose

The first dimension of our taxonomy addresses the specific software mechanisms that enable compositional adaptation. Table 2 lists several key techniques with brief descriptions and examples. Mehmet Aksit and Zièd Choukair[8] provide an excellent discussion of such methods.

All of the techniques in Table 2 create a level of indirection in the interactions between program entities. Some techniques use specific software design patterns to realize this indirection, whereas others use AOP, reflection, or both. The two middleware techniques both modify interaction between the application and middleware services, but they differ in the following way: Middleware interception is not visible to the application, whereas integrated middleware provides adaptive services invoked explicitly by the application.

We use the term *composer* to refer to the entity that uses these techniques to adapt an application. The composer might be a human—a software developer or an administrator interacting with a running program through a graphical user interface—or a piece of software—an aspect weaver, a component loader, a runtime system, or a metaobject. Indeed, autonomic computing promises that, increasingly, composers will be software components.

When and where the composer modifies the program determines the *transparency* of the recomposition. Transparency refers to whether an application or system is aware of the "infrastructure" needed for recomposition. For example, a middleware approach to adaptation is transparent with respect to the application source code if the application does not need to be modified to take advantage of the adaptive features. Different degrees of transparency (with respect to application source, virtual machine, middleware source, and so on) determine both the proposed solution's portability across platforms and how easily it can add new adaptive behavior to existing programs.[10]

When to compose

Second, we differentiate approaches according to when the adaptive behavior is composed with the business logic. Generally speaking, later composition time supports more powerful adaptation methods, but it also complicates the problem of ensuring consistency in the adapted program. For example, when composition occurs at development, compile, or load time, dynamism is limited but it is easier to ensure that the adaptation will not produce anomalous behavior. On the other

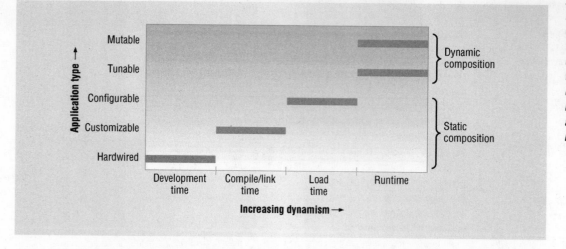

**Figure 3.
Classification
for software
composition using
the time of
composition or
recomposition as
a classification
metric.**

hand, while runtime composition is very powerful, it is difficult to use traditional testing and formal verification techniques to check safety and other correctness properties. Figure 3 illustrates the use of composition time as the classification metric for adaptive applications. The vertical axis lists application types that implement either static or dynamic composition. *Static* composition methods take place at development, compile, or load time, whereas *dynamic* composition refers to methods that a composer can apply at runtime.

Static composition. If an adaptive program is composed at development time, then any adaptive behavior is *hardwired* into the program and cannot be changed without recoding.

Alternatively, a developer or user can implement a limited form of adaptation at compile time or link time by configuring the application for a particular environment. For example, aspect-oriented programming languages such as AspectJ enable weaving of aspects into programs during compilation. Aspects might implement an environment-specific security or fault-tolerance policy. Such *customizable* applications require only recompilation or relinking to fit to a new environment.

Configurable applications delay the final decision on the algorithmic units to use in the current environment until a running application loads the corresponding component. For example, the Java virtual machine (JVM) loads classes when a Java application first uses them. Although we consider load-time composition a type of static composition, it offers more dynamism than other static methods. When the application requests the loading of a new component, decision logic might select from a list of components with different capabilities or implementations, choosing the one that most closely matches the current needs. For example, if a user starts an application on a handheld computer, the runtime system might load a minimal display component to guarantee proper presentation.

Other load-time approaches work by dynamically modifying the class itself as it is loaded. For example, to provide runtime monitoring and debugging capabilities, Kava enables the JVM to modify the bytecode as it loads a class.

Dynamic composition. The most flexible approaches to compositional adaptation implement it at runtime. A composer can replace or extend algorithmic and structural units during execution without halting and restarting the program. We differentiate two types of approaches according to whether or not the composer can modify the application's business logic.

Tunable software prohibits modification of code for the business logic. Instead, it supports fine-tuning of crosscutting concerns in response to changing environmental conditions, such as dynamic conditions encountered in mobile computing environments. An example is the fragment object model used in AspectIX, which enables runtime tuning of a Corba application's distribution behavior.

In contrast, *mutable software* allows the composer to change even the program's imperative function, enabling dynamic recomposition of a running program into one that is functionally different. For example, in the OpenORB middleware platform, all objects in the middleware and application code have reflective interfaces, so at runtime the reflective application can change virtually any object in any way, including modifying its interface and internal implementation. While very powerful, in most cases the developer must constrain this flexibility to ensure the system's integrity across adaptations.

Where to compose

The final dimension in which we compare approaches to compositional adaptation centers on where in the system the composer inserts the adaptive code. The possibilities include one of the middleware layers (see Figure A in the "Middleware and Adaptation" sidebar) or the application code itself. In this survey, we do not discuss changes to the operating system; however, we note that operating system extensibility is an active research area. Moreover, adaptations in cross-layer frameworks

> **Introducing adaptive behavior in higher middleware layers enables portability across virtual machines.**

such as DEOS and Grace involve the cooperation of the operating system, middleware, and application.

Middleware layers. Projects involving compositional adaptation at the host-infrastructure middleware layer generally fall in one of two groups. One approach is to construct a layer of adaptable communication services. ACE is an early example that used service wrappers and C++ dynamic binding to support adaptable interprocess communication and event handling services. Ensemble provides a layered architecture that enables a distributed application to select a particular communication protocol.

The second approach is to provide a virtual machine with facilities to intercept and redirect interactions in the functional code. For example, JVM and common language runtime (CLR) facilitate dynamic recomposition through reflection facilities provided by the Java language and .NET platform, respectively. R-Java supports metaobjects by adding a new instruction to the Java interpreter, while Prose and Iguana/J use aspect weaving to add behavioral reflection to the standard JVM. In general, approaches in this category are very flexible with respect to dynamic reconfiguration in that they allow new code to be introduced at runtime. However, they use customized virtual machines to provide transparency to the application, which may reduce portability.

Introducing adaptive behavior in higher middleware layers—distribution, common services, and domain-specific services—enables portability across virtual machines. These approaches typically involve middleware components that intercept messages associated with remote method invocations and redirect or modify them in a manner that accounts for current conditions. For some frameworks, the application developer constructs explicit calls to adaptive middleware services. Examples include Orbix, Orbix/E, ORBacus, CIAO, and Boeing Bold Stroke. QuO uses wrappers around Corba stubs and skeletons to gain control of the call sequence, whereas IRL and ACT use Corba portable interceptors to do so. Portable interceptors serve as "generic" hooks that a composer can use at runtime to load other types of interceptors. Since a user can load a portable interceptor using a command-line parameter, this approach enables the composer to integrate adaptive components into the program without modifying either the application or the middleware code.

Application code. Although middleware approaches support transparent adaptation, they apply only to programs that are written against a specific middleware platform. A more general approach is for developers to implement compositional adaptation in the application program itself.

Two main techniques are available. The first is to program all or part of the application code using a language that directly supports dynamic recomposition. Some languages, such as CLOS or Python, provide support inherently, while others have been extended to support adaptation. For example, Open Java, R-Java, Handi-Wrap, PCL, and Adaptive Java all extend Java to include new keywords and constructs that enhance the adaptive code's expressiveness. However, this approach requires the developer to use these features explicitly in constructing the program.

The second technique is to weave the adaptive code into the functional code. AspectJ and Composition Filters weave adaptive behavior into existing applications at compile time. In contrast, tools such as TRAP/J use a two-step approach to enable dynamic recomposition. In the first step, an aspect weaver inserts generic interception hooks, in this case implemented as aspects, into the application code at compile time. In the second step, a composer dynamically weaves new adaptive components into the application at runtime, and a metaobject protocol uses reflection to forward intercepted operations to the adaptive components. This approach offers a way to add adaptive behavior to existing applications transparently with respect to the original code. Such a capability is important as users expect legacy applications to execute effectively across an increasingly diverse computing infrastructure.

KEY CHALLENGES

Despite many advances in mechanisms to support compositional adaptation, the full potential of dynamically recomposable software systems depends on fundamental advances on four other fronts.

Assurance

Recomposable software design requires a programming paradigm that supports automated checking of both functional and nonfunctional system properties.[11]

To help ensure the adapted system's correctness, developers must first certify all components for correctness with respect to their specifications. They can obtain this certification either by selecting components that have already been verified and validated offline using traditional techniques, such as testing, inspection, and model checking, or by generating code automatically from specifications. The certification can include nonfunctional requirements, such as security and performance, as well as functional requirements.

Second, techniques are needed to ensure that the system still executes in an acceptable, or *safe*, manner during the adaptation process. Our group and others are using dependency analysis to address this problem. In addition, developers can use high-level contracts[12] and invariants to monitor system correctness before, during, and after adaptation.

Security

Whereas assurance deals primarily with system integrity, security addresses protection from malicious entities—preventing would-be attackers from exploiting the adaptation mechanisms. In addition to verifying component sources, an adaptive software system must protect its core from attackers. Various well-studied security mechanisms are available, such as strong encryption to ensure the confidentiality and authenticity of messages related to adaptation.

However, the system must also hide adaptation management from would-be intruders and prevent them from impeding or corrupting the adaptation process. A comprehensive approach to this problem must ensure the integrity of the data used in decision-making and conceal the adaptive actions, perhaps by obscuring them within other system activities.

Interoperability

Distributed systems that can adapt to their environment must both adapt individual components and coordinate adaptation across system layers and platforms. Software components are likely to come from different vendors, so the developer may need to integrate different adaptive mechanisms to meet an application's requirements. The problem is complicated by the diversity of adaptive software approaches at different system layers. Even solutions within the same layer are often not compatible.

Developers need tools and methods to integrate the operation of adaptive components across the layers of a single system, among multiple computing systems, and between different adaptive frameworks.

Decision making

Adaptive systems respond to a dynamic physical world. They must act autonomously, modifying software composition to better fit the current environment while preventing damage or loss of service. Decision-making software uses input from software and hardware sensors to decide how, when, and where to adapt the system. Interactive systems may even require the decision maker to learn about and adapt to user behavior.

Some researchers have constructed software decision makers using rule-based approaches or control theory. Others have designed decision makers whose actions are inspired by biological processes, such as the human nervous system and emergent behavior in insect species that form colonies.

These approaches to decision making in adaptive software have been effective in certain domains, but environmental dynamics and software complexity have limited their general application. More extensive research in decision making for adaptive software is needed. Future systems must accommodate high-dimensional sensory data, continue to learn from new experience, and take advantage of new adaptations as they become available.

> **The system must also hide adaptation management from would-be intruders.**

Many of the mechanisms for compositional adaptation are available now, and we expect their use to increase as programmers become more familiar with adaptive software technologies and society comes to expect computer systems to manage themselves. There is a potential downside, however, in the lack of supporting development environments. Compositional adaptation is powerful, but without appropriate tools to automatically generate and verify code, its use can negatively impact—rather than improve—system integrity and security.

The computer science community must build development technologies and tools, well grounded in rigorous software engineering, to support compositional adaptation. This foundation will raise the next generation of computing to new levels of flexibility, autonomy, and maintainability without sacrificing assurance and security. ∎

Acknowledgments

We express our gratitude to the many individuals who have contributed to this emerging area of study. Discussions with researchers associated with many of the projects listed in Table 1 have greatly improved our understanding of this area. We also thank the faculty and students in the Software Engineering and Network Systems Laboratory at

Michigan State University for their contributions to RAPIDware, Meridian, and related projects.

This work was supported in part by National Science Foundation grants CCR-9901017, CCR-9912407, EIA-0000433, EIA-0130724, and ITR-0313142, and by the US Department of the Navy, Office of Naval Research, under grant no. N00014-01-1-0744.

Further information

Our group is participating in compositional adaptation research through two projects: RAPIDware (www.cse.msu.edu/rapidware) addresses adaptive software for protecting critical infrastructures, and Meridian (www.cse.msu.edu/meridian) addresses automated software engineering for mobile computing. Among other artifacts, these projects produced ACT, Adaptive Java, and TRAP/J. The technical report on our taxonomy is a "living document" available through the RAPIDware URL.

References

1. M. Weiser, "Hot Topics: Ubiquitous Computing," *Computer*, Oct. 1993, pp. 71-72.
2. J.O. Kephart and D.M. Chess, "The Vision of Autonomic Computing," *Computer*, Jan. 2003, pp. 41-50.
3. G.S. Blair et al., "An Architecture for Next-Generation Middleware," *Proc. IFIP Int'l Conf. Distributed Systems Platforms and Open Distributed Processing* (Middleware 98), Springer, 1998, pp. 191-206.
4. D.L. Parnas, "On the Criteria to Be Used in Decomposing Systems into Modules," *Comm. ACM*, Dec. 1972, pp. 1053-1058.
5. K. Czarnecki and U. Eisenecker, *Generative Programming*, Addison-Wesley, 2000.
6. G. Kiczales et al., "Aspect-Oriented Programming," *Proc. European Conf. Object-Oriented Programming* (ECOOP), LNCS 1241, Springer-Verlag, 1997, pp. 220-242.
7. P. Maes, "Concepts and Experiments in Computational Reflection," *Proc. ACM Conf. Object-Oriented Programming Systems, Languages, and Applications* (OOPSLA), ACM Press, 1987, pp. 147-155.
8. M. Aksit and Z. Choukair, "Dynamic, Adaptive, and Reconfigurable Systems Overview and Prospective Vision," *Proc. 23rd Int'l Conf. Distributed Computing Systems Workshops* (ICDCSW03), IEEE CS Press, May 2003, pp. 84-89.
9. C. Szyperski, *Component Software: Beyond Object-Oriented Programming*, 2nd ed., Addison-Wesley, 2002.
10. P.K. McKinley et al., "A Taxonomy of Compositional Adaptation," tech. report MSU-CSE-04-17, Dept. Computer Science and Engineering, Michigan State Univ., 2004.
11. N. Venkatasubramanian, "Safe 'Composability' of Middleware Services," *Comm. ACM*, June 2002, pp. 49-52.
12. A. Beugnard et al., "Making Components Contract Aware," *Computer*, July 1999, pp. 38-45.

Philip K. McKinley is a professor in the Department of Computer Science and Engineering at Michigan State University. His research interests include adaptive middleware, mobile computing, pervasive computing, distributed systems, and group communication. McKinley received a PhD in computer science from the University of Illinois at Urbana-Champaign. He is a member of the IEEE Computer Society and the ACM. Contact him at mckinley@cse.msu.edu.

Sayed Masoud Sadjadi is a PhD candidate in the Department of Computer Science and Engineering at Michigan State University. His research interests include adaptive software, middleware, pervasive computing, autonomic computing, and sensor networks. Sadjadi received an MS in software engineering from Azad University at Tehran. He is a student member of the IEEE Computer Society and the ACM. Contact him at sadjadis@cse.msu.edu.

Eric P. Kasten is a PhD candidate in the Department of Computer Science and Engineering and a software developer in the National Superconducting Cyclotron Laboratory, both at Michigan State University. His research interests include autonomic computing and learning algorithms for adaptable software. Kasten received an MS in computer science from Michigan State University. He is a member of the IEEE Computer Society and the ACM. Contact him at kasten@cse.msu.edu.

Betty H.C. Cheng is a professor in the Department of Computer Science and Engineering at Michigan State University. Her research interests include formal methods for software engineering, component-based software development, object-oriented analysis and design, embedded systems development, and visualization. Cheng received a PhD in computer science from the University of Illinois at Urbana-Champaign. She is a senior member of the IEEE Computer Society and a member of the ACM. Contact her at chengb@cse.msu.edu.

Generating Efficient Security Software from Policies*

Scott D. Stoller and Yanhong A. Liu

Computer Science Dept., State University of New York at Stony Brook

December 7, 2005

Abstract

In today's widely distributed large-scale computer systems, there is a growing need to establish and enforce enterprise-wide security policies. This has stimulated development and deployment of more scalable and expressive security policy frameworks, notably role-based access control (RBAC) and trust management. Clear, precise, high-level specifications of these frameworks and policies help assure their correct design, implementation, and use.

Our work addresses the challenge of generating efficient, high-assurance implementations of security policy frameworks and policies from simple, declarative, high-level specifications. We are developing implementation methods for high-level languages that analyze and transform such specifications to automatically produce efficient implementations. This is a significant advance over the state of the art, which is time-consuming and error-prone manual coding of implementations.

Categories and Subject Descriptors: K.6.5 [Management of Computing and Information Systems]: Security and Protection; D.4.6 [Operating Systems]: Security and Protection — Access Controls

Keywords: security policy, role-based access control, trust management, distributed system security, logic programs, program optimization

1 Introduction

In today's widely distributed large-scale computer systems, there is a growing need to establish and enforce enterprise-wide security policies. In particular, precise access control policies are essential for ensuring confidentiality and integrity of information. In this context, the limitations of access control lists—one of the simplest and most widely used forms of access control—are becoming increasingly evident. This has stimulated development and deployment of more powerful security policy frameworks, notably role-based access control (RBAC) and trust management. In RBAC, roles are abstractions that ease management of security policies in large systems [SCFY96, Ame04]. Trust management supports decentralized management of security policies [BFIK99].

---

*This work was supported in part by ONR under grants N00014-04-1-0722 and N00014-02-1-0363 and NSF under grants CCR-0306399 and CCR-0311512. Authors' address: Computer Science, SUNY, Stony Brook, NY 11794-4400, USA. Email: {stoller,liu}@cs.sunysb.edu

Correct design, implementation, and use of security policy frameworks and policies are essential for achieving overall system security. Clear, precise, high-level specifications of these frameworks and policies can play a valuable role. Such specifications offer several benefits: they can be inspected and analyzed for errors; they facilitate communication and negotiation between vendors and purchasers; and they help software application developers, security policy developers, and system administrators correctly understand and use the framework or policy. For these benefits to be fully realized, the implementations of the policy frameworks and policies must be known to conform to the specifications. Moreover, the implementations must be efficient; otherwise, they will not be used.

Our work addresses the challenge of generating efficient, high-assurance implementations of security policy frameworks and policies from high-level specifications. Our goal is to allow the designers to specify the policy frameworks and policies in a simple and declarative way, without concern for efficiency. We are developing implementation methods for high-level languages that analyze and transform such specifications to automatically produce efficient implementations.

This is a significant advance over the state of the art, which is manual coding of implementations. Even when starting with a high-level specification, manual coding of an efficient implementation is a time-consuming and error-prone task. Specifications are aimed to be clear and easy to understand, while implementations are aimed to be efficient. Efficiency often requires designing appropriate algorithms and sophisticated primary and auxiliary data structures and maintaining the data structures at all relevant steps of the algorithm. This makes the implementation significantly longer and more complicated than the specification. By performing such design and implementation automatically, our methods offer increased productivity and higher assurance of correctness. Our method encourages use of abstraction and separation of efficiency from other concerns and thereby helps lead to clearer and simpler specifications.

We give a brief introduction to RBAC and trust management and an overview of our methods for efficient implementation of specifications, and then briefly describe our initial results for applying our methods to implement RBAC and trust management, including how our methods led us to identify a number of errors and unnecessary complications in the ANSI standard for RBAC [Ame04] and develop a corrected and simplified specification for RBAC.

2   Security Policy Frameworks

We look at RBAC and trust management, because RBAC is increasingly widely used and trust management is increasingly important. The concepts underlying them are fundamental in other frameworks as well.

2.1   Role-Based Access Control (RBAC)

RBAC is a well known framework that significantly eases management of security policies in large systems [SCFY96, Ame04]. A role is an abstraction associated with a set of permissions, typically the permissions needed to perform the tasks associated with a position in an organization. An RBAC policy specifies, among other things, the roles that each user may adopt, and the permissions associated with each role. A study commissioned by NIST shows that RBAC can significantly reduce the cost of security policy administration and forecasts that by 2006, between 30 and 50 percent of employees in the service sector and between 10 and 25 percent of employees in nonservice sectors will be managed by RBAC systems [GOK02].

Many operating systems, database systems, and middleware systems support some form of RBAC. However, terminology, features, interfaces, and handling of special cases vary widely. This causes difficulties for application developers, policy writers, and procurement officers. This motivated the development of ANSI INCITS Standard 359-2004 [Ame04], which provides system-independent formal models and functional specifications for core RBAC and three extensions, expressed in a set-based specification language.

The model for core RBAC consists of sets of operations, objects, permissions (to perform operations on objects), roles, users, and sessions (a user must create a session and activate a role in it, in order to use the permissions associated with that role), and several relations built on these sets. The relations associate permissions with roles, users with the roles they can activate, users with the sessions they created, and sessions with the roles activated in them. The functional specification defines commands that query and update these sets and relations. For example, there are commands to add and remove roles, grant a permission to a role, and check whether an operation on an object is permitted in a session. The three extensions are role hierarchy, static separation of duty constraints, and dynamic separation of duty constraints.

An implicit assumption underlying RBAC is the existence of senior security officers (administrators) who are completely trusted system-wide. Administrative RBAC [SBM99] extends RBAC to support junior security officers, who are trusted by the senior security officers to manage specified parts of the policy, but it does not eliminate this assumption. Consequently, RBAC is not directly suitable for large enterprises, coalitions, etc., which contain interacting computer systems with no globally trusted administrators.

2.2   Trust Management

Trust management is designed to offer flexible solutions for decentralized management of security policies [BFIK99]. In particular, it does not assume the existence of globally trusted principals. Trust management has three characteristic features: each policy statement is associated with a principal, called its source or issuer; each principal's policy specifies which sources it trusts for which kinds of statements, thereby delegating some authority to those sources; and policies may refer to arbitrary attributes of and relationships between principals, resources, and other objects.

For example, a database server's policy might include the statement: the database server says x may read the database if the Human Resources Department says b is x's boss, and b says x may read the database. This expresses that the database server trusts the Human Resources Department for information about is-boss-of relationships, and trusts a person's boss regarding that person's permission to read the database. This policy cannot be expressed in RBAC.

Trust management policies can be expressed naturally in rule-based languages. Such languages facilitate declarative descriptions; they naturally support user-defined attributes and relations; and they allow recursive definitions, which arise when hierarchical structures are involved. Several trust management frameworks, including [Jim01, DeT02, LMW02, LGF03, BS04, NOW04], have policy languages based on Datalog [GMUW02], a classic rule-based query language for databases. For example, the sample policy statement above can be expressed as the rule

$$\texttt{DBserver.hasPermission}(x, \texttt{Read(DB)}) :- \texttt{HumanRsrcs.isBossOf}(b, x), \ b.\texttt{hasPermission}(x, \texttt{Read(DB)}).$$

where a comma between premises denotes conjunction, and $s.r(args)$ means source s says relationship r holds between arguments *args*.

Trust management is much younger than RBAC and is not yet widely deployed, but it will be increasingly needed in large enterprises and coalitions, driven by increasing inter-dependence between computer systems with limited mutual trust, as a result of increasing computer system integration and increasing sharing of resources and information. Security of such organizations will depend critically on the ability to precisely specify trust relationships between these systems.

3   Methods for Efficient Implementation of Specifications

This section gives an overview of three methods we are developing for efficient implementation of specifications. Specifically, the methods are for implementation of relational rules, implementation of a powerful construct for pattern-based retrieval from relations, and optimization of operations on sets and relations in object-oriented languages. Sets and relations are fundamental for representing data and facts; rules are important for representing knowledge and queries over them; and objects support updates and provide structure.

3.1   From Rules to Efficient Implementations

Our method for implementation of rule-based languages, described in [LS03], automatically transforms sets of rules in Datalog-like languages into specialized algorithms and lightweight implementations, and performs an automated complexity analysis that provides time and space guarantees for the generated algorithms. A key feature of our approach is generation of data structures and code specialized to the given rules.

The transformation is based on a general method for efficient fixed-point computation. Starting from a given set of rules and facts, the set of derivable facts can be computed by repeatedly deriving new facts from existing facts using the rules, until no more new facts can be derived. This is a fixed-point computation. Our transformation exploits three key ideas to compute the fixed point efficiently: (1) perform a minimum update in each iteration, by considering one new derived fact at a time; (2) maintain appropriate auxiliary maps, serving as indices, based on the structure of the rules, and update them incrementally in each iteration; and (3) use appropriate combinations of indexed and linked data structures to implement each set and map, based on how it is used.

The generated implementations have guaranteed optimal time complexity and associated space complexity, in the sense that only useful combinations of information that lead to the invocation of a policy rule are considered, and each such combination is considered exactly once. The method computes the worst-case time and space complexities, as formulas. These are independent of the order of rules in the program and the order of hypotheses within each rule. In contrast, in previous systems, including highly optimized systems such as GNU Prolog (http://www.gnu.org/software/gprolog/) and XSB (http://xsb.sourceforge.net/), the running time of a program can vary dramatically depending on the order of rules or the order of hypotheses. It is very difficult for users to determine which order will lead to more efficient execution, because the answer depends on implementation details.

We implemented our method in two prototype tools, both written in the programming language Python (http://www.python.org/). One reads rules and generates efficient C code. The other reads rules and generates programs in a pseudo-code language similar to a subset of Python. Our tool called Patton translates that pseudo-code language into C++ [RL05].

We extended the method to handle three extensions to Datalog—stratified negation, unsafe rules, and simple constraints [LS05].

3.2 Efficient Implementation of Retrieval from Relations

Specifications and programs involving sets and relations can often be expressed more clearly and concisely using a simple and powerful construct that we call pattern-based retrieval from relations, also called partially-bound retrieval from relations. Given a tuple pattern with some bound variables and some unbound variables, and given a set of tuples, representing a relation, pattern-based retrieval finds and iterates over the tuples that match the pattern, binding the unbound variables based on the match. Pattern-based retrieval can be used in `for` loops, `while` loops, and set comprehensions. It can also be used in `if` statements, to test whether a matching tuple exists.

For example, suppose the relation `PR` (permission-role assignment) contains a tuple `[op, obj, r]` if role `r` has permission to perform operation `op` on object `obj`. The ANSI standard for RBAC [Ame04] defines a function `RoleOperationsOnObject(role, object)`, which returns the set of operations that the given role has permission to perform on the given object. Using a `for` loop with pattern-based retrieval, we can express this function clearly and concisely in Python extended with pattern-based retrieval as follows; note that `role` and `object` are bound, and `op` is unbound, in this pattern-based retrieval.

```
def RoleOperationsOnObject(role, object):
    result = set()
    for op, object, role in PR:
        result.add(op)
    return result
```

Straightforward implementations of pattern-based retrieval iterate over the entire set of tuples to find the tuples that match. This is inefficient if a small fraction of the tuples match. Our method, described in [RL05], automatically introduces and maintains auxiliary maps (indices), that allow matching tuples to be found directly. All operations that add or remove elements from the set of tuples are intercepted, and the indices are updated appropriately. With our method, the amortized cost of a pattern-based retrieval is O(1) per retrieved tuple.

We originally implemented this method in Patton [RL05] (the name was chosen because it is a well-known name that sounds similar to "pattern"), whose pseudo-code language supports pattern-based retrieval, which significantly eases the translation from rules to C++ described in Section 3.1. We later implemented this method in a tool called Halsey [RL05] (the name acknowledges ONR's support of this research), which translates Python extended with pattern-based retrieval into standard Python.

3.3　Incrementalization Across Object Abstraction

Object abstraction supports the separation of what operations are provided by systems and components from how the operations are implemented, and is essential in enabling the construction of complex systems from components. Unfortunately, clear and modular implementations have poor performance when expensive query operations are repeated, while efficient implementations that incrementally maintain these query results are much more difficult to develop and to understand, because the code blows up significantly, and is no longer clear or modular.

For example, consider the `CheckAccess` operation in RBAC, which determines whether a given operation on a given object is permitted in a given session. A straightforward implementation of the specification of `CheckAccess` in the ANSI standard [Ame04] iterates over all roles, searching for a role that is activated in the given session and has the desired permission. A much more efficient implementation is possible: if we incrementally maintain the union of the sets of permissions associated with the active roles in the session, then `CheckAccess` simply tests for membership in that set. This requires incrementally updating that set when a role is activated or deactivated or a permission is granted to or revoked from a role. This makes the code considerably longer, more complicated, less modular, and harder to understand and maintain.

We developed a powerful and systematic method, described in [LSG+05], that first allows components to be specified by straightforward and modular implementations in an object-oriented language; then does an analysis, across object abstraction, to identify expensive queries and updates to their parameters (i.e., data on which the query result depends); and finally derives sophisticated and efficient implementations by incrementally maintaining the results of repeated expensive queries with respect to updates to their parameters. For the above example, our method successfully produces the efficient implementation of `CheckAccess` from the straightforward implementation.

We implemented this method in a prototype tool called InvTS (Invariant-driven Transformation System), which optimizes queries over sets and objects in Python. InvTS incorporates analyses that identify queries and updates in a specialized rule-based transformation system to generate the optimized program.

4　Implementing RBAC

Existing implementations of RBAC are hand-coded, and are large and complicated compared to specifications. For example, NIST's reference implementation of RBAC for Web servers, called RBAC/Web (http://csrc.nist.gov/rbac/#software), contains over 1000 lines of Perl that implement RBAC functionality described in the ANSI standard for RBAC [Ame04]. We specified RBAC, based on the ANSI standard, in a high-level object-oriented language with sets and relations, similar to a subset of Python. Our specification of the RBAC functionality implemented in RBAC/Web is about 100 lines. Since our specification language is similar to Python, it was easy to translate our specification of RBAC into Python for the following experiments.

We applied InvTS, our prototype tool for incrementalization, to our specification of core RBAC in Python, to obtain an efficient implementation of it. The experiments reported in [LWG$^+$06] confirm the effectiveness of our method, showing improvement from polynomial time in the straightforward implementation, to constant time in the incrementalized implementation, for `CheckAccess`.

An additional benefit of our approach is that it led to a simplified and corrected specification of RBAC. While re-writing the ANSI standard specification of RBAC following the principle of separating what from how, we found and eliminated a number of errors and complications, some of which are likely caused by interaction with efficiency concerns. For example, in RBAC with role hierarchy, the specification in the standard stores and incrementally maintains the reflexive-transitive closure of the role inheritance relationship. This makes some operations more efficient, but it requires inverting (undoing) the reflexive-transitive closure in other operations, and that calculation is defined incorrectly in the standard. In our approach, the user writes a simpler specification that stores the role inheritance relationship (not its reflexive-transitive closure) and hence never uses that calculation, and efficiency is achieved through automated optimizations.

We also re-wrote part of the specification of core RBAC—specifically, the administrative commands and supporting system functions—using pattern-based retrieval [RL05]. To write an efficient implementation without pattern-based retrieval, the programmer must introduce several auxiliary maps and updates to them; for example, in the command to delete a user, auxiliary maps are needed to efficiently find tuples with information about that user. With pattern-based retrieval, those auxiliary maps and the updates to them are introduced automatically.

We also specified all of the query functions, i.e., functions that do not perform updates, in core RBAC and hierarchical RBAC using rules. Our prototype tools for generating C and C++ code from rules can be used to produce efficient implementations of them.

5   Implementing Trust Management

A significant obstacle to deployment of trust management systems with rule-based policy languages is the lack of suitable implementations of such languages. Simple interpreters are easy to implement but have poor performance, especially for rule sets containing recursive definitions. Development of an optimized implementation is a large undertaking, and the result is sophisticated but heavy-weight systems, such as the logic-programming system XSB (http://xsb.sourceforge.net/), which are not easily deployed for trust management [LMW02]. Worse yet, as discussed above, even in the best existing highly-optimized logic programming systems, such as GNU Prolog and XSB, the running time of a program can vary dramatically and almost unpredictably depending on the order of rules in the program or the order of hypotheses within each rule.

Our method for generating efficient lightweight implementations from rules is well suited to implementation of trust management policies. In addition, the time and space complexities of the generated code are independent of the orders of rules and hypotheses. To demonstrate the suitability and effectiveness of our method in the context of trust management, we are applying it to a substantial case study, namely, a security policy for electronic health records [Bec05], based on a policy developed by the United Kingdom's National Health Service [Nat03].

6   Conclusion and Future Work

We are developing methods and tools that provide a powerful infrastructure for efficient implementation of security policy frameworks, policies, and many other systems. Compared to manual coding, our methods and tools offer significantly increased productivity and higher assurance of correctness, because they eliminate the need for time-consuming and error-prone manual optimizations. We are demonstrating this by applying our methods and tools to RBAC and trust management.

In ongoing work, we are improving our methods and tools, finishing specifications and implementations of RBAC and trust management, and more thoroughly evaluating the effectiveness of our methods on them.

An important direction for future work is to develop a security policy framework based on relations and objects as well as rules. Rules are often well suited for expressing queries, but they are poorly suited for expressing updates to relations. Also, policies in current trust management frameworks lack structure; object orientation will allow natural and meaningful structuring. Once a suitable language has been developed, methods and tools for analysis, verification, and efficient implementation will be needed to support it for practical use.

References

[Ame04]   American National Standards Institute (ANSI), International Committee for Information Technology Standards (INCITS). Role-based access control. ANSI INCITS Standard 359-2004, February 2004.

[Bec05]   Moritz Y. Becker. A formal security policy for an NHS electronic health record service. Technical Report UCAM-CL-TR 628, University of Cambridge, Computer Laboratory, March 2005.

[BFIK99]   Matt Blaze, Joan Feigenbaum, John Ioannidis, and Angelos D. Keromytis. The role of trust management in distributed systems. In *Secure Internet Programming*, volume 1603 of *Lecture Notes in Computer Science*, pages 185–210. Springer-Verlag, 1999.

[BS04]   Moritz Y. Becker and Peter Sewell. Cassandra: Flexible trust management, applied to electronic health records. In *Proc. 17th IEEE Computer Security Foundations Workshop (CSFW)*, pages 139–154. IEEE Computer Society Press, 2004.

[DeT02]   John DeTreville. Binder, a logic-based security language. In *Proc. 2002 IEEE Symposium on Security and Privacy*, pages 105–113. IEEE Computer Society Press, 2002.

[GMUW02]   Hector Garcia-Molina, Jeffrey D. Ullman, and Jennifer Widom. *Database Systems: The Complete Book.* Prentice-Hall, 2002.

[GOK02]   Michael P. Gallaher, Alan C. O'Connor, and Brian Kropp. The economic impact of role-based access control. Planning Report 02-1, National Institute of Standards and Technology (NIST), March 2002. Available at http://csrc.nist.gov/rbac.

[Jim01]   Trevor Jim. SD3: A trust management system with certified evaluation. In *Proc. 2001 IEEE Symposium on Security and Privacy*, pages 106–115. IEEE Computer Society Press, 2001.

[LGF03]   Ninghui Li, Benjamin N. Grosof, and Joan Feigenbaum. Delegation logic: A logic-based approach to distributed authorization. *ACM Transaction on Information and System Security*, 6(1):128–171, 2003.

[LMW02]   Ninghui Li, John C. Mitchell, and William H. Winsborough. Design of a role-based trust management framework. In *Proc. 2002 IEEE Symposium on Security and Privacy*, pages 114–130. IEEE Computer Society Press, 2002.

[LS03]   Yanhong A. Liu and Scott D. Stoller. From Datalog rules to efficient programs with time and space guarantees. In *Proceedings of the 5th ACM SIGPLAN International Conference on Principles and Practice of Declarative Programming*, pages 172–183, Aug. 2003.

[LS05]   Yanhong A. Liu and Scott D. Stoller. Querying complex graphs. In *Proceedings of the 8th International Symposium on Practical Aspects of Declarative Languages*, LNCS, Charleston, South Carolina, Jan. 2005. Springer-Verlag, Berlin.

[LSG+05]   Yanhong A. Liu, Scott D. Stoller, Michael Gorbovitski, Tom Rothamel, and Yanni Ellen Liu. Incrementalization across object abstraction. In *Proc. ACM SIGPLAN 2005 Conference on Object-Oriented Programming, Systems, Languages and Applications (OOPSLA)*. ACM Press, October 2005.

[LWG+06]   Yanhong A. Liu, Chen Wang, Michael Gorbovitski, Tom Rothamel, Yongxi Cheng, Yingchao Zhao, and Jing Zhang. Core role-based access control: Efficient implementations by transformations. In *Proceedings of the ACM SIGPLAN 2006 Workshop on Partial Evaluation and Semantics-Based Program Manipulation*, Jan. 2006.

[Nat03]   National Health Service of the United Kingdom. Output based specification for integrated care record service version 2, August 2003. Available via http://www.dh.gov.uk/.

[NOW04]   Wolfgang Nejdl, Daniel Olmedilla, and Marianne Winslett. Peertrust: Automated trust negotiation for peers on the semantic web. In *Proc. Workshop on Secure Data Management (SDM 2004)*, volume 3178 of *Lecture Notes in Computer Science*, pages 118–132. Springer-Verlag, 2004.

[RL05]   Tom Rothamel and Yanhong A. Liu. The efficient implementation of partially bound retrieval. Technical Report DAR-05-23, SUNY at Stony Brook, Computer Science Dept., July 2005.

[SBM99]   Ravi Sandhu, Venkata Bhamidipati, and Qamar Munawer. The ARBAC97 model for role-based administration of roles. *ACM Transactions on Information and Systems Security (TISSEC)*, 2(1):105–135, February 1999.

[SCFY96]   Ravi Sandhu, Edward Coyne, Hal Feinstein, and Charles Youman. Role-based access control models. *IEEE Computer*, 29(2):38–47, February 1996.

Role-Based Access Control:
A Corrected and Simplified Specification*

Yanhong A. Liu   Scott D. Stoller

Computer Science Dept., State Univ. of New York at Stony Brook, Stony Brook, NY 1179·
{liu,stoller}@cs.sunysb.edu

Abstract

This paper describes a corrected and simplified specification of role-based access control (RBAC) based on the specification in the ANSI standard for RBAC. We give a complete specification of core RBAC, explaining the methodology we used in developing it; we then give a complete specification of hierarchical RBAC, with an additional option for managing the relationship on roles; and we also describe a specification of constrained RBAC, making extension relationships among RBAC components clear. We compare our specification with the standard and point out errors and unnecessary complications we found. We also describe the principles for developing clear and simpler specifications, and summarize our method and results for generating efficient implementations.

1 Introduction

Role-based access control (RBAC) is a framework for controlling user access to resources based on roles. It can significantly reduce the cost of security policy administration and is increasingly widely used in large organizations. The ANSI standard for RBAC was developed "in recognition of a need among government and industry purchasers of information technology products for a consistent and uniform definition of role-based access control features"[Ame]. It was approved in 2004 after several rounds of public review [SFK00, JT00, FSG+01], building on much research during the preceding decade (e.g., [FK92, GB98]), although the idea of roles in access control can be traced back at least two decades [LHM84].

The standard has four components: core RBAC defines core functionalities on permissions, users, sessions, and roles, while the other three components are extensions that add support for a hierarchy of roles, constraints on the roles of a user, and constraints on the active roles in a session, respectively. The functionalities are specified formally and precisely in a set-based specification language, Z [ISO, Spi92].

Because of the importance of RBAC and the ANSI standard for it, we are using them as an application in our research on optimization by incrementalization [LSG+05]. Our basic idea is to start with straightforward but likely inefficient implementations of the functionalities and generate sophisticated and efficient implementations following a systematic optimization method.

Our powerful optimization method allows one to write clear and modular specifications that may contain expensive queries if executed straightforwardly, and automatically generate efficient, though not clear or modular, implementations by incrementally maintaining the results of expensive queries with respect to updates to the data they depend on. This enables us to separate "what" from "how" in specifying the

---

*This work was supported in part by ONR under grants N00014-04-1-0722 and N00014-02-1-0363 and NSF under grant CCR-0306399.

functionalities in a system like RBAC, and arrive at clearer and simpler specifications that have higher assurance of correctness.

Following this approach, we found a number of errors and complications in the standard. Most of them appear to be caused by interaction with efficiency concerns. For example, the `AddInheritance` command in limited hierarchical RBAC can never add any inheritance because its pre-condition, which uses an incorrect definition to retrieve immediate inheritance from transitive inheritance, is always false. For another example, five of the seven mapping functions defined in the core RBAC reference model are unnecessary, and so are the updates to `assigned_users` and `assigned_permissions` in all core RBAC administrative commands.

This paper presents a corrected and simplified specification of RBAC. We use an object-oriented language with high-level operations over sets and relations and with a straightforward execution semantics; the language is also easier to read and write than Z. We use the same names and pre-conditions for commands and functions as in the standard.

We give a complete specification of core RBAC, explaining the methodology we used in developing it. We then give a complete specification of hierarchical RBAC, with an additional option for managing the relationship on roles. We also describe a specification of constrained RBAC, making extension relationships among RBAC components clear. Finally, we compare our specification with the standard and point out errors and unnecessary complications we found; we describe in particular the principles for developing clearer and simpler specifications more extensively, summarize our method and results for generating efficient implementations, and discuss future work.

The rest of this paper is organized as follows. Section 2 gives an overview of the ANSI standard for RBAC, and defines the language we use for the specification. Sections 3, 4, and 5 specify core RBAC, hierarchical RBAC, and constrained RBAC, respectively. Section 6 contains discussions and comparison with the standard. Section 7 concludes.

2 Preliminaries

ANSI standard for RBAC. The ANSI standard for RBAC has the following four components, where SSD (static separation of duties) and DSD (dynamic separation of duties) are also called constrained RBAC.

- core RBAC: core support for functionalities relating permissions, users, sessions, and roles.

- hierarchical RBAC: added support for a hierarchy of roles.

- SSD: added support for constraints on the roles of a user.

- DSD: added support for constraints on the active roles in a session.

For each component, the standard defines a reference model and a set of functionalities. The reference model refers to the basic data manipulated in the component, such as the set of roles, the set of users, and the relationship between roles and users. The functionalities are divided into four categories:

- administrative commands: commands for administrators to update RBAC sets and relations that are static, i.e., that are independent of user sessions.

- supporting system functions: functions that support user activities which are dynamic, i.e., that are performed as part of user sessions.

- review functions: mandatory functions for administrators to query RBAC sets and relations.

- advanced review functions: additional, optional functions for administrators to query RBAC sets and relations.

The standard uses the Z specification language [ISO, Spi92] to formally define the commands and functions, though the reference models and the relationships among components are described in English. We use the following language instead of Z for reasons explained below.

Language. Figure 1 defines the specification language used in this paper, where X^*, X^+, and $X^?$ denote that X occurs 0 or more, 1 or more, and 0 or 1 times, respectively.

A specification is a set of classes, each defining a set of fields and a set of methods, possibly with pre-conditions. Types may be specified not only for fields but also for variables, method parameters, and return values, although we omit those types from the grammar. We generally omit types when they can be inferred from the specification. Note the types for sets and tuples, the special **for** statement, and the expression for

$$
\begin{array}{lcl}
spec & ::= & class^+ \\[4pt]
class & ::= & \texttt{class } classname \ (\texttt{extends } classname^+)^? \\
 & & \quad (fieldname : type)^* \\
 & & \quad (methodname\,(varname^*) : (\texttt{pre-condition}: expr\,;\,)^? stmt\,)^* \\[4pt]
type & ::= & \texttt{set}(type) \mid \texttt{tuple}(type^+) \mid classname \mid \texttt{int} \mid \ ... \\[4pt]
stmt & ::= & \texttt{for } (varname \ \texttt{in} \ expr)^+ \mid expr : stmt \\
 & & \quad \mid \ expr\,.\,methodname\,(expr^*) \mid \texttt{return } expr \\
 & & \quad \mid \ expr\,.\,fieldname \ = \ expr \mid varname = expr \mid stmt\ stmt \mid \ ... \\[4pt]
expr & ::= & \{expr : (varname \ \texttt{in} \ expr)^+ \mid expr\} \\
 & & \quad \mid \ expr\,.\,methodname\,(expr^*) \\
 & & \quad \mid \ expr\,.\,fieldname \mid varname \mid expr \ \texttt{and} \ expr \mid \ ...
\end{array}
$$

$classname$, $fieldname$, $methodname$, $varname$: identifiers

Figure 1: Language.

set comprehension. We make substantial use of sets and tuples because they are well suited for high-level specifications.

For the loop **for** v_1 **in** $e_1, ..., v_k$ **in** $e_k \mid e : s$, each variable v_i enumerates elements of the set value of expression e_i, and for each combination of values of v_1 through v_k, if the value of Boolean expression e is **true**, then execute s. We read the entire statement as "for each v_1 in $e_1, ...,$ and v_k in e_k such that e, do s". We omit $\mid e$ when e is **true**.

For the set comprehension $\{e_0 : v_1$ **in** $e_1, ..., v_k$ **in** $e_k \mid e\}$, each variable v_i enumerates elements of the set value of expression e_i, and for each combination of values of v_1 through v_k, if the value of Boolean expression e is **true**, then the value of expression e_0 is an element of the resulting set. We read the expression as "the set of e_0 where v_1 is from $e_1, ...,$ and v_k is from e_k such that e". We omit $\mid e$ when e is **true**.

We use the following kinds of expressions for other operations on sets and tuples. We use standard infix set notation instead of object-oriented notation, although we express them in ASCII.

$\{x_1, ..., x_k\}$	a set with elements $x_1, ..., x_k$
$[x_1, ..., x_k]$	a tuple with elements $x_1, ..., x_k$
$\{[x_1, y_1], ..., [x_k, y_k]\}$	a binary relation, i.e., a set of 2-tuples, i.e., pairs
$S + T,\ S - T$	union and difference, respectively, of sets S and T
S subset T	whether S is a subset of or equal to T
x in S, x notin S	whether or not, respectively, x is an element of S
exists x in $S \mid e$	whether some element x in S satisfies condition e
forall x in $S \mid e$	whether every element x in S satisfies condition e
$\#S$	number of elements in S

They are mostly like expressions on sets and tuples in SETL [SDDS86]. We abbreviate **forall** x **in** $S \mid$ (**forall** y **in** $T \mid e$) as **forall** x **in** S, y **in** $T \mid$ e, and abbreviate **forall** x **in** S, y **in** $S \mid$ e as **forall** x, y **in** $S \mid$ e; similarly for **exists**.

Other statements and expressions are as in popular object-oriented languages such as Java. Only side-effect-free methods may be invoked in expressions, and their bodies are always of the form **return** $expr$.

We use the convention that this.*methodname*(*expr* *) and this.*fieldname* are abbreviated as *methodname*(*expr* *) and *fieldname*, respectively. We abbreviate **and** as a comma. We use indentation to indicate scoping. We use // to begin a comment that lasts till the end of the line.

Our language differs from the Z specification language used in the ANSI standard for RBAC in four main ways: (1) it supports modularity and inheritance, which is needed for describing a system with multiple components where a component may extend others, (2) it is executable—the semantics of a specification corresponds to a straightforward implementation of the specification, (3) it is easy to read, especially set comprehension, since the subexpressions appear in the same order as in a natural English description, and (4) it is easy to write, since it uses only ASCII characters.

3 Specification of core RBAC

We specify the core RBAC component as a class CoreRBAC, whose fields specify the reference model, and whose methods specify the functionalities.

```
class CoreRBAC:
  ... // reference model
  ... // functionalities
```

We define the following sets and relations for the reference model of core RBAC, explained below.

```
OBJS:      set(Object)                                    // an operation-object pair
OPS:       set(Operation)                                 // is called a permission.
USERS:     set(User)
ROLES:     set(Role)
PR:        set(tuple(tuple(Operation,Object),Role)) // PR subset (OBJS * OPS) * ROLES
UR:        set(tuple(User,Role))                          // UR subset USERS * ROLES
SESSIONS:  set(Session)
SU:        set(tuple(Session,User))                       // SU subset SESSIONS * USERS
SR:        set(tuple(Session,Role))                       // SR subset SESSIONS * ROLES
```

A system has sets of objects, operations, users, roles, and sessions; their elements are of types Object, Operation, User, Role, and Session, respectively. A operation-object pair, called a permission, denotes an allowed operation on an object. A permission-role pair in PR denotes a permission assigned to a role. A user-role pair in UR denotes a user assigned to a role. A session-user pair in SU denotes a session and the unique user of the session. A session-role pair in SR denotes a session and a role active in the session.

We define below the functionalities summarized in the following table for core RBAC.

Categories	Core RBAC Functionalities
administrative commands	add/delete user/role, assign/deassign user, grant/revoke permission
supporting system functions	create/delete session, add/drop active role, check access
review functions	assigned users/roles
advanced review functions	role/user permissions, session roles/permissions, role/user ops on obj

Administrative commands. Adding an element to a set of users or roles (AddUser, AddRole) can be specified in a similar way; same with adding an element to a relation (AssignUser adding to UR, and GrantPermission adding to PR, except that the latter uses nested tuples).

```
AddUser(user):
  pre-condition: user notin USERS;
  USERS = USERS + {user}
```

```
AddRole(role):
  pre-condition: role notin ROLES;
  ROLES = ROLES + {role}

AssignUser(user,role):
  pre-condition: user in USERS, role in ROLES, [user,role] notin UR;
  UR = UR + {[user, role]}

GrantPermission(operation, object, role):
  pre-condition: operation in OPS, object in OBJS, role in ROLES,
                 [[operation,object],role] notin PR;
  PR = PR + {[[operation,object],role]}
```

Deleting an element is symmetric to adding an element, but possibly with two kinds of additional updates. First, if an element is deleted from a set, then from all relations defined using the set, all pairs that contain the deleted element must be deleted. Second, `DeleteUser`, `DeleteRole`, and `DeassignUser` may affect `SESSIONS`, because sessions are created by users and have active roles, and must satisfy the constraint that a session can have a role only if the user of the session is assigned that role. Specifically, `DeleteUser` may either delete associated sessions or leave the sessions to terminate normally; `DeleteRole` and `DeassignUser` have a third option of deleting only the specified role from the sessions. As in the standard, we formally specify only the first option, i.e., deleting all associated sessions, for all three operations, illustrating both kinds of additional updates; the other two options are simpler to specify.

```
DeleteUser(user):
  pre-condition: user in USERS;
  UR = UR - {[user,r]: r in ROLES}     // maintain UR
  for s in SESSIONS | [s,user] in SU:  // maintain SESSIONS
    DeleteSession(user,s)              // DeleteSession is defined below
  USERS = USERS - {user}              // update last for pre-condition of DeleteSession

DeleteRole(role):
  pre-condition: role in ROLES;
  PR = PR - {[[op,obj],role]: op in OPS, obj in OBJS}         // maintain PR
  UR = UR - {[u,role]: u in USERS}                           // maintain UR
  for s in SESSIONS, u in USERS | [s,u] in SU, [s,role] in SR: // maintain SESSIONS
    DeleteSession(u,s)
  ROLES = ROLES - {role}                  // update last for update of SR in DeleteSession

DeassignUser(user, role):
  pre-condition: user in USERS, role in ROLES, [user,role] in UR;
  UR = UR - {[user,role]}
  for s in SESSIONS | [s,user] in SU, [s,role] in SR: // maintain SESSIONS
    DeleteSession(user,s)

RevokePermission(operation, object, role):
  pre-condition: operation in OPS, object in OBJS, role in ROLES,
                 [[operation,object],role] in PR;
  PR = PR - {[[operation,object],role]}
```

Supporting system functions. `CreateSession` creates a session for a user with an initial set of active roles; it first checks that the user is assigned those roles, and then adds the appropriate elements to SU, SR, and SESSIONS. DeleteSession deletes all elements of SU, SR, and SESSIONS that are associated with the session.

```
CreateSession(user, session, ars):
  pre-condition: user in USERS, session notin SESSIONS,
                 ars subset AssignedRoles(user); // AssignedRoles is defined below
  SU = SU + {[session,user]}
  SR = SR + {[session,r]: r in ars}
  SESSIONS = SESSIONS + {session}

DeleteSession(user, session):
  pre-condition: user in USERS, session in SESSIONS, [session,user] in SU;
  SU = SU - {[session,user]}
  SR = SR - {[session,r]: r in ROLES} // maintain SR
  SESSIONS = SESSIONS - {session}
```

Adding and deleting active roles adds to and deletes from SR, respectively; adding an active role also checks that the user of the session is assigned that role. Note the last condition calls AssignedRoles, as done in CreateSession, but it can also be written as user in AssignedUsers(role) or as [user,role] in UR.

```
AddActiveRole(user, session, role):
  pre-condition: user in USERS, session in SESSIONS, role in ROLES,
                 [session,user] in SU, [session,role] notin SR,
                 role in AssignedRoles(user);
  SR = SR + {[session,role]}

DropActiveRole(user, session, role):
  pre-condition: user in USERS, session in SESSIONS, role in ROLES,
                 [session,user] in SU, [session,role] in SR;
  SR = SR - {[session,role]}
```

CheckAccess checks whether an operation on an object is allowed in a session, i.e., whether the session has an active role that is assigned the operation-object pair as a permission.

```
CheckAccess(session, operation, object):
  pre-condition: session in SESSIONS, operation in OPS, object in OBJS;
  return exists r in ROLES | [session,r] in SR, [[operation,object],r] in PR
```

Review functions and advanced review functions.   These functions are queries on the basic sets and relations.

Most of them (AssignedUser, AssignedRoles, RolePermissions, SessionRoles) are over one relation, i.e., given a value for the left or right component of a relation, find all associated values for the other component in the relation. For example, the first two are review functions defined by:

```
AssignedUsers(role):
  pre-condition: role in ROLES;
  return {u: u in USERS | [u,role] in UR}

AssignedRoles(user):
  pre-condition: user in USERS;
  return {r: r in ROLES | [user,r] in UR}
```

Two functions (UserPermissions, SessionPermissions) are over two relations, i.e., given a value for one component of a relation, equate the other component of the relation with one component of a second relation, and find all associated values for the other component of the second relation. Two other functions (`RoleOperationsOnObject`, `UserOperationsOnObject`) require nested tuples but are otherwise similar to the above functions. All advanced review functions are defined below:

```
RolePermissions(role):
  pre-condition: role in ROLES;
  return {[op,obj]: op in OPS, obj in OBJS | [[op,obj],role] in PR}

UserPermissions(user):
  pre-condition: user in USERS;
  return {[op,obj]: r in ROLES, op in OPS, obj in OBJS | [user,r] in UR, [[op,obj],r] in PR}

SessionRoles(session):
  pre-condition: session in SESSIONS;
  return {r: r in ROLES | [session,r] in SR}

SessionPermissions(session):
  pre-condition: session in SESSIONS;
  return {[op,obj]: r in ROLES, op in OPS, obj in OBJS | [session,r] in SR, [[op,obj],r] in PR}

RoleOperationsOnObject(role, object):
  pre-condition: role in ROLES, object in OBJS;
  return {op: op in OPS | [[op,object],role] in PR}

UserOperationsOnObject(user, object):
  pre-condition: user in USERS, object in OBJS;
  return {op: r in ROLES, op in OPS | [user,r] in UR, [[op,object],r] in PR}
```

4   Specification of hierarchical RBAC

Hierarchical RBAC allows a role to inherit permissions from other roles without being granted those permissions directly. The ANSI standard for hierarchical RBAC has two sub-components: general hierarchy, which allows multiple inheritance, and limited hierarchy, which allows only single inheritance. For both of them, the standard requires that the inheritance relation be acyclic.

We consider the same two subcomponents, for consistency with the standard. However, we see little motivation for limited hierarchy. Single inheritance in object-oriented languages avoids the problem of a class inheriting conflicting definitions of a method, but that problem does not arise in role hierarchy. While inheriting from more than one role may give a role too much power, a role may acquire too much power from other operations anyway, so other controls, such as separation of duties in constrained RBAC, are used to prevent this.

We also consider a third option, which we call unrestricted inheritance, where the inheritance relation is unrestricted and thus may contain cycles. Although managerial hierarchies are acyclic, roles and their relationships do not always mimic managerial hierarchies, and the extra flexibility from allowing cycles may be useful. A cycle means that all the roles in the cycle are in an equivalence class and indeed have the same permissions.

For general and limited hierarchical RBAC, we define the following two classes, one for each of the subcomponents, where the new and redefined parts are specified below.

```
class GeneralHierarchicalRBAC extends CoreRBAC:
  ... // new inheritance relation in reference model
  ... // new and redefined functionalities
class LimitedHierarchicalRBAC extends GeneralHierarchicalRBAC:
  ... // redefined functionalities
```

The third option discussed above could be defined as a new subcomponent that extends core RBAC, and general hierarchical RBAC could extend it instead of core RBAC.

We define the inheritance relation INH to be a set of role pairs given explicitly by administrators, not the reflexive-transitive closure of the role pairs given.

```
INH: set(tuple(Role,Role))
```

A pair [r1,r2] in INH denotes that r1 inherits from r2; the implication is that r1 should in effect have all the permissions that r2 has, without having to be assigned them directly. We call r1 the heir and r2 the bearer. We use INH* to denote the transitive-reflexive closure of INH. The acyclicity requirement is

$$\texttt{forall r1, r2 in ROLES | [r1,r2] in INH*, [r2,r1] in INH*} \Rightarrow \texttt{r1=r2}$$

and the single inheritance requirement is

$$\texttt{forall r, r1, r2 in ROLES | [r,r1] in INH, [r,r2] in INH} \Rightarrow \texttt{r1=r2}$$

The functionalities of general hierarchical RBAC are the same as those of core RBAC except for the changes summarized in the following table, where + indicates additional functionalities, and ∓ indicates redefined functionalities.

Categories	General Hierarchical RBAC Functionalities
administrative commands	+ add/delete inheritance, + add ascendant/descendant
supporting system functions	∓ create session, ∓ add active role
review functions	+ authorized users/roles
advanced review functions	∓ role/user permissions, ∓ role/user ops on obj

The functionalities of limited hierarchical RBAC are the same as those of general hierarchical RBAC except for a modification to the administrative command AddInheritance. In fact, all functionalities except for AddInheritance are the same for unrestricted inheritance, general hierarchy, and limited hierarchy, so we describe them together below.

The administrative command AddInheritance simply adds a new pair to INH for unrestricted inheritance; for general hierarchy, its precondition checks acyclicity, and for limited hierarchy, also checks single inheritance. DeleteInheritance simply removes a pair from INH. AddAscendant and AddDescendant are self explanatory, although we would call them AddHeir and AddBearer, respectively.

```
AddInheritance(heir,bearer): // for unrestricted inheritance
   pre-condition: heir in ROLES, bearer in ROLES, [heir,bearer] notin INH;
   INH = INH + {[heir,bearer]}

AddInheritance(heir,bearer): // for general hierarchy
   ... // same as above except to add, in the pre-condition,
       // [bearer,hier] notin INH*, to check acyclicity

AddInheritance(heir,bearer): // for limited hierarchy
   ... // same as above except to also add, in the pre-condition,
       // not exists r in ROLES | [heir,r] in INH, to check single inheritance

DeleteInheritance(heir,bearer):
   pre-condition: heir in ROLES, bearer in ROLES, [heir,bearer] in INH;
   INH = INH - {[heir,bearer]}

AddAscendant(heir,bearer):
   AddRole(heir)
```

```
AddInheritance(heir,bearer)

AddDescendant(bearer,heir):
  AddRole(bearer)
  AddInheritance(heir,bearer)
```

The supporting system functions `CreateSession` and `AddActiveRole` are minimally modified to call a new review function; this change allows a user to activate inherited roles. Following the standard, the function `CheckAccess` is inherited from core RBAC and does not use the inheritance relation; to use a permission from inherited roles, a user must find an authorized role that is assigned that permission and explicitly activate that role for the session during `CreateSession` or using `AddActiveRole`.

```
CreateSession(user, session, ars):
  ... // same as in CoreRBAC except that, in the precondition,
      // AssignedRoles is replaced with AuthorizedRoles, which is defined below

AddActiveRole(user, session, role):
  ... // same change as for CreateSession above
```

New review functions (`AuthorizedUsers`, `AuthorizedRoles`) and redefined advanced review functions (`RolePermissions`, `UserPermissions`, `RoleOperationsOnObject`, `UserOperationsOnObject`) use the inheritance relation together with UR and PR. Note that `SessionRoles` and `SessionPermissions` are inherited from core RBAC and do not use the inheritance relation, consistent with the definition of `CheckAccess`.

```
AuthorizedUsers(role):
  pre-condition: role in ROLES;
  return {u: heir in ROLES, u in USERS | [heir,role] in INH*, [u,heir] in UR}

AuthorizedRoles(user):
  pre-condition: user in USERS;
  return {r: heir in ROLES, r in ROLES | [user,heir] in UR, [heir,r] in INH*}

RolePermissions(role):
  pre-condition: role in ROLES;
  return {[op,obj]: bearer in ROLES, op in OPS, obj in OBJS |
                    [role,bearer] in INH*, [[op,obj],bearer] in PR}

UserPermissions(user):
  pre-condition: user in USERS;
  return {[op,obj]: heir in ROLES, bearer in ROLES, op in OPS, obj in OBJS |
                    [user,heir] in UR, [heir,bearer] in INH*, [[op,obj],bearer] in PR}

RoleOperationsOnObject(role, object):
  pre-condition: role in ROLES, object in OBJS;
  return {op: bearer in ROLES, op in OPS |
              [role,bearer] in INH*, [[op,object],bearer] in PR}

UserOperationsOnObject(user, object):
  pre-condition: user in USERS, object in OBJS;
  return {op: heir in ROLES, bearer in ROLES, op in OPS | [user,heir] in UR,
              [heir,bearer] in INH*, [[op,object],bearer] in PR}
```

5   Specification of constrained RBAC

Constrained RBAC supports separation of duty, whose purpose is to reduce fraud by limiting the power of individual users (statically constrained) or individual sessions (dynamically constrained), so fraud can be perpetrated only through collusion among multiple users or multiple sessions.

Static separation of duty.   A static separation of duty (SSD) constraint is characterized by a name, used to identify it in administrative commands, a set `rs` of roles, and a natural number `n`, called the cardinality, such that `1 <= n <= #rs-1`. In our specification, the meaning of an SSD constraint is that a user can be assigned to `n` or fewer roles from `rs`. We find this interpretation more intuitive than the one in the standard, which says that `2 <= n <= #rs` and that a user can be assigned to fewer than `n` roles from `rs`. Our formal model of an SSD constraint includes a set `SsdNAMES` of SSD constraint names, a relation `SsdNR` that relates a name in `SsdNAMES` to a role in the associated role set, and a relation `SsdNC` that relates a name in `SsdNAMES` to its unique associated cardinality.

```
SsdNAMES:  set(SsdName)
SsdNR:     set(tuple(SsdName, Role))
SsdNC:     set(tuple(SsdName, int))
```

SSD constraints can be added to core RBAC or general or limited hierarchical RBAC. In core RBAC with SSD constraints, the assignment of roles to users must satisfy

```
forall u in USERS, [name,n] in SsdNC |
   #{r: r in AssignedRoles(u) | [name,r] in SsdNR} <= n
```

In general or limited hierarchical RBAC with SSD constraints, the user assignment and inheritance relation must satisfy the same constraints except with `AssignedRoles` replaced with `AuthorizedRoles`.

The functionalities are described below. We omit the detailed definitions because they are straightforward aside from the points explained.

Core RBAC with SSD constraints extends core RBAC. All administrative commands are inherited except that `AssignedUser` is redefined to also check that the updated user assignment would satisfy the SSD constraints. New administrative commands (`Create/DeleteSsdSet`, `Add/DeleteSsdRoleMember`, `SetSsdSetCardinality`) are added to create, modify, and delete SSD constraints; the non-deletion commands check that the new or updated SSD constraint would be satisfied, and that the cardinality would be in the required range. New review functions (`SsdRoleSets`, `SsdRoleSetRoles`, `SsdRoleSetCardinality`) are introduced to query SSD constraints. Supporting system functions and advanced review functions are simply inherited.

General hierarchical RBAC with SSD constraints is defined similarly, except that (1) it extends general hierarchical RBAC and redefines also command `AddInheritance` to check that the SSD constraints would be satisfied, and (2) it also extends core RBAC with SSD constraints and redefines non-deletion commands. These redefinitions simply use `AuthorizedRoles` in place of `AssignedRoles`.

Limited hierarchical RBAC with SSD constraints extends general hierarchical RBAC with SSD constraints except that `AddInheritance` is redefined to add a check for single inheritance.

Dynamic separation of duty.   A dynamic separation of duty (DSD) constraint is also characterized by a name, a set `rs` of roles, and a cardinality `n` such that `1 <= n <= #rs-1`. In our specification, the meaning is that a session can have `n` or fewer roles from `rs` that are active. Our interpretation of the cardinality is different than the interpretation in the standard, just like for SSD constraints. Our formal model of DSD constraints is very similar to our model of SSD constraints.

```
DsdNAMES: set(DsdName)
DsdNR:    set(tuple(DsdName, Role))
DsdNC:    set(tuple(DsdName, int))
```

DSD constraints can be added to core RBAC, general or limited hierarchical RBAC. In all of them, the following condition must be satisfied.

```
forall s in SESSIONS, [name,n] in DsdNC |
  #{r: r in SessionRoles(s) | [name,r] in DsdNR} <= n
```

Core RBAC with DSD constraints extends core RBAC. All administrative commands are inherited. New administrative commands are added to create, modify, and delete DSD constraints, just as for SSD above, except that DSD constraints are checked instead of SSD constraints. All supporting system functions are inherited except that `CreateSession` and `AddActiveRole` are redefined to also check that the DSD constraints would be satisfied. New review functions are introduced to query DSD constraints, similar to those for SSD above. Advanced review functions are simply inherited.

General hierarchical RBAC with DSD constraints is defined similarly, except that (1) it extends general hierarchical RBAC and simply inherits all definitions, and (2) it extends core RBAC with DSD constraints and redefines `CreateSession` and `AddActiveRole` to use `AuthorizedRoles` in place of `AssignedRoles`.

Limited hierarchical RBAC with DSD constraints extends general hierarchical RBAC with DSD constraints except that `AddInheritance` is the same as in limited hierarchical RBAC.

6 Discussion and comparison with the ANSI standard

We discuss the principles we use for developing clearer and simpler specifications with higher assurance for correctness. Compared with the standard, we corrected a number of errors and eliminated a number of complications and redundancies, most of which appear to be caused by efficiency considerations.

Maintaining basic, not derived, sets and relations. For clarity and simplicity, only basic data should be maintained in specifications, where basic data refers to data given and modified externally, in contrast to derived data that can be computed from basic data. Following this principle, we found an error in hierarchical RBAC, unnecessary complications in core RBAC and hierarchical RBAC, and omissions in the standard.

The error is that the pre-condition of the `AddInheritance` command in limited hierarchical RBAC is always false, due to the incorrect definition of the inheritance relation in terms of its reflexive-transitive closure. The standard maintains the derived relation INH* (denoted RH in the standard) instead of the basic relation INH. This makes some functionalities more efficient, but it requires giving a definition of INH in terms of INH*. The definition given in Section 5.2 of the standard is incorrect, because it does not remove the reflexive relationships and therefore does not completely undo the effects of the reflexive-transitive closure. This makes the pre-condition of `AddInheritance` in limited hierarchical RBAC always false, and could also affect other uses of the direct inheritance relation. The most straightforward remedy is to maintain the basic relation INH and use INH* as needed, as done in Section 4 of this paper. Fixing the incorrect definition is not as good a remedy, because it results in an unnecessarily complicated specification. Maintaining INH instead of INH* yields much simpler definitions of `AddInheritance` and `DeleteInheritance`.

Maintaining INH instead of INH* also provides a more natural semantics for `DeleteInheritance`. For example, consider this sequence of calls: `AddInheritance(r1,r2)`, `AddInheritance(r1,r3)`, `AddInheritance(r2,r3)`, `DeleteInheritance(r2,r3)`. With our specification, the last two calls cancel each other out exactly; in other words, `AddInheritance` and `DeleteInheritance` are inverses. With the definition in the standard, the call to `DeleteInheritance` also removes the inheritance relation between r1 and r3.

The other main unnecessary complications in core RBAC are that five of the seven mapping functions defined in the reference model (`assigned_users`, `assigned_permissions`, `Op`, `Ob`, and `avail_session_perms`) are unnecessary, and so are all updates to `assigned_users` and `assigned_permissions` in all administrative commands, so we eliminated them. These mapping functions are not used in the rest of the specification. In fact, the functions corresponding to `assigned_users`, `assigned_permissions`, and `avail_session_perms` are also defined as review or advanced review functions, called `AssignedUsers`, `RolePermissions`, and `SessionPermissions`, respectively; the other two can be defined as review functions too if needed. Note that incrementally updating the result of a query, such as `AssignedUsers`, is needed only for efficiency reasons, because the result can always be computed from scratch; such updates need not be specified because they can be derived from the query and how the data it depends on are updated, as we do in [LSG$^+$05].

Similarly, we removed the two mapping functions, `authorized_permissions` and `authorized_users`, in the reference model of hierarchical RBAC. Another small simplification we made to core RBAC is that we removed the set PERMS, which equals OPS × OBJS, so the few uses of PERMS are replaced with uses of OPS and OBJS.

Omissions of functionalities were found because our design principle allows one to freely update and query basic data as needed; we did not add them to the specifications earlier to avoid distraction from the main concepts. First, basic data is given and updated externally, so functionalities should be provided for appropriate updates. The standard lacks commands to add and delete objects and operations. These commands can be defined similarly to commands for adding and deleting users and roles. Similarly, some query functions seem needed but not provided. For example, in hierarchical RBAC, since a user must explicitly activate an inherited role to use its permissions, one needs a function `PermissionRoles` to find the set of roles granted a given permission and, furthermore, a function `UserPermissionRoles` to find the set of roles authorized to the user and granted the given permission:

```
PermissionRoles(operation,object):
  pre-condition: operation in OPS, object in OBJS;
  return {r: r in ROLES | [[operation,object],r] in PR}


UserPermissionRoles(user,operation,object):
  pre-condition: user in USERS, operation in OPS, object in OBJS;
  return {r: r in ROLES | r in AuthorizedRoles(user), [[operation,object],r] in PR}
```

Query functions should probably also include most of the mapping functions in the standard that do not have corresponding review or advanced review functions. For example, one other mapping function in core RBAC (besides the five eliminated), called `session_users` (though could perhaps be called `session_user`), maps a session to its unique user; this could be a useful review function.

There are two related problems. First, some of the query functions are needed by users as well as administrators, so it is not clear whether they should classified as supporting system functions or review or advanced review functions. Second, it is not clear what criteria are used in the standard to distinguish review functions from advanced review functions. For example, `SessionPermissions` is essentially the operation needed for efficient `CheckAccess` (discussed with other simplifications below), but it is only an optional advanced review function, not a mandatory review function.

Using relations instead of mapping functions.   Relations should generally be used instead of mapping functions. Relations can be updated more readily, and information in them can easily be used as mappings from any components to other components. In particular, a binary relation can be easily used as two mapping functions—from left to right, and right to left. Following this principle, we replaced the two other mapping functions in core RBAC (besides the five eliminated), `session_user` and `session_roles`, with relations SU and SR, respectively. This simplified maintenance of these values in all supporting system functions and uses of these values in deletion commands, as discussed below. We also replaced mapping functions with relations in constrained RBAC, which gives similar benefits.

To illustrate the benefit of easy maintenance, consider the command `AddActiveRole(user, session, role)`. In the standard, it updates `session_roles` by retrieving the current value of `session_roles(session)` inserting `role` in the returned set to obtain the new set of active roles, removing the current entry for this session from `session_roles`, and then adding an entry to `session_roles` that maps this session to the new set of active roles. The formula to do this is too long to fit on one line. In our specification, the update is simply `SR = SR + {[session,role]}`.

To illustrate the benefit of binary relations being easily usable in both directions, consider `DeleteRole`, which calls `DeleteSession` to delete sessions in which the role being deleted is active. There is an error in the standard here: `DeleteSession` has two parameters, a user and a session, but the call site in `DeleteRole` passes only one argument, namely, the session. To fix this, `user_sessions` (which is not defined but is used in multiple functionalities in the standard) needs to be used in reverse to find the associated user. Using a function in reverse is awkward. In our specification, the relation `SU` can easily be used in both directions.

For statically constrained RBAC, the standard represents SSD constraints as a set `SSD` of names together with mapping functions `ssd_set` and `ssd_card` that map each name to the associated role set and cardinality, respectively. We replaced the two mapping functions with two relations, `SsdNR` and `SsdNC`. This leads to simplified specifications of the functionalities for manipulating SSD constraints; the simplifications are similar to those described above. We did a similar replacement for DSD constraints in dynamically constrained RBAC.

Other simplifications.   One kind of simplification is to replace a complicated formula with a more straight-forward, shorter, and logically equivalent formula. Another kind of simplification is to call other defined functions, instead of repeating the bodies of those functions. One can also combine these two kinds of simplifications.

We did the first kind of simplification for all the more complicated functionalities of statically constrained RBAC. Specifically, in administrative commands, both redefined commands (`AssignUser` and `AddInheritance`) and three of the five new commands (`CreateSsdSet`, `AddSsdRoleMember`, `SetSsdSetCardinality`) contain similar conditions that check whether the attempted operation would lead to the user assignment violating the SSD constraints. As written in the standard, all of these conditions are hard to read, because they involve a triple or quadruple subscript and an implicit universal quantification over `subset`, and because they are structured much differently than the informal explanation of SSD constraints in Section 5.3.1 of the standard. In our specification, all of these conditions are replaced with simpler ones based closely on the informal explanation, like our formula for SSD constraints in Section 5 of this paper.

We did the second kind of simplification in the pre-condition of `CreateSession` and `AddActiveRole` in core RBAC and hierarchical RBAC. For example, the pre-condition of `CreateSession(user,session,ars)` in core RBAC checks whether `user` is assigned all of the roles in `ars`. In the standard, this condition includes repeating the body of the review function `AssignedRoles`. In our specification, that expression is replaced with a call to `AssignedRoles`; this generally makes the specification shorter and easier to read. The benefit shows up more when `CreateSession` in hierarchical RBAC needs a more complicated pre-condition, and one can simply replace `AssignedRoles` with `AuthorizedRoles` in the definition. Similarly, also for consistency, we call `AssignedRoles` and `AuthorizedRoles` in the pre-condition of `AddActiveRole` in core RBAC and hierarchical RBAC, respectively. Note that the standard uses the mapping function `authorized_users` in the pre-condition of `AddActiveRole` in hierarchical RBAC; `user in authorized_users(role)` equals `user in AuthorizedUsers(role)`, which equals our `role in AuthorizedRoles(user)`.

For combining both kinds of simplifications, consider `CheckAccess(session,operation,object)`, which returns the Boolean value of the following expression.

```
exists r in ROLES | [session,r] in SR, [[operation,object],r] in PR
```

This expression equals at least the following three expressions that use advanced review functions, although, here, the bodies of those functions are not exactly the same as the replaced fragments; the last one clearly looks neatest:

```
exists r in ROLES | [session,r] in SR, [operation,object] in RolePermissions(r)
exists r in SessionRoles(session) | [operation,object] in RolePermissions(r)
[operation,object] in SessionPermissions(session)
```

One could also use a review or advanced review function in the definition of another function; even when such rewrite does not yield a more concise definition, one might find that in an extended component, only the first function has to be redefined instead of both. For example, if in core RBAC one uses `RolePermissions` and `RoleOperationsOnObject` in the definitions of `UserPermissions` and `UserOperationsOnObject`, respectively, then in hierarchical RBAC, only the first two have to be redefined, not all four. We did not do these rewrites, since we felt that they are not more straightforward, even though they look neater—one must understand the functions called to understand the caller.

Implementation. Our specification can be translated straightforwardly into a programming language that supports objects and classes as well as sets and tuples. We chose Python (http://www.python.org/), which has excellent support for these. This provides an executable specification, useful for validation and prototyping. This straightforward implementation is inefficient, because it always computes expensive queries, such as the set of roles satisfying the conditions in `CheckAccess`, from scratch.

We have developed a powerful method for optimization by incrementalization, which analyzes programs to identify expensive queries and updates to their parameters, i.e., values on which the query result depends, and transforms the programs to incrementally maintain the results of expensive queries with respect to updates to their parameters [LSG+05]. We applied a prototype implementation of this method for Python to our straightforward implementation of core RBAC, and obtained an efficient implementation. The incrementalized implementation incrementally maintains the result of expensive queries, including the set of roles satisfying the conditions in `CheckAccess`, and the results of all review and advanced review functions, such as `AssignedUsers`. The experiments reported in [LSG+05] confirm the effectiveness of this method, showing improvements from polynomial time in the straightforward implementation, to constant time in the incrementalized implementation, for `CheckAccess`.

An executable specification of core RBAC is at ftp://ftp.cs.sunysb.edu/pub/liu/coreRBAC.py. We plan to make an executable specification of the entire RBAC available.

7   Conclusion

To summarize, this paper shows how a corrected and simplified specification can be developed following important principles. In addition to correcting a number of errors, we made the following main simplifications to the specification in the standard. For core RBAC, we eliminated five of the seven mapping functions and maintenance of `assigned_users` and `assigned_permissions` in all administrative commands, replaced the two other mapping functions with relations and simplified their maintenance in all supporting system functions. For hierarchical RBAC, we eliminated the two mapping functions, maintain the direct inheritance relation instead of the transitive inheritance relation, and simplified `AddInheritance` and `DeleteInheritance`. In constrained RBAC, we simplified the SSD constraints, and thus all the commands and functions that check them, and we replaced two mapping functions with relations, which also leads to simplified definitions of some functionalities.

Remaining issues. There are several ways that our current specification and the RBAC model could be further improved.

First, for specifying `DeleteUser`, `DeleteRole`, and `DeassignUser`, the standard informally describes multiple acceptable alternatives but formally specifies only one of them, and we did the same. The other alternatives should also be formally specified, but more importantly, the challenge is to find the best way to specify all the alternatives declaratively, instead of calling `DeleteSession` in a loop.

A related issue is that most administrative commands perform a primary update accompanied by secondary updates needed to preserve consistency among the sets and relations. For example, in `DeleteUser`, the update to `USERS` is accompanied by an update to `UR` and a sequence of calls to `DeleteSession`, which updates `SU`, `SR`, and `SESSIONS`. A better approach would be to express the consistency constraints explicitly and declaratively, and systematically derive the secondary updates needed to preserve them.

In many applications, separation of duty constraints are most naturally expressed in terms of permission to perform multiple specified operations on a single object or in a single transaction. It would be useful to extend the specification to support this. Such separation of duty constraints cannot be reliably enforced by the static or dynamic separation of duty constraints in the current specification, because they can be circumvented by updates to the user-role assignment and use of multiple sessions, respectively.

Finally, formal verification of correctness properties of the specification would provide even higher assurance of its correctness.

Acknowledgment

Michael Gorbovitski implemented the method for optimization by incrementalization; he also first used `AssignedRoles` in the pre-condition of `CreateSession`. Tom Rothamel helped with experiments for optimization by incrementalization. Hongxu Cai implemented a clean version of core RBAC and hierarchical RBAC in Python and described a number of inconsistencies in the standard. They all helped confirm some of the errors and complications found in the standard. Amit Sasturkar provided helpful comments on a draft of this paper. Chen Wang found an error in the specification in a draft of this paper.

References

[Ame]   American National Standards Institute, Inc. Role-based access control. ANSI INCITS 359-2004. http://csrc.nist.gov/rbac/.

[FK92]   D. Ferraiolo and R. Kuhn. Role-based access control. In *Proceedings of the NIST-NSA National Computer Security Conference*, pages 554–563, 1992.

[FSG+01] David F. Ferraiolo, Ravi Sandhu, Serban Gavrila, D. Richard Kuhn, and Ramaswamy Chandramouli. Proposed NIST standard for role-based access control. *ACM Transactions on Information and Systems Security*, 4(3):224–274, 2001.

[GB98]   A. Gavrila and J. Barkley. Formal specification for RBAC user/role and role relationship management. In *Proceedings of the 3rd ACM Workshop on Role Based Access Control*, pages 81–90, 1998.

[ISO]   International Organization for Standardization. Z formal specification notation – Syntax, type system and semantics. ISO/IEC 13568:2002.

[JT00]   T. Jaeger and J. Tidswell. Rebuttal to the NIST RBAC model proposal. In *Proceedings of the 5th ACM Workshop on Role Based Access Control*, pages 66–66, Berlin, Germany, July 2000.

[LHM84] Carl E. Landwehr, Constance L. Heitmeyer, and John McLean. A security model for military message systems. *ACM Trans. Comput. Syst.*, 2(3):198–222, 1984.

[LSG+05] Yanhong A. Liu, Scott D. Stoller, Michael Gorbovitski, Tom Rothamel, and Yanni E. Liu. Incrementalization across object abstraction. In *Proceedings of the 20th ACM Conference Object-Oriented Programming, Systems, Languages, and Applications*, San Diego, California, Oct. 2005.

[SDDS86] J. T. Schwartz, R. B. K. Dewar, E. Dubinsky, and E. Schonberg. *Programming with Sets: An Introduction to SETL*. Springer-Verlag, New York, 1986.

[SFK00] R. Sandhu, D. Ferraiolo, and R. Kuhn. The NIST model for role-based access control: Towards a unified standard. In *Proceedings of the 5th ACM Workshop on Role-Based Access Control*, pages 47–63, Berlin, Germany, July 2000.

[Spi92] J. M. Spivey. *The Z Notation: A Reference Manual*. Prentice-Hall, 2nd edition, 1992.

Analysis, Modeling, and Simulation
for Networked Systems[†]

Mostafa Bassiouni

Vicki M. Bier

Pascale Carayon

Jagdish Chandra

Ratan K. Guha

Sara B. Kraemer

Stephen M. Robinson

Daniel G. Schwartz

Sara Stoecklin

Abstract

This paper summarizes the work of a DOD University Research Initiative project focused on the development of models, tools, and environments for better understanding and management of networked, interacting systems comprising critical national infrastructure, including computer and information systems. Several threats to the reliability and security of these systems arise from causes that may be either deliberate (intrusion, malicious damage) or non-deliberate (human error, environmental hazards). The project involves eleven senior investigators at four universities, as well as numerous graduate students, and it covers a topical breadth unusual for an effort of this size.

1 Introduction

Many key elements of our critical infrastructures, including those relevant to DOD, use computer and information systems and software for interfacing and coordination of subsystems representing different functions of the overall system. As a result, they are exposed to severe reliability and security problems. These issues are not limited just to external threats and malicious intrusions, but also include human failures or environmental conditions, to which many of these systems are equally susceptible. In order to better understand both the benefits of and the vulnerabilities in such interdependent systems, there is a need for versatile models, robust analysis tools, and interactive simulation environments. Developing these model, tools, and environments is the focus of a DOD URI project whose work is summarized in this paper. The project comprises a number of subject area teams, each involving one or more of the eleven senior investigators along with graduate students from the participating universities (Florida State University, The George Washington University, the University of Central Florida, and the University of Wisconsin-Madison).

[†] The research reported here was sponsored by the U. S. Army Research Office under Grant DAAG19-01-1-0502.

Our focus in this project is on networked information systems including computer and communication architectures. In particular, for the past three years our interdisciplinary team has concentrated on the following broad but interrelated topics:

1. Identification, detection, and characterization of vulnerabilities and failures in networked systems,
2. Threat analysis and risk management in networked information systems,
3. Human factors analysis in information assurance,
4. Distributed simulation and trade-off studies,
5. Program integration and information exchange.

This paper presents an overview of our work in the first four of these areas, together with references to papers giving additional detail.

2 Identification, detection, and characterization of vulnerabilities and failures in networked systems

The connections within an entity composed of networked systems introduce new complexity into the effort to understand ways in which the entity may fail, or may be vulnerable to attack by hostile forces. This part of the research program attempts to develop concepts and tools to deal with this complexity. In this section we discuss three areas of such development: risk management strategies for events that may have low probability but can cause great disruption or damage, identifying and characterizing optimal strategies for defense against sabotage, and stability analysis using stochastic dynamic hybrid system models.

2.1 Risk management strategies for high consequence/low probability events

In managing risks due to high-consequence, low-probability events, risk assessment is necessary (Zimmerman and Bier, 2002), since more intuitive approaches to risk management using trial and error are likely to incur high costs. In this context, risk assessment refers to "a systematic approach to organizing and analyzing scientific knowledge and information for potentially hazardous activities or for substances that might pose risks under specified circumstances" (National Research Council, 1994). The overall objective of risk assessment is to estimate the risk of adverse health, safety, environmental, economic, and other effects of particular hazards, which can include hazardous chemicals, biological agents, etc. Here, "hazard" has been defined as "An act or phenomenon that has the potential to produce harm or other undesirable consequences to humans or what they value" (Stern and Fineberg, 1996). Risk assessment involves identifying and quantifying the steps by which a particular hazard can result in one or more adverse effects.

In the security context, the concepts of "vulnerability" and "threat" are closely related to that of risk. In particular, the National Research Council (2002) defines "vulnerability" as "an error or a weakness in the design, implementation, or operation of a system."

"Threat" is then defined as "an adversary that is motivated to exploit a system vulnerability and capable of doing so," and "risk" as "the likelihood that a vulnerability will be exploited, or that a threat may become harmful." Thus, in the security context, the definition of risk is limited to that of intentional threats, unlike the more general definition given above.

Kaplan and Garrick (1981) define "risk" as involving "both uncertainty and some kind of loss or damage." Thus, fundamentally, risk depends both on the probability or frequency of an adverse outcome, and on the severity of that outcome. Kaplan and Garrick (1981) state that the goal of a risk assessment is to answer three questions: "What can go wrong?"; "How likely is it that that will happen?"; and "If it does happen, what are the consequences?"

Risk assessment and risk management are generally considered to be distinct functions. For example, the National Research Council (1983) recommends that regulatory agencies maintain a clear distinction between risk assessment and risk management, so that the scientific findings embodied in risk assessments are distinguished from the value judgments that appropriately influence the choice of risk-management options. However, in practice, most risk assessments do include the identification and evaluation of possible risk-reduction measures, so risk assessment and risk management are usually integrated in some fashion. In particular, Stern and Fineberg (1996) recommend an "analytic-deliberative" process, in which "analysis informs deliberation" (to ensure that judgments and choices are well informed), but "deliberation frames analysis" (so that interested stakeholders can have an input into the scope of the risk assessment).

The process of risk assessment begins with hazard identification. This is followed by the assessment of accident occurrence frequencies, and then by consequence analysis (including, for example, the use of dose-response models). Relevant consequence measures might include: the structural response of a building to an impact or explosion; the costs associated with property damage, loss of use, and facility repair; the amount of hazardous material or energy released to the environment as a result of an adverse event; and the numbers of fatalities or other health effects.

Bier (1997) and Zimmerman and Bier (2002) summarize the process of probabilistic risk assessment (PRA) for complex engineered systems. To structure the list of possible scenarios for what can go wrong, PRA models are generally hierarchical in nature. Fault trees and event trees are commonly used to represent the combinations of component failures that could lead to an accident or other adverse outcome (McCormick, 1981). While the two techniques are equivalent, in that either of them can be used to represent the same system or subsystem, each technique has slightly different strengths and weaknesses (Pate-Cornell, 1984). Available data sources are then used to help quantify the various quantities that appear in the risk model. Bayesian statistics (Martz and Waller, 1982) and expert opinion (Bier and Lin, in review) are frequently used for data analysis in support of risk assessments, since Bayesian statistics are well suited to the analysis of sparse data. Recent empirical work by Bier and Lin (in review) has shed light on the calibration of expert judgments, and some of the factors affecting the extent of that calibration. After the initial risk assessment has been completed, the model can then be used for risk management purposes--e.g., to identify the dominant contributors to risk, and assess the benefits of risk reduction options (such as design and procedure changes). The application of PRA has resulted in a number of examples of successful risk management; a few examples are given in Garrick (1987).

Of course, risk assessment can be of little use in protecting against events (such as the World Trade Center disaster) that had not been adequately anticipated. Since September 11th, a number of past experiences have been identified that could perhaps have helped to identify the risk of such an attack if their implications had been fully grasped. For example, Barnett (2001) states:

> After the disaster, it was widely (and truthfully) reported from the aviation community that no one there imagined an event like the one that happened. But could that circumstance reflect a failure of our imaginations? There were, after all, lots of events that could be interpreted as precursors of the calamity… all the elements of the Sept. 11 catastrophe--the idea of using planes as weapons, suicidal individuals in the cockpit, and a willingness to take thousands of innocent lives-- had historical precedent.

While it would of course be wrong to expect perfect foresight on the part of risk managers, the fact that past experience had foreshadowed the possibility of the World Trade Center and other disasters points out the need for good methods of learning from past experience. The seminal paper by March et al. (1991) discusses numerous strategies for "learning from samples of one or fewer," which is often necessary in order to successfully avoid severe events. Collection, reporting, and analysis of data on near-miss events or "precursors" to severe events (Bier, 1998; Phimister et al., 2004) are important steps to facilitate learning from past experience. For example, Phimister et al. (2004) note that reporting of near misses is valuable for several purposes, including model development in support of risk assessments, monitoring of system safety, and ensuring awareness of possible risks; see also van der Schaaf (1992). Methods of precursor analysis (Bier, 1998; Phimister et al., 2004) provide one strategy for using information about prior events in estimating the frequencies of extreme events. Other approaches have been discussed in Bier et al. (1999).

2.2 Characterizing optimal defensive strategies for sabotage risk

Protection from a knowledgeable and adaptable adversary is a fundamentally different challenge than protection against accidents or acts of nature. For example, earthquakes do not get stronger or smarter just because we have defended our buildings against them. However, if one's adversaries know or can easily learn about one's defensive measures and detection technologies, then they can actively choose to either bypass or circumvent those measures. For example, prior to September 11th, metal-screening devices were believed to have substantially increased the safety and security of commercial air travel; however, the box cutters used by the terrorists on September 11th to gain control of the hijacked airplanes may have fallen just below the detection settings of such screening devices.

Therefore, unlike in applications of risk analysis to problems such as the risk of nuclear power accidents, the relationship of recommended risk-reduction actions to the dominant risks emerging from the analysis is not straightforward. In most applications of risk analysis, risk-reduction actions follow the usual "80/20 rule" (originally due to Pareto)— the decision maker can review a list of possible actions, ranked based on the magnitude of risk reduction per unit cost, and choose the most cost-effective, typically getting something on the order of 80% of the benefit for perhaps 20% of the cost. This does not work so well in the security context (especially if the potential attacker can readily observe system defenses), since the effectiveness of investments in defending one component can depend critically on whether other components have also been hardened (or, conversely, if the attacker can easily identify alternative targets that have not yet been hardened).

As noted by Dresher (1961), optimal allocation of defensive resources requires that "each of the defended targets yield the same payoff to the attacker." Thus, even if some components can be hardened quite inexpensively, focusing protective investments only on those can lead to wasted resources, if adversaries instead choose to attack targets that cannot be hardened as cost-effectively. In other words, critical assets must be defended against all possible attacks, which is much more difficult than just shoring up a few "weak links." As a result, Ravid (2001) has concluded that security improvements are generally more costly than safety improvements: "investment in defensive measures, unlike investment in safety measures, saves a lower number of lives (or other sort of damages) than the apparent direct contribution of those measures."

Models that take the (series or parallel) structure of the system into account include Bier and Abhichandani (2003) and Bier et al. (in press). These models have some interesting implications in practice. First, of all, they demonstrate the potential value of secrecy (and even deception) for security, since defensive measures may be less effective if they are widely known (or can be easily discovered by adversaries). As just one example, the proposal to sterilize mail to protect against future anthrax attacks might have been an effective defensive strategy if the installation of sterilization equipment could have been kept secret. However, this would probably not be possible in our open society, especially given the outcry of public concern about the threat of anthrax spores being sent through the mail. If installation of anthrax-sterilization equipment were public knowledge, this would likely only cause future attackers to find a different (and possibly more effective) means of delivery instead of the public mail. In that case, the initially proposed $40 million of sterilization equipment might never have sterilized a single anthrax spore!

Similarly, the work by Bier and colleagues shows that the optimal strategy for reducing vulnerability to intentional hazards depends critically on the assumptions made regarding attacker behavior and motivations. Consider the question of what attackers decide to do when a few "signature" buildings have been fortified to protect them against prospective attacks. If attackers simply move on to target progressively less well defended buildings, then expensive methods of protecting signature buildings may not actually be effective at protecting the public health and safety. Methods so expensive that they can be employed only in those few buildings that are perceived to be most "at risk" would clearly protect people and assets in those particular buildings, but might yield little overall benefit to public health and safety benefit if attackers simply target other buildings. In that case, only methods inexpensive enough for widespread application, and/or mobile (such as emergency response capabilities), would substantially reduce overall levels of societal risk. By contrast, if attackers are interested only in the few highest-profile targets, then expensive methods of protecting those few targets may be potentially worthwhile from a societal as well as a private viewpoint.

For series systems, the results to date still represent weakest-link models, in the sense that at equilibrium the defender invests in only those components that are most vulnerable (i.e., have the highest probability of being successfully attacked), or would cause the highest expected damage given an attack (taking into account both the success probability of an attack and the value of the component). However, ongoing work by Bier and colleagues is addressing the development of models in which the optimal defensive strategy would allow for the possibility of defender hedging in equilibrium. In particular, in the proposed model, attackers and defenders are assumed to have different valuations for the various potential targets. Moreover, the model assumes that attackers can observe defensive investments perfectly (which is conservative, but perhaps not overly so), but that defenders are uncertain about the attractiveness of each possible target to the attackers. While this model allows for the possibility of defensive hedging at equilibrium, it is interesting to note that such hedging does not always occur. In particular, it will often be optimal for the defender to put no investment into some targets that have a non-zero probability of being attacked—especially when the defender is highly budget constrained and the various potential targets differ greatly in their values to the defender (both of which seem likely to be the case in practice).

It is clearly also important to extend the current results to model more complicated system structures, with both parallel and series subsystems. Ongoing work by the author and colleagues is beginning to address this challenge, at least under particular assumptions. In addition, it would be nice to extend the existing models to address the case in which the success probability of an attack on a particular component need not be a convex function of the resources invested to defend that component (making it possible, for example, to analyze "discrete" security measures that require some minimal level of investment in order to be effective). Finally, it would of course be worthwhile to extend our models to include the dimension of time, rather than the current static or "snapshot" view of system security. This would allow us to model imperfect attacker information (including, for example, Bayesian updating of the probability that an attack will succeed based on a past history of successful and failed attacks), as well as the possibility of multiple attacks over time.

2.3 Stability analysis of hybrid dynamic models of networked systems

Many infrastructure systems such as power grids, transportation systems, and communication networks (and the interdependencies among them) can be modeled as stochastic hybrid dynamical systems. Stability analysis of such models enables one in the assessment of dynamic reliability and resilience of such complex systems to various exogenous factors. We have investigated stability of such network-centric dynamical systems that might be subject to external disturbances and/or structural perturbations.

Here we are interested not only in the models of time evolution (both continuous and discrete/event driven) of any specific system or sub-system, but also the dynamic interdependencies among various sub-systems, abrupt changes in states such as due to any change in network configuration as a result of structural changes or external disturbances, and modeling of uncertainty at various phases of design and operation. Topics relating to optimal control of such hybrid systems have been treated extensively as controlled switching diffusions.

Our goal in Chandra and Ladde (2004) is to investigate various stability behaviors of such network-centric dynamical systems that might be subject to structural perturbations. In our model, the switching mechanism described by a finite state Markov process in the stochastic hybrid system decomposes the problem in both continuous space and the time domain. In the case of the former, it decomposes it into a finite number of regions, each endowed with a stochastic system of differential equations. In each such region, we can associate either a scalar or a vector Lyapunov function. We can then estimate the properties of solution processes of the governing equations using an appropriate framework of differential inequalities and comparison tools. Finally, by employing decomposition/aggregation techniques, we are able to derive rigorous estimates on the solution processes of the overall system.

In this paper, we have developed a framework for stability analysis of a class of stochastic hybrid dynamic systems. The primary motivation for this work comes from the need to develop predictive models of various failure modes in such complex interacting dynamical systems. We are also interested in the assessment of reliability and performance under dynamic environments. With this in mind, we intend to pursue some related control problems utilizing the framework developed in this paper. Currently, we are investigating constructive strategies for the design of control processes that will ensure that the solution processes of such stochastic hybrid systems remain in a specified performance region. Also, dynamic reliability of such complex network systems is of considerable practical interest for the assessment of robust and resilient performance under both stochastic disturbances and structural degradation.

3 Threat analysis and risk management in networked information systems

Information systems are a specific example of entities comprising networked, interacting systems, and moreover this category of system has critical importance for military operations and homeland defense. In this section we highlight work in two areas related to information systems: enhancing fault-tolerance and robustness in mobile wireless communication networks, and the use of case-based reasoning tools for improving security of information systems.

3.1 Fault tolerant and robust mobile wireless networks

3.1.1 A hybrid totally mobile wireless architecture for survivable communications

The "ad-hoc" wireless architecture is widely used in military maneuvers and in situations of emergencies or natural disasters. It provides rapidly deployable communications services without requiring a wired backbone infrastructure. The ad-hoc architecture does not guarantee connectivity and does not scale well on large geographic areas. The cellular network architecture, on the other hand, relies on a wired backbone infrastructure and uses a single-hop wireless routing paradigm. The cellular model has the advantage of reliable routing and good scalability but does not offer rapid deployment of communications services nor does it facilitate the dynamic movement of the network infrastructure after installation.

We have designed and evaluated a new hybrid wireless architecture [Bassiouni *et al.* 2000, 2004; Cui and Bassiouni 2001, 2002a, 2002b] that combines the advantages of the ad-hoc and the cellular wireless models. This hybrid network model provides "communications-on-the-move" services with enhanced flexibility and scalability. In the hybrid network model, specialized mobile routers are used to achieve continued connectivity and fast forwarding. A mobile router has functionality similar to a cellular base station, but has no wired connections. In its simplest form, the mobile router could be a truck-mounted transceiver box with rechargeable battery. Satellite links or backbone wireless channels are used for communications among the mobile routers while short-hop wireless channels are used for communications between each mobile router and its users (mobile hosts or terminals). When the mobile hosts move, the mobile routers would also move to ensure the continuity of coverage and improve the quality of service for active connections.

1 Movement strategies

Mobile routers coordinate their movements to achieve the best coverage for their users. The movement of mobile routers can be controlled by human operators or can be robotically automated within the context of self-organizing configurable networks. Different movement coordination strategies can be used to control the movement of automated mobile routers. In our comprehensive simulation model, we implemented the "Center of Gravity" movement strategy. In this strategy, the mobile hosts periodically measure or estimate their position coordinates (e.g., using GPS) and emit them to their mobile router. Each mobile router calculates the gravimetric center of its hosts then moves towards this center. More sophisticated movement strategies involving interactions among the routers and/or the use of external advisory signals can be used to achieve better coordination and enhanced availability.

2. Two-tier hybrid model

Our detailed simulation tests have shown that improved performance and increased reliability can be obtained by arranging the mobile routers into a hierarchy of two levels. Routers at the lower level have a standard range of coverage and are devoted to servicing individual groups of users (called swarms). Routers at the higher level have a larger transmission range and are used to provide "umbrella" coverage for multiple swarms. By tuning the power level of their transmitter, the mobile routers can adjust their range of coverage and switch from one level of the hierarchy to the other. The umbrella routers at the higher level of the hierarchy can be rotated over time to balance power consumption. Similarly, the number of the routers in the lower level can be increased or decreased to adapt to swarm splitting or merging.

3. Recovery protocols

To improve the reliability and resiliency of the hybrid network architecture, mechanisms must be put in place to ensure that the operations of the mobile routers can survive environmental hazards or hostile attacks. In order to be able to handle faults of mobile routers when they occur, the network must be equipped with robust fault tolerance and recovery protocols. Below we elaborate on some of the recovery protocols that we have designed and evaluated.

3.1. The dual recovery protocol

In the dual backup restoration protocol, an extra backup router is assigned to each swarm. The backup router exchanges state-update messages with the primary router in order to be able to accurately mirror its state. The backup router follows the movement of its primary as close as practicable. If the primary router malfunctions, its backup can take over promptly and re-establish links to the hosts served by the primary.

The dual backup protocol is simple and provides definite performance gains in face of hostile attacks and threat conditions. In particular, the dual backup protocol provides the fastest recovery when a backup router survives the destruction of its primary router. However, one disadvantage of the dual backup protocol is that the primary router and its backup are likely to be destroyed together (e.g., they enter a mine field together). Furthermore, the dual backup protocol does not provide optimal utilization of the backup resources in the long run. As more primary routers get knocked out and are replaced by their backups, several swarms will operate without backups thereby degrading the gracefulness of future recovery.

3.2. The distributed recovery protocol

Rather than strictly dedicating a backup router to each primary mobile router, the backup routers are carefully scattered among the primary mobile routers. When a primary router fails, one or more of the nearby backup routers is dispatched to provide coverage for the set of mobile terminals originally covered by the failed router. This protocol is called "the distributed recovery protocol". It is flexible and does not require dedicating a backup router for each primary router.

3.3. Performance evaluation of recovery protocols

Both simulation and analytical (birth-death Markov) models were developed to evaluate the different recovery protocols for the hybrid wireless network architecture. In the analytical models, exponential distributions were assumed for the time between failures (TBF) of mobile routers, the repair time of failed routers, the interarrival times of new calls to a primary router and the call duration time. The simulation model used 36 primary mobile routers serving 1800 mobile terminals. The number of standby mobile routers in the simulation was changed from zero (i.e., no recovery) to 36 (i.e., the number of primary mobile routers). The distributed recovery protocol has given better performance especially in the case when failed routers can be repaired and put back into service after some repair time. Our simulation tests have also shown that the second-tier architecture further improves the performance of the distributed recovery protocol.

3.1.2 Strategies for reliable and resilient mobile wireless networks

Section 3.1.1 describes recovery protocols for hybrid mobile wireless architectures that combine the advantage of ad-hoc (mobile nodes) and cellular models. Such architectures provide an essential ingredient "communication-on-the-move" service in dynamic battlespace with enhanced flexibility and stability. In order to ensure reliability and robustness of such systems, we have investigated the resiliency of such architectures by considering strategies for optimal deployment (number and location) of back-up routers that would ensure reliable performance in such interdependent mobile systems.

Basically, in this architecture, specialized mobile routers (usually placed in moving trucks) are used to achieve continued connectivity and fast message forwarding. Satellite links or backbone wireless channels are used for communication between each mobile router, while short-hop wireless channels are used for communication between each mobile router and its users (mobile hosts). When mobile hosts move, the mobile routers also move (following certain dynamic path) to ensure the continuity of coverage and improve the quality of service for active connections.

What happens if any of the mobile routers fails, either due a natural hazard or a malicious attack? In order to overcome such exigencies and design fault-tolerant architectures of mobile routers, the network of routers could be equipped with robust fault-tolerant and recovery protocols. These protocols normally entail adding redundant hardware and (back-up) routers, requiring extra overhead for achieving satisfactory operations. The cost-benefit analysis for enhancing reliability and resilience in such mobile architectures presents some challenging technical problems. Specifically, in Chandra and Landon (2004), we consider development of strategies for optimal deployment (number and location) of back-up mobile routers that achieve enhanced reliability and resilience in the overall performance of mobile architecture.

Our basic premises are as follows: In order for back-up routers to avoid the similar (fate) hazard as the primary, they need to keep a "safe" distance from them. On the other hand, they cannot be too far from the primary routers, if they were to be functionally useful. Thus, the optimal deployment strategies will lead to constrained optimization problems, where the cost functions are derived from various reliability models and taking into consideration dependencies among various routers. A back-up router could be available to more than one primary router, thus requiring a careful analysis of geometry of feasible regions of accessibility.

While in this paper, our primary focus has been on explicit and implementable strategies for multiple primary routers that are relatively stationary, our current and future work will consider moving primary routers under various mobility models (both deterministic and stochastic).

3.2 Case-based reasoning and data mining for cybersecurity

Case-based reasoning (CBR) is a generic problem-solving methodology that has been used for a wide variety of applications in business, industry, government, and defense. It provides a formalized procedure for reasoning from "lessons learned." A *case* is record of past experience, comprised of a *problem-solution* pair, where a problem is represented as a collection of *features*. Cases are stored in a *case archive*. When a new problem arises from the environment, its features are identified and fed into a search engine, which scans the case archive for cases that are similar to the given problem, based on some *similarity measure*. The most similar cases are retrieved and used as the basis for formulating a solution to the present problem. This new problem-solution pair then becomes a new case for entry into the archive. The proposed solution is applied to the environment, and a measure of its success/failure is noted and stored in the archive along with the case. In this manner, the archive grows and the overall system performance improves through use over time.

To date virtually all cased-based reasoning systems have been tailor made for their particular application. This means that a considerable programming effort has been required for development of each such system. The first phase of our work has aimed at alleviating this burden.

Our approach has been to apply a modern software engineering technique known as "reflective," or "adaptive," architectures, to create a generic software framework that abstracts out the domain-independent components of an arbitrary case-based reasoner. This framework can then be easily and quickly instantiated to create a specific case-based reasoner for a wide variety of different types of application domains. The upshot is that, given our framework, developers have the ability to create a new case-based reasoner that is tailored to any new problem domain with very minimal additional programming. To obtain this level of abstractions, the cases are encoded in XML, where the case features and solution descriptions are defined by an XML schema. Given the schema, one can employ Sun Microsystems' Java XML Binding (JAXB) package to automatically generate the needed Java source code for parsing the XML documents. Merging these new classes with the CBR framework produces the core components of a search engine for scanning the given XML case archives and applying the appropriate similarity measure.

It is the latter that employs the reflective aspect of our framework. For each case feature there is a *comparator*, a Java method that determines whether, or to what extent, the feature's value for a given problem situation matches the corresponding feature's value for a case in the archive. A similarity measure is then a combination of the results produced by the feature comparators. What comparators are to be used for what case features is recorded in a *meta-data dictionary*, and this is applied dynamically during search to determine which comparators to apply for each case. One implements a new similarity measure simply by adding new comparators into the existing collection, making appropriate entries in the meta-data dictionary, and if necessary, defining a new comparator combination rule. The system also generates the graphical user interface from the metadata.

As a proof of concept we have replicated the well-known "Snort" [Snort (undated)] intrusion detection system (IDS), which is rule-based, as a case-based system. This in turn has been delivered to Ratan Guha's group at University of Central Florida for incorporation into their simulations of ad hoc wireless networks. In addition, we have explored prospects for using case-based reasoning in the human factor research undertaken by Pascale Carayon at University of Wisconsin.

In the second phase of our work we have continued to delve into the problems of intrusion detection for networked computer systems. This aims at developing a multi-sensor monitoring system that captures alerts from a wide variety of different types of intrusion detection systems (network based, host based; misuse detection, anomaly detection) and identifies patterns of such alerts as representing real attacks. The objective in this is to synthesis the information provided by the various sensors (IDSs) thereby providing a more accurate attack identification. Individual sensors, acting alone, are known to suffer from varying rates of false positives (alerts raised when no attack is taking place) and false negatives (neglecting to raise an alert when a real attack is occurring). We expect to alleviate this problem by combining the results of arbitrarily many individual sensors of various types.

Preliminary results with just Snort, i.e., looking at patterns of Snort alerts per session, rather than individual alerts per packet, indicate that this new approach can significantly improve the overall performance. The current effort is aimed at developing a proof of concept system that monitors just Snort, which will then be extended to include monitoring of one or more host-based IDS's (e.g., stide [Forrest *et al.*, (1996)]).

Data mining is being used to generate the case archive for the monitoring system. For this we are using the well-known DARPA data sets provided by MIT's Lincoln Labs. This contains both network (tcp dump) data and host (audit) data, where the two types of data have been correlated according to "sessions". This is important for our monitoring system inasmuch as it is necessary to correlate network sessions with host sessions in order to determine that the alerts being raised by the various sensors pertain to the same login session. In those data sets, however, much of this correlation was performed manually. Accordingly, for the purposes of the monitoring system, we are developing means by which this correlation can be automated. Moreover, inasmuch as this correlation requires a considerable amount of preprocessing of the raw data, we are exploring the possibility of implementing this activity on a computer cluster or grid.

Part of the DARPA data is being used to train the system, and part will be used to test it to test it. We expect to have a prototype proof of concept system in operation by the end of the granting period, April 2006. Publications documenting our progress to date are Schwartz et al. (2002), Guha et al., (2002), Yilmaz et al., (2003), Long et al., (2004), Patel et al., (2004), Stoecklin et al., (2004).

4   Human factors analysis in information assurance

People often find it easy to imagine threats to a critical infrastructure system arising from saboteurs, hijackers, or computer hackers. Also easy to visualize, though often less newsworthy, are threats originating from natural causes: storms or other severe weather occurrences, or events due to causes such as structural failure, corrosion, or rust. Human error, on the other hand, seems to come to mind less often as a threat to such systems. Even when it does, the first reaction is often to try to assign blame to some individual. The concept that human error is a systemic cause of danger to infrastructure, and that often the organization is more responsible for the occurrence of error than are the individual humans in it, seems difficult for people to absorb. Our project has devoted substantial resources to investigating the human component of danger to critical infrastructure systems, including information systems, and in this section we describe some of that work and give numerous references giving additional detail of various studies.

4.1   Human and organizational issues in computer and information security

In this area of research, we aim to identify and describe the human and organizational factors associated with computer and information security. These factors may have an impact on computer and information security, such as the occurrence of security vulnerabilities and breaches (Carayon, Kraemer, & Bier, to be published). For example, a network administrator at a large organization is partly responsible for a host of Windows updates on the organization's information system. Since her security responsibilities are a fraction of her total duties as an administrator, and in addition to a heavy workload, she struggles to keep up with all of the updates and patches related to Windows systems. During a time when the network administrators are performing large system repairs, almost all of her work time is devoted to these duties. Consequently, she does perform her usual monitoring of updates and a critical patch is not performed. A vulnerability now exists on the Windows systems and the network administrators are not aware of it. Because of time constraints and workload associated with the job of network administration, the patch may or may not be recognized.

According to the National Research Council Computer Science and Telecommunications Board (2002) it is important to distinguish between accidental causes and deliberate causes. Accidental causes are natural or human but non-deliberate (e.g., human error). Deliberate causes result from conscious human choice (e.g., terrorism). In the computer and information security literature, these are referred as 'attacks'. Models of human error can be used to identify and characterize vulnerabilities of computer and information systems. It has been argued that "Human error is usually not a useful explanation for security problems. Usually either operational or management practice is at fault" (Computer Science and Telecommunications Board-National Research Council, 2002). However, this assertion does not consider the rich human error literature, in particular with regard to 'latent' organizational failures (Reason, 1990). The human error literature has explored the cognitive mechanisms involved in human errors, but has also emphasized the role of human and organizational factors in contributing to the creation of error-prone conditions. This research can be applied to understand human errors involved in computer and information security and to identify the mechanisms that attackers could be using.

One of our primary goals in this research is to identify the critical human and organizational factors associated with computer and information security and describe them in a systematic framework. As described in the preceding paragraphs, job and organizational design factors such as task load, time constraints, and prioritization of work duties have an effect on an organization's level of security. We are attempting to identify these factors and describe the pathways that lead to security vulnerabilities and breaches.

We have conducted several research activities to reach this goal. Firstly, we have collaborated with Professor Raj Veeramani and the Global E-Commerce Consortium at the University of Wisconsin. In this collaboration, we organized a work group of security professionals in private industry. The working group has identified key computer and information security vulnerabilities, the human and organizational factors associated with those vulnerabilities, and best practices (Carayon & Kraemer, 2003a). We have also examined this problem from a human error perspective. Using the human error taxonomies provided by the cognitive and psychological sciences, we interviewed 11 network administrators and three security professionals on the role of human error and its place in computer and information security. These interviews substantiated a conceptual framework of how human and organizational factors are related to errors committed by network administrators and end users (Carayon & Kraemer, 2002; Kraemer & Carayon, submitted). Finally, we have developed and pilot tested a human factors evaluation method for computer and information security, the Human Factors Vulnerability Analysis (HFVA). HFVA is a method to extract the human and organizational factors associated with a technical security vulnerability identified through an automated vulnerability system scan (Carayon & Kraemer, 2003b). This research was done in collaboration with Professor Vernon and her colleagues at the computer laboratories in the Computer Sciences and Computer Aided Engineering Departments at the University of Wisconsin. Professor Vernon provided technical data generated from a Nessus audit and we followed up with a pilot test of HFVA. The pilot test consisted of interviews with the labs' network administrators. The pilot test produced data on feasibility of HFVA and two case studies of technical vulnerabilities (Kraemer & Carayon, 2003).

4.2 Human factors analysis of red teams and applications to infrastructure protection

In this area of our research, we have focused on red team performance and its application to infrastructure protection. The Department of Defense has recognized that red teaming has long been a valuable, if underutilized, tool for deepening the understanding of the adversaries the United States faces in the war on terrorism (Defense Science Board Task Force, 2003). In particular, red teaming is valuable in understanding adversary's capabilities and potential responses to United States' initiatives (Defense Science Board Task Force, 2003). In order to expand and improve the experience base of system defenders, a developed understanding of the strategies and tactics employed by red teams is critical to warding off attacks on computer and information systems.

The use of red teams are important mechanisms for detecting system vulnerabilities and hence enhancing security, since the product of their work is an analysis of the security system from an adversary's perspective (Schudel & Wood, 2000). The organization may then use this information to improve their current security system against future attacks. We have ongoing collaboration efforts with Sandia National Laboratories' Information Design Assurance Red Team (IDART™). In our preliminary research with IDART™, we have focused on the area of red team performance (Carayon, Duggan, & Kraemer, 2003; Carayon & Kraemer, 2004). Specifically, we have identified measures of red team performance (Kraemer, Carayon, & Duggan, 2004), factors that contribute to and hinder red team performance, and factors that can be used in a trade-off analysis between red team performance and automated security methods.

In our second phase of research with IDART™, we will expand on our previous research concerning the identification of human and organizational factors in computer and information security. The preliminary conceptual framework we have begun to create describes the possible organizational pathways that an attacker may use to execute an attack. In this phase, we will interview red team members to identify the human and organizational vulnerabilities they find when performing assessments. Our goal is to analyze this information into a systematic, usable framework that red teams may use in understanding the human and organizational factors that may be exploited in an attack. Such a tool may be used when red teams perform their assessments. This tool would provide a taxonomic framework of the exploitable human and organizational factors related to the computer and information vulnerabilities they find when performing system analyses. Further, the information provided in this research may be applicable to case-based reasoning systems. A case-based reasoning system will capture and catalogue computer and information security vulnerabilities, associated human and organizational factors, and solutions implemented. The strength of such a system lies in the documentation of security incidents, vulnerabilities, strategies for attacks, and solutions implemented, and therefore this information is not lost for future assessments or left to the cognition of the red team.

5 Distributed simulation and trade-off studies

In this section we describe three areas of study involving simulation, optimization, and other means of understanding and deciding on tradeoffs in system design and operation. Again, these emphasize our unifying theme of networked, interacting systems. The first is an approximation method for reducing the number of expensive simulation runs needed in optimizing networked stochastic systems. The second is a game-theoretic approach to allocating bandwidth in wireless LANS. The third area is a simulation testbed for modeling and analyzing wireless network performance.

5.1 Stochastic optimization of networked systems via approximation

Many systems of interest in logistics, manufacturing, and other areas can be represented by stochastic networks. Generally these networks contain various parameters, for example in the distributions governing service at the nodes, and it is often possible to adjust these parameters at some cost. For example, one may obtain faster service by investing in improvements to the entity performing the service, such as a production machine, a refueling station on an airfield, etc.

This raises the question of how one might best improve a measure of network performance, such as expected throughput, if improvement funds are limited. In other words, for a given budget how can one change the parameters in the model in order to obtain the best performance attainable at that budget level? This is a problem of stochastic optimization.

As the systems involved are usually complex, the normal way of measuring performance is by building and running a simulation model of the system. This method has the advantage that, by expending enough computing resources, one can usually estimate relevant system performance measures quite accurately. However, it has at least two disadvantages:

- It may be slow, especially for complex systems;
- It provides a snapshot of the system's performance with whatever parameter settings are in force during the simulation, but unless the user does additional work it does not indicate how one might change those settings to improve selected performance measures.

In a series of papers [Granger, Krishnamurthy and Robinson 2001, 2004a, 2004b] we have applied to this problem an approach originally introduced in [Whitt 1983]. This approach approximates the traffic process in the stochastic network by renewal processes, and it models performance measures of individual stations in the network in terms of the first two moments of those renewal processes. These so-called two-moment approximations lead to a system of nonlinear equations which, when solved, provides estimates of the performance measures of interest. We have augmented this approach by applying some recently developed enhancements described in [Krishnamurthy 2002;

Krishnamurthy, Suri, and Vernon 2002] to enable modeling of fork-join constructs among other improvements, and have applied the resulting methodology to several military logistics problems. The papers [Granger, Krishnamurthy and Robinson 2001, 2004a] describe air logistics networks, while [Granger, Krishnamurthy and Robinson 2004b] shows how to model airfield operations for the purpose of detecting bottlenecks and improving the system. In these applications we have observed that the approximations are both sufficiently accurate for system improvement and/or optimization, and extremely fast compared to simulation. Speedup factors of 60 or more were not uncommon in the examples we ran. Further work to extend the applicability of this method is now in progress.

5.2 A game theoretic approach for fair sharing of bandwidth in wireless local area networks (WLANs)

In distributed systems like WLANs, medium access is essentially contention-based. This presents an opportunity to model the medium access in a WLAN as a non-cooperative game: "access game". In Rakshit and Guha 2004a, we have computed optimal strategies for users playing the "access game" in an incomplete information scenario. The main emphasis of our work is to design the "access game" in such a fashion as to achieve fairness in bandwidth sharing in a WLAN. Battery power constraints are also incorporated in designing the access game.

As collision in unavoidable in a distributed system, we define fairness as follows [Rakshit and Guha, 2004b, 2004c, 2004d; Guha and Rakshit, 2004a, 2004b]: if the probability of success in accessing the medium is proportional to the weightages of the users, then fairness is achieved. IEEE802.11 is the most widespread Medium Access Protocol used for WLANs and recent research has shown that this MAC protocol cane be modeled as p-persistent Carrier Sense Multiple Access (p-CSMA) MAC protocol. Therefore, in designing the access game we assume that the users employ p-CSMA in accessing the medium. We now briefly discuss the design of the "access game".

5.2.1 Description of the "Access Game"

"Access Game" is a single-shot medium access game. At the beginning of each transmission period, users/players have two choices: "transmit" and "wait". If exactly one user transmits, then that user succeeds in transmission. If more than one user contends for the medium, there is collision. The payoffs of the access game have two components: Quality of Service (QoS) and Battery Power (BP). For WLAN, QoS component is more important than the BP component. If a user transmits and succeeds, then it gains bandwidth but loses some battery power in transmitting the packet. Therefore, the payoff for "success" has a positive QoS component and a negative BP component. If a user transmits and fails, it loses battery power for contention but does not gain any bandwidth. Therefore, the payoff for failure has negative components for both QoS and BP. Finally if the user waits, then no or minimal battery power is expended. Therefore, the payoff for "wait" has a positive BP component and negative QoS component. As QoS is more important than BP, the payoff for "success" is higher than the payoff for "wait", which in turn is higher than the payoff for "failure". It can be however argued that in other types of distributed networks, BP is not important at all or BP is more important than QoS. These situations have been analyzed in [Rakshit and Guha 2004b, 2004c].

As the outcome of the "access game" is probabilistic in nature, a user's utility function is defined as the expected payoff from the scenarios described above. The objective of each user is to maximize its own utility function. We analyze the "access game" with two equilibrium solution concepts from non-cooperative game theory: Nash Equilibrium (NE) and Constrained Nash Equilibrium (CNE). Both these solutions are obtained under the assumption that the "access game" is a complete information game i.e. users have all the necessary information about all other users.

5.2.2 Solution concepts

NE is the most celebrated solution concept in non-cooperative game theory and our analysis shows [Rakshit and Guha 2004b, 2004c] that each access game has a unique NE. Unfortunately; this unique NE does not necessarily correspond to "fairness" in bandwidth sharing for a given set of payoffs or more specifically, for a given set of payoff ratios. Therefore, we compute the CNE of the "access game". For CNE, users are given the fairness criteria as the set of constraints. Therefore, CNE is essentially a constrained optimization problem where users optimize their individual utility function with fairness criteria as a set of constraints. The difference with the usual constrained optimization problem is that the optimization is done in a distributed fashion by individual users without any centralized computation. If the utility functions are concave, then equilibrium exists and it is shown that the utility functions in our case are concave in nature. Therefore, the CNE exists. Moreover, it is also shown that the CNE of the "access game" is also unique [Rakshit and Guha 2004d]. Consequently, there is a unique set of transmission probabilities that simultaneously maximizes the utility function satisfies the fairness criteria.

5.2.3 Complete information, incomplete information and approximation

In the above analysis, the key assumption was that users have complete information about the number of other users in the system. However, this is not usually the case in distributed systems where users do not know about the other users in the system. We have presented a simple approximation scheme [Guha and Rakshit 2004a, Rakshit and Guha 2004c] to remove this problem so that the above analysis can be used in realistic situations. The key to our approximation is the fact that there is usually a central entity (R, henceforth) in WLANs. R acts as a gateway between the WLAN and the outside world and at the same time functions as a registration authority, i.e. users inform R while entering and leaving the system. The approximation scheme is described below and it has two essential components: information gathering and information dissemination.
Users are divided into a fixed number of classes and a user of a particular class has pre-determined weightage.

When a user of a particular class joins the system, it informs R and R increases the number of users in the corresponding class by one. When a user leaves the system, it informs R and R decreases the number of users in the corresponding class by one (information gathering).

At the beginning of each transmission period, R broadcasts the number of users in different classes (information dissemination). As the users of the system know the number of different classes and the weightage assigned to the users in a particular class, the information broadcast by R helps users to compute their transmission probabilities optimally.

5.3 An architecture for wireless network distributed simulation

5.3.1 Introduction

The Wireless Network Distributed Simulation (WINDS) framework is a flexible simulation test-bed targeting a wide range of wireless networks with intrusion detection systems. The framework is cross-platform, Java-based, GUI-driven and can be used as a wireless network simulator for a variety of purposes, such as routing in ad hoc networks, mobility models of totally mobile wireless networks, and Bluetooth Pico-nets. We have currently used an implementation of WINDS architecture as a test-bed for our Agent-based Intrusion Detection System for Ad Hoc Wireless Networks [Kachirski and Guha 2003; Guha and Kachirski 2002; Guha et al. 2002]. The objectives of this project were to reduce redundant software design efforts in the area of wireless network simulation, establish a framework general enough to be used for simulations of many wireless network-related mechanisms, and provide for common base for the experimentation with various wireless technologies.

5.3.2 Architecture of the system

The architecture of wireless simulation framework is based on a building-block approach. Researcher implements an algorithm or a prototype from modules that receive inputs in the form of events, process them, and then generate outputs (events, log entries, GUI updates). The entire wireless network is built from objects – wireless nodes, event generator, and communication channels. Connections between wireless nodes are maintained by the connections module incorporated into the simulation engine. Any type of wireless network is supported and can be configured – both ad hoc and infrastructure wireless networks. Object-oriented approach is central to the generality and flexibility of the system and allows users of our framework to reuse, share and catalog simulation components by modifying or replacing appropriate classes. Our framework also includes customizable user interface that can be easily adapted to a specific problem via code [Kachirski and Guha 2004].

Originally developed as a single-processor version, the wireless simulator architecture consists of four key modules, each comprised of a number of components:

GUI (graphical user interface)
Simulator Core Module

Simulation engine
Simulation objects
Network Traffic Module
Packet pre-processor
Packet generator
Data Logging Module
Data parser
CSV file generator

The GUI module displays state of the simulation in real-time, also allowing the user to control simulation flow and adjust operational parameters. The simulation engine controls an internal clock and synchronizes every event in the system among simulation objects. Programmatically implemented as a high-priority thread, the simulation engine runs in a loop continuously, driving execution of all other components of the simulation. Simulation objects execute independently and are time-synchronized via the simulation engine clock. Our simulation framework has a few pre-defined simulation objects – wireless node, base station, ad hoc routing algorithm. User-defined objects can also be incorporated by defining template for such an object and registering with simulation controller. In addition, user objects can incorporate code written in C++ for computationally-intensive tasks. Network traffic for our framework is generated by the Network Packet Processor, which reads a pre-processed packet data file in XML format, and forwarding each packet to the appropriate simulation object at specified time stamp. At the end of the simulation run, these results are first pre-processed by a Data Parser to format data suitable for import into the mathematical analysis and graphing software.

5.3.3 Distributed implementation of the architecture

The single-processor version of the simulation system suffices for small-scale simulations of wireless networks. However, we have had significant reduction in performance when simulations of 200 or more wireless nodes were in progress. So we have extended this architecture on a cluster computer with 64 processors. All the objects in the simulation are equally distributed among the processors. During simulation execution, each of the processors performs computations relevant to objects assigned to it. Communication between objects is handled by the communication broker that invokes an appropriate communication channel based on object location. Each processor has dedicated memory space, and can access data concurrently on a network file subsystem. Inter-processor communication is conducted via high-speed Ethernet switch at 100Mbps. Other WINDS simulation framework features include:

Fault-tolerant distributed simulation system design – one of the advantages of using a cluster computer for distributed simulations is the availability of a large number of processors interconnected by a high-speed network. We incorporate the option for a fault-tolerant simulation system, mirroring each processor's functionality on another processor, thus achieving a high degree of fault tolerance and consistency in a distributed simulation.

Automatic simulation clock rate adjustment, based on the slowest system – The design of our WINDS framework allows researchers to utilize heterogeneous computer systems widely spread-out geographically. Thus, the performance of the simulation execution may suffer considerably from out-of-order delivery of inter-processor communication units, and lost network packets. We incorporate resource-monitoring functionality in our simulation framework, that monitors performance details of each individual computer and adjust simulation execution to accommodate slow systems with low network bandwidth / high network congestion / high resource utilization.

Efficient simulation object distribution – The round-robin mechanism of simulation object distribution did not provide the optimal arrangement. We organize simulation objects in hierarchies (e.g., a tree structure for interconnecting processors) to minimize network communication.

References

1. A. Barnett, The Worst Day Ever: The Sept. 11 Catastrophe Raises Many Troubling Questions, *OR/MS Today,* December 2001, http://lionhrtpub.com/orms/orms-12-01/worstdayfr.html.

2. M. Bassiouni and W. Cui, Enhancing Terminal Coverage and Fault Recovery in Configurable Cellular Networks Using Geolocation Services. Book chapter in *Next Generation Wireless Networks: Defining Applications and Services*, edited by S. Tekinay, Kluwer Publishing, pp. 231 - 254, December 2000

3. M. Bassiouni, W. Cui and B. Zhou, Fast Routing and Recovery Protocols in Hybrid Ad-hoc Cellular Networks. Book Chapter in *Wireless Communications Systems and Networks*, edited by M. Guizani, Kluwer Publishing, pp. 685-697, June 2004

4. V. M. Bier, An Overview of Probabilistic Risk Analysis for Complex Engineered Systems, in V. Molak (editor), *Fundamentals of Risk Analysis and Risk Management.* Boca Raton, FL: CRC Press, 1997.

5. V. M. Bier, Accident Sequence Precursors and Probabilistic Risk Analysis. University of Maryland, College Park, Maryland, 1998.

6. V. M. Bier and V. Abhichandani, Optimal Allocation of Resources for Defense of Simple Series and Parallel Systems from Determined Adversaries. In *Risk-Based Decisionmaking in Water Resources X,* pp. 59-76. Reston, VA: American Society of Civil Engineers, 2003.

7. V. M. Bier, Y. Y. Haimes, J. H. Lambert, N. C. Matalas, and R. Zimmerman, A Survey of Approaches for Assessing and Managing the Risk of Extremes, *Risk Analysis,* Volume 19, 1999, pp. 83-94.

8. V. M. Bier and S.-W. Lin, 2004. A Study of Expert Overconfidence, submitted to *Decision Analysis.*

9. V. M. Bier, A. Nagaraj, and V. Abhichandani, 2004. Protection of Simple Series and Parallel Systems with Components of Different Values, *Reliability Engineering & System Safety,* in press.

10. Carayon, P., Duggan, R., & Kraemer, S., 2003. A Model of Red Team Performance. In H. Luczak & K. J. Zink (Eds.), *Seventh International Symposium on Human Factors in Organizational Design and Management.* Aachen, Germany.

11. Carayon, P., & Kraemer, S., 2002. Macroergonomics in WWDU: What about computer and information system security? Paper presented at the 6th International Scientific Conference on Work With Display Units - WWDU 2002 - World Wide Work, Berlin, Germany.

12. Carayon, P., & Kraemer, S., 2003a. Human factors in e-security: The business viewpoint (Technical Report 184). Madison, WI: Center for Quality and Productivity Improvement.

13. Carayon, P., & Kraemer, S., 2003b. Using accident analysis methods in computer security: The development of the Human Factors Vulnerability Analysis (HFVA), *Proceedings of the XVth Triennial Congress of the International Ergonomics Association and the 7th Joint Conference of Ergonomics Society of Korea/Japan Ergonomics Society.* Seoul, Korea.

14. Carayon, P., & Kraemer, S., 2004. Red team performance: Summary of findings (Technical Report). Madison, WI: Center for Quality and Productivity Improvement.

15. Carayon, P., Kraemer, S., & Bier, V., 2004. Human factors issues in computer and e-business security. In A. Labbi (Ed.), *Predictive Modeling for e-Business Risk Management* (forthcoming).

16. J. Chandra and G. Ladde, 2004. Stability analysis of stochastic hybrid systems. *International Journal of Hybrid Systems* (to appear)

17. J. Chandra and J. Landon, 2004. Towards a reliable and resilient mobile wireless architecture. Submitted to *IEEE Journal of Reliability.*

18. Computer Science and Telecommunications Board-National Research Council. *Cybersecurity Today and Tomorrow: Pay Now or Pay Later.* Washington, DC: National Academy Press, 2002.

19. W. Cui and M. Bassiouni, Adaptive Recovery Protocols for Multi-layer Ad-Hoc Networks in Theater of Non-uniform Failure Rate. *Proceedings of the 16th AeroSense SPIE Conference on Digital Wireless Communications,* April 2002b

20. W. Cui and M. Bassiouni Channel Planning and Fault Recovery in Hierarchical Hybrid Cellular Networks with Mobile Routers. *Proceedings of IEEE Wireless Local Networks- 26th LCN Conference,* pp. 646-652, November 2001

21. W. Cui and M. Bassiouni Analysis of Hierarchical Cellular Networks with Mobile Base Stations. *Journal of Wireless Communications and Mobile Computing,* John Wiley & Sons Publishing, Volume 2, pp. 131-149, March 2002a

22. Defense Science Board Task Force. (2003). The role and status of DoD red teaming activities. Washington, D. C.: Office of the Under Secretary of Defense for Acquisition, Technology, and Logistics.

23. M. Dresher, *Games of Strategy: Theory and Applications.* Englewood Cliffs, NJ: Prentice-Hall, 1961.

24. Forrest, S., Hofmeyr, S.A., Somayaji, A., and Longstaff, T.A., A sense of self for unix processes, *Proceedings of 1996 IEEE Symposium on Computer Security and Privacy* (1996), pp 120-128.

25. B. J. Garrick, Examining the Realities of Risk Management, in V. T. Covello, L. B. Lave, A. Moghissi, and V. R. R. Uppuluri (editors), *Uncertainty in Risk Assessment, Risk Management, and Decision Making.* New York, NY: Plenum, 1987.

26. J. Granger, A. Krishnamurthy, and S. M. Robinson, Stochastic modeling of airlift operations. In: B. A. Peters, J. S. Smith, D. J. Medeiros, and M. W. Rohrer, eds., *Proceedings of the 2001 Winter Simulation Conference,* pp. 432 – 440

27. J. Granger, A. Krishnamurthy, and S. M. Robinson, Approximation and optimization for stochastic networks. In: K. Marti, Y. Ermoliev, and G. Pflug, eds., *Dynamic Stochastic Optimization,* pp. 67–79. Springer-Verlag (Lecture Notes in Economics and Mathematical Systems No. 532), Berlin 2004a

28. J. Granger, A. Krishnamurthy, and S. M. Robinson, 2004b. Rapid improvement of stochastic networks using two-moment approximations. Accepted by *Mathematical and Computer Modelling.*

29. R. Guha, O. Kachirski, 2002, "Intrusion Detection Using Mobile Agents in Wireless Ad Hoc Networks", *Proceedings of the IEEE Workshop on Knowledge Media Networking, KMN'02,* pp. 153-160.

30. Guha, R., Kachirski, O., Schwartz, D.G., Stoecklin, S., and Yilmaz, E., Case-based agents for packet-level intrusion detection in ad hoc networks, *Seventeenth International Symposium on Computer and Information Science (ISCIS'02)*, Orlando, FL, October 28-30, 2002, pp. 315-320.

31. Guha, R.K., and Rakshit, S., 2004a, Selfish users and distributed MAC protocols in wireless local area networks (WLANs), to appear in the Proceedings of APIEMS2004, Australia, Dec. 2004.

32. Guha, R.K., and Rakshit, S., 2004b, Medium Access and Fair Bandwidth Sharing in WLAN, to appear in the Proceedings of ACST2004, Nov. 2004, US Virgin Islands.

33. O. Kachirski and R. Guha, Effective Intrusion Detection Using Multiple Sensors in Wireless Ad Hoc Networks, *Proceedings of 36th HICSS Conference,* 2003, pp. 57-64.

34. O. Kachirski, R. Guha, Extending Architecture for Wireless Network Distributed Simulation (WINDS) – *Proceedings of the 2004 European Simulation Multiconference (ESM'04),* Magdeburg, Germany (June 2004)

35. Kaplan, S., and B. J. Garrick, On the Quantitative Definition of Risk, *Risk Analysis,* Volume 1, 1981, pp. 11-27.

36. Kraemer, S., & Carayon, P. (2003). A human factors vulnerability evaluation method for computer and information security. In H. F. a. E. Society (Ed.), *Proceedings of the Human Factors and Ergonomics Society* (pp. 1389-1393). Denver, CO.

37. Kraemer, S., & Carayon, P. (2004). A human factors model of human error in computer and information security. Submitted to *Interacting with Computers.*

38. Kraemer, S., Carayon, A., & Duggan, R. (2004). Red team performance for improved computer and information security. In H. F. a. E. Society (Ed.), *Proceedings of the Human Factors and Ergonomics Society.* New Orleans, LA

39. Krishnamurthy, A., *Analytical Performance Models for Material Control Strategies in Manufacturing Systems.* Ph.D. Dissertation, Department of Industrial Engineering, University of Wisconsin-Madison, Madison, WI, July 2002

40. A. Krishnamurthy, R. Suri and M. K. Vernon. Two-moment Approximations for the Variability Parameter of the Departure Process from a Fork/Join Station with General Inputs. Technical report, Department of Industrial Engineering, University of Wisconsin, Madison, Wisconsin, 2002.

41. Long, J., Stoecklin, S., Schwartz, D.G., and Patel, M., Adaptive similarity measures in case-based reasoning, *The 6th IASTED International Conference on Intelligent Systems and Control (ISC 2004)*, August 23-25, 2004, Honolulu, Hawaii.

42. J. G. March, L. S. Sproull, and M. Tamuz, Learning from Samples of One or Fewer, *Organization Science,* Volume 2, 1991, pp. 1-13.

43. H. F. Martz and R. A. Waller, *Bayesian Reliability Analysis.* New York, NY: Wiley, 1982.

44. N. J. McCormick, *Reliability and Risk Analysis: Methods and Nuclear Power Applications.* San Diego, CA: Academic Press, 1981.

45. Patel, M., Stoecklin, S., Schwartz, D.G., Graphical user interface using a reflective architecture and XML, *The 2004 International Conference on Software Engineering Research and Practice (SERP'04)*, Las Vegas, NV, June 21--24, 2004, pp. 648-651.

46. Rakshit, S. and Guha, R.K., 2004a, Optimal Strategies in MAC Protocols, ICC2004, Paris.

47. Rakshit, S., and Guha, R.K., 2004b, Access Games: A Game Theoretic Framework for Fair Bandwidth Sharing in Distributed Systems. Submitted for INFOCOM2005.

48. Rakshit, S. and Guha, R.K., 2004c, Fair Bandwidth Sharing in Distributed Systems: a Game-Theoretic Approach. Submitted to *IEEE Transaction on Computers*

49. Rakshit, S. and Guha, R.K., 2004d, A Non-Cooperative Game-Theoretic Model for the Medium Access and Fair Bandwidth Sharing in WLAN. Submitted to *Wiley Journal of Wireless Communications and Mobile Computing.*

50. Reason, J. (1990). *Human Error.* Cambridge: Cambridge University Press.

51. Schudel, G., & Wood, B. (2000). Modeling behavior of the cyber-terrorist. Paper presented at the Conference Proceedings: Research on Mitigating the Insider Threat to Information Systems-#2., Santa Monica, California.

52. Schwartz, D.G., Stoecklin, S., and Yilmaz, E., A case-based approach to network intrusion detection, *Fifth International Conference on Information Fusion (IF'02)*, Annapolis, MD, July 7-11, 2002, pp. 1084-1089.

53. Snort, http://www.snort.org/

54. Stoecklin, S., Schwartz, D.G., Yilmaz, E., and Patel, M., A metadata architecture for case-based reasoning, *The 2004 International Conference on Artificial Intelligence (IC-AI'04)*, Las Vegas, NV, June 21-24, 2004, pp. 790-794.

55. W. Whitt, The Queuing Network Analyzer, *Bell Systems Technical Journal,* 62: 2779–2815, 1983.

56. Yilmaz, E., Stoecklin, S., and Schwartz, D.G., Toward a generic case-based reasoning framework using adaptive software architectures, *The 2003 International Conference on Information and Knowledge Engineering (IKE'03)*, Las Vegas, NV, June 23-26, 2003, Volume II, pp. 512-513.

Protection of simple series and parallel systems with components of different values

Vicki M. Bier[a,*], Aniruddha Nagaraj[a], Vinod Abhichandani[b]

[a]Department of Industrial Engineering, University of Wisconsin-Madison, 1513 University Avenue, Madison, WI 53706-1572, USA
[b]E6794 Ochsner Rd., Plain, WI 53577, USA

Received 29 December 2003; accepted 5 June 2004

Abstract

We apply game theory, optimization, and reliability analysis to identify optimal defenses against intentional threats to system reliability. The goals are to identify optimal strategies for allocating resources among possible defensive investments, and to develop qualitative guidelines that reflect those strategies. The novel feature of the approach is the use of reliability analysis together with game theory and optimization to study optimal management of intentional threats to system reliability. Thus, this work extends and adapts the existing body of game-theoretic work on security to systems with series or parallel structures. The results yield insights into the nature of optimal defensive investments that yield the best tradeoff between investment cost and security. In particular, the results illustrate how the optimal allocation of defensive investments depends on the structure of the system, the cost-effectiveness of infrastructure protection investments, and the adversary's goals and constraints.
© 2004 Published by Elsevier Ltd.

Keywords: Parallel systems; Defensive investments; Cost-effectiveness; Series systems; Game theory; Optimization

1. Introduction

After the September 11, 2001, terrorist attacks on the World Trade Center and the Pentagon, and the anthrax attacks in the United States, there has been an increased interest in strategies for protecting assets of value (including human life) against attacks by an intelligent and adaptable adversary. Even before that, there were calls for greater attention to critical infrastructure protection, including computer security; see, for example, the President's Commission on Critical Infrastructure Protection [1].

Protecting against intentional attacks is fundamentally different from protecting against 'acts of nature' or 'accidents'. For example, an earthquake will not become stronger or 'smarter' just because we have fortified our buildings to protect against it. On the other hand, an intelligent and determined adversary may adopt a different offensive strategy to circumvent (or destroy) our protective security measures. Therefore, a good defensive strategy must consider the adversary's behavior. To illustrate, if we harden one point of entry into a system, the adversary may target an alternative point of entry instead. Therefore, Schneier [2] notes in the context of internet security that "the attacker has an advantage. He can choose when and how to attack".

The requirement to take the behavior of adversaries into account means that attacker goals and motivations must be considered in selecting defensive strategies [3]. One important characteristic is whether an adversary is opportunistic or determined. Opportunistic adversaries are looking for easy targets, and therefore may be deterred if their current target proves to be too difficult or costly to attack. Ordinary vandals and some types of computer hackers fall into this category. By contrast, realistic levels of difficulty or cost will not necessarily deter a determined attacker. Determined adversaries can include terrorists, military adversaries, or even some unethical business adversaries.

Defending against opportunistic adversaries is less difficult than defending against determined attackers. For example, if an organization is convinced that its adversaries

* Corresponding author. Fax: +1-608-265-9094.
E-mail address: bier@engr.wisc.edu (V.M. Bier).

are opportunistic, it may be acceptable simply to adopt security measures that are better than the average for similar companies or systems, since the organization's defenses need only be strong enough to discourage possible attacks. By contrast, defending something of value from a truly determined attacker is much more difficult.

We now compare the optimal strategies for defending simple systems, configured either in series or in parallel, against attacks by knowledgeable and determined adversaries. In particular, we extend the model of Bier and Abhichandani [4] to reflect the fact that components may have inherent values, in addition to their instrumental value in ensuring the functionality of the system. For example, such inherent values may include the economic losses and/or loss of life that would result if a component is destroyed or rendered inoperable (even if the system as a whole is still operable), as well as the cost of repairing the component. Our new model still includes the original model of Ref. [4] as a special case.

The goals of this work are to identify optimal strategies for allocating resources among possible defensive investments, and to develop qualitative guidelines that reflect those strategies. The intent is to frame the problem and provide qualitative insights. Thus, the model presented here is not intended primarily for real-world operational application with specific numerical parameter values. That said, however, numerical estimates of the model parameter could in principle be obtained using expert judgment.

2. Problem formulation and notation

Whereas Bier and Abhichandani [4] assumed that the attacker will maximize the success probability of an attack, here we assume that the attacker will maximize the expected damage of an attack on the system. This revised objective function incorporates the inherent values of the components. For example, in the original model [4], the attacker is assumed to be indifferent regarding whether a single component in a parallel system is disabled, while the new model assumes that the attacker would in general prefer to disable some of the components in a parallel system (as reflected by the inherent values of those component), even if unsuccessful at disabling the entire system. However, this model reduces to one in which the attacker maximizes the probability of successfully disabling the system when the inherent values of all components are set to zero.

We retain the assumption in Ref. [4] that attacks against different components succeed or fail independently. We allow attacks to take place either sequentially or simultaneously, since the timing of an eventual system failure is assumed not to be an important consideration. Although clearly somewhat restrictive, this assumption is likely to be more nearly satisfied in systems that already have such basic reliability and security measures as spatial separation and functional diversity.

We consider both series and parallel systems. Redundant components that provide alternative means to perform the same task, such that only one component must be functional in order for the task to be performed successfully, are considered to be functionally in parallel to each other. Similarly, components that are all necessary to perform a single task are functionally in series. Of course, real-world systems may consist of a large number of components in complex combinations of series and parallel configurations, or even more general graph topologies. In this paper, we discuss simple series and parallel systems as a building block toward understanding optimal strategies for the security of more complex systems. For both series and parallel systems, we consider cases both with and without defender budget constraints. Additionally, in the series case, we consider different levels of attacker knowledge, and different assumptions about the maximum possible number of attacks.

We summarize below the notation used in this paper:

C	Total budget constraint of the defender (where applicable).
C_i	Investment by the defender in hardening of component i.
$P_i(C_i)$	Probability of success of an attack on component i, as a function of the investment C_i expended to strengthen that component. The $P_i(C_i)$ are assumed to be convex, monotonically decreasing, strictly positive, continuous, twice differentiable, and invertible (with differentiable inverses).
V	Value of system functionality to the defender; i.e. the loss (in dollar terms) incurred by the defender if the system is disabled.
V_i	Inherent value of component i; i.e. the loss incurred by the defender if component i is disabled (irrespective of whether the system is disabled).
$D(C_1, C_2, \ldots, C_n)$	Conditional expected damage experienced by the defender given an attack on the system, as a function of the defensive investment C_i.
$F(C_1, C_2, \ldots, C_n)$	Objective function that the defender wishes to minimize.
α	Probability of an attack on the system.

3. Components in parallel

Consider a parallel system of n components that works perfectly if at least one of the n parallel components works. Since the components are redundant, every component must be disabled to disable the entire system. The damage caused by disabling the system is V. Disabling component i also causes damage V_i for $i = 1, \ldots, n$, even if the system as a whole is not disabled.

We assume here that the attacker can attack each component only once. This may at first seem to be unduly restrictive. However, the model can be parameterized to allow for multiple attacks against component i, simply by setting the success probability $P_i(C_i)$ to reflect the probability that at least one attack on component i will succeed out of the maximum possible number of attacks (which could in principle be infinite). We assume that the defender does not care whether the attacks occur simultaneously or sequentially, and is concerned only about the expected damage caused by the attacker and the cost of the defensive investments.

3.1. Constrained case

In this case, we assume that the defender has limited resources, and wishes to minimize the expected damage due to an attack, subject to the given budget constraint. We begin by considering a two-component system for which the expected damage (conditional on an attack) is

$$D(C_1, C_2) = V_1 P_1(C_1) + V_2 P_2(C_2) + V P_1(C_1) P_2(C_2)$$

and the defender seeks to minimize

$$F(C_1, C_2) = D(C_1, C_2)$$
$$= V_1 P_1(C_1) + V_2 P_2(C_2) + V P_1(C_1) P_2(C_2) \quad (1)$$

subject to the constraints

$$C_1 + C_2 \leq C \quad \text{and} \quad C_1, C_2 \geq 0$$

Here, V_i might represent the cost of repairing component i (regardless of whether the system as a whole is still functional), while V is the loss incurred by the defender when the entire system is disabled.

Since the objective function is not in general convex, it may have multiple local minima. However, since the objective function is monotonically decreasing, the constrained minimum must occur along the line $C_1 + C_2 = C$, so, at the minimum, we will have $C_2 = C - C_1$. Substituting this into Eq. (1), differentiating with respect to C_1, and equating the result to zero, we get

$$\frac{\partial F(C_1, C - C_1)}{\partial C_1} = V_1 P_1'(C_1) - V_2 P_2'(C - C_1) + V P_1'(C_1)$$
$$\times P_2(C - C_1) - V P_1(C_1) P_2'(C - C_1)$$
$$= 0$$

Thus, if a local optimum exists for $0 < C_1 < C$, it must satisfy

$$\frac{P_1'(C_1)}{V_2 + V P_1(C_1)} = \frac{P_2'(C - C_1)}{V_1 + V P_2(C - C_1)} \quad (2)$$

Since the objective function is monotonically decreasing, a point satisfying this condition is either a (local) minimum or

an inflection point. To see this, we take the second derivative of the objective function, $\partial^2 F(C_1, C - C_1)/\partial^2 C_1$, yielding:

$$V_1 P_1''(C_1) + V_2 P_2''(C - C_1) + V P_1''(C_1) P_2(C - C_1)$$

$$+ V P_1(C_1) P_2''(C - C_1) - 2 V P_1'(C_1) P_2'(C - C_1)$$

Since the $P_i(C_i)$ are monotonically decreasing and convex, the first derivatives are strictly negative and the second derivatives are strictly positive. Therefore, the second partial derivative of the objective function will be positive (and the corresponding solution will be a local minimum) if the term $2 V P_1'(C_1) P_2'(C - C_1)$ is sufficiently small. If the second derivative of the objective function is zero, then the point satisfying the first-order condition will be an inflection point. If the second derivative is negative, then the corresponding solution will be a saddle point and there can be multiple optima (e.g. at $C_1 = C$ and $C_2 = C$).

3.1.1. Special cases

1. Let $P_i(C_i) = a_i e^{-bC_i}$ for $i = 1, 2$, and let $V_1 = V_2$. Assuming that C_1 and C_2 are greater than zero at optimality, then the only point on the line $C_1 + C_2 = C$ that satisfies the first-order condition for optimality is $C_1 = [\ln(a_1/a_2) + bC]/2b$, so there is a unique optimum. If $a_1 = a_2$, then the optimum will occur at $C_1 = C_2 = (C/2)$; otherwise, the component with the higher initial probability a_i of being disabled should get the larger investment. For sufficiently large values of a_1/a_2 (i.e. if attacks against component 1 have a much higher initial probability of success than attacks against component 2), we will have $C_1 = C$ at optimality; likewise, for sufficiently small values of a_1/a_2 (i.e. if component 2 is more vulnerable), we will have $C_2 = C$ at optimality.

2. Let the $P_i(C_i)$ be log-convex (which implies, roughly speaking, that the success probability of an attack against component i decreases faster than exponentially in the level of investment). In this case, the defender's objective function will be convex. Therefore, if a feasible point satisfying Eq. (2) exists, it will be a global minimum. However, it is still possible that a feasible point satisfying Eq. (2) may not exist, in which case the global optimum will occur where C_1 equals either zero or C.

3. Let there exist $C_1 > 0$ satisfying Eq. (2). If V_1 increases to $\hat{V}_1$ and there exists a new $\tilde{C}_1 > 0$ satisfying Eq. (2), then we must have $\tilde{C}_1 > C_1$. Thus, increasing the inherent value of a component that is already receiving positive investment at optimality can only increase the optimal level of investment in that component.

3.1.2. Extension to systems with more than two components

For a parallel system with n components, an attacker must disable all components in order to disable the system.

As in the two-component case, we assume that the attacker causes damage V_i if component i is disabled, and additional damage V if the system as a whole is disabled. The defender again seeks to minimize the conditional expected damage given all attack,

$$F(C_1, C_2, ..., C_n) = D(C_1, C_2, ..., C_n)$$

$$= \sum_{i=1}^{n} V_i P_i(C_i) + V \prod_{i=1}^{n} P_i(C_i) \tag{3}$$

subject to the constraints

$$\sum_{i=1}^{n} C_i \leq C \quad \text{and} \quad C_i \geq 0, \quad i = 1, 2, ..., n$$

As before, the objective function is not in general convex, so there may be multiple optima, but since the objective function is monotonically decreasing, the optimum must be on the constraint $\sum_{i=1}^{n} C_i = C$. A candidate for the optimal solution must satisfy the Karush–Kuhn–Tucker conditions [5]:

$$P_i'(C_i) \left[V_i + V \prod_{j \neq i} P_j(C_j) \right] + \lambda \geq 0$$

$$C_i \left[P_i'(C_i) \left(V_i + V \prod_{j \neq i} P_j(C_j) \right) + \lambda \right] = 0$$

$$C_i \geq 0, \quad \lambda > 0, \quad i = 1, 2, ..., n$$

If a component receives investment $0 < C_i < C$ at optimality, we have

$$P_i'(C_i) \left[V_i + V \prod_{j \neq i} P_j(C_j) \right] = -\lambda \tag{4}$$

This implies that if $C_i, C_j > 0$ for $i \neq j$, then

$$P_i'(C_i) \left[V_i + V \prod_{k \neq i} P_k(C_k) \right] = P_1'(C_j) \left[V_j + V \prod_{k \neq j} P_k(C_k) \right] \tag{5}$$

When $V_i = V_j = 0$, Eq. (5) simplifies to the result obtained in Ref. [4].

Note that the optimum may involve not spending anything on one or more components if they are too costly to harden relative to their value. Any such components receiving zero investment need not satisfy Eq. (4).

Graphically, the feasible set of this optimization problem is the hyperplane defined by $C_1 + \cdots + C_n = C$ and $C_i \geq 0$. If the optimum occurs in the interior of this region, then Eq. (5) will be satisfied for all pairs of variables. More generally, every component i for which $C_i > 0$ at optimality will satisfy Eq. (4). Additionally, at optimality, Eq. (5) must be satisfied by all pairs of variables satisfying $C_i, C_j > 0$.

3.2. Unconstrained case

In this case, we assume that the defender has an unlimited budget, and can spend as much as is justified to harden the components. For a parallel system with n components, the conditional expected damage to the system is given by $D(C_1, C_2, ..., C_n) = \sum_{i=1}^{n} V_i P_i(C_i) + V \prod_{i=1}^{n} P_i(C_i)$. The defender seeks to minimize the unconditional expected damage plus the total investment cost:

$$F(C_1, C_2, ..., C_n)$$

$$= \alpha \left[\sum_{i=1}^{n} V_i P_i(C_i) + V \prod_{i=1}^{n} P_i(C_i) \right] + \sum_{i=1}^{n} C_i$$

The Karush–Kuhn–Tucker conditions for the optimal solution are

$$\alpha P_i'(C_i) \left[V_i + V \prod_{k \neq i} P_k(C_k) \right] + 1 \geq 0$$

$$C_i \left[\alpha P_i'(C_i) \left(V_i + V \prod_{k \neq i} P_k(C_k) \right) + 1 \right] = 0$$

$$C_i \geq 0, \quad i = 1, 2, ..., n$$

Therefore, if $C_i > 0$ for some i, then we must have

$$P_i'(C_i) \left[V_i + V \prod_{k \neq i} P_k(C_k) \right] = \frac{-1}{\alpha} \tag{6}$$

which also implies (as in the constrained case)

$$\frac{P_i'(C_i)}{V_j + V \prod_{k \neq j} P_k(C_k)} = \frac{P_j'(C_j)}{V_i + V \prod_{k \neq i} P_k(C_k)}$$

for $C_i, C_j > 0$. Note that if the probability of an attack increases, then the investment in components already receiving positive investment also increases.

3.2.1. Special case

Let the $P_i(C_i)$ be identical, and let $V_i = v$ for all i. Then Eq. (6) implies that for all $i \neq j$ such that $C_i, C_j > 0$, there will exist a critical point with $C_i = C_j$. However, this will not necessarily be the global minimum unless the objective function is convex.

3.3. Interpretation of results

1. If the $P_i(C_i)$ are log-convex for all i, the objective functions in both the constrained and unconstrained cases will be convex, ensuring the existence of a global minimum (possibly with one or more $C_i = 0$).
2. Eqs. (4) and (6) imply that at optimality, the marginal reductions in conditional expected damage of an attack

associated with increased investment in all components already receiving positive investment must be equal.

3. In the unconstrained case, for sufficiently small values of α, it will not be cost-effective to invest in defending any components, and the global minimum will be $C_i = 0$ for all i. As the attack probability α increases, it will become worthwhile to invest in the defense of one or more components, and eventually in all components. (In the constrained case, at least one component will always receive positive investment at optimality.)

4. The optimal allocation of resources for defense depends critically on the cost-effectiveness of defending the various components; the optimal solution may involve not defending one or more components if they cannot be defended sufficiently cost-effectively. Thus, the defender can choose which components to harden based on the cost-effectiveness of doing so, and need not invest in components that are extremely costly to defend.

4. Components in series

Here, we consider a system with components in series. In a series system, if even one component fails, the entire system is disabled. Some systems, like long oil pipelines or electricity transmission lines, are physically in series. One can also view multiple failure modes for a single component as being in series.

As before, we assume that the defender wants to achieve either the minimum expected damage given an attack (within a budget constraint), or an optimal tradeoff between expected damage and defensive cost, taking into account attacker behavior. However, the attacker no longer has to disable all components in order to succeed, but has a choice of which component(s) to attack. We assume that the attacker's goal is to maximize expected damage. The optimal defense will depend on the attacker's constraints (whether the attacker is limited to attacking a single component, or can target multiple components), and the attacker's knowledge of the system.

We consider two cases where the attacker has perfect knowledge about system's defenses: one in which the attacker is limited to a single attack on a single component; and one in which the attacker can attack each component once. The assumption of perfect attacker knowledge may be reasonable when the attacker has access to inside information, or when information about defenses is readily observable. The assumption that the attacker can target only a single component is not fully general, but can be realistic in some circumstances (e.g. because of attacker resource constraints, or if a failed attack would lead to the attacker being detected and disabled). We also consider a case where the attacker has no knowledge of the system's defenses, and is limited to a single attack on a single component. For each, we consider the defender's optimization problem both with and without budget constraints.

4.1. Perfect attacker knowledge of defenses—single attack

As stated above, we assume here that the attacker's objective is to choose the component that will maximize the expected damage. In this case, the defender's best strategy is to bring the expected damage resulting from an attack against each component equal to each other (or as close to each other as possible or justifiable). To see this, consider a two-component system, and assume without loss of generality that $(V + V_1)P_1(0) \leq (V + V_2)P_2(0)$, so that

$$\max\left[(V + V_1)P_1(0), (V + V_2)P_2(0)\right] = (V + V_2)P_2(0)$$

Clearly, any investment in component 1 will make no difference to system security unless component 2 has been hardened. Thus, defensive investments should be allocated so that levels of damage expected from attacks against all components are made equal to each other or as close as possible given the budget constraint (or as close as justifiable given the attack probability α).

4.1.1. Constrained case

Here, the defender is assumed to have a finite budget C available. For a two-component system, the objective function to be minimized is given by

$$F(C_1, C_2) = \max\left[(V + V_1)P_1(C_1), (V + V_2)P_2(C_2)\right]$$

Since the objective function is monotonically decreasing, the minimum will occur where $C_1 + C_2 = C$. Assume without loss of generality that initially $(V + V_1)P_1(0) \leq (V + V_2)P_2(0)$. Define $\tilde{C}$ such that $(V + V_1)P_1(0) = (V + V_2)P_2(\tilde{C})$. Thus, $\tilde{C}$ is the level of expenditure required to equalize the expected damage of attacks against the two components.

If the budget constraint is such that $C \leq \tilde{C}$, then the optimal strategy for the defender is to use the entire budget to improve component 2. When the budget constraint is reached, $(V + V_1)P_1(0)$ will still be less than or equal to $(V + V_2)P_2(\tilde{C})$, so the defender should not harden component 1 at all.

If $C > \tilde{C}$, the defender should first invest $\tilde{C}$ in component 2 to set the expected damage caused by attacks against the two components equal, and then invest further in both components in such a manner that the expected damage caused by attacks against them remains the same. At optimality, we will have $(V + V_1)P_1(C_1) = (V + V_2)P_2(C_2)$. By the monotonic nature of the objective function, the optimum will occur at $C_1 + C_2 = C$.

Extending to systems with more than two components, the defender must again allocate the defensive resources in such a manner that all $(V + V_i)P_i(C_i)$ are equal to each other (or as close to each other as possible given the budget constraint). As before, the constrained minimum will occur where $C_1 + \cdots + C_n = C$. Resources must initially be utilized to try to bring the component(s) with the highest expected damage to par with the second highest. If that can be achieved, those components can be further strengthened to be at par with the third highest, and so on. If the defender is able to equalize all expected values before reaching the budget constraint, any remaining resources should then be allocated in such a manner that all $(V + V_i)P_i(C_i)$ remain equal. If $C_i, C_j > 0$ at optimality, then we must have $(V + V_i)P_i(C_i) = (V + V_j)P_j(C_j)$, and $(V + V_k)P_k(C_k) \leq (V + V_i)P_i(C_i)$ for all k such that $C_k = 0$, $C_i > 0$.

4.1.2. Unconstrained case

The conditional expected damage given a single attack on the system is

$$D(C_1, C_2, ..., C_n) = \max_{i=1,2,...,n} \left[(V + V_i)P_i(C_i) \right]$$

Since there is no budget constraint, we assume that the defender will optimize the unconditional expected damage plus the cost of defensive investments:

$$F(C_1, C_2, ..., C_2) = \alpha \max_{i=1,2,...,n} \left[(V + V_i)P_i(C_i) \right] + \sum_{i=1}^{n} C_i$$

This function is convex. Thus, any local optimum must be a global minimum. For sufficiently small values of α, it will not be cost-effective to invest resources to defend any component, and the global minimum will occur at $C_i = 0$ for all i. As α becomes larger, it will eventually become worthwhile to invest in defense.

If the global minimum is such that $C_i > 0$ for all i, then at optimality we must have $(V + V_1)P_1(C_1) = (V + V_2)P_2(C_2) = ... = (V + V_n)P_n(C_n)$. Substituting this into the objective function, we can rewrite it as

$$F(C_1, C_2, ..., C_n) = \alpha(V + V_1)P_1(C_1) + \sum_{i=1}^{n} C_i$$

The revised objective function is differentiable for all non-negative C_1. Moreover, since the objective function is convex, differentiating with respect to C_1 and setting the result to zero implies that the global minimum must satisfy $(V + V_1)P_1'(C_1) = -1/\alpha$. More generally, if $C_i > 0$ at optimality for all i, then

$$(V + V_i)P_i'(C_i) = \frac{-1}{\alpha} \tag{7}$$

At optimality, the marginal reduction in the conditional expected damage to the system by investing all incremental amounts in those components already receiving some investment will be inversely proportional to the attack probability α. If α increases, those components already being defended will receive more investment.

Special case: If $V_i = V_j$ and $P_i(\cdot) = P_j(\cdot)$ for all $i \neq j$, then from Eq. (7), we have at optimality $C_1 = ... = C_n$, and each C_i must satisfy $(V + V_i)P_i'(C_i) = -n/\alpha$.

4.1.3. Interpretation of results

For a series system, if the attacker knows about the system's defenses, the defender has less flexibility than for a parallel system. In particular, the defender can no longer choose to invest only in the most cost-effective components, since the attacker can simply choose to attack those components that were not defended. This is consistent, for example, with the observation by Woo [7] that "al-Qaeda...is sensitive to target hardening". In the constrained case, the optimal allocation of resources does not depend on the derivatives $P'(C_i)$ at all, since if all the C_i are positive at optimality, then we must have $(V + V_1)P_1(C_1) = (V + V_2)P_2(C_2) = \cdots = (V + V_n)P_n(C_n)$, and the total level of investment C is already determined by the budget constraint. In the unconstrained case, the optimal solution depends on the derivatives of the $P_i(C_i)$, but those derivatives now influence only the total level of investment $C_1 + \cdots + C_n$, not the values of the individual C_i (for $C_i > 0$), since if $C_i, C_j > 0$ at optimality, we must have $(V + V_i)P_i(C_i) = (V + V_j)P_j(C_j)$. This greatly limits the defender's flexibility.

Dresher [6], discussing optimal allocation of defenses in the military context, notes that "It is necessary that each of the defended targets yield the same payoff to the attacker" at optimality. Even if some components can be hardened inexpensively, focusing protective investments on only those will lead to wasted resources if adversaries can choose to attack components that are more costly to harden. This suggests that defense will generally be more costly when the adversary knows about the system defenses.

4.2. Perfect attacker knowledge—multiple attacks

Here, the attacker is not limited to attacking a single component, but can attack each component in the system once. We allow attacks to take place either sequentially or simultaneously, but assume that components fail or survive independently of each other. Every component i that is successfully disabled is assumed to cause damage V_i, in addition to the damage V if at least one component (and therefore the system as a whole) is disabled. Thus, the conditional expected damage is given by

$$D(C_1, C_2, ..., C_n) = \sum_{i=1}^{n} V_i P_i(C_i) + V \left[1 - \prod_{i=1}^{n} (1 - P_i(C_i)) \right]$$

As before, we consider two cases, with and without a budget constraint for the defender.

4.2.1. Constrained case

When there is a budget constraint, the defender is assumed to minimize the conditional expected damage, given by

$$F(C_1, C_2, ..., C_n) = \sum_{i=1}^{n} V_i P_i(C_i) + V \left[1 - \prod_{i=1}^{n} (1 - P_i(C_i)) \right] \tag{8}$$

subject to $\sum_{i=1}^{n} C_i \leq C$, and $C_i \geq 0$. Since the objective function is monotonically decreasing, the optimum will occur on the hyperplane $C_1 + \cdots + C_n = C$. A candidate for the optimal solution must satisfy:

$$P_i'(C_i)\left[V_i + V \prod_{j \neq i}(1 - P_j(C_j))\right] + \lambda \geq 0$$

$$C_i\left[P_i'(C_i)\left(V_i + V \prod_{j \neq i}(1 - P_j(C_j))\right) + \lambda\right] = 0$$

$$C_i \geq 0, \text{ and } \lambda > 0$$

So if $C_i, C_j > 0$ at optimality, then we must have

$$P_i'(C_i)\left[V_i + V \prod_{k \neq i}(1 - P_k(C_k))\right]$$
$$= P_j'(C_j)\left[V_j + V \prod_{k \neq j}(1 - P_k(C_k))\right] \qquad (9)$$

This result is similar to Eq. (5) of the parallel case, except for the product term. This reflects the fact that in a parallel system, the attacker causes damage V only if *all* components are disabled, whereas in the series case the attacker must disable only one component to cause damage V.

4.2.2. Unconstrained case

In the unconstrained case, the defender minimizes the sum of the unconditional expected damage due to attacks and the total cost of investments:

$$F(C_1, C_2, ..., C_n) = \alpha \min_{i=1,2,...,n}\left[\sum_{i=1}^{n} V_i P_i(C_i)\right.$$
$$\left. + V\left(1 - \prod_{i=1}^{n}(1 - P_i(C_i))\right)\right] + \sum_{i=1}^{n} C_i$$

An optimal solution must satisfy the Karush–Kuhn–Tuckcr conditions:

$$\alpha P_i'(C_i)\left[V_i + V \prod_{j \neq i}(1 - P_j(C_j))\right] + 1 \geq 0$$

$$C_i\left[\alpha P_i'(C_i)\left(V_i + V \prod_{j \neq i}(1 - P_j(C_j))\right) + 1\right] = 0$$

$$C_i \geq 0$$

So, if $C_i > 0$ at optimality, then we must have

$$P_i'(C_i) = \frac{-1}{\alpha\left[V_i + V \prod_{j \neq i}(1 - P_j(C_j))\right]} \qquad (10)$$

If $C_i, C_j > 0$ at optimality, then C_i and C_j must also satisfy Eq. (9).

4.2.3. Interpretation of results

To minimize the conditional expected damage given an attack on the system, the defender seeks to minimize the product of convex functions in the parallel case, and seeks to maximize the product of concave functions in the case of

series systems subjected to multiple attacks. Thus, the general properties of the optimal solutions will be similar in these two cases; e.g. there can be multiple optima. Because the attacker can target multiple components, the optimal defensive strategy also no longer focuses exclusively on the component(s) that cause the highest expected damage if attacked. Other components may also merit positive investment, since the investment may pay off if the attacker is unsuccessful in disabling the components with the highest expected damage.

If the $P_i(C_i)$ are sufficiently small, then we can write

$$1 - \prod_{i=1}^{n}(1 - P_i(C_i)) \approx \sum_{i}^{n} P_i(C_i)$$

In this case, the objective function in Eq. (8) is approximately convex, and therefore solutions satisfying the Karush–Kuhn–Tucker conditions will be at or near a global minimum.

If $P_i(C_i) \gg P_j(C_j)$ for all $j \neq i$ and for all $C_i \leq C$, then we can write

$$1 - \prod_{i=1}^{n}(1 - P_i(C_i)) \approx P_i(C_i)$$

In this case, if $V_i \gg V_j$, the objective function (8) can be approximated as:

$$F(C_1, C_2, ..., C_n) \approx (V + V_i)P_i(C_i)$$

Thus, the optimal solution in this case will be similar to the optimal solution in the case of series systems subject to only a single attack.

As in Section 4.1.2, Eq. (10) implies that the optimal investment in component i is increasing in the estimated probability of attack α; moreover, the optimal investment in any given component may be zero if the attack probability α is sufficiently small. The derivatives $P_i'(C_i)$ influence not only the total investment $C_1 + \cdots + C_n$, but also the allocation of that total investment to each component. This implies, as in the parallel case, that the optimal allocation of resources to series systems subject to attacks on all components depends on the cost-effectiveness with which the various components can be defended.

4.3. No attacker knowledge—single attack

When the attacker has no information about the system's defenses, we assume that the attacker will target one component at random, without regard to the defensive investments C_i or the functions $P_i(C_i)$. Consider a system with n components, and suppose that any attack will target component i with probability q_i, such that $q_i \geq 0$ and $q_1 + \cdots + q_n = 1$. The expected damage to the system will then be $D(C_1, C_2, ..., C_n) = \sum_{i=1}^{n} q_i(V + V_i)P_i(C_i)$. This is clearly convex, by convexity of the P_i and non-negativity of the q_i, V, and V_i.

4.3.1. Constrained case

Here, the defender has a resource constraint C, and is assumed to minimize the conditional expected damage to the system,

$$F(C_1, C_2, ..., C_n) = \sum_{i=1}^{n} q_i(V + V_i)P_i(C_i)$$

By the monotonicity of the objective function, the global minimum will occur at, $C_1 + \cdots + C_n = C$. Since the objective function is convex, a candidate for the global minimum must satisfy the Karush–Kuhn–Tucker conditions:

$$q_i(V + V_i)P_i'(C_i) + \lambda \geq 0,$$

$$C_i[q_i(V + V_i)P_i'(C_i) + \lambda] = 0,$$

$$C_i \geq 0, \ \lambda > 0$$

If $C_i, C_j > 0$ at optimality, then we must have

$$q_i(V + V_i)P_i'(C_i) = q_j(V + V_j)P_j'(C_j) \qquad (11)$$

Thus, at optimality, the marginal reduction in the conditional expected damage given an attack from an incremental amount of investment in any component already receiving positive investment is the same.

Special case: If $P_i(\cdot) = P_j(\cdot)$, then the component with the higher value of $q_i(V + V_i)$ should receive more investment at optimality.

4.3.2. Unconstrained case

Here, the defender is assumed to minimize the sum of the unconditional expected damage from attacks and the total cost of investment,

$$F(C_1, C_2, ..., C_n) = \alpha \left[\sum_{i=1}^{n} q_i(V + V_i)P_i(C_i) \right] + \sum_{i=1}^{n} C_i$$

The objective function is still convex, and the Karush–Kuhn–Tucker conditions satisfied by the global minimum are

$$\alpha q_i(V + V_i)P_i'(C_i) + 1 \geq 0,$$

$$C_i[\alpha q_i(V + V_i)P_i'(C_i) + 1] = 0,$$

$$C_i \geq 0$$

It is straightforward to see that if $C_i > 0$ at optimality, then we must have

$$P_i'(C_i) = \frac{-1}{\alpha q_i(V + V_i)} \qquad (12)$$

4.3.3. Interpretation of results

1. The conditional probabilities q_i cannot be considered in isolation. A higher probability of attack against component i than component j may not warrant a higher level of investment in component i, if component j has a sufficiently large inherent value V_j.
2. When the attacker is limited to attacking a single component in a series system, the defender has greater flexibility if the attacker has no knowledge of defenses than if the attacker has perfect information. This indicates the potential value of secrecy to improve cost-effectiveness of defenses.
3. Increases in the value of the product αq_i will increase the optimum value of C_i, at least for any component already receiving positive investment. In addition, an increase in the expected damage $V + V_i$, will increase the optimum investment in component i. The optimal levels of investment in different components can be determined independently of each other, as there is no budget constraint to induce coupling between them.

5. Conclusions and future work

Our results support the overall conclusion of Ref. [4], that defending series systems against knowledgeable and determined attackers can be extremely difficult. However, by incorporating the inherent values of components into our model, we recognize that in a parallel system, damage can be inflicted even if an attacker fails to disable the entire system. The results also emphasize the importance of redundancy as a defensive strategy (especially if attacks against redundant components succeed or fail independently of each other). Thus, O'Hanlon et al. [8] note: "Protection should be concentrated on the largest, most critical plants and nodes in the national system, especially ones that lack adequate redundant systems". Finally, our results suggest that secrecy (and even deception) can be important ways of improving security, especially for series systems.

We also suggest that the defender should consider the expected damage caused by attacks against various components, and not only their inherent values. In other words, if one component is more valuable than another, but has a lower probability of being successfully attacked, then the more vulnerable but less valuable component may be more likely to be attacked, and hence merit greater investment. This makes sense given the observation by Woo [7] that "Osama bin Laden has expected very high reliability levels for martyrdom operations". This is in contrast to the recommendation of O'Hanlon et al. [8], who state: "In our view, policy-makers should focus primarily on those targets at which an attack would involve a large number of casualties, would entail significant economic costs, or would critically damage sites of high national significance". Our results suggest that some high-value targets with a low probability of being successfully attacked may not merit investment, while other (less valuable but more vulnerable) targets may merit defending.

Obviously, many real-world systems have complex architectures, so it is important to extend this work to such systems, rather than purely series or parallel systems. Finding optimal attack strategies for arbitrary systems is NP-hard in general, as can be shown from the results in Ben-Dov [9] and Cox et al. [10,11]. Therefore, we may develop near-optimal heuristic attack strategies, and identify optimal or near-optimal defenses against such attacks. It is also worthwhile to extend our models to include time, rather than the current static or 'snapshot' view of system security. This would allow us to model imperfect attacker information (including Bayesian updating of the probability that an attack will be successful), as well as multiple attacks over time.

Acknowledgements

This material is based upon work supported in part by the US Army Research Laboratory and the US Army Research Office under grant number DAAD19-01-1-0502, and by the US National Science Foundation under grant number DMI-0228204. Any opinions, findings, and conclusions or recommendations expressed herein are those of the authors and do not necessarily reflect the views of the sponsors.

References

[1] President's Commission on Critical Infrastructure Protection. Critical foundations: protecting America's infrastructures. Washington, DC, http://www.ciao.gov/resource/pccip/PCCIP_Report.pdf; October 1997.

[2] Schneier B. Managed security monitoring: network security for the 21st century. Counterpane Internet Security, Inc.; 2001 http://www.counterpane.com/msm.pdf.

[3] Schudel G, Wood A. Modeling behavior of the cyber-terrorist. In: Anderson R, Bozek T, Longstaff T, Meitzler W, Skroch M, Van Wyk K, Conference Proceedings: Research on Mitigating the Insider Threat to Information Systems—#2. Santa Monica, CA: Rand; 2000.

[4] Bier V, Abhichandani V. Optimal allocation of resources for defense of simple series and parallel systems from determined adversaries, Proceedings of the Engineering Foundation Conference on Risk-Based Decision making in Water Resources X. Santa Barbara, CA: American Society of Civil Engineers; 2002.

[5] Hillier F, Lieberman G. Introduction to operations research, 4th ed. Oakland, CA: Holden-Day; 1986.

[6] Dresher M. Games of strategy: theory and applications. Englewood Cliffs, NJ: Prentice-Hall; 1961.

[7] Woo G. Insuring against al-Qaeda, Insurance Project Workshop, http://www.nber.org/confer/2003/insurance03/woo.pdf, National Bureau of Economic Research, Inc., Cambridge, MA; January 31 and February 1, 2003.

[8] O'Hanlon M, Orszag P, Daalder I, Destler M, Gunter D, Litan R, Steinberg J. Protecting the American homeland: a preliminary analysis. Washington, DC: Brookings Institution; 2002 http://www.brook.edu/fp/research/projects/homeland/pthindex.htm.

[9] Ben-Dov Y. Optimal testing procedures for special structures of coherent systems. Mgt Sci 1981;27:1410–20.

[10] Cox L, Qiu Y, Kuehner W. Heuristic least-cost computation of discrete classification functions with uncertain argument values. Ann Oper Res 1989;21:1–30.

[11] Cox L, Chiu S, Sun X. Least-cost failure diagnosis in uncertain reliability systems. Reliab Eng Syst Safety 1996;54:203–16.

CHAPTER 4

Malicious Mobile Code

Ralph Wachter and Gary Toth

Mobile code is software obtained from remote systems, transferred across a network, and downloaded and executed on a local system without the need for installation or execution by the recipient. Most Internet interactions use some form of mobile code. It is pervasive in a distributed computing environment. As a result, the rapid spread of viruses, worms, and other exploits are all too common.

New technologies depend on the seamless, safe, and secure use of mobile code. Mobile code, including agent technology, shows great promise for distributed computing but introduces significant risk for misuse. In the current computing environment that relies on commercial off-the-shelf software and Internet connectivity, the concern is creating computer systems that can be protected from malicious mobile code attacks.

As early as the 1970s, the research community, supported by the Department of Defense and the intelligence community, identified the need for operating systems that could enforce confidentiality and integrity policies and could protect from malicious code. Unable to keep pace with the rapid advance of affordable technology, the development of trusted operating systems fell behind, so the military and intelligence communities instead turned their focus to the safe and secure use of commodity products.

Today, mitigation tools and strategies are reactive, developed only in response to the release of a new exploitation, giving the attackers a time advantage. In efforts to mitigate malicious code for mobile software, several research teams have produced results ranging from sound theoretical frameworks to prototypes that are almost ready for fielding.

This chapter presents technical papers from three projects focused on defending against malicious code by:

- Effective detection and response to malicious code
- Understanding of threat and vulnerability
- Building resilience and self-recovery systems
- Establishing safe environments for mobile code
- Trusted and authenticated mobile code

Professor Schneider and a team at Cornell University undertook research in language-based security and produced security policies and corresponding enforcement mechanisms to establish trust in systems and applications software. These enforcement mechanisms include in-lined reference monitors for application-level safety, type systems for ensuring the safety of legacy languages and for end-to-end confidentiality, and secure languages for firmware, used to ensure secure system boot. They created the following tools: Cyclone, In-lined Reference Monitors, and JIF Confidentiality and Integrity Enforcement, while establishing interactions with AT&T, Inc., Sun Microsystems, Inc., and the Microsoft Corporation. The paper "Language-Based Security for Malicious Mobile Code" provides a good summary of this team's research results.

The summary paper titled "Safe Execution of Mobile and Untrusted Code: The Model-Carrying Code Project" discusses the software prototype developed by the research team lead by Professor Sekar at the State University of New York at Stony Brook. The prototype embodies a new approach, known as model-carrying code (MCC), which allows users to benefit from benign mobile code while mitigating the risks from mobile malicious code. MCC tools, languages, and verifiers enable developers to build behavioral models of their mobile code, and users to verify that mobile code is compliant with their security policy. The code runs in a recoverable, monitored execution environment, which validates that the code satisfies its accompanying model. If the code does not conform to the model, the state of the system before execution is restored. So the responsibility for safe execution is shared by the code producer and the code consumer. Computer Associates, a leading vendor of security software, developed the model-carrying code technology into a management tool and platform for an enterprise environment.

Professor Whittaker at the Florida Institute of Technology took a behavioral approach in the Gatekeeper project to virus detection with an undo capability. This approach provides a greater capability for detection while significantly reducing the number of false positives. A small business was spawned to sell both Gatekeeper products. The early work has been incorporated into the Harris Corporation's STAT security software tools. The context paper "Behavioral Detection of Malicious Code" summarizes the work carried out by this MURI team.

Language-Based Security for Malicious Mobile Code

Fred B. Schneider

fbs@cs.cornell.edu

Dexter Kozen

kozen@cs.cornell.edu

Greg Morrisett

greg@eecs.harvard.edu

Andrew C. Myers

andru@cs.cornell.edu

Abstract

Classical operating system architecture provides support for only a limited class of coarse-grained security policies. Furthermore, system software has grown too large and complicated to be considered trustworthy. To address these shortcomings, we have explored the application of *programming language* technology, including advanced type-systems, proof systems, analyses, and compilers for realizing new classes of security policies and for reducing or relocating the trusted computing base.

Categories and Subject Descriptors

D.3.3 [Programming Languages]: Language Constructs and Features

D.4.6 [Operating Systems]: Security and Protection

F.3.1 [Logics and Meanings of Programs]: Specifying and Verifying and Reasoning about Programs

K.6.5 [Management of Computing and Information Systems]: Security and Protection

General Terms

Languages, Security, Verification

Keywords:

in-lined reference monitor, static analysis, type systems, proof-carrying code, secure information flow, firmware

1 Introduction

The need for secure computing first became apparent in the early 1970's, when the high cost of hardware forced users to share standalone computers by multiplexing processor time. Concurrent processes had to be isolated from each other in order to prevent the bugs of one process from disrupting the execution of another. Different processes resided in separate regions of memory and used the processor during disjoint time intervals. Security policies governed access to shared resources, such as long-term storage, so that they could be shared in a safe and controlled way. The operating system, through a hardware-based *reference monitor*, enforced these policies by intercepting critical operations and blocking them if necessary. Reference monitors and mechanisms enforcing program isolation were small and understandable, so one could be confident that these security policies would be enforced.

Today's operating systems are much more complex than those of the 1970's. They consist of tens of millions of lines of code and must be frequently updated with patches, new device drivers, and other modules received over the Internet. The extensions might come from authenticated sources, but it is difficult to design code that works correctly in every context. There is little basis for confidence in such large pieces of code that evolve rapidly with frequent updates. It is no surprise that with alarming regularity, attackers exploit logic and coding errors to compromise confidentiality, integrity, or availability of computing systems.

Application software that runs above the operating system is also frequently updated by extensions, often packaged as applets or scripts. Content received over the Internet, such as email messages and web pages, typically includes active elements that are executed upon receipt, often without a user's knowledge or ability to intervene. As a result, users today are susceptible to a new class of attacks—attacks not against the operating system but against applications. Since applications run with the privileges of a user, these attacks have access to confidential data and can easily compromise the integrity of the host and data. Virus scanners have proven effective for blocking some known attacks of this form, but they cannot detect previously unseen or obfuscated threats.

In short, today's computers run a collection of software that is dynamically changing, and users often cannot determine what software is actually being executed, what caused it to execute, or what it might do. Classical operating system mechanisms for isolation and reference monitors provide only limited protection, because they do not distinguish between legitimate application code running on behalf of the user and code provided by an attacker. Furthermore, system software has grown too large and complicated to be considered trustworthy. New technology is needed to build systems that are secure and that we can trust.

2   Language-Based Security

The efforts of this project focus on rich classes of security policies and corresponding enforcement mechanisms that can be used to establish trust in system and application software, regardless of origin. Such mechanisms must remain effective despite the ever-increasing size of operating systems and the constant changes that system and application software must undergo. The enabling technologies come from research in *programming languages*, including semantics, type systems, program logics, compilers, and runtime systems. We believe that research in these areas is capable of delivering the flexible, general, and high-performance enforcement mechanisms we seek as well as providing a basis for assurance in the resulting enforcement mechanisms. Here is our rationale.

- The functionality of any hardware-based mechanism can always be achieved by software alone, since one can build an interpreter that does the same checks as the hardware. If the overhead of interpretation is too great, the performance gap can be closed by using compilation technologies, such as just-in-time compilers, partial evaluation, runtime code generation, and profile-driven feedback optimization. Furthermore, unlike hardware realizations, software implementations can be more easily extended or changed to meet new, application-specific demands as the context changes. Indeed, in Section 3, we describe an approach that allows application-specific policies to be easily specified and dynamically composed.

- Modern high-level languages, including Java and ML, provide linguistic structure such as modules, abstract data types, and classes that allow programmers to specify and encapsulate application-specific abstractions. The interfaces of these abstractions can then be used to enrich the vocabulary of the security framework with application-specific concepts, principles, and operations.

- Code analysis, including type checking, dataflow analysis, abstract interpretation, and proof checking, can be leveraged to reason statically about the runtime behavior of code. This allows us to enforce policies, such as restrictions on information flow, that are impossible to implement using runtime mechanisms such as reference monitors. Program analysis also allows further code optimization to eliminate unnecessary dynamic checks. The program analyzer, which could well be a large and complex piece of code, can be replaced in a trusted computing base (TCB) by a proof checker, which will typically be much smaller.

In short, by analyzing code before it executes, runtime checks are avoided, a wider class of policies can be enforced, and the trusted computing base can be relocated. By modifying code before it executes, policies that involve application-specific abstractions and arbitrary program interfaces can be enforced. Finally, by using high-level language abstractions, we can effectively enrich the vocabulary of the security policy and its enforcement mechanisms.

The idea of using languages and compilers to help enforce security policies is not new. The Burroughs B-5000 system required applications to be written in a high-level language (Algol), and the Berkeley SDS-940 system employed object-code rewriting as part of its system profiler. More recently, the SPIN [5], Vino [52, 47], and Exokernel [13] extensible operating systems have relied on language technology to protect a base system from a limited set of attacks by extensions. What is new in our work is the degree to which language semantics provides the leverage. We have examined integrated mechanisms that work for both high- and low-level languages, that are applicable to an extremely broad class of fine-grained security policies, and that allow flexible allocation of work and trust among the elements responsible for enforcement.

In the following, we report on four specific focus areas where we have successfully applied language technology to increase the system security: in-lined reference monitors for application-level safety properties (Section 3), type systems for ensuring safety of low-level legacy languages (Section 4), type systems for end-to-end confidentiality and integrity (Section 5), and secure languages for firmware (Section 6).

3 Inlined Reference Monitors

SFI (software fault isolation) employs program modification to rewrite binaries so that only reads, writes, or branches to appropriate locations in a program's address space are allowed [51]. This *memory safety* security policy is useful for protecting a base system (e.g., a kernel) from certain misbehavior by extensions as well as for protecting different users' programs from each other. Though traditionally enforced by address translation hardware, supporting memory safety by program modification has two advantages: (i) it reduces the overhead of cross-domain procedure calls and (ii) it can implement a more-flexible memory-safety model.

SFI-inserted code can be viewed as a reference monitor that has been "in-lined" into a *target application*. This observation led us to investigate the fundamental limits and engineering issues associated with using in-lined reference monitors (IRMs) in general. With the IRM approach, a security policy is specified in a declarative language, and a general-purpose tool is used to rewrite code for the target application, inserting tests and state to enforce the policy.

Schneider proved that the class of properties that can be enforced by a reference monitor (in-lined or otherwise) is restricted to safety properties[1] and that any enforceable safety property could, at least in principle, be enforced by an execution monitor [46].

In subsequent work, Morrisett, Schneider and their graduate student Hamlen revisited the framework to consider issues of computability and the more general class of *program rewriters* as policy enforcement mechanisms [23]. In this revised model, a program rewriter is allowed to replace faulty or malicious code with any new behavior, as long as that behavior respects the intended policy. Intuitively, IRMs are a special case of rewriters that replace faulty code with "halt". The framework allowed us to compare different enforcement mechanisms, including static analyses, IRMs, and program rewriters and show formally that rewriters can enforce strictly more policies than the other approaches.

The rewriting approach is particularly attractive from a methodological perspective, because it allows composition and analysis of policies. The conjunction of two policies is enforced by passing the target application through the rewriter twice in succession—once for each policy. By keeping policy separate from program, we can more easily reason about and evolve the security of a system. Furthermore, now that the class of security policies that can be enforced by rewriting is characterized in a mathematically rigorous way, it is ideal for use in connection with other language-based approaches, which exploit formal semantics and analysis.

The rewriting approach also has been shown to be practical. Two generations of prototypes have been built and a third is under construction. The first prototype, SASI (Security Automata SFI Implementation), handled Intel's x86 and Java's JVM architectures [15]; the second, PSLang (Policy Specification Language) and PoET (Policy Enforcement Toolkit), demonstrates the extent to which object-code type annotations are helpful but works only on JVML. The PSLang/PoET prototype gives competitive performance for the implementation of Java's stack inspection security policy [14].

A disadvantage with both SASI and PoET/PSLang is that they depend crucially upon the correctness of the rewriter. Our third prototype, called Mobile and which is being developed for Microsoft's .NET framework, overcomes this limitation. The Mobile rewriter produces modified code along with a set of annotations that allows a third party checker to easily verify that the resulting code respects the policy. Thus, the rewriter is removed from the trusted computing base in favor of a (simpler) trusted type-checker. In this respect, Mobile is a *certified* rewriter that leverages the ideas of proof-carrying code [38].

---

[1]In the literature on concurrent program verification, *safety properties* correspond to closed sets and *liveness properties* correspond to dense sets. Every property is thus the conjunction of a safety and a liveness property [45]

4   Type Systems for Legacy Languages

High-level languages, such as Java, C#, and ML provide compelling security and reliability benefits. In particular, a type-safe language automatically ensures both object-level memory isolation and a form of control-flow isolation, which are necessary to ensure the integrity of any reference monitor. Nevertheless, most of today's security-critical software is written in type-*unsafe* languages. For example, all major operating systems including Windows, Mac OS X, Linux, etc. are written in C. Consequently, attackers have been able to leverage coding flaws including buffer overruns, integer overflows, and format string mismatches—all flaws that would be prevented in a type-safe language—to break into machines.

Given that operating systems consist of tens of millions of lines of code, it is simply too expensive for vendors to throw away the code and start over in a type-safe language. Even if they could afford to do so, there are strong technical reasons that prevent the use of today's type-safe languages in domains such as operating systems, real-time systems, and embedded systems. In large part, this is because today's type-safe languages, unlike C and C++, do not provide the degree of control over data representations, memory management, predictability, and code performance that is needed for these settings.

4.1   Type-Safe C Code

We have developed a type-safe dialect of C known as Cyclone[2] for use in systems programming. When compared to bug-finding tools such as Lint, SPLint, Prefix and Prefast, the primary advantage of Cyclone is that it makes a strong *guarantee* of type safety that is enforced through a combination of (a) an advanced type system, (b) sophisticated static analyses, (c) language extensions, and (d) run-time checks inserted by the compiler. The type-safety guarantee ensures that a wide class of attacks, including buffer overruns, format string attacks, and integer overflow attacks cannot be used to subvert the integrity of a service. Just as importantly, the static type system ensures that common coding errors (e.g., accessing an uninitialized variable) are caught early.

Of course the safety provided by Cyclone or any other type-safe language has a price. Figure 1 shows the performance of Cyclone and Java code normalized to the performance of C code for most of the micro-benchmarks in the *Great Programming Language Shootout*.[3]

The average over all of the benchmarks (plotted on the far right) shows that Cyclone is about 60% slower than GCC, whereas Sun's Java VM is about 6.5 times slower. For larger, more realistic benchmarks we see even less overhead for Cyclone. For example, our Cyclone port of the Boa Web server[4], adds only about 3% overhead [25]. And of course, we found and fixed a number of errors in the various programs we have ported, including buffer overruns, that could lead to successful penetrations.

In addition to time, programmers worry about other resources such as space. Most type-

---

[2]The Cyclone compiler, tools, and documentation are freely available at `http://www.eecs.harvard.edu/~greg/cyclone/`.

[3]See `http://shootout.alioth.debian.org/`. The benchmarks were run on a dual 2.8GHz/2GB Red Hat Enterprise workstation. We used Cyclone version 0.8.2 with the -O3 flag, Sun's Java client SDK build version 1.4.2_05-b04, and GCC version 3.2.3 with the -O3 flag. Each reported number in Figure 1 is the median of 11 trials.

[4]`http://www.boa.org`

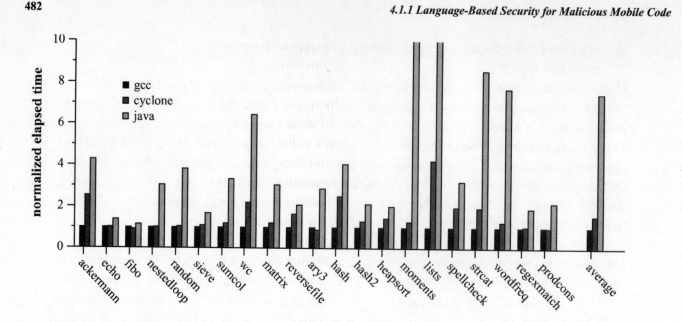

Figure 1: Great Programming Language Shootout Performance for C, Cyclone, and Java

safe languages, including Java, take resource control away from the programmer. For instance, memory management in Java is handled automatically by a garbage collector. In contrast, Cyclone provides the low-level control over data layout and memory management needed to build kernels and embedded systems. In particular, it provides a sophisticated region-based type system [22] coupled with an ownership model [25] that yields type-safe, real-time, programmer-controlled memory management. In addition, because the language has no hidden type-tags and uses the same data representations and calling conventions as C, it is easy to interface Cyclone code with legacy libraries.

We have found that with respect to space, there are again overheads when using Cyclone as compared to C, but these overheads are much less than for Java. For instance, the C version of the *heapsort* benchmark had a maximum resident working set size of 472 pages, the Cyclone version used 504 pages, and the Java version used 2,471. In general, by supporting safe manual memory management, Cyclone is able to significantly reduce space overheads present in garbage-collected languages [25].

There is another cost to achieving safety, namely, the cost of porting a program from C to a safe language. Porting a program to C# or Java involves a complete rewrite for anything but the simplest programs. In contrast, most of the Shootout benchmarks, and indeed larger programs such as the Boa web server, can be ported to Cyclone by touching 5 to 15 percent of the lines of code. To achieve the best performance, programmers may have to provide additional information in the form of *extended type qualifiers* or *assertions* that are statically checked by the compiler. Of course, the number of lines of code that changed tells us little about how hard it is to make those changes. In all honesty, this can still be a time-consuming and frustrating task. Nevertheless, it is considerably easier than rewriting the program from scratch in a new language.

CCured [39] is another dialect of C that provides a strong type safety guarantee. Like Cyclone, CCured uses a combination of static analysis and run-time checks to ensure object-level type safety. It is generally easier to port an application from C to CCured because the analysis is almost fully automatic. However, CCured implicitly adds meta-data to objects to support run-time checks and relies upon a garbage collector to manage memory. Finally, CCured cannot easily support a multi-threaded environment. These shortcomings make it difficult to use CCured in critical systems such as kernels, embedded, or real-time systems.

Other tools, such as Evans's SPLint [16], Microsoft's Prefix [6] and SLAM [3], and Engler's Metal [12] provide support for sophisticated static analysis or software model checking. These tools can detect bugs at compile time that Cyclone cannot, but most of them, including Prefix, SPLint and Metal are *unsound* because they make optimistic assumptions. For instance, the analyses used in Metal ignore the potential for aliasing or interactions among multiple threads, which is of course common in systems programs. In turn, this may cause the tool to miss a potential bug because the semantics are not accurately modeled. In short, all of these tools are extremely good for finding bugs, but not ensuring their absence. In contrast, Cyclone either reports a static error or inserts a dynamic check for each potential error and can thus provide guarantees.

4.2 Type-Safe Machine Code

Java is by far the most widely appreciated example of a language in which type safety is used to provide security. The functionality of a Java-enabled system, such as a Web browser, can be dynamically extended by downloading Java code (applets) to be executed within the context of the system. In fact, a browser does not accept Java source code directly, but rather, JVML bytecodes (generated by a compiler) that are better suited for direct execution. Therefore, the security of the browser does not depend on the type safety of Java source, but rather the type safety of the executable JVML code.

Before executing potentially malicious JVML code, the browser invokes a verifier to check the type-consistency of the bytecode with respect to an interface that mediates access to the browser internals. The process of type-checking is meant to ensure that the applet code is isolated from the surrounding context of the browser, and that access to browser resources is mediated through the provided interface. Different security policies can be realized by changing this interface. For example, applets from a trusted source (e.g., the local machine) may be given access to the file system, whereas applets from an untrusted source (e.g., another host) may not.

Though more flexible than traditional OS-based mechanisms, the JVML type system is not without shortcomings. First, the type system is relatively weak by modern standards. For instance, it provides no notion of parametric polymorphism. Second, the JVML is a relatively high level CISC machine language tailored for Java. As such, it is ill-suited for compiling other type-safe languages including Cyclone. For example, because JVML provides no support for tail calls, it makes a poor target language when compiling functional languages. Finally, the official specification of the JVML type system is an informal English description and provides no model for ensuring soundness, though recent work has provided formal specifications of important fragments of the language [48, 10, 43, 20, 17, 18, 40]. Even if such formal models can be constructed, it would be a daunting task to prove the correctness of a production JVML verifier, JIT compiler, and runtime. Hence, the JVML model requires trusting a rather large set of components that in practice have proven unreliable [28].

To address some of the shortcomings of the JVML, we have studied and developed advanced type systems for concrete machine languages. A by-product of this work is called

Typed Assembly Language (TAL) [31, 32]. Unlike the JVML, TAL is based on a low-level RISC-like machine model and consequently is better suited for compiling a variety of source languages, not just Java. Furthermore, the type system of TAL is powerful enough that many more checks can be done statically and thus compilers can produce more efficient code. For example, a general class of array bounds checks can be statically verified by the current TAL type checker, whereas the JVML type system requires run-time tests.

The current TAL implementation has been tailored for the widely deployed Intel x86 line of processors. On those machines, TAL code can be executed without translation, so the TCB does not include an interpreter or compiler. Like the JVML, key fragments of the TAL type system and semantics have a formal model, and a soundness result has been proven.

5 Type Systems for End-to-End Security

Type safety is essential to secure programming. However, code may contain vulnerabilities or malicious code that can lead to security violations without compromising type safety. Malicious programs may simply violate confidentiality (secrecy) by leaking sensitive information. And programs often contain vulnerabilities that enable attackers to violate confidentiality or integrity. This has been an ongoing problem for various web services. For example, the Hotmail email service has at times had vulnerabilities that permitted users to improperly read each others' mail.

Systems are secure only if they protect the confidentiality and integrity of the data they manipulate. Ideally we would like to be able to state high-level security requirements and have them automatically checked for programs. This would be useful both for users downloading possible malicious programs, and for program designers who want assurance that they have met the security requirements.

We have been exploring policies based on *information flow* (e.g., [19, 11]), which are attractive because they govern *end-to-end* use of information within a system. Information flow policies are therefore more expressive than ordinary (discretionary) access control, which regulates which principals (users, machines, programs, or other entities) can read or modify the data at particular points during execution, but do not track how information propagates.

We have been most interested in enforcing two fundamental information security properties: confidentiality, which requires that information not be released improperly, and integrity, which requires that information be computed properly from trustworthy information sources. To understand where information propagates, it is useful to have access to a program-level representation of the computation using the information. Previous run-time schemes for tracking information flow, such as mandatory access control, lacked precision and imposed substantial time and space overhead.

5.1 Mostly-Static Information Flow Control

A compile-time analysis of programs can check that information flows within programs in accordance with confidentiality and integrity requirements. In fact, this static analysis can be described as a type system in which the type of data in the program carries not only information about the structure of the data (such as `int`), but also carries security restrictions on the use of the data. Such a language is said to have *security types*. The program does not have to be trusted to enforce the security policy; only the type checker must be trusted.

Security types are provided by our programming language Jif [34] (for Java Information Flow), which extends the Java language with support for specification and analysis of information flow. The Jif compiler checks information flow, then translates the Jif program to an equivalent Java program with extra embedded annotations that carry security information. Thus, run-time space and time overhead are small. Jif has been publicly available now for a few years and has been used by several other research projects. While a number of other related languages have been designed for theoretical studies (e.g., [50, 24, 54, 4, 42]), Jif remains the most complete and powerful implementation of static information flow analysis, and it has also influenced other language designs.[5]

5.2   Security Labels

Jif programs contain labels based on the *decentralized label model* (DLM) [35], in which principals can express ownership of information-flow policies. This model works well for systems incorporating mutual distrust, because labels specify on whose behalf the security policy operates. In particular, label ownership is used to control the use of *selective declassification* [41], a feature needed for realistic applications of information-flow control.

In this model, a *principal* is an entity (e.g., user, process) that can have a security concern. These concerns are expressed as labels, which state confidentiality or integrity policies that apply to the labeled data. Principals can be named in these policies as owners of policies and as readers of data.

For example, a security label specifying confidentiality is written as $\{\texttt{o}:\texttt{r}_1,\texttt{r}_2,\ldots,\texttt{r}_n\}$, meaning that the labeled data is owned by principal $\texttt{o}$, and that $\texttt{o}$ permits the data to be read by principals $\texttt{r}_1$ through $\texttt{r}_n$ (and, implicitly, $\texttt{o}$). A label is a security policy controlling the uses of the data it labels; only the owner has the right to weaken this policy.

Labels on data create restrictions on the use of that data. The use of high-confidentiality data is restricted to prevent information leaks, and the use of low-integrity data is restricted to prevent information corruption. The label on information may be securely changed from label L_1 to label L_2 if L_2 specifies at least as much confidentiality as L_1, and at most as much integrity as L_1. This label relationship is written as $L_1 \sqsubseteq L_2$.

For example, if a Jif program contains variables x_1 and x_2 with labels L_1 and L_2 respectively, then an assignment $x_2 = x_1$ is permitted only if $L_1 \sqsubseteq L_2$. Otherwise, the assignment transfers the information in x_1 to a location with a weaker security label. For labels in the DLM, this relationship can be checked at compile time, so the labels of x_1 and x_2 are not represented at run time.

Recently, we have shown how to extend the DLM to include policies for information availability [59]. Because information flow analysis is essentially a dependency analysis, a static information flow analysis can determine how system availability depends on availability of inputs.

---

[5]More information on this approach can be found in our frequently-cited survey of work on language-based information flow security [44].

5.3   Beyond Zero Information Flow

The usual formalization of information security is in terms of *noninterference*, a formal statement that no information flow occurs from one security level to another. Noninterference is mathematically elegant, but real programs need to release some information as part of their proper functioning. For example, a password program leaks a little information about passwords because a guesser learns at least that the password is not the guessed password. To characterize the security of real systems, more notions of security are needed that are more expressive and general than noninterference.

Recent results show substantial progress toward this goal. We identified a property called *robustness* that generalizes noninterference by ensuring that information release, while permitted, cannot be affected by untrusted attackers [53]. Further, we proved that robustness can be enforced by a static program analysis that permits information release only at high-integrity program points [36]. This analysis is built into recent versions of Jif.

Another way to generalize noninterference is to control the quantity of information that is released by a system. A standard approach has been to model the quantity of information in terms of the reduction in the uncertainty of the attacker [11, 29, 21]. We have shown that *accuracy* can be used a quantitative information metric, avoiding troubling anomalies that arise in the uncertainty-based approach [9].

One further promising approach to generalizing noninterference is to add policies for downgrading and erasure [7, 8]. Downgrading policies say when downgrading can be used to weaken noninterference; dually, erasure policies say when information erasure must be used to strengthen noninterference. Erasure policies require that the system "forget" information at a given security level.

5.4   Automatic Partitioning of Secure Distributed Systems

Distributed systems make security assurance particularly difficult, as these systems naturally cross administrative and trust boundaries; typically, some of the participants in a distributed computation do not trust other participants or the computing software and hardware they provide. Systems meeting this description include clinical and financial information systems, business-to-business transactions, and joint military information systems. These systems are distributed precisely *because* they serve the interests of mutually distrusting principals. The open question is how programmers should build distributed systems that properly enforce strong security policies for data confidentiality and integrity.

We introduced automatic program partitioning and replication [56, 57, 58] as a way to solve this problem. As depicted in Figure 2, the Jif/split compiler automatically partitions high-level, non-distributed code into distributed subprograms that run securely on a collection of host machines that are trusted to varying degrees by the participating principals. (Such hosts are *heterogeneously trusted*.) A partitioning is secure if the security of a principal can be harmed only by the hosts the principal trusts. Thus, partitioning of the source program is driven by a high-level specification of security policies and trust.

Both code and data are partitioned to ensure that data and computation are not placed on a machine where confidentiality or integrity might be violated. Sometimes there is no single machine that is sufficiently trusted to protect the integrity of data or computation; in that case,

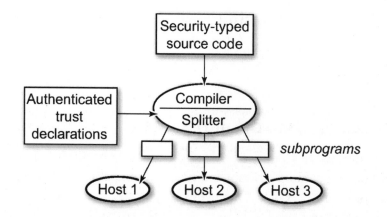

Figure 2: Program partitioning

the partitioning process may replicate the data or computation across several hosts. Results are only considered to be high integrity when all the replica hosts agree on its value.

A number of distributed programs have been implemented using automatic program partitioning and replication, including a variety of online auction programs, a banking simulation, and the game of Battleship. Static information flow checking caught a number of bugs in our implementations of these programs. We compared the distributed programs generated automatically by Jif/split with carefully hand-coded versions of the same programs; the results suggested that the run-time performance of Jif/split programs is reasonable; the hand-coded programs are more efficient primarily because they can exploit concurrency. We have studied information flow in the presence of concurrency [55], but Jif does not yet support concurrent programming because concurrency can create covert timing channels.

6 Secure Languages for Firmware

Firmware is low-level driver code associated with hardware devices whose purpose is to provide an interface by which the system can operate the device. On a typical computing platform, firmware is composed of many interacting modules. There is usually some central kernel support, as well as device drivers supplied by the manufacturers of the various hardware components. A driver for a particular device may be used to initialize the device, perform diagnostic checks, establish communication with other devices connected to it, allocate system resources, and other similar tasks. Often the drivers reside in ROM on the devices themselves and are loaded at boot time.

Because these device drivers are normally considered part of the trusted computing base, they constitute a significant security risk. They execute in privileged mode and have essentially unrestricted access to other devices and the entire hardware configuration. They could easily circumvent any operating system-based security mechanism. A malicious driver would have virtually limitless potential to cause irreparable damage, introduce channels for clandestine access, install arbitrary software, or modify the operating system.

Compounding the worry is that most drivers are written by third-party device manufacturers and may come from various subcontractors of unknown origin. Many of these devices and their associated firmware are mass-produced overseas, outside the purview of any domestic authority. It would be well within the capability of a determined adversary to exploit this vulnerability on a massive scale.

Attempts to address this security issue generally fall into two categories: *authentication-based* and *language-based*.

6.1   Authentication-Based Approaches

In an authentication-based approach, an attempt is made to ensure the integrity of firmware via digital signatures or chain-of-custody and physical protection. This strategy requires that the firmware was originally benign. This belief is typically based on trust in the supplier or in some detailed inspection of the code by a (human) certifying authority. It simply ensures that the code has not been tampered with after it was approved. This strategy can preserve an existing relationship of trust, but it cannot establish new trust. Examples of this approach are the driver-certification scheme currently used by Microsoft and the AEGIS system [2].

The authentication-based approach is currently the preferred strategy in practice today. However, its use is not without cost. There may be a large, far-flung network of vendors for whom trust must be established. Moreover, there are mechanisms for automatically updating device drivers and firmware with patches via the Internet. Firmware that is updated regularly needs to be reexamined each time.

6.2   The Language-Based Approach

In the language-based approach, firmware modules are written in a type-safe language and compiled to an annotated bytecode form. Each time a firmware module is loaded, it is automatically and invisibly verified against a standard security policy by a trusted verifier. The compiled code and the compiler that produced it need not be trusted. This approach is similar to proof-carrying code and related techniques [37, 38, 30, 33, 27].

In this project, we have developed a prototype called *BootSafe* [1, 49]. The system operates in the context of the Open Firmware standard [26], an IEEE standard for boot firmware that was developed in the mid 1990's and is now in widespread use. Both Sun Microsystems and Apple use boot firmware that conforms to the standard. Several commercial implementations of Open Firmware are available.

The Open Firmware standard is based on the Forth programming language. Currently, device drivers are written in Forth and compiled to *fcode*, a low-level, mostly machine-independent bytecode language similar to the Java virtual machine language. Every Open Firmware-compliant boot kernel must include an fcode interpreter or virtual machine.

The BootSafe architecture consists of several major subsystems:

- J2F, an annotating Java bytecode to Forth fcode compiler;

- a stand-alone verifier;

- an API and runtime support library consisting of various Java classes and interfaces.

BootSafe-compliant device drivers are written in Java. They may extend system classes provided by the API that implement standard functionality and provide access to Open Firmware services. They may also be required to implement certain Java interfaces in the API that specify functionality necessary to conform to the Open Firmware standard. Java thus provides an enforcement mechanism that is absent in Forth.

The Java driver is compiled to bytecode using any standard off-the-shelf Java compiler. The BootSafe compiler J2F is then used to compile the (typed) Java bytecode to annotated fcode. The fcode driver can then be shipped with the hardware device. In Open Firmware, the driver is burned into ROM and stored on the device itself.

When the system boots, the boot kernel recursively probes the system bus to determine the hardware configuration and initialize devices. At that time, each device is probed to see if there is an on-board driver. If so, it is loaded into main memory, linked against the runtime support library, and executed. Just before execution, the verifier checks the driver to ensure compliance with the security policy.

The security policy used in BootSafe is a standard, baked-in policy appropriate for device drivers. Besides basic memory and control-flow safety, the security policy asserts that device drivers may not access other devices, may only access system memory and bus addresses allocated to them through a strictly controlled allocation and deallocation procedure, and may otherwise interact with the system only through a strict interface provided by the API.

Our prototype contains fully operational and verified Open Firmware-compliant boot drivers written in Java for a network card and a 1.4Mb floppy disk drive.

6.3   Limitations

Language-based techniques, while a strong countermeasure to malicious firmware, cannot protect against all forms of attack. For example, certain denial-of-service attacks and malicious hardware are difficult or impossible to detect. However, they do raise the bar by making it more difficult for drivers to operate devices maliciously.

7   Putting It Together

In-lined reference monitors, advanced type systems, and certifying compilers are promising approaches to system security. Each allows rich instantiations of the Principle of Least Privilege; each involves only a small and verifiable trusted computing base. Moreover, our language-based security approaches seem ideally suited for use in extensible and component-based software—a domain not served well by traditional operating system reference monitors.

We have solved a large number of both theoretical and practical engineering problems for these separate areas of language-based security. Moreover, we have demonstrated that they can work together to achieve more than the sum of the parts. For example, in the Mobile rewriter, by coupling IRM-style rewriting with certifying compilation, we are able to eliminate the need for a trusted rewriter. By leveraging the type-safety of the Microsoft intermediate language, we are able to avoid the dynamic overheads of protecting the integrity of the in-lined reference monitor. At the same time, we were able to augment the ideas of proof-carrying code to provide for a more dynamic and flexible policy language.

The possible ways to combine rewriting, static analysis, and certification are endless, and the tradeoffs are complex. We believe that a key underlying theme is the relocation of function and trust in the TCB. It seems easier to insert run-time checks than to do analysis before execution is started. Yet, static analysis can lead to better performance, because it occurs offline and deals better with non-safety properties such as availability and integrity. It also seems easier and requires a smaller TCB to check proofs than to create them.

References

[1] Frank Adelstein, Dexter Kozen, and Matt Stillerman. Malicious code detection for open firmware. In *Proc. 18th Computer Security Applications Conf. (ACSAC'02)*, pages 403–412, December 2002.

[2] William A. Arbaugh, David J. Farber, and Jonathan M. Smith. A secure and reliable bootstrap architecture. In *Proc. 1997 Symposium on Security and Privacy*, pages 65–71. IEEE, May 1997.

[3] Thomas Ball and Sriram Rajamani. The SLAM project: Debugging system software via static analysis. In *Twenty-Ninth ACM SIGPLAN/SIGACT Symposium on Principles of Programming Languages*, pages 1–3, Portland, OR, January 2002.

[4] Anindya Banerjee and David A. Naumann. Secure information flow and pointer confinement in a Java-like language. In *IEEE Computer Security Foundations Workshop (CSFW)*, June 2002.

[5] Brain Bershad, Stefan Savage, Przemyslaw Pardyak, Emin Sirer, Marc Fiuczynski, David Becker, Craig Chambers, and Susan Eggers. Extensibility, safety and performance in the SPIN operating system. In *Proc. 15th ACM Symp. on Operating System Principles (SOSP)*, pages 267–284, Copper Mountain, December 1995.

[6] William Bush, Jonathan Pincus, and David Sielaff. A static analyzer for finding dynamic programming errors. *Software – Practice and Experience*, 30(7):775–802, June 2000.

[7] Stephen Chong and Andrew C. Myers. Security policies for downgrading. In *Proc. 11th ACM Conference on Computer and Communications Security*, pages 198–209, October 2004.

[8] Stephen Chong and Andrew C. Myers. Language-based information erasure. In *Proc. 18th IEEE Computer Security Foundations Workshop*, June 2005.

[9] Michael R. Clarkson, Andrew C. Myers, and Fred B. Schneider. Belief in information flow. In *Proc. 18th IEEE Computer Security Foundations Workshop*, June 2005.

[10] Alessandro Coglio, Allen Goldberg, and Zhenyu Qian. Towards a provably-correct implementation of the JVM bytecode verifier. In *Proceedings of the OOPSLA'98 Workshop on the Formal Underpinnings of Java*, Vancouver, B.C., October 1998.

[11] Dorothy E. Denning. *Cryptography and Data Security*. Addison-Wesley, Reading, Massachusetts, 1982.

[12] Dawson Engler, Benjamin Chelf, Andy Chou, and Seth Hallem. Checking system rules using system-specific, programmer-written compiler extensions. In *Proceedings of the Fourth USENIX Symposium on Operating Systems Design and Implementation*, October 2000.

[13] D.R. Engler, M.F. Kaashoek, and J. O'Toole. Exokernel: An operating system architecture for application-level resource management. In *Proc. 15th ACM Symp. on Operating System Principles (SOSP)*, Copper Mountain, 1995.

[14] U. Erlingsson and F.B. Schneider. Irm enforcement of java stack inspection. In *IEEE Symposium on Security and Privacy*, Oakland, California, May 2000. To appear.

[15] Ulfar Erlingsson and Fred B. Schneider. SASI enforcement of security policies: A retrospective. In *Proceedings of the New Security Paradigms Workshop*, Ontario, Canada, September 1999.

[16] David Evans and David Larochelle. Improving security using extensible lightweight static analysis. *IEEE Software*, 19(1):42–51, January 2002.

[17] S. Freund and J. Mitchell. A type system for object initialization in the Java bytecode language. In *Proc. Conf. on Object-Oriented Programming, Systems, Languages, and Applications*, pages 310–328. ACM Press, 1998.

[18] S. Freund and J. Mitchell. Specification and verification of Java bytecode subroutines and exceptions. Technical report, Computer Science Department, Stanford University, 1999.

[19] Joseph A. Goguen and Jose Meseguer. Security policies and security models. In *Proc. IEEE Symposium on Security and Privacy*, pages 11–20, April 1982.

[20] Allen Goldberg. A specification of Java loading and bytecode verification. In *Proc. 5th ACM Conf. on Computer and Communications Security*, San Francisco, California, October 1998.

[21] James W. Gray, III. Towards a mathematical foundation for information flow security. In *Proc. IEEE Symposium on Security and Privacy*, pages 21–34, 1991.

[22] Dan Grossman, Greg Morrisett, Trevor Jim, Michael Hicks, Yanling Wang, and James Cheney. Region-based memory management in Cyclone. In *Proceedings of the ACM SIGPLAN Conference on Programming Language Design and Implementation*, June 2002.

[23] Kevin Hamlen, Greg Morrisett, and Fred B. Schneider. Computability classes for enforcement mechanisms. *ACM Transactions on Programming Languages and Systems*. To appear.

[24] Nevin Heintze and Jon G. Riecke. The SLam calculus: Programming with secrecy and integrity. In *Proc. 25th ACM Symp. on Principles of Programming Languages (POPL)*, San Diego, California, January 1998.

[25] Michael Hicks, Greg Morrisett, Dan Grossman, and Trevor Jim. Experience with safe manual memory management in cyclone. In *Proceedings of the ACM International Symposium on Memory Management (ISMM)*, pages 73–84, October 2004.

[26] IEEE. *IEEE Standard for Boot (Initialization Configuration) Firmware: Core Requirements and Practices*, 1994. Standard 1275-1994.

[27] Dexter Kozen. Efficient code certification. Technical Report 98-1661, Computer Science Department, Cornell University, January 1998.

[28] Gary McGraw and Edward Felten. *Hostile Applets, Holes and Antidotes*. John Wiley and Sons, New York, 1996.

[29] Jonathan K. Millen. Covert channel capacity. In *Proc. IEEE Symposium on Security and Privacy*, Oakland, CA, 1987.

[30] Greg Morrisett, Karl Crary, Neal Glew, Dan Grossman, Richard Samuels, Frederick Smith, David Walker, Stephanie Weirich, and Steve Zdancewic. TALx86: A realistic typed assembly language. In *Second Workshop on Compiler Support for System Software*, Atlanta, May 1999.

[31] Greg Morrisett, David Walker, Karl Crary, and Neal Glew. From System F to typed assembly language. In *Proc. 25th ACM Symp. on Principles of Programming Languages (POPL)*, pages 85–97, San Diego California, USA, January 1998.

[32] Greg Morrisett, David Walker, Karl Crary, and Neal Glew. From System F to typed assembly language. *ACM Transactions on Programming Languages and Systems*, 21(3):528–569, May 1999.

[33] J. Gregory Morrisett, David Walker, Karl Crary, and Neal Glew. From System F to typed assembly language. *ACM Transactions on Programming Languages and Systems*, 21(3):527–568, 1999.

[34] Andrew C. Myers. JFlow: Practical mostly-static information flow control. In *Proc. 26th ACM Symp. on Principles of Programming Languages (POPL)*, San Antonio, TX, USA, January 1999.

[35] Andrew C. Myers and Barbara Liskov. Protecting privacy using the decentralized label model. *ACM Transactions on Software Engineering and Methodology*, 9(4):410–442, October 2000.

[36] Andrew C. Myers, Andrei Sabelfeld, and Steve Zdancewic. Enforcing robust declassification. In *Proc. 17th IEEE Computer Security Foundations Workshop*, pages 172–186, June 2004.

[37] George Necula and Peter Lee. Safe kernel extensions without run-time checking. In *Proceedings of Operating System Design and Implementation*, pages 229–243, Seattle, October 1996.

[38] George C. Necula. Proof-carrying code. In *Proc. 24th Symp. Principles of Programming Languages*, pages 106–119. ACM SIGPLAN/SIGACT, January 1997.

[39] George C. Necula, Scott McPeak, and Westley Weimer. CCured: Type-safe retrofitting of legacy code. In *Proceedings of the ACM SIGPLAN/SIGACT Symposium on Principles of Programming Languages*, pages 128–139, 2002.

[40] R. O'Callahan. A simple, comprehensive type system for Java bytecode subroutines. In *Proc. 26th ACM Symp. on Principles of Programming Languages (POPL)*, pages 70–78, January 1999.

[41] François Pottier and Sylvain Conchon. Information flow inference for free. In *Proc. 5nd ACM SIGPLAN International Conference on Functional Programming (ICFP)*, pages 46–57, 2000.

[42] François Pottier and Vincent Simonet. Information flow inference for ML. In *Proc. 29th ACM Symp. on Principles of Programming Languages (POPL)*, pages 319–330, 2002.

[43] Zhenyu Qian. A formal specification of Java(tm) virtual machine instructions for objects, methods, and subroutines. In J. Alves-Foss, editor, *Formal Syntax and Semantics of Java(tm)*. Springer Verlag LNCS, 1998.

[44] Andrei Sabelfeld and Andrew Myers. Language-based information-flow security. *IEEE Journal on Selected Areas in Communications*, 21(1):5–19, January 2003.

[45] Fred B. Schneider. *On Concurrent Programming*. Springer-Verlag, New York, 1997.

[46] Fred B. Schneider. Enforceable security policies. *ACM Transactions on Information and System Security*, 2(4), March 2000.

[47] Margo Seltzer, Y. Endo, Chris Small, and K. Smith. Dealing with disaster: Surviving misbehaved kernel extensions. In *USENIX Symposium on Operating Systems Design and Implementation*, pages 213–227, Seattle, Washington, October 1996.

[48] Raymie Stata and Martín Abadi. A type system for java bytecode subroutines. In *Proc. 25th ACM Symp. on Principles of Programming Languages (POPL)*, San Diego, January 1998.

[49] Matt Stillerman and Dexter Kozen. Demonstration: Efficient code certification for open firmware. In *Proc. 3rd DARPA Information Survivability Conference and Exposition (DISCEX III)*, volume 2, pages 147–148. IEEE, IEEE Computer Society, Los Alamitos, CA, April 2003.

[50] Dennis Volpano, Geoffrey Smith, and Cynthia Irvine. A sound type system for secure flow analysis. *Journal of Computer Security*, 4(3):167–187, 1996.

[51] Robert Wahbe, Steven Lucco, Thomas Anderson, and Susan Graham. Efficient software-based fault isolation. In *Proc. 14th ACM Symp. on Operating System Principles (SOSP)*, pages 203–216, Asheville, December 1993.

[52] E. Yasuhiro, J. Gwertzman, M. Seltzer, C. Small, Keith A. Smith, and D. Tang. VINO: The 1994 fall harvest. Technical Report TR-34-94, Harvard Computer Center for Research in Computing Technology, 1994.

[53] Steve Zdancewic and Andrew C. Myers. Robust declassification. In *Proc. 14th IEEE Computer Security Foundations Workshop*, pages 15–23, Cape Breton, Nova Scotia, Canada, June 2001.

[54] Steve Zdancewic and Andrew C. Myers. Secure information flow and CPS. In *Proc. 10th European Symposium on Programming*, volume 2028 of *Lecture Notes in Computer Science*, pages 46–61, 2001.

[55] Steve Zdancewic and Andrew C. Myers. Observational determinism for concurrent program security. In *Proc. 16th IEEE Computer Security Foundations Workshop*, pages 29–43, Pacific Grove, California, June 2003.

[56] Steve Zdancewic, Lantian Zheng, Nathaniel Nystrom, and Andrew C. Myers. Untrusted hosts and confidentiality: Secure program partitioning. In *Proc. 18th ACM Symp. on Operating System Principles (SOSP)*, pages 1–14, Banff, Canada, October 2001.

[57] Steve Zdancewic, Lantian Zheng, Nathaniel Nystrom, and Andrew C. Myers. Secure program partitioning. *ACM Transactions on Computer Systems*, 20(3):283–328, August 2002.

[58] Lantian Zheng, Stephen Chong, Andrew C. Myers, and Steve Zdancewic. Using replication and partitioning to build secure distributed systems. In *Proc. IEEE Symposium on Security and Privacy*, pages 236–250, Oakland, California, May 2003.

[59] Lantian Zheng and Andrew C. Myers. End-to-end availability policies and noninterference. In *Proc. 18th IEEE Computer Security Foundations Workshop*, June 2005. To appear.

Malicious Code Detection for Open Firmware

Frank Adelstein, Matt Stillerman
ATC-NY
33 Thornwood Drive, Suite 500
Ithaca, NY 14850-1250, USA
{fadelstein,matt}@atc-nycorp.com

Dexter Kozen
Department of Computer Science
Cornell University
Ithaca, New York 14853-7501, USA
kozen@cs.cornell.edu

Abstract

Malicious boot firmware is a largely unrecognized but significant security risk to our global information infrastructure. Since boot firmware executes before the operating system is loaded, it can easily circumvent any operating system-based security mechanism. Boot firmware programs are typically written by third-party device manufacturers and may come from various suppliers of unknown origin. In this paper we describe an approach to this problem based on load-time verification of onboard device drivers against a standard security policy designed to limit access to system resources. We also describe our ongoing effort to construct a prototype of this technique for Open Firmware boot platforms.

1. Introduction

Our critical infrastructure for transportation, communication, financial markets, energy distribution, and health care is dangerously dependent on a computing base vulnerable to many forms of malicious attack and software failure. The consequences of a coordinated attack on our information infrastructure could be devastating [22]. One serious vulnerability that has largely been ignored up until now is *malicious boot firmware.*

Most computing devices are powered up by a *boot sequence*—a series of computational steps in which the hardware is initialized and the operating system loaded and started. *Boot firmware* is the program that controls this process. Boot firmware typically runs in privileged mode on bare hardware. It has essentially limitless access to peripheral devices. The boot program runs before the operating system is loaded, prior to the start of most security measures. Thus malicious boot firmware has the potential to cause very serious harm. This harm falls into three general categories:

- It could prevent the computer from booting, thus effecting a denial of service.

- It could operate devices maliciously, thereby damaging them or causing other harm.

- It could corrupt the operating system as it is loaded.

This last form of attack is perhaps the most serious, since most other security measures depend on operating system integrity. Even the most carefully crafted security mechanisms implemented at the operating system, protocol, application, or enterprise levels can be circumvented in this manner.

On a typical computing platform, the boot firmware is composed of many interacting modules. There is usually a *boot kernel*, which governs the bootup process, as well as boot-time device drivers supplied by the manufacturers of various components. The purpose of a boot driver is to initialize the device, perform diagnostic checks, establish communication with other devices connected to it, allocate system resources, and other similar tasks. The driver often resides in ROM on the device itself and is loaded and run at boot time.

To interact successfully, these pieces must respect well-defined abstraction boundaries and communicate only via standardized interfaces. Yet at boot time, the pieces all run in the same address space in privileged mode. There is no isolation and no external enforcement of good citizenship. It would be well within the means of determined opponent to introduce malicious code into a device driver for a keyboard or mouse, for example.

One line of defense is to ensure the integrity of firmware via digital signatures [2] or chain-of-custody and physical protection. This strategy requires that we assume that the boot firmware was originally benign. Such a belief could be based on trust in the supplier or in some detailed examination of the code. It simply ensures that the code has not been changed after it was approved. Thus, the strategy is a means for preserving an existing relationship of trust, but not of establishing trust.

Reprinted from *18th Annual Computer Security Applications Conference, Proceedings* (December 9-13 2002). 403–412.

This strategy could be costly in practice. There may be a large, far-flung network of vendors for whom trust must be established. Moreover, there are mechanisms for automatically updating device drivers and firmware with patches via the Internet. Firmware that is updated regularly would need to be reexamined each time.

In this paper we describe an alternative technique that provides a basis for trust in boot firmware, regardless of its source. The technique involves automatic verification of boot firmware modules as they are loaded. We also describe ongoing work to construct a prototype verification system using this technique for computers compliant with the Open Firmware boot standard.

Our verification technique is based on *Efficient Code Certification (ECC)* proposed in [6]. ECC is related to other recent language-based approaches to the security of mobile code [12, 15]. Each time an untrusted firmware module is loaded, it is verified against a standard security policy. Inexpensive static checks on the compiled code suffice to guarantee dynamic properties of the program. Among other things, the security policy asserts that device drivers must access other devices only through a strict interface and must only access memory or bus addresses allocated to them.

ECC verification relies on a certifying compiler that produces particularly well-structured and annotated code, so that the verifier can analyze it statically. The verification step essentially prevents the compiler from being bypassed, spoofed, or counterfeited. Confidence in the safety of verified device drivers only requires trust in the verifier, not in the compiler nor the code it produces. By "trust" here we mean that the user must have some other rational basis for believing in the integrity and correctness of the verifier – that it is in the *trusted computing base (TCB)*. The compiler and its output, on the other hand, do not have to be in the TCB. Any device driver code, whether produced by the compiler or not, must be verified.

This technique, while a strong countermeasure to malicious firmware, cannot protect against all forms of attack. For example, certain denial-of-service attacks and malicious hardware are difficult or impossible to detect by this method. However, it does raise the bar by making it more difficult to operate devices maliciously at boot time. Our approach is complementary to existing and proposed schemes that employ digital signatures, trusted suppliers, and code inspection. Those techniques would be appropriate to protect the integrity of the TCB, which will be relatively static.

Our prototype, currently under development, is compliant with the Open Firmware standard [5] and operates in that context. Open Firmware is an IEEE standard for boot firmware that was developed in the mid 1990's and is by now in fairly widespread use (e.g., by Sun and Apple). Several commercial implementations are available. One key feature of Open Firmware that is responsible for its power and flexibility is its incorporation of boot-time device drivers and other modules written in *fcode*, a machine-independent compiled form of the Forth programming language. Open Firmware boot systems include an fcode interpreter, allowing a single implementation of fcode-based firmware to be reused across multiple platforms. The fcode driver is typically stored in ROM on the device itself and reloaded into main memory during the boot cycle. It is these fcode device drivers that are the subject of verification in our prototype.

The verifier is part of the Open Firmware boot kernel and is loaded from boot ROM when the machine powers up. The verifier, along with the fcode interpreter and other parts of the Open Firmware kernel, are considered part of the trusted computing base. The complementary protection schemes mentioned above will be appropriate for protection of this software because it is assumed to be static and supplied by a single vendor.

The security policy is a combination of type safety and various architectural constraints. The policy is designed to rule out the most obvious forms of attack. The constraints are a formalization of conventions that all legitimate fcode programs should adhere to, as well as restrictions that make verification easier without imposing undue limitations on the programmer. Those conventions are not strict requirements of Open Firmware, yet any firmware that violates them would likely be incorrect or malicious. For instance, each device driver conventionally operates its own device directly, and accesses the other devices only via their drivers.

A cornerstone of the ECC technique is a certifying compiler. Our prototype compiler translates Java Virtual Machine code (bytecode) to Forth fcode. We expect developers to use Java as the source language and compile to Java bytecode with a standard Java compiler such as the `javac` compiler from Sun Microsystems as the first stage. We are also developing a Java API so that these programs can access Open Firmware services and data structures. This API is not just a matter of convenience—it is a key element in our eventual assurance argument. The API presents a safer interface than the standard one; we will verify that untrusted code uses this interface and does not bypass it.

2   Open Firmware

Open Firmware is a standard for boot firmware platforms [5]. This standard enables vendors to write machine-independent and instruction set-independent boot firmware, including boot-time drivers. The major advantage to this approach is that Open Firmware-compliant firmware will work across a wide range of hardware. Sun Microsystems Open Boot works this way and was the inspiration for this standard.

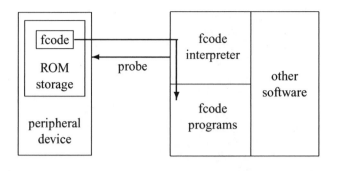

Figure 1. Fcode Loading in Open Firmware

Manufacturers of peripherals need only write one boot-time device driver. The same driver will work with any Open Firmware implementation on any platform. This driver is stored in ROM on the device itself.

The major tasks of boot firmware are:

- to determine the physical configuration of the host and peripherals and build the device tree data structure to represent this,

- to initialize those devices that require it, and

- to load the operating system (or runtime program) and start it running.

Open Firmware provides an abstract model of this process. A hardware-specific adaptation layer whose interface is defined in the standard supports this abstraction.

A key feature of Open Firmware is the incorporation of an interpreter for Forth fcode (Fig. 1). Forth is a stack-based programming language with a long history of use on microprocessors. Fcode is a standard compiled form of Forth that is very compact. Forth programs are called *words*, and a compiler that produces fcode from Forth is called a *tokenizer*. The mapping from Forth to fcode is completely defined in the Open Firmware standard.

Open Firmware boot systems contain an fcode interpreter. Such systems dynamically load and execute fcode modules during the boot cycle. Our system uses ECC-style verification, described in Section 3 below, to detect unsafe fcode programs.

Portions of the boot firmware (other than the adaptation layer) can be written in Forth and will run identically on different hardware platforms. This software will employ the standard boot data structures and hardware abstractions. In particular, peripheral devices are all accessed through a standard API consisting of a set of Forth words that each device of a particular type must define. The boot-time driver for each device is supplied in the form of an fcode program that when executed causes all required words to be defined appropriately. It also builds the portion of the device tree

that represents this device. That fcode program is stored in ROM on the device itself. Open Firmware defines a standard method to retrieve the driver-defining code from any device. During the boot process, all of these programs are retrieved and executed, thus constructing an API for each device.

3 ECC

The ECC project (for Efficient Code Certification) [6] was conceived as a way to improve the runtime efficiency of small, untrusted, run-once applications such as applets and active messages while still ensuring safe execution. *Run-once* means that the cost of verification cannot be amortized over the lifetime of the code, so certificates should be as concise and easy to verify as possible.

ECC guarantees certain dynamic safety properties of compiled code by performing efficient static checks. In particular, it permits implementation of a module that, at boot-time, verifies the safety of the boot firmware before it is run. This technique relies on certain general mathematical theorems that relate the control flow safety, memory safety, and stack safety of a running program to the block structure of its compiled form. As a practical matter, the technique relies on a certifying compiler that produces particularly well-structured code, so that a verifier can perform appropriate static checks just prior to runtime. The user need only trust the verifier, which is a particularly simple program that can be persuasively validated by inspection.

ECC attempts to identify the minimum information necessary to ensure a basic but nontrivial level of code safety and to encapsulate this information in a succinct certificate that is easy to produce and to verify. Performance and ease of implementation are important concerns. ECC is able to ensure

- control flow safety—the program never jumps to a random location in the address space, but only addresses within its own code segment containing valid instructions;

- memory safety—the program does not access random places in memory, but only valid locations in its own data segment, system heap memory explicitly allocated to it, or valid stack frames; and

- stack safety—the state of the stack is preserved across subroutine calls.

These safety conditions are mutually dependent in the sense that none of them are safe unless all of them are safe. This level of safety is roughly comparable to that provided by Java bytecode verification. It also entails other ancillary safety properties such as checking the number and types of function call arguments.

A prototype certifying compiler for the Scheme language to Intel Architecture (x86) machine code and a corresponding verifier have been developed [6].

The system does not rely on general theorem provers or typing mechanisms. Although less flexible than other language-based approaches such as PCC or TAL [18, 12], certificates are compact and easy to produce and to verify. The certificate can be produced by the code supplier during the code generation phase of compilation and verified by the consumer at load time. Both operations can be made automatic and invisible to both parties.

Drawbacks to ECC include platform-dependence and fragility with respect to compiler optimization. Simple local optimizations such as tail recursion elimination can be handled. Preliminary experiments indicate that the sizes of the certificates produced by the ECC prototype range from 6% to 25% of the size of the object code. This seems to indicate a substantial improvement over PCC, although a fair comparison would require a more careful analysis to take all variables into account. The verification process is very efficient. It is linear time except for a sorting step to sort jump destinations, but since almost all jumps are forward and local, a simple insertion sort suffices.

4. The BootSafe System

In this section we describe in some detail our prototype, called *BootSafe*. We hope to convince the reader, as we are ourselves convinced, that this is a sound and commercially viable approach to protection against an important class of malicious boot firmware.

Our objective is to detect malicious fcode programs during the Open Firmware boot cycle as they are loaded, in order to prevent them from executing.

Detection is based on ECC verification as described in Section 3 above. However, verification will go beyond the basic safety properties of the original ECC prototype. This will require a meaningful security policy for fcode programs—essentially a conservative definition of program safety—and a means of enforcing that policy. Devising an effective policy is difficult because it is hard to foresee all the ways that an attacker could harm us.

The BootSafe system consists of a Java-to-fcode certifying compiler J2F and a corresponding fcode verifier (Fig. 2).

The following sections detail our approach to compilation and verification. Following that are sections containing some background information.

4.1   Compilation

The compilation of a Java program to fcode is a two-stage process. In the first stage, Java source is compiled down to Java Virtual Machine (VM) code, also known as

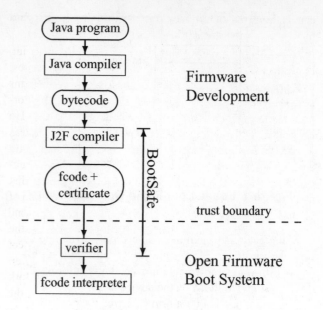

Figure 2. The BootSafe System

bytecode. For this purpose we can use any existing Java compiler, such as the javac compiler available from Sun Microsystems. For the second stage, we are implementing a compiler J2F that maps Java VM code to Forth VM code, also known as fcode. Thus we can leverage existing compilers for Java. In addition, we will be able to leverage the Java bytecode verifier, as explained below.

The translation from Java VM to Forth VM is relatively straightforward in many ways, although there are some design challenges. One such challenge is to design an appropriate object encoding and method dispatch mechanism. Since Forth contains no prior support for objects, we must design the object encoding from scratch. This goal has already been achieved.

Another issue is the class loading and initialization strategy. The standard Java strategy loads and initializes classes at their first active use. This is known as lazy initialization. For applications in boot firmware, lazy initialization is less desirable because it imposes a runtime overhead that could play havoc with real-time constraints that boot-time drivers are often subject to during diagnostic testing of devices. We thus prefer an eager initialization strategy to avoid this overhead. We have designed and implemented a load-time static analysis method that computes initialization dependencies among Java classes based on the static call graph of the class initializers [7]. We can use the computed dependencies to order the classes for initialization at load time. This is a departure from standard Java semantics, but a valuable one for this application. In addition to avoiding the runtime overhead of lazy initialization, it gives a clearer picture of the dependencies involved in class initialization, and can flag a variety of erroneous circularities that the standard lazy method lets pass.

Our J2F compiler can currently compile with int, boolean, and char types, String and StringBuffer classes, user-defined classes, and arrays of these types. It performs both static and instance method dispatch correctly. It incorporates our eager class initialization strategy as described in the preceding paragraph. The output of our J2F compiler is a working Forth program. The Forth code produced, along with a runtime support module of our design, can be successfully read and interpreted by the Forth interpreter that is part of SmartFirmware (a commercial implementation of Open Firmware). In the future we will utilize a backend mapping to fcode, and all verification will be done on the fcode, allowing us to produce a much more compact object involving Forth execution tokens instead of text. However, throughout the prototyping phase, we will continue to work with Forth source code so as to make it easier to debug the design of our J2F compiler and BootSafe verifier.

In the near future we will fill out the existing J2F prototype to handle a variety of other built-in types and library classes, eventually moving toward a significant and robust subset of Java, perhaps full Java minus only support for reflection and concurrency. It is also not clear that it will be necessary to support the double-word types long and double for applications in firmware. The elimination of these two types would result in a substantial simplification, since they requires special handling.

One significant advantage of Java over Forth is that the Open Firmware architecture is naturally object-oriented. Objects and inheritance can be used to great advantage in modeling the device tree and the various devices that comprise it. For example, the standard API of a PCI bus can be represented as an abstract class that manufacturers can subclass in order to implement drivers for their specific products. In fact, we will *require* such subclassing as one of the architectural constraints, mentioned above, that lead to enforcement of the security policy.

4.2 Verification

Sun has defined a form of safety verification for JVM bytecode as part of its definition of the JVM. Our verification will build on this, verifying analogous properties of fcode programs that have been translated from bytecode, as well as some new checks that are peculiar to the Open Firmware environment.

Verification consists of a general device-independent part that applies to all drivers and a device-specific part that may vary depending on the kind of device. The overall security policy we will eventually enforce is three-tiered. Enforcement of each tier depends on the previous ones.

Tier 1: Basic safety policy. This basic level corresponds to that which is commonly called type-safety in the literature on language-based security. It has a fixed platform- and application-independent description involving memory safety, control flow safety, and stack safety that are all interrelated. This level corresponds roughly to the level of safety provided by the Java bytecode verifier. It is also the easiest of the three levels to design and implement, because we can leverage the design of the Java bytecode verifier in our fcode verifier. Since we are translating from Java, it is possible to mimic the behavior of the Java bytecode verifier fairly directly, supplying the necessary typing information in the form of an attached certificate, as in the ECC prototype. Since we have a formal description of the Java verification process, we can supply in the certificate whatever extra information we need that may be present in the Java bytecode, then build our verifier to perform the same checks as the Java verifier. Thus the established type safety of Java and the existence of well-documented bytecode verification algorithms are a huge advantage that will save us much design time.

Tier 2: Device encapsulation policy. Each peripheral device is operated directly or indirectly only by its own device driver. Each device driver provides the only interface (API) for the rest of Open Firmware to access the corresponding device. Drivers that must access their devices through a chain of other devices, such as buses, must do so in a highly controlled and prespecified manner that is verifiable. Such forms of indirect access typically involve some form of address translation that is set up by the Open Firmware *mapin* procedure whose application can be tightly controlled. Although there is no software mediation at the time of the actual device access, it is possible for the verifier to check that the mapin procedure is called according to a highly constrained and recognizable pattern and that all bus addresses subsequently accessed by the driver are within the memory range allocated to that device by mapin. This is more or less comparable to an array bounds check in Java.

Tier 3: Prevention of specific forms of harm. In this tier, we enforce conventions that any reasonable device driver should adhere to. In so doing, we rule out many of the routes by which malicious fcode could cause harm. For instance, device drivers, once they are loaded, should never be redefined—there is no legitimate reason to do so. Such redefinition is otherwise legal within fcode, and would be a very attractive attack mechanism.

Enforcement of tier 2 and 3 policies will be based on architectural constraints—restricting the interaction of modules with one another and constraining the interfaces. This enables two strategies for enhancing safety: ruling out interactions that should never happen in legitimate firmware, and require that services are accessed via wrappers that perform run-time checks. Some Java language features such as private, protected, and final methods can be of great benefit here. For instance, by requiring that untrusted code is a subclass of a trusted class, we can ensure that final methods of the trusted class cannot be overridden in the subclass.

5. Related Work

In this section we discuss the mechanisms, such as cryptography and mediated access, that have been most commonly used to address security threats and their practical limitations for guarding against malicious firmware. We then discuss other important examples of language-based security mechanisms (Java, proof carrying code, and typed assembly language) and the tradeoffs involved in deciding which is appropriate for a particular application.

5.1 Non-Language-Based Mechanisms

Traditional approaches to the security problem include: mediated access or proxy execution, cryptography, code instrumentation, and trusted compilation.

Mediated access or proxy execution, probably the oldest and most widespread system security mechanism, proceeds by isolating critical operations and data in a system kernel, the only code privileged to access these operations and data directly. All other processes gain access only by using the kernel as a proxy, after communicating their desires by message. This not only prevents untrusted code from corrupting the system, but also allows the kernel to monitor all access, perform authentication, or enforce other safety policies.

Cryptography discourages access to sensitive data during transit across an untrusted network and can also be used for authentication.

Code instrumentation, software fault isolation (SFI), and sandboxing [24] alter (instrument) machine code so that critical operations can be monitored during execution in order to enforce a security policy. The monitor is invisible (except for performance costs) so long as execution follows the policy, but intervenes to protect the system when a violation is detected. Schneider [20, 21] extends this idea to handle any security policy that can be expressed by a finite-state automaton. For example, one can express the condition, "No message is ever sent out on the net after a disk read," with a two-state automaton. These automata are called *security automata*. The code is instrumented so that every instruction that could potentially affect the state of the security automaton is preceded by a call to the automaton. Security automata give considerable flexibility in the specification of safety policies and allow the construction of specialized policies tailored to a consumer's particular

needs. The main drawback is that some runtime overhead is incurred for the runtime calls to simulate the automaton.

Trusted compilation is the practice of compiling locally using a trusted compiler.

None of these mechanisms are well suited to firmware. Firmware typically runs before the system kernel is even loaded. Mediation can be provided only by the BIOS, which operates in a relatively austere environment unequipped for proxy execution: firmware drivers associated with installed components are typically given direct access to critical system components. It is desirable to allow this capability without compromising security.

Code instrumentation is also costly. The runtime check required before every sensitive operation could contribute substantially to runtime overhead. Some runtime checks can be eliminated if program analysis determines that they are unnecessary, but this is also a costly undertaking and could contribute substantially to load time overhead. Moreover, even the most sophisticated analysis techniques are necessarily incomplete, because safety properties are undecidable in general.

Trusted compilation of the firmware would have to be redone every time a system is booted, incurring not only a performance penalty but the additional complexity of including the compiler in the trusted computing base. Also, trusted compilation does not by itself supply any justification for trust in the source code that is being compiled.

5.1.1 Cryptographic Authentication (AEGIS)

We have already noted that authentication alone cannot ensure that untrusted code is safe to run. Clearly, however, it can provide some protection. The most sophisticated authentication architecture for firmware is provided by AEGIS [2]. The prototype has been designed as a minimal change to the boot process of the IBM PC that provides a layered sequence of authentication checks of untrusted BIOS code and CMOS, then expansions cards, then the operating system boot blocks, etc., throughout the boot process. It also provides a mechanism for attempting to recover from a failed integrity check by obtaining a replacement module from a trusted source.

5.2 Language-Based Mechanisms

Compilers for high-level programming languages typically accumulate much information about a program during the compilation process. This information may take the form of type information or other constraints on the values of variables, structural information, or naming information. This information may be obtained through parsing or program analysis and may be used to perform optimizations or to check type correctness. After a successful compilation, compilers traditionally throw this extra information away, leaving a monolithic sequence of instructions with no apparent structure or discernible properties.

Some of this extra information may have implications regarding the safety of the compiled object code. For example, programs written in type-safe languages must type-check successfully before they will compile, and assuming that the compiler is correct, any object code compiled from a successfully typechecked source program should be memory-safe. If a code consumer only had access to the extra information known to the compiler when the program was compiled, it might be easier to determine whether the code is safe to run.

Code certification refers to the idea of retaining extra information from a program written in a high-level language in the object code compiled from it. This extra information—called a certificate—is created at compile time and packaged with the object code. When the code is downloaded, the certificate is downloaded along with it. The consumer can then run a verifier, which inspects the code and the certificate to verify compliance with a security policy. If it passes the test, then the code is safe to run. The verifier is part of the consumer's trusted computing base; the compiler, the compiled code, and the certificate need not be.

5.2.1   Java

Perhaps the first large-scale practical instance of the language-based approach was the Java programming language [8]. Javas language-based mechanism is designed to protect against malicious applets. The Java runtime environment contains a bytecode verifier that is supposed to ensure the basic properties of memory, control flow, and type safety. In addition, a trusted security manager enforces higher-level safety policies such as restricted disk I/O. The Java compiler produces platform-independent virtual machine instructions or bytecode that can be verified by the consumer before execution. The bytecode is then either interpreted by a Java virtual machine (VM) interpreter or further compiled down to native code.

Early versions of Java contained a number of highly publicized security flaws [3]. For example, a subtle defect in the Java type system allowed an applet to create and control a partially instantiated class loader. The applet could then use this class loader to load, say, a malicious security manager that would permit unlimited disk access.

Some authors [3, 9] blamed these problems on the lack of an adequate semantic model for Java. Steps to remedy this situation have since been taken [1, 19]. Despite these initial failings, the basic approach was a significant step forward in practical programming language security. It not only pointed the way toward a simple and effective means

of providing a basic level of security, but also helped direct the attention of the programming language and verification community to critical security issues resulting from the rise of the Internet.

The machine-independent bytecode produced by the Java compiler is still quite high-level, and that is a disadvantage. Once downloaded, the bytecode must either be interpreted by a Java VM interpreter or compiled to native code by a just-in-time (JIT) compiler. Either technique incurs a runtime penalty. If the safety certificate represented in the bytecode were mapped down to the level of native code by a back-end Java VM compiler, then the same degree of safety could be ensured without the runtime penalty, because the code supplier could do the back-end compilation before downloading. This would trade the platform independence of Java VM for the efficiency of native code.

5.2.2   Proof Carrying Code (PCC)

Proof carrying code (PCC) [13, 14, 15, 16, 17, 18] is a strategy for producing and verifying formal proofs that code meets general security policies. The software supplier does the hard work of generating the proof, and the software consumer checks the proof before the code is run. The security policy is expressed in first-order logic augmented with symbols for various language and machine constructs.

The most general version of PCC is somewhat more complicated, involving a two-phase interaction between the supplier and the consumer. In the first phase of this protocol, the supplier produces and delivers a program consisting of annotated object code. The annotations consist of loop invariants and function pre- and post-conditions, and make the next phase of the protocol easier. The consumer formulates a safety policy and uses an automated tool to generate, from the policy and the annotated program, a *verification condition*. The verification condition is a logical formula that implies that the program satisfies its security policy. In the second phase of the protocol, the supplier proves the verification condition and sends the proof back to the consumer. The consumer runs a proof checker to check that the proof is valid.

The verification condition generator is part of the consumer's trusted computing base—in a sense, it *defines* the security policy—but some communication cost can be saved by having the supplier generate the verification condition using the same verification condition generator that the consumer uses. The consumer then checks that the verification condition produced by the supplier is the same as the one produced locally.

A certifying compiler produces the initial annotation of the code, using information from the program source and program analysis during compilation. The Touchstone compiler [14] is a certifying compiler for a type-safe subset of C. It admits many common optimizations such as dead code elimination, common subexpression elimination, copy propagation, instruction scheduling, register allocation, loop invariant hoisting, redundant code elimination, and the elimination of array bounds checks.

The advantages of the PCC approach are its expressiveness and its ability to handle code optimizations. In principle, any security policy that can be constructed by a verification condition generator and expressed as a first-order verification condition can be handled. The main disadvantages are that it is a two-phase protocol, that it involves weighty machinery such as a full-fledged first-order theorem prover and proof checker, and that proof sizes are quite large, roughly 2.5 times the size of the object code for type safety and even larger for more complicated safety policies. Given the limited space available on boot firmware, this size penalty alone makes PCC inappropriate for our problem.

5.2.3 Typed Assembly Language (TAL)

Typed assembly language (TAL) [4, 9, 10, 12] can be viewed as a specialized form of proof-carrying code devoted to verifying a form of type safety. It is a language-based system in which type information from a strongly-typed high-level language is preserved as compilation transforms the source through a platform-independent typed intermediate language (TIL) [11, 23] down to the level of the object code itself. The result is a type annotation of the object code that can be checked by an ordinary type checker. In this special case, proof checking is reduced to type checking.

TAL is not as expressive as PCC, but it can handle any security policy expressible in terms of the type system. This includes memory, control flow, and type safety, among others. TAL is also robust with respect to compiler optimizations, since type annotations can be transformed along with the code. TAL proofs, though much smaller than proofs in PCC, are still significantly larger than those needed by ECC.

Proof size can be traded off against the complexity of the verifier, but that increases and complicates the amount of trusted code.

6. Current Project Status

The long-term goal of this project is to adapt the ECC technique to the analysis of Open Firmware fcode programs to detect malicious boot software. We are implementing a certifying compiler and verifier necessary for this method. The ECC-based verifier will then be incorporated into an existing commercial implementation of the Open Firmware standard in order to provide practical malicious boot firmware detection to the marketplace.

At present, we have a working prototype of the J2F compiler for Java Virtual Machine (JVM) bytecode to Forth fcode for a single-threaded subset of the Java language. This subset is appropriate for writing device drivers and other firmware modules. It provides access to Open Firmware services through an API currently being designed. The compiler will output a certificate appropriate to the verification tasks described below. The API takes advantage of the natural object-oriented structure of the Open Firmware device tree and allows access to Open Firmware services from within Java programs.

The BootSafe verifier will initially verify only basic type safety, roughly at the level provided by ECC and by the Java bytecode verifier. This initial version operates as a stand-alone program.

We have successfully compiled sample device drivers for a block-oriented storage device and a PCI bus. These are good representatives of typical devices in current use. These drivers can run under SmartFirmware (a commercial Open Firmware implementation) in simulation mode.

7. Conclusions and Future Work

As noted, typical boot firmware is an amalgam of many pieces, including libraries, the main boot program, and boot-time device drivers from various vendors. To interact successfully, these pieces must respect well-defined abstraction boundaries and communicate only via standardized interfaces. Yet at boot time, the pieces all run in the same address space. There is no isolation and no external enforcement of good citizenship. The existing Open Firmware standard does not address this problem. It only helps non-malicious designers by defining the standard for device interaction and process management during bootup.

Our approach has the potential to guarantee that all of the pieces of boot firmware are good citizens: that they respect each other's boundaries and interact only via published standardized interfaces. Moreover, this guarantee is refreshed each time the boot program runs with inexpensive static checks. Rechecking each time counters the threat of substituting malicious boot firmware components for approved ones.

We believe Open Firmware is the right context because it is a clear, well-designed, and widely used standard. We have designed a Java-to-fcode certifying compiler and built an early prototype. Our current effort is directed toward making this novel form of protection a practical reality by integrating the verifier with a commercial implementation of Open Firmware.

Although we our developing our techniques in the context of the Open Firmware standard, there is nothing to prevent non-Open Firmware compliant boot firmware from being made verifiable using similar techniques.

Among the large-scale issues still to be addressed are:

- the design of a Java API for Open Firmware that is both convenient to use and supports the kind of verification that we require;

- enhancement of the verifier to verify compliance of fcode programs with the second-order security policy (this version of the verifier will run as a stand-alone program and will be directly integrated with Smart-Firmware);

- modification of the J2F compiler to accommodate the refined Open Firmware API and enhanced verification.

Acknowledgments

We are indebted to T. J. Merritt for valuable ideas and comments and to David Baca and Kori Oliver for their assistance with the implementation. We also thank the anonymous reviewers for their suggestions. This work was supported in part by DARPA contracts DAAH01-02-C-R080 and DAAH01-01-C-R026, NSF grant CCR-0105586, and ONR Grant N00014-01-1-0968. The views and conclusions contained herein are those of the authors and should not be interpreted as necessarily representing the official policies or endorsements, either expressed or implied, of these organizations or the US Government.

References

[1] M. Abadi and R. Stata. A type system for Java bytecode subroutines. In *Proc. 25th Symp. Principles of Programming Languages*, pages 149–160. ACM SIGPLAN/SIGACT, January 1998.

[2] William A. Arbaugh, David J. Farber, and Jonathan M. Smith. A secure and reliable bootstrap architecture. In *Proc. 1997 Symposium on Security and Privacy*, pages 65–71. IEEE, May 1997.

[3] Drew Dean, Ed Felten, and Dan Wallach. JAVA security: From HotJava to Netscape and beyond. In *Proc. Symp. Security and Privacy*. IEEE, May 1996.

[4] N. Glew and G. Morrisett. Type-safe linking and modular assembly language. In *Proc. 26th Symp. Principles of Programming Languages*, pages 250–261. ACM SIGPLAN/SIGACT, January 1999.

[5] IEEE. *IEEE Standard for Boot (Initialization Configuration) Firmware: Core Requirements and Practices*, 1994. Standard 1275-1994.

[6] Dexter Kozen. Efficient code certification. Technical Report 98-1661, Computer Science Department, Cornell University, January 1998.

[7] Dexter Kozen and Matt Stillerman. Eager class initialization for Java. In W. Damm and E.R. Olderog, editors, *Proc. 7th Int. Symp. Formal Techniques in Real-Time and Fault Tolerant Systems (FTRTFT'02)*, volume 2469 of *Lecture Notes in Computer Science*, pages 71–80. IFIP, Springer-Verlag, Sept. 2002.

[8] Tim Lindholm and Frank Yellin. *The JAVA virtual machine specification*. Addison Wesley, 1996.

[9] G. Morrisett, K. Crary, N. Glew, D. Grossman, R. Samuels, F. Smith, D. Walker, S. Weirich, and S. Zdancewic. TALx86: A realistic typed assembly language. In *Proc. Workshop on Compiler Support for System Software*, pages 25–35. ACM SIGPLAN, May 1999.

[10] G. Morrisett, K. Crary, N. Glew, and D. Walker. Stack-based typed assembly language. In Xavier Leroy and Atsushi Ohori, editors, *Proc. Workshop on Types in Compilation*, volume 1473 of *Lecture Notes in Computer Science*, pages 28–52. Springer-Verlag, March 1998.

[11] G. Morrisett, D. Tarditi, P. Cheng, C. Stone, R. Harper, and P. Lee. The TIL/ML compiler: Performance and safety through types. In *1996 Workshop on Compiler Support for Systems Software*, 1996.

[12] Greg Morrisett, David Walker, Karl Crary, and Neal Glew. From System F to typed assembly language. In *25th ACM SIGPLAN/SIGSIGACT Symposium on Principles of Programming Languages*, pages 85–97, San Diego California, USA, January 1998.

[13] George C. Necula. Proof-carrying code. In *Proc. 24th Symp. Principles of Programming Languages*, pages 106–119. ACM SIGPLAN/SIGACT, January 1997.

[14] George C. Necula. *Compiling with proofs*. PhD thesis, Carnegie Mellon University, September 1998.

[15] George C. Necula and Peter Lee. Safe kernel extensions without run-time checking. In *Proc. 2nd Symp. Operating System Design and Implementation*. ACM, October 1996.

[16] George C. Necula and Peter Lee. The design and implementation of a certifying compiler. In *Proc. Conf. Programming Language Design and Implementation*, pages 333–344. ACM SIGPLAN, 1998.

[17] George C. Necula and Peter Lee. Efficient representation and validation of proofs. In *Proc. 13th Symp. Logic in Computer Science*, pages 93–104. IEEE, June 1998.

[18] George C. Necula and Peter Lee. Safe, untrusted agents using using proof-carrying code. In Giovanni Vigna, editor, *Special Issue on Mobile Agent Security*, volume 1419 of *Lect. Notes in Computer Science*, pages 61–91. Springer-Verlag, June 1998.

[19] Robert O'Callahan. A simple, comprehensive type system for Java bytecode subroutines. In *Proc. 26th Symp. Principles of Programming Languages*, pages 70–78. ACM SIGPLAN/SIGACT, January 1999.

[20] Fred B. Schneider. Towards fault-tolerant and secure agentry. In *Proc. 11th Int. Workshop WDAG '97*, volume 1320 of *Lecture Notes in Computer Science*, pages 1–14. ACM SIGPLAN, Springer-Verlag, September 1997.

[21] Fred B. Schneider. Enforceable security policies. Technical Report TR98-1664, Computer Science Department, Cornell University, January 1998.

[22] Fred B. Schneider, editor. *Trust in Cyberspace*. Committee on Information Systems Trustworthiness, Computer Science and Telecommunications Board, National Research Council. National Academy Press, 1999.

[23] D. Tarditi, G. Morrisett, P. Cheng, C. Stone, R. Harper, and P. Lee. TIL: A type-directed optimizing compiler for ML. In *Conf. Programming Language Design and Implementation*. ACM SIGPLAN, 1996.

[24] R. Wahbe, S. Lucco, T. E. Anderson, and S. L Graham. Efficient software-based fault isolation. In *Proc. 14th Symp. Operating System Principles*, pages 203–216. ACM, December 1993.

Safe Execution of Mobile and Untrusted Code:
The Model-Carrying Code Project

R. Sekar   C.R. Ramakrishnan   I.V. Ramakrishnan   Scott Smolka

Samik Basu   Sandeep Bhatkar   Abhishek Chaturvedi   Daniel DuVarney

Zhenkai Liang   Yow-Jian Lin   Dipti Saha   Weiqing Sun   Prem Uppuluri

V.N. Venkatakrishnan   Wei Xu   Mohan Channa   Yogesh Chauhan

Kumar Krishna   Shruthi Krishna   Vishwas Nagaraja   Divya Padmanabhan

Department of Computer Science,
Stony Brook University, Stony Brook, NY 11794.

Abstract

Starting from the Melissa email virus of 1999, threats posed by software from untrusted sources have grown enormously. Untrusted code can install spyware, steal confidential information, including identities and financial information. Even worse, it can turn an unsuspecting user's computer into a so-called "zombie" that can be commandeered by an attacker to carry out criminal activities, including the launching of attacks on other systems on the Internet. These threats can all be eliminated by simply preventing users from accessing any untrusted code or data. However, such an approach isn't practical: users have become accustomed to a wealth of information as well as software on the Internet that have significantly simplified their day-to-day activities and tasks and enhanced their productivity. Thus, the goal of our model-carrying code (MCC) project was to develop an infrastructure and software tools that enable users to access benign mobile code, while bounding their risks due to malicious mobile code. Our approach enables code producers and consumers to collaborate in order to achieve security, yet it doesn't impose a significant burden on either one of them. This paper provides an overview of the MCC approach, surveys the scientific contributions of the project, and summarizes its practical outcomes.

Categories and Subject Descriptors

D.4.6 [**Operating Systems**]: Security and Protection, *Invasive software*
K.6.5 [**Computing Milieux**]: Management of computing and Information Systems, *Security and Protection,*Unauthorized access

General Terms

Security, Verification

Keywords

mobile code security, malicious code, sand-boxing, security policies

1   Introduction

The Model-Carrying Code (MCC) project began in 2001, just as the threat of cyber attacks due to untrusted content on the Internet began to rise. In the preceding decade, the primary threat to enterprise networks were perceived to be coming from the Internet. To counter this threat, most research (as well as products) focused on building a "hard exterior shell" around these networks, using technologies such as firewalls and intrusion detection systems. Unfortunately, such technologies aren't effective against cyber attacks launched from inside an enterprise. While it may be justifiable to assume that insiders weren't likely to intentionally attack their own networks, there is a high risk that they may do so *unwittingly*. The Melissa email virus of 1999, which took the form of an email attachment, was the first large-scale cyber attack that relied on this approach. When the recipient attempted to view this attachment, malicious code embedded within the attachment was executed, causing copies of the virus to be sent to many other users. Several copycat attacks followed, and it soon became clear that mobile code (and content from untrustworthy sources) posed a real and serious threat to Internet security.

The rising trend of threats posed by untrustworthy mobile code has accelerated sharply in the last couple of years. This increase began with attacks embedded in maliciously crafted web pages that compromised popular browsers such as the Internet Explorer, and made it possible for attackers to execute arbitrary code on the computers running these browsers. Similar high-profile attacks included malicious code embedded in different types of image files, multimedia content, word-processing documents, and so on. The rising popularity of peer-to-peer networks such as KaZaA and instant-messaging software has only compounded the situation by providing other conduits for spreading cyber-attacks via malicious code.

Some previous efforts in mobile code security have focused on the dangers posed by mobile code, and developed techniques to prevent damage due to them. Often, these techniques posed undue restrictions on mobile code and prevented it from providing much useful functionality. In contrast, the MCC project is based on the observation that the vast majority of code and content downloaded over the Internet is *benign*. Thus, MCC's goal is to ensure that users can benefit from *benign mobile code* while minimizing the risks posed by malicious code. Its focus is on *practical* and *usable* solutions that are deployable in the near-term to secure the large base of existing software, while posing minimal burden on mobile code producers and consumers.

1.1   State of the Art in Mobile Code Security

Current approaches to mobile-code security fall into two categories: *content inspection* and *behavior confinement*. Content-inspection techniques analyze potentially malicious content (whether it be data or code) in order to determine if it is indeed malicious. Their key benefit is *convenience*: little effort is required by mobile-code producers or consumers to make use of these tools. Their main drawback, which significantly limits their use, is the difficulty of detecting malicious code. Antivirus technologies [65] rely on detecting unique bit patterns ("signatures") that have previously been found only in malicious code. This approach, however, is ineffective for screening out malicious code that has not been seen before. Even worse, automated code-morphing tools are now available that can transform malicious code in ways that preserve their function, but alter the bit-patterns in them. These tools are being improved at a rapid rate, and will likely make signature-based detection ineffective in the future.

A second approach for content inspection is based on mathematical reasoning about the runtime behavior of code. Such reasoning can potentially infer all possible actions of mobile code, and can be used to discard code that may exhibit unsafe behavior. To be usable, such mathematical reasoning should be automated into a code-scanning software tool. Although major advances have been made in the area of automated reasoning and formal verification [13], the problem of verifying nontrivial properties of modern COTS (commercial, off-the-shelf) software continues to be intractable. The problem is further compounded by the fact that in the case of mobile code, such reasoning has to be done on binary code, which is much harder to analyze than source code.

Behavior confinement, otherwise known as *sandboxing*, is employed in the Java programming language [26] and several research tools. It is based on limiting the actions of mobile code so that it cannot cause any harm. Its benefits and drawbacks are complementary to that of content inspection. In particular, behavior confinement avoids the hard problem of reasoning about *all possible* behaviors of software. Instead, it inspects the actions that are actually performed during *a particular* execution of mobile code, and blocks any actions deemed risky. Its drawback is that by the time the risky behavior is observed, some damage may already be done. For instance, consider a file-compression program that replaces a file with a compressed version of its contents. By the time malicious behavior is detected, the program may have already erased the original file. Less worrisome, but still problematic, is the fact that the program may have created a number of intermediate files that need to be cleaned up manually after the risky behavior is detected and the program has terminated.

In summary, content-inspection approaches are *convenient* but do not provide a general solution for malicious software, whereas behavior-confinement approaches are *broadly applicable* but *difficult-to-use*. In contrast, the MCC approach aims to provide a convenient yet broadly applicable solution. A second drawback of existing approaches, shared by content inspection as well as behavior confinement, is the effort needed to characterize "risky behavior," which differs depending on the functionality of mobile code. For example, an instant-messaging program needs to communicate with remote hosts on the Internet. On the other hand, one would not expect an image viewer, operating on a local file, to access the network. Network communication represents risky behavior for such a program, as it may be used maliciously to send sensitive documents. The MCC project is the first one to provide practically useful tools to tackle this *security-policy specification* problem.

1.2 The MCC Approach

The MCC approach is aimed at combining the benefits of content inspection and behavior confinement approaches, while mitigating their drawbacks. In the vast majority of cases, MCC blocks the execution of unsafe mobile code even before it begins, thereby retaining the convenience of content-inspection approaches. Even when safety cannot be accurately determined before execution, but is observed subsequently at runtime, MCC eliminates the need for manual cleanup actions by incorporating automated recovery procedures. MCC avoids the computational intractability associated with content-inspection approaches by employing a judicious combination of runtime-monitoring techniques with automated analysis and reasoning.

One of the primary innovations in the MCC approach is the introduction of an intermediate level of abstraction, called a *model*, to bridge the semantic gap between low-level binary code and high-level security concerns of code consumers. Such a model captures the security-relevant aspects of code behavior, while abstracting away most other details that relate to the function of the code. Code consumers download mobile code together with its behavior model, and hence the term "model-carrying code." These models are used by an automated verification procedure to determine if the code satisfies the consumer's notion of safety. Since MCC models are hundreds (or thousands) of times smaller than programs, and considerably simpler, fully automated verification is feasible. Moreover, since models get generated by mobile code producers, the model generation process can benefit from the availability of source code, as well as the test suites used by the code producer.

In addition to tackling computational difficulties, the introduction of models in MCC provides another important benefit: it provides a way for code consumers and producers to collaborate to achieve security, while at the same time decoupling their concerns. This contrasts with previous approaches that placed the responsibility entirely with the code producer [40], or with the code consumers [26]. In particular, our approach doesn't burden producers with issues of "safety." Indeed, the definition of safety can vary from one consumer to another, and is best left to the consumer. Similarly, consumers don't need to predict the access needs of an application, which is best left to the code producer that wrote the code and understands its functionality as well as implementation. Producers simply encode this information about the access requirements of mobile code using a model. Armed with this model, a consumer can use automated verification tools to check if a piece of mobile code satisfies the specific safety concerns of interest to him/her.

The definition of safety in MCC is still based on *security policies*, but unlike previous approaches, MCC brings a considerable degree of automation to the policy-selection process. Indeed, suitable families of security policies can be preselected by security administrators so that naive users do not have to make complex security-related decisions. More sophisticated users are assisted in policy selection by the automated verification process, which can automatically suggest policy refinements that are consistent with the behavior of a given piece of mobile code.

The techniques developed in the MCC project are being incorporated into software tools that are placed at the entry points for mobile code and/or content downloaded over the Internet. Specifically, they are being incorporated into software installers, through which explicitly downloaded and installed software enters the system, and email/web browsers, through which implicitly downloaded code and content enter the system. These tools are being released as open-source software over the Internet. The list of currently available tools can be found on the project home page at http://seclab.cs.sunysb.edu/mcc/.

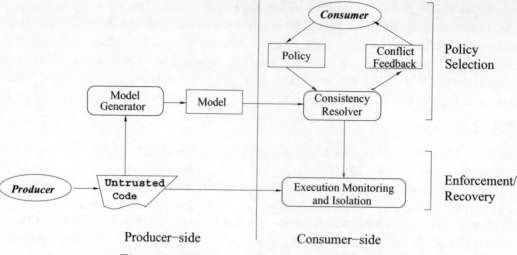

Figure 1: The Model-Carrying Code Framework

1.3   Paper Organization

The rest of this paper is organized as follows. Section 2 provides a high-level technical overview of the MCC approach. The research carried out in the MCC project falls into four main areas: *security policies, model extraction, consistency resolution,* and *enforcement.* These research efforts are summarized in Sections 3, 4, 5 and 6, with pointers to other papers that contain in-depth treatments of these efforts.

Another important outcome of MCC research has been the development of a new generation of techniques to counter *buffer overflow* attacks, which account for about 75% of security vulnerability advisories issued by leading organizations such as the US-CERT. A related development is that of automatic generation of signatures to block fast-spreading, Internet-wide attacks such as Code Red and Slammer. These research efforts are described in Section 7.

2   Overview of the MCC Approach

Execution of mobile/untrusted code has become an integral part of the everyday Internet experience. It appears in many forms, such as "active web pages" (e.g. pages with Java, Javascript, VBScript, or ActiveX content), content viewers and players (e.g., RealPlayer, FlashPlayer, Acrobat, and image viewers), games, P2P applications, and freeware/shareware or commercial applications that provide utility functions (e.g., photo album organizers, file compression and format conversion utilities, instant messengers, document search tools and related browser plug-ins). Moreover, complex content, such as images and documents, share some of the properties of code — in particular, maliciously crafted content can exploit vulnerabilities in the software that operates on this content to execute arbitrary code.

The MCC approach is designed so that users can enjoy all of the functions and benefits provided by benign mobile code and content, while adequately protecting themselves from the risks posed by malicious mobile code. The key idea in MCC (see Figure 1) is the introduction of program behavioral *models* that help bridge the semantic gap between (very low-level) binary code and high-level security concerns of consumers. These models successfully capture security-related properties of the code, but do not capture aspects of the code that pertain only to its functional correctness. The model is stated in terms of security-relevant operations made by the code and the operands of these operations.

While models can be created manually, doing so would be a time-consuming process. Code producers are unlikely to spend the additional effort needed to generate models, and requiring them to do so would hinder the widespread adoption of the MCC approach. To address this problem, we have developed techniques that can *automatically generate* the required models during software testing.

A code consumer receives both the model and the program from the producer. The consumer wants assurance that the code will satisfy a certain security policy. The use of a security behavior model enables us to decompose this assurance argument into two parts:

- *policy satisfaction:* check whether the model satisfies the policy, i.e., the behaviors captured by the model are a subset of the behaviors allowed by the policy.

- *model safety:* check whether the model is a safe approximation of program behavior, i.e., the behaviors of the program are a subset of the behaviors of the model.

Together, policy satisfaction and model safety imply that the behavior exhibited by the program is a subset of the behavior permitted by the policy.

It should be noted that model safety is a necessary step whenever the code consumer does not trust the model provided by the code producer. In particular, the model provided by a producer may be incorrect either due to malice, or unintentional errors.

In principle, policy satisfaction as well as model safety can be established using automated verification techniques. In practice, however, we resort to runtime enforcement for ensuring model safety due to the difficulties in verifying properties of low-level (binary) code.

The policy selection component in Figure 1 is concerned with policy satisfaction, whereas the enforcement component is concerned with model safety. Policy selection uses automated verification; since models are much simpler than programs, complete automation of this verification step is possible. If the model is *not* consistent with the policy, the consistency resolver generates a compact and user-friendly summary of all consistency violations. The consumer can either discard the code at this point, or refine the policy in such a way that would permit execution of the code without posing undue security risks. Alternatively, a system administrator may preconfigure acceptable policies (and their refinements) for a given computer system, so that naive users don't have to make these decisions.

If the refined policy is consistent with the model, then the model and the code are forwarded to the enforcement module. Our current implementation of enforcement is based on runtime interception of security-sensitive operations made by untrusted code, specifically, system calls made by the program to access resources administered by the underlying operating system. If the enforcement component detects a deviation from the model, then the execution of the untrusted code is terminated. An alternative to model enforcement is to directly enforce the consumer's security policy.

As mentioned earlier, runtime monitoring and behavior enforcement suffers from the drawback that if a violation occurs at runtime, then the offending code will need to be terminated. Not only has the user wasted time with the malicious code, but in addition, she may have to manually clean up the "mess" left behind by the aborted application. This may entail recovering files that may have been deleted by the application, deleting files created by the application, and so on. To mitigate this problem, we have developed a new approach in the MCC project called *isolated execution* (see Section 6.1) that automates the recovery process, so that runtime aborts don't inconvenience users.

Although the primary focus of the MCC implementation has been on untrusted programs executing on the UNIX operating system, techniques from our approach could be easily adapted for different execution environments such as Java or Microsoft's Common Language Runtime (CLR). As a first step in this direction, we have performed some preliminary work in defining security policies in terms of security-relevant method calls in Java, and in implementing policy enforcement via bytecode rewriting [60].

3   Security Policies

We have developed a language for security policy specification called BMSL. As compared to previous research in security policy languages [19, 50, 26, 55], BMSL is more expressive and hence allows specification of a larger class of policies. Specifically, BMSL policies can restrict not only individual security-relevant operations, but also constrain the sequence in which they can be issued. Moreover, these policies can express complex constraints regarding the operands to these operations.

We have developed a compilation algorithm for BMSL policies that generates efficient policy-enforcement engines from high-level policy specifications. The performance of these enforcement engines is largely insensitive to the size or complexity of policies, thereby allowing users to focus on correctness of their specifications rather than their computational efficiency. Another key feature of BMSL is its mathematical foundation [58], including a precise semantics, and a formal proof that enforcement engines are faithful to this semantics. This factor, together with a new type system designed for the language, decreases the likelihood of specification errors in security policies. These results are explained at depth in [58]. Application of this language to the related problem of intrusion detection (via policy enforcement) can be found in [59]. Finally, [60] describes the application of BMSL to the definition and enforcement of policies on Java programs.

We have developed a methodology for classifying applications into categories such that all applications in a given category can share the same policies. This method is well-integrated into the tools used for software installation and execution so that policy development and management can be largely automated. These results are promising in that they make it possible to apply MCC on a large scale, where it can manage the policies for a large number of diverse applications. This result also lays the foundation for applying MCC policy development and refinement framework more broadly, for instance, in the context of security-hardened operating systems such as SELinux [55] that require security policies to be developed for every application.

4 Model Extraction

We have developed efficient algorithms that can generate security behavior models quickly, even for large programs. These algorithms generate models that are a hundred to a thousand times smaller than the programs from which they are derived, a fact that has been instrumental in making the MCC approach practical even for large programs. A high-level overview of our approach to model extraction can be found in [53], while an in-depth presentation can be found in [11]. The latter paper also discusses the application of these models to the problem of intrusion detection. It shows that MCC models are richer and more powerful as compared to models of program behavior used in previous intrusion detection techniques [21, 52, 20, 23, 22]. Specifically, these models can capture sequencing relationships among security-relevant operations made by a program, as well the dependencies and relationships between the operands of different operations in a sequence. This richness enables our models to detect a range of attacks that were outside the scope of these approaches.

5 Consistency Resolution

We have developed a number of techniques for verifying that the model carried by a piece of mobile code is consistent with the code consumer's security policies. The approach we advocate for this problem is *model checking* [12, 46], which explores the different configurations (or states) the model may find itself in during execution. For example, the model may specify an execution where the contents of an arbitrary file F are read, followed by sending and receiving data over the network, followed by the writing of F. In this execution, we can identify a number of configurations: before F is read, after the read but before the network activity, the configurations due to the individual actions over the network, and the ones before and after F is written. Verification of models involves inspection of all the configurations (and sequences of configurations) that are possible in the model, and checking whether the policies are satisfied in these configurations (and configuration sequences).

Although there are many advanced model-checking techniques for the verification of systems of varying size and complexity [29, 17, 4, 28], the models derived from mobile code typically possess features that existing techniques cannot handle automatically. First, such models, as well as their policies, may specify data values over unbounded domains (e.g., the above model treats arbitrary files). Model-checking techniques typically require that the set of possible states is finite, and verification techniques that can handle infinite state spaces typically require assistance from the user to complete the verification. These restrictions make existing verification techniques inapplicable in the context of MCC.

In our research, we made a key observation that made these problems amenable to an elegant solution: that the behaviors of models do not change drastically when the data values change. In many cases, the models are in fact *data independent*, meaning that the control behavior of the model (i.e., its actions) are independent of the data values themselves. In [49] we described an automatic technique to verify properties of such models and corresponding policies. Our approach considers a set of configurations at a time, represented by a single *constraint*: every solution to the constraint represents a configuration in the set. For a large class of models, including all data-independent ones, the number of distinct constraints describing its set of reachable configurations is finite, thereby making complete verification possible. For a larger class of models, we developed simple approximation techniques where the set of configurations represented by a constraint may under- or over-approximate the set of possible configurations, thereby making it possible to conservatively analyze the models for policy violations in finite time.

Another feature of mobile code models that is not treated by traditional model-checking techniques is the presence of function calls and recursion. These features also lead to a potentially infinite set of configurations. In [5] we describe an efficient technique for verifying such models. A key benefit of our approach is that it provides improved accuracy as compared to previous approaches.

Finally, a policy may be satisfied when only one instance of a mobile code is executed at any time, but may be violated when two instances are run simultaneously. Model-checking techniques can be used to verify properties only when the number of simultaneous executions is bounded and very small. In [6] we describe a technique that overcomes this drawback for certain classes of systems. In fact, our technique can verify properties of an *infinite* family of systems, i.e., an unbounded number of simultaneous executions. The key idea is to compute the condition each instance imposes on the remainder of the system in order to satisfy a policy. By observing the sequence of such conditions and evaluating how this sequence converges, we can estimate whether an arbitrary number of instances satisfies the policy.

Policy refinement comes into play when consistency resolution fails, i.e., the model violates some security policy. In this case, the policy may be more strict than is necessary and it becomes useful to provide feedback to the user regarding the failure so that the policy can be appropriately refined. Such feedback is given in terms of *counter-examples*: execution sequences of the model that demonstrate the policy violation. Previous verification techniques were geared towards providing one counter-example at a time. While this is a reasonable approach when verifying correctness properties, it is too cumbersome in the context of MCC. For instance, users may be told that the program violates a policy because it opens a file F_1, and if they accept this, then they are told that the policy is still violated because a file F_2 is opened, and so on. In contrast, we have developed new approaches [7, 8] that can efficiently compute *all* counter examples, and thus present all violations in one shot to the user. This enables users to make more informed decisions on how to relax their policies, while also reducing the time spent in the refinement process.

6 Runtime Enforcement

We have developed techniques to enforce compatibility of mobile code with its model, or the consumer's security policies. Our original enforcement approach was based entirely on intercepting operating system requests made by an application, and validating them against the model (or policy). This approach, however, has its drawbacks, one of which is related to recovery after attacks, and another of which is related to privacy policies. We subsequently addressed this shortcoming using the concept of *isolated execution* described below.

6.1 Isolated Execution

A purely enforcement-based approach causes significant inconvenience to a user *if* untrusted code is aborted at runtime. Specifically, we need to restore the system state so that it is *as if the aborted execution never took place*. It is cumbersome to manually identify the set of restoration actions to be performed. It is further complicated in realistic systems where a number of applications are running concurrently with the untrusted code, since we don't want to undo the effects of these applications. To address this problem, we have developed a new approach, called *isolated execution*, that enables automatic recovery from runtime aborts. The main idea is to isolate the effects of mobile code, such as the files created or deleted, from the rest of the system. In effect, the mobile code operates on a "private copy" of the entire file system, allowing any and all operations on this copy. If this execution is to be aborted, we simply discard the private copy. If it is successful, then we provide techniques to merge the results of the execution into the host file system. In addition to permitting automated and painless recovery from program aborts, the approach also expands the classes of security policies that can be supported within the MCC framework. In particular, policies are no longer required to be stated in terms of operations made by the mobile code, but can be given in terms of the system state resulting from these operations. Indeed, a policy can be based entirely on the system state at the end of mobile-code execution.

Based on the concept of isolated execution, we have developed a stand-alone tool (independent of MCC) called *Alcatraz* for safe execution of potentially malicious applications [37]. An important advantage of Alcatraz is that most programs can run successfully within Alcatraz. This is in stark contrast with other behavior confinement approaches [26, 25, 1, 51], which cause most programs with substantive functionality to fail. Moreover, it permits users to manually inspect the changes made by mobile code before accepting the changes. This is helpful since our security policies can control only the operations performed on different files, but not the resulting changes to underlying file data.

Recently, we have shown that isolation can provide the basis for *safe execution environments* (SEE) within which users can "try out" operations that can potentially break their computer system. For instance, they can try out new software patches, new software packages, system configuration changes, vulnerability testing tools, and so on. If the result is satisfactory, they can continue on. Otherwise, they can recover back to the original system state at the touch of a button. Additional details on SEE can be found in [57].

6.2   Enforcing Privacy Policies Via Source-Code Rewriting.

It is well known that policies involving dissemination of private data cannot be enforced simply by examining the operations made by an application [50]. It is necessary to examine the flow of sensitive data within the application. Work to date in this area has focused primarily on compile-time techniques, called static analysis, to analyze all possible behaviors of a programs, and reject it if there is a potential for a leak [16, 2, 63, 39, 48]. Unfortunately, this approach hasn't proved very practical for all but the simplest programs due to the fact that the analysis must simultaneously consider all possible execution paths and data values, and be conservative, reporting an information leak if there is even a single path along which a leak could occur. At runtime, the leaking path could well be infeasible due to conditions that cannot be determined at compile-time. As an example, consider a program that incorporates a bug report feedback to a vendor. If this crash report contains sensitive information (or data derived from sensitive information), a static analysis based approach would simply reject this program. In contrast, a runtime based approach can abort execution of the program when it is about to send a bug report. Based on this intuition, we have developed a source-code transformation to enforce information-flow policies [62]. We have formally established that the generality offered by our technique can be achieved *without* having to relax the privacy guarantees [24] provided by previous approaches based on compile-time analysis techniques.

Recently, we have refined and scaled this technique so that it can be applied to stop "injection attacks" that have become the biggest source of problems for web applications. In these attacks, an attacker exploits weaknesses in web applications to "smuggle" illegal requests to backend servers (e.g., a database server) past the validation checks performed by the application. We have shown that this class of attacks can be accurately and automatically detected using our approach, which carefully tracks information flow through a web application. We have developed a preliminary implementation of this approach for the C language, and the results to date are very promising. Additional details about this technique can be found in [67].

7   Techniques for Preventing Memory Errors

About 75% of all security vulnerabilities reported in recent years by organizations such as US-CERT have been due to a specific software bug called *buffer overflow*, or more generally, a memory error. Memory errors cause the memory space of a program to be corrupted, often in ways that can be controlled by an attacker. By appropriately manipulating the input to a vulnerable program, attackers can corrupt its memory in such a manner that malicious code (or data) embedded in the input is copied into the program's memory space and executed (or used). Although buffer overflows have been well-publicized, and in spite of extensive efforts by software vendors to fix these vulnerabilities, they continue to be discovered at an alarming rate. Moreover, even when defensive techniques are developed to address specific types of attacks that exploit buffer overflows [14, 18], newer attack types (that are sometimes even more versatile than the older attacks) have continued to emerge.

From the perspective of attacker, buffer overflows are very attractive since memory errors are pervasive in large-scale software, and are very hard to track down and eliminate. Thus, there is an endless supply of vulnerabilities that can be discovered and exploited. Moreover, when they are exploited, attackers are able to execute arbitrary code of their choice, thus giving them a great deal of flexibility and power. For these reasons, memory errors will likely remain the principal source of cyber attacks in the foreseeable future. Indeed, all of the Internet worms that have been reported in the past few years, including Code Red and Slammer, have exploited buffer overflows. Moreover, just within the last year, buffer-overflow vulnerabilities have been revealed in web browsers, image and document viewers, and multimedia players. These vulnerabilities allow attackers to infiltrate into computers that simply download a web page, image, document or play a song. These developments highlight the need for comprehensive solutions that can defeat all types of buffer-overflow attacks, whether they use previously known or novel strategies.

7.1 Program Transformation Techniques to Detect All Memory Errors

Although several techniques have been developed for detecting memory errors [27, 3, 44, 31, 47, 41, 30], they suffer from one or more of the following problems: inability to detect all memory errors, requiring extensive modifications to existing C programs, changing the memory management model of C to use garbage collection, and excessive performance overheads. As a result, these techniques aren't suitable to be applied to the vast base of existing software programs. We have therefore developed a new approach [68] for memory error detection that addresses these drawbacks. Our approach can detect *all* memory errors. It makes very conservative assumptions, thereby preserving compatibility with most legacy C code. It still imposes significant performance overheads, although it represents at least a four-fold improvement over previous techniques that preserve C's explicit memory management model [31, 47, 44]. Our ongoing research is focused on program optimization techniques to further reduce these overheads.

7.2 Randomization Based Techniques for Preventing Buffer Overflow Attacks

Although dynamic detection techniques such as those described above provide the most comprehensive protection from memory errors, they do impose significant performance overheads. Moreover, they can impact compatibility with precompiled libraries for which source code is unavailable. These factors have fueled the development of alternative solutions specialized for security, i.e., techniques for detecting memory errors that lead to attacks, rather than trying to capture all memory errors. Early work in this direction was focused on a specific type of attack called stack-smashing [14]. Subsequently, other types of attacks were discovered that necessitated the development of techniques specialized for those types of attacks [15]. Clearly, playing catch-up with attackers is not the best way to solve the problem, especially in the context of attacks with very serious consequences such as memory errors. Therefore, we developed the first solution, called *address obfuscation* [9], that offered broad protection against all common types of memory error attacks[1].

Address obfuscation, alternatively called address-space randomization (ASR), operates by randomizing the locations of objects (such as program variables) within the memory space of an application. As a result, attackers can no longer predict the memory locations that need to be corrupted for a successful attack. We provided a comprehensive analysis of the strengths and vulnerabilities of randomization, and identified new randomization-targeted attacks that can be successful in some cases. Based on this analysis, we have recently developed a more comprehensive randomization approach [10] that provides probabilistic protection against all memory error exploits, whether they be known or novel. Our approach is implemented as a fully automatic source-to-source transformation which is compatible with legacy C code. The address-space randomizations take place at load-time or runtime, so the same copy of the binaries can be distributed to everyone; this ensures compatibility with today's software distribution model. Experimental results

---

[1] The same basic technique was also independently discovered by the PaX project [45], and aspects of this approach have since become an integral part of some recent distributions of the Linux operating system.

demonstrate that our randomization techniques incur low performance overheads.

7.3   Automated Signature Generation to Counter Automated Attacks

It is widely recognized that large-scale attacks, such as those launched by worms and zombie farms, pose a grave threat to our network-centric society. Existing approaches such as software patches are simply unable to cope with the volume and speed with which new vulnerabilities are being discovered. We have recently developed a new approach that can provide effective protection against a vast majority of these attacks. Our approach uses a forensic analysis of a victim server memory to correlate attacks to inputs received over the network, and *automatically* develop a signature that characterizes inputs that carry attacks. The signatures tend to capture characteristics of the underlying vulnerability (e.g., a message field being too long) rather than the characteristics of an attack, thereby making it effective against variants of attacks. Our approach introduces low overheads (under 10%), does not require access to source code of the protected server, and has successfully generated signatures for all of the attacks that we studied in our experiments, without producing false alarms. Signature generation is fast, taking a few milliseconds at most. This enables such filters to be deployed very quickly, thereby providing protection against fast-spreading worms. The techniques we have developed in this regard are described in detail in [35] and [36]. As compared with most recent research in automated generation of attack signatures [54, 43, 33, 69, 64, 66], our approach can generate generalized signatures from a single attack instance. In experiments, we have shown that it produces no false positives, and is able to defeat variants of an attack that exploit the same underlying vulnerability. We have deployed these signatures in the Snort intrusion detection system [56] to filter out attacks in the network.

8   Summary

In this project, we have developed a new approach called model-carrying code for safe use of untrusted code. Unlike previous approaches that were focused mainly on malicious code containment, MCC makes no judgment regarding the inherent risks associated with untrusted code. It simply provides the infrastructure and tools needed by code consumers to make risk versus reward decisions regarding untrusted code.

We have established the practicality of MCC by developing a software prototype. This prototype has been used on many moderate to large COTS applications in use today, and provides good runtime performance. More importantly, we have shown that MCC can be incorporated in a seamless fashion into tools that serve as conduits for untrusted code, including software installers, email handlers, and web browsers. We have developed an effective and convenient user interface for management and control of MCC. This management infrastructure can provide a highly simplified user-interface for naive users that can be tailored by security administrators. At the same time, these tools provide a much richer set of functionalities to security-savvy users.

In addition to mobile/untrusted code security, we developed solutions to several other important problems in computer security, including: security policy languages, policy verification and refinement, efficient policy enforcement, automatic extraction of security behavior models and their use in host-based intrusion detection, debugging memory errors, buffer-overflow defense, accurate detection of a wide range of attacks, automated generation of attack signatures, and so on. We have developed and publicly released several software tools that implement these solutions, including:

- *RPMShield* for secure software installation,
- *Alcatraz* for safe execution of untrusted code,
- *Tracer,* which provides the infrastructure for system-call interception and runtime enforcement in MCC.
- *Address-space randomization tools* that produce address-space randomized programs from source code
- *Memory-Safe C* tool for transforming C programs to detect all memory errors at runtime

In addition, several other tools, including the complete MCC infrastructure and management tools, are in the final stages of development and are slated for release in the near future. The latest information related to this project, including publications and software releases, can be found at the project web page at `http://seclab.cs.sunysb.edu/mcc/`.

References

[1] Acharya, A. and Raje, M. 2000. Mapbox: Using parameterized behavior classes to confine applications. In *USENIX Security Symposium*.

[2] G. R. Andrews and R. P. Reitman. An axiomatic approach to information flow in programs. *ACM Transactions on Programming Languages and Systems (TOPLAS)*, 2(1):56–75, Jan. 1980.

[3] Todd M. Austin, Scott E. Breach, and Gurindar S. Sohi. Efficient detection of all pointer and array access errors. In *Proceedings of the ACM SIGPLAN'94 Conference on Programming Language Design and Implementation (PLDI)*, pages 290–301, Orlando, Florida, 20–24 June 1994. *SIGPLAN Notices* 29(6), June 1994.

[4] Thomas Ball and Sriram K. Rajamani. The SLAM toolkit. In *Computer Aided Verification CAV*, New York-Berlin-Heidelberg, July 2001.

[5] S. Basu, K.N. Kumar, R.L. Pokorny, and C.R. Ramakrishnan. Resource constrained model checking for recursive programs. In *Tools and Algorithms for the Construction and Analysis of Systems(TACAS)*, 2002.

[6] Samik Basu and C. R. Ramakrishnan. Compositional analysis for verification of parameterized systems. In *Ninth International Conference on Tools and Algorithms for the Construction and Analysis of Systems (TACAS)*, volume 2619 of *Lecture Notes in Computer Science*, pages 315–330, Warsaw, Poland, April 2003. Springer.

[7] Samik Basu, Diptikalyan Saha, Yow-Jian Lin, and Scott A. Smolka. Generation of all counter-examples for push-down systems. In *Formal Techniques for Networked and Distributed Systems (FORTE)*, 2003.

[8] Samik Basu, Diptikalyan Saha, and Scott A. Smolka. Localizing program errors for Cimple debugging. In *Formal Techniques for Networked and Distributed Systems (FORTE)*, 2004.

[9] Sandeep Bhatkar, Daniel C. DuVarney, and R. Sekar. Address obfuscation: An efficient approach to combat a broad range of memory error exploits. In *Proceeding of 12th USENIX Security Symposium*, 2003.

[10] Sandeep Bhatkar, R. Sekar, and Daniel C. DuVarney. Efficient techniques for comprehensive protection from memory error exploits. In *Proceeding of 14th USENIX Security Symposium*, 2005.

[11] Abhishek Chaturvedi, Sandeep Bhatkar and R. Sekar. Improving attack detection in host-based ids by learning properties of system call arguments. Technical report SECLAB-05-03, Secure Systems Lab, Department of Computer Science, Stony Brook University, Available at http://seclab.cs.sunysb.edu/pubs.htm, 2005.

[12] E. M. Clarke and E. A. Emerson. Design and synthesis of synchronization skeletons using branching-time temporal logic. In D. Kozen, editor, *Proceedings of the Workshop on Logic of Programs*, Yorktown Heights, volume 131 of *LNCS*, pages 52–71. Springer-Verlag, 1981.

[13] E. M. Clarke and J. M. Wing. Formal methods: State of the art and future directions. *ACM Computing Surveys*, 28(4), December 1996.

[14] Crispan Cowan, Calton Pu, Dave Maier, Jonathan Walpole, Peat Bakke, Steve Beattie, Aaron Grier, Perry Wagle, Qian Zhang, and Heather Hinton. StackGuard: Automatic adaptive detection and prevention of buffer-overflow attacks. In *Proc. 7th USENIX Security Conference*, pages 63–78, San Antonio, Texas, jan 1998.

[15] Crispin Cowan, Matt Barringer, Steve Beattie, and Greg Kroah-Hartman. Formatguard: Automatic protection from printf format string vulnerabilities. In *USENIX Security Symposium*, 2001.

[16] D. E. Denning and P. J. Denning. Certification of programs for secure information flow. *Comm. of the ACM*, 20(7):504–513, July 1977.

[17] D. L. Dill. The Murφ verification system. In Computer Aided Verification, 1996, pages 390–393.

[18] Hiroaki Etoh and Kunikazu Yoda. Protecting from stack-smashing attacks. Published on World-Wide

Web at URL http://www.trl.ibm.com/projects/security/ssp/main.html, June 2000.

[19] David Evans and Andrew Tywman. Flexible policy directed code safety. In *IEEE Symposium on Security and Privacy*, 1999.

[20] Henry Hanping Feng, Oleg M. Kolesnikov, Prahlad Fogla, Wenke Lee, and Weibo Gong. Anomaly detection using call stack information. In *IEEE Symposium on Security and Privacy*, 2003.

[21] S. Forrest, S. A. Hofmeyr, A. Somayaji, Intrusion Detection using Sequences of System Calls, Journal of Computer Security Vol. 6 (1998) pg 151-180.

[22] D. Gao, M. K. Reiter, and D. Song. Gray-box extraction of execution graphs for anomaly detection. In *USENIX Security Symposium*, pages 103–118, San Diego, CA, USA, August 2004.

[23] J. T. Giffin, S. Jha, and B. P. Miller. Efficient context-sensitive intrusion detection. In *Network and Distributed System Security Symposium*, San Diego, CA, February 2004.

[24] J. Goguen and J. Meseguer. Security policies and security models. In *IEEE Symposium on Security and Privacy*, 1982.

[25] Ian Goldberg, David Wagner, Randi Thomas, and Eric A. Brewer. A secure environment for untrusted helper applications: confining the wily hacker. In *USENIX Security Symposium*, 1996.

[26] L Gong, M Mueller, H Prafullchandra, and R Schemers. Going beyond the sandbox: An overview of the new security architecture in the Java development kit 1.2. In *USENIX Symposium on Internet Technologies and Systems*, 1997.

[27] Reed Hastings and Bob Joyce. Purify: A tool for detecting memory leaks and access errors in C and C++ programs. In USENIX Association, editor, *Proceedings of the Winter 1992 USENIX Conference*, pages 125–138, Berkeley, CA, USA, January 1992. USENIX.

[28] Thomas A. Henzinger, Ranjit Jhala, Rupak Majumdar, George C. Necula, Grégoire Sutre, and Westley Weimer. Temporal-safety proofs for systems code. In *Computer Aided Verification CAV*, 2002.

[29] G. J. Holzmann. The model checker SPIN. *IEEE Transactions on Software Engineering*, 23(5):279–295, May 1997.

[30] Trevor Jim, Greg Morrisett, Dan Grossman, Micheal Hicks, James Cheney, and Yanling Wang. Cyclone: a safe dialect of C. In *USENIX Annual Technical Conference*, Monterey, CA, June 2002.

[31] Robert W. M. Jones and Paul H. J. Kelly. Backwards-compatible bounds checking for arrays and pointers in C programs. In M. Kamkar and D. Byers, editors, *Third International Workshop on Automated Debugging*. Linkoping University Electronic Press, 1997.

[32] Hyang-Ah Kim and Brad Karp. Autograph: Toward automated, distributed worm signature detection. In *Proceedings of 13th USENIX Security Symposium*, 2004.

[33] Christian Kreibich and Jon Crowcroft. Honeycomb - creating intrusion detection signatures using honeypots. In *Proceedings of 2nd Workshop on Hot Topics in Networks (HotNets-II)*, 2003.

[34] K. Krishna, W. Sun, P. Rana, T. Li, and R. Sekar. V-NetLab: A cost-effective platform to support course projects in computer security. *Colloquium for Information Systems Security Education*, 2005.

[35] Z. Liang and R. Sekar. Automated, sub-second attack signature generation: A basis for building self-protecting servers. In *ACM conference on Computer and Communications Security (CCS)*, 2005.

[36] Zhenkai Liang, R. Sekar, and Daniel C. DuVarney. Automatic synthesis of filters to discard buffer overflow attacks: A step towards realizing self-healing systems. In *USENIX Annual Technical Conference*, 2005.

[37] Zhenkai Liang, VN Venkatakrishnan, and R. Sekar. Isolated program execution: An application transparent approach for executing untrusted programs. *Annual Computer Security Applications Conference*, 2003.

[38] J. McLean. A general theory of composition for trace sets closed under selective interleaving functions. In *IEEE Symposium on Security and Privacy*, pages 79–93, May 1994.

[39] A. C. Myers. JFlow: Practical mostly-static information flow control. In *ACM Symposium on Prin-*

ciples of Programming Languages (POPL), pages 228–241, January 1999.

[40] G. Necula and P. Lee, Proof-carrying code. In *ACM Symposium on Principles of Programming Languages (POPL)*, 1997.

[41] George C. Necula, Scott McPeak, and Westley Weimer. CCured: type-safe retrofitting of legacy code. In *Symposium on Principles of Programming Languages (POPL '02)*, pages 128–139, Portland, OR, January 2002.

[42] James Newsome, Brad Karp, and Dawn Song. Polygraph: Automatically generating signatures for polymorphic worms. In *Proceedings of IEEE Symposium on Security and Privacy*, 2005.

[43] James Newsome and Dawn Song. Dynamic taint analysis for automatic detection, analysis, and signature generation of exploits on commodity software. In *Proceedings of 12th Annual Network and Distributed System Security Symposium (NDSS)*, 2005.

[44] Harish G. Patil and Charles N. Fischer. Efficient run-time monitoring using shadow processing. In Mireille Ducasse, editor, *Proceedings of the 2nd International Workshop on Automated and Algorithmic Debugging*, St. Malo,

[45] PaX ASLR. Published on World-Wide Web at URL http://pageexec.virtualave.net.

[46] J. P. Queille and J. Sifakis. Specification and verification of concurrent systems in Cesar. In *Proceedings of the International Symposium in Programming*, volume 137 of *Lecture Notes in Computer Science*, Berlin, 1982. Springer-Verlag.

[47] Olatunji Ruwase and Monica S. Lam. A practical dynamic buffer overflow detector. In *Network and Distributed System Security Symposium (NDSS)*, February 2004.

[48] A. Sabelfeld and A. C. Myers. Language-based information-flow security. *IEEE J. Selected Areas in Communications*, 21(1), January 2003.

[49] Beata Sarna-Starosta and C. R. Ramakrishnan. Constraint-based model checking of data-independent systems. In *International Conference on Formal Engineering Methods (ICFEM)*, volume 2885 of *Lecture Notes in Computer Science*, pages 579–598, Singapore, November 2003. Springer.

[50] Fred B. Schneider. Enforceable security policies. *ACM Transactions on Information and System Security (TISSEC)*, 3(1), 2001.

[51] Scott, K. and Davidson, J. 2002. Safe virtual execution using software dynamic translation. In *Proceedings of Annual Computer Security Applications Conference*.

[52] R. Sekar, M. Bendre, P. Bollineni, and D. Dhurjati. A fast automaton-based approach for detecting anomalous program behaviors. In *IEEE Symposium on Security and Privacy*, 2001.

[53] R. Sekar, V.N. Venkatakrishnan, Samik Basu, Sandeep Bhatkar and Daniel C. DuVarney. Model-carrying code: A practical approach for safe execution of untrusted applications. In *ACM Symposium on Operating Systems Principles (SOSP'03)*, Bolton Landing, New York, October 2003. ACM Press.

[54] Sumeet Singh, Cristian Estan, George Varghese, and Stefan Savage. Automated worm fingerprinting. In *Proceedings of 6th Symposium on Operating System Design and Implementation (OSDI)*, 2004.

[55] P. Loscocco and S. Smalley. Integrating flexible support for security policies into the linux operating system. In *USENIX Annual Technical Conference (FREENIX Track)*, 2001.

[56] Snort. Open source network intrusion detection system. http://www.snort.org.

[57] Weiqing Sun, Zhenkai Liang, R. Sekar, and VN Venkatakrishnan. One-way isolation: An effective approach for realizing safe execution environments. *ISOC Network and Distributed Systems Symposium*, 2005.

[58] Prem Uppuluri. *Intrusion Detection/Prevention Using Behavior Specifications*. PhD thesis, Stony Brook University, 2003.

[59] Prem Uppuluri and R Sekar. Experiences with specification based intrusion detection. In *proceedings of the Recent Advances in Intrusion Detection conference*, October 2001.

[60] V.N. Venkatakrishnan, Ram Peri, and R. Sekar. Empowering mobile code using expressive security

policies. In *New Security Paradigms Workshop (NSPW)*, 2002.

[61] V. N. Venkatakrishnan, R. Sekar, T. Kamat, S.Tsipa and Z.Liang. An approach for secure software installation. In *Proceedings of USENIX System Administration Conference*, 2002.

[62] V.N. Venkatakrishnan, Daniel C. DuVarney, Wei Xu and R. Sekar. A program transformation technique for enforcement of information flow properties. Technical report SECLAB-04-01, Secure Systems Lab, Department of Computer Science, Stony Brook University, Available at http://seclab.cs.sunysb.edu/pubs.htm, 2004.

[63] D. Volpano, G. Smith, and C. Irvine. A sound type system for secure flow analysis. *Journal of Computer Security*, 4(3):167–187, 1996.

[64] Ke Wang and Salvatore J. Stolfo. Anomalous payload-based network intrusion detection. In *Proceeding of 7th International Symposium on Recent Advances in Intrusion Detection (RAID)*, 2004.

[65] Anti-virus software, In Wikipedia, available at `http://en.wikipedia.org/wiki/Antivirus`

[66] J. Xu, P. Ning, C. Kil, Y. Zhai, and C. Bookholt. Automatic diagnosis and response to memory corruption vulnerabilities. In *ACM CCS*, 2005.

[67] Wei Xu, Sandeep Bhatkar, and R. Sekar. Practical dynamic taint analysis for countering input validation attacks on web applications. Technical report SECLAB-05-04, Secure Systems Lab, Department of Computer Science, Stony Brook University, Available at http://seclab.cs.sunysb.edu/pubs.htm, 2005.

[68] Wei Xu, Daniel C. Duvarney, and R. Sekar. An efficient and backwards-compatible transformation to ensure memory safety of C programs. In *ACM SIGSOFT International Symposium on Foundations of Software Engineering*, California, November 2004.

[69] V. Yegneswaran, J. Giffin, P. Barford, and S. Jha. An architecture for generating semantics-aware signatures. In *USENIX Security*, 2005.

Model-Carrying Code: A Practical Approach for Safe Execution of Untrusted Applications[*]

R. Sekar   V.N. Venkatakrishnan   Samik Basu   Sandeep Bhatkar   Daniel C. DuVarney

Department of Computer Science

Stony Brook University, Stony Brook, NY 11794.

Email: {sekar, venkat, bsamik, sbhatkar, dand}@cs.sunysb.edu

ABSTRACT

This paper presents a new approach called *model-carrying code* (MCC) for safe execution of untrusted code. At the heart of MCC is the idea that untrusted code comes equipped with a concise high-level model of its security-relevant behavior. This model helps bridge the gap between high-level security policies and low-level binary code, thereby enabling analyses which would otherwise be impractical. For instance, users can use a fully automated verification procedure to determine if the code satisfies their security policies. Alternatively, an automated procedure can sift through a catalog of acceptable policies to identify one that is compatible with the model. Once a suitable policy is selected, MCC guarantees that the policy will not be violated by the code. Unlike previous approaches, the MCC framework enables code producers and consumers to collaborate in order to achieve safety. Moreover, it provides support for policy selection as well as enforcement. Finally, MCC makes no assumptions regarding the inherent risks associated with untrusted code. It simply provides the tools that enable a consumer to make informed decisions about the risk that he/she is willing to tolerate so as to benefit from the functionality offered by an untrusted application.

Categories and Subject Descriptors

D.4.6 [**Operating Systems**]: Security and Protection, — *Invasive software* ; K.6.5 [**Computing Milieux**]: Management of computing and Information Systems, Security and Protection, Unauthorized access

General Terms

Security, Verification

Keywords

mobile code security, policy enforcement, sand-boxing, security policies

[*]This research is supported mainly by an ONR grant N000140110967, and in part by NSF grants CCR-0098154 and CCR-0208877, and an AFOSR grant F49620-01-1-0332.

1. INTRODUCTION

There has been significant growth in the use of software from sources that are not fully trusted — a trend that has accelerated since the advent of the Internet. Examples of untrusted or partially trusted software include: document handlers and viewers (e.g., Real Audio, ghostview), games, peer-to-peer applications (e.g., file sharing, instant messaging), freeware, shareware and trialware, and mobile code (applets, JavaScript, ActiveX).

Contemporary operating systems provide little support for coping with such untrusted applications. Although support for *code-signing* has been introduced into recent OSes, this technique is useful only for verifying that the code originated from a trusted producer. If the code originated from an untrusted or unknown producer, then code-signing provides no support for safe execution of such code. The users (henceforth called *code consumers*) are faced with the choice of either losing out on the potential benefits provided by such code by not running it, or exposing themselves to an unacceptable level of risk by running the code with all of the privileges available to the code consumer.

The lack of OS-level support for safe execution of untrusted code has motivated the development of a number of alternative approaches. These approaches can be divided into *execution monitoring* [14, 12, 31, 33, 18, 1, 19] and static analysis [29, 28, 7, 11, 34, 24]. With execution monitoring, policy violations are detected at runtime, at which point the consumer can be prompted to see if he/she is willing to grant additional access rights to the program, or instead wishes to simply terminate it. In the former case, the consumer is being asked to make decisions on granting additional access to a program without knowing whether these accesses will allow the program to execute successfully, or simply lead to another prompt for even more access. On the other hand, terminating the program causes inconvenience, since the user may have already spent a significant amount of time searching/acquiring the untrusted code, or in providing input to it. In addition, the consumer may have to perform "clean up" actions, such as deleting temporary files created by the program or rolling back changes to important data.

Static analysis-based techniques do not suffer from the inconvenience of runtime aborts. However, from a practical perspective, static analysis techniques are effective only when operating on the source code of programs. Typically, code consumers deal with binary code, which makes it difficult (if not impossible) for them to statically verify whether the code satisfies their policy. Although proof-carrying code (PCC) [29] can, in principle, allow such verification to be applied to binaries, practical difficulties have limited its application to primarily type and memory safety properties. Thus, for the vast majority of code distributed in binary form, and the vast majority of safety policies which concern resource accesses

Reprinted with permission from *ACM Symposium on Operating Systems Principles, Proceedings of the Nineteenth ACM Symposium on Operating Systems Principles, SESSION: Safely executing untrusted code.* 2003. 15–28.

519

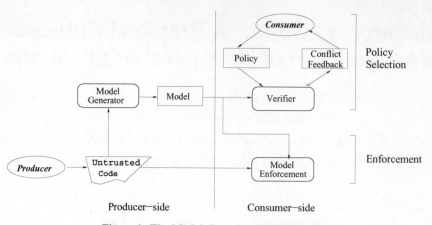

Figure 1: The Model-Carrying Code Framework

made by untrusted programs, static analysis-based approaches do not provide a practical solution for safe execution.

The new approach presented in this paper, called model-carrying code (MCC), combines the convenience of static analysis-based approaches such as PCC (i.e., the reduction or elimination of runtime aborts) with the practicality of execution-monitoring (i.e., the ability to enforce a rich class of consumer-specified security policies). It is inspired by the PCC approach, and shares with it the high-level idea that untrusted code is accompanied by additional information that aids in verifying its safety. With MCC, this additional information takes the form of a *model* that captures the security-relevant behavior of code, rather than a proof. Models enable code producers to communicate the security needs of their code to the consumer. The code consumers can then check their policies against the model associated with untrusted code to determine if this code will violate their policy. Since MCC models are significantly simpler than programs, such checking can be fully automated.

Models serve the important purpose of decoupling the concerns of code producers and consumers. Code producers need not guess security policies of different consumers, nor do they need to expend resources on the generation of proofs in response to requests from consumers. Similarly, code consumers no longer need to tackle the difficult problem of correctly guessing the security needs of an untrusted application. Moreover, they need not reveal their security policies to code producers that they do not trust. Thus, MCC provides a framework for code producers and consumers to collaborate to achieve safe execution of untrusted code. This contrasts with previous execution-monitoring approaches [19, 14, 18, 12] that place the burden of security entirely on the code consumer, and PCC, which places the burden entirely on the code producer.

MCC enables code consumers to try out different security policies of interest to them *prior to the execution of untrusted code,* and select one that can statically be proved to be consistent with the model associated with a piece of untrusted code. This contrasts with purely execution monitoring-based approaches, wherein the consumer needs to deal with repeated runtime aborts (and associated clean-up efforts) to try out different policies; and with PCC, where the only policies that can be statically checked are those for which proofs have been furnished by the code producer.

When a consumer's policy is violated by a model, MCC provides a concise summary of all violations, rather than providing them one by one. By capturing all policy violations in one shot, MCC helps avoid repeated policy violation prompts that are associated with execution monitoring-based approaches. Moreover, this summary is of considerable help in navigating the policy space and identifying the refinement that is most suitable for a given piece of code. Thus, MCC provides support not only for policy enforcement, but

also *policy selection* — a problem that has not been addressed by previous research in this area.

1.1 Overview of Approach

The key idea in our approach (see Figure 1) is the introduction of program behavioral *models* that help bridge the semantic gap between (very low-level) binary code and high-level security policies. These models successfully capture security-related properties of the code, but do not capture aspects of the code that pertain only to its functional correctness. The model is stated in terms of the security-relevant operations made by the code, the arguments of these operations, and the sequencing relationships among them. In our current implementation, these operations correspond to system calls, but alternatives such as function calls are also possible.

While models can be created manually, doing so would be a time-consuming process that would affect the usability of the approach. Therefore, we have developed a *model extraction* approach that can automatically generate the required models. Since the model extraction takes place at the producer end, it can operate on source code rather than binary code. It can also benefit from the test suites developed by the code producer to test his/her source code.

The code consumer receives both the model and the program from the producer. The consumer wants to be assured that the code will satisfy a security policy selected by him/her. The use of a security behavior model enables us to decompose this assurance argument into two parts:

- *policy satisfaction:* check whether the model satisfies the policy, i.e., the behaviors captured by the model are a subset of the behaviors allowed by the policy. This can be expressed symbolically as

$$\mathcal{B}[M] \subseteq \mathcal{B}[P]$$

where P denotes a policy, M denotes a model, and $\mathcal{B}$ is a function that maps a policy (or a model) to the set of all behaviors satisfied by the policy/model.

- *model safety:* check if the model captures a safe approximation of program behavior — more precisely, that any behavior exhibited by the program is captured by the model:

$$\mathcal{B}[A] \subseteq \mathcal{B}[M]$$

Here, A denotes an application, and $\mathcal{B}$ and M have the same meaning as before.

Together, these two imply that $\mathcal{B}[A] \subseteq \mathcal{B}[P]$, i.e., the application A satisfies the security policy P.

Note that model safety is a necessary step whenever the code consumer does not trust the model provided by the code producer.

In particular, the producer may provide an incorrect model either due to malice, or errors/omissions in the model extractor (e.g., failure to account for all possible program behaviors).

In principle, policy satisfaction as well as model safety can be established using static analysis or verification techniques. In practice, however, we resort to runtime enforcement for ensuring model safety due to the difficulties in verifying properties of low-level (binary) code.

The policy selection component in Figure 1 is concerned with policy satisfaction, whereas the enforcement component is concerned with model safety. The policy selection component uses automated verification (actually, model-checking [8]). Since models are much simpler than programs, complete automation of this verification step is possible. If the model is *not* consistent with the policy, the verifier generates a compact and user-friendly summary of all consistency violations. The consumer can either discard the code at this point, or refine the policy in such a way that would permit execution of the code without posing undue security risks.

The policy selection step requires that a consumer be knowledgeable about security issues. Consumers that do not possess this level of knowledge can rely on their system administrator to pre-specify the policy to be used with an untrusted application at its installation time, or provide a set of choices that the user can select prior to execution of the code.

If the refined policy is consistent with the model, then the model and the code are forwarded to the enforcement module. Our current implementation of enforcement is based on system call interception. If the enforcement component detects a deviation from the model, then the execution of the untrusted code is terminated. An alternative to model enforcement is to directly enforce the consumer's security policy, as discussed further in Section 5.

Although execution monitoring, by itself, has the drawbacks mentioned earlier, its use in MCC does not entail the same drawbacks. Note that any enforcement violation in MCC indicates that either the code producer intentionally supplied an incorrect model, or that the model extractor was faulty. The predominance of benign code over malicious code on the Internet indicates that most code producers are not malicious, and hence they will not intentionally provide incorrect models. We expect violations due to model extractor errors to be unlikely as well. Thus, in the vast majority of cases, MCC enables code consumers to use untrusted code *safely* (i.e., their security policy will not be violated) and *conveniently* (i.e., there will be no runtime aborts). In a small minority of cases, where a runtime violation is experienced, safety is still retained, but convenience may be lost.

Although this paper focuses on untrusted programs executing on a UNIX operating system, techniques from our approach could be easily adapted for different execution environments such as Java or Microsoft's Common Language Runtime (CLR) environment (part of its .NET initiative). As a first step in this direction, we have done some preliminary work in defining security policies in terms of security-relevant method calls in Java, and implementing policy enforcement via bytecode rewriting [36].

1.2 Organization of the Paper

We begin our description of the MCC approach with an overview of the MCC policy language in Section 2. Next, in Section 3, we describe our approach for extracting models from programs. The policy selection component is described in Section 4, while enforcement is described in Section 5. Our implementation of the above four components is described in Section 6, together with performance results that establish the practicality of MCC. Finally, concluding remarks appear in Section 7.

2. SECURITY POLICIES

Enforcement in MCC relies on execution monitoring, and hence only *enforceable security policies* [31] are of interest. Such policies are limited to *safety properties*. With other kinds of properties such as those involving information flow [42] and covert channels [23], enforcement is either impossible or impractical, and hence they are not considered in this paper.

Common examples of enforceable policies include access-control and resource-usage policies. Java 2 security model [19] supports standard access-control policies, but can handle applications that consist of code from multiple producers. Naccio [14] supports specification of both access control and resource usage policies. The security automaton formalism [31] can support safety properties that involve sequencing relationships between operations. However, this formalism (and the associated language PoET/PSLang [13]) does not provide the ability to remember argument values such as file descriptors for subsequent comparisons with arguments of other operations. We have shown in [36, 33] that this ability to remember arguments enhances the expressive power of the policy language significantly. Accordingly, our policy language is based on *extended finite state automata* (EFSA) that extend standard FSA by incorporating a finite set of state variables to remember argument values. For instance, we can associate a write operation with the file name involved in writing by recording the return value from an open operation (a file descriptor), and comparing it with the argument of the write operation. Below, we describe this policy language and illustrate it through examples.

2.1 Security Policy Language

We model behaviors in terms of externally observable *events*. In modern operating systems, security-related actions of programs must be ultimately effected via system calls. For this reason, system calls constitute the event alphabet in our policies. Naturally, it is possible to define behaviors in terms of operations other than system calls, such as arbitrary function calls. Higher level policies can often be stated more easily and accurately in terms of function calls. For instance, a policy that permits a program P to make name server queries can be stated as "program P is allowed to use the function gethostbyname" rather than the more complicated (and less precise) version "program P is allowed to connect to IP address xyz on port 53." On the downside, enforcement of such policies will require secure interception of arbitrary function calls, which is not possible in general for binary code.

We use the term *history* to refer to a sequence of events. A history includes events as well as their arguments. A *trace* is a history observed during a single execution of a program. The behavior of a program A, denoted $\mathcal{B}(A)$, is defined to be the set of all traces that may be produced during any execution of A.

Policies capture properties of traces. They are expressed using EFSA. Like security automata, EFSA express negations of policies, i.e., they accept traces that violate the intended policy. The state of an EFSA is characterized by its *control state* (the same notion as the "state" of an FSA), plus the values of (a finite set of) state variables. State variables can take values from possibly infinite domains, such as integers and strings. Each transition in the EFSA is associated with an event, an enabling condition involving the event arguments and state variables, and a set of assignments to state variables. For a transition to be taken, the associated event must occur and the enabling condition must hold. When the transition is taken, the assignments associated with the transition are performed.

EFSA-based policies are expressed in our Behavior Monitoring Specification Language (BMSL). BMSL permits EFSA to be described by defining states, start and final states, and transition rules.

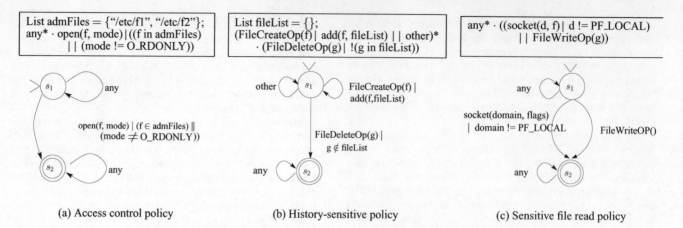

(a) Access control policy   (b) History-sensitive policy   (c) Sensitive file read policy

Figure 2: Examples of REE policies and their equivalent EFSA representation

BMSL also permits a dual representation of EFSA using *Regular Expressions over Events (REE)* [33]. Just as EFSA extend FSA with state variables, REEs extend regular expressions with state variables. For simple policies, REEs tend to be much more concise and "text-friendly" than EFSA. Hence in practice, we write most of our policies using REEs. The BMSL compiler can translate policies into an EFSA form that is used by the verifier. The EFSA form may also be used for policy enforcement, as we have done in the past for the purposes of intrusion detection [4]. [35] establishes the equivalence of EFSA and REE, so the two notations can be freely mixed in BMSL. (This capability of BMSL is analogous to the ability to mix regular expressions and state machine constructs in Lex.) Further details on REEs and EFSA, including their formal semantics, matching complexity and expressive power can be found in [35]. Below, we provide a short description of BMSL.

Events. Events may be further classified as follows:

- *Primitive events:* There are two primitive events associated with each system call, one corresponding to the system call invocation and the other to its exit. The invocation event has the same name as the system call, while the return event has an "_exit" appended to its name. The arguments of the entry event include all of the arguments at the point of call. The arguments to an exit event include all of the arguments at the point of return, plus the value of the return code from the system call.
- *Abstract events:* Abstract events can be used to denote classes of primitive events, e.g., we may define FileModificationOps as an event that corresponds to a set of events that modify files. More generally, abstract events may be defined using the notation $event(args) = pat$, where $event$ denotes the abstract event name, and pat is defined below.

Patterns. The simplest patterns, called *primitive patterns,* are of the form $e(x_1, ..., x_n)|cond/asg$, where $cond$ is a boolean-valued expression on the event arguments $x_1, ..., x_n$ and state variables, and asg contains zero or more assignments to state variables. The scope of event arguments is limited to the primitive pattern within which it occurs.

Compound patterns are obtained by composing primitive patterns using operators similar to those in regular expressions. The meaning of compound patterns is best explained by the following definition of what it means for a history H to satisfy a pattern:

- *event occurrence:* $e(x_1, ..., x_n)|cond$ is satisfied by the event

history consisting of the single event $e(v_1, ..., v_n)$ if and only if $cond$ evaluates to $true$ when variables $x_1, ..., x_n$ are replaced by the values $v_1, ..., v_n$.
- *alternation:* $pat_1||pat_2$ is satisfied by H if either pat_1 or pat_2 is satisfied by H.
- *sequencing:* $pat_1 \cdot pat_2$ is satisfied by an event history H of the form $H_1 H_2$ provided H_1 satisfies pat_1 and H_2 satisfies pat_2.
- *repetition:* $pat*$ is satisfied by H iff H is empty, or is of the form $H_1 H_2$ where H_1 satisfies pat and H_2 satisfies $pat*$.
- *negation:* $!pat$ is satisfied by H iff pat is not satisfied by H. (The use of negation is not permitted in BMSL if pat involves sequencing or repetition.)

The notion of satisfaction extends in the obvious way when state variables are included, and the details can be found in [35].

We say that a history H matches a policy pat provided that *some prefix* of H satisfies pat.

2.2 Illustrative Examples

Often, it is convenient to group similar events into one abstract event. For instance, there are a number of system calls that can result in the creation or modification of a file, such as open, creat, and truncate. By defining an abstract event:

```
FileWriteOp(f) = (open(f, mode) | writeFlags(mode))
                 || creat(f) || truncate(f)
```

we can use FileWriteOp subsequently to denote any of these operations. For readability, we have abstracted a test on the value of mode into a call to a function writeFlags, which returns true whenever the mode corresponds to opening the file for writing. We have also omitted trailing arguments to creat and truncate as we are not interested in their values.

Figure 2 illustrates three simple policy examples using REE as well as EFSA notation. Note that the special event *any* stands for any event, while *other* stands for an event other than those matching the rest of the transitions on the same state. Since a history H matches an REE whenever a prefix of H satisfies the REE, the REE patterns do not need to have the *any* transitions that occur in the final state of the EFSA policies.

Figure 2(a) is a simple *access control* policy that prevents writes to all files, and reads from any of the files in a set admFiles. Note that the operator || is overloaded so that it can represent pattern alternation as well as the boolean-or operation. If any of these prohibited operations are performed by a program, then the automaton makes a transition from the start state (marked with a ">" symbol) to the final state (marked with a double circle). For any other operations, the transition marked "any" is taken, i.e., the EFSA stays in the start state.

Resource usage policies can also be expressed using EFSA very easily. For instance, a state variable can be used to keep track of the number of open file descriptors, and deny further opens when too many files are open. We do not dwell on resource usage examples in this paper since resource usage properties are not very amenable to fully automated verification.

Figure 2(b) illustrates a *history-sensitive* policy that allows an untrusted application to remove only those files that it previously created. This policy illustrates the use of a list variable `fileList` to remember the names of files that were created by an application. (Here, `FileCreateOp` is an abstract event that should have previously been defined to denote successful returns from all system calls that may create a file.) Any file that the application attempts to delete is checked in this list, and if absent, a policy violation is flagged. Another example of a history-sensitive policy is one that requires an application to close all the files it opened before executing another program. In REE, this policy is expressed as:

$$\text{any* } \cdot \text{ open\_exit(f, fd)|(fd > 0) / (FD = fd)}$$
$$\cdot \text{ (!close(g)|(g == FD))* } \cdot \text{ execve()}$$

Note that this policy uses only a single state variable FD, but the nondeterministic nature of matching will ensure that a policy violation is reported when any successfully opened file remains open at the time of the `execve` system call.

Figure 2(c) shows the "no network accesses and no file write operations" policy. This policy prevents an application from sending information to an untrusted remote site or write it to an output file. A possible scenario for the use of this policy is the case when an application needs to operate on confidential information.

3. MODEL GENERATION

The problem of generating abstract models from programs has been studied by several researchers in software model-checking [3, 20, 26, 21, 9, 10, 5]. However, very few of these approaches are fully automated, and furthermore, they generate distinct models which are customized for each property to be proved. Property-specific customization greatly simplifies the model, and makes it possible to prove complex properties that could not be proved otherwise. However, in MCC, the code producer generating the model is unaware of consumer security policies. Hence, a *single* model must be generated that is usable for almost all policies. For this reason, some of the previous works in generating program behavior models for intrusion detection are more closely related to MCC model generation than the software model-checking approaches. In particular, [38] develops an approach to derive automata models of program behavior from source code. This approach can generate FSA as well as PDA (push-down automata) models. The principal difficulty in applying this approach to MCC is its inability to systematically reason about system call arguments. Clearly, it is not enough to know that *something* is being written by a program — we need to identify the object being modified by the write. For this reason, an EFSA (or EPDA) model is more appropriate than an FSA (or PDA) model. Moreover, the model generation step needs to capture values of system call arguments, as well the relationships among the arguments of different system calls. For instance, the model should associate a `write` operation with the file being written by capturing the relationship that the file descriptor argument of the `write` is the same as the return value of a previous `open` operation. In the rest of this section, we describe a new technique for generating such models in the context of MCC.

3.1 Model Generation Approaches

MCC models are intended to capture program behavior, which was defined in the previous section to be the set of all possible sequences of security-relevant operations made by a program. In order to capture all possible sequences of operations, our model extraction approach preserves the looping and branching structure present in programs, while abstracting away details such as assignments to internal variables. Figure 3 illustrates a model for a sample program. Note that in Figure 3, S0 through S5 denote system calls.

As the above example shows, FSA provide a convenient representation for MCC models, concisely preserving the looping and branching structures within the program. However, the example of Figure 3 omits system call arguments for the sake of simplicity. When argument properties are incorporated into the model, EFSA (rather than FSA) become more natural. It is also possible to use pushdown automata (PDA) for expressing models, which have the benefit of capturing call-return relationships, and hence are more accurate. However, this added accuracy may not be fully useful, since enforcement of PDA models would require secure interception of all function calls made by a program, which is not possible for arbitrary binaries. On the other hand, one important advantage PDA have over FSA is their modularity, i.e., the PDA model of one procedure in a program does not depend on the models of other procedures invoked by it. This factor enables models of different program components (such as libraries) to be extracted independently, and then be composed together to obtain the overall model for the program. Accurate models can hence be synthesized even when the code comes from multiple sources — the most common case of this occurring when an executable from an untrusted producer uses dynamically linked libraries resident on the consumer's workstation (e.g., `libc`).

One approach to model extraction is to use a program analysis technique, such as that described in [38, 7]. The main benefit of this approach is that, if the model generation process strictly avoids unsound assumptions, then the models will be conservative — in this case, using the notation of Section 1.1, we are guaranteed that for an application A and its model M derived by source code analysis, $\mathcal{B}(A) \subseteq \mathcal{B}(M)$. The drawback is that, due to the limitations of source code analysis, M may include execution sequences that can, in fact, never be performed by A. This may lead to a spurious policy violation report from the verifier.

To overcome the spurious violation problem, models may be generated from actual program behaviors observed under different test conditions. The downside of this approach is that program behaviors that are not observed during model generation may not be captured in the model. This may lead the verifier to conclude that a program satisfies a policy, when it actually does not. To minimize this possibility, as many program behaviors as possible should be exercised during the learning process. This can be accomplished using a comprehensive test suite, which the code producer most likely will have already developed for testing purposes. Depending on the comprehensiveness of the test suite, there may still be a probability that the application deviates from its model. In such cases, the MCC enforcement mechanism will terminate the program. Note that in this case, safety is still preserved, but the convenience (of not having runtime aborts) is lost. Fortunately, this happens only in the (hopefully very small) fraction of runs that deviate from the model.

We are currently pursuing the extraction of EFSA models using execution monitoring, and EPDA (standard PDA extended with state variables) models from source code. In both cases, the main focus of our research has been in tracking data flow relationships affecting critical system call arguments such as the resource ac-

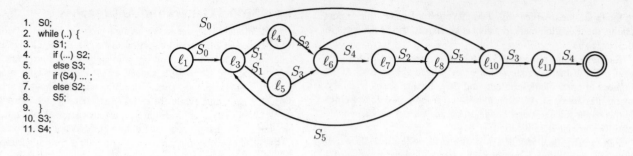

```
 1.  S0;
 2.  while (..) {
 3.      S1;
 4.      if (...) S2;
 5.      else S3;
 6.      if (S4) ... ;
 7.      else S2;
 8.      S5;
 9.  }
10.  S3;
11.  S4;
```

Figure 3: A sample program and its model

cessed using a system call. Currently, our implementation of source-code model extraction is not mature enough, so our description below focuses on execution monitoring-based model extraction.

3.2 Model Generation via Execution Monitoring

In the context of intrusion detection, a number of techniques have been developed for extracting program behavior models in terms of system calls [16, 40, 32, 6, 15, 27, 25]. Some of these techniques [16] learn a finite set of fixed-length strings of system calls, while some others are capable of learning (a finite set of) variable-length strings [40]. We developed a new approach in [32] that is capable of representing an infinite number of strings of unbounded length using a finite-state automaton. Another approach [6] for learning FSA has been developed recently. [15] builds on [32] to develop an approach that learns PDA models rather than FSA models, but this approach incurs significantly higher overheads.

While FSA can serve as a starting point for MCC models, they are not sufficient by themselves — in particular, MCC models need to capture crucial information, such as file names or network addresses that will be referenced by security policies. The main focus of MCC research in model extraction has been to develop a *fully automated* algorithm for extracting such argument relationships. This contrasts with human-assisted approaches such as [2], where a programmer was required to identify the subsequences within an execution trace within which such argument relationship will be attempted. Moreover, our approach is aimed at learning relationships involving complex data types such as file names, whereas [2] is concerned only with integer arguments. Below, we describe our approach for model extraction via machine learning from execution traces. We first provide a brief overview of our approach for learning FSA from system call sequences [32], and then proceed to describe the extensions to this algorithm for learning argument relationships.

3.2.1 Overview of FSA Learning Algorithm

It is well-known that learning FSA from strings (execution traces, in our case) is a computationally hard problem [30]. The primary difficulty is that the strings, by themselves, do not give any clue as to the state of the automaton. For instance, if we see a string $abcda$, we cannot determine whether the two a's in the string correspond to the same state of the automaton or different states. The key insight behind the technique of [32] is that we can indeed obtain state-related information if we knew the location from where the system call was made. Based on this call location information, an FSA is constructed as follows. Whenever a system call is made from program location ℓ_i, we first create a new automaton state labeled ℓ_i if it is not already present. In addition, if S' was the previous system call and was made from location ℓ_{i-1}, then an edge labeled with

S' is created from the previous system call location ℓ_{i-1} to ℓ_i. Using this approach, Figure 3 illustrates the model learned from the following two execution traces.

- $\frac{S_0}{\ell_1} \frac{S_3}{\ell_{10}} \frac{S_4}{\ell_{11}}$
- $\frac{S_0}{\ell_1} \frac{S_1}{\ell_3} \frac{S_2}{\ell_4} \frac{S_4}{\ell_6} \frac{S_5}{\ell_8} \frac{S_1}{\ell_3} \frac{S_3}{\ell_5} \frac{S_4}{\ell_6} \frac{S_2}{\ell_7} \frac{S_5}{\ell_8} \frac{S_3}{\ell_{10}} \frac{S_4}{\ell_{11}}$

In these traces, the notation $\frac{S}{\ell_i}$ denotes that the system call S is being made from the line ℓ_i. (For illustrative purposes, line numbers are used in place of locations of machine instructions in this example.) Note that automaton states are labeled with the location from where each system call was made.

The simple description given above needs to be extended when we take into account the fact that most programs make extensive use of libraries. For instance, system calls are usually made from wrapper functions provided by libc. In this case, note that each system call will be made from exactly one location in libc, and hence the automaton will not capture useful information about the executable that is making these system calls. To address this problem, our learning algorithm ignores the program locations within libraries, instead using the location within the executable from where these library calls were invoked. This requires a "walk" up the program stack at the point of system call. We describe an implementation of the stack-walk for Linux/x86. Implementations for a different OS/architecture will typically be very similar. On Linux/x86 the EBP (extended base pointer) register is used to chain together activation records of a caller and callee functions. Specifically, the return address for the current procedure is found at the location (EBP+4), while the base pointer of the caller is stored at the location (EBP). The range of locations within the executable can be found by reading the pseudo file /proc/*pid*/maps, where *pid* denotes the process identifier for the monitored process. Using this information, the stack frame is traversed up from the point of the system call until a return address R within the executable is located. This location R is used in the model as the location from where this system call was made.

3.2.2 Learning Argument Values

Before describing the algorithm for learning system call argument values, it is necessary to provide an overview of the implementation architecture of the model extractor. The model extractor consists of an online and an offline component. The online component consists of a runtime environment to intercept system calls and a logger that records these system calls and their arguments into a file. The logger incorporates some level of knowledge about what system call arguments (and return values) are useful for model extraction, and whether any preprocessing is necessary on these arguments. For instance, the logger converts file and directory name arguments into a canonical form before recording them. Similarly, it extracts the IP address and port information from sockets and records them explicitly. It ignores some system call arguments and return values, such as buffers returned by the read system call, most fields of the structure returned by stat system call, etc. The offline component consists of two parts: the EFSA learning algorithm, and a log file parser.

The extension of the FSA algorithm to learn system call argument values proceeds as follows. First, we may be interested in absolute values of arguments. For instance, a model should capture names of specific files opened by an application. To accomplish this, our algorithm records system call argument values together with each system call in the FSA. If there are multiple invocations of a system call along an edge in the FSA, the model extractor collects argument values from each of the invocations. If the number of such values crosses a threshold, then an aggregation algorithm is employed to summarize the values, rather than listing each one. In principle, the learning algorithm should support different aggregation operations, but in practice, we have so far found the need for only two such operations: the longest common prefix operation for file names, and the union operation for sets represented using bit vectors, e.g., file open modes or permissions. For each system call argument type, a configuration file specifies the threshold point when aggregation will be used, and the aggregation operation to be used for that type. For file name arguments, the threshold can be specified as a function of the file name prefix. For instance, we can set a threshold of 2 for files of the form /tmp/*, while using a threshold of 10 for files of the form /etc/*.

We point out that the use of the basic FSA approach, and in particular, the use of program location information, is crucial for the success of this approach. Without this information, we could potentially be forced to summarize argument values across all system calls with the same name. Alternatively, we may try to partition system calls with the same name into subsets that yield good aggregation, but such subset construction algorithms will likely be expensive. If the algorithm needs to incorporate relationships among the arguments of a single system call, e.g., the fact that a certain file name is always opened in read-only mode, then the subset construction will become even more complex. In effect, the program location information, provides an efficient and effective way to construct such subsets. Its effectiveness stems from the fact that system calls made by the same point of code in a program are more likely to be related than those made from different program locations.

3.2.3 Learning Argument Relationships

The most interesting aspect of model extraction is our approach for learning temporal relationships between arguments of *different* system calls. We observed that such relationships are crucial for tracking many security-related properties. For instance, in order to relate a write system call to the file being written, we need to associate the file descriptor argument of write with the return value of a previous open system call. Similarly, to track the remote location from which data was read by a process, we need to associate the socket argument of a recv or read with the return value of a preceding accept or argument of connect. Finally, to identify the child process to which a signal is being sent by a parent process, one needs to relate the return value of fork with the return value of wait.

One of the main difficulties in learning system call argument relationships is in identifying which pairs of system calls need to be considered. A naive approach, which considers every possible pair, will be unacceptably inefficient. Such an algorithm will have complexity that is quadratic in the size of the trace, which is typically of the order of 10^3 to 10^7 events, depending upon the comprehensiveness of the test suites used in generating the traces. Even worse, such an approach can generate relationships that are quadratic in the size of the trace. However, we would like the number of relationships learned to be of the same order as the size of FSA, which is typically in the range of a few hundred states.

To overcome the above difficulties, we rely on the observation that we are typically interested in specific relationships among arguments of the same kind. For instance, we are interested in the equality relationship between file descriptor arguments, but not in inequalities or other relationships. Moreover, it is meaningless to compare file descriptors with process identifiers. Based on this observation, our approach is to specify, through a configuration file, the "kind" of a system call argument, and the relationships of interest involving arguments of this kind. (Note that return values are treated as if they are additional arguments to a system call.) In our implementation, we currently support equality relationships among integral and string types, and prefix and suffix relationships over strings.

Once the relationships of interest are specified, they can be learned as follows. First, a distinct (EFSA) state variable is associated with each (system call, invocation location, argument number) triple. Note that because of the way system calls are traced back to locations in the executable, multiple system calls that are made from a library function f invoked by the executable at location ℓ will all appear as transitions from the state corresponding to ℓ. Thus it is possible to have multiple system calls that are all executed from the same location ℓ, and hence the need to consider system call numbers in addition locations. (This means that there will be two distinct variables corresponding to the file name argument of an open system call that are made from two different locations in the program.)

Each variable that is a candidate for an equality relationship is stored in a hash table, indexed by its most recent value. The hash tables for different kinds of arguments will be different, e.g., a separate hash table will be maintained for file descriptors and process ids. At any point during learning, associated with each file descriptor value fd will be the list of variables (of file descriptor type) whose most recent value was fd. When another system call with a file descriptor variable v with value fd' is made, the learning algorithm will look up fd' in the table, and obtain the associated list V of variables. If this is the first time v has been seen, then the relationship information associated with v is set to V. This indicates that every variable in V is equal to v. If it is not the first time, then there will already be a set V' of variables that was associated with v the last time v was encountered during learning. We associate $V \cap V'$ with v and proceed. (This means that the relationships may weaken over many runs, but cannot be strengthened. Finally, the previous value fd_{old} of v is deleted from the hash table, and v is added to the hash table entry for fd'.)

For prefix and suffix relationships, a trie data structure is used in place of the hash table. (A trie can be viewed as a tree-structured finite-state automaton for matching strings.) In particular, when a variable v is encountered in the trace with value s, we traverse down a path in the trie that matches s. If there is a complete match for s, and this match takes us to a state S in the trie, then the variables associated with S are candidates for equality with v. Each variable v' associated with any descendant state S' of S is a candidate for the relationship $prefix(v, v') = v$ and $prefix(v, v') = s$. Similarly, any variable v'' associated with an ancestor state S'' of S is a candidate for the relationship $prefix(v, v'') = v''$ and $prefix(v, v'') = s''$, where s'' is the string corresponding to state S''. Finally, any variable v''' associated with a descendant state S''' of an ancestor state of S (such as S'') is a candidate for the re-

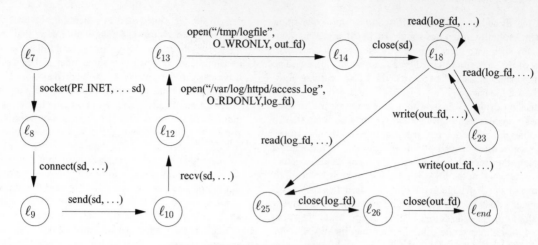

Figure 4: Model EFSA for Figure 5

lationship $prefix(v, v''') = s''$. If only a (possibly empty) prefix of s is present in the trie, then the treatment is similar, except that there will be no descendant states (such as S') mentioned above.

Once the candidates for relationship with the current instance of v are identified, they are compared with the candidates for the previous occurrence of v in the trace, and only the common relationships are preserved. At this point, note that v would be stored in a state S_{old} which corresponds to its previous value s_{old}. v is then deleted from S_{old}, and inserted into S. The state S_{old} is deleted if it is no longer associated with any variables, and the same is done for the ancestors of S_{old}. The new state S is created if it is not already present.

For suffix relationships, the exact same algorithm is used, but the tries are constructed after reversing the strings. In addition, to improve the speed of the algorithm, we can restrict the lengths of paths from S to states S', S'' and S''' described above.

The final step of the algorithm is to prune redundant relationships. Suppose that a program whose current location is ℓ_0 opens a file, and performs read operations on this file from n different program locations $\ell_1, ..., \ell_n$. Let $x_0, x_1, ..., x_n$ be the corresponding state variables. The above algorithm will associate the set $\{x_1, ..., x_n\}$ with x_0, $\{x_0, x_2, ..., x_n\}$ with x_1 and so on. Obviously, this is redundant information — for instance, we can associate $\{x_0\}$ with x_1, $\{x_1\}$ with x_2 and so on. Note that such pruning is difficult to perform during the learning phase itself. This is because premature pruning can lose information. For instance, the first two occurrences of x_2 may have been equal to both x_1 and x_0, but subsequent occurrences may be equal only to x_0. If the relationship was pruned pre-maturely, it is possible to have retained $\{x_1\}$ with x_2. In this case, when it is subsequently discovered that x_1 is not equal to x_2, this relationship is lost, and thus we are left with no relationships involving x_2.

We use the example shown in Figure 5 to illustrate model extraction. This program is a simplified version of a hypothetical freeware program which analyzes web server logs for unusual activity. (Our experience with a *real* program that analyzes web logs is described in Section 6.) In particular, the log entries are compared against signatures of known attacks. Since the signature set is constantly updated as new attacks are discovered, it is better for the analyzer program to download these signatures from a central server rather than encoding them within the analyzer program. Hence, the first step in the execution of the example program is to connect to this signature server over the network, and download a set of sig-

natures. It then opens the log file, and matches each line in the log file with the signatures. To simplify the example, we have used just a single pattern as a signature. In addition, we do not check error cases. Any matches are written into an output file. The lines of code where system calls are made by the program are marked with the symbol "◄" in Figure 5.

Figure 4 shows an abstracted version of the EFSA learned by the above algorithm for the example program. The abstracted details include the following. The learning algorithm makes a number of system calls at program start up, which correspond to calls made by the (dynamic) program loader such as /lib/ld-linux.so. In addition, the need to allocate heap storage may lead to additional system calls. These details have been abstracted away, and the argument relationships are represented in a human-readable form to

```
1.  int main(int argc, char *argv[]) {
2.      int sd, rc, i, log_fd,out_fd,flag = 1;
3.      struct sockaddr_in remoteServAddr;
4.      char recvline[SIG_SIZE+1], *request = "...";
5.      char buf[READ_SIZE];

6.      init_remote_server_addr(&remoteServAddr,...);
7.      sd = socket(PF_INET,SOCK_STREAM,0);  ◄
8.      connect(sd,(struct sockaddr*)&remoteServAddr,sizeof(...));  ◄
9.      send(sd, request, strlen(request)+1,0);  ◄
10.     recv(sd, recvline, SIG_SIZE,0);  ◄
11.     recvline[SIG_SIZE] ='\0';
12.     log_fd = open("/var/log/httpd/access_log",O_RDONLY);  ◄
13.     out_fd = open("/tmp/logfile",O_CREAT|O_WRONLY);  ◄
14.     close(sd);  ◄
15.     while (flag!=0) {
16.         i = 0;
17.         do {
18.             rc=read(log_fd,buf+i,1);  ◄
19.             if (rc == 0) flag =0;
20.         } while (buf[i++] != '\n' && flag != 0);
21.         buf[i]='\0';
22.         if (strstr(buf,recvline) !=0)
23.             write(out_fd,buf,strnlen(buf,READ_SIZE)+1);  ◄
24.     }
25.     close(log_fd);  ◄
26.     close(out_fd);  ◄
27.     return 0;
28. }
```

Figure 5: A Freeware Program for Web Log Analysis

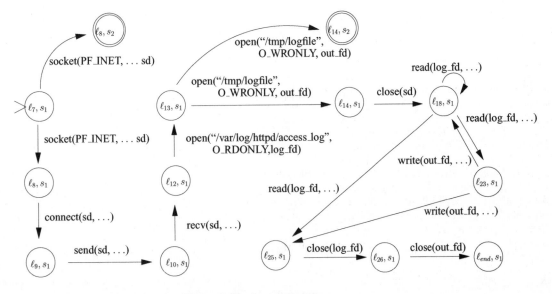

Figure 6: Product Automaton

obtain Figure 4 from the EFSA learned by the above algorithm. In the figure, each state label ℓ_i corresponds to program line i.

4. VERIFICATION

Verification is concerned with determining whether or not a model M satisfies a security policy P. Formally, we need to check whether behaviors captured by M is a subset of behaviors permitted by the policy P — $\mathcal{B}[M] \subseteq \mathcal{B}[P]$ where M, B and P were introduced earlier. Noting that the policy automaton actually represents the negation $\overline{P}$ of P, we simply need to determine if $\mathcal{B}[M] \cap \mathcal{B}[\overline{P}] = \phi$. Thus, our verification approach is to build the product automaton $M \times \overline{P}$, which will accept the intersection of the behaviors accepted by M and $\overline{P}$. If there are feasible paths in this product automaton that lead to final (i.e., violating) states of $\overline{P}$, then the policy is violated and $M \times \overline{P}$ is a representation of all such violations.

All common operations, such as computing the product of two automata and checking it for reachability, have well-known solutions in the case of FSA, but become complex in the case of EFSA due to the presence of infinite domain variables. We begin by computing the EFSA product in much the same way as an FSA product construction. Specifically, the product automaton $MP = M \times \overline{P}$ is constructed as follows:

- The state variable set of MP is the union of the state variables of M and $\overline{P}$.
- The start state of MP is a tuple (ℓ_0, s_0), where ℓ_0 and s_0 are the start states of M and $\overline{P}$, respectively. Similarly, the final state set is $F_{MP} \subseteq F_M \times F_{\overline{P}}$, where F_M is the set of *all* states in M and $F_{\overline{P}}$ denotes the set of *final* states in $\overline{P}$.
- Whenever there exists a transition from a state ℓ to ℓ' in M on event e with condition C_1 and assignment A_1, and a transition from s to s' in $\overline{P}$ on the same event e with condition C_2 and assignment A_2, then (and only then) there is a transition from (ℓ, s) to (ℓ', s') in MP on condition $C_1 \wedge C_2$ with assignment $A_1 \cup A_2$.

A transition in the product automaton is said to be enabled only when the associated condition $C_1 \wedge C_2$ is satisfiable. Given that our EFSA is defined over infinite-domain variables representing strings and integers, the problem of determining satisfiability of arbitrary constraints appearing as enabling conditions of transitions is un-

decidable in general. We therefore focus on a tractable subset of constraints over infinite-domain variables; specifically equality ($=$) and disequality ($\neq$) relationships between the variables. The model checker relies on an underlying constraint processing system to decide the satisfiability of these constraints. The constraint processing system maintains a store of conjunctions of constraints between the variables. A product transition is feasible if the corresponding enabling conditions are satisfiable in the existing store present in the constraint processing system. In this case, the constraint store is updated by adding the enabling conditions. Otherwise, the transition is considered infeasible.

As alluded before, EFSA are defined over infinite-domain variables. Hence, the model checker empowered with the constraint solver, as described above, is incapable of inferring the satisfiability of constraints in some cases, e.g. range ($\geq$) constraints over integer variables or prefix constraints over strings. Such situations are handled conservatively as follows. If the arguments to the constraint are sufficiently defined then the constraint processing system evaluates them. Otherwise it considers these "undecided" constraints as satisfiable and adds them to the existing constraint store. This strategy results in the incompleteness of the constraint-based model checker due to the generation of infeasible paths in the product automaton. Such infeasible paths, in general, could lead to spurious policy violation sequences. However, we have not experienced such spurious reports in the programs we have considered so far.

Consider the example program and the corresponding model in Figures 5 and 4 respectively. In order to verify whether the model conforms to the policy (see Figure 2(c)) of no socket and write-to-file operations, a product (Figure 6) of the model automaton and the policy automaton is constructed. Two violating traces are obtained in the model — (a) the transition from (ℓ_7, s_1) to (ℓ_8, s_2) in the model consisting of `socket(PF_INET,...,sd)` and (b) the transition sequence from (ℓ_{13}, s_1) to state (ℓ_{14}, s_2) due to the `open` operation of a file in `O_WRONLY` mode.

4.1 Conflict presentation

One important aspect of the verifier is to give a comprehensive view of why/how a violation of the policy occurred. This information is crucial for policy selection.

Owing to the size of the product (which is of the order of the size of the model), presentation of the product "as is" does not provide a clear and precise view of the violations in the model. The product automaton is hence presented to the user by projecting it onto the policy automaton, because the root cause of policy violation (leading to a final state of the policy automaton) can be attributed to the sequences of policy-specified actions that are present in the model.

Note that the product contains all violating paths in the model. During projection, we combine common aspects of multiple violating paths. Frequently, this combination requires merging transitions that are associated with different conditions on event arguments. For instance, open events corresponding to opening different files may all need to be combined. We use an approach similar to the model extraction algorithm for doing this combination: If the number of different argument values is small, we retain the set of possible values. If it exceeds a certain threshold, then they are combined using an appropriate aggregation technique. For instance, the file names { /tmp/a1, /tmp/a2, /tmp/a3, /etc/xyz, /var/f1, /var/f2 } may be combined into { /tmp/a*, /etc/xyz, /var/f1, /var/f2 }. Using this approach produces the following summary of conflicts from Figure 6:

- open operation on file /tmp/logfile in write mode,
- socket operation involving the domain PF_INET

The refinement for the first violation is relatively obvious — the user can simply permit write access to files in /tmp. For the second violation, we relax the policy to permit network access, as long as these accesses are completed before reading any sensitive files. The list of sensitive files needs to be specified, but we can assume that any file that the consumer does not consider to be "public" is classified as sensitive. In particular, this means that the web log file is considered sensitive. The new policy with these refinements is shown in Figure 7.

The ability of the conflict presentation technique to summarize the violations provides help to a user in identifying suitable policies. One approach that can provide additional assistance to a consumer in policy selection is based on catalogs of acceptable policies. Given such a catalog, the verifier can search this catalog to identify a policy that is compatible with a given piece of code. The conflict summary can provide direction to this search, so that the verifier does not have to consider all policies in the catalog.

5. ENFORCEMENT

Runtime monitoring consists of intercepting system calls, obtaining the argument values to these system calls, and matching them against models of expected behavior of the untrusted application. Recall that we enforce models (not policies), which are large nondeterministic automata. To avoid having to simulate the nondeterminism, which can lead to high overheads, we simply use the program counter value to determinize the transitions. Policy enforcement based on system call interception is a well-understood topic [18, 33, 17], so we do not describe it any further here.

If the application violates the behavior captured by the model, the enforcement module aborts the program. When this happens, there are only two possibilities:

- producer intentionally misrepresented the program behavior, or
- the model does not capture all possible program behaviors. (This can happen when models are constructed through runtime monitoring, but the test cases used for these runs were not sufficiently comprehensive.)

In the first case, termination is the right choice. Since the second case is indistinguishable to a consumer from the first case, the only safe response is to terminate the application in this case as well.

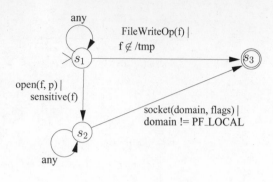

Figure 7: Refined Policy

While runtime aborts cause inconvenience, we point out that safety is not violated, since the program is aborted before it violates a security policy. Moreover, either of the above two cases are likely to be rare, given (a) the predominance of benign software in the Internet, and (b) the fact that a consumer, in a single run, is not very likely to uncover new behaviors unless the code producer did a very poor job of testing his/her code.

Note that within the MCC framework, it is possible to enforce policies, rather than models. However, since the model EFSA captures a subset of behaviors permitted by the policy EFSA, some behaviors that would violate the model EFSA would go undetected during policy enforcement. It is questionable whether a consumer wants to allow such behaviors, which the producer, in some sense, has identified as illegitimate. For instance, consider an untrusted application that reads image files, and saves them back with a preview image included in the file. A policy that allows execution of this application needs to grant write-access to such a file. However, it is possible that a third-party attacks this program and causes it to simply delete the image file. In this case, previous experience in applying such models in intrusion detection [32, 39] suggests that it is very likely that such attacks will be prevented by model enforcement, while it will be missed by policy enforcement.

A possible benefit of policy enforcement is that it may be simpler than model enforcement. Even though model EFSA are much larger than policy EFSA, they are deterministic, and hence can be efficiently enforced. The enforcement algorithm is also simple, as it simply needs to (a) keep track of the most recently encountered value of every state variable, and (b) before making a state transition, perform the relationship checks associated with the transition. Policy automata, although smaller, are nondeterministic. This factor requires them to potentially keep an unbounded number of previous values encountered for a state variable, and perform checks with respect to each such value. Although we have not encountered this worst case behavior in our previous work in intrusion prevention [33, 4], the mere possibility shows that policy enforcement is not necessarily simpler than model enforcement..

Another possible reason for favoring policy enforcement over model enforcement is that the soundness of the approach will no longer depend on the correctness of the verifier. However, since the verifier is already very simple, we believe that the reduction in the size of the trusted computing base achieved as a result of such a choice is not compelling.

6. IMPLEMENTATION

In this section, we summarize the status of our implementation, and describe the results of applying MCC to some common programs such as instant messengers, web log analyzers, and docu-

Application	Program Size (KB)	Model Size			Enforcement Overhead		Verification	
		States	Transitions	Relationships	Interception only	Total	Time (msec.)	Space (MB)
xpdf 1.0	906	125	455	305	2%	30%	1.00	0.5
gaim 0.53	3173	283	937	432	2%	21%	1.80	0.7
http-analyze 2.4.1.3	333	158	391	247	0%	2.4%	0.70	0.4

Figure 8: Results on Generation, Verification and Enforcement of Models

ment viewers. These programs range in size from a few thousand lines to tens of thousands of lines of source code.

Security Policies. As mentioned previously, security policies are specified in our BMSL language [4]. A compiler for this language, which produces EFSA from BMSL specifications, has been described in an earlier paper [33]. As shown in the policy examples discussed so far, policy automata tend to be very small (2 to 6 states).

Model generation. We have implemented model generation using execution monitoring. Our implementation learns system call argument values as described in Section 3.2.2. Argument relationship learning has been implemented for equality relationships for arguments such as file descriptors, and prefix/suffix relationships for strings such as pathnames. The sizes of the models, in terms of number of states, transitions and relationships, are shown in Figure 8.

In terms of the time needed to learn the models — we first note that model generation is an offline process, hence we have not attempted to optimize it. Currently, the logging of system calls is done using user-level system call interception, built with the `ptrace` facility on Linux. The frequent context switches involved in this approach, together with the need to fetch system call argument data, introduces significant overheads, which range from 40% to 200%. However, since learning itself is an offline activity, this overhead is quite acceptable. The logger and system call interceptor are implemented in C and C++ and have a combined size of 9 KLOC.

Different applications tend to generate different volumes of system calls. For instance, `xpdf` and `gaim` generate a large number of system calls, while `http-analyze` generates much fewer calls in each run. These two factors balance each other out. We used training traces in the range of 10^3 to 10^5 system calls for all programs.

The current implementation of model extraction is not optimized for performance, since model extraction is an offline process. For this reason, model extraction is relatively slow, taking of the order of few minutes for traces of size of the order of 10^5 system calls on a machine with a 800 MHz Pentium III processor running Red Hat Linux 7.3 with 384 MB of memory. The size of the learning algorithm implementation is about 6000 lines.

Verifier. The verifier is implemented in XSB [41] Prolog, a version of Prolog that supports "memoization" of query results using a technique called tabling. Tabling avoids redundant subcomputations — instead, previously saved results of queries are reused. This factor greatly simplifies the implementation of verification and program analysis techniques, which involve so-called *fixpoint* computation. The analysis can be specified using a set of recursive rules, leaving the tabling technique to automatically compute the fixpoint. This facility enables the verifier to be implemented using about 300 lines of Prolog code. This code implements the automata

product construction, as well as the constraint-handling operations described in Section 4. The constraint processing system interprets equality constraints using Prolog's variable unification mechanism and handles disequality constraints by storing them in the form of a list.

We have verified the application models described above using policies similar to the ones described in Section 2. Here, we present a brief description of the policies corresponding to each of the applications. Figure 8 tabulates the results of verification.

- *PDF viewer* application. We use conventional sandboxing policies on the PDF viewer application. Such a policy prevents the application from creating any new files (except in the `/tmp` directory), disallows it from overwriting files, restricts network connections and prevents it from executing other applications. No violations were reported for these policies. Thus, for applications such as document viewers, it appears that MCC is as simple to use as sandboxing approaches.

- *http-analyze* application. The http-analyze application [22] is a real application which is similar to the abstract log analyzer example discussed earlier. We generated the model of the program by learning its behavior and verified it against the refined policy shown in Figure 7. Recall that this policy disallows the application from (a) writing to non-temporary directories, and (b) performing network operations after reading sensitive files. The second part of the policy is not violated by the model. The first part of the policy is violated, since the application creates a file called `index.html` in the current directory, and two subdirectories called `btn` and `www`, and several files in each of these subdirectories. The model extraction process summarizes this information, so that the following violations are reported by the verifier:

  - attempt to create directories: `btn` and `www`
  - attempt to write files: `index.html`, `btn/*` and `www/*`

  The policy is refined to permit these accesses, and then the application is run successfully.

- *Gnu instant messaging* application. The model for Gaim application is verified against a "no file access" policy that disallows reading/writing of any files except for those that are commonly accessed by graphical user interface applications. The policy is violated by the model. Projecting the product on the policy, a violating trace in the model is obtained — an `open` operation is performed on `.gaim` (read/write mode), `.imrc` (read mode) and `.gaimrc` (write mode) files in the user's home directory. The policy is relaxed by restricting file access of the user's home directory to only `.gaim`, `.gaimrc` and `.imrc`. The refined policy is not violated by the model.

All these experiments were conducted RedHat Linux 7.2 running on a 1.7GHz Xeon with 2GB of memory. As figure 8 shows, verification takes only milliseconds, and has low memory requirements, thus making it practical.

Model enforcement. The enforcement system uses an in-kernel module to perform system call interposition. Whenever the application performs a system call, the enforcement module makes the corresponding transition on the model automaton, thereby keeping track of the system state. Figure 8 shows that the runtime overheads for model enforcement are moderate— 2% to 30%. Much of this overhead arises from the stalk walk required to obtain the program location from where system calls are made. Often, this requires 10 or more stack frames to be traversed. Our current stack traversal algorithm is conservative, and cross-checks every return address found on the stack with the calling instruction. Moreover, no systematic performance tuning has been attempted yet. These factors lead to the moderate overhead. With improved implementation of the stack walk and performance tuning, these overheads may be cut down by a factor of two or more.

The variation in overheads across applications results from the variations in the frequencies of system calls made by these applications. The http-analyze application performs very few system calls, whereas xpdf and gaim make a large number of system calls.

6.1   Discussion

We make the following remarks based on our implementation experience so far.

6.1.1   Usability and Practicality

As illustrated with the xpdf application, for applications that are amenable to sandboxing types of policies, MCC seems to be as simple to use as execution-monitoring approaches. Indeed, the added expressive power of MCC policies can be expected to allow more applications to execute without raising violations during either the verification or the runtime stage. For instance, consider a policy that permits an untrusted application to create new directories, and to overwrite files in the directory created by it. Clearly, such a policy requires the use of state variables to remember the name of directories created by the untrusted application, and hence can be expressed as an EFSA, but not using the policy languages used in previous execution monitoring-based approaches.

The http-analyze example demonstrates the effectiveness of MCC in minimizing policy violation alerts. A naive execution monitoring-based approach would have resulted in close to 100 runtime prompts, corresponding to each file created by this application. Even a more intelligent system, which requests write access for entire directories after a number of violations (say, 3) have been reported for files in that directory, would result in 7 user alerts. It is our experience that users "give up" after perhaps 3 such prompts, and either discard the code, or click "yes to all."

While MCC improves over previous techniques in offering some guidance for policy refinement, there is much room for improvement. One possibility that we plan to consider in the future is that of having the verifier automatically search through a hierarchy of safety policies to find one that is suitable for a particular application. In addition, we need to improve the understandability of violations of security policies that involve nontrivial temporal relationships.

These comments on the usability of MCC, together with performance results reported above, validate our claim that MCC is indeed practical.

6.1.2   System complexity

System complexity is an important consideration in security, as complexity leads to errors that can impact security. A careful examination of MCC shows that although it is realized using several components, including a policy language compiler, model genera-

atively simple. Where there was a choice between simplicity and generality, we have usually favored simplicity, in order that we be able to build a reasonably robust system with modest implementation resources. Even the verifier, which is often considered a complex piece of software, is very simple in MCC — only 300 lines of code, written in a declarative language. The compiler is of moderate size (15 KLOC), but much of this complexity arises from the fact that BMSL is designed to be a general purpose event monitoring language that is capable of monitoring diverse events, and complex data types such as network packet data. If one were to separate the code that would be needed for EFSA policies of the kind described in this paper, then it would perhaps be half the current size. The model enforcer is also simple, consisting of only 2500 lines of code. The model extractor, which consists of the implementation of the learning algorithm, the logger and the system call interceptor, is about 15000 lines of code. Thus the total system size is of the order of 33 KLOC.

Not all of the MCC components are critical for security. In particular, the correctness of the model extractor does not impact the safety of MCC. If the implementation of other components is tightened up to eliminate features unneeded for MCC, then the size of security-critical components of MCC can be brought down to below 10 KLOC. On the other hand, it should be noted that safety depends on many non-MCC components, including the underlying OS, the gcc compiler and related tools, and the XSB system. All these components must be considered part of the trusted computing base, in addition to the BMSL compiler, verifier and model enforcer.

6.1.3   Standardization

In order to enable the widespread deployment of MCC or a similar approach, a significant amount of work in standardization will be required in addition to technical solutions. Currently, the policy language uses events that are closely tied to an operating system. Moreover, several choices are made regarding which system call arguments are important, and what relationships involving them need to be preserved in a model. These need to be standardized as well, if we are to achieve interoperability and compatibility across different OSes and/or users. Finally, note that many policies need to be parameterized. For instance, we need to express the fact that a certain application may open a file in the consumer's home directory. Developing a uniform way to identify such parameters, and naming them is another important aspect of standardization. (Once such parameters are standardized, it is simple to incorporate them into MCC — the logging component of the model generator needs to ensure that system call arguments such as filenames are expressed in a parameterized form. The policies also need to be stated in a parameterized form.)

6.2   Integration into Existing Systems

It is our objective that typical users should not be required to change their ways in order to benefit from MCC. To accomplish this objective, we integrate MCC into the tools that are used in the process of explicit installation, implicit downloading, or execution of untrusted code.

Explicit installation of code. We have incorporated the MCC approach into a tool called *RPMshield* [37], an enhancement of the RedHat Package Manager (RPM) software installation tool. This tool applies the MCC approach to the installation phase, wherein it is ensured that the installation of a package does not clobber files belonging to other packages, and that the installation scripts observe consumer-specified policies. Some of the concrete problems addressed by this enhancement include: clobbering of manually edited configuration files during package upgrades, and execution of arbitrary pre- and post-installation scripts. In the case of untrusted packages, these scripts can cause arbitrary damage, whereas with RPMshield, they cannot.

During installation, an untrusted application is associated with a set of allowable policies. In addition, it is flagged to indicate whether these policies should be silently enforced (which would be the case if the policy selection took place during installation) or whether the MCC user interface is to be invoked for policy selection during each run.

Implicitly downloaded code. The two principal mechanisms for implicit code downloading are email attachments, and web content. We integrate the MCC approach into these environments by defining a new content type, `application-mcc`, corresponding to model-carrying code. The MCC policy selection user-interface is then invoked for handling instances of such content, ensuring a smooth integration with diverse email readers and browsers.

Execution of untrusted code. The above installation and/or downloading process ensures that untrusted code will always be executed under MCC control. In particular, execution occurs within the secure enforcement environment, and with or without the support of the policy selection user-interface.

Untrusted code without a model. To facilitate the adoption of MCC, our user interface supports the execution of code without accompanying models. In such cases, a consumer-specified policy is silently enforced on the application. This may not be convenient or suitable for all applications, but it certainly works well for applications such as document handlers. Alternatively, third parties could generate models for such programs and these models could be downloaded and used for policy selection.

7. CONCLUSION

In this paper, we have presented model-carrying code, a promising solution to the problem of running untrusted code. Unlike previous approaches that were focused mainly on malicious code containment, MCC makes no assumptions on the inherent risks posed by untrusted code. It simply provides tools that consumers can use in order to make informed decisions about the risks that they are willing to tolerate so as to enjoy the functionality provided by untrusted code.

We demonstrated that MCC is practical by showing that several small to moderate size programs can be successfully handled. MCC does not require users to switch to a new programming language, nor does it require them to change their ways in terms of how they download or run untrusted code. Instead, MCC is incorporated in a transparent fashion into tools that serve as conduits for untrusted code, including software installers, email handlers, and browsers.

MCC achieves a practical balance between the security-related obligations of the producer and the consumer, thereby avoiding placement of an undue burden on either party. The producer can generate a model for an application and supply it to several consumers with different security concerns. Similarly, consumers can develop and enforce policies that address their security concerns without having *a priori* knowledge about security needs of diverse applications. Thus, MCC provides a scalable framework for permitting the networked distribution of end-user software applications while addressing security concerns.

The MCC approach is complementary to existing approaches such as PCC and code-signing, and can be gainfully combined with them. For instance, a code producer may provide a proof of model safety with the code. In this case, the consumer can statically check

the correctness of this proof; runtime enforcement of models is unnecessary. Similarly, digital signatures may be combined with MCC by having the producers digitally sign their models to indicate that they certify the safety of the model. If a consumer trusts this representation by the producer, then they can skip the enforcement step. Since model safety does not rely on runtime enforcement in both cases, there is a scope for expanding the classes of properties that can be supported by MCC to include liveness and information flow. Moreover, runtime aborts can be avoided.

Acknowledgments

We thank Yow-Jian Lin for several discussions on model extraction and verification, and for feedback on earlier drafts of the paper; C.R. Ramakrishnan, Scott Smolka and Diptikalyan Saha for several discussions on verification; I.V. Ramakrishnan for overall discussions on MCC and RPMshield; Prem Uppuluri for discussions regarding the policy language and compiler; and Wei Xu for discussions regarding model extraction from source code. We also acknowledge Weiqing Sun for his support with system call interposition environment for model enforcement, Mohan Krishna and Shruthi Murthy for support with the policy compiler, Abhishek Chaturvedi for support with model extraction, Tapan Kamat for support with RPMShield, and Zhenkai Liang for support with system call interposition for model extraction. Finally, we thank the anonymous reviewers for their insightful comments that led to significant improvements in the content and organization of this paper.

8. REFERENCES

[1] Anurag Acharya and Mandar Raje. Mapbox: Using parameterized behavior classes to confine applications. In *USENIX Security Symposium*, 2000.

[2] G. Ammons, R. Bodik, and J.R. Larus. Mining specifications. In *ACM Symposium on Principles of Programming Languages (POPL)*, 2002.

[3] Thomas Ball and Sriram K. Rajamani. The SLAM toolkit. In *Computer Aided Verification CAV*, New York-Berlin-Heidelberg, July 2001.

[4] T. Bowen, D. Chee, M. Segal, R. Sekar, T. Shanbhag, and P. Uppuluri. Building survivable systems: An integrated approach based on intrusion detection and damage containment. In *DARPA Information Survivability Conference (DISCEX)*, 2000.

[5] Guillaume Brat, Klaus Havelund, SeungJoon Park, and William Visser. Java pathfinder: Second generation of a Java model checker. *Post-CAV 2000 Workshop on Advances in Verification*, 2000.

[6] C.C Michael and Anup Ghosh. Simple, state-based approaches to program-based anomaly detection. *ACM Transactions on Information and System Security (TISSEC)*, 5(3), 2003.

[7] Hao Chen and David Wagner. MOPS: an infrastructure for examining security properties of software. In *ACM conference on Computer and Communications Security (CCS)*, 2002.

[8] E M Clarke, E A Emerson, and A P Sistla. Automatic verification of finite-state concurrent systems using temporal logic specifications. In *ACM Transactions on Programming Languages and Systems (TOPLAS)*, volume 8(2), 1986.

[9] James Corbett, Matthew Dwyer, John Hatcliff, Corina Pasareanu, Robby, Shawn Laubach, and Hongjun Zheng. Bandera: extracting finite-state models from Java source

code. In *22nd International Conference on Software Engineering (ICSE)*, 2000.

[10] Daniel C. DuVarney and S. Purushothaman Iyer. C Wolf — a toolset for extracting models from C programs. In *International Conference on Formal Techniques for Networked and Distributed Systems (FORTE)*, 2002.

[11] Dawson Engler, Benjamin Chelf, Andy Chou, and Seth Hallem. Checking system rules using system-specific, programmer-written compiler extensions. In *USENIX Symposium on Operating Systems Design and Implementation (OSDI)*, 2000.

[12] Ulfar Erlingsson and Fred B. Schneider. SASI enforcement of security policies: A retrospective. In *New Security Paradigms Workshop (NSPW)*, 1999.

[13] Ulfar Erlingsson and Fred B. Schneider. IRM enforcement of Java stack inspection. In *IEEE Symposium on Security and Privacy*, 2000.

[14] David Evans and Andrew Tywman. Flexible policy directed code safety. In *IEEE Symposium on Security and Privacy*, 1999.

[15] Henry Hanping Feng, Oleg M. Kolesnikov, Prahlad Fogla, Wenke Lee, and Weibo Gong. Anomaly detection using call stack information. In *IEEE Symposium on Security and Privacy*, 2003.

[16] S. Forrest, S. A. Hofmeyr, A. Somayaji, and T. A. Longstaff. A sense of self for UNIX processes. In *IEEE Symposium on Security and Privacy*, 1996.

[17] Timothy Fraser, Lee Badger, and Mark Feldman. Hardening COTS software with generic software wrappers. In *IEEE Symposium on Security and Privacy*, 1999.

[18] Ian Goldberg, David Wagner, Randi Thomas, and Eric A. Brewer. A secure environment for untrusted helper applications: confining the wily hacker. In *USENIX Security Symposium*, 1996.

[19] L Gong, M Mueller, H Prafullchandra, and R Schemers. Going beyond the sandbox: An overview of the new security architecture in the Java development kit 1.2. In *USENIX Symposium on Internet Technologies and Systems*, 1997.

[20] Thomas A. Henzinger, Ranjit Jhala, Rupak Majumdar, George C. Necula, Grégoire Sutre, and Westley Weimer. Temporal-safety proofs for systems code. In *Computer Aided Verification CAV*, 2002.

[21] G.J. Holzmann and Margaret H. Smith. Software model checking - extracting verification models from source code. In *Formal Methods for Protocol Engineering and Distributed Systems*, Kluwer Academic Publ., 1999.

[22] Http-analyze application. Available from http://www.http-analyze.org/.

[23] Butler W. Lampson. A note on the confinement problem. *Communications of the ACM*, 16(10), 1973.

[24] David Larochelle and David Evans. Statically detecting likely buffer overflow vulnerabilities. In *USENIX Security Symposium*, 2001.

[25] Wenke Lee and Sal Stolfo. Data mining approaches for intrusion detection. In *USENIX Security Symposium*, 1997.

[26] David Lie, Andy Chou, Dawson Engler, and David L. Dill. A simple method for extracting models from protocol code. In *Proceedings of the 28th Annual International Symposium on Computer Architecture*, 2001.

[27] Christoph Michael and Anup Ghosh. Using finite automata to mine execution data for intrusion detection: A preliminary report. In *Recent Advances in Intrusion Detection (RAID)*, 2000.

[28] Andrew C Myers and Babara Liskov. Protecting privacy using the decentralized label model. *ACM Transactions on Software Engineering Methodology*, 1999.

[29] G Necula. Proof-carrying code. In *ACM Symposium on Principles of Programming Languages (POPL)*, 1997.

[30] L. Pitt and M. Warmuth. The minimum consistency DFA problem cannot be approximated within any polynomial. In *ACM Symposium on Theory of Computing (STOC)*, 1989.

[31] Fred B. Schneider. Enforceable security policies. *ACM Transactions on Information and System Security (TISSEC)*, 3(1), 2001.

[32] R. Sekar, M. Bendre, P. Bollineni, and D. Dhurjati. A fast automaton-based approach for detecting anomalous program behaviors. In *IEEE Symposium on Security and Privacy*, 2001.

[33] R Sekar and Prem Uppuluri. Synthesizing fast intrusion prevention/detection systems from high-level specifications. In *USENIX Security Symposium*, 1999.

[34] Umesh Shankar, Kunal Talwar, Jeffrey S. Foster, and David Wagner. Detecting format-string vulnerabilities with type qualifiers. In *USENIX Security Symposium*, 2001.

[35] Prem Uppuluri. *Intrusion Detection/Prevention Using Behavior Specifications*. PhD dissertation, Department of Computer Science, Stony Brook University, 2003.

[36] V.N. Venkatakrishnan, Ram Peri, and R. Sekar. Empowering mobile code using expressive security policies. In *New Security Paradigms Workshop (NSPW)*, 2002.

[37] V.N. Venkatakrishnan, R. Sekar, S. Tsipa, T. Kamat, and Z. Liang. An approach for secure software installation. In *USENIX System Administration conference (LISA)*, 2002.

[38] D. Wagner and D. Dean. Intrusion detection via static analysis. In *IEEE symposium on security and privacy*, 2001.

[39] David Wagner and Paolo Soto. Mimicry attacks on host-based intrusion detection systems. In *ACM conference on Computer and Communications Security (CCS)*, 2002.

[40] Andreas Wespi, Herv Debar, Marc Dacier, and Mehdi Nassehi. Fixed- vs. variable-length patterns for detecting suspicious process behavior. *Journal of Computer Security (JCS)*, 8(2/3), 2000.

[41] XSB. The XSB logic programming system v2.3, 2001. Available from http://www.cs.sunysb.edu/~sbprolog.

[42] Steve Zdancewic, Lantian Zheng, Nathaniel Nystrom, and Andrew C. Myers. Untrusted hosts and confidentiality: Secure program partitioning. In *ACM Symposium on Operating Systems Principles (SOSP)*, 2001.

Behavioral Detection of Malicious Code

William Allen[†], Richard Ford[†], Jens Gregor[*], Gerald Marin[†], Mike Thomason[*], James Whittaker[†]

[†]Florida Institute of Technology,
[*]University of Tennessee

Abstract

Despite the growing threat posed by Malicious Mobile Code, current solutions are not capable of providing sufficient protection from new threats. In this paper, we provide an overview of the problem and different approaches to remediation. We then introduce the idea of behavioral virus suppression coupled with a robust undo technology. Using this approach, we illustrate a new and reliable method of not only detecting but also removing previously unseen viruses. Finally, we describe our network-based detection algorithms and explore their application in a distributed version of our virus suppression solution.

Keywords: Computer security; information security; malicious code; virus

Introduction

Virus, worm, trojan, spyware…these are words that have become far too common in everyday language. Sadly, the language of "Malicious Mobile Code" (MMC) has become a regular part of computing vocabulary, and while users reluctantly tolerate its presence, the scope of the problem is vast.

Unfortunately, the problems that *underlie* MMC are even worse than they might appear at first glance. MMC is capable of causing far more damage than decreased productivity or deleted data: MMC provides a perfect vector for attacks against government agencies and defense organizations. Such attacks can have distinct – and unpleasant – real world consequences. MMC erodes the very foundations of trusted computing, and as such *must* be stopped.

In this article, we will provide a brief history of MMC, where it came from, and what risks it poses. After dispelling some of the prevalent MMC myths, we will then look at current solutions, how they fall short, and, most importantly, what steps we have taken to improve them.

Malicious Mobile Code: Past, Present and Future

Before embarking on a brief journey through history, a few definitions are in order. First, we can define a virus as follows (from [Virus-L95]):

> A computer virus is a self-replicating program containing code that explicitly copies itself and that can "infect" other programs by modifying them or their environment such that a call to an infected program implies a call to a possibly evolved copy of the virus.

A worm is somewhat similar, but is entirely self-contained. Again, borrowing from the Virus-L FAQ [Virus-L95]:

> A computer WORM is a self-contained program (or set of programs), that is able to spread functional copies of itself or its segments to other computer systems (usually via network connections).

Defining a Trojan horse turns out to be much more difficult. The "traditional" definition, taken from the "Orange Book" [NCSC87] is:

> Trojan horse-a computer program with an apparently or actually useful function that contains additional (hidden) functions that surreptitiously exploit the legitimate authorizations of the invoking process. An example is a program that makes a "blind copy" of a sensitive file for the creator of the Trojan horse.

As can be seen, the most important component of this definition is what the user *expects* – note the words "hidden" and "surreptitiously". Thus, the label Trojan is entirely subjective. This rather blurred view of the world carries over to the related problems of Adware and Spyware. While the industry has yet to adopt a widely-held definition of these terms, they are generally considered to describe software that the user would not want, which either displays advertisements or surreptitiously gathers information about computer usage and browsing habits.

Armed with these definitions, it is interesting to briefly examine the evolution of MMC since its inception. The first virus, *Elk Cloner* was discovered on the Apple in 1982 [Lammer93]. This virus did not garner much publicity – so little, in fact, that many people consider the *Brain* virus – discovered in 1986 [Lammer93] – to be the "first" virus. Like most common early viruses, *Brain* was spread from machine to machine when an infected diskette was inadvertently left in the boot drive at boot time. Once the machine was infected, all disks subsequently used in the machine would be infected. Disks were not the only infection vector possible: other viruses could infect executable files. Once again, when these files were carried to another machine and executed, the virus would spread.

Despite the prevalence of some of the early boot sector viruses (most notably, *Form* and *Stoned*) it still took a long time for a virus to make its way around the world. Users rarely exchanged executable files, and infected diskettes only became active if they were booted from. In order to spread more quickly, virus writers needed to target something that was frequently exchanged. Microsoft provided the perfect target in the form of Office documents.

With the benefit of hindsight, the design flaw in Office exploited by the virus writers seems astonishingly obvious, but at the time of the first macro virus (a virus embedded in an office document using the ability of the document to launch macros in the host program) both users and researchers were caught off-guard. This virus, named *Concept*, was discovered by Sarah Gordon in 1995 [Gordon95], and used the auto-macro function of Word to execute code. Thus, simply opening an infected Word document was enough to infect your machine. Worse yet, auto-execution was not a programming error that could be easily fixed, but dangerous functionality that had been intentionally – but ill-advisedly – included. Because of this, fixing the problem turned out to be difficult, as many users had already designed products around this "auto-macro" capability. *Concept* quickly spread worldwide, outstripping boot viruses in terms of prevalence. Macro viruses had come of age.

Despite the success of macro viruses, speed of spread was still limited by user action; a virus could only spread from machine to machine when a user shared in infected object. However, the exported APIs from Office allowed for a far more aggressive approach: having the virus actively send itself to all members of the user's address book. In March of 1999 the *Melissa* virus did just this, filling up corporate mail boxes worldwide in a space of a few hours [CERT99].

Even though worms that used email to spread sound like a worst case scenario, a worm that requires no user interaction to spread is far more virulent. The Internet Worm of 1988 was a precursor to the chaos brought about by the *CodeRed* worm of 2001. This marked the onset of an avalanche of new worms primarily targeting the popular Windows operating system. At the time of writing the most dramatic of these was *SQL.Slammer*, which caused a measurable perturbation in Border Gateway Protocol statistics – a measure of the connectivity of the Internet [Griffin03].

Historically, viruses and worms – MMC in general – have been a huge problem for government, corporate and home computer users… and the situation does not seem to be getting any better. Increasing connectivity, ubiquity of computing and a strong interest in computer exploitation all continue to make the problem worse. It is within the bounds of possibility that a worm could literally bring the Internet down; indeed some experts believe this is a question of when, not if.

Given this rather gloomy forecast, it seems prudent to examine why it is that MMC seems so capable of avoiding our best efforts at stopping it.

Current Solutions

In order to understand why MMC is so effective, it is best to begin with a solid understanding of how current countermeasures work. At a high level, we can break this discussion down to two general areas: virus-specific detection, which deals with detection of those viruses we already know about, and generic virus detection, which attempts to detect previously unknown viruses.

Virus-specific detection tends to focus on detecting attributes of a particular virus. For example, when MMC first emerged, anti-virus software vendors often searched files for a particular hexadecimal string, i.e., the "signature" of the infection. If this string was found the file was deemed infected. As virus writers became more sophisticated, viruses often changed their appearance between infections. This property, known as polymorphism, significantly added to the complexity of detection algorithms, but in essence the approach is still to look for properties of the virus in a particular file. Most anti-virus vendors are quite efficient at creating and distributing these signatures for new viruses, but even the best process tends to leave a vulnerability window between the time a virus begins to spread and the time that it is detected and a signature distributed to infected networks.

Given that a worm can become pandemic in a matter of minutes this window of vulnerability is an area of considerable concern. There has been a tremendous amount of interest in developing techniques which can detect MMC that has never been seen before; this is known as generic virus detection.

When considering such detection it is important to consider two important quantities: the rate of *false positives* and the rate of *false negatives*. A false positive is when an uninfected object is incorrectly identified as infected, and a false negative is when an infected object is incorrectly identified as clean. In both causes, misidentification can cause problems. When considering false negative rates it is important to consider how many objects there are on a system. A false positive rate of 0.1% may sound impressive, but in practice such a solution is unusable. On the computer being used to write this article, for example, there are currently just under 110,000 files; a false positive rate of 0.1% would correspond to about 110 being incorrectly classed as infected.

The challenge with false negatives is somewhat different. Even if a generic virus detection rate has a 10% false negative rate, the result is still that 9 out of 10 new viruses might be caught. This is still useful, though far from a complete solution; however, it does clearly illustrate the reduction of false positives is the "holy grail" of generic virus detection: 90% detection is better than even a 0.1% false positive rate.

Perhaps the earliest approach used for generic detection was to use the fact that a virus makes changes to objects it infects. Thus, a checksum could be used to alert the user to those files that have been modified. While this technique has a very low false negative rate, it is important to realize that it is *change detection* not virus detection. Thus, files that are detected are not necessarily infected, but may have been changed by an entirely legitimate process. This complicating factor makes checksumming alone an impractical approach to generic virus detection.

Another technique that was common in the early days of anti-virus technology, and is still used today, is heuristics. This approach uses different attributes of a file to determine if it is "virus-like". If it is sufficiently virus-like, the user is alerted and the file is marked as infected. The problem with this sort of virus detection is that it is relatively easy for the virus writer to reverse engineer the ways in which the heuristics work. In essence, the virus writer has near infinite time to try and beat the heuristic detection. Once this is accomplished, he or she can release their creation knowing it avoids detection. Basically, all these static detection techniques can be reduced to the halting problem, as demonstrated by Cohen in his seminal work [Cohen94]. Because of this, behavioral detection is an attractive alternative to these techniques.

By watching the behavior of a suspicious file does it is relatively easy to determine if it possesses harmful properties. Unfortunately, this approach is often applied post-fact; that is, the behavior blocker can only tell if something bad has happened *after* something bad has happened. Thus, there is a natural tendency to try and detect malicious activity quickly. This is in tension with the desire to reduce false positives. The longer a program is observed, the more accurate the detection is.

Gatekeeper II: Detection and Removal

The challenge with behavioral detection has always been balancing damage reduction with detection accuracy. As discussed previously, the longer a process runs, the better a behavioral system understands the impact of a program, but the more damage the program has the opportunity to inflict. Our solution to this problem is both innovative and simple: couple a behavioral classifier with a robust undo technology. This effectively breaks the tension between early detection (low damage) and late detection (high reliability), making a behavioral approach significantly more attractive.

We chose to break up the problem into three distinct areas: the underlying interception technology and infrastructure, the detection mechanisms, and network-based modeling and understanding of attacks. As such, we will continue our discussion following these categories, before synthesizing them into a single solution.

Infrastructure and Interception

The overall design of Gatekeeper II (GKII) depends heavily on its ability to monitor processes within the Win32 system. (Although these techniques are applicable – often more simply – on other operating systems, we focus on Windows because it is the most often attacked.) Figure 1 shows a schematic diagram of the system. As can be seen, GKII consists of a monitoring engine, a meta-engine that preprocesses intercepted data and reconciles the results of the different components, and "matching engines," which are basically classifiers that attempt to determine if a process is benign or malicious.

Interception is handled by our HEAT Technology (Hostile Environment Application Testing) which is capable of intercepting all API calls made by the program to its environment, including file system call, kernel calls, and calls to any third party object or library [Whittaker02]. The calls are then preprocessed to place them in a meaningful context and passed down to multiple different classifiers – these are discussed in the next section. It is worth noting that HEAT does not require any changes to be made to the monitored executable or host operating system; monitoring is achieved automatically and transparently at runtime.

These intercepted calls represent every external behavior enacted by the monitored process and are the data on which we are able to determine whether a process is benign or malicious, the system also passes this information to our Undo engine. This engine provides the ability to "roll back" the changes made to the system by a process or a process hierarchy. Thus, if a process is determined to be harmful it can be safely stopped and its actions undone.

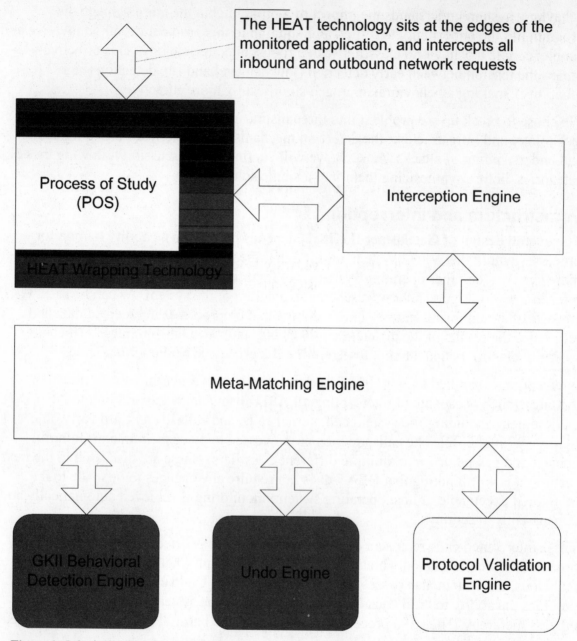

Figure 1: Schematic diagram of GKII. The Process of Study (POS) is wrapped at runtime by our HEAT technology. This effectively buffers the process from the rest of the system. System Calls are monitored in real time and matched with a number of different engines.

Detection

One of the benefits of the GKII approach is the ability to use multiple classification mechanisms to detect the presence of malicious code. To date, we have pursued two different strategies, but several more are planned. In our first behavioral engine, we score processes based on the system calls they issue and the behaviors their calls represent (such as modifying system files or opening sockets). In our Probabilistic Suffix Tree (PST) engine, we use a statistical method to examine the relative probability of sequences of system calls.

The idea for the behavioral engine arose from pre-existing work at Florida Tech. Essentially, it was noticed that if one examined those viruses in the wild, a number of very similar high-level behaviors emerged. These common behaviors were fairly rare in legitimate programs, and as such, were potentially good indicators of malicious intent.

Once a list of behaviors was constructed, the first incarnation of our anti-virus product was born: IMP ("Identify, Monitor, and Protect") [Whittaker2002]. Our experience with building and designing this led us to the creation of Gatekeeper and its successor, GKII.

The technology underlying the PST engine is a little bit more difficult to grasp than the intuitively clear process of matching behaviors to processes. Instead of focusing on what particular actions were taken, the PST technique focuses on the probability of particular call sequences in legitimate code. Unlike the behavioral approach which involves training on both viral and benign samples, the PST engine only requires training on benign traces [DeCerqueira03]. Thus, a process is never truly labeled malicious but rather "not benign" – a subtle, but important difference. This engine is described in detail in [Mazeroff04].

Results from the system to date have been very encouraging. Detection results are presented in detail in [Ford04] along with experiment design details. However, by way of summary, GKII currently detects over 90% of viruses it has never seen before, with a very low false positive rate.

Network-based Modeling and Detection

Although the current instance of GKII is capable of detecting and mitigating MMC that is executing locally, it is unable to detect malicious network traffic, such as Denial-of-Service (DoS) attacks and worms, as it is host-based. One of the goals of the distributed Gatekeeper project is to add network monitoring in the form of agents or sensors which detect and communicate "suspicious" behavior to Gatekeeper. This could include a high volume of traffic directed towards a specific host or subnet (which might indicate a DoS attack) or a high volume of outbound traffic from a specific host (which could indicate a worm or other viral activity).

Much work has been done to detect known patterns of malicious activity, but recent events (*Blaster, SQL.Slammer,* etc.) have shown that some attacks spread too quickly to rely on pattern-based detection techniques. The detection of unknown, or "zero-day", attacks requires anomaly-based detection techniques, and our efforts have been directed towards developing new methods for detecting malicious behavior in network traffic.

The techniques that we have developed to date were based on the observation that high-bandwidth attacks, such as flooding DoS-type attacks and rapidly-spreading worms, produce a high volume of homogeneous traffic while network environments generally consist of a more heterogeneous mix of protocols. We further observed that this malicious traffic could, if its arrival rate were high enough, significantly disrupt the normal distribution of traffic flows. Our detection techniques were based on two measures of traffic characteristics, self-similarity and fractal dimension. Leland, et al. [Leland94] established that LAN traffic normally exhibits a self-similar property and our research showed that high-bandwidth attacks could disrupt that expected behavior, thus indicating abnormal activity [Allen03]. Ayedemir, et al. [Ayedemir01] demonstrated that the fractal dimension of LAN traffic (which is related to its self-similar properties) could be measured and our work has shown that certain types of network attacks can significantly alter the fractal dimension of network traffic [Allen03].

These two detection techniques rely on inherent characteristics of normal network traffic and, therefore, can be used to detect previously unknown types of high-bandwidth attack. We hope to show that sensors, implementing the above detection algorithms, can be used to report the presence of disruptive activity in a network environment to network-aware Gatekeeper nodes.

Note that, at this time, the network side processing is done principally to alert specific GateKeeper-protected machines of likely malicious activity. In the long run, the intent is to use IDS techniques to allow GateKeeper to focus its attention on high probability processes. Given the dynamic changes that may occur in normal network traffic, this approach may send false alarms to GateKeeper, but network traffic will never be blocked while new traffic templates are being estimated. If the network alert techniques can ultimately be shown to work real-time with acceptable false alarm rates, then they may be integrated into GateKeeper as additional detection engines. Note that false alarms are much less of a problem in this system than usual because GateKeeper can correlate network alerts with host activity before acting on those alerts.

While the host-based version of Gatekeeper could be tested by introducing malicious code into an isolated machine, reliably and safely testing a network-aware and/or distributed version of Gatekeeper is problematic. Placing instrumented hosts in a real network environment exposes them to unknown attackers and exposes the entire network, and potentially the entire Internet, to the MMC used to test the Gatekeeper nodes. Running tests in an isolated network is safer, but means that the experiments will be carried out in an unrealistic environment and the results may not transfer well to the real world.

To provide a realistic network environment for testing Gatekeeper's ability to detect network-based attacks and for testing the distributed version of Gatekeeper, the network team is building a system that will enable synthetically-generated traffic to be run "live" in a laboratory environment. This network testing environment consists of three components. The first, based on a technique developed by Dr. Marin, models traffic from real networks and uses those models to generate synthetic traffic in a laboratory setting [Luo04]. The traffic models are derived from a combination of the classical statistical distributions for LAN traffic [Paxson95] and empirical models that use hybrid modeling techniques and heavy-tailed distributions to create accurate, detailed models of protocols such as FTP, SSH and HTTP. Real traffic traces were captured from the CS department LAN at UCF and models were produced for five common network protocols. Those models were used to produce simulation traces which have been successfully compared with the actual traffic, demonstrating the accuracy of the modeling techniques.

Dr. Allen has led the development of the MAGNA (Modeling and Generating Network Attacks) tool [Allen04] which uses state-based models of network attacks to generate synthetic attack traffic. This tool can be used to execute both DoS and Worm-like attacks in a test bed network under controlled conditions. MAGNA also supports the creation of new variants of known attacks or novel network-based attacks.

We have also built a scheduling and control system that can be used to run experiments in a laboratory network by combining our traffic modeling technique (used to generate attack-free background traffic) with the attacks executed by MAGNA. This system, which we call HONEST (Hands-On Network Environment for Security Testing), provides a user-friendly GUI interface, detailed logging of generated events, remote configuration of client/server interaction and automatic capture of the generated network traffic. Figure 2 shows the system design for the test bed environment.

During the next year, we will work to refine the HONEST and MAGNA tools and to produce additional attack-free traffic models so that lab environments can be created that contain a mix of realistic background traffic and labeled attacks. These environments will then be used in testing and refining Gatekeeper's ability to detect network-based malicious activity.

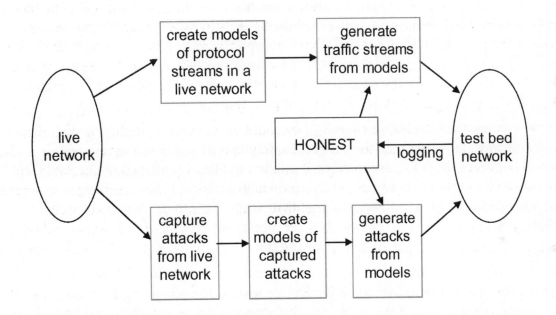

Figure 2: Schematic diagram for testing a distributed version of Gatekeeper using the MAGNA and HONEST tools

The Big Picture

The preceding sections have presented several of the building blocks needed for a robust and reliable virus suppression system. However, we have yet to build a comprehensive solution that integrates these components. In this section, we will describe our future work, which aims to tie these parts together.

Part of the challenge with any virus suppression system is dealing with the few samples that actually slip through the net; any host-based system is not likely to be perfect, and will inevitably miss some samples. To this end, it is our desire to tie together the network tools and host-based tools to create a system which is capable of determining when a virus or worm has been missed.

Because worms represent the most obvious threat to a defended system, we have primarily focused on coordinated defense against worms. One way to proceed is to detect an active worm on the network and to use this knowledge to modify the way in which other GKII installations work. Such a system would be capable of modifying its parameters based upon the actual state of the network. This property of self-organization allows the system to deal with perturbations cooperatively.

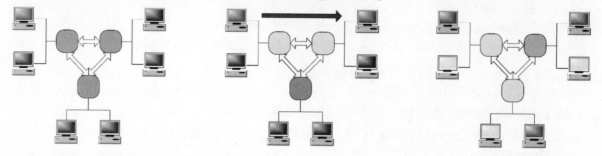

Figure 3: Schematic diagram of distributed GKII in action. (a) Shows a single infected machine (RED), with GKII monitoring nodes installed on uninfected machines (BLUE) and network devices (GREEN). (b) The infection spreads, raising suspicion levels on the path of the infection (YELLOW and ORANGE) (c) The network reconfigures itself to combat the new threat, raising its warning status globally due to the new infection.

Figure 3 shows a schematic for the integrated system. As can be seen, the host-based behavioral systems exchange an overall measure of the "threat" to the system. Should a worm subvert the host node, the network node is capable of detecting the breach as the worm begins to spread. This would be broadcast to other uninfected nodes, and their threat level adjusted with respect to that particular protocol. Thus, changes can be made on a per-protocol basis, allowing the system to tune itself to meet the current threat landscape.

Such integrated systems that are capable of changing their defensive stance in real time are difficult to predict. For this reason, we have built two test tools: Hephaestus, a virus spread simulator [Shirey04], and HONEST, a system for generating realistic network traffic [Cooper05]. Our goal is to build a hybrid system that combines the best of behavioral detection with network-based threat measurement. With our existing work complete, such a simulation is within reach during our current research window.

Conclusions

As we have seen, MMC presents an ever-increasing threat to the future of trustworthy computing. Self-replicating code now has the ability to become ubiquitous in minutes after its release and current static analysis tools are ill-placed to ever provide a solution to an evolving threat.

Our research has extended the state of the art in behavioral approaches to virus detection *and removal*. In addition, we are in the process of creating a system that combines the best of host-based detection with a more network-centric solution. Our belief is that this approach will make it extremely difficult to create a worm that spreads successfully at a high speed.

Aside from the problem of speed of spread, many open problems remain in the field of MMC. Further research is needed in the difficult area of real time spyware detection and removal.

References

Allen03 Allen W.H., Marin G.A., *On the Self-similarity of Synthetic Traffic for the Evaluation of Intrusion Detection Systems*, in Proceedings of the IEEE International Symposium on Applications and the Internet, Jan, 2003

Allen04 Allen W.H., and Marin G.A., *MAGNA: Modeling And Generating Network Attacks*, in Proceedings of the IEEE Conference on Local Computer Networks, Nov. 2004

Ayedemir01 Ayedemir M., Bottomley L., Coffin M., Marin G.A., *Two tools for network traffic analysis*, Computer Networks, vol. 36, no. 2-3, 2001

CERT99 CERT Advisory CA-1999-04 Melissa Macro Virus, March 27, 1999

Cohen94 Cohen F.B., *A Short Course on Computer Viruses*, 2nd edition. John Wiley & Sons, New York, 1994

Cooper05 Cooper M., *HONEST: Hands-On Networking Environment for Security Testing*, Master's Thesis, Florida Institute of Technology, 2005

DeCerqueira03 De Cerqueira V.P., *Graphical user interface for malicious mobile code fingerprinting*, Master's Thesis, Univ. Tennessee, 2003

Ford04 Ford R.A., Wagner M., and Michalske J., *Gatekeeper II: New Approaches to Generic Virus Prevention.* From the proceedings of the International Virus Bulletin Conference, Chicago, 2004

Gordon95 Gordon S., *What a (Winword) Concept*, Virus Bulletin, September 1995

Griffin03 Griffin T., and Zhuoqing M., *Internet Routing Streams*, Workshop on the Management and Processing of Data Streams, 2003

Lammer93 *The Survivor's Guide to Computer Viruses*, Ed. Victoria Lammer, Virus Bulletin Ltd ISBN 0-9522114-0-8, 1993

Leland04 Leland W., Taqqu M., Willinger W., and Wilson D., *On the Self-Similar Nature of Ethernet Traffic*, IEEE-ACM Transactions on Networking, vol. 2 no. 1, Feb. 1994

Luo04 Luo S., Marin G.A., *Generating Realistic Traffic for Security Experiments*, in Proceedings of the IEEE SouthEast Conference, Mar. 2004

Mazeroff04 Mazeroff G., *Probabilistic Suffix Models for Windows Application Behavior Profiling: Framework and Initial Results*. Master's Thesis. University of Tennessee, 2004

NCSC1987 National Computer Security Center, *A Guide to Understanding Discretionary Access Control in Trusted Systems*, NCSC-TG-003-87, 1987

Paxson95 Paxson V., and Floyd S., *Wide-Area Traffic: The Failure of Poisson Modeling*, IEEE-ACM Transactions on Networking, vol. 3 no. 3, June 1995

Shirey04 Shirey C.B., *Modeling the Spread and Prevention of Malicious Mobile Code via Simulation*, Masters Thesis, Florida Institute of Technology, 2004

Virus-L95 VIRUS-L/comp.virus Frequently Asked Questions v2.00, maintained by Nick Fitzgerald. Downloaded from http://www.faqs.org/faqs/computer-virus/faq/ July 2005, authored 1995

Whittaker02 Whittaker J.A., and De Vivanco A., *Neutralizing Windows-based malicious mobile code*, Proceedings of the 17th ACM Software Applications Conference (ACM-SAC), pp. 242-246, Madrid, Spain, 2002

Gatekeeper II: New Approaches to Generic Virus Prevention

Richard Ford Ph.D., Florida Institute of Technology,
Matt Wagner, Microsoft Corporation,
Jason Michalske, Florida Institute of Technology,
(rford, matt, jmich)@se.fit.edu

Abstract

The need for reliable detection of rapidly spreading worms and viruses has never been higher; malicious mobile code such as SQL.Slammer has proven that an epidemic can occur far faster than developers can react using existing technology. Thus, there has been significant interest in developing fast and reliable techniques for detecting previously unseen malicious code.

In this paper, we extend the work carried out under the Gatekeeper project, a behavioral virus detection engine with undo capability. New techniques to provide for higher virus detection rates with lower false positive rates are described for the first time, and a demonstration of the new Gatekeeper tool is given, showing detection rates that are extremely high with low processor overhead and minimal false positives. Directed attacks against Gatekeeper are considered, and novel defenses described.

Introduction

Viruses and worms have become a fact of online life. Almost every user has a story to tell about a worm or virus that they have been attacked by, and few adults are oblivious to the online dangers posed by today's rapid malware. With outbreak times reduced to minutes as opposed to weeks or days, however, today's virus-specific detection techniques are straining to keep up with the rapidly changing threat landscape. Indeed, significant work has been done showing that specific solutions are essentially unable to keep up with worms that spread as rapidly Slammer or even faster [Williamson2003]. Clearly, some level of protection from such new viruses and worms is urgently needed.

In this paper, we examine Gatekeeper II, a proactive virus detection engine that uses behavioral techniques to reduce spread rate. Although several aspects of the Gatekeeper project have been published elsewhere [Ford2004, Wagner2003], we first present an overview of the basic Gatekeeper technology. We then discuss improvements made in Gatekeeper II. Detection and removal results are provided and interpreted. Finally, we discuss some of the weaknesses of behavioral systems such as Gatekeeper, and how these vulnerabilities can be mitigated in the future.

Gatekeeper I Overview

Gatekeeper II (GKII) represents a significant step forward from its predecessor, Gatekeeper I (GKI), despite the fact that many parts of the underlying technology are essentially unchanged. In order to understand GKII in context, we first present a brief discussion of the GKI system, which contained several important improvements over traditional behavioral antivirus products.

At the simplest level, Gatekeeper consists of three key components: an interception engine, a matching engine, and an undo engine. The interception engine is responsible for intercepting and gating – in a allow/deny manner – Win32 API calls made by a process that is currently being monitored. Allow/Deny or go/no-go decisions are based on the output of a separate Matching Engine used for arbitration. This determines if a particular series of actions appears to be hostile in nature; if they are deemed benign, system operation continues as normal. However, if the call sequence received by the matching engine is found to be suspicious – that is, if the threat level of the process crosses a certain critical threshold – the process that generated the calls is halted, and all its actions optionally undone.

Detection results for GKI were highly encouraging. Very high (>90% of those viruses in the wild in May of 2003) detection rates were observed within the training set, with only minimal false positives. Essentially, GKI proved that a behavioral system was capable of reliable virus/non-virus discrimination under real-world conditions.

The relative effectiveness of Gatekeeper compared to previous behavioral implementations can be attributed to the following innovations:

1. **Late Detection**. When examining a process behaviorally, the longer the process runs the more accurately a detection system is likely to accept or reject samples. Hostile samples will display more "hostile" behavior, whereas benign samples will show that they are harmless. Arbitration of borderline cases – the ones that typically cause a false positive – can be postponed until any malicious operation is clear. However, the longer a malicious process is allowed to execute, the more likely it is that damage to the system will occur. By implementing a robust undo engine, detection of samples can be postponed, allowing more behaviors to be examined before a detection decision must be made.

2. **Improved Training**. By automating the training process of Gatekeeper, an optimum solution can be created that does not depend on the knowledge of any domain expert. This training technique removes the reliance on domain expertise, and allows for the extraction of underlying patterns that may be counterintuitive.

3. **"Missing State" Detection**. Many behavioral systems attempted to identify malicious code by what it *did* – that is, by the accesses and modifications it made to the system. Although this method is acceptable for detection purposes, it is also prone to false positives. Gatekeeper makes accept/reject decisions based upon not only the actions carried out by a process but also what good behaviors actions are *absent*. For example, many HTTP requests made to different servers without any preceding DNS lookup are more suspicious than the same requests made with each IP being generated by a DNS request. Although the mechanism used for this process is simplistic, it is highly effective.

GKII: Improvements to the Gatekeeper Model

Despite the strong results obtained from the original Gatekeeper project, we believe there are several significant areas of possible improvement. Aside from simple architectural enhancements that improve speed and portability, the following key changes to the system have been made:

1. Added an object-ownership engine,

2. Enhanced parsing of return codes,

3. Added an object caching engine,

4. Designed a Multiple Matching Engine architecture, supporting the inclusion of a Fractal Dimension and Probabilistic Suffix Tree (PST) Engine,

5. Added the ability to determine executable type at runtime,

6. Improved the genetic training algorithm.

Each improvement directly affects the way in which Gatekeeper II determines if a process hierarchy is hostile or not. Within the following sections, each improvement is outlined, and its benefits enumerated. Due to space constraints, we touch on some issues briefly; full details of the many improvements in GKII can be found in an upcoming publication.

The Ownership Engine

One of the issues with behavioral systems is that they are usually unaware of the relationships between files. That is, if a program creates an object – be that a file, registry key, or child process – there is a strong likelihood that that object will be later referenced or modified by subsequent invocations of that program. Similarly, if a file has only been used by one set of programs and a different executable modifies that file, it may be reasonable to wonder what operations the new program is carrying out. Thus, we may consider the ownership of system objects to be a useful metric in determining the intent and threat of actions.

The driving force behind the implementation of the ownership tracking was a false positive in GKI when running Internet Explorer, which occasionally decides to delete its entire cache of saved pages on startup. *Prima facie* these multiple file deletions *look* like a viral payload. However, when one notes that all these files were created by that same executable, their deletion seems far less threatening. Thus, our belief was that scoring process' threat levels based on ownership of files would be highly advantageous in terms of reliability of classification.

Results from the ownership engine have been highly encouraging. Previous work on detection of malcode by anomalous registry access, for example, has shown that malcode can have a different pattern of access than normal programs [Heller2003]. However, this method is limited, as it relies on *knowing* the objects to be protected. In addition, this classification is too narrow to be effective either from a false positive or false negative perspective. We believe our approach is stronger, as it relies on less prior knowledge of the malcode. Furthermore, we can take a hybrid approach, as it is possible to add behaviors to Gatekeeper that specifically assign additional threat values based upon the access of certain keys.

The hardest problems we faced when designing the ownership engine were overinstalls and updates. Consider the process of updating an application. This process is likely to modify existing executable files on the disk, as well as check certain registry keys. As the installer or updater is new to the system, it will not "own" any of the files that are changed. However, most of the keys will be changed within a certain hierarchy – that is, if many files are modified, all those files are in the same ownership chain. Thus, when we observe a large number of files being modified or deleted that are in the same ownership hierarchy, we should consider the possibility that we are intercepting an update or overinstall.

This idea allows threat to be modified for multiple file deletions/modifications within the same ownership hierarchy, and helps minimize the number of false positives triggered by overinstalls and updates.

The Failure Monitor

One of the weaknesses of the original Gatekeeper was that it was not "smart" in terms of understanding return codes: it was aware of API calls, but not of the reasons why they succeeded or failed. GKII significantly enhances GKI's ability to interpret whether a call succeeded or failed, thereby significantly enhancing the ability to detect viruses.

Consider a network-aware worm that is attempting to randomly access the network for vulnerable hosts. When socket open calls are issued by the virus, we might expect the failure rate of these calls to be high, as many target IP addresses are either unpopulated or are not listening on the target port. A web browser, however, will also make many calls to socket open, but we might expect both a different pattern – more calls to the same destination, and a different ratio of success to failure. Thus, both the ratio and type of failures associated with a particular call are important in terms of detection.

There are several drawbacks with our implemented approach in this area, all of which could negatively impact detection. First, by dealing specifically with more cases, the number of variables to be considered when tuning detection is greatly increased. Second, threats based on multiple failures are currently combined linearly; there is no reason that this should be the best approach. Additional research on how actions in general are combined is desirable, and is likely to lead to better detection results, and enhanced false positive rejection. Finally, as implemented, GKII knows only about pass/fail results; it is not tuned for the different *causes* of failure, which can also be indicative of hostile action. If sufficient detection is not achieved within this version of the Failure Monitor, we believe that an even more granular approach may be advantageous.

Object Caching

One weakness of the original Gatekeeper was that its memory of actions taken on objects, and the relation of handles to particular objects was somewhat weak. That is, Gatekeeper would "forget" the association between handles and actual objects in certain circumstances, allowing for particular directed attacks against the detection mechanism, and decreasing granularity of logging. This loss of information reduced the effectiveness of some of the behavioral detection.

In GKII we have added a generic object cache which maps handles to actual objects. This allows for modifications and changes to be tracked on a per-object basis, as opposed to simply noting that a particular call was made to a less-than-known entity. Once again, the addition of object caching helps both from a performance standpoint and from a detection standpoint. Initial results are encouraging, and show that the presence of the object caching engine allows for more accurate tuning of detection/rejection weights.

Multiple Matching Engines

The internal architecture of GKII is significantly different from the preceding version. One of the areas we have considered most is the problem of directed attacks. To this end, we have added support for multiple matching engines within GKII. By creating such an architecture, we believe that the process of passing off malicious code as benign is significantly complicated.

Due to the ongoing development process, the results presented are taken from only one matching engine. However, the current architecture is able to support any number of parallel matching engines, whose output is combined into one normalized threat level.

The benefit of this architecture is that one can use more than one technique in order to determine the risk posed by a sample. In particular, two other matching engines have been considered: an engine that examines system calls for self-similarity and an engine that uses a PST to determine whether call sequence execution is anomalous when compared to a training set of known benign sequences. An engine developed by Mazeroff et al. [Mazeroff2003] is currently being integrated with the main GKII project; results are expected in late 2004.

Another engine currently under development is based upon the concept of fractal dimension of call traces [Allen2003]. Using this particular engine, we hope to determine the presence of benign loop injection. This technique relies on the self-similarity of call sequences. Changes to the degree of self-similarity can be a good indicator of the presence of viral code, especially worms, which attempt to access as many hosts as possible during their infection cycle. In tests against attacks embedded in network traffic, promising results were obtained; if this technique were effective only against network-aware code, it would still present a significant step forward in terms of virus prevention.

By coupling the output of these, we believe the difficulty of creating code specifically designed to evade detection will significantly increase. We are presently awaiting additional results from this approach, and will present them in a future publication.

Executable Type Determination

As the GKII system is behavioral at the Win32 level, it monitors system calls only, even if those calls are generated by an interpreter. For example, if a Visual Basic Script is executed, GKII intercepts all calls made by the script interpreter. Given that this process adds a particular signature of calls, it is possible to determine what type of executable is being monitored by examining both the pattern and content of intercepted calls.

Determining the executable type is particularly important when examining viruses written in high-level interpreted languages like Virus Basic Script. For such a virus, a single line of script can generate multiple calls at a Win32 level. However, from a virus detection standpoint, it is not these calls that are important, but the higher level VBS APIs that matter. By training the system separately on viruses written in different languages, detection weights can be tuned to provide for optimal detection within a particular execution environment, as opposed to a general solution that attempts to detect *all* viruses via the same set of call sequences. As a trivial example, the Visual Basic Scripting Engine is always invoked by a certain set of calls when it is instantiated. This sequence is neither good nor bad: it is simply an artifact of the execution method. Thus, an optimal detection algorithm will not generate threat data from such sequences of calls; rather it will use the order and content of these calls to determine that the code is running from within a particular interpreter.

Preliminary results appear to be encouraging; however, it should be noted that the results presented in this paper were produced with this feature disabled.

Genetic Algorithm and Trainer

Finally, because of the size of the GKII training parameter space, we have made some significant enhancements to our training algorithm. As it is difficult to manually sort through traces and weight benign/malicious behaviors, we have created a simple system that provides for both random modification of "genes" (where each gene represents the weight, either positive or negative, of a particular behavior), as well as limited crossover of genes between successful generations. As we believe there is a low level of coupling between the different genes, we have a strong degree of confidence that the global optimum solution is being discovered, as opposed to a local minimum.

Data for the training consists of a number of benign traces gathered on several machines as well as traces obtained from a large number of "In the Wild" viruses.

Future work in the training area will enable the training algorithm determine its own behaviors from call traces; this allows a malicious behavior set to be extracted without requiring a human to spot the pattern by either domain expertise or analysis of a large number of samples.

Test Methodology and Results

Although experimental results from GKI were encouraging, our experience building the system exposed several areas where we could improve the reliability of virus detection. In particular, we were concerned about reducing the false positive rate, as even small numbers of false positives are extremely damaging in terms of practical application.

When we examined the causal factors behind GKI's false positives, we discovered a fairly consistent trend: in each case, the threat level was being artificially driven up by programs that were deleting or modifying files which they owned – that is, files that had either been creating during this invocation of the program, or during previous runs of the program. A good example of this was Internet Explorer, which sometimes chooses to delete its entire cache on startup; GKII would observe these multiple deletions and determine that such wide-scale destruction of data with no user prompting was evidence of malicious intent.

GKII was designed to address this type of false positive by the addition of the ownership engine described earlier. The addition of this engine also allows the GK training process to more aggressively weight certain actions, and thereby improves detection results.

To test the reliability of GKII, we conducted the following experiment. Using 73 behavioral traces from viruses from the December 2002 WildList, and 27 long traces of function calls generated by benign processes – including scenarios that caused false positives in GKI – we used our genetic algorithm to train GKII. After training, the false positive count on the training data was 0, with 69 detections (94.5%). In the case of the four missed viruses, failure of detection was not related to theoretical shortcomings of GKII, but to issues associated with either bugs or failure to monitor certain actions. In each case, these issues should be easily resolved.

With these weights frozen, we then used viruses introduced to later WildLists to test GKII's performance on viral samples that were unknown at the time of training. The results of this test are shown in Table 1.

The experiment then continued by executing the new viruses reported to the WildList for each month from January 2003 through March 2004. Of the 151 new viruses, 126 were detected (83.4%) without any modification to the threat weights. Of the 25 viruses that were not detected, the false negatives appear to be caused by monitoring issues as opposed to a weakness in the GKII detection algorithm.

Month	Possible	# Detections	Percent
Jan 03	11	10	90.9
Feb 03	2	2	100.0
Mar 03	3	3	100.0
Apr 03	13	10	76.9
May 03	5	5	100.0
Jun 03	21	20	95.2
Jul 03	9	7	77.8
Aug 03	0	0	0.0
Sep 03	13	12	92.3
Oct 03	9	8	88.9
Nov 03	4	2	50.0
Dec 03	3	3	100.0
Jan 04	13	9	69.2
Feb 04	2	2	100.0
Mar 04	43	33	76.7
Total	**151**	**126**	**83.4**

Table 1: Detection results from GKII when examining previously unseen viruses found in the wild.

These results prove that GKII can provide reliable virus detection given samples that differ from those in the training set.

Weaknesses of the Gatekeeper Approach

Although the Gatekeeper approach has many benefits, it is not without certain weaknesses. In this section, we will examine what we consider to be the two most important unresolved problems: undo issues and targeted attacks.

Undo Issues

Although the undo technology within Gatekeeper is very powerful, there are several issues that cannot be adequately handled. Essentially, they can be broken into two types of problems: non-reversible actions, and race conditions within the Undo Engine.

In the first class of problems, Gatekeeper is clearly unable to reverse actions that affect other machines, such as opening connections to remote machines or sending email. While this is not ideal, from a macroscopic standpoint some leakiness of protection is acceptable: if Gatekeeper were ubiquitous, the overall suppression of virus spread would be sufficient to prevent an epidemic.

In the second class of problems, the solution is more difficult. Consider the following scenario. Two programs both make modifications to the same file. After time t Gatekeeper determines that the changes from Program A were hostile, and desires to reverse the modified file to its previous state. However, this is not possible, because if the modified code is reversed to the time prior to its original modification, the changes made by Program B are lost. If only the changes made by Program A are undone, the file is left in an uncertain condition as it is possible that some structural changes made by Program B relied on the changes made by Program A Thus, in this instance there is no reliable way to reverse the observed changes.

It is our belief that this problem is impossible to solve analytically, as the necessary information is simply not available. It is impossible to know with surety that the changes made by Program B were not as a direct consequence of the changes made by Program A. However, while this is clearly an important theoretical problem, we question how often this issue would occur in practice. Virus detection is likely to be an exception to normal operation, and so for most programs, undo problems are a non-issue. Even when a virus is detected, a second program must access the changed files before the Undo Engine is invoked for the problem to occur. It is our belief that this scenario will occur very rarely; in such a circumstance, the user would be warned, and prompted for further information about the ultimate decision.

Based upon the arguments here, we believe that these challenges to the Undo Engine are important, but not sufficient to render the approach impractical.

Targeted Attacks

One of the areas that is most difficult to resolve is the challenge of a targeted attack – that is, an attack where a virus writer creates a virus that is designed to either evade Gatekeeper's monitoring engine, or to avoid detection based upon GKII's rule set. This type of attack is very dangerous, as the attacker holds all the advantages: each attack can be tried repeatedly and modified until a weakness in the detection mechanism can be found. A virus or worm could then be released that is known to be immune to GKII.

We have taken a number of countermeasures within GKII in order to make this type of attack is more difficult to carry out; however, we acknowledge that GKII's defenses could be breached by a determined attacker.

Perhaps the most important defense against directed attack is GKII's tight integration with the Win32 API. As such, attempts to unhook GKII's monitoring components can be intercepted and denied at runtime. Due to the strong control of the program of study's interactions with the underlying operating system, evasion of the monitoring engine will be no trivial task. Finally, advances in trusted computing, such as *Microsoft's* NGSCB, should provide a secure reference monitor from which it should be possible to retrieve and process information (see [Microsoft2004] for an overview of NGSCB's features).

The addition of multiple detection engines is also a significant hurdle for an attacker to overcome; techniques that evade detection by one engine are likely to peak the threat level in another. For example, a virus that randomly inserts "harmless" Win32 calls into an attack is highly likely to appear suspicious when examined from a PST standpoint.

Lastly, we suggest that the ultimate goal of GKII is arguably not to create an antivirus solution that is bulletproof –such a solution is demonstrably impractical – but to create a solution that significantly raises the bar in terms of the knowledge required to evade detection by generic techniques. If one of the side-effects of the GKII deployment is that virus writers must write viruses that spread more slowly in order to minimize behavioral signatures, the problem once again becomes amenable to solution by existing reactive techniques.

Suggestions for Further Work

The largest problem with generic virus detection is its tendency to become stuck in a continual update cycle, as is the case with virus-specific techniques. As a virus writer finds a way to evade the detection method of a product, those methods will be patched and a solution provided.

We believe that there is a dearth of solid work in creating future-proof antivirus solutions – that is, solutions where it is not "free" for an attacker to experiment with impunity. We have proposed such "distributed" anti-virus systems elsewhere [Ford2004a], but essentially it is our belief that focus needs to shift from atomic end point protection, which is by its nature highly susceptible to being reverse engineered, to more holistic solutions that attempt to protect the network itself. As GKII's detection in the absence of targeted attacks is very high, it is clear that at least in principle it is possible to provide for reliable virus suppression. The next step in improvement is to make it difficult to reverse engineer the underlying algorithm with impunity.

Any system that provides atomic endpoint protection in a standalone environment will be susceptible to a reverse engineering attack: an aggressor can simply isolate the system and study it until it is understood. If it were possible to distribute a protection scheme, however, it would be significantly more difficult to create a virus or worm that was known to be effective on a macroscopic scale. Such an undertaking is not likely to be easy, as it requires defenders to anticipate potential attacks; however, it is crucial that the Internet is not left vulnerable to carefully-crafted directed attacks by well-capitalized attackers.

Conclusion

GKII represents an important improvement in state-of-the-art behavioral detection. By operating at runtime, it is immune to polymorphism and entry point obfuscation. Additionally, it is excellent at preventing worms that result from buffer overruns, where the malcode is not actually present at the time of execution, but is contained in the application data.

Improvements over GKI have been examined; these provide for better discrimination between good and bad behaviors as well as improved performance. Experimental results show good tracking of detection as a function of time, indicating that the update cycle of Gatekeeper is likely to be significantly longer than for current antivirus products.

We believe that generic detection techniques represent the *only* way forward for virus suppression. Current solutions are fraught with problems and are unlikely to be scaleable to the low reaction times required to manage rapid malware. By proving that generic virus detection is possible, further work in *distributed* virus suppression is encouraged – this approach is required for long-term virus resilience of our networks.

We would like to thank Geoff Mazeroff for helpful discussions in the preparation of this paper, and the Office of Naval Research (Award Number N00014-01-1-0862) for support in the ongoing development of Gatekeeper.

Bibliography

Allen2003 Allen W.A., *Analysis, Detection and Modeling of Attacks in Computer Communications Networks*, PhD Dissertation, University of Central Florida, August 2003

Ford2004 Ford, R.A., Thompson H.H., *The Future of Proactive Virus Detection*. From the Proceedings of the EICAR Conference, Luxembourg 2004

Ford2004a Ford R.A., *The Wrong* Stuff, Preprint. To be published in IEEE S&P 2004

Heller2003 K.A. Heller, K.M. Svore, A. Keromytis, S.J. Stolfo, *One Class Support Vector Machines for Detecting Anomalous Windows Registry Accesses*, in the proceedings of the workshop on Data Mining for Computer Security (at IEEE ICDM-2003).

Mazeroff2003 G. Mazeroff, V. De Cerqueira, J. Gregor, and M. Thomason. *Probabilistic Trees and Automata for Application Behavior Modeling*, in Proceedings of the 41st Annual ACM Southeast Conference, 2003. Savannah, GA. 2003.

Microsoft2004, Microsoft, *Next Generation Secure Computing Base*, available online at http://www.microsoft.com/resources/ngscb/default.mspx 2004

Wagner2004, Wagner M., *Behavior Oriented Detection of Malicious Code at Run-Time*, M.Sc. thesis, Florida Institute of Technology. Available online at http://www.se.fit.edu/gatekeeper/papers/bodmalcode.pdf 2004

Williamson2003 Williamson M., Leveille J., *An Epidemiological Model of Virus Spread and Cleanup*. From the Proceedings of the Virus Bulletin Conference, 2003.

CHAPTER 5

Dependable Critical Information Infrastructure for Command and Control

Robert Herklotz and Chris Arney

Dependable critical information infrastructure for command and control focuses on mathematics, science, and engineering that will eventually lead to applications and technologies that protect the military's critical command and control systems. The military's command and control network infrastructure must provide authentic, accurate, secure and reliable services under a full range of conditions and threats. This initiative develops predictive techniques for network protection and enhances network situational awareness in command and control systems. Essential to this work are the development of proper performance metrics, the establishment of a base-line theoretical mathematical foundation, the implementation of case studies in the form of multidisciplinary prototypes, and empirical analysis of the performance metrics to link the theory to the practice in this area of information assurance application. The project researchers use robust, adaptive, computationally efficient techniques for analyzing high-speed, high-fidelity networks like those used in command and control. Techniques for detecting attacks, masquerading, covert data transfer, data corruption or subversion, and unauthorized use of resources are all important to insure a dependable infrastructure. In addition, these techniques must adapt to and discover new attack methodologies, determine if newly identified attack methodologies are present, trace subtle or recently uncovered attacks, support post-incident forensic analysis, and characterize general network behavior and performance.

As networking and high-speed interconnectivity become more essential to command-and-control capabilities, it is important that the network be as free of vulnerabilities as possible. The ability to detect anomalies in network behavior or the presence of unauthorized traffic in very high-speed networks is a key enabler for protecting the information infrastructure from compromise. Without the commitment to implement continual infrastructure protection, the threats quickly outstrip protections. Two critical components for progress in this area are the development of methodology for measuring infrastructure protection capability (that is, people, practices, and technology) and the development of tools to help those responsible for protection of the infrastructure to monitor the level of protection. This work involves modeling and simulation (M&S) of complex computer-based infrastructures (like command-and-control networks), calibration of M&S processes with empirical and experimental results, and performing operations research assessments to determine when and how to use the tools and methodologies.

Other important research issues include threat pattern identification and extrapolation, intrusion forecasting, automated profiling and prediction, alarm thresholds, and adaptation. The trade-offs between monitoring, analysis and reporting techniques and system performance and efficiency are important topics in this investigation. To be successful, these techniques need to provide real-time support and be scalable and applicable to very high-speed dynamic distributed networks. The result of this research effort is the ability to generate a network status report and forecast, and then to use that knowledge to automatically modify the behavior of network assets to mitigate the effects of actual and anticipated threats. This process is critical to command and control networks.

This chapter presents technical papers from four CIP MURI teams working on the following aspects of dependable critical information infrastructure for command and control:

- Establishment of full situation awareness
- Effective networked command and control
- Deceptive data detection and deceptive behavior modeling

The paper "Applications of Feedback Control in Information Network Security" by the Harvard MURI team describes a new and promising feedback control methodology for complex network protection and a hierarchical architecture for networks intended to maximize security. The guiding principle of this research is that network defense must be automated—manual intervention is too slow and unreliable. The paper "Anomaly Detection Using Call Stack Information" by Feng *et al.* describes a call stack methodology for detecting anomalies (intrusions). The authors show results of their experiments and compare their methods with other approaches. As is often the case, better security systems can be formed by layering and combining methods, but performance will always suffer in such circumstances. Both papers show the value of establishing proper performance metrics and the synergy of combining theoretical and empirical analysis.

The summary paper "Detecting Deception in the Military Infosphere: Improving and Integrating Detection Capabilities with Automated Tools" by the University of Arizona team presents their latest work on detecting and countering deceptions. The paper "Adaptable Situation-Aware Secure Service-Based (AS^3) Systems" presents their research on the situation awareness model in service-based systems. Based on this model, situation-aware agents are developed to incorporate situation-awareness and adaptive coordination in service-based systems. The Cornell MURI team has been working on diffuse computing and the summary paper titled "Software Quality and Infrastructure Protection for Diffuse Computing" captures their research outcomes.

Software Quality and Infrastructure Protection
for Diffuse Computing

J. Feigenbaum, J.Y. Halpern, P.D. Lincoln, J.C. Mitchell, A. Scedrov,* J.M. Smith,† and P. Syverson

Abstract

Diffuse computing is concerned with managing and maintaining a computational infrastucture that is distributed among many heterogeneous nodes that do not trust each other completely and may have differing incentives, needs, and priorities. As commercial, academic, civilian, government, and military systems become increasingly diffuse, the challenges of providing reliable and trustworthy diffuse systems become increasingly important.

Diffuse computational systems require new software design and engineering methodologies. Components are combined on an as-needed basis, but, given the increasing scale and complexity of modern distributed systems such as the WWW, the rigorous methodological support has failed to materialize in any form. With the local autonomy that characterizes large-scale distributed systems, global design and analysis may in fact be impossible.

In this paper we survey the research partially supported by OSD/ONR CIP/SW URI "Software Quality and Infrastructure Protection for Diffuse Computing" through ONR Grant N00014-01-1-0795. We develop fundamental understanding, models, algorithms, and network testbed, in order to reduce cost, improve performance, and provide higher reliability for networked operations across untrusted networks. We take a synergistic approach, combining several complementary thrusts: incentive-compatibility in distributed computation, authorization mechanisms, infrastructure and secure communication protocols, privacy and anonymity, and networking. We study a market system of autonomous agents that realistically model the behavior of a large-scale distributed system. Rules imposed on the market system ("mechanism design") allow global desiderata to be achieved in spite of local autonomy. In this way, the behavior of the software as a system can be described formally in spite of incomplete knowledge. We carry out the initial development of such a methodology and the construction of a multi-institutional experimental platform upon which we can prototype this software-quality methodology. This will open up a whole new range of "global" software-design techniques that work in today's and tomorrow's systems.

These advances, leading to new software technology, will ensure greater confidence in critical national infrastructures that depend so much on information technology.

Keywords: incentive-compatibility, authorization, network protocols, privacy, anonymity, networking. ACM Computing Classification: C.2.2 Network Protocols, F.2.2 Nonnumerical Algorithms and Problems, F.3.1 Specifying and Verifying and Reasoning about Programs, E.3 Data Encryption, C.2.1 Network Architecture and Design, K.6.5 Security and Protection.

---

*P.I. of the project. University of Pennsylvania, Philadelphia, PA 19104. scedrov@math.upenn.edu

†The work reported by J.M. Smith was completed before December 31, 2003.

‡External collaborator.

1   Diffuse computing

Advances in networking, web services, business infrastructure, and mass market demands have led to the emergence of a new computing paradigm that we will refer to as *diffuse computing*. In this paradigm, the focus is shifting from self-contained computers and client-server clusters to constellations of services that work together. Already, private companies provide free email management and storage, free mailing list and web page management, free storage for digital photo collections, and other web-based services that obviate the need for individuals to install, maintain and host software to provide these functions. On a larger, corporate scale, more and more computing services are being outsourced. Web-site hosting, caching, network delivery, and other services are provided by contract organizations that manage and maintain the required software, hardware, and network connectivity. On a more dynamic level, mobile code mechanisms and dynamic service platforms such as Jini, http://www.jini.org/, allow the installed code of a running system to change rapidly, in the process of performing a single or multiple simultaneous tasks. Driven by the potential for improved functionality, better interoperability, and the need for networked operations in all walks of life, the common "computer system" used by an individual or organization no longer consists of an identifiable set of applications running on an identifiable hardware configuration linked to the network through a single point of access or firewall. Instead, daily computing draws on a constellation of services provided by various sites on the network, each autonomously administered and updated by the provider of the service.

A related phenomenon is the rapid rise in prominence of peer-to-peer software systems, in which a single task may be distributed among a dynamically changing set of available computers, linked through network paths of different capacity. Prominent and emerging peer-to-peer examples include *distributed.net*, http://www.distributed.net/index.html.en, an organization allowing thousands of computers around the world to participate in mathematics and cryptography challenges, the *Folding@Home* project, please see information available on http://www.stanford.edu/group/pandegroup/Cosm/, distributing a "screen saver" that allows users to contribute computing resources to protein-folding simulations, and the *Casino-21* project http://www.climate-dynamics.rl.ac.uk/˜hansen/casino21.html in which more than 20,000 people worldwide already have volunteered to contribute their personal computers' off-hours power to a scientific experiment that will attempt to forecast the climate of the 21st century.

Staggering computational power and information resources can be assembled from a collection of small to moderate sized computing devices, coordinated over a network: distributed.net's computing power is more than 160,000 PCs working 24 hours a day, 7 days a week, 365 days a year! From a positive standpoint, pressing world problems can conceivably be solved by peer-to-peer systems. On a smaller scale, a collection of networked personal devices, carried on the body and/or installed in a vehicle, can work together to provide significant coordinated computing power as needed, making the whole greater than the sum of its parts, not only in power but in reliability and resistance to faults or corruption.

Diffuse computing has other advantages besides computational power. It also provides mobility, scalability, ease of maintenance, and fault tolerance. Mobility follows from the diffuse nature of the medium. If an individual draws computing services from a network, then those services may be preserved as the individual (or computing device, or an embedded computer) moves around physically or around the network. Scalability arises from the ability to switch vendors or aggregate services. For example, if information storage and retrieval is outsourced to a storage vendor, then a client may buy more storage if more is needed, or aggregate the services of more than one vendor if greater reliability through replication is desired. Maintenance becomes the obligation of service providers, who may accrue resulting economies of scale. Dynamic service installation also simplifies maintenance in a way that usefully decouples subsystems: if a client caches an interface implemented in mobile code, and refreshes periodically, this automatic process keeps the client current with upgrades, bug fixes, and performance enhancements provided by the service. By using homogeneous peer-to-peer designs without a centralized server, systems no longer are vulnerable to a single point of failure.

Given these advantages, it seems clear that diffuse computing is here to stay. In time, we expect individuals and organizations to be able to draw all of their computing needs from a diffuse collection of network-available services, including information aggregation, information storage and retrieval, and high-powered compute services that provide compute cycles on a contract basis. Diffuse computing not only has an appeal for individuals and private enterprises who may draw on a collection of internet services, but also provides a useful computational model for a large organization that is heterogeneous and geographically distributed. The concept of diffuse computing is further validated by the related subsequent developments such as *grid computing*, see http://www.grid.org and http://www.worldcommunitygrid.org, among others.

Unfortunately, along with all of its benefits, diffuse computing also opens the door to enormous risks. The same principle that allows difficult number-theoretic problems to be solved by distributed.net also allows a similar coalition to flood parts of the network with massive denial-of-service attacks, crack codes of banks or government installations, process surveillance information without the knowledge of innocent individuals running innocuous screen savers, and so on. The 2000 "tribal flood network" distributed denial-of-service attack using a coordinated network of compromised machines illustrates the potential for network-based attack, see http://www.securiteam.com/securitynews/5YP0G000FS.html. In addition, diffuse computing heightens security concerns, since an individual or operational unit cannot trust the providers of some or all of the services they rely upon.

In short, diffuse computing offers great potential to those who will understand its strengths and pragmatic operational properties, and great risk to those who fail to understand the potential threats and employ conceivable countermeasures.

We undertake a comprehensive study of the software infrastructure needed for diffuse computing. We combine several complementary thrusts: incentive-compatibility in distributed computation, authorization mechanisms, infrastructure and communication protocols, privacy and anonymity, and networking. One particular focus is the study of market systems of autonomous agents that realistically model the behavior of large-scale distributed systems. Rules imposed on the market system ("mechanism design") allow global desiderata to be achieved in spite of local autonomy. We carry out the initial development of such a software-quality methodology, including a systematic, formal treatment of underlying models, algorithms, and data structures, and the construction of a multi-institutional experimental platform upon which we can prototype it. This will open up a whole new range of "global" software-design techniques that work in today's and tomorrow's systems.

These advances, leading to new software technology, will ensure greater confidence in critical national infrastructures that depend so much on information technology.

2 Challenges in diffuse software infrastructure

In this section, we consider in more detail some of the issues involved in designing appropriate software for diffuse systems and our work.

2.1 Market-based computation

In designing efficient, distributed algorithms and network protocols, computer scientists typically assume that users are either *cooperative* (*i.e.,* that they follow the protocol) or that they are faulty. The fault-tolerance community has considered various fault models, ranging from *crash* failures (where a faulty process simply crashes and does not take part in the protocol thereafter) to *Byzantine* failures (where a faulty process may actively try to disrupt a protocol) [17]. In contrast, game theorists design market mechanisms in which it is assumed that users are neither cooperative nor adversarial but rather *selfish*: They respond to well-defined incentives and will deviate from the protocol only for tangible gain. Until recently, computer scientists ignored incentive-compatibility, and game theorists ignored computational efficiency. Recent work on *algorithmic mechanism design* [36, 15] combines computational complexity and incentive-compatibility. We consider the combination of various fault and attacker models with incentive compatibility. That is, we consider resource-restricted selfish attacker behavior within a fault model containing simple as well as Byzantine faults. We use game-theoretic principles in designing efficient algorithms for the allocation of scarce resources in a diffuse computing environment. In addition, we explore the completely open question of whether user-privacy concerns can be "layered" on top of incentive-compatibility or whether privacy has to be combined with other desiderata in the original mechanism design. In the information-assurance community, Meadows is developing methods to make cryptographic protocols more resistant to denial of service by trading off the cost to defender against the cost to the attacker [33]. The work on market-based computation partially supported by this project includes [14, 16, 35]. In an example of an interaction between project sites made possible by this project, the work [35] at Stanford was motivated and influenced by [14, 16], which had been carried out at Yale and other institutions. In another example of cross-site collaboration, this research led to the recent work on rational secret sharing and multiparty computation [21] coauthored by faculty from Cornell and a student from Stanford, with additional support by the follow-up CIP/SW project "Trustworthy Infrastructure, Mechanisms, and Experimentation for Diffuse Computing" described on `http://www.cis.upenn.edu/group/spyce/timedc/`.

2.2   Authorization management

In centralized computing systems, and even in distributed systems that are closed or relatively small, authorization to use resources (*e.g.,* databases, web pages, corporate network gateways, *etc.*) is broken down into *authentication* ("who made this request?") and *access control* ("is the requestor authorized to use the resource?"). An emerging body of work on *trust management* (see, *e.g.,* [37, 13, 6, 29]) recognizes that this traditional approach will not work in the type of diffuse computing environment that we address in this proposal. We adopt the trust-management approach, in which a request may be accompanied by one or more "credentials," and the authorization question becomes "do these credentials prove that this request complies with the policy governing this resource?". In particular, we investigate the open or partially open issues of nonmonotonic policies, tools for formal analysis of security policies, and credential-storage and credential-retrieval. The work on authorization management partially supported by this project includes [22, 23, 31, 30].

2.3   Protocols for diffuse computation and secure communication

Diffuse computation requires new network protocols for locating and for maintaining an inventory of diffuse services and for secure and reliable communication among components of a diffuse system. Relevant research topics include:

1. *Developing efficient service-discovery protocols,* which allow components of a diffuse system to maintain contact and efficient routing among a dynamically changing set of cooperating components,

2. *Developing efficient service search techniques* that allow one component to find data or computational services from cooperating components,

3. *Developing secure and authenticated communication protocols* for diffuse services, including integration methods for applying distributed authorization management concepts,

4. *Extending and applying protocol design and analysis methods* to diffuse service protocols and related network protocols such as group key management and secure multicast protocols, and

5. *Developing new specification techniques* appropriate for specifying diffuse protocols, that take into account costs and uncertainty.

Reliable, secure communication is a cornerstone of assured diffuse computation since distributed services must be able to communicate reliably in the face of network unreliability, network-based interference or attack.

One of our efforts in this area is the cross-site collaboration on internet routing protocols [25, 26], which began while the authors were students at Penn and at Yale, respectively, partially supported by this project. The work on various aspects of network security protocol analysis partially supported by this project includes [7, 10] and a Penn-Stanford collaboration [34, 9, 11]. This work has led to security analysis and improvements of widely deployed protocols such as IEEE 802.11i wireless LAN [24] and PKINIT, a public-key version of Kerberos 5 [8]. In this regard we continue to be active on the IEEE and IETF standards boards. In the case of PKINIT our work [8] revealed a flaw requiring an August 2005 Microsoft security patch for Windows 2000, Windows XP, and Windows 2003.

2.4 Privacy and anonymity

Exponential growth in digital information gathering, storage, and processing capabilities inexorably leads to conflict between well-intentioned government or commercial datamining, and fundamental privacy interests of individuals and organizations. We develop a mechanism that provides cryptographic fetters on the mining of personal data, enabling efficient mining of previously-negotiated properties, but preventing any other uses of the protected personal data [27]. This in turn led to the recent work on privacy-preserving sharing and correlation of security alerts [32] partially supported by the follow-up CIP/SW project "Trustworthy Infrastructure, Mechanisms, and Experimentation for Diffuse Computing", which is described on http://www.cis.upenn.edu/group/spyce/timedc/. We also provide a framework for reasoning about information-hiding requirements in multiagent systems and for reasoning about anonymity in particular [19, 20]. Furthermore, we explore some reasons why diffuse anonymity systems are particularly hard to deploy, enumerate the incentives to participate either as senders or also as nodes, and build a general model to describe the effects of these incentives [1]. We introduce a new cryptographic technique which leads to new types of functionality in mixnet architectures [18]. We also investigate anonymity network topologies [12]. Dr. Syverson of the Naval Research Laboratory, one of the coauthors of this work, is an external collaborator of the project.

2.5 Networking

Increases in scale, complexity, dependency and security for networks have motivated increased automation of activities. Technology derived from active networking research can be used to develop a series of *network monitoring* systems. This approach allows users to customize the monitoring function at the lowest possible level of abstraction to suit a wide range of monitoring needs: we use operating-system mechanisms that result in a programming environment providing a high degree of flexibility, retaining fine-grained control over security, and minimizing the associated performance overheads [4, 3, 5]. We also investigate *proxy-based transcoding*, which adapts Web content to better match client capabilities (such as screen size and color depth) and last-hop bandwidths. Traditional transcoding breaks the end-to-end model of the Web, because the proxy does not know the semantics of the content. *Server-directed transcoding* preserves end-to-end semantics while supporting aggressive content transformations [28]. We also develop techniques for measuring Internet path properties, and we use these techniques to study network performance and protocol behavior. Our current focus in this regard is on *network tomography* tools that allow us to measure network-internal delays [2]. Researchers supported by this project who contributed to advances in networking include Dr. Knutsson, a postdoctoral researcher at Penn, and Mr. Anagnostakis, a graduate student at Penn. Networking research on this project has influenced both the theoretical research on anonymity systems [1] described above, as well as the treatment of congestion control in the design of implemented Navy systems such as Onion Routing, `http://www.onion-router.net/`.

The full list of publications stemming from our work on this project from its inception in May 2001 to date includes more than 70 publications and 5 software prototypes, all available on the project web site `http://www.cis.upenn.edu/spyce/`, which also includes a more detailed version of this survey.

We would like to thank Dr. Ralph Wachter of the Office of Naval Research for his most valuable advice and guidance. We would also like to thank Cynthia Dwork, Tim Griffin, and Vitaly Shmatikov for inspiring and productive scientific discussions and for their contribution to the project.

References

[1] A. Acquisti, R. Dingledine, and P. Syverson. On the economics of anonymity. In R.N. Wright, editor, *Financial Cryptography, FC 2003*, volume 2742 of *LNCS*. Springer Verlag, 2003.

[2] K. G. Anagnostakis and M. B. Greenwald. A hybrid direct-indirect estimator of network internal delays. In *Proc. of ACM SIGMETRICS'04*, 2004.

[3] K. G. Anagnostakis, M. B. Greenwald, S. Ioannidis, and S. Miltchev. Open Packet Monitoring on FLAME: Safety, Performance and Applications. In *Proceedings of the 4th International Working Conference on Active Networks (IWAN'02)*, December 2002.

[4] K. G. Anagnostakis, S. Ioannidis, S. Miltchev, J. Ioannidis, Michael B. Greenwald, and J. M. Smith. Efficient packet monitoring for network management. In *Proceedings of the 8th IFIP/IEEE Network Operations and Management Symposium (NOMS)*, pages 423–436, April 2002. (an earlier extended version of this paper is available as UPenn Technical Report MS-CIS-01-28, September 2001).

[5] K. G. Anagnostakis, S. Ioannidis, S. Miltchev, J. Ioannidis, and J. M. Smith. Efficient packet monitoring for network management. Technical Report MS-CIS-01-28, Computer and Information Science, The University of Pennsylvania, September 2001.

[6] M. Blaze, J. Feigenbaum, J. Ioannidis, and A. Keromytis. The role of trust management in distributed system security. In J. Vitek and C. Jensen, editors, *Secure Internet Programming: Security Issues for Distributed and Mobile Objects*, pages 185–210. Springer LNCS 1603, 1999.

[7] F. Butler, I. Cervesato, A. D. Jaggard, and A. Scedrov. An Analysis of Some Properties of Kerberos 5 Using MSR. In *Proceedings of the 15th Computer Security Foundations Workshop*, 2002.

[8] I. Cervesato, A. Jaggard, A. Scedrov, J.-K. Tsay, and C. Walstad. Unbinding AS-REP from AS-REQ in PKINIT. In *IETF-63, Kerberos Working Group*, 2005. http://www3.ietf.org/proceedings/05aug/slides/krb-wg-1.pdf.

[9] R. Chadha, J. C. Mitchell, A. Scedrov, and V. Shmatikov. Contract signing, optimism, and advantage. *Journal of Logic and Algebraic Programming, Special issue on Modelling and Verification of Cryptographic Protocols*, 64(2):189–218, 2005.

[10] A. Datta, A. Derek, J.C. Mitchell, and D. Pavlovic. A derivation system and compositional logic for security protocols. *Journal of Computer Security*, 13:423–482, 2005.

[11] A. Datta, A. Derek, J.C. Mitchell, A. Ramanathan, and A. Scedrov. Games and the impossibility of realizable ideal functionality. In S. Halevi and T. Rabin, editors, *3-rd Theory of Cryptography Conference (TCC 2006)*. Springer LNCS, 2006. Accepted for publication.

[12] R. Dingledine, V. Shmatikov, and P. Syverson. Synchronous batching: From cascades to free routes. In D. Martin and A. Serjantov, editors, *Privacy Enhancing Technologies, PET 2004*.

[13] C. Ellison. SPKI Certificate Documentation. http://world.std.com/~cme/html/spki.html.

[14] J. Feigenbaum, C. Papadimitriou, R. Sami, and S. Shenker. A BGP-based mechanism for lowest-cost routing. In *Proceedings of the 21st ACM Symposium on Principles of Distributed Computing (PODC '02)*, pages 173–182. ACM Press, New York, 2002.

[15] J. Feigenbaum, C. Papadimitriou, and S. Shenker. Sharing the cost of multicast transmissions. *Journal of Computer and System Sciences*, 63:21–41, 2001.

[16] J. Feigenbaum, R. Sami, and S. Shenker. Mechanism design for policy routing. In *Proceedings of the 23rd Symposium on Principles of Distributed Computing (PODC'04)*, pages 11–20. ACM Press, New York, 2004.

[17] M. J. Fischer. The consensus problem in unreliable distributed systems. Technical Report RR-273, Yale University, 1983. Also appears in *Foundations of Computation Theory*, ed. M. Karpinski, Lecture Notes in Computer Science, Vol. 185, Springer Verlag, 1983, pp. 127–140.

[18] P. Golle, M. Jakobsson, A. Juels, and P. Syverson. Universal re-encryption for mixnets. In Tatsuaki Okamoto, editor, *Topics in Cryptology – CT-RSA 2004*, volume 2964 of *LNCS*. Springer Verlag, 2004.

[19] J. Y. Halpern and K.R. O'Neill. Anonymity and information hiding in multiagent systems. In *Proc. 16-th IEEE Computer Security Foundations Workshop (CSFW)*, pages 75–88, 2003.

[20] J.Y. Halpern and K.R. O'Neill. Anonymity and information hiding in multiagent systems. *Journal of Computer Security*. To appear.

[21] J.Y. Halpern and V. Teague. Rational secret sharing and multiparty computation: Extended abstract. In *STOC*, pages 623–632, 2004.

[22] J.Y. Halpern and V. Weissman. Using first-order logic to reason about policies. In *Proc. 16-th IEEE Computer Security Foundations Workshop (CSFW)*, pages 187–201, 2003.

[23] J.Y. Halpern and V. Weissman. A formal foundation for XrML. In *Proc. 17-th IEEE Computer Security Foundations Workshop (CSFW)*, pages 251–263, 2004.

[24] C. He and J.C. Mitchell. Security analysis and improvements for IEEE 802.11i. In *11-th Annual Network and Distributed System Security Symposium (NDSS '05)*, 2005.

[25] A. Jaggard and V. Ramachandran. Robustness of class-based path-vector systems. In *Proc. 12-th International Conference on Network Protocols (ICNP)*. IEEE Computer Society Press, Los Alamitos, 2004.

[26] A. Jaggard and V. Ramachandran. Toward the design of robust interdomain routing protocols. *IEEE Network*, 19 (6), 2005.

[27] S. Jarecki, P. Lincoln, and V. Shmatikov. Negotiated privacy. In M. Okada, B. Pierce, A. Scedrov, H. Tokuda, and A. Yonezawa, editors, *Software Security - Theories and Systems. Mext-NSF-JSPS International Symposium, ISSS 2002*, volume 2609 of *LNCS*, pages 96–111. Springer Verlag, 2003.

[28] B. Knutsson, H. Lu, J. Mogul, and B. Hopkins. Architecture and performance of server-directed transcoding. *ACM Transactions on Internet Technology (TOIT)*, 3(4):392–424, November 2003.

[29] N. Li. *Delegation Logic: A Logic-based Approach to Distributed Authorization*. PhD thesis, New York University, September 2000.

[30] N. Li, J.C. Mitchell, and W.H. Winsborough. Beyond proof-of-compliance: Security analysis in trust management. *Journal of the ACM*. Accepted for publication.

[31] N. Li, J.C. Mitchell, and W.H. Winsborough. Beyond proof-of-compliance: Safety and availability analysis in trust management. In *IEEE Symp. on Security and Privacy, Oakland*, 2003.

[32] P. Lincoln, P. Porras, and V. Shmatikov. Privacy-preserving sharing and correlation of security alerts. In *Proc. 13-th USENIX Security Symposium*. USENIX Association, 2004.

[33] C. Meadows. A cost-based framework for analysis of denial of service in networks. *Journal of Computer Security*, 9 (1-2):143–164, 2001. Available in preprint form at http://chacs.nrl.navy.mil/publications/CHACS/CRYPTOindex.html.

[34] J.C. Mitchell, A. Ramanathan, A. Scedrov, and V. Teague. A probabilistic polynomial-time process calculus for the analysis of cryptographic protocols. *Theoretical Computer Science*, 2006. Accepted for publication.

[35] J.C. Mitchell and V. Teague. Autonomous nodes and distributed mechanisms. In M. Okada, B. Pierce, A. Scedrov, H. Tokuda, and A. Yonezawa, editors, *Software Security - Theories and Systems. Mext-NSF-JSPS International Symposium, ISSS 2002*, volume 2609 of *LNCS*, pages 58–83. Springer Verlag, 2003.

[36] N. Nisan and A. Ronen. Algorithmic mechanism design. *Games and Economic Behavior*, 35:166–196, 2001.

[37] R.L. Rivest and B. Lampson. Cryptography and Information Security Group Research Project: A Simple Distributed Security Infrastructure. www.toc.lcs.mit.edu/~cis/sdsi.html.

Games and the Impossibility of Realizable Ideal Functionality

Anupam Datta
Stanford University
danupam@cs.stanford.edu

Ante Derek
Stanford University
aderek@cs.stanford.edu

John C. Mitchell
Stanford University
jcm@cs.stanford.edu

Ajith Ramanathan
Stanford University
ajith@cs.stanford.edu

Andre Scedrov
University of Pennsylvania
scedrov@math.upenn.edu

Abstract

A cryptographic primitive or a security mechanism can be specified in a variety of ways, such as a condition involving a game against an attacker, construction of an ideal functionality, or a list of properties that must hold in the face of attack. While game conditions are widely used, an ideal functionality is appealing because a mechanism that is indistinguishable from an ideal functionality is therefore guaranteed secure in any larger system that uses it. We relate ideal functionalities to games by defining the *set* of ideal functionalities associated with a game condition and show that under this definition, which reflects accepted use and known examples, bit commitment, a form of group signatures, and some other cryptographic concepts do not have any realizable ideal functionality.

Reprinted with kind permission of Springer Science and Business Media from *Third Theory of Cryptography Conference, TCC 2006*, New York, NY, March 2006. *Lecture Notes in Computer Science*, Vol. 3876. pages 360–369. Copyright Springer-Verlag 2006.

1   Introduction

Many security conditions about cryptographic primitives are expressed using a form of game. For example, the condition that an encryption scheme is semantically secure against chosen ciphertext attack (IND-CCA2) [5] may be expressed naturally by saying that no adversary has better than negligible probability to win a certain game against a challenger. In this definition, the game itself clearly identifies the information and actions available to the adversary, and the condition required to win the game identifies the properties that must be preserved in the face of attack. Another way of specifying security properties uses ideal functionalities [1,7,20,27]. In this approach, referred to by some authors as Universal Composability (UC), an idealized way of achieving some goal is presented, possibly using mechanisms such as authenticated channels and trusted third parties that are not basic primitives in practice. An implementation is then considered secure if no feasible attacker can distinguish the implementation from the ideal functionality, in any environment. An advantage of this approach is that indistinguishability from an ideal functionality leads to composable notions of security [4,7,27]. In contrast, if a mechanism satisfies a game condition, there is no guarantee regarding how the mechanism will respond to interactions that do not arise in the specified game.

In this paper, we develop a framework for comparing game specifications and ideal functionalities, and prove some negative results about the existence of ideal functionalities in certain settings. While most known primitives have game-based definitions (see, e.g., [33]), it has proven difficult to develop useful ideal functionalities for some natural primitives. Some interesting issues are explored in [2,8], which describe a series of efforts to develop a suitable ideal functionality for digital signatures. In brief, there is a widely accepted game condition for digital signatures, existential unforgeability against chosen message attacks, formulated in [18]. However, there are many possible ideal functionalities that are consistent with this game condition. For example, a functionality could either explicitly disclose information about messages that were signed in the past, or not disclose this information. More generally, given a game condition, it is often feasible to formulate various functionalities that satisfy the game condition yet reveal varying kinds of "harmless" information that does not seem relevant to the goals of the mechanism.

If we have a game or set of games that define a concept like secure encryption, digital signature, or bit-commitment, then we would like to identify precisely the set of possible ideal functionalities associated with each game condition. Since an ideal functionality is intended to be evidently secure by construction, we propose that an *ideal* functionality must satisfy the given game condition on information-theoretic grounds, rather than as a result of computational complexity arguments. Applied to encryption, for example, this means that an ideal functionality for encryption must not provide *any* information about bits of the plaintext to the adversary. Our definition of *ideal functionality* for a set of game conditions is consistent with the all examples we have found in the literature, and reflects the useful idea that it should be easier to reason about systems that use an ideal functionality than about systems that use a real functionality. Using our definition, we show that while bit-commitment may be specified using games, there is no realizable ideal functionality for bit-commitment. This may be seen as a negative result about specification using ideal functionality, since there are constructions of bit-commitment protocols that are provably correct under modest cryptographic assumptions (see, e.g., [17]). We also show that there is no realizable ideal functionality for other reasonable and implementable cryptographic primitives, including a form of group signatures and a form of symmetric encryption with integrity guarantees, under certain conditions that allow the encryption key to be revealed after it is used.

The intuition behind our impossibility result is relatively simple. Illustrated using bit-commitment, a good commitment scheme must have two properties: the commitment token must not reveal any information about the chosen bit, while subsequent decommitment must reveal a verifiable relationship between the chosen bit and the commitment token. These are contradictory requirements because the first condition suggests that tokens must be chosen randomly, while the second implies that they are not. Similar "decommitment" issues arise in symmetric encryption or keyed hash, if the encryption key is revealed after some messages using the key have been sent on the visible network. At a more technical level, our proof by contradiction works by showing that if there was a realization of the ideal functionality for bit-commitment, it could be transformed into a protocol for bit-commitment that achieves perfect hiding and binding without using a trusted third party. However, it is well known that such a protocol does not exist [17]. While impossibility results for group signatures and symmetric encryption could be proved by instantiating the general proof method, we present simpler proofs by reducing bit-commitment to these primitives.

In a previous study of ideal functionality for bit commitment, Canetti and Fischlin show that a particular ideal functionality for bit-commitment is not realized by any real protocol [9]. In related work, Canetti [7] shows that particular functionalities for ideal coin tossing, zero-knowledge, and oblivious transfer are not realizable. Canetti et al [12] show that a class of specific functionalities for secure multi-party computation are not realizable, while Canetti and Krawczyk [10] compare indistinguishability-based and simulatability-based definitions of security in the context of key-exchange protocols. Our results are more general since we prove that, given a *game* definition of a primitive, there is *no* realizable ideal functionality associated with that game condition. In addition, our proof is different in that it provides a reduction to a previous negative result independent of universal composability [17], and appears to apply immediately to many primitives. A related issue is the choice of so-called "setup assumptions," such as public-key infrastructure, and common reference string. Our negative results hold under some setup assumptions, such as the absence of shared private information, or the presence of presence of a trusted certificate authority (or PKI), and fail for other setup assumptions, such as the assumption of a common reference string. This is expected, since [9] construct a realizable ideal functionality in the common reference string model. We have yet to characterize precisely the set of possible setup assumptions under which our negative results hold.

While our general proof could be carried out using a number of computational models, we adopt a setting based on a form of process calculus. One advantage of this setting over interacting Turing machines [7, 17, 18] is a straightforward way of modularizing games that use a functionality. This is useful for defining primitives that are protocols, as opposed to local functions, by games. In principle, some version of our proof could be carried out using some version of Turing machines, augmented with separate function-call-and-return tapes for interacting with some form of oracle that performs public communication visible to the adversary.

Preliminary definitions are presented in Section 2, followed definitions of bit-commitment functionalities and the main impossibility proof in Section 3. Reductions from other primitives are given in Section 4, with concluding remarks in Section 5.

2 Preliminaries

2.1 Probabilistic Process Calculus

Process calculus is a standard framework for studying concurrency [23, 34] that has proved useful for reasoning about security protocols [1, 31]. This is more of a "software" model than a "machine" model, since process calculus expressions are a form of program defining a concurrent system. Two main organizing ideas in process calculus are actions and channels. *Actions* occur on channels and are used to model communication flows. *Channels* provide an abstraction of the communication medium. In practice, channels might represent an IP address and port number in distributed computing, or a region of shared memory in a parallel processor.

A probabilistic polynomial-time process calculus (PPC) for security protocols is developed in [21, 24, 25] and updated in more recent papers [30, 31]. The syntax consists of a set of *terms* that represent local sequential probabilistic polynomial-time computation and do not perform any communication with other processes, process *expressions* that can communicate with other processes, and *channels* that are used for communication. Terms contain variables that receive values over channels. There is also a special variable η called the *security parameter*. Each expression defines a set of *processes*, one for each choice of value for the security parameter. Each channel name has a bandwidth polynomial in the security parameter associated with it. The bandwidth ensures that no message gets too large and, thus, ensures that any expression can be evaluated in time polynomial in the security parameter.

Syntax of PPC   Expressions of PPC are constructed from the following grammar.

$$\mathcal{P} ::= \oslash \;\Big|\; \nu(c)\mathcal{P} \;\Big|\; \mathsf{in}(c, x).(\mathcal{P}) \;\Big|\; \mathsf{out}(c, \mathrm{T}).(\mathcal{P}) \;\Big|\; [\mathrm{T}].(\mathcal{P}) \;\Big|\; (\mathcal{P} \mid \mathcal{P}) \;\Big|\; !_{q(\eta)}(\mathcal{P})$$

Intuitively, $\oslash$ is the *empty process* taking no action. A process $\mathsf{in}(c, x).\mathcal{P}$ with an *input* operator waits until it receives a value for input variable x on the channel c and then proceeds with process $\mathcal{P}$. Similarly, an *output* $\mathsf{out}(c, \mathrm{T}).\mathcal{P}$ transmits that value of T on the channel c and then proceeds with $\mathcal{P}$. Channel names that appear in an input or an output operation can be either public or private, with a channel being private if it is bound by the *private-binding* operator, ν and public otherwise. Actions on a private channel bound by a ν are not observable outside the scope of the ν operator. Hence private channels can be used to provide a form of secure communication. The *match* operator [T], a form of "if", executes the expression that follows it iff T evaluates to 1. The *parallel composition* operator, |, applied to two expressions allows them to evaluate concurrently, possibly communicating over any shared channels. The *bounded replication* operator has bound determined by the polynomial q affixed as a subscript. The expression $!_{q(\eta)}(\mathcal{P})$ is expanded to the $q(\eta)$-fold parallel composition $\mathcal{P} \mid \cdots \mid \mathcal{P}$ before evaluation. There is also a syntactic notion of context in PPC. A *context* $\mathcal{C}[\,\cdot\,]$ is an expression with a hole $[\,\cdot\,]$ such that we can substitute any expression into the hole and obtain a well-formed expression. Contexts may be used to represent the environment or adversary that interacts with a protocol or process.

Evaluating PPC expressions   To evaluate an expression in PPC we choose a probabilistic scheduler that selects communication steps. We then evaluate every term and match that is not in the scope of an input expression. When we can no longer evaluate terms and matches, we select a pair of input and output expressions on the same channel according to the scheduler, erase the output expression and substitute the value transmitted by the output (truncated suitably by the bandwidth of the channel) for the variable bound by the input. This procedure is repeated until no communication steps are possible. Further discussion, and explanation of a number of issues related to probabilistic scheduling, are explained in [15, 16, 30, 31].

Equivalence relations over PPC   Two equivalence relations over PPC will prove useful for studying security issues. The first relation, *computational observational equivalence*, written $\cong$, relates two expressions just when, in any context, the difference between the distributions they induce on observable behavior (messages over public channels) is negligible in the security parameter η. Formally $\mathcal{P} \cong \mathcal{Q}$ just when $\forall$ contexts $\mathcal{C}[\ \cdot\ ].\forall$ observables o:

$$\text{Prob}\left[\text{evaluating } \mathcal{C}[\mathcal{P}] \text{ produces } o\right] - \text{Prob}\left[\text{evaluating } \mathcal{C}[\mathcal{Q}] \text{ produces } o\right] \text{ is negligible in } \eta$$

Since the evaluation of all expressions and contexts in PPC are guaranteed to terminate in polynomial-time, $\cong$ is a natural way to state that two expressions are computationally indistinguishable to a poly-time attacker. The second relation, *information-theoretic observational equivalence*, written $=$, relates two expressions just when they induce exactly the same distribution on observable behavior in all contexts. Formally $\mathcal{P} = \mathcal{Q}$ just when $\forall$ contexts $\mathcal{C}[\ \cdot\ ].\forall$ observables o:

$$\text{Prob}\left[\text{evaluating } \mathcal{C}[\mathcal{P}] \text{ produces } o\right] - \text{Prob}\left[\text{evaluating } \mathcal{C}[\mathcal{Q}] \text{ produces } o\right] = 0$$

As a consequence, we can use $=$ to state that two expressions are indistinguishable even to unbounded attackers.

2.2   Function calls and returns

Process calculus allows processes to be programmed in a modular way, with one process relying on another for certain computations or actions. For example, one process P might wish to send a number bit-by-bit on a channel d. This can be done by writing another process Q that handles all the communication on channel d for P. This process Q receives a number n on some channel c used only for communication between P and Q, and then sends the bits of n on a channel d as required. If P wants a return value, such as notification that Q has finished sending the message, then P can execute an input action on channel c immediately after sending the number n to Q. This pattern of sends and receives essentially works like an ordinary remote procedure call and return. If the channel c is private, we can think of this as a remote procedure call between one process and another on the same processor, through a loopback interface, or a remote procedure call between two processors behind a firewall that makes LAN traffic invisible to an external attacker.

We will refer to the pattern of sends and receive just described for processes P and Q as a *function call and return*. Function calls and returns turn out to be a very useful concept in structuring games that specify properties of cryptographic primitives. To give a relatively concise notation, we will write $\mathsf{Call}^\eta(\langle\mathtt{params}\rangle, \mathbb{C})$ returns $\langle\mathtt{vars}\rangle.\mathcal{P}$ for a call that sends (outputs) parameters **params** on calling channels $\mathbb{C}$, and then waits to receive (input) return values $\langle\mathtt{vars}\rangle$ before executing process $\mathcal{P}$. To emphasize that a function call and return hides the structure of Q from the calling process P, we sometimes refer to this as a *black-box call*. Since PPC provides private channels, a function call and return will always be done on a private channel to avoid exposing the parameters or return values to an adversary.

For every function call and return to proceed, there must be a process that waiting to receive the call and then send a return value. Rather than write out all the input and output actions associated with responding to a remote procedure call, we will simply write $\mathsf{Impl}[\mathbb{C}, \mathbb{D}]$ for a process that responds to blackbox calls on channels $\mathbb{C}$, possibly using channels in $\mathbb{D}$ for some other purpose.

For example, the process Q described above has the form $\mathsf{Impl}[c, d]$. since it receives function calls on channel c and performs public communication on channel d.

2.3   Interfaces and cryptographic primitives

In this paper, a *cryptographic primitive* is defined by an interface and a set of required security or correctness conditions that are expressible using the interface. The *interface* is the set of actions defined and applicable to the primitive, expressed as a set of function calls and returns. For example, the interface to an encryption primitive consists of calls to three probabilistic functions: key-generation, encryption, and decryption. A correctness condition for encryption is that the decryption of an encryption under the correct key returns the message encrypted. A semantically-secure encryption primitive must also satisfy a security condition stating that no probabilistic polynomial-time adversary can win a game that involves guessing which of two messages has been encrypted.

A *protocol* for a primitive is process that responds to a set of function calls and supplies the associated returns, without using any additional private communication. For example, RSA can be formulated as an encryption protocol that implements key-generation, encryption, and decryption. A *functionality* for a primitive similarly supports the given interface, but may use additional private communication (such as used for a trusted third party; see Section 3.3). These restrictions on private communication are meant to prevent abusing the security associated with private channels, which are not a realistic primitive on the open public network. However, there are no restrictions on the way a functionality can communicate or reveal information to the adversary. For example, a functionality for signatures [8] could let the attacker choose the bitstrings for signatures.

An *ideal functionality* for an interface and a set of game conditions is a functionality that satisfies the correctness conditions with high probability and satisfies the security conditions in an information-theoretic way (i.e., against an unbounded adversary).

2.4   Universal Composability

Universal composability [7, 9, 11–13] involves a protocol to be evaluated, an ideal functionality, two adversaries, and an environment. The protocol realizes the ideal functionality if, for every attack on the protocol, there exists an attack on the ideal functionality, such that the observable behavior of the protocol under attack is the same as the observable behavior of the ideal functionality under attack. Each set of observations is performed by the same environment. The intuition here is that the ideal functionality "obviously" possess a desired security property, possibly because the ideal functionality is constructed using a central authority, trusted third party, or private channels. Therefore, if a protocol is indistinguishable from an ideal functionality, the protocol must have the desired security property. In previous work, that which makes an ideal functionality "ideal" appears not to have been characterized precisely. Universal composability can be expressed as an equivalence relation in process calculus [15, 16], definitions relevant to this paper are summarized in Appendix A.

3   Functionalities for Bipartite Bit-Commitment

A bipartite bit-commitment protocol allows a principal A to commit on a bit b to the principal B. However, B gains no information about the bit b until A later opens the commitment. We therefore formulate bit-commitment using four function calls, one call for each principal in each phase of the commitment. After defining the interface for bipartite bit-commitment, we define the game conditions for bit commitment and prove that no ideal functionality for these game conditions is realizable. We stress that the game conditions for bit-commitment as formulated in this paper are equivalent to standard security notions [17, 26], and that they can be realized using standard cryptographic assumptions such as the existence of pseudorandom functions [26].

3.1 Commitment interface

A bipartite bit-commitment scheme provides four function calls:

$$\mathsf{SendCommit}^\eta(b, \mathbb{C}) \text{ returns } \langle \sigma \rangle \qquad \mathsf{GetCommit}^\eta(\mathbb{C}) \text{ returns } \langle \sigma \rangle$$
$$\mathsf{Open}^\eta(\sigma, \mathbb{C}) \text{ returns } \emptyset \qquad \mathsf{Verify}^\eta(\sigma, \mathbb{C}) \text{ returns } \langle \mathbf{r} \rangle$$

The initiator A commits to a bit using the call $\mathsf{SendCommit}^\eta(b, \mathbb{C})$ returns $\langle \sigma \rangle$, which communicates the commitment value over the channels in $\mathbb{C}$. Some state information σ is generated that can, amongst other things, be used to differentiate between different commitments and is needed to open the corresponding commitment. A responder B may receive a commitment from A by executing a call $\mathsf{GetCommit}^\eta(\mathbb{C})$ returns $\langle \sigma \rangle$ over the channels in $\mathbb{C}$, which may also returns some state information σ.

In the decommitment phase, the initiator A may open the commitment using the function call $\mathsf{Open}^\eta(\sigma, \mathbb{C})$ returns $\emptyset$, which uses the state information from the initial call to indicate which commitment is to be opened. The responder B can then verify the committed value by making the call $\mathsf{Verify}^\eta(\sigma, \mathbb{C})$ returns $\langle \mathbf{r} \rangle$. If verification succeeds, $\mathbf{r}$ contains the value of the committed bit. Otherwise, $\mathbf{r}$ is a symbol $\perp$ indicating failure.

3.2 Commitment correctness and security conditions

There are three conditions—correctness, hiding, and binding—on bit-commitment [17, 26]. After explaining each condition, we show that each can be stated as an equivalence. The equivalences are written using $\cong$, which give the game condition required of any implementation. With $\cong$ replaced by $=$, the same equivalences can be used to state the information-theoretic properties required for an ideal functionality. More precisely, an *ideal functionality for bipartite bit-commitment* is an implementation for the four function calls listed in the interface above such that the correctness property below is satisfied with high probability, and the hiding and binding properties of bipartite bit-commitment below are satisfied with an information-theoretic equivalence. It is easy to verify that the concrete functionality considered in [9] is an instance of the ideal functionality for bipartite bit-commitment.

Given a game condition, there is a canonical way of writing it as an indistinguishability between expressions. The basic idea is that, since $\cong$ quantifies over all contexts, any successful attack on the game condition can be translated into a similarly successful context that distinguishes between the two sides of the equivalence. Conversely, since all expressions and contexts in PPC are guaranteed to evaluate in polynomial time and since the class of terms is precisely the class of probabilistic poly-time functions, every successfully distinguishing context can be translated into a successful attack on the corresponding game conditions.

Hiding An implementation Impl is *hiding* if for an honest initiator, no adversary can gain, with non-negligible advantage, information about the committed bit. In other words, probability

P_{Adv} that the attacker Adv, after interacting with an honest initiator committing to a randomly chosen bit b, successfully guesses the bit b should be close to a half. Writing this property as an equivalence yields:

$$\nu(\mathbb{C}, c).(\mathsf{Impl}[\mathbb{C}, \mathbb{D}] \mid \mathsf{out}(c, \mathsf{rand}) \mid \mathsf{in}(c, b).\mathsf{SendCommit}^{\eta}(b, \mathbb{C}) \text{ returns } \langle \sigma \rangle.\mathsf{in}(d, b').\mathsf{out}(dec, b' \stackrel{?}{=} b))$$
$$\cong \quad \nu(\mathbb{C}, c).(\mathsf{Impl}[\mathbb{C}, \mathbb{D}] \mid \mathsf{out}(c, \mathsf{rand}) \mid \mathsf{in}(c, b).\mathsf{SendCommit}^{\eta}(b, \mathbb{C}) \text{ returns } \langle \sigma \rangle.\mathsf{in}(d, b').\mathsf{out}(dec, \mathsf{rand}))$$

Both expressions select a random bit and commit to it. The adversary (expressed as a context) interacts with the commitment protocol and tries to guess the committed-to value. The difference between the two expressions is that the LHS tests, over the channel dec, whether the adversary's guess matches the chosen bit, while the RHS assumes, again over the channel dec, that the adversary fails with probability $1/2$. Clearly, any successfully distinguishing context must guess the bit with non-negligible advantage, thereby proving the existence of an adversary that violates the hiding property. Hence, we can naturally express the hiding condition that for all Adv, the probability $P_{Adv} - \frac{1}{2}$ is negligible in η as a process calculus equivalence. To say that an implementation is perfectly or information-theoretically secure we require that $\forall Adv \colon P_{Adv} - \frac{1}{2} = 0$, which is the same as replacing $\cong$ by $=$ in the equivalence above.

Binding   The *binding* property is that no adversary can open a commitment to an arbitrary value. This condition can be restated using a game in which the adversary commits to a challenger (an honest responder), who then picks a random b and challenges the adversary to open the commitment to b. As an equivalence, it is stated as:

$$\nu(\mathbb{C}, d)(\mathsf{GetCommit}^{\eta}(\mathbb{C}) \text{ returns } \langle \sigma \rangle.\mathsf{out}(d, \mathsf{rand}) \mid$$
$$\mathsf{in}(d, b).\mathsf{out}(c, b).\mathsf{Verify}^{\eta}(\sigma, \mathbb{C}) \text{ returns } \langle \mathbf{r} \rangle.\mathsf{out}(dec, \mathbf{r} \stackrel{?}{=} b) \mid \mathsf{Impl}[\mathbb{C}, \mathbb{D}])$$
$$\cong \quad \nu(\mathbb{C}, d)(\mathsf{GetCommit}^{\eta}(\mathbb{C}) \text{ returns } \langle \sigma \rangle.\mathsf{out}(d, \mathsf{rand}) \mid$$
$$\mathsf{in}(d, b).\mathsf{out}(c, b).\mathsf{Verify}^{\eta}(\sigma, \mathbb{C}) \text{ returns } \langle \mathbf{r} \rangle.\mathsf{out}(dec, \mathsf{if} \ \mathbf{r} \stackrel{?}{=} \bot \ \mathsf{then} \ \mathsf{false} \ \mathsf{else} \ \mathsf{rand}) \mid \mathsf{Impl}[\mathbb{C}, \mathbb{D}])$$

Here both expressions wait for a commitment, and then challenge the adversary to open the commitment to a randomly chosen bit. The LHS tests whether the adversary successfully does so, whilst the RHS assumes that if the attempt to open does not fail (i.e., the result of Verify is not $\bot$) the adversary fails with probability $1/2$. Perfect binding is expressed by replacing $\cong$ with $=$ in the equivalence above.

Correctness   An implementation Impl is *correct* if an honest responder is able to verify an opened commitment by an honest initiator with overwhelming probability. This correctness property may be expressed as the process calculus equivalence.

$$\nu(\mathbb{C}, c)(\mathsf{out}(c, \mathsf{rand}) \mid \mathsf{in}(c, b).$$
$$\mathsf{SendCommit}^{\eta}(b, \mathbb{C}) \text{ returns } \langle \sigma_I \rangle.\mathsf{Open}^{\eta}(\sigma_I, \mathbb{C}) \text{ returns } \emptyset.\mathsf{in}(d, b').\mathsf{out}(dec, b \stackrel{?}{=} b') \mid \mathsf{Impl}[\mathbb{C}, \mathbb{D}]) \mid$$
$$\nu(\mathbb{C}')(\mathsf{GetCommit}^{\eta}(\mathbb{C}') \text{ returns } \langle \sigma_R \rangle.\mathsf{Verify}^{\eta}(\sigma_R, \mathbb{C}') \text{ returns } \langle \mathbf{r} \rangle.\mathsf{out}(d, \mathbf{r}) \mid \mathsf{Impl}[\mathbb{C}', \mathbb{D}])$$
$$\cong \quad \nu(\mathbb{C}, c)(\mathsf{out}(c, \mathsf{rand}) \mid \mathsf{in}(c, b).$$
$$\mathsf{SendCommit}^{\eta}(b, \mathbb{C}) \text{ returns } \langle \sigma_I \rangle.\mathsf{Open}^{\eta}(\sigma_I, \mathbb{C}) \text{ returns } \emptyset.\mathsf{in}(d, b').\mathsf{out}(dec, \mathsf{true}) \mid \mathsf{Impl}[\mathbb{C}, \mathbb{D}]) \mid$$
$$\nu(\mathbb{C}')(\mathsf{GetCommit}^{\eta}(\mathbb{C}') \text{ returns } \langle \sigma_R \rangle.\mathsf{Verify}^{\eta}(\sigma_R, \mathbb{C}') \text{ returns } \langle \mathbf{r} \rangle.\mathsf{out}(d, \mathbf{r}) \mid \mathsf{Impl}[\mathbb{C}', \mathbb{D}])$$

Here, both expressions pick a random bit, commit to it, and then try to open it. The LHS checks whether the verifier obtained the correct value for the bit, whilst the RHS assumes that the verifier gets the right value all the time.

3.3   Impossibility of Bit-Commitment

In this section, we show that no ideal functionality for bit-commitment can be realized. This generalizes the impossibility result for one particular functionality given in [9]. Other plausible bit-commitment functionalities can be constructed by adjusting the level of information and possible actions provided to the attacker by the functionality. For example, the functionality may let the attacker change the identity of the committer, hence making the commitment unauthenticated. Alternatively, the functionality may let the attacker change the committed bit if the attacker manages to correctly guess an internal secret of the functionality (since this is a low probability event, correctness still holds). Our proof shows that all of these variants (as well as further variants discussed in [9]) and their combinations are not realizable. Although we have not yet obtained a general characterization, our theorem applies under some setup assumptions, and fails in the common reference string model in accordance with the construction given in [9].

Our proof by contradiction roughly works as follows: given a real protocol $\mathcal{P}$ that realizes an ideal functionality $\mathcal{F}$ for bit-commitment, we construct another real protocol $\mathcal{Q}$ which provides the same correctness guarantee. However, in protocol $\mathcal{Q}$ all calls to the bit-commitment interface by principals are handled by copies of $\mathcal{F}$. As a consequence, $\mathcal{Q}$ provides perfect hiding and binding, which is a contradiction.

In order to state the theorem formally, we require some definitions. We say that $\mathcal{P}$ is a *real protocol* if each instance of $\mathcal{P}$ only communicates with one principal over a set of private channels. Intuitively, since it cannot communicate with two separate parties over private channels hidden from the adversary, a real protocol cannot act as a secure trusted third party. We say that a protocol $\mathcal{P}$ for bit-commitment is *terminating* when the following expression will, with high probability, produce the messages "go" and "done".

$$\nu(\mathbb{C})(\mathsf{SendCommit}^\eta(b, \mathbb{C}) \text{ returns } \langle \sigma_I \rangle.\mathsf{in}(c, z).\mathsf{Open}^\eta(\sigma_I, \mathbb{C}) \text{ returns } \emptyset.\mathsf{in}(d, z) \mid \mathcal{P}[\mathbb{C}, \mathbb{D}] \mid$$
$$\nu(\mathbb{C}')(\mathsf{GetCommit}^\eta(\mathbb{C}') \text{ returns } \langle \sigma_R \rangle.\mathsf{out}(c, \text{``go''}).\mathsf{Verify}^\eta(\sigma_R, \mathbb{C}') \text{ returns } \langle \mathbf{r} \rangle.\mathsf{out}(d, \text{``done''}) \mid \mathcal{P}[\mathbb{C}', \mathbb{D}])$$

Intuitively, if the function calls are implemented with $\mathcal{P}$, in the absence of the attacker two honest parties should be able to first finish the commitment stage, synchronize, and then finish the decommitment stage.

Theorem 1. *If $\mathcal{F}$ is an ideal functionality for bilateral bit-commitment, then there does not exist a terminating real protocol $\mathcal{P}$ that securely realizes $\mathcal{F}$.*

Before giving the proof, the following two lemmas will be useful. The first lemma states the well known fact [17] that perfect hiding and binding protocols for bit-commitment do not exist without a trusted third party. We omit the proof here. The second lemma states that any realization of $\mathcal{F}$ will also be correct for bit-commitment. The proof sketch is in Appendix B. Similarly, any realization of $\mathcal{F}$ will enjoy complexity-theoretic hiding and binding guarantees; however, we do not require this fact for the impossibility result.

Lemma 2. *There does not exist a terminating real protocol $\mathcal{P}$ which is correct with high probability, and both perfectly hiding and perfectly binding.*

Lemma 3. *If $\mathcal{P}$ is a terminating real protocol that securely realizes $\mathcal{F}$, then $\mathcal{P}$ is correct with high probability.*

Proof of Theorem 1. We assume that $\mathcal{P}$ securely realizes $\mathcal{F}$. It follows that for any configuration involving principals making use of $\mathcal{P}$, there exists a simulator $\mathcal{S}$ such that replacing the calls to $\mathcal{P}$ with calls to the simulator in conjunction with the functionality yields an indistinguishable configuration.

Consider the following real configuration when the environment plays the role of the responder honestly. It selects a bit and sends that bit to the initiator. The initiator then commits to

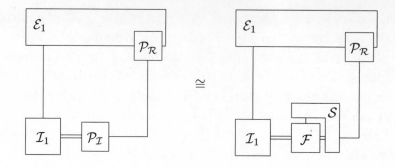

Figure 1: Configurations for the first step

that bit using a copy of the implementation $\mathcal{P}_{\mathcal{I}}$. The responder is corrupted by the adversary to simply forward messages to the environment. After corrupting the responder, the adversary simply forwards messages. The environment then honestly plays the responder's role using a copy of the real implementation $\mathcal{P}_{\mathcal{R}}$. At the conclusion of the commitment phase, the environment initiates decommitment by instructing the initiator to open. The environment then verifies the initiator's attempt to open, and then decides if the bit the initiator opened to was the bit the environment selected at the start of the run. The programs of the four principals are given below, where $\mathsf{Forward}(\mathbb{C} \leftrightarrow \mathbb{D})$ is an expression that forwards in an order-preserving way messages received on the channels $\mathbb{C}$ to channels $\mathbb{D}$ and vice versa:

$$
\begin{aligned}
\mathcal{E}_1 &\equiv \nu(\mathbb{C}, c)(\mathsf{out}(c, \mathsf{rand}) \mid \mathsf{in}(c, b).\mathsf{out}(\mathrm{IO}_I, b).\mathsf{GetCommit}^\eta(\mathbb{C}) \text{ returns } \langle \sigma \rangle.\mathsf{out}(\mathrm{IO}_I, \mathsf{open}). \\
&\qquad \mathsf{Verify}^\eta(\mathbf{r}, \mathbb{C}) \text{ returns } \langle \sigma \rangle.\mathsf{out}(dec, b \overset{?}{=} \mathbf{r})) \\
\mathcal{I}_1 &\equiv \nu(\mathbb{C}')(\mathsf{in}(\mathrm{IO}_I, b).\mathsf{SendCommit}^\eta(b, \mathbb{C}') \text{ returns } \langle \sigma' \rangle.\mathsf{in}(\mathrm{IO}_I, x).\mathsf{Open}^\eta(\sigma', \mathbb{C}') \text{ returns } \emptyset) \\
\mathcal{A}_1 &\equiv \mathsf{Forward}(\mathrm{Net}_I \leftrightarrow \mathrm{Net}_R) \\
\mathcal{R}_1 &\equiv \mathsf{Forward}(\mathrm{IO}_R \leftrightarrow \mathrm{Net}_R)
\end{aligned}
$$

This real configuration and its corresponding ideal configuration are shown in Figure 1 on the left and right, respectively (omitting the forwarders for clarity). Let us consider the ideal configuration. Here, the initiator uses the ideal functionality $\mathcal{F}$, whilst the environment continues using the real protocol. A simulator $\mathcal{S}$ must exist such that it can "convert" the messages of the functionality into messages that $\mathcal{P}_{\mathcal{R}}$ understands and vice versa. This simulator sits between $\mathcal{P}_{\mathcal{R}}$ and $\mathcal{F}$ and is connected to $\mathcal{F}$ via the bit-commitment interface and the unspecified interface of $\mathcal{F}$. Since $\mathcal{P}$ securely realizes $\mathcal{F}$, it follows that the configurations are indistinguishable. Furthermore, by Lemma 3 the environment in the real configuration must register success with high probability, since the adversary does nothing. Whence the expression $\mathcal{Q}$ consisting of $\mathcal{F}$ and $\mathcal{S}$ wired in the way that they are must be able to commit to $\mathcal{P}_{\mathcal{R}}$ and, then, successfully open the commitment.

Let us now consider another real configuration (Figure 2) where the initiator is corrupted to be a forwarder but the responder is honest. As before, the adversary, after corrupting the initiator, does nothing. The environment selects a bit and then runs the initiator's role directly. However, instead of using $\mathcal{P}$ to implement the initiator's role, the environment uses the expression $\mathcal{Q}$ from the first part of the argument. To commit, the environment sends the bit to the functionality whose messages are then translated by the simulator into messages suitable for the copy of the implementation $\mathcal{P}_{\mathcal{R}}$ used by the honest responder. After committing, the environment waits for a receipt from the responder, before decommitting. It then waits for the responder to send the bit it believes the initiator committed to and the environment checks that the bit it received was the same as the bit to which it committed. The responder, for its part, receives a commitment, sends a receipt to the environment, then verifies a commitment, and forwards the result to the

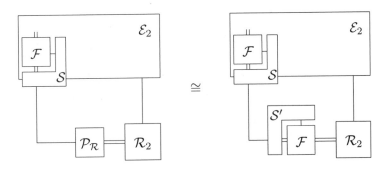

Figure 2: Configurations for the second step

environment. The programs are given below:

$$\mathcal{E}_2 \equiv \nu(\mathbb{C}, c)(\mathsf{out}(c, \mathsf{rand}) \mid \mathsf{in}(c, b).\mathsf{SendCommit}^\eta(b, \mathbb{C}) \text{ returns } \langle\sigma\rangle.\mathsf{in}(\mathrm{IO}_R, x).$$

$$\mathsf{Open}^\eta(\sigma, \mathbb{C}) \text{ returns } \emptyset.\mathsf{in}(\mathrm{IO}_R, b')\mathsf{out}(dec, b \stackrel{?}{=} b') \mid \mathcal{Q}[\mathbb{C}, \mathrm{IO}_R])$$

$$\mathcal{R}_2 \equiv \nu(\mathbb{C}')(\mathsf{GetCommit}^\eta(\mathbb{C}') \text{ returns } \langle\sigma'\rangle.\mathsf{out}(\mathrm{IO}_R, \mathsf{receipt}).\mathsf{Verify}^\eta(\mathbf{r}, \mathbb{C}') \text{ returns } \langle\sigma'\rangle.\mathsf{out}(\mathrm{IO}_R, \mathbf{r}))$$

$$\mathcal{A}_2 \equiv \mathsf{Forward}(\mathrm{Net}_I \leftrightarrow \mathrm{Net}_R)$$

$$\mathcal{I}_2 \equiv \mathsf{Forward}(\mathrm{IO}_I \leftrightarrow \mathrm{Net}_I)$$

In this scenario, the simulator $\mathcal{S}'$ sits between the expression $\mathcal{Q}$ (consisting of simulator $\mathcal{S}$ and functionality) and the functionality $\mathcal{F}$. Again, from secure realizability, Lemma 3, and the fact that $\mathcal{Q}$ looks like an initiator running the implementation $\mathcal{P}$, we know that in the real configuration, the environment will, with high probability, register a success. Therefore, so must the ideal configuration, whence the expression $\mathcal{Q}'$ consisting of $\mathcal{F}$ and $\mathcal{S}'$ must correctly play the role of the responder running the implementation $\mathcal{P}$.

If we look at the ideal configuration, we notice that the functionality is no longer working as a trusted third party. Every message is run through the simulators $\mathcal{S}$ and $\mathcal{S}'$. Thus, we have an implementation of bit-commitment that is a real protocol. The initiator executes the code given by the expression $\mathcal{Q}$ while the responder executes the code given by the expression $\mathcal{Q}'$. From the above argument it follows that the implementation $\mathcal{Q} \mid \mathcal{Q}'$ is a correct implementation. Furthermore, the $\mathcal{Q} \mid \mathcal{Q}'$ has to be information-theoretically hiding and binding because of the way they make use of the functionality. For example, to commit to a bit, the caller passes the bit to the functionality which, by definition, reveals no information about the bit regardless of the other parties in the configuration until the open step. Thus, we have a correct with high probability, and information-theoretically hiding and binding implementation of the bit-commitment interface that does not make use of trusted third parties. This contradicts Lemma 2. □

4 Generalization of the Impossibility Result and Other Examples

In this section we state a more general impossibility result: if $\mathcal{G}$ is a functionality and P is a protocol which uses $\mathcal{G}$ to achieve bit-commitment with perfect hiding and binding, then the functionality $\mathcal{G}$ cannot be realized. Intuitively, the functionality $\mathcal{G}$ together with protocol P constitutes an ideal functionality for bit-commitment $\mathcal{F}$, and any realization of $\mathcal{G}$ will lead to the realization of $\mathcal{F}$. Therefore, we would expect that all primitives that can be used to build bit-commitment are not realizable as functionalities. We illustrate this by showing that certain (rather strong) variants of symmetric encryption and group signatures cannot have realizable ideal functionalities. Due to space constrains, the security definitions are mostly informal and proof sketches have been moved to Appendix B.

Hybrid Protocols   We will consider implementations of primitives which, in addition to public channels, may use a particular functionality. Let $\mathcal{G}$ be any functionality, *a $\mathcal{G}$-hybrid protocol P* for a primitive is an implementation of the primitive's interface which does not make use of the trusted third party except maybe by making calls to $\mathcal{G}$'s interface. We will write $P[\mathcal{Q}]$ to denote an instance of P where are calls to $\mathcal{G}$'s interface are handled by the implementation $\mathcal{Q}$ (real or ideal).

Theorem 4. *If $\mathcal{G}$ is a functionality and P is a terminating $\mathcal{G}$-hybrid protocol for bit-commitment which is correct with high probability and provides perfect hiding and perfect binding, then no protocol realizes functionality $\mathcal{G}$.*

Symmetric Encryption   Symmetric encryption primitive is defined by the standard interface for key generation, encryption and decryption.

$$\mathsf{KeyGen}^\eta(\mathbb{C}) \text{ returns } \langle K \rangle \quad \mathsf{Encrypt}^\eta(K, p, \mathbb{C}) \text{ returns } \langle c \rangle \quad \mathsf{Decrypt}^\eta(K, c, \mathbb{C}) \text{ returns } \langle p \rangle$$

In addition to the obvious correctness property, we assume, as in [3], that the encryption scheme is CCA-secure and that it provides ciphertext integrity. Provably secure schemes with respect to these two properties exist under reasonable assumptions [32]. Informally, we can describe the properties as follows:

- *CCA-security* means that it is hard for an adaptive attacker with access to the decryption oracle to distinguish the plaintext from a random value of the same length given the ciphertext. *Perfect CCA-security* means that the probability of success is exactly half.

- *Integrity of ciphertexts* means that it is hard for an attacker to find a ciphertext c which will successfully decrypt unless that ciphertext has been produced by the encryption algorithm for some key and plaintext. *Perfect integrity of ciphertexts* means that the probability of an attacker finding such a ciphertext is zero.

Corollary 5. *If $\mathcal{F}$ is a functionality for symmetric encryption providing perfect CCA-security and perfect integrity of ciphertext then $\mathcal{F}$ cannot be realized.*

Group Signatures   Group signature primitive is defined by the interface for key generation, group signing, group signature verification and opening. For simplicity we will assume that the group is always of size two.

$$\mathsf{GKeyGen}^\eta(\mathbb{C}) \text{ returns } \langle gpk, gmsk, gsk_0, gsk_1 \rangle \quad \mathsf{GSign}^\eta(m, gsk, \mathbb{C}) \text{ returns } \langle sig \rangle$$
$$\mathsf{GVerify}^\eta(gpk, m, sig, \mathbb{C}) \text{ returns } \langle result \rangle \qquad \mathsf{GOpen}^\eta(gmsk, m, sig, \mathbb{C}) \text{ returns } \langle identity \rangle$$

In addition to the obvious correctness properties, we assume that the group signature scheme provides anonymity and traceability even against dishonest group managers. This is a stronger security requirement than the version principally considered in [6] (though [6] does briefly discuss this variant); [6] also shows that schemes with these properties exist if trapdoor permutations exist. Informally, we can describe the properties as follows:

- *Anonymity* means that it is hard for an adaptive attacker with access to an opening oracle to recover the identity of the signer given a signature and a message, even if the attacker has all the signing keys. *Perfect anonymity* means that the probability of success is exactly half (assuming, as we do, only two possible signers).

- *Traceability* means that it is hard for an attacker that adaptively corrupts a coalition of signers and has access to a signing oracle to produce a valid message-signature pair that opens to a signer not in the coalition, even when the group manager is dishonest. *Perfect traceability* means that the probability of an attacker forging such a signature is zero.

Corollary 6. *If $\mathcal{F}$ is a functionality for group signatures providing perfect anonymity and perfect traceability then $\mathcal{F}$ cannot be realized.*

5 Conclusion and Future Directions

We articulate accepted practice in the literature by giving a precise definition of an *ideal* functionality satisfying any given game specification: An ideal functionality must be a process or a set of processes that realize the game conditions in an information-theoretic, rather than computational complexity, sense. Using this definition we show that bit commitment, group signatures, and other cryptographic concepts that are definable using games do not have any realizable ideal functionality. This proof appears applicable to other functionalities, and to a range of so-called "setup assumptions." However, we have not yet characterized the applicable setup assumptions precisely.

An appealing property of indistinguishability-based specifications is the connection with composability: if a real security mechanism is indistinguishable from an ideal one, then any larger system using the real mechanism will behave in the same way as the same system using the ideal mechanism instead. In light of the limitations on indistinguishability-based specifications explored in this paper, there are several modifications to the basic theory that might provide useful forms of composability. One direction is to relax or modify the requirements for ideal functionality. For example, information-theoretic equivalence could be replaced with the indistinguishability of random systems in the sense of [22]. This would allow adaptive, computationally unbounded distinguishers to query the system at most polynomially many times in the security parameter. Another possible direction involves the modification of the Universal Composability framework recently considered in [28, 29], which allows a commitment functionality. In the modified framework, parties are typed in a certain way, and the typing must be respected by the simulator. On the other hand, since the intuition for some of these directions is not clear, it may be more productive to develop methods for stating and proving *conditional* forms of composability. More precisely, primitives and protocols could be guaranteed to operate securely only in environments that satisfies certain conditions. Games currently provide a very limited form of conditional composability, since a game condition provides guarantees for any system whose actions can be regarded as (or reduced to) moves in a relevant game. We also consider the work on protocol composition logic [14, 19] a potentially relevant form of conditional composability, since protocols or primitives proved correct in that framework carry guarantees that apply to any environment respecting certain invariants expressed explicitly in the logic.

References

[1] Martín Abadi and Andrew D. Gordon. A calculus for cryptographic protocols: the spi calculus. *Information and Computation*, 143:1–70, 1999. Expanded version available as SRC Research Report 149 (January 1998).

[2] Michael Backes and Dennis Hofheinz. How to break and repair a universally composable signature functionality. In *Information Security, 7th International Conference, ISC 2004, Proceedings*, volume 3225 of *Lecture Notes in Computer Science*, pages 61–72. Springer-Verlag, 2004.

[3] Michael Backes and Birgit Pfitzmann. Symmetric encryption in a simulatable Dolev-Yao style cryptographic library. In *CSFW '04: Proceedings of the 17th IEEE Computer Security Foundations Workshop*, pages 204–218. IEEE Computer Society, 2004.

[4] Michael Backes, Birgit Pfitzmann, and Michael Waidner. A general composition theorem for secure reactive systems. In *TCC '04: Proceedings of the 1st Theory of Cryptography Conference*, volume 2951 of *Lecture Notes in Computer Science*, pages 336–354. Springer-Verlag, 2004.

[5] Mihir Bellare, Alexandra Boldyreva, and Silvio Micali. Public-key encryption in a multi-user setting: Security proofs and improvements. In *Advances in Cryptology - EUROCRYPT 2000, International Conference on the Theory and Application of Cryptographic Techniques, Proceeding*, volume 1807 of *Lecture Notes in Computer Science*, pages 259–274. Springer-Verlag, 2000.

[6] Mihir Bellare, Daniele Micciancio, and Bogdan Warinschi. Foundations of group signatures: Formal definitions, simplified requirements, and a construction based on general assumptions. In *Advances in Cryptology - EUROCRYPT 2003, International Conference on the Theory and Applications of Cryptographic Techniques, Proceedings*, volume 2656 of *Lecture Notes in Computer Science*, pages 614–629. Springer-Verlag, 2003.

[7] Ran Canetti. Universally composable security: A new paradigm for cryptographic protocols. In *FOCS '01: Proceedings of the 42nd IEEE symposium on Foundations of Computer Science*, page 136, 2001. Full version available at http://eprint.iacr.org/.

[8] Ran Canetti. Universally composable signature, certification, and authentication. In *CSFW '04: Proceedings of the 17th IEEE Computer Security Foundations Workshop*, pages 219–233. IEEE Computer Society, 2004.

[9] Ran Canetti and Marc Fischlin. Universally composable commitments. In *Advances in Cryptology - CRYPTO 2001, 21st Annual International Cryptology Conference, Proceedings*, volume 2139 of *Lecture Notes in Computer Science*, pages 19–40. Springer-Verlag, 2001.

[10] Ran Canetti and Hugo Krawczyk. Analysis of key-exchange protocols and their use for building secure channels. In *Advances in Cryptology - EUROCRYPT 2001, International Conference on the Theory and Application of Cryptographic Techniques, Proceeding*, volume 2045 of *Lecture Notes in Computer Science*, pages 453–474. Springer-Verlag, 2001.

[11] Ran Canetti and Hugo Krawczyk. Universally composable notions of key exchange and secure channels. In *Advances in Cryptology - EUROCRYPT 2002, International Conference on the Theory and Application of Cryptographic Techniques, Proceeding*, volume 2332 of *Lecture Notes in Computer Science*, pages 337–351. Springer-Verlag, 2002.

[12] Ran Canetti, Eyal Kushilevitz, and Yehuda Lindell. On the limitations of universally composable two-party computation without set-up assumptions. In *Advances in Cryptology - EUROCRYPT 2003, International Conference on the Theory and Applications of Cryptographic Techniques, Proceedings*, volume 2656 of *Lecture Notes in Computer Science*, pages 68–86. Springer-Verlag, 2003.

[13] Ran Canetti, Yehuda Lindell, Rafail Ostrovsky, and Amit Sahai. Universally composable two-party and multi-party secure computation. In *STOC '02: Proceedings of the 34th annual ACM symposium on Theory of computing*, pages 494–503. ACM Press, 2002.

[14] Anupam Datta, Ante Derek, John C. Mitchell, and Dusko Pavlovic. A derivation system and compositional logic for security protocols. *Journal of Computer Security*, 13:423–482, 2005.

[15] Anupam Datta, Ralf Küsters, John C. Mitchell, and Ajith Ramanathan. On the relationships between notions of simulation-based security. In *TCC '05: Proceedings of the 2nd Theory of Cryptography Conference*, volume 3378 of *Lecture Notes in Computer Science*, pages 476–494. Springer-Verlag, 2005.

[16] Anupam Datta, Ralf Küsters, John C. Mitchell, Ajith Ramanathan, and Vitaly Shmatikov. Unifying equivalence-based definitions of protocol security. In *2004 IFIP WG 1.7, ACM SIGPLAN and GI FoMSESS Workshop on Issues in the Theory of Security (WITS 2004)*, 2004.

[17] Oded Goldreich. *Foundations of Cryptography: Basic Tools*. Cambridge University Press, 2000.

[18] Shafi Goldwasser, Silvio Micali, and Charles Rackoff. The knowledge complexity of interactive proof systems. *SIAM Journal on Computing*, 18(1):186–208, 1989.

[19] Changhua He, Mukund Sundararajan, Anupam Datta, Ante Derek, and John C. Mitchell. A modular correctness proof of TLS and IEEE 802.11i. In *ACM Conference on Computer and Communications Security*, 2005. To appear.

[20] Patrick Lincoln, John C. Mitchell, Mark Mitchell, and Andre Scedrov. A probabilistic poly-time framework for protocol analysis. In *ACM Conference on Computer and Communications Security*, pages 112–121, 1998.

[21] Patrick D. Lincoln, John C. Mitchell, Mark Mitchell, and Andre Scedrov. Probabilistic polynomial-time equivalence and security protocols. In *Formal Methods World Congress, vol. I*, number 1708 in Lecture Notes in Computer Science, pages 776–793. Springer-Verlag, 1999.

[22] Ueli M. Maurer. Indistinguishability of random systems. In *Advances in Cryptology - EUROCRYPT 2002, International Conference on the Theory and Application of Cryptographic Techniques, Proceeding*, volume 2332 of *Lecture Notes in Computer Science*, pages 110–132. Springer-Verlag, 2002.

[23] Robin Milner. *Communication and Concurrency*. International Series in Computer Science. Prentice Hall, 1989.

[24] John C. Mitchell, Mark Mitchell, and Andre Scedrov. A linguistic characterization of bounded oracle computation and probabilistic polynomial time. In *FOCS '98: Proceedings of the 39th Annual IEEE Symposium on the Foundations of Computer Science*, pages 725–733. IEEE Computer Society, 1998.

[25] John C. Mitchell, Ajith Ramanathan, Andre Scedrov, and Vanessa Teague. A probabilistic polynomial-time calculus for the analysis of cryptographic protocols (preliminary report). In *17th Annual Conference on the Mathematical Foundations of Programming Semantics*, volume 45. Electronic notes in Theoretical Computer Science, 2001.

[26] Moni Naor. Bit commitment using pseudorandomness. *Journal of Cryptology*, 4(2):151–158, 1991.

[27] Birgit Pfitzmann and Michael Waidner. Composition and integrity preservation of secure reactive systems. In *ACM Conference on Computer and Communications Security*, pages 245–254, 2000.

[28] Manoj Prabhakaran and Amit Sahai. New notions of security: Achieving universal composability without trusted setup. In *STOC '04: Proceedings of the 36th annual ACM symposium on Theory of computing*, pages 242–251. ACM Press, 2004.

[29] Manoj Prabhakaran and Amit Sahai. Relaxing environmental security: Monitored functionalities. In *TCC '05: Proceedings of the 2nd Theory of Cryptography Conference*, volume 3378 of *Lecture Notes in Computer Science*, pages 104–127. Springer-Verlag, 2005.

[30] Ajith Ramanathan, John C. Mitchell, Andre Scedrov, and Vanessa Teague. Probabilistic bisimulation and equivalence for security analysis of network protocols. Unpublished, see `http://www-cs-students.stanford.edu/~ajith/`, 2003.

[31] Ajith Ramanathan, John C. Mitchell, Andre Scedrov, and Vanessa Teague. Probabilistic bisimulation and equivalence for security analysis of network protocols. In *Foundations of Software Science and Computation Structures, 7th International Conference, FOSSACS 2004, Proceedings*, volume 2987 of *Lecture Notes in Computer Science*, pages 468–483. Springer-Verlag, 2004.

[32] Phillip Rogaway, Mihir Bellare, John Black, and Ted Krovetz. OCB: A block-cipher mode of operation for efficient authenticated encryption. In *CCS '01: Proceedings of the 8th ACM Conference on Computer and Communications Security*, pages 196–205. ACM Press, 2001.

[33] Victor Shoup. Sequences of games: a tool for taming complexity in security proofs. Cryptology ePrint Archive, Report 2004/332, 2004. `http://eprint.iacr.org/2004/332`.

[34] Robert J. van Glabbeek, Scott A. Smolka, and Bernhard Steffen. Reactive, generative, and stratified models of probabilistic processes. *International Journal on Information and Computation*, 121(1), August 1995.

A Universal Composability

Universal composability [7, 9, 11–13] involves a protocol to be evaluated, an ideal functionality, two adversaries, and an environment. The protocol realizes the ideal functionality if, for every attack on the protocol, there exists an attack on the ideal functionality, such that the observable behavior of the protocol under attack is the same as the observable behavior of the idealized functionality under attack. Each set of observations is performed by the same environment. The intuition here is that the ideal functionality 'obviously' possess a desired security property, possibly because the ideal functionality is constructed using a central authority, trusted third party, or private channels. Therefore, if a protocol is indistinguishable from an ideal functionality, the protocol must have the desired security property. In previous work, that which makes an ideal functionality "ideal" appears not to have been characterized precisely.

Universal composability can be expressed as a relation in process calculus [15, 16]. To give a form appropriate for the present paper, let $\mathcal{P}_1, \ldots, \mathcal{P}_n$ be n principals. We will assume that for some k, every principal $\mathcal{P}_i$ $(i > k)$ is in collusion with the adversary. Given an expression $\mathcal{P}$, we will write $\mathcal{P}[\mathbb{C}]$ to denote an instance of P running over the channels in $\mathbb{C}$. We say that an implementation Impl *securely realizes* a functionality $\mathcal{F}$ just when for any real world adversary $\mathcal{A}$, there exists a simulator $\mathcal{S}$ such that for any environment $\mathcal{E}$:

$$\nu(\mathbb{C}_1, \ldots, \mathbb{C}_k)(\mathcal{P}_1[\mathbb{C}_1, \mathbb{D}] \mid \cdots \mid \mathcal{P}_n[\mathbb{C}_n, \mathbb{D}] \mid \mathsf{Impl}[\mathbb{C}_1, \mathbb{D}] \mid \cdots \mid \mathsf{Impl}[\mathbb{C}_k, \mathbb{D}]) \mid \mathcal{A}[\mathbb{C}_{k+1}, \ldots, \mathbb{C}_n, \mathbb{D}] \mid \mathcal{E}$$
$$\cong \nu(\mathbb{C}_1, \ldots, \mathbb{C}_k)(\mathcal{P}_1[\mathbb{C}_1, \mathbb{D}] \mid \cdots \mid \mathcal{P}_n[\mathbb{C}_n, \mathbb{D}] \mid \mathcal{F}[\mathbb{C}_1, \ldots, \mathbb{C}_k, \mathbb{D}]) \mid \mathcal{S}[\mathbb{C}_{k+1}, \ldots, \mathbb{C}_n, \mathbb{D}] \mid \mathcal{E}$$

Here the first[1] k principals are assumed to be honest, and the remainder are assumed to be dishonest and acting in collusion with the adversary. To prevent the adversary/simulator from unfairly interfering with communications between the honest principals and the implementations (real or ideal), we make the links between the honest principals and the implementations private. Specifically, participant $\mathcal{P}_i$ uses private channels $\mathbb{C}_i$ to communicate with the implementation (real or ideal). The set of network channels $\mathbb{D}$ is used for communication between different participants. Both the adversary and the simulator have access to these channels.

Secure realisability requires that if we replace the real implementations Impl with an ideal implementation $\mathcal{F}$ (the functionality), there exists a simulator (that can interact with $\mathcal{F}$) which

---

[1]Since parallel composition is associative, the order in which we write the processes does not matter, and we may assume without loss of generality that the k honest principals occur first in the list.

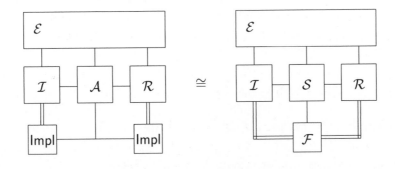

Figure 3: Real and ideal configurations with two honest participants

makes the ideal and real configurations indistinguishable. Another way to state this is that every real attack can be translated, using the simulator, into an attack on the functionality. We note that the principals that act in collusion with the attacker execute arbitrary programs and, in the ideal world, interact directly with the simulator (which mounts the ideal attack). Example configurations with two honest participants $\mathcal{I}$ and $\mathcal{R}$ are given in Figure 3.

B Proof Sketches

Proof sketch of Lemma 3. Consider a configuration consisting of an honest initiator running the implementation $\mathcal{P}$, an honest responder running the implementation $\mathcal{P}$, and an adversary that does nothing. The initiator waits for a bit from the environment and then commits to that bit. It then waits for a message from the environment and then opens its commitment. The responder, after receiving a commitment, sends a receipt to the environment. After a successful verification of an attempt to open the commitment, it sends the opened-to value to the environment. The environment selects a bit, sends it to the initiator and waits for a receipt from the responder. Once it gets this message, it instructs the initiator to open its commitment, and then waits for the responder to reveal the bit to which the initiator committed. If that bit matches the bit the environment selects at the start of the run, the environment registers success. Otherwise it registers failure.

By the terminating property of $\mathcal{P}$, we know that this run will complete. The ideal configuration has the initiator talking to the functionality which talks directly to the responder. Though a simulator exists in the ideal configuration, it can do nothing since both the initiator and responder are connected directly to the functionality. By virtue of the functionality's correctness, we know that in the ideal configuration the environment will register success with high probability. Since $\mathcal{P}$ securely realizes $\mathcal{F}$, the environment must register success in the real configuration with high probability. Whence the correctness of $\mathcal{P}$ is established. $\qquad\square$

Proof sketch of Theorem 4. Assume that P is a terminating $\mathcal{G}$-hybrid protocol for bit-commitment, which is correct with high probability and provides perfect hiding and binding. A functionality $\mathcal{F} = P[\mathcal{G}]$ is clearly an ideal functionality for bit-commitment. Let Q be a real protocol which is a realization of $\mathcal{G}$, consider a real protocol $R = P[Q]$ in which all the calls of P to the functionality $\mathcal{G}$ are implemented with Q. We claim that R is a secure realization of $\mathcal{F}$. Choose any real configuration for R, consisting of an attacker A, and parties $P_1, \ldots, P_n$. We need to show that there is a simulator S such that for any environment E this configuration is indistinguishable from one where parties call functionality $\mathcal{F}$ instead of R. This configuration is also a real configuration for the protocol Q. Therefore, there is a simulator such that when all calls to Q are replaced with calls to $\mathcal{G}$, the two configurations are indistinguishable for any environment. Since this ideal configuration is exactly the ideal configuration for $\mathcal{F}$ we are done with the proof, because by Theorem 1 there can be no protocol realizing any ideal functionality for bit-commitment. □

Proof sketch of Corollary 5. Assume that $\mathcal{F}$ is an ideal functionality for symmetric encryption and construct a $\mathcal{F}$-hybrid protocol for bit-commitment providing perfect hiding and binding. The initiator can commit to b by generating a new key, encrypting b and sending the ciphertext via public channel. To open the commitment, initiator sends the key. This protocol provides perfect hiding because of the perfect CCA-security provided $\mathcal{F}$, and provides perfect binding because of the perfect integrity of ciphertexts provided by $\mathcal{F}$. By Theorem 4, functionality $\mathcal{F}$ cannot be realized. □

Proof sketch of Corollary 6. Construct a $\mathcal{F}$-hybrid protocol for bit-commitment providing perfect hiding and binding. The initiator can commit to b by generating all the group keys, signing a random message with b's signing key, and then sending, as the signature, the tuple consisting of the b's signature, the message, the group public key, and all the signing keys. To open the commitment, the initiator sends the group manager's secret key. This protocol provides perfect hiding because of the perfect anonymity provided $\mathcal{F}$, and provides perfect binding because of the perfect traceability provided by $\mathcal{F}$. By Theorem 4, functionality $\mathcal{F}$ cannot be realized. □

Adaptable Situation-Aware Secure Service-Based (AS³) Systems

¹S. S. Yau, ¹H. Davulcu, ²S. Mukhopadhyay, ¹D. Huang, ¹Y. Yao, and ¹H. Gong

¹*Arizona State University, Tempe, AZ 85287-8809, USA*
¹*{yau, hasan.davulcu, dazhi.huang, yisheng.yao, haishan.gong}@asu.edu}*

²*West Virginia University, Morgantown, WV, USA*
²*supratik.mukhophadyay@mail.wvu.edu*

Abstract

Service-based systems are distributed systems which have the major advantage of enabling rapid composition of distributed applications, regardless of the programming languages and platforms used in developing and running different components of the applications. In these systems, various capabilities are provided by different organizations as services interconnected by various types of networks. The services can be integrated following a specific workflow to achieve a mission goal for users. For large-scale service-based systems involving multiple organizations, high confidence and adaptability are of prime concern in order to ensure that users can use these systems anywhere, anytime with various devices, knowing that their confidentiality and privacy are well protected and the systems will adapt to satisfy their needs in various situations. Hence, these systems must be adaptable, situation-aware and secure. In this paper, an approach to rapid development of adaptable situation-aware secure service-based (AS³) systems is presented. Our approach enables users to rapidly generate, discover, and compose services into processes to achieve their goals based on the situation and adapt the composed processes when situation changes.

Keyword:

Adaptable situation-aware secure service-based systems, adaptive workflow synthesis, AS³ logic, AS³ calculus, distributed trust management, hierarchical situation awareness, security, service-oriented architecture

1. Introduction

Service-based systems are distributed computing systems with the major advantage of enabling rapid composition of distributed applications, regardless of programming languages and platforms used in developing and running different components of the applications. In service-based systems, various capabilities are provided by different organizations as *services*, which are software/hardware entities with well-defined interfaces to provide certain capability over wired or wireless networks. The services can be integrated following a specific *workflow*, which is a series of cooperating and coordinated activities designed to carry out a well-defined process to achieve a mission goal for users. Our MURI project, "Adaptable Situation-Aware Secure Service-based (AS³) Systems" aims at conducting basic research on automating the development, deployment and operations of robust and secure service-based systems to achieve declaratively specified mission goals with multiple QoS requirements in dynamic and unreliable environments.

The motivation of our project is to facilitate the rapid adoption of service-based systems in many large-scale distributed systems, such as Grid and Global Information Grid (GIG), for various distributed applications including collaborative scientific and engineering work, e-business, healthcare, military, and homeland security. For these large-scale service-based systems, *high confidence* and *adaptability* are of prime concern. It is very important to ensure that users can use these systems anywhere, any time using various devices (ranging from handheld devices to PCs), knowing that their confidentiality and privacy are well protected and the systems will adapt to their needs in various situations. Therefore, these systems must have the following properties:

(1) *Adaptability*. In these systems, services may become unavailable due to distributed denial-of-service attacks or system failures, and new processes may be created in runtime to fulfill users' new mission goals. Hence, the systems must have the capabilities to change their configurations to provide high availability, or to adapt their behavior to satisfy the new goals in dynamic environments.

(2) *Situation awareness* (SAW). SAW is the capability of being aware of situations and adapting the system's behavior based on situation changes [Yau02a-b]. SAW is essential for high confidence and adaptable service-based systems since it is needed for determining adaptive processes to achieve users' goals, and enforcing flexible security policies.

(3) *Security*. To provide high confidence to users, these systems must have the capabilities of authenticating users and service providers, verifying the integrity of services, protecting the confidentiality of information, controlling the access to services based on security policies, and detecting malicious services and users.

Although various techniques have been developed to improve the security and provide dynamic service composition of service-based systems [IBM04a-c, OAS04a-b], so far there are no effective enabling techniques for developing *Adaptable Situation-aware Secure Service-based* (AS³) *Systems*. In our MURI project, we are developing a declarative unifying logic-based approach to developing service-based systems with situation awareness, distributed security policy management and enforcement, and adaptive workflow management while preserving overall correctness and consistency of the systems. In this paper, we will outline our accomplishments:

(a) An AS³ logic for supporting the specification, verification and synthesis of AS³ systems with various QoS requirements, such as security, SAW and real-time.

(b) An AS³ calculus for providing a formal programming model for AS³ systems.

(c) Declarative models of hierarchical SAW and security policies, and mappings between model representations and AS³ logic specifications for supporting requirement analysis and converting requirements to AS³ logic specifications.

(d) An agent-based distributed trust management approach for effectively managing and enforcing situation-aware security policies.

(e) Adaptive workflow synthesis using domain-specific knowledge as the situation evolves during the workflow execution.

2. An Example

To illustrate the effectiveness of our approach to developing AS³ systems with the necessary adaptability, situation awareness and security, and to demonstrate their applications in enhancing and protecting critical infrastructure of our society, we have developed a demonstration AS³ system for road emergency response. This AS³ system, as shown in Figure 1, connects the Intelligent Transportation System (**ITS**), Police Departments (**PD**), Fire Departments (**FD**), and Ambulance Services (**AMS**), for maintaining traffic safety and coordinating various first responders (**ITS**, **PD**, **FD** and **AMS**) in emergency situations. **ITS**, **PD**, **FD** and **AMS** provide various capabilities as services in the system. A Mission Planner (**MP**) service in the system is used to automatically synthesize workflows using these services to fulfill various mission goals. For the clarity of presentation, we use the following *Accident Response* scenario, which does not enumerate all situations in a real-world accident scenario, to illustrate the need for adaptability, situation awareness and security provided by AS³ system.

A 911 call center gets a report of a serious accident at location **L** in the city during the rush hour. In response to such a situation, the following workflow shown in Figure 2 is automatically generated by the **MP** to coordinate field rescue operations and mitigate the effects of the accident. The following is a step-by-step description of the control flow logic in the workflow:

(1) Two Police Patrol Cars (**CAR**), a Fire Engine (**FE**) and an Ambulance (**AMB**) are dispatched to **L**. An Emergency Road Closure (**ERC**) service provided by the **ITS** is also invoked to *display road closure messages* on the big screens along the affected roads.

(2) Upon arriving at **L**, the police officers *set up a perimeter* to secure the accident site, and inform the **FE** and **AMB** that the accident site is secure.

(3) The fire fighters and/or paramedics start to *rescue* the passengers trapped in the damaged vehicles. In case that the vehicles are severely damaged, the fire fighters need to use special equipments to break into the vehicles before the passengers can be safely moved out of the vehicles.

(4) Once the passengers are out of the damaged vehicles, the paramedics on the AMB start to *assess the status* of the injured passengers for deciding the appropriate medical care for them.

(5) The paramedics carefully put the injured passengers on the **AMB** and take them to a nearby hospital. Meanwhile,, the **FE** also leaves **L** after the fire fighters finish their work.

(6) The police officers remove the perimeter, and the **CAR**s leave **L**. Meanwhile:

- The **ERC** provided by the **ITS** is invoked again to notify drivers in nearby roads that the road closure has ended.

In the AS³ system, a set of coordination agents will be automatically generated to monitor the situations, execute the abovementioned workflow, and adapt the workflow when necessary. The constraints that the workflow needs to satisfy include the following:

❖ All the responders should arrive at the accident site within fifteen minutes.

❖ Any **CAR**, **FE**, or **AMB** that are serving at one accident site should not be dispatched to another accident site before completing their jobs at the accident site.

❖ Injured passengers in critical conditions should be brought to a nearby hospital within fifteen minutes after they are rescued from their damaged vehicles, or their lives may not be saved.

❖ Any coordination **agent** should only follow the commands from a trusted **MP**, being authenticated and delegated by a trusted party (the proper authority).

❖ Only after **CAR**s leaves from **L**, **ERC** can end the road closure.

In a perfect world, the above workflow would execute successfully and perform all the needed tasks to complete the rescue operations. However, various things may go wrong during execution. For examples, a service may fail to terminate successfully, an unperceived exception condition may arise at run-time or more resources may be needed in order to fulfill a user's goal. Since it is almost impossible to identify all control and correction steps before execution time, it must be possible to adapt the workflow at run-time with *dynamic reconfiguration constraints* such as follows:

❖ **Resource failure**: An ambulance can transport at most two injured passengers at the same time, and hence the **MP** should send another ambulance within five minutes to carry additional injured passengers.

❖ **Failure due to unreliable data**: Inaccurate sensory or situation information such as the reported number of injured passengers.

❖ **Service failure:** If the police fails to set up a perimeter within five minutes after the 911 call center gets an accident report, FE and AMB can enter the accident site regardless a police perimeter has been set up or not.

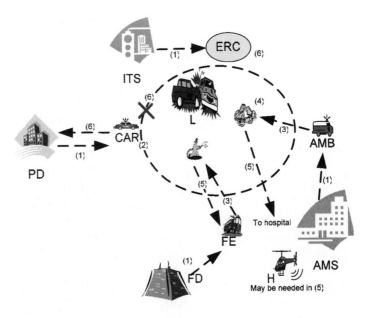

Figure 1. The motivating example

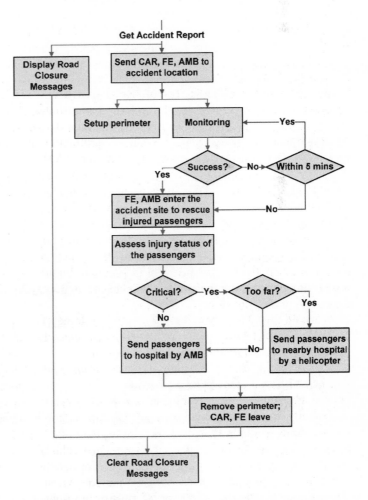

Figure 2. The workflow in the motivating example

❖ **Exception Condition:** If the paramedics determine that one or more of the injured passengers are in *critical condition* in Step (5), and the accident site is too far from any nearby hospitals, a helicopter (H) is discovered and used to transport the passenger in critical condition to a selected hospital.

3. Background

The interdisciplinary research in this project is related to the following research areas: deliberative and reactive systems, languages and formalisms for service modeling and composition, distributed trust management, situation awareness, and workflow planning and scheduling. In this section, the background of these related research areas will be discussed.

3.1 Deliberative and Reactive Systems

Deliberative systems (also referred as *deliberative agents*) are systems based on the "Sense-Plan-Act" (SPA) model [Ark98], in which agents sense the environment, jointly plan their actions, and act cooperatively to achieve a well-defined goal [Dav94, Dor97, Nam01]. Such systems usually consist of a planner and a world model [Dav94, Dor97, Nam01]. In the world model, the actions and events in the world are represented symbolically, usually using some logic like first-order logic based situation calculus [McC69]. The planner utilizes some AI planning techniques [Abe04, Bac01, Cha87] to generate a sequence of actions that needs to be performed to achieve the goal based on the world model. Although deliberative systems can generate complicated coordinated actions and allow learning and prediction, the difficulty in modeling the world and keeping the world model up-to-date and the high computational complexity in planning makes deliberative systems not suitable for applications requiring real-time response in dynamic environments.

Reactive systems (also referred to as *reactive agents*), on the contrary, do not require any world model and planning. A reactive system works in a stimulus-response manner, for which a set of "Sense-Act" rules are defined to control the reaction of the system to the event sensed by the system [Bro91ab, Nie03]. This type of system utilizes simple low-level reactions based on the information collected from environments to obtain complex, goal-related and intentional behavior [Bro91ab, Nie03]. Reactive systems can provide very fast response to the events detected. But due to the lack of a world model and a planner, reactive systems can only act according to the pre-defined rules, and cannot plan actions ahead of time. Furthermore, pure reactive systems do not provide any learning capability. Hence, reactive systems are not adaptive.

Much research has been done to develop *hybrid systems* (combinations of reactive and deliberative systems) to take advantages of both types of systems and overcome their limitations [Bly93, Nwa96, Nou97, Woo02, Urd03, Vas04]. In hybrid systems, techniques of deliberative systems are used at the top layer to perform high-level planning and learning, while techniques of reactive systems are used at the bottom layer to drive the low-level reactions to environment changes. However, an intermediate layer must be added to mediate reactive and deliberative layers due to the significant differences between the two types of techniques. Currently, there is no unifying formal approach to developing such kind of systems.

The AS³ systems proposed in our project can be considered as hybrid systems. In this project, we will develop a declarative unifying logic-based approach to developing AS³ systems with hierarchical SAW for reactive behavior and adaptive workflow management for goal-directed actions.

3.2 Languages and Formalisms for Service Modeling and Composition

Service-Oriented Architecture (SOA) aims at facilitating seamless integration, interoperability and deployment of distributed applications. SOA is increasingly deployed for building distributed service-oriented systems. SOA promotes component reuse as well as provides separation of concerns by separating the business logic of an application from the implementation details of the individual interactions of the components. A service can be viewed as a stand-alone software/hardware module performing a specific function. For example, a sensor can be viewed as a stand-alone hardware module that provides the service of "sensing its environment". Services can run on spatially distributed individual nodes of a network. The functionalities provided by a service are implemented by one or more methods that may themselves use functionalities of other services. Services can be dynamically discovered and invoked. A service has an interface that is exposed to the environment and is used by other modules for invoking functionalities provided by it. The implementation details of the service as well as its location are supposed to be hidden from the users. A service registers itself with a service registry that allows other modules to locate the service as well as obtain information about its interface. New services having complex functionalities can be created by composing existing services. SOA loosely couples its individual constituent modules. Services and the clients that can access them can communicate with each other either asynchronously (documented-oriented) or synchronously (remote procedure call).

In web-service-based SOA, services communicate with clients through well established XML-based protocols like SOAP (Simple Object Access Protocol). The enabling technologies for developing such SOA include XML,

WSDL (Web Services Definition Language) [W3C], SOAP (Simple Object Access Protocol) [New02], and UDDI (Universal Description Discovery and Integration) [New02]. The XML framework provides a language and techniques for defining and processing semi-structured data. WSDL provides an XML-based language for describing web services interfaces. A WSDL file not only describes a service interface, but also provides a set of locations for accessing the service. SOAP provides a framework for XML-based messaging. It is essentially a protocol for one-way message transmission, but a remote procedure call-like mechanism can be emulated. UDDI provides a directory for registering and discovering web services. Web services register themselves with a UDDI registry by sending a SOAP message. Once registered, the UDDI registry includes the URL of a WSDL file that contains the description of the web service. When a client queries the UDDI registry using a SOAP message, it receives the WSDL file corresponding to the web service that directs it how to format a SOAP message that reaches the service. On receiving the SOAP message, the SOAP processor at the service end can map it to an input to the method implementing the required functionality referred in the message. The output of the method (if any) is formatted as a SOAP message and sent back to the client. An alternative to using WSDL, SOAP and UDDI is ebXML (Electronic Business XML) that provides a framework for negotiation between services.

Other popular languages for describing web services include ontology-based languages like RDF (Resource Description Framework). RDF follows XML syntax and provides a data model for representing services/resources.

3.3 Situation awareness

Situation awareness (SAW) is the capability of being aware of situations and adapting the system's behavior based on situation changes [Yau02a-b]. A *situation* is a set of context attributes over a period of time that is relevant to future system behavior. A *context* is any instantaneous, detectable, and relevant property of the environment, the system or users, such as time, location, wind velocity, temperature, available bandwidth, invocation of action, and a user's schedule [Yau02a-b]. *Hierarchical situation awareness (H-SAW)* is the capability of being aware of situations in different abstract levels and properly reacting to situation changes. In service-based systems, it is often desirable that the services can be discovered and invoked dynamically based on situations, so that the effort of the users to find suitable services can be greatly reduced and the systems can provide better quality of services to the users. However, to achieve SAW in distributed service-based systems, such as AS³ systems, we will encounter a number of challenging issues, such as dynamic system infrastructure, the need for high scalability, and heterogeneous and unreliable resources. Therefore, systematic approaches for developing situation-aware service-based systems are needed. Furthermore, the approaches should be easy to use, and can be easily adapted to various application domains.

Situation awareness has been studied in artificial intelligence [Rus03], human-computer interactions [Car83] and data fusion community [Hal01]. Existing work may be divided into two categories. One focuses on modeling and reasoning SAW [Mcc69, Pin94, Mcc00, Mat03a-b, Pla03], and the other focuses on providing toolkit, framework or middleware for development and runtime support for SAW [Dey01, Rom02, Ran03, Cha03, Yau02a,b]. These notable work can hardly meet the challenges due to lack of a systematic way to deal with the increasingly dynamic operating environments of service-based systems. In our approach, a declarative model is developed to help application developers analyze and specify SAW requirements. A logic is developed to formally specify the declarative model and support the automated synthesis of calculus terms through theorem proving. The calculus terms will be further compiled into distributed software agents to perform runtime context acquisition and situation analysis.

3.4 Distributed Trust Management

Trust is "the capacity to commit oneself to fulfilling the legitimate expectations of others, is both the constitutive virtue of, and the key causal precondition for the existence of any society" [Dun84]. In our daily life, we frequently make trust decisions, directly or indirectly. For example, when we take a taxi, we trust the taxi driver will take us to the destination safely and charge us a reasonable fare. In AS³ systems, service providers and service users form virtual societies, in which we face information overloads, increased uncertainty and risk of using services provided by third-parties. Therefore, trust plays an essential role for ensuring successful and secure interactions among members. We refer *trust management* to an approach to collecting, specifying, analyzing, and presenting evidences to make decisions on whether a principal is trusted. When applied to AS³ systems, evidences include (1) *security policies*, which are detail statements that embody the goals of protecting security-critical services, (2) *credentials*, which represent delegations of trust among principals, and (3) *current system situation*. The system situational information can facilitate the system to determine if the principal should be trusted in the system. For example, whether a principal has successfully logged on the system before may help decide if the principal should be trusted now or not. A *principal* is an entity with a unique identity in AS³ system that requests permissions for accessing certain services. An *entity* is any concrete or abstract object in an AS³ system, including a user, a process, a service, or a computation/communication resource. In AS³ system, each principal may potentially interact with any other principal. For better manageability, a set of principals with some common properties (such as roles) may be organized as a *group*. A *group* may be externally identified as a single organizational principal.

The trust management for AS³ system should be flexible, scalable and adaptable to the changing environments and user requirements and provide security support for dynamic service discovery and execution. Existing security solutions for service-based systems [Nak02, Nae03, IBM04c, OAS04a] and trust management approaches in distributed systems [Bla96,99, Chu97, Jim01, Li03, Gav04] can hardly meet this challenge due to lack of a systematic way to deal with the increasingly dynamic operating environments of service-based systems. A distributed trust management (DTM) framework, together with a formal model, is essential to provide a systematic approach to specifying and enforcing security policies, including authentication, access control and delegation policies. Such a DTM framework supports reasoning the trust relationship among principals based on security policies, credentials and current system situation, and allows direct authorization of security-critical actions in the dynamic environments of AS³ systems.

3.5 Workflow Planning and Scheduling

Planning techniques [Sri04] have been used to schedule dynamically changing workflows. The classical planning problem [Nau04] is specified by describing the initial state of the world, the desired goal state, and a set of deterministic actions. The objective of planning is to find a sequence of these actions, which, when executed from the initial state, lead the agents to the goal state. Each action has preconditions to be satisfied in order to execute it, and has effects after the execution of that action. For instance, in the "travel" domain, **fly(Phoenix, San Diego)** is an action. "A person must be located in Phoenix" to do that action is a precondition, and after flying to San Diego, "the person's location will be changed to San Diego" is the effect. A problem is composed of the initial state and the goal state [Kam97].

Classical planners are simply state transition systems with the restrictive assumption of implicit time and resources. This restricted model is quite useful for studying the logics and computational aspects of planning with simple state-transition operators. However, in many applications, this resrticted model is not realistic for the following reasons:

- **Quality of Service Requirements:** In reality, actions do occur over a time span and there exists certain resources. Furthermore, the goals in a plan are often meaningful only if they are achieved within a time limit. In a dynamic environment, various events may be expected to occur at future time periods. Hence, actions have to be located in time with respect to expected events and to goals [Bac01].

- **Lack of Domain Knowledge:** Classical planners are also domain independent, that is, they cannot take advantage of domain knowledge [Nau99]. In planning problems, search spaces are all exponential in size, and blind search in any of them is ineffective. Hence, a key problem facing planning systems is that of guiding or controlling search. Domain knowledge is the way that we can embed *control information* [Bac00].

- **Execution Time Problems:** Since classical planning techniques assume static goals and environment with complete and reliable domain information, in real-world problems most of the generated plans will fail. The failures are due to various execution time problems such as dynamic external environment [Abe04], incomplete domain information [Gar02], and unreliable situation information [Kro03, 04].

For workflows with timing and resource constraints, the workflows need to be properly scheduled with appropriate resources being assigned to them. Classical scheduling algorithms, such as Rate Monotonic and Earliest Deadline First, depend on *a priori* knowledge of workload and systems, and hence they can only be used in predictable environments [Liu73, Sta88]. Dynamic scheduling systems, such as Spring, provide performance guarantees upon new task arrivals with on-line admission control, but still require *a priori* task set characterizations [Zha87]. Feedback control real-time scheduling can provide robust performance guarantees in unpredictable environments, but also requires *a priori* task set characterizations and is not designed for workflow scheduling [Abd97, Cac00, Lu01, Lu02]. Logic-based workflow scheduling techniques can be used to handle multiple constraints on workflow execution, but cannot deal with unpredictable environments [Sen02, Dav98]. Grid workflow scheduling techniques can provide performance guarantees for workflows in Grid, but are specially designed for scientific computing (computation intensive, high parallelism, little coordination) [Yan03, Her04, Kea04, Wic04, Yu04].

4. Overview of Our Approach to AS³ Systems

The concept of AS³ systems is to satisfy these requirements using a declarative unifying logic-based approach, which can also be applied to general service-based systems. In this section, we will present an overview of our approach and highlight what we have accomplished so far.

As depicted in **Figure 3**, our approach to developing, deploying and operating an AS³ system consists of the following steps:

S1) Using our declarative models of H-SAW and security policies to analyze and specify SAW and security requirements for the AS³ system.

S2) Using AS³ logic to declaratively specify mission goals and services in the AS³ system, and automatically translating the model representations generated in **S1)** to AS³ logic specifications.

S3) Using our AS³ logic proof system and the distributed workflow scheduler to automatically synthesize and schedule workflows, which achieve the specified mission goals. A set of software agents described in AS³ calculus terms is generated by the proof system and the scheduler. These agents include H-SAW agents for

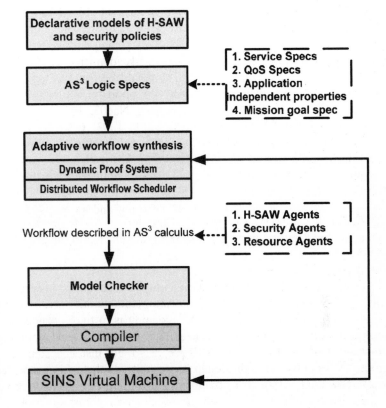

Figure 3. Our overall approach and research aspects

monitoring and executing the synthesized workflows, security agents for enforcing security policies, and resource agents for allocating and scheduling workflows

S4) Verifying the generated agents using a model checker, and compiling the verified agents to executable SINS* agents running on SINS Virtual machines [Bha03].

Our approach includes the development of the following major components:

(1) Develop a formal programming and specification model, involving a calculus and a logic, to support the specification, verification and synthesis of AS³ systems with various QoS requirements.

We have developed an AS³ calculus to provide a process calculus-based formal programming model for AS³ systems. The AS³ calculus can model timeouts and failures, and has well-defined operational semantics that involves interactions of external actions and internal computations. The external actions include communication between processes, logging in and out of groups/domains. The internal computations are (possibly asynchronous) invocations of named services. Continuation passing [App92] is used to provide semantics of asynchronous service invocations. The AS³ calculus allows modeling various QoS requirements and dynamic adaptation at runtime by processes. In particular, it provides a hierarchical domain-based security model, which requires two processes to move into the same named domain before they are allowed to communicate with each other. The AS³ calculus also has a well-defined equational theory that allows for modeling redundancy for fault-tolerance as well as formal reasoning using a simulation relation.

We have also developed an AS³ logic, which is a hybrid normal modal logic [Bla03] for specifying AS³ systems. The logic has both temporal and spatial modalities for expressing situation information as well as modalities for expressing communication, service invocation, logging in and out of groups/domains. These modalities provided by AS³ logic allow declarative specification of services and mission goals (step **S2**). The logic provides atomic formulas for expressing relations among variables and nominals for identifying agents. The vocabulary of the logic does not include function symbols, but has nominals that identify agents and constant symbols that are interpreted

---

 * SINS (Secure Infrastructure for Networked Systems) [Bha03] is a secure agent-based middleware for reactive systems developed at the US Naval Research Laboratory. SINS Virtual Machine provides the execution environment for software agents developed based on SINS.

over a domain. Models for the logic are (annotated) processes in the AS³ calculus. The AS³ logic allows declarative specification of QoS requirements, such as security, situation awareness and real-time requirements (step **S2**). A novel proof system of AS³ logic allows the synthesis of AS³ calculus terms from declarative specifications in AS³ logic (step **S3**) using a Curry-Howard style isomorphism [Bar84] interpreting proofs as processes, as well as allowing checking consistency of specifications. The synthesized AS³ calculus terms represent executable workflows that implement the specification and can be compiled to directly execute on the SINS virtual machine [Bha03]. The AS³ calculus, together with the AS³ logic and the Curry-Howard style isomorphism-based synthesis mechanism for AS³ calculus terms, provides a logical framework for designing, validating, and implementing AS³ systems.

(2) **Develop declarative models of QoS requirements for AS³ systems, and mappings between model representations and AS³ logic specifications.**

Since the AS³ logic developed in (1) is a modal logic, which is difficult to be used by developers who are not experts in logic, it is necessary that the developers can analyze and specify their requirements using some declarative models to achieve rapid development of AS³ systems. The model representations of the requirements should then be automatically mapped to appropriate AS³ logic specifications. We have developed models of H-SAW [Yau05c] and security policies [Yau05a-b] (step **S1**), and the associated mappings to AS³ logic specifications (step **S2**).

❖ **A declarative model for H-SAW in AS³ systems.**

H-SAW in an AS³ system is the capability of the AS³ system being aware of situations in different abstract levels, which correspond to a command and control hierarchy formed by users or agents, and properly reacting to situation changes. H-SAW is essential for AS³ systems because it is needed for enforcing security policies and for adapting workflows when the situation changes. We consider a service as a process, which can accept inputs from other processes and produce outputs. Hence, a service-based system can be considered as a collection of parallel processes, each of which can send/retrieve data to/from other processes. Modeling H-SAW in AS³ systems consists of two aspects: (1) modeling situations, and (2) modeling the relations between situations and processes.

In our model for H-SAW, a situation is either an atomic situation or a composite situation. An ***atomic situation*** is defined as a term composed of operations on context instances and constants. Since context acquisition and operations on contexts are highly domain-specific and often involve low-level system processes, our model does not include the ways contexts are collected and the semantics of operations on contexts. Instead, we assume that each context is collected periodically by invoking at least one service in a service-based system, and a service can collect a context and also implement operations for preprocessing this context. A ***composite situation*** is composed of other situations through the usage of situation operators. The situation operators in our model include not only normal logical connectives (negation, conjunction, disjunction), but also temporal ("ever" and "always") and knowledge ("know") operations. The incorporation of these operators enables developers to model complex situations requiring reasoning on time and knowledge of agents. In particular, our model can be used to express the situation that timestamped common knowledge [Hal90] is attained among distributed processes.

In our model, the relations between situations and processes are defined, which allow service providers and developers to specify the situations that trigger, allow or prohibit the execution of processes in AS³ systems. These relations also enable application developers to model control structures in processes, which are commonly used in service coordination. We have also developed a mapping between our declarative model and AS³ logic specifications for H-SAW, so that the AS³ logic specifications can be automatically generated (step **S2**) once the model representations for H-SAW requirements are generated by developers. Currently, we are analyzing and comparing the expressiveness of various models for SAW, and improving the expressiveness of our model to capture a wider variety of SAW requirements.

❖ **A declarative model for security policies in AS³ systems.**

Our security policy model is a declarative model that abstracts the concepts, such as "service", "Principal", "Delegation", "Permission" and "TrustPolicy", and relations among concepts, such as "Trust", "CanAccess", and "Delegate", in the security policies. We have also identified a fragment of AS³ logic for specifying security policies, and developed algorithms for checking consistency, redundancy, and service accessibility. This model is needed to provide a logic-based approach to specifying and reasoning security policies, including authentication, access control and delegation policies. Our security policy model provides a general, yet simple, security policy specification approach for specifying security policies. It can be used for specifying RBAC-based access control policies, such as the specification done by Lee and Stoller [Lee06] by considering a role as a group of principals with some common properties, granting permissions to groups, and allocating principals to groups. Hierarchical RBAC can be done in our DTM framework by having subgroups in groups, and constrained RBAC can be simply specified using situation awareness constraints. Besides RBAC, our DTM framework provides the following two useful features for AS3 systems: (i) automated synthesis of security policy enforcement agents from declarative security policy specifications, and (ii) no restrictions to centralized security policy repository. Security policies are distributed to many security policy enforcement agents, which collaboratively checking or evaluating the access decision in a distributed manner. To provide dynamic and flexible trust management in AS³ systems, we have incorporated context and action history in dynamic evaluation of trust relationships among entities [Yau05a], and hence support dynamic constrained authorization. Currently, we are analyzing and comparing the expressiveness of various models for DTM, and improving the expressiveness of our models to capture a wider variety of DTM requirements.

(3) **Develop the following enabling techniques for building and operating AS³ systems based on the results from (1) and (2).**

AS³ systems require adaptive situation-aware behavior in the presence of system failures, overload, or damages and rapid reconfiguration in order to achieve users' dynamic mission goals. AS³ systems also need to securely access to critical information infrastructure of distributed services based on flexible security policies. To support the rapid development and operations of AS³ systems, we have developed a set of enabling techniques used in step **S3**, including a deductive knowledge-based planner for synthesizing workflows from declarative specified goals, H-SAW agents for adaptable service coordination, and agent-based distributed trust management for managing and enforcing security policies. In the following, we will summarize these techniques:

3a) Deductive Knowledge-Based Adaptive Planner with AS³ logic. Knowledge-based planning systems are generally based on a philosophy of using whatever domain knowledge is available to solve the planning problem. This knowledge may include (i) services and goal structures, (ii) various kinds of QoS and security constraints, (iii) situation awareness, (iv) search control techniques, and (v) interaction with humans when their expertise is needed [Liu03]. In our previous work [Dav04], we demonstrated the use of logic for modeling and reasoning about Web service contracts. Specifically, we presented a logic, called *CTR-S*, which captures the dynamic aspects of contracting for services involving two or more parties in a potentially adversarial situation. In [Dav04], we assumed that we started with a complete specification of the workflow plan and the services comprised. However, our framework enabled reasoning with contract execution, which amounts to enforcement of dynamically evolving contractual temporal constraints. We consider that the goals and environment are dynamically evolving, and do not assume the existence of complete and reliable domain information. We utilize the AS³ logic and its proof system to enable synthesis and reasoning with adaptive workflows. In the following, we will briefly discuss two specific aspects of our research in this area:

(i) **Enforcing Customizable Failure Semantics using Dynamic Reconfiguration Constraints**: We utilize AS³ logic as a programming language for expressing knowledge about service behavior as well as domain specific reconfiguration constraints that must be enforced during adaptation from run-time failures.

(ii) **Dynamic Proof Theory**: We are developing a dynamic proof theory of AS³ logic in order to efficiently and correctly enforce dynamic reconfiguration constraints on adaptive workflow templates. The dynamic proof theory will be based on a static proof theory of AS³ logic that we have already developed.

3b) H-SAW agents for adaptable service coordination. H-SAW agents are automatically synthesized from the AS³ logic specifications of H-SAW requirements using the proof system of AS³ logic. H-SAW agents perform the following tasks: (i) Distributed context acquisition and processing by invoking the services that provide and process contexts. (ii) Distributed situation analysis. Based on our model for H-SAW, situations are organized in a hierarchical structure that reflects the composition relations among situations. Hence, distributed SAW agents are also organized hierarchically. Situations analyzed by low-level SAW agents are used by high-level agents to compose more abstract situations. This not only helps us obtain a view of current situation at different abstract levels, but also facilitates situation information sharing among SAW agents. (iii) Autonomous service coordination by invoking certain services based on recognized situations.

3c) Agent-based distributed trust management for efficiently and effectively managing and enforcing security policies. Our agent-based distributed trust management technique is to synthesize security agents and interceptors from the security policy specifications using the proof system of AS³ logic, and deploy the security agents and interceptors on a secure agent platform, such as the SINS [Bha03], to enforce security policies. The interceptors will intercept the service requests and invoke the corresponding security agents to perform trust decision evaluation and enforce the trust decisions. SINS is currently used in our prototype system. It is based on distributed agent technology and a synchronous programming language, called Secure Operations Language (SOL) also developed at NRL [Bha02].

3d) Distributed workflow scheduling for efficiently scheduling, deploying and executing workflow with dependencies on situations and security policies. Failure sometimes can be caused due to unreliable situation information or changing resource requirements. To accommodate such dynamic information during the execution of multiple workflow instances, it is desirable to transform the original workflow specifications into new workflow specifications that incorporate all resource management and timing constraints into the control flow graph itself such that a constraint solver can be used at runtime to allocate resources and adaptively adjust the allocation as the resource requirements and situation change at run-time, without unnecessarily modifying the control-flow strategies. We are currently developing a constraint-based system for finding feasible schedules and resource assignments for multiple concurrent workflow instances with timing and resource constraints, and generating resource agents to control the resource allocation at runtime.

5. Future Challenges

In the future, the research problems of automating the development, deployment and operations of AS³ systems with QoS guarantees can be generalized to the problems of rapidly composing and executing applications satisfying various QoS requirements using distributed components in large, distributed and heterogeneous environments. The solution of these generalized problems will enable "computing-on-demand", and hence will greatly improve the usability and survivability of national or global computing infrastructures, like Grid. In order to achieve this, many research issues need to be addressed, such as developing new virtual machines (or middleware) to support application composition on these computing infrastructures, generating more effective modeling languages and techniques for expressing and automated reasoning with service semantics and QoS requirements, developing system services for performance monitoring and estimation and more robust and adaptive algorithms for distributed scheduling and resource management.

Acknowledgment

This work is supported by the DoD/ONR under the Multidisciplinary Research Program of the University Research Initiative, Contract No. N00014-04-1-0723. The authors appreciate many useful discussions with Ramesh Bharadwaj of Naval Research Laboratory.

References

[Abd97] T. F. Abdelzaher, E. M. Atkins, and K. G. Shin, "QoS Negotiation in Real-Time Systems and its Application to Automatic Flight Control," *IEEE Real-Time Technology and Applications Symposium*, June 1997.

[Abd00] A. Abdul-Rahman and S. Hailes, "Supporting Trust in Virtual Communities," *Proc. the 33rd Hawaii International Conference on System Sciences*, 2000, pp. 6007-6015.

[Abe04] D. Aberdeen, S. Thiébaux, and L. Zhang, "Decision-Theoretic Military Operations Planning," *ICAPS-04*, 2004.

[App92] A.W. Appel, "Compiling with continuations," Cambridge University Press, 1992.

[Ark98] R.C. Arkin, "Behavior-based Robotics", MIT Press, 1998.

[Bac00] F. Bacchus and F. Kabanza, "Using Temporal Logics to Express Search Control Knowledge for Planning," *Artificial Intelligence*, vol. 116(1-2), 2000, pp. 123-191.

[Bac01] F. Bacchus and M. Ady, "Planning with Resources and Concurrency: A Forward Chaining Approach," *Int'l Joint Conf. on Artificial Intelligence (IJCAI-2001)*, 2001, pp. 417-424.

[Bar84] H. P. Barendregt, "The Lambda Calculus (Studies in Logic and the Foundations of Mathematics)", North Holland, 1984.

[Bha02] R. Bharadwaj, "SOL: A Verifiable Synchronous Language for Reactive Systems," *Proc. Synchronous Languages, Applications, and Programming (SLAP' 02)*, http://chacs.nrl.navy.mil/publications/ CHACS/2002/2002bharadwaj-entcs.pdf

[Bha03] R. Bharadwaj, "Secure Middleware for Situation-Aware Naval C² and combat Systems," *Proc. 9th Int'l Workshop on Future Trends of Distributed Computing System (FTDCS 2003)*, 2003, pp. 233-240.

[Bla96] M. Blaze, et al., "Decentralized Trust Management," *Proc. IEEE Symposium on Privacy and Security*, Oakland, 1996, pp. 164-173.

[Bla99] M. Blaze, et al., "The KeyNote Trust Management System (version 2)," *RFC2704*, 1999.

[Bla03] P. Blackburn, M. de Rijke and Y. Venema, "Modal Logic", Cambridge University Press, 2003.

[Bly93] Jim Blythe and W. Scott Reilly, "Integrating Reactive and Deliberative Planning in a Household Robot", Technical Report CMU-CS-93-155, Carnegie Mellon University, School of Computer Science, May 1993.

[Bro91a] Rodney Brooks, "Integrated systems based on behaviors", In Proceedings of AAAI Spring Symposium on Integrated Intelligent Architectures, Stanford University, March 1991. Available in SIGART Bulletin, Volume 2, Number 4, August 1991.

[Bro91b] Rodney Brooks, "Intelligence without reason", In Proc. of IJCAI-91. Morgan Kaufmann, San Mateo, 1991.

[Cac00] M. Caccamo, G. Buttazzo, and L. Sha, "Capacity Sharing for Overrun Control," *IEEE Real-Time Systems Symposium*, Orlando, FL, December 2000.

[Car83] S. Card, T. Moran and A. Newell, "The Psychology of Human-Computer Interaction," *Lawrence Erlbraum Associates*, 1983.

[Cha87] David Chapman. "Planning for conjunctive goals", Artificial Intelligence, 32:333–378, 1987.

[Cha03] A. T .S. Chan and Siu Nam Chuang, "MobiPADS: A Reflective Middleware for Context-Aware Computing," In *IEEE Transactions on Software Engineering*, vol. 29(12), Dec 2003, pp. 1072-1085.

[Che01] R. Chen and W. Yeager, "Poblano - a distributed trust model for peer-to-peer networks," *Technical report*, Sun Microsystems, 2001.

[Chu97] Y. Chu, et al., "REFEREE: Trust Management for Web Applications," *World Wide Web J.*, vol.2(3),1997,pp.127-139.

[Dav94] Davidsson, P., "Concepts and autonomous agents", LU--CS--TR: 94--124, Department of computer science, Lund University, 1994

[Dav98] H. Davulcu, M. Kifer, C.R. Ramakrishnan, and I.V. Ramakrishnan. "Logic based modeling and analysis of work flows," *Proc. ACM Symp. on Principles of Database Systems*, June 1998, pp. 25-33.

[Dav04] H. Davulcu, et al., "CTR-S: A Logic for Specifying Contracts in Semantic Web Services," *Proc. 13th Int'l WWW Conf.*, 2004, pp.144-153.

[Dey01] A. K. Dey and G. D. Abowd, "A Conceptual Framework and a Toolkit for Supporting the Rapid Prototyping of Context-Aware Applications," *Human-Computer Interaction*, vol. 16(2-4), 2001, pp. 97-166.

[Dor97] J. E. Doran, et al, "On Cooperation in Multi-Agent Systems", The Knowledge Engineering Review, 12(3), 1997.

[Gar02] A.Garland and N. Lesh, "Continuous Plan Evaluation with Incomplete Action Descriptions," *Proc. 3rd Int'l NASA Workshop on Planning and Scheduling for Space*, Houston, 2002.

[Gav04] R. Gavriloaie, W. Nejdl, D. Olmedilla, K. Seamons, and M. Winslett, "No registration needed: How to use declarative policies and negotiation to access sensitive resources on the semantic web", In *1st First European Semantic Web Symposium*, 2004

[Hal90] J. Halpern and Y. Moses, "Knowledge and common knowledge in a distributed enviroment," *J. ACM*, vol. 37(3), 1990, pp. 549-587.

[Hal01] David L. Hall and James Llina, "Handbook of Multisensor Data Fusion," *CRC Press*, 2001.

[Her04] R. Hernandez, D. Vanderster and N. Dimopoulos, "Resource Management and Knapsack Formulations on the Grid," *Proc. 5th Int'l Workshop on Grid Computing*, November 2004, pp. 95-101.

[IBM04a] Business Process Execution Language for Web Services. http://www-128.ibm.com/developerworks/library/specification/ws-bpel/

[IBM04b] WS-Security. http://www-106.ibm.com/developerworks/webservices/library/ws-secure/

[IBM04c] WS Security Policy. http://www-106.ibm.com/developerworks/library/ws-secpol/

[Jim01] T. Jim, "SD3: A Trust Management SystemWith Certified Evaluation", In *IEEE Symposium on Security and Privacy*, May 2001.

[Kam97] S. Kambhampati, "Refinement Planning as a Unifying Framework for Plan Synthesis," *AI Magazine*, vol. 18(2), 1997, pp. 67-97.

[Kea04] K. Keahey, K. Doering, and I. Foster, "From Sandbox to Playground: Dynamic Virtual Environments in the Grid," *Proc. 5th Int'l Workshop on Grid Computing*, November 2004, pp. 34-42.

[Kro03] R. van der Krogt, M. de Weerdt, and C. Witteveen, "A resource based framework for planning and replanning," *Web Intelligence and Agent Systems*, vol. 1(3/4), 2003, pp. 173-186.

[Kro04] R. van der Krogt and M. de Weerdt, "The two faces of plan repair," *Proc. 16th Belgium-Netherlands Conf. on Artificial Intelligence (BNAIC-04)*, 2004, pp. 147-154.

[Li03] N. Li and J. Mitchell, "RT: A Role-Based Trust Management Framework," *Proc. 3rd DARPA Information Survivability Conf. and Exposition* (DISCEX '03), Apr. 2003.

[Liu73] C. L. Liu and J. W. Layland, "Scheduling Algorithms for Multiprogramming in a Hard Real-time Environment," *J. ACM*, vol. 20(1), 1973, pp. 46-61.

[Liu03] Donghong Liu, "Knowledge-based planning systems and HTN planners," 2003.

[Lu01] C. Lu, "Feedback Control Real-time Scheduling", *Ph.D. thesis*, University of Virginia, May 2001.

[Lu02] C. Lu, J. A. Stankovic, G. Tao and S. H. Son, "Feedback Control Real-Time Scheduling: Framework, Modeling, and Algorithms," *Real-Time Systems Journal*, vol. 23(1/2), 2002, pp. 85-126.

[Mat03a] C. J. Matheus, et al., "A Core Ontology for Situation Awareness," *Proc. 6th Int'l Conf. on Information Fusion*, 2003, pp. 545-552.

[Mat03b] C. J. Matheus, et al., "Constructing RuleML-Based Domain Theories on top of OWL Ontologies," *Proc. 2nd Int'l Workshop on Rules and Rule Markup Languages for the Semantic We*b, 2003, pp. 81–94.

[McC69] J. McCarthy and P. J. Hayes, "Some Philosophical Problems from the Standpoint of Artificial Intelligence," *Machine Intelligence 4*, 1969, pp. 463-502.

[McC00] J. McCarthy., "Situation Calculus with Concurrent Events and Narrative", *http://wwwformal.stanford.edu/jmc/narrative/ narrative.html*, 2000.

[Nae03] Naedele M., "Standards for XML and Web services security," *Computer*, Vol.36, Iss.4, 2003, pp.96-98.

[Nak02] Nakamur Y., Hada S. and Neyama R., "Towards the integration of Web services security on enterprise environments," *Proc. of Symp. on Applications and the Internet (SAINT) Workshops (2002)*, 2002, pp.166-175

[Nam01] Brian Mac Namee, Pádraig Cunningham, "A Proposal for an Agent Architecture for Proactive Persistent Non Player Characters", *Proc. 12th Irish Conference on Artificial Intelligence and Cognitive* Science pp. 221-232, 2001.

[Nau99] D. Nau, Y. Cao, A. Lotem, and H. Muñoz-Avila, "SHOP: Simple Hierarchical Ordered Planner," *Proc. 16th Int'l Joint Conf. on Artificial Intelligence (IJCAI 99)*, 1999, pp. 968-975.

[Nau04] D. Nau, M. Ghallab, and P. Traverso, "Automated Planning: Theory and Practice," Morgan Kaufmann, 2004.

[New02] E. Newcomer, "Understanding Web Services," Addison Wesley, 2002.

[Nie03] Niederberger C., Gross M. , "Hierarchical and Heterogeneous Reactive Agents for Real-Time Applications", Computer Graphics Forum, September 2003, vol. 22, no. 3, pp. 323-331

[Nou97] Nourredine Bensaid and Philippe Mathieu, "A hybrid architecture for hierarchical agents", pages 91-95. Griffith University, Gold-Coast, Australia, February 1997.

[Nwa96] Hyacinth S. Nwana, "Software Agents: An Overview", *Knowledge Engineering Review*, Vol. 11, No 3, pp. 205-244, October/November 1996.

[OAS04a] "OASIS eXtensible Access Control Markup Language (XACML) TC," http://www.oasis-open.org/committees/tc_home.php?wg_abbrev=xacml.

[OAS04b] OASIS Security Services TC, "Security Assertion Markup Language (SAML)," http://www.oasis-open.org/committees/tc_home.php?wg_abbrev=security.

[Pin94] J. A. Pinto, "Temporal Reasoning in the Situation Calculus," *PhD Thesis*, University of Toronto, 1994.

[Pla03] D. Plaisted, "A Hierarchical Situation Calculus," *J. Computing Research Repository (CoRR)*, 2003.

[Ran03] A. Ranganathan and R. H. Campbell, "A Middleware for Context-Aware Agents in Ubiquitous Computing Environments," *Proc. ACM/IFIP/USENIX Int'l Middleware Conf.*, 2003, pp. 143-161.

[Rom02] M. Roman, C. Hess, R. Cerqueira, A. Ranganathan, R. Campbell and K. Nahrstedt, "A middleware infrastructure for active spaces," *IEEE Pervasive Computing*, vol. 1(4), 2002. pp. 74–83.

[Rus03] S. Russell and P. Norvig, "Artificial Intelligence: A modern Approach," 2nd ed., *Prentice Hall*, 2003.

[Sen02] P. Senkul, M. Kifer, and I. H. Toroslu, "A Logical Framework for Scheduling Workflows under Resource Allocation Constraints," *Proc. 28th Int'l Conf. on Very Large Data Bases (VLDB'02)*, 2002, pp. 694-705.

[Shm05] V. Shmatikov and C. Talcott, "Reputation-Based Trust Management," *J. Computer Security (Special issue on selected papers of WITS '03)*, vol. 13, no. 1, 2005, pp.167-190.

[Sri04] Biplav Srivastava and Jana Koehler. Planning with Workflows - An Emerging Paradigm for Web Service Composition. Workshop on Planning and Scheduling for Web and Grid Services held in conjunction with (ICAPS 2004), Canada, June 2004.

[Sta88] J. A. Stankovic and K. Ramamrithitham (Eds), "Hard Real-Time Systems," *IEEE Press*, 1988.

[Urd03] C. Urdiales, et al, "Hierarchical planning in a mobile robot for map learning and navigation", in *Autonomous Robotic Systems - Soft Computing and Hard Computing Methodologies and Applications*, D. Maravall, D. Ruan and C. Zhou (eds), Springer Verlag Pub pp. 165-188, 2003

[Vas04] Vasco Pires, Miguel Arroz, Luis Custódio, Logic Based Hybrid Decision System for a Multi-robot Team, *8th Conference on Intelligent Autonomous Systems*, 2004

[W3C] W3C, "Web Services Description Language (WSDL) 1.1," *http://www.w3.org/TR/wsdl*

[Wic04] A. Bose, B. Wickman, and C. Wood, "MARS: A Metascheduler for Distributed Resources in Campus Grids," *Proc. 5th Int'l Workshop on Grid Computing*, November 2004, pp. 110-118.

[Woo02] Mike Wooldridge, "An Introduction to Multiagent Systems by Michael Wooldridge", ISBN 0 47149691X, John Wiley & Sons (Chichester, England), February 2002

[Xio04] L. Xiong and L. Liu, "PeerTrust: Supporting Reputation-Based Trust for Peer-to-Peer Electronic Communities," *IEEE Trans. Knowl. Data Eng.* Vol. 16 No.7, 2004, pp.843-857.

[Yan03] L. Yang, J. M. Schopf and I. Foster, "Conservative Scheduling: Using Predicted Variance to Improve Scheduling Decisions in Dynamic Environments," *Proc. Supercomputing 2003*, November 2003.

[Yau02a] S. S. Yau, et al., "Development of Situation-Aware Application Software for Ubiquitous Computing Environments," *Proc. 26th Ann. Int'l Computer Software and Applications Conf. (COMPSAC 2002)*, 2002, pp. 233-238.

[Yau02b] S. S. Yau, et al., "Reconfigurable Context-Sensitive Middleware for Pervasive Computing," *IEEE Pervasive Computing*, vol. 1(3), 2002, pp. 33-40.

[Yau05a] S. S. Yau, et al., "Situation-Aware Access Control for Service-Oriented Autonomous Decentralized Systems," *7th Int'l Symp. on Autonomous Decentralized Systems*, 2005, pp.17-24.

[Yau05b] S. S. Yau, et al., "An Adaptable Security Framework for Service-based Systems," *10th IEEE Int'l Workshop on Object-oriented Real-time Dependable Systems*, pp.28-35.

[Yau05c] S. S. Yau, D. Huang, H. Gong and H. Davulcu, "Situation-awareness for Adaptable Service Coordination in Service-based Systems," *Proc. 29th Annual Int'l Computer Software and Applications Conference (COMPSAC 2005)*, 2005, pp. 107-112.

[Yu02] B. Yu and M. P. Singh, "An evidential model of distributed reputation management," *1st Int'l Joint Conference on Autonomous Agents and MultiAgent Systems*, 2002.

[Yu04] J. Yu and R. Buyya, "A Novel Architecture for Realizing GridWorkflow using Tuple Spaces," *Proc. 5th Int'l Workshop on Grid Computing*, November 2004, pp. 119-128.

[Zha87] W. Zhao, K. Ramamritham and J. A. Stankovic, "Preemptive Scheduling Under Time and Resource Constraints," *IEEE Transactions on Computers*, vol. 36(8), 1987.

Automated Agent Synthesis for Situation Awareness in Service-based Systems

S. S. Yau, H. Gong, D. Huang, W. Gao, and L. Zhu

Arizona State University, Tempe, AZ 85287-8809, USA

{yau, haishan.gong, dazhi.huang, w.gao, luping.zhu}@asu.edu

Abstract

Service-based systems have many applications, such as collaborative research and development, e-business, health care, environmental control, military applications, and homeland security. In dynamic service-oriented computing environment, situation awareness (SAW) is needed for system monitoring, adaptive service coordination and flexible security policy enforcement. Furthermore, various application software systems in such environments often need to reuse situational information for providing better quality of service. Hence, to greatly reduce the development effort of situation-aware application software in service-based systems as well as supporting runtime system adaptation, it is necessary to automate the development of reusable and autonomous software components, called SAW agents, for context acquisition, situation analysis and reactive behavior of the systems. In this paper, an automated agent synthesis approach for SAW in service-based systems is presented. This approach is based on AS^3 calculus and logic, and our declarative model for SAW.

Keywords: Service-based systems, automated agent synthesis, situation awareness agents, AS^3 calculus and logic.

1. Introduction

Service-based systems have been applied in many areas, such as collaborative research and development, e-business, health care, environmental control, military applications and homeland security, due to their capability of enabling rapid composition of distributed applications, regardless of the programming languages and platforms used in developing and running the applications [1]. In these systems, situation awareness (SAW), which is the capability of being aware of situations and adapting the system's behavior based on situation change [2, 3], is often needed for system monitoring, adaptive service coordination and flexible security policy enforcement [4].

Consider a service-based system, which has access to a set of services, including a rescue center, rescue ships, helicopters and medical ships, for various sea rescue operations. The following "sea rescue" example is presented to demonstrate the importance of SAW in a service-based system, and to illustrate our approach:

0) The rescue center (*rc*) receives an SOS message from a ship (*bs*) indicating that *bs* has an accident and some passengers are seriously injured.

1) Upon detecting such a situation, *rc* is responsible for locating proper services to rescue the injured passengers.

2) Based on the *bs*'s location and the status of various rescue services, *rc* notifies a helicopter H_A, which can reach *bs* quickly, to pick up the injured passengers and send them to a nearby hospital.

3) Before H_A arrives at *bs*, the weather bureau reports that the wind near *bs* is too strong for H_A to perform the rescue operation safely. Hence, H_A returns to its base, and *rc* notifies a nearby medical ship to go to *bs* to provide emergency medical treatment for passengers.

In this example, situational information, such as SOS messages, weather and status of rescue services, is required for *rc* to coordinate the rescue operation. Furthermore, most situational information in this example, such as the status of injured passengers and weather report, can be shared with or reused in other applications of this system, such as searching for missing ships.

The sharing and reusing of situational information are common requirements of many service-based systems, such as Global Information Grid, which need dynamic coordination and adaptation. Hence, it is necessary to provide reusable SAW capability in service-based systems. To greatly reduce the development effort of situation-aware application software in service-based systems as well as supporting runtime system adaptation, it is necessary to automate the development of reusable and autonomous software components, called *SAW agents*, for runtime context acquisition, situation analysis and triggering reactive behavior of the systems.

In this paper, we will present an approach to automated synthesis for SAW agents in service-based systems. Our approach is based on our declarative SAW model [5], and AS^3 calculus and logic for rapid development of Adaptable Situation-Aware Secure Service-Based (AS^3) systems [4].

Reprinted with permission from *30th Annual International Computer Software and Applications Conference (COMPSAC'06)*. pp 503–512.

SAW requirements are analyzed and graphically specified using our SAW model, and automatically translated into declarative AS³ logic specifications, from which AS³ calculus terms defining SAW agents are synthesized. By automating the synthesis of SAW agents, situation awareness capability can be rapidly developed and adapted in service-based systems.

2. Current State of the Art

Substantial work has been done on SAW in artificial intelligence, human-computer interactions and data fusion community. Existing approaches may be divided to two categories: One focuses on modeling and reasoning SAW [6-12], and the other on providing toolkit, framework or middleware for development and runtime support for SAW [2, 3, 13-16].

In the first category, Situation Calculus [6] and its variants [7-8] represent dynamic domains. However, the definitions of "situation" used in Situation Calculus and its variants are quite different. McCarthy [6] considers a situation as a complete state of the world, while Reiter *et al.* [8] considers a situation as a state of the world resulting from a finite sequence of actions. McCarthy's definition leads to the Frame problem because a situation cannot be fully described. Reiter's definition [8] makes a situation totally determined by executed actions. GOLOG [7] aims at developing applications in dynamic domains. However, it cannot handle sensing actions and no development support is provided. Some conceptual models for SAW, such as core SAW ontology [9, 10], CoBrA Ontology [11] and SAW-OWL-S [12], have been developed. But these models are limited to representing and reasoning of SAW requirements.

In the second category, Context Toolkit [13] provides a set of ready-to-use context processing components for developing context-aware applications. GAIA [14, 15], which is a distributed middleware infrastructure provides development and runtime support for context-aware applications in ubiquitous computing environment. MobiPADS [16] is a reflective middleware designed to support dynamic adaptation of context-aware services based on application's runtime reconfiguration. RCSM [2, 3] provides the capabilities of context acquisition, situation analysis and situation-aware communication management, and a middleware-based situation-aware application software development framework. However, no existing approaches can have automated synthesis of software components for runtime support for SAW in service-oriented computing environment.

3. Background

In this section, we will highlight the architecture of our AS³ systems [4], where SAW agents are used to provide

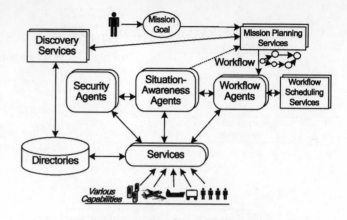

Fig. 1. The architecture of an AS³ System

runtime support for context acquisition and situation analysis [5]. We will also summarize the key concepts of our declarative SAW model [5], and AS³ calculus and logic [18], based on which our agent synthesis approach is developed.

AS³ systems are collections of services, users, processes and resources, which act to achieve users' goals under dynamic situations without violating their security policies. Fig. 1 shows the architecture of an AS³ system, in which organizations publish their various capabilities as services. Each service provides a set of invocable methods as "actions" in the AS³ system. *SAW Agents* collect context data periodically, analyze situations based on context data and executed action results, trigger appropriate actions based on situations to provide reactive behavior of the system, and provide situational information to other agents for situation analysis, service coordination, and security policy enforcement. *Security Agents* enforce relevant security policies in a distributed manner based on the current situation. *Mission Planning Service* and *Workflow Scheduling Service* generate and schedule workflows to achieve users' goals based on security policies, situations and available resources. *Workflow Agents* coordinate the execution of workflows based on situational information.

3.1 A Model for SAW

In our SAW model, we have defined the essential constructs like contexts, situations and relations among situations and actions [5]. Our SAW model is language-independent and can be translated to specifications of various formal languages, such as F-Logic and AS³ Logic. To facilitate rapid modeling of SAW requirements, we have developed graphical representations for the constructs in our SAW model with a supporting GUI tool for developers to model SAW requirements. Fig. 2 illustrates the graphical representation of situation "ready to dispatch a helicopter to accident location" in our "sea rescue" example. Boxes represent the entities in the model.

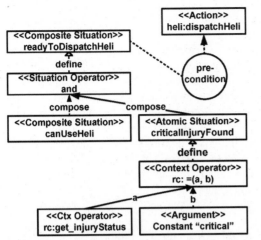

Fig. 2. Partial graphical representations of the example

The type of an entity is quoted by "<<" and ">>". Solid lines with arrowheads connect entities for composition or definition. Circles represent relations among situations and actions. In addition, the entities are associated with various attributes, such as context types and termination conditions of situation analysis. These attributes are required for synthesizing SAW agents.

3.2 AS³ Calculus and Logic

AS³ calculus [18] is based on classical process calculus [19]. AS³ calculus can model timeouts, failures, service invocations, and communications. Part of the syntax of AS³ calculus used in this paper is shown in Table 1. A (recursive) process can be the inactive process, parallel composition of processes, a nominal identifying a process, or a process performing an external action or an internal computation. Continuation passing [20] is used to provide semantics of asynchronous service invocations. In Table 1, $I{:}l_i(y)^\wedge cont$ denotes the invocation of the method l_i of a

service I with parameter y and continuation *cont*. External actions involve input and output actions (as in the ambient calculus [21]) on named channels. Internal computation involves beta reduction, conditional evaluation for logic control, and service invocations.

AS³ logic [18] has both temporal and spatial modalities for expressing situation information, as well as modalities for expressing communication and service invocation. It provides atomic formulas for expressing relations among variables and nominals for identifying agents. AS³ logic allows declarative specification of QoS requirements, such as security, SAW and real-time requirements. Models for the logic are processes in the AS³ calculus. Part of the syntax of AS³ logic to be used in this paper is shown in Table 2. In addition, we can use primitive connectives and modalities in Table 2 to define the following useful connectives and modalities:

- Eventually: $diam(\varphi) := E(T\ U\ \varphi)$
- Universal quantification on time: $\forall t\ \varphi := \neg\exists t\neg\varphi$

4. Our Approach

Our approach to automated agent synthesis for SAW in service-based systems consists of the following four steps:
Step 1) Use our SAW model to analyze and model SAW requirements. The process of analyzing and modeling SAW requirements will be described in Sec. 4.1.
Step 2) Translate model representations to AS³ logic specifications.
Step 3) Synthesize SAW agents in AS³ calculus terms automatically from AS³ logic specifications.
Step 4) Compile AS³ calculus terms to executable Java codes. A compiler for this purpose has been developed to generate executable SAW agents on SINS (Secure Infrastructure for Networked Systems) platform [22].

We have developed the following four system services

Table 1. Part of the syntax of AS³ calculus

P::=	//Processes	E::=	//External actions
zero	(inactive process)	*ch(x)*	(input from a named channel)
P *par* P	(parallel composition of processes)	*ch<x>*	(output to a named channel)
I(x_1, …, x_n)	(process identifier with parameters)		
E.P	(external action)	C::=	//Internal computations
C.P	(internal computation)	let *x*=D instantiate P	(beta reduction)
P_1 *plus* P_2	(nondeterministic choice)	if *exp* then P else P'	(conditional evaluation)
time t.P	(timeout)		
		D::= $I{:}l_i(y)^\wedge cont$-	(method invocation)

Table 2. Part of the syntax of AS³ logic

φ_1, φ_2 ::=		formula	$E(\varphi 1\ U\ \varphi 2)$	until
T		true	$E(\varphi 1\ s\ \varphi 2)$	since
U		nominal	$k(u; \varphi)$	knowledge of u
pred(x_1,…,x_n)		atomic formula	serv(x;u;σ;φ)	invocation of service σ using
x ~ c		atomic constraint		input x by φ and returning u
	// ~::= > | < | ≤ | ≥ | =, c is a natural number		$\exists t\ \varphi$	existential quantification on time
φ1 || φ2		disjunction	$<u>\ \varphi$	behavior after sending message
ㄱφ		negation	φ1 ∧ φ2	conjunction

to facilitate the evaluation of situations:

a) *appendHistory(SituName, SituData, Timestamp, AgentName)* stores situational information and removes outdated data. Data related to a situation is co-located with the SAW agent monitoring the situation.

b) *chkSituP(SituName, ω, ε, AgentName)* checks whether the situation was true sometime within [*now-ω, now-ω+ε*], where *now* is the current time, *ω* is an offset from *now*, and *ε* is the length of the time period to be checked.

c) *chkSituH(SituName, ω, ε, AgentName)* checks whether the situation was always true within [*now-ω, now-ω+ε*].

d) *retrieveRelatedData(SituName, ω, ε, AgentName, Type)* retrieves related data of the situation.

Due to limited space, the design and implementation of these services are omitted here.

4.1 Specifying SAW Requirements

❖ Analyzing SAW Requirements

Based on the ontology of our SAW model [5], developers can analyze the SAW requirements as follows:

i) Identify the relevant services, and the contexts and context operators provided by the services.

ii) Identify situations and the relations among situations and actions (methods provided by services).

iii) If the identified situations contain any situation operators, decompose them to atomic situations [5].

iv) The atomic situations are constructed using the identified contexts and context operators.

❖ Specifying SAW Requirements

After requirement analysis, developers can construct the graphical representations of these SAW requirements (see Sec. 3.1), and generate AS³ logic specifications from the graphical representations using our SAW modeling tool without any knowledge about AS³ logic.

The generation of AS³ logic specifications for SAW requirements is straightforward. The specifications usually contain three parts: service specifications, situation specifications and reactive behavior specifications.

* Service specifications: Each method of a service *σ* is described by the method signature *m(a;b; σ;φ)* and a modality *serv(x;u; σ;φ)* in AS³ logic as follows:

$$m(a;b; \sigma;\varphi) \rightarrow serv(x;u; \sigma;\varphi)$$

The method signature *m(a;b; σ;φ)* describes a method *m* of service *σ* with input *a* and output *b*. The modality *serv(x;u; σ;φ)* describes an event indicating that the agent *φ* invokes service *σ* with input *x* and returns *u* as output. This formula provides a mapping between service implementations and context operators. For example, the following specification describes a method of service *rc* for collecting the context "injStat":

get_injuryStatus(int(ALoc); str(Stat); rc; saw_rcAgent)
→ serv(loc(ALoc); injStat(Stat); rc; saw_rcAgent)

In this specification, the variables *ALoc* and *Stat* used in the modality *serv* are typed using their context types *loc* and *injStat*, whereas the same variables used in the method signature of *get_injuryStatus* are typed using the data types *int* and *str*. This allows developers to map the context types, which are platform-independent and only used for high-level reasoning on SAW, to the actual data types supported by the low-level execution platform.

* Situation specifications: For a situation *S*, which is represented by a node N_s in the graphical representations, a formula with the following form will be generated in the AS³ logic specifications:

Definition → diam(k([x₁, ..., xₙ, S], AGENT)),

where $x_1, ..., x_n$ are the related contexts, *AGENT* is the name of the SAW agent monitoring *S*, *k([x₁, ..., xₙ, S], AGENT)* denotes *S* and will be used anywhere this situation is referred to, and *Definition* contains a set of operations for collecting related contexts and analyzing *S*. The entire formula means that *AGENT* will eventually have the knowledge about *S* if *AGENT* performs all the operations specified in *Definition*.

Definition of situation *S* is generated from subgraph G_S linked to node N_s through a "definition" arc. By traversing G_S, necessary operations for analyzing *S* are translated to the corresponding AS³ logic formulas as follows:

(i) For the situation operators in our model [5], ¬, ∧ and ∨ are provided in AS³ logic; *P* (sometimes) and *H* (always) are defined using the existential and universal quantifications on time in AS³ logic; and *Know* is represented using *k(u; φ)*.

(ii) The context operators are translated to AS³ logic formulas using *serv(x;u; σ; φ)* and atomic constraints.

Attributes defined on situations, including the frequency of checking situations and the conditions for terminating the execution of an SAW agent, are also described in the specifications. For example, a situation "a seriously injured passenger has been found" is analyzed by *saw_rcAgent* every 10 time units until the situation *rescueSuccess* becomes true. AS³ logic specification for this situation is as follows:

serv(loc(ALoc);injStat(Stat);rc;saw_rcAgent) ∧ Stat = 'critical'
→ diam(k([loc(ALoc), injStat(Stat), criticalInjuryFound],
monitor_until(10, rescueSuccess), saw_rcAgent))

* Reactive behavior specifications: The "trigger" relation in our SAW model describes the reactive behavior of the system. Specification of a trigger relation in AS³ logic is a simple formula in the format *trigger(S, M)*, where *M* is triggered when *S* is true. Fig. 3 shows partial SAW specifications in the "sea rescue" example.

4.2 Automated Synthesis of SAW Agents

Instead of directly synthesizing SAW agents in platform-dependent programming languages, such as C++, Java and C#, our automated agent synthesis method first synthesizes the AS^3 calculus terms, which define SAW agents. The main advantage of using AS^3 calculus is to provide us platform-independent models of the agents, which capture the essential processes of context acquisition, situation analysis and action triggering. These models can later be used in verifying the synthesized agents. Platform-specific compilers can be developed to compile AS^3 calculus terms to executables on different platforms. We have developed a compiler to compile AS^3 calculus terms to agents on SINS platform [22]. Here, we will focus on the synthesis algorithms of SAW agents in AS^3 calculus terms.

❖ **Defining SAW agents using AS^3 calculus**

Before presenting the synthesis algorithms, we need to first examine how SAW agents are defined using AS^3 calculus. Fig. 3 shows the specifications of the SAW agent, *saw_heliAgent*, in our "sea rescue" example. Fig. 4 depicts the AS^3 calculus terms of *saw_heliAgent*. The main process of *saw_heliAgent* is defined by L15-L17 in Fig. 4. L16 instantiates two sub-processes (*withinRange_Agent* and *canUseHeli_Agent*) in parallel to analyze two situations AS2 and CS2 in Fig. 3. An input action for collecting the information of "accidentDetected" situation is performed in L16 before instantiating

	/* service specifications */
SERV1)	*get_windVelocity([int(ALoc), int(Time)]; int(Vel); rc; saw_rcAgent)*
	→ *serv([loc(ALoc), int(Time)]; windVel(Vel); rc; saw_rcAgent)*
SERV2)	*withinRange(int(ALoc); bool(Result); heli; saw_heliAgent)*
	→ *serv(loc(ALoc); bool(Result); heli; saw_heliAgent)*
SERV3)	*backToBase([ ];[ ];heli; SAW_heliAgent)*
	→ *serv([ ];[ ]; heli; saw_heliAgent)*
	/* atomic situation specifications */
AS1)	*serv([int(ALoc), int(Time)];windVel(Vel);rc;saw_rcAgent) ∧ Vel < 10*
	→ *diam(k([int(Time), windVel(Vel), lowWindVelocity], monitor_until(10, rescueSuccess), saw_rcAgent))*
AS2)	*serv(loc(Aloc); bool(Result); heli; saw_heliAgent) ∧ Result = true*
	→ *diam(k([withinRange], monitor_until(50, rescueSuccess), saw_heliAgent))*
	/* composite situation specifications*/
CS1)	*∀Time CurrentTime-30 < Time < CurrentTime*
	∧ k([int(Time), windVel(Vel), lowWindVelocity], monitor_until(10, rescueSuccess), saw_rcAgent)
	→ *diam(k([lowWindForAWhile], monitor_until(-1, rescueSuccess), saw_heliAgent))*
CS2)	*k([loc(ALoc), accidentDetected], saw_rcAgent)*
	∧ k([lowWindForAWhile], saw_rcAgent)
	∧ k([withinRange], saw_heliAgent))
	→ *diam(k([loc(ALoc), canUseHeli], monitor_until(-1, rescueSuccess), saw_heliAgent))*
	/* reactive behaviorspecifications */
RB1)	*trigger(k([loc(Aloc), windVel(Vel), not(canUseHeli)], saw_heliAgent), serv([ ];[ ]; heli; saw_heliAgent))*

Fig. 3. Part of the SAW specifications in the example

L1	**fix** withinRange_Agent(integer ALoc) =
L2	**let** bool Result = heli:withinRange(integer ALoc) **instantiate**
L3	**if** Result = true
L4	**then ch** withinRange<true>
L5	**else ch** withinRange<false>.
L6	(**time** 50. withinRange_Agent(integer ALoc)
L7	**plus ch** rescueSuccess(string Status) . **zero**)
	‖
L8	**fix** canUseHeli_Agent =
L9	**ch** accidentDetected(integer ALoc, bool S0) . **ch** lowWindForAWhile(bool S1) **par ch** withinRange(bool S2).
L10	**if** S0=true && S1 = true && S2 = true
L11	**then ch** canUseHeli<integer ALoc, integer Vel, true>
L12	**else** {**ch** canUseHeli<integer ALoc, integer Vel, false> . heli:backToBase()}.
L13	{canUseHeli_Agent(integer ALoc, bool S0)
L14	**plus ch** rescueSuccess(string Status) . **zero** }
	‖
L15	**fix** saw_heliAgent =
L16	{ **ch** accidentDetected(integer ALoc, bool S0) . withinRange_Agent(integer ALoc) } **par** canUseHeli_Agent) .
L17	saw_heliAgent

Fig. 4. An example SAW agent in the "sea rescue" example.

winthinRange_Agent. L17 recursively executes the *saw_heliAgent*.

The sub-process *canUseHeli_Agent* is defined by L8-L14. *canUseHeli_Agent* first collects information on situations "accidentDetected" (S0), "lowWindForAWhile" (S1), and "withinRange" (S2) in L9. Then, the result of analyzing situation "canUseHeli" is generated based on the truth value of S0, S1 and S2 (L10-L12). In addition, method "backToBase" is triggered in L12.

This example illustrates the following important aspects of defining SAW agents using AS^3 calculus:

(a) The input and output actions in AS^3 calculus are used to model communications among SAW agents. When an SAW agent determines the truth value of a situation, named S, it sends all the related contexts and the truth value of S through a communication channel also named S. All other agents interested in S will receive the information from channel S. Hence, SAW agents can be easily reused since new applications can easily obtain situational information based on the names of situations.

(b) The parallel composition and non-deterministic choice (see Table 1) in AS^3 calculus are used when multiple input action need to be performed by an SAW agent without predefined execution orders. Which operator should be used is determined by our agent synthesis algorithms.

(c) The method invocation and conditional evaluation in AS^3 calculus are used to model operations on contexts.

(d) The timeout and recursive processes in AS^3 calculus are used to model periodical context acquisition and situation analysis.

❖ **Agent Synthesis Algorithms**

Given a set of SAW specifications, our SAW agent synthesis process consists of the following three steps:

P1) For each atomic situation, synthesize a sub-process to analyze the situation using **SynAtom** algorithm.

P2) For each composite situation, generate a sub-process to analyze the situation using **SynComp** algorithm.

P3) For each SAW agent, synthesize its main process to initialize the sub-processes for analyzing situations monitored by the agent using **SynMain** algorithm.

We will use the example shown in Fig. 4 to illustrate the above process. As specified in Fig. 3, *saw_heliAgent* monitors two situations: "withinRange" (AS2) and "canUseHeli" (CS2). Hence, in **P1)**, sub-process *withinRange_Agent* for analyzing "winthinRange" is synthesized using **SynAtom**.

Initially, the list aL_2 for storing the operations for analyzing (AS2) is empty. Since the first atomic formula *serv(loc(Aloc); bool(Result); heli; saw_heliAgent)* in (AS2) matches the case in line 4 of **SynAtom**, the corresponding method signature shown in (SERV2) is found and appended to aL_2. The list $reqL_2$ for storing the required for analyzing (AS2) and the list $acqL_2$ for storing the contexts collected by *saw_heliAgent* are also updated. Now, we

have $reqL_2 = [loc(Aloc)]$, $acqL_2 = [bool(Result)]$, $aL_2 = [withinRange(int(ALoc);bool(Result);heli;saw\_heliAgent)]$.

SynAtom algorithm:

0 **For** each atomic situation specification aS_i:
   $Def_i \rightarrow k([x_0, \ldots, x_m, aS_i], monitor\_until(f_i, cond_i), A_0)$

1 Initialize an empty list aL_i to store the operations for analyzing aS_i, and two empty lists $reqL_i$ and $acqL_i$ to store the required and acquired variables of aS_i.

2 **For** each atomic formula T_j in Def_i

3 **switch**(T_j)

4 **case** T_j is $serv(I_j;O_j;S_j;A_0)$, find the method signature M_j from the specification of service S_j by matching I_j and O_j, and add M_j to aL_i. Append I_j and O_j to $reqL_i$ and $acqL_i$ respectively.

5 **case** T_j is $K(O_j;SM_j;A_0)$, where SM_j is a service name concatenated with a method name, add a an input action to aL_i, and append O_j to $acqL_i$

6 **case** T_j is an atomic constraint, generate an *if-then-else* statement for T_j and append it to aL_i:

6a Generate the constraint evaluation for T_j,

6b Add the output action $ch\ aS_i(x_0, \ldots, x_n, \textbf{\textit{true}})$ in the "*then*" branch, and add the output action $ch\ aS_i(x_0, \ldots, x_n, \textbf{\textit{false}})$ in the "*else*" branch

6c Iterate reactive behavior specifications to find actions to be triggered in aS_i or $\neg aS_i$, and add the method invocations to the "*then*" or "*else*" branch

7 Get input perimeters for instantiating this sub-process by removing all variables in $acqL_i$ from $reqL_i$

8 Append the following statement for recursion and termination to the end of aL_i:
   $(\ time\ f_i.aS_i(req_i)\ plus\ ch\ cond_i(bool\ Status)\ .\ zero)$

Since the second atomic formula *Result = true* in (AS2) matches the case in line 6 of **SynAtom**, an *if-then-else* statement is generated following lines 6a-6c. Now, $aL_2 = [withinRange(int(ALoc); bool (Result); heli; saw\_heliAgent), if Result=true then ch withinRange<true> else ch withinRange<false>]$.

Since there is no more atomic formula in (AS2), the loop from line 2 to line 6 ends. Since $reqL_2$ contains variable $ALoc$, which is not in $acqL_2$, an input parameter is declared for *withinRange_Agent* (L1 in Fig. 4).

Next, AS^3 calculus terms for the operations currently in aL_2 need to be generated and properly ordered. The calculus term for *withinRange(int(ALoc); bool(Result); heli; saw_heliAgent)* is the following beta reduction in AS^3 calculus:

let bool Result=heli:withinRange(integer ALoc) instantiate P

where P denotes a process of subsequent operations.

In this example, the subsequent operation is the *if-then-else* statement in aL_2 since variable *Result* used in the *if-then-else* statement is the output from method *withinRange*. Hence, *P* is replaced by the *if-then-else* statement, and L2-L5 in Fig. 4 are generated.

Finally, since *monitor_until(50, rescueSuccess)* is specified in (AS2), L6-L7 in Fig. 4 are generated following line 8 of *SynAtom*.

In **P2)**, a sub-process for analyzing "canUseHeli" (CS2) is generated using *SynComp* algorithm.

By scanning (CS2), the following formulas are found:

- $k([loc(ALoc), accidentDetected], saw\_rcAgent)$

SynComp algorithm:

0   **For** each composite situation specification cS_i:
     $Def_i \rightarrow k([x_0, \dots, x_n, cS_i], monitor\_until(f_i, cond_i), A_0)$

1   **If** cS_i is defined using situation operator *P* or *H*, go to Line 6; otherwise continue to Line 2

2   **For** each formula $k([c_0, \dots, c_j, S_j], A_j)$ in Def_i,

3   Generate an input action $ch\ S_j\ (x_0, \dots, x_n, S_j\_result)$ to get the information of S_j

4   Generate a condition expression $condExp_j$ for S_j:

4a   **If** S_j is the name of a situation, then generate $(S_j\_result = true)$

4b   **If** S_j is in the form $not(S_j')$, where S_j' is the name of a situation, then generate $(S_j\_result = false)$

5   Concatenate all the input actions using "**par**" or "**plus**", generate the corresponding conditional evaluation as follows and then go to Line 7:

5a   For a conjunction ($\land$) in Def_i, the corresponding input actions are concatenated using "**par**", and the condition expressions are concatenated using "**and**"

5b   For a disjunction ($\lor$) in Def_i, the corresponding input actions are concatenated using "**plus**", and the condition expressions are concatenated using "**or**"

6   **If** cS_i is defined using situation operator *P* or *H*, Def_i has the following form:
     $\forall T\ CurrentTime - \varpi < T < CurrentTime - \varpi + \varepsilon$
     $\land\ k([c_0, \dots, c_j, S_j], A_j)$

6a   Generate an input action to get the information of S_j

6b   Get current time *ts*, generate statement for invoking service $appendHistory(S_j, value\ of\ S_j, ts, A_j)$

6c   Generate statement for invoking service $chkSituP(S_j, \varpi, \varepsilon, A_j)$ or $chkSituH(S_j, \varpi, \varepsilon, A_j)$

6d   Generate statement for invoking service $retrieveRelatedData(S_j, \varpi, \varepsilon, A_j)$

7   Generate *if-then-else* statements with the generated conditional evaluations, and placed them after all the input actions. Output actions for sending the situation analysis result and actions to be triggered are added on proper branches as in *SynAtom*

8   Generate statement for recursion and termination as in *SynAtom*

- $k([lowWindForAWhile], saw\_rcAgent)$
- $k([withinRange], saw\_heliAgent)$

Hence, the corresponding input actions and condition expressions, which are generated following lines 3-4 of *SynComp*, are given below:

Input Actions	Condition Exp.
ch accidentDetected(integer ALoc, bool S0)	S0 = true
ch lowWindForAWhile(bool S1)	S1 = true
ch withinRange(bool S2)	S2 = true

As shown in L9-L12 in Fig. 4, following lines 5a-5b of *SynComp*, the input actions are concatenated using **par**, and the subsequent condition evaluation is generated. Finally, L13-L14 in Fig. 4 are generated since *monitor_until(-1, rescueSuccess)* is specified in (CS2).

After the generation of *withinRange_Agent* for (AS2), and *canUseHeli_Agent* (CS2), the main process of *saw_heliAgent* is synthesized using *SynMain*.

Now, we would like to highlight the main idea of *SynMain*. If a situation monitored by an SAW agent depends on context data collected by other SAW agents, proper input actions will be generated by *SynMain*, and the data retrieved by input actions will be used to instantiate the sub-process for monitoring the situation. The input actions and subsequent instantiation statement of sub-processes are concatenated using **par**.

For (AS2), its required input list $reqL_2$ contains variable $ALoc$. By searching the situation specifications, situation "accidentDetected" provides the value of $ALoc$. Hence, an input action in L16 in Fig. 4 is synthesized to collect $ALoc$. Then, the sub-process for analyzing situation "withinRange" (AS2) is instantiated with an input parameter ($ALoc$) in L16 in Fig. 4. Similarly, we can also generate the instantiation statement for the sub-process that monitors situation "canUseHeli" (CS2).

Finally, the instantiation statements for the two sub-processes are composed using **par** in L16 in Fig. 4. A recursion statement is added at the end of *saw_heliAgent*.

5. Evaluations

To evaluate the applicability of our approach, we have investigated the computational cost of each step in our approach based on analytical results and a case study. A Prolog-based implementation of our agent synthesis algorithms, and a compiler developed using GENTLE, are used in our case study. In the following descriptions, the number of situations used in the definition of a composite situation is called *Composition Factor* (*CF*).

For Step 1), we consider a novice user and an expert user to use our SAW modeling tool to model the SAW requirements of an application with 19 services, 10 atomic situations, 5 composite situations (average *CF = 2.2*) and 21 relations for reactive behavior. The time spent by the users is shown in the following table:

	Studying the tool	Modeling			
		Service	Atomic situ.	Comp. situ.	Relation
Novice	35 min.	35 min.	30 min.	8 min.	20 min.
Expert	-	10 min.	10 min.	5 min.	5 min.

Hence, we can expect that an average user will spend about 1, 2 and 0.5 minutes in modeling a service, an atomic situation and a relation, respectively, using our tool. The time needed for modeling a composite situation increases as CF increases. However, we expect that developers can often keep CF small by reusing situations previously defined in the specifications of new situations.

For Step 2), the complexity of the translation from model representations to AS^3 logic specifications is $O(G)$, where G is the size of the graphical representations for SAW requirements. For Step 3), the complexity of the entire agent synthesis process is dominated by the complexity of **SynAtom**, which is $O(m*(m+n)*x)$, where m is the number of atomic situations, n is the number of services, and x is the maximum length of the specifications of atomic situations. This shows that our agent synthesis process is efficient (has polynomial time complexity), and has good scalability. In our case study, Steps 2) to 4) together only took less than 10 seconds.

6. Conclusions and Future Work

In this paper we have presented an approach to automated agent synthesis for SAW in service-based systems. Our approach is based on our SAW model and AS^3 calculus and logic. Service and SAW specification formats in AS^3 logic have been presented. Algorithms for automated synthesis of SAW agents have been described. SAW agents synthesized using our approach can analyze atomic situations based on the results of various context operations provided in a service-based system, and the logical or temporal composition of situations. Currently, the SAW agents are capable of analyzing truth-value based situation. Future work in this direction includes consistency and redundancy checking on SAW specifications, development of support for agent deployment and agent mobility, and extensions for handling fuzzy situations.

Acknowledgment

This work is supported by the DoD/ONR under the Multidisciplinary Research Program of the University Research Initiative, Contract No. N00014-04-1-0723.

References

[1] Web Services Architecture. Available at: http://www.w3.org/TR/2004/NOTE-ws-arch-20040211/.

[2] S. S. Yau, Y. Wang and F. Karim, "Development of Situation-Aware Application Software for Ubiquitous Computing Environments", *Proc. 26th IEEE Int'l Computer Software and App. Conf.*, 2002, pp. 233-238.

[3] S. S. Yau, et al, "Reconfigurable Context-Sensitive Middleware for Pervasive Computing," *IEEE Pervasive Computing*, vol. 1(3), 2002, pp. 33-40.

[4] S. S. Yau, et al, "Adaptable Situation-Aware Secure Service Based Systems", *Proc. 8th IEEE Int'l Symp. on Object-oriented Real-time distributed Computing*, 2005, pp. 308-315.

[5] S. S. Yau, et al, "Situation-Awareness for Adaptable Service Coordination in Service-based Systems", *Proc. 29th Annual Int'l Computer Software and App. Conf.*, 2005, pp. 107-112.

[6] J. McCarthy and P. J. Hayes, "Some Philosophical Problems from the Standpoint of Artificial Intelligence", *Machine Intelligence 4*, 1969, pp. 463-502.

[7] H. J. Levesque, et al, "GOLOG: A logic programming language for dynamic domains", *J. Logic Programming*, vol. 31(1-3), 1997, pp. 59 -84.

[8] R. Reiter, *"Knowledge in Action: Logical Foundations for Specifying and Implementing Dynamical Systems"*, MIT Press, 2001.

[9] C. J. Matheus, M. M. Kokar, and K. Baclawski, "A Core Ontology for Situation Awareness", *Proc. 6th Int'l Conf. on Information Fusion*, 2003, pp. 545 –552.

[10] C. J. Matheus, et al, "Constructing RuleML-Based Domain Theories on top of OWL Ontologies", *Proc. 2nd Int'l Workshop on Rules and Rule Markup Languages for the Semantic We*b, 2003, pp. 81–94.

[11] H. Chen, T. Finin, and A. Joshi. "An Ontology for Context-Aware Pervasive Computing Environments". *Special Issue on Ontologies for Distributed Systems, Knowledge Engineering Review*, vol.18, Sep. 2003, pp. 197-207.

[12] S. S. Yau and J. Liu, "Incorporating Situation Awareness in Service Specifications", *Proc. 9th IEEE Int'l Symp. on Object-oriented Real-time distributed Computing*, 2006, pp. 287-294.

[13] A.K. Dey, and G.D. Abowd, "A Conceptual Framework and a

Toolkit for Supporting the Rapid Prototyping of Context-aware Applications", *Human-Computer Interaction*, vol. 16(2-4), 2001, pp. 97-166.

[14] M. Roman, et al., "A middleware infrastructure for active spaces," *IEEE Pervasive Computing*, vol. 1(4), 2002, pp. 74-83.

[15] A. Ranganathan, and R.H. Campbell, "A Middleware for Context-aware Agents in Ubiquitous Computing Environments", *Proc. ACM Int'l Middleware Conf.*, 2003, pp. 143-161.

[16] A.T.S. Chan, and S.N. Chuang, "MobiPADS: a Reflective Middleware for Context-aware Computing," *IEEE Trans. on Software Engineering*, vol. 29(12), 2003, pp. 1072-1085.

[17] P. Blackburn, M. deRijke, and Y. Venema, *Modal Logic*, Cambridge University Press, 2003.

[18] S. S. Yau, et al., "Automated Agent Synthesis for Situation-Aware Service Coordination in Service-based Systems," *Technical Report, ASU-CSE-TR-05-008*, August, 2005. http://dpse.eas.asu.edu/AS3/papers/ASU-CSE-TR-05-009.pdf

[19] A. J. R. J. Milner, *Communicating and Mobile Systems: the π-Calculus*. Cambridge University Press, 1999.

[20] A. Appel, "Compiling with Continuations." Cambridge University Press, 1992

[21] L. Cardelli and A. D. Gordon, "Mobile Ambients," *Theoretical Computer Science*, vol. 240(1), 2000, pp. 177-213.

[22] R. Bharadwaj, "Secure Middleware for Situation-Aware Naval C2 and combat Systems," *Proc. 9th Int'l Workshop on Future Trends of Distributed Computing System (FTDCS 2003)*, 2003, pp. 233-240.

DETECTING DECEPTION IN THE MILITARY INFOSPHERE: IMPROVING AND INTEGRATING DETECTION CAPABILITIES WITH AUTOMATED TOOLS

Judee K. Burgoon
Jay F. Nunamaker, Jr.
University of Arizona

Joey F. George
Florida State University

Mark Adkins
John Kruse
University of Arizona

David Biros
Oklahoma State University

INTRODUCTION

A major threat to the success of military operations in the 21st century is the failure to detect and counter deception in the joint battlespace infosphere. Success depends on the joint forces achieving information superiority. This requires safeguarding the infosphere against manipulation, infiltration, and deception by adversaries. Yet achieving high information assurance is complicated not only by the very speed, complexity, volume, and globality of communications and information exchange that the infosphere now affords but also by the fallibility of human deception detection, a vulnerability exacerbated by new information technologies. Although automating deception detection is an appealing prospect, the complexity of detecting and countering deceptions that involve humans as source, conduit, or target defies a completely automated solution.

A more promising approach is to integrate improved human detection with automated tools. Reported here are the results to date of a five-year, multi-institutional research program designed to pursue this end. Its objectives were to (1) synthesize multiple theories to create a model of deception and detection processes, (2) identify through experimental and longitudinal research reliable indicators of deceit under varying task and communication conditions, (3) identify information-processing biases that affect the accuracy of human deception detection, (4) develop and test prototypes for automated tools to augment human detection, (5) develop and test a multi-pronged, computer-assisted training program to improve detection abilities, and (6) document lessons learned. The research was undertaken by teams of researchers at the University of Arizona, Michigan State University, Florida State University, Baylor University, and Wright-Patterson Air Force Base Division of Information Technology. In this report, we first review the issues motivating the research, then summarize the highlights from work directed toward the first four objectives to set the stage for the accompanying published article.

STATEMENT OF THE PROBLEM

The explosive emergence of new communication and information technologies portends profound changes in the conduct of military operations in the 21st century, with unprecedented capacities for the rapid, real-time, global exchange of messages and complex information needed for battlefield success and information superiority. The sheer volume, complexity, and speed of information transmission and communication, and our lack of knowledge of unintended as well as intended capabilities of newly adopted tools and systems, pose accompanying risks to information assurance–risks of biased and erroneous intelligence, of inability to fuse data and ideas into operational concepts, of inadequate assessment of alternative interpretations, of faulty and catastrophic decision-making. If implementation is not accompanied by deeper understanding, training, and tools to mitigate these risks. A major threat to information assurance is deception.

Deception and Vulnerability of Joint Battlespace Infosphere

Broadly defined, *deception* refers to messages and information knowingly transmitted to create a false conclusion [1]. Deception comes in many guises. It includes not just lies and fabrications but also evasions, equivocations, exaggerations, misdirections, deflections, and concealments. In fact, the latter forms of deceit are far more common than outright lies [2, 3]. Field informants may omit critical details about suspicious activities. Disinformation campaigns may misdirect attention to bogus operations and away from real ones. Intelligence analysts may be equivocal about their confidence in their data or the thoroughness of their analysis. All of these forms of diverging from "the truth, the whole truth, and nothing but the truth" may compromise all stages of data-gathering and information fusion wherever humans are involved as information sources, conduits, or recipients.

Extensive social science research has confirmed that humans are very adroit at dissembling yet very poor at detecting deceit. The consistent and notoriously low estimates of human accuracy in detecting detection [4-6] point to human decision-makers as the weakest link in any C4I system. For example, Biros, Zmud and George [7] demonstrated how personnel specialists could be spoofed into making erroneous decisions when the data in their Personnel Concept III (PC-III) system was manipulated. Similar results were found in other studies at Wright-Patterson Air Force Base Division of Information Technology, where participants in Airborne Warning and Control System simulations were easily spoofed into believing friendly aircraft were foes and adversaries were friendly aircraft, and a "red team" attack resulted in email message receivers giving up login IDs and passwords to a bogus email request. These studies demonstrate that military members are susceptible to such forms of deception as spoofing and social engineering. It underscores the conclusion that humans are the weakest link in the infosphere. Coping with human fallibility thus remains a major problem to tackle.

Human deception detection is hampered by several factors: the lack of a reliable, stable, and uniform set of indicators of deceit; information-processing biases that lead humans to regard incoming communications as truthful; tendencies to rely on nondiagnostic indicators when deceit is suspected; and tendencies of heightened suspicion to backfire, leading to "false positives" (i.e., judging truthful and valid information as deceptive [5, 8-18]. Even highly trained law enforcement and military personnel have often shown little better than chance accuracy in detecting deception [19, 20]. These already serious difficulties are likely to become *magnified* when messages and information are derived from IT artifacts such as computers and networks. Information technologies such as email, wireless voice communication, teleconferencing, and computer agents that aggregate data from unauthenticated sources may exacerbate detection challenges, not only because operators, analysts, and decision-makers may be unaware of how deceit can be perpetrated in the new infosphere and but also because new technologies introduce additional cognitive biases, such as placing undue trust on information delivered via computers or mass media [21-25]. Too, the accelerated pace of information exchange, especially under the physically and cognitively taxing conditions that characterize wartime and combat operations other than war, may heighten reliance on heuristic processing (use of mental shortcuts) that divert attention from diagnostic information to invalid indicators, thereby further eroding detection accuracy. Reliance on visual interfaces, for example, ironically can make detection worse rather than better [2, 26]. Opportunities for deceivers to plan, rehearse, and edit their messages prior to transmission may place recipients at a further disadvantage [27].

Automated Approaches

Clearly, deception and its detection pose a significant threat to information superiority. The first line of defense in information assurance thus must begin with hardening the infosphere against deception entering the knowledge engine at the data capture stage and secondarily having strategies and tools to flag, probe, and counter deceptive information that evades initial detection. The current research program was intended to offer a complementary approach to current emphasis on intrusion detection systems (IDS). Although it is appealing to try to replace human detectors with completely automated tools, it is unrealistic and infeasible to expect that artificial intelligence solutions can compensate fully for errors in human judgment. Past instruments (e.g., the Voice Stress Analyzer and the polygraph) have suboptimal detection rates. Moreover, even if a dependable set of indicators could be verified, automated systems could not replace the extraordinary (if underutilized) human capacity to recognize, integrate, and interpret subtle and highly variable behavioral anomalies. And, humans cannot be removed from the full data and information fusion chain. At best, then, computer-based tools should augment more finely honed human detection strategies and skills.

Our approach to tackling this complex problem has been to develop a theoretical model that is informed by multiple disciplines, to test for reliable indicators of deceit through controlled experiments, to identify variables (e.g., mode of communication, suspicion, cognitive biases) that influence accurate detection, and to develop prototypes for automated detection of these indicators that can augment human judgments. A major emphasis has been on investigating deception and its detection under conditions like those facing today's joint forces. The voluminous research on deception conducted to date has not been very informative because none of it has been conducted utilizing the kinds of computer-mediated systems and human-computer interfaces undergirding the joint battlespace infosphere and much of it has entailed fairly sterile, static, and inconsequential tasks (e.g., students telling short, innocuous lies recorded for later judging by human "detectors") that bear little resemblance to the tasks faced by military personnel responsible for information assurance. The research reported herein included not only far more realistic tasks and longer interactions, but also military personnel as research participants. Simultaneously, we have worked to develop automated tools for processing the identified reliable verbal and nonverbal indicators. We summarize each of these research efforts next.

SYNOPSIS OF RESEARCH OBJECTIVES AND FINDINGS

Objective 1: Creating an Integrated Model of Deception Detection

The scientific examination of human deception has a long history. Over a century of research and theorizing has seen physiognomic, physiological and psychological models all advanced as the best approach to tell if someone is lying. Yet accurate rates have remained poor. We have taken a behavioral approach, searching for the most diagnostic indicators of deceit and extending the research domain into the arena of electronic communication. Four theories and models have framed our research: *interpersonal deception theory* (IDT), and *channel expansion theory* (CET), *expectancy violations theory* (EVT) and *signal detection theory* (SDT).

IDT [28, 29] can be contrasted to more psychological explanations for deceptive communication in emphasizing the strategic and dynamic nature of deception displays and the mutual influence between sender and receiver that occurs in interpersonal encounters [30, 31]. Although initially applied to face-to-face deception, IDT's principles and findings apply as well to mediated forms of communication, such as email, voice communication, and videoconferencing, and to multi-person communication. The original version of IDT [28] articulated assumptions about deception and about interpersonal communication upon which the theory was founded. It then advanced a number of empirically testable statements and presented the results of numerous experimental tests in face-to-face contexts (see [29] for a summary). We combined this theory with CET to better account for deceptive behavior and its detection when transmitted via electronic media.

CET [32, 33] was developed to draw attention, beyond features of actors, to features of transmission channels, features of messages, and the information exchange process itself. CET argues that the information bandwidth of an interface is not fixed and is not based solely on the objective characteristics of the medium. Rather, as participants develop experience with each other, the channel, the message topic, and the communication context, they will perceive the channel as being better able to handle rich, equivocal, socio-emotional messages. While CET encompasses all communications media, it is especially apropos for computer-mediated environments such as email and chat, both known to "filter out" certain information cues (e.g., tone of voice), which may make the latter stages of the data fusion process more difficult. This argues for taking a longer, longitudinal view on how deceivers and detectors adapt to information technology–on the sender side, to use leaner media to their advantage in evading detection; on the receiver side, to acquire greater acuity in detecting deception.

Our integrated theoretical model, published and elaborated in [32], merges features of IDT with CET (see Figure 1). Testable hypotheses are derivable from the relationships depicted, in combination with the assumptions and propositions of IDT.

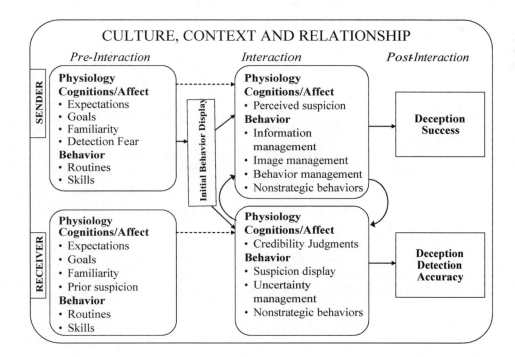

Figure 1. Model merging IDT and CET.

A further innovation of the merged model is the analysis of medium characteristics that must be taken into account as influences on deceptive encoding and decoding. Drawing upon numerous analyses of media characteristics (e.g., [32, 33]) we have concluded that the following are especially germane for deception research: synchronicity, symbol variety, cue multiplicity, tailorability, reprocessability, and rehearsability (ability to plan, edit, or mentally rehearse one's messages before transmission).

Two other theories that in tandem have guided the work are EVT and SDT. EVT [34-38] explains and predicts the consequences of deviations from expected or normal behavior. It differentiates between behavioral confirmations (behavior that matches expectations) and behavioral violations (behavior that deviates noticeably from expectations), and identifies factors that result in confirmations or violations being positive or negative. Many of the behaviors identified as potentially reliable indicators of deceit qualify as negative violations because they deviate from normal conversational patterns and evoke suspicion. EVT and IDT together predict that people attune to these violations, even if only subconsciously. Thus, recognition of violations becomes a key principle for identifying suspicious behavior and alerting humans to such behavior.

SDT [14] provides the classification model for distinguishing hits (judging actual deception as deceptive or truthful messages as truthful), misses (judging deception as truthful), and false alarms (judging truthful behavior as deceptive). An updated model of our approach based on these three theories is shown in Fig. 2 in which we distinguish between deviations from general norms, which would be applicable to making judgments about unknown others, and deviations from personal norms, which would be applicable to making judgments about single individuals for whom a personal history of behavior is available.

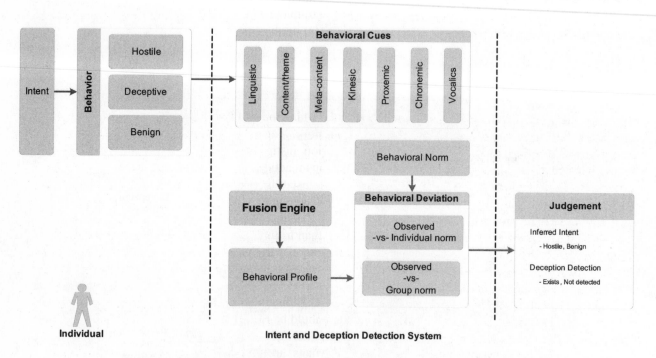

Figure 2. Model employing expectancy violations as signal threshold.

In this model, we envision deception that is multimodal, with numerous cues that are candidates for analysis. Linguistic cues include features like word selection, phrasing, and sentence structure. Content/theme cues are taken from the meaning of the sender's words. Meta-content cues are derived from features that are related to content—e.g., number of details—but can be calculated without contextual information. Kinesic cues concern the way a person moves. Proxemic cues concern the distancing and spacing patterns between people. Chronemic cues concern a person's use of time. For example, a person might establish dominance by arriving late to a meeting. Paralinguistic cues are features of the voice other than the words. From these cues, any deviation between observed behavior and past individual or general norms is noted. The deviations from multiple types of cues and from multiple communications channels are then fed into a fusion engine which weighs the importance of each indicator and compounds the most salient ones into a judgment of deception or truth. Our research, described next, has centered on identifying which indicators are most useful, separately or in combination, for identifying deception and which can be automated.

Objective 2: Identifying Reliable Indicators of Deceit

Detecting deception is a difficult task for most, in that people are right little more than half the time [5]. Too often the behaviors that lay people stereotypically associate with deception are in fact not diagnostic, that is, they do not actually reflect how deceivers behave [5, 39]. To try to improve these odds, scores of scholars and hundred of publications have been dedicated to uncovering reliable verbal and nonverbal behaviors produced by perpetrators of deceit. Among the ones that have proven to be reliable in brief face-to-face encounters are increased blinking, higher voice pitch, more pauses, longer response latencies, shorter message duration, increased self-grooming, more passive statements, more negative statements, and more distancing of the storyteller from the story told [40].Unfortunately, research has seldom examined which of these indicators are present under mediated forms of communication or that appear during the lengthier kinds of communication that take place in real-world contexts. Likewise, research has seldom had deceivers actually interact with those who are judging their truthfulness and seldom involved high stakes or jeopardy. Adding complexity is the fact that deception cues are highly transitory and changeable over time, so that cues evident early in an interchange may differ substantially from those evident later [41]. We therefore conducted rigorous laboratory and field tests to identify single and multiple indicators that reliably distinguish truthful communication from deceptive communication and the conditions under which those patterns remain constant or change.

Taxonomy of Deception Indicators

To aid in the identification of indicators we developed a taxonomy [42] that groups verbal and nonverbal indicators into five classes: arousal, emotions, memory, cognitive load, and communicator tactics. *Arousal and emotion indicators* assume that deception instigates physiological arousal and negative emotional states, producing involuntary and unconscious reactions that can be telltale signs to perceptive observers. They include voice pitch, blinking, pupil instability, adaptor gestures such as scratching, rubbing, hand-wringing or hair-twisting, restless movements, and micromomentary facial expressions. Many of these indicators are absent or inaccessible in mediated communication. *Cognitive load indicators* assume that deceiving is more cognitively demanding than truth-telling. Verbal or nonverbal indicators of cognitive difficulties may serve as indirect signs of potential deception. These include longer and more frequent pausing, speech dysfluencies, cessation of gesturing, gaze aversion, shorter utterances, simpler and less diverse language, less complex sentences, and uncertain language. *Memory indicators* assume that truthful memories should be more extensive and richly detailed than imagined or fabricated events, so language and gestures associated with such accounts should be richer than deceptive ones. *Communicator strategies and tactics* encompass all the ways in which deceivers deliberately manage their verbal and nonverbal behavior to appear credible. Because humans are quite facile at "running off" deceptive routines, strategic communication does not require a lot of conscious thought, and deceivers may readily shift from one strategy to another as a conversation progresses. Predicting likely tactics thus requires knowledge of various contingencies impinging on the deceiver and cognizance of the likely adaptations that will be made over time.

Empirical Verification of Reliable Indicators

Our laboratory and field experiments on verifying reliable indicators of deceit were intended to identify general patterns of truth and deception as well as to take into account different moderator variables and temporal adjustments. To date, we have completed 18 experiments and field tests with nearly 2150 subjects at University of Arizona, Michigan State University, and Florida State University. These efforts have yielded rich data sets that offer insights into important knowledge about the reliability and consistency of deception indicators in face-to-face and electronic communication and that represent extraordinarily rich corpora for future exploration. Following is a brief synopsis of seven different types of investigations we have conducted, beginning with those focused on text-based communication, progressing through several different formats for obtaining multimodal interview data, and ending with group deliberations. These research endeavors are enabling us to analyze deceptions across a broad spectrum of communications and from situations with real jeopardy.

Desert Survival Experiments

The desert survival experiments [43, 44] were performed to analyze deceptive communication in same-time versus different-time text-based communication. Pairs conducted a decision-making task. Imagining that their jeep had overturned in the Kuwaiti desert, they were to arrive at a consensus ranking of 12 items they should salvage in terms of their usefulness to survival, utilizing as part of their discussion Army manual information on surviving in the desert. In half of the groups, one person introduced faulty and deceptive information. Communication was conducted by means of email or chat, and all text was submitted to automated linguistic analysis.

These experiments confirmed that many linguistic indicators reliably differentiate truth and deception. Deceptive messages were longer, less complex, less imagistic, had less diverse vocabulary and content, were richer in details, used more expressive, informal, distancing and uncertain language, used more group references than self references, and used more modal verbs and modifiers. Many of the relationships are opposite to those found in face-to-face deception and that same-time communication differs from delayed communication. Comparisons of classification accuracies among neural networks, decision trees, discriminant analysis, and logit regression showed high accuracy with all of them.

Security Force Squadron Police Statements

To test the applicability of automated linguistic analysis to statements from actual suspects and witnesses, we obtained a large corpus of written statements collected at air force bases by SFS personnel. Statements relate to everything from on-base thefts to auto accidents.

The statements are being automatically tagged and the linguistic analysis tools are being tested for success in discriminating between statements from innocent respondents and statements from guilty ones. Preliminary results show accuracies of up to 78% in correctly classifying deceptive statements, with five data mining methods achieving accuracies of 70% or greater. This is an exceptionally strong improvement over the average accuracy of 51% found in past deception research.

Deceptive Interviews

A series of investigations conducted as part of the original development of IDT included one subjected to secondary analysis as part of the current research effort. In the experiment, nontraditional students and community members were interviewees who responded to 12 questions during which they alternated between giving blocks of truthful and blocks of deceptive answers. Interviewers adopted one of three interviewing styles indicative of different levels of suspicion and involvement.

The videotaped interviews have been transcribed for automated linguistic analysis and are being manually coded on multiple nonverbal behaviors. Viability for automated nonverbal analysis is being assessed. Results reported previously in [45] confirmed that deceivers were less involved verbally and nonverbally initially but increased their level of involvement sufficiently over the course of the interview to approximate the behavior of truthtellers by the end of the interview. Recent results showed that nearly all of the 23 linguistic and meta-content features were influenced by deception or deception order. Initially, deceivers were more detached and subdued, and used more depersonalized, redundant, and complex language than truthtellers. Over time, however, they adapted their communication to be more like truthtellers and were best able to do so if they started the interview with a baseline of truthful behavior. These findings underscore the strategic nature of deception and the difficulty of detecting it under dynamic real-world conditions.

Mock Theft Experiments

A pilot and main experiment [46, 47] utilized a staged theft in which some participants "stole" a wallet from a classroom while others were simply present during the theft.. All participants were then interviewed by untrained and trained interviewers via chat, audio conferencing, or face-to-face interaction. Interviewer ratings, trained coder assessments of verbal and nonverbal behavior, and automated analysis of language, meta-content, and kinesics were all gathered. A companion observer study included third-party assessments of senders' trustworthiness and estimates of interviewee innocence or guilt.

Results to date have been voluminous. Deceptive messages were shorter, less complex, and distanced senders from their messages. Contrary to expectations, deceptive messages had more specific sensory details than did truthful ones. Automated blob analysis and manual codings of kinesic behaviors showed that deceivers gestured less, used fewer adaptors, moved their heads less, and kept their hands together longer—all evidence that deceivers were less behaviorally active than truthtellers. Analysis of vocalic indicators revealed that deceivers had fewer silent pauses, but more speech dysfluencies (other than vocalized pauses) than did truthtellers. Other behaviors differed depending on modality and phase of the interview. Although deception was generally more arousing and cognitively difficult than truth, this was not the case with text communication. Also, deceivers were more motivated and exercised more control over their behavior than truthtellers. As with past research, human interviewers were made very judgments (41% correct classification of truth and deception by untrained interviewers, 50% correct classification by trained interviewers). Third-party naïve observers were also very inaccurate, showing pronounced truth and visual biases. Best discrimination and accuracy occurred in the audio modality. As evidence of the viability of automating detection, a combination of six features correctly classified 79% of the cases.

Real-Jeopardy Behavioral Analysis Interviews

Experimentally generated data often lack the high motivation and jeopardy found in real-world circumstances. To determine ecological validity and triangulate results with automated and human-coded behavior, we obtained videotapes of criminal suspects for whom ground truth was known. A standard protocol, the Behavioral Analysis Interview, was followed. Manual and automated analysis of kinesic behavior was conducted on these interviews. All manually coded behaviors differentiated truth from deception, and a single behavior—adaptors (self-touch behaviors)—produced 100% accurate classification of deceivers in a cross-validation analysis (see Figure 2). These results validate the behavioral patterns generated in mock theft and support the use of these particular behaviors (illustrators, adaptors, and head movements) in automated detection tools.

Classification Results (b,c)

		Guilt	Predicted Group Membership		Total
			0	1	
Original	Count	0	9	3	12
		1	1	12	13
	%	0	75.0	25.0	100.0
		1	7.7	92.3	100.0
Cross-validated(a)	Count	0	9	3	12
		1	0	13	13
	%	0	75.0	25.0	100.0
		1	.0	100.0	100.0

a Cross validation is done only for those cases in the analysis. In cross validation,
   each case is classified by the functions derived from all cases other than that case.
b 84.0% of original grouped cases correctly classified.
c 88.0% of cross-validated grouped cases correctly classified.

Figure 3. BAI classification results using discriminant analysis, with adaptor gestures as predictor.

Resume Faking Experiments

Another context for deception detection is employment interviews for security forces. The resume faking experiments were constructed to investigate interactive, dyadic deceptive communication using business students' false resumes. Students were randomly assigned to interviewer or applicant roles, with the applicants having submitted resumes that had been intentionally falsified. The interviews were conducted via text chat, e-mail, computer-mediated audio, or audio with chat. Half of the interviewers were warned of the possibility that the resumes had been enhanced; the other interviewers were not warned. Interviewer detection performance was compared to that of third-party observers. Text and audio are being manually coded and will be subjected to automated text analysis.

Results indicated that, regardless of the medium used, the vast majority of the deceptive information went undetected. Interviewers using richer media were better at detecting deception than were those using leaner media. Observers were more accurate when in text than audio mode and when forewarned.

StrikeCOM Experiments

Virtually no research has examined deception under conditions of attempting to deceive multiple receivers and using different communication modes. The StrikeCOM experiments [48] were performed to analyze deceptive communication in chat, audio, and face-to-face communication and with the greater complexity of expanded team size. Participants in some experiments were U. S. Air Force ROTC cadets who used StrikeCOM to conduct mock air operations. StrikeCOM is an online, turn-based simulation of a C3ISR (Command, Control, Communication, Intelligence, Surveillance, Reconnaissance) task. The object of the game is to find and destroy enemy camps that have been hidden on a game board. Three-person teams must effectively work together to find the enemy camps. Each player controls different intelligence assets. In some games, one team member was instructed to be deceptive and purposefully mislead the team away from the enemy camps. In other games, one team member was also made suspicious.

All interactions between team members were recorded. Verbal and nonverbal behaviors of all three members are being analyzed. Results to date indicate that team members became distrustful of deceivers, yet deceivers' information was still accepted and resulted in poorer team performance. This suggests that humans often do not act on their suspicions and continue to show biased information processing. On feature of deceiver communication that may have raised suspicions was the speech acts they used. Their utterances included acts indicative of uncertainty, such as questions or backchannels (see Figure 3, which shows differences in the arrayed speech acts between deceptive and nondeceptive team members).

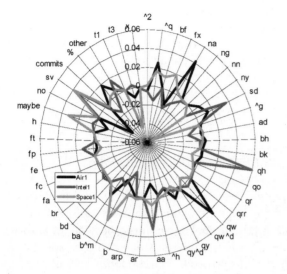

Figure 4. Speech act profiling showing greater uncertainty by deceiver (Space role) than by nondeceivers (Intel and Air roles) from StrikeCOM experiment.

Group Resource Allocation Task

This last set of experiments also explored deceptive computer-mediated communication under the conditions of attempting to deceive multiple receivers at once. Additional interests were the influence of proximity between team members and the impact of being made suspicious about possible deceit. Groups conducted a resource allocation task. Dependent variables of interest, beyond the choice of language and content, were the amount of deception voluntarily submitted during group discussions and the success of deceivers in undermining group performance.

Like StrikeCom, results showed that deception went undetected most of the time—only 9% of deceptive statements were recognized as such—and deceivers succeeded in getting their way 72% of the time. Deceivers also lied more over computers than face-to-face and lied more when faced with suspicious receivers, indicating that they adapted to receiver communication and went on the offensive.

Objective 3: Identify Information-Processing Biases

We have noted that deception is commonplace in all quarters of human conduct. Its very frequency should cause people to become attuned to such behavior and detect it accurately. Yet this is not the case. Accuracy rates distinguishing truth from deception are notoriously dismal, even among trained professionals [1-4]. One reason is that, without knowledge of deceptive cues, humans tend when making judgments of honesty to rely on cognitive heuristics, or mental shortcuts, many of which are based on faulty logic and thus unreliable [5-7, 28]. The most robust of these heuristics is the truth bias, which is a tendency to overestimate the truthfulness of others [8-10]. Another likely culprit in inaccurate detection is the visual bias [11], which shows that humans tend to give primacy to visual information and a concomitant tendency to overlook more diagnostic information in other modalities such as the voice or text. Yet a third bias has been variously labeled the nonverbal conspicuousness or expectancy violation bias [12], which is a tendency to pay undue attention to novel, unusual, or conspicuous behaviors. The objective of this facet of our research project was to examine the effects of truth, visual, and expectancy violations heuristics in judging truth and deceit under different modalities.

In one experiment we conducted, judgments were made by observers who saw, heard, or read one of the interviews from the mock theft experiment. Observers in the text condition had access to only the transcript of a given interview; observers in the audio condition heard a recorded interview and so had access to both the words and the voice; observers in the audiovisual condition watched a videotaped interview and so had access to the words, voice, and visual nonverbal cues.

The predicted truth bias was supported: judgments and ratings of truthfulness far exceeded actual truthfulness of far more of the interviewees were judged as truthful than were actually truthful. The visual bias was also supported: far more of the interviewees were judged as truthful by judges in the video condition, followed by those in the audio condition and finally the text condition. These biases confirm that human judgment is error-prone and that modality affects error rates. Automated tools are one means of offsetting these biases.

Objective 4: Develop and Test Prototypes for Automating Detection

Our efforts to develop a suite of tools for automating deception detection began with an intensive search and review of all commercial off-the-shelf (COTS) software packages, including analysis tools, document management tools, parsers, and repository applications that might be applicable to our mission, as well as reviewing relevant hardware options. Our review and evaluation indicated that some could be applied to specific areas of the research but that none of them wholly met our needs. Subsequently, we devised a software development plan.

It soon became apparent that we would require a number of distinct, but related applications. This suite of tools, entitled "Agent99 Suite" was envisioned to include Trainer, Analyzer, Parser, and Client components. By employing a modular architecture, using Java, a web-enabled-AF Portal compliant language that would provide for XML data exchange, we could ensure the interoperability and portability of our tools. Following are brief descriptions of the different tools comprising the Agent99 Suite.

Agent99 Analyzer

The first tool in the Agent99 Suite is the Analyzer. To provide a basis of comparison for automated deception detection approaches we need accurate and reliable assessments of behavior. In most circumstances, this means using human coders to observe and record behaviors that may or may not be indicative of deception. These records can then be correlated both with known findings of truthfulness and the judgments of automated systems. Specifically, it lets coders watch videos or listen to audio tracks while automatically recording the times of particular behaviors. Users can navigate back and forth through the tracks and make multiple passes to collect data on elusive behaviors. Analyzer opens up potential for building and validating the other tools in the suite.

Agent99 Trainer

Agent99 Trainer was designed to provide self-paced instruction, practice and feedback in a web-based or CD-ROM application. It includes an Virtual Classroom module that includes a Watch Lecture module featuring a multi-media expert lecture video that is synchronized with PowerPoint presentation slides and a lecture transcript. An outline-type navigation menu allows users to select and access the topics and multimedia examples on demand. A Search Tool includes Keyword Search and Ask-A-Question (AAQ). These return relevant video segments in the lecture video. An Assessment Tool includes pop-up quizzes at certain breakpoints to facilitate user evaluation and immediate feedback through correct answers.

Agent99 Parser

From the outset, the research team recognized that the analysis of textual messages would be an important line of inquiry. One of the first steps required for the lexical analysis of text is to break down the content into sentences, and identify the component parts-of-speech. We determined that the tool should also be able to provide stemming, named entity and dependency relation identification, and analysis to fine granularity. Moreover, to maintain flexibility the parser would need to rely on standardized linguistic tags. Specifically, we were interested in using the Penn Treebank tags as they have become the de facto standard for research in this area. Following is an example of text marked with Penn Treebank tags.

> We/PRP can/MD never/RB be/VB satisfied/VBN as/RB long/RB as/IN our/PRP$ children/NNS are/VBP stripped/VBN of/IN their/PRP$ selfhood/NN and/CC robbed/VBN of/IN their/PRP$ dignity/NN by/IN signs/NNS stating/VBG "for/VBG|NN white/NN|VB only."/NNPS We/NNPS cannot/VBP be/RB satisfied/VBN as/RB long/RB as/IN a/DT Negro/NNP in/IN Mississippi/NNP cannot/VBP vote/NN and/CC a/DT Negro/NNP in/IN New/NNP York/NNP believes/VBZ he/PRP has/VBZ nothing/NN for/IN which/NN to/TO vote./VB

More than a dozen parser tools were tested. Although the proprietary Iskim software was most accurate, we selected Grok as the foundation for our parser. Grok presented superior flexibility and cost because it offered open source code, is trainable for different domains, is freely distributable, and receives continued upgrades from the open source community.

After using Grok for the core textual analysis, Agent99 Parser performs a number of aggregations and counts to characterize the text. We have found that deceivers can be expected to utilize language in patterns that can be revealed through such simple indicators as words per sentence, lexical complexity and reading level. Agent99 Parser derives such deception indicators simply and reliably.

Agent99 Client

Often, deceivers utilize strategies and techniques that cannot be uncovered through counts and aggregation. For more complex lexical analysis we must move beyond the simple tools offered by the Parser. The Agent99 Client tool uses machine learning techniques such as decision trees and neural networks to analyze text. Once again, we have been able to harness free and open source software to meet our ends. The GATE (General Architecture for Text Engineering) toolset performs all of the tasks accomplished by the Grok software and a few more. It is quite flexible and allows the addition of new lexical and grammatical bases of evaluation.

After performing the GATE investigation on the data, the Agent99 Client uses Weka, yet another open source software application, to perform advanced statistical and machine learning analyses. Weka can easily be set up to execute any number of algorithms for machine learning and solving real-world data mining problems through the use of data pre-processing, classification, regression, clustering, association rules and visualization. The extensive use of GATE and Weka has freed our research group from building our own analysis tools and has afforded us the opportunity to instead focus on identifying and detecting reliable deception cues.

AutoID

The final thrust of the automation efforts is the automation of deception detection in video. This program known as Automated Intent Detection (AutoID) was initiated as part of a Department of Homeland Security research project and continued under the auspices of the MURI research. The point of this research agenda is to leverage the current states of the art in both kinesics (i.e., the study of movement) and video motion detection. Although this effort is ambitious, we maintain that by combining and extending both areas of inquiry one can significantly lower the barriers to analyzing large corpora of video for deception cues.

General metrics are extracted from the video using a method called blob analysis. We utilize a refined method of blob analysis developed by the Computational Biomedicine Imaging and Modeling Center (CBIM) at Rutgers University. This method uses color analysis, eigenspace-based shape segmentation and Kalman filters to track head and hand positions throughout the video segment. The figure below shows a video frame that has been subjected to blob analysis. The head and both hands are isolated as separate "blobs"—ellipses for which height and width can be measured.

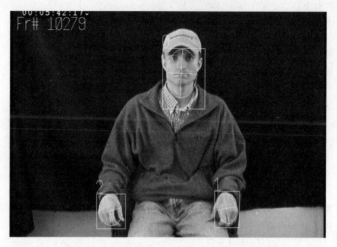

Figure 5. Video frame after blob analysis.

A number of features can be extracted or inferred from the relatively simple metrics produced by the blob analysis. Many of these features attempt to capture some of the key elements that people would look for when trying to detect deception. However, a number of additional features that typically aren't used by humans (e.g. distance of movement per frame) are extracted because they are potentially useful in an automated environment. For example, a human will be able to detect motion, but will not be able to accurately gauge the speed and angle of the movement. In our research, we have found that deceivers typically gesture less, but more rapidly.

The automated extraction of non-verbal behavioral cues associated with deception overcomes many of the weaknesses which hinder other methods of deception detection. It is not invasive and can be done without cooperation from the subject. This method allows flexibility, could provide prompt feedback, and does not require specially trained humans.

SUMMING UP

This multi-faceted, multi-disciplinary research program has produced a very rich yield to date. Our research has created an enhanced framework for understanding deception and its detection. We have revised interpersonal deception theory and combined it with channel expansion theory to produce a much more robust model that has high applicability to deception over electronic communication. As well, we have located our research within the familiar frame of signal detection theory and considered how violations of communication expectations can function as a higher-order principle guiding development of automated tools for detecting deception in human communication.

Our taxonomy of deception indicators has provided a parsimonious approach to grouping multi-modal deception indicators for analysis. Our numerous laboratory and field experiments have confirmed a host of reliable text-based and nonverbal deception indicators while also raising cautionary notes about the important effects of modalities, tasks, suspicion, and interaction dynamics in moderating deception displays. For example, certain practices such as warnings can improve detection. Mock theft and desert survival experiments have confirmed differences in how deception is perpetrated under text versus face-to-face communication in ways that give deceivers extra advantages. Whereas brevity is commonplace in FtF deception, deceivers using text produce much longer messages that also appear truthful. Our StrikeCom experiments found deceivers were able to undermine performance, especially in textual modes of communication.

Notwithstanding, it appears that many reliable indicators are available that are also amenable to automation and so may be incorporated into computer-assisted detection tools. Text-based indicators include message length, syntactic and lexical complexity, lexical diversity, specificity, certainty, immediacy, affect, and dominance. Nonverbal indicators include cues and patterns related to arousal, expressiveness, and dominance. We have found that neural networks, multiple discriminant analysis, and Bayesian analysis offer promise for identifying clusters of cues that accurately predict truth or deception.

Additionally, we have confirmed the influence of several cognitive heuristics and biases on detection accuracy. Visual bias and truth bias are among the two that reduce detection accuracy. These findings highlight major considerations in automating deception detection.

Notwithstanding, much progress has been made toward developing prototypes that can augment humans' ability to detect deception. Continued identification of which indicators should be most reliable under which conditions will place within grasp the end goal of implementing real-time systems to alert end users to suspicious incoming communications.

WORKS CITED

[1] D. B. Buller and J. K. Burgoon, "Interpersonal deception theory," *Communication Theory*, vol. 6, pp. 203-242, 1996.

[2] B. M. DePaulo, D. A. Kashy, S. E. Kirkendol, M. M. Wyer, and J. A. Epstein, "Lying in everyday life," *Journal of Personality & Social Psychology*, vol. 70, pp. 979-995, 1996.

[3] R. E. Turner, C. Edgley, and G. Olmstead, "Information control in conversations: Honesty is not always the best policy," *Kansas Journal of Speech*, vol. 11, pp. 69-89, 1975.

[4] C. Bond, and B.M. DePaulo, "Accuracy of deception judgments," *Personality and Social Psychology Review*, In press.

[5] T. H. Feeley and, M. A. deTurk, "Global Cue Usage in Behavioral Lie Detection," " *Communication Quarterly*, vol. 43, pp. 420-430, 1995.

[6] G. R. Miller and J. K. Burgoon, "Factors influencing judgments of witness credibility and truthfulness," in *The psychology of the courtroom*, N. L. Kerr and R. M. Bray, Eds. New York: Academic Press, 1982, pp. 169-194.

[7] D. Biros, R. Zmud, and J. George, "Inducing sensitivity to deception in order to improve decision making performance: A field study," *MIS Quarterly*, vol. 26, pp. 119-144, 2002.

[8] J. K. Burgoon, D. B. Buller, and W. G. Woodall, *Nonverbal Communication: The Unspoken Dialogue*. New York: McGraw-Hill, 1996.

[9] K. Fiedler and I. Walka, "Training lie detectors to use nonverbal cues instead of global heuristics," *Human Communication Research*, vol. 20, pp. 199-223, 1993.

[10] T. Levine, H. S. Park, and S. McCornack, "Accuracy in detecting truths and lies: Documenting the 'veracity effect'," *Communication Monographs*, vol. 66, pp. 125-144, 1999.

[11] T. R. Levine, L. N. Anders, J. Banas, K. L. Baum, K. Endo, A. D. S. Hu, and N. C. H. Wong, "Norms, expectations, and deception: A norm violation model of veracity judgments," *Communication Monographs*, vol. 67, pp. 123-137, 2000.

[12]   A. Tversky and D. Kahneman, "Judgement under uncertainty - Heuristics and biases.," *Science*, vol. 185, pp. 1124-1131, 1974.

[13]   A. Vrij, "Interviewing to detect deception.," in *Handbook of the Psychology of Interviewing* A. Memon, and Bull, R., Ed. Chichester, UK: John Wiley & Sons Ltd., 1999.

[14]   A. Vrij, *Detecting lies and deceit: The psychology of lying and its implications for professional practice.* Chichester, UK: Wiley, 2000.

[15]   A. Vrij, *Detecting lies and deceit: The psychology of lying and the implications for professional practice.* . Chichester: Wiley & Sons, 2000.

[16]   A. Vrij, L. Akehurst, and P. Morris, "Individual differences in hand movements during deception," *Journal of Nonverbal Behavior*, vol. 21, pp. 87-103, 1997.

[17]   A. Vrij, L. Akehurst, S. Soukara, and R. Bull, "Detecting deceit via analyses of verbal and nonverbal behavior in children and adults," *Human Communication Research*, in press.

[18]   A. Vrij, K. Edward, and R. Bull, "Stereotypical verbal and nonverbal responses while deceiving others," *Personality and Social Psychology Bulletin*, vol. 27, pp. 899-909, 2001.

[19]   J. Burgoon, D. Buller, A. Ebesu, and P. Rockwell, "Interpersonal deception: V. Accuracy in deception detection," *Communication Monographs*, vol. 61, pp. 303-325, 1994.

[20]   P. Ekman, M. O'Sullivan, W.V. Friesen, and K. Scherer, "Invited article: Face, voice, and body in detecting deceit," *Journal of Nonverbal Behavior*, vol. 15, pp. 125-136, 1991.

[21]   J. George and J. Carlson, "Group support systems and deceptive communication," presented at 32nd Hawaii International Conference on Systems Sciences, Maui, HI, 1999.

[22]   R. P. Hart, *Seducing America: How television charms the modern voter*. New York: Oxford, 1994.

[23]   C. Nass, B. J. Fogg, and Y. Moon, "Can computers be teammates?," *International Journal of Human-Computer Studies*, pp. 669-678, 1996.

[24]   C. Nass, J. Steuer, and E. R. Tauber, "Computers are Social Actors.," Boston, MA, 1994.

[25]   C. M. Nass, Y. Moon, "Machines and mindlessness: Social responses to computers," *Journal of Social Issues*, vol. 56, pp. 81-104, 2000.

[26]   M. Zuckerman and R. Driver, "Telling lies: Verbal and nonverbal correlates of deception," in *Nonverbal Communication: An Integrated Perspective*, A. W. Siegman and S. Feldstein, Eds. Hillsdale, NJ: Erlbaum, 1985, pp. 129-147.

[27]   J. O. Greene, H.D. O'Hair, M.J. Cody, and C. Yen, "Planning and control of behavior during deception," *Human Communication Research*, vol. 11, pp. 335-364, 1985.

[28]   D. B. Buller, J.K. Burgoon, "Interpersonal deception theory," *Communication Theory*, vol. 6, pp. 203-242, 1996.

[29]   J. K. Burgoon, Buller, D.B., "Interpersonal deception theory," in *Readings in persuasion, social influence and compliance-gaining*, J. S. S. R. H. Gass, Ed. Boston: Allyn & Bacon, 2004, pp. 239-264.

[30]   J. K. Burgoon, D.B. Buller, C.H. White, W. Afifi, and A.L.S. Buslig, "The role of conversational involvement in deceptive interpersonal interactions," *Personality and Social Psychology Bulletin*, vol. 25, pp. 669-686, 1999.

[31]   C. H. White and J. K. Burgoon, "Adaptation and communicative design: Patterns of interaction in truthful and deceptive conversations," *Human Communication Research*, vol. 27, pp. 9-37, 2001.

[32]   J. Carlson and R. Zmud, "Channel Expansion Theory and the Experiential Nature of Media Richness Perceptions," *Academy of Management Review*, vol. 42, pp. 153-170, 1999.

[33]   R. C. King and W. Xia, "Media appropriateness: Effects of experience on communication media choice," *Decision Sciences*, vol. 28, pp. 877-910, 1997.

[34]   J. K. Burgoon, "Cross-cultural and intercultural applications of expectancy violations theory," in *Intercultural communication theory*, R. L. Wiseman, Ed. Thousand Oaks, CA: Sage, 1995, pp. 194-214.

[35]   J. K. Burgoon and M. Burgoon, "Expectancy theories.," in *Handbook of language and social psychology*, P. R. H. Giles, Ed., 2nd ed. Sussex, England: John Wiley & Sons, 2001, pp. 79-101.

[36]   J. K. Burgoon and J. L. Hale, "Nonverbal expectancy violations: Model elaboration and application to immediacy behaviors," *Communication Monographs*, vol. 55, pp. 58-79, 1988.

[37]   J. K. Burgoon and B. A. LePoire, "Effects of communication expectancies, actual communication, and expectancy disconfirmation on evaluations of communicators and their communication behavior," *Human Communication Research*, vol. 20, pp. 67-96, 1993.

[38]   J. K. Burgoon and J. B. Walther, "Nonverbal expectancies and the evaluative consequences of violations," *Human Communication Research*, vol. 17, pp. 232-265, 1990.

[39]   G. Miller and J. Stiff, *Deceptive communication*. Newbury Park, CA: Sage Publications, Inc., 1993.

[40]   D. B. Buller, J. K. Burgoon, A. Buslig, and J. Roiger, "Interpersonal deception: VIII. Nonverbal and verbal correlates of equivocation from the Bavelas et al. (1990) research," *Journal of Language and Social Psychology*, vol. 13, pp. 396-417, 1994.

[41]   D. B. Buller, J. B. Stiff, and J. K. Burgoon, "Behavioral adaptation in deceptive transactions: Fact or fiction?," *Human Communication Research*, vol. 22, pp. 589-603, 1996.

[42]   J. K. Burgoon, "Nonverbal measurement of deceit," in *The sourcebook of nonverbal measures: Going beyond words.*, V. Manusov, Ed. Hillsdale, NJ: Erlbaum, in press.

[43]   J. Q. Burgoon and T. Qin, "The Dynamic nature of deceptive verbal communication," *Journal of Language and Social Psychology*, in press.

[44]   L. Zhou, J. K. Burgoon, D. Twitchell, and J. F. Nunamaker, Jr., "Automated linguistics-based cues for detecting deception in text-based asynchronous computer-mediated communication: An empirical investigation," *Group Decision and Negotiation*, vol. 13, pp. 81-106, 2004.

[45]   J. Burgoon, D. Buller, C. White, W. Afifi, and A. Buslig, "The role of conversational involvement in deceptive interpersonal interactions," *Personality and Social Psychology Bulletin*, vol. 25, pp. 669-685, 1999.

[46]   J. K. Burgoon, J.P. Blair, and E. Moyer, "Effects of communication modality on arousal, cognitive complexity, behavioral control and deception detection during deceptive episodes," presented at Annual Meeting of the National Communication Association, Miami Beach, Florida, 2003.

[47]   J. K. Burgoon, J. P. Blair, T. Qin, and J. F. Nunamaker, Jr., "Detecting deception through linguistic analysis," presented at Proceedings of the Symposium on Intelligence and Security Informatics, Tucson, AZ, 2003.

[48]   D. P. Twitchell, K. Wiers, M. Adkins, J.K. Burgoon, and J.F. Nunamaker, Jr. "StrikeCOM: A multi-player online strategy game for researching and teaching group dynamics," presented at Hawaii International Conference on System Sciences, Big Island, Hawaii, 2005.

PUBLICATIONS TO DATE

Adkins, M., Kruse, J., & Younger, R.E. (2004). A language technology toolset for development of a large group augmented facilitation system. In R. H. Sprague, Jr. (Ed.) *Proceedings of the Thirty-Seventh Hawaii International Conference on Systems Sciences*, Los Alamitos, CA: IEEE Computer Society Press.

Adkins, M., Younger, R. E., & Schwarz, R. (2003). Information technology augmentation of the skilled facilitator approach. In R. H. Sprague, Jr. (Ed.) *Proceedings of the 36th Hawaii International Conference on Systems Sciences*, Maui, HI. Los Alamitos, CA: IEEE Computer Society Press.

Adkins, M., Twitchell, D.P., Burgoon, J.K., & Nunamaker, J.F., Jr. (2004). Advances in automated deception detection in text-based computer-mediated communication. *Proceedings of the SPIE Defense and Security Symposium,* Orlando, Florida.

Allspach, L. E., & Burgoon, J.K. (2003). Nonverbal displays. *Encyclopedia of human emotions.* New York: Macmillan.

Biocca, F., Harms, C., & Burgoon, J. K. (2004). Criteria and scope conditions for a theory and measure of social presence. *Presence: Teleoperators and Virtual Environments.*

Briggs, R. O., deVreede, J.G., Nunamaker, J.F. Jr., & Sprague, R.H., Jr. (in press). Information system success. *Journal of Management Information Systems.* 19 (4), 5-8.

Briggs, R. O, deVreede, J.G., & Nunamaker, J. F., Jr. (in press). Thinklets-a comparable unit of analysis for experiments, *Journal of Management Information Systems*, 19(4).. 31-64. (Best Paper from HICSS Conference 2001)

Buller, D. B., & Burgoon, J. K. (1994). Deception: Strategic and nonstrategic communication. In J. A. Daly & J. M. Wiemann (Eds.), *Strategic interpersonal communication* (pp. 191-223). Hillsdale, NJ: Erlbaum.

Buller, D. B., & Burgoon, J. K. (1996). Interpersonal deception theory. *Communication Theory, 6*, 203-242.

Buller, D. B., & Burgoon, J. K. (1997). Emotional expression in the deception process. In P. A. Andersen & L. K. Guerrero (Eds.), *Communication and emotion* (pp. 381-402). Orlando, FL: Academic Press.

Buller, D. B., Burgoon, J. K., Buslig, A., & Roiger, J. (1994). Interpersonal deception: VIII.Nonverbal and verbal correlates of equivocation from the Bavelas et al. (1990) research. *Journal of Language and Social Psychology, 13*, 396-417.

Buller, D. B., Burgoon, J. K., Buslig, A., & Roiger, J. (1996). Testing interpersonal deception theory: The language of interpersonal deception. *Communication Theory, 6*, 268-289.

Buller, D. B., Burgoon, J. K., White, C., & Ebesu, A. S. (1994). Interpersonal deception: VII. Behavioral profiles of falsification, concealment, and equivocation. *Journal of Language and Social Psychology, 13*, 366-395.

Buller, D. B., Stiff, J. B., & Burgoon, J. K. (1996). Behavioral adaptation in deceptive transactions: Fact or fiction. *Human Communication Research, 22*, 589-603.

Burgoon, J. K. (1991). Relational message interpretations of touch, conversational distance, and posture. *Journal of Nonverbal Behavior, 15*, 233-258.

Burgoon, J. K. (1992). Applying a comparative approach to nonverbal expectancy violations theory. In J. Blumler, K. E. Rosengren & J. M. McLeod (Eds.), *Comparatively speaking: Communication and culture across space and time* (pp. 53-69). Beverly Hills, CA: Sage.

Burgoon, J. K. (1993). Interpersonal expectations, expectancy violations, and emotional communication. *Journal of Language and Social Psychology, 12*, 30-48.

Burgoon, J. K. (1995). Cross-cultural and intercultural applications of expectancy violations theory. In R. L. Wiseman (Ed.), *Intercultural communication theory (International and Intercultural Communication Annual* (Vol. 19, pp. 194-214). Thousand Oaks, CA: Sage.

Burgoon, J. K. (in press, a). Nonverbal measurement of deceit. In V. Manusov (Ed.), *The sourcebook of nonverbal measures: Going beyond words*. Hillsdale, NJ: Erlbaum.

Burgoon, J. K. (in press, b). Revisiting the motivation impairment effect: Illumination or illusion? Manuscript accepted for publication in *Communication Yearbook*.

Burgoon, J. K., Adkins, M., Kruse, W. J., Jensen, M. L., Deokar, A. Twitchell, D.P., Nunamaker, J. F., Jr., Lu, S., Metaxas, D. M., & Younger, R. E. (2004) The decision for detecting intent. *Proceeding of the Global Business and Finance Research Conference,* London.

Burgoon, J. K., Adkins, M., Kruse, W. J., Jensen, M. L., Deokar, A. Twitchell, D. P., Lu, S., Metaxas, D. M., Nunamaker, J. F., Jr., & Younger, R. E. (2004) Moving toward intent detection: A tool-based approach. *IEEE proceedings from the Conference on Intelligent Transportation Systems*. Washington, D.C. IEEE.

Burgoon, J. K., & Bacue, A. (2003). Nonverbal communication skills. In B. R. Burleson & J. O. Greene (Eds.), *Handbook of Communication and Social Interaction Skills* (pp. 179-219). Mahwah, NJ: Erlbaum.

Burgoon, J. K., Blair, J. P., Qin, T., & Nunamaker, J. F., Jr. (2003). Detecting deception through linguistic analysis. *Proceedings of the Symposium on Intelligence and Security Informatics*. Berlin: Springer-Verlag.

Burgoon, J. K., Blair, J. P. & Strom, R. (2005). Heuristics and modalities in determining truth versus deception. *Proceedings of the 38th Hawai'i International Conference on System Sciences.* Los Alamitos: IEEE.

Burgoon, J. K., Bonito, J. A., Stoner, G. M. & Dunbar, N. E. (2003). Trust and deception in mediated communication. *Proceedings of the 36th Hawai'i International Conference on System Sciences.* Maui, HI. Los Alamitos: IEEE.

Burgoon, J. K., Bonito, J. B., & Kam, K. (In press). Communication and trust under face-to-face and mediated conditions: Implications for leading from a distance. In S. Weisband & L. Atwater (Eds.), *Leadership at a Distance*. Mahwah, NJ: LEA.

Burgoon, J. K., & Buller, D. B. (2004). Interpersonal deception theory. In J. S. Seiter & R. H. Gass (Eds.), *Readings in Persuasion, Social Influence and Compliance-gaining* (pp. 239-264). Boston: Allyn & Bacon.

Burgoon, J. K., Buller, D. B., Blair, J. P.., & Tilley, P. (in press). Sex differences in presenting and detecting deceptive messages. In D. Canary & K. Dindia (Eds.)*, Sex Differences and Similarities in Communication, 2e.* Mahwah, NJ: LEA.

Burgoon, J. K., Buller, D. B., White, C. H., Afifi, W. A., & Buslig, A. L. S. (1999). The role of conversational involvement in deceptive interpersonal communication. *Personality and Social Psychology Bulletin, 25,* 669-685.

Burgoon, J. K., Chen, F., & Twitchell, D. (in press). Deception and its detection under synchronous and asynchronous computer-mediate communication. *Group Decision and Negotiation.*

Burgoon, J. K., & Ebesu Hubbard, E. (in press). Expectancy violations theory and interaction adaptation theory. In W. Gudykunst (Ed.), *Theorizing About Intercultural Communication.* Thousand Oaks: Sage.

Burgoon, J. K., Marett, K., & Blair, J. P. (2004). Detecting deception in computer-mediated communication. In J. F. George (Ed.), *Computers in Society: Privacy, Ethics & the Internet* (pp. 154-166). Upper Saddle River, NJ: Prentice-Hall.

Burgoon, J. K., & Nunamaker, J. (2004). Toward computer-aided support for the detection of deception. *Group Decision and Negotiation, 13,* 1-4.

Burgoon, J. K., & Nunamaker, J. F. (2004). Toward computer-aided support for the detection of deception: Volume 2. *Group Decision and Negotiation, 13,* 107-110.

Cao, J., Crews, J. M., Lin, M., Burgoon, J. K., Deokar, A., & Nunamaker, J. F. Jr. Computer-based training: What users want. In preparation for *Human-Computer Interaction (HCI).*

Cao, J., Crews, J. M., Lin, M., Burgoon, J. K., & Nunamaker, J. F., Jr. (2003). Can people be trained to better detect deception?: Instructor-led vs. web-based training. Accepted for *2003 Americas Conference on Information Systems (AMCIS 2003), Tampa, Florida.* Recommended for publication in a special issue of the *Journal of SMET Education: Innovations and Research.*

Cao, J., Crews, J., Lin, M., Burgoon, J., & Nunamaker, J. F., Jr. (2003). Designing Agent99 Trainer: A learner-centered, web-based training system for deception detection. *Proceedings of the Symposium on Intelligence and Security Informatics.* Berlin: Springer-Verlag.

Cao, J., Crews, J. M., Lin, M., Burgoon, J. K., & Nunamaker, J. F. Jr. (2003). Can People Be Trained to Better Detect Deception? Instructor-Led vs. Web-Based Training. *Proceedings of the Ninth Americas Conference on Information Systems (AMCIS 2003),* Tampa, Florida.

Cao, J., Crews, J. M., Lin, M., Burgoon, J. K., & Nunamaker, J. F. Jr. (2003). Designing Agent99 Trainer: A Learner-Centered, Web-Based Training System for Deception Detection. *Proceedings of the first NSF/NIJ Symposium on Intelligence and Security Informatics (ISI 2003),* Tucson, AZ, 358-365.

Cao, J., Crews, J. M., Nunamaker, J. F., Jr., Burgoon, J. K., & Lin, M. (2004). User experience with Agent99Trainer: A usability study. *Proceedings of the 37th Hawai'i International Conference on System Sciences,* Kona, HI. Los Alamitos: IEEE.

Cao, J., Lin, M., Deokar, A., Burgoon, J., Crews, J., & Adkins, M. (2004) Computer-based training for deception detection: What users want? In H. Chen, R. Miranda, D.D. Zeng, C. Demchak, J. Schroeder, T. Madhusudan (Eds.) *Intelligence and Security Informatics*. Springe-Verlag, Berlin.

Cao, J., Lin, M., Deokar, A., Burgoon, J. K., Crews, J. M., & Adkins, M. (2004). Computer-based Training for Deception Detection: What Users Want. *Proceedings of the second NSF/NIJ Symposium on Intelligence and Security Informatics (ISI 2004)*, Tucson, AZ.

Cao, J., Crews, J. M., Nunamaker, J. F. Jr., Burgoon, J. K., & Lin, M. (2004). User experience with Agent99 Trainer: A usability study. *Proceedings of 37th Annual Hawaii International Conference on System Sciences (HICSS 2004)*, Kona, HI. Los Alamitos: IEEE.

Cao, J. & Zhang, D. (2001). An intelligent learning assistant in multimedia-based interactive e-learning. *Proceedings of the Seventh Americas Conference on Information Systems (AMCIS 2001)*, Boston, Massachusetts, 127-133.

Cao, J., Roussinov, D., Robles-Flores, J. A., & Nunamaker, J. F. Jr. (2005) Automated question answering from videos: NLP vs. pattern matching. *Proceedings of the 38th Annual Hawaii International Conference on System Sciences (HICSS 2005)*, Kona, HI. Los Alamitos: IEEE.

Carlson, J.R. & George, J.F. (2004). Media appropriateness in the conduct and discovery of deceptive communication: The relative influence of richness and synchronicity. *Group Decision and Negotiation*, 13(2), 2004, 191-210.

Carlson, J.R., George, J.F., Burgoon, J.K., Adkins, M., & White, C. H. (2004). Deception in computer-mediated communication. *Group Decision and Negotiation*, 13, 5-28.

Crews, J. M., Cao, J., Lin, M., Burgoon, J. K., & Nunamaker, J. F. Jr. (under review). Training people to better detect deception: Instructor-led Vs. web-based training. *Journal of Science, Math, Engineering, and Technology Education Innovations and Research (SMET)*.

DePaulo, B., Lindsay, J., Malone, B., Muhlenbruck, L., Charlton, K., & Cooper, H. (2003). Cues to deception. *Psychological Bulletin, 129*, 74-118.

Dunbar, N. E., & Burgoon, J. K. (in press). Nonverbal measurement of dominance. In V. Manusov (Ed.), *The Sourcebook of Nonverbal Measures: Going Beyond Words*. Hillsdale, NJ: Erlbaum.

Dunbar, N. E., & Burgoon, J. K. (in press). Perceptions of power and interactional dominance in interpersonal encounters. *Journal of Social and Personal Relationships*

Dunbar, N. E., Ramirez, A., Jr., & Burgoon, J. K. (2003). Interactive deception: Effects of participation on participant-receiver and observer judgments. *Communication Reports, 16*, 23-33.

George, J. F., (2004) The theory of planned behavior and Internet purchasing. *Internet Research*, 14(3), 198-212.

George, J. F. (2004). Introduction to the social issues of computing. In George, J.F. (Ed.) *Computers in Society: Privacy, Ethics & the Internet.* Upper Saddle River, N.J.: Prentice-Hall, 6-13.

George, J. F., Biros, D. P., Adkins, M., Burgoon, J. K., & Nunamaker, J. F., Jr. (2004) Testing various modes of computer-based training for deception detection. In H. Chen, R. Miranda, D.D. Zeng, C. Demchak, J. Schroeder, T. Madhusudan (Eds.) *Intelligence and Security Informatics* (pp. 411-417). Berlin: Springer-Verlag.

George, J. F., Biros, D. P., Burgoon, J. K., & Nunamaker, J. F., Jr. (2003). Training professionals to detect deception. *Proceedings of the Symposium on Intelligence and Security Informatics*. Berlin: Springer-Verlag.

George, J. F., & Carter, P., (2004). Computer-based performance monitoring. In George, J.F. (Ed.) *Computers in Society: Privacy, Ethics & the Internet.* Upper Saddle River, N.J.: Prentice-Hall, 110-120.

George, J.F. & Marett, K. (2004). Inhibiting deception and its detection. *Proceedings of the 37th annual Hawaii Conference on Systems Science*, Kona, HI. Los Alamitos: IEEE.

George, J. F., Marett, K., Burgoon, J. K., Crews, J., Cao, J., Lin, M., & Biros, D. P. (2004). Training to detect deception: An experimental investigation. *Proceedings of the 37th Hawai'i International Conference on System Sciences*, Kona, HI. Los Alamitos: IEEE.

George, J.F., Marett, K. & Tilley, P. (2004). Deception detection under varying electronic media and warning conditions. *Proceedings of the 37th Annual Hawaii Conference on System Sciences*, Kona, HI. Los Alamitos: IEEE.

Hale, J. L. & Burgoon, J. K. (in press). Nonverbal measurement of relational communication. In V. Manusov (Ed.), *The Sourcebook of Nonverbal Measures: Going Beyond Words*. Hillsdale, NJ: Erlbaum.

Lin, M., Cao, J., Burgoon, J. K., & Nunamaker, J. F. Jr. (2004). Agent99 Trainer: A computer-based training system for deception detection. In preparation for *IEEE Computer*

Lin, M., Chau, M., Cao, J., & Nunamaker, J. F. Jr. (conditionally accepted). Automated video segmentation for lecture videos. *The International Journal of Technology and Human Interaction (IJTHI)*. Athens, Greek: Idea Group Publishing.

Lin, M., Crews, J. M., Cao, J., Nunamaker, J. F. Jr., & Burgoon, J. K. (2003). AGENT99 Trainer: Designing a Web-Based Multimedia Training System for Deception Detection Knowledge Transfer. *Proceedings of the Ninth Americas Conference on Information Systems (AMCIS 2003)*, Tampa, Florida.

Lowry, P.B., Albrecht, C.C., Nunamaker, J.F., Jr., & Lee, J.D. (2003), Evolutionary development and research on Internet-based collaborative writing tools and processes to enhance e-writing in an e-government setting, *Decision Support Systems*, 34(3), 229-252.

Marett, L.K. & George, J.F., (2004). Deception in the case of one sender and multiple receivers. *Group Decision and Negotiation*, 13(1), 29-44.

Meservy, T. O., Jensen, M. L., Kruse, J., Burgoon, J. K., & Nunamaker, J. F. (2005). Automatic extraction of deceptive behavioral cues from video. *Intelligence and Security Informatics: Proceedings of the Third Symposium on Intelligence and Security Informatics ISI 2005, Atlanta, GA, USA.* Berlin: Springer-Verlag.

Nunamaker, J. F., Jr. & Briggs, R. (Eds.) (In press) Collaboration technology research: Current topics and applications. *Advances in Management Information Systems (AMIS), Volume II*, M.E. Sharpe, Inc.

Nunamaker, J. F., Jr. & Briggs, R. (Eds.) (In press). Collaboration technology research: Foundations. *Advances in Management Information Systems (AMIS)*, Volume 1, M.E. Sharpe, Inc.

Qin, T., Burgoon, J. K., & Nunamaker, J. F., Jr. (2004). An exploratory study on promising cues in deception detection and application of decision trees. *Proceedings of the 37th Hawai'i International Conference on System Sciences,* Kona, HI. *Los Alamitos: IEEE.*

Romano, N.C., Bauer, Chen, H., and Nunamaker, J.F., Jr. (2003). A web-based collaborative approach to attitude solicitation, analysis, sense-making & visualization, *Management Information Systems Journal,* 19(4), 213-246.

Thatcher, J. B., & George, J. F. (2004). Commitment, trust, and social involvement: An exploratory study of antecedents to web shopper loyalty. *Journal of Organizational Computing and E-Commerce,* 14(4).

Twitchell, D., Adkins, M., Nunamaker, J.F., Jr., & Burgoon, J.K. (2004). Using speech act theory to model conversations for automated classification and retrieval. *Proceedings from Language Action Perspective Working Conference,* Rutgers University, NJ.

Twitchell, D., Zhou, L., Burgoon, J. K., Nunamaker, J. F., Jr., Qin, T., & Broneck, K. (2003). Linguistic indicators of deceit in electronic communication. *Proceedings of the 36th Hawai'i International Conference on System Sciences.* Maui, HI. Los Alamitos: IEEE.

Twitchell, D., Zhou, L., Burgoon, J. K., Nunamaker, J. F., Jr., Qin, T., & Broneck, K. (in press). Linguistic indicators of deceit in electronic communication. *Group Negotiation and Decision-Making.*

White, C. H., & Burgoon, J. K. (2001). Adaptation and communicative design: Patterns of interaction in truthful and deceptive conversations. *Human Communication Research, 27,* 9-37.

Zhang, D., & Nunamaker, J.F., Jr. (2003). An NLP Approach to video indexing & retrieval, *IEEE Transactions on Multimedia.* 6(3), 450-458

Zhou, L., Burgoon, J. K., & Twitchell, D. (2003). A longitudinal analysis of language behavior of deception in e-mail. *Proceedings of the Symposium on Intelligence and Security Informatics.* Springer-Verlag.

Zhou, L., Burgoon, J. K., Twitchell, D., & Nunamaker, J. F., Jr. (2004). Automating linguistics-based cues for detecting deception in text-based asynchronous computer-mediated communication. *Group Decision and Negotiation, 13,* 81-106.

Zhou, L., Burgoon, J. K., Twitchell, D. P., Qin, T., & Nunamaker, J. F., Jr.(2004). Toward the automatic prediction of deception: An empirical comparison of classification methods. *Journal of Management Information Systems, 20 (4),* 129-136.

Zhou, L., Twitchell, D., Qin, T., Burgoon, J. K., & Nunamaker, J. F., Jr. (2003). An exploratory study into deception detection in text-based computer-mediated communication. *Proceedings of the 36th Hawai'i International Conference on System Sciences. Los Alamitos: IEEE.*

Detecting Concealment of Intent in Transportation Screening: a Proof-of-Concept

Judee K. Burgoon, Douglas P. Twitchell, Matthew L. Jensen, Mark Adkins, John Kruse, Amit Deokar, Shan Lu, Dimitris N. Metaxas, Jay F. Nunamaker Jr., Robert E. Younger

Abstract—Past research in deception detection at the University of Arizona has guided the investigation of concealment detection. A theoretical foundation and model for the analysis of concealment detection is proposed. The visual and verbal channels are the two avenues of concealment detection studied. Several available test beds for visual intent analysis are discussed and a proof-of-concept study exploring nonverbal communication within the context of concealment detection is shared. Additionally, two methods that may aid in verbally detecting deception during the interviews characteristic of secondary screening are introduced. Message feature mining uses message features or cues combined with machine learning techniques to classify messages according to their deceptive potential. Speech act profiling, a method for quantifying and visualizing entire conversations, has shown promise in aiding deception detection. These methods may be combined and are intended to be a part of a suite of tools for automating deception detection.

I. INTRODUCTION

Safeguarding the homeland against deception and infiltration by adversaries who may be planning hostile actions poses one of the most daunting challenges in the 21st century. Achieving high information assurance is complicated not only by the speed, complexity, volume, and global reach of communications and information exchange that current information technologies now afford, but also by the fallibility of humans in detecting hostile intent. All too often, the people protecting our borders and public spaces are handicapped by untimely and incomplete information, overwhelming flows of people and materiel, and the limits of human vigilance. Moreover, the vulnerabilities posed by human agents are often exacerbated by the very same technologies that enable amassing the glut of information.

The interactions and complex interdependencies of information systems and social systems render the problem difficult and challenging. We simply do not have the wherewithal to specifically identify every potentially dangerous individual around the world. Although completely automating concealment detection is an appealing prospect, the complexity of detecting and countering hostile intentions defies a fully automated solution. A more promising approach is to integrate improved human detection with automated tools that augment other biometric systems for behavioral analysis, the end goal being a system that singles out individuals for further scrutiny in a manner that reduces false positives and false negatives. Such an approach is needed to assist the transportation systems and border security personnel who have to counter high stake situations routinely.

Transportation and border security systems have a common goal: allow law-abiding people to pass through checkpoints and detain those people with hostile intent. These systems employ a number of security measures aimed at accomplishing this goal. The methods and technologies described in this paper may prove to be useful in prescreening, primary screening, and secondary screening activities.

The usefulness of any method of transportation security must be evaluated. The U.S. Federal Aviation Administration (FAA) has utilized nine criteria for evaluating such systems. These criteria are aimed at ensuring the best methods and technologies are deployed in U.S. airports, and the methods reviewed in this paper are given a precursory evaluation based on the nine criteria.

In this paper, we present our current research efforts in the direction of developing automated tools to identify concealment and deception. The paper is organized as

Portions of this research were supported by funding from the U. S. Air Force Office of Scientific Research under the U. S. Department of Defense University Research Initiative (Grant #F49620-01-1-0394) and by the U. S. Department of Homeland Security (Cooperative Agreement N66001-01-X-6042). The views, opinions, and/or findings in this report are those of the authors and should not be construed as official Department of Defense or Department of Homeland Security positions, policies, or decisions.

J. K. Burgoon, M. Adkins, J. Kruse, M. L. Jensen, A. Deokar, D. P. Twitchell, and J. F. Nunamaker are with The Center for the Management of Information at The University of Arizona, Tucson, AZ 85721 USA (phone: 520-621-2640; fax: 520-621-2641; e-mails: jburgoon@cmi.arizona.edu, madkins@cmi.arizona.edu, jkruse@cmi.arizona.edu, mjensen@cmi.arizona.edu, adeokar@cmi.arizona.edu, dtwitchell@cmi.arizona.edu, jnunamaker@cmi.arizona.edu,).

S. Lu and D. Metaxas are with the Computational Biomedicine Imaging and Modeling Center at Rutgers University, New Brunswick, NJ 08854 USA (e-mails: shanlu@cs.rutgers.edu, dnm@cs.rutgers.edu).

R. Younger is with the Space and Naval Warfare Systems Center, San Diego, CA 92152 USA (e-mail: younger@spawar.navy.mil) follows: Section II discusses the relationship between deception, concealment, internal state and behavior. Section III explains the model and the methodology we follow to identify concealment based on suspicion level. Sections IV and IV.C discuss verbal and nonverbal methods for concealment detection respectively. Section VI describes how these technologies might be used for aviation security, and Section VII evaluates the methods based on FAA criteria. Finally, Section VIII concludes and future research work is proposed.

II. Deception, Concealment, Intent and Behavior

Deception is defined as a message knowingly transmitted with the intent to foster false beliefs or conclusions [1]. Over the past two and a half years, the Center for the Management of Information (CMI) at the University of Arizona has conducted over a dozen experiments to study deception with over 2000 subjects [2-5]. These experiments have been instrumental in understanding the factors influencing deception, and have guided the building of automated tools for detecting deception and the creation of training for security personnel [6, 7]. Since a person will most likely be deceptive about hostile intentions, research in deception detection has led to the question of whether or not concealed malicious intent can be inferred from cues in communication.

For those who guard our transportation systems, identifying deception is a difficult daily task. Opportunities for travelers to deceive occur frequently in the screening process and it is the responsibility of those who monitor travelers to root out deceivers who may be engaged in illegal or terrorist activities. This task is made even more complicated by the brief interactions between agents and travelers, tremendous flow of people using transportation systems, and by the limits of human attention.

The quest for the perfect lie detector or truth serum has been long and has resulted in only a few modest successes. The most common and probably most controversial method of deception detection is use of the polygraph, commonly known as the "lie-detector test." In a summary of laboratory tests, Vrij reports that the polygraph is about 82% accurate at identifying deceivers [8]. The National Academy of Science, however, concluded that such experimental numbers are often overestimates of actual results, especially in personnel screening [9]. Although it is not admissible in court, the polygraph is useful in some investigations for identifying potential suspects. The problem is, however, the polygraph is a very invasive procedure and one that evokes fear in those subjected to it. Investigators must have a good reason for subjecting someone to a polygraph test and the subject must agree to take the test. Therefore, even though the polygraph is relatively accurate compared to

other methods, its invasive quality renders it useless in most everyday situations.

Other techniques, such as the Statement Validity Analysis (SVA) methods Criteria Based Content Analysis (CBCA) and Reality Monitoring (RM), are based on the content of interviews with subjects rather than the physiological arousal as with the polygraph. Because both of these methods require an interview with the subject suspected of being deceptive, they are still intrusive, yet not as physically invasive as the body-sensor-addled polygraph. Both methods also require trained interviewers for conducting the interview and highly skilled analysts for reviewing the statements and reaching a judgment. Neither method provides immediate feedback. CBCA is based on what is known as the Undeutsch-Hypothesis [10, 11], which states that a statement derived from actual memory will differ in content and quality from a statement derived from fantasy. CBCA uses a set of criteria to evaluate this hypothesis. Trained investigators rate a criminal statement against each criterion using a three-point scale. RM uses a list of criteria that overlaps somewhat with CBCA, but operates under a different hypothesis: truthful or real memories are likely to contain perceptual, contextual, and affective information while deceptions or fabrications are likely to contain cognitive operations (thoughts and meanings). In a face-to-face study of 73 nursing students, Vrij found that use of CBCA and RM to detect deception was successful at rates of 79.5% and 64.1% respectively [12].

Not all deception detection methods are invasive. Computerized Voice Stress Analysis (CVSA), for example is a technique that analyzes the voice pitch changes as a measure of arousal. The technique has shown to be roughly equivalent in accuracy to the polygraph [13], but as with the polygraph, this method will not be useful in situations where deception is not accompanied by physiological arousal.

Despite the research in face-to-face deception and the success of SVA in some studies, most people remain unable to detect deception in face-to-face media at a rate higher than chance [14]. Several possible reasons have been given for the lack of detection accuracy including truth bias, visual distraction, situational familiarity, and idiosyncratic behaviors that cloud true deception cues (See [14]:79-81, 98-99 for more detail).

Searching for deceptive cues in behavior has led us to examine the one of the roots of deception, intensions that the sender wants to conceal. The intent of a person, whether benign or hostile, is closely tied to his or her internal state. Internal states may be manifest by any of a number of behaviors. However, a single behavior could indicate a number of internal states as demonstrated in Fig. 1. The relationship between one behavior and multiple internal states renders the task of identifying concealment of intent particularly challenging. Hence, our current research focuses on understanding these mappings and leveraging experience in the area of deception detection to produce methods which identify whether the true intent of a person is being concealed.

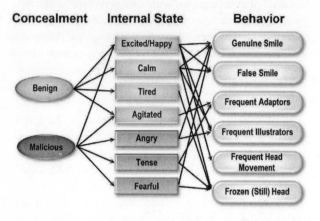

Fig. 1 Relationship between concealment, internal state and behavior

III. THEORETICAL FOUNDATION

Several theories and models offer useful perspectives on the linkage between concealment and overt behavioral manifestations that elicit trust or suspicion. Three theories that are especially germane—interpersonal deception theory, expectancy violations theory, and signal detection theory—are integrated to produce a model of suspicious and trust-eliciting verbal and nonverbal communication. Additionally, we are developing a theory-guided taxonomy for clustering verbal and nonverbal behaviors into appropriate groupings of suspicious and non-suspicious behavior in order to identify those who have the highest probability of concealed malicious intent.

Interpersonal deception theory (IDT) is a key theory for mapping behavioral cues into general behavioral characteristics of deception [15]. IDT depicts the process-oriented nature of interpersonal deception and the multiplicity of pre-interactional, interactional, and outcome factors that are thought to influence it. Among its relevant precepts is the assumption that deception is a strategic activity subject to a variety of tactics for evading detection. It also recognizes the influence of receiver behaviors on sender displays, and it views deception as a dynamic and iterative process, a game of moves and countermoves that enable senders to make ongoing adaptations that further hamper detection. Consequently, a theory of suspicious and trust-eliciting behavior must take into account a variety of moderator variables, each of which may spawn a different behavioral profile.

Expectancy violations theory (EVT) is concerned with what nonverbal and verbal behavior patterns are considered normal or expected, what behaviors constitute violations of expectations, and what consequences violations create [16]. Its proponents contend that specific behavioral cues are less diagnostic than whether a sender's behavior conforms to or violates expected behavioral patterns and that receivers are more likely to attune to such violations. In other words, it is more useful to classify communication according to whether it includes behavioral anomalies, deviations from a baseline, or discrepancies among indicators. Behavioral patterns which include deviations and anomalies are predicted to influence receiver judgments of credibility and deceit. The theory distinguishes between positive and negative violations. Positive violations may actually foster perceived trustworthiness and credibility, whereas negative violations should foster suspicion. Expectancy violations theory is thus relevant to the process of comparing the behavioral profiles against the expected norms.

The process of interpreting different verbal and nonverbal cues and clustering them together in the form of behavioral characteristics to contrast with the expected behavioral characteristics is non-trivial and challenging, considering the large variation in the behaviors of different human beings. The key segments of this dynamic process are the characteristics of actors, features of transmission channels, features of messages, and the information exchange process itself.

Finally, a threshold for deriving the level of suspicion or trust is based on signal detection theory (SDT). Developed by Green and Swets [17], SDT defines two sets of probabilities in a signal detection test, in which two possible stimuli types must be discriminated. In the context of intent identification, the two possible stimuli types are concealment and openness. If the actual intent is hostile and the output judgment is suspicion, the trial is a "hit." If the actual intent is benign and the output is judged suspicion, it is a "false alarm." If the actual intent is hostile but the judgment is one of trust, it is a "miss." Finally, if the actual intent is trustworthy and the judgment is one of trust, it is a correct decision as shown in Table I.

TABLE I
POSSIBLE JUDGMENTS FROM SDT

		Judgment	
		Suspicion	**Trust**
Conceal-ment	**Hostile**	"Hit"	"Miss"
	Benign	False Alarm	Correct Decision

According to SDT, the output of such a binary test is based on the value of a decision variable, which in the context of concealment identification is the suspicion level. The threshold value of the decision variable is called the criterion. For humans, the selection of a criterion is not only related to the value of actual stimuli but also related to their psychological characteristics. In other words, the criterion is a function of perceived stimuli, which, in the context of concealment detection, are the behavioral profile deviations. The SDT calculation methods described in [18] can be used to study the distribution of the values of the suspicion level variable across the behavioral profile deviations to determine the actual intent of the individual can be considered as input for the model, which is demonstrated in the form of the behavioral cues, either verbal or nonverbal. These behaviors include linguistic, content, meta-content, kinesic, proxemic, chronemic, and paralinguistic cues. The behaviors are influenced by the interaction of sender and receiver actions, cognitions and their mutual influence.

Linguistic cues include features like word selection, phrasing, and sentence structure. Content/Theme cues are taken from the meaning of the sender's words.

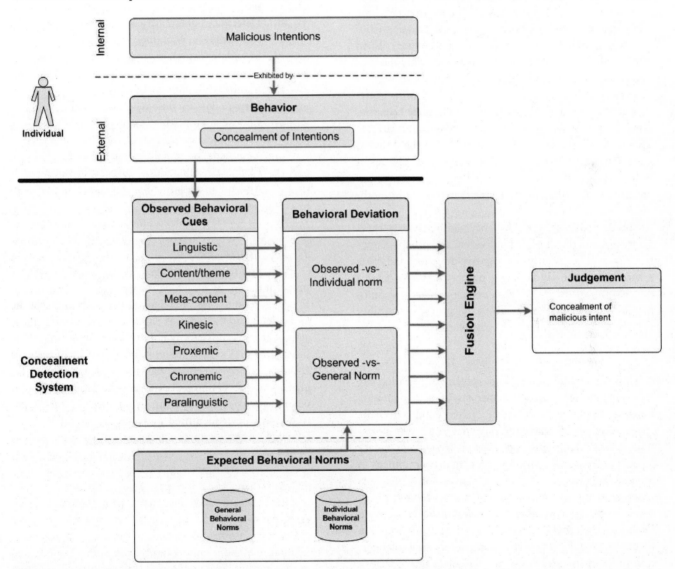

Fig. 2 Model of concealment detection based on observed behavioral cues. The behavioral cues are compared to norms for that individual and to general norms. Deviations are noted and combined to produce a judgment on the suspicion of concealment.

appropriate criterion for the final decision making.

We have integrated these multidisciplinary theories and models into a single systemic framework that guides our experimental work and tool development. The model is shown in Fig. 2. It is a decision model for judging how trustworthy an individual is on a trust-suspicion spectrum, based on demonstrated behavioral cues. The

Meta-content cues are derived from the types of topics the content addresses. For example, Reality Monitoring is based on meta-content. Kinesic cuse are found in the way a person moves. Proxemic cues are determined from the distance a person is to other people and other objects. For example, sitting in the back row of a meeting might indicate disinterest in the meeting. Chronemic cues concern a person's use of time. For example, a person might establish dominance by arriving late to a meeting. Paralinguistic cues are obtained from groups of linguistic features. An example is a person demonstrating other-centeredness by consistently not referring to himself or herself.

The observed behavioral characteristics of the sender can be compared to the normal or expected characteristics stored in a repository. Unexpected deviations may indicate concealment of malicious intent.

First the immediate behavioral characteristics are compared with the individual's historical characteristics across multiple episodes within a given context. When individual-level histories are not available, only the second set of expectations will be utilized. This second set of expectations is comprised of a general profile of expected behavior across people within the same scenario. For example, when guilty suspects are questioned face-to-face, they may show a combination of verbal brevity, vocal tension, and over control of movement. The result is that such individuals typically look more tense, unpleasant, aroused, and submissive than those with nothing to hide.

The deviation between the observed behavioral characteristics and the expected individual and group characteristics in either positive or negative directions indicates a suspicion level. By setting a proper threshold on this deviation measure and given a certain context, the automated tool will thus be able to indicate the probability that the sender is suspicious or trustworthy.

IV. VERBAL CUES AND LINGUISTIC ANALYSIS

Message feature mining and speech act profiling are two methods for automated analysis of verbal interactions. Both of these methods, given good automatic speech recognition, have the potential to aid transportation security by giving screeners, especially secondary screeners feedback concerning potential concealment in security interactions. To work effectively in a transportation security context such as airport screening, effective speech recognition software would be required to deploy these verbal deception and concealment detection methods. We do not discuss automatic speech recognition in this paper; however, we feel that current speech recognition technologies would be sufficient for the requirements of the verbal detection methods since neither require complete word recognition and the probabilistic nature of both means that any speech recognition errors are simply (but, of course, undesirably) added to the total error of the system.

A. Message Feature Mining

Message feature mining [7] is a method for classifying

messages as deceptive or truthful based on content-independent message features. It can be divided into two major steps, extracting features and classification, each with its own sub-steps. Table II is a summary of the procedure.

TABLE II
SUMMARY OF INTENT-BASED TEXT CLASSIFICATION PROCEDURE

1) Extract Features.
   a) Choose appropriate features for deceptive intent.
   b) Determine granularity of feature aggregation (i.e. sentence, paragraph, etc.).
   c) Calculate features over desired text portions.
2) Classify.
   a) Manually classify documents.
   b) Prepare data for automatic classification.
   c) Choose appropriate classification method.
   d) Train model on portion of data.
   e) Test model on remaining data.
   f) Evaluate results and modify features, granularity, and/or classification method to improve results.

1) Extracting Features

Extracting features includes choosing appropriate features for deception on which the messages will be classified, determining the granularity of feature aggregation, and calculating the features on the desired text. Of these steps, the most difficult is choosing the appropriate features. Potentially there are an infinite number of possible features. Choosing those that are most appropriate for classifying deception or concealment requires knowledge of the deception domain. A number of general features have been identified and may be useful in many contexts. These features are discussed below in Section 3) below.

2) Classifying Messages

Classifying the messages starts with manually classifying the messages in the training set, preparing data for automatic classification, choosing an appropriate classification method, training and testing the model, and evaluating the results. Because unsupervised learning may or may not create clusters based on deception, message feature mining uses supervised learning and manual classification of the training and testing sets. Once the data set is manually classified, it needs to be cleaned and formatted for input into the machine learning algorithms.

After the data are ready for classification, an appropriate classification method or set of methods must be chosen. There are a number of methods to choose from, each with its own advantages and disadvantages [19].

Furthermore, most machine learning methods have a number of parameters (such as number of hidden nodes in neural networks) that adjust the behavior of the models, resulting in a very large number of possible models. Choosing a set of methods to use can be daunting; however, some methods that seem to have withstood the test of time include inductive decision trees and neural networks. After the method or set of methods is chosen, it is a simple task to train and test the data and obtain the accuracy results. Once obtained, the results can be used as a feedback tool for modifying the features, the granularity, and/or the classification methods in an effort to improve the results.

3) The Desert Survival Study

The Desert Survival study was designed with two purposes in mind: first to test message feature mining with a set of cues to deception and second to create a data repository for testing automated deception detection tools. To this end, the study utilized the Desert Survival Problem [20], which provides an environment for group communication and produced a set of deceptive and truthful messages. This set of messages provided a test bed for determining deceptive cues and testing message feature mining for deception detection.

The Desert Survival Problem places groups of two in a situation where they must rank 12 items according to how important that item is to survive in the desert. Before beginning the task, group members are given expert advice on how to survive in the desert and a member of the group is instructed to be deceptive. Group members discuss the items and come to a consensus on how to rank the items. The deceptive member is encouraged to change the group's consensus contrary to his or her own opinion. A more detailed explanation can be found in [3] and [2].

TABLE III
EXAMPLE FEATURES (ADAPTED FROM [3])

- Word quantity
- Average sentence length [21]
- Passive voice ratio $\frac{\text{total \# of passive verbs}}{\text{total \# of verbs}}$
- Emotiveness [21]:
  $$\frac{\text{total \# adjectives} + \text{total \# of adverbs}}{\text{total \# of nouns} + \text{total \# of verbs}}$$
- Content word diversity:
  $\frac{\text{total \# of unique content words}}{\text{total \# of content words}}$, where content words primarily expresses lexical meaning (not function words).

The data consists of all of the messages sent by all of the participants each day of the study. Each message is

considered a document and is classified as deceptive or truthful based on whether the participant was instructed to be deceptive. Table III gives the operational definitions for a sample of 5 of the 23 features used in the Desert Survival study. All of the features are explained in [3].

4) Experimental Findings

Zhou et. al. [3, 22] used the Desert Survival problem in a study with groups of two. One of the subjects in some of the pairs was instructed to deceive his or her partner by recommending a ranking counter to their actual opinion. Using the automated message feature mining technique the researchers were able to obtain approximately 80% accuracy at detecting deceptive messages and subjects—much better than the 50% baseline accuracy of guessing. Although the technology is not perfect, it has a number of possible uses. For example, in a situation where deception is suspected, large email archives could be searched for messages that exhibit deceptive cues reducing the investigators' workload. As noted earlier, coupled with automatic speech recognition, it could provide an aid to interviewers in secondary screening.

B. Speech Act Profiling

Speech act profiling [23] is a method of analyzing and visualizing conversations and participants behavior according to how they converse rather than the subject of the conversation. Since people may deceive in any domain, it is useful to have an analysis technique that is domain independent. Speech act profiling provides a domain independent analysis of conversations by combining the concepts of speech act theory, automated speech act classification, and fuzzy logic.

Speech act theory posits that any utterance (usually a sentence) contains a propositional content part, c, and an illocutionary force, f [24]. The propositional content is the meaning of the words which created the utterance. For example, the statement *it's cold in here* has the propositional content that the room or area where the speaker is located is cold. The illocutionary force, however, is the intent of the speaker's assertion that something about the world is true. That is, the speaker is *doing* something by speaking, which in this case is asserting. Speakers can do many things with an utterance. They can assert, question, thank, declare, insult, order, and even make substantial changes in the world such as marry a couple or inaugurate an president. There might be more than one illocutionary force or speech act associated with an utterance, and the real act is determined by the context where the words are uttered. With the previous example, *it's cold in here*, if uttered by a general in the army to a private might be an order to turn up the thermostat rather than just a simple statement. Thus, every utterance has several illocutionary act potentials, each dependent on the context. From here on, the illocutionary force or act potentials are labeled as speech acts.

Speech acts are important in deception detection for two reasons. First, they are the means by which deception is transmitted; and second, they provide a mechanism for studying deception in conversations in a content independent manner. Deceptive speakers may express more uncertainty in their messages than truthtellers [25], and this uncertainty can be detected in the type of speech acts speakers use. For example, uncertain speakers should tend to use more *opinions, maybe expressions*, and *questions* than truthtellers.

TABLE IV
SELECTED SPEECH ACTS FOUND IN THE SPEECH ACT PROFILES
(ADAPTED FROM [26])

Tag Name	Tag	Example
STATEMENT-NON-OPINION	sd	I'm in the legal department.
ACKNOWLEDGE (BACKCHANNEL)	b	Uh-huh.
STATEMENT-OPINION	sv	I think it's great
AGREE/ACCEPT	aa	That's exactly it
ABANDONED, TURN-EXIT OR UNINTERPRETABLE	%	So,-
APPRECIATION	ba	I can imagine
YES-NO-QUESTION	qy	Do you have to have special training?
YES-ANSWER	ny	Yes.
WH-QUESTION	qw	Well, how old are you?
NO ANSWERS	nn	No.
AFFIRMATIVE NON-YES ANSWER	na	It is.
MAYBE/ACCEPT-PART	maybe	Something like that

Speech acts are important and technically useful since a method has been created to automatically identify them [27]. This method uses a manually annotated corpus of conversations to train n-gram language models and a hidden Markov model, which in turn identify the most likely sequence of speech acts in a conversation. Using the principles of fuzzy logic, the probabilities from the hidden Markov model can be taken as degrees to which an utterance belongs to a number of fuzzy sets representing the speech acts. Speech act profiling aggregates these fuzzy sets together and subtracts from them a

"normal" conversation profile (created from the training corpus) to create a profile for an entire conversation. An example profile is shown in Fig. 3. Additionally, Table IV shows a selection of 12 of the speech acts from the total set of 42 used in [27].

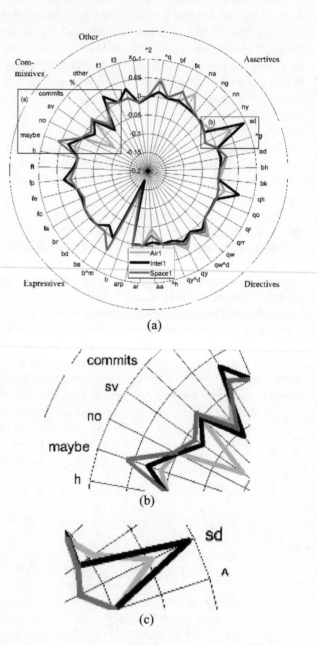

Fig. 3 (a) Sample speech act profile showing submissive and uncertain behavior by the deceiver as indicated by the (b) greater number of MAYBE/ACCEPT-PARTs (maybe) and OPINIONS (sv) and (c) fewer STATEMENTs (sd)

Fig. 3 is a speech act profile created from all of the utterances from a single multi-player online game, Strike-Com [28]. One of the players, Space1, has been told to deceptively steer the group away from bombing the correct locations (the goal of the game) as well as to conceal his intentions. In this particular game the profile indicates that the participant playing Space1 is uncertain compared to the other participants, Air1 and Intel1, as indicated by the greater number of MAYBE/ACCEPT-PARTs (maybe) and OPINIONS (sv) as magnified in Fig. 3(b) and fewer STATEMENTs (sd) as magnified in Fig. 3(c). An example of this uncertain language is shown in the excerpt in Table V. Early in the game, Space1 hedges the comment "i got a stike on c2" with the comment "but it says that it can be wrong..." Later Space1 qualifies his advocacy of grid space e3 with "i have a feeling." In reality there was no target at e3, and Space1 was likely attempting to deceive the others as instructed. In DePaulo et. al.'s meta-analysis of deception [25], vocal and verbal impressions of uncertainty by a listener were significantly correlated with deception. That is, when deception is present, the receiver of the deceptive message often notices uncertainty in the speaker's voice or words. Since the voice channel isn't available in chat, any uncertainty would have to be transmitted and detected using only the words. The uncertainty transmitted in the words is picked up by the profile in Fig. 3 in the form of a high proportion (relative to the other players) of MAYBE/ACCEPT-PARTs (maybe) and OPINIONs (sv) and a low proportion of STATEMENTs (sd).

TABLE V
EXCERPT OF CONVERSATION REPRESENTED BY THE SPEECH ACT
PROFILE IN FIG. 3

Speaker	Utterance
Space1	i got a stike on c2.
Space1	but it says that it can be wrong...
...	....
Space1	i have a feeling theres on at e3... also , on the next turn we need to check columns one and two.

1) Experimental Findings

To test speech act profiling's ability to aid in deception detection, Twitchell et. al. [29] identified those speech acts that were related to uncertainty and summed their proportions for each participant in each conversation. They found that the deceptive participants in the conversations were significantly more uncertain than their fellow players. This result shows that using speech act profiling as part of deception detection in text-based synchronous conversations is promising. Besides uncertainty, other groupings of speech acts could be tested such as dominant or submissive behavior, which has also been identified with deception [25].

When coupled with automated speech recognition, speech act profiling may also show promise while interviewing suspected transportation security threats (further

detailed in Section VI). The profile in Fig. 4 shows a conversation from the SwitchBoard corpus that indicates an interview is occurring. Speaker B is questioning Speaker A as indicated by the greater than normal number of WH-QUESTIONS (qw) and YES-NO-QUESTIONS (qy) by Speaker B and the greater than normal number of STATEMENTs (sd) by Speaker A. If Speaker A were attempting to conceal malicious intent, the profile might reveal the concealment by showing higher proportion of MAYBE/ACCEPT-PARTs (maybe) and OPINIONs (sv) and a lower proportion of STATEMENTs (sd) than we see with this interview where no deception or concealment occurs.

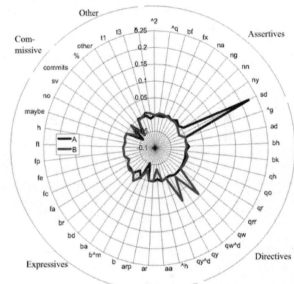

Fig. 4 A speech act profile of an interview with no deception or concealment

C. Future Steps for Verbal Analysis

Speech act profiling could be improved by using a set of hidden Markov models that represent concealment conversational patterns. Example conversations with each speech act manually annotated would be manually categorized, and the conversations from each category used to train the corresponding hidden Markov model in a process similar to the one currently used in speech act profiling [23, 27]. New conversations to be classified are run through each hidden Markov model. When one of the models produces an output probability beyond an empirically derived threshold, the conversation could be labeled as containing concealment.

V. CONCEALMENT DETECTION FROM NONVERBAL CUES

As with the verbal analysis, the analysis of nonverbal behavioral characteristics of a sender requires a rich data set. The research team has compiled data from its past and current research projects to form test beds which are good examples of human behavior. The available data sets are briefly described below along with the experiment designs to illustrate their richness and potential for this research.

A. Pre-Polygraph Interview Data Set

Because experimentally generated data often lack the high motivation and severity of consequences found in real-world circumstances, we have obtained videotapes of criminal suspects being subjected to pre-polygraph interviews. Some interviewees were found guilty based on confession or by independent corroborating evidence, while others were exonerated. This test bed enables controlling for the degree of nervousness common for anyone subjected to criminal interviews from the behavior patterns uniquely associated with criminal conduct. We believe that the criminals' behavior will be a valid surrogate for concealing or deceptive behavior evidenced in other contexts.

B. Mock Theft Experiment Data Set

The Mock Theft experiment [4, 5] was designed to reveal cues that can be used in detecting deception. In this experiment, some participants played the role of a thief while others where simply present during the theft. All participants were subsequently interviewed by untrained and trained interviewers via text chat, audio conferencing, or face-to-face interaction. A companion observer study includes third-party assessments of senders' trustworthiness and thus can serve as a second form of independent verification of whether the interviewees' language, content, and nonverbal behavior appeared trustworthy or suspicious.

C. Airport Scenario Data Set

Four actors were hired to assist in performing a proof-of-concept study to determine the feasibility of identifying behavioral states from gestures and body movement. They participated in scenarios designed to simulate airport screening procedures. The scenarios included seated interaction, standing interaction, queuing, and locomotion. Within each scenario, each actor was asked to demonstrate three states: relaxed, agitated, and over-controlled.

D. Machine Learning Training Set

Seven employees of CMI created a set of videos used to train machine learning tools to identify gestures. Twenty gestures involving the fingers, hands, arms, trunk and head were repeated 10-12 times by each participant.

E. Data Set Analysis

In an effort to test the concept of automatically identifying nonverbal cues that arouse suspicion, the CMI at the University of Arizona and the Center for Computational Biomedicine, Imaging and Modeling (CBIM) at Rutgers University conducted a proof-of-concept study. This study investigated methods used in identifying agitated, relaxed, and over-controlled behaviors from nonverbal cues in a video segment. The results of this proof-of-concept study are illustrated below.

1) Location Estimation of the Head and Hands

Central to the recognition of nonverbal signals including individual gestures in video is the ability to recognize and track body parts such as the head and hands. This issue has been investigated in the past (see [30]) and CBIM's use of "blob analysis" provides a useful approach to examining human movement [31, 32]. Using color analysis, eigenspace-based shape segmentation, and Kalman filters, we have been able to track the position, size, and angle of different body parts with great accuracy. Fig. 5 shows a single frame of video which has been subjected to blob analysis. The ellipses in the figure represent the body parts' position, size, and angle.

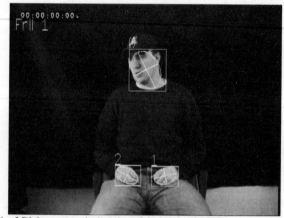

Fig. 5 Blobs capture the location of the head and hands

Blob analysis extracts hand and face regions using the color distribution from an image sequence. A three-dimensional look-up-table (3-D LUT) is prepared to set the color distribution of the face and hands. This 3-D LUT is created in advance using skin color samples. After extracting the hand and face regions from an image sequence, the system computes elliptical "blobs" identifying candidates for the face and hands. The 3-D LUT may incorrectly identify candidate regions which are similar to skin color, however these candidates are disregarded through fine segmentation and comparing the subspaces of the face and hand candidates. Thus, the most face-like and hand-like regions in a video sequence are identified. From the blobs, the left hand, right hand and face can be tracked continuously. For a detailed description of this process, refer to [33].

From each blob, a number of measurements are recorded for each frame in an image sequence. As demonstrated in Fig. 6, the center of the blob is captured as x and y coordinates. These coordinates are based on the pixels contained in each frame. Further, the lengths of the major and minor axes of the ellipse are recorded in pixels. Finally, the angle of the major axis of the blob is recorded. Table VI contains a small example data stream from a single blob.

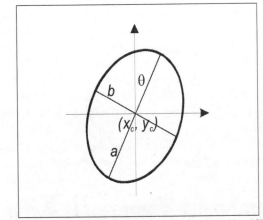

Fig. 6 An example of a blob that surrounds the hands and head [34]

TABLE VI

MEASUREMENTS FROM THE HEAD BLOB. SIMILAR MEASUREMENTS ARE COLLECTED FROM THE HAND BLOBS [34]

Frame	X	Y	Major Axis Length	Minor Axis Length	Major Axis Angle
1	322	149	90	63	0.48
2	322	149	90	63	0.48
3	323	149	88	64	0.46
4	323	148	89	65	0.49

From positions and movements of the hands and face we can make further inferences about the trunk and relations to other people and objects. This allows the identification of gestures, posture and other body expressions [33, 34].

Although methods based on color analysis offer a great deal of precision in tracking the head and hands, there are drawbacks to such an approach. First, the process is more time intensive than other gesture recognition methods and color analysis requires complex initialization not found with other methods [35]. Further, the process can be disrupted by significant occlusion such as a subject wearing gloves.

Despite these drawbacks, color analysis provides much greater accuracy in estimating the location of body parts, than other methods. In a controlled setting such as indoors at an airport checkpoint, color analysis offers an effective foundation on which behavioral analysis is possible.

2) Determining Behavioral State from Gestures

Some behaviors associated with deception might be classified into two groups: agitation and over-control. Related to agitation are manifestations of nervousness and fear [36]. One example of nervous behavior is fidgeting [37]. Although, the link between fidgeting and deception is still debated, dePaulo's meta-analysis reviewing numerous studies on deception found a significant relationship between undirected fidgeting and deception, although it questions the role of self-touches and object touches in predicting deception [25].

Liars may be aware of behavioral cues, such as fidgeting, which might reveal their deception. In an effort to suppress deceptive cues and appear truthful, liars may overcompensate and dramatically reduce all behavior [8, 25]. Such tenseness and over-control can be seen in decreased head movements [38], leg movements [39] and hand and arm movements [12].

Using our model presented in Fig. 2, a baseline of behavior was established for agitated, relaxed and over-controlled behavioral states using the airport scenario data set. The airport scenarios were then subjected to blob analysis and resultant data from each video frame, as well as the velocity of the hands' movements, the frequency of the hands touching the face, and the frequency of the hands coming together were used to calculate the behavioral state associated with the movement.

Fig. 7 graphically displays some sample data taken from the one of the actors as well as sample frames from the video segments. The figure shows the change in position and velocity of the head and hands for each frame of video. In the agitated state, change in hand velocity and hand positions is rapid and frequent. In the controlled state, change in head and hand positions is slow and infrequent and the relaxed state shows moderate changes in position and velocity.

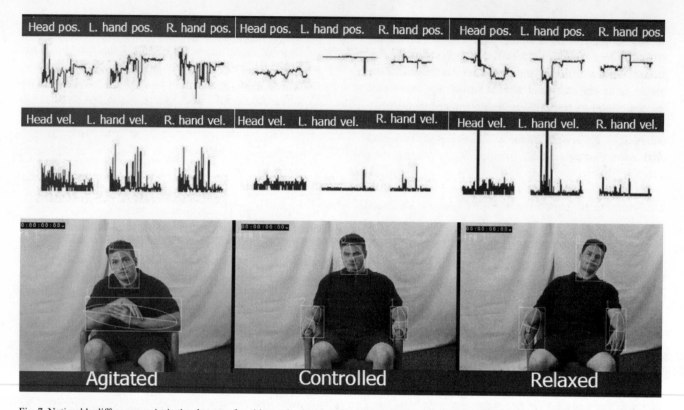

Fig. 7 Noticeable differences exist in the changes of position and velocities of the hands and head between the states.

The data captured in the blob analysis from the video clips from the airport scenarios was then used to calculate the behavioral state associated with the movement. The state is calculated in Equation (1).

$$\text{State} = [W_1 * F_1 + W_2 * (F_2 + F_3)] * F_0 \qquad (1)$$

Where F_1, F_2, F_3 represent the features that describe the head (F_1) and the velocity of the two hands (F_2, F_3). W_1 and W_2 are the weight variables that are determined by the number of times the hands touch the face, and the hands touch each other. F_0 is the normalization factor which adjusts the state to range from $0.0 - 1.0$ [33].

Based on this training data provided by the actors, we roughly classified the movements into three states with the thresholds shown in Table VII.

TABLE VII
BEHAVIORAL STATES OF ACTORS

State	State Values
Controlled	$0.0 < \text{State} < 0.2$
Relaxed	$0.2 < \text{State} < 0.7$
Agitated	$0.7 < \text{State} < 1.0$

These thresholds were then tested on subjects from the Mock Theft Experiment where interviewees displayed relaxed and over-controlled behavior. State was accurately determined for all of the interviewees that were tested using the state equation.

Clearly, automatically judging behavioral states is very difficult. While this proof-of-concept study is simplistic in calculating behavioral states from observed movement, it does show that such an approach may be possible. In order to gain more acceptable results, a more flexible model must be created for behavioral state determination and more features and cues should be included in the model.

3) Future Steps in Concealment Detection

While blob analysis may be a useful approach in detecting concealment, large hurdles exist for actual deployment of such a system. In order to analyze the behavior of people and detect concealment in an actual transportation setting, a near real-time, automated system is necessary. In building a near real-time system, there are serious challenges to overcome such as video-rate processing and automatic detection and recovery from failures. Currently, the processing time of blob analysis reaches about 15 frames per second at a 320x240 resolution. Sampling every other frame has been proposed as a solution however, considering the improvement of computer technology, a faster processing rate may be expected with time.

Another issue confounding the creation of a near real-time system is the considerable effort required to create the training skin samples. This task becomes even more onerous when dealing with large numbers of people that would be present in a public area such as an airport. This problem is currently being explored and a combination of natural images and computer-synthesized samples may be a possible solution to this issue.

In addition to technical issues in concealment detection, obstacles exist in extracting behavioral cues which might indicate concealment. Although initially identified cues that were described in Equation (1) show promise, efforts are currently underway to investigate additional kinesic cues which may be useful in automatically identifying concealment. These efforts are based on work from the psychological and communication disciplines and match reliable deceptive cues with features that can be identified in blob analysis. Promising cues that can be automatically identified are location of gestures in relation to the body and total amount of gestureal activity.

VI. APPLICATION TO TRANSPORTATION SECURITY

Both verbal and nonverbal methods for concealment and deception detection have the potential to be useful in transportation security. In airport and border screening at least one instance of face-to-face verbal interaction occurs. With adequate speech recognition—which is continuously improving—message feature mining and speech act profiling along with other verbal methods such as voice stress analysis could be combined to aid primary screeners in detecting those persons attempting to conceal hostile intent. However, since relatively little is often said in a primary screening, the verbal methods should have greater success in secondary screening where an interview-style conversation occurs. The nonverbal methods described above could also aid during the primary and secondary screening activities, but, additionally, could be of great service during pre- and post-screening surveillance.

A. The Airport Scenario

A possible application for these methods is in an airport scenario. Aviation security is perhaps the most familiar transportation security scenario. Most security systems are implemented in levels. No single level of security is expected to apprehend all attempts at a security breach. Instead, each level lowers the probability that a breach will occur. Aviation security operates on this principle. The layers begin with law enforcement agencies searching out and apprehending potential threats to aviation security. They end with such measures as reinforced cockpit doors, flight crew training, and professional air marshals. Between these layers lies security in the airport itself.

Fig. 8 depicts some of the major layers involved in passenger screening at airports. The first layer, ticket purchase, might occur inside or outside the airport, and the transaction sometimes occurs with a verbal exchange. This verbal exchange has the potential to be subject to analysis; however, any analysis would likely only be able to be done post hoc since training ticket agents to use a deception detection system would be extremely challenging. In the U.S. after the ticket purchase, passenger information obtained through the ticket purchase is sent to a system called the Computer Assisted Passenger Prescreening System (CAPPS) [40]. This system checks the passenger information against watch lists of known threats to U.S. security and assigns the travelers with security risk rating based on confidential criteria. Some of the information sent to CAPPS is also collected at check-in time, the next layer.

Check-in provides another layer where passengers are screened using CAPPS and verbal analysis could but is unlikely to be used for the same reasons as the ticket purchase layer. Nonverbal analysis, however, could begin at this point. Cameras placed around the airport could track the movements of individuals at most layers of the security process. Surveillance while travelers are waiting immediately before screening could provide the best opportunity for identifying concealment using blob analysis. At this point, travelers are slowed and often stopped in their progress toward their gate, reducing the need to track forward movement and allowing a controlled environment. Screening areas could be designed so that only one person is in the field of view of the camera at one time. Additionally, the anxiety of being screened may elicit more of the behaviors of interest from a suspect than at other areas of the airport. Although pre-screening may be the most productive area, surveillance and nonverbal analysis could continue through the remainder of the process until boarding.

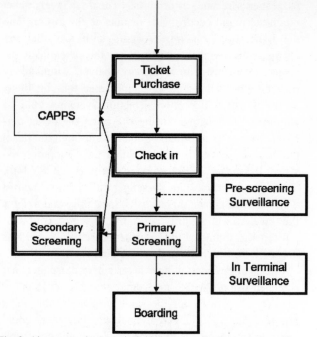

Fig. 8 Airport security layers. Bolded boxes indicate layers amenable to nonverbal analysis. Double-bordered boxes indicate layers that could be subject to both verbal and nonverbal analysis.

Unlike the verbal analysis, nonverbal analysis does not require the airline or security agents to interact with the concealment detection system. Instead, trained experts in a control room could use the system to create alerts when suspicious activity occurs, which would require further manual analysis to ascertain any threat.

Recognizing deception becomes even more critical when a suspicious individual has been identified during primary screening, which may happen at a ticketing counter or metal detector or through preliminary verbal or nonverbal analysis. Often such an individual is asked to undergo some form of secondary screening. The secondary screening usually takes the form of an interview-style conversation where the suspicious individual is asked several pointed questions. During the interview, the agent must decide the validity of the individual's responses and whether the individual should be allowed to proceed. Because even trained interviewers have difficulty detecting deception it would be useful for the interviewer to be augmented with unbiased feedback concerning the deceptive potential of the interviewees.

Although the verbal methods are being developed using transcribed interviews, they could utilize speech recognition software for real time interview analysis as shown in Fig. 9. At primary screening , potential interviewees are screened using methods such as metal detectors, brief questioning, or nonverbal concealment detection. During secondary screening if the interviewee doesn't admit guilt to any offense, the interviewer must determine whether the interviewee is being deceptive.

There are a number of interviewing methods used by law enforcement and others to attempt to detect deception. These interviewing methods are augmented by a computerized deception detection system. The system uses automatic speech recognition to convert the speech into usable text. The text is then run through a number of deception detection algorithms which can aid the interviewer in determining deception. For example, if the interviewee attempts to equivocate in response to the questions posed, a deception detection algorithm could detect the uncertainty expressed and alert the interviewer. The interviewer could then use this information to pursue a more extensive line of questioning than he or she would have done otherwise. The nonverbal blob analysis could be used in the same fashion—analyzing behavior and providing feedback to the trained interviewer.

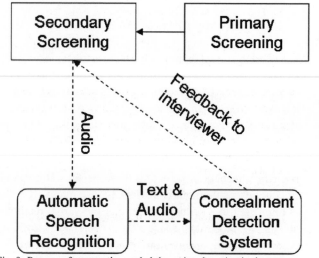

Fig. 9 Process of augmenting verbal deception detection in the secondary screening portion of Fig. 8. Suspect travelers are referred to secondary screening where they are interviewed. The audio stream from the interview is captured converted to text and fed into the concealment detection system. The system then gives feedback to the interviewer.

The security scenario at border crossings is similar to the airport scenario. Instead of ticketing, check-in, screening, and boarding, border crossing typically only has primary and secondary screening. The verbal and nonverbal analyses could be used during these screenings and nonverbal analysis could be used during pre- and post-screening. Indeed, as mentioned in Section VIII, an experiment is currently being setup to test blob analysis at a border crossing.

VII. EVALUATION

The FAA has established a set of criteria for evaluating technologies for aviation security [41]. These nine criteria were developed over a number of years using several private consulting firms. A useful exercise is to evaluate the methods presented in this paper against the FAA criteria. The nine criteria are (1) technical credibility, (2) comprehensiveness, (3) usefulness, (4) usability, (5) ease of implementation, (6) flexibility, (7) applicability, (8) subjective judgments, and (9) total life-cycle cost. Definitions of these criteria are cited in each sections [41]. Most of the criteria cannot be fully applied until an actual system exists. Despite this limitation the methods are rated as far as possible against each of the criteria. Currently, the deception and concealment detection methods described in this paper are not developed enough to create a deployable system.

A. Technical Credibility

The degree to which the methodology is technically sound and provides reproducible results. This criterion reflects the inherent scientific and technical quality of the methodology and the level of technical credibility in its application to the assessment problem. This includes proper treatment of uncertainty

Although some laboratory experiments have been performed, neither of the methods described in this paper have been adequately test in the field to ensure they are technically sound and create reproducible results; however, as described, they show great promise. On the other hand, the methods are grounded in respected and thoroughly tested theories.

B. Comprehensiveness

The degree to which the methodology addresses important dimensions of the airport security planning process: evaluating countermeasure tradeoffs, risk assessment, and cost/benefit analysis

Issues such as countermeasure tradeoffs, risk assessment, and cost/benefit analysis have not yet been addressed with the concealment detection methods. These will need to be addressed in the future.

C. Usefulness

The degree to which the outputs of the process/methodology are (a) understandable, (b) meaningful, and (c) useful for making decisions.

Both the verbal and nonverbal methods provide outputs that are understandable, meaningful, and useful for making decisions. The intent of a system implementing message feature mining, speech act profiling, and blob analysis is to provide the user with probabilities that a person is deceptive or is concealing malicious intent. This information could be used to further question a suspected security threat.

D. Usability

The concept of usability encompasses three dimensions: (a) user skill level needed to successfully apply the methodology, (b) adequacy of the user interface, and (c) ease of data entry for and application of the model to generate results.

For those using concealment and deception detection in primary screening, the training required to use the methods would be minimal. The system should automatically recommend to primary screeners when to refer a traveler to secondary screening. Secondary screeners would be required to have a higher skill level since, as indicated in Fig. 9, the interviewer would have to skillfully use the information from the system to attain the highest accuracy.

E. Ease of Implementation

The degree of intrusiveness and/or difficulty involved in gathering required input information. There are two dimensions: (a) the availability of the required information and (b) if available, the time involved in gathering and preparing the required information.

The information needed to make these systems work is not difficult to gather. Cameras, microphones, CPUs, and user interfaces are the equipment required. Besides secondary screening, the behaviors observed are public behaviors and no privacy intrusion is needed.

F. Flexibility

This criterion addresses issues related to the safety of the traveling public. It is measured by the degree to which the methodology could accommodate (a) the range of airport sizes, configurations, and complexities and (b) the range of threat scenarios of interest.

Conceivably, these technologies could be implemented in almost any airport configuration. Higher accuracies may be obtained in the visual analysis if changes are made to the screening and prescreening areas, but these changes would not be drastic or expensive. The verbal and nonverbal methods are mostly suitable against security threats that follow the normal passenger movement routine in an airport. It is not useful against those that would infiltrate secure areas or attempt to get inside through employment.

G. Applicability

The degree to which the methodology is applicable to other operational, but not public-safety related, security interests - theft (e.g., baggage theft, pilferage, or concession theft) and criminal activities.

These methods are not particularly suitable for non-public safety related interests such as theft. They could be used for interviews of suspected thieves, but the benefits of using this kind of system may not be worth the implementation efforts.

H. Subjective Judgment

> The degree to which subjective judgments are used in the VA process

Subjective judgments are part of the concealment detection methods. The system would likely be designed so most subjective judgments are limited to secondary screening, but maximization of accuracy requires that human judgment be a part of the process.

I. Total Life-Cycle Cost

> The total life cycle cost for three years. There are three components: hardware, software, and technical support.

Most costs would be derived from the training required to allow the security personnel to operate the system.

VIII. CONCLUSION

The concealment detection methods described in this paper should only be part of a comprehensive system for preventing hostile threats to transportation systems specifically and to the homeland generally. Each part of the system represents a layer of security that reduces the probability of threatening actions. As part of an integrated system, concealment detection as described here should be tested both independently and together with other security measures.

A. Future Steps

It is evident that the concealment detection methods are not at developed enough to provide an adequate scientific or operational evaluation. Much needs to be done to improve and to validate the concealment detection model and methods.

The development of a fusion engine to combine the nonverbal cues with previously identified text-based and audio indicators is one way to strengthen reliability in concealment detection and is depicted in the model in Fig. 2. The data streams from each type of indicator of concealment, both verbal and nonverbal, will be fed into a fusion engine and the engine will merge the probabilities of malicious concealment based on the weight of reliability for each method.

One issue in field testing any concealment detection system in airports is the relative rarity of perpetrators engaged in concealment with malicious intent. Border crossings in the U.S., on the other hand, are replete with offenders attempting to smuggle narcotics or themselves across the border. Numerous arrests are made each day at U.S. borders. This high level of criminal activity represents a potentially valuable data collection opportunity for studying concealment. To this end, it would be useful to conduct studies and establish baselines for specific behaviors on border crossings. The data gathered would be extremely rich in behavioral cues and would provide another ecologically valid test bed where subjects should have high motivation due to serious possible consequences. The lessons learned in the border context could then be transferred to the airport context where criminal activities are less abundant, but potentially more dangerous.

With data from contextually valid sources such as interviews with people who have high motivation to deceive, one could investigate cues that security and law-enforcement officers use to determine probability of concealed hostile intent. Rich data sets may also be available for training and testing machine learning tools in applicable settings where contextual constraints such as lighting, space and equipment issues are present.

Although the idea of attaining high information assurance by automatically detecting deception and concealment seems appealing, a much more realistic goal is the development of a tool to assist humans in their judgment of these behaviors. The creation of a tool is possible through adherence to a theoretically-based model and use of realistic data sets. Although the proof-of-concept study presented here is a small first step, our approach shows promise in understanding the detection of concealment.

History has shown that transportation systems are particularly vulnerable to security threats, and although much has been done to mitigate threats to the transportation system, still more can be done. Concealment of physical objects has been and continues to be a major priority, but concealment of intent is an area that may also be fruitful for increasing security. Concealment detection focusing on behavioral characteristics automatically tracked using blob analysis, message feature mining, and speech act profiling could be effective means for adding additional transportation security.

REFERENCES

[1] D. Buller and J. Burgoon, "Interpersonal deception theory," *Communication Theory*, vol. 6, pp. 203-242, 1996.

[2] L. Zhou, J. K. Burgoon, J. F. J. Nunamaker, and D. P. Twitchell, "Automated linguistics based cues for detecting deception in text-based asynchronous computer-mediated communication: An em-

pirical investigation," *Group Decision and Negotiation*, vol. 13, pp. 81-106, 2004.

[3] L. Zhou, D. P. Twitchell, T. Qin, J. K. Burgoon, and J. F. Nunamaker Jr., "An Exploratory Study into Deception Detection in Text-Based Computer-Mediated Communication," presented at Thirty-Sixth Annual Hawaii International Conference on System Sciences (CD/ROM), Big Island, Hawaii, 2003.

[4] J. K. Burgoon, J. P. Blair, and E. Moyer, "Effects of Communication Modality on Arousal, Cognitive Complexity, Behavioral Control and Deception Detection During Deceptive Episodes," presented at Annual Meeting of the National Communication Association, Miami Beach, Florida, 2003.

[5] J. K. Burgoon, J. P. Blair, T. Qin, and J. F. Nunamaker, "Detecting Deception Through Linguistic Analysis," presented at NSF/NIJ Symposium on Intelligence and Security Informatics, 2003.

[6] J. George, D. P. Biros, J. K. Burgoon, and J. Nunamaker, "Training Professionals to Detect Deception," presented at NSF/NIJ Symposium on "Intelligence and Security Informatics", Tucson, AZ, 2003.

[7] M. Adkins, D. P. Twitchell, J. K. Burgoon, and J. F. Nunamaker Jr., "Advances in Automated Deception Detection in Text-Based Computer-Mediated Communication," presented at Proceedings of the SPIE Defense and Security Symposium, Orlando, Florida, 2004.

[8] A. Vrij, *Detecting Lies and Deceit: the psychology of lying and implications for professional practice*. Chichester: John Wiley \& Sons, 2000.

[9] B. o. B. Committee to Review Scientific Evidence on the Polygraph, Cognitive, and Sensory Sciences and Committee on National Statistics, Division of Behavioral and Social Sciences and Education, National Research Council of the National Academies., "The polygraph and lie detection." Washington, D.C.: National Academies Press, 2003.

[10] M. Steller and G. K\"ohnken, "Criteria-Based Content Analysis," in *Psychological methods in criminal investigation and evidence*, D. C. Raskin, Ed. New York: Springer-Verlag, 1989, pp. 26-181.

[11] U. Undeutsch, "The development of statement reality analysis," in *Credibility Assessment*, U. Undeutsch, Ed. Dordrecht, The Netherlands: Kluwer, 1989, pp. 101-121.

[12] A. Vrij, K. Edward, K. P. Roberts, and R. Bull, "Detecting deceit via analysis of verbal and nonverbal behavior," *Journal of Nonverbal Behavior*, vol. 24, pp. 239-263, 2000.

[13] R. G. Tippett, "A Comparison Between Decision Accuracy Rates Obtained Using the Polygraph Instrument and the Computer Voice Stress Analyzer in the Absence of Jeopardy," vol. 2003: Florida Department of Law Enforcement, 1994.

[14] G. R. Miller and J. B. Stiff, *Deceptive Communication*. Thousand Oaks, CA: Sage Publications, 1993.

[15] J. K. Burgoon, D. B. Buller, L. K. Guerrero, and W. A. Afifi, "Interpersonal deception: XII, information management dimensions underlying deceptive and truthful messages," *Communication Monographs*, vol. 63, pp. 50-69, 1996.

[16] J. K. Burgoon, "A communication model of personal space violations: Explication and an initial test," *Human Communication Research*, vol. 4, pp. 129-142, 1978.

[17] a. S. J. A. Green D. M., *Signal Detection Theory and Psychophysics*: New York: Wiley, 1966.

[18] H. Stanislaw, Todorov, N, "Calculation of signal detection theory measures," *Behavior Research Methods, Instruments, & Computers*, vol. 31, pp. 137-149, 1999.

[19] T. M. Mitchell, *Machine Learning*. New York: McGraw-Hill, 1997.

[20] J. C. Lafferty and P. M. Eady, *The Desert Survival Problem*. Plymouth, Michigan: Experimental Learning Methods, 1974.

[21] J. K. Burgoon, M. Burgoon, and M. Wilkinson, "Writing Style as Predictor of Newspaper Readership, Satisfaction and Image," *Journalism Quarterly*, vol. 58, pp. 225-231, 1981.

[22] L. Zhou, D. P. Twitchell, T. Qin, J. K. Burgoon, and J. F. Nunamaker Jr., "Toward the Automatic Prediction of Deception - An

empirical comparison of classification methods," *Journal of Management Information Systems*, vol. 20, pp. 139-166, 2004.

[23] D. P. Twitchell and J. F. Nunamaker Jr., "Speech Act Profiling: A probabilistic method for analyzing persistent conversations and their participants," presented at Thirty-Seventh Annual Hawaii International Conference on System Sciences (CD/ROM), Big Island, Hawaii, 2004.

[24] J. R. Searle, "A Taxonomy of Illocutionary Acts," in *Expression and Meaning: Studies in the Theory of Speech Acts*. Cambridge, UK: Cambridge University Press, 1979, pp. 1-29.

[25] B. M. DePaulo, B. E. Malone, J. J. Lindsay, L. Muhlenbruck, K. Charlton, and H. Cooper, "Cues to Deception," *Psychology Bullitin*, vol. 129, pp. 75-118, 2003.

[26] D. Jurafsky, E. Shriber, and D. Biasca, "Switchboard \uppercase{SWBD-DAMSL} Shallow-Discourse-Function Annotation Coders Manual, \uppercase{D}raft 13." http://www.colorado.edu/ling/jurafsky/ws97/manual.august1.html , 1997.

[27] A. Stolcke, K. Reis, N. Coccaro, E. Shriberg, R. Bates, D. Jurafsky, P. Taylor, C. Van Ess-Dykema, R. Martin, and M. Meteer, "Dialogue Act Modeling for Automatic Tagging and Recognition of Conversational Speech," *Computational Linguistics*, vol. 26, pp. 339-373, 2000.

[28] D. P. Twitchell, K. Wiers, M. Adkins, J. K. Burgoon, and J. F. J. Nunamaker, "StrikeCOM: A Multi-Player Online Strategy Game for Researching and Teaching Group Dynamics," presented at Hawaii International Conference on System Sciences (CD/ROM), Big Island, Hawaii, 2005.

[29] D. P. Twitchell, J. F. Nunamaker Jr., and J. K. Burgoon, "Using Speech Act Profiling for Deception Detection," presented at Lecture Notes in Computer Science: Intelligence and Security Informatics: Proceedings of the Second NSF/NIJ Symposium on Intelligence and Security Informatics, Tucson, Arizona, 2004.

[30] D. M. Gavrila, "The Visual Analysis of Human Movement: A Survey," *Computer Vision and Image Understanding*, vol. 73, pp. 82-98, 1999.

[31] K. Imagawa, S. Lu, and S. Igi, "Color-Based Hands Tracking System for Sign Language Recognition," presented at Proceedings of 3rd International Conference on Automatic Face and Gesture Recognition, 1998.

[32] S. Lu, D. Metaxas, D. Samaras, and J. Oliensis, "Using Multiple Cues for Hand Tracking and Model Refinement," presented at IEEE CVPR 2003, Madison, Wisconsin, 2003.

[33] S. Lu, G. Tsechpenakis, D. N. Metaxas, M. L. Jensen, and J. Kruse, "Blob Analysis of the Head and Hands: A Method for Deception Detection," presented at Thirty-Eighth Annual Hawaii International Conference on System Sciences, Big Island, Hawaii, 2005.

[34] J. K. Burgoon, M. Adkins, J. Kruse, M. L. Jensen, A. Deokar, D. P. Twitchell, S. Lu, D. N. Metaxas, J. F. Nunamaker Jr., and R. E. Younger, "An Approach for Intent Identification by Building on Deception Detection," presented at Thirty-eighth annual Hawaii International Conference on System Sciences, Big Island, Hawaii, 2005.

[35] C. Wren, A. Azarbayejani, T. Darrell, and A. Pentland, "Pfinder: Real-Time Tracking of the Human Body," *IEEE Transactions on Pattern Analysis and Machine Intelligence*, vol. 19, pp. 780-785, 1997.

[36] P. Ekman, *Telling Lies*. New York: W. W. Norton \& Company, 1985.

[37] M. Zuckerman, B. M. DePaulo, and R. Rosenthal, "Verbal and nonverbal communication of deception," in *Advances in Experimental Social Psychology*, L. Berkowitz, Ed. New York: Academic, 1981, pp. 1-59.

[38] D. Buller, J. Burgoon, C. White, and A. Ebesu, "Interpersonal Deception: VII. Behavioral Profiles of Falsification, Equivocation and Concealment," *Journal of Language and Social Psychology*, vol. 13, pp. 366-395, 1994.

[39] P. Ekman, "Lying and Nonverbal Behavior: Theoretical Issues and New Findings," *Journal of Nonverbal Behavior*, vol. 12, pp. 163-176, 1988.

[40] "Aviation Security: Computer-Assisted Passenger Prescreening System Faces Significant Implementation Challenges," United States Government Accountability Office. GAO-04-385.

[41] R. Lazarick, "Airport Vulnerability Assessment - A Methodology Evaluation," presented at IEEE 33rd Annual International Conference on Security Technology, 1999.

Applications of Feedback Control in Information Network Security

David L. Pepyne, Weibo Gong, Yu-Chi (Larry) Ho, Christos G. Cassandras,
Wenke Lee, Avrom Pfeffer, and Hong Liu

November 1, 2004

Abstract

This paper describes an application of feedback control based methods to the security problem of complex information networks. The results presented can be characterized as extending and applying system theoretic tools to one of the most difficult challenges in computer science and engineering of our age.

Contents

1 Introduction

In 1961, President J.F. Kennedy put forth a challenge to scientists and engineers when he asked the nation to "commit itself to achieving the goal, before this decade is out, of landing a man on the Moon and returning him safely to the Earth." And in 1969 the world paused and watched in wonder those fuzzy black and white television images as Neal Armstrong took "one small step a for man; one giant leap for mankind". A similar challenge was made in 1996 when President Clinton signed Presidential Decision Directive #63 (PDD#63). In doing so he challenged the scientists and engineers of today to solve what has become one today's most pressing challenges — the security of our critical infrastructures.

Meeting the challenge of manned interplanetary space travel required solving some of the most difficult engineering problems of the 1960's — how to balance a rocket more than 300 feet tall on top of a pillar of flame producing millions of tons of thrust, how to navigate a vehicle through hundreds of thousands of miles of empty space to pinpoint accurate planetary insertion, and how to communicate the triumphs of the mission back to ground control and an admiring public. The space race of the 1960's completed the formalization of what has become known as *systems and control theory*. One of the core ideas of this theory is the *feedback principle* — a closed-loop cycle of observation and corrective adjustment. This simple, but enormously powerful, principle is ubiquitous both in manmade and natural systems. Feedback is the principle behind the thermostat on the wall, the flight control in an airplane, and the homeostatic regulatory mechanisms in our bodies. Feedback allows these systems to compensate for uncertainties due to variation in the system's components and to react to disturbances from the outside environment. Thus our house stays warm even as the furnace ages and as the outside temperature goes up and down, an airplane is able to fly just as well with 10 passengers as with 100, in turbulence and in calm sky, and our bodies are able to supply our muscles with the blood and oxygen they need whether we are sitting behind a desk or sprinting the 100 meter dash. Focusing on what is becoming perhaps the most important global infrastructure — the Internet — the goal of this paper is to illustrate through several important examples how an approach based on the feedback principle can be applied towards meeting the challenge of critical infrastructure security.

2 Background

As our social, economic, government and defense systems become more tightly entangled in the WWW, there is an increasing risk should the Internet fail due to attack. One reason is simply that as we migrate services to the Internet, we inevitably begin to dismantle the existing ways of administering those services. How many times have we heard the apology "the computer is down, please come back later"? While this example is inconvenient, when it is the food delivery network, energy supply, medical services, law enforcement, and defense that breaks down when the Internet fails, the consequences can be catastrophic. Thus, the protection and security of the Internet has been elevated to a level at least on par, if not higher, than the physical protection of our airports, public buildings, highways, ports, pipelines, water supplies, power grids, and borders. In short, the protection of the Internet is critical to the defense of our homeland.

Conceived during the height of the Cold War, the Internet was designed to survive a Soviet nuclear attack. This ability is achieved through a packet based design with path redundancy and a dynamic packet routing protocol that can quickly reroute packets around failed and damaged components.

Much more potentially damaging than physical attacks, however, are what we call *information attacks.* These are attacks, not against the physical equipment that makes up the Internet, but against the data transmitted through and stored in the Internet and against the software programs that run on the computers that are connected to the Internet. Such information attacks exploit the capabilities and vulnerabilities of the Internet and its users to eavesdrop on conversations, steal data, corrupt files, deny access to information services, or just cause time and money consuming inconvenience. The most publicly familiar information attacks include email virus attachments and unsolicited junk email (a.k.a. SPAM).

Not only can information attacks be much more effective than physical attacks, but for a attacker, they are much simpler, safer, and cheaper. Physical attacks require the attacker's physical presence at the attack location, which puts the attacker at risk of being caught. Information attacks, in contrast, can be launched from the comfort of an easy chair or while sipping a steaming cup of coffee in an Internet cafe half a world away from attacker's victim. Physical attacks can be labor intensive and often require specialized skills, such as lock picking and bomb making. With today's ever growing library of "hacking for dummies" instructions and toolkits available for immediate download right from the Internet, less and less sophistication is needed to carry out an information attack. Physical attacks can incur travel costs and expensive hard to get tools and materials, whereas all that is required for a successful Internet attack is a couple hundred dollar computer and some time and patience. Finally, because the Internet was not originally designed to deal with information attacks, criminals are quickly discovering that — unlike dealing with guards, fences, security cameras, motion sensors, and locks — the Internet can be extremely easy to attack.

2.1   Trends in Information Attacks

Almost from the day the first two computers were networked together (and even before that for those readers who remember floppy disk viruses), people have been devising ways to use one computer to attack another. As computers, networking technologies, the population of computer users, have evolved, so too have the attackers, their methods, and their goals.

The first generation of attacks were largely human on computer attacks where a person sitting at a terminal would seek out and try to break into other computers connected to the network. Getting so-called "root access" with which an attacker could create user accounts and view and modify files was the Holy Grail of such attacks. The hacker Kevin Mitnik got his fame this way.

The second generation of attacks occurred soon after the WWW brought a curious public flocking to the Internet. Early attacks on the WWW involved modifying Web page content in sometimes embarrassing ways — the usual targets were DoD and government websites, the the White House website being a popular victim. Within a short time, however, there was a shift from webpage defacement to attacks to make webpages inaccessible. As with attacks to modify webpages, these so-called denial-of-service (DoS) attacks were typically launched against popular, high profile websites such as CNN, Yahoo, and Amazon. Because this second generation attacks tended to target high profile Web sites, the Holy Grail of these WWW attacks seemed to have been "honorable" mention on the evening television news.

DoS attacks range from simple one-on-one, where a fast computer overwhelms a slower one, to many-on-one, where a gang of computers attack in numbers to overwhelm a victim (cf. [1]). These many-on-one attacks, called *Distributed Denial-of-Service* (DDoS) attacks, marked a turning point in attack trends. As a prerequisite for a DDoS attack an attacker must first covertly compromise a distributed collection of "zombie" computers with a malware (malicious software) program that allows these computers to be remotely controlled through the Internet by the attacker. In fact, the third generation of Internet attacks, which was characterized by worms and email viruses, seemed precisely aimed at devising mechanisms for spreading such zombie-maker programs. Analogous to biological viruses, worms and email viruses computer malware programs that are capable of self-replication. The first thing a worm or email virus will do is send a copy of itself to as many other computers that it can find. Worms do this by sending copies of themselves to randomly selected Internet addresses. Email viruses do this by sending themselves to email addresses it finds in the infected victim's email address book or (even more creative) by using the infected victim's computer to search the Web for target email addresses. The main difference between worms and viruses is that worms are fully automated and do not require any human assistance to spread, while email viruses typically require a human to click the virus email attachment. Thus, while a worm requires that there exist an unpatched exploitable vulnerability (such as a buffer overflow vulnerability in a Web service), an email virus attachment needs only to use a little social engineering to entice a human to click it. In either case, the spreading rate of a worm or email virus can be exponential — the Blaster worm spread throughout the entire Internet in a matter of minutes, the Melissa email virus in a matter of days [44, 45, 46, 47].

While the first three generations of attacks seemed to have come largely from hackers who did it for its "intellectual challenge", today we are entering a fourth generation of attacks whose intent is criminal. Considering who uses the Internet and what the Internet used for, the incentives for engaging in cybercrime are quite compelling. First, there has been an exponential increase in the number of people using the Internet. Moreover, these users are among the world's most wealthy. Secondly, there has been exponential increase in the amount of commercial activity taking place on the Internet; every day billions of dollars flow through it links. For some companies, the Internet is the only way they do business (e.g., e-Bay and Amazon).

The techniques employed by the forth generation of attackers have the following goal — to exploit our human vulnerabilities or the vulnerabilities of our computer and communication technologies in order to get information of value from us or to capture the resources that will enable attacks against others. This includes stealing passwords, credit card, bank account, and social security numbers. On-line identity theft, the Internet equivalent of having your pocket picked, is becoming rampant with more than 33 million people victimized so far [13]. Other fourth generation attacks bear the signatures of organized crime. There have been reports of Mafia style "cyberextortion" against businesses engaged in on-line gambling, banking, credit card processing, and even against companies planning initial public offerings. The ruse here is tens of thousands of dollars payment as "protection" money against a business crippling DDoS attack (see also, [12]). There are also what one might call "hijack" attacks, where attackers compromise computer resources and use them for all nature of nefarious "businesses" such as hosting porn sites and SPAM distribution. Some "entrepreneurial" attackers are even renting out compromised computers as "gangs for hire" to clients who, for example, might want to "rough up" an on-line competitor with a DDoS attack.

Thus, beyond the obvious cyberterrorism or cyberwar attacks designed to destabilize the engines of our society, we each face the more immediate threat that we could suffer real financial loss or our computers could be hijacked for criminal purpose whenever we connect to the on-line cyberworld.

2.2 Attack Methods

The means by which cybercriminals exploit computer and human vulnerabilities range from covert, virtually undetectable computer engineering methods, to almost laughable social engineering methods that appeal to your deepest or darkest desires.

Computer Engineering Attacks. The most common way to extract information from individuals involves "infecting" their computer with *spyware*, a computer program that runs quietly in the background covertly monitoring a user's activities and in some cases transmitting them to a remote attacker database. The spyware problem has become so widespread that it is claimed *every* computer that has ever been connected to the Internet already has *some* form of spyware running on it, all the way from "benign" browser cookies to malicious keystroke loggers. Similarly, the Mafia style, resource hijacking, and entrepreneurial attacks also require that an attacker first infect some computers, generally with some form of *network aware shellcode* [16]. Such shellcode lets an attacker execute operating system instructions (execute, read, write, delete) and thus allows an attacker to run malware that examines, modifies, and steals files, *spyware* that logs keystrokes for passwords and personal information. Alternatively, shellcode can allow the attacker to make a computer into a remotely controlled zombie that serves up pornography or music files, participates in a DDoS attack, becomes a SPAM server, serves to redirect messages to defeat traceback, and so on. Such shellcode can be downloaded from the Internet for virtually every computer operating system that is in use today. The primary methods for disseminating shellcode are worm attacks, email virus attacks, and recently through a Browser vulnerability that can be made to interpret an image file on a Web site as a program. On the other hand, if the potential financial payoff is large enough, organized criminals can simply hire a staff of professional hackers to manually break into systems, and there is some evidence that this is happening.

Social Engineering Attacks. These attacks, also sometimes referred to as *phishing*, try to entice a user to voluntarily give up the desired personal information. Social engineering attacks might ask an unsuspecting user to fill out a fake Web form to sign up for a really cool service or to collect a "valuable prize".

2.3   Security Policies

To defend an information system from attack, we need to try to eliminate or at least reduce the chance that our individual or system vulnerabilities will be exploited by attackers. The first step in security generally involves specifying a *security policy*. A security policy is a set of rules to define what it is that users and programs are and are not authorized to do [14], [15]. Typically, a security policy is evaluated against the following five security criteria:

1. *Confidentiality* - information in a computer, as well as information transmitted between computers, should be revealed only to authorized individuals;

2. *Integrity* - information in a computer, as well as information transmitted between computers, should be free from unauthorized modification or deletion;

3. *Availability* - authorized users of a computer or computer network should not be denied access when access is desired;

4. *Authorized Use* - only authorized individuals should be allowed to use a computer system and then only in a prescribed manner;

5. *Message Authentication* - one should be able to be sure that the individual who the system claims sent a message did indeed transmit it.

While some of these criteria can be achieved by technological means — e.g., by using encryption for confidentiality, error detection and correction for integrity, passwords and biometrics for authorized use, and certificates for message authentication — the bulk of a security policy will consist of rules that the human users are supposed to follow — e.g., pick a good password and keep it safe, keep your computer updated with the most current system patches, don't log into the corporate network from your home computer, don't let your laptop out of your sight, and so forth. Thus, in a sense a security policy is really nothing more than a set of laws. And like laws, a security policy only applies to those who follow them; security policy only describes appropriate behavior it cannot directly regulate it. Thus, a security policy cannot prevent a user from making a mistake that compromises security, nor can a security policy prevent corrupt or disgruntled insiders or malicious outside attackers from deliberately violating the policy. Consequently, just as we have police to enforce laws in the real world, we need tools to do the same in the cyberworld.

Common cybersecurity tools for preventing attacks include encryption, virus programs, and firewalls. Encryption is to the information world what locks and keys are to the physical world. Virus tools and firewalls are to the information world what security guards and security screeners are to the physical world. Most of us use these security tools on a daily basis. The problem with encryption is that it is generally not possible to know if the encryption key has been stolen, making encryption only as secure as its keys. The problem with prevention methods like virus programs and firewalls is that they can generally only block attacks that have *a priori* been determined to be bad.

Detecting new attacks coming from outside an organization's enterprize network is the goal of an *intrusion detection system* (IDS), whereas detecting new attacks coming from inside the network (e.g., from a person otherwise authorized to use a computer network) is the goal of a *misuse detection system* (MDS). IDS and MDS are typically statistics based systems that either look for activity that is statistically similar to prior observed attack behavior or look for activity that deviates statistically from prior observed "normal" behavior. One problem with IDS and MDS is the difficulty building good models, in the first case due to a lack of attack data, in either case due to current limitations in the state of the art in statistical model building. But another real problem with IDS and MDS is that since they are generally statistics based, they can generally only detect an attack only after it has been ongoing for some period of time (e.g., until sufficient data has been observed to drive the confidence interval below some threshold value). Thus, our virus software, firewalls, IDS, and MDS defenses can be helpless against attacks that only require a single packet (like the Slammer worm) or a single connection (like most operating system exploits that, for example, install a spyware or a zombie program). An important part of any security policy, therefore, involves periodic patching our computers with the latest software bug and security vulnerability fixes. As the lead time between the discovery of a vulnerability and its exploit by attackers continues to decrease (we are approaching the point "zero day" point, where the vulnerability is exploited almost simultaneously with its announcement) many organizations are trying to automate the patching process (despite all the potential vulnerabilities such a process introduces).

The above security tools are typically designed to protect individual computers. Since they are not generally coordinated, they are limited in their ability to protect against network wide attacks such as the worms, viruses, and DDoS attacks. These network wide attacks are coordinated attacks that will likewise generally require coordinated detection and defense — locally a computer cannot generally tell if a packet is an isolated anomaly or part of a coordinated attack against the network infrastructure. Currently network wide attacks are generally handled *manually* by IT administrators. The problem with manual defense is that it is generally much too slow to be effective against the automated attacks coming from zombies. Zombies are fast, they are tireless, and, since they are indifferent to being destroyed (after all the zombie is running on someone else computer), zombies are fearless.

2.4   The Nature of the Security Challenge

The nature of the security challenge is as much a people challenge as a technical challenge.

People Challenges. Security is about risk and risk management. As described above, the risks in the on-line world are increasing and can be expected to do so for the foreseeable future. One of the chief challenges with security is the subjective nature of risk. Generally speaking, our behavior depends on our perceptions of the risks associated with the behavior. In the real world, for example, our perceptions of risk cause us to lock our homes and cars, and cause us to keep our credit cards carefully protected and out of public view. However, one challenge with cybersecurity is that there are just too many people who simply either do not know the risks they are taking or have unrealistically low perceptions of the risks. For example, many people do not keep their computers updated with the most current operating system bug fixes and patches. However, what most people do not realize is that there is a persistent level of attack traffic on the Internet, generated by automated attack programs running on compromised zombie computers, always scanning for additional vulnerable computers to recruit. The level of attack traffic is so high in fact that it is estimated that if one were to connect a "clean" but unpatched Windows computer to the Internet, it would be discovered and compromised in a little as 16 minutes.

Only way to change people's perceptions of risk is through education. On the Internet a single indiscretion can have serious, even life-altering consequences. A single click of a virus email attachment can unknowingly expose your every keystroke to a peeping Tom. One unpatched vulnerability and your computer can become an attacker's zombie. Ask a user who is negligent about security — Do you want your credit card numbers stolen? Do you want your computer hosting a porn site? Do you want someone watching your every key stroke? Do you want your computer used as a SPAM mailer? The danger of underestimating the risks is that these things can and are happening, and most users will not even know they have been compromised until it is much too late. When Internet security is phrased in this way, users risk perceptions change fast.

But even so, the lack of *objective, observer independent* metrics for measuring security also introduces another difficulty. Lack of objective metrics for security makes it hard to demonstrate that a security expense really improves security. This makes security a hard sell, particularly since security generally conflicts with performance, which the bean counters can measure in objective, quantifiable ways.

Technical Challenges. In addition to the people challenges, security is also confronted by many unsolved technical challenges. First, a security system must stand up against mistakes by careless or uncooperative users and against persistent, determined, intelligent attackers. Thus, a security system must be evaluated not only against its functional requirements (does the system do what it is supposed to do?), but it must also be evaluated to ensure that there are *no circumstances* which would allow security to be compromised (can the system allow something bad to happen?). For example, is there feature that an attacker can exploit to take advantage of a careless user? Email attachments are a feature (as opposed to a bug or a programming error) that are exploited by email viruses. Is there some combination of inputs that might allow an attacker to install a zombie program on a computer? An example here is the *buffer overflow vulnerability.* By overwriting a buffer with more data than it expects, an overflow occurs which causes the operating system execute the buffer contents as a program, thereby allowing an attacker to take remote control of the computer.

The challenge is that while functional testing can be done in a systematic and comprehensive way, exception testing generally cannot. So the usual approach to exception testing is via human penetration testing (*Red Teaming*). Here a team of "friendly" hackers (sometimes called *Red Hats* as opposed to malicious *Black Hats*) apply various abnormal inputs to a system in search of exceptions. The problem with Red Teams is that these tests be biased by the team's assumptions, prejudices, motives, knowledge, and experience.[1] Moreover, penetration testing is by necessity almost always incomplete. The theoretical reason for this is simply that the number of possible inputs grows exponentially. Thus, except for

---

[1]In an attempt to remove some of this bias, we developed SPREADER [17]. SPREADER simulates how threats propagate and affect a networking environment. This tool is designed to assist researchers in understanding how security vulnerabilities and exploits propagate. SPREADER can also be used as an "automated Red Team" to launch simulated attacks against a simulation of a network to assist security administrators in understanding where their network's vulnerabilities lie.

very small systems, even with automated penetration testing tools it will never be possible to test all possible inputs as our networks continue to grow in size. Exception testing is a co-NP problem that no amount of technology development will be able to overcome. What's more, even if it were possible to test all combinations of inputs to a system, the No Free Lunch Theorem (NFLT) and our papers [18], [19], [20] showed the general limits of "security performance".

Perhaps the biggest technical challenge with Internet security may be that the Internet is based on a technology that at its core had no provisions for security. Thus, the security applications we develop may be limited by the infrastructure. The logical follow-on is that structure and architecture of system design will be of paramount importance. Thus theoretical foundational research reinforces practical conclusions reached via experience. For example, hierarchical system can provide many advantages. In addition many schemes that do not scale up well can be used on subunits of hierarchical systems (divide and conquer is the only antidote against exponential growth. Another logical conclusion is the need for simple decentralized solutions to complex system problems (versus single all-encompassing grand solutions). This conclusion is further reinforced by the many successful examples of "coping with complexity" in nature and in everyday human enterprize using simple strategies. Our individual research efforts follow from and can be understood from these two considerations.

2.5   Contributions

It is without question that the Internet has become our most critical information infrastructure. The Internet now either directly or indirectly influences every aspect of our social, business, government, and defense activity. Thus, in a literal sense, our well-being depends on the well-being of the Internet. But anyone who uses it or reads the news knows the Internet is a risky place with new vulnerabilities and attacks being reported almost every other day.

While it is important to educate people about the methods attackers are using and about the risks they face on-line, what is really needed are solutions to manage those risks. There are many technical challenges to overcome, technical challenges that will mean that the risks can never be completely eliminated, and that the best we can do is manage them more intelligently.

What our analysis of attack trends and methods made clear is that defense must be automated, it must be continuous, it must be immediate, and it must be adaptive to a constantly shifting attack landscape. This is necessary to deal with the increasing number of attacks by zombie computers. Since these attacks are running at the speed of computers, they operate at speeds way beyond the abilities of human first responders.

Many defense systems have been proposed such as virus programs, firewalls, intrusion and misuse detection, and encryption. Different from these, the centerpiece of this paper is a new automated approach based on the feedback principle. Specific contributions to be described in subsequent sections include the following:

1. For attacks that require only a single brief connection we propose a feedback system for operating systems that warns a user every time a never before seen program attempts to run on their computer, forcing the user to close the loop to control what programs are allowed to run (Section 4.2).

2. For self-propagating epidemic style worm attacks that attackers are using to spread malicious software (malware) programs we propose an adaptive feedback worm defense system (Section 4.3).

3. To defend against denial-of-service (DoS) attacks that can cripple or shut down an on-line service we propose several defense systems based on the feedback principle, one

of which involves a distributed cooperative feedback control method that dissipates the attack throughout a network of routers (Section 4.4).

4. Every new technology introduces new vulnerabilities. Wireless technologies are particularly vulnerable, particularly the next generation of mobile wireless technologies that are just now becoming popular. Section 5 describes some of the issues and how feedback strategies can be used to defend mobile wireless networks.

5. Among the most difficult problems with information network security is detection. Arguing that quick detection of network wide attack requires a coordinated network of security sensors, we propose a Bayesian network based framework for sensor networks.

6. It is well-known from designing high performance systems that the structure (architecture) of the system is critical. The same we argue is true for security — certain network architectures are more manageable and hence easier to secure than others. This is a key open research issue which we touch on in Section 7.

3   Feedback Defense for Network Attack

Generally speaking, a defense system against network attacks contains two components — a *detection* component and a *filtering* component. The detection component tries to find out which incoming or outgoing traffic at a checkpoint belongs to an attack. Based on the detection results, the filtering component implements an appropriate defense mechanism to stop the attack traffic from going through the defense perimeter.

The performance of such a defense system is determined the values of a set of parameters. The values of these parameters determine, for example, the detection accuracy. Typical implementations used a fixed set of parameters, usually chosen in ad hoc ways. Our innovation is to use the feedback principle to drive the *attack severity* to zero with more aggressive filtering when the attack severity is high and less when it is low by adjusting the parameters so as to optimize the tradeoff between *false alarm* rate (related to performance) and *miss* rate (related to security) [23].

Motivation for the idea comes from techniques used in epidemic disease control, such as during the 2003 SARS incident. There a feedback like strategy was used to take more aggressive quarantine on suspicious patients when the epidemic in their area was more severe. Then as the the epidemic faded, quarantine action became much more lenient, even though those suspicious patients had the same symptom as the patients quarantined before. Other motivation comes from biological systems and the feedback they use to protect themselves when under stress or when attacked by a virus. There feedback causes a cell to "hypermutate" (raise its mutation rate) when under stress in an attempt to find a state immune to the stress. Similarly, you get a fever that goes up and down in response to the level of a bacterial infection in an attempt to "filter" out the invader.

3.1   A general framework for feedback defense

As we will now describe, our feedback defense system for network defense works as follows. A *detector* component classifies incoming traffic as normal or attack and estimates the attack severity. A *filter* component blocks all traffic classified as attack. The performance of the system is determined by the detector's false alarm and miss probabilities. False alarms hurt performance by causing non-attack traffic to be filtered. Misses hurt security by allowing attack traffic to pass into the system. The detector's *receiver operating characteristic* (ROC) curve describes the relationship between these two probabilities. Based on the observed attack severity, an *optimizer* component dynamically adjusts the values of the detector's parameters in an attempt to find the optimal compromise between these two conflicting probabilities. In this way we obtain a closed loop regulator for attack severity.

To describe the general framework (see [23] for details), let us represent the *"attack severity"* at any time t by $\pi(t)$, which we take to be the ratio of attack incidents to total network traffic incidents observed by the defense system at time t. In a DDoS attack, for example, an incident might be an incoming TCP connection request; for a worm attack, an incident might be a TCP/SYN packet.

No detection system is perfect and all occasionally make errors. A *false alarm* (false positive) is said to occur when a normal (legitimate) network incident is mislabelled as an attack incident. A *miss* (false negative) is said to occur when the system fails to detect an attack incident, mislabelling it as a normal network incident. For a given detector, let $P_p(t)$ denote its *false positive probability* and $P_n(t)$ its *false negative probability*.

Fig. 1 is a plot of a typical *receiver operating characteristic* (ROC) curve, which describes a fundamental trade-off relationship between these two probabilities (when one is large the other small).

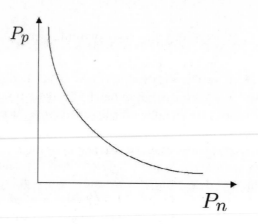

Figure 1: Trade-off between the probability of false positive and false negative for a general detection system.

Let us associate costs with each of the two types of errors. Define the cost of a false positive as c_p. This represents the performance cost associated with the filter blocking non-attack traffic that it should have allowed to pass. Define the cost of a false negative as c_n. This is the security cost associated the filter allowing attack traffic which it should have blocked to pass into the system. In terms of these two costs, we can define the instantaneous overall cost introduced by the defense system at time t as,

$$C(t) = c_p P_p(t)[1 - \pi(t)] + c_n P_n(t)\pi(t) \tag{1}$$

The "feedback defense principle" means that a defense system should adjust the parameters of the detector and filter (to generate appropriate $P_n(t), P_p(t)$) to minimize the cost $C(t)$ in (1) according to the estimated attack severity $\pi(t)$. Therefore, such a defense system is a feedback control system based on the feedback of $\pi(t)$ to optimize:

$$C(t) = \min_{P_p(t), P_n(t)} \{c_p[1 - \pi(t)]P_p(t) + c_n\pi(t)P_n(t)\} \tag{2}$$

The architecture of such a feedback defense system is illustrated in Fig. 2. The system operates in discrete time, where at time step $k + 1$, the optimal value for the parameters $P_n(k + 1), P_p(k + 1)$ computed based on the estimated attack severity during the time interval $k - 1$ to k is applied to the defense system to be used during the next time interval k to $k + 1$.

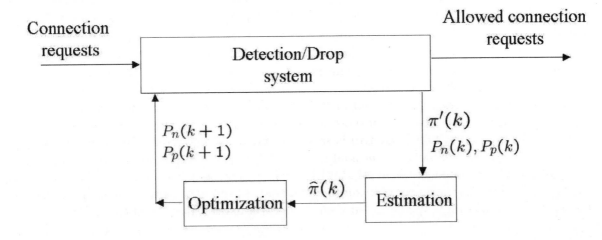

Figure 2: Feedback defense system architecture.

A key component in Fig. 2 is the *estimation* block. The goal of the estimation block is to use the observed attack severity $\pi'(k)$ to obtain the estimate $\hat{\pi}(k)$ of the true attack severity $\pi(k)$. Due to false positives and false negatives, there will always be some error between the estimated attack severity $\hat{\pi}(k)$ and the true attack severity $\pi(k)$. However, consider the following estimator for $\pi(k)$,

$$\hat{\pi}(k) = \frac{\pi'(k) - P_p(k)}{1 - P_n(k) - P_p(k)} \qquad (3)$$

Define $N(k)$ as the number of network incidents observed during the time interval k to $k+1$. Then assuming the detection system's classification decisions are made independently for each observed network incident, then the mean and variance of the estimated attack severity $\hat{\pi}$ (omitting k from all variables) are respectively,

$$E[\hat{\pi}] = \pi \qquad (4)$$

$$Var[\hat{\pi}] = \frac{P_p(1 - P_p)(1 - \pi) + P_n(1 - P_n)\pi}{(1 - P_n - P_p)^2} \cdot \frac{1}{N} \qquad (5)$$

Equation (4) shows that the estimation formula (3) generates an *unbiased* estimate of the true attack severity π. The variance shown in (5) provides a guideline for determining how long the discrete time interval should be in order to obtain a specified estimation accuracy. Specifically, for an estimator with performance defined by P_n, P_p, we can use the variance equation (5) to determine the number of network incidents N to observe before updating the estimate $\hat{\pi}$. In this way, we obtain an adaptive algorithm for obtaining an unbiased estimate of the attack severity π.

The next sections describe several applications of this general framework for feedback defense. These are for illustration only and do not represent the full potential of the feedback principle for security. This is a subject that remains to be fully explored.

3.2 Feedback Defense in Individual Computers

As described in Section 2, most Internet attacks are directed against the computers connected at the "edges" of the network, e.g., via a worm, email, or hacker attack to install spyware or make it a zombie.

The difficulty with current operating systems is that in an effort to make them "user friendly" they have become almost completely opaque to the user so that it is next to impossible to even know what programs are running on a computer at any given time. Moreover, with the speed of modern processors, the vast sizes of today's hard drives, and the huge bandwidth of broadband connections, most users won't even be able to notice when there is an attack program running in the background, and thus will have no idea that they have been compromised. Thus, it would seem that a particularly simple way to gain a great deal of protection would be to install feedback into operating systems so that users choose what programs will be allowed to run.

This is an idea rooted in social metaphors. A key concept in most societies is that of *ownership*. When you own something, you should be able to control what it does. Thus, just like we control who we allow to enter our homes (plumbers, painters, nannies, cleaning people, etc.), we should be in control over what programs enter and run on our individual computers. Moreover, just as the metaphor of locks and keys helps design cryptographic systems, social metaphors such as ownership may prove useful for in designing systems that are more natural to use and hence more natural to secure. [2]

In [22], we developed a simple operating system plug-in that we call ProgramID. The basic idea of ProgramID is to give individual users more control over what programs are allowed to run on their computers. When a new program tries to execute for the first time, it is blocked from running by ProgramID, and the computer user is asked if they really want the program to run or not. The user will be required to give the program specific permission to execute, in which case a cryptographic hash of the program will be computed for future identification the next time the program is executed, and as protection against malicious modification. [3]

The challenge of course is the "detection" component of the feedback loop. For programs such as word processors, spreadsheets, and so on, that are used everyday, answering the question of whether or not to allow the program to run is easy. For others such as dynamically linked libraries, drivers, and so on, answering this question is more difficult for a typical user. Thus, even though users will occasionally make classification errors and will give a malicious program permission to run, what an idea like ProgramID does is the following. First, it provides an interactive level of protection against attacks such as email attachments, malicious web pages, and so on. Second, it provides a component part of what we should have — a malware "most wanted list". Such blacklists work very well for real-world law enforcement, and although they do introduce some vulnerabilities, they could be expected to work well in the cyberworld as well.

3.3 TCP-based worm infection and Port scan attack

As described, worms constitute one of the primary ways that attackers distributed malware. Port scans are what attackers use to determine what services are running on a network in a search for vulnerabilities to exploit. Since both of these activities typically involve a single packet, they cannot generally be stopped by traditional virus programs, firewalls, or IDS. Their effects, however, can be reduced with a feedback defense system as we next describe.

On a local network, port scan attacks and TCP-based worm infection have the same property: both attacks send a large number of connection requests to empty (unused) IP space in the local network. We call these connection requests "illegal requests". People have presented many detection and filtering approaches based on the above property, such as the "threshold random walk" detection approach [25][26].

---

[2]The idea of using social metaphors in computer engineering has also been explored in the context of SPAM in [21].

[3]In this respect, ProgramID is similar to the freeware *Tripwire* software (see *www.tripwire.org*).

Because these attacks only work if the attacker uses their true source address, once such an attack is detected, a defense system can put the attackers source IP address in a "blacklist" to block further attacks from it.

In [23] we proposed two types of feedback defense systems for these attacks. The first one detects attack sources based only on observed illegal requests: for each illegal request, the defense system labels its source as an attacker with a probability p, which can be adjusted by the feedback system. Such a detection approach is very light-weight and has no privacy issues since it requires no information about normal traffic. Therefore, it is suitable for defense on high-speed links and for use by Internet Service Providers.

Denote by Z the number of illegal requests observed during a discrete time interval. Since $P_p = p, P_n = 1 - p$, one possible form of the feedback optimization function for the defense system is:

$$C = \min_p \{c_p \cdot p + c_n(1-p)Z\} \tag{6}$$

where $c_p \cdot p$ corresponds to the false positive cost (assuming that a constant number of normal hosts send illegal requests to the local network) and $c_n(1-p)Z$ corresponds to the false negative cost.

The second feedback defense system detects attack sources based on both normal requests and illegal requests. The detection method uses the modified threshold random walk presented in [26]: each source has a non-negative counter which increases by one if the source sends an illegal request and decreases by one if the source sends a normal request; a source is determined to be an attacker when its counter reaches a value n. For such a defense system, we can define the feedback optimization function as:

$$C = \min_n \{c_p \cdot \frac{1}{n} + c_n \cdot n \cdot Z\} \tag{7}$$

where c_p/n corresponds to false positive cost and $c_n \cdot n \cdot Z$ corresponds to false negative cost.

3.4   Denial of Service Attacks

As described, Denial of Service (DoS) attacks constitute one of the major threats to the current Internet. In a DoS attack, a malicious agent exploits the weakness of network protocols to flood a target node and exhaust its resources.

The problem with DoS attacks is that they are among the easiest to launch (e.g., with the many automated attack tools, such as TFN, TFN2K and Trinoo [2]), but among the hardest to defeat. Existing methods proposed to defend against DoS attacks can be classified into two categories: *precaution* methods and *reaction* methods. Precaution methods are designed to stop a DoS attack at its source. Reaction methods refer to passive approaches which are taken by the victim of the attack. Generally, there are two precautions that we can take to defend against DoS attacks: (*i*) keep computers from being compromised so attackers cannot use them in DDoS attacks (e.g., via installing IDS software and keeping patches updated [6] ,[3],[7]), and (*ii*) with egress filtering to prevent DoS traffic from entering the Internet. For example, many DoS attacks use "spoofed" (fake) source addresses, which an ISP can detect and filter out as part of its security policy. Reaction methods can be divided into three phases: detecting the attack, identifying the attacker, and blocking "bad" packets. The most popular reaction methods are ICMP (Internet Control Message Protocol) traceback [10], packet marking [4],[9], route-based filtering [8], and the pushback strategy [5].

In what follows, we describe several ways the feedback principle can be effectively applied to the DoS problem.

3.4.1   SYN flood DDoS attack

Most servers can simultaneously only serve a finite number of connections. In a SYN flood attack an attacker floods a server with a large number of connection reques and then never responds when the server answers the request. It is like someone calling you on the phone and leaving the line open. When a legitimate caller tries to connect, they cannot because all connections are already in use.

While it is relatively easy to know when we are under SYN flood DDoS attack (i.e., there are a large number of half-open connections), defense is hard, since in order to defend against such an attack, a defense system must be able to detect an incoming SYN attack packet based only on its packet header, when all fields in the packet header can be arbitrarily modified (spoofed) by the attacker.

The "Hop-Count Filtering" (HCF) technique presented in [24] is a promising way to identify SYN flood DDoS attack traffic. HCF defines "hop-count" as the number of routers a connections must pass through to reach another host. HCF calculates the hop-count of an incoming SYN packet to a server based on the packet's TTL field, and then compares this hop-count value against the real hop-count to that source — the real hop-count is derived based on previous successful connections from the source. If these two hop-count values are not consistent, this SYN packet is labelled as an attack and filtered out by the defense system.

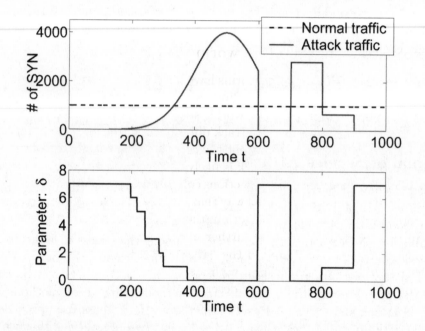

Figure 3: Feedback defense against SYN flood DDoS attack.

We conducted a simulation experiment for our feedback defense system. In the experiment, we assume a server receives a constant 10,000 number of normal TCP/SYN packets per minute; the SYN flood attack varies its attacking intensity. Fig. 3 shows the attack scenario and how the feedback defense system adaptively adjusts its detection/filtering performance by automatically tuning its detection aggressiveness — δ decreases as the detection point on the trade-off curve shown in Fig. 1 moves from the right to the left, i.e., the detection becomes more aggressive. In the experiment, $0 \leq \delta \leq 8$ and $c_n = c_p$.

Fig. 4 shows the results of the estimate $\hat{\pi}$ as a function of time. It shows that our estimation formula (3) provides accurate estimation results.

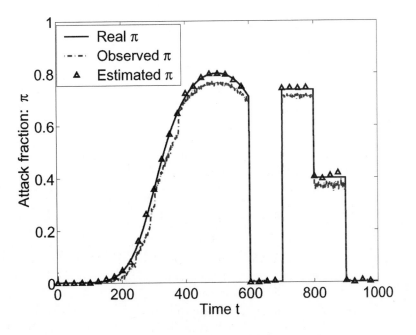

Figure 4: Estimation of attack severity π.

3.4.2 DDoS attack initiated by worm infected hosts

In recent years, several wide-spreading worms have included a payload programmed to launch a DoS attack against specific websites. Since a wide-spreading worm can infect hundreds of thousands of computers all over the world, such a worm does not have to use spoofed packets in its attack, which makes this attack different from the SYN flood attack. As more networks install egress filters which prevent the computers on the network from sending out spoofed packets, this type of DDoS attack is likely to become more popular in future worms.

For such a DDoS attack, normal connections can be distinguished from attack connections by relying on statistical differences in the way that humans behave vs. how automated attacks behave. Upon detecting an attack connection, the defense system can put the attack source IP address into a "blacklist" to block further attacks from the infected source. For such an attack, each "incident" calculated in the "attack severity" π corresponds to a source IP address that tries to set up a connection with a server.

In our feedback defense system design described in [23], we assume that we have deployed such a defense system with a trade-off curve shown in Fig. 1. In each discrete time interval, the defense system has the probability $(1 - P_n)$ of detecting an attack source, which means that an attack source will be detected after a geometrically distributed period of time. We designed the feedback defense system based on the general objective function (2). Our experiments show that such a feedback defense system can adaptively tune its parameters to achieve good performance no matter whether it is under light attack or under heavy attack.

3.4.3 Distributed Congestion Control for DoS Defense

As a final example of a feedback strategy for DoS attack, we describe a defense strategy consisting of a queue-length based local detection mechanism and a feedback control scheme for systematically regulating the sending rate at nodes upstream from the attack target. Our goal is to detect *potential* DoS attacks before they cause significant damage to the network, identify *real* attacking sources, and reduce the damage caused by attacks. Our approach described in [43] shares many features with the so-called *pushback* strategy for

DoS attack [5]. Pushback can be regarded as a special kind of congestion control, where congestion is defined as "too many packet drops on a particular node" [11],[5]. An advantage of the pushback strategy is that it prevents upstream node resources from being wasted on packets that will be dropped downstream. However the pushback strategy also has several limitations: sometimes, pushback may increase the damage done to legitimate, but bursty, flows; in addition, the pushback strategy does not provide a way to identify the attacking source. The feedback approach described next overcomes these limitations.

We designed our DoS defense method to have the following properties: (i) it must detect DoS attacks at an early stage, (ii) it must control and reduce the damage caused by the DoS attack quickly, (iii) it must identify the attacking source accurately, and (iv) it must provide a way to optimize network performance while it is reacting to the attack. The proposed feedback control based DoS defense strategy is aimed at combining these features. Feedback control, for our purpose, means using buffer content information at the attack's target node in order to control rates of upstream nodes. Like the pushback strategy [5], our DoS defense strategy also includes a local detection mechanism and a feedback control mechanism.

The local detection mechanism. The local ACC (Aggregate-based Congestion Control) agent in the pushback strategy [5] uses the dropping history (information obtained from dropped packets) to detect the attack. In our defense strategy, however, the detection mechanism uses the local queue content to detect a potential DoS attack. Using the dropping history is easy to implement, but it prevents us from detecting an attack until it has already caused congestion at the target node. Using the instantaneous queue content gives us the ability to detect the attack before it does any harm to the network.

The proposed local detection mechanism includes two parts: (i) a rule used to detect a potential attack, and, once this is triggered, (ii) a method used to identify a "suspect" flow, where flow is defined to be a group of packets with the same destination address. Now, let's define $x(t)$ as the queue length of the target node and T_1, T_2 as two threshold parameters such that $T_2 < T_1 < B$, where B is the queue capacity. If the local queue length $x(t)$ exceeds T_1, we regard this event as a signal of a potential attack and initiate a DoS defense mechanism. Subsequently, if $x(t)$ drops below T_2, we regard this as a signal that the potential attack is under control and stop the DoS defense mechanism. To formalize this scheme, we define two states for the target node: (i) state 1 is the *normal* state, in which no DoS attack is detected, and (ii) state 2 is the DoS *defense* state, in which a DoS attack is detected. Accordingly, we need to define two events at the target node: (i) s is a "start defense mode" event that occurs when $x(t)$ reaches T_1 from below and the current target state is 1, (ii) e is an "end defense mode" event that occurs when $x(t)$ reaches T_2 from above and the current state is 2. After detecting a potential DoS attack, the next step is to identify the *suspect flow*. In our strategy, the queue content is used to identify the "suspect" attacking flow as follows. First, the target node groups packets in the queue according to their destination address. Second, if an event s occurs, the group with the largest number of packets is identified as the "suspect" flow. After detecting a potential DoS attack and identifying the suspect flow, the target node will send a message to all upstream nodes. This message contains the ID (destination address) of the suspect flow and a parameter p which represents an *admission probability* to be used by upstream nodes as described in the next section. This admission probability p is a crucial parameter in the DoS defense mechanism.

In summary, our local detection mechanism operates as follows: (i) If an event s occurs, the target node sets its state to 2 and then (a) identifies the flow with the highest number in the queue as the "suspect" flow, (b) Sends a signaling message to upstream nodes, (ii) If an event e occurs, the target node sets its state to 1 and sends messages to upstream nodes to stop the DoS defense. The local detection mechanism is the core of our DoS defense strategy. It is responsible for the detection, identification of the suspect flow, and it also controls (through the parameter p) the behavior of upstream nodes, which is further described next.

Feedback control mechanism. We will now discuss how upstream nodes react to a potential attack. The basis of the DoS defense strategy is feedback information used to control the sending rate of an upstream node as a function of the queue length at a given node, starting with the target node. Let us start with the simple case of two nodes in series, and define $x_1(t)$ and $x_2(t)$ to be the queue length of the downstream and upstream node at time t respectively. For simplicity, we will subsequently drop t and refer to x_1 and x_2 as the instantaneous queue lengths. Next, we define $\beta_2(x_1)$ to be the service rate of the upstream node, which is given by

$$\beta_2(x_1) = s(x_1; p)r_2 \tag{8}$$

where r_2 is the maximum service rate of this node and $s(x_1; p)$ is a *feedback function*. In our DoS defense strategy, if the downstream node is the target node, we use the following hysteresis feedback function:

$$\beta_2(x_1) = \begin{cases} r_2 & \text{if the target node state is 1} \\ pr_2 & \text{if the target node state is 2} \end{cases} \tag{9}$$

One advantage of the hysteresis feedback function lies in providing great savings in communication costs between nodes, since it only requires that the target node sends a feedback message when an e or s event occurs. Another benefit is that it can control the queue length jittering at the target node to a desired degree, regulated by the parameters T_1, T_2.

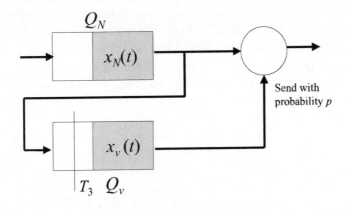

Figure 5: The *p-holding* policy.

It follows from the discussion above that when the target node state becomes 2, the sending rate of the suspect flow at the upstream node is reduced from r_2 to pr_2. In order to implement this feedback control mechanism at the upstream nodes of the target node there are two possibilities: (i) drop the suspect packets with probability $1 - p$, or (ii) send the suspect packets with probability p or otherwise hold them at the upstream node. Since congestion is often caused by legal flooding flows, such as video streams, these may be misidentified as suspect flows by the local detection mechanism. At the same time, an attacker may also forge some feedback messages to force upstream nodes drop some legal packets. Thus, option (ii) above is preferable and we adopt what we term a $p - holding$ policy in order to give suspect packets a chance to reach their destination instead of dropping them indiscriminately. Fig. 5 depicts the $p - holding$ policy. As seen in the figure, the queue at a node upstream from the target is reconfigured to consist of two queues: Q_N represents a *normal* queue and Q_V represents a *virtual* queue with corresponding lengths $x_N(t)$ and $x_V(t)$. The $p-$holding policy operates as follows: (i) When the upstream node receives a feedback message, it creates the virtual queue Q_V. (ii) If a packet belongs to the suspect flow, when it reaches the head of Q_N it is inserted into the tail of Q_V ; otherwise, it is immediately forwarded downstream. (iii) The first packet in Q_V is sent with probability p, otherwise it is held in Q_V. (iv) If $x_V \geq T_3$, the node begins to feed back the value of p to all its upstream nodes. (v) If Q_N reaches its capacity and a new packet arrives, this new packet is admitted and a packet from the head of Q_V is dropped. (vi) When an e event occurs at the target node, then Q_N and Q_V are merged by inserting all packets of Q_V to the head of Q_N.

In order to formalize this process, we define three states for upstream nodes (unlike the target node, which only has two): (i) state 1 is the normal state, in which no DoS attack is detected, (ii) state 2 is a DoS defense state, in which the upstream node receives a message from the target node and begins to limit the sending rate of the suspect flow, and (iii) state 3 is another DoS defense state, in which the current node asks upstream nodes to also limit their sending rates of the suspect flow. Accordingly, we define an event w to occur when $x_V(t) \geq T_3$ and to mean "propagate defense mode". After receiving a feedback message, an upstream node will change its own state 1 to state 2 and begin to use the p-holding policy to control the suspect flow. Moreover, if the node finds $x_V(t)$ exceeding T_3 (w event), it enters state 3 and sends further feedback messages to its upstream nodes.

Simulation Results: Fig. 6 depicts a DDoS attack scenario for simulation purposes. Source 1 is a normal TCP (transport control protocol) source whose sending rate is 10 packets/sec. The destination of source 1 is node 17. Source 2 is a normal source whose destination is node 18. Node 7 is the edge node connecting to these two normal sources. Nodes 3-6 are the attack sources whose sending rates are 2.5 packets/sec each. The destination of the attacking packets is node 17. Nodes 8 and 9 are the edge routers connecting to these attacking sources. Service rates of node 7, 8 and 9 are 20 packets/sec, and the service rate of node 13 is 40 packets/sec. The service rates of the target node 15 is 10 packets/sec. Node 15 is the edge node connecting to node 17 and called the target node here. In the simulation, we set the queue capacity of all nodes to $B = 80$, and the thresholds to $T_1 = 60$, $T_2 = 10$ and $T_3 = 20$.

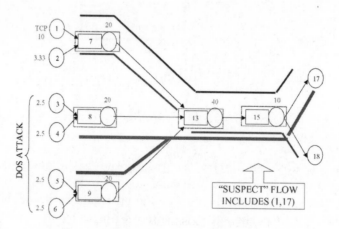

Figure 6: A DDos scenario.

Fig. 7 shows the loss rates at the target node. Note that the loss rates of both flows are relatively high when no DoS defense strategy is being used; they are both almost 0 when the defense strategy is used.

For upstream nodes, Fig. 8 gives the loss rates for both flows when our defense strategy is being used. Looking at Fig. 8 and 7, it is obvious that congestion is pushed back from the target node to upstream nodes. At the same time, this defense strategy protects the normal flow, since the loss rate of the suspect flow is much larger at the upstream node 13. Fig. 9 provides another interesting result: it shows that the throughput of the upstream node

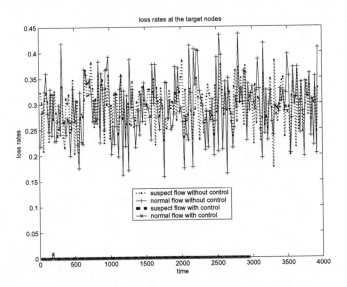

Figure 7: Loss rates at the target node.

oscillates around the throughput of the target node, a direct consequence of the feedback control.

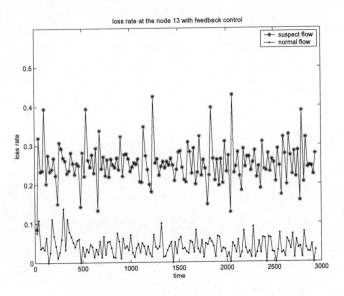

Figure 8: Loss rates at node 13.

Fig. 10 shows the suspect packet arrival rates at the edge routers. The edge node connecting to the normal source (node 7) experiences an obvious arrival rate drop for the suspect flow, which is caused by the TCP flow control mechanism. However edge nodes connecting to attacking sources do not experience such a significant drop, since these attacking flows do not obey any kind of end–to–end protocol. Therefore, by looking at the arrival rate of the suspect flow at the edge node, we may identify the real attacking sources. In summary, these results illustrate the effectiveness of the defense mechanism against *distributed* DoS attacks.

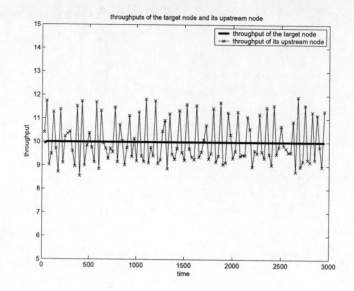

Figure 9: Throughputs of the target node and its upstream node.

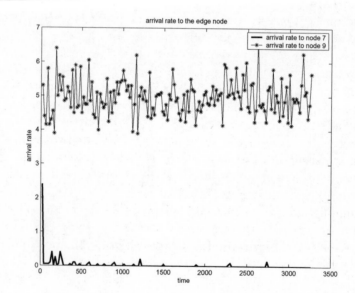

Figure 10: Arrival rate of suspect flow at the edge node.

4   Emerging Challenges — Mobile Ad-Hoc Wireless Networks

In devising defense, we must keep in mind that attack methods are correlated to the underlying technology. For example, in reviewing the history of attack trends in Section 2, we see that they were largely driven by the available technology. Computer memory, disk, and processing capabilities have been growing exponentially (Moore's law). Networking has gone from the days when most people connected only intermittently to the Internet via modems, to today where "always on" broadband and cable modems are the standard. Soon "anywhere, anytime" high-speed wireless will dominate.

With slow intermittent modem connections, attacks tended to be local one-on-one — hacker and webpage defacing — attacks. One-on-one DoS attacks worked when server speeds were much slower than they are today. Worm attacks rose as the number of different services — and therefore number of possible vulnerabilities — multiplied. DDoS attacks only became feasible once a sufficient fraction of the Internet's users had broadband connections, since these were necessary to ensure that there would always be an adequate population of available zombies. High-speed processors and high-speed connections were also needed to hide the performance drains caused by the zombie programs and their activities.

The rapid proliferation of wireless networks and mobile computing applications is changing the landscape of network security. The nature of mobility creates new vulnerabilities that do not exist in a fixed wired network, and yet many of the proven security measures turn out to be ineffective. Therefore, the traditional way of protecting networks with firewalls and encryption software is no longer sufficient. We need to develop new architecture and mechanisms to protect the wireless networks and mobile computing applications.

The history of security research has taught us a valuable lesson — no matter how many intrusion prevention measures are inserted in a network, there are always some weak links that one could exploit to break in. Intrusion detection presents a second wall of defense and it is a necessity in any high-survivability network.

The vast difference between the fixed network where current intrusion detection research is taking place and the mobile ad-hoc network (**MANET**) makes it very difficult to apply intrusion detection techniques developed for one environment to another. The most important difference is perhaps that the latter does not have a fixed infrastructure, and todays network-based intrusion detection systems (IDSs), which rely on real-time traffic analysis, can no longer function well in the new environment. Compared with wired networks where traffic monitoring is usually done at switches, routers and gateways, the mobile ad-hoc environment does not have such traffic concentration points where the IDS can collect audit data for the entire network. Therefore, at any one time, the only available audit trace will be limited to communication activities taking place within the radio range, and the intrusion detection algorithms must be made to work on this partial and localized information.

Our research attempts to develop intrusion detection techniques for mobile ad-hoc networks. Specifically, we have focused on the following tasks:

- Vulnerability and attack analysis
- Anomaly detection approaches
- Distributed and cooperative IDS architecture

4.1   Vulnerability and Attack Analysis

We note that since MANET uses a TCP/IP stack, many well-known attacks can be applied to MANET but existing security measures in wired networks can address these attacks. On the other hand, some protocols, especially routing protocols, are MANET specific. Very few attack instances of these protocols have been well studied. We propose a new attack

	Routing Messages	*Data Packets*	*Routing Table Entries*
Confidentiality	Location disclosure	Data disclosure	N/A
Integrity	Add Fabrication	Fabrication	Add route
Delete	Interruption	Interruption	Delete route
Change	Modification	Modification	Change Route Cost Rushing
Availability	Flooding	Flooding	Routing Table Overflow

Table 1: Taxonomy of Anomalous Basic Events.

analysis approach by decomposing a complicated attack into a number of basic components called basic events. Every basic event consists of causally related protocol behavior and uses resources solely within a single node. It is easier to study the protocol behavior more accurately from the point of view of a single node. Specifically, we study the basic routing behavior in MANET. We propose a taxonomy of anomalous basic events for MANET, which is based on potential targets that attackers can compromise and the security goals that attackers attempt to compromise for each target.

We identify an anomalous basic event by two components, its target and operation. The routing behavior of MANET typically involves three elements or targets: routing messages, data packets and routing table (or routing cache) entries. Furthermore, we need to study what are the possible attack operations on these targets. Individual security requirements can be identified by examining the following well-known security goals: Confidentiality, Integrity and Availability. We summarize possible combinations of routing targets and operations in the following table:

We examine the basic and complex MANET attacks noted in the literature, and find that they can all be expressed as some combination of the anomalous basic events listed in the above table.

For a more detailed description of this research, please refer to [27].

4.2   Anomaly Detection

Attack analysis provides a basis for designing detection models. We use both specification-based and statistical-based approaches. First, normal basic events of the protocol can be modelled by an extended finite state automaton (EFSA) according to the protocol specifications. The EFSA can detect anomalous basic events that are direct violations of the specifications. Statistical learning algorithms, with statistical features, i.e., statistics on the states and transitions of the EFSA, can train an effective detection model to detect those anomalous basic events that are temporal and statistical in nature.

We choose one of the most popular MANET routing protocols, AODV, as a case study. We develop specifications in the form of an EFSA from the AODV IETF draft. The states and transitions of the EFSA specify the behaviors of the major routing functions, in terms normal basic events. There are three types of violations in EFSA: invalid state, incorrect transition, and unexpected action. We show that the specification-based anomaly detection model, using the EFSA, can detect the following anomalous events as violations of the EFSA: interruption of data packets, interruption of routing messages, add route of routing table entries, delete route of routing table entries, change route cost of routing table entries, fabrication of routing messages.

In order to construct a statistics-based anomaly detection model, statistical features are computed periodically based on the specified statistics from a running EFSA, and stored in audit log for further inspection. We use a number of off-line audit logs (known as training data) which contain attacks matching the anomalous basic events. They are processed by the RIPPER machine learning algorithm. The output anomaly detection model is a set of detection rules. We show that our statistics-based model can detect the following anomalous basic events; flooding of data packets, flooding of routing messages, modification of routing messages, and rushing of routing messages.

For a more detailed description of this research, please refer to [27].

4.3 Cluster-Based IDS Architecture

MANET nodes typically have limited battery power, thus it is not efficient to make each MANET node always a monitoring node, especially when the threat level is low. Instead, a cluster of neighboring MANET nodes can randomly and fairly elect a monitoring node, the clusterhead, for the entire neighborhood. In other words, the responsibility of intrusion detection is shared among nodes in the cluster.

We have developed cluster formation and maintenance algorithms. A cluster is defined as a group of nodes that are close to each other. The criteria of close is that a node in the cluster, the clusterhead, has all other members, known as citizens, in its 1-hop vicinity. It is imperative that clusterhead assignment be fair and secure. By fairness, we mean that every node should have a fair chance to serve as a clusterhead. Note that fairness has two components, fair election, and equal service time. We currently do not consider differentiated capability and preference (such as criteria based on network or CPU load, unless they can be verifiable) and assume that every node is equally eligible. Thus, fair election implies randomness in election decision, while equal service time can be implemented by periodical fair re-election. By security, we mean that none of the nodes can manipulate the selection process to increase (or decrease) the chance for it (or another node) to be selected. Obviously, if randomness of the election process can be guaranteed, then security is also guaranteed. We show that our protocols guarantee both the fairness and security.

The clusterhead is selected to perform IDS functions for the whole cluster. It instructs the cluster citizens on how the feature computation is to take place. There are several schemes on how and where features are computed and transmitted.

LFSS (Local Feature Set Scheme): for each feature sampling period, a randomly selected cluster member (which can be the clusterhead itself) is requested to transmit its whole feature set to the clusterhead.

CLFSS (Clusterhead-Assisted Local Feature Set Scheme): the clusterhead computes some of the features, more specifically, traffic-related features. The citizens are still responsible for computing and transmitting route and location related features to the clusterhead.

Our experiments showed that CLFSS is significantly superior in terms of CPU usage and network overhead than LFSS. Its detection accuracy is just a little worse than LFSS and a little worse than the per-node based detection scheme [Table 1].

For a more detailed description of this research, please refer to [28].

5 Graphical Models for Early Detection

A key ingredient in a feedback defense system is the detection component. New methods are needed to detect new attacks — particularly network wide attacks. This is a difficult sensor fusion problem. Here we describe a framework that we are developing for this purpose.

Early detection of potential attacks is crucial in the defense against malicious security violations. Only when an attack is detected can defensive measures be taken. There is always a delay between the detection of an attack and the deployment of defensive measures. By detecting the attack as early as possible, the total delay before defensive measures have been taken can be minimized. Since attacks often exhibit a rapid increase in activity, even a small improvement in detection time can lead to a dramatic decrease in the number of targets affected.

Graphical models [36] provide a powerful, expressive and computationally tractable framework for reasoning about and detecting network attacks. Graphical models are a family of representation languages, of which the best known is Bayesian networks [41]. The idea behind graphical models is that the world is represented by a set of state variables, and relationships between the variables are modelled by a graph. There is an edge in the graph between two variables that are probabilistically dependent on each other. Edges may be directed, as in Bayesian networks, or undirected, as in Markov random fields [35]. The power of graphical models lies in their ability to decompose complex probability distributions over many variables into local terms that depend only on a small number of variables. This capability is highly relevant to network security, where we must handle uncertainty regarding a large number of variables.

Graphical models can integrate information from the network as a whole. Many attacks, such as worms and distributed denial of service attacks, are present throughout the network. Even when the level of traffic directed at a site through a particular node is fairly small, it may be possible to combine information from all the nodes to reach the conclusion that a distributed denial of service attack is taking place. In our model, each node maintains beliefs about the probability of an attack on the network as a whole, as well as the probability of an attack on its site. An undirected graphical model is used, in which each node is connected to its neighbors in the network. The belief potential over a pair of neighboring nodes is designed to represent the fact that if one is under attack, the other is also likely to be under attack.

This model consists of a massive distributed inference network. Existing inference algorithms for Bayesian networks include exact inference algorithms such as Pearl's polytree algorithm [41], bucket elimination [32] and the junction tree algorithm [38], and approximate inference algorithms such as likelihood weighting [42], Gibbs sampling [34] and loopy belief propagation [39]. These and other algorithms are generally not designed for distributed networks, and have not been applied to networks of the scale of the Internet. There is therefore a need for efficient, distributed inference mechanisms for very large scale graphical models.

Of all the existing algorithms for graphical models, the one that shows most promise for implementation on the Internet is loopy belief propagation. In loopy belief propagation, each node maintains beliefs about the probability distribution over the variables represented at the node. Nodes pass messages to their neighbors. The message sent by a node to its neighbor captures any local evidence at the node, as well as summarizing all of the information received from the other neighbors of the node. When a node receives messages from all its neighbors, it updates its beliefs and sends new messages to its neighbors. In this way information is propagated throughout the network, and all the nodes base their beliefs on information collected from the network as a whole.

We have shown [30] that loopy belief propagation has a number of properties that make it a very attractive algorithm for network security. The first property is that it is a naturally distributed algorithm. It is based on a message-passing paradigm, and each node can update its beliefs and propagate messages completely independently from the others. It therefore works well in an asynchronous environment. Furthermore, the algorithm works well even in a heterogeneous environment in which different nodes have vastly different capabilities, and propagate information at very different rates. It turns out that in such an environment, the more powerful nodes take up the slack of the less powerful nodes, so that the least powerful nodes are not the limiting factor on the performance of the algorithm.

The second attractive property of loopy belief propagation that we have discovered is its robustness to failure. In our experiments, we systematically knocked out nodes from the network so that they failed to send messages and participate in the belief propagation process. We found that as nodes were knocked out, the damage was limited to the vicinity of those nodes. Neighbors of the knocked out nodes had approximately 10% error in their beliefs, while nodes further away had almost no error. This property persisted even when 20% of the nodes in the network were knocked out, as long as there remained at least one path through the network so that information from one point in the network could be communicated to any other point. This graceful degradation property of the algorithm makes it very attractive to the Internet setting, where participation in any propagation scheme is likely to be only partial, and where nodes will come and go on a regular basis.

A third property we found of loopy belief propagation is that it is responsive to changes in the environment. When an environment variable changes, the network quickly adapts to form new beliefs based on the changed situation. This is even the case when the environment changes frequently, more quickly than the convergence time of the algorithm. In fact, we found that even if the environment changes 30 times within the convergence time of the algorithm, the algorithm is still able to track the changes quite well, with only a relatively small error. While the error grows as the speed of environmental change increases, it only grows gradually, and the network remains stable even in the face of very rapid environmental change. This is another graceful degradation property that is likely to be very important for the Internet.

On the other hand, while we have shown that loopy belief propagation is responsive to environmental changes, it does not track the dynamics of the environment. It considers each instance as a separate instance in time, disconnected from the previous instance. In reality, it would be much better to explicitly model the system dynamics, with one time instance related to the next. For example, a medium level of suspicion of attack in two adjacent time instances would be cause for high level of suspicion. This kind of intertemporal reasoning is important for network security. Therefore we need a framework that is capable of modelling the dynamics of the environment that retains the good properties of loopy belief propagation.

One possibility for such a modelling framework are *asynchronous dynamic Bayesian networks*. As its name implies, these are based on dynamic Bayesian networks [31], which are temporal models in which the dynamics of the environment are captured by a transition model from one time instance to the next. This transition model is decomposed into variables and the relationships between them, in a manner similar to Bayesian networks. However, ordinary dynamic Bayesian networks are fully centralized, and the algorithms for reasoning about them [37], [29], [33], rely on centralized processing of beliefs about the state of the network at any time. In contrast, asynchronous dynamic Bayesian networks are fully distributed and asynchronous, relying on the belief propagation process.

The basic idea is that each node updates its beliefs asynchronously and sends messages to its neighbors at the time that it updates. A node produces its belief about the current state of the system at the time at which it updates. To do this, it combines the messages received from its neighbors, which are each time-stamped, as well as its own previous beliefs about its state, and propagates them through the system dynamics. Because the time lag between updates is variable, we can no longer use a fixed, discrete-time transition model as in ordinary dynamic Bayesian networks. Instead, we use a continuous time model based on continuous time Bayesian networks [40]. In our framework, the belief update process works as follows. Suppose that a node X last updated at time t_0, and has received messages from its neighbors at intervening times $t_1, t_2, \ldots, t_{n-1}$, and is now updating its belief at time t_n, The update procedure begins by propagating the old belief about X forward through the system dynamics to time t_1. It then integrates the message received at time t_1 to obtain an intermediate belief about X. This belief is then propagated through the dynamics to time t_2, at which point the message from t_2 is integrated, and so on. Finally the belief at time t_{n-1} is propagated forward to produce the final belief at time t_n. Based on this belief, node X sends a new message to its neighbors, time-stamped t_n.

6   Hierarchical System Structure

There is growing theoretical and empirical evidence to suggest that system architecture is the key to efficient management and effective security. In the 2001 RAND I3P workshop, researchers agreed that the No. 1 greatest impact to the future of the Internet would be the development of "Security Management Friendly Network Architectures". We argue that a hierarchical system structure, such as the one illustrated in Fig. 11, is the right architecture for the future Internet and various network services.

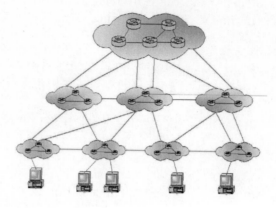

Figure 11: Hierarchical system architecture illustration.

A hierarchical system structure eliminates the "cross tier" links that "flatten" the network relationships. It follows more closely the organizational structure of most enterprizes. In addition, its clear structure facilitates modeling, testing (Red Teaming) and management decomposition (authority, duties, capabilities, responsibilities). Contrast this to "flat" networks, which make it very hard to track attack sources, to block attack traffic, to assign authority and responsibility for network administrators or ISPs. Moreover, hierarchical systems scale up well as the number of nodes grows (divide and conquer is the only antidote against exponential growth).

A hierarchical network structure not only means that the Internet routing should be hierarchical, but also means that the logical structure of network services, such as email, should also follow a hierarchical structure.

Let us use email as one example. Suppose each organization has only one "entrance" email server that responsible for sending and receiving emails to other organizations. If internal email servers of an organization reside on a lower-level tiers of the hierarchy and only communicate with each other and the organization's entrance email server, then it is much easier to authenticate email servers and email senders, to determine who is responsible for an email virus attack or spam attack, and to block email-borne attack traffic.

Another example is enterprise network security segmentation. A large enterprise network can be divided into many big subnetworks to constrain what network traffic can travel between those subnetworks, which are administrated by the enterprise-scale security staff. Each subnetwork can be further segmented into many smaller subnetworks, each of which is administrated by local administrators. In this way, the enterprise-scale security staff will not be overwhelmed with complex security tasks, while at the same time, local administrators will have the flexibility to adjust local network policy on their own.

As a final example, our work on intrusion detection in ad-hoc wireless networks demonstrated that a hierarchical structure consisting of clusters of nodes managed by designated dynamically assigned cluster leaders can offer many security advantages by its ability to divide and conquer the security management burden [28].

Further developing the theoretical underpinnings for observations such as these is an open research problem.

7   Summary and Conclusions

The Internet has become essential to our current way of life, making it our most important information infrastructure. Internet attack trends have gone from humans breaking into computers for the fun of it, to very fast automated attacks against individuals and the infrastructure for criminal gain. Identify theft is the Internet equivalent of a street mugging. DDoS attacks are being used for cyberextortion and to put on-line companies out of business. Gangs of compromised computers are being marketed as mercenaries for hire. These attacks are being facilitated by an infrastructure that was never designed with security and by technology developments such as always on broadband, wireless access points, and opaque and vulnerable operating systems and application software. These attacks are becoming easier through the availability of "kiddie scripts" that even a novice can download right off the Internet. In particular, today there is "shellcode" for every operating system that attackers can download. If successfully installed on a machine via some unpatched vulnerability, this shellcode gives a remote user complete control to install spyware to get more information or to use as part of a gang for SPAM or DDoS attack against the infrastructure. It is claimed that virtually every computer on the Internet has some form of spyware already on it.

Given the above we strongly argue that network defense must be automated. Attacks today cannot generally be stopped manually. Automated attacks are hard to stop because so often there is no longer anyone who controls them. Automated attacks are fast, they are persistent, and they are easily reproduced if one is destroyed.

In this paper we introduced the feedback principle as a systematic way to design network defense systems. Beginning with the computers at the edges, we should be able to know and control what programs/services are running. There should be feedback between a computer and its "owner"; no program should run without permission from the computer's owner. For this purpose we proposed ProgramID to help detect spyware, email viruses, and the "footprints" of attacks such as changes to files and file structures. Moving out into the network, we then proposed several ways that the feedback principle can be used for DDoS and worm defense. Future uses of the Internet will make heavy use of MANETS, which have a unique set of security challenges. As discussed, these too can be tackled with the feedback principle. If you can't detect an attack you can't stop it. Arguing that detection must be a coordinated effort, we proposed a sensor framework based on Bayesian graphical networks. Finally, we closed with a fundamental question, that of determining the "right" architecture for security. This is an open question, but we showed that a hierarchy has many desirable features.

8   Acknowledgements

The work described in this paper was supported in part by the U.S. Army Research Office under contract number DAAD 19-01-1-0610. The authors are also indebted to the late Dr. Julian Wu and his successor Dr. Robert Launer for their excellent management, guidance, and advice.

References

[1] S. Cai, Y. Liu and W. Gong, "Client-Controlled Slow TCP and Denial of Service," *Proceedings of the 43rd IEEE Conference on Decision and Control,* Dec. 2004.

[2] Rocky KC Chang, "Defending against Flooding-Based Distributed Denial-of-Service Attacks: A Tutorial," *IEEE Communication Magzine*, Vol. 40(10):42-51, 2002.

[3] Bernard Fortz, J. Rexford, and M. Thorup, "Traffic engineering with traditional IP routing protocols," *IEEE Communication Magzine*, Vol. 40(10):118-124, 2002.

[4] H.Burch and W.Cheswick,"Tracing anonymous packets to their approximate source," *Proceedings of USENIX LISA*, 2000.

[5] R. Mahajan, S.M. Bellovin, S. Floyd, John Ioannidis, Vern Paxson, and Scott Shenker, "Controlling high bandwidth aggregates in the network," *Technical report*, ACIRI, 2001.

[6] Constantine Manikopoulos and Symeon Papavassiliou, "Network intrusion and fault detection: A statistical anomaly approach,"*IEEE Communication Magzine*, Vol. 40(10):76-82, 2002.

[7] Richard M. Mortier, "Multi-timescale internet traffic engineering," *IEEE Communication Magzine*, Vol. 40(10):125-131, 2002.

[8] K. Park and H. Lee, "On the effectiveness of route-based packet filtering for distributed DoS attack prevention in power-law internets," *In Proceedings of ACM SIGCOMM*, 2001.

[9] S. Savage, D. Wetherall, A. Karlin, and T. Anderson, "Network support for IP traceback," *ACM Tran. on Networking*, 9(3):226-237, 2001.

[10] S.M.Bellovin, "ICMP traceback messages," *Internet draft*, 1998.

[11] Y. Xiong, S. Liu, and Peter Sun, "On the defense of the distributed denial of service attacks: An on-off feedback control approach," *IEEE Transactions on Systems, Man, and Cybernetics-Part A: Systems and Humans*, Vol. 31:282-293, 2001.

[12] J. Swartz, "Crime explodes as legions of strong-arm thugs, sneaky thieves log on," *USA Today*, October 21, 2004.

[13] "Stop Thieves from Stealing You," *Consumer Reports*, pp. 12-17, October 2003.

[14] C.P. Pfleeger and S.L. Pfleeger, "Security in Computing (3rd ed.)," *Prentice Hall*, 2002.

[15] G.B. White, E.A. Fisch, and U.W. Pooch, "Computer System and Network Security," *CRC Press*, 1996.

[16] I. Arce, "The Shellcode Generation," *IEEE Security & Privacy Magazine*, Vol. 2. No. 5, pp. 72-76, Sept.-Oct. 2004.

[17] K. Kotapati, V. Venkararaman, and H. Liu, "A System for Network Vulnerability Assessment and Defense," *Proc. of the ISAS Sixth World Multi-Conference on Systemics, Cybernetics, and Informatics* (ISAS-SCI 2002), pp. 1254-1258, Orlando, FL, July 14-18, 2002.

[18] Y.-C. Ho and D.L. Pepyne, "Simple Explanation of the No-Free-Lunch Theorem and Its Implications," *Journal of Optimization Theory and Applications*, Vol. 115, No. 3, pp. 549-570, December 2002.

[19] Y.-C. Ho, Q.C. Zhao and D.L. Pepyne, "The No Free Lunch Theorem, Complexity and Computer Security," *IEEE Trans. on Automatic Control*, Vol. 48, No 5., pp. 783-793, May 2003.

[20] Y.-C. Ho and D.L. Pepyne, "A Conceptual Framework for Optimization and Distributed Intelligence," *Proc. 43rd IEEE Conference on Decision and Control*, 2004.

[21] B. Whitworth and E. Whitworth, "Spam and the Social-Technical Gap," *IEEE Computer*, Vol. 37, No. 10, October 2004.

[22] Y.-C. Ho, D.L. Pepyne, Q. Zhao, H. Liu, Q. Yu and B. Dukes, "ProgramID," *Journal of Discrete Event Dynamic Systems: Theory and Applications*, Vol. 14, pp. 381-393, 2004.

[23] C. Zou, N. Duffield, W. Gong and Don Towsley, "Adaptive Defense Against Various Network Attacks," submitted 2004.

[24] C. Jin, H. Wang, and K. G. Shin, "Hop-count Filtering: and effective defense against spoofed DDoS traffic," *Proceedings of 10th ACM Conference on Computer and Communications Security* (CCS'03), October 2003.

[25] J. Jung, V. Paxson, A. W. Berger, and H. Balakrishnan, "Fast portscan detection using sequential hypothesis testing," *In Proceedings of the IEEE Symposium on Security and Privacy*, May 2004.

[26] N. Weaver, S. Staniford, and V. Paxson, "Very fast containment of scanning worms," *In Proceedings of 13th USENIX Security Symposium*, August 2004.

[27] Y. Huang and W. Lee, "Attack Analysis and Detection for Ad Hoc Routing Protocols," *Proceedings of the 7th International Symposium on Recent Advances in Intrusion Detection* (RAID 2004), 2004.

[28] Y. Huang and W. Lee, "A Cooperative Intrusion Detection System for Ad Hoc Networks," *Proceedings of the ACM Workshop on Security of Ad Hoc and Sensor Networks* (SASN 03), 2003

[29] X. Boyen and D. Koller, "Tractable inference for complex stochastic processes," *Uncertainty in Artificial Intelligence* (UAI), 1998.

[30] C. Crick and A. Pfeffer, "Loopy belief propagation as a basis for communication in sensor networks," *Uncertainty in Artificial Intelligence* (UAI), 2003.

[31] T. Dean and K. Kanazawa, "Probabilistic temporal reasoning," *Proceedings of the National Conference on Artificial Intelligence* (AAAI), 1988.

[32] R. Dechter, "Bucket elimination: A unifying framework for probabilistic inference," *Learning in Graphical Models*, MIT Press, 1999.

[33] A. Doucet, "On sequential simulation-based methods for Bayesian filtering," *Technical Report, Cambridge University Department of Engineering, CUED/F-INFENG/TR.* 310, 1998.

[34] S. Geman and D. Geman, "Stochastic relaxation, Gibbs distributions and the Bayesian Restoration of Images," *IEEE Transactions on Pattern Analysis and Machine Intelligence*, 6, pp. 721-741, 1984.

[35] J. M. Hammersley and P. Clifford, "Markov fields on finite graphs and lattices," *Unpublished manuscript*, 1971.

[36] M. I. Jordan, "Learning in Graphical Models", *MIT Press*, 1999.

[37] U. Kjaerulff, "dHugin: A computational system for dynamic time-sliced Bayesian networks," *International Journal of Forecasting, Special Issue on Probability Forecasting*, 11, pp. 89-111, 1995.

[38] S. L. Lauritzen and D. J. Spiegelhalter, "Local computations with probabilities on graphical structures and their application to expert systems," *Journal of the Royal Statistical Society*, 50, 157-224, 1988.

[39] K. P. Murphy, Y. Weiss and M.I. Jordan, "Loopy belief propagation for approximate inference: An empirical study," *Uncertainty in Artificial Intelligence* (UAI), 1999.

[40] U. Nodelman, C. R. Shelton, and D. Koller, "Continuous time Bayesian networks," *Uncertainty in Artificial Intelligence* (UAI), 2002.

[41] J. Pearl, "Probabilistic Reasoning in Intelligent Systems," *Morgan Kaufmann*, 1988.

[42] M. Shwe and G. Cooper, "An empirical analysis of likelihood-weighting simulation on a large, multiply connected medical belief network," *Computers and Biomedical Research*, 24, pp. 453-475, 1991.

[43] X. Wu and C.G. Cassandras, "A Feedback Control Defense Strategy for Denial-Of-Service Attacks" *Proceedings of the 43rd IEEE Conference on Decision and Control,* Dec. 2004.

[44] C. C. Zou, W. Gong and D. Towsley, "Code Red Worm Propagation Modeling and Analysis", *Proceedings of 9th ACM Conference on Computer and Communications Security (CCS'02),* October 2002.

[45] C. C. Zou, L. Gao, W. Gong and D. Towsley, "Monitoring and Early Warning for Internet Worms", *Proceedings of 10th ACM Conference on Computer and Communications Security (CCS'03),* October 2003.

[46] C. C. Zou, W. Gong and D. Towsley, "Worm Propagation Modeling and Analysis under Dynamic Quarantine Defense", *Proceedings of ACM CCS Workshop on Rapid Malcode (WORM'03),* October 2003.

[47] C. C. Zou, D. Towsley and W. Gong, "Email Worm Modeling and Defense", *Proceedings of 13th International Conference on Computer Communications and Networks (ICCCN'04)",* October 2004.

Anomaly Detection Using Call Stack Information

Henry Hanping Feng[1], Oleg M. Kolesnikov[2], Prahlad Fogla[2], Wenke Lee[2], and Weibo Gong[1]

[1] *Department of Electrical and Computer Engineering*
University of Massachusetts
Amherst, MA 01003
{hfeng, gong}@ecs.umass.edu

[2] *College of Computing*
Georgia Institute of Technology
Atlanta, GA 30332
{ok, prahlad, wenke}@cc.gatech.edu

Abstract

The call stack of a program execution can be a very good information source for intrusion detection. There is no prior work on dynamically extracting information from call stack and effectively using it to detect exploits. In this paper, we propose a new method to do anomaly detection using call stack information. The basic idea is to extract return addresses from the call stack, and generate abstract execution path between two program execution points. Experiments show that our method can detect some attacks that cannot be detected by other approaches, while its convergence and false positive performance is comparable to or better than the other approaches. We compare our method with other approaches by analyzing their underlying principles and thus achieve a better characterization of their performance, in particular, on what and why attacks will be missed by the various approaches.

1 Introduction

A lot of research has focused on anomaly detection by learning program behavior. Most of the methods proposed were based on modeling system call traces. However, there has not been much improvement on system call based methods recently in part because system calls themselves only provide limited amount of information. Invoking system calls is only one aspect of program behavior. We can also use other aspects, such as the information contained in the call stack, for intrusion detection purposes.

There is prior work on using finite state automata (FSA) to model program behavior. Wagner et al. proposed to statically generate a non-deterministic finite automaton (NDFA) or a non-deterministic pushdown automaton (NDPDA) from the global control-flow graph of the program [17]. The automaton was then used to monitor the program execution online. Sekar et al. proposed to generate a compact deterministic FSA by monitoring the program

execution at runtime [16]. Both methods were proposed as system-call-based. However, what is really appealing is that both implicitly or explicitly used the program counter information to construct states. The program counter (PC) indicates the current execution point of a program. Because each instruction of a program corresponds to a distinct PC, this location information may be useful for intrusion detection.

In addition to the current PC, a lot of information can be obtained about the current status and the history (or the future, depending on how it is interpreted) of program execution from the call stack, particularly in the form of return addresses. Thus, the call stack can be a good information source for intrusion detection. However, to the best of our knowledge, there is no prior work on dynamically extracting information from the call stack and effectively using this information to detect exploits.

In this paper, we propose a new anomaly detection method, called *VtPath*, that utilizes return address information extracted from the call stack. Our method generates the abstract execution path between two program execution points, and decides whether this path is valid based on what has been learned on the normal runs of the program. We also developed techniques to handle some implementation issues that were not adequately addressed in [16], using techniques that are much simpler than those described in [17].

Based on our understanding of the principles behind VtPath and the approaches in [17, 16], we believe the VtPath method can detect some attacks that cannot be detected by the other approaches. We developed several attacks in our experiments to verify that this is indeed the case. Our experimental results also show that the VtPath method has similar convergence and false positive performance as the deterministic FSA based approach.

Another contribution of this paper is that we attempt to compare the various approaches by analyzing their underlying principles and thus achieve a better characterization of their performance, particularly on what and why attacks

Reprinted from *Symposium on Security and Privacy*, 2003. Proceedings. (May 11–14 2003). 62–75.

675

will be missed by the various approaches.

The rest of the paper is organized as follows. Section 2 describes the related research. Section 3 presents the Vt-Path method. Section 4 discusses important implementation issues. Section 5 presents experimental evaluation results. Section 6 presents the comparison of the VtPath method to other approaches. Section 7 summarizes the paper and discusses future work.

2 Related Work

The *callgraph* model Wagner et al. proposed characterizes the expected system call traces using static analysis of the program code [17]. The global control-flow graph is naturally transformed to a NDFA. This automaton is nondeterministic because in general which branch of choices will be taken cannot be statically predicted. The NDFA can then be used to monitor the program execution online. The operation of the NDFA is simulated on the observed system call trace non-deterministically. If all the non-deterministic paths are blocked at some point, there is an anomaly. It was stated that there were no false alarms because all possible execution paths were considered in the automaton.

Wagner et al. pointed out that the callgraph model allows some impossible paths. Basically, if a function is called from one place but returns to another, the model will allow the impossible path, which should not occur in any normal run. We refer to this as the *impossible path* problem. To solve it, Wagner et al. proposed a complex pushdown automaton model, called the *abstract stack* model, in which the stack forms an abstract version of the program call stack. Namely, everything but the return addresses is abstracted away. We use a similar virtual stack structure for our method, but we avoid the complex generation and simulation of pushdown automata. In addition, our method dynamically extracts information from call stack at runtime, while both of the above models only dynamically monitor system calls.

One main problem of the above models is that the monitor efficiency is too low for many programs. The monitor overhead is longer than 40 minutes per transaction for half of the programs in their experiments [17]. This is because of the complexity of pushdown automata and the non-determinism of the simulation. Also, too much non-determinism may impair the ability to detect intrusions. This problem is not well addressed in the paper. There may be scalability problem too because of the human efforts in refining models for some libraries.

Giffin et al. refined the ideas behind the above models [7]. Their approach applies static analysis on binary executables, so it is not dependent on any programming language, but on working platforms. They developed many optimization and obfuscation techniques to improve the preci-

sion and efficiency. In particular, "inserting null calls" is their main technique to largely decrease the degree of non-determinism and help solve the impossible path problem, and consequently, increase the precision. This technique requires the rewriting of the executables and the change of the call name space. This may be appropriate for remote execution systems, which is the application context of their approach. However, this technique may be inappropriate or undesired under the common host-based anomaly detection environment. In addition, Giffin et al. reported high efficiency (low overhead) in their experiments. They added large delay per real system call to simulate network round trip time (RTT), and small delay (4 magnitudes lower than the simulated RTT delay) for each null call inserted. It is possible that most of the run time was spent on the simulated RTT delay, and the relative overhead appeared small even if many null calls were added. In particular, the network delay for thousands of null calls inserted is only comparable to the delay for one real system call. The relative overhead may not appear so small under the common host-based anomaly detection environment with no network delay involved.

The method proposed by Sekar et al. does not have the problems related to non-determinism. Instead of statically analyzing the source code or binary, the method (we call it the FSA method) generates a deterministic FSA by monitoring the normal program executions at runtime. Each distinct program counter at which a system call is made is a state. System calls are used as the labels for transitions. The FSA can then be used to monitor the program execution online. If the stack crashes, or a state or transition does not exist, there may be an anomaly. There are false positives also because some legal transitions or states may never occur during training. Because each transition is deterministic, the efficiency is high and the method will not miss intrusions due to non-determinism. The FSA method also suffers from the impossible path problem mentioned earlier in this section. This problem was not addressed in the paper. Also, some implementation issues were not adequately addressed. The way DLLs were handled is so simple that some intrusions on the DLLs may be missed. We will have a more detailed discussion on these issues later in the paper.

Ashcraft et al. proposed to use programmer-written compiler extensions to catch security holes [1]. Their basic idea is to find violations of some simple rules using system-specific static analysis. One example of these rules is "integers from untrusted sources must be sanitized before use". While we agree that their method or this kind of methods can be very useful in finding programming errors, we do not think it is a panacea that can solve all the problems. A lot of security requirements are subtle and cannot be described in simple rules. For example, their range checker can only guarantee "integers from untrusted sources are checked for range", but not "checked for the right range", because "the right range" is very subtle and too instance-specific to be developed for each instance of untrusted integers. As a result, sometimes we can decide whether an action should be permitted only by checking whether this action occurs before in normal situations. We think dynamic monitoring based anomaly detection methods, such as our method and the FSA method, are still important even if there are many static bug removers. In fact, these two kinds of approaches are good complements to each other. The static methods can remove many logically obvious bugs, and because we cannot remove all the bugs, dynamic monitoring can help detect the exploits on the remaining holes. Another problem with Ashcraft's approach is that the rules have to be system-specific because "one person's meat is another person's poison". The human efforts to develop these rules may not be as easy. If the rules developed are not precise enough to generate low false positives, the programmers will just think of some ways to bypass the rule checking.

There are many methods that only model system call traces. The N-gram method models program behavior using fixed-length system call sequences [8, 5]; data mining based approaches generate rules from system call sequences [12, 11]; Hidden Markov Model (HMM) and Neural Networks were used [19, 6]; algorithms originally developed for computational biology were also introduced into this area. In [20], Wespi et al. presented a novel technique to build a table of variable-length system call patterns based on the Teiresias algorithm. Teiresias algorithm was initially developed for discovering rigid patterns in unaligned biological sequences [14, 4]. This algorithm is quite time and space consuming when applied on long traces containing many maximal patterns. Wespi et al. announced that their method worked better than N-gram. However, N-gram generated the highest scores it could possibly generate on all their intrusion traces. This may suggest the attacks they chose are inherently easy to detect. So although Wespi's method generated higher looking scores, this does not necessarily mean it works better.

Cowan et al. proposed a method, called StackGuard, to detect and prevent buffer overflow attacks [2, 3]. Stack-Guard is a compiler technique for providing code pointer integrity checking to the return address. The basic idea is to place a "canary" word next to the return address on the stack, and check if this word was modified before the function returns. This is a good idea and may work well with buffer overflow attacks, but it is not effective in detecting many other kinds of attacks.

All methods described above have their advantages and disadvantages. In the next section, we will develop a new method that combines some advantages of the automaton based methods while avoiding their problems. Our method trains the model by monitoring at runtime, so it is closer to

the FSA method.

3   The VtPath Model

Although closely related, our method has many properties that the FSA method does not possess. It uses call stack history as well as the current PC information. This can help detect more intrusions. It explicitly lists which function boundaries a transition traverses. This makes the model more precise. Our method is able to handle many implementation issues, such as signal handling. These issues were not considered for the FSA method. Also, our method handles DLL functions just like statically linked functions. This avoids the potential problems for the FSA method related to its unnecessary simplification. Our model is called VtPath because one main concept we use is called virtual path.

3.1   Background

Each instruction corresponds to a distinct program counter. However, it is neither necessary nor possible in efficiency to follow all these program counters. The FSA method records the program counter information at each system call. This is a good choice because system calls are where the program interacts with the kernel. In our approach, we also record program counter information at each system call. In the future, we may record information at other places as well, for example, when each jump or function call instruction is executed. We make the following assumption:

Assumption *The program counter and call stack can be visited with low runtime overhead when each system call is made.*

Using kernel-level mechanism to intercept system calls can achieve low runtime overhead. Our experiments later will show the overhead for pure algorithm execution is actually very low.

We will discuss how to handle DLLs later in the paper. In this section we assume all the functions that the program invokes are statically linked. We use relative program counters because the program may be loaded at different places for different runs, but the relative positions within program memory space will remain the same.

3.2   Virtual Stack Lists and Virtual Paths

As each system call is made, we extract the system call name and the current PC, as the FSA method does. In addition, we also extract all the return addresses from the call stack into a *virtual stack list* $A = \{a_0, a_1, \ldots, a_{n-1}\}$, where n is the number of frames in the call stack, and a_{n-1} is the return address of the function last called. The current

PC is then added into the list A as item a_n. For example, assume a function $f()$ is called within the $main()$ function. Then there are three elements in the virtual stack list when a system call in function $f()$ is made. a_0 and a_1 are the return addresses of $main()$ and $f()$, respectively; a_2 is the current PC. The virtual stack list denotes a history of all unreturned functions.

Our model uses a *virtual path* to denote a transition between two system calls. Assume $A = \{a_0, a_1, \ldots, a_n\}$ and $B = \{b_0, b_1, \ldots, b_m\}$ are the virtual stack lists for the current and the last system calls, respectively. Note that the two system calls may be called in different functions. We compare the lists A and B from the beginning, until we find the first subscript l so that $a_l \neq b_l$. As shown in Figure 1, the virtual path between the two system calls is defined as:

$$P = b_m \rightarrow Exit; \ldots; b_{l+1} \rightarrow Exit; b_l \rightarrow a_l;$$
$$Entry \rightarrow a_{l+1}; \ldots; Entry \rightarrow a_n \quad (1)$$

where $Entry$ and $Exit$ are two specially defined PCs denoting the entry and exit points of any function.

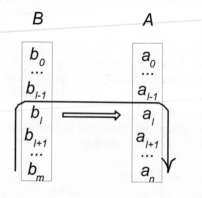

Figure 1. The virtual path from the last system call to the current system call, whose virtual stack lists are B and A, respectively.

The definition of the virtual path abstracts the execution between two system calls. The program sequentially returns from some functions (corresponding to the return addresses b_{m-1} to b_l), and then gradually enters some other functions (corresponding to the return addresses a_l to a_{n-1}). We traverse the virtual stack lists back to a common function (corresponding to the return address a_{l-1} and b_{l-1}, which are equal), below which both system calls are made.

For recursive functions, the control flows generally are very data-driven. The virtual stack lists obtained may be different for each distinct set of parameters, which results in a lot of distinct virtual paths. This could make training harder to converge or result in higher false positive rates. We modified our method to avoid this problem. A common property of recursion in virtual stack lists is that the same

return address occurs repeatedly. When our method finds out that a pair of return addresses are the same, all the return addresses between them are removed from the virtual stack list, including one end of the pair. This reflects the fact that we only record each function at most once in the call history.

3.3 Training Phase

During training, we use a hash table, called RA (return address) table, to save all the return addresses ever occurred in the virtual stack lists of system calls. If the return address is the last item in a virtual stack list (the current PC item), the corresponding system call number is saved with it. Another hash table, called VP (virtual path) table, is used to save all the virtual paths. Virtual paths are denoted in a compact string form.

The return addresses and virtual paths are gradually added during many normal program runs. For each run, we assume there is one null system call with empty virtual stack list before the first real system call, and another one after the last real system call. The virtual path between the null system call and the first real system call, whose virtual stack list is $A = \{a_0, a_1, \ldots, a_n\}$, is:

$$P = Entry \rightarrow a_0; \ldots; Entry \rightarrow a_n \quad (2)$$

The virtual path between the last real system call, whose virtual stack list is $B = \{b_0, b_1, \ldots, b_m\}$, and the null system call is:

$$P = b_m \rightarrow Exit; \ldots; b_0 \rightarrow Exit; \quad (3)$$

3.4 Online Detection Phase

After training, we can use the hash tables to monitor the program execution online. As each system call is made, we record its virtual stack list. Like in the training, we also assume there are null system calls at the beginning and the end of the program run. There may be several types of anomaly phenomena:

- If we cannot get the virtual stack list, the stack must be corrupted. This is a *stack anomaly*. This kind of anomalies often happens during a coarse buffer overflow attack.

- Assume the current virtual stack list is $A = \{a_0, a_1, \ldots, a_n\}$. We check whether each item is in the RA table. If any return address is missing, this is a *return address anomaly*.

- If a_n does not have the correct system call, this is a *system call anomaly*.

- We generate the virtual path between the last and the current system call according to the equations (1), (2) or (3). If the virtual path is not in the VP table, this is a *virtual path anomaly*.

One problem for the FSA method is that the intruder could possibly craft an overflow string that makes the call stack looks not corrupted while it really is, and thus evading detection. Using our method, the same attack would probably still generate a virtual path anomaly because the call stack is altered. Our method uses and saves more information in training, so it is harder for attacks to evade detection.

3.5 Impossible Path Problem

Our method can help solve the impossible path problem mentioned before. Assume the attacker can somehow modify the return address within a function $f()$, so that the program enters function $f()$ from one call point and exits from another. This will not trigger an alarm for the FSA method because all the transitions are legal. Our experiments later will show carefully designed attacks exploiting this problem can fool callgraph and abstract stack methods as well. This kind of attacks can help the intruder because some critical part of the program could be jumped, for example, some permission checking code. The intruder can also use the technique to repeat the execution of some program part to create race conditions.

Our method will disallow the virtual path between the last system call before the call stack alteration point and the first system call after the alteration point. This is because in the call stack, the return addresses of function $f()$ for these two system calls will be different. These two return addresses will be included, resulting in an invalid virtual path.

4 Implementation Issues

Wagner et al. addressed some implementation issues for their statically generated models [17]. If not handled properly, these issues will also affect the effectiveness of the dynamic monitoring approaches. However, Sekar et al. only addressed one of the issues regarding DLLs [16]. Moreover, we believe that their method simplifies the behavior of DLLs so much that many intrusions on these DLLs may be missed. We find that some of these implementation issues are much easier to handle at runtime than at static analysis because some information is only available at runtime. Wagner et al. also pointed out this as the second principle in their paper [17].

4.1 Non-Standard Control Flows

For optimization and convenience, some non-standard control flows, such as function pointers, signal handlers and *setjmp()* function, are often used in programming. Wagner et al. stated that these features are always used in real applications of interests for intrusion detection [17]. They also found that function pointers and *setjmp()* are extensively used in some library functions.

Signals A signal handler is a function that is invoked when the corresponding signal is received. The program suspends the current execution and turn to the signal handler. It continues the execution from the suspended point after the signal handler returns. It is hard to consider signal handling in the model because a signal may occur anytime during the program execution. The problem is further complicated if signal handlers can be called within each other. If we treat signal handler calls as ordinary function calls in training, there will be false positives when signals occur at new places.

When the first system call in a signal handler is executed, we save the information about the last system call, including its virtual stack list. The last system call is then set to the null system call. When the signal handler returns, we restore the information about the last system call. This framework can be easily extended for the multi-level signal handler case. Each execution of signal handlers is treated like a program run. The same techniques used for training and online detection before can still be applied here with signal handlers.

For Linux, when a signal handler is called upon the receipt of a signal, a *sigreturn* system call is inserted into the stack frame. It will be called when the signal handler returns, to clean up the stack so that the process can restart from the suspended point. If we find a new *sigreturn* system call in the call stack when a system call is made, we know a signal handler was executed. If we encounter *sigreturn*, the signal handler just returned. Our method is simpler than Wagner's method because it does not need to monitor the signals received or signal handler registrations.

***setjmp()/longjmp()* calls and function pointers** The *setjmp()/longjmp()* library functions are useful for exception and error handling. The *setjmp()* call saves the stack context and environment for later use by *longjmp()*, which restores them. After the *longjmp()* call is finished, the execution continues as if the corresponding *setjmp()* call just returned. Function pointers are used to dynamically choose a function to call at runtime.

It is hard to handle them statically because it is hard to predict statically the value of a function pointer, or which *setjmp()* call is corresponding to a *longjmp()* call. Wagner et al. can only come up with some rough solutions that make the model more permissive than necessary or add more nondeterminism because their methods do not train at runtime. For our method, there is no such problem because it does not need to be aware of function pointers or the library calls. In detection phase, if a new function is called through a function pointer, or a new *longjmp()/setjmp()* pair appears, our method will generate an anomaly. It is reasonable to generate an anomaly here because some new situations have happened that never occurred before in training.

4.2 Dynamically Linked Libraries

One problem for both our method and the FSA method is related to dynamically linked libraries (DLLs). The difficulty is that the functions within DLLs may be loaded at different relative locations (comparing to the static portion) for different program runs, so the program counters may change from run to run. The methods Wagner et al. proposed do not have the above problem because they do not use PC information for online monitoring.

The FSA method tried to solve this problem by traversing the stack back to the statically linked portion. Using the virtual stack list concept, this means that the FSA method uses the last item in the list that is in the statically linked portion as the state. The behavior of a function in DLLs is simplified to a list of system calls that can be generated by this function and all functions it called. There will be states that have many transitions pointing to themselves labeled with these system calls. This simplifies the model for DLLs a lot. However, intrusions may also occur in the DLLs. For example, the intruder may install the Trojan version of a DLL. The FSA method may make the model for DLLs too simple to detect these intrusions. As detailed in a later section, for security critical daemon programs in our experiments, most system calls are actually made in DLLs.

We model the functions in DLLs just like any statically linked function. During training, we use a "block" lookup table to save the information for each executable memory block of each forked process, including the start address, the block length, the name (with full path) and the offset of the file from which the memory block was loaded. We use the block length, file name and offset but not the start address to match the same memory blocks in different runs. When we get a return address, we can use the block lookup table to decide which memory block it is in and what the relative PC within the block is. These two pieces of information together can uniquely distinguish a return address. Each return address is denoted by a global block index and an offset within the block.

There can be another kind of anomaly: *block anomaly*. This happens when we cannot match a memory block to any memory block occurred during training. This can be because the intruder is trying to load another DLL.

For Linux, there is a pseudo file named "maps" under the process's information pseudo file system "/proc". This file contains all the memory block information we need. There are structures containing similar information under other flavors of UNIX, such as Solaris.

Using the above approach, we can match a dynamically loaded code block to the same code blocks in other runs, although this block may be loaded to a different place. A return address can be uniquely distinguished, and the functions in DLLs can be modeled and checked just like statically linked functions.

4.3 Threads

Currently, there are many different ways to implement threads. As far as we can distinguish which thread generates a system call, there is no problem for applying our method on multi-threaded applications. For Linux, different threads actually have different process IDs, so we can distinguish threads by distinguishing their IDs. For other flavors of UNIX, we can try to find other ways to distinguish threads.

5 Experimental Evaluation

In this section, we present results from our experiments. We first describe the experiments on comparing VtPath with FSA in terms of convergence time, false positives, overhead, and detection of common root exploits. We then describe the experiments on evaluating the effectiveness of VtPath against some attacks, including impossible path exploits, that can evade several other detection models, and discuss the lessons learned.

5.1 Experiments on Comparing VtPath with FSA

Sekar et al. conducted experiments on normal data for some security-critical daemon programs [16]. They showed FSA uniformly worked better than N-gram in the sense of convergence speed, false positive rates and overhead. We conducted similar experiments to compare our VtPath method with FSA.

If all functions are statically linked, for the same program run, whenever there is a new transition for FSA, there is also a new virtual path for VtPath. This is because the virtual path contains all the information of the corresponding transition. So generally speaking, virtual paths are more specific than transitions. For VtPath, we should expect a slower convergence speed, a higher false positive rate and a higher detection rate. When DLLs are involved, the situation is somewhat complicated. As FSA simplifies DLL behavior model, it should have even faster convergence speed, fewer false positives, and lower detection rate. But there are situations where the simplification may also increase the convergence time and false positives. This is because one intra DLL function transition may map to different transitions at different DLL function call points, due to stack traverse to the statically linked portion. The situation becomes severe if some frequently called DLL functions have many intra-function transitions. For programs using a lot of signal handling, the convergence time and false positive rates of VtPath will benefit from its signal handling mechanism.

We conducted experiments on security critical daemon programs ftpd and httpd. We used the original FSA implementation from the authors, and compared VtPath with it. For fairness, all the comparison was based on data collected from the same program runs. The experiments were conducted on a RedHat 7.2 workstation with dual Pentium III 500MHz processors. We used WebStone 2.5 benchmark suite to generate HTTP traffic [13]. The files and visiting distribution were copied from our laboratory web server. For FTP experiments, we wrote some scripts using the "expect" tool. These scripts can execute commands that mimic some common user activities, such as downloading or uploading files and directories. The scripts were randomly executed to exercise the FTP server. The files were copied from one lab user's home directory.

We found out some bugs in the original FSA implementation, which contributed to higher false positive rates and slower convergence. We modified the programs and created our own FSA implementation. We will present our results for the VtPath implementation and both FSA implementations.

5.1.1 Convergence

The training process is considered as converged if the normal profile stops increasing (i.e., with no new behavior added). The convergence speed is important because the faster the training converges the less time and effort are needed. For FSA, the normal profile consists of states and transitions. There is always a new transition whenever there is a new state because the state is a part of the corresponding transition. The above statements are also true for VtPath if we use "return address" instead of "state" and "virtual path" instead of "transition". Therefore, we believe that the number of virtual paths or transitions is a good metric to measure convergence speed because the profile stops increasing if this number stops increasing. These numbers are plotted against the numbers of system calls used for training, which are presented in logarithmic scale.

We made a program to start the daemon program, and simultaneously record the traces for both methods. When the number of system calls made exceeds a preset limit, the program stops the daemon program. By this way, we generate traces with different lengths. We apply these traces incrementally starting from the shortest traces for training

on both methods. Every time a trace is applied, the profile is copied and the convergence metric is calculated.

Figure 2 shows the results for ftpd. The solid line with star marks is for VtPath; the dashed line with square marks is for our FSA implementation; the dotted line with circle marks is for the original FSA implementation. The interesting thing is that the number of virtual paths actually increases more slowly than the number of transitions. This may be due to the DLL or signal handling related issues discussed at the beginning of this section. The original FSA implementation generates even more number of transitions. For VtPath and our FSA implementation, the profile increase stops after about 5M system calls are processed. The httpd experiments show similar results in terms of the comparisons between the methods.

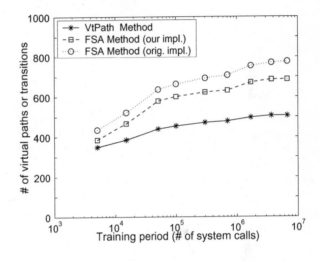

Figure 2. Convergence on ftpd

In our httpd experiments, less than 1% of the system calls are actually made in the statically linked portion. For more than 30% of the system calls, FSA has to go back at least 3 call stack frames to find a return address in statically linked portion. This means at least 3 levels of DLL functions are called for 30% of the system calls. These facts may suggest that DLLs are very important, and the simplification of DLL behavior by FSA may have severely impaired its detection capability.

5.1.2 False Positives

For ftpd experiments, we collect several normal testing traces ranging from 1M to several million system calls for each method, with a script execution distribution slightly different from what was used for the convergence experiments. As Sekar et al. argued in [16], this is to account for the fact that things may change between the training and detecting times. We use the profiles saved in the convergence experiments to analyze these testing traces. Like what Sekar et al. did in [16], each mismatched return address (state) or virtual path (transition) is counted as a false positive. The false positive rates are calculated as the number of false positives over the number of system calls in each trace, and averaged over the several testing traces for each method.

Figure 3 shows the relationship between the average false positive rate and the number of system calls used for training for `ftpd` experiments. Note both axes are in logarithmic scale. VtPath has almost the same false positive rates as our FSA implementation. Actually, using the profiles corresponding to more than 1M system calls, there is no false positives on all testing traces. The original FSA implementation generates much higher false positive rates at most points. Our `httpd` experiments show similar results in terms of comparisons between the methods.

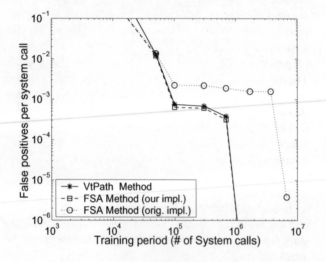

Figure 3. False positive rates on `ftpd`

5.1.3   Runtime and Space Overhead

We use the same user-level mechanism to intercept system calls as FSA. As pointed out by Sekar et al. [16], this mechanism incurs relatively high runtime overhead. They estimated that system call interception incurs 100% to 250% runtime overhead, while the overhead of their algorithm execution is only about 3%. For real applications, we want to use kernel-level mechanisms that incur much lower system call interception overhead. In this section, we only compare the algorithm execution overhead for both methods.

We use the average process time per system call stop to evaluate the algorithm runtime overhead. In our experiments, for FSA, the value is about 350 milliseconds for training and 250 milliseconds for detection. For VtPath, the value is about 150 milliseconds for both training and detection. It is interesting that the VtPath algorithm actually executes faster because, theoretically, it should be a little bit slower since it needs to do more work. The reason may

be that we paid much attention on efficiency for our VtPath implementation.

The space overhead for VtPath, however, is higher than FSA. This is because it needs to save more information of call stack. For our `ftpd` experiments, the profiles that the FSA code creates are about 10K bytes, while the profiles that the VtPath code creates are about 30K bytes. These profiles should require less spaces when loaded into memory because the profiles saved on disk are human readable.

5.1.4   Detection of Common Exploits

We have also tested VtPath and FSA against several recent local and remote root exploits, namely efstool (local root), dhcpd v3.0.1rc8, and gdm v2.0beta1-4. Both VtPath and FSA successfully detected all of these exploits in our experiments.

5.2   Impossible Path Exploits and Beyond

We implemented two example attacks, including an impossible path exploit first introduced in [17], to demonstrate the effectiveness of the VtPath approach. The attacks were realized and tested on a RedHat 7.3 machine.

We evaluate the implementation of our approach as well as related approaches such as abstract stack, N-gram, callgraph, and FSA, under the same conditions to determine how effective the approaches are against the test attacks we develop. In our experiments, we use working implementations of N-gram and FSA we received from the authors (the bugs we found do not impair the detection ability of FSA for our test attacks). For abstract stack and callgraph, we do not have access to the implementations and thus we do all the tests manually using the algorithms described in [17].

Our approach is able to detect both attacks 1 and 2 described below. None of the other approaches we analyze detect either of them. We have also tested our approach against the mimicry attacks described in [18]. We find that our approach as well as FSA is able to detect the mimicry attacks. However, we find a way to improve the mimicry attacks to make them invisible to FSA. We achieve this by manipulating the stack contents that are analyzed by FSA implementation in such a way that FSA will mistakenly trace back to a legitimate system call in the text segment. The *masked mimicry attack* we develop will not be detected by the FSA implementation. VtPath, however, will still be able to detect both the original and the masked mimicry attack. We plan to describe our improvements of mimicry attacks to evade IDS in a separate paper.

In Section 5.2.3 and Section 5.2.4, we will present our critique of the attacks 1 and 2 we implemented and consider some general ideas behind the possible attacks against the detection models discussed in this paper.

5.2.1 Attack 1

As mentioned earlier, due to the lack of precision of many program execution models, it may be possible for an attacker to jump a security-critical section of a program code without being detected by IDS. We refer to the class of attacks that exploits this vulnerability as impossible path exploits (IPEs). The attack 1 we implement belongs to the IPE class. To the best of our knowledge, this is the first working implementation of the IPE attack.

Attack description. The attack works as follows. Consider *login_user()* function, shown in Figure 4. There are two possible execution paths in this function because of the *if()* statement. If *is_regular(user)* returns true, path number one is followed. Otherwise, path number two is followed. Suppose the function read_next_cmd() called at (I) contains an overflow at the *strcpy()* statement. Then, an attacker can substitute the return address of the function so that the *read_next_cmd()* returns to (II), the address where the other read_next_cmd() would otherwise return.

```
void  read_next_cmd(){
  uchar input_buf[64];
  umask(2);            // sys_umask()
  ...
  // copy a command
  strcpy( &input_buf[0], getenv( "USERCMD" ));
  printf( "\n" );      // sys_write()
}
void login_user(int user){
  if( is_regular(user)){
    // unprivileged mode
    read_next_cmd(); // (I), this function will
                     // be overflowed
    ...
    // handle commands allowed to a regular user
    return;
  }
  // privileged mode
  read_next_cmd();    // (II), this function call
                      // will be skipped
  // —> this is where the control will be
  // transferred after a ret in read_next_cmd() at (I)
  seteuid(0);
  system( "rsync /etc/master.passwd ok@aeou.com:/ipe" );
  // and other privileged commands accessible only to
  // superuser
}
```

Figure 4. Pseudo code for attack 1

None of the existing models except VtPath will be able to differentiate between the *sys_write()* called when *read_next_cmd()* at (I) is called and the *sys_write()* called when *read_next_cmd()* at (II) is called. Consequently, be-

cause of imprecision of the models, including the ones for N-gram, abstract stack, callgraph, and FSA, after the jump an IDS would not detect an anomaly. The IDS would think the program has followed a legitimate execution path number two.

VtPath can detect the attack since in addition to verifying program counters and state transitions, it also sees stack context for both invocations of *read_next_cmd()*. More specifically, it can see an invalid virtual path from *sys_umask()* to *sys_write()* in *read_next_cmd()* at (I), as the return address of *read_next_cmd()* is changed by the overflow in *strcpy()*.

5.2.2 Attack 2

Attack description. This attack works as follows. *f()*, shown in Figure 5, is called from main() twice for the following two operations - checking a user name and checking a password. *f()* selects which operation to perform based on its parameter. The parameter is saved in a variable, *mode*. The variable is modified by an attacker when the adjacent local buffer, *input*, is overflowed. The local buffer is overflowed with a valid username and trailing zeros so that when *f(1)* is called, the value of mode is changed to zero. Under attack, instead of checking a user name and then checking a password, *f()* checks a user name twice. As a result, an attacker obtains access without knowing a password.

This attack will be detected by VtPath because it will see an invalid path between the *sys_close()* when *f(1)* is called and the following *sys_write()* in *main()*. N-gram, abstract stack and callgraph models will not be able to detect the attack because both branches in *f()* have the same system calls and the system call sequence stays unchanged during the attack. FSA will miss the attack because the transition from *sys_close()* to *sys_write()* is a valid FSA transition.

5.2.3 Observations

Based on the two attacks we described above, we can make the following general observations. First, both attacks require a way to change the control flow of a program. For our sample attacks we use buffer overflows. We realize that buffer overflows are not always possible and will eventually become a less significant threat. However, we believe our choice is justified given that over two-third of CERT's advisories in recent years were buffer overflows [15].

Second, programs that are vulnerable need to have a specific structure allowing, for example, a critical section to be jumped. In attacks described above, we show two examples of the possible program structures that can be exploited, namely a security-critical *if()* or a function whose argument controls execution and can be overflowed. For the IPE in Attack 1, it is also necessary that there be a function that is called from more than one point in a program.

```
f(int arg){
  int  mode = arg;        // this variable is overflowed
  char input[10];
  fopen();                // sys_open(), open passwd file
  // overflow, changes 'mode' variable => execution flow
  scanf("%s", &input[0] );
  if( mode == CHECK_UNAME ){ // check username?
   fread();                // sys_read(), read from passwd file
   fclose();               // sys_close()
   if( is_valid_user(input) ) ret = 1; else ret = 0;
  }
  else if( mode == CHECK_PASSWD ){ // check password?
   fread();                // sys_read(), read from passwd file
   fclose();               // sys_close()
   if( is_valid_pass(input) ) ret = 1; else ret = 0;
  }
  return ret;
}
void main(){
  printf( prompt );        // sys_write()
  ret=f(0);                // (I), read/check username
  if( ret ) ret = f(1);    // (II), read/check password
                           // if username was correct
  printf( "Authenticated\n" ); // sys_write()
  if( ret )
   execve( "/bin/sh" );       // superuser mode
}
```

Figure 5. Pseudo code for attack 2

```
f(){
...

// read in some large string z, syscalls are fine here
f0();

// important: f1() has no system calls
// it copies z to x, z is larger than x, so x is overflowed;
// after the ret instruction, the overflow code can
// jump anywhere within f(), as long as it is between
// f1() and the next system call;
// for example, the code can jump to IP1
f1();

if( cond ){
 // regular user privileges
 ...
 return;
}
...
IP1:
// superuser privileges
execve( "/bin/sh" );
}
```

Figure 6. Pseudo code for granularity attack

When the control flow of a vulnerable program is changed as in Attack 1, the function is exploited and a jump occurs.

5.2.4 Generalizations

The attacks we describe here have a common property in that they take advantage of the inherent limitations, or the insufficient level of granularity, of the IDS model. The information (or audit data) as well as the modeling algorithm used by an IDS model can be inadequate in a such a way that some attacks do not manifest as anomalies. For instance, attackers can exploit the fact that many anomaly-based IDS only check their program behavior models at a time of a system call [16, 17, 8]. Consider the example in Figure 6. This attack will not be detected by any of the approaches we described so far. VtPath will also be unable to detect the attack unless the IP1 is somewhere else in the program at a different level of nestedness so that there is an anomaly in the stack contents that can be detected.

As [10, 9] proposed and [17] pointed out, it is important that the intended behavior of a program is taken into account in a model. If a program comes with a complete specification of its intended behavior, any attack that causes the program to behave differently or violating the specification can be detected, provided that an IDS can check the pro-

gram behavior against the specification precisely. For our purposes, such an IDS will be considered to have a *maximal* level of granularity because it can detect all attacks that cause the program to deviate from its intended behavior. In most cases, an IDS has an inadequate level of granularity and thus there are always attacks on the program that can evade detection.

5.2.5 Importance of IPEs

We recognize that a successful execution of the attacks we described above is contingent upon quite a few variables and may not always be possible. It can be tempting to dismiss the problem of IPEs altogether as having little relevance since finding an existing piece of code that is exploitable may not be easy. Besides, as with many other attacks, the attacker is constrained by the need to perform reconnaissance and to have access to the details of the environment on the attacked host, particularly the IDS and other protection tools used.

We must point out, however, that instead of looking for vulnerable code, attackers can introduce IPE-vulnerable code into open source products in the form of innocent improvements or legitimate bug fixes. In contrast to other security flaws that attackers may attempt to inject, changes needed for IPEs can be made very subtle, which makes them less likely to be detected by code inspection. One of the reasons is that it is typically the structure of the code that makes it vulnerable to IPE, not the actual commands. Furthermore, it seems natural to assume that attackers will do everything in their power to disguise the IPE-vulnerable code. This can be done, for example, by gradually shaping the structure of a program code over series of patches.

6 A Comparison of System Call Based Anomaly Detection Approaches

In this section, we compare several anomaly detection methods based on their underlying principles. These methods include N-gram, FSA, VtPath, callgraph, abstract stack, and the method Wespi et al. proposed [20] (We call it Var-gram because it uses variable length N-gram patterns). The principles of the methods proposed in [7] are the same as those of callgraph and abstract stack; thus, our analysis on callgraph and abstract stack can also be applied to these methods. Our comparison is based on the algorithmic approaches of the models as well as the types of information they use. We analyze their performance characteristics in terms of false positives, detection capability, space requirement, convergence time, and runtime overhead.

We also realize that the performance of the methods can vary a lot due to their implementation details, such as issues regarding signals, DLLs and system call parameters. For example, some detection approaches are equipped with mechanisms to predict static system call parameter values. These mechanisms can also be applied to other detection approaches with appropriate modification, either through static analysis or dynamic monitoring. We can also develop appropriate mechanisms regarding other implementation issues for each approach. In this section, we ignore all the implementation issues, and focus on the underlying principles.

State based approach and information captured. We can model the execution of a program using a state diagram. At the start of the program, the system is in the start state. At each event occurrence, the system transits from one state to another. At any point, it is in a valid state if and only if the start state was valid and all the intermediate transitions were also valid. Consider an instantiation of the monitored program. To capture the normal behavior, the model tries to capture the valid states and valid state transitions by monitoring the behavior of the program at different event points. The model should also ignore the variables that are specific to that particular run of the program. It tries to learn the behavior of program by generalizing the observed instances of the program. However, it is not feasible to monitor the program at every event. For the approaches we study here, the states of the system are recorded only at the point of system calls. The decision to monitor only at system calls is justifiable because many attacks can manifest at the system call level.

Possible variables which could be considered while defining the states of the system include "contents of data heap", "registers", "code segment", "program stack", "system call and its arguments" and other system variables. The objective of a model is to record only the relevant state variables. Using the state transition diagram of each run during the training period, we would like to build a generalized state transition diagram which represents the normal behavior of the program. Data heap and register values are highly specific to that particular run of the program and do not generalize well, so we can ignore them. Code segment might be useful in some cases. System calls and their arguments are certainly useful. Although some arguments of some system calls are worth recording, many arguments can have many possible values, resulting in a model with slow convergence and high overhead. Call stack is important for learning the flow of program. In general, using more information to develop the intrusion detection model helps in attaining better detection rate. But it may also cause higher runtime overhead and more false positives.

N-gram and Var-gram choose to record only the system calls. N-gram records fixed-length sequences of system calls that occurred in the training data. Var-gram extracts variable-length sequences of system calls that occur repeatedly. FSA chooses to store the current system call along with its PC. The involvement of PCs makes it possible to distinguish system calls with the same name but called at different locations (location sensitive). VtPath keeps additional entries from the call stack, which further distinguishes system calls called in different contexts (context sensitive). N-gram can achieve some characteristics of location or context sensitive by using larger N. We believe that VtPath has better tradeoff considering the performance of N-gram, FSA, and VtPath in experiments. Although they are state based, abstract stack and callgraph models use a different approach of learning the behavior of the program by statically analyzing the source code. They only concern about system calls at detection time as N-gram and Var-gram do.

False positives False positives depend on how well the model captures the normal behavior of a program while ignoring the information that does not generalize well. Callgraph and abstract stack models do not have any false positive because they are statically derived from the source code, and all possible paths of execution are encoded in the grammar of the model. N-gram and Var-gram record sequences of system calls that occur in the training data. Any path which is not covered in the training set may produce a new sequence, thus raising a false positive. For N-gram, the probability of the alert depends largely on the size of N.

The larger N is, the higher is the probability that new paths will generate new N-length sequences. FSA tries to model programs more accurately by taking into account the locations of system calls. This is logical because the location of a system call determines what system call will be executed. The model may generate a false positive if any valid system call location or any valid transition between system call locations is not covered in training. VtPath on the other hand models the program more strictly because valid transitions must have valid return address combinations as well. So it should generate a little bit more false positives than FSA. Both FSA and VtPath essentially use diagrams. Comparing to N-gram, the location or context sensitive property will increase false positives, but on the other hand the digram property will decrease false positives when comparing to N-gram with large N.

Detection capability In Section 5.2, we presented a few specific attacks which will be missed by some detection approaches while detected by others. Detection capability of an IDS depends on its granularity, which in turn is determined by the amount of relevant information the IDS is storing and its modeling technique. An IDS with more granularity should have better detection capability.

All the approaches we study here try to model the system call behavior of the program. Any attack that introduces a new system call or causes very noticeable changes in the system call sequences (e.g., common buffer overflow attacks) should be detected by all the approaches. It is easier for FSA and VtPath to find Trojan horses because program counters for system calls and return addresses for function calls will probably change with the change in the code, while system call sequences may not. FSA and VtPath can also detect all the attacks where any system call is made from invalid points. All other approaches will miss these attacks if the system call sequences do not change. VtPath provides another level of protection because it is hard to jump or skip to another place in the program by changing return addresses while avoiding detection. Attacks which have no effect on system call sequences and return addresses will evade all the approaches discussed here (if no frequency or parameter value information is used).

For N-gram and Var-gram, the detection capability depends on the statistical regularity of normal data and also the properties of attack, in particular, how much the attack sequences deviate from that normal behavior. However, there is no concrete research done on what types of attack can be detected by N-gram and Var-gram. Due to the context-insensitive treatment of function calls, callgraph model allows IPE. As a result, all attacks that follow any of these IPEs will go undetected. Abstract stack model tries to remove this imprecision by including some context-sensitive information. However, our experiments showed that carefully designed IPEs can still evade detection by it.

The non-determinism may impair the detection capability for both callgraph and abstract stack models. FSA checks the transition between the PCs of two system calls. It suffers from the same problems of the context-insensitive property as callgraph. In particular, IPE can evade FSA. VtPath stores all the system call points and all the allowed virtual execution paths. It can be evaded if an attack changes the call stack but somehow changes the virtual path to another valid one.

Space requirement For N-gram and Var-gram, the main space requirement is to store the system call sequences. That depends on the number of different sequences and also on the data structure used for storage. For example, storing sequences in the form of array generally takes more space, whereas tree structure takes less. For callgraph and abstract stack models, the space requirement is proportional to the number of NDFA transitions or the size of context free grammars (CFGs), which is proportional to the number of positions where function calls or system calls are made in the program code. For FSA, the memory requirement is proportional to the number of transitions in the automaton. The upper bound on number of transitions is proportional to the square of the number of places system calls are made in the program code. But in general, the number of transitions should be comparable to that of callgraph. For VtPath, the space requirement is driven by the number of virtual paths. In the extreme case, the number of virtual paths that pass function boundaries can be exponential to the number of function calls in program code. However, in general, the number of virtual paths is at the same level as the number of transitions for FSA or callgraph.

Convergence time By convergence time, we mean the amount of training time or data required to have a stable model. N-gram converges when most of the possible sequences are encountered in the training data set. This depends on the value of N. As N increases, the size of required training data increases, possibly exponentially. Var-gram converges when most of the "wanted" patterns appear repeatedly and are extracted. The Teiresias algorithm Var-gram uses is not suitable for incremental training usage, so we can only check the convergence by training on data sets with different sizes separately and comparing the resulting patterns. For FSA, we need to cover most of the possible states and possible transitions. It is not necessary to go through each path of execution. It therefore needs less data and time to form the stable model. Abstract stack and callgraph models do static analysis of the source code, so they do not require any training data. Also they need just one pass of the program. VtPath converges when most of the possible virtual paths are covered. This will require a somewhat larger data set than FSA. But as it is essentially based on diagrams with call stack attached, it should take less training data and time than N-gram with large N.

Runtime overheads Runtime overhead of IDS is due to system call interception and processing time of the IDS model. Because system call interception overhead is similar for all the models, here we discuss only the processing time of a model for each system call. N-gram and Var-gram need to check if there are matches in the database for the system call sequences starting from the current point. Using a trie structure, this can be done in time linear to the sequence length. For FSA (or VtPath), at each system call we need to check if it has a valid state (or valid return addresses) and there is a valid transition (or valid virtual path). Using a hash table this will take constant time.

Non-determinism will aggravate the runtime overhead for callgraph and abstract stack. In the callgraph model, there could be multiple paths from the current state. Using efficient techniques, we can cover all the next possible valid states in the time proportional to the number of states. So for each system call, the upper bound of time overhead is proportional to the number of states. In abstract stack model, for each system call we need to go through each possible path in the CFG to determine the possible next states and the stack contents. This may take exponential time in some cases.

7 Summary

Call stack can be very useful for intrusion detection purposes. In this paper, we developed a new method that can dynamically extracts return address information from the call stack and use it for anomaly detection. Our experiments show that this method is effective in terms of both detection ability and false positive rates. We also compared various related approaches to achieve a better understanding on what and why attacks will be missed by these approaches.

The main advantages of FSA and VtPath are that they are deterministic and location (context) sensitive. The main advantages of callgraph and abstract stack are that they can remove all false positives and do not require training. We may be able to combine these methods together and have all these advantages. Using binary analysis techniques similar to those in [7], we can extract and generate all the possible system calls (with the corresponding PCs), return addresses, and virtual paths from executables. The profile generated can then be used to dynamically monitor program executions. We can avoid false positives because the profile is generated by techniques similar to other static analysis techniques compared in this paper. The determinism and location sensitive properties are also kept. We will conduct more research on this subject in the future.

ACKNOWLEDGEMENTS We would like to thank Yong Huang for providing some related material and discussions. We would also like to thank John Levine for suggestions and corrections. The work reported in this paper is supported in part by ARO contract DAAD19-01-1-0610 and NSF contracts CCR-0133629 and CCR-0208655. The contents of this work are solely the responsibility of the authors and do not necessarily represent the official views of the U.S. Army and NSF.

References

[1] K. Ashcraft and D.R. Engler, "Using Programmer-Written Compiler Extensions to Catch Security Holes", *IEEE Symposium on Security and Privacy*, Oakland, CA, 2002.

[2] C. Cowan, C. Pu, D. Maier, H. Hinton, P. Bakke, S. Beattie, A. Grier, P. Wagle and Q. Zhang, "Stack-Guard: Automatic Adaptive Detection and Prevention of Buffer-Overflow Attacks", *7th USENIX Security Symposium*, San Antonio, TX, 1998.

[3] C. Cowan, P. Wagle, C. Pu, S. Beattie and J. Walpole, "Buffer Overflows: Attacks and Defenses for the Vulnerability of the Decade", *DARPA Information Survivability Conference and Expo*, Hilton Head Island, SC, 2000.

[4] A. Floratos and I. Rigoutsos, "On the Time Complexity of the TEIRESIAS Algorithm", *Research Report 98A000290*, IBM, 1998.

[5] S. Forrest, S.A. Hofmeyr, A. Somayaji and T.A. Longstaff, "A Sense of Self for Unix Processes", *IEEE Symposium on Computer Security and Privacy*, Los Alamos, CA, pp.120-128, 1996.

[6] A. Ghosh and A. Schwartzbard, "A study in using neural networks for anomaly and misuse detection", *8th USENIX Security Symposium*, pp. 141-151, 1999.

[7] J.T. Giffin, S. Jha and B.P. Miller, "Detecting Manipulated Remote Call Streams", *11th USENIX Security Symposium*, 2002.

[8] S.A. Hofmeyr, A. Somayaji, and S. Forrest, "Intrusion Detection System Using Sequences of System Calls", *Journal of Computer Security*, 6(3), pp. 151-180, 1998.

[9] C. Ko, "Execution Monitoring of Security-Critical Programs in Distributed Systems: A Specification-based Approach". *PhD thesis*, UC Davis, 1996.

[10] C. Ko, G. Fink and K. Levitt, "Automated Detection of Vulnerabilities in Privileged Programs by Execution Monitoring", *10th Computer Security Applications Conference*, Orlando, Fl, pp.134-144, 1994.

[11] W. Lee and S. Stolfo, "Data Mining Approaches for Intrusion Detection", *7th USENIX Security Symposium*, San Antonio, TX, 1998.

[12] W. Lee, S. Stolfo, and P. Chan, "Learning Patterns from Unix Process Execution Traces for Intrusion Detection", *AAAI Workshop: AI Approaches to Fraud Detection and Risk Management*, 1997.

[13] Mindcraft, "WebStone Benchmark Information", http://www.mindcraft.com/webstone/.

[14] I. Rigoutsos and A. Floratos, "Combinatorial Pattern Discovery in Biological Sequences: The TEIRESIAS Algorithm", *Bioinformatics*, 14(1), pp. 55-67, 1998.

[15] B. Schneier, "The Process of Security", *Information Security*, April, 2000, http://www.infosecuritymag.com/articles/april00/columns_cryptorhythms.shtml.

[16] R. Sekar, M. Bendre, P. Bollineni, and D. Dhurjati, "A Fast Automaton-Based Method for Detecting Anomalous Program Behaviors", *IEEE Symposium on Security and Privacy*, Oakland, CA, 2001.

[17] D. Wagner and D. Dean, "Intrusion Detection via Static Analysis", *IEEE Symposium on Security and Privacy*, Oakland, CA, 2001.

[18] D. Wagner and P. Soto, "Mimicry Attacks on Host-Based Intrusion Detection Systems", *ACM Conference on Computer and Communications Security*, 2002.

[19] C. Warrender, S. Forrest, and B. Pearlmutter, "Detecting Intrusions Using System Calls: Alternative Data Models", *IEEE Symposium on Security and Privacy*, pp. 133-145, 1999.

[20] A. Wespi, M. Dacier and H. Debar, "Intrusion Detection Using Variable-Length Audit Trail Patterns", *3rd International Workshop on the Recent Advances in Intrusion Detection*, LNCS 1907, Springer, pp. 110-129, 2000.